lonely planet

East Africa

Hugh Finlay
Geoff Crowther

D0180384

East Africa

4th edition

Published by
Lonely Planet Publications
Head Office: PO Box 617, Hawthorn, Vic 3122, Australia
Branches: 155 Filbert St, Suite 251, Oakland, CA 94607, USA
               10 Barley Mow Passage, Chiswick, London W4 4PH, UK
               71 bis rue du Cardinal Lemoine, 75005 Paris, France

Printed by
SNP Printing Pte Ltd, Singapore

Photographs by

Bethune Carmichael	Geoff Crowther	Dawn Delaney
Greg Elms	David Else	Hugh Finlay
Greg Herriman	Roger Jones	Debra Tan
David Wall	Tony Wheeler	

Front cover: Maasai tribesman in silhouette (Pete Turner, The Image Bank)
Safari Guide title page: David Wall
Tribal Groups & Cultures title graphic: Steve Barnes

First Published
September 1987

This Edition
June 1997

Although the authors and publisher have tried to make the information as accurate as possible, they accept no responsibility for any loss, injury or inconvenience sustained by any person using this book.

National Library of Australia Cataloguing in Publication Data

Crowther, Geoff, 1944- .
East Africa.

4th ed.
Includes index.
ISBN 0 86442 449 3.

1. Africa, East – Guidebooks. I. Finlay, Hugh. II. Title.
(Series: Lonely Planet travel survival kit).

916.76044

text © Lonely Planet 1997, except Kenya © Hugh Finlay 1997
maps © Lonely Planet 1997
photos © photographers as indicated 1997

Hugh Finlay

After deciding there must be more to life than civil engineering, Hugh took off around Australia in the mid-70s, working at everything from spray painting to diamond prospecting, before hitting the overland trail. He joined Lonely Planet in 1985 and has written *Jordan & Syria*, co-authored *Nepal* and contributed to other LP guides including *Africa*, *India* and *Australia*. He lives in central Victoria, Australia, with his partner Linda and his daughters Ella and Vera.

Geoff Crowther

Born in Yorkshire, England, Geoff took to his heels early on in search of the miraculous, taking a break from a degree in biochemistry. The lure of the unknown took him to Kabul, Kathmandu and Lamu in the days before the overland companies began digging up the dirt along the tracks of Africa.

In 1977 he wrote his first guide for Lonely Planet – *Africa on the cheap*. He has also written *South America on a shoestring* and *Korea & Taiwan*, and has co-authored guides to *India* and *Malaysia, Singapore & Brunei*.

From the Authors

From Hugh In addition to many of the people listed below (particularly Philip and Alastair at Flight Centres), I would also like to thank the following people for their help and hospitality in Kenya and Uganda: Hans-Peter Erismann, Julia Crombie (African Pearl Safaris), James Bakeine & Dorothy Tukamushaba (Nile Safaris), James Crockford, Ms Monica Mbabazi, Rulan Desai (Kilimanjaro Safari Club), Ian Vincent (Kilimanjaro Buffalo Lodge), Jane & Julia Barnley (Sirikwa Safaris), Sheldon Guenther, Raj Shah (Naiberi River Camp Site) and Max Cheli (Tortilis Camp). Many thanks also to fellow Lonely Planet author David Else for his trekking information and last-minute updates.

From Geoff Geoff would like to thank the following people for their friendship, help, encouragement, hospitality and constructive criticism:

Alice Jane Njoki Chege, a Kikuyu from Kiambu and a consummate linguist, contributed to the research with a disarming panache and vitality which was highly encouraging.

Graeme 'Tommo' Thomson of Flight Centres, Nairobi, who digs up the dirt, hugs the forefront of innovative long-distance safaris and offers good service.

Malcolm 'Le Baron' Gascoigne of Yare Safaris, Nairobi: his humour is contagious and his enthusiasm for life infectious.

Philip Jackson helped substantially with the textual detail of this guide on numerous occasions and always had facts and figures to hand.

Kris Zachrisson, of Tour Africa Safaris,

climbed Mt Kenya with me; I couldn't have had a better companion.

Terry Rice, Stephen Laiser, Oliver Davidson and Augustino Mtemi of Arusha, for a superb 'Welcome back, Geoff!', free maps and heaps of information.

Alastair Brown, an English reprobate of a mechanic, and Musa Hassan Mussa, who introduced me to everyone in Arusha and was always there to help and advise.

Jim Shaner, an American who knew MS-DOS almost as well as he knew Somali and rescued me from a Windows labyrinth.

Kate Rousseau, who made a sterling, last-minute trip to Rwanda to help research and update that chapter.

Ashley Chosun Crowther, my son, who sent me a drawing and a happy birthday message.

This Book

Geoff researched and wrote the first *East Africa*, and Hugh and Geoff have both updated the editions since. They returned to the region to work on this fourth edition and also to research and update *Kenya*, which appears in full in this guide. Hugh updated Uganda, most of Kenya and coordinated the project. Geoff updated Tanzania, Eastern Zaïre, Rwanda (with a little help) and parts of Kenya. Civil unrest kept us out of Burundi altogether.

From the Publisher

Cathy Lanigan edited this book with assistance from Anne Mulvaney, Michelle Coxall, Miriam Cannell, Janet Austin, Justin Flynn, Katrina Browning, Liz Filleul, Chris Wyness, Lindsay Brown and Jane Rawson. Chris Klep was responsible for cartography and design and Geoff Stringer, Verity Campbell, Trudi Canavan, Indra Kilfoyle, Rachael Scott and Janet Watson assisted with

mapping. Thanks to Valerie Tellini for the layout and Geoff Stringer for designing the chapter ends. Matt King did the Safari Guide illustrations and other illustrations were provided by Margaret Jung, Valerie Tellini and Miriam Cannell. Simon Bracken designed the cover and Adam McCrow was responsible for the back cover cartography. Sharon Benson did the indexing.

Thanks

Thanks to all the travellers who found the time and energy to write us to us from all over the world with their suggestions and comments, your names appear on page 714.

Warning & Request

Things change – prices go up, schedules change, good places go bad and bad places go bankrupt – nothing stays the same. So, if you find things better or worse, recently opened or long since closed, please tell us and help make the next edition even more accurate and useful.

We value all of the feedback we receive from travellers. Julie Young coordinates a small team who read and acknowledge every letter, postcard and email, and ensure that every morsel of information finds its way to the appropriate authors, editors and publishers.

Everyone who writes to us will find their name in the next edition of the appropriate guide and will also receive a free subscription to our quarterly newsletter, *Planet Talk*. The very best contributions will be rewarded with a free Lonely Planet guide.

Excerpts from your correspondence may appear in updates (which we add to the end pages of reprints), new editions of this guide, in our newsletter *Planet Talk*; or in the Postcards section of our Web site – so please let us know if you don't want your letter published or your name acknowledged.

Contents

UGANDA

Map Legend

BOUNDARIES

International Boundary

Provincial Boundary

ROUTES

Freeway

Highway

Major Road

Unsealed Road or Track

City Road

City Street

Railway

Underground Railway

Tram

Walking Track

Walking Tour

Ferry Route

Cable Car or Chairlift

AREA FEATURES

Parks

Built-Up Area

Pedestrian Mall

Market

Christian Cemetery

Non-Christian Cemetery

Reef

Beach

Mountain Range

HYDROGRAPHIC FEATURES

Coastline

River, Creek

Rapids, Waterfalls

Lake, Intermittent Lake

Canal

Swamp

SYMBOLS

✪ CAPITAL	National Capital		✪	⛽	Embassy, Petrol Station
◉ Capital	Regional Capital		✈	✛	Airport, Airfield
CITY	Major City		🏊	✿	Swimming Pool, Gardens
● City	City		❖	🐘	Shopping Centre, Zoo
● Town	Town		⚘	⛱	Winery or Vineyard, Picnic Site
● Village	Village		←	A25	One Way Street, Route Number
■ ▼	Place to Stay, Place to Eat		🏛	⚐	Stately Home, Monument
☕ 🍴	Cafe, Pub or Bar		🏰	▣	Castle, Tomb
✉ ☎	Post Office, Telephone		⌒	⛪	Cave, Hut or Chalet
❶ ⑤	Tourist Information, Bank		▲	☀	Mountain or Hill, Lookout
⬤ 🅿	Transport, Parking		🗼	⚓	Lighthouse, Shipwreck
🏛 ⌂	Museum, Youth Hostel		)(	◉	Pass, Spring
🏕 🏕	Caravan Park, Camping Ground		🏖	⛳	Beach, Golf Course
✝ ✚	Church, Cathedral			⁙	Archaeological Site or Ruins
☪ ✡	Mosque, Synagogue				Ancient or City Wall
卐 卐	Buddhist Temple, Hindu Temple				Cliff or Escarpment, Tunnel
✚ ★	Hospital, Police Station				Railway Station

Note: not all symbols displayed above appear in this book

Introduction

If your vision of Africa is of elephants crossing the plain below Kilimanjaro, an Arab dhow sailing into Zanzibar, a million pink flamingos, Maasai tribespeople guarding their cattle, then East Africa is where this vision becomes reality.

This book covers a small group of countries of absorbing interest and diversity. Whatever your interests, East Africa has plenty to see, experience and consider.

Kenya and Tanzania are the heart of African safariland. Some of the most famous reserves are found here, and in a trip to these countries you will probably see everything from rhinos to lions, hippos to baboons, wildebeest to flamingos. Safaris are an experience in themselves, but the reserves are also spectacular, such as the Ngorongoro park in Tanzania, which is in the crater of a colossal extinct volcano, or the Amboseli park in

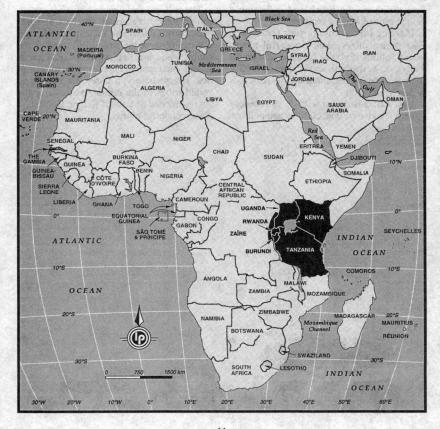

Kenya, which has Mt Kilimanjaro as a spectacular backdrop.

The reserves of Kenya and Tanzania are the region's best known natural attractions, but certainly not the only ones. The superb Ruwenzori Mountains sprawl across the border between Uganda and Zaïre, while further south are some of the most active volcanoes in Africa, particularly in the Parc Nacional des Volcans in Rwanda. And Rwanda is, of course, famous for its scattered groups of mountain gorillas, which you can also visit. Scuba divers will find plenty to interest them along the coast and around the offshore islands, while other visitors may find lazing on the beach and collecting a suntan quite enough exercise.

If lazing isn't a word in your vocabulary, East Africa offers some wonderful mountains to climb. If you're fit, an assault on Mt Kenya or, best of all, snowcapped Mt Kilimanjaro, the highest mountain in Africa, is within your reach.

East Africa isn't just wildlife and scenery – there are also people, cultures and politics.

Politically the region offers as wide a span of Africa's problems and aspirations as you could ask for. At one extreme there's Kenya, where Africa really works and where stability and progress have been the norm, a situation very different from so many other African nations. Tanzania illustrates where the best of African intentions can go disastrously awry, Zaïre is a victim of pure, untrammelled greed, while Rwanda and Burundi are painful examples of the horrors of tribal animosity. Uganda is the shining light in the area – the bad old days are well and truly over, peace and stability have returned and there's a new optimism.

The cultures and people of the region are equally interesting. Along the coast, and particularly on islands like Zanzibar and Lamu, you can observe the strong influence of the Arabs, who came first as traders and later as slavers and remained in the region for centuries. Everywhere you'll see the many and varied tribes of the region, particularly the strong-minded Maasai of Kenya. Go there – it's a wonderful region.

Regional Facts for the Visitor

PLANNING

When to Go

The main tourist season in East Africa is January and February, as the weather at this time of year is generally considered to be the best – hot and dry. It's also when you'll find the largest concentrations of bird life on the Rift Valley lakes, and when the animals in the game parks tend to congregate more around the watercourses as other sources dry up, making them easier to spot.

From July to September could be called the 'shoulder season' as the weather is still dry and it's the time of that visual extravaganza – the annual wildebeest migration into the Masai Mara National Reserve (Kenya) from the Serengeti (Tanzania).

During the long rains (from March to May) and the short rains (from October to December) things are much quieter – places tend to be less full and accommodation prices come down. The rains generally don't affect your ability to get around and see things, it's just that you may well get rained on, especially in the late afternoon.

What Kind of Trip?

East Africa is a compact region which is relatively easy to get around. For this reason many travellers choose to travel independently, using a combination of public transport, organised safaris and occasional vehicle hire. For anyone on a budget, organised safaris are the best option for getting to the game parks, although in Uganda the opportunities are limited and safaris are expensive. The main bases from which to take a safari are Nairobi (Kenya) and Arusha (in northern Tanzania). See the Organised Vehicle Safaris sections in the Kenya and Tanzania chapters for full details on the pros and cons of taking a safari of this kind.

Maps

There are a number of maps which cover the region. The Hallwag 1:2,000,000 *Kenya & Tanzania* also includes Uganda, Rwanda, Burundi and eastern Zaïre.

Michelin's 1:4,000,000 *Africa – Central & South* also gives good regional coverage, although on a smaller scale.

The best map of all would probably be the recent Bartholomew's 1:2,500,000 *Kenya & Tanzania*.

Lonely Planet's *Kenya travel atlas* provides the handiest, most accurate maps available and is a great companion to this guidebook.

What to Bring

Bring the minimum. Many travellers in East Africa find once they actually get there that they have far too much gear. This is not only an uncomfortable inconvenience, it also means that instead of taking back some special reminders of the region you'll be taking back the same extra pullover and jeans that you set off with. Unless it's absolutely essential, *leave it at home!*

A rucksack (backpack) is far more practical than an overnight bag, and is essential if you plan to do any trekking or walking. It is worth buying a good-quality bag right at the start – African travel soon sorts out the good stuff from the junk, and if it's the latter you've opted for, you'll be cursing it the whole way.

What type of pack you buy is largely a matter of personal preference. We find that the travel packs with the straps which zip into a compartment in the back are excellent. Although expensive, they are a compromise solution to a number of problems; however, they are not really suited for specialised activities such as trekking or serious walking.

A day pack is a worthwhile item, if only for keeping your camera dry and out of the incredible dust which seems to permeate every crack and crevice when you're on safari. For these reasons and for security, it needs to be one which zips shut. Quite a few travellers use the local *kiondos* (woven baskets) which are fine if they suit your purpose.

A sleeping bag is more or less essential if you are travelling overland beyond East Africa or planning to climb mountains, but within the region itself there are enough hotels for you not to need one. On the other hand, carrying a sleeping bag and closed-cell foam mat does give you a greater degree of flexibility and means that if you take a safari you know you'll have adequate gear. Sleeping bags are the one thing which all camping safari companies require you to provide.

There's always much discussion about the pros and cons of carrying a tent, and basically it boils down to what sort of travelling you want to do, and how much weight you're prepared to carry. As with a sleeping bag, a tent is not necessary if you're just travelling from town to town, but carrying your own portable shelter opens up a stack of exciting possibilities. The same applies to carrying a stove and cooking gear, so give some careful thought to what you want to do, and how. On the other hand, the full range of camping equipment can be hired from various places in Kenya, but not in Tanzania or Uganda.

Quite a few travellers carry a mosquito net, and with the risk of malaria there is no doubt that this is not a bad idea, although with judicious use of insect repellent and mosquito coils, you should have few problems. On the topic of insect repellent, bring a good supply and make sure that whatever you bring has as the active ingredient diethyl toluamide, commonly known as DEET. This has been found to be the most effective against mosquitoes. Brands which have this include Mijex and Rid. Mosquito coils are what the locals use (when they use anything at all, that is) to keep the mozzies at bay, and local brands such as Doom are available in even the smallest stores.

Clothes need to be both practical and to take into account local sensibilities. Although this region straddles the equator, the large variations in altitude lead to equally large variations in climate. The coast is hot and steamy year-round, while Nairobi and the western highlands of Kenya get decidedly cool in the evenings in July and August, so you need to carry one decent warm pullover as well as warm-weather gear. A windproof and waterproof jacket also comes in handy, particularly during the rainy seasons. Most travellers seem to get around in T-shirts and shorts, which is fine in most areas, but you should be more circumspect on the Muslim-dominated coast, particularly on Lamu and Zanzibar. Here women should wear tops that keep the shoulders covered and skirts or pants which reach at least to the knees. Shorts on men are likewise not particularly appreciated. Civil servants, officials and embassy staff, likewise, do not appreciate scantily dressed travellers and will treat you with disdain.

Overlooked by many people but absolutely indispensable is a good pair of sunglasses. The amount of glare you experience in the bright tropical light is not only uncomfortable but can damage your eyes. A hat which shades your face and neck is also well worth considering, and a water bottle is worth any slight inconvenience it may cause. It needs to be unbreakable, have a good seal, and hold at least one litre.

Also important are little things which can make life just that bit more comfortable: a Swiss Army pocketknife, a small sewing kit (including a few metres of fishing line and a large needle for emergency rucksack surgery), a 10m length of light nylon cord for a washing line and a handful of clothes pegs, and half a tennis ball makes a good fits-all washbasin plug.

Most toiletries – soap, shaving cream, shampoo, toothpaste, toilet paper, tampons – are available throughout the region.

The one thing that you're really going to appreciate is a pair of binoculars, whether they be pocket ones or larger field binoculars. When out in the game parks you can put them to constant use and they are essential for identifying the dozens of species of mammals and birds that you'll come across. If you don't plan on going to the game parks they are still handy just for the scenery, or perhaps for trying to spot that potential lift coming over the horizon when you're stuck out in the middle of nowhere.

HIGHLIGHTS

The region probably offers the greatest variety in the smallest area of anywhere in Africa. Top of the list is game-viewing, which is best in Kenya and Tanzania, although the mountain gorillas in Uganda are starting to draw more and more visitors. Next come the Swahili culture and beaches of the coast, and opportunities for snorkelling and scuba diving.

Mountain trekkers – in fact all lovers of the great outdoors – will be well satisfied with the range of activities and sights. Mt Kilimanjaro (Tanzania), Mt Kenya (Kenya) and the amazing Ruwenzori Mountains (Uganda) all offer superb trekking, while the national parks of all three countries are top class.

Uganda is certainly the baby of the region when it comes to tourism (in 1995 there were only 175,000 visitors), but with recent stability and growth it is poised to become a major destination.

See the Facts for the Visitor sections in the country chapters for more details on their highlights.

VISAS & DOCUMENTS
Passport

If you already have a passport, make sure it's valid for a reasonably long period of time and has plenty of blank pages on which stamp-happy immigration officials can do their stuff. If it's more than half full and you're going to need a lot of visas, get a new passport before you set off. This way you won't have to waste time hanging around in a capital city somewhere while your embassy issues you with a new one. In some countries there is the option of getting a normal-sized passport or a 'jumbo' passport. Get the larger one. US nationals can have extension pages stapled into otherwise full passports at any of their embassies.

Visas

Visas are obtained from the embassy or consulate of the appropriate country either before you set off or along the way. It's best to get them along the way, especially if your travel plans are not fixed, but keep your ear to the ground regarding the best places to get them. Two different consulates of the same country may have completely different requirements; the fee may be different, one consulate might want to see how much money you have whereas another won't, one might demand an onward ticket while another won't even mention it, one might issue visas while you wait and another might insist on referring the application back to the capital (which can take weeks).

Whatever you do, don't turn up at a border without a visa unless you're absolutely sure visas aren't necessary or you can get one at the border. If you get this wrong you'll find yourself tramping back to the nearest consulate, and in some countries, this can be a long way.

You'll occasionally come across some tedious, petty-power freak at an embassy or consulate whose sole pleasure in life appears to be making as big a nuisance of themselves as possible and causing you the maximum amount of delay. If you bite the carrot and display your anger or frustration, the visa will take twice as long to issue. But if you want that visa, don't display any emotion – pretend you have all day to waste.

Consular officials sometimes refuse point-blank to stamp a visa on anything other than a completely blank page, so make sure your passport has plenty of them.

Another important fact to bear in mind about visas is their sheer cost. None are free and some are outrageously expensive (Zaïre, for instance). Unless you carry a passport from one of the Commonwealth or European Community (EC) countries, you'll need visas, and if you're on a tight budget, the cost can make a hole in your pocket. It's a good idea to make a rough calculation of what the visa fees are going to amount to before you set off, and allow for it. Make sure you have plenty of passport-size photographs for visa applications – 12 should be sufficient.

Some countries demand you have a ticket out of the country before they will issue you with a visa or let you into the country. So long as you intend to leave from the same place you arrived, there is no problem, but if you want to enter at one point and leave from another, this can be a headache. Fortunately, having to show an onward ticket seems to be rare in East Africa, and usually only happens when arriving by air. If they do insist on you having an onward ticket but you want to spend the minimum possible (and have it refunded without problems), try buying a Miscellaneous Charges Order (MCO) from an international airline for, say, US$100.

The other way to get around the onward ticket requirement is to buy the cheapest ticket available out of the country and then get it refunded later on. If you do this, make sure you can get a refund without having to wait months. Don't forget to ask specifically where it can be refunded, since some airlines will only refund tickets at the office where you bought them, some only at their head office.

See individual country chapters for details on visa requirements and the addresses of embassies and consulates.

Travel Insurance

A travel insurance policy to cover theft, loss and medical problems is a wise idea. See Predeparture Planning in the Health section of this chapter for details about insurance.

Driving Licence & Permits

If you're taking your own transport or are thinking of hiring a vehicle to tour certain national parks, get hold of an International Driving Permit (IDP) before you set off. Any national motoring organisation will fix you up with this, provided you have a valid driving licence for your own country. The cost of these permits is generally about US$5. On the other hand, a national driving licence seems to suffice for hiring a vehicle in most countries.

Student Card

An International Student Identity Card (ISIC) or the graduate equivalent is useful in many places and can save you a bit of money, though its usefulness diminishes with each passing year. Possible concessions include airline tickets, train fares and reduced entry charges to museums and archaeological sites. If you're not strictly entitled to a student card, it's often possible to get one if you book a flight with one of the 'bucket shop' ticket agencies that have proliferated in some European and North American cities. The deal usually is that you buy an airline ticket and they'll provide you with a student card.

International Health Certificate

Whoever supplies you with your vaccinations will provide you with an International Health Certificate with the necessary stamps. In most places you won't be asked to present it, but border officials often see it as a good way of catching people out. The Kenya/Ethiopia border at Moyale and Zanzibar have both been a problem in the past.

MONEY
Costs

It's very difficult to predict what a trip to East Africa is going to cost, since so many factors are involved: how fast you want to travel, what degree of comfort you consider to be acceptable, how much sightseeing you want to do, whether you intend to hire a vehicle to explore a game park or rely on other tourists to give you a lift, whether you're travelling alone or in a group and a host of other things.

There's only one thing which remains the same in Africa, and that's the pace of change – it's fast. Inflation and devaluations can wreak havoc with your travel plans if you're on a very tight budget. You should budget for at least US$20 per day in this region. This should cover the cost of basic but reasonable accommodation, food in local cafes, and public transport. It won't include the cost of getting to Africa, safaris in game parks or major purchases in markets. On the other hand, if you stay in one place for a while and cook your own food, you can reduce daily costs considerably, because you won't be

The Maasai are the most well known of East Africa's tribal people, and their name is synonomous with their striking red dress and beaded jewellery. They also have a reputation as fierce warriors; young male warriors (*morani*) can look startling with ochre covered faces.

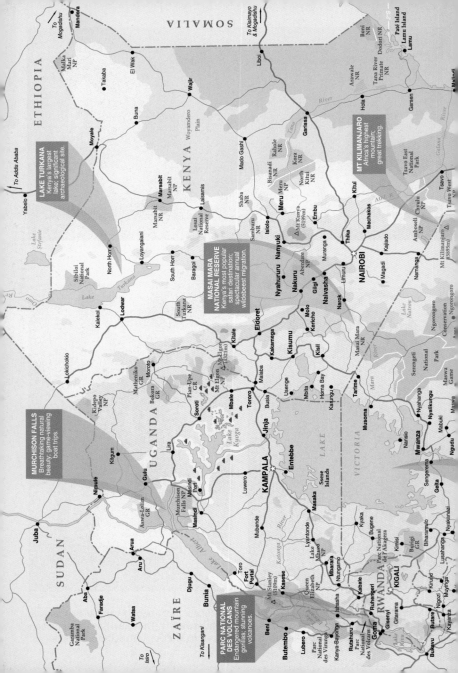

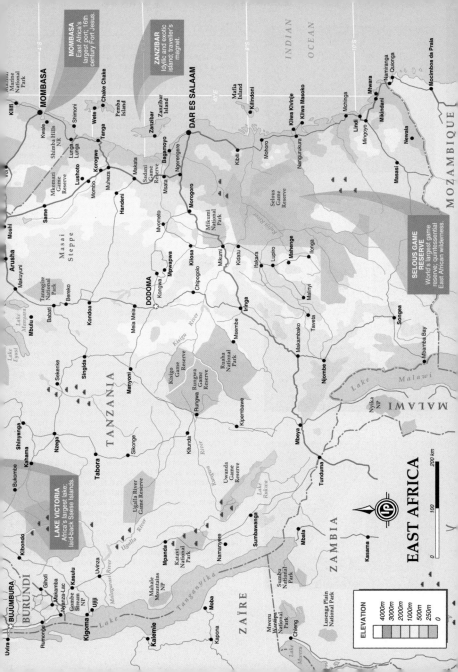

MOMBASA
East Africa's largest port; 16th century Fort Jesus.

ZANZIBAR
Idyllic and exotic island; traveller's magnet.

SELOUS GAME RESERVE
World's largest game reserve; quintessential East African wilderness.

LAKE VICTORIA
Africa's largest lake; laid-back Ssese Islands.

EAST AFRICA

ELEVATION
4000m
3000m
2000m
1000m
500m
250m
0

0   100   200 km

INDIAN OCEAN

MOZAMBIQUE

MALAWI

ZAMBIA

ZAÏRE

BURUNDI

TANZANIA

Mombasa
Kilifi
Kwale
Shimoni
Chake Chake
Wete
Pemba Island
Zanzibar
Zanzibar Island
DAR ES SALAAM
Mafia Island
Kilindoni
Tanga
Lunga Lunga
Shimba Hills NR
Korogwe
Lushoto
Mombo
Muheza
Makata
Sadani Game Reserve
Msata
Ngerengere
Bagamoyo
Kibiti
Mohoro
Kilwa Kivinje
Kilwa Masoko
Lindi
Mingoyo
Mtwara
Mikindani
Mnamiranga
Quionga
Mocimboa da Praia
Nangurukura
Newala
Masasi
Mchinga
Same
Moshi
Arusha
Makuyuni
Tarangire National Park
Bereko
Babati
Mbulu
Lake Manyara
Lake Eyasi
Handeni
Mvomero
Morogoro
Kilosa
Chipogolo
Mpwapwa
Kongwa
DODOMA
Mkumi National Park
Mkumi
Kidatu
Itakara
Lupiro
Mahenge
Ilonga
Selous Game Reserve
Rufiji River
Mela Mela
Kondoa
Singida
Sekenke
Manyoni
Sikonge
Kisigu River
Kisigo Game Reserve
Rungwa Game Reserve
Ruaha National Park
Msembe
Iringa
Malinyi
Tavata
Makambako
Njombe
Songea
Mbamba Bay
Lake Malawi
Nyika NP
Shinyanga
Nzega
Kahama
Bukombe
Tabora
Ugalla River Game Reserve
Ugalla River
Kitunda
Kipembawe
Rungwa River
Uwanda Game Reserve
Lake Rukwa
Mbeya
Tunduma
Mbala
Sumbawanga
Kasama
Namanyere
Katavi National Park
Mpanda
Mahale Mountains NP
Uvinza
Kigoma
Ujiji
Malagarasi River
Lake Tanganyika
Kalemie
Moba
Kapona
Chienji
Sumbu National Park
Mweru Wantipa National Park
Lusenga Plain National Park
Lake Mweru
BUJUMBURA
Rumonge
Uvira
Gihofi
Mabamba
Makamba
Gombe Stream NP
Nyanza-Lac
Kibondo

Dhows

DAVID ELSE

Dhows have been sailing along the coast of East Africa for centuries and, until fairly recently, were the principal trading vessels used between the eastern coast of the continent and the Persian Gulf and India. They once numbered in the thousands but, since the turn of the century, they have declined rapidly in the face of competition from steamships. These days only a few make the journey to the Gulf. Those that remain confine themselves to sailing between the mainland and the offshore islands and between the islands themselves, and even then only in certain areas. Their romantic appeal, nevertheless, remains and a dhow trip around the Lamu archipelago is an extremely popular activity among travellers.

Essentially, all dhows are wooden vessels, either planked or dug out, along with a rudder, mast and lateen (triangular) sail. Like all sail boats, unless motorised they're completely dependent on the wind. Unlike boats with only square sails, they're capable of tacking into the wind.

Dhows are differentiated by size and shape. The largest are known as *jahazi*, which are planked, ocean going vessels with broad hulls and ruggedly designed to be capable of withstanding constant bumping along rocky shores and submerged coral reefs. They can have either one or two lateen sails. Most have woven coconut fibre matting fixed to their sides to reduce splash and a wooden 'eye' attached to each side of the bow below a decorated or carved tailboard. Dhows of this type built in the Lamu archipelago often have a perpendicular bow whereas those from Zanzibar have sloping bows. A jahazi often has a toilet hanging off the stern of the boat.

Motorised versions of the jahazi are known as *mtaboti* or *mchaboti*. The only difference is that these have an inboard motor instead of a sail.

TONY WHEELER

Smaller craft go under a generic name of *mashua* and there are many different types. Around Lamu they're usually known as *kijahazi*. These dhows differ from the jahazi in being smaller, much narrower in the hull and having only one sail. They can be remarkably fast given a favourable wind and are the ones you're most likely to use for trips around Lamu.

Another common type of dhow, smaller still, is the *dau la mwao* – a sort of dugout canoe with a narrow hull, small mast and no keel which sits low in the water and is frequently used for transporting soil, sand and coral rag building blocks. Most do not have a square stem. A variation of this type from the Kizingitini area is the *mtori* which is somewhat smaller and faster and fitted with a keel. Decoration on the mwao and the mtori is restrained. It's interesting to note that the mwao is the nearest surviving relative to the *dau la utango* which was the most common type of dhow found along the coast during the 19th century.

There are excellent models of the various types of the dhow in the Lamu museum. ■

TONY WHEELER

paying for transport and you'll get a better deal on the cost of accommodation.

Which Currency?

Be careful which currency you take with you, as some are difficult or even impossible to change. US dollars, Canadian dollars, UK pounds, French francs, German marks, Swiss francs and Italian lire are all readily accepted. Australian and New Zealand dollars can be difficult to change, except in Nairobi, as the exchange rate may not be known. You don't get this problem with North American and European currencies.

See individual country chapters for exchange rates.

Travellers' Cheques & Cash

For maximum flexibility, take the larger slice of your money in travellers' cheques and the rest in cash – say up to US$500. American Express, Thomas Cook and Citibank cheques are the most widely used and their offices generally offer instant replacement in the event of loss or theft. Keep a record of the cheque numbers and the original bill of sale for the cheques in a safe place, in case you lose your cheques. Replacement is a whole lot quicker if you can produce this information. Even so, if you don't look clean and tidy, or they don't believe your story for some reason or another, replacement can take time, since quite a few travellers have sold their cheques on the black market, or simply pretended to lose them, and then demanded a replacement set. This is particularly so with American Express cheques. You should avoid bringing cheques from small banks which only have a few overseas branches, as you'll find them very difficult, if not impossible, to change in many places.

Make sure that you buy a good range of cheque denominations – such as US$10, US$20, US$50 and US$100 – so that you don't get stuck changing large denomination bills for short stays or for final expenses. Plenty of small cheques are essential for Tanzania if you don't want to end up with a mountain of local currency, since all mid-range and top-end accommodation and all national park fees have to be paid in hard currency. This particularly thorny issue is discussed in greater detail in the Money section of the Tanzania Facts for the Visitor chapter, and you're well advised to read it *before* you leave home.

Carrying a credit card and a personal chequebook is an excellent way of having funds to hand. With these, you can generally withdraw up to US$150 in cash per day and up to US$1000 in travellers' cheques per week from any branch of the credit card company or participating banks. This virtually dispenses with the need to buy travellers' cheques in your home country, though you should take some, since you can only avail yourself of this service during banking hours.

With a Visa card, for example, any main branch of Barclays Bank will let you have the local equivalent of US$150 per day without contacting your bank. For any amount over US$150, they'll fax your bank before giving you the money. You don't need a cheque account to do this. Similarly, American Express offices will issue US dollar travellers' cheques up to a certain limit (usually US$5000 every 20 days) against one of their cards and a personal cheque drawn on your bank. If you don't have a personal chequebook but you do have a credit card, there's usually no problem. Simply present your card and ask for a counter cheque. This is fine even if you don't have an actual cheque account but do have, say, a deposit account. What will happen in that case is that the bank will bounce the cheque which you signed for American Express, and American Express will send you a demand for the money or bill your American Express account. If you're on a long trip, you'll have to arrange for someone back home to pay the monthly accounts.

There are American Express offices or agents in Nairobi, Mombasa, Kampala and Dar es Salaam.

National Westminster Eurocheque cards are another possibility. With one of these and a personal cheque, you can withdraw up to UK£100 a day at selected banks in Kenya,

Tanzania and Uganda. Nominated banks in Kenya are those of the Kenya Commercial Bank at both Kencom House and Kipande House in Nairobi, at Treasury Square in Mombasa, and in Kisumu and Nakuru; the National Bank of Kenya's main branches in Nairobi and Mombasa; and the Standard Chartered Bank's main branches in Nairobi and Mombasa. In Tanzania, Eurocheque cards can be used at the head office of the National Bank of Commerce in Dar es Salaam, and in Uganda at the head offices of either the Stanbic or Uganda Commercial banks in Kampala.

Credit Cards

American Express, Diner's Club, Visa and MasterCard are all widely recognised credit cards which can be used to pay for accommodation, food, airline tickets, books, clothing and other services in most large towns, especially in Kenya (though less so in neighbouring countries). Even Kenyan Railways accepts Visa cards for railway tickets.

Credit cards also have their uses when 'sufficient funds' are demanded by immigration officials before they will allow you to enter a country. It's generally accepted that you have 'sufficient funds' if you have a credit card.

International Transfers

If you run out of money while you're abroad and need more, ask your bank back home to send a draft to you (assuming you have money back home to send). Make sure you specify the city and the bank branch. Transferred by cable or telex, money should reach you within a few days. If you correspond by mail, the process will take at least two weeks, often longer. Remember that some countries will only give you your money in local currency; others will let you have it in US dollars or another hard currency. Find out what's possible before you request a transfer; you could lose a fair amount of money if there's an appreciable difference between the official and unofficial exchange rates. Kenya

is probably the best place to transact this sort of business.

Black Market

You cannot always change travellers' cheques in small places or, of course, when the banks are closed. You should bring some cash with you though, because it allows you to take advantage of any street rate of exchange (black market). Sometimes you can change travellers' cheques on the black market, but this isn't always the case.

During the 1980s, you could get considerably more for your hard currency on the street in Uganda, Tanzania and Zaïre than you could at the banks. The difference in Kenya was minimal. This has all changed with the introduction of foreign exchange bureaus and there's no longer a black market in Kenya, Tanzania or Uganda.

In Rwanda and Burundi, virtually everyone changes on the street (assuming they have cash), since there's a significant difference between the bank rate and the street rate.

Zaïre's economic situation is totally crazy, and any comment about the currency would be outdated as soon as it's made. You'd have to be lobotomised to go to a bank in this country. Zaïre does have a strong black market.

The black market is a thorny issue. Some people regard it as morally reprehensible, even economic sabotage. It's certainly predatory, but some countries used to overvalue their currency to a degree that was totally Mickey Mouse.

You'll have to make up your own mind about which side of the moral fence you stand on, but one thing is for sure – you won't meet many budget travellers who don't use the black market where there's a significant difference between the bank and street rates. And you'll meet plenty of officials – some of them in remarkable positions of authority and in full view of everyone around – who will make it plain that they're interested in swapping local currency for hard cash.

This doesn't mean that you should be

blasé and incautious. Quite the opposite. Discretion is the name of the game.

When changing on the black market, have the exact amount you want to change available – avoid pulling out large wads of notes. Be very wary about sleight of hand and envelope tricks. Insist on personally counting out the notes that are handed to you. Don't allow yourself to be distracted by supposed alarms like 'police' and 'danger'. In many countries you won't have to take part in this sort of mini-drama, as money is generally changed in certain shops or with merchants at a market, so it's a much more leisurely process. Whatever else you do, *don't* actually change on the street, as you may be set up by a police undercover agent.

Treat all the official and black market rates given in this book as a guide only. They are correct at the time the book goes to press, but coups, debt crises, devaluations and IMF 'structural adjustment programs' can alter the picture dramatically. You must check out all prices and exchange rates with your fellow travellers along the way. They are your best source of current information.

Bargaining

Many purchases involve some degree of bargaining. This is always the case with things bought from a market, street stall or craft shop. Bargaining may also be necessary for hotels and transport in some places, though these are often fairly standard and you won't be paying any more than the local people. Food and drink bought at restaurants don't usually involve any bargaining – the prices will be written on the menu.

Where bargaining is the name of the game, commodities are looked on as being worth what their owners can get for them. The concept of a fixed price would invoke laughter. If you cop out and pay the first price asked, you'll not only be considered a halfwit but you'll be doing your fellow travellers a disservice, since this will create the impression that all travellers are equally stupid and are willing to pay outrageous prices. You are expected to bargain – it's part of the fun of going to Africa. All the same,

no matter how good you are at it, you'll never get things as cheaply as local people do. To traders and hotel and cafe owners, you represent wealth – whatever your appearance.

In most cases bargaining is conducted in a friendly, sometimes exaggeratedly extroverted manner, though there are occasions when it degenerates into a bleak exchange of numbers and leaden handshakes. Decide what you want to pay or what others have told you they've paid, and start off at a price at least 50% lower than this. The seller will inevitably start off at a higher price, sometimes up to 100% higher, than they are prepared to accept. This way you can both end up appearing to be generous.

There will be times when you simply cannot get a shopkeeper to lower the prices to anywhere near what you know the product should be selling for. This probably means that a lot of tourists are passing through and if you don't pay those outrageous prices, some mug will. Don't lose your temper bargaining. There's no need to. You can always walk away and come back another day or go to a different shop. It's just theatre.

POST & COMMUNICATIONS

Have letters sent to you c/o Poste Restante, GPO, in whatever city or town you will be passing through. Alternatively, you can use the mail holding service operated by American Express offices and their agents, if you have their cheques or one of their credit cards. Plan ahead – it can take up to two weeks for a letter to arrive even in capital cities, and sometimes much longer in smaller places.

Most embassies will not hold mail and will forward it to the nearest poste restante.

The poste restante services in most of East Africa are pretty reliable. Mail is generally held for four weeks – sometimes more, sometimes less – after which it is returned to the sender. The service is free in most places, but in others (Tanzania, Rwanda, Burundi), there is a small charge for each letter that you collect.

As a rule you need your passport as proof of identity. In large places where there's a lot of traffic, the letters are generally sorted into alphabetical order, but in smaller places, they may all be lumped together in the one box. Sometimes you're allowed to sort through them yourself; sometimes a post office employee will do this for you.

If you have not received expected letters, ask them to check under every conceivable combination of your given name, surname, any other initials and even under 'M' (for Mr, Ms, Miss, Mrs). This sort of confusion isn't as widespread as many people believe, though most travellers have an improbable story to tell about it. If there is confusion, it's generally because of bad handwriting on the envelope or language difficulties. If you want to make absolutely sure that the fault won't be yours, have your friends address letters with your surname in block letters and underlined.

Avoid sending currency notes through the post. They'll often be stolen by post office employees no matter how cleverly you disguise the contents. There are all sorts of ways of finding out whether a letter is worth opening. Still, some people do successfully get cash sent through the mail.

For more Post & Communication information, see that section in each individual country chapter.

BOOKS

You can walk into any decent book shop in Europe, America or Australasia and find countless books on western and eastern history, culture, politics, economics, religion/philosophy, craft and anything else you care to name. Finding the same thing for Africa is somewhat more difficult, except in specialist book shops. Things are improving, however, but so far only in the large-format, hardback, photo-essay genre.

What you will be hard-pressed to find is a good selection of novels, plays and biographies by contemporary African authors, many published by the African branches of major western publishers. Heinemann's African Writers Series offers a major collection of such works but they're generally only available in large African cities. In East Africa, the book shops of Nairobi carry an excellent selection but the choice is considerably more limited in Tanzania and Uganda. In western countries, they're to be found only in specialist book shops.

Most books are published in different editions by different publishers in different countries. As a result, a book might be a hardcover rarity in one country while it's readily available in paperback in another. Fortunately, book shops and libraries search by title or author, so your local book shop or library is best placed to advise you on the availability of the recommendations that follow.

Lonely Planet

Lonely Planet's *Africa on a shoestring* covers more than 50 African countries, concentrating on practical information for budget travellers. *Kenya* is available as a separate guidebook, but also appears in full in the book you are reading.

Lonely Planet's *Trekking in East Africa* by David Else covers a selection of treks and expeditions in the mountains and wilderness areas of Kenya, Tanzania, Uganda and Malawi, and has plenty of advice and general information about trekking in this part of the world.

For coverage of Kenya and northern Tanzania you can't go past Lonely Planet's *Kenya travel atlas*. And Lonely Planet's *Swahili phrasebook* will help you solve most of your basic language problems in East Africa.

Guidebooks

Insight Kenya, edited by Mohammed Amin & John Eames, is another of the popular APA guidebook series with many excellent photographs and a lively text. It concentrates more on the country's history, its peoples, cultures, sights and wildlife than on practical information and is a good book to read either before you go or while you're there.

Guide to Mt Kenya & Kilimanjaro, edited by Iain Allan, has been written and added to over the years by dedicated enthusiasts, but is mainly directed at skilled trekkers and mountaineers. It contains information on the rock and ice routes, but also has some (very dated) trail descriptions, maps, photographs, and descriptions of fauna, flora, climate and geology, even mountain medicine.

The *Camping Guide to Kenya* covers every camp site in Kenya – the cities, national parks and mountain areas – and contains information and advice for campers and backpackers venturing off the main routes into the more remote areas of Kenya.

Mountain Walking in Kenya covers a selection of walking routes through the mountain and highland regions of Kenya, including everything from easy strolls around Lake Naivasha to longer hikes on Mt Kenya. There's an equipment guide as well as accurate maps and colour photographs.

Travellers' & Other Accounts
Dian Fossey's research with the mountain gorillas of Rwanda is recounted in her book *Gorillas in the Mist*. *The White Nile* by Alan Moorehead is a superbly evocative account of the exploration of the upper Nile and the rivalry between the European powers. *Journey to the Jade Sea* by John Hillaby recounts this prolific travel writer's epic trek to Lake Turkana in northern Kenya in the days before the safari trucks began pounding up the dirt there. Other books to look for include *Initiation* by JS Fontaine, *A Bend in the River* by VS Naipaul and *Travels in the Congo* by André Gide.

Two women's accounts of life in East Africa earlier this century have been recent best sellers. *Out of Africa* by Karen Blixen (Isak Dinesen) has also been made into a hugely popular movie. *West with the Night* by Beryl Markham has also been a major best seller. *Last of the Free* by Gareth Patterson is the story of the raising and ultimate release into the wild of three lion cubs left by George Adamson.

Inveterate traveller, Dervla Murphy, recounts her bicycle trip from Kenya to Zimbabwe in *The Ukimwi Road*, a book equally revealing about the impact of HIV/AIDS on the people of Africa.

Unhappy Valley by Bruce Berman & John Lonsdale takes a fresh look at the colonial history of Kenya, while Nigel Pavitt's *Kenya – The First Explorers* has some good photos and extracts from the early European explorers to visit the area.

Safari – A Chronicle of Adventure by Bartle Bull tells the tale of the whole safari business from the early days to today.

History, Politics & Economics
There are numerous books on the history of Africa which include *The Penguin Atlas of African History* by Colin McEvedy, *A Short History of Africa* by Roland Oliver & JD Fage, and *The Story of Africa* by Basil Davidson. Also excellent reading is *The Africans – A Triple Heritage* by Ali A Mazrui, which was published in conjunction with a BBC TV series of the same name.

For the origins and development of the coastal Swahili culture and how it has been affected by the arrival of the Portuguese in the Indian Ocean, the standard work is *The Portuguese Period in East Africa* by Justus Strandes. For a radical African viewpoint of the effects of colonialism in general, Walter Rodney's *How Europe Underdeveloped Africa* is well worth a read.

Worthwhile contemporary accounts include the extremely readable but rather discouraging *The Africans* by David Lamb. Or there's *The Making of Contemporary Africa* by Bill Freund, and *A Year in the Death of Africa* by Peter Gill. On contemporary Kenyan politics, it's well worth reading Oginga Odinga's *Not Yet Uhuru*, and *Detained – A Prison Writer's Diary* by Ngugi wa Thiong'o, for a view radically different from that put out by the Kenyatta and Moi regimes.

Not exclusively about Africa, but very relevant to bilateral and multilateral aid issues, is the *Lords of Poverty* by Graham Hancock, an exposé of the bungling and waste perpetrated by the UN, IMF, World Bank and others.

The *Africa Review*, an annual production by World of Information, offers an overview of the politics and economics of every African country as well as detailed facts and figures. It's well balanced and researched and makes no attempt to curry favour with any particular regime.

Flora & Fauna

A Field Guide to the Larger Mammals of Africa by Jean Dorst & Pierre Dandelot, together with *A Field Guide to the Birds of East Africa* by JG Williams & N Arlott, should suffice for most people's purposes in the national parks and wildlife reserves.

General

There are some excellent but quite expensive photo-essay hardbacks which you may prefer to look for in a library, such as *Journey though Kenya*, by Mohammed Amin, Duncan Willets & Brian Tetley. There is a companion volume entitled *Journey through Tanzania* by the same authors.

Other colourful books on the region include *Africa Adorned* by Angela Fisher; *Ivory Crisis* by Ian Parker & Mohammed Amin; *Isak Dinesen's Africa* by various authors; *Africa: A History of a Continent* by Basil Davidson; and *Through Open Doors: A View of Asian Cultures in Kenya* by Cynthia Salvadori. Salvadori also co-authored with Andrew Fedders *Peoples & Cultures of Kenya*.

In addition to the above, there has recently been a flurry of large-format, hardback books on the various tribal societies of Kenya, especially the Maasai and Samburu, which you'll see in the book shops of Nairobi and Mombasa.

ONLINE SERVICES

As with everything, the World Wide Web has a wealth of information – and a lot of dross – on Africa. Lonely Planet has its own web site with a bulletin board and a postcard section, with information about East Africa from other travellers. Its address is: www.lonelyplanet.com.

The following places are also somewhere to start looking, with interesting information and good links to related sites.

Africa Online
    www.africaonline.com
    www.africaonline.com/AfricaOnline/
        newsstand.html
University of Pennsylvania African Studies Dept
    www.sas.upenn.edu

PHOTOGRAPHY
Film & Equipment

The availability of film varies, from a wide range in Nairobi to virtually nothing in small towns. Kampala and Dar es Salaam also have a decent range these days, but the best bet is still to bring what you need with you. Processing (slides and colour negatives) is reliable in Nairobi; elsewhere it's probably best to hang on to them.

For serious wildlife photography a SLR (single lens reflex) camera which can take long focal length lenses is necessary. If all you have is a little generic 'snapomatic' you may as well leave it behind; although they are becoming more sophisticated these days, the maximum focal length is around 110 mm – still too small for getting decent shots.

Zoom lenses are best for wildlife photography as you can frame your shot easily to get the best composition. This is important as the animals are constantly and often quickly on the move. The 70 to 210 mm zoom lenses are popular and the 200 mm is really the minimum you need to get good close-up shots. The only problem with zoom lenses is that with all the glass (lenses) inside them, they absorb about 1½ 'f' stops of light, which is where the 200 and 400 ASA film starts to become useful.

Telephoto (fixed focal length) lenses give better results than zoom lenses but you're limited by having to carry a separate lens for every focal length. A 400 or 500 mm lens brings the action right up close, but again you need the 200 or 400 ASA film to make the most of them. You certainly need a 400 or 500 mm lens if you're keen on photographing bird life.

Another option is to carry a 2x teleconverter, which is a small adaptor which fits between the lens and the camera body, and doubles the focal length of your lens, so a

200 mm lens becomes 400 mm. These are a good cheap way of getting the long focal length without having to buy expensive lenses. They do, however, have a couple of disadvantages. The first is that, like the larger lenses themselves, a teleconverter uses about 1½ 'f' stops of light. Another disadvantage is that, depending on the camera and lens, teleconverters can make it extremely difficult to focus quickly and precisely, which is an important consideration when both you and the animals are on the move.

When using long lenses a tripod can be extremely useful, and with anything greater than about 300 mm it's a necessity. The problem here is that in the confined space of the hatch of a minibus (assuming you'll be taking an organised safari) it is impossible to set up the tripod, especially when you are sharing the space with at least three or four other people. Miniature tripods are available and these are useful for setting up on the roof of the van, although you can also rest the lens itself on the roof, provided that the van engine is switched off to kill any vibration.

Whatever combination of camera, lenses and accessories you decide to carry, make sure they are kept in a decent bag which will protect them from the elements, the dust and the knocks they are bound to receive. It's also vital to make sure that your travel insurance policy includes your camera gear if it is stolen.

Photographing People

As is the case in any country where you are a tourist, this is a subject which has to be approached with some sensitivity. People such as the Maasai and the Samburu have had so many rubbernecks pointing cameras at them for so many years that they are utterly sick to death of it – with good reason. There are even signs up in Namanga and Amboseli saying that it is prohibited to take photos of the Maasai. This doesn't mean that you can't, but just that you'll have to pay for it. Much as you may find this abhorrent, it is nevertheless an aspect of the tourism industry you'll just have to accept – put yourself in their position and try to think what you'd do.

It is of course possible to take pictures of people with zoom lenses but, most of the time, what's the point? By paying or giving some sort of gift, you'll not only get a better picture by using a smaller lens but you'll have some interaction with your subject. You might even get an invitation to see the family (and possibly photograph them).

TIME

Time in Kenya, Uganda and Tanzania is GMT/UTC plus three hours year-round; in Rwanda, Burundi and eastern Zaïre it's GMT/UTC plus two hours. See the warning regarding Swahili time in the Time section of the Kenya Facts for the Visitor chapter.

ELECTRICITY

The countries of the region use the 240V system. The power supply varies – from reliable in Kenya to widely fluctuating in Tanzania.

Power sockets also vary widely, but are usually of the three-square-pin variety as used in the UK, although some older buildings have round-pin sockets. Bring a universal adaptor if a power supply is important to you.

HEALTH

Travel health depends on your predeparture preparations, your day-to-day health care while travelling and how you handle any medical problem or emergency that does develop. While the list of potential dangers can seem quite frightening, with a little luck, some basic precautions and adequate information, few travellers experience more than upset stomachs.

Travel Health Guides

There are a number of books on travel health you may consider taking:

Staying Healthy in Asia, Africa & Latin America, Dirk Schroeder, Moon Publications, 1994. Probably the best all-round guide to carry, as it's compact but very detailed and well organised.

Travellers' Health, Dr Richard Dawood, Oxford University Press, 1995. Comprehensive, easy to read, authoritative and is also highly recommended, although it's rather large to lug around.

Where There is No Doctor, David Werner, Macmillan, 1994. A very detailed guide which is intended for someone, like a Peace Corps worker, going to work in an underdeveloped country, rather than for the average traveller.

Travel with Children, Maureen Wheeler, Lonely Planet Publications, 1995. Includes basic advice on travel health for younger children.

There are also a number of excellent travel health sites on the Internet. Lonely Planet's home page (http://www.lonelyplanet.com), has links to the World Health Organisation, Centers for Diseases Control & Prevention in Atlanta, Georgia, and Stanford University Travel Medicine Service at http://www.lonelyplanet.com/health/health.htm/h-links.htm.

Predeparture Planning

Health Insurance A travel insurance policy to cover theft, loss and medical problems is a good idea. There is a wide variety of policies available and your travel agent will be able to make recommendations. The policies handled by STA Travel and other student travel organisations are usually good value. Some travel insurance policies offer lower and higher medical-expense options but the higher ones are chiefly for countries such as the USA which have extremely high medical costs. Check the small print:

1. Some policies specifically exclude 'dangerous activities' which can include scuba diving, motorcycling, and even trekking. If such activities are on your agenda you don't want that sort of policy. A locally acquired motor-cycle licence may not be valid under your policy.
2. You may prefer a policy which pays doctors or hospitals direct rather than you having to pay on the spot and claim later. If you have to claim later make sure you keep all documentation. Some policies ask you to call back (reverse charges) to a centre in your home country where an immediate assessment of your problem is made.
3. Check that the policy covers ambulances or an emergency flight home. If you have to stretch out you will need two seats and somebody has to pay for them!

Medical Kit It is wise to carry a small, straightforward medical kit. The kit should include:

- Aspirin or paracetamol (acetaminophen in the USA) – for pain or fever.
- Antihistamine (such as Benadryl) – useful as a decongestant for colds and allergies, to ease the itch from insect bites or stings, and to help prevent motion sickness. There are several antihistamines on the market, all with different pros and cons (eg a tendency to cause drowsiness), so it's worth discussing your requirements with a pharmacist or doctor. Antihistamines may cause sedation and interact with alcohol so care should be taken when using them.
- Antibiotics – useful if you're travelling well off the beaten track, but they must be prescribed and you should carry the prescription with you. Some individuals are allergic to commonly prescribed antibiotics such as penicillin or sulpha drugs. It would be sensible to always carry this information when travelling.
- Loperamide (eg Imodium) or Lomotil are good for diarrhoea; prochlorperazine (eg Stemetil) or metaclopramide (eg Maxalon) for nausea and vomiting. Anti-diarrhoea medication should not be given to children under the age of 12.
- Rehydration mixture – for treatment of severe diarrhoea. This is particularly important if travelling with children, but is recommended for everyone.
- Antiseptic such as povidone-iodine (eg Betadine), which comes as a solution, ointment, powder and impregnated swabs – for cuts and grazes.
- Multivitamins – are a worthwhile consideration, expecially for long trips when dietary vitamin intake may be inadequate.
- Calamine lotion or Stingose spray – to ease irritation from bites or stings.
- Bandages and Band-aids – for minor injuries.
- Scissors, tweezers and a thermometer (note that mercury thermometers are prohibited by airlines).
- Cold and flu tablets and throat lozenges.
- Insect repellent, sunscreen, chap stick and water purification tablets.
- A couple of syringes, in case you need injections in a country with medical hygiene problems. Ask your doctor for a note explaining why they have been prescribed.

Ideally antibiotics should be administered only under medical supervision and should never be taken indiscriminately. Take only the recommended dose at the prescribed intervals and continue using the antibiotic for the prescribed period, even if the illness seems to be cured earlier. Antibiotics are quite specific to the infections they can treat. Stop immediately if there are any serious reactions and don't use the antibiotic at all if you are unsure that you have the correct one.

In East Africa, if a medicine is available at all it will generally be available over the counter and the price will be much cheaper than in the west. However, be careful if buying drugs, particularly where the expiry date may have passed or correct storage conditions may not have been followed. Bogus drugs are not uncommon and it's possible that drugs which are no longer recommended, or have even been banned in the west, are still being dispensed.

Health Preparations Make sure you're healthy before you start travelling. If you are embarking on a long trip make sure your teeth are OK; there are lots of places where a visit to the dentist would be the last thing you'd want.

If you wear glasses take a spare pair and your prescription. Losing your glasses can be a real problem, although in many places you can get new spectacles made up quickly, cheaply and competently.

If you require a particular medication take an adequate supply, as it may not be available locally. Take the prescription or, better still, part of the packaging showing the generic rather than the brand name (which may not be locally available), as it will make getting replacements easier. It's wise to have a legible prescription or a letter from your doctor with you to show that you legally use the medication.

Immunisations Vaccinations provide protection against diseases you might meet along the way. For some countries no immunisations are necessary, but the further off the beaten track you go the more necessary it is to take precautions.

It is important to understand the distinction between vaccines recommended for travel in certain areas and those required by law. Essentially the number of vaccines subject to international health regulations has been dramatically reduced over the last 10 years. Currently yellow fever is the only vaccine subject to international health regulations. Vaccination as an entry requirement is usually only enforced when coming from an infected area.

Occasionally travellers face bureaucratic problems regarding cholera vaccine even though all countries have dropped it as a health requirement for travel. In some situations it may be wise to have the vaccine despite its poor protection, eg for the trans-Africa traveller.

On the other hand a number of vaccines are recommended for travel in certain areas. These may not be required by law but are recommended getting for your own personal protection.

All vaccinations should be recorded on an International Health Certificate, which is available from your physician or government health department.

Plan ahead for getting your vaccinations: some require an initial shot followed by a booster, while some vaccinations should not be given together. It is recommended you seek medical advice at least six weeks prior to travel.

Most travellers from western countries will have been immunised against various diseases during childhood but your doctor may still recommend booster shots against measles or polio, diseases still prevalent in many developing countries. The period of protection offered by vaccinations differs widely and some are contraindicated if you are pregnant.

In some countries immunisations are available from the airport or government health centres. Travel agents or airline offices will tell you where. Vaccinations include:

Tetanus & Diphtheria Boosters are necessary every 10 years and protection is highly recommended.

Polio A booster of either the oral or injected vaccine is required every 10 years to maintain our immunity from childhood vaccination. Polio is a very serious, easily transmitted disease which is still prevalent in many developing countries.

Typhoid Available either as an injection or oral capsules. Protection lasts from one to five years depending on the vaccine and is useful if you are travelling for long in rural, tropical areas.

Hepatitis A The most common travel-acquired illness which can be prevented by vaccination. Protection can be provided in two ways – either with the antibody gamma globulin or with a vaccine called Havrix 1440. Havrix 1440 provides long-term immunity (possibly more than 10 years) after an initial injection and a booster at 6 to 12 months. It may be more expensive than gamma globulin but certainly has many advantages, including length of protection and ease of administration. It is important to know that, being a vaccine, it will take about three weeks to provide satisfactory protection – hence the need for careful planning prior to travel. Gamma globulin is not a vaccination but a ready-made antibody which has proven very successful in reducing the chances of hepatitis infection. It should be given as close as possible to departure because it is at its most effective in the first few weeks after administration and the effectiveness tapers off gradually between three and six months.

Hepatitis B Travellers at risk of contact (see Infectious Diseases, later) are strongly advised to be vaccinated, especially if they are children or will have close contact with children. The vaccination course comprises three injections given over a six month period, then boosters every three to five years. The initial course of injections can also be given over as short a period as 28 days if more rapid protection is required.

Yellow Fever Protection lasts 10 years and is recommended for East Africa; it is a requirement for entering Zanzibar and Pemba. It is also a requirement for many countries when returning home. You usually have to go to a special yellow fever vaccination centre. Vaccination is not recommended during pregnancy but if you must travel to a high-risk area it is probably advisable.

Meninogococcal Meningitis Vaccination is recommended for travellers to East Africa. A single injection will give good protection against the A, C, W and Y groups of the bacteria for at least a year. The vaccine is not, however, recommended for children under two years because they do not develop satisfactory immunity from it.

Rabies Pretravel rabies vaccination involves having three injections over 21 to 28 days and should be considered by those who will spend a month or longer in a country where rabies is common, especially if they are cycling, handling animals, caving, travelling to remote areas, or are children (who may not report

a bite). If someone who has been vaccinated is bitten or scratched by an animal they will require two booster injections of vaccine.

Cholera Not required by law but occasionally travellers can face bureaucratic problems on some border crossings eg Burundi. Protection is poor and it lasts only six months. It is contraindicated in pregnancy.

Smallpox Smallpox has now been wiped out worldwide, so immunisation is no longer necessary.

Basic Rules

Care in what you eat and drink is the most important health rule; stomach upsets are the most likely travel health problem (between 30 and 50% of travellers in a two week stay experience this) but the majority of these upsets will be relatively minor. Don't become paranoid; trying the local food is part of the experience of travel, after all.

Water The number one rule is *don't drink the water* and that includes ice. If you don't know for certain that the water is safe always assume the worst. Reputable brands of bottled water or soft drinks are generally fine, although in some places bottles refilled with tap water are not unknown. Only use water from containers with a serrated seal – not tops or corks. Take care with fruit juice, particularly if water may have been added. Milk should be treated with suspicion, as it is often unpasteurised. Boiled milk is fine if it is kept hygienically. Tea or coffee should also be OK, since the water should have been boiled.

Water Purification The simplest way of purifying water is to boil it thoroughly. Vigorously boiling for five minutes should be satisfactory; however, at high altitude water boils at a lower temperature, so germs are less likely to be killed.

Simple filtering will not remove all dangerous organisms, so if you cannot boil water it should be treated chemically. Chlorine tablets (Puritabs, Steritabs or other brand names) will kill many but not all pathogens, including giardia and amoebic cysts. Iodine is very effective in purifying water and is available in tablet form (such as Potable Aqua), but follow the directions carefully and remember that too much iodine can be harmful.

If you can't find tablets, tincture of iodine (2%) can be used. Four drops of tincture of iodine per litre or quart of clear water is the recommended dosage; the treated water should be left to stand for 20 to 30 minutes before drinking. Iodine crystals can also be used to purify water but this is a more complicated process, as you have to first prepare a saturated iodine solution. Iodine loses its effectiveness if exposed to air or damp so keep it in a tightly sealed container. Flavoured powder will disguise the taste of treated water and is a good idea if you are travelling with children.

Micropur water filters are useful for long trips. They filter out parasites, bacteria and viruses, and although expensive they are more cost effective than buying water.

Food Salads and fruit should be washed with purified water or peeled where possible. Ice cream is usually OK if it is a reputable brand name, but beware of Third World street vendors and of ice cream that has melted and been refrozen. Thoroughly cooked food is safest but not if it has been left to cool or if it has been reheated. Shellfish such as mussels, oysters and clams should be avoided as well as undercooked meat, particularly in the form of mince. Steaming does not make shellfish safe for eating.

If a place looks clean and well run and if the vendor also looks clean and healthy, then the food is probably safe. In general, places that are packed with travellers or locals will be fine, while empty restaurants are questionable. The food in busy restaurants is cooked and eaten quite quickly with little standing around and is probably not being reheated.

Nutrition If your food is poor or limited in availability, if you're travelling hard and fast and therefore missing meals, or if you simply lose your appetite, you can soon start to lose weight and place your health at risk.

Make sure your diet is well balanced.

Eggs, tofu, beans, lentils (dhal in India) and nuts are all safe ways to get protein. Fruit you can peel (bananas, oranges or mandarins for example) is usually safe (melons can harbour bacteria in their flesh and are best avoided) and a good source of vitamins. Try to eat plenty of grains (including rice) and bread. Remember that although food is generally safer if it is cooked well, overcooked food loses much of its nutritional value. If your diet isn't well balanced or if your food intake is insufficient, it's a good idea to take vitamin and iron pills.

In hot weather make sure you drink enough – don't rely on feeling thirsty to indicate when you should drink. Not needing to urinate or very dark yellow urine is a danger sign. Always carry a water bottle with you on long trips. Excessive sweating can lead to loss of salt and therefore muscle cramping. Salt tablets are not a good idea as a preventative, but in places where salt is not used much, adding salt to food can help.

Everyday Health Clean your teeth with purified water rather than straight from the tap. Avoid climatic extremes: keep out of the sun when it's hot, dress warmly when it's cold. Avoid potential diseases by dressing sensibly. You can get worm infections through walking barefoot or dangerous coral cuts by walking over coral without shoes. You can avoid insect bites by covering bare skin when insects are around, by screening windows or beds and by using insect repellents. Seek local advice: if you're told the water is unsafe due to jellyfish, crocodiles or bilharzia, don't go in. In situations where there is no information, discretion is the better part of valour.

Medical Problems & Treatment
Potential medical problems can be broken down into several areas. Firstly there are the problems caused by extremes of temperature, altitude or motion. Then there are diseases and illnesses caused through poor environmental sanitation, insect bites or stings, and animal or human contact. Simple

cuts, bites and scratches can also cause problems.

Self-diagnosis and treatment can be risky, so wherever possible seek qualified help. Although we do give drug dosages in this section, they are for emergency use only. Medical advice should be sought where possible before administering any drugs.

In Nairobi an embassy or consulate can usually recommend a good place to go for such advice. So can five-star hotels, although they often recommend doctors with five-star prices. (This is when that medical insurance really comes in useful!) In some places standards of medical attention are so low that for some ailments the best advice is to get on a plane and go somewhere else.

Vital Signs

A normal body temperature is 98.6°F or 37°C; more than 2°C (4°F) higher is a 'high' fever. A normal adult pulse rate is 60 to 80 beats per minute (children 80 to 100, babies 100 to 140). You should know how to take a temperature and a pulse rate. As a general rule the pulse increases about 20 beats per minute for each 1°C rise in fever.

Respiration (breathing) rate is also an indicator of illness. Count the number of breaths per minute: between 12 and 20 is normal for adults and older children (up to 30 for younger children, 40 for babies). People with a high fever or serious respiratory illness (like pneumonia) breathe more quickly than normal. More than 40 shallow breaths a minute usually means pneumonia. ∎

Environmental Hazards

Sunburn In the tropics, the desert or at high altitude you can get sunburnt surprisingly quickly, even through cloud. Use a sunscreen and take extra care to cover areas which don't normally see sun – eg your feet. A hat provides added protection, and you should also use zinc cream or some other barrier cream for your nose and lips. Calamine lotion is good for mild sunburn.

Prickly Heat Prickly heat is an itchy rash caused by excessive perspiration trapped under the skin. It usually strikes people who have just arrived in a hot climate and whose pores have not yet opened sufficiently to cope with greater sweating. Keeping cool but bathing often, using a mild talcum powder or even resorting to air-conditioning, may help until you acclimatise.

Heat Exhaustion Dehydration or salt deficiency can cause heat exhaustion. Take time to acclimatise to high temperatures and make sure you get sufficient liquids. Wear loose clothing and a broad-brimmed hat. Do not do anything too physically demanding.

Salt deficiency is characterised by fatigue, lethargy, headaches, giddiness and muscle cramps and in this case salt tablets may help. Vomiting or diarrhoea can deplete your liquid and salt levels. Anhydrotic heat exhaustion, caused by an inability to sweat, is quite rare. Unlike the other forms of heat exhaustion it is likely to strike people who have been in a hot climate for some time, rather than newcomers.

Heat Stroke This serious, sometimes fatal, condition can occasionally occur if the body's heat-regulating mechanism breaks down and the body temperature rises to dangerous levels. Long, continuous periods of exposure to high temperatures can leave you vulnerable to heat stroke. You should avoid excessive alcohol or strenuous activity when you first arrive in a hot climate.

The symptoms are feeling unwell, not sweating very much or at all and a high body temperature (39 to 41°C). Where sweating has ceased the skin becomes flushed and red. Severe, throbbing headaches and lack of coordination will also occur, and the sufferer may be confused or aggressive. Eventually the victim will become delirious or convulse. Hospitalisation is essential, but meanwhile get victims out of the sun, remove their clothing, cover them with a wet sheet or towel and then fan continually.

Fungal Infections Fungal infections, which

occur with greater frequency in hot weather, are most likely to occur on the scalp, between the toes or fingers (athlete's foot), in the groin (jock itch or crotch rot) and on the body (ringworm). You get ringworm (which is a fungal infection, not a worm) from infected animals or by walking on damp areas, like shower floors.

To prevent fungal infections wear loose, comfortable clothes, avoid artificial fibres, wash frequently and dry carefully. If you do get an infection, wash the infected area daily with a disinfectant or medicated soap and water, and rinse and dry well. Apply an antifungal cream or powder like the widely available Tinaderm. Try to expose the infected area to air or sunlight as much as possible and wash all towels and underwear in hot water as well as changing them often.

Hypothermia Too much cold is just as dangerous as too much heat, particularly if it leads to hypothermia. If you are trekking on Mt Kenya be prepared.

Hypothermia occurs when the body loses heat faster than it can produce it and the core temperature of the body falls. It is surprisingly easy to progress from very cold to dangerously cold due to a combination of wind, wet clothing, fatigue and hunger, even if the air temperature is above freezing. It is best to dress in layers; silk, wool and some of the new artificial fibres are all good insulating materials. A hat is important, as a lot of heat is lost through the head. A strong, waterproof outer layer is essential, as keeping dry is vital. Carry basic supplies, including food containing simple sugars to generate heat quickly and lots of fluid to drink. A space blanket is something all travellers in cold environments should carry.

Symptoms of hypothermia are exhaustion, numb skin (particularly toes and fingers), shivering, slurred speech, irrational or violent behaviour, lethargy, stumbling, dizzy spells, muscle cramps and violent bursts of energy. Irrationality may take the form of sufferers claiming they are warm and trying to take off their clothes.

To treat mild hypothermia, first get the person out of the wind and/or rain, remove their clothing if it's wet and replace it with dry, warm clothing. Give them hot liquids – not alcohol – and some high-kilojoule, easily digestible food. Do not rub victims, instead allow them to slowly warm themselves. This should be enough to treat the early stages of hypothermia. The early recognition and treatment of mild hypothermia is the only way to prevent severe hypothermia, which is a critical condition.

Altitude Sickness Acute Mountain Sickness or AMS occurs at high altitude and can be fatal. The lack of oxygen at high altitudes (over 2500m) affects most people to some extent. It may be mild (benign AMS) or severe (malignant AMS) and occurs because less oxygen reaches the muscles and the brain at high altitude, requiring the heart and lungs to compensate by working harder. Symptoms usually develop during the first 24 hours at altitude but may be delayed up to three weeks. Symptoms of benign AMS include headache, lethargy, dizziness, difficulty sleeping and loss of appetite. Malignant AMS may develop from benign AMS or without warning and can be fatal. Symptoms include breathlessness, dry cough (which may progress to the production of pink, frothy sputum), severe headache, lack of coordination and balance, confusion, irrational behaviour, vomiting, drowsiness and unconsciousness.

In benign AMS the treatment is to remain resting at the same altitude until recovery, usually a day or two. Paracetamol or aspirin can be taken for headaches. If symptoms persist or become worse, however, descent is necessary; even 500m can help. The treatment of malignant AMS is immediate descent to a lower altitude. There are various drug treatments available but they should never be used to avoid descent or enable further ascent by a person with AMS.

There is no hard-and-fast rule as to how high is too high: AMS has been fatal at altitudes of 3000m, although 3500 to 4500m is the usual range. A number of measures can be adopted to prevent acute mountain sickness:

- Ascend slowly – have frequent rest days, spending two to three nights at each rise of 1000m. If you reach a high altitude by trekking, acclimatisation takes place gradually and you are less likely to be affected than if you fly direct.
- The altitude at which a person sleeps is an important factor. It is always wise to sleep at a lower altitude than the greatest height reached during the day. Also, once above 3000m, care should be taken not to increase the sleeping altitude by more than 300m per day.
- Drink extra fluids. Mountain air is dry and cold and moisture is lost as you breathe.
- Eat light, high-carbohydrate meals for more energy.
- Avoid alcohol as this may increase the risk of dehydration.
- Avoid sedatives.
- The drugs acetazolamide (Diamox) and dexamethasone have been recommended for prevention of AMS. They can reduce the symptoms, but they also mask warning signs; severe and fatal AMS has occurred in people taking these drugs. In general they are not recommended for travellers.

Motion Sickness Eating lightly before and during a trip will reduce the chances of motion sickness. If you are prone to motion sickness try to find a place that minimises disturbance – near the wing on aircraft, close to midships on boats, near the centre on buses. Fresh air usually helps; reading and cigarette smoke don't. Commercial motion-sickness preparations, which can cause drowsiness, have to be taken before the trip commences; when you're feeling sick it's too late. Ginger (available in capsule form) and peppermint (including mint-flavoured sweets) are natural preventatives.

Infectious Diseases

Diarrhoea A change of water, food or climate can all cause the runs; diarrhoea caused by contaminated food or water is more serious. Despite all your precautions you may still get a mild bout of travellers' diarrhoea but a few rushed toilet trips with no other symptoms is not indicative of a serious problem. Moderate diarrhoea, involving half-a-dozen loose movements in a day, is more of a nuisance.

Dehydration is the main danger with any diarrhoea, particularly for children where dehydration can occur quite quickly. Fluid replacement remains the mainstay of management. Weak black tea with a little sugar, soda water, or soft drinks allowed to go flat and diluted 50% with water are all good. With severe diarrhoea a rehydrating solution is necessary to replace minerals and salts. Commercially available ORS (oral rehydration salts) are very useful; add the contents of one sachet to a litre of boiled or bottled water. In an emergency you can make up a solution of eight teaspoons of sugar to a litre of boiled water and provide salted cracker biscuits at the same time. You should stick to a bland diet as you recover.

Lomotil or Imodium can be used to bring relief from the symptoms, although they do not actually cure the problem. Only use these drugs if absolutely necessary – eg if you *must* travel. Lomotil and Imodium are not recommended for children under 12 years. Under all circumstances fluid replacement is the most important thing to remember. Do not use these drugs if the person has a high fever or is severely dehydrated.

In certain situations antibiotics may be indicated:

- Watery diarrhoea with blood and mucous. (Gut-paralysing drugs like Imodium or Lomotil should be avoided in this situation.)
- Watery diarrhoea with fever and lethargy.
- Persistent diarrhoea not improving after 48 hours.
- Severe diarrhoea, if it is logistically difficult to stay in one place.

The recommended drugs (adults only) would be either norfloxacin 400 mg twice daily for three days or ciprofloxacin 500 mg twice daily for three days.

The drug bismuth subsalicylate has also been used successfully. It is not available in some countries. The dosage for adults is two tablets or 30ml and for children it is one tablet or 10ml. This dose can be repeated every 30 minutes to one hour, with no more than eight doses in a 24 hour period.

The drug of choice in children would be co-trimoxazole (Bactrim, Septrin, Resprim) with dosage dependent on weight. A five day course is given. This is a sulpha drug and must not be used by people with a known sulpha allergy.

Ampicillin has been recommended in the past and may still be an alternative.

Giardiasis The parasite causing this intestinal disorder is present in contaminated water. The symptoms are stomach cramps, nausea, a bloated stomach, watery, foul-smelling diarrhoea and frequent gas. Giardiasis can appear several weeks after you have been exposed to the parasite. The symptoms may disappear for a few days and then return; this can go on for several weeks. Tinidazole, known as Fasigyn, or metronidazole (Flagyl) are the recommended drugs for treatment. Either can be used in a single treatment dose.

Dysentery This serious illness is caused by contaminated food or water and is characterised by severe diarrhoea, often with blood or mucus in the stool. There are two kinds of dysentery. Bacillary dysentery is characterised by a high fever and rapid onset; headache, vomiting and stomach pains are also symptoms. It generally does not last longer than a week, but bacillary dysentery is highly contagious.

Amoebic dysentery is often more gradual in the onset of symptoms, with cramping abdominal pain and vomiting less likely; fever may not be present. Amoebic dysentery is not a self-limiting disease: it will persist until treated and can recur and cause long-term health problems.

A stool test is necessary to diagnose which kind of dysentery you have, so you should seek medical help urgently. In case of an emergency the drugs norfloxacin or ciprofloxacin can be used as presumptive treatment for bacillary dysentery, and metronidazole (Flagyl) for amoebic dysentery.

For bacillary dysentery, norfloxacin 400 mg twice daily for seven days or ciprofloxacin 500 mg twice daily for seven days are the recommended dosages.

If you're unable to find either of these drugs then a useful alternative is co-trimoxazole 160/800 mg (Bactrim, Septrin, Resprim) twice daily for seven days. This is a sulpha drug and must not be used by people with a known sulpha allergy.

In the case of children co-trimoxazole is a reasonable first-line treatment. For amoebic dysentery, the recommended adult dosage of metronidazole (Flagyl) is one 750 mg to 800 mg capsule three times daily for five days. Children aged between eight and 12 years should have half the adult dose; the dosage for younger children is one-third the adult dose.

An alternative drug to Flagyl is Fasigyn (tinidazole), taken as a two gram daily dose for three days. Alcohol must be avoided during treatment and also for 48 hours after treatment.

Cholera Cholera vaccination is not very effective. The bacteria responsible for this disease are waterborne, so attention to the rules of eating and drinking should protect the traveller.

Outbreaks of cholera are generally widely reported, so you can avoid such problem areas. The disease is characterised by a sudden onset of acute diarrhoea with 'rice water' stools, vomiting, muscular cramps and extreme weakness. You need medical help – but treat for dehydration, which can be extreme, and if there is an appreciable delay in getting to hospital then begin taking tetracycline. The adult dose is 250 mg four times daily. It is not recommended for children aged eight years or under nor for pregnant women. An alternative drug is Ampicillin. Remember that while antibiotics might kill the bacteria, it is a toxin produced by the bacteria which causes the massive fluid loss. Fluid replacement is by far the most important aspect of treatment.

Viral Gastroenteritis This is caused not by bacteria but, as the name suggests, by a virus. It is characterised by stomach cramps, diarrhoea, and sometimes by vomiting and/or a slight fever. All you can do is rest and drink lots of fluids.

Hepatitis Hepatitis is a general term for inflammation of the liver. There are many causes of this condition: drugs, alcohol and infections are but a few.

Viral hepatitis can be divided into two groups on the basis of how it is spread. The first route of transmission is via contaminated food and water (leading to hepatitis A and E) and the second route is via blood and bodily fluids (resulting in hepatitis B, C and D).

Hepatitis A This is a very common disease in most countries, especially those with poor standards of sanitation. Most people in developing countries are infected as children; they often don't develop symptoms, but do develop lifelong immunity. The disease poses a real threat to the traveller, as people are unlikely to have been exposed to hepatitis A in developed countries.

The symptoms are fever, chills, headache, fatigue, feelings of weakness and aches and pains, followed by loss of appetite, nausea, vomiting, abdominal pain, dark urine, light-coloured faeces, jaundiced skin and the whites of the eyes may turn yellow. You should seek medical advice, but in general there is not much you can do apart from resting, drinking lots of fluids, eating lightly and avoiding fatty foods. People who have had hepatitis must forego alcohol for six months after the illness, as hepatitis attacks the liver and it needs that amount of time to recover.

The routes of transmission are via contaminated water, shellfish contaminated by sewerage, or foodstuffs sold by food handlers with poor standards of hygiene.

Taking care with what you eat and drink can go a long way towards preventing this disease. But this is a very infectious virus, so if there is any risk of exposure, additional cover is highly recommended.

Hepatitis E This is a very recently discovered virus, of which little is yet known. It appears to be rather common in developing countries, generally causing mild hepatitis, although it can be very serious in pregnant women.

Care with water supplies is the only current prevention, as there are no specific vaccines for this type of hepatitis. At present it doesn't appear to be too great a risk for travellers.

The following strains are spread by contact with blood and bodily fluids:

Hepatitis B This is also a very common disease, with almost 300 million chronic carriers in the world. Hepatitis B, which used to be called serum hepatitis, is spread through contact with infected blood, blood products or bodily fluids, for example through sexual contact, unsterilised needles and blood transfusions, or via small breaks in the skin. Other risk situations include having a shave or tattoo in a local shop, or having your body pierced. The symptoms of type B are much the same as type A except that they are more severe and may lead to irreparable liver damage or even liver cancer. Although there is no treatment for hepatitis B, a cheap and effective vaccine is available; the only problem is that for long-lasting cover you need a six month course. People who should receive a hepatitis B vaccination include anyone who anticipates contact with blood or other bodily secretions, either as a healthcare worker or through sexual contact with the local population, particularly those who intend to stay in the country for a long period of time.

Hepatitis C This is another recently defined virus. It is a concern because it seems to lead to liver disease more rapidly than hepatitis B.

The virus is spread by contact with blood – usually via contaminated transfusions or shared needles. Avoiding these is the only means of prevention, as there is no available vaccine.

Hepatitis D Often referred to as the 'Delta' virus, this infection only occurs in chronic carriers of hepatitis B. It is transmitted by blood and bodily fluids. Again there is no vaccine for this virus, so avoidance is the best prevention. The risk to travellers is certainly limited.

Typhoid Typhoid fever is another gut infection where contaminated water and food are responsible. Vaccination against typhoid is not totally effective and it is one of the most dangerous infections, so medical help must be sought.

In its early stages typhoid resembles many other illnesses: sufferers may feel like they have a bad cold or flu on the way, as early symptoms are a headache, a sore throat and a fever which rises a little each day until it is around 40°C or more. The victim's pulse is often slow relative to the degree of fever present and gets slower as the fever rises – unlike a normal fever where the pulse increases. There may also be vomiting, diarrhoea or constipation.

In the second week the high fever and slow pulse continue and a few pink spots may appear on the body; trembling, delirium, weakness, weight loss and dehydration are other symptoms. If there are no further complications, the fever and other symptoms will slowly diminish during the third week. However you must get medical help before this because pneumonia (acute infection of the lungs) or peritonitis (perforated bowel) are common complications, and because typhoid is very infectious.

The fever should be treated by keeping the victim cool and dehydration should also be watched for.

The drug of choice is ciprofloxacin at a dose of one gram daily for 14 days. It is quite expensive and may not be available. The alternative, chloramphenicol, has been the mainstay of treatment for many years. In many countries it is still the recommended antibiotic but there are fewer side effects with Ampicillin. The adult dosage is two 250 mg capsules, four times a day. Children aged between eight and 12 years should have half the adult dose; younger children should have one-third the adult dose.

People who are allergic to penicillin should not be given Ampicillin.

Worms These parasites are most common in rural, tropical areas and a stool test when you return home is not a bad idea. They can be present on unwashed vegetables or in undercooked meat and you can pick them up through your skin by walking in bare feet. Infestations may not show up for some time, and although they are generally not serious, if left untreated they can cause severe health problems. A stool test is necessary to pinpoint the problem and medication is often available over the counter.

Tetanus This potentially fatal disease is found worldwide, occurring more commonly in undeveloped tropical areas. It is difficult to treat but is preventable with immunisation. Tetanus occurs when a wound becomes infected by a germ which lives in soil and in the faeces of horses and other animals, so clean all cuts, punctures or animal bites. Tetanus is also known as lockjaw, and the first symptom may be discomfort in swallowing, or stiffening of the jaw and neck; this is followed by painful convulsions of the jaw and whole body.

Rabies Rabies is a fatal viral infection found in many countries and is caused by a bite or scratch by an infected animal. Dogs are noted carriers as are monkeys and cats. Any bite, scratch or even lick from a warm-blooded, furry animal should be cleaned immediately and thoroughly. Scrub with soap and running water, and then clean with an alcohol or iodine solution. If there is any possibility that the animal is infected medical help should be sought immediately to prevent the onset of symptoms and death. In a person who has not been immunised against rabies this involves having five injections of vaccine and one of immunoglobulin over 28 days starting as soon as possible after the exposure. Even if the animal is not rabid, all bites should be taken seriously as they can become infected or can result in tetanus.

A rabies vaccination is now available and should be considered if you are in a high-risk category – eg if you intend to explore caves (bat bites can be dangerous), work with animals, or travel so far off the beaten track that medical help is more than two days away.

Meningococcal Meningitis This is a bacterial infection of the lining of the brain. Sub-Saharan Africa is considered the 'meningitis belt' and the meningitis season falls at the time most people would be attempting the overland trip across the Sahara – the northern winter before the rains come.

This very serious disease attacks the brain and can be fatal. A scattered, blotchy rash, fever, severe headache, sensitivity to light and neck stiffness which prevents forward bending of the head are the first symptoms. Death can occur within a few hours, so immediate treatment is important.

Treatment is large doses of penicillin given intravenously, or, if that is not possible, intramuscularly (ie in the buttocks). Vaccination offers good protection for over a year, but you should also check for reports of current epidemics.

Tuberculosis (TB) Tuberculosis is a bacterial infection which is widespread in many developing countries. It is usually transmitted from person to person by coughing but may be transmitted through consumption of unpasteurised milk. Milk that has been boiled is safe to drink, and the souring of milk to make yoghurt or cheese also kills the bacilli. Typically many months of contact with the infected person are required before the disease is passed on so it is not considered a serious risk to travellers.

The usual site of the disease is the lungs, although other organs may be involved. Most infected people never develop symptoms. In those who do, especially infants, symptoms may arise within weeks of the infection occurring and may be severe. In most, however, the disease lies dormant for many years until, for some reason, the infected person becomes physically run down. Symptoms include fever, weight loss, night sweats and coughing. Vaccination against tuberculosis may prevent serious disease so is recommended especially for young children who are likely to be heavily exposed to infected people.

Schistosomiasis Also known as bilharzia, this disease, is carried in water by minute worms. The larvae infect certain varieties of freshwater snails found in rivers, streams, lakes and behind dams. The worms multiply and are eventually discharged into the water surrounding the snails.

They attach themselves to your intestines or bladder, where they produce large numbers of eggs. The worm enters through the skin, and the first symptom may be a tingling and sometimes a light rash around the area where it entered. Weeks later, when the worm is busy producing eggs, a high fever may develop. A general feeling of being unwell may be the first symptom; once the disease is established abdominal pain and blood in the urine are other signs. The infection often causes no symptoms until the disease is well established (several months to years after exposure) and damage to internal organs irreversible.

Avoiding swimming or bathing in fresh water where bilharzia is present is the main method of preventing the disease. Even deep water can be infected. If you do get wet, dry off quickly and dry your clothes as well. Seek medical attention if you have been exposed to the disease, even if you don't have any symptoms, and tell the doctor your suspicions, as bilharzia in the early stages can be confused with malaria or typhoid. If you cannot get medical help immediately, praziquantel (Biltricide) is the recommended treatment. The recommended dosage is 40 mg/kg in divided doses over one day. Niridazole is an alternative drug.

Diphtheria Diphtheria can be a skin infection or a more dangerous throat infection. It is spread by contaminated dust contacting the skin or by the inhalation of infected cough or sneeze droplets. Frequent washing and keeping the skin dry will help prevent skin infection. The mainstay of treatment of the diphtheria throat infection is an intravenous infusion of diphtheria antitoxin. The antitoxin is produced in horses so may be associated with allergic reactions in some people. Because of this it must be administered under close medical supervision.

Antibiotics such as erythromycin or penicillin are then given to eradicate the diphtheria bacteria from the patient so that it is not transmitted to others. A vaccination is available to prevent the throat infection.

Sexually Transmitted Diseases Sexual contact with an infected sexual partner spreads these diseases. While abstinence is the only 100% preventative, using condoms is also effective. Gonorrhoea, herpes and syphilis are the most common of these diseases; sores, blisters or rashes around the genitals, discharges or pain when urinating are common symptoms. Symptoms may be less marked or not observed at all in women. Syphilis symptoms eventually disappear completely but the disease continues and can cause severe problems in later years. The treatment of gonorrhoea and syphilis is with antibiotics.

There are numerous other sexually transmitted diseases, for most of which effective treatment is available. However, there is no cure for herpes and there is also currently no cure for AIDS.

HIV/AIDS HIV, the Human Immunodeficiency Virus, may develop into AIDS, Acquired Immune Deficiency Syndrome. HIV is a huge problem in East Africa, and the statistics are frightening. Not only are the health services being stretched way beyond limits – it's estimated that 50% of Kenyan hospital cases are HIV-related – but life expectancy is dropping rapidly, and it has been estimated that by the turn of the century Kenya will have one million AIDS orphans.

Any exposure to blood, blood products or bodily fluids may put the individual at risk. In many developing countries transmission is predominantly through heterosexual sexual activity. This is quite different from industrialised countries where transmission is mostly through contact between homosexual or bisexual males, or via contaminated needles shared by IV drug users. Apart from abstinence, the most effective preventative is always to practise safe sex using condoms. It is impossible to detect the HIV-positive status of an otherwise healthy-looking person without a blood test.

HIV/AIDS can also be spread through infected blood transfusions; donors in Kenya are rarely screened for HIV/AIDS. It can also be spread by dirty needles – vaccinations, acupuncture, tattooing and ear or nose piercing can be potentially as dangerous as intravenous drug use if the equipment is not clean. If you do need an injection, ask to see the syringe unwrapped in front of you, or better still, take a needle and syringe pack with you overseas – it is a cheap insurance package against infection with HIV.

Fear of HIV infection should never preclude treatment for serious medical conditions. Although there may be a risk of infection, it is very small indeed.

Insect-Borne Diseases

Malaria This serious disease is spread by mosquito bites. It is extremely important to take malarial prophylactics. Symptoms include headaches, fever, chills and sweating which may subside and recur. Without treatment malaria can develop more serious, potentially fatal effects.

Antimalarial drugs do not prevent you from being infected but kill the parasites during a stage in their development.

There are a number of different types of malaria. The one of most concern is falciparum malaria which is responsible for the very serious cerebral malaria. It is the predominant form in many malaria-prone areas of the world. Contrary to popular belief cerebral malaria is not a new strain.

The problem in recent years has been the emergence of increasing resistance to commonly used antimalarials like chloroquine, maloprim and proguanil. Newer drugs such as mefloquine (Lariam) and antibiotics such as doxycycline (Vibramycin, Doryx) are often recommended for chloroquine and multi-drug resistant areas. Expert advice should be sought, as there are many factors to consider when deciding on the type of antimalarial medication, including the area to be visited, the risk of exposure to malaria-carrying mosquitoes, your medical history, and your age and pregnancy status. It is also important to discuss the side-effect profile of the medication, so you can work out some level of risk versus benefit ratio. It is also very important to be sure of the correct dosage of the medication prescribed to you. Some people have inadvertently taken weekly medication (chloroquine) on a daily basis, with disastrous effects. While discussing dosages for prevention of malaria, it is often advisable to include the dosages required for treatment, especially if your trip is through a high-risk area that would isolate you from medical care.

The main messages are:

1. Primary prevention must always be in the form of mosquito-avoidance measures. The mosquitoes that transmit malaria bite from dusk to dawn and during this period travellers are advised to:
   - wear light-coloured clothing
   - wear long pants and long sleeved shirts
   - use mosquito repellents containing the compound DEET on exposed areas (overuse of DEET may be harmful, especially to children, but its use is considered preferable to being bitten by disease-transmitting mosquitoes)
   - avoid highly scented perfumes or aftershave
   - use a mosquito net – it may be worth taking your own
2. While no antimalarial is 100% effective, taking the most appropriate drug significantly reduces the risk of contracting the disease.
3. No-one should ever die from malaria. It can be diagnosed by a simple blood test. Symptoms range from fever, chills and sweating, headache and abdominal pains to a vague feeling of ill-health, so seek examination immediately if there is any suggestion of malaria.

Contrary to popular belief, once a person contracts malaria he/she does not have it for life. Two species of the parasite may lie dormant in the liver but they can also be eradicated using a specific medication. Malaria is curable, as long as the person seeks medical help when symptoms occur.

Antimalarial drugs are available in pharmacies in Nairobi. Lariam (mefloquine) costs KSh 1200 for four tablets; Paludrine (proguanil) tablets are KSh 15 each.

Dengue Fever There is no prophylactic available for this mosquito-spread disease; the main preventative measure is to avoid mosquito bites. A sudden onset of fever, headaches and severe joint and muscle pains are the first signs before a rash starts on the trunk of the body and spreads to the limbs and face. After a further few days, the fever will subside and recovery will begin. Serious complications are not common but full recovery can take up to a month or more.

Yellow Fever This disease is endemic in East Africa. This viral disease is transmitted to humans by mosquitoes; the initial symptoms are fever, headache, abdominal pain and vomiting. There may appear to be a brief recovery before the disease progresses to more severe complications, including liver failure. There is no medical treatment apart from keeping the fever down and avoiding dehydration, but yellow fever vaccination gives good protection for 10 years.

Typhus Typhus is spread by ticks, mites or lice. It begins with fever, chills, headache and muscle pains followed a few days later by a body rash. There is often a large painful sore at the site of the bite and nearby lymph nodes are swollen and painful. Treatment is with tetracycline, or chloramphenicol under medical supervision.

Tick typhus is spread by ticks. Seek local advice on areas where ticks pose a danger and always check your skin carefully for ticks after walking in a danger area such as a tropical forest. A strong insect repellent can help, and serious walkers in tick areas should consider having their boots and trousers impregnated with benzyl benzoate and dibutylphthalate.

Sleeping Sickness In parts of tropical Africa tsetse flies can carry trypanosomiasis or sleeping sickness. They pass it on by biting large, warm-blooded animals and are responsible for the lack of horses and cows in some areas. The tsetse fly is about twice the size of a housefly and recognisable by the scissor-like way it folds its wings when at rest. Only a small proportion of tsetse flies carry the disease but it is best to try to avoid being bitten; there is no immunisation. The flies are attracted to large moving objects such as safari buses, to perfume and aftershave, and to colours like dark blue. Swelling at the site of the bite, five or more days later, is the first sign of infection; this is followed within two to three weeks by fever. The illness is serious but responds well to medical attention.

Cuts, Bites & Stings

Cuts & Scratches Skin punctures can easily become infected in hot climates and may be difficult to heal. Treat any cut with an antiseptic such as povidone-iodine. Where possible avoid bandages and Band-aids, which can keep wounds wet. Coral cuts are notoriously slow to heal and if they are not adequately cleaned small pieces of coral can become embedded in the wound. Avoid coral cuts by wearing shoes when walking on reefs, and clean any cut thoroughly with sodium peroxide if available.

Bites & Stings Bee and wasp stings are usually painful rather than dangerous. Calamine lotion or Stingose spray will give relief and ice packs will reduce the pain and swelling. There are some spiders with dangerous bites but antivenenes are usually available. Scorpion stings are notoriously painful although not fatal in this part of the world. Scorpions often shelter in shoes or clothing.

Snakes To minimise your chances of being bitten always wear boots, socks and long trousers when walking through undergrowth where snakes may be present. Don't put your hands into holes and crevices, and be careful when collecting firewood.

Snake bites do not cause instantaneous death and antivenenes are usually available. Keep the victim calm and still, wrap the bitten limb tightly, as you would for a sprained ankle, and then attach a splint to immobilise it. Then seek medical help, if possible with the dead snake for identification. Don't attempt to catch the snake if there is even a remote possibility of being bitten

again. Tourniquets and sucking out the poison are not useful and are now comprehensively discredited.

Bedbugs & Lice Bedbugs live in various places, but particularly in dirty mattresses and bedding. Spots of blood on bedclothes or on the wall around the bed can be read as a suggestion to find another hotel. Bedbugs leave itchy bites in neat rows. Calamine lotion or Stingose spray may help.

All lice cause itching and discomfort. They make themselves at home in your hair (head lice), your clothing (body lice) or in your pubic hair (crabs). You catch lice through direct contact with infected people or by sharing combs, clothing and the like. Powder or shampoo treatment will kill the lice and infected clothing should then be washed in very hot water.

Leeches & Ticks Leeches may be present in damp rainforest conditions; they attach themselves to your skin to suck your blood. Trekkers often get them on their legs or in their boots. Salt or a lighted cigarette end will make them fall off. Do not pull them off, as the bite is then more likely to become infected. An insect repellent may keep them away. You should always check your body if you have been walking through a potentially tick-infested area as ticks can cause skin infections and other more serious diseases. If a tick is found attached, press down around the tick's head with tweezers, grab the head and gently pull upwards. Avoid pulling the rear of the body as this may squeeze the tick's gut contents through the attached mouth parts into the skin, increasing the risk of infection and disease. Smearing chemicals on the tick will not make it let go and is not recommended.

Women's Health

Gynaecological Problems Poor diet, lowered resistance due to the use of antibiotics for stomach upsets and even contraceptive pills can lead to vaginal infections when travelling in hot climates. Maintaining good personal hygiene, and wearing skirts or loose-fitting trousers and cotton underwear will help to prevent infections.

Yeast infections, characterised by a rash, itch and discharge, can be treated with a vinegar or lemon-juice douche, or with yoghurt. Nystatin, miconazole or clotrimazole suppositories are the usual medical prescription. Trichomoniasis and gardnerella are more serious infections; symptoms are a smelly discharge and sometimes a burning sensation when urinating. Male sexual partners must also be treated, and if a vinegar-water douche is not effective medical attention should be sought. Metronidazole (Flagyl) is the prescribed drug.

Pregnancy Most miscarriages occur during the first three months of pregnancy, so this is the most risky time to travel as far as your own health is concerned. Miscarriage is not uncommon, and can occasionally lead to severe bleeding. The last three months should also be spent within reasonable distance of good medical care. A baby born as early as 24 weeks stands a chance of survival, but only in a good modern hospital. Pregnant women should avoid all unnecessary medication, but vaccinations and malarial prophylactics should still be taken where possible. Additional care should be taken to prevent illness and particular attention should be paid to diet and nutrition. Alcohol and nicotine, for example, should be avoided.

WOMEN TRAVELLERS
Sexual harassment of women is far less prevalent in East Africa than in many countries.

White women come under the category of 'tourists' and enjoy a somewhat dubious though privileged status. If you're a white woman, you may get the occasional hassle but it's rarely persistent if treated with the cold shoulder. There are certain areas in Nairobi where you wouldn't want to walk alone at night, but that applies equally to men, though usually for different reasons.

In country areas women need to exercise caution and not place themselves in situations where if a problem arose they would not be able to alert someone. Attacks on foreign women (and indeed, men) are on the increase, especially in Kenya, and the attacks often happen in isolated places.

GAY & LESBIAN TRAVELLERS
In this part of the world the official attitude towards homosexual activities is one of disdain if not outright hostility. In practice, it's a different matter but discretion is the better part of valour, as homosexual acts are illegal and penalties are harsh. People will approach you on occasion and, in some places, it's pretty obvious what's going on.

DISABLED TRAVELLERS
Think seriously before coming to East Africa if you fit into this category. There are no facilities whatsoever and you'd find it particularly difficult – if not impossible – to get onto public transport let alone into your room at a hotel with no lifts. Likewise, there are no suitable toilet facilities.

TRAVEL WITH CHILDREN
This presents few problems other than those you would encounter anywhere else in the world. Africans in general are very friendly, helpful and protective towards children (and their mothers). On the other hand, if you want reasonable toilet and bathroom facilities, you'd be advised to stay in a mid-range hotel. You'd also be well advised to avoid feeding your children street food. Canned baby foods, powdered milk, disposable nappies and the like are available in most large supermarkets in the major towns and cities but not elsewhere. Your major concern if they get sick is good medical facilities. These are few and far between. Your fallback here is a pharmacy. Most of these stock the usual range of medicines and you will not need a doctor's prescription to buy them.

Most hotels will not charge you for a child under two years of age and for those between two and 12 years old sharing the same room as their parents it's usually 50% of the adult rate. You'll often get a cot thrown in for this price. Likewise, most reasonable restaurants will cater for children – smaller portions at a comparable price.

For more information and hints on travelling with children, see *Travel with Children* by Maureen Wheeler, Lonely Planet Publications, 1995.

DANGERS & ANNOYANCES

Travel in this area is relatively trouble free if you stay clear of certain areas warned about in parts of this book. There is the risk of petty theft, and this mainly occurs in Nairobi and other tourist areas of Kenya. However, elsewhere also keep your wits about you.

BUSINESS HOURS

Government offices are open Monday to Friday from 8 or 8.30 am to 1 pm, and 2 to 5 pm. Some private businesses are also open on Saturday mornings from around 8.30 am to 12.30 pm.

Banking hours are Monday to Friday from 9 am to 2 pm. Banks are also open on the first and last Saturday of the month from 9 to 11 am. Foreign exchange bureaus are open much longer hours, but still only open on weekdays.

ACTIVITIES

East Africa offers the visitor a few special-interest activities. Following is a summary of these activities; for more details, see the Activities section in some of the country chapters.

Safaris

This is probably the number one attraction of a visit to East Africa. Kenya has traditionally been the base for budget safaris, but these days there is also a good range of options in Tanzania, especially in Arusha.

Gorilla Tracking

Right up there in popularity with safaris are gorilla-tracking trips. The main centre for this was always the Parc Nacional des Volcans, but after the problems there in 1994 the focus shifted to Djomba in Zaïre, just across the border from Uganda. In the last couple of years, the gorillas at Bwindi National Park have become the favoured option, but the problem here is the shortage of permits.

Rwanda is safe enough to travel in at the moment and a steady trickle of visitors are visiting the gorillas there once again. Eastern Zaïre is very volatile and the situation changes rapidly, so make sure you have up to date advice before heading for Djomba.

Trekking & Mountain Climbing

Again, there are excellent opportunities for trekkers, the main ones being Mt Kilimanjaro (Tanzania), Mt Kenya (Kenya) and the Ruwenzori Mountains (Uganda). On the Ruwenzoris and Kilimanjaro you have to travel with an organised group or licensed operator; on Mt Kenya you can go solo or just hire porters and/or guides as you see fit.

White-Water Rafting

There are a couple of options – one operating out of Nairobi, the other out of Kampala.

Snorkelling & Scuba Diving

In both Kenya and Tanzania you can don a mask and snorkel, or the full scuba gear, and dive on the reefs. There are operators in both countries offering scuba courses, and in recent years Zanzibar has become a major dive centre.

WORK

It's difficult, though by no means impossible, for foreigners to find jobs. The most likely areas in which employment might be found are in the safari business, teaching, advertising and journalism but, except for teaching, it's unlikely you'll see jobs advertised and the only way you'll find out about them is to spend a lot of time getting to know resident expatriates. You will also need to be able to prove that you have the relevant qualifications and/or experience in the field. Basically the rule of thumb is that if an African can do the job there's no need to hire a foreigner.

The most fruitful area in which to look for work, assuming that you've had some experience and have the relevant skills, is the 'disaster industry'. Nairobi and, to a lesser extent, Kampala and Kigali, are awash with UN and other aid agencies servicing the famines in Somalia and southern Sudan and the refugee camps along the Kenyan border with those countries, and the relief efforts in Rwanda and eastern Zaïre. But remember that the work is tough, often dangerous and the pay low. To find such work you would, again, have to spend a lot of time getting to know the expatriates involved in this.

Work permits and resident visas are not the easiest of things to arrange either. A prospective employer may be able to arrange them relatively painlessly but, usually, you would find yourself spending a lot of money and time at immigration.

ACCOMMODATION

Except in Burundi and Rwanda, where options for cheap accommodation are very limited, you can usually find somewhere cheap to stay, even in the smallest towns. Options include a wide choice of budget hotels, youth hostels (Kenya only), religious missions and camp sites. Some of these places (religious missions) may be free, but if they are, please leave a donation (otherwise it won't be long before they no longer welcome travellers – as has happened in other parts of Africa).

In budget hotels, what you get depends largely on what you pay for, though in general, they're good value. You can certainly expect clean sheets and shared showers, but you don't always get a fan or mosquito net and, if you're paying rock-bottom prices, the showers will be cold.

Very cheap hotels often double as brothels, but so do many other more expensive hotels. Theft from hotel rooms generally isn't a problem, though only a fool would tempt fate by leaving money and other valuables lying around unattended for hours at a time. If a place looks safe, it generally is. Check the door locks and the design of keys. Many cheap hotels also have a full-time doorman or even a locked grille and they won't let anyone in who is not staying there.

Obviously, you need to take care in dormitory-type accommodation, since you can't lock anything up (unless there are lockers). All in all, the chances of being mugged in a dark alley at night in a dubious part of a city or along a deserted stretch of beach are far greater than having your gear stolen from a hotel room.

Top of the range hotels, like the Hilton, are only really found in the major cities, and prices and facilities are as you would expect for this type of place. Other large towns usually have at least one mid-range or better place to stay, and at these you can expect to pay from US$15/20 for a single/double room with private facilities.

Camping

There are camp sites of a sort all over East Africa but the facilities offered vary tremendously. Some are nothing more than a patch of dirt without even a tap. Others are purpose-built. Where there's nothing, religious missions will often allow you to camp in their compounds – usually for a small fee. Don't simply camp out in the bush or on a patch of wasteland in a town or city, however. You are asking for problems, and if you leave your tent unattended, there'll be nothing left in it when you get back. In small villages off the beaten track, ask permission first from someone in authority before setting up your tent.

FOOD
Local Food

For the main part, East African cuisine consists largely of stodge filler with beans or a (tough) meat sauce and is really just survival food for the locals – maximum filling-up potential at minimum cost. It is still possible to eat cheaply and well although the lack of variety becomes tedious after awhile. People with carnivorous habits are far better served by the local food than vegetarians.

The most basic local eateries (usually known as *hotelis*) hardly warrant being called restaurants. These places usually have a limited menu and are open only for lunch – the main meal of the day. If you're on a tight budget you'll find yourself eating in these places most of the time. However, if you have the resources, even in the smaller towns it's usually possible to find a restaurant that offers more variety and better food at a higher price. Often these places are connected with the mid-range and top-end hotels.

The only place where any sort of distinctive African cuisine (other than Kenya's *nyama choma*, or barbecued goat's meat) has developed is on the coast where the Swahili dishes reflect the history of contact with Arabs and other Indian Ocean traders – coconut and spices are used heavily and the results are generally excellent.

As might be expected with the large number of Asians in the region, there are also large numbers of Indian restaurants. In addition, many hotels are owned by Indians and the choice of food available on their menus reflects this. If you like Indian cuisine, you'll have no problems even in the smaller towns, though most of these restaurants are confined to the major cities. Indian food also offers the best choice for vegetarians.

Sambusas are probably the most common snack and are obvious descendants of the Indian samosa. They are deep-fried pastry triangles stuffed with spiced mince meat. Occasionally you come across sambusas with vegetable fillings, but this is usually only in the Indian restaurants. If you can find them freshly made and still warm, sambusas can be excellent. However, more often by the time you get them, they are at least several hours old, are cold and have gone limp and greasy from the oil saturation.

Another item that fits into the pure starch category is that curious beast known as the *mandazi*. It's a semisweet, flat doughnut and, once again, when they're fresh they can be very good. They are usually cooked and eaten at breakfast time – often dunked in tea. Should you decide to eat one later in the day, chances are it will be stale and hard.

Something that you don't come across very often but which makes an excellent snack meal is *mkate mayai* (literally 'bread eggs'). This was originally an Arab dish and is now found in countries as far ranging as Kenya and Singapore. Basically it's a wheat dough which is spread into a thin pancake, filled with minced meat and raw egg and then folded into a neat parcel and fried on a hotplate.

Seemingly on every second street corner someone is trying to make a few bob selling corn cobs roasted on a wire grille over a bed of hot coals. Another street-corner snack is deep-fried yams, eaten hot with a squeeze of lemon juice and a sprinkling of chilli powder.

Main Dishes Basically it's meat, meat and more meat, accompanied by starch of some sort. The meat is usually in a stew with perhaps some potato or other vegetables thrown in, and is often as tough as an old boot. Beef, goat and mutton are the most commonly eaten meats.

The starch comes in four major forms: potatoes, rice, mashed plantains *(matoke)* and maize meal *(ugali* in Kenya, *posho* in Uganda). The maize meal is cooked up into a thick porridge until it sets hard. It's then served up in flat bricks. It's incredibly stodgy, almost totally devoid of any flavour and tends to sit on the stomach like a royal corgi, but most Kenyans swear by it. Naturally, you must try it at least once and some travellers actually get to like it, but don't hold your breath! The main thing it has going for it is that it's cheap.

Roast chicken and steak are popular dishes in the more up-market restaurants of the bigger towns. Food in this sort of place differs little from what you might get at home. Cooked red kidney beans are always an alternative to meat and are widely available in local eateries.

Menus, where they exist in the cheaper places, are usually just a chalked list on a board on the wall. In better restaurants they are usually just in English.

The following food list gives some of the main words you are likely to come across when trying to decipher Swahili menus or buy food in the market.

Useful Words

boiled	*chemka*
bread	*mkate*
butter	*siagi*
cup	*kikombe*
curry	*mchuzi*
egg(s)	*yai (mayai)*
food	*chakula*
fork	*uma*
fried	*kaanga*
glass	*glasi*
hot/cold	*moto/baridi*
hot (spicy)	*hoho*
Indian bread	*chapati*
knife	*kisu*
napkin	*kitambaa*
pepper	*pilipili*
plate	*sahani*
raw	*mbichi*
ripe	*mbivu*
roast	*choma*
salt	*chumvi*
sauce	*mchuzi*
soup	*supu*
sugar	*sukari*
sweet	*tamu*
table	*mesa*
teaspoon	*kijiko*
yoghurt	*maziwalala*

Vegetables & Grains

aubergine	*biringani*
cabbage	*kabichi*
capsicum	*pilipili baridi*
carrots	*karoti*
cassava	*muhogo*
garlic	*vitunguu saumu*
kidney beans	*maharagwe*
lettuce	*salad*
maize-meal porridge	*ugali, posho*
mashed plantains	*matoke*
onions	*vitunguu*
plantains	*ndzi*
potatoes	*viazi*
rice	*wali*
spinach (boiled)	*sukuma wiki*
tomatoes	*nyana*
vegetables	*mboga*
vegetable stew	*mboga*

Meat & Fish

beef	*nyama ya ngombe*
crab	*kaa*
fish	*samaki*
kebabs	*mushkaki*
lobster	*kamba*
meat	*nyama*
meat stew	*karanga*
mutton, goat	*nyama ya mbuzi*
pork	*nyama ya nguruwe*
squid	*ngisi*
steak	*steki*

Fruit

This is where East Africa really excels. Because of the region's varied climate, there's an excellent array of fruits. The tropical ones are especially good. Depending on the place and the season you can buy mangoes, papaya, pineapple, watermelon, oranges, guavas, custard apples, bananas (many varieties) and coconuts. Prices are cheap and the quality very high.

bananas	*ndizi*
coconut (green)	*dafu*
coconut (ripe)	*nazi*
custard apples	*stafeli*
dates	*tende*
fruit	*matunda*
grapefruit	*madanzi*
guava	*pera*
limes	*ndimu*
mangoes	*maembe*
oranges	*machungwa*
papaya	*paipai*
passionfruit	*pasheni*
pineapples	*mananasi*
sugar cane	*miwa*
watermelon	*tikiti*

Fast Food

Fast food has taken off in a big way in Kenya (less so elsewhere) and virtually every town has a place which serves food that rates high in grease and low in price. Fried chips with lashings of lurid tomato sauce are a basic filler, but sausages, eggs, fish and chicken are also popular. In Nairobi there are literally dozens of these places, and they can be handy places to pick up a snack.

Vegetarian

Vegetarians are not well catered for. Away from the main cities there are virtually no vegetarian dishes to accompany the starch. Beans are going to figure prominently in any vegetarian's culinary encounters in East Africa! Buying fresh fruit and vegetables in the market can help relieve the tedium.

Self-Catering

Preparing your own food is a viable option if you are camping and carrying cooking gear. Every town has a market and there's usually an excellent range of fresh produce available.

DRINKS
Nonalcoholic Drinks

Locally produced soft drinks (*sodas*) are widely available and pretty cheap. Also good are the excellent fresh fruit juices, which are more refreshing, better for you and are also inexpensive.

Alcoholic Drinks

Beer If you like beer you'll love East Africa. The amber fluid is probably the most widely available commodity in the entire region! The locally produced product varies from country to country, but is generally pretty good. The only problem is that in Kenya most Kenyan beer drinkers prefer to take it warm, so getting a cold beer can be a task.

The most widely available import is Castle Lager from South Africa, but its availability depends on local import laws.

Local Brews Locally produced alcohol is available throughout the region. The *pombe* (fermented banana or millet beer) is usually fine; distilled liquors can be lethal.

Getting There & Away

Many travellers get to East Africa overland as part of a much lengthier journey through the continent. Due to the civil war in Sudan, however, it is not possible to go overland down the Nile valley between Sudan and either Uganda or Kenya. The furthest you will get coming down from the north is Khartoum. From there to Kenya the only route is out east through Eritrea and Ethiopia, and this has become a popular option in recent times, although the Sudan/Eritrea border is subject to closures as the two governments don't see eye to eye over a number of issues.

At the time of writing, travelling the overland route from West and Central Africa through Zaïre is not possible. You should, however, keep your eye on the situation, as it could radically change overnight.

There are no problems coming up from the south between Zambia or Malawi and Tanzania.

Trying to find a passage on a ship to Africa these days is virtually a waste of time. There are no regular passenger services and you won't get onto a freight ship without a merchant sailor's ticket. Don't believe any of the rumours that there are such ships.

AIR

Unless you are coming overland, flying is just about the only – and the most convenient – way of getting to East Africa. Nairobi is the main hub for flights and the route on which you are most likely to get a relatively cheap ticket, but it's also worth checking out cheap charter flights to Mombasa from Europe.

Buying an ordinary economy-class ticket is not the most economical way to go, but it does give you maximum flexibility and the ticket is valid for 12 months.

Students and those under age 26 can often get discounted tickets, so it's worth checking first with a student travel bureau to see if there is anything on offer. Another option is an advance-purchase ticket, which is usually between 30 and 40% cheaper than the full economy fare but has restrictions. You must purchase your ticket at least 21 days in advance (sometimes more) and you must stay away for a minimum period (usually 14 days) and return within 180 days (sometimes less). The main disadvantage is that stop-overs are not allowed and if you have to change your dates of travel or destination, there will be extra charges to pay. Stand-by fares are another possibility. Some airlines will let you travel at the last minute if there are seats available just before departure. These tickets cost less than the economy fare but are usually not as cheap as the advance-purchase fares.

Of all the options, however, the cheapest way to go is via the so-called 'bucket shops'. These are travel agencies which sell discounted tickets and advertise in newspapers and magazines. Airlines only sell a certain percentage of their tickets through bucket shops, so the availability of seats can vary widely, particularly in the high season. You have to be flexible with these tickets, though if the agency is sold out for one flight, it can generally offer you something similar in the near future.

Most of the bucket shops are reputable organisations, but be careful, as there is always the occasional fly-by-night operator who sets up shop, takes your money for a bargain-basement ticket and then either disappears or issues you with an invalid or unusable ticket. Check what you are buying carefully before you hand over money.

The USA

In the USA, the best way to find cheap flights is by checking the Sunday travel sections in the major newspapers, such as the *Los Angeles Times* or *San Francisco Examiner-Chronicle* on the west coast and the *New York Times* on the east coast. The student travel bureaus are also worth trying – STA Travel or Council Travel.

North America is a relative newcomer to the bucket-shop traditions of Europe and

Asia, so ticket availability and the restrictions attached to them need to be weighed against what is on offer with the more normal advance-purchase or economy fares.

Return tickets to Nairobi from New York (Air France) cost US$2600 in the low season (1 November to 14 December, 16 January to 24 March, 11 to 14 April) and US$3000 in the high season (15 December to 15 January, 25 March to 10 April, 15 June to 30 September). From Los Angeles, a return ticket (British Airways) costs US$1920 in the low season and US$2300 in the high season. If you shop around, it's possible to get one-way tickets from New York to Nairobi for as little as US$650 in the low season, and return tickets for US$1300 also in the low season.

From Canada, Air France offers flights from Toronto to Nairobi for US$2850 in the low season and US$2953 in the high season.

It may well be cheaper in the long run to fly first to London from the east coast of the USA using Virgin Atlantic (from around US$251 one way in the low season), or stand-by on the other airlines for a little more, and then buy a bucket-shop ticket from there to Kenya with or without stopovers, but you must do your homework to be sure of this. All the main magazines which specialise in bucket-shop advertisements in London will mail you copies so you can study current prices before you decide on a course of action.

Australia & NZ

For Australians and New Zealanders there are a number of route options to Africa. There are direct connections with Qantas from Perth to Harare (Zimbabwe) and Johannesburg twice a week, and with South African Airways direct to Johannesburg, also twice a week. A return ticket from Sydney or Melbourne to Harare costs around A$1700 to A$2000, depending on the season. From there to Nairobi, Entebbe or Dar es Salaam it's going to cost an additional A$800 or so for a return ticket.

Another option between Australia and Africa is the weekly Air Mauritius flight from Perth to Mauritius, from where there

are twice-weekly flights to Nairobi. The fare is A$2000 from Sydney or Melbourne, and you can have a stopover in Mauritius if you wish.

The most recent routing from the east coast of Australia is with EgyptAir, which flies to Cairo from Sydney twice a week, with twice-weekly connections to Nairobi or Entebbe. Return fares from Sydney or Melbourne range from A$1866 to A$2144 depending on the season.

Other cheap options to Nairobi include going via Bombay with Air India, or via Karachi with PIA. The return fare with Air India from Sydney or Melbourne ranges from A$2075 to A$2429 depending on the season. PIA offers tickets for A$1655 in the low season and A$2030 in the high season.

It obviously makes sense for Australasians to think in terms of a RTW ticket or an Australia/New Zealand to Europe round-trip ticket with stopovers in Asia and Africa. It shouldn't be too much trouble for a travel agency to put together a ticket which includes various Asian stopovers plus a Nairobi stopover. Having Nairobi added to such a ticket bumps up the price a little and you may have to go through several travel agencies before you get satisfaction as many of them know very little about deals via Africa.

It's probably best to start your search for a ticket by looking in the travel section of the Saturday issue of either the *Sydney Morning Herald* or the *Age* and by visiting a student travel bureau.

The UK

In London there are several newspapers with lots of bucket-shop ads which will give you a good idea of current fares, as well as specialist magazines catering entirely to the travel industry.

Trailfinder is a magazine put out three times a year by Trailfinders (☎ (0171) 938 3366), 194 Kensington High St, London W8 7RG. Trailfinders can fix you up with all your ticketing requirements for anywhere in the world as well as insurance, immunisation and books. They've been in business for years and can be highly recommended. All the staff are experienced travellers, so they speak your language. Trailfinders is open Monday to Saturday from 9 am to 6 pm (until 7 pm on Thursday).

The Africa Travel Centre (☎ (0171) 387 1211), 21 Leigh St, London WC1H 9QX, specialises in travel to and around Africa. It has discounted flight prices to most major cities in Africa, as well as information on what safaris are available, along with costs. You can book all your safaris in advance here, as well as your airline ticket. Office hours are Monday to Friday from 9.30 am to 5.30 pm and Saturday from 10 am to 2 pm. As with Trailfinders, they're highly recommended for your Africa needs.

The price of airline tickets from London to Nairobi is around UK£220 one way and UK£350 return. The corresponding fares to Dar es Salaam are UK£265/400 respectively.

The airlines used are generally Aeroflot and other Eastern European and Middle Eastern airlines, but this isn't always the case. Both Trailfinders and Africa Travel Centre can organise you with multi-stopover tickets which include Kenya and other African destinations.

There are also 'open jaws' tickets available (fly into one city/country and out of another). A specialist in this sort of fare is the Africa Travel System (☎ (0171) 630 5434), Glen House, Stag Place, Victoria, London SW1E 5AG. It offers tickets such as London to Nairobi and Entebbe to London with Sabena for UK£633 in the low season and UK£927 in the high season, London to Nairobi and Dar es Salaam to London with EgyptAir for UK£633 (low) and UK£927 (high), and London to Nairobi and Lilongwe to London with EgyptAir/Ethiopian Airlines for UK£794 (low) and UK£865 (high). On these tickets, you make your own travel arrangements between Nairobi and your place of departure.

Africa Travel System can also arrange tickets which take you east to Australasia after Africa, at prices comparable to anything you'll be offered at the bucket shops in Nairobi.

There is no advantage in buying a one-way ticket to Nairobi and then another one-way ticket back to Europe from there. You'll end up paying more than if you bought a return ticket in the first place. You may also run foul of immigration on arrival in Kenya without an onward ticket and be forced to buy one on the spot – an expensive exercise in lack of forethought.

A round-the-world (RTW) ticket is another economical option if that's what you want to do and have the time, but very few of these include African stopovers: Johannesburg is the most common. Starting and finishing in London with stopovers in Johannesburg, Perth, Sydney, San Francisco, Orlando and Washington, you're looking at around UK£800.

Don't take advertised fares as the gospel truth. To comply with truth-in-advertising laws, UK companies must be able to offer *some* tickets at their cheapest quoted price but they might only have one or two of them each week. If you are not one of the lucky ones, you could find yourself looking at tickets which cost up to UK£50 more (one way or return). The best thing to do, therefore, is to start looking into tickets well before your intended departure date so you have a very good idea of what is available.

Remember that discounted tickets cannot generally be paid for with a credit card. You must pay with cash or with a bank cheque.

Elsewhere in Africa

Both Ethiopian Airlines and Kenya Airways operate regular and direct flights between Nairobi and Addis Ababa. Ethiopian also flies from Addis to Bujumbura, Entebbe, Kigali and Dar es Salaam.

Kenya Airways and Sudan Airways operate direct flights between Khartoum and Nairobi. Sudan Airways also has weekly flights between Khartoum and Entebbe.

The only direct connection between Tanzania (Dar es Salaam) and Lusaka is by Aero Zambia. This is a private company which has offices in Nairobi but not, as yet, in Dar es Salaam. Make enquiries at a travel agency.

There are also direct connections from Nairobi to:

Accra (Ghana) with Ethiopian Airways
Antananarivo (Madagascar) with Air Madagascar
Brazzaville (Congo) with Ethiopian Airways
Cairo (Egypt) with EgyptAir
Harare (Zimbabwe) with Air Zimbabwe
  and Kenya Airways
Johannesburg (South Africa) with South African
  Airways, Kenya Airways, and Olympic Airways
Kinshasa (Zaïre) with Ethiopian Airways
Lagos (Nigeria) with Ethiopian Airways
Lilongwe (Malawi) with Kenya Airways
  and Air Malawi
Mauritius with Air Mauritius

Asia

You may safely assume that flying is the only feasible way of getting between the Indian subcontinent and Kenya. There are plenty of flights between East Africa and Bombay, due to the large Indian population in the region. There are bucket shops of a sort in New Delhi, Bombay and Calcutta, and most of the discounted tickets will be with Air India.

Typical fares from Bombay to Nairobi are around US$584 return with either Ethiopian Airlines, Kenya Airways or Pakistan International Airlines (PIA; via Karachi).

In Nairobi there are travel agencies offering tickets to Karachi, Islamabad, New Delhi, Bombay and Calcutta. Most of these will be with Air India or PIA.

LAND

There are a number of routes into East Africa from other parts of the continent. See the Getting There & Away sections in the country chapters for details of crossings.

Ethiopia

The border crossing at Moyale is frequently used by travellers and overland trucks and presents few problems. Beware that when crossing into Kenya you will be asked for your vaccination card here which must have valid cholera and yellow fever stamps. Those without cards are refused entry into Kenya.

The only transport between Moyale and Marsabit are trucks. These take two to four

days and cost KSh 500 to Marsabit and KSh 600 to KSh 1000 to Isiolo.

All vehicles, including buses travelling between Marsabit and Isiolo or Marsabit and Moyale, must travel in convoy to minimise the danger of attack from *shiftas* (bandits).

There are buses going north from the Ethiopian side of Moyale but they start early at around the break of dawn. A few km out of town, you'll encounter the first of many police checkpoints. At the border, ensure your passport is stamped both by immigration (at the checkpoint) and customs (100m further on), otherwise you will be sent back to the border from here. If there are any Tupperware smugglers on board (seriously!), then expect a long delay. Customs rules allow passengers to bring in only one item of any particular sort per person so don't be too surprised if you're asked to wear a sweater or carry an umbrella. It's a bizarre sight, seeing up to 60 people turfed off the bus by the police, all of them with the same umbrella design – but perfectly legal.

Malawi

The one crossing point here is between Karonga and Mbeya, at the top of Lake Malawi, via Tukuyu and Kyela. A daily bus from Karonga to the border at Iponga on the Songwe River departs between 2.30 and 3 pm and takes about four hours. The bus goes via Kaporo, where you get your Malawi exit stamp. The border closes at 6 pm, which means you'll get there too late to cross and will have to stay the night. You'll find this most inconvenient, as there are no facilities whatsoever – no food, accommodation or running water. Nor will you be allowed to sleep on the bus, so bring what you need to make an uncomfortable night tolerable. The bus returns to Karonga at 6 am the next day.

In the morning you cross over to the Tanzanian side, after which it's about seven km to the main Kyela to Mbeya road. You'll have to hitch a ride or walk this stretch. Once on the main road, buses to Mbeya (about a five-hour trip) pass two or three times a day, but it's often more convenient to hitch a ride. There's no need to go into Kyela along this route, as the town is five km south-east of the junction and so in the wrong direction for Mbeya.

Going in the opposite direction from Tanzania, take a bus from Mbeya going to Kyela (TSh 1000) but get off at the turn-off to the border. Alternatively, take a bus to Tukuyu, which is on the same road (TSh 800, about three hours), and then another to Kyela (TSh 400, 1½ hours), again alighting at the turn-off to the border. At the turn-off you will find several youths with bicycles, who will perch you on the back and pedal away at a suicidal rate to the border for TSh 500. The border closes at 6 pm but it's still worth going there. Kyela is a dump and you'll probably be allowed to sleep on the verandah of the immigration office. There's food here and cold beers. Change money with the bicycle boys.

In the morning, you cross the border, but because there's a one hour time difference between Tanzania and Malawi, by the time the Tanzanian border post opens, the bus to Karonga will have already left, so you'll have to hitch to the Malawi customs post (15 km). Should you manage to overtake the bus, it costs MK 3 from the Malawi customs post to Karonga and takes 30 minutes.

Don't attempt to cross this border on a Sunday, as there's hardly any traffic and you'll have to do a lot of walking.

The Metro International bus does the Dar es Salaam-Lilongwe run once a week on Tuesdays, which takes about 24 hours and costs TSh 26,900. The route takes you via Morogoro, Iringa, Mbeya, Karonga, Rumphi, Mzuzu and Kasungu. The road is in good condition. Bookings must be made by 5.30 am on the Monday before departure. You would seriously have to be in a hurry to take this bus without a break but Metro does have good buses.

Mozambique
A few hardy travellers make the journey through northern Mozambique, entering Tanzania at Namiranga on the Rovuma River (the border). From Pemba (Mozambique) to Moçimboa the road is a nightmare but there

is regular transport (the trip takes 10 hours). In Moçimboa there is one basic *pousada* where you can stay overnight. From Moçimboa there is at least one pick-up daily to the border (five hours), leaving at 5 am.

Once through the Mozambique border post, there is a half-hour walk to the Rovuma River where you cross by boat (10 minutes) and continue on to Mtwara (there is only irregular transport).

Somalia
There's no way you can get overland from Kenya to Somalia at present (unless you're part of a refugee aid convoy). Even if you attempted it, the Kenyan police or the army would turn you back. Moreover, the entire border area is infested with well-armed Somali shifta making any attempt to cross it a dangerous and foolhardy venture.

Sudan
As with Somalia, there's no way you can get overland between Kenya and Sudan at present. The furthest north you're going to get is Lokichokio, and you'll be lucky to get that far unless you're with a refugee aid convoy.

Similarly, the route through northern Uganda is also out of the question.

Zambia
Bus The usual route is on the TAZARA railway, but there's also road transport from Mbeya to Tunduma on the Tanzania-Zambia border. From the border, you walk to Nakonde on the Zambian side and take a bus from there to Kasama and Lusaka. Not many people use the road route.

Train The TAZARA railway runs between Dar es Salaam and Kapiri Mposhi, in the heartland of the Zambian copper belt, via Mbeya and Tunduma/Nakonde. The line was built by the Chinese in the 1960s and passes through some of the most remote countryside in Africa, including part of the Selous Game Reserve. It is Zambia's most important link with the sea, but unfortunately, maintenance hasn't matched the energy with which the Chinese first constructed the railway. As a result, schedules can be erratic. There are usually five trains per week in either direction, two express and three ordinary.

The express trains depart from Dar es Salaam on Tuesday and Friday at 5.55 pm and the ordinary trains on Monday, Thursday and Saturday at 9 am. The journey takes between 42 and 48 hours and the fares (in Tanzanian shillings) from Dar es Salaam are as follows:

Station	1st Class	2nd Class	3rd Class
Mbeya	19,400	12,700	7600
Kasama	27,800	18,200	10,900
Mpika	32,500	21,300	12,800
Kapiri Mposhi	42,000	27,500	16,500

Tickets should be booked in advance in Dar es Salaam at the TAZARA railway station on Pugu Rd. This is not the same station as the one in central Dar es Salaam, where Central Line trains arrive and depart. The TAZARA station is about halfway to the airport. Get there on an airport bus from the junction of Sokoine Drive and Kivukoni Front, opposite the Cenotaph and Lutheran church. A taxi will cost TSh 3000 to TSh 4000.

Book tickets at least five days ahead. Don't expect any 1st or 2nd-class tickets to be available beyond this point, unless you have 'contacts' such as government officials and diplomats. It's remarkable how easy it is to get a 1st class ticket the day before departure if you know someone like this! Third-class tickets are sold only on the day of departure.

Student discounts of 50% are available for International Student Identity Card (ISIC) holders, though getting authorisation for this can be time-consuming. The normal procedure is to pick up a form from the TAZARA station and take it to the Ministry of Education beside State House, where you fill in more forms and get the appropriate rubber stamp. Then you take the form back to the TAZARA station and buy your ticket. It's a lot of fuss for a few dollars!

Men and women can only travel together in 1st and 2nd class if they occupy an entire compartment. Bedding is complimentary in 1st and 2nd class.

Meals are usually available on the train and can be served in your compartment, though food supplies generally run out towards the end of a journey. If this happens, there are always plenty of food and drink vendors at the stations en route. Don't take photographs on this train unless you have discussed the matter beforehand with the police.

BOAT
Zambia

The historic vessel, the MV *Liemba*, which is owned and operated by Tanzanian Railways, connects the Zambian port of Mpulungu with the Tanzanian port of Kigoma and Bujumbura in Burundi. See the Tanzania Getting There & Away chapter for full details.

Mozambique

A boat called the *Edma* makes the trip between Pemba (Mozambique) and Mtwara (Tanzania) via Ibo Island (sometimes) and Moçimboa. It doesn't run to any set schedule so you need to make enquiries to pin it down.

TAKING YOUR OWN VEHICLE
Carnets

When bringing a foreign-registered vehicle into countries in East Africa, it must be covered by a *carnet de passage*. The purpose of a carnet is to allow an individual to take a vehicle into a country where duties would normally be payable, without the necessity of having to pay those duties. It's a document which guarantees that if a vehicle is taken into a country but not exported, then the organisation which issued it will accept responsibility for payment of import duties. Carnets can only be issued by national motoring organisations and before they will issue such a document they have to be absolutely sure that if the need to pay duties ever arises they would be reimbursed by the individual to whom the document is issued.

The amount of import duty can vary quite

a lot, but generally, it's between one and 1½ times the new value of the vehicle.

The motoring organisation will calculate the highest duty payable of all the countries that you intend to visit and arrive at what is known as an 'indemnity figure'. This amount must be guaranteed to the motoring organisation by the individual before carnet documents are issued.

If duties ever become payable – for example, if you take the vehicle into a country but don't export it again – the authorities of that country will demand payment of duties from the motoring organisation. It, in turn, would surrender the indemnity it was holding.

If this were a bank indemnity then the bankers would hand over the deposit they were holding. In the case of an insurance company, they would have to settle the claim. In the case of the latter the insurance company has the right of recovery from an individual of the amount it has had to pay out.

To get a carnet you first need to make an application to a motoring organisation. They will issue you with an indemnity form for completion either by a bank or an insurance company. Once this is completed and a bond deposited with a bank or a premium paid to an insurance company, the motoring organisation issues a carnet. The cost of the carnet itself is minimal. The whole process generally takes about a week to complete.

DEPARTURE TAXES

The airport departure tax for international flights from Kenya or Tanzania is US$20. In Tanzania you must pay this in foreign currency (cash); in Kenya, cash, travellers' cheques and local currency are all accepted. Local currency can be reconverted into US dollars at the airports on presentation of a bank receipt proving you changed sufficient hard currency into local shillings.

In Uganda, the departure tax for international flights is US$23, payable in either foreign or local currency.

WARNING
The information in this chapter is particularly vulnerable to change: prices for international travel are volatile, routes are introduced and cancelled, schedules change, special deals come and go, and rules and visa requirements are amended. Airlines and governments seem to take a perverse pleasure in making price structures and regulations as complicated as possible. You should check directly with the airline or a travel agent to make sure you understand how a fare (and ticket you may buy) works. In addition, the travel industry is highly competitive and there are many lurks and perks.

The upshot of this is that you should get opinions, quotes and advice from as many airlines and travel agents as possible before you part with your hard-earned cash. The details given in this chapter should be regarded as pointers and are not a substitute for your own careful, up-to-date research. ■

Getting Around

AIR

There's a good network of internal flights within Kenya but much less so in Tanzania, Uganda, Rwanda, Burundi and Zaïre. Most of the internal sectors are serviced by the respective national carrier, but in Kenya and Tanzania there are also quite a few private companies which operate light aircraft (six to eight-seater twin-propeller planes).

BUS, MINIBUS & TAXI

Buses are usually quicker than trains or trucks. In Kenya, where there's a good network of sealed roads, you may have the choice of going by so-called 'luxury' bus or by ordinary bus over certain routes. The luxury buses cost more but are not always quicker than the ordinary buses.

In Tanzania there's also a choice of 'luxury' and ordinary buses, but only on the main routes: Arusha to Moshi and Dar es Salaam, and Dar es Salaam to Mombasa. Uganda has ordinary buses only. There are very few full-size buses in Burundi and Rwanda – minibuses are the rule. In Zaïre, buses and minibuses are few and far between, so you will be reliant on trucks for transport in most areas.

Most East African countries rely heavily on minibuses (known as *matatus* in Kenya, *taxis* in Uganda, *dalla-dallas* in Tanzania)
for transport. They're generally more expensive than ordinary buses but are quicker. In Kenya and Tanzania, you can expect them to be packed to bursting point. Due to overloading, excessive speed, poor maintenance and driver recklessness, matatus in Kenya are not the safest way of getting around. In fact, they can be downright dangerous, and newspaper reports of matatu crashes are a regular feature. In Uganda, Rwanda and Burundi, however, travelling in minibuses is much safer.

Most countries also have share-taxis (which take up to five or six passengers and leave when full) and private taxis. You can forget about private taxis if you're on a budget, but share-taxis should definitely be considered. They can cost up to twice as much as the corresponding bus fare but in some places are only slightly more expensive than a matatu, and they're certainly quicker and more comfortable. They're also considerably safer than matatus.

TRUCK

For many travellers, trucks are the favoured means of transport. They may be the *only* form of transport in some areas. They're not only the cheapest way of getting from A to B as a rule, but you also get an excellent view from the top of the load.

Road Conditions

The main roads of Kenya, Uganda, Rwanda and Burundi are sealed and generally in a good state of repair, though you'll occasionally encounter the odd rough patch. However, the main roads of Tanzania are often in an appalling state (with the exceptions of the Namanga to Moshi, Moshi to Dar es Salaam and Dar es Salaam to Morogoro roads). The situation is similar in Zaïre.

Roads in far-flung rural areas of all East African countries may well be in a bad state of repair, so breakdowns and getting stuck, especially in the wet season, are a regular feature of any journey. Desert roads in north and north-east Kenya may just be a set of tyre tracks left in the sand or dust by previous trucks. Don't pay too much attention to red lines drawn on maps in places like this. Many roads are impassable in the wet season, and on some of them a convoy system may be in operation, so it's only possible to travel at certain times of the day. ■

For most regular runs there will be a 'fare', which is more or less fixed and is what the locals pay – but check this out before you agree to a price. Sometimes it's possible to get the truckie to lower the price if there's a group of you. Trucks are generally cheaper than buses over the same distance, but not always. Most of the time you'll be on top of the load, though you can sometimes travel in the cab for about twice what it costs on top.

There are trucks on main routes to most places every day, but in the more remote areas they may only run once or twice a week. Many lifts are arranged the night before departure at the 'truck park' – a compound/dust patch that you'll find in almost every African town. Just go there and ask around for a truck which is going your way. If the journey is going to take more than one night or one day, ask about food and drink.

TRAIN

Kenyan trains are excellent and are the preferred method of transport where they are available. Tanzanian trains are considerably slower but are still the preferred means of transport, since many roads are in such bad shape that going by bus is a generally uncomfortable experience. Ugandan trains are even slower, and long delays are common. The system has been allowed to run down badly over the last few years and passenger services have been curtailed. Burundi, Rwanda and eastern Zaïre have no railways.

Third class is usually very crowded and uncomfortable and you may have thieves to contend with, so it's not generally recommended. Second class is preferable and will cost you about the same as a bus over the same distance. Travelling 1st class will cost you about double what a bus would cost but does give you a considerable measure of privacy and comfort.

HITCHING

In Kenya, but less so in the other countries of East Africa, resident expatriates and aid workers with their own vehicles seem to be reasonably generous about offering free lifts.

Remember that sticking out your thumb in many African countries is the equivalent of an obscene gesture, though allowances are generally made for foreigners. Wave your hand up and down instead.

A word of warning about lifts in private cars. Smuggling across borders does go on, and if whatever is being smuggled is found, you may be arrested even though you knew nothing about it. Most travellers manage to convince police that they were merely hitching a ride and had nothing to do with the smuggler (passport stamps are a good indication of this), but the convincing can take days.

Free lifts on trucks are the exception rather than the rule, though it depends on the driver. You may have to wait a long time until a free lift comes along, so it's often not worth bothering trying for one.

Although many travellers hitchhike, it is not a totally safe way of getting around. Just because we explain how hitching works does not mean we recommend it.

BOAT

There are quite a few possibilities for travelling by boat, either on the lakes inland or along the coast. In particular, there are some amazingly venerable old steamships operating on the lakes. A trip on the MV *Liemba* on Lake Tanganyika is quite an experience.

There are international connections on Lake Victoria (Uganda-Tanzania and Kenya-Tanzania) and Lake Tanganyika (Burundi-Tanzania-Zambia and Tanzania-Zaïre), but there are no international connections on Lake Victoria between Kenya and Tanzania, or on Lake Kivu between Zaïre and Rwanda.

Along the coast, there are dhows and a catamaran between Kenya and Tanzania (Mombasa to Pemba, Zanzibar and Dar es Salaam). Between Dar es Salaam and Zanzibar, there's a choice of dhow, regular motorised boat, catamaran and hydrofoil. Further down the coast, there's a fairly regular ship between Dar es Salaam and Mtwara, calling at most small ports en route.

Safari Guide

ANTELOPES

Bongo
(Tragelaphus eurycerus)
Swahili: *bongo*

The large, striped bongo antelope is rarely seen. About your only chance of sighting one is in Aberdare National Park. They live close to water in dense forest, only leaving the forest cover to graze at night in open clearings.

The bongo stands around 120 cm high at the shoulder and measures around 250 cm from head to tail. Mature males are a beautiful dark mahogany-brown colour, while the females are a much lighter reddish-brown. Both sexes have distinctive vertical white stripes on the body, never less than nine, never more than 14. Horns are sported by both males and females, and these are slightly spiralling (lyre shaped) with yellow tips, with those on the male being slightly shorter and sturdier than on the female.

The bongo grazes mainly on leaves and will often stand on its hind legs to increase its reach. It also digs for roots with its horns. Bongo are usually found in small family herds although bulls often lead a solitary existence, meeting up with other animals only to mate.

Bushbuck
(Tragelaphus scriptus)
Swahili: *pongo*

Although the small bushbuck antelope exists in fairly large numbers in most of Kenya's game parks, it is a shy, solitary animal and is rarely sighted.

Standing at about 80 cm at the shoulder, the bushbuck is chestnut to dark brown in colour with a variable number of white vertical stripes on the body between the neck and rump, as well as (usually) two horizontal white stripes lower down which give the animal a 'harnessed' appearance. There are also a number of white spots on the upper thigh and a white splash on the neck. Females are reddish brown. Horns are usually only grown by males but females have been known to grow them on rare occasions. They are lyre shaped with gentle spirals and average about 30 cm in length.

Bushbuck are rarely found in groups of more than two and prefer to stick to areas with heavy brush cover. When startled they take off and crash loudly through the undergrowth. They are nocturnal animals and browsers yet rarely move far from their chosen spot. Though shy and elusive they can be aggressive and dangerous when cornered. Their main predators are leopard and python.

Kirk's Dik Dik
(Madoqua kirki)
Swahili: *dik dik*

Kirk's dik-dik is the more common of the two dik-diks found in Kenya (the other is Gunther's dik-dik, found only in Marsabit National Park & Reserve) and is commonly seen in Nairobi, Tsavo, Amboseli and Masai Mara reserves. Its name comes from the 'zic-zic' call it makes when alarmed.

The dik-dik is a tiny antelope, standing only around 35 cm at the shoulder. It is a reddish-brown colour on the back, with lighter flanks and white belly. Size is usually the easiest way to identify a dik-dik, but other telltale marks are the almost total lack of a tail and the tuft of dark hair on the forehead. Horns (found on the males only) are so short (around six cm) that they are often lost in the hair tuft.

Dik-dik are usually seen singly or in pairs and are often found in exceedingly dry places – it seems they don't have a great dependence on water. They are territorial creatures, each pair occupying an area of around five hectares. They are mainly nocturnal but can be seen grazing in acacia scrub in the early morning and late afternoon; like so many animals they rest in the heat of the day.

The females bear a single offspring twice a year. After six months the young dik-dik reaches sexual maturity and is then driven out of the home territory.

Common or Bush Duiker
(Sylvicapra grimmia)
Swahili: *nsya*

This is the most common of the duikers, of which there are at least 10 species. Even so, they are not often sighted as they are largely nocturnal, usually only live in pairs and prefer areas with good scrub cover. They are known to exist in Marsabit, Tsavo, Nairobi, Amboseli, Meru and Masai Mara reserves.

The duiker stands only 60 cm at the shoulder, is a greyish light-brown colour with white belly and a dark brown vertical stripe on the face. The horns (males only) are short (around 20 cm), pointed, and grow straight.

Duikers are widely distributed and can be found in a variety of habitats ranging from open bush to semi-desert and up to the snow line of the highest mountains except for bamboo forest and rainforest. This ability to survive in many different habitats explains their survival in cultivated areas where other herbivorous species have been exterminated.

They are almost exclusively browsers and only rarely eat grasses though they appear to supplement their diet with insects and guinea fowl chicks. They are capable of doing without water for long periods but will drink it when available.

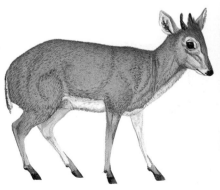

Eland
(Tragelaphus oryx)
Swahili: *pofu*

The eland looks similar to some varieties of cattle seen on the Indian subcontinent, and is found in Nairobi, Marsabit, Tsavo and Masai Mara parks/reserves.

The biggest of the antelopes, the eland stands about 170 cm at the shoulder and a mature bull can weigh up to 1000 kg. Horns are found on both sexes and these are spiralled at the base, swept straight back and grow to about 65 cm. Males have a much hairier head than the females, and their horns are stouter and slightly shorter. They are a light greyish-brown in colour, and bear as many as 15 vertical white stripes on the body, although these are often almost indistinguishable on some animals.

The eland prefers savannah scrub to wide open spaces, but also a·.oids thick forest. It grazes on grass and tree foliage in the early morning and late afternoon, and is also active on moonlit nights. It needs to drink once a day, but can go for a month or more without water if its diet includes fodder with high water content.

Eland are usually found in groups of around six to 12, but there may be as many as 50 in a herd. A small herd normally consists of several females and one male, but in larger herds there may be several males, and there is a strict hierarchy. Females reach sexual maturity at around two years and can bear up to 12 calves in a lifetime. The young are born in October-November.

Gerenuk
(Litocranius walleri)
Swahili: *swala tiga*

The gerenuk is probably the easiest of all antelopes to identify because of its inordinately long neck, which accounts for its Swahili name, *swala tiga*, meaning giraffe-gazelle. Its distribution is limited to Meru, Samburu, Tsavo and Amboseli national parks.

Growing to around 100 cm at the shoulder, the gerenuk is a dark fawn colour on the back which becomes much lighter on the sides and belly. The horns (found on the male only) curve gently backward and grow up to 40 cm long.

The gerenuk's habitat ranges from dry thorn bush country to semidesert and its food consists mainly of the tender leaves and shoots of acacia bushes. It is quite capable – in the same way as a goat – of standing on its hind legs and using one of its forelegs to pull down the higher branches of bushes to get at the leaves and shoots. Also like goats, they are quite capable of doing without water.

Grant's Gazelle
(Gazella granti)
Swahili: *swala granti*

This is one of the most common antelopes and exists in large numbers in Nairobi, Amboseli, Masai Mara, Tsavo and Marsabit reserves.

Grant's gazelle are most easily identified by their colouring and long horns: sandy brown on the back, clearly demarcated from a lighter colour on the flanks and white belly, and white around the tail and hind legs. They are not a large gazelle, standing around 90 cm at the shoulder. Horns are found on both sexes and are heavily ridged with around 25 rings; in the male they grow to around 60 cm (although they often appear longer because of the relatively small body) and curve gracefully and evenly up and back, usually with some outward curving as well; in the female the horns are much shorter but follow the same pattern.

You usually come across herds of Grant's gazelle in open grassy country where there is some forest cover, although they are also occasionally found in heavily wooded savannah country. Herd size is usually between 20 and 30, with one dominant male, does and young. Food consists mainly of leaves and grass. As water is obtained through dietary intake these gazelles do not need to drink.

Greater Kudu
(Tragelaphus strepsiceros)
Swahili: *tandala mkubwa*

The greater kudu is one of the largest of the antelopes but it's a rare sight and only found in any numbers in Marsabit National Park & Reserve. Elsewhere, kudu prefer hilly country with fairly dense bush cover. The kudu stands around 1.5 metres at the shoulder and weighs up to 250 kg, yet it's a very elegant creature, light grey in colour, with broad ears and a long neck. The sides of the body are marked by six to 10 vertical white stripes and there is a white chevron between the eyes. Horns are carried only by the males and are both divergent and spiralling.

Kudu live in small herds of up to four or five females with their young but these often split up during the rainy season. The males are usually solitary though occasionally they band together into small herds.

They are mainly browsers and only seldom eat grasses but are capable of eating many types of leaves which would be poisonous to other animals.

Although somewhat clumsy animals when on the move, they are capable of clearing well over two metres when jumping.

Hartebeest
(Alcelaphus buselaphus)
Swahili: *kongoni*

The hartebeest is a medium-sized antelope and is found in Nairobi, Tsavo, Amboseli and Masai Mara parks. It is easy to recognise as it has a long, narrow face and distinctively angular short horns (on both sexes) which are heavily ridged. Colouring is generally light brown on the back, becoming paler towards the rear and under the belly. The back slopes away from the humped shoulders. They prefer grassy plains for grazing but are also found in lightly treed savannah or hills.

The hartebeest feeds exclusively on grass, and usually drinks twice daily, although it can go for months without water if necessary.

They are social beasts and often intermingle with animals such as zebras and wildebeest. Their behaviour is not unlike the wildebeest's, particularly the head tossing and shaking.

Sexual maturity is reached at around 2½ years and calving goes on throughout the year, although there are peak periods in February and August. Predators are mainly the large cats, hyena and hunting dogs.

Impala
(Aepyceros melampus)
Swahili: *swala pala*

The graceful impala is one of the most common antelopes and is found in virtually all national parks and reserves in large numbers.

A medium-sized antelope, it stands about 80 cm at the shoulder. The coat is a glossy rufous colour though paler on the flanks with the underparts, rump, throat and chin being white. A narrow black line runs along the middle of the rump to about halfway down the tail and there's also a vertical black stripe on the back of the thighs but, unlike in Grant's gazelle, this does not border the white buttocks. It's also distinguishable from Grant's gazelle by having a tuft of long black hair above the heels of the hind legs. Only the males have horns which are long (averaging 75 cm), lyre-shaped and curve upwards as they spread.

Impala are gregarious animals; each male has a 'harem' of up to 100 females, though more usually around 15 to 20. Males without a 'harem' form bachelor groups. Fierce fighting occurs between males in rutting season, otherwise they're quite placid animals.

One of the most noticeable characteristics of impala is their speed and prodigious ability at jumping. They are quite capable of clearing 10m in a single jump lengthwise or three metres in height and this they frequently do even when there are no obstacles in their path.

Impala are both browsers and grazers and are active during the day and by night. They are quite highly dependent on water but are capable of existing on just dew for fairly long periods. Their main predators are leopard, cheetah and hunting dogs.

HUGH FINLAY

Klipspringer

(Oreotragus oreotragus)
Swahili: *mbuzi mawe*

The distinctive klipspringer inhabit rocky outcrops in Tsavo, Amboseli, Masai Mara, Marsabit and Meru reserves.

Standing about 50 cm at the shoulder, they are easily recognised by their curious 'tip-toe' stance (the hooves are designed for balance and grip on rocky surfaces) and the greenish tinge of their speckled coarse hair. Horns (found on the male only) are short (10 cm) and widely spaced.

Klipspringer are most often seen on rocky outcrops, or in the grassland in the immediate vicinity, and when alarmed they retreat into the rocks for safety. They are amazingly agile and sure-footed creatures and can often be observed bounding up impossibly rough rock faces. These antelope can also go entirely without water if there is none around, getting all they need from the greenery they eat. They are most active just before and after midday, and single males often keep watch from a good vantage point. The klipspringer is usually found in pairs, or a male with two females, and inhabits a clearly defined territory.

Klipspringer reach sexual maturity at around one year, and females bear one calf twice a year. Calves may stay with the adult couple for up to a year, although young males usually seek their own territory earlier than that.

Predators are mainly the leopard and the crowned eagle, but also include jackal and baboon.

Lesser Kudu

(Tragelaphus imberbis)
Swahili: *tandala ndogo*

The lesser kudu is a smaller model of the greater kudu, the major differences being the lack of a beard, more numerous and more pronounced vertical white stripes on the body, and two white patches on the underside of the neck. As with the greater kudu, only the males have horns. The coat colour varies from brownish grey to blue-grey. It stands around a metre high at the shoulder.

Kudu usually live in pairs accompanied by their fawns though females occasionally form small herds. They are very shy animals and spend much of the day hiding in dense bush, only moving out of cover to feed in the early morning and at dusk. This makes them difficult to spot.

Kudu are browsers and feed on a mixture of leaves, young shoots and twigs and, though they drink regularly if water is available, they are capable of doing without it for relatively long periods – more so than the greater kudu.

The most likely places you will find them are Tsavo and Marsabit national parks where they prefer the drier, more bushy areas.

Oribi
(Ourebia ourebi)
Swahili: *taya*

Not unlike a duiker in appearance, the small oribi is relatively uncommon, and your best chance of spotting one is in the Masai Mara reserve.

The oribi's most distinguishing mark, although you'll need binoculars to spot it, is a circular batch of naked black skin below the ear – it is actually a scent gland. Another useful indicator is the tuft of black hair on the tip of the short tail. Otherwise the oribi is a uniform golden brown with white on the belly and insides of the legs. Short straight horns about 10 cm in length are found on the males only.

Oribi usually graze in grassy plains with good shelter. If water is available they will drink willingly but can also go without it entirely. When alarmed they bolt and then make bouncing jumps with a curious action – all four legs are kept completely stiff. It is thought this helps them to orient themselves in places with poor visibility. After 100m or so they stop and assess the danger.

Oribi are usually found in pairs and are territorial. Sexual maturity is reached at around one year, and the females bear one calf twice a year.

Being quite small, the oribi have many predators, including the larger cats.

Oryx
(Oryx gazella callotis)
Swahili: *choroa*

The fringe-eared or Kilimanjaro oryx *(Oryx gazella callotis)* is found in Kenya's Amboseli and Tsavo national parks and is a large antelope standing around 120 cm at the shoulder. The coat is a sandy fawn with a black spinal stripe which extends to the tip of the tail. The underparts are white and separated from the lower flanks by another black stripe. There are also two black rings just above the knee of the forelegs.

The related galla oryx *(Oryx gazella gallarum)* is reddish-grey and is most commonly seen in the Marsabit reserve and along the Tana River. (Note that the oryx species name may also be referred to as *beisa*.)

Both types of oryx have ovate, pointed ears with the main distinguishing feature being, as the name suggests, a tuft of black hair on the ears of the fringe-eared one. Oryx are easy to distinguish from other antelopes due to their straight, very long and heavily ridged horns which are carried almost parallel. Both the males and females have horns. These horns come into their own when the animal is forced to defend itself. Held down between the forelegs, they are formidable weapons and used to impale an enemy.

Oryx are principally grazers but will also browse on thorny shrubs. They are capable of doing without water for long periods but will drink daily if it is available.

Herds vary from five to 40 individuals and sometimes more though the bulls are usually solitary. Oryx are often found in association with zebra and Grant's gazelle.

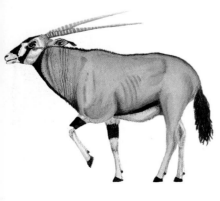

Reedbuck
(Redunca redunca)
Swahili: *tohe*

The best places to spot the dusty brown reedbuck is in Nairobi and Amboseli national parks, and they are occasionally seen in Tsavo National Park.

The reedbuck is a medium-sized antelope, standing around 80 cm high at the shoulder. The most distinctive features are the forward curving horns (found on the males only) and the bushy tail. The underbelly, inside of the thighs, throat and underside of the tail are white.

The reedbuck frequents open grassy plains or hills and is never found more than around eight km from a water supply. It is very territorial and is found in small groups of up to 10 animals. The groups usually consist of an older male and accompanying females and young. Its diet consists almost exclusively of grass but does include some foliage.

At mating time males fight spiritedly. After reaching sexual maturity at around 1½ years, females bear one calf at a time.

The bohor reedbuck's main predators include the big cats, hyena and hunting dogs.

Roan Antelope
(Hippotragus equinus)
Swahili: *korongo*

The roan antelope is one of Kenya's less common antelope species. The best place to see one is in the Shimba Hills National Reserve, where they have been translocated from other parts of the country, although there are still a few small herds in Masai Mara.

The roan is the third largest of the antelopes after eland and kudu. It measures up to 150 cm at the shoulder and bears a striking resemblance to a horse. The coat varies from reddish fawn to dark rufous with white underparts and there's a conspicuous mane of stiff, black-tipped hairs which stretches from the nape to the shoulders. Under the neck, there's another mane of sorts consisting of long dark hairs. The ears are long, narrow and pointed with a brown tassel at the tip. The face is a very distinctive black and white pattern. Both sexes have curving backswept horns which can measure up to 70 cm.

Roan are aggressive by nature and fight from a very early age – a characteristic which frequently deters predators. For most of the year they live in small herds of up to 20 and sometimes more, led by a master bull, but in the mating season, the bulls become solitary and take a female out of the herd. The pair stay together until the calf is born after which the females form a herd by themselves. They eventually return to their former herd. Herds congregate during the dry season.

Being principally grazers, roan rarely move far when food is plentiful but they are susceptible to drought and during such periods they may be constantly on the move.

Sable Antelope
(Hippotragus niger)
Swahili: *pala hala*

Also found only in the Shimba Hills National Reserve, the sable antelope is slightly smaller than its cousin the roan, but is more solidly built. The colouring is dark brown to black, with white face markings and belly. Both sexes carry long backswept horns which average around 80 cm, those of the male being longer and more curved.

The sable antelope is active mainly in the early morning and late afternoon, and is found in herds of up to 25 and sometimes more in the dry season. They are territorial and each group occupies a large area, although within this area individual males have demarcated territories of up to 30 hectares. Sable feed mainly off grass but leaves and foliage from trees account for around 10% of their diet.

Females start bearing calves at around three years of age, and the main calving times are January and September.

Like the roan, the sable is a fierce fighter and has been known to kill lions when attacked. Other predators include the leopard, hyena and hunting dog.

Sitatunga
(Tragelaphus spekei)
Swahili: *nzohe*

The sitatunga is a swamp antelope with unusual elongated hooves which give it the ability to walk on marshy ground without sinking. It is restricted solely to the Saiwa Swamp National Park near Kitale, and it's well worth a visit to this small, walkers-only park.

Very similar to the bushbuck in appearance, except that the coat of the male is much darker and the hair of both sexes much longer and shaggier, the sitatunga stands something over one metre at the shoulder. The females have a lighter, reddish coat and the males have twisted horns up to 90 cm long. It is a fairly shy antelope and sightings are not all that common. A good swimmer, the sitatunga will often submerge itself almost completely when alarmed.

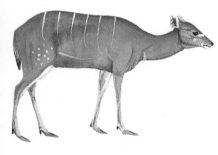

It feeds largely on papyrus and other reeds and is usually nocturnal though in places where it remains undisturbed it can be diurnal. Animals normally live singly or in pairs but sometimes come together in small herds numbering up to 15.

Thomson's Gazelle
(Gazella thomsonii)
Swahili: *swala tomi*

The small and frisky Thomson's gazelle is instantly recognisable by the black slash across the side which separates the brown back from the white underbelly. They are very common in the plains country, such as in Amboseli, Masai Mara and Nairobi reserves, but rare in different habitats such as Tsavo National Park.

Standing around 60 cm at the shoulders, the 'Tommy' is one of the smaller antelopes. Horns on the male grow to about 30 cm and almost straight with just a gentle curve towards the tips; in the female the horns are straighter and much shorter. Another easy to identify characteristic is the short black tail which seems to be constantly twitching. Along with the oribi, Tommys also do the stiff-legged bouncing jump when alarmed.

Group size varies: one old (largely territorial) male may be accompanied by anything from five to 50 females, or there may be herds of up to 500 young males without territory. When food is plentiful the herds tend to be smaller and more territorial. In times of drought herds of several thousand may gather and roam for food. They are often found in close proximity to other animals, including wildebeest and Grant's gazelles.

Sexual maturity is reached at around one year but males only mate after establishing their own territory, which occurs sometime after two years of age. Calving occurs throughout the year though tends to peak at the end of the rainy season.

Being a small animal, Tommys have many predators, including the big cats, hunting dogs, hyena and serval.

HUGH FINLAY

HUGH FINLAY

TONY WHEELER

Topi
(Damaliscus lunatus)
Swahili: *nyamera*

The topi is not unlike the hartebeest in appearance, but is a dark almost purplish colour and has black patches on the rear thighs, front legs and face. Its horns, which are found on both sexes, also differ in shape from the hartebeest in curving gently up, out and back. Although fairly widely distributed in East Africa, in Kenya it is only found in Masai Mara where it exists in large numbers.

A highly gregarious antelope which lives in herds numbering from 15 up to several hundred individuals, topi congregate at certain times of year in gatherings of up to 10,000 in preparation for a migration to fresh pastures. They are often found mingling with wildebeest, hartebeest and zebra.

In the mating season, bulls select a well-defined patch of ground which is defended against rivals and this is where mating takes place. At this time females are free to wander from one patch to another. After mating, the herds split into single-sex parties.

Topi are exclusively grazers and prefer flood plains which support lush pasture though they are capable of thriving on dry grasses which other antelopes will not eat. When water is available they drink frequently but they are also capable of surviving long periods without water so long as there is sufficient grass available.

Their main predator is the lion.

HUGH FINLAY

Waterbuck
Defassa or common waterbuck
(Kobus ellipsiprymnus)
Swahili: *kuru*

The defassa waterbuck is a fairly solid animal and is easily recognisable by its thick, shaggy, dark brown coat, and white inner thighs. It is fairly common and easily seen in Nairobi and Nakuru national parks, and in Masai Mara. A second variety, the ringed waterbuck (also *Kobus ellipsiprymnus*), so-called because of the white ring around its rump, is also seen in Marsabit, Tsavo and Amboseli parks. Both varieties have white facial and throat markings.

Only the males have horns, and these curve gradually outwards then grow straight up to a length of about 75 cm. As you might expect from the name, waterbuck are good swimmers and readily enter the water to escape from predators. Their habitat is always close to water, and males have marked territories by the water's edge. Females and younger males tend to wander at random through male territories. Herds are small and usually consist of cows, calves and one mature bull – the other bulls live in small groups apart from the herd.

The bulk of the waterbuck's diet is grass but it does eat some of the foliage of trees and bushes.

Sexual maturity is reached at just over one year, although a male will not become the dominant bull in the herd until around five years of age.

Waterbuck are usually only preyed on when other food is scarce. The reason being that when mature the flesh is tough and has a distinct odour. Predators such as lion, leopard and hunting dogs go for the young calves and females.

HUGH FINLAY

TONY WHEELER

Wildebeest (Gnu)
Blue wildebeest or brindled gnu
(Connochaetes taurinus)
Swahili: *nyumbu*

Wildebeest are to the African savannah what the bison once were to the North American prairies. Numbering in their millions in certain areas, particularly Masai Mara and over the border in Serengeti, they are unmistakable for their prehistoric appearance. Wildebeest (also known as blue wildebeest or brindled gnu) are well known for their eccentric behaviour which includes loud snorting, tossing and shaking of the head, bucking, running around in circles and rolling in the dust (thought to be a reaction to the activity of the botfly larva which manage to find their way right up into their nostrils). They are heavily built with a massive head and wild mane, are somewhat clumsy, and have been described as having the forequarters of an ox, the hind parts of an antelope and the tail of a horse.

Their sheer numbers, nevertheless, are testimony to their superb adaptation to the environment.

Almost entirely grazers, they are constantly on the move in search of good pasture and water, and their annual migration between the Serengeti and Masai Mara (and vice versa) has to be one of the world's most spectacular sights. Thousands lose their lives in this annual event – drowning in rivers, being taken by crocodiles and other predators or just through sheer exhaustion. The migration north from Serengeti takes place in July and the return trip from Masai Mara in October.

They're very gregarious animals and are usually seen in large herds numbering up to tens of thousands in association with zebra, Thomson's gazelle and other herbivores.

During the mating season, groups of up to 150 females and their young are gathered together by one to three bulls which defend a defined territory against rivals even when on the move. There's apparently no hierarchy among the bulls and, at the end of the mating season, the breeding herds are reabsorbed into the main herds.

Although they graze in a scattered fashion without any apparent social organisation during the rainy season, they coalesce around water holes and remaining pasture in the dry season. Wildebeest prefer to drink daily and will walk up to 50 km to secure water but are capable of surviving for up to five days without it. They're also a noisy animal when grazing, constantly producing a series of snorts and low-pitched grunts.

Their main predators are lions, cheetahs and hunting dogs though hyena are also very partial to young calves.

TONY WHEELER

BIRDS

Flamingo
(Phoenicopterus minor, Phoenicopterus ruber)
Swahili: *heroe*

Flamingo are found by the million in Kenya. They are attracted by the proliferation of algae and crustaceans which thrive in the soda lakes of Baringo, Bogoria, Nakuru and Magadi in the Rift Valley, and Lake Natron across the border in Tanzania.

There are always some birds at each lake but large concentrations seem to move capriciously from one to another over a period of years. Lake Nakuru is the current hot spot but this may well change. It is thought that the changing water levels may be one reason why they change locations. Whatever lake they are presently at, the best time of the year for flamingo viewing is in January-February when they form huge pink masses around the shores of the lakes.

Flamingo have a complicated and sophisticated system for filtering the foodstuffs out of the water. This is because the highly alkane water would be toxic if consumed in large quantities. The deep-pink lesser flamingo, *Phoenicopterus minor*, filters algae and diatoms out of the water by vigorous suction and expulsion of the water in and out of its beak several times per second. The minute particles are caught on fine hairlike protrusions which line the inside of the mandibles. This is all done with the bill upside down in the water. The suction is created by the movement of the thick and fleshy tongue which lies in a groove in the lower mandible and works to and fro like a piston. Where the *Phoenicopterus minor* obtains its food largely by sweeping its head to and fro and filtering the water, the greater flamingo, or *Phoenicopterus ruber,* is more a bottom feeder and supplements its algae diet with small molluscs, crustaceans and other organic particles from the mud. It has been estimated that one million lesser flamingo consume over 180 tons of algae and diatoms daily!

GREG HERRIMAN

TONY WHEELER

Ostrich
(Struthio camelus)
Swahili: *mbuni*

The very distinct and instantly identifiable ostrich is the largest living bird. It is widely distributed throughout the savannah plains of Kenya, and so is most widely seen in the southern parks and reserves – Masai Mara, Amboseli and Tsavo.

The adult ostrich stands around 2.5m high and weighs as much as 150 kg. The neck and the legs are bare, and all these areas of bare skin turn bright red in breeding males. The bushy plumage on the males is black, with white feathers in the redundant wings and the tail. The females are a uniform greyish brown and are slightly smaller and lighter than the males. The ostrich's long and strong legs can push it along at up to 50 km/h.

The Ostrich tends to be territorial and is rarely seen in groups of more than six individuals. It feeds on leaves, flowers and seeds of a variety of plants. When feeding, the food is gradually accumulated in the top of the neck and then passes down to the stomach in small boluses, and it's possible to see these masses of food actually moving down the neck.

The ostrich breeds in the dry season, and the males put on quite an impressive courtship display. Having driven off any possible rival males, the male trots up to the female with tail erect, then squats down and rocks from side to side, simultaneously waving each wing in the air alternately. Just for good measure the neck also waves from side to side. The males may couple with more than one female, in which case the eggs of all the females (up to five) are laid on the same nest, and so it may contain as many as 30 eggs. The eggs are incubated by the major female (the one first mated with) by day, and by the male at night. The other female birds have nothing further to do with the eggs or offspring.

TONY WHEELER

Vulture
Nubian vulture
(Torgos tracheliotus)
Swahili: *gushu*

Vultures are a large, eagle-like bird belonging to the Accipitridae family, of which hawks and eagles are also members. There are a whole range of different species, the most common ones in Kenya being the Egyptian *(Neophron percnopterus)*, hooded *(Necrosyrtes monachus)* and white-headed vulture *(Trigonoceps occipitalis)*. Others include Ruppell's vulture *(Gyps ruppellii)*, a common nester in Kenya's Hell's Gate National Park, and also the white-backed vulture *(Gyps bengalensis)*, found in all East African national parks. Vultures prefer savannah country with high concentrations of game.

These large birds, with a wing span of up to three metres and weighing up to five kg, feed almost exclusively by scavenging. They are fairly inefficient fliers and so rely to a large degree on finding rising hot-air thermals on which to glide and ascend. For this reason you won't see them in the air until well into the morning when the upcurrents have started.

African vultures have no sense of smell and so depend totally on their excellent eyesight, and that of their colleagues, for locating food. Once a kill or a fallen animal has been sighted a vulture will descend rapidly and await its turn at the carcass. Of course other vultures will follow the first downwards and in this chain reaction they may come from as far afield as 50 km. They are very efficient feeders and can rapidly strip flesh from bone, although they are not good at getting a start on a completely intact carcass. A large group of vultures (and they congregate in groups, often of up to 100) can strip an antelope to the bone in half an hour. Because they are poor fliers, however, vultures often cannot fly with a belly full of food and so after gorging will retreat a short distance and digest their meal.

HUGH FINLAY

BUFFALO

(Syncerus caffer)
Swahili: *mbogo*

The buffalo is another animal which appears in great numbers in all the major parks, with the exception of Nairobi National Park.

The massive animal is said to be the most dangerous (to humans) of all African animals and should be treated with caution, although for the most part they will stay out of your way. Females protecting young calves, and solitary rogue bulls, are the most aggressive, and having 800 kg of angry animal thundering towards you is no joke.

Both sexes have the distinctive curving horns which broaden and almost meet over the forehead, although those in the female are usually smaller. The buffalo's colour varies from dark reddish brown to black.

Buffalo are often found in herds of 100 or more and never stray too far from water, especially in the dry season. When food and water are plentiful the herds often disperse. They are territorial in that they have a home range of about 50 km outside of which they don't stray.

TONY WHEELER

CARNIVORES

Cheetah
(Acinonyx jubatus)
Swahili: *duma*

The cheetah is one of the most impressive animals you can hope to see – sleek, streamlined and menacing. It's found in small numbers in all of Kenya's major game reserves – Nairobi, Amboseli, Masai Mara, Tsavo, Samburu, Buffalo Springs, Marsabit and Meru.

Similar in appearance to the leopard, the cheetah is longer and lighter in the body, has a slightly bowed back and a much smaller and rounder face. It stands around 80 cm at the shoulder, measures around 210 cm in length (including the tail) and weighs anything from 40 to 60 kg.

When undisturbed, the cheetah hunts in early morning or late evening, although these days with the number of tourist vehicles around, it is often found hunting at midday when the rubbernecks are back in the lodges stuffing their faces and the poor animal has a chance to stalk some dinner undisturbed. This forced change in habit is particularly stressful for the cheetah as it relies on bursts of tremendous speed for catching its prey, and this speed (up to 110 km/h) is only sustainable for a very short time. Obviously, as the midday heat is much greater than morning or afternoon, hunting for the cheetah becomes much more difficult. During a hunt the cheetah stalks its prey

HUGH FINLAY

as close as possible and then sprints for 100 metres or so; if by that time it hasn't caught its victim, it will give up and try elsewhere. The prey (usually small antelope) is brought to the ground often with a flick of the paw to trip it up. Other food includes hare, jackal and young wart hog.

Cheetah cubs reach maturity at around one year but stay with the mother much longer than that as they have to learn hunting and survival skills. Cubs are usually born in litters numbering from two to four, and the main breeding period is from March to December.

The cheetah rarely fights but predators (mainly of cubs) include lion, leopard and hyenas.

Civet

(Viverra civetta or Civetticus civetta)
Swahili: *fungo*

The civet is a medium sized omnivore around 40 cm high at the shoulder and 90 cm long (excluding the tail), with some canine features and short, partially retractile claws. Its coat of long coarse hair is basically grey but with a definite and variable pattern of black spots over most of the body, along with two black bands stretching from the ears to the lower neck and two black bands around the upper part of the hind legs. The tail is bushy at the base becoming thinner towards the tip, held out straight when the animal is on the move, and black except for three to four greyish bands near the base. The head is mostly greyish white and the ears are quite small, rounded and tipped with white hairs.

Civet are solitary, nocturnal animals which hide in thickets, tall grass or abandoned burrows during the day and so are rarely sighted. The most likely places to spot one are in Marsabit or Tsavo West reserves, although they are also known to inhabit Nairobi, Amboseli and Masai Mara.

It has a very varied diet consisting of rodents, birds and their eggs, reptiles, amphibians, snails, insects (especially ants and termites) as well as berries, the young shoots of bushes and fruits.

Litters consist of up to four cubs and these have a similar, though slightly darker colouring.

The other conspicuous feature of the civet is the presence of musk glands in the anal region which produce a foul-smelling oily substance used to mark territory. This musk is used in the manufacture of perfumes; in Western countries it is collected from animals held in captivity.

Genet
Small spotted or common genet
(Genetta genetta)
Swahili: *kanu*

Unlike the civet, the genet distinctly resembles the domestic cat though the body is more elongated and the tail longer and bushier. The coat is long and coarse with a prominent crest along the spine. The basic colour varies from grey to fawn and is patterned from the neck to the tail with roundish dark brown to blackish spots. The tail is banded with nine to 10 similarly coloured rings and has a whitish tip. The large-spotted or rusty-spotted genet *(Genetta tigrina)*, is similar in appearance to the common genet, but has a brownish-black spinal stripe and larger spots.

The genet lives in savannah and open country and is a very agile tree climber but not frequently sighted since it is entirely nocturnal. During the day it sleeps in abandoned burrows, rock crevices, hollow trees or up on high branches and seems to return to the same spot each day. The animals live singly or in pairs.

Its prey is generally hunted on the ground though it will climb trees to seek out nesting birds and their eggs. Like the domestic cat, it stalks prey by crouching flat on the ground. Its diet consists of a variety of small animals (mostly rodents), birds, reptiles, insects and fruits. It is well known for being a wasteful killer, often eating only a small part of the animals it catches.

Litters typically consist of two to three kittens. Like the domestic cat, the genet spits and growls when angered or in danger.

Hunting Dog
(Lycaon pictus)
Swahili: *mbwa mwitu*

The hunting dog is the size of a large domestic dog and is found in all the reserves, or where there is a high concentration of game animals.

The dog's unusual coloration makes it quite an ugly creature – the black and yellowish splotches are different in each animal, ranging from almost all black to almost all yellow. The only constant is the white tail tip. Prominent physical features are the large rounded ears.

Hunting dogs tend to move in packs ranging from four or five up to as many as 40. They are efficient hunters and work well together. Once the prey has been singled out and the chase is on, a couple of dogs will chase hard while the rest pace themselves; once the first two tire another two step in and so on until the quarry is exhausted. Favoured animals for lunch include gazelle, impala and other similar sized antelope. They rarely scavenge, preferring to kill their own.

Hunting dog cubs are usually born in grass-lined burrows in litters averaging seven, although litters of up to 15 are not unheard of. By six months they are competent hunters and have abandoned the burrow. The hunting dog has no predators, although unguarded cubs sometimes fall prey to hyena and eagle.

Hyena
(*Crocuta crocuta*)
Swahili: *fisi*

The spotted hyena is a fairly common animal throughout most of Kenya and especially where game is plentiful. Bearing a distinct resemblance to dogs, it is a large, powerfully built animal with a very sloping back, broad head and large eyes but with rather weak hindquarters. The sloping back is what gives the animal its characteristic loping gait when running. Its coat is short, dull grey to buff and entirely patterned with rounded blackish spots except on the throat. Its powerful jaws and teeth enable it to crush and swallow the bones of most animals except the elephant.

Hyena are mainly nocturnal animals but are frequently seen during the day, especially in the vicinity of lion or cheetah kills impatiently waiting for their turn at the carcass along with vultures. Otherwise, the days are spent in long grass, abandoned aardvark holes or in large burrows which they dig out up to a metre below the surface of the soil. It's a very noisy animal and when camping out in the bush at night you'll frequently hear its characteristic and spine-chilling howl which rises quickly to a high-pitched scream. This is only one of the sounds which the spotted hyena emits. Another is the well known 'laugh', though this is generally only produced when the animal finds food or is mating.

The hyena has highly developed senses of smell, sight and sound, all important in locating food (carrion or prey) and for mutual recognition among pack members and mating pairs.

TONY WHEELER

Hyena are well known as scavengers and can often be seen following hunting lions and hunting dogs, usually at a respectable distance, though they will occasionally force these animals to abandon their kill. On the other hand, although carrion does form an important part of their diet, hyenas are also true predators and are more than capable of bringing down many of the larger herbivores. To do this they often form packs to run down wildebeest, zebra and gazelle, and are able to reach speeds of up to 60 km/h. They also stalk pregnant antelope and, when the female gives birth, snatch and kill the newly born foal and occasionally the mother too. Domestic stock are also preyed on.

In the mating season, hyena assemble in large numbers especially on moonlit nights. All hell breaks loose on these occasions and the noise is incredible. The gestation period is about 110 days and litters number up to four though usually less. The young are born in the mother's burrow. The pups are weaned at around six weeks old and become independent shortly afterwards.

Humans are the hyena's main enemy, though lions and hunting dogs will occasionally kill or mutilate hyenas if they get too close to a kill. Although they are reputed to be cowardly, you're advised to keep your distance from them as they do occasionally attack humans sleeping in the open.

TONY WHEELER

GEOFF CROWTHER

Jackal
Common or golden jackal
(Canis aureus)
Swahili: *bweha*

There are two species of jackal found in Kenya: the common or golden jackal, and the black-backed jackal *(Canis mesomelas)*, which is a common sight in the major reserves. The black back which gives it its name is usually more silvery than black, is wide at the neck and tapers to the tail. The golden jackal is similar, though without the back markings. Although the jackal is in fact a dog, its bushy tail and long ears are more like a fox.

The jackal is mostly a scavenger and so is commonly seen in the vicinity of a kill. The jackal will hunt for itself – insects, small mammals, birds, and the occasional small antelope. They are also found around human settlements and will attack sheep, poultry and calves.

Jackal are territorial and a pair will guard an area of around 250 hectares. Cubs are born in litters of five to seven and, although they don't reach maturity until almost a year old, they usually leave the parents when just two months old.

Enemies of the black-backed jackal include the leopard, cheetah and eagle.

Leopard
(Panthera pardus)
Swahili: *chui*

The leopard is perhaps the most graceful and agile of the large cats. A powerfully built animal which uses cunning to catch its prey, it is present in all the major game reserves but is difficult to find as it is nocturnal and spends the day resting on branches of trees, often up to five metres above the ground. It is as agile as a domestic cat in climbing such trees and this is also where it carries its prey so that it's out of the way of other scavengers which might contest the kill.

The leopard's coat is usually short and dense with numerous black spots on a yellowish background. The underparts are white and less densely spotted. In addition, the coats of leopards found in open country are generally lighter than those in wooded country.

Leopard are solitary animals except during the mating season when the male and female live together. The gestation period is three months and a litter usually consists of up to three cubs. They prey on a variety of birds, reptiles and mammals including large rodents, rock hyrax, wart hog, smaller antelopes and monkeys (especially baboon), and occasionally take domestic animals such as goat, sheep, poultry and dogs. This wide range of prey explains why they are still able to survive even in areas of dense human settlement long after other large predators have disappeared. But their presence is generally unwelcome since they occasionally turn human-eater. It also explains why they are found in very varied habitats ranging from semidesert to dense forest and as high as the snow line on Mt Kenya and Kilimanjaro.

HUGH FINLAY

Lion
(Panthera leo)
Swahili: *simba*

Lion are one of the main attractions of the game reserves and are found in all the main ones. They spend most of the day lying under bushes or in other attractive places and when you see a pride stretched out in the sun like this, they seem incredibly docile. It is possible to drive up very close to them in a vehicle – they either don't sense humans or realise that humans in vehicles are not a threat. Whatever the case, don't be tempted to get out of a vehicle at any time in the vicinity of a lion. Loud noises and sudden movement also disturb them. They're at their most active for around four hours in the late afternoon, then spend the rest of the time laying around.

Lion generally hunt in groups, with the males driving the prey towards the concealed females who do most of the actual killing. Although they cooperate well together, lions are not the most efficient hunters – as many as four out of five attacks will be unsuccessful. Their reputation as human-eaters is largely undeserved as in most circumstances they will flee on seeing a human. However, once they have the taste for human flesh, and realise how easy it is to make a meal of one, lions can become habitual killers of people. This mostly occurs among the old lions which no longer have the agility to bring down more fleet-footed animals.

Lion are territorial beasts and a pride of one to three males and accompanying females (up to 15) and young will defend an area of anything from 20 to 400 sq km, depending on the type of country and the amount of game food available.

Lion cubs are born in litters averaging two or three. They become sexually mature by 1½ years and males are driven from the family group shortly after this. Lions reach full maturity at around six years of age. Unguarded cubs are preyed on by hyena, leopard, python and hunting dogs.

GREG HERRIMAN

TONY WHEELER

GREG HERRIMAN

Mongoose
Banded mongoose
(Mungos mungo)
Swahili: *kicheche*

The banded mongoose (the one most commonly found in Kenya) is usually seen in groups in Tsavo, Amboseli and Masai Mara reserves. It is brown or grey in colour and is easily identifiable by the dark bands across the back which stretch from the shoulder to the tail. The animal is about 40 cm in length and weighs between 1.3 and 2.3 kg.

Mongoose are very sociable animals and live in packs of between 30 and 50 individuals which stay close to one another when foraging for prey. They are often very noisy, having a wide variety of sounds which they use to communicate with each other. When threatened they growl and spit in much the same manner as a domestic cat. Being diurnal animals, they prefer sunny spots during the day but retire to warrens – rock crevices, hollow trees and abandoned anthills – at night. A pack frequently has several warrens within its territory.

The mongoose's most important source of food are insects, grubs and larvae but they also eat small amphibians, reptiles, birds' eggs, fruits, berries and birds. Their main predators are birds of prey though they are also taken by lion, leopard and hunting dogs. Snakes rarely pose a danger since these would-be predators are attacked by the entire pack and the snake is frequently killed.

Mongoose are one of the creatures which have become very habituated to humans in some places and come right up to the game lodges scavenging for scraps.

Serval
(Felis serval)
Swahili: *mondo*

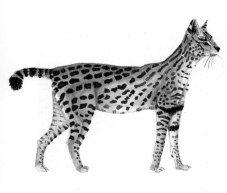

The serval is a wild cat, about the size of a domestic cat but with much longer legs. It is found in all the major game reserves in Kenya.

The serval's colouring is a dirty yellow with large black spots which follow lines along the length of the body. Other prominent features are the large upright ears, the long neck and the relatively short tail. It stands about 50 cm high and measures 130 cm including the tail. Being a largely nocturnal animal, the serval is usually only seen in the early morning or late evening. It lives on birds, hares and rodents and is an adept hunter – it catches birds in mid-flight by leaping into the air.

Serval cat young are born in litters of up to four and although independent at one year, don't reach sexual maturity until two years of age.

ELEPHANT

GEOFF CROWTHER

(Loxodonta africana)
Swahili: *ndovu* or *tembo*

Everyone knows what an elephant looks like so a description of them is unnecessary except perhaps to mention that African elephants are much larger than their Asian counterparts and that their ears are wider and flatter. A fully grown bull can weigh up to 6½ tonnes and sometimes more. In Kenya they are found in all the major game parks with the exception of Nairobi National Park where they would be too destructive to the environment to make their long term presence viable. They have been encountered as high as 3600m on the slopes of Mt Kenya.

The tusks on an old bull can weigh as much as 50 kg each, although 15 kg to 25 kg is more usual. The longest tusks ever found on an elephant in Kenya measured 3.5m! Both the males and females grow tusks, although in the female they are usually smaller. An elephant's sight is poorly developed but its senses of smell and hearing are excellent.

Elephant are gregarious animals and are usually found in herds of between 10 and 20 individuals consisting of one mature bull, a couple of younger bulls, cows and calves, though herds of up to 50 individuals are sometimes encountered. Old bulls appear to lose the herding instinct and often lead a solitary existence, only rejoining the herd for mating. Herds are often very noisy since elephant communicate with each other by a variety of sounds, the most usual ones being various rumbles produced through the trunk or mouth. The most well known elephant sound, however, is the high-pitched trumpeting which they produce when frightened or in despair and when charging.

HUGH FINLAY

Herds are on the move night and day in order to secure sufficient water and fodder, both of which they consume in vast quantities – the average daily food intake of an adult is in the region of 250 kg. They are both grazers and browsers and feed on a wide variety of vegetable matter including grasses, leaves, twigs, bark, roots and fruits and they frequently break quite large trees in order to get at the leaves. Because of this destructive capacity, they can be a serious threat to a fragile environment especially in drought years and are quite capable of turning dense woodland into open grassland over a relatively short period of time. Because of Africa's rapidly increasing human population and the expansion of cultivated land, they also come into conflict with farmers when they destroy crops such as bananas, maize and sugar cane.

The other essential part of an elephant's diet are various mineral salts which they obtain from 'salt licks'. These are dug out of the earth with the aid of their tusks and swallowed in considerable quantities.

Elephant breed year-round and the period of gestation is 22 to 24 months. Expectant mothers leave the

HUGH FINLAY

GREG HERRIMAN

herd along with one or two other females and select a secluded spot where birth occurs. They rejoin the herd a few days later. Calves weigh around 130 kg at birth and stand just under a metre high. They're very playful and guarded carefully and fondly by their mothers until weaned at two years old. After that, they continue to grow for a further 23 years or so, reaching puberty at around 10 to 12 years. An elephant's life span is normally 60 to 70 years though some individuals reach the ripe old age of 100 and even longer.

GIRAFFE

Rothschild's Giraffe
(Giraffa camelopardalis rothschild)
Swahili: *twiga*

Rothschild's giraffe, one of three types of giraffe common to East Africa, is found in western Kenya around Lake Baringo, and Uganda. The Masai giraffe *(Giraffa camelopardalis tippelskirchi)* is more widespread in Kenya and is found in all the parks south and west of Nairobi. Rothschild's is paler and more thickset than the Masai, with less-jagged patches, and is usually unmarked below the knee. The Masai giraffe has irregular, star-shaped patches and is usually buff-coloured below the knee. However, it is often difficult to identify a particular giraffe type because individual and regional variations in colour and pattern are wide.

The average male stands around 5.5m; females are mere midgets at 4.5m. Horns are found on both sexes, but are merely short projections of bone covered by skin and hair. These are all that's left of what would once have been antlers. Despite the fact that the giraffe has such a huge neck, it still has only seven vertebrae – the same number as humans.

TONY WHEELER

Reticulated Giraffe
(Giraffe camelopardalis reticulata)
Swahili: *twiga*

The reticulated giraffe differs from the Masai and Rothschild's giraffes in both colouring and pattern. It is a deeper brown and its body has a much more regular 'tortoiseshell' pattern, with white rather than buff-coloured outlines. It is found in the north and north-east of the country – Meru, Marsabit and Samburu reserves. You can easily come across them at the side of the road between Isiolo and Marsabit but probably the biggest herds are to be seen in Samburu and Buffalo Springs reserves.

Giraffe graze mainly on acacia tree foliage in the early morning and afternoon; the rest of the time they rest in the shade. At night they also rest for a couple of hours, either standing or lying down.

GEOFF CROWTHER

HIPPOPOTAMUS

GEOFF CROWTHER

(Hippopotamus amphibius)
Swahili: *kiboko*

In Kenya the hippo is found in greatest numbers in Masai Mara but can also be observed at Amboseli, Nairobi and Tsavo national parks and at Lake Baringo. At Tsavo there is a submarine viewing tank but the hippo are not very cooperative and seem to have deserted the immediate area.

Hippo are too well known to need description except to note that these huge, fat animals with enormous heads and short legs vary between 1350 kg and 2600 kg when fully grown. Their ears, eyes and nostrils are so placed that they remain above water when the animal is submerged.

Hippo generally spend most of the day wallowing in shallow water, coming out to graze only at night. They are entirely herbivorous and feed on a variety of grasses in pastures up to several km away from their aquatic haunts. They are voracious feeders and can consume up to 60 kg of vegetable matter each night. They urinate and defecate in well-defined areas – often in the water in which case they disperse the excreta with their tails.

GEOFF CROWTHER

Hippo are very gregarious animals and live in schools of 15 to 30 individuals though, in certain places, the schools can be much larger. Each school consists about equally of bulls and cows (with their calves) and, like other herd animals, there's an established hierarchy. Hippos may appear to be placid but they fight frequently among themselves for dominance and this is especially so among the males. The wounds inflicted in such fights are often quite horrific and virtually every hippo you see will bear the scars of such conflicts. They're not normally dangerous to humans unless cornered or frightened but you should definitely keep your distance. They may look sluggish but they are capable of running at considerable speed.

Hippo breed all year and the period of gestation is around 230 days. The cows give birth to a single calf either in the water or on land and suckle it for a period of four to six months after which it begins to graze on a regular basis. Sexual maturity is reached at about four years old and the life span is about 30 years (longer in captivity).

GEOFF CROWTHER

The only natural predators of hippo are lion and crocodile which prey on the young. Though hippo occasionally foul up fishing nets, they're considered to be beneficial since their wallowing stirs up the bottom mud and their excreta is a valuable fertiliser which encourages the growth of aquatic organisms.

GEOFF CROWTHER

HYRAX or DASSIE

(Procavia capensis)
Swahili: *pimbi*

The species of hyrax you're most likely to encounter (especially on Baboon Cliffs in Nakuru National Park but also in Nairobi, Tsavo, Masai Mara and Marsabit reserves) is the cape rock hyrax *(Procavia capensis)* or cape dassie. It's a small but robust animal about the size of a large rabbit with a short and pointed snout, large ears and thick fur. The tail is either absent or reduced to a stump.

Hyrax are extremely sociable animals and live in colonies of up to 60 individuals, usually in rocky, scrub-covered locations. They're diurnal, feeding mostly in the morning and evening on grass, bulbs and roots, and on insects such as grasshoppers and locusts. During the rest of the day they can be seen sunning themselves on rocks and chasing each other in play. Where habituated to humans, they are often quite tame but in other places, when alarmed, they dash into rock crevices uttering shrill screams. Their senses of hearing and sight are excellent.

Hyrax breed all year and the period of gestation is about seven months – a remarkably long period for an animal of this size. Up to six young are born at a time and the young are cared for by the whole colony. Predators include leopard, hunting dogs, eagle, mongoose and python.

Despite being such a small creature, hyrax are more closely related to the elephant than any other living creature by virtue of certain common physical traits.

PRIMATES

Baboon
(Papio cynocephalus)
Swahili: *nyani*

The yellow baboon is just one of at least seven subspecies of baboon and is the one most commonly sighted in Kenya. The other relatively common one is the olive baboon *(Papio anubis),* most often seen in Nairobi National Park. The main difference between the two is that the olive baboon has long facial hair and a mane on the shoulders, especially the males.

Baboon have a dog-like snout which gives them a much more aggressive and less human-like facial appearance than most other primates. They are usually found in large troops (of up to 150 animals, with a dominant male) which will have a territorial area ranging from two to 30 sq km. They spend most of the time on the ground searching for insects, spiders and birds' eggs. The baboon have also found that the lodges in the game parks are easy pickings, especially when

GEOFF CROWTHER

idiotic tourists throw food to them so they can get a good snap with the Instamatic.

Eastern Black & White Colobus
(Colobus guereza caudatus)
Swahili: *mbega*

This forest-dwelling colobus monkey is a handsome creature found only in the forest parks – Mt Kenya, Mt Elgon, Aberdare and Saiwa Swamp.

The monkey is basically black but has a white face, bushy white tail and a white 'cape' around the back which flows out behind when the monkey moves through the trees – an impressive sight. An average colobus measures about 140 cm, of which about 80 cm is tail, and weighs from 10 kg to 23 kg.

The black and white colobus spends most of its time in the forest canopy and is easily missed unless you keep a sharp eye out. It is unusual for them to leave the trees; they get most of their water from small puddles formed in the hollows of branches and trunks. Colobus monkey are usually found in troops of up to 12 animals, consisting of a dominant male, females and young. Newborn monkeys are initially white, gaining their adult coat at around six months.

Greater Bushbaby
(Galago crassicaudatus)
Swahili: *komba*

Looking more like an Australian possum, the bushbaby is in fact a small monkey and is about the size of a rabbit. It is found in all major reserves, although being a nocturnal creature it is rarely sighted by day. The head is small with large rounded ears and, as might be expected on a nocturnal animal, relatively large eyes. The thick fur is dark brown and the bushbaby sports a thick bushy tail. Your average bushbaby measures around 80 cm in length, of which the tail is around 45 cm, and weighs less than two kg.

The lesser bushbaby *(Galago senegalensis)* is about half the size of the greater bushbaby. It is a very light grey in colour and has yellowish colouring on the legs.

Vervet
Green monkey or grivet
(Cercopithecus aethiops)
Swahili: *tumbili*

The playful vervet is the most common monkey in Kenya and is seen in parks and reserves throughout the country. It is easily recognisable with its black face fringed by white hair, and yellowish-grey hair elsewhere except for the underparts which are whitish. The males have an extraordinary bright blue scrotum.

Vervets are usually found in groups of up to 30 and are extremely cheeky and inquisitive – they are often very habituated to humans. Normally they live in woodland and savannah but never in rainforest or semidesert areas.

TONY WHEELER

RHINOCEROS

(Diceros bicornis)
Swahili: *kifaru*

One of Africa's most sought-after species by poachers, the numbers of black rhino in Kenya have fallen dramatically in the past, though they are now once again on the increase, thanks to some determined conservation efforts. They are now thought to number around 500, compared with around 20,000 in 1970!

Rhino are one of the more difficult animals to sight, simply because they're so few in numbers compared to other wildlife. They are seen in Amboseli quite often, and also in Masai Mara, Tsavo East (rarely), Nairobi National Park and Nakuru. Rhino usually feed in the very early morning or late afternoon; at other times they tend to keep out of sight.

The eyesight of the rhino is extremely poor and it relies more on its keen senses of smell and hearing. Usually when alarmed it will flee from perceived danger, but if it decides to charge it needs to be given a wide berth, though with its poor eyesight chances are it'll miss its target anyway. Rhinos have been known to charge trains and even the carcasses of dead elephants!

A rhino's territory depends on the type of country and the availability of food, and so can be as little as a couple of hectares or as much as 50 sq km. The diet consists mainly of leaves, shoots and buds of a large variety of bushes and trees.

Rhino reach sexual maturity by five years but females do not usually become pregnant for the first time until around seven years of age. Calves weigh around 40 kg at birth and by three months of age weigh around 140 kg. Adult animals weigh in at anything from 1000 kg to 1600 kg! They are solitary animals, only coming together for some days during mating. Calves stay with the mother for anything up to three years, although suckling generally stops after the first year.

GREG HERRIMAN

GREG HERRIMAN

WART HOG

(Phacochoerus aethiopicus)
Swahili: *ngiri*

Although there are a number of wild-pig species in Kenya, the one you're most likely to see is the wart hog. It is found in all the major parks – Amboseli, Masai Mara, Nairobi, Tsavo, Meru, Marsabit and Samburu.

The wart hog gets its name from the somewhat grotesque wart-like growths which grow on its face. They are usually found in family groups of a boar, a sow and three or four young. Their most (or perhaps only) endearing habit is the way they turn tail and trot away with their thin tufted tails stuck straight up in the air like some antenna.

The males are usually bigger than the females, measuring up to one metre and weighing as much as 100 kg. They grow upper and lower tusks; the upper ones curve outwards and upwards and grow as long as 60 cm; the lower ones are usually less than 15 cm.

Wart hog live mainly on grass, but also eat fruit and bark, and, in hard times, will burrow with the snout for roots and bulbs. They rest and give birth in abandoned burrows or sometimes excavate a cavity in abandoned termite mounds. The young are born in litters of up to eight, although two to four is far more usual.

TONY WHEELER

TONY WHEELER

ZEBRA

(Equus burchelli, Equus grevyi)
Swahili: *punda milia*

TONY WHEELER

Zebra are one of the most common animals in the Kenyan parks and are widely distributed. You'll find them in great numbers in Nairobi, Tsavo, Amboseli, Samburu, Buffalo Springs, Maralal and Marsabit reserves as well as Masai Mara where they are present in the thousands.

Zebra often intermingle with other animals, most commonly the wildebeest but also topi and hartebeest.

There are two species to be seen in Kenya, the most common being Burchell's zebra which is found in all the western and southern parks all the way up to Samburu and Maralal. In the more arid north-west and north-east, however, the most common species is the Grevy's zebra which differs from Burchell's in having much narrower and more numerous stripes, prominent, broad, rounded ears, and a pure white underbelly.

GEOFF CROWTHER   GREVY'S

Some taxonomists classify Burchell's zebra into various 'races' or subspecies but this is a contentious issue since it is impossible to find two zebras exactly alike even in the same herd. What is more certain is that although Burchell's and Grevy's zebra often form mixed herds over much of their range, they do not interbreed in the wild.

Zebra are grazers but will occasionally browse on leaves and scrub. They need water daily and rarely wander far from a water hole, though they appear to have considerably more resistance to drought than antelope.

Reproductive rituals take the form of fierce fights between rival stallions for control of a group of mares. The gestation period is about 12 months and one foal is born at a time.

The most usual predator is the lion, though hyena and hunting dogs will occasionally take zebra too.

GEOFF CROWTHER

Kenya

Introduction

In past centuries, the main visitors to Kenya were the Arab traders who plied their dhows along the eastern coast of Africa. These days it's tourists and adventurers who come to visit Kenya in large numbers – currently around one million annually – and it's little wonder as it has an amazing variety of attractions to offer.

For many people Kenya means wildlife and in this field alone it is one of the best places in Africa. Millions of wildebeest on their annual migration, and equally large numbers of pink flamingos massing on the shores of the Rift Valley soda lakes are breathtaking sights. For sheer majesty it's hard to beat the sight of a herd of elephants crossing the plains with Africa's most famous mountain, the evocative snowcapped Kilimanjaro, rising in the background. Kenya is the heart of safari country and a trip through a few of Kenya's spectacular reserves is a memorable experience.

If relaxation is on your mind then head for the coast. Mombasa is a town with a history, and from here any of the superb picture-postcard beaches are easily accessible. But without doubt the highlight of the coast is the island of Lamu, where the Arab influence is evident and the pace of life definitely a few steps behind the rest of the country – the perfect place to unwind for a week, or two...

Those people who are seeking more energetic pursuits will find no shortage of challenges – Kenya has some excellent mountains to climb, especially the popular Mt Kenya with its unusual alpine flora, and the much less visited Mt Elgon in the west on the Ugandan border. Organised camel treks through Kenya's semidesert north also attract a steady stream of hardy souls.

The heart of this relatively prosperous country is the bustling capital, Nairobi. It is a modern and efficient city where things work and business can be taken care of in a snap – a far cry from so many other African countries where even simple things like a telephone call can be a major exercise. Added to this is the fact that Kenya has excellent air connections with Europe, Asia and elsewhere in Africa, making it the ideal place for a short visit, or the starting or finishing point for a longer sojourn in Africa. Either way it's a great place – don't miss it.

Facts about the Country

HISTORY
The Birthplace of Humanity

Thanks to the Leakey family's now famous digs in Olduvai Gorge (Tanzania) and around Lake Turkana (Kenya), the Rift Valley which runs through the centre of Kenya has been established as the 'cradle of humanity'. The Leakeys' discoveries of several hominoid skulls, one of which is estimated to be 2½ million years old, have radically altered the accepted theories on the origin of humans.

Before the East African digs, the generally accepted theory was that the ancestors of modern humans were of two different species: ape-like *Australopithecus africanus* and *Australopithecus robustus*. It was believed that one of these species died out while the other gave rise to *Homo sapiens*. The Leakey discoveries suggested that there was a third contemporary species, *Homo habilis*, and that it was this one which gave rise to modern humans while both the Australopithecus species died out, leaving no descendants. The dust has yet to settle on this anthropological issue.

Early Settlement

This area of Africa has people from all over the country – Kenya is home to almost every major language in Africa. Even Khoisan, the 'click' language spoken by the Bushmen and Hottentots in southern Africa, has its representatives, although these days they are only a tiny community close to the Tana River near the coast. This diversity is clear evidence that Kenya has been a major migratory pathway over the centuries.

The first wave of immigrants were the tall, nomadic, Cushitic-speaking people from Ethiopia who began to move south around 2000 BC. They were pastoralists and depended on good grazing land for their cattle and goats, so when the climate began to change and the area around Lake Turkana became more arid, they were forced to

KENYA

Area: 582,645 sq km
Population: 28.2 million
Population Growth Rate: 2.9%
Capital: Nairobi
Head of State: President Daniel arap Moi
Official Languages: Swahili, English
Currency: Kenyan shilling
Exchange Rate: US$1 = 54 KSh
Per Capita GNP: US$320
Inflation: 46%
Time: UTC + 3

resume their migration south. They got as far as central Tanzania.

A second group of pastoralists, the Eastern Cushitics, followed them in around 1000 BC and occupied much of central Kenya. The rest of the ancestors of the country's medley of tribes arrived from all over Africa between 500 BC and 500 AD, though there was still much movement and rivalry for land right up to the beginning of the 20th century. Even today it hasn't ended completely: the Bantu-speaking people (such as the Gusii, Kikuyu, Akamba and Meru) arrived from West

Africa, while the Nilotic speakers (such as the Maasai, Luo, Samburu and Turkana) came from the Nile Valley in southern Sudan.

Arab & Persian Traders

While migrations were going on in the interior, Muslims from the Arabian peninsula and Shirazis from Persia (now Iran) began to visit the East African coast from the 8th century AD onwards. They came to trade, convert and settle, rather than conquer as they had done in North Africa and Spain. Their dhows would head down on the northeast monsoon bringing glassware, ironware, textiles, wheat and wine, and return with ivory, slaves, tortoiseshell and rhino horn.

This trade soon extended right across the Indian Ocean to India and beyond. (Even China entered the fray at one point early in the 15th century, with a fleet of 62 ships and an escort of some 37,000 men, after the king of Malindi had sent the Chinese emperor a gift of a giraffe!) Many of the traders stayed to settle and intermarry with the Africans. As a result, a string of relatively affluent and Islamic-influenced coastal towns sprang up along the East African coast from Somalia to Mozambique, acting as entrepôts for the cross-Indian Ocean trade. Though there was naturally rivalry between these towns from time to time, up until the 16th century life was relatively peaceful. All this was to be rudely shattered with the arrival of the Portuguese.

Portuguese Invaders

While the Spanish Crown was busy backing expeditions to the Americas, the Portuguese were determined to break the Ottoman Turks' grip on trade with the Far East, particularly the trade in spices – worth more than their weight in gold in Europe. Throughout the 15th century, the Portuguese had been exploring further and further down the western coast of Africa until, in 1498, they finally rounded the Cape of Good Hope and headed up the east coast under the command of Vasco da Gama.

They were given a hostile reception both at Sofala on the Mozambique coast and at Mombasa, but were lucky to find a friendly sultan at Malindi who provided them with a pilot who knew the route to India. Da Gama was back again with another expedition in 1502, after selling the first expedition's cargo of spices in Portugal and reaping a small fortune.

The main Portuguese onslaught began with Dom Francisco de Almeida's armada of 23 ships and some 1500 men in 1505. Sofala was looted and burned to the ground, Kilwa was occupied and garrisoned, and Mombasa was taken after a naval bombardment and fierce street fighting. Mombasa was sacked again by Nuña da Cunha in 1528. Despite attempts by the Ottoman Turks to wrest control back from the Portuguese in 1585 and 1589, the Arab monopoly of Indian Ocean trade had been broken.

After the original onslaught, there followed two centuries of harsh colonial rule. Tribute was demanded and levies were imposed on all non-Portuguese ships visiting the coastal towns. Severe retribution was the punishment for the slightest offence. Economic exploitation came hand in hand with a drive to convert the local population to Catholicism, but the Portuguese never had much success at this, and whenever an outpost was abandoned, those who had been 'converted' reverted to Islam. Mombasa came to be the principle Portuguese outpost following the construction of Fort Jesus there in 1593.

The Portuguese made their task easier by playing one sultan off against another, but their grip over the East African coast was always tenuous as their outposts had to be supplied from Goa in India, where the viceroy had his headquarters. Delays were inevitable. The colonial bureaucracy also became moribund because offices were sold to the highest bidder. And, in the final analysis, Portugal was too small a country and lacked sufficient resources to effectively hold on to a worldwide empire.

The beginning of the end came in 1698 when Fort Jesus fell to the Arabs after a siege lasting 33 months. By 1720, the Portuguese had packed up and left the Kenyan coast for good.

Omani Dynasties

The Arabs remained in control of the East African coast until the arrival of the British and Germans in the late 19th century. The depredations of the Portuguese period, however, had exacted a heavy price and the constant quarrelling among the Arab governors who succeeded them led to a decline in the trade and prosperity which the East African coast had once enjoyed. Political and economic recovery had to wait until the beginning of the 19th century.

Throughout the 18th century, Omani dynasties from the Persian Gulf entrenched themselves along the East African coast. They were nominally under the control of the Sultan of Oman, but this control was largely ineffective until Seyyid Said came to the Omani throne in 1805.

The Omanis had built up a relatively powerful navy during the latter part of the 18th century, and Seyyid Said used it to bring the East African dynasties into line. In 1822 he sent an army to subdue Mombasa, Paté and Pemba, which were then ruled by the Mazrui clan.

The Mazruis appealed to Britain for help, which it provided the following year in the form of two warships on a survey mission. The commander of one of these ships, Captain Owen, decided to act first and ask questions later, so the British flag was raised over Fort Jesus and a protectorate was declared. A small garrison was left in charge, but three years later the British government repudiated the protectorate and the flag was hauled down. Seyyid Said reasserted his control the following year, garrisoned Fort Jesus and began to lay out clove plantations on Zanzibar. In 1832 he moved his court to Zanzibar.

19th Century Colonialism

By the mid-19th century, several European nations were showing an interest in the East African coast, including the British and the Germans. The British were interested in the suppression of the slave trade, and when Seyyid Said moved to Zanzibar they set up a consulate on the island. Later an agreement was reached between the British and the Germans as to their spheres of interest in East Africa. Part of the deal was that the Sultan of Zanzibar would be allowed to retain a 16-km-wide strip of the Kenyan coastline under a British protectorate. The agreement remained in place right up until independence, when the last Sultan of Zanzibar, Seyyid Khalifa, then ceded the territory to the new government.

The Kenyan interior, particularly the Rift Valley and the Aberdare highlands, remained impregnable to outsiders until the 1880s because it was occupied by Maasai pastoralists. Their reputation as a proud warrior tribe had been sufficient to deter Arab slavers and traders and European missionaries and explorers up to that date. But with the rest of Africa being combed by European explorers, Kenya's turn was soon to follow.

Notable early explorers who lived to tell the tale were Gustav Fischer (a German whose party was virtually annihilated by Maasai at Hell's Gate on Lake Naivasha in 1882), Joseph Thomson (a Scot who reached Lake Victoria via the Rift Valley lakes and the Aberdares in 1883) and Count Teleki von Szek (an Austrian who explored the Lake Turkana region and Mt Kenya in 1887). James Hannington, an Anglican bishop who set out in 1885 to set up a diocese in Uganda, wasn't quite so fortunate. He discovered Lake Bogoria (known as Lake Hannington during colonial days) but was killed when he reached the Nile.

By the late 19th century, the Maasai were considerably weakened and their numbers reduced by years of civil war between two opposing factions, the Ilmaasai and the Iloikop. The dispute was about which of the two were the true descendants of Olmasinta, the legendary founder of the tribe. Rinderpest (a cattle disease), cholera, smallpox and famine had also taken their toll between 1880 and 1892. Because of this, the British were able to negotiate a treaty with Olonana (known as Lenana today), the *laibon* ('chief' or 'spiritual leader') of the Maasai. Armed with this treaty, the British were able to construct the Mombasa-Uganda railway through the heart of the Maasai grazing lands. The approximate halfway point of this railway is where Nairobi stands today.

White Settlement

With the railway completed and the headquarters of the colonial administration moved from Mombasa to Nairobi, white settlers began to move into the fertile highlands north of Nairobi in search of farming lands. Their interests clashed with those of the Maasai, prompting the colonial authorities to pressure Olonana into restricting the Maasai to two reserves, one on either side of the new railway. Though this was a blow to Maasai independence, worse was to follow – the white settlers soon wanted the northern reserve as well. In 1910 and 11, those Maasai who lived there were forced to trek south, despite Olonana's objections.

Though it's probably true that it was the Maasai who had the greatest amount of land taken from them by the white settlers, the Kikuyu, a Bantu agricultural tribe which occupied the highlands around the western side of Mt Kenya and the Aberdares, also suffered. The Kikuyu came to nurse a particular grievance about the alienation of land by white settlers later on in the 20th century (see African Nationalism later in this section). Many of the numerically larger tribes such as the Luo and Luyha and the tribes of the north-east were hardly affected, if at all.

White settlement in the early years of the 20th century was led by Lord Delamere, a pugnacious gentleman-farmer from Cheshire, England. Since he was not familiar with the land, its pests and its wildlife, his first ventures – into sheep farming and, later, wheat growing – were disastrous. By 1912, however, following the move to the highlands, Delamere and his followers had put the colony onto a more realistic economic footing by establishing mixed agricultural farms. Other European settlers established coffee plantations about the same time, including Karen Blixen and her hunter husband, Bror. Her memoirs are to be found in the book *Out of Africa*, which has been made into a very successful film starring Meryl Streep and Robert Redford.

White settlement of Kenya was interrupted by WWI, during which some two-thirds of the 3000 white settlers formed impromptu cavalry units and went off in search of Germans in neighbouring Tanganyika, leaving their wives behind to manage the farms. The soldiers were not entirely successful but they did eventually manage to drive the German forces into Central Africa with some able assistance from Jan Smut's South African units. However, General von Lettow-Vorbeck's intrepid unit of 155 Germans and 3000 Africans remained undefeated when the armistice was signed in November 1918. It was during a skirmish between the two armies in January 1917 that Captain Frederick Selous (after whom the national park in Tanzania was named) was killed. Under the Treaty of Versailles, Germany lost Tanganyika and the British were given a mandate by the League of Nations to administer the territory.

Settlement of Kenya resumed after the war under a scheme where veterans of the European campaign were offered land in the highlands, either at rock-bottom prices or on long-term loans. The effect of this was to raise the white settler population to around 9000 by 1920. By the 1950s it had reached 80,000.

African Nationalism

While all this was going on, more and more Kikuyu were migrating to Nairobi or being drawn into the colonial economy in one way or another. They weren't at all happy about the alienation of their land and this led to the formation of a number of associations whose principle concern was the return of land to the Kikuyu.

One of the early leaders of the Kikuyu political associations was Harry Thuku. Shortly after he was arrested for his activities by the colonial authorities in March 1922, a crowd of Africans gathered outside the Nairobi Central Police Station where he was being held. Reports differ as to what happened next, but by the time the police had stopped shooting, between 21 and 100 people had been killed.

Thuku was eventually exiled to Kisimayo and was only finally released from jail in 1930 after he had agreed to cooperate with the colonial authorities. His cooperation cost him his leadership of the Kikuyu movement since he was thenceforth regarded as a collaborator. This early Sharpeville led to the politicisation of the Kikuyu and was the start of a sustained campaign for political, social and economic rights. (Sharpeville refers to the notorious massacre by police of unarmed black demonstrators in 1960 in the town of the same name in South Africa. It signalled the beginning of the armed struggle by the African National Congress (ANC) against the apartheid regime.)

While Harry Thuku's star was on the wane, that of another member of the tribe was on the rise. His name was Johnstone Kamau, later changed to Jomo Kenyatta, and he was to become independent Kenya's first president. Kenyatta was born in 1892 in the highlands north of Nairobi, the son of a peasant farmer. He spent the early years of his life as a shepherd tending his father's flocks. When he was in his teens he ran away to a nearby Church of Scotland mission school where he picked up an education.

At the age of 29 he moved to Nairobi. He worked there as a court interpreter and watermeter reader but his real skills lay elsewhere – as an orator. He soon became the secretary for propaganda of the East Africa Association, which had been set up to campaign for land reform, better wages, education and medical facilities for Africans. At this time, Africans were barred from hotels and restaurants and were only considered for the most menial jobs within the colonial administration.

Although it was official British government policy to favour African interests over those of the settlers in the event of conflicts, this was often ignored in practice because of the dominance of Lord Delamere's lobby in the whites-only legislative council. Recognising this, Kenyatta soon moved to join the more outspoken Kikuyu Central Association as its secretary-general.

Shortly afterwards, in 1929, with money supplied by Indians with communist connections, he sailed for London to plead the Kikuyu case with the British colonial secretary. Though the colonial secretary declined to meet him, Kenyatta teamed up with a group called the League Against Imperialism which took him to Moscow and Berlin and then back to Nairobi. He returned to London the following year and remained there for the next 15 years. He spent his time perfecting his oratory with Trafalgar Square crowds, studying revolutionary tactics in Moscow, visiting cooperative farms in Scandinavia and building up the Pan-African Federation with Hastings Banda (who later became the president of Malawi) and Kwame Nkrumah (who later became the president of Ghana). By the time he returned to Kenya in 1946, he was the recognised leader of the Kenyan liberation movement.

During WWII, the Belgian, British, French and Italian governments all recruited African troops to fight. The overall effect on Africans (as well as soldiers from other colonised peoples) was a realisation that the Europeans were not omnipotent. They could be defeated or, at the least, forced to come to terms with African aspirations for the same benefits and opportunities as their European overlords. Africans had also been trained in the use of arms. When the war ended, therefore, the returning soldiers were in no mood to accept the status quo and began to actively campaign for change.

The main African political organisation involved in the confrontation with the colonial authorities was the Kenya African Union (KAU), first headed by Harry Thuku and then by James Gichuru who himself stood down in favour of Kenyatta on the latter's return from Britain. The Kikuyu Central Association had been banned in 1940 along with many other similar organisations.

Mau Mau Rebellion

As the demands of the KAU became more and more strident and the colonial authorities less and less willing to make concessions, oath-taking ceremonies began to spread among various tribes like the Kikuyu, Maasai and Luo. Some of these secret oaths bound the participants to kill Europeans and their African collaborators. The Mau Mau was one such secret political society which bonded its members, willingly or otherwise, to the organisation via oath-taking ceremonies. Formed in 1952, it consisted mainly of Kikuyu tribespeople, and its aim was to drive white settlers out of Kenya.

The first blow was struck early in 1953 with the killing of a white farmer's entire herd of cattle. This was followed, a few weeks later, by the massacre of 21 Kikuyu loyal to the colonial government. The Mau Mau rebellion had started. The government declared an emergency and began to gather the tribespeople into 'protected villages', surrounded by barbed wire and booby-trapped trenches, which they were forbidden to leave during the hours of darkness. Some 20,000 Kikuyu 'home guards' were recruited to assist British army units brought in to put down the rebellion and to help police the 'protected villages'. By the time the rebellion came to an end in 1956 with the defeat of the Mau Mau, the death toll stood at over 13,500 Africans – Mau Mau guerrillas, civilians and troops – and just over 100 Europeans, 37 of whom were settlers. In the process, an additional 20,000 Kikuyu had been thrown into detention camps where many died of disease or exposure.

Only a month after the rebellion started, Kenyatta and several other KAU leaders were arrested and put on trial as the alleged leaders of the Mau Mau. It's very doubtful that Kenyatta had any influence over the Mau Mau commanders, let alone that he was one of their leaders, but he was, nevertheless, sentenced to seven years jail in the remote Turkana region after a trial lasting five months. He was released in 1959 but was immediately sent to Lodwar under house arrest.

The rebellion shook the settlers to the roots and gave rise to a number of white political parties with opposing demands, ranging from partition of the country between blacks and whites to the transfer of

power to a democratically elected African government. It should have been obvious to anyone with eyes to see that the latter view would have to prevail in the end, but it wasn't adopted as official policy until the Lancaster House Conference in London in 1960. The rebellion did lead, however, to an exodus of white settlers who packed their bags and headed off to Rhodesia, South Africa and Australia. At the conference, independence was scheduled for December 1963 and the British government agreed to provide the new Kenyan government with US$100 million in grants and loans so that it would be able to buy out European farmers in the highlands and restore the land to the tribes from whom it had been taken.

In the meantime a division occurred in the ranks of the KAU between those who wanted a unitary form of government with firm centralised control in Nairobi and those who favoured a federal setup in order to avoid Kikuyu domination. The former renamed their party the Kenya African National Union (KANU) and the latter split off under the leadership of Ronald Ngala to become the Kenya African Democratic Union (KADU). Many of the white settlers, who had come to accept the inevitable, supported the KADU.

Kenyatta was released from house arrest in mid-1961 and assumed the presidency of the KANU. Despite his long period of incarceration by the colonial authorities, he appeared to harbour no resentment against the whites and indeed set out to reassure the settlers that they would have a future in the country when independence came. At a packed meeting of settlers in Nakuru Town Hall in August 1963, he asked them to stay, saying that the country needed experience and that he didn't care where it came from. He assured them of the encouragement and protection of the new government and appealed for harmony, saying that he wanted to show the rest of the world that different racial groups were capable of living and working together. It did the trick. Kenyatta's speech transformed him, in the eyes of the settlers, from the feared and reviled spiritual leader of the Mau Mau into the venerable *mzee* ('respected elder') of the post-independence years.

Most of the white settler farms have been bought out by the government over the subsequent years and the land divided up into small subsistence plots which support 15 to 20 people. This may well have appeased the pressure for land redistribution in a country with one of the world's highest birth rates, but it has led to a serious decline in agricultural production (and therefore a diminishing tax base for the government) and has threatened to damage the region's delicate ecology. By 1980, Kenya was forced to import half the grain it needed, whereas in 1975 it was self-sufficient. The government is keen to halt the break-up of the settler farms which remain, but the prospects of being able to do this in a land-hungry nation are not good. In any case, many of the vast properties held by former white settlers were snapped up by prominent Kikuyu politicians in the years following independence. Many black radicals in Kenya regarded this as a betrayal of the independence struggle and the stand-off continues to this day.

Independence

The two parties, KANU and KADU, formed a coalition government in 1962, but after the May 1963 elections, KANU and Kenyatta came to power. Independence came on 12 December 1963 with Kenyatta as the first president. He ruled Kenya until his death in 1978. Under Kenyatta's presidency, Kenya developed into one of Africa's most stable and prosperous nations. Unlike many other newly independent countries, there was no long string of coups and counter-coups, military holocausts, power-crazy dictators and secessionist movements. It wasn't all plain sailing, but Kenyatta left the country in a much better state than he found it and, although there were excesses, they were minor by African standards. By the time he died, there were enough Kenyans with a stake in their country's continued progress to ensure a relatively smooth succession to the presidency – violence and instability would

have benefited few people. Kenyatta's main failings were that he was excessively biased in favour of his own tribe and that he often regarded honest criticism as tantamount to treason. Opponents of his regime who became too vocal for comfort frequently 'disappeared'.

Control of the government and large sectors of the economy still remain in the hands of the Kikuyu, to the social and financial detriment of other ethnic groups. Corruption in high places remains a problem and once prompted JM Kariuki, a former Mau Mau fighter and later an assistant minister in the government, to remark that Kenya had become a nation of '10 millionaires and 10 million beggars'. There are indeed great disparities in wealth. Many destitute squatters and unemployed people, especially in

Jomo Kenyatta became independent Kenya's first president in 1963. He led the country until his death in 1978.

Nairobi, have little hope of ever finding employment – but this is hardly a problem peculiar to Kenya. The accumulation of wealth and land by a handful of top politicians and their business associates and the concurrent dispossession and impoverishment of tens of thousands of their fellow countrymen is a theme frequently addressed by the more politically aware of Kenya's novelists and, in some cases, has led to their exile.

In 1964, Kenya effectively became a one-party state following the voluntary dissolution of the opposition KADU party. With it died the party's policy of federalism, and the two chamber legislature became the single chamber legislative assembly. However, when Oginga Odinga, a Luo, was purged from the KANU hierarchy in 1966, due to allegations that he was plotting against the government, he formed his own opposition party, the Kenya People's Union. The party was later banned and Odinga was jailed. He was released when he agreed to rejoin KANU, but was imprisoned again in 1969 on spurious charges. After his release in 1971 he was banned from running for public office until 1977.

Tom Mboya, an intelligent young Luo who was widely regarded as future presidential material, was murdered by a Kikuyu gunman in 1969. The ambitious Mboya was feared by influential Kikuyu, who felt that he had designs on succeeding Kenyatta as president. JM Kariuki, a very popular Kikuyu who spoke out stridently and often about the new black elite and their corrupt practices, met a similar fate: he was assassinated in 1975. Other politicians who opposed Kenyatta – however mildly – found themselves arrested and held for long periods, often without trial.

The 1980s

Kenyatta was succeeded by Daniel arap Moi, Kenyatta's Vice President. A member of the Tugen tribe, Moi was regarded by Kikuyu power brokers as a suitable front man for their interests. He lacked the charisma and cult following of Kenyatta, and so was even

less willing to brook criticism of his regime. The early years of his regime were marked by the arrest of dissidents, the disbanding of tribal societies and the closure of universities. There were allegations of conspiracies to overthrow the government, the details of which were often so labyrinthine that they could have come straight out of a spy novel. Whether these conspiracies were real or just a convenient façade to justify Moi's consolidation of power is hard to tell, since names and details were rarely released.

What certainly *was* real was the attempted coup by the Kenyan air force in August 1982. It was put down by forces loyal to the government, but by the time it was over about 120 people were dead and there had been widespread looting of the major shopping areas. Twelve ringleaders were subsequently sentenced to death and 900 others received jail sentences. The entire Kenyan air force was disbanded and replaced by a new unit.

Since then, other alleged conspiracies have come to light but, again, the details are rarely made known. The most publicised of these clandestine opposition groups was Mwakenya, which supposedly centred around a number of lecturers at Nairobi University along with the exiled novelist and playwright Ngugi wa Thiong'o. Certainly Ngugi has made his opposition to the Kenyan government quite plain, but there is little evidence to support the claim that he was a leading light of the movement.

President Moi was re-elected in March 1987 in an election which was most notable for the controversial voting system it employed. Candidates could only run in the secret ballot election after gaining a set percentage of the vote in a preliminary election whereby voters queued behind the candidate of their choice. If the candidate gained more than 70% of the queue vote, they were automatically elected and did not have to take part in the secret ballot election. The outcome was that at least 45 constituencies had no secret ballot as the candidate who had received over 70% of the turnout in the queue vote was automatically elected (it didn't matter that in one case the turnout was less than 9% of registered voters). In other constituencies, the number of candidates was significantly reduced because the nominees failed to win sufficient support at the preliminary election.

After the election, Moi expanded his cabinet to 33 ministers – many on the basis of political patronage – and, as a result, the government's (and therefore Moi's) position seemed totally secure. With the fall of a couple of outspoken politicians in the 1987 elections (amid allegations of vote rigging) it seemed unlikely that parliamentary opposition to Moi on major issues in the immediate future would be anything more than a whisper. Perhaps more significantly, changes to the constitution were rushed through parliament unopposed in late 1987, giving Moi increased presidential powers, including the right to dismiss senior judges and public servants without redress. The independence of the judiciary had been a much-admired cornerstone of the Kenyan political system ever since independence and the changes were viewed with alarm by many sections of society.

From this point on there ceased to be any effective political opposition within the parliamentary system and the party further strengthened its hold by augmenting the ranks of the KANU Youth Wing, who essentially served as pro-government vigilantes. They were frequently unleashed to disrupt demonstrations, harass opposition figures and maintain a climate of intimidation among those who might have similar sympathies. Many opposition political leaders were detained without trial during this period, including Mwai Kibaki and Kenneth Matiba.

Yet the government was unable to silence various leaders of the Christian churches (especially the bishops of the Anglican church), who increasingly turned their sermons into political speeches. They were supported by an outspoken critic of government nepotism, Professor Wangui Mathai, the leader of the Green Movement. All of these people were vilified by both the president and various ministers and there were calls for their removal and even arrest on charges of sedition. Mathai probably suffered most, as she was thrown out of her modest offices on University Way and forced to endure a public character assassination blitz, whose script could have been put together from the trash scrawled on toilet walls.

But times were changing. Multiparty politics was sweeping Africa and Kenya was not to escape.

The 1990s

With the collapse of Communism in Eastern Europe and the break up of the Soviet Union, the west's attention was abruptly refocused. It was no longer necessary to prop up corrupt African regimes in the name of containing Communism.

The Kenyan government quickly found itself under intense pressure from the donor countries to introduce a multiparty system and to name a date for elections if it wanted aid to be maintained. Though it prevaricated, the government – faced with a foreign debt of some US$9 billion, a downturn in the economy and determined grass-roots opposition in the form of FORD (Forum for the Restoration of Democracy) – was forced to capitulate. To drive the point home, aid was suspended by virtually all Western countries in early 1992.

Suddenly, everyone was talking politics everywhere and anywhere and there emerged a clear consensus that FORD would sweep to victory in any election, assuming it could get its act together and that the elections were reasonably free and fair. Unfortunately, the opposition shot itself in the foot in the lead-up to the elections. The principle players were Oginga Odinga, Kenneth Matiba and Mwai Kibaki. Originally all members of FORD, but unable to stomach the idea of anyone but themselves being the new president, they split the party into three – FORD-Kenya (Oginga Odinga), FORD-Asili (Kenneth Matiba) and the Democratic Party or DP (Mwai Kibaki). From that point on, they had no chance.

In the meantime, Moi, according to the IMF/World Bank, authorised the printing of

KSh 9 billion bank notes (over US$250 million), unsupported by foreign currency or gold reserves. He used these to line the pockets of his supporters and blatantly buy votes for the ruling party (KANU). In the lead-up to the elections, the newspapers were full of pictures and stories of *wananchi* ('peasants and workers') lining up to collect their KSh 500 and KANU-emblazoned T-shirt and cap. Moi knew that full stomachs would buy votes even if the economy collapsed shortly after the elections – which it virtually did.

He also played the tribal card for all it was worth in his home area, allowing the Kalenjin to wreak havoc among Kikuyu settlers in the area. Hundreds were killed and injured in these tribal clashes and thousands left homeless and destitute. Hardly anything has been done since to rehabilitate these people, and violence continues to simmer. The violence succeeded in driving Kikuyu (who were clearly not going to vote for KANU) from Kalenjin areas (Moi's home ground).

Another blatant ploy was to postpone the election until the final week of December and to ensure that it fell on a normal working day. Had it not finally been declared a public holiday about a week in advance, tens of thousands of registered voters, particularly in Nairobi and other major towns, would have been unable to travel back to the place where they were registered in order to vote. Moi was aware that he had little support in the Nairobi area and among the Kikuyu, as the election results were to show. His support among the Luo was also tenuous.

To curry the favour of the donor nations, international observers were brought in to monitor a cross section of the polling stations and to decide whether the elections had been free and fair. As far as the voting itself went, the elections were fair to a greater rather than a lesser degree, though the various opposition parties, predictably, denied this. The trouble was, the observers were flown in only days before the election and, by then, the dirty deeds had been done. Moi and KANU swept to victory, but with only one-third of the total vote. Clearly, the opposition

would have won if they had presented a united front, but vanity and ambition got in the way.

Vanity and ambition also resurfaced shortly after the elections as several MPs, unable to stomach the prospect of life on the opposition benches, cynically defected to the KANU and were welcomed with glee. Loyalty to the voters who had elected them on an opposition ticket was apparently of no concern to these MPs. The press cried foul, accusing KANU of having bought them. They were probably right but the evidence was, naturally, scant.

In many ways, though, KANU needn't have bothered, as the opposition went on to make complete fools of themselves by literally coming to blows over which of the three leaders was to occupy the leader of the opposition's chair in the parliament. It was a pathetic display of childish fractiousness and it's still going on today. All of the opposition parties, but particularly FORD-Kenya and FORD-Asili, have frequently been shaken to their foundations by some very transparent blood-letting over leadership. In an early 1996 by-election, the voter turn-out was an incredible 4.5%! KANU 'won', of course, but what a hollow victory!

In 1995, a new party was launched to draw all the opposition under one umbrella and agree on a single presidential candidate to contest the next elections. The party was Safina, founded by Richard Leakey (whom Moi had sacked as director of the Kenya Wildlife Service), Raila Odinga (Oginga Odinga's son and the FORD-Asili MP for Langata constituency), Paul Muite (a prominent lawyer) and other vocal opposition MPs. Moi was well aware of Leakey's international reputation and his ability to raise election funding from overseas. The party was refused registration and Leakey was vilified almost daily for weeks. He was accused of being a white supremacist and neocolonialist, harassed wherever he went and, on one occasion, beaten up. Whites should stay out of Kenyan politics and concern themselves only with business, Moi thundered. Apparently, being a Kenyan-born citizen bestowed no political rights on anyone who happened to be white. It was racism at its best.

Despite all the invective, Safina has made some headway in bringing the opposition together – except for Mwai Kibaki (DP) – but, equally it may lead to nothing, given the personalities of the protagonists.

Meanwhile, KANU has been doing its best to silence any credible contenders for State House other than the present incumbent. In 1990 the erudite former minister for Foreign Affairs, Dr Robert Ouko, was murdered shortly after returning from the USA, and the inquiry into his death has dragged on inconclusively ever since. The same goes for Koigi Wamwere, who was held in remand in a Nakuru jail for years and was only acquitted in 1996 of a charge of attacking a police station with the intent of stealing weapons. Likewise, Professor George Saitoti, the Vice President, after an unwise slip of the tongue regarding his presidential aspirations, was forced to utterly debase himself in public and beg for forgiveness for even thinking about it. But the *pièce de résistance* was KANU's 1996 announcement that it was planning to change the constitution to allow Moi another term in office if he wins the next election (at present he is barred from a further term as president).

A great deal depends on the outcome of the next election (scheduled for December 1997) and, as far as the continuation of aid is concerned, something serious has to be done about clearing up the backlog of corruption and embezzlement cases involving billions of Kenyan shillings. Most of these cases have been going on for years with no resolution in sight. The Goldenberg, Trust Bank and Kamlesh Pattni scandals· alone amount to close to KSh 20 billion.

And political survival is not the government's only concern. Kenya still has one of the highest population growth rates of any country in the world (around 3%). The strain on health and educational facilities is already showing, and the situation seems unlikely to improve. Add to this the hundreds of thousands of people of working age who

are unable to find work, and you have a recipe for increased social turmoil and political instability.

GEOGRAPHY

Kenya straddles the equator and covers an area of some 583,000 sq km, which includes around 13,600 sq km of inland water in the form of part of Lake Victoria. It is bordered to the north by the arid bushlands and deserts of Ethiopia and Sudan, to the east by Somalia and the Indian Ocean, to the west by Uganda and Lake Victoria, and to the south by Tanzania. The main rivers in Kenya are the Athi/Galana and the Tana.

The country can be roughly divided into four main zones: the coastal belt, the Rift Valley and central highlands, western Kenya, and northern and eastern Kenya.

Coastal Belt

This area covers some 480 km of Indian Ocean littoral, including coral reefs and beaches, the Lamu archipelago, the Tana River estuary (Kenya's principal river) and a narrow, low-lying and relatively fertile strip of land suitable for agriculture. Beyond this, the terrain rises fairly steeply towards the central plateau and gives way to bushland and scrub desert.

Rift Valley & Central Highlands

These regions form the backbone of the country and it's here that Kenya's scenery is at its most spectacular. The lake-studded Rift Valley runs the whole length of the country from Lake Turkana to Lake Magadi and is peppered with the cones of extinct volcanoes. It's bounded on the eastern side by the thickly forested slopes of the Aberdare mountains and, further to the east, by the massif of Mt Kenya – Africa's second highest mountain at 5199m. This is the most fertile area of the country and the lower slopes of the mountains are intensively cultivated. Nairobi, the capital, sits at the southern end of the central highlands.

Western Kenya

The west of the country consists of an

undulating plateau stretching from the Sudanese border to Tanzania in the south. The area around the shores of Lake Victoria is particularly fertile, well watered and intensively cultivated, and is also home to Mt Elgon (Kenya's second highest mountain at 4321m). Further south the land gradually merges into scrub and savannah, and is suitable only for cattle grazing; however, it's here that Kenya's largest and most popular wildlife sanctuaries are situated – Masai Mara, Amboseli and Tsavo. To the south of Amboseli rises the spectacular massif of Mt Kilimanjaro – Africa's highest mountain (5895m).

Northern & Eastern Kenya

These two regions cover a vast mountainous area of bushland, scrub and desert, where rainfall is sparse and the land is suitable only for cattle grazing. It's this area where Kenya is at its wildest and most untouched by the modern world.

GEOLOGY

The major geological feature in Kenya is the Great Rift Valley, a huge depression which extends for nearly 5000 km down to Mozambique in south-eastern Africa.

The valley system consists of a series of troughs and areas of uplift known as swells. The troughs, generally 40 to 55 km wide, are found along parallel fault lines, and make up most of the lakes and escarpments in East Africa. The swells form on either side of the troughs, and it's here that the mighty peaks of Kilimanjaro, Mt Kenya and Mt Elgon are found – all extinct volcanoes. The floor of the Rift Valley is still dropping, although at the rate of a few mm per year you are hardly likely to notice!

The Rift Valley is certainly not one long, well-formed valley with huge escarpments either side, although this classic geography does occur in places (the Rift Valley Province is one such location). Sometimes there are a series of small scarps, or even just a single scarp on one side (such as the Nkuruman Escarpment east of Masai Mara). In some cases uplift has occurred between parallel fault lines, leading to the formation of spectacular mountain ranges such as the Ruwenzoris on the Uganda-Zaïre border.

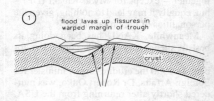

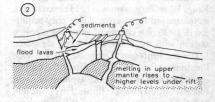

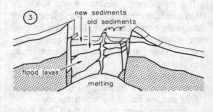

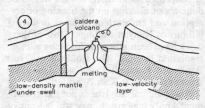

Extensive volcanic activity (as shown above) resulted in East Africa's Rift Valley, one of the world's most extensive rifts. The volcanic activity produced Mt Kilimanjaro, Mt Kenya and Mt Elgon.

CLIMATE

Because of Kenya's diverse geography, temperature, rainfall and humidity vary widely, but there are effectively four zones about which generalisations can be made.

The undulating plateau of western Kenya is generally hot and fairly humid with rainfall spread throughout the year, falling mostly in the evenings. The greatest precipitation is usually during April when a maximum of 200 mm may be recorded, while the lowest falls are in January with an average of 40 mm. Temperatures range from a minimum of 14°C or 18°C to a maximum of 30°C to 34°C.

The central highlands and Rift Valley enjoy perhaps the most agreeable climate in the country, though there's quite a variation between the hot and relatively dry floor of the central Rift Valley and the snow-covered peaks of Mt Kenya. Rainfall varies from a minimum of 20 mm in July to 200 mm in April and falls essentially in two seasons – March to May (the 'long rains') and October to December (the 'short rains'). The Aberdare mountains and Mt Kenya are the country's main water catchment areas, and falls of up to 3000 mm per year are often recorded. Average temperatures vary from a minimum of 10°C or 14°C to a maximum of 22°C to 26°C.

The vast semi-arid bushlands, deserts and lava flows of northern and eastern Kenya are where the most extreme variations in temperature are to be found, ranging from highs of up to 40°C during the day in the deserts, dropping down to 20°C or less at night. Rainfall in this area is sparse and when it does fall it often comes in the form of violent storms. July is generally the driest month and November the wettest. The average annual rainfall varies between 250 and 500 mm.

The fourth climatic zone is the coastal belt, which is hot and humid all year round, though tempered by coastal sea breezes. Rainfall ranges from a minimum of 20 mm in February to a maximum of 300 mm in May. The annual average is between 1000 mm and 1250 mm. Average temperatures vary little throughout the year, ranging from a minimum of 22°C to a maximum of 30°C.

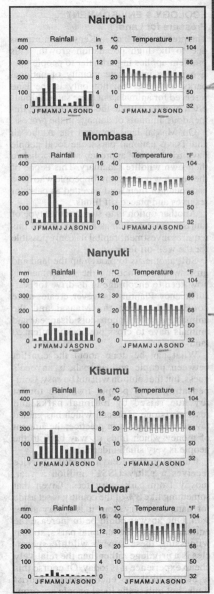

KENYA

ECOLOGY & ENVIRONMENT
Pressure for Land

The pressure for land in Kenya is enormous due to the high population growth. This problem applies in particular to people who live in the immediate vicinity of national parks and reserves: not only is the land reserved for animals, but these same animals often wander outside the parks, causing tremendous amounts of damage in the process.

On Maasai land between the Amboseli and Tsavo national parks, the local people have tried a new approach and established their own wildlife sanctuary. This is one of the very few options left for people who have had much of their land gazetted as parks or reserves and placed off limits.

Another option is to start another type of tourism project, such as a lodge, but as this requires investment capital it is only possible for the well-off few.

Still another is to plough up the land and grow wheat, something the government is now keen to encourage in its drive for self-sufficiency. Planting, however, creates more conflicts between the Maasai and the animals, as wildlife corridors disappear and animals have to cross previously unfenced land.

What can be done about the conflict between people and animals is anyone's guess, but the solution will not be easy. Compensating local people from the tourist revenue raised by national parks and reserves is one approach which has gained favour recently. But in practice, the amount of money which finds its way back to the people is very small indeed.

Currently, the Kenya Wildlife Service receives a paltry US$13 million a year, mostly from park entry fees. Given that something like 8% of the country is set aside for nature conservation, it is a very small sum. One answer could be to increase the entrance fees to the national parks, so that witnessing these superb wildlife spectacles is a privilege rather than the relatively cheap experience it is today. Of course this is hardly likely to encourage the tourist trade, but unless the local people are prop-

erly compensated for their land, it's not inconceivable that the great wildlife reserves of Kenya will become little more than large 'safari parks', reminiscent of those found in the West.

Environmental Problems

It is the tourist industry which is the cause of some of Kenya's major environmental problems, and once again, tough measures are called for. Parks such as Amboseli and Masai Mara are crisscrossed with tracks and crawling with tourist minibuses. The problem is particularly bad in the Mara, where minibuses seem to go pretty much where they please, as regulations are not policed by the local Narok council that administers the reserve.

The lodges within the parks themselves also create problems. Foremost among these is their use of firewood, a valuable and scarce resource – a recent survey found that each of the lodges and tented camps around Masai Mara used, on average, 100 tonnes of firewood in a year.

FLORA & FAUNA
Flora

Kenya's flora is notably diverse because of the country's wide range of physiographic regions. The vast plains of the south are characterised by distinctive flat-topped acacia trees, interspersed with the equally distinctive bottle-shaped baobab trees and thorn bushes.

On the slopes of Mt Elgon and Mt Kenya the flora changes with altitude. Thick evergreen temperate forest grows between 1000 and 2000m, giving way to a belt of bamboo forest up to about 3000m. Above this height is mountain moorland, characterised by the amazing groundsel tree *(Dendrosencio)*, with its huge cabbage-like flowers, and giant lobelias with long spikes. In the semidesert plains of the north and north-east, the vegetation cover is unremarkable yet very characteristic – thorn bushes seem to go on forever. In the northern coastal areas mangroves are prolific and the trees are cut for export, mainly to the Middle East for use as

Wildlife Conservation

As Kenya relies so heavily on tourism for income, and because it's the animals which people have chiefly come to see, the government has placed a high priority on wildlife conservation and the eradication of poaching. To this end, in the late 1980s it appointed well-known palaeontologist Richard Leakey (son of Louis Leakey famed for discovering ancient human fossil remains in the Rift Valley in the 1950s) as head of the Kenya Wildlife Service.

Following Leakey's appointment, corrupt wildlife officials were sacked and the anti-poaching units beefed up, to the extent that 200 US-trained paramilitary personnel were deployed in 1990 on shoot-to-kill patrols. The measures have had a large degree of success, despite the fact that Richard Leakey was sacked in 1994 and replaced by an individual with a much lower profile. Extremely stiff penalties for poaching are now in effect.

Yet despite the risks, poaching still goes on, although on a much smaller scale than in previous years. It's easy to see the reasons for poaching. There is big money in ivory and rhino horn, and as long as the Taiwanese government and various Arab governments – notably the two Yemens, Oman and Kuwait – refuse to ban their importation, the slaughter of Kenya's wildlife is likely to continue. One kg of ivory is worth about US$300 wholesale and rhino horn is US$2000 a kg (or up to US$30,000 for a single horn). In the Middle East rhino horn is prized for dagger handles whilst in China and Korea, in powdered form, it's a supposed aphrodisiac.

Although poaching had been going on for many years, it took on a new dimension in 1972 as a result of the drought in north-eastern Africa which rendered some 250,000 Somali pastoralists destitute as their sheep, goats and camels died by the million. Many drifted south, armed with weapons ranging from bows and arrows to WWII guns, and found poaching to be a suitable antidote to poverty. Meanwhile, corruption in the Kenya Wildlife Service deepened, with officials taking bribes in return for turning a blind eye to the poachers' activities. By 1976, it was plain that the number of elephants being slaughtered by poachers far exceeded those dying as a result of drought and deforestation and it was estimated that there were over 1300 poachers operating within Tsavo National Park alone.

Worse was yet to come. In 1978, waves of Somalis hungry for ivory and rhino horn, and encouraged by official corruption, swept across the border and into the national parks, only this time they came with modern automatic weapons issued to them by the Somali government during the 1977 war with Ethiopia. They killed everything in their path including any Kenyan tribal poachers they came across. By the end of the decade, some 104,000 elephants (about 62% of the total) and virtually the entire rhino population had been slaughtered.

There was little improvement during the early 1980s despite the setting up of anti-poaching patrols armed with modern weapons, high-speed vehicles and orders to shoot on sight. Part of the reason was the patrols' reluctance to engage the Somalis, who have a reputation for toughness and uncompromising violence. By 1989, however, following the murder of George Adamson by poachers in the Kora National Reserve (as he was saving the lives of orphaned wildlife) as well as attacks on tourists in other national parks, the Kenyan government signalled its determination to seriously address the problem. ■

Minimising Your Impact

In their quest for the perfect photo opportunity, some drivers do crazy things. A healthy dose of common sense goes a long way, but too many drivers are under too much pressure to please their clients, with little regard for the effects on the wildlife. In the interests of the animals, please observe the following:

- Never get too close to the animals and back off if they are getting edgy or nervous. On a safari I once took, a female cheetah (with cub) became extremely agitated when she was totally surrounded and hemmed in by a dozen minibuses, all full of excited visitors trying to get their 'shot'. She reacted by dropping the cub and bolting.
- Never get out of your vehicle, except at designated points where this is permitted. The animals may look tame and harmless enough, but this is not a zoo – the animals are wild and you should treat them as such.
- Animals always have the right of way. Don't follow predators as they move off – you try stalking something when you've got half a dozen minibuses in tow.
- Keep to the tracks. One of the biggest dangers in the parks today is land degradation from too many vehicles crisscrossing the countryside. Amboseli's choking dust is largely a result of this. Likewise, Masai Mara in November 1992 looked, from the air, as though the East African Rally had been run entirely in the park. There were tyre tracks literally everywhere and they were clearly acting as drainage channels for the rain. If that continues, there won't be much grassland left.
- Don't light fires except at camp sites, and dispose of cigarettes with care.
- Don't litter the parks and camp sites. Unfortunately, the worst offenders are often the safari drivers and cooks who toss everything and anything out the window, and leave camp sites littered with all manner of crap. It won't do any harm to point out to them the consequences of what they're doing, or clean it up yourself. ∎

---

scaffolding; mangrove wood is termite resistant and is in high demand.

Fauna

Kenya has such a dazzling array of wildlife that game-viewing in the national parks is one of the main attractions of a visit to this country. All of the 'big five' (lion, buffalo, elephant, leopard and rhino) can be seen in at least two of the major parks, and there's a huge variety of other less famous but equally impressive animals.

To aid identification of animals while you're game-spotting on safari, refer to the Safari Guide on page 53. For a full treatment of Kenya's animals, Collins' *A Field Guide to the Mammals of Africa* has excellent colour plates to aid identification, as does the smaller *A Field Guide to the Larger Mammals of Africa*, also by Collins. The main trouble with both these books is the relatively poor index (which lists many animals only by their Latin names) and the frequent placement of colour plates far from the actual description of the animals in question. *Animals of East Africa* has good descriptive notes of the animals' habits and appearance, but the sketches are not the greatest and the notes on distribution are out of date.

The bird life is equally varied and includes ostriches, vultures and eagles, a wide variety of water birds such as flamingos, storks, pelicans, herons, ibis and cormorants, and others such as the yellow weaver birds which you'll see everywhere. The best reference guide for twitchers is *A Field Guide to the Birds of East Africa* by John G Williams. It is widely available in Kenya.

Endangered Species

Most of Kenya's major predators and herbivores have become endangered because of the continuous destruction of their natural habitat by people in search of agricultural and grazing land – particularly that adjacent to the national parks and game reserves.

The black rhino is probably Kenya's most endangered species, and its population has been ravaged by poachers over the years. Fortunately, it has been the subject of some major conservation efforts in recent years and its numbers are once again on the rise, although there are still very few in the wild. Rhino sanctuaries, complete with electric fencing, have been established in Tsavo and Lake Nakuru national parks, and the Aberdares is also due to be fenced in the future.

While the elephant is not technically endangered, it is still the target of poachers and large numbers are killed each year. Following the international ban on ivory, which was enforced by the UN Convention on International Trade in Endangered Species (CITES) in 1989, the number of elephants killed illegally in Kenya fell from over 2000 in 1988-89 to just over 200 in 1992-93.

GOVERNMENT & POLITICS

Kenya is a multiparty state, with the Kenya African National Union (KANU) being the ruling party. The major opposition parties (in order of numbers of seats held) are FORD-Asili, FORD-Kenya and the Democratic Party (DP). The government consists of the president, who holds executive power, and a single legislative assembly which consists of 188 members, the attorney general, the speaker, and 10 members who are nominated by the president. There's a high degree of political patronage.

The judiciary were, until 1987, independent of government pressure and free to interpret both the constitution and the laws passed by the legislative assembly. In that year, however, parliament rushed through a bill giving the president the right to dismiss judges without recourse to a tribunal, thus effectively silencing them as a source of opposition. The unpopular measure has yet to be repealed.

As far as the independence and freedom of action of government ministers is concerned, it would be fair to say that it's very limited. Indeed, it would not be inappropriate to slightly misquote Louis XIV's classic statement: 'L'état? C'est Moi!'

ECONOMY

The cornerstone of Kenya's capitalist economy is agriculture, which employs around 80% of the population, contributes some 29% of the GDP and accounts for over 50% of the country's export earnings. The principal food crops are maize, sorghum, cassava, beans and fruit, while the main cash crops are coffee, tea, cotton, sisal, pyrethrum and tobacco. The bulk of the food crops are grown by subsistence farmers on small plots of land, whereas most of the cash crops originate from large, privately owned plantations employing contract labour (though there's a significant input from smaller growers). Coffee and tea are the largest of the agricultural export earners with annual production being around 120,000 tonnes and 160,000 tonnes respectively.

While such figures might be a healthy sign for the country's balance of payments, there's a great deal of discontent among the small farmers and labourers, who are paid a pittance for the tea and coffee they produce or pick. In 1989-90, the country witnessed riots over this paltry sum. The dispute was handled badly by the Kenya Tea Development Authority (KTDA), and although several heads rolled and price increases were promised, it was all too little too late. Small growers regularly have to wait up to a year or more to be paid. The situation is similar in the coffee sector and exacerbated by internationally imposed quotas which limit Kenya's ability to dispose of its stockpile.

On the other hand, tourism has replaced coffee as the country's largest export earner, although arrivals have dropped off since 1992 due to the tribal clashes in western Kenya, and the nation's perceived political instability and general lack of security. Each year around 700,000 people visit Kenya, contributing more than US$200 million to the country's economy.

In addition to agriculture and tourism, Kenya has a relatively well developed industrial base which accounts for some 20% of GDP, though the bulk of this industry is concentrated around Nairobi and Mombasa. The principal products include processed food, beer, vehicles and accessories, construction materials, engineering, textiles, glass and chemicals. Initially, this sector of the economy was developed with import substitution in mind, but the bias has now changed in favour of joint-venture, export-oriented industries as a result of the increasing deficit in the balance of payments and IMF loan conditions. (The IMF have returned to Kenya after being thrown out in March 1993.) Kenya's external debt of around US$8 billion is still considered to be low, but the most worrying aspect is the high proportion of the country's foreign exchange earnings which go into servicing foreign debt – currently around 35%.

Mining is a relatively small contributor to GNP and is centred around the extraction of soda and fluorspar for export. There are other minerals, which include silver, gold, lead and limestone, but these have yet to be developed commercially.

Kenya's major export trading partners are the UK (17%), the EU (45%), the USA (about 5%) and Germany (12%).

Some 70% of domestic energy requirements are imported, but geothermal projects are being developed: there are four hydroelectric plants in operation along the Tana River and a hydroelectric plant was recently completed in the Turkwel Gorge. Kenya's major sources of imports are the EU (39%), the UK (about 18%), Japan (9%), Germany (8%) and the USA (5%).

POPULATION & PEOPLE

Kenya's population stands at around 28 million and is made up almost entirely of Africans, with small (although influential) minorities of Asians (about 80,000), Arabs (about 40,000) and Europeans (about 40,000). The population growth rate of around 3% is one of the world's highest and is putting great strain on the country's ability to expand economically and to provide reasonable educational facilities and other urban services.

Africans

There are more than 70 tribal groups among the Africans, although the distinctions between many of them are already blurred and are becoming more so as Western cultural values become more ingrained. Traditional values are also disintegrating as more and more people move to the larger towns, family and tribal groups become scattered and the tribal elders gradually die off. See the Tribal Groups & Cultures section on p. 106 for more information.

Yet even though the average African may have outwardly drifted away from tribal traditions, the tribe is still the single most important part of a person's identity. When two Africans meet and introduce themselves they will almost always say right at the outset what tribe they are from. Although nominally Christian for the most part, a surprising number of people still practise traditional customs. Some of the more brutal customs, such as clitoridectomy (female circumcision), were outlawed by the British, usually with the aid of the local missionaries, but circumcision still remains the main rite to pass from childhood to adulthood for boys.

The most important distinguishing feature between the tribes is language. The majority

Kenya has one of the world's highest population growths, so you'll encounter plenty of children.

of Kenya's Africans fall into one of two major language groups: the Bantu and the Nilotic. The Bantu people arrived in East Africa in waves from West Africa over a period of time from around 500 BC. Among the Bantu the largest tribal groups are the Kikuyu, Meru, Gusii, Embu, Akamba, Luyha and Mijikenda.

The Nilotic speakers migrated to the area from the Nile Valley some time earlier but then had to make room for the migrations of Bantu-speaking people. Nilotic speaking groups include the Maasai, Turkana, Samburu, Pokot, Luo and Kalenjin. Together, these tribal groups account for more than 90% of the total African population in Kenya. The Kikuyu and the Luo are by far the most numerous groups, and between them hold practically all the positions of power and influence in the country.

A third language grouping, and in fact the first migrants into the country, are the Cushitic speakers, who occupy the north-east of the country and include such tribes as the El-Molo, Somali, Rendille and the Galla.

On the coast, Swahili is the name given to the local people who, while having various tribal ancestries, have in common the fact that they have been mixing, trading and intermarrying both among themselves and with overseas immigrants for hundreds of years.

Asians

The economically important Asian minority is made up largely of people of Indian descent whose ancestors originated from the western state of Gujarat and from the Punjab. Unlike the situation in Uganda, sense prevailed and the Asians here were not thrown into exile, largely because their influence was too great. (Uganda is still trying to get its economy back on track.)

India's connections with East Africa go back centuries to the days when hundreds of dhows used to make the trip between the west coast of India or the Persian Gulf and the coastal towns of East Africa every year. In those days, however, the Indians came as traders and only a very few stayed to settle. This all changed with the building of the Mombasa-Uganda railway at the turn of the century. In order to construct it, the British colonial authorities brought in some 32,000 indentured labourers from Gujarat and Punjab. When their contracts expired many of them decided to stay and set up businesses. Their numbers were augmented after WWII with the encouragement of the British.

Since they were an industrious and economically aggressive community, the Indians soon controlled large sectors of the economies of Kenya, Tanzania and Uganda as merchants, artisans and financiers. Not only that, but they kept very much to themselves, regarding the Africans as culturally inferior and lazy. Few gave their active support to the black nationalist movements in the run-up to independence, despite being urged to do so by Nehru, India's prime minister. And when independence came, like many of the white settlers, they were very hesitant to accept local citizenship, preferring to wait and see what would happen. To the Africans, therefore, it seemed they were not willing to throw in their lot with the newly independent nations and were there simply as exploiters.

As is well known, Uganda's Idi Amin used this suspicion and resentment as a convenient ruse to enrich himself and his cronies. Uganda's economy collapsed shortly after the expulsion of the Asian community, since Amin's henchmen were incapable of running the industries and businesses which the Asians had been forced to leave.

For a time in the 1970s it seemed that there was little future for Asians in Africa. Governments were under heavy pressure to 'Africanise' their economies and job markets. Even in Kenya thousands of shops owned by Asians who had not taken out Kenyan nationality were confiscated in the early 1970s and Asians were forbidden to trade in the rural areas. Those days appear to have passed and African attitudes towards Asians have mellowed. What seemed like a widespread demand that they should go 'home' has been quietly dropped; the lesson of what happened to the economy of Uganda when the Asians were thrown out is one reason for this.

TRIBAL GROUPS & CULTURES

Kenya is home to more than 70 tribal groups; this section provides an introduction to some of these people and their diverse cultures.

Akamba

The region east of Nairobi towards Tsavo National Park is the traditional homeland of the Akamba people *(Ukambani)*. They migrated here from the south several centuries ago in search of food, mainly the fruit of the baobab tree which was accorded great nutritional value.

The Akamba were great traders and ranged all the way from the coast to Lake Victoria and up to Lake Turkana. Ivory was one of the main barter items but locally made products such as beer, honey, iron weapons and ornaments were also traded. They used to obtain food stocks from the neighbouring Maasai and Kikuyu, as their own low-altitude land was relatively poor and couldn't sustain the increasing population which followed their arrival in the area.

In colonial times the Akamba were highly regarded by the British for their intelligence and fighting ability and were drafted in large numbers into the British army. Thousands lost their lives in WWI. When it came to land, however, the British were not quite so respectful and tried to limit the number of cattle the Akamba could own (by confiscating them) and also settled more Europeans in Ukambani. The Akamba response was the formation of the Ukamba Members Association, which marched en masse to Nairobi and squatted peacefully at Kariokor Market in protest. After three weeks the administration gave way and the cattle were eventually returned to the people.

All adolescents go through initiation rites to adulthood at around the age of 12, and have the same age-set groups common to many of Kenya's peoples. The various age-set rituals involve the men, and the women to a lesser extent, gaining seniority as they get older.

Young parents are known as 'junior elders' *(mwanake* for men, *mwiitu* for women) and are responsible for the maintenance and upkeep of the village. Once his children are old enough to become junior elders themselves, the mwanake goes through a ceremony to become a 'medium elder' *(nthele)*, and later in life a 'full elder' *(atumia ma kivalo)* with the responsibility for death ceremonies and administering the law. The last stage of a person's life is that of 'senior elder' *(atumia ma kisuka)* with responsibility for the holy places.

Akamba subgroups include Kitui, Masaku and Mumoni.

Gusii

The Gusii inhabit an area in the western highlands east of Lake Victoria. The area is dominated by Nilotic-speaking groups with just this pocket of the Bantu-speaking Gusii.

Being a relatively small group, the Gusii were always on the move following influxes of other groups into their existing lands. After migrating to the Mt Elgon area sometime before the 15th century, the Gusii were gradually pushed south by the advancing Luo, and over the next couple of centuries came into conflict with the Maasai and the Kipsigis. They finally settled in the hills here as the high ridges were easier to defend. Having fought hard for their autonomy, the Gusii were unwilling to give it up to the British and suffered heavy losses in conflicts early this century. Following these defeats, the men were conscripted in large numbers into the British army.

The Gusii family typically consists of a man, his wives and their married sons, all living together in a single compound. Large families serve two purposes: with high infant mortality rates the survival of the family is assured, and the large numbers facilitate defence of the family enclosure. Initiation ceremonies are performed for both boys and girls, and rituals accompany all important events. Death is considered not to be natural but the work of 'witchcraft'. The Gusii were primarily cattle keepers but also practised some crop cultivation, and millet beer was often important at big occasions.

As is the case with many of Kenya's ethnic groups, medicine men *(abanyamorigo)* had a highly privileged and respected position. Their duty was to maintain the physical and mental wellbeing of the group – doctor and social worker combined. One of the more bizarre practices was (and still is) the removal of sections of the skull or spine to aid maladies such as backache or concussion.

Kalenjin

'Kalenjin' is a name formulated in the 1950s to describe the group of peoples previously called the Nandi by the British. The Nandi tag was erroneous as the people were all Nandi-speakers (one of many dialects) but were not all Nandis; the other groups included Kipsigis, Marakwet, Pokot and Tugen (arap Moi's people). The word *kalenjin* means 'I say to you' in Nandi.

The Kalenjin people occupy the western edge of the central rift valley area which includes Kericho, Eldoret, Kitale, Baringo and the Mt Elgon area. They first migrated to the area west of Lake Turkana from southern Sudan around 2000 years ago and gradually filtered south as the climate changed and the forests dwindled.

Although originally pastoralists, most Kalenjin groups took up agriculture. Some, however, such as the Okiek, stuck to the forests and to a hunter-gatherer existence. Beekeeping was a common activity and the honey was used not only in trade but also for brewing beer.

As with most tribes, Kalenjin have age-sets into which a man is initiated after circumcision and remains for the rest of his life. Polygamy was widely practised. Administration of the law is carried out at the *kok* – an informal gathering of the clan's elders and other interested parties in the dispute. Unusually, the doctors were usually women and they used herbal remedies in their work. Other specialist doctors practised trepanning – taking out pieces of the skull to cure certain ailments – which is also practised by the Bantu-speaking Gusii of the Kisii district.

Kikuyu

The Kikuyu number more than three million and their heartland is the area around Mt Kenya. The original Kikuyu are thought to have migrated to the area from the east and north-east over a period of a couple of hundred years from the 16th century, and were actually part of the group known as Meru. Basically they overran the original occupants of the area such as the Athi and the Gumba, although intermarriage and trading did take place.

The Kikuyu's new land was bordered by the Maasai and although there were periods of calm between the two groups, there were also times when raids were carried out against each other's property and cattle. Both groups placed a high value on cattle. Intermarriage was not uncommon between them and they share a number of similarities – particularly in dress, weaponry, and dancing – as a result of their intermingling.

The administration of the clans *(mwaki)*, made up of many family groups *(nyumba)*, was originally taken care of by a council of elders with a good deal of importance being placed on the role of the witch doctor, medicine man and the blacksmith. Traditionally the Kikuyu god (Ngai) is believed to reside on Mt Kenya *(Kirinyaga* – the 'mountain of brightness', 'mountain of whiteness' or 'black and white peak spotted like ostrich feathers')* which accounts for the practice of orientating Kikuyu homes with the door facing Mt Kenya.

Initiation rites for both boys and girls are important ceremonies and consist of circumcision in boys and cliterodectomy in girls (the latter now rarely practised), accompanied by elaborate preparations and rituals. Each group of youths of the same age belong to an 'age-set' *(riika)* and pass through the various stages of life (with associated rituals) together.

Subgroups of the Kikuyu include Embu, Ndia and Mbeere.

Luo

The Luo people live in the west of the country on the shores of Lake Victoria. Along with the Maasai, they migrated south from the Nile region of Sudan around the 15th century. Although they clashed heavily with the existing Bantu-speaking people of the area, intermarriage and cultural mixing occurred.

The Luo are unusual amongst Kenya's ethnic groups in that circumcision is not practised in either sex. The tradition was replaced by something that one can imagine being almost as painful – the extraction of four or six teeth from the bottom jaw. Although it is not a common practice these days, you still see many middle-aged and older people of the region who are minus a few bottom pegs.

Although originally cattle herders, the Luo have adopted fishing and subsistence agriculture. The family group consists of the man, his wife (or wives) and their sons and daughters-in-law. The house compound is enclosed by a fence, and includes separate huts for the man and for each wife and son. (There is a good reconstruction of a Luo homestead in the grounds of the Kisumu Museum.)

The family group is a member of a larger grouping of families *(dhoot)*, several of which in turn make up a group of geographically related people *(ogandi)* each led by a chief *(ruoth)*. Collectively the ogandi constitute the Luo tribe. As is the case with many tribes, great importance is placed on the role of the medicine man and the spirits.

Maasai

It is the Maasai more than anyone who have become a symbol of 'tribal' Kenya. With a reputation (often exaggerated) as fierce warriors and a supercillious demeanour, the Maasai have largely managed to stay outside the mainstream of development in Kenya and still maintain their cattle herds in the area south of Nairobi straddling the Tanzanian border.

They first came to the region from the Sudan and eventually came to dominate a large area of central Kenya until, in the late 19th century, they were decimated by famine and disease, and their cattle herds routed by rindepest. Up until the Masai Mara National Reserve was created in the early 1960s, the Maasai had plenty of space for their cattle grazing, but at a stroke much of this land was put off limits. As their population increased (both the cattle and the Maasai) pressure for land became intense and conflict with the authorities constant. Settlement pro- grammes have only been reluctantly accepted as Maasai traditions scorn agriculture and land ownership is a foreign concept.

Another consequence of the competition for land is that many of the ceremonial traditions can longer be fulfilled. Part of the ceremony where a man becomes a warrior *moran* involves a group of young men around the age of 14 going out and building a village *manyatta* after their circumcision ceremony. Here they spend as long as eight years alone, and while the tradition and will survives, the land is just not available.

Tourism provides an income to some, either through selling everyday items (gourds, necklaces, clubs and spears), dancing or simply posing for photographs. However, while a few can make a lot of money from tourism the benefits are not widespread.

The colourful Maasai live a nomadic lifestyle, wan- dering throughout the year, with their main source of food being their cattle.

DAVID ELSE

Meru

The Meru arrived in the area north-east of Mt Kenya from the coast sometime around the 14th century following invasions of that area by Somalis from the north. The group was led by a chief known as the *mogwe* up until 1974 when the incumbent converted to Christianity and denied his son from inheriting the role. A group of tribal elders *(njuuri)* were all-powerful and along with the mogwe and witch doctor would administer justice as they saw fit – which often consisted of giving poison-laced beer to an accused person. Other curious practices included holding a newly born child to face Mt Kenya and then blessing it by spitting on it, and witch doctors might eliminate one of their rival's sons by putting poison on the circumcision blade.

Subgroups of the Meru include the Chuka, Igembe, Igoji, Tharaka, Muthambi, Tigania and Imenti.

Samburu

Closely related to the Maasai, and in fact speaking the same language, the Samburu occupy an arid area directly north of Mt Kenya. It seems that when the Maasai migrated to the area from Sudan, some headed east (and became the Samburu) while the bulk of them continued south to the area they occupy today.

As is often the case, age-sets are an integral part of the society and the men pass through various stages before becoming a powerful elder at the top of the ladder. Circumcision is practised in both sexes; with the girls it is only done on the day of marriage, which is usually when she is around 16 years old. Men are often in their thirties by the time they pass out of warriorhood and become elders qualified to marry.

Samburu males go through the stages of being junior and then senior warriors, followed by junior and finally senior elders.

DAVID ELSE

Swahili

Although the people of the coast do not have a common heritage, they do have a linguistic link – Kiswahili (commonly referred to as Swahili), a Bantu-based language which evolved as a means of communication between Africans and foreign traders such as Arabs, Persians and the Portuguese. As might be expected with such diverse input, the Swahili language borrows words from Arabic, Hindi, Portuguese and even English. The word *swahili* is a derivative of the Arabic word for coast – *sahel.*

Arab traders first started plying the coast in their sailing dhows sometime before the 7th century, arriving with the north-east monsoon and sailing home on the south-west monsoon. The main exports were ivory, tortoiseshell and leopard skins, while items such as glass beads from India and porcelain from as far afield as China found their way here.

After the 7th century Islam became a strong influence as traders began settling along the coast. Today the majority of the coastal people are Muslims, although it's a world away from the puritanical forms of Islam which prevail in some places in the Middle East.

Swahili subgroups include Bajun, Siyu, Pate, Mvita, Fundi, Shela, Ozi, Vumba and Amu (residents of Lamu).

Turkana

The Turkana are another of Kenya's more colourful (and warlike people). Originally from the Karamajong district of north-eastern Uganda, the Turkana number around 250,000 and live in the virtual desert country of Kenya's north-west. Due to their isolation, the Turkana are probably the least affected by the 20th century of all Kenya's people.

Like the Samburu and the Maasai (with whom they are linguistically linked), the Turkana are cattle herders first, although more recently they have taken up fishing the waters of Lake Turkana and even growing the occasional crops, weather permitting. But unlike the other two tribes, the Turkana have discontinued the practice of circumcision.

The traditional dress of the Turkana people is amazing, as is the number of people who still wear it – catching a bus up in the north-west is a real eye-opener for a first-time visitor. The men cover part of their hair with mud which is then painted blue and decorated with ostrich and other feathers. The main garment they wear, despite the blast-furnace heat of the region is a woollen blanket (usually a garish modern checked one) which is worn around the shoulder.

Traditional accessories include a small wooden stool carved out of a single piece of wood (used either as a pillow or a stool), a wooden stick with a distinctive shape, and a wrist knife. Both the men and the women wear with great flourish the lip plug through the lower lip. The women wear a variety of beaded and metal adornments, much of it indicating to the trained eye events in the woman's life. A half skirt of animal skins and a piece of block cloth are the only garments worn, although those days pieces of colourful cloth are not uncommon for use as baby slings.

Tattooing is also common and usually has special meaning. Men are tattooed on the shoulders and upper arm each time they kill an enemy – the right shoulder for killing a man, the left for a women; it's surprising the number of men you still see with these markings. Witch doctors and prophets are held in high regard and tattooing on someone's lower stomach is usually a sign of witch doctors' attempts to cast out an undesirable spirit rather than any sort of decoration.

KENYA

EDUCATION

Primary school education is provided free by the government, but is not compulsory. Over 5½ million children attend around 15,000 primary schools, while the country's 2500 or so secondary schools cater to around 600,000 students.

There are four universities, with a total enrolment of around 35,000 students: the University of Nairobi (established in 1956) and Kenyatta University (1972), both in Nairobi; Egerton University (1939) in Nakuru; and Moi University (1984) in Eldoret.

Illiteracy runs at the alarmingly high rate of around 30%.

ARTS
Music

Indigenous Kenyan pop music does exist, but it is nowhere near as well known as styles such as *soukous* from Zaïre, which dominate the local scene.

The style known as *benga* is the contemporary dance music of Kenya today. It originated among the Luo people of western Kenya, and became popular in the area in the 1950s. It has since spread throughout the country.

The music is characterised by clear electric guitar licks and a bass rhythm. The guitar in the modern bands takes the place of the traditional *nyatiti* (folk lyre), while the bass guitar replaces the drum, which originally was played by the nyatiti player with a toe ring. Some well-known exponents of benga include Shirati Jazz, Victoria Jazz and Ambira Boys.

Popular bands today play a mix of music, heavily influenced by benga, soukous and Western music, with lyrics generally in Swahili. These include bands such as Them Mushrooms and Safari Sound.

The live-music scene in Nairobi is quite fluid, but good places to try include the International Casino at Museum Hill, the Sirona Hotel in Parklands and the Landmark Hotel in Westlands. There are a number of places in the suburbs, but you'll need a taxi or your own transport. Try the Bombax Club at Dagoretti Corner on the Langata Road, the Cantina Club at the entrance to Wilson Airport and the Simba Saloon at the Carnivore Restaurant just past Wilson Airport. The *Daily Nation* has good listings on weekends, but doesn't usually give the addresses of the advertised places.

Literature

Heinemann's African Writers Series has arguably the best range of contemporary African authors (see the list of writers included in the series inside each book). Two of Kenya's best authors are Ngugi wa Thiong'o and Meja Mwangi, whose books are a good introduction to what's happening in East African literature at present. Ngugi is uncompromisingly (but somewhat dogmatically) radical, and his harrowing criticism of the neocolonialist politics of the Kenyan establishment landed him in jail for a year, lost him his job at Nairobi University and forced him into exile. His books, surprisingly, are not banned in Kenya even though he was considered a dangerously subversive thorn in the side of the government. Meja Mwangi sticks more to social issues and urban dislocation but has a brilliant sense of humour which threads its way right through his books. All the titles below are published by Heinemann.

Titles worth reading by Ngugi wa Thiong'o include *Petals of Blood*, *A Grain of Wheat*, *Devil on the Cross* and *Weep Not Child*. Titles by Meja Mwangi include *Going Down River Road, Kill me Quick* and *Carcass for Hounds*. All these titles are published by Heinemann.

Another author whose books are well known even outside Africa is Chinua Achebe. Although Achebe is a Nigerian and his material is drawn from his experiences in that country, many of the themes and issues are relevant to contemporary East Africa. His most famous title is *Things Fall Apart* (Heinemann, 1958). *Ant Hills of the Savannah*, a much more recent publication, is also well worth reading.

Another Nigerian author who writes about similar themes is Elechi Amadi. Try his *The Concubine*.

For writing by women in Africa try

Witch doctors are an important component of Kikuyu traditional beliefs and the doctors are held in high regard.

Most Samburu tribespeople lead a traditional lifestyle. Their culture is very similar to the Maasai with whom they share the same language.

Unwinding Threads, a collection of short stories by many different authors from all over the continent.

SOCIETY & CONDUCT
Refugees & the Dispossessed

As Kenya is a relatively stable country, with opportunities to make a living or at least receive hand-outs from tourists, it is a natural magnet for refugees from strife-torn neighbouring countries. Nairobi, Mombasa and, to a lesser degree, the coastal resort towns are the favoured destinations. You'll come across plenty of refugees on your travels, although it's relatively easy for these people to remain anonymous if they can make enough money to stay off the streets.

There's nothing remarkable about this – it happens all over the world. What is remarkable in Kenya is the number of single young mothers – many of them are Kenyan but there are also those from Uganda, Sudan, Ethiopia and Rwanda. The break up of many traditional communities as a result of colonial policies that were designed to bring people into the money economy, and the continuation of this system under postcolonial regimes, has led to the large-scale movement of people to urban areas. Most arrive with nothing and are forced to live in overcrowded shantytowns (some 60% of Nairobi's population lives in these places) with little hope of anything resembling a steady job with reasonable pay. As a result, all the symptoms of urban alienation can be found in these places, and drunkenness, theft and rape (particularly of schoolgirls) are fairly commonplace. But such problems aren't confined to the major urban areas: they appear to be fairly widespread everywhere outside of traditional tribal areas.

As far as the girls are concerned, once they become pregnant they're expelled from school (in other words, it's the end of their educational prospects) and, as likely as not, rejected by their families too. In 1986, the number of young girls who found themselves in this position was 11,000 (according to official figures) and the number has been rising steadily ever since. The options for such girls are extremely limited. A few shelters do exist (usually run by Christian organisations), but it's only the lucky few who get in; for the rest, it's very poorly paid domestic work or the flesh market.

Laws regarding the responsibilities of paternity in Kenya either don't exist or are hardly ever enforced – it's definitely a man's world – and establishment Kenyan society remains tight-lipped about the problem. What society remains even more tight-lipped about is the practice of well-to-do Kenyan families recruiting little girls from the bush as domestic servants. Those recruited are even more circumspect.

Though clothed and fed and, if lucky, paid a pittance which varies between US$1 and US$16 a month, these children work on average 15 to 17 hours a day with no days off. Some get no pay at all, with just food and clothing provided in lieu of salary. The reason their parents push them into this hellish existence, apart from the wages which they expect to recoup, is the hope that their children will acquire a training and education of sorts. The reality is often quite different. These girls are often raped by either the man of the house or his sons and thrown out when they become pregnant; as likely as not, those girls also join the flesh market.

Whatever you may think of prostitution, life without a good income is hard in Kenya. Minimal accommodation rentals, even in rough areas of Nairobi, are around US$50 a month; in better areas it's much more. Add decent clothes and footwear and medical attention when necessary, and that's a lot of money to be made, even to make ends meet – let alone save anything. It's not surprising, therefore, that those who do manage to get their heads above water head for the bars and discos frequented by expatriate workers and tourists, since it's more lucrative and there is the vague possibility of marriage or, at least, a long-term friendship.

Of course, it isn't just pregnant young girls who find themselves dispossessed. The conditions under which young boys have to work in the coffee, sisal and rice plantations are equally onerous and many find their way onto the streets of Nairobi (so-called 'parking boys'), Mombasa and the coast ('beach boys'), along with other jobless adult males.

Blaming the government for this state of affairs is all too easy for those from rich Western countries but is, to a large degree, unfair. Because of Kenya's high birth rate and the limited funds available, the government is already flat out keeping pace with the demand for schools and hospitals, developing the transport infrastructure and paying interest on its foreign loans. Given this, it's unlikely that much can be done in the foreseeable future for those who fall under the category of Kenya's dispossessed.

Cultural Considerations

Dress Despite their often exuberant and casual approach, Kenyans are generally quite conservative, and are particularly concerned with modesty in dress. Many travellers seem to get around in T-shirts and shorts, which is acceptable (just) in most areas, but you should be more circumspect on the Muslim-dominated coast, particularly in Lamu. Here women should wear tops that keep the shoulders covered and skirts or pants which reach at least to the knees. Shorts on men are likewise not particularly appreciated.

When doing official business with people such as civil servants and embassy staff, your position will be much enhanced if you're smartly dressed and don't look like you've just spent five weeks in the back of a truck (even if you have!).

Child Prostitution Child prostitution is prevalent in Kenya, particularly in Nairobi and the tourist areas of the coast where so-called 'sex tourism' is big business. Although the government is signatory to at least one UN convention aimed at protecting children, it has been less than vigorous in tackling the problem.

It is illegal to engage in sexual activity with children under the age of 14 (!), and even though people caught doing so may be

dealt with leniently in Kenya, they may also be liable to legal action in their own country.

Photographing People Kenya's wildly photogenic tribal people are generally less than wildly enthusiastic about being photographed, and with good reason. See Photography in the Regional Facts for the Visitor chapter for more information.

RELIGION

It's probably true to say that most Kenyans outside the coastal and eastern provinces are Christians of one sort or another, while most of those on the coast and in the eastern part of the country are Muslim. Muslims make up some 30% of the population. In the more remote tribal areas you'll find a mixture of Muslims, Christians and those who follow their ancestral tribal beliefs.

Christianity

As a result of intense missionary activity from colonial times to the present, just about every Christian sect is represented in Kenya, from Lutherans and Catholics to Seventh Day Adventists and Wesleyans. The success which all these sects have enjoyed would be quite mind-boggling if it were not for the fact that they have always judiciously combined Jesus with education and medicine – two commodities in short supply until recently in Kenya. Indeed, there are still many remote areas of Kenya where the only place you can get an education or medical help is at a mission station, and there's no doubt that those who volunteer to staff them are dedicated people.

On the other hand, the situation is often not as simple as it might at first appear. As with Catholicism in Central and South America, which found it necessary to incorporate native deities and saints into the Roman Catholic pantheon in order to placate local sensibilities, African Christianity is frequently a combination of traditional and Christian beliefs. This is especially so where a tribe has strong ancestral beliefs. There are also many pure, home grown African Christian sects which owe no allegiance to any of the major Western cults. The only thing they have in common is the Bible, though their interpretation of it is often radically different. It's worth checking out a few churches while you're in Kenya, and even if you can't understand the words, you'll certainly be captivated by what only Africans can do with such beauty and precision – unaccompanied choral singing.

The upsurge of home grown Christian sects has much to do with cultural resurgence, the continuing struggle against neocolonialism, and the alienation brought about by migration to urban centres far from tribal homelands. Some of these sects are distinctly radical and viewed with alarm by the government. The Tent of the Living God, for instance, was denounced by the president as being anti-Christ and three of its leaders were arrested at a gathering in Eastleigh, Nairobi, in late January 1990. The charges against them were thrown out of court the following week and the men released, but the government's action was perhaps an indication of how it intends to deal with such perceived threats to the status quo in the future.

It isn't just the radical sects which worry the government, however. During the agitation for the introduction of a multiparty political system, even mainstream church leaders took to criticising the government from the relative safety of their pulpits. Many were denounced and some came so close to the bone that they were accused of treason and there were calls for their arrest, although none were actually arrested.

Islam
Most Muslims belong to the Sunni branch of the faith and, as a result, the Sunni communities have been able to attract substantial Saudi Arabian funding for schools and hospitals along the coast and elsewhere.

Only a small minority belong to the Shia branch of Islam and most are to be found among the Asian community. On the other hand, Shiites have been coming to East Africa from all over the eastern Islamic world for centuries, partially to escape per-

secution but mainly for trading purposes. They didn't come here to convert souls, and there was a high degree of cooperation between the schismatic sects and the Sunnis, which is why there's a total absence of Shiite customs in Swahili culture today.

Among the Asian community there are representatives of virtually all Shiite sects, but the most influential are the Ismailis – followers of the Aga Khan. As with all Ismailis, they represent a very liberal version of Islam and are perhaps the only branch of the faith which is strongly committed to the education of women at all levels and their participation in commerce and business. It's obvious that the sect has prospered well in Kenya, judging by all the schools and hospitals dedicated to the Aga Khan which you will come across in most urban centres.

Hinduism
Hinduism is a self-contained religion which concerns only those born into it. You'll come across a considerable number of temples in the larger urban areas where most people of Indian origin live. There are literally scores of different sects of Hinduism to be found in Kenya – too numerous to mention here – and many are economically quite influential.

For a superb and very detailed account of each and every Asian-derived sect of both Islam and Hinduism see *Through Open Doors – A View of Asian Cultures in Kenya*, by Cynthia Salvadori. This is a large-format, hardback book with many illustrations, and is on sale in most of Nairobi's bookshops.

LANGUAGE
English and Swahili (correctly known as Kiswahili) are the official languages and are taught in schools throughout Kenya, but there are many other major tribal languages, including Kikuyu, Luo, Kikamba, Maasai and Samburu as well as a plethora of minor tribal languages. Most urban Kenyans and even tribal people involved in the tourist industry speak English so you shouldn't experience too many problems making yourself understood. Italian and German are also spoken by many Kenyans but usually only

among those associated with the tourist trade on the coast.

It's extremely useful, however, to have a working knowledge of Swahili, especially outside urban areas and in remote parts of the country, since this will open doors and enable you to communicate with people who don't speak English. It's also the most common language which speakers of different tribal languages use to communicate with each other. Even tribespeople who haven't been to school will usually be able to speak *some* Swahili. If you're planning on visiting Tanzania you'll find it extremely useful, as it's now the official language there (though English is still used extensively).

Another language you'll come across in Kenya, one which is spoken almost exclusively by the younger members of society, is Sheng. Essentially a patois, it's a fairly recent development and, like Swahili, is still evolving. It's composed of a mixture of Swahili and English along with a fair sprinkling of Hindi, Gujarati, Kikuyu and several other Kenyan tribal languages. It originated in the colonial days as a result of the employment of African nannies by whites to look after their children.

Unless you can speak reasonable Swahili, you probably won't realise Sheng is being spoken since it does sound quite similar to Swahili. One of the indications that it's being spoken is the initial greeting between friends. The greeting will be *'Sassa!'*. The response to this can be, *'Besht'*, *'Mambo'* or *'Fit'* (pronounced almost like 'feet'). There is then an option to continue in Sheng or any other mutually intelligible language. For more Swahili terms see Food in Regional Facts for the Visitor. Lonely Planet's *Swahili phrasebook* by Robert Leonard gives you a more complete overview.

Pronunciation

Vowels Swahili vowels are pronounced as follows:

a	as the 'a' in 'father'
e	between the 'e' in 'better' and the 'a' in 'may'
i	as the 'ee' sound in 'bee'
o	as the 'o' in 'old'
u	as the 'oo' in 'too'

Double vowels, or any two vowels together, are pronounced as two separate syllables. There are no diphthongs as in English. Thus *saa* (time/hour) is pronounced 'sa-a', and *yai* (egg) is pronounced 'ya-i'.

Consonants Some consonants require a bit of explanation:

dh	as the 'th' in 'this'
ky	as the 'ch' in 'chat'
th	as the 'th' in 'thing'
ny	as the 'ñ' in Spanish *señora*
ng'	as the 'ng' in 'sing'
gh	like a 'g', but more of a gargle
r	in English closer to a 'd', but 'r' will also be understood

Word Stress

In words where there are more than two syllables, the stress generally falls on the second last syllable.

Greetings & Civilities

It is considered rude to speak to someone without first greeting them, so even if you only want directions, you should greet the person first. It's the English equivalent of 'excuse me'.

Hello.	*Jambo* or *Salama*

(There is also a respectful greeting used for elders: *shikamoo*. The reply is *marahaba*.)

Welcome.	*Karibu*
Goodbye.	*Kwaheri*
Thank you.	*Asante*
Thanks very much.	*Asante sana*
You're welcome.	*Karibu*
Yes.	*Ndiyo*
No.	*Hapana*

Small Talk

How are you?	*Habari?*
I'm fine, thanks.	*Nzuri.*
What's your name?	*Unaitwa nani?*

My name is ...	*Jina langu ni*
Where are you from?	*Unatoka wapi?*
I come from ...	*Mimi ninatoka*
Where do you live?	*Unakaa wapi?*
I live in ...	*Ninakaa*
How are things in ...?	*Habari ya ... ?*
Fine.	*Nzuri*
No problem.	*Hakuna matata*
It is ...	*Ninaitwa ...*
How was the journey?	*Habari ya safari?*
I don't understand.	*Nisamehe sifahamu.*
white people	*Wazungu*
white person	*Mzungu*

Getting Around

I want to go to ...	
Mimi nataka kwenda ...	
Is this the way to ... ?	
Hii njia ya ... ?	
How much to go to ... ?	
Shillingi ngapi kwenda ... ?	

When does the ... leave?	*... inakwenda saa ngapi?*
bus	*basi*
train	*treni*
truck/car	*gari*
boat	*boti*
share taxi	*gari ndogo*

Drive slowly.	*Endesha pole pole.*
Wait a minute.	*Ngoja kidogo.*
Stop here.	*Simama hapa.*

ticket	*tikiti*
airport	*kiwanja cha ndege*
bus station	*stesheni ya basi*
railway station	*stesheni ya treni*
taxi	*teksi*
right	*kwa kulia*
left	*kwa kushoto*

Accommodation

Where is a ... ?	*Wapi ... ?*
hotel	*hoteli ya kulalia*
very good hotel	*hoteli mzuri sana*
guesthouse	*nyumba ya wageni*

Do you have a room for ... ?	*Kuna rumu ya ... ?*
one person	*mtu moja*
two people	*watu wahili*

How much is the room?	
Rumu ni shillingi ngapi?	
I'd like to see the room.	
Nataka kuona rumu tafadhali.	
Is there hot water?	
Kuna maji ya moto?	

for one day	*kwa siku moja*
for a week	*kwa wiki mzima*
shower	*shawa*
bath	*bafu*
fan	*feni*
sheet	*shiti*
towel	*tauli*
key	*ufunguo*
noisy	*kelele*

Around Town

Where is a/the ...?	*Wapi ... ?*
bank	*benki*
hotel	*hoteli ya kulalia*
hospital	*hospitali*
police station	*stesheni ya polisi*
post office	*posta*
restaurant	*hoteli ya chakula*
toilet	*choo*

On Safari

Look there.	*tazama pale*
What is there?	*iko nini pale?*
What animal is that?	*huyo mnyama gani?*

antelope	*pofu/kulungu*
bird	*ndege*
crocodile	*mamba*
elephant	*ndovu/tembo*
gazelle	*swala/swara/paa*
giraffe	*twiga*
hippopotamus	*kiboko*
hyena	*fisi*
lion	*simba*
monkey	*tumbili*
rhinoceros	*kifaru*
snake	*nyoka*

KENYA

water buffalo	*nyati*
zebra	*punda milia*

Shopping

Where is a/the ... ?	*Wapi ... ?*
chemist/pharmacy	*duka la dawa*
bookshop	*duka la vitabu*
grocery	*duka*
market	*sokoni*

I want to buy ...	*Mimi nataka kununua ...*
Do you have ... ?	*Kuna ... ?*
There is.	*Kuna*
There isn't.	*Hakuna*
How much?	*Ngapi?*
This is very expensive.	*Hii ni bei ghali sana.*

too big	*kubwa*
too small	*kidogo*
more	*zaidi*

clothing	*nguo*
insect repellent	*dawa ya mdudu*
laundry detergent	*omo*
mosquito coil	*dawa ya mbu ya kuwashia*
soap	*sabuni*
toilet paper	*karatasi ya choo*
toothpaste	*dawa ya meno*

Time

Bear in mind that Swahili time and Western time differ by six hours, although unless you get right out into the small towns this should be no cause for confusion.

What is the time?	*Saa ngapi?*
It's 8 o'clock.	*Saa nane.*
When?	*Saa ngapi?*
today	*leo*
tomorrow	*kesho*
yesterday	*jana*
hour	*saa*
week	*wiki*
month	*mwezi*
year	*mwaka*

Days of the Week

Monday	*Jumatatu*
Tuesday	*Jumanne*
Wednesday	*Jumatano*
Thursday	*Alhamisi*
Friday	*Ijumaa*
Saturday	*Jumamosi*
Sunday	*Jumapili*

Numbers

1	*moja*
2	*mbili*
3	*tatu*
4	*nne*
5	*tano*
6	*sita*
7	*saba*
8	*nane*
9	*tisa*
10	*kumi*

The 'teens' are *kumi na ...* (10 plus ...), the 20s *ishrini na ...* (20 plus ...) and so on. The hundreds are *mia*, and the thousands *elfu*.

11	*kumi na moja*
12	*kumi na mbili*
20	*ishrini*
30	*thelathini*
40	*arobaini*
50	*hamsini*
60	*sitini*
70	*sabini*
80	*themanini*
90	*tisini*
100	*mia*
200	*mia mbili*
1000	*elfu*
2126	*elfu mbili mia moja ishrini na sita*

Health & Emergencies

I am ill.	*Mimi mgonjwa.*
Please call a doctor.	*Tafadhali wewe umwite daktari.*
I hurt here.	*Ninaumwa hapa.*
I'm pregnant.	*Nina mimba.*
pharmacy	*duka la dawa*

dentist	*daktari la meno*	Watch out!	*angalia*
doctor	*daktari*	Leave me alone!	*niache*
hospital	*hospitali*	I'm lost.	*nimepotea*
medicine	*dawa*	I've been robbed.	*nimeibiwa*

Facts for the Visitor

PLANNING
When to Go

There are a number of factors to take into account when considering what time of year to visit Kenya. The main tourist season is January and February, as the weather at this time of year is generally considered to be the best – hot and dry. It's also when you'll find the largest concentrations of bird life on the Rift Valley lakes, and the animals in the game parks tend to congregate more around the watercourses as other sources dry up, making them easier to spot.

From June to September could be called the 'shoulder season' as the weather is still dry and it's the time of that visual extravaganza – the annual wildebeest migration from the Serengeti into the Masai Mara National Reserve.

During the long rains (from March to May) and the short rains (from October to December) things are much quieter – places tend to be less full and accommodation prices come down. The rains generally don't affect your ability to get around and see things (although Amboseli National Park can be flooded out), it's just that you may well get rained on, especially in the late afternoon. This is especially so in the highlands and the west of the country.

Maps

The *Tourist Map of Kenya*, printed and published in Kenya, gives good detail as does the *Kenya Route Map*. Lonely Planet's *Kenya Travel Atlas* gives excellent coverage of the country, is in book form (so won't fall apart) and includes maps of the most popular national parks and reserves.

Macmillan publishes a series of maps to the game parks and these are not bad value at KSh 250 each.

The Public Map Office next to the Kenyatta Conference Centre in Nairobi has a stock of government survey maps covering the whole country. The most popular ones (Mt Kenya, Mt Elgon and those covering the game parks) are often out of stock but it's worth getting hold of these maps if possible.

The only trouble with maps published by the Survey of Kenya other than those available in the book shops is that they're not available to the general public without official authorisation. This is hard to get and takes time so, if you're a tourist with limited time, you can forget it. Even people with credentials, such as Kenyan residents and members of the Mountain Club of Kenya (MCK), have great difficulty or simply find it impossible to get hold of detailed maps of the country.

HIGHLIGHTS

Without doubt it is the game parks which attract people to Kenya – the wildlife viewing here is still probably the best and most easily accessible in Africa. The Masai Mara National Reserve is the number one attraction, but other parks such as Amboseli, Tsavo and Samburu also provide great viewing. Bird-watchers will also be well satisfied with a visit to Kenya. The Rift Valley lakes of Baringo, Bogoria, Naivasha and Nakuru are all excellent for bird-watching.

For the really adventurous, Kenya offers some exciting prospects. Trekking the snowy heights of Mt Kenya, the second-highest peak in Africa, is a superb experience and one which doesn't require specialised equipment. Other options include camel (or even donkey) safaris with Samburu tribespeople in the semiarid regions of the north; hiking safaris; and ballooning. People looking for activities requiring slightly less energy will find the beaches of the coast the perfect place to chill out for awhile. And it need not be purely hedonistic, as there is a rich history and the strong Swahili coastal culture to delve into. For other highlights see the table on pages 122-3.

TOURIST OFFICES
Local Tourist Offices
Considering the extent to which the country relies on tourism, it's incredible to think that there's not even a tourist office in Nairobi! There's not much available in the way of printed information either, though there are a couple of free pamphlets which go some way toward filling the gap. They are the monthly *Tourist's Kenya*, and the quarterly *What's On*, which also covers Uganda and Tanzania. Both contain articles on subjects of tourist interest plus selective listings of hotels, restaurants, airlines, embassies, banks, safari and car-hire companies, train and boat schedules, and a considerable amount of advertising (which is why they're free). You can pick them up at the larger hotels and at travel agencies.

The only tourist offices in the country are those in Mombasa on Moi Ave (☎ (011) 311231) and in Malindi on Lamu Rd.

Tourist Offices Abroad
The Ministry of Tourism maintains several overseas offices including:

France
    5 Rue Volney, Paris 75002
    (☎ (01) 4260-6688; fax 4261-1884)
Germany
    Hochstrasse 53, 6 Frankfurt A M
    (☎ (069) 282552; fax 239239)
Hong Kong
    1309 Liu Chong Hing Bank Building, 24 Des Voeux Rd, Central (☎ 2523-6053)
Japan
    Yurakucho Building, 1-10 Yurakucho, 1 Chome, Chiyoda-ku, Tokyo (☎ (03) 214-4595)
Sweden
    Birger Jarlsgatan 37, 11145 Stockholm
    (☎ (08) 218300; fax 200030)
Switzerland
    Bleicherweg 30, CH8039 Zurich
    (☎ (01) 202-2244; fax 202-2256)
UK
    25 Brook's Mews (off Davies St), Mayfair, London (☎ (0171) 355-3144; fax 495-8656)
USA
    9100 Wilshire Blvd, Los Angeles, CA 90212 (☎ (213) 274-6634; fax 859-7010)
    424 Madison Ave, New York, NY 10017 (☎ (212) 486-1300; fax 688-0911)

VISAS & DOCUMENTS
Visas
Visas are required by all except nationals of Commonwealth countries (excluding nationals of Australia, New Zealand and Sri Lanka and British-passport holders of Indian, Pakistani and Bangladeshi origin), Denmark, Ethiopia, Germany, the Republic of Ireland, Italy, Norway, Spain, Sweden, Turkey and Uruguay. Those who don't need visas are issued a Visitor's Pass on entry which is valid for a stay of up to six months. Three months is the average, but it depends what you ask for.

The cost of a three-month visa is roughly the local equivalent of US$30, though this does vary. Two photos (sometimes three) are required but you normally do not have to show an onward ticket or a letter from a travel agent confirming that you have booked one. Visas remain valid for three months from the date of issue. Apply well in advance for your visa especially if doing it by mail – it can take up to two weeks in some countries (eg Australia). Kenyan visa applications are simple and straightforward in Tanzania and Uganda, and payment is accepted in local currency.

Visas are also available on arrival at Jomo Kenyatta international airport in Nairobi for US$20. Transit visas issued at the airport are valid for three days only and are definitely not extendable.

So long as your visa remains valid you can visit either Tanzania or Uganda and return without having to apply for another visa. This does not apply to visiting any other countries.

Visa Extensions Visas can be renewed in Nairobi at the immigration office (☎ (02) 332110), Nyayo House (ground floor), on the corner of Kenyatta Ave and Uhuru Highway; at the office in Mombasa (☎ (011) 311745); or in Kisumu at immigration on the 1st floor of Reinsurance Plaza, corner of Jomo Kenyatta Highway and Oginga Odinga Rd, during normal office hours.

A three-month, single-entry visa costs US$30. No onward tickets or 'sufficient

HIGHLIGHTS

	REGION	COMMENTS
Historical		
Fort Jesus Mombasa's Portuguese fort, built in 1593 changed hands nine times between 1631 and 1875; it's now a museum.	The Coast	The Old Town's biggest attraction is well worth a visit, especially Omani house in the fort's north-western corner.
Gedi The mysterious and extensive ruins of this Arab-Swahili town are among the principal historical monuments on the coast.	The Coast	Excavations indicate that the town was founded in the 13th century and was inexplicably abandoned in the 17th or 18th century.
Lamu The island is home to Kenya's oldest town which has changed little over the centuries.	The Coast	Access is by diesel-powered launch from the mainland. Shela beach is one of the most relaxing places you'll ever visit.
Activities		
Diving/Snorkelling Diving is excellent at the marine national parks of Malindi and Watamu. It's even better at the Shimoni and Wasini islands, although they are less accessible and developed.	The Coast	You can rent a glass-bottom boat at Malindi to see the amazing variety of coral and fish.
White-Water Rafting A day trip from Nairobi starts above the Sagana on the Athi River, finishing above the Masinga Dam. An exciting three-day trip takes you from Yatta Gap to Tsavo Safari Camp.	Around Nairobi	Of the two major rivers in Kenya, the Athi/Galana and Tana, only the former has substantial rapids, chutes and waterfalls.
Beaches The beach at Diani is one of the best; Tiwi Beach is more low-key and camping on the beach is available. Lamu boasts some of the finest beaches on the coast.	The Coast	Beaches south of Mombasa are white coral sand and are protected by a coral reef that excludes sharks.
Trekking Mt Kenya (5199m) is Africa's second highest mountain and its gleaming and eroded snow-covered peaks act as a magnet for trekkers, particularly from mid-January to late February and late August to September.	The Central Highlands	Mt Kenya's highest peaks, Batian and Nelion, can only be reached by mountaineers, but trekkers can reach the third highest, Point Lenana (4985m). The views are simply stunning.
Dhow Trips The main form of travel around the Lamu archipelago, which boasts more dhows than anywhere else off the East African coast. Dhows began to be used as a form of transport from the 8th century onwards.	The Coast	One of Kenya's most worthwhile and memorable experiences; make sure you take a hat and sunblock as there is rarely any shade on board.

	REGION	COMMENTS
Safaris		
Wildlife Safaris		
They typically start and end in either Nairobi or Mombasa and are conducted through Kenya's world-renowned national parks; there are usually two, sometimes three, game drives per day.	National Parks & Reserves	All budgets are catered for: camping safaris for the budget-conscious to lodge and tented camp sites for those who want luxury.
Balloon Safaris		
Hot-air balloon flights depart daily from both Keekorok Lodge and Fig Tree Lodge in Masai Mara National Reserve and include a champagne breakfast on the plains.	Western Kenya	Not to be missed, a silent dawn glide is an absolutely superb way of viewing the savannah plains and the animals, without the intrusion of vehicles and dozens of other tourists.
Cycling Safaris		
The best options are a three-day Masai Mara combined trip (walking/cycling) or a six-day trip, again through the heart of Maasai land.	Various	Doing your own thing entails confronting the dangers of cycling along main roads in Kenya and the major off-road problems of punctures from thorn trees.
Camel Safaris		
Most of them take place in the Samburu and Turkana tribal areas between Isiolo and Lake Turkana.	Northern Kenya	A superb way of getting off the beaten track and into areas where vehicle safari's don't go. An unrivalled desert experience among the nomads of Kenya's north.
National Parks & Reserves		
Masai Mara National Reserve		
The highlight is no doubt the annual wildebeest migration when literally millions of these ungainly beasts move north from the Serengeti in July and August in search of lush grass, before turning south again around October.	Western Kenya	Virtually everyone who visits Kenya goes to this 320 sq km of open grassland dotted with flat-topped Acacia trees. This is the Kenyan section of the Serengeti Plains and wildlife abounds.
Amboseli National Park		
The best reasons for visiting this park are its dramatic setting against the backdrop of Mt Kilimanjaro, and the chance of spotting a black rhino.	Southern Kenya	Although there's not the huge profusion of game found in the Masai Mara, the game here is easy to spot. There are also huge herds of elephants.
Kakamega Forest Reserve		
A superb slab of virgin tropical rainforest in the heart of an intensively cultivated agricultural area. Home of a number of primates and over 330 species of birds.	Western Kenya	The forest itself comprises a number of habitats but is generally very dense. This reserve is well worth the mimimal effort required to get to it.
Lake Baringo		
Of Kenya's 1200 different species of birds, more than 450 species have been sighted at this freshwater lake. The lake has many islands (two of them inhabited).	The Rift Valley	A spectacular sight and a very mellow place to visit. One of the islands is called 'Devil's Island' and locals claim it is haunted.

funds' are demanded. Remember that you don't need a re-entry visa if you're only going to visit Tanzania or Uganda *as long as your visa remains valid*. Staff at the immigration offices are generally friendly and helpful.

Getting Other Visas in Kenya Since Nairobi is a common gateway city to East Africa and the city centre is easy to get around, many travellers spend some time here picking up visas for other countries. See Embassies below for details of addresses and office hours.

Burundi
> The embassy is currently not issuing visas and will tell you to get one on arrival at the border.

Ethiopia
> In theory, the embassy here only issues visas to people who have no Ethiopian embassy in their own country. In practice, anyone can get one, although you may have to explain why you didn't get one before leaving home. One-month visas cost US$63, require one photo and take 48 hours to issue. Applications must be submitted before noon.

Rwanda
> Double-entry, seven-day transit visas cost KSh 1500; one-month visas cost KSh 2000, require two photos and are delivered the same day if you apply before noon. If you are travelling overland, it's much cheaper (US$20) to get a visa on arrival at the border.

Somalia
> The embassy does not presently function and, in fact, anyone can get into Somalia without a visa.

Sudan
> Visas are difficult to get because of the civil war and all applications have to be referred to Khartoum. An onward ticket is necessary, so get one of these before you apply.

Tanzania
> The cost of a visa depends on your nationality and ranges from US$55 for British nationals, US$45 for Americans, US$26 for Japanese, US$16 for Germans, to US$10 for others. One photo is required and visas take half an hour to issue. Visas are also available on arrival at Namanga, Kilimanjaro airport (Arusha), Dar es Salaam airport and at Zanzibar.

Uganda
> Most nationalities don't require visas. For those that do they cost up to US$25, require two photos and are delivered the same day if you apply before noon.

Zaïre
> Visa fees are the same for all nationalities. Single-entry/multiple-entry visas cost KSh 2500/4000 for a month; KSh 4500/6000 for two months; and KSh 6500/7500 for three months. Two photos are required and visas are delivered the same day if you apply before 11 am.

EMBASSIES

Kenya has diplomatic representation in many countries. Where there is no Kenyan embassy or high commission, visas can be obtained from the British Embassy or high commission.

Kenyan Embassies Abroad

Kenya maintains the following embassies and consulates abroad:

Australia
> QBE Building, 33 Ainslie Ave, Canberra, ACT 2601 (☎ (06) 247-4788; fax 257-6613)

Belgium
> 1-5 Avenue de la Joyeuse, 1040 Brussels (☎ (02) 230-3065; fax 230-8462)

Canada
> 415 Laurier Ave, Ottawa, Ontario, KIN 6R4 (☎ (613) 563-1773; fax 233-6599)

Egypt
> 7 El Mohandes Golal St, Mohandessen, Giza, Cairo (☎ (091) 345-3628; fax 344-3400)

Ethiopia
> Fikre Miriam Rd, PO Box 3301, Addis Ababa (☎ (01) 610303; fax 611433)

France
> 3 Rue Cimarosa, 75116 Paris (☎ (01) 4553-3500; fax 4553-9532)

Germany
> Villichgasse 17, 5300 Bonn-Bad Godesburg 2, Micael Plaza (☎ (0228) 356042; fax 358428)

India
> E-66 Vasant Marg, Vasant Vihar, 110057 New Delhi (☎ (011) 687-6538; fax 687-6550)

Italy
> Via Icilio No 14, 00153 Rome (☎ (06) 578-1192; fax 5742-2788)

Japan
> 24-3 Yakumo, 3 Chome, Meguru-ku, Tokyo 152 (☎ (03) 723-4006; fax 723-4488)

Netherlands
> Niewe Parklaan 21, 2597 The Hague (☎ (070) 350-4215; 355-3594)

Nigeria
> 52 Oyinkan Abayomi Drive, Ikoyi, PO Box 6464, Lagos (☎ (01) 682768; fax 685532)

Pakistan
> Sector G-613, House 8, St 88, PO Box 2097, Islamabad (☎ (051) 211243; fax 212542)

Rwanda
PO Box 1215, Kigali (☎ 82774; fax 86234)

South Africa
302 Brooke St, Menlo Park, Pretoria
(☎ (012) 342-5066)

Sudan
Street 3 Amarat, PO Box 8242, Khartoum
(☎ 43758; fax 452264)

Sweden
Birger Jarlsgatan 37, 2tr, 10395 Stockholm
(☎ (08) 218300; fax 209261)

Tanzania
NIC Investment House, Samora Ave, PO Box
5231, Dar es Salaam (☎ (051) 46362; fax 46519)

Uganda
Plot No 2030, Muyenga Kansanga Rd, PO Box
5220, Kampala (☎ (041) 267386; fax 267369)

UK
45 Portland Place, London W1N 4AS
(☎ (0171) 636-2371; fax 323-6717)

USA
2249 R St NW, Washington DC 20008
(☎ (202) 387-6101; fax 462-3829)

Zaïre
4002 Ave de l'Ouganda, BP 9667, Zone
Degombe, Kinshasa (☎ (012) 33205)

Zambia
Harambee House, 5207 United Nations Ave, PO
Box 50298, Lusaka (☎ (01) 227938; fax 263150)

Zimbabwe
95 Park Lane, PO Box 4069, Harare
(☎ (04) 792901; fax 723042)

Foreign Embassies in Kenya

Countries which maintain diplomatic missions in Kenya include:

Australia
Riverside Drive, Nairobi (PO Box 39341); open
weekdays 7.45 am to 4.30 pm and Friday 7.45 am
to 12.30 pm (☎ 445034; fax 444617)

Belgium
Limuru Rd, Muthaiga, Nairobi (PO Box 30461);
open weekdays 8.30 am to 12.30 pm
(☎ 741564; fax 741568)
Mitchell Cotts Building, Mombasa
(☎ 220231; fax 312617)

Burundi
Development House, Moi Ave, Nairobi (PO Box
44439); open Monday to Friday 8.30 am to 12.30
pm and 2 to 5 pm (☎ 218458; fax 219005)

Canada
Comcraft House, Haile Selassie Ave, Nairobi
(PO Box 30481); open 7.30 am to 4 pm
(☎ 214804; fax 226987)

Denmark
HFCK Building, Koinange St, Nairobi (PO Box

40412); open weekdays 7.45 am to 3 pm
(☎ 331088; fax 331492)

Djibouti
Comcraft House, Haile Selassie Ave, Nairobi
(PO Box 59528); open weekdays 8.30 am to 3
pm (☎ 339633; fax 339168)

Egypt
Harambee Plaza, Haile Selassie Ave, Nairobi (PO
Box 30285); open 9 am to 3.30 pm
(☎ 225991; fax 21560)

Eritrea
Rehema House, Westlands, Nairobi (PO Box
38651); open weekdays 8.30 am to 12.30 pm and
2 to 5.30 pm (☎ 443163; fax 443165)

Ethiopia
State House Ave, Nairobi (PO Box 45198); open
8.30 am to 12.30 pm and 2 to 5 pm
(☎ 723027; fax 723401)

France
Barclays Plaza, Loita St, Nairobi (PO Box 41784);
open 8.30 am to noon (☎ 339783; fax 220435)

Germany
Williamson House, 4th Ngong Ave, Nairobi (PO
Box 30180); open 8.30 am to 12.30 pm
(☎ 712527; fax 714886)
Palli House, Nyerere Ave, Mombasa
(☎ 314732; fax 314504)

Greece
IPS Building, Kimathi St, Nairobi (PO Box
30543); open 9 am to 2 pm
(☎ 340722; fax 216044)

India
Jeevan Bharati Building, Harambee Ave, Nairobi
(PO Box 30074); open 8.30 am to 1 pm and 1.30
to 4.30 pm (☎ 222566; fax 334167)

Israel
Bishops Rd, Nairobi (PO Box 30107); open 8 am
to 1 pm and 2 to 5 pm (☎ 722182; fax 715966)

Italy
Jubilee Building, Moi Ave, Mombasa
(☎ 314705; fax 316654)

Japan
ICEA Building, Kenyatta Ave, Nairobi (PO Box
60202); open 8.30 am to 12.30 pm and 2 to 4.30
pm (☎ 332955; fax 216530)

Malawi
Waiyaki Way, Westlands, Nairobi (PO Box
30453); open 9 am to 12.30 pm and 2 to 4.30 pm
(☎ 440569; fax 440568)

Mauritius
Union Towers, Moi Ave, Nairobi; open 8.30 am
to 12.30 pm and 2 to 5 pm; this is also the Air
Mauritius office (☎ 330215)

Mozambique
159 Kyuna Road, Kyuna, Nairobi (PO Box
66923); open weekdays 9 am to noon
(☎ 581857; fax 582478)

Netherlands
Uchumi House, Nkrumah Ave, Nairobi (PO Box

41537); open 9 am to 12.30 pm
(☎ 227111; fax 339155)
ABN Bank Building, Nkrumah Rd, Mombasa
(☎ 311043)

New Zealand
Minet-ICDC House, Mamlaka Rd, Nairobi
(☎ 722467; fax 722549)

Pakistan
St Michael's Rd, Westlands, Nairobi (PO Box
30045); open 8.30 am to 1 pm and 1.30 to 3.30
pm (☎ 443911; fax 443803)

Rwanda
International House, Mama Ngina St, Nairobi
(PO Box 48579); open 8.30 am to 12.30 pm and
2 to 5 pm (☎ 334341; fax 336365)

Seychelles
Agip House, Waiyaki Way, Westlands, Nairobi;
open 9 am to noon and 2.30 to 4 pm
(☎ 445599; fax 441150)

Somalia
There is currently no functioning Somali embassy.

South Africa
Lonrho House, Standard St, Nairobi (PO Box
42441); open weekdays 8.30 am to 12.30 pm and
1.30 to 4.30 pm (☎ 228469; fax 223687)

Spain
Bruce House, Standard St, Nairobi (PO Box
45503) (☎ 335711; fax 332858)

Sudan
Minet-ICDC House, Mamlaka Rd, Nairobi (PO
Box 74059); open 8.30 am to 3.30 pm
(☎ 720853)

Sweden
International House, Mama Ngina St, Nairobi
(PO Box 30600); open 8.30 am to 5 pm
(☎ 229042; fax 218908)
Alba Petroleum, Miji Kenda Rd, Mombasa
(☎ 314065; fax 492804)

Tanzania
Continental House, corner of Uhuru Highway
and Harambee Ave, Nairobi (PO Box 47790);
open 8.30 am to noon (☎ 331056; fax 218269)
Palli House, Nyerere Ave, Mombasa; open weekdays from 8.30 am to 12.30 pm and 2.30 to 5 pm.
(☎ 229595; fax 227077)

Uganda
Uganda House, Baring Arcade, Kenyatta Ave,
Nairobi (PO Box 60853); open 8.30 am to 12.30
pm and 1.30 to 5 pm (☎ 330801; fax 330970)

UK
Upper Hill Rd, Nairobi (PO Box 30465); open
8.30 to 11.30 am and 1.30 to 3.30 pm
(☎ 716064; fax 712233)

USA
Moi Ave, Nairobi (PO Box 30137); open 7.30 am
to 12.30 pm and 1.15 to 4.15 pm
(☎ 334141; fax 340838)

Zaïre
Electricity House, Harambee Ave, Nairobi (PO
Box 48106); open 8.30 am to 12.30 pm and 2 to
5 pm (☎ 229771)

Zambia
Nyerere Rd, Nairobi (PO Box 48741);
(☎ 724796; fax 718494)

Zimbabwe
Minet-ICDC House, Mamlaka Rd, Nairobi (PO
Box 30806); open 8.30 am to 12.30 pm and 2 to
4.30 pm (☎ 721045; fax 726503)

MONEY
Costs
The cost of budget accommodation in Kenya
is very reasonable so long as you're happy
with communal showers and toilets. Clean
sheets are invariably provided and sometimes you'll also get soap and a towel. For
this you're looking at KSh 200 a single and
KSh 300 a double and up. If you want your
own bathroom, costs rise to around KSh 300
a single and KSh 450 a double. Prices can be
slightly cheaper on the coast but more expensive in Nairobi.

There are plenty of small cafes in every
town, usually concentrated in a certain area.
They cater to local people and you can get a
traditional meal for around KSh 100 or KSh
200. Often the food isn't up to much but
sometimes it can be excellent. For just a little
bit more, the Indian restaurants are great
value. Some offer all-you-can-eat lunches
for around KSh 250. The food is not only
tasty but you won't need to eat for the rest of
the day either. A splurge at a better-class
restaurant will set you back between KSh
500 and KSh 1000.

The price of beer and soft drinks depends
entirely on where you buy them. They're
cheapest bought from a supermarket (around
KSh 35 for a beer). Using this as a benchmark figure, you would be paying around
30% more for them in a basic bar, slightly
more than double in a better-class bar or
restaurant, and up to eight times as much in
a five-star hotel!

Public transport is very reasonable and the
trains are excellent value. To travel from one
end of Kenya to the other (Mombasa to
Malaba) on the train in 2nd class is going to
cost you KSh 3750. In 3rd class it's less than

half that. Bus prices are about halfway between the 3rd and 2nd-class train fares.

The thing that is going to cost you most in Kenya is safaris. A three-day safari, for instance, with companies which cater for budget travellers is from around US$180; seven days costs from US$400. This includes transport, food, hire of tents, national park entry fees, camping fees and the wages of the guides and cooks. In other words, more or less everything except a few drinks and tips.

Car hire is even more expensive and is probably out of reach of most budget travellers. A 4WD Suzuki costs from KSh 4600 per day with unlimited mileage; petrol is extra. If you don't want 4WD then a small car, such as a Nissan Sunny, costs around KSh 3200 per day.

Note: The prices used in this book are as quoted by the organisation concerned, and may sometimes be in dollars and sometimes in Kenyan shillings. Whether costs are quoted in US$ or KSh makes no difference as payment is always in local currency.

Carrying Money

Never carry large amounts of cash around, especially if you have a preference for money belts which are worn outside your clothes. Those worn under your clothes are much less enticing to would-be thieves, of which there are no shortage. See the Dangers & Annoyances section later in this chapter for a complete run-down on personal security precautions.

Currency

The unit of currency is the Kenyan shilling (KSh), which is made up of 100 cents. Notes in circulation are KSh 1000, 500, 200, 100, 50, 20 and 10; there are new ('copper') coins of KSh 1, 5 and 10. These are quite small and as yet not in wide circulation. Old ('silver') coins are much bigger and heavier, and come in the denominations of KSh 5 (seven-sided) and KSh 1, and 50, 10 and 5 cents. Note that most public telephones in Nairobi and other major towns have been modified to only accept 'copper' coins; a major pain as they are not that easy to find.

Currency Exchange

After a period of instability in the early 90s, the Kenyan shilling has stabilised, and now hovers around the US$1 = KSh 50 to KSh 60 mark.

USA	US$1	=	KSh 54
UK	UK£1	=	KSh 93
France	1FFr	=	KSh 10
Germany	DM1	=	KSh 33
Australia	A$1	=	KSh 41

While most major currencies are accepted in Nairobi and Mombasa, once away from these two centres you'll run into problems with currencies other than US dollars, pounds sterling, French francs and German marks.

If you are going to be travelling elsewhere in East Africa, play it safe and carry dollars – it makes life much simpler.

Changing Money

With the deregulation of the money supply, foreign exchange bureaus have popped up all over the place, and these are the preferred places to change money these days. Their rates are competitive, and they don't charge commission. The rates for the main bureaus in Nairobi are published in the *Daily Nation* newspaper.

Banks will change money, but they charge commission, in some cases pretty steep ones. They also take a lot longer than the foreign exchange (forex) bureaus, are open shorter hours and are generally less convenient.

Black Market

The deregulation of the money supply has knocked the black market on the head. Despite this, you still get characters sidling up beside you in Nairobi or Mombasa and whispering the magic words: 'Change money?'. While they might promise enticing rates, in reality they can't offer any more than the banks or forex bureaus, and are just trying to lure you into a situation where they can relieve you of some of your cash. Give them a big miss.

Tipping & Bargaining

With such an active tourist industry, Kenya is a country where tipping is expected. Obviously there's no need to tip in the very basic African eateries or hotels, on *matatus* (local minibuses) or when using other public transport. In better restaurants 5 to 10% of the bill is the usual amount, although in these a service charge of 10% will often have been included on the bill (though it's debatable whether the employees ever get it).

If you take a safari then it's also expected that you tip your driver, guide and cook. The majority of employees in this industry earn low wages so be as generous as you feel able to. Around KSh 150 per day per employee is about the right amount. This is the cost per person, and how much you give obviously depends on whether they have worked well to make your safari enjoyable.

POST & COMMUNICATIONS

The Kenyan postal system is run by the government Kenya Posts & Telecommunications Corporation (KPTC; known disparagingly as 'kaput'). Despite this, the postal system is very reliable. Letters sent from Kenya rarely go astray but do take up to two weeks to reach Australia or the USA. Incoming letters to Kenya take around a week to reach Nairobi.

Parcels or books sent by surface mail take up to 4½ months to arrive – but they do get there.

Postal Rates

The air-mail rates (in KSh) for items posted from Kenya are:

Item	Africa	Europe	USA & Australia
letter	17.50	20.00	25.00
postcard	9.50	13.00	17.50
aerogram	14.50	14.50	14.50

Sending Mail

Kenya is a good place from which to send home parcels of goodies, or excess gear. In the main post office in Nairobi you'll often see at least a couple of people busily taping and wrapping boxes to send home. You have to take the parcel *unwrapped* to be inspected by customs at the post office not later than 3.30 pm. You then wrap and send it. The process is very simple and, apart from wrapping the parcel, takes only a few minutes.

Receiving Mail

Letters can be sent care of poste restante in any town. Virtually every Africa overland traveller uses Nairobi as a mail drop and so the amount of mail in poste restante here is amazing. The vast majority finds its way into the correct pigeonholes though there's naturally the occasional mistake, mostly entirely the fault of the letter-writer. Make sure your correspondents write your name in block capitals and underline the surname.

Some travellers use the American Express Clients Mail Service and this can be a useful alternative to poste restante. Officially you are supposed to have an Amex card or be using their travellers' cheques to avail yourself of the service but no check of this is made at the office in Nairobi. The postal addresses in Nairobi and Mombasa are:

American Express Clients Mail Service
Express Kenya Ltd, PO Box 40433, Nairobi
Express Kenya Ltd, PO Box 90631, Mombasa

The Nairobi office is in Bruce House on Standard St (☎ (02) 334722), while the Mombasa office is on Nkrumah Rd (☎ (011) 312461).

Telephone

The phone system works reasonably well, although it can take a number of attempts to get an international connection depending on the time of day.

International Calls International calls from Kenya are fiercely expensive. To Europe or the USA the rate is US$3 per minute, to Australia and New Zealand it's US$4 per minute. From a private phone it's marginally cheaper.

International calls are easy to make from major towns where you can either go through the operator or dial yourself on a private line.

Phone cards are available at the Nairobi Extelcoms office and at the Kenyatta Conference Centre in denominations of KSh 200, KSh 400 and KSh 1000 but the supply is erratic. There are card phones in Posta Rd near the main post office in Nairobi, and another two in the Extelcoms office on Haile Selassie Ave. There are also two in the lobby of the Kenyatta Conference Centre and these are by far the best as there's little background noise there. Mombasa, Malindi, Lamu, Nakuru and Kisumu each have at least one card phone at their main post office.

Operator-connected calls are also easy to make. The Extelcoms office in Nairobi is open from 8 am to midnight. Again, the Kenyatta Conference Centre is the best place to ring from as there's an international call office in the lobby and this is much quieter and less frantic than the Extelcoms office. It is only open until 6 pm, however.

In other towns, calls can be made from the post office, although there may be some delay in getting through to the international operator in Nairobi.

It's possible to make reverse-charge (collect) calls only to the UK, Europe and the USA.

Calls put through a hotel operator from your room will be loaded at between 25 and 50% so check what they're going to charge you before making a call.

Local Calls Local and long-distance (STD) calls are also quite straightforward. There are public phone boxes in every town and these all seem to work. The only problem is that there aren't enough of them, especially in Nairobi where you'll often find a queue of four or five people at each box. Local calls cost KSh 3, while STD rates vary depending on the distance. Call boxes in Nairobi accept only new ('copper') KSh 1 or KSh 5 coins. Elsewhere the boxes are slowly being converted, and will usually have 'copper coins

only' scribbled on them in black marker pen if they have been converted.

When making a local call, make sure you put a coin into the slot first (regardless of what you insert after that). If you don't, you may have problems making your call.

Calls to Tanzania and Uganda are only long-distance calls, not international. The telephone codes for the main towns and cities in Kenya are as follows:

Diani Beach	0127
Eldoret	0321
Isiolo	0165
Kakamega	0331
Kericho	0361
Kilifi	0125
Kisii	0381
Kisumu	035
Kitale	0325
Lamu	0121
Malindi	0123
Maralal	0368
Mombasa	011
Nairobi	02
Naivasha	0311
Nakuru	037
Nanyuki	0176
Nyahururu	0365
Nyeri	0171
Thika	0151
Voi	0147
Watamu	0122

E-mail
E-mail is still in its early stages, and thus far there are two providers in Nairobi, one of which is set up for taking casual e-mail. See the Nairobi chapter for details.

NEWSPAPERS & MAGAZINES
Tabloid newspapers are printed in both English and Swahili. Of the three English-language papers, the best is the *Daily Nation*, which has both local and overseas coverage, and is worth reading on a daily basis if you want to get a feel for what's happening in the country. It has the best cartoons and does not shirk from criticising the government and

exposing corruption, but balances this with a similar attitude towards the opposition parties. The others are the *Kenya Times* (the KANU party rag) and the *Standard*.

There is also a good range of locally produced magazines in both English and Swahili. Principal among these is the *Weekly Review* which is the Kenyan equivalent of *Time/Newsweek*. Radicals berate this magazine saying that it is a tool of government propaganda but it does, nevertheless, discuss issues in much greater detail than any of the daily newspapers and it's well worth a read.

The *East African* is a decent weekly paper published by the Nation group, which is also available in Uganda.

The *East African Chronicle* is an interesting business weekly. Probably the best for in-depth articles which pull no punches is the *Economic Review*, which is also a weekly paper.

Foreign newspapers (up to a week old) in English, French, Italian and German are readily available in Nairobi and Mombasa but vary greatly in price depending on where you buy them.

Current affairs magazines such as *Time, Newsweek, New African* and *South* are also widely available at a controlled price which is printed on the front cover. *New African* is the best of the bunch if you're looking for

---

Films

With its wide, sweeping landscapes and superb scenery, Kenya has been the location for many feature films. Unfortunately the quality of the films does not always match the quality of the backdrop!

Films shot in Kenya include the 1950s Tarzan movies, *King Solomon's Mines* in 1950, the pretty awful *White Mischief*, featuring Sarah Miles and John Hurt, and the 1985 film depiction of the life of Karen Blixen, *Out of Africa*, which starred Robert Redford and Meryl Streep.

A more recent offering is the 1990 *Mountains of the Moon*, which dramatised the historic journey of Burton and Speke in their search for the source of the Nile. ■

---

detailed coverage of African affairs and events. It's published monthly.

RADIO & TV

The Kenyan Broadcasting Corporation (KBC) has radio transmissions in English, Swahili and more specialised languages such as Hindi and African languages.

The BBC World Service and Voice of America transmit to East Africa on short wave around 12 hours a day and have programs in English and Swahili. The *Daily Nation* prints the programs each day. Although frequencies change from time to time, the main ones to try if you have a short-wave radio include 17885, 15420 and 9630 kHz.

There are two TV channels – KBC and KTN. The latter is better except that it no longer produces its own independent news programs but takes them from KBC. Many programs are imported from Europe, the USA and Australia.

M-Net cable TV from South Africa is the most recent addition to the scene in Kenya. Most mid-range and better hotels subscribe to the service, so you can watch CNN, BBC and a host of movie and sports channels.

PHOTOGRAPHY

Film

You'll find Kodak and Fuji 64, 100, 200 and 400 ASA slide film readily available in Nairobi and Mombasa, but 800 ASA is harder to find. The same is true for colour-negative film.

As an indication of price, 36-exposure slide film in Nairobi costs KSh 400, 36-exposure colour print film is KSh 200.

Camera Hire & Repair

If you don't have the inclination or the resources to buy expensive equipment but you know a bit about photography, it is possible to hire SLR cameras and lenses in Nairobi. The best place to do this is Expo Camera Centre (☎ (02) 221797), Jubilee Exchange, Mama Ngina St. It's busy here every day of the working week, both with local businesses and tourists, so you can trust it must be reliable and that the prices are competitive.

Expo also has a well-equipped repair shop where you can leave an ailing camera to be repaired with confidence. They do an excellent job but they're not cheap (neither is anyone else).

Film Processing

There are plenty of one-hour film-processing labs in Nairobi, and at least one in all other major towns. They can handle any film speeds. The cost is reasonable and the results just as good as what you'd get back home. Three good places are Expo Camera Centre, Camera Experts and the lab next to the Coffee House, all on Mama Ngina St. The lab also has a wide variety of film for sale.

Developing of print films is not cheap at around US$15 for 36 exposures. Developing and mounting of slide film is cheap, however, and it saves you the worry of taking exposed film through dodgy airport X-ray machines. It costs KSh 285 for a roll of 36 and takes four hours, but can only be done in Nairobi.

TIME

One thing that must be borne in mind is that Swahili time is six hours out of kilter with the way we tell the time, so that noon and midnight are 6 o'clock *(saa sitta)* Swahili time, and 7 am and 7 pm are 1 o'clock *(saa moja)*. Just add or subtract six hours from the time you are told and hopefully from the context you'll be able to work out whether the person is talking about am or pm! You don't come across this all that often unless you speak Swahili but you still need to be prepared for it.

DANGERS & ANNOYANCES

It is a sad fact that crime is rife in Kenya, and it ranges from petty snatch theft and mugging right on up through violent armed robbery and car-jacking, and even goes into the white-collar ranks and above. Rarely does one come across a country where such lawlessness is so ingrained that it's basically

accepted as part of life. It certainly doesn't help that the authorities are not only unable but also seem unwilling to do anything to clean the place up. Indeed it could be argued that the authorities are among the worst offenders.

As a visitor to Kenya this means that, while there is no need to be paranoid that every person you see or meet is a potential crook, you definitely need to keep your wits about you at all times. From a visitor's point of view, the situation is worse in the areas with the highest concentration of tourists, namely Nairobi, Mombasa and the coast. Simple snatch thefts and robbery with minimal force are the most common problems, and many, many people are relieved of their valuables on a daily basis. The worst instances involve armed robbery or other violence which has ended in the death of some tourists. The problem is certainly not limited to attacks on tourists, but obviously they make pretty juicy targets.

This is a great shame and certainly mars many peoples' visit to Kenya. There are some wonderful people in Kenya, but unfortunately many visitors are forced onto the defensive for so much of the time they simply never get to meet them. Instead they come away with a very negative view of the country. This is hugely damaging to Kenya's tourism industry (its number one foreign exchange earner) and is to a large extent responsible for the dramatic slump in tourism numbers the country now finds itself experiencing. As long as the authorities are prepared to sit back and continue to cream off as much as they can while doing nothing to ensure the safety of visitors (let alone local Kenyans) they run the risk of killing the golden goose. Not only that but they also run the risk of the entire country ultimately sliding into the sort of chaotic mire which characterises many African countries but which, up until now, Kenya has managed to avoid.

Theft

The time when you face the biggest risk is within the first couple of days of arriving in the country. The people who make a living by relieving people of their possessions can often spot new arrivals by their uncertain movements and general unfamiliarity with the place. This is particularly true in Nairobi, and in fact the number of people who get their passports and money knocked off on the No 34 public bus in from the airport is amazing. The thieves use the 'instant crowd' technique – you'll find yourself jostled and before you know it your bag or money-belt strap has been slashed. Unless you are familiar with the place, it's probably better to pay out the KSh 900 for a taxi.

Never leave your gear unattended anywhere as chances are it won't be there when you get back, no matter how short a time you are away. In hotel rooms your gear is generally quite safe but use your common sense – in some places (particularly the real cheapies/brothels) the door locks are purely cosmetic. In Nairobi the danger of theft from your hotel room has to be weighed against the real risk of having your possessions ripped off on the street. If your hotel and room are secure, it's probably safer to leave valuables there. If you are going out raging at night, only carry as much money as you're likely to need, and leave everything else in your hotel. If your hotel has safety deposit boxes, leave your valuables there.

The place to carry your passport, money and other precious documents is in a pouch against your skin, either around your waist or your neck. Neither method is foolproof but both give a measure of security and make it much harder to lose things. Leather pouches are far more comfortable to have against your skin than synthetic ones, and the moisture from perspiration is far less likely to turn your documents into a soggy pulp.

Small pouches and other wallets worn on the outside of your clothes are like flashing beacons to a thief, as are the ubiquitous money belts ('bum bags'), yet they continue to be immensely popular. Advertise your valuables, and someone will be watching you. Day packs, especially in Nairobi, instantly classify you as a tourist (and probably one who hasn't been around too long).

Elsewhere, they're not quite such a beacon. Minimise the risk by wearing them on your front rather than your back.

Never walk the streets of Nairobi or Mombasa wearing jewellery or a watch which is clearly visible – snatch thefts are very commonplace at any hour of the day, even in seemingly safe places.

If you are the victim of a snatch theft, think twice before yelling 'Thief!' Nairobi people hate thieves, pursue them with a vengeance and, if they can catch them, mete out instant, brutal and often lethal punishment on the spot. One or more thieves lose their lives every day in Nairobi in this way. The police may intervene, but not always.

Confidence Tricks In Nairobi the chances are you'll come across people who play on the emotions and gullibility of foreigners. People with tales about being 'refugees' can sound very convincing as they draw you into their net but they all end up asking for money. If you do give any, expect to be 'arrested' by 'plain-clothes police', complete with fake ID cards, who then extract a 'fine' from you on the basis that 'it's illegal to give money to foreigners'. Stories such as this abound and the number of travellers who get taken in – sometimes to the tune of hundreds of dollars – is legend. The best policy is to ignore all such requests for money even though you'll occasionally be turning down a genuine request for help.

Another trick in Nairobi is the envelope full of money which gets dropped on the footpath in front of you. The idea is that, as you are reaching to pick it up, someone else (the accomplice of the person who dropped it) grabs it and then suggests to you that, as you both found it, you should go somewhere and share your 'good luck'. If you go along the only thing that will be shared is your money in a side alley somewhere.

Another tried and tested con trick starts out with a 'student' approaching you with a photocopied sponsorship form headed by the name of a school. They tell you their school needs funds to buy equipment and ask you to give a donation. Look at the form and you'll find the names of two or three wonderfully philanthropic foreigners who have apparently donated vast amounts of Kenyan shillings to this worthy cause. If you fall for this then you need your head examined. If the person proves persistent, ask them to go along with you to a telephone to confirm that the request is genuine and that the person is a registered student at the school in question. The story changes each week. Whatever works gets pumped for all it's worth.

In Nakuru they don't lack ingenuity either. A trick that has been popular for years involves tourists with cars. Locals splash oil on your wheels, then tell you that your wheel bearings, differential or something else has failed, and then direct you to a nearby garage where their friends will 'fix' the problem – for a substantial fee. We've even had reports of oil being splashed on the back wheels and then the driver being told that the rear differential had failed even though the car was front wheel drive! Another vehicle trick is that people on the side of the road will gesticulate wildly to you as you are driving along, indicating that your front wheels are wobbling. Chances are that if you stop you'll be relieved of your valuables.

Mugging

Foreigners (and even experienced expatriates) do occasionally get mugged, but if you're sensible the chances of it happening to you are small. There are certain places in Nairobi and on the coast where it's not recommended to walk at night, but other than that it's just a matter of common sense: don't go out drinking in the nightclubs or bars carrying your valuables and then go rolling home down the street; don't wear your wealth, or you become a very tempting target. Leave valuable jewellery at home, keep cameras out of sight and don't pull out wads of money to pay for something. Always have enough small change for everyday transactions handy and keep the rest concealed. Take a cue from the taxi drivers of Nairobi who stash their money in at least half a dozen places on their body and in various articles of clothing.

Lastly, be wary on crowded matatus. It's not the ragamuffins you should watch but those who appear to be well dressed and on their way home from work. Plenty of these people work the matatus and you, as a tourist, are just one of their targets. Kenyans get hit, too.

And, if you do get mugged, don't listen to anyone who swears blind that he/she can get back what you've lost because they know 'the scene'. You'll end up several hours later being told a sob story or simply never see the person again.

Police: Friend or Foe?

For visitors from western countries it comes as something of a surprise to find the local police force are not seen by the local people as protectors and upholders of law and order.

Any encounter between police and civilians is likely to end with money changing hands, regardless of the situation. Basically, they are a major cause of hassle to be avoided at all cost; you should keep your head down and hope they don't notice you.

A good example of police excess occurred on the busy Thika road just outside Nairobi late in 1996. Traffic police caused severe chaos when, for two hours, they stopped motorists and demanded a 'Christmas present' of KSh 500 (US$10) from each! ■

PUBLIC HOLIDAYS

January
  New Year's Day (1st)
March-April
  Good Friday
  Easter Monday
May
  Labour Day (1st)
June
  Madaraka Day (1st)
October
  Moi Day (10th)
  Kenyatta Day (20th)
December
  Independence Day (12th)
  Christmas Day (25th)
  Boxing Day (26th)

ACTIVITIES
Scuba Diving
Malindi, Watamu, Shimoni and Wasini Island are the spots for scuba diving, the latter two being preferred. At Watamu, diving is from a boat not far offshore. A typical anchor dive is made at 12m to 15m depth. Visibility is often only fair and in fact Kenyan diving visibility has a poor reputation due to the plankton in the water. There are, however, usually plenty of fish even if the coral is not that spectacular. For more information contact the Dive Shop at the Driftwood Club in Malindi, or the Ocean Sports Hotel at Watamu. Possibilities at Shimoni and Wasini Island, in the extreme south, are covered in The Coast chapter.

Windsurfing
Most of the resort hotels south and north of Mombasa have sailboards for hire, and the conditions are ideal – the waters are protected by offshore reefs and the winds are usually reasonably strong and constant. The going rate at most places seems to be about KSh 250 per hour, it will cost you more if you need instruction.

Beaches
One of the great attractions of Kenya is the superb beaches which line the coast. Many travellers find themselves staying much longer than they anticipated. This is real picture postcard stuff – coconut palms, dazzling white sand and clear blue water. The only problem is that for the most part the resort hotels have a virtual monopoly on accommodation, although there are a couple of budget options both south and north of Mombasa.

The beach at Diani is one of the best although it's lined solidly with resort hotels. Tiwi Beach, between Diani and Mombasa, is much more low-key and you can camp right on the beach at the Twiga Lodge. There are similar possibilities north of Mombasa, although at certain times of year seaweed accumulates on the beach in huge quantities. Lamu doesn't suffer this problem and has some of the best beaches on the coast.

Desert Grandeur
There's the opportunity to experience this on either side of Lake Turkana and for a considerable distance south of there on the eastern side of the lake. For most travellers, this is one of the highlights of their trip to Kenya.

On the western side, access to the lake is easy with a bitumen road all the way from Kitale, and there's at least one bus and often a matatu or two every day in each direction. If you're heading up this way then don't miss the opportunity of exploring the Cherangani Hills east of the Kitale-Lodwar road using the Marich Pass Field Studies Centre as your base. Either side offers many challenging possibilities. The Turkana, Samburu and Rendille tribespeople are fascinating and, like the Maasai, have hung onto their traditional ways. It's certainly an area which you shouldn't miss.

Trekking & Walking
Mt Kenya is the obvious one, but other promising and relatively unexplored territory includes Mt Elgon on the Uganda border, the Cherangani Hills north of Kitale, the Mathews Range and Ndoto Mountains north of Isiolo, and even the Ngong Hills close to Nairobi. For more information refer to the relevant chapters in this book or contact the Mountaineering Club of Kenya (MCK) at its clubhouse at Wilson airport (meetings every Tuesday at 8.30 pm – visitors welcome), or in Nairobi (☎ (02) 501747), PO Box 45741, Nairobi.

Gliding
The Gliding Club of Kenya has its headquarters in Mweiga near Nyeri in the Aberdares, and there are flights every day except Monday. For more information contact the Gliding Club of Kenya (☎ (0156) 22467), PO Box 926, Nyeri.

Ballooning
Balloon safaris in the game parks are an absolutely superb way of seeing the savannah plains and of course the animals, but without the intrusion of vehicles and dozens of other tourists doing the same thing.

The most popular of these trips is in the Masai Mara National Reserve. The hot-air balloons depart daily from both Keekorok Lodge and the Fig Tree Lodge just after dawn and return around mid-morning. The flight includes a champagne breakfast on the plains. The cost is US$360. Bookings can be made through Adventures Aloft (☎ (02) 220592), Eagle House, Kimathi St, PO Box 40683, Nairobi; the Fig Tree Lodge; Block Hotels (☎ (02) 540780), PO Box 47557, Nairobi; or directly at Keekorok Lodge.

There's another outfit which offers balloon trips in Taita Hills Game Reserve. Bookings for this can be made through the Hilton International (☎ (02) 334000), PO Box 30624, Nairobi.

Fishing

The Kenya Fisheries Department operates a number of fishing camps in various parts of the country. They are really only an option if you have your own transport as the sites are off the main roads. Before you head off you need to get a fishing licence from the Fisheries Department. Advance bookings are not taken so it's just a matter of turning up at the site. For full details of the exact locations of the camps, see the Fisheries Department in Nairobi; the office is near the Nairobi National Museum.

White-Water Rafting

Rafting is still in its infancy in Kenya, perhaps because of the limited possibilities – there are only two major rivers, the Athi/Galana and the Tana. The Tana flows through relatively flat country so it's sluggish and unsuitable for rafting. The Athi/Galana, on the other hand, has substantial rapids, chutes and waterfalls. The only outfit which can fix you up with a trip down this river is operated by Mark Savage (☎ (02) 521590), PO Box 44827, Nairobi. He has two units of the Avon Ranger 3 river rafts.

A day trip from Nairobi consists of putting in just above Sagana on the Athi River and finishing about four km above the Masinga Dam. The trip starts with about two km of mild rapids, followed by six km of smooth

water and then two km of Grade 4-plus rapids without a breather and another two km of the same grade but with a few calm stretches for bailing out. This is followed by portage around a waterfall and a further 13 km of smooth water to the take-out point.

There's also an exciting three-day trip available from Yatta Gap on the Athi down to Tsavo Safari Camp (74 km).

ACCOMMODATION

Kenya has a good range of accommodation from the very basic KSh 150 a night budget hotels to luxury tented camps in the national parks for up to US$500 a night!

Kenyan residents should bear in mind that most places have separate rates for residents, and these are often considerably less than the nonresident rates. Rates quoted throughout this book are nonresident rates unless otherwise stated.

Camping

There are enough opportunities for camping that it is worth considering bringing a tent. It is also possible to hire camping equipment in Nairobi and elsewhere but it's not the sort of lightweight gear you could carry without a vehicle.

There are camp sites in just about every national park and game reserve and these are usually very basic. There'll be a toilet block with a couple of pit toilets, and usually a water tap, but very little else. Private sites are few and far between but where they do exist they offer more in the way of facilities. Often it's possible to camp in the grounds of a hotel but this is not an option in the bigger towns where space is limited.

Camping out in the bush is also possible though you would be advised to ask permission first. On the coast this is not advisable and sleeping on the beaches would be just asking for trouble.

Just in case you thought that the tented camps in the game parks might be a cheap option – forget it. They are luxury camps with all the facilities laid on, and high prices. The 'tents' barely justify the name – they usually just have canvas or mosquito netting for walls, but otherwise have a roof and bathroom. High, shoulder and low-season pricing policies apply equally to these places as to the top-end hotels.

Hostels

The only youth hostels affiliated with the International Youth Hostels Federation (IYHF) are in Nairobi and Malindi. If you like youth hostels, they are fine, but they are not so cheap and there are better options available.

There are other places which call themselves 'youth hostels' but are not members of the federation. Some are good, others less so.

Hotels

Real bottom-end hotels (known everywhere as boardings & lodgings – 'hotels' are often only restaurants) are generally brothels first and hotels second. This in itself is not a problem as long as you don't mind the noise, disruption and general atmosphere. Most places don't mind renting out rooms all night, although in some you get distinctly strange looks when they discover that not only do you want the room for the whole night, but that you want to spend it alone! These places are also not all that clean – you'll have to ask for clean sheets, and the shared bathrooms smell – and the rooms are often claustrophobic cells. On the other hand, you do occasionally come across cheap places which are clean and pleasant places to stay, so don't dismiss them totally; there's usually at least one cheap boarding & lodging in each town. On the plus side, they are cheap; expect a single/double room to cost around KSh 150/250.

Things improve dramatically if you have a dollar or two more to spend, though there are always exceptions. For KSh 300/500 a single/double, you will usually get a clean room with private bath (soap and towel supplied). These places often have a restaurant and bar (usually noisy). The only real advantages you get over the cheap places are your own bathroom and toilet and a degree of security.

Those who prefer a mid-range hotel are well catered for. If you're willing to spend KSh 600 to KSh 1000 a night then you can expect all the basic comforts and sometimes even touches of luxury such as towels, soap and toilet paper, clean sheets and beds, a table and chair; and often a telephone and room service.

At the top end of the market, accommodation ranges from better than the average mid-range to the five-star international chain hotels which provide the lot with prices to match. These start at around KSh 1200/1500 for a single/double and head up from there. Some of these places are old colonial buildings with bags of atmosphere, but most are modern and vary from characterless to the luxurious. The resort hotels on the coast and the lodges in the game parks also fall into this category, although some of the latter are superb places to stay if you can afford it – having animals come to drink at the salt lick in front of your lodge as you sit on the verandah sipping a cool drink is just great, but pleasures such as this can set you back up to US$300 per person for full board, depending on the season.

If you intend to stay in any of the top-end hotels, it's important to know that the price depends on the season. The high season generally runs from 16 December to 31 March and from 1 July to 31 August. The shoulder season is from 1 September to 15 December and the low season from 1 April to 30 June. There's generally an additional supplement over the Christmas and New Year periods.

Although most mid-range and top-end places quote prices in US dollars, payment in local currency is the accepted thing.

FOOD

The food in Kenya is the same as that found across the region. The one major dish which is unique to the country is the national obsession known as *nyama choma* (barbecued goat's meat). In recent years it has become almost a fetish among Africans and expatriates alike and, to cater for the demand, dozens of places have opened up offering just that. Sometimes it's good; sometimes it's tough as old leather. What you get is what you choose from a refrigerated selection of various cuts which you buy by the kg. Once it's barbecued, it's brought to your table by a waiter and sliced into bite-sized pieces along with a vegetable mash (often *matoke*, which are plantains). It's not a cheap option but not expensive either.

The trouble with nyama choma, if you've had any culinary experience, is that in no way does it resemble (except in the most expensive establishments) anything similar to marinated and seasoned barbecued meat. Most of the time, you'll take years off the life of your teeth chewing it and end up spending more time with a toothpick than you spent eating.

Nevertheless, the Kenyan middle class regard an invitation to nyama choma (and copious quantities of Tusker lager) as a special night out. So don't let us put you off – try it! Maybe this is how Africans keep their beautiful, healthy teeth.

DRINKS
Nonalcoholic Drinks
Tea & Coffee Despite the fact that Kenya grows some of the finest tea and coffee in the world, getting a decent cup of either can be difficult.

Tea *(chai)* is the national obsession and is drunk in large quantities. It bears little resemblance to what you might be used to but as long as you look on it as just a different hot drink and not actually tea it can be quite good. Be warned that it is generally very milky and horrendously sweet. Chai is made the same way in Kenya as it is in India: all the ingredients (tea, milk and masses of sugar) are put into cold water and the whole lot is brought to the boil and stewed. Finding a good honest cup of tea is virtually impossible outside the fancy restaurants. For tea without milk ask for *chai kavu*.

Coffee is similarly disappointing. Instant coffee is generally used, and in small quantities, so, once again, you're looking at a sweet, milky concoction. However, as each cup is individually made it's somewhat

easier to order one tailored to your own liking.

Soft Drinks All the old favourites are here, including Coke, Pepsi and Fanta, and they go under the generic term of soda. As with beer, prices vary depending on where you buy. In most places you pay around KSh 15 per bottle but in the more exclusive places you can pay up to KSh 70.

Juice There are no such predictable prices for freshly squeezed fruit juices which range from KSh 30 to KSh 150 per glass.

The main juice you'll find available everywhere is passionfruit juice. It is always fresh and very good. It is known locally simply as passion, although it seems a little odd asking a waitress whether she has passion and how much it costs!

Alcohol
Beer Kenya has a thriving local brewing industry and formidable quantities of beer are consumed. It's probably true to say that beer is the most widely available manufactured product in the country. Go to just a tiny group of *dukas* (local stores) by the side of the road somewhere and chances are one of them will either be a bar, or it will stock beer. Sure, it won't be cold, but even in the most up-market places beer is available both chilled and warm. 'Why warm?' you might ask as your face wrinkles in horror! The answer is because most Kenyans appear to prefer it that way.

The beer names are White Cap, Tusker and Pilsner (all manufactured by Kenya Breweries Ltd) and they're sold in 500 ml bottles. They are basically the same product with different labels (though there is a discernible difference in taste) but most people end up sticking to just one brand. The same company manufactures export-quality 300 ml beers – Export and Premium – and these are slightly stronger and more expensive. Kenbrew is a stronger beer which has gained popularity recently. Guinness is also available but tastes and looks nothing like the genuine Irish article.

Lastly, Kenya Breweries also has a draught version of Tusker which is very good but only available in a few places. Check the price before ordering – in some places it's cheaper than the bottled variety; in others it costs more (sometimes considerably more).

Beers are cheapest bought from a supermarket – a 500 ml bottle will cost you around KSh 35. Bought from a normal bar, you are looking at KSh 70. Bought at a bar in a five-star hotel it can cost you up to KSh 200.

Wine Kenya has a fledgling wine industry and the Lake Naivasha colombard wines are said to be quite good. This is something that cannot be said about the most commonly encountered Kenyan wine – papaya wine. It tastes foul and even the smell is unbearable.

On the other hand, you can get cheap imported European and even Australian wine by the glass for around KSh 150 in Nairobi restaurants. This is expensive when compared to the price of beer but is actually not too bad.

Local Brews Although it is strictly illegal to brew or distil liquor this doesn't stop it going on. *Pombe* is the local beer and is usually a fermented brew made with bananas or millet and sugar. You may get the chance to sample it here and there and it shouldn't do you any harm. The same cannot be said for the distilled drinks, known locally as *chang'a*, as these are often very effective poisons – inefficient/amateur distilling techniques ensure various percentages of methyl alcohol creep into the brew. They'll blind you if you're lucky; kill you if you're not. Avoid them!

ENTERTAINMENT
Cinemas

There are cinemas in Nairobi, Mombasa and other major towns. The fare varies from Indian masala to trashy Hollywood ultra-violence. The Nairobi cinemas usually have fairly recent Hollywood releases. The price is a bargain, usually around KSh 100 or less.

Discos

Africans love to party and you'll always find a disco in the main towns. Nairobi has half a dozen, and they are great places to spend an evening. Single men may find that in some places they are outnumbered by unattached African women. Once again, entry is cheap.

Bars

Almost equal to the African love of dancing is the African love of beer – they consume massive amounts of the stuff, and there are bars everywhere. These range from flash five-star places where waiters wear bow-ties, to local dukas where the beer is warm, the floor earthen and the noise level high.

THINGS TO BUY

Kenya is an excellent place for souvenirs, although much of the cheap stuff is just pure junk mass-produced by hand for the tourist trade. Look carefully at what's available before parting with your money.

Nairobi and Mombasa are the main centres but many of the items come from the various regions, so it's often possible to pick them up at source.

The best buys include *makonde* carvings, sometimes made from ebony (but often softer woods stained with boot polish), *kiondos* (woven sisal baskets), jewellery and tribal souvenirs, including colourful Maasai beaded jewellery, the decorated *calabash* (dried gourds) and spears and shields. There are also batiks, local sarongs (*kangas* and *kikois*), soapstone carvings from Kisii in the west of Kenya, and paintings.

It's possible to pick up something which will look good in your living room without spending a fortune but, these days, something of genuine quality and artistry is going to cost real money because there are many skilful artists who produce works of genuine art (as opposed to tourist tat) and know there are quite a few tourists around who are discerning and will pay big bucks for quality. This particularly applies to makonde carvings, jewellery and paintings. In some cases, they can cost thousands of US dollars.

If you're interested in quality artwork, spend time doing the rounds of the shops and galleries which deal in it.

CRAFT OF KENYA

You'll find some beautiful local craft work in Kenya, including:

Fabrics & Batik

Kangas and *kikois* are the local sarongs and serve many purposes. Kangas are colourful prints on thin cotton. Each bears a Swahili proverb and they are sold in pairs, one to wrap around your waist and one to carry a baby on your back, though you can buy one if you prefer. Biashara St in Mombasa is the kanga centre in Kenya, and you'll pay upwards of KSh 200 for a pair, depending on quality.

Kikois are made of a thicker cotton and just have stripes. They are originally from Lamu and this is still the best place to buy them, although the kanga shops in Mombasa also stock them. They are also made into travellers' clothes in Lamu.

Batik cloth is another good buy and there's a tremendous range, but the better prints are not cheap. The cheapest are printed on cotton and you can expect to pay around KSh 400 for one measuring about one metre square, but the price also varies depending on the artist. Batiks printed on silk are of superior quality and the prices are usually in the thousands rather than hundreds of shillings.

Makonde

Makonde carvings, which are made from ebony, a very black and very heavy wood, are the best pieces of woodcarving to buy and also the most expensive. This genre of carving had its origins in the highlands on either side of the Ruvuma River in southern Tanzania, but, because of its popularity, has been copied by other carvers all over East Africa. Created with inspiration, attention to detail and an appreciation of the life force which motivates its imagery, makonde is a superbly unique art form. Unfortunately, too many imitators create inferior products. Much of what is passed off as ebony is actually lighter (and cheaper) wood blackened with Kiwi boot polish; it's further degraded by the often slapdash quality of the carving. A quality piece of makonde carving is always superbly finished.

Before you buy any of this type of carving, do the rounds of the expensive craft shops in Nairobi and see what it ought to look like. Better still, buy it in Tanzania where it's much cheaper anyway. And, when you've seen the real thing, don't become too obsessed with ebony: there are some excellent Kenyan carvers who use local hardwoods and employ Kiwi boot polish as the finish.

Basically, there are two forms of this art – the traditional and the modern – and they're instantly distinguishable. The modern stuff is pure Modigliani, though the carvers have doubtless never heard of the man or seen any of his works.

The best pieces are to be found in the expensive craft shops and were probably made in Tanzania, but you shouldn't pass up the opportunity of having a good look at what is hawked around the bars of Nairobi. Some of it is good; most of it is rubbish. If you're interested, heavy bargaining is necessary.

Sisal Baskets

Sisal baskets, or *kiondos*, are probably the most distinctive Kenyan souvenir and are now popular and widely available in the West. They are still an excellent buy and the range is staggering – take a look in the market in Nairobi (although prices there are expensive). They come in a variety of sizes, colours and configurations with many different straps and clasps. Expect to pay around KSh 100 for a basic basket, and up to around KSh 300 for a large one with a leather 'neck'. Some of the finer baskets have the bark of the baobab tree woven into them and this bumps up the price considerably.

Soapstone

Soapstone carvings from Kisii in the west of Kenya are the main sculptural offering on sale. The soft, lightly coloured soapstone is carved into dozens of different shapes, from ashtrays to elephants. The best place for buying Kisii soapstone carvings is not in Kisii, as you might expect, but in Kisumu on Lake Victoria. The only problem is that it's extremely heavy and a kg or two of dead weight in your rucksack is not something to be taken lightly.

Elephant Hair Bracelets

On the streets of Nairobi you'll undoubtedly be approached by hawkers trying to sell you 'elephant hair' bracelets. Despite all the protestations to the contrary, these bracelets are made from reed grass (which is then covered in boot polish), from slivers of cow horn, or simply from plastic. You can safely assume that none of them are the real McCoy. ■

Getting There & Away

AIR

Tanzania

Nairobi to Dar es Salaam One of the cheapest regular options in air travel between Tanzania and Kenya is the flight between Dar es Salaam and Nairobi (US$139 one way) though you must add the US$20 departure tax to this price. There's usually one flight per day in either direction on each sector by Air Tanzania or Kenya Airways. The flights are usually easy to get on if you book a day or two in advance.

Mombasa to Zanzibar Another very popular flight is the three times weekly service between Mombasa and Zanzibar by Kenya Airways and Air Tanzania, which costs US$69 one way plus US$20 departure tax. In the high season flights need to be booked as far in advance as possible as there's heavy demand for seats.

Eagle Aviation also flies this route twice a week.

Other Routes Eagle Aviation flies three times a week between Mombasa and Kilimanjaro (for Arusha and Moshi). Precision Air Services (☎ (02) 210014 in Nairobi) flies between Nairobi and Kilimanjaro (US$127) and between Mombasa and Kilimanjaro (US$127) twice a week.

Air Victoria (☎ (02) 602491) and Western Airways (☎ (02) 503743), both with offices at Wilson airport, between them fly from Mwanza to Nairobi (US$175 and US$150 respectively) five times a week.

LAND

Tanzania

Bus There are several land connections by bus between Kenya and Tanzania.

Mombasa to Dar es Salaam Hood Bus/Cat Bus has departures from Mombasa to Dar es Salaam via Tanga on Monday, Tuesday and Friday at 9 am. In the opposite direction, buses depart Dar es Salaam for Mombasa via Tanga on Tuesday, Wednesday and Friday at 9 am. Officially, the journey from Mombasa to Tanga takes about eight hours and to Dar es Salaam about 12½ hours but, in practice, it can take as long as four hours to clear all 50 or so passengers through both border posts at Horohoro/Lunga Lunga so the journey time may be that much longer. The fare between Mombasa and Dar es Salaam is KSh 400 (TSh 4000 in the opposite direction). The bus office in Dar es Salaam is on Msimbazi St, close to the Kariakoo Market and the Caltex station. In Mombasa, it's on Kenyatta Ave.

The road between Dar es Salaam and Tanga is surfaced and in good condition but from there to the border it's diabolical. From the border to Mombasa you're back on a good tarmac road.

No-one but a masochist would do this journey the hard way by taking a bus first to Tanga followed by another one from there to the border and yet another from there to Mombasa. For a start, there's a six-km walk between the two border posts and hitching is well-nigh impossible. Once on the Kenyan side, however, there are frequent matatus for the one-hour journey to Mombasa. Doing it this way could take you the best part of two days.

Nairobi to Arusha & Moshi Between Nairobi and Arusha there's a choice of normal buses and minibus shuttles. All of them go through the border posts without a change.

The minibus shuttles between Nairobi and Arusha vary slightly in price but all take the same amount of time (four hours). One of the cheapest is Riverside Shuttle (☎ (057) 8323 in Arusha) which has its office next to the Chinese restaurant on Sokoine Rd in Arusha. It departs Nairobi daily at 8.30 am from opposite the Norfolk Hotel on Harry Thuku Rd, and from Arusha daily at 2 pm. The fare is TSh 7000 or KSh 1000 and the shuttle will drop you at any downtown hotel at either end on request. Simply tell the driver where you want to get off. At the Nairobi end, the driver will also drop you at Jomo Kenyatta international airport on request.

Slightly more expensive is the Davanu Shuttle (☎ (057) 4311 in Arusha; (02) 222002 in Nairobi) which has offices at Windsor House, 4th Floor, University Way, Nairobi, and at the Adventure Centre, Goliondoi Rd, Arusha. It departs Nairobi for Arusha daily at 8.30 am and 2 pm and Arusha for Nairobi daily at 8 am and 2 pm. The fare is TSh 8000 or KSh 1000. As with Riverside, Davanu will drop you at any downtown hotel at either end on request. Be careful with both companies regarding fares as they will initially attempt to charge you the equivalent of US$25 (Riverside) and US$30 (Davanu) if you're a nonresident. Simply telling them you're going to check out prices with their rivals usually does the trick.

Much cheaper is Arusha Express, which operates full-sized buses and has its office among the cluster of bus companies down Accra Rd in Nairobi. In Arusha, the office is at the bus station. It operates a daily service leaving Nairobi at 8.30 am and costs KSh 400 or TSh 3000 and takes about four hours. It returns to Nairobi the same day at around 2 pm.

Getting through customs and immigration on all the above buses is straightforward. The only snag you might encounter is being approached by touts who claim to work for the bus company and are employed to get you through the border crossing. This they will do (unnecessary) and in the process claim that officially you have to change US$50 to enter Tanzania, and will offer a ridiculous exchange rate. Don't fall for it.

It's also easy, but less convenient, to do this journey in stages and, since the Kenyan and Tanzanian border posts are next to each other at Namanga, there's no long walk involved. There are frequent matatus (TSh 700) and share-taxis (TSh 1300) from Arusha to Namanga every day. The taxis normally take about 1½ hours, though there are a number of kamikaze drivers who are

totally crazy and will get you there in just one hour. From the Kenyan side of the border, there are frequent matatus (KSh 200, three hours) and share-taxis (KSh 300, two hours) to Nairobi, which go when full. Both have their depot outside the petrol station on Ronald Ngala St, close to the junction with River Rd in Nairobi.

Nairobi to Dar es Salaam Direct buses between Nairobi and Dar operate roughly every second day from each city. In Nairobi the buses park up outside the Arusha Express office in Accra Rd, and will have a sign on the bus door giving departure time (some travel by day, others at night); tickets can be booked with the bus crew who hang out on the bus.

The journey takes 10 to 12 hours and costs KSh 1000.

Voi to Moshi The crossing between Voi and Moshi via Taveta is also reliable as far as transport goes (buses, matatus and share-taxis), as long as you go on a Wednesday or Saturday, which are the market days in Taveta. A matatu between Voi and Taveta (along a bumpy road) takes 2½ hours and costs KSh 200. From Taveta to Holili (the Tanzanian border), however, it's a three-km walk, but there are also *boda-boda* (bicycle taxis) for TSh 300. From Holili there are plenty of matatus and share-taxis to Moshi. A matatu from Holili to Moshi will cost you TSh 400 and take about 45 minutes.

Kisii to Musoma/Mwanza There are no direct buses between Kenya and Tanzania through the Isebania border post and doing it in stages is a pain in the arse. The road between Mwanza and Musoma is terrible and between there and the border it's diabolical. Once over the border, it's plain sailing on tarmac roads but you'll need a night's sleep at Kisii before continuing. There's very little traffic on the road between Isebania and Musoma so give yourself plenty of time and don't count on lifts with overland companies, the UN or other NGOs. Ideally, you need your own vehicle.

KENYA

Serengeti to Masai Mara If you look at any detailed map of the Serengeti National Park and Masai Mara National Reserve, you'll see that there's a border crossing between Bologonja and Sand River, and so you would assume it's possible to cross here. It is if you're crossing *from* Kenya *to* Tanzania, assuming you have the appropriate vehicle documentation (insurance and temporary entry permit). But officially, it isn't possible to cross in the opposite direction because you must pay the park entry fee to Masai Mara and you must pay it in Kenyan shillings, which you ought not to have since, under Kenyan currency regulations, you're not allowed to export them. And the nearest place where you *might* be able to change money is at Keekorok Lodge, 10 km away. Just imagine! In practice, the border guards/park officials are very helpful, so if you just happen to have a sufficient stash of Kenyan shillings to pay the park entry fees, then like Nelson with his blind eye at Trafalgar, it's a question of 'I see no ships'. There is, of course, no public transport along this route.

Train Through service to Tanzania has recently recommenced, with a once-weekly connection between Voi and Moshi. From Voi the departure is on Saturday at 5 am, arriving in Moshi at 11.30 am. The return trip leaves Moshi at 2 pm, arriving in Voi at 7.10 pm. The fare from Voi to Taveta is KSh 330/175 in 1st/2nd class; Voi to Moshi is KSh 475/255.

Uganda

The main border post which most overland travellers use is Malaba, with Busia being an alternative if you are coming from Kisumu.

Bus Akamba operates three direct buses between Nairobi and Kampala daily which cost KSh 900 (USh 18,000). Buses depart at 7 am and 7 pm, and the journey takes around 12 to 14 hours. Its office in Kampala is on Dewinton St; in Nairobi on Lagos Rd. Akamba also has it's daily Royal service, which is real luxury with large seats similar to 1st class in an aircraft. There are only three

in each row! Tickets cost KSh 2100 (USh 42,000), and the price includes a meal at the halfway point (Eldoret).

Mawingo also operates daily buses at 3 pm. These are marginally cheaper than Akamba (USh 16,000 from Kampala), but are more crowded and take up to 15 hours.

Doing the journey in stages, there are frequent taxis until the late afternoon between Kampala (USh 5000, three hours) or Jinja (USh 5000, two hours) and Malaba (Uganda). There are also frequent taxis in either direction between Tororo and Malaba which cost USh 250 and take less than one hour. The road is in excellent condition, although it does mean that the drivers can get up to terrifying speeds. Luckily, there's not much traffic on this road except close to Kampala.

The Ugandan and Kenyan border posts are about one km from each other at Malaba and you can walk or take a boda-boda.

On the Kenyan side there are daily buses by different companies between Malaba and Nairobi which depart at around 7.30 pm arriving at about 5.30 am the next day. The fare is KSh 450 with Akamba. If you prefer to travel by day there are plenty of matatus between Malaba and Bungoma which take about 45 minutes. If you stay in Bungoma overnight there are plenty of cheap hotels to choose from. From Bungoma there are several daily buses to Nairobi which leave at about 8 am and arrive about 5 pm the same day.

The other entry point into Kenya from Uganda is via Busia further south. There are frequent taxis between Jinja and Busia and between Busia and Kisumu. Akamba has direct buses on this route which connect Kisumu and Kampala. The buses leave Kisumu daily at noon, and cost KSh 600.

Train The recent increase in East African cooperation has led to the reintroduction of a classic rail journey, between Nairobi and Kampala. This is an excellent way to travel between the two capitals, and the border crossing is a breeze as the immigration officials come through the train and you don't even have to leave your compartment. The Kenyan Railways train is hauled by Kenyan locomotives and staffed by Kenyan crew on the Kenyan side; Ugandan locos and crew take over on the Ugandan side. The spirit of cooperation is not total, however: the picture of Moi in the buffet car remains up the whole way and Museveni doesn't get a look in!

Departure from Nairobi is at noon on Tuesday, arriving in Kampala on Wednesday at 9.30 am. The fare is KSh 4400/3520 in 1st/2nd class, which includes bedding and meals. From Kampala the departure is at 4 pm on Wednesday, arriving in Nairobi at 2.40 pm on Thursday, and the fares are USh 57,850/35,300 in 1st/2nd class. The train is often subject to delays of anything up to six hours.

There are also trains from Nairobi to the border at Malaba via Nakuru and Eldoret on Friday and Saturday at 3 pm, arriving at Malaba the next day at 8 am. The fares are KSh 2630/1820 in 1st/2nd class including meals and bedding. In the opposite direction they leave Malaba on Saturday and Sunday at 4 pm, arriving in Nairobi the following morning.

BOAT
Tanzania
Sea It's possible to go by dhow between Mombasa, Pemba and Zanzibar but sailings are very infrequent these days. Make enquiries in Mombasa at the dhow registrar's office on Government Square in the Old Town (entry to the compound will cost you KSh 5 which is payable at an office on the right-hand side of the entrance gate) and find out when the next dhow is going.

More reliable is the ferry, MS *Sepideh*, operated by Zanzibar Sea Ferries Ltd (☎ (054) 33725 in Zanzibar, (051) 38025 in Dar es Salaam, 56210 in Pemba and (011) 311486 in Mombasa), which connects Mombasa with Tanga, Pemba, Zanzibar and Dar es Salaam. The schedule varies according to the season but it's usually twice a week in either direction. The fares are US$65 Mombasa-Dar es Salaam, US$50 Mombasa-Zanzibar, and US$40 Mombasa-Tanga or Mombasa-Pemba.

Lake Victoria Until early 1996 there was a steamer service which connected Kisumu (Kenya) with Mwanza (Tanzania) on Lake Victoria on a once-weekly basis but the ship which serviced this route (the MV *Bukoba*) sank in May 1996. It's likely that the schedules of the other two boats – the MV *Victoria* and the MV *Serengeti* – will have been altered so that the two ports are connected again but you'll have to make enquiries. Even when the two ports were connected, cancellations were frequent.

Originally the boat left Mwanza at 6 pm on Thursday, arriving in Kisumu at 10 am the following day, then departed at 6 pm on Friday arriving back in Mwanza at 10 am on Saturday. The fare from Kisumu was KSh 1200/950/600 in 1st/2nd/3rd class. Make enquiries at the port office from 8 am to noon and 2 to 4 pm weekdays.

LEAVING KENYA
The airport departure tax for international flights is US$20. This is payable in US dollars cash, or the equivalent in other major foreign currencies or Kenyan shillings.

Getting Around

AIR

Kenya Airways

Kenya Airways, the national carrier, connects the main cities of Nairobi, Mombasa, Kisumu and Malindi. It's advisable to book in advance and essential to reconfirm 48 hours before departure if you're coming from either Malindi or Kisumu and have to connect with an international flight from either Nairobi or Mombasa airports. Otherwise you may well find that your seat has been reallocated. The flight schedules and fares can be found in the respective city chapters.

The main Kenya Airways booking office in Nairobi is in the Barclays Plaza building on Loita St (☎ (02) 823456).

Private Airlines

There are also a number of private airlines operating light aircraft which connect the main cities with smaller towns and certain national parks. The airlines are Air Kenya Aviation (☎ (02) 501421), Prestige Air Services (☎ (02) 501211), and Eagle Aviation (☎ (02) 603593, and they all operate out of Nairobi's Wilson Airport and/or Mombasa's Moi Airport.

These airlines connect Nairobi with Mombasa, Kisumu, Nanyuki, Malindi, Lamu and the national parks/reserves of Amboseli, Masai Mara and Samburu. Flight schedules can be found under the relevant sections.

BUS

Kenya has a network of regular buses, matatus (normally minibuses), share-taxis and normal private taxis. The cheapest form of transport is by bus, followed by matatu, share-taxi (Peugeot services) and lastly private taxi (expensive). There's not a great deal of difference in journey times between normal buses and matatus, but there's a huge difference in safety.

Bus fares are generally about halfway between what you would pay on the railways

in 2nd class but journey times are quicker. Unlike the trains, which usually travel at night, many buses travel during the day so you may prefer to take a bus if you want to see the countryside. All but one of the bus companies are privately owned but some of them run better buses than others. Akamba Bus Service has the most comprehensive network, and has a pretty good safety record. The government bus line, KBS Stagecoach, runs modern buses, including some double-deckers, to the main towns and is also reliable and safe. Of the other private companies, Coastline, Goldline and Malindi Bus are also OK.

Some Kenyan towns have what you might call a 'bus station', although this is often nothing more than a dirt patch. In others each bus company will have its own terminus though these are often close to each other. There are exceptions and these are indicated on the street maps. Matatu and share-taxi ranks sometimes use the same stations as buses but this isn't always the case, especially in Nairobi.

There are also a number of private 'shuttle buses' which connect Nairobi with Mombasa and with Arusha and Moshi in Tanzania. They're more comfortable than ordinary buses since they only take around 18 passengers but they are at least two to three times more expensive than ordinary buses. Their schedules can be found in the Nairobi and Mombasa sections.

MATATU

The way that most local people travel is by vehicles known as matatus. (The name comes from 'three', because when matatus first started running it cost three coins to travel.) These can be anything from small, dilapidated Peugeot 504 pick-ups with a cab on the back, to shiny, brightly painted 20-seat minibuses complete with mega-decibel stereos, as found in Nairobi. The majority of those which do the long-distance runs,

Matatus

Matatus are not just transport. They are Kenya's contribution to world culture. These gaudily painted minibuses, featuring 200-decibel stereo systems pumping out disco beats at bone-conduction level have a crew of three: the driver, who normally hasn't slept for three days, keeping himself going by chewing *miraa* shoots (from a bush which contains a natural amphetamine); the conductor, who extracts fares from reluctant passengers; and the tout, a veritable Daddy Cool whose aerial gymnastics on the outside of the minibus ought to be an Olympic event. The tout performs these antics to attract customers.

All Nairobi matatus are individually named and some of the popular ones on the Eastleigh run include 'Public Enemy', 'Undertaker', 'Get in & Die', 'Florida 2000', 'You Move with the Best', and 'You Die Like the Rest'. Driving standards and the frequency of fatal accidents justify these names, yet despite this, matatus are still the preferred mode of local transport. ■

however, are white Nissan minibuses. Most matatu drivers are under a lot of pressure from their owners to maximise profits so they tend to drive recklessly and overload their vehicles. They also put in long working days. Stories about matatu smashes and overturnings in which many people are killed or injured can be found daily in the newspapers. Of course, many travellers use them and, in some cases, there is no alternative, but if there is (such as a bus or train) then take that in preference. The Mombasa to Nairobi road is notorious for smashes.

As in most East African countries, you can always find a matatu which is going to the next town or further afield so long as it's not too late in the day. Simply ask around among the drivers at the park. Matatus leave when full and the fares are fixed. It's unlikely you will be asked for more money than the other passengers.

TRAIN

Kenyan trains are a very popular form of travel, despite the fact that the rolling stock, tracks and other essential works have been allowed to deteriorate. The trains generally run on time and are considerably safer than travelling by bus or matatu. Passenger lines run from Mombasa on the coast to Malaba on the Kenya-Uganda border via Voi, Nairobi, Nakuru and Eldoret with branch lines from Nakuru to Kisumu and Voi to Taveta. The other branch lines, which do not operate passenger services are the Nairobi to

Nanyuki, Gilgil to Nyahururu, or Eldoret to Kitale branches.

Classes

First class consists of two-berth compartments with a washbasin, drinking water, a wardrobe and a drinks service. There's a lockable door between one compartment and the adjacent one so, if there are four of you travelling together, you can make one compartment out of two, if you wish. They're usually very clean. What you cannot do is lock the door of your compartment from the outside when you go for meals.

Second class consists of four-berth compartments with a washbasin and drinking water supply. Third class is seats only. All the compartments have fans. Sexes are separated in 1st and 2nd class unless you book the whole compartment. Again, compartments aren't lockable from the outside, so don't leave any valuables lying around and maybe padlock your rucksack to something.

Third class can get a little wearing on the nerves on long journeys especially if they are overnight (which most are). Second class is more than adequate in this respect and 1st class is definitely a touch of luxury as far as budget travel goes.

Reservations

You must book in advance for both 1st and 2nd class – two to three days is usually sufficient – otherwise you'll probably find that there are no berths available and you will have to go 3rd class. Visa credit cards are accepted for railway bookings. If you're in Malindi and planning on taking the train from Mombasa to Nairobi, bookings can be made with travel agencies and major hotels in Malindi, or by calling the station yourself. Compartment and berth numbers are posted up about 30 minutes prior to departure.

Meals & Bedding

Most trains have a dining car which provide dinner and breakfast. Meals on the trains used to be quite an experience with plentiful and cheap four-course meals served on starched white linen by smartly dressed waiters. Sadly, these days the meals are nothing special, and the level of service is generally mediocre but that's of little consequence since you pay for them anyway in the price of the ticket whether you want them or not. Cold beer is available at all times either in the dining car or you can have it delivered to your compartment.

Bedding is provided in 1st and 2nd class and is also included in the price of your ticket.

CAR & 4WD

If you are bringing your own vehicle to Kenya you should get a free three-month permit at the border on entry, so long as you have a valid *carnet de passage* for it. If you don't have a carnet you should be able to get a free one-week permit at the border on entry after which you must get an 'authorisation permit for a foreign private vehicle' at Nyayo House, Kenyatta Ave, Nairobi, which costs a few dollars but a lot of time queuing. Before you do this, however, get in touch with the Automobile Association of Kenya which is in the Hurlingham shopping centre (signposted) in Nairobi.

When you are driving your own vehicle there are certain routes in north-east Kenya where you must obtain police permission before setting out. This is just a formality but there will be a roadblock to enforce this. The main stretch where this applies is between Isiolo and Marsabit where all transport must travel in convoy at a particular time of day

unless you're turning off to go somewhere else (such as Samburu National Park, Wamba or Maralal).

Foreign registered vehicles with a seating capacity of more than six people are not allowed into Kenyan game parks and reserves. The regulation is in force mainly to keep out the overland trucks.

Road Conditions

Kenyan roads are generally in good condition and many are excellent but, to a degree, it depends on which party the local member of parliament belongs to. If it's KANU (the ruling party) they'll be good, elsewhere watch out for potholes. The main exception to this is the Mombasa to Malaba road via Nairobi (the A104). This is the main road through the country and it not only takes Kenyan traffic but all of the heavy trucks bound for Uganda, Rwanda, Burundi and eastern Zaïre so it takes a constant battering. There are many long excellent sections but, equally, there are others in need of repair – especially between Nairobi and Mombasa. If a truck forces you off the road along one of the narrow sections on this road you can virtually say goodbye to your entire suspension and, possibly, your life. Drive very carefully along this road and at all costs avoid driving at night.

The roads in the north and north-east and in the national parks are all gravel, usually in a reasonable state of repair though there are long sections of corrugated gravel in some parts. Driving on these, at the necessary speed to avoid wrecking a vehicle, can be agony on your kidneys after several hours, especially if you're on a bus which has had a double set of unyielding springs fitted to it. Naturally, there are washouts on some of these gravel roads during the rainy seasons and, under these circumstances, journey times can be considerably longer. If a bridge gets washed out, you'll either have to turn back or wait.

Right up in the north on the eastern side of Lake Turkana, especially in the Kaisut and Chalbi deserts, you can make good headway in the dry season, and the roads (which would be better described as tracks) are often surprisingly smooth and in good condition. This is certainly true of the road from Wamba to North Horr via Parsaloi, Baragoi, South Horr and Loyangalani, except for the *luggas* (dry riverbeds) between Wamba and Parsaloi for which you'll need 4WD.

After rain, however, it's another story, particularly on the flat parts of the deserts. They turn into treacherous seas of mud, often as much as a metre deep in places. Only a complete fool would attempt to drive in these circumstances without 4WD, sand ladders, adequate jacking equipment, shovels, a tow rope or wire, drinking water and spare metal jerry cans of fuel. This is particularly true of the stretches of track between North Horr and Maikona and on any of the tracks leading off the Marsabit to Isiolo road through the Losai National Reserve.

To get out of the mud, if you're really stuck, you're going to be entirely dependent on the small number of vehicles which *may* pass by and *may* stop and help (they won't want to get stuck either), or on a passing herd of camels. It's going to cost you money either way. Not only that, but you can sometimes drive for hours only to find that it's impossible to cross a river, which may not even exist in the dry season, and have to drive all the way back again. Fuel is very difficult to find in this region and is usually only available at mission stations for up to three times what you would pay for it in Nairobi – and they'll only sell you a limited amount. Make adequate preparations if you are driving your own vehicle.

Fuel Costs
In Nairobi, petrol costs KSh 35 per litre; diesel is somewhat cheaper at KSh 27.

Car & 4WD Rental
Hiring a vehicle to tour Kenya (or at least the national parks) is a relatively expensive way of seeing the country but it does give you freedom of movement and is sometimes the only way of getting to the more remote parts of the country. On the other hand, if you're sharing costs, it's quite a feasible option.

There are a number of factors to take into consideration before deciding what type of vehicle to take and which company to go through, and there's no real substitute for sitting down with pen and paper and working out as near as possible what the total cost will be. To do this you'll need as many hire-charge leaflets as you can get hold of and a distances table.

The other major consideration is what type of vehicle is going to be suitable to enable you to get where you want to go. At times other than the rainy season, a 2WD vehicle may be perfectly adequate in some parts of the country including Masai Mara Game Reserve, Amboseli and Tsavo national parks (at least on the main access routes of the latter), but it won't get you to the east side of Lake Turkana and would restrict your movements in the Aberdare and Meru national parks and the Buffalo Springs and Samburu game reserves. Most companies also have a policy of insisting that you take a 4WD vehicle if you're going upcountry and off the beaten track.

Rental Costs This is something of a minefield since the daily/weekly base rates vary quite a lot as do the km (mileage) charges. What initially looks cheap often works out just as expensive as anything else. To give you some idea of average costs, the base rates for a 2WD saloon car are between KSh 950 to KSh 1500 per day plus KSh 8.50 to KSh 15 per km (usually with a daily minimum of either 50 or 100 km) plus collision damage waiver insurance (CDW) of between KSh 600 and KSh 900 per day and theft protection insurance waiver (TPW) of around KSh 600 per day (see Insurance later). Daily unlimited km rates vary between KSh 3900 (one day) and KSh 3200 (eight to 30 days) plus the two insurance rates quoted above.

In the next category, an average small 4WD vehicle such as a Suzuki Sierra costs between KSh 1200 and KSh 1500 per day plus KSh 12 to KSh 15 per km (usually with a daily minimum of either 50 or 100 km) plus CDW of between KSh 600 and KSh 900 per day and TPW of around KSh 600 per day. Daily unlimited km rates vary between KSh 4600 (two to seven days) and KSh 3200 (eight to 30 days) but conditions may apply here depending on how many km you want (see Minimum Mileage Conditions later). The lower price includes, say, 500 km and the higher price, say, 1200 km. To these daily rates you must add KSh 600 to KSh 800 CDW per day plus around KSh 600 TPW per day but, again, some companies include the insurance costs in these rates; others do not.

In the highest category – a 4WD Isuzu Trooper or Mitsubishi Pajero, for example – daily rates vary between KSh 2000 and KSh 2500 plus KSh 25 and KSh 30 per km (usually with a daily minimum of 50 or 100 km) plus CDW of between KSh 900 and KSh 1100 per day and TPW of around KSh 750. Daily unlimited km rates vary between KSh 5100 (two to seven days) and KSh 7400 (eight to 30 days) but conditions may apply depending on how many km you want. To these rates you must add KSh 900 to KSh 1100 CDW per day plus around KSh 750 to KSh 900 per day TPW per day but, again, some companies include the insurance costs in these rates.

Value Added Tax Whatever the total charges come to on your hire – hire rate, insurance, fuel top-up, km charges, etc – you will be charged 15% value added tax (VAT) on top of the lot. You can argue the hind leg off a donkey about the patently obvious fact that VAT has already been previously added to some of the costs but you'll be wasting your breath. The Kenyan tax man doesn't understand such logic and anyone who runs a company in Kenya knows this too so they're not going to leave themselves short. End of story. This is Kenya.

Minimum Mileage Conditions Some of the so-called 'unlimited' km rates are not quite that. Some have a ceiling of 500 to 1200 km per week free after which you pay the excess at the normal km rate. Some companies also offer the option of 500 km or 1200 km per week free of charge with corresponding

lower or higher base rates. If you are renting on a daily basis, some companies have a 50 km or 100-km minimum charge, regardless of whether you travel this far or not. If you're not planning on going too far then it may be more economical to opt for the lower free km rate.

Insurance The only way to cover yourself against damage to the hire vehicle and other property is to take out Collision Damage Waiver (CDW) insurance. The thing to really look out for here is the excess payable by you in the event of a collision. With the larger and generally more reputable companies (Avis, Hertz, Europcar, Central, among others) it's generally around KSh 2500 and a very generous KSh 2000 with Central. With others (Glory, Market, Payless, Habib's, et al.), however, it's as high as KSh 40,000, and this is over and above the KSh 600 to KSh 1100 or so you pay per day for insurance in the first place! What sort of CDW insurance leaves you liable for KSh 40,000 excess? Insurance? What insurance!? You *must* establish what the excess is before renting a vehicle or you could be in for a nasty shock if someone stoves into you and writes the car off. Even if the excess is high, however, it's essential to be insured and remember that tyres, tools and windscreens are always excluded from CDW insurance.

The other insurance you must have is Theft Protection Waiver (TPW). Some companies include this in the CDW insurance; many do not. As with CDW, you must know whether you are insured for this as car theft is becoming increasingly common in Kenya, and if your vehicle is ripped-off and you're not insured, you'll be up for the full value of the vehicle. Do you know how much vehicle is worth in Kenya? Don't even think about it. Not only that, but without such insurance, some companies stipulate that you will be liable, 'up to the value stated by the company'. In other words, think of a number and double it. That leaves you with no legal rights except to pay what they demand. Even if you have TPW, some of the cheaper car hire companies have an excess of KSh 40,000 which you are liable for. The more expensive companies do not and, yet again, Central comes out on top with a liability of just KSh 2000.

Deposits There's a wide variation in the deposits charged on hired vehicles. It's usually the estimated total hire charges (base rate and km) plus whatever the excess is on the CDW. You can cover this with either cash or signed travellers' cheques (returnable). The most convenient way to do it is by using a credit card.

Drivers' Licences & Minimum Age An international driver's licence or your own national driving licence is standard. Some companies stipulate a minimum age of 23 years but with others it is 25. There are occasionally stipulations about endorsements on licences (clean licences preferred) and that you must have been driving for at least two years. You will also need acceptable ID such as a passport.

Maintenance Although it's not always the case, it's probably true to say that the more you pay for a vehicle, the better condition it will be in. It's worth paying attention to this, especially if you're planning on going a long way. It doesn't necessarily mean that all the cheaper companies neglect maintenance but, as our feedback mail indicates, some certainly do.

The other factor related to maintenance is what the company will do for you (if anything) in the event of a major breakdown. The major companies *may* deliver you a replacement vehicle and make arrangements for recovery of the other vehicle at their expense, but with most companies you'll be entirely responsible for getting the vehicle fixed and back on the road. Only when you return it will you be refunded and you'll need receipts to prove what you spent.

Seasonal Discounts It's a good idea to do some footwork during the low season as some of the more expensive companies offer

substantial discounts of up to 40% on their normal rates during this period.

One-Way Rates If you want to hire a vehicle in one place and drop it off in another there will be additional charges to pay. These vary depending on the vehicle, the company and the pick-up and drop-off locations. With some companies it's free but in most cases it would be wise to count on KSh 7500 between Nairobi and Mombasa and KSh 1500 between Mombasa and Malindi.

Driving to Tanzania Only the larger (and more expensive) companies cater for this and there are additional charges. Briefly, these are about KSh 12,000 for documentation, insurance, permits etc.

Rental Agencies At the top end of the market are two companies:

Avis
> Koinange St, Nairobi (☎ (02) 336794)
> Moi Ave, Mombasa (☎ (011) 223048)
> Sitawi House, Malindi (☎ (0123) 20513)
> Two Fishes Hotel, Diani Beach (☎ (0127) 2101)
> Jomo Kenyatta International Airport, Nairobi (☎ (02) 822186)

Hertz
> Muindi Mbingu St, Nairobi (☎ (02) 331960)
> Jomo Kenyatta International Airport, Nairobi (☎ (02) 822339)
> Moi Ave, Mombasa (☎ (011) 316333)
> Moi International Airport, Mombasa (☎ (011) 433211)
> Moi Ave, Malindi (☎ (0123) 20040).

In much the same league but somewhat less expensive on weekly rates is Europcar at Bruce House, Standard St, Nairobi (☎ (02) 334722), and also in the Times building, Nkrumah Rd, Mombasa (☎ (011) 215917), and in Malindi (☎ (0123) 30556). It also has branch offices at Jomo Kenyatta International Airport in Nairobi (☎ (02) 822348), Moi International Airport in Mombasa (☎ (011) 433780), and at Diani Sea Lodge at Diani Beach (☎ (0127 2114).

Somewhat cheaper but very reliable companies with well-maintained vehicles include:

Central Rent-a-Car
 Fedha Towers, Standard St, Nairobi
 (☎ (02) 222888; fax 339666)
Glory Car Hire
 Diamond building, Tubman Rd, Nairobi
 (☎ (02) 2250224; fax 331533)
 Moi Ave, Mombasa (☎ (011) 313561/221159)
 Ngala building, Lamu Rd, Malindi
 (☎ /fax (0123) 20065)
Habib's
 Agip House, Haile Selassie Ave, Nairobi
 (☎ (02) 220463)
Market Car Hire
 Market Service Station, on the corner of Koinange
 & Banda Sts, Nairobi (☎ (02) 225797)
Payless Car Hire
 Hilton Hotel, Nairobi
 (☎ (02) 223581; fax 223584)
 Mombasa (☎ (011) 222629; fax 221282)
 Malindi (☎ (0123) 31643; fax 31645)
 Diani (☎ (0127) 2276)

Central Rent-a-Car is certainly the best in this category with a well-maintained fleet of fairly new vehicles and a good back-up service. Its excess liability on CDW is also the lowest (KSh 2000), and its insurance rates include *both* TPW and CDW insurance.

Glory has some decent cars but also has some real bombs. Market and Payless are owned by the same people and their excess liability on CDW would leave you penniless if you did have an accident (KSh 40,000), but then so would Glory which has the same excess.

BICYCLE

Bicycles are basically only in use in cities and there's not many of them. Virtually everybody travels by matatu. Anyone foolish enough to risk cycling along main roads in Kenya must be considered suicidal. The exception would be in the countryside and off the main roads. Always assume that the vehicle approaching you from behind is going to knock you off the road so get off it before it reaches you. This obviously makes cycling tedious but it's better than ending up on a mortuary slab.

The hills of Kenya are not particularly steep but can be long and hard. You can expect cover around 80 km per day in the hills of the western highlands, somewhat more where the country is flatter. Be wary of cycling off road as punctures from thorn trees are a major problem.

HITCHING

Hitching is usually good on the main roads and may well be preferable to travelling by matatu, but if you are picked up by an African driver and are expecting a free lift then make this clear from the outset. Most will expect a contribution at least. Hitching to the national parks, on the other hand, can be very difficult since most people either go on a tour or hire their own vehicle. Apart from that, once you get to the park lodges or camping areas, you will be entirely dependent on persuading other tourists with their own vehicles to take you out with them to view game since walking in the parks is generally forbidden. Although many travellers hitchhike, it is not a totally safe way of getting around. Just because we explain how hitching works does not mean we recommend it.

BOAT
Lake Victoria Ferry
Ferries connect Kisumu with Kendu Bay and Homa Bay, and Homa Bay with Mfangano Island, but the service is very limited. The schedule for the lake ferries can be found in the Kisumu section.

Dhow
Sailing on a dhow along the East African coast is one of Kenya's most worthwhile and memorable experiences. There's nothing quite like drifting along the ocean in the middle of the night with the moon up high, the only sounds the lapping of the waves against the side of the boat and subdued conversation. It's enjoyable at any time of day, even when the breeze drops and the boat virtually comes to a standstill.

There are no creature comforts aboard these dhows so when night comes you simply bed down wherever there is space. You'll probably get off these boats smelling of fish since fish oil is used to condition the timbers of the boat – nothing that a shower won't remove! Take drinking water and food with you although fish is often caught on the way and cooked up on deck over charcoal. Just imagine yourself on Magellan's or Francis Drake's circumnavigation of the world and you'll have it about right except it will only take a few days instead of three years and you won't have to do any pillaging! Dhows can be picked up in Lamu but there are also possibilities in Mombasa.

Many of the smaller dhows these days have been fitted with outboard motors so that progress can be made when there's no wind. The larger dhows are all motorised and some of them don't even have sails.

If you have the money (US$60), check out the Tamarind Dhow cruises which leave from the Tamarind Restaurant in Nyali on the mainland opposite Mombasa island – see the Mombasa section for details.

Safaris

ORGANISED VEHICLE SAFARIS

There are essentially two types of organised safaris – those where you camp and those where you stay in game lodges or luxury tented camps at night. Whichever you choose, safaris typically start and end in either Nairobi or Mombasa, though there are a number of exceptions to this. Apart from transfer to and from Nairobi or Mombasa and driving from one park to another, once you're in a park you'll be taken on a number of game drives – usually two and sometimes three per day. Each drive typically lasts two to 2½ hours and the best (in terms of sighting animals) are those in the early morning and late afternoon when the animals are at their most active. The vehicles used for these drives are six to eight-seater minibuses with roof hatches, Land Rovers, or open-sided trucks.

As a general rule, you'll be left to your own devices between late morning and around 3 pm (except for lunch) though, if you're on a camping safari, you may well be taken to a lodge in the early afternoon to

relax over a cold beer or have a swim in the pool. You may also be taken to a lodge after the late-afternoon game drive for the same thing before returning to camp for dinner.

Camping Safaris

Camping safaris cater for budget travellers, for the young (or young at heart) and for those who are prepared to put up with discomfort. They are no-frills safaris, with none of life's little luxuries such as flush toilets, running water or iced drinks. Such safaris can be quite demanding depending on where you go, and you'll be expected to lend a hand. You'll end up sweaty and dusty and there may well be no showers available – even cold ones. On the other hand, you're in for an authentic adventure in the African bush with nothing between you and the animals at night except a sheet of canvas and the embers of a dying fire. It's not at all unusual for elephants or hippos to trundle through the camp at night, or even the occasional lion, and, so far, no-one has been eaten or trampled on.

Another plus for these safaris is that you'll probably find yourself with travellers from the four corners of the earth. Truck safaris may have as many as half a dozen different nationalities on board.

The price of your safari will include three meals a day cooked by the camp cook(s), though on some safaris you'll be expected to lend a hand in the preparation and clean up. Food is of the 'plain but plenty' variety.

The price will also include all the necessary camping gear except a sleeping bag which you must provide or hire locally. The tents provided sleep two people as a rule and you'll be expected to erect and dismantle it yourself, though there are some safaris where the camp is taken on ahead of you and the tents erected by the staff, or where companies have permanent tented camps sites. If you're a single traveller, you'll be expected to share a tent with someone else. If you don't want to do that then you'll be up for a 'single supplement' of between 20% to 25% on the price of the safari which will secure you a tent of your own. Mosquito nets are generally not provided so you'll have to hire one yourself or bring along insect repellent either in the form of coils or a skin cream.

You'll need to bring clothing and footwear sufficient to cover you for hot days and cold nights but the amount of baggage which you'll be allowed to bring is limited. Excess gear can usually be stored at the safari company's offices. Don't forget to bring along a torch (flashlight) and pocket-knife – the company will provide kerosene lanterns for the camp but it's unlikely they'll be left on all night.

There are also a number of somewhat more expensive camping safaris available which utilise permanent camp sites with pre-erected tents fitted with mosquito nets, beds and sheets and which have showers.

Remember that at the end of one of these safaris your driver/guide and the cook(s) will expect a reasonable tip. This is only fair since wages are low and these people will have made a lot of effort to make your trip a memorable one. Be generous here. Other travellers are going to follow you and the last thing anyone wants to find themselves closeted with is a disgruntled driver/guide who couldn't care less whether you see game or not. A good tipping guide is around KSh 150 per guide/cook per person per day – in other words, what you would spend on a round of drinks between just two people.

Lodge & Tented Camp Safaris

The other type of safari is for those who want luxury at night and in between game drives. The accommodation is in game lodges or luxury tented camps. There are plenty of beautifully conceived and superbly located lodges in the main national parks where you can expect a fully self-contained room, cottage or tent, cuisine of an international standard, a terrace bar with ice-cold drinks, a swimming pool and videos and plenty of staff to cater for all your requirements. Many of these lodges overlook a watering hole or salt lick so you can sit on the viewing terrace and watch the animals from there. The watering hole or salt lick will usually be floodlit at night. Some of the lodges put out bait or salt

to encourage certain animals to visit the spot and while this is often very contrived, it usually guarantees you a sighting of animals which you'd be very lucky to see otherwise, leopards in particular.

There's obviously a considerable difference in price for these safaris as opposed to camping, and most of the people who go on them are package tourists with expectations and attitudes of mind quite dissimilar to those who opt for a camping safari. For them it's essentially a holiday rather than in-depth involvement in Africa, its people and wildlife. It's the African bush at arm's length. On the other hand, if you have the money, it's worth staying at the occasional lodge just for the contrast and many lodges do go to great lengths to bring Africa as close as possible to you in terms of design, location and decor.

Lodge safaris will cost you up to four times what a camping safari costs, sometimes considerably more. Luxury tented camps are no less expensive than lodges and the more exclusive ones cost up to twice as much as a lodge. They are for people to whom money is no object and who want to experience what it must have been like in the days of the big-game hunters, except that they'll be stalking game with cameras rather than guns.

Routes

Whether you take a camping safari or a lodge safari, there's a whole plethora of options available ranging from two days to 15 days and, in some cases, up to six weeks, though the longer trips would take you to neighbouring countries as well. If possible, it's best to go on a safari which lasts at least five days and preferably longer since otherwise a good deal of your time will be taken up driving to and from the national parks and Nairobi. You'll also see a great deal more on a longer safari and have a much better chance of catching sight of all the major animals. Remember that sightings of any particular animal cannot be guaranteed but the longer you spend looking, the better your chances are. A longer safari will also give you the opportunity of having some involvement with the local tribespeople.

A three-day safari typically takes you either to Amboseli or Masai Mara. A four-day safari would take you to Amboseli and Tsavo, to Amboseli and Masai Mara or to Samburu and Buffalo Springs but you'd be pushing it to get three parks in four days. A five-day safari would take you to Amboseli and Tsavo, or to Masai Mara and Lake Nakuru; whereas a six-day safari would take you to lakes Nakuru, Bogoria and Baringo plus Masai Mara, or to Lake Nakuru, Masai Mara and Amboseli. On a seven-day safari, you could expect to visit at least two of the Rift Valley lakes plus Masai Mara and Amboseli, whereas on an 11-day safari you would take in two or more of the Rift Valley lakes plus Masai Mara, Amboseli and Tsavo; or Samburu and Buffalo Springs, Meru, Lake Nakuru and Masai Mara.

Most of the safari companies cover the above standard routes but some also specialise in different routes designed to take you off the beaten track. There are, for instance, safaris which take in Masai Mara, Lake Victoria, Mt Elgon, Saiwa Swamp and Nakuru, and others which take in Mt Kenya, Samburu and Buffalo Springs, Nyahururu, Lake Nakuru and Masai Mara. Other safaris visit Shaba, rather than Samburu and Buffalo Springs, where you'll hardly see another vehicle. There are also others which will take you to Marsabit National Park in the far north, but they're very few and are generally part of a safari to Lake Turkana.

Some companies also offer safaris to Lake Turkana which range from six to 10 days. The shorter trips take one or other of the standard routes – Nairobi, Nakuru, Nyahururu, Maralal, Baragoi, South Horr and Loyangalani or Nairobi, Isiolo, Maralal, Baragoi, South Horr and Loyangalani. The longer trips detour from this route and take you to either or both of Samburu and Buffalo Springs National Reserves and either Meru National Park or Shaba National Reserve. There are also combination safaris which include a vehicle safari to Lake Turkana and a camel safari in the Mathews Range or the Ndoto Mountains. A full description of the options available can be found in the Lake Turkana Safaris section later on.

Costs

There's a lot of competition for the tourist dollar among the safari companies, and prices for the same tour are very similar. The trouble is, there are now so many safaris to choose from which offer similar itineraries and options that it's not that easy to compare prices. It depends what you want, though it's still generally true that the longer you go for, the less it costs per day.

For camping safaris with no frills you are looking at an all-inclusive price of around US$70 to US$80 per day on a reducing scale the longer you are out. The price includes transport, food (three meals per day), park entry and camping fees, tents and cooking equipment. The price per day for safaris over 11 days tends to rise somewhat since there's a lot more organisation involved and you'll be going to remote areas where there are no services available so everything has to be trucked in.

Unfortunately, the situation is not as simple as the above suggests. While it may be OK to use the above figure as a benchmark, prices vary widely. A three-day safari to Amboseli and Masai Mara or Amboseli and Tsavo varies from US$180 to US$570. A five-day safari to Amboseli and Masai Mara or to the Rift Valley and Amboseli varies from US$300 to US$800; and a seven-day safari to Amboseli, Masai Mara and the Rift Valley or to Amboseli, Masai Mara and Samburu varies from US$400 to US$1000 or more. In other words, you must do some legwork. Collect as many company leaflets as you can (about a morning's work), decide where you want to go, compare prices, work out what's included and what isn't, and then make your choice. Remember that, generally, you get what you pay for. A high degree of personal involvement in camp chores and a willingness to eschew creature comforts usually guarantees a low price. If you want the opposite, it will cost you more. No-one works for nothing.

The prices for safaris which involve staying in lodges or tented camps are considerably higher. Here you're looking at a minimum of US$180 per person per night in the lodges and up to US$350 in the luxury tented camps.

The above prices are based on the assumption that you will share accommodation (a tent or room) with one other person. If you don't want to do this then you'll have to pay what's called a 'single room supplement'. This is generally around 20% to 25% extra and sometimes up to 50%.

Departure Frequency

This varies a lot from company to company and depends on the season. In the high season, many companies have daily or every second day departures to the most popular game parks – Amboseli, Masai Mara and Tsavo – since there's high demand. To the less frequented parks such as Samburu and Buffalo Springs, Shaba and Meru, they generally leave only once or twice per week. Safaris to Lake Turkana are usually only once weekly. In addition, most companies will leave for any of the most popular game parks at any time so long as you have a minimum number of people wanting to go – usually four. In the low season, there are fewer departures.

It obviously makes a lot of sense to either book ahead or to get a group together rather than just turn up and expect to leave the very next morning. Advance booking is essential for the Lake Turkana safaris since they're heavily subscribed. It's also essential for any of the more exotic options described in the Other Safaris section.

Choosing a Company

There is no doubt that some safari companies are better than others. The main factors which make for the difference are the quality and type of vehicles used, the standard of the food, and the skills and knowledge of the drivers/guides. It's equally true that any company can take a bunch of people on safari one week and bring them back fully satisfied, and yet the following week take a different set of people on the same safari and end up with a virtual mutiny. That's an extreme example, but whether a company gets praised or condemned can hinge on something as simple as a broken spring which involves having to wait around for most of the day whilst a replacement vehicle is sent out from Nairobi.

The other major factor to take into consideration before you decide to go with any particular company is whether they actually operate their own safaris with their own vehicles or whether they are just agents for other safari companies. If they're just agents then obviously part of what you pay is their commission but the most important thing here is, if anything goes wrong or the itinerary is changed without your agreement, you have very little comeback and you'll be pushing shit uphill to get a refund. We get letters about this all the time from travellers to whom this has happened.

Unfortunately, the situation isn't that easy to avoid. It's a minefield working out which are genuine safari companies and which are just agencies. Go into any office in Nairobi and, naturally, they all have their own vehicles and, of course, they'll compensate you at the end of the safari if anything goes seriously wrong. Not so if they're just agents. They will already have paid the lion's share of what you gave them to the company which actually provided the vehicles and staff so that gives them very little room to manoeuvre. Likewise, there's no way that the actual safari company is going to provide the agency with a refund.

It's perfectly obvious that quite a few so-called safari companies are merely agencies. Simply pick up half a dozen leaflets from various companies and compare the wording – you'll find that quite a few are identical!

On the other hand, quite a lot of genuine safari companies put out leaflets giving the impression that they do every conceivable safari under the sun. They don't. They may well do quite a lot of them with their own vehicles and staff and take personal responsibility for them but, in many cases, especially as regards Mt Kenya treks, gorilla safaris to Uganda/Zaïre and the national parks of Tanzania (Serengeti, Ngorongoro, Lake Manyara, Mt Kilimanjaro etc), they will be on-selling to another company or a Tanzanian company which specialises in these. This doesn't mean they're out to rip you off. If a company operates its own safaris, it has a reputation to look after and it will only be on-selling to companies that it trusts and which have a record at least the equal of its own.

If you find shopping around too daunting you might consider going to a travel agent (see the Travel Agents section in the Nairobi chapter). However, if you are looking for a real bottom-end safari, you are likely to get a better price by shopping around as negotiation is then possible.

Another aspect of Kenya's safari business is that there's a good deal of client swapping between companies whose vehicles are full and those which aren't. You may find yourself on a certain company's safari which is not the one you booked through. The reputable companies won't do this without informing you but the agents certainly will. Getting swapped onto another company's safari isn't necessarily a bad thing but make sure that the safari you booked and paid for is what you get. There is an organisation called the Kenyan Association of Tour Operators (KATO) to which most reputable safari companies belong so you have *some* recourse to appeal in case of conflict but it's essentially a paper tiger.

Despite the pitfalls mentioned here, there are many reliable companies offering camping safaris which have their own vehicles and an excellent track record. The following companies have been listed alphabetically, and are not in any order of preference, reliability or cost.

This is by no means an exhaustive list of companies which offer camping safaris nor is there necessarily any implication that others are unreliable – though some are. On the other hand, we do get hundreds of letters from travellers every year describing their experiences with various safari companies. Some get consistently good reports and others get variable reports, but there are some which get consistently bad reports. If you do choose a company not listed here don't blame us if you get into strife but do tell us what the problem was and what was done about it (if anything).

Best Camping Tours
2nd floor, Nanak House, corner of Kimathi and Banda Sts, PO Box 40223, Nairobi (☎ 229667; fax 217923)
This is a popular and reliable company which offers budget camping safaris on all the main routes including Amboseli or Masai Mara (three to four days); Amboseli and Tsavo (four days); Amboseli, Tsavo, the Rift Valley lakes and Masai Mara (eight days); Mt Kenya, Samburu, Nakuru and Masai Mara (eight days); Amboseli, Mt Kenya, Samburu, Nakuru and Masai Mara (eight days); and many other options. Average cost is around U$80 per day.

Blackwing Safaris
PO Box 42532, Nairobi (☎/fax 891241)
This small company caters for discerning clients who want flexibility and quality and who don't want to be crammed into the usual safari minibus. Safaris are only three clients or less at a time and can be arranged for any duration within Kenya or Tanzania. Safaris cost a standard US$360 a day per person assuming a minimum of five days but this includes the lot – all transport, transfer to and from Nairobi airport, first and last nights at the Boulevard Hotel in Nairobi, all food and drink (including beer, wine and spirits), all park entry and camping fees, and the full range of camping and safari equipment.

Bushbuck Adventures
Gilfillan House, Kenyatta Ave, PO Box 67449, Nairobi (☎ 212975; fax 218735; e-mail bushbuck@arcc.or.ke)
Bushbuck is a small company and its emphasis is on passenger comfort and conservation. It's relatively expensive but part of the profits go back into conservation projects. Its main emphasis is on customised safaris for individuals and groups. The price ranges from US$390 per day for a one person safari to US$160 per person for 12 people (in two vehicles).

Come to Africa Safaris Ltd
3rd floor, Rehema House, between Kaunda and Standard Sts, PO Box 69513, Nairobi (☎ 213186; fax 213254)
This company covers most of the national parks in Kenya (as well as Tanzania) and also has its own permanent tented camp – the Mara Hippo Camp – in Masai Mara. All its safaris cost a standard US$70 per person per day, and are popular among budget travellers.

Exotic Safaris

1st floor, South Wing, Uniafric House, Koinange St, PO Box 54483, Nairobi (☎ 338811; fax 245767) We receive consistently good reports of this company, which offers a full range of safaris along the standard routes. It also offers an eight-day Turkana safari – see later.

Gametrackers Camping Safaris

1st floor, Kenya Cinema Plaza, Moi Ave, PO Box 62042, Nairobi (☎ 338927, 222703; fax 330903) Also long-established and reliable, this company offers a whole range of both camping and lodge safaris. It also offers a number of much longer safaris such as a four-week Mountain Gorilla Safari (US$890), a five-week Southern Africa Safari (US$855), and a nine-week Africa in Depth Safari (US$1425). It also covers the national parks of Tanzania, Mt Kenya treks, Lake Turkana and a camel safari (details of the last three below).

Departures for the shorter trips vary between once a week and 10 times a month. For the longer trips it's usually once a week and for the four and five-week safaris it's once a month.

Ketty Tours

Moi Ave (PO Box 82391), Mombasa (☎ 315178; fax 311355)

This company specialises partly in short tours of the coastal region (Wasini, Shimba Hills, Gedi etc) but it also offers camping safaris to all the usual parks ranging from two to 10 days. The average cost per person per day is US$80.

Safari-Camp Services

Barclays Plaza, PO Box 44801, Nairobi (☎ 330130; fax 212160)

This company was one of the first in Kenya and has been operating successfully for two decades. You'll hear nothing but praise about them. It was also the originator of the legendary 'Turkana Bus'. Safari Camp Services is very much concerned with authenticity, good organisation and value for money.

Its Turkana Bus is one of the best (see below) and its Wildlife Bus, which visits Samburu, Lake Nakuru and Masai Mara is just as good (seven days, US$505, departures once a fortnight on Saturday). There are also 'lodge-equivalent' camping safaris for those who prefer somewhat better facilities.

Safari Camp Services also takes in camel safaris (see below), the coast, and Lake Nakuru and Masai Mara (five days, US$360, departs once a fortnight).

Safari Seekers

5th floor, Jubilee Insurance Exchange building, Kaunda St, PO Box 9165, Nairobi (☎ 226206; fax 334585)

Ground floor, Diamond Trust Arcade, Moi Ave, PO Box 88275, Mombasa (☎ 220122; fax 228277). This company has been operating for some years and

gets consistently good reports. It also has its own permanent camp sites in Amboseli, Samburu and Masai Mara. Safari Seekers offers both camping and lodge safaris in Kenya (ex-Nairobi and Mombasa) and Tanzania (ex-Arusha) as well as mountain climbing in Kenya. All of these it operates itself. Camping safaris cost US$80 to US$85 per person per day all inclusive except for sleeping bags (US$10 per person per trip). Departures are at least once a week or anytime assuming a minimum of four people. Safari Seekers also offer a choice of 10 lodge/ luxury tented camp safaris which will depart any day assuming a minimum of two people and average US$230 per person per day all inclusive.

Special Camping Safaris Ltd

Karen Shopping Centre, PO Box 51512, Nairobi (☎ /fax 882541)

This small company offers Amboseli and Tsavo (four days, US$350), Masai Mara (four days, US$350), Masai Mara and the Rift Valley lakes (six days, US$510), and a Game Safari 'special' which takes in Masai Mara, Lakes Naivasha, Nakuru, Bogoria and Baringo, Maralal, Samburu and Mt Kenya (10 days, US$800). It also has a 10-day Turkana expedition (details below). Departures are once a week for the shorter trips and once a fortnight for the longer ones.

Savuka Tours & Safaris

3rd floor, Pan Africa House, Kenyatta Ave, PO Box 20433, Nairobi (☎ 725907, 725108)

This outfit is not a member of KATO but we've had good reports of it from its customers. It has a permanent camp site in Masai Mara.

Tour Africa Safaris Ltd

3rd Mezzanine floor, Corner House, cnr Mama Ngina and Kimathi Sts, PO Box 34187, Nairobi (☎ 336767; fax 338271)

Ground floor, NSSF House, Nkrumah Rd, Mombasa (☎ 316172; fax 316197)

TAS specialises in longer distance safaris such as to the gorillas in Zaïre, Tanzanian national parks and southern African countries, but it does have two safaris exclusively in Kenya. The first is the 'Big Simba Expedition' which takes in Lake Nakuru and Masai Mara and involves staying at TAS' exclusive luxury tented camp in the Mara (five days, US$395, departures once a week). The other is a seven-day 'Wildlife Safari' which takes in Samburu, Lake Nakuru and Masai Mara.

Up-Market Companies If you don't want to camp but prefer to stay in a lodge each night then check out:

Abercrombie & Kent Ltd

6th & 7th floor, Bruce House, Standard St, PO Box 59749, Nairobi (☎ 228700; fax 215752)

African Tours & Hotels
Utalii House, Uhuru Highway, PO Box 30471, Nairobi (☎ 336858; fax 218109)
Nkrumah Rd, PO Box 90604, Mombasa (☎ 223509; fax 311022)
Inside Africa Safaris
Wabera St between Mama Ngina and Kaunda Sts, PO Box 59767, Nairobi (☎ 223304; fax 215448)
Pollman's Tours & Safaris
Koinange St, PO Box 45895, Nairobi (☎ 544373; fax 544639)
Taveta Rd, PO Box 84198, Mombasa (☎ 312565; fax 314502)
United Touring Company
Fedha Towers, cnr Muindi Mbingu and Kaunda Sts, PO Box 42196, Nairobi (☎ 331960; fax 331422)
Moi Ave, PO Box 84782, Mombasa (☎ 316333; fax 314549)
Vacational Tours & Travel Ltd
Nairobi Hilton, PO Box 44401, Nairobi (☎ 337392; fax 210530)

In this category Inside Africa Safaris come up consistently cheaper, assuming a minimum of eight people, than the others but its safari options are limited to the Aberdares, Amboseli, Masai Mara, Lake Nakuru and Samburu plus a number of coastal trips (eg Shimba Hills and Taita Hills), and none of its safaris is longer than six days. Also, its prices rise dramatically if there are less than eight in the group. As an example, its price for a four-day Masai Mara and Lake Nakuru safari is US$495 per person assuming eight people but US$690 if you're a group of only three people and US$580 if you're a group of five people. By contrast, UTC's price for the same thing is a standard US$815 (high season) and US$635 (low season) and Abercrombie & Kent's price for the same thing is US$574 (high season) and US$518 (low season). Pollman's prices are about intermediate between Inside Africa and UTC/Abercrombie & Kent.

As with camping safaris, however, things are not quite as simple as the above might indicate. UTC's and Abercrombie & Kent's prices assume double occupancy of a room or tent. If you're a single traveller and don't want to share then you'll be up for 'single room supplement' which is typically 10% extra on top of the above rates.

Departure frequency is another factor to take into consideration. UTC and Abercrombie & Kent have daily departures on their shorter safaris and guaranteed weekly departures on their longer trips whereas Inside Africa, which is a much smaller company, will not guarantee regular departures unless your group is large enough (or willing to pay the higher prices for a smaller group).

OTHER SAFARIS
Lake Turkana Safaris
There can be few travellers who come to Kenya who do not relish the idea of what amounts to a pilgrimage through the semi-arid wilds of Samburu and up to the legendary Lake Turkana (The Jade Sea). To get an idea of the sort of country you will pass through on this journey, refer to the East of Turkana section in the Northern Kenya chapter.

These safaris all use open-sided 4WD trucks which take up to 18 people along with two to three staff (cook, driver and courier) and you will need to set aside a minimum of seven days to complete the journey. There are others which take longer (10 days) and give you a better appreciation of this part of Kenya and its peoples, and there are even longer ones which incorporate a camel safari. All of them terminate at Loyangalani on the shores of Lake Turkana before returning south. The routes taken are fairly standard but what you see en route depends on how long the safari lasts. Some take in Lake Bogoria and Lake Baringo and others take in Samburu and Buffalo Springs national reserves: others take in both of these. Virtually all of them pass through Maralal where you spend the night.

The following list of recommended safari companies which offer trips to Lake Turkana is listed alphabetically and not in any order of preference or price.

Bushbuck Adventures
Barclays Bank building, Kenyatta Ave, PO Box 67449, Nairobi (☎ 212975; fax 218735)
Bushbuck offers Lake Turkana safaris but it keeps well away from the usual route, instead taking in the Matthew's Range, the Ndoto Mountains and Shaba National Game Reserve. It also offers a

longer 'Northern Frontier Expedition' which takes in Samburu, the Ndoto Mountains, Lake Turkana and North Horr and, like the previous tour, keeps well away from the usual route.

Exotic Safaris & Travel

1st floor, Uniafric House, Koinange St, PO Box 54483, Nairobi (☎ 338811; fax 245767)

Exotic offers an eight-day Turkana safari which goes via Lake Baringo and South Horr on the way north, and Maralal and Samburu National Reserve on the way back. The price is US$455 all inclusive except for sleeping bags, and departures are any day assuming a group of four people or more.

Gametrackers

1st floor, Kenya Cinema Plaza, Moi Ave, PO Box 62042, Nairobi (☎ 338927; fax 330903)

This company offers two eight-day options to Lake Turkana and one of the options takes in Marsabit National Park – the only company to do this. The first option takes in Lake Baringo, South Horr, Lake Turkana, the Nabuyotom volcano on the southern shore of the lake (by power boat), Maralal and the Samburu National Reserve. It costs US$415 and there are two departures per month. The other option goes first to Samburu National Reserve (two days) and then heads for Marsabit after which it crosses the Chalbi Desert and over to Lake Turkana. From Lake Turkana it returns to Nairobi via Maralal. This safari costs US$415 and departs twice a month.

Gametrackers also offers a combined Lake Turkana and camel safari that lasts 10 days – see below under 'Camel Safaris'.

Safari Camp Services

PO Box 44801, Barclays Plaza, Nairobi (☎ 28936, 330130; fax 212160)

This is the group that blazed the trail 20 years ago and recently celebrated its 1000th departure. There are two options: the Turkana Bus and the Vanishing Africa safari. The Turkana Bus is the economy option and takes in Maralal, Lake Turkana, Wamba and Samburu National Reserve. It takes seven days, costs around US$400, and departures are two to five times a month, depending on the season. Vanishing Africa is somewhat more up-market and uses Land Cruisers for transport. This 14-day safari takes in Masai Mara, lakes Naivasha, Nakuru and Baringo, Maralal, South Horr, Lake Turkana, and Samburu National Reserve and utilises lodge accommodation wherever possible – private camp sites elsewhere. As a result, it's considerably more expensive at US$2870 and only departs once a month. The prices are all inclusive except for a sleeping bag and alcoholic drinks.

Safari Camp Services also offers a combined Turkana Bus safari with a camel safari in the Matthews Range/Ndoto Mountains which lasts 14 days in total and costs US$799 all inclusive.

Special Camping Safaris

Gilfillan House, Kenyatta Ave, PO Box 51512, Nairobi (☎ 338325; fax 211828)

This company takes the usual route but its safari lasts 10 days and takes in a night on the slopes of Mt Kenya. The cost is US$600 and there are two departures each month except during April, May and November when there are no departures.

Yare Safaris

1st floor, Union Towers, Mama Ngina St, PO Box 63006, Nairobi (☎ /fax 214099)

Yare offers three Turkana options: the Turkana Charge (for those in a big hurry – six days, US$390), the Turkana Run (for those in slightly less of a hurry – seven days, US$370) and the Turkana Trail (for those with more time at their disposal – 10 days, US$530). Departures are fortnightly throughout the year. Yare has a good reputation and is a popular choice.

Camel Safaris

This is a superb way of getting right off the beaten track and into areas where vehicle safaris don't or cannot go. Camel safaris offer maximum involvement in areas of Kenya which the 20th century has hardly touched, if at all. Most of them take place in the Samburu and Turkana tribal areas between Isiolo and Lake Turkana and you'll have plenty of opportunity to become accustomed to the pace of nomadic life and to mingle with the indigenous people. You'll also encounter wildlife though, naturally, sightings of any particular animal and in what numbers cannot be guaranteed.

You have the choice of riding the camels or walking alongside them (except in a few spots where you will be forced to dismount). The camels are led by experienced Samburu *morani* (warriors) and accompanied by English-speaking guides of the same tribe who are well-versed in bush lore, botany, ornithology and local customs. Most travelling is done as early as possible in the cool of the day and a camp site established around noon. Following lunch, you are free to relax during the heat of the day and, in the evening, while the sleeping arrangements and dinner are being organised by the staff, take a walk (along with a guide if you choose). Hot showers are normally available before drinks and dinner are served around a camp fire.

All the companies provide a full range of camping equipment (two-person tents, as a rule) and ablution facilities, but they vary in what they require you to bring along. Some even provide alcoholic drinks, though normally you pay extra for this. The typical distance covered each day is between 15 and 18 km so you don't have to be super fit. Far more important is flexibility and a good positive attitude, since no two safaris are exactly alike.

Yare Safaris also host the annual Maralal International Camel Derby from its lodge and camp site at Maralal. The derby includes a full day of races in Maralal on the Saturday of the last week of October, plus a longer 18-day endurance race. For full details see the Maralal section in the Northern Kenya chapter.

The following list of recommended companies which offer camel safaris has been listed alphabetically, and not in any order of preference or price.

Camel Trek Ltd
PO Box 15076, Nairobi (☎ 891079; 891716)
Camel Trek is a small, reliable company which has treks starting from Isiolo. Departures are weekly from mid-December through March, and from July to mid-October, and the cost is US$644 for a five-day safari and US$517 for three-nights. Return transport from Nairobi is available for US$55.

Desert Rose Camels
PO Box 44801, Nairobi (☎ 228936; fax 212160)
Safaris cover the Matthews Range, Ndoto Mountains and Ol Doinyo Nyiru between Wamba and South Horr. The exact route depends on the season, the number of days you have available and personal interests. You will be accompanied by experienced Samburu camel handlers and guides. All baggage, camping equipment and food and drink are transported by camels. There are, of course, camels for riding, too.
Desert Rose prefer a minimum of six days for a safari and for this the rates are US$160 per person per day (10 people) going gradually up to US$226 per person per day (five people) and US$424 (two people) and US$752 (one person). These rates include all food and drink (including wine and beer), camping equipment, and a medical kit.

Gametrackers
1st floor, Kenya Cinema Plaza, Moi Ave (PO Box 62042), Nairobi (☎ 338927; fax 330903)
This company offers a 10-day combined camel safari and vehicle safari, which starts and finishes in Nairobi, but the camels are used exclusively for transporting baggage: you have to walk alongside them. The trip takes in the Ndoto Mountains and Lake Turkana (reached by vehicle). There are departures twice a month (on a Monday) except during April, May and November and the cost is US$550 per person which includes all transport, food and camping equipment (except sleeping bags).

Yare Safaris Ltd
1st floor, Union Towers, Mama Ngina St, PO Box 63006, Nairobi (☎/fax 214099)
Yare offers a seven-day safari although only five days are actually spent on safari since the first and last days involve transfer from and to Nairobi. Overnight accommodation the night before and after the trek is in double self-contained *bandas* (thatched huts) at Yare's Maralal club and camp site. The actual trek starts at Barsalinga on the Ewaso Nyiro River (which flows through Samburu and Buffalo Springs game reserves) and it leaves every Saturday. You may walk or ride as you wish but a support vehicle carrying the bulk of your luggage, the tents and supplies plus any personal needs such as beer, spirits and soft drinks will go ahead of the camels to the next camp site. This is not an arduous safari but neither is it luxury. A flexible and positive attitude of mind is the most important thing to have. The cost is US$450 per person which includes everything except a sleeping bag, items of a personal nature and alcoholic drinks (which you can purchase at the club before departure).

Walking & Cycling Safaris

For the keen walker and those who don't want to spend all their time in a safari minibus, there are a number of options.

Bike Treks
PO Box 14237, Nairobi (☎ 446371; fax 442439)
This company offers both walking and cycling as well as combined walking/cycling safaris. Its shortest safari is a three-day Masai Mara combined trip which costs US$285 and includes transport to and from Nairobi, all camping equipment, food and bicycles but excludes park fees and tips. A more substantial safari is the six-day walking trip (US$720) in the Loita plains and hills of Maasailand west and south of Narok which includes a full day game viewing drive in the Masai Mara Game Reserve.
For cyclists, there's a six-day safari, again through

the heart of Maasailand including a full day's game drive in Masai Mara Game Reserve which costs US$720 including everything except park entry and public camp-site fees and tips. A minimum of three people guarantees departure on any of these safaris.

Bushbuck Adventures

Barclays Bank building, PO Box 67449, Nairobi (☎ 212975; fax 218735)

This company also offers what is essentially a 14-day walking safari which takes in the Aberdare and Mt Kenya national parks including an ascent of Mt Kenya. The last few days are spent touring Shaba National Reserve in a Land Rover. The cost is US$2270 per person all-inclusive.

Gametrackers

1st floor, Kenya Cinema Plaza, Moi Ave, PO Box 62042, Nairobi (☎ 338927; fax 330903)

This company offers a four-day walking safari into the Aberdare National Park. There are up to five departures each month except during May and November when there are none and the cost is US$315 per person (minimum five people).

Hiking & Cycling Kenya

4th floor, Arrow House, Koinange St, PO Box 39439, Nairobi (☎ 218336; fax 228107)

This company specialises in hiking safaris although they all involve some transport by road and/or boat. All are camping safaris. Its 10-day safari takes you to Lake Turkana in the footsteps of Count Teleki. On the way back to Nairobi, by vehicle, you visit Maralal and Samburu National Reserve.

There's also a 14-day walking and boating safari which takes in the Mara River, Lake Nakuru, Mt Elgon, the Cherangani Hills and Lake Turkana. It also includes game drives through Masai Mara and a visit to the remote Sibiloi National Park (by boat) at the north-eastern end of Lake Turkana. This is a very interesting package and one of the few opportunities you will have to visit Sibiloi (hardly any other safari company includes this park on their itineraries).

Samburu Trails Trekking Safaris

PO Box 56923, Nairobi (☎ 505139; fax 502739)

This company offers walking safaris in Samburuland. There are two options, both starting from Isiolo. These are comfortable safaris with everything provided including tents, camp beds and bedding, safari showers, tables and chairs. All the equipment is transported by donkeys so it's a good idea to keep your personal baggage down to a minimum. The cost is US$125 per person per day (or US$60 per person for larger groups) and it's suggested you set aside a minimum of five days for either trek.

Sirikwa Safaris

PO Box 332, Kitale

This outfit is run by Jane & Julia Barnley from their farmhouse/guesthouse and camping site about 20 km outside Kitale on the Lodwar road. They can arrange bird-watching trips to the Cherangani Hills along with a guide (KSh 600 per day for a guide) as well as trips to Saiwa Swamp National Park, Marich Pass, Mt Elgon and the Kongelai Escarpment.

White-Water Rafting

For a totally different safari experience, there's white water-rafting.

Savage Wilderness Safaris Ltd

PO Box 44827, Nairobi (☎ 521590; fax 501754)

This outfit is the only one of its kind in Kenya. Depending on water levels, rafting trips of up to 450 km and of three weeks duration can be arranged, though most trips last between one and four days during which you cover up to 80 km.

One of the most popular short trips (one day's duration) is on the Tana River, north-east of Nairobi. The first of the rapids is only class (or grade) 3 followed by three km of class 2 and 3 (ideal for learning some of the basic skills needed to tackle the larger rapids further on). That's followed by six km of calm scenic water where birdlife abounds. The last six km are the most exciting, consisting of class 3, 4 and, at certain water levels, class 5 rapids interspersed with short sections of calmer water. This trip departs anytime there are two or more customers and costs US$95 per person.

Another of the popular short trips is the three-day adventure on the Athi River, south-east of Nairobi between Tsavo East and West national parks. These trips leave any day of the week subject to a minimum of four passengers and cost US$320 per person with additional days at US$45.

The last rafting possibility is along the Ewaso Nyiro River, north-west of Isiolo. This trip takes a minimum of three days. It's a scenic river all the way and there's plenty of wild game to be seen. This trip costs US$380 per person with additional days at US$105.

The above prices are inclusive of transport, high quality food, soft drinks, beer, and, where applicable, tents, airbeds and sleeping bags. You are also provided with all necessary equipment – life jackets, helmets etc. National park entry and camping fees are not included but the usual itineraries do not enter parks.

The most exciting times to go on these white-water rafts are from late October to mid-January and from early April to late July when water levels are at their highest. The Tana River generally maintains a higher water level longer than the Athi.

Balloon Safaris

Viewing a game park from the vantage point of a hot-air balloon is a magnificent experience which you won't ever forget – but it is expensive! The experience of floating silently above the plains with a 360° view of everything beneath you, without safari buses competing for the best photo opportunity, is incomparable. It's definitely worth saving for.

The flights typically set off at dawn and go for about 1½ hours after which they put down and you tuck into a champagne breakfast. After that, you'll be taken on a game drive in a support vehicle and returned to your lodge. At present, these flights are only available in the Masai Mara and they cost around US$360.

Adventures Aloft
Eagle House, Kimathi St, PO Box 40683, Nairobi (☎ 221439)
This company operates out of Mara Fig Tree Lodge and you can either book in Nairobi, at the Fig Tree Lodge, or any other lodge in Masai Mara.

Balloon Safaris Ltd
Wilson Airport, PO Box 43747, Nairobi (☎ 502850)
This company operates out of Keekorok Lodge so you can either book through Block Hotels in Nairobi (☎ 540780; fax 540821) or at Keekorok Lodge or any other lodge in Masai Mara. The flights depart from Keekorok Lodge.

Flying Safaris

These safaris essentially cater only for the rich and those interested in sport fishing. They centre around Rusinga Island in Lake Victoria. A light aircraft collects you from your nearest Masai Mara airstrip in the early morning and returns you in time for lunch or an afternoon game drive. In the meantime a motorboat takes you out on Lake Victoria where you can feed and photograph African Fish-Eagles and go fishing for Nile perch – the largest freshwater fish in Africa. Angling gear is provided. Bookings can be made through Lonrho Hotels Kenya (☎ 216940; fax 216796), PO Box 58581, Nairobi.

Mt Kenya Climbs

All the details of organised climbs up this mountain are to be found in the Mt Kenya section in the Kenya National Parks & Reserves chapter.

SAFARIS FURTHER AFIELD

Quite a few companies in Nairobi offer safaris to the Tanzanian game parks of Lake Manyara, Ngorongoro Crater, Serengeti and Tarangire but most of them are just agencies for Tanzanian safari companies based in Arusha so you might as well go there and organise things yourself. It would certainly cost less than doing it in Kenya since you won't be paying the agency's commission. On the other hand, there are a few companies in Nairobi which specialise in long distance safaris to the north, west and south of Kenya. While most of these take in up to three of the Kenyan national parks, the main focus is elsewhere. The options here range from two to eight weeks, the longer ones taking you to Zimbabwe, Botswana or South Africa.

One of the most popular of these long-range safaris is to the mountain gorillas of Zaïre/Uganda. A two-week trip there would typically go through Kenya and Uganda and return the same way, taking in several of the Kenyan and Ugandan national parks along the way. A three-week trip would take you first to the gorillas via Uganda (including several national parks along the way) and return to Kenya by looping through Tanzania along the southern shore of Lake Victoria taking in the Serengeti and Ngorongoro.

Another possibility is a safari to Ethiopia taking in all the major sights (Addis Ababa, Lalibela, Gondar, Axum etc). This is possible in four weeks but is something of a rush. Better are the five and six-week safaris taking in Lake Turkana and Marsabit National Park on the way up to the Ethiopian border at Moyale. These trips start and finish in Nairobi.

The trips going south are usually one way and generally terminate in either Harare (Zimbabwe) or Cape Town (South Africa). Depending on the amount of time you wanted to spend, they would take you through Tanzania, Malawi, Zimbabwe, Botswana, Namibia and South Africa. Some of the longer trips might include a visit to the gorillas before heading south.

Recommended companies offering extended safaris include the following.

Gametrackers

1st floor, Kenya Cinema Plaza, Moi Ave, PO Box 62042, Nairobi (☎ 338927; fax 330903)

This company offers a four-week Gorilla Safari to Zaïre via Uganda on the outward journey and returning via Tanzania, taking in several national parks. The cost is US$890 plus a group kitty of US$250 plus the cost of visas and national park fees (US$325), a total of US$1465. Departures are monthly except in August and November.

Its five-week Southern Africa Safari takes in Tanzania, Zanzibar, Malawi, Zimbabwe and Botswana including several national parks. The tour terminates in Harare. This costs US$855 plus a group kitty of US$165 plus the cost of visas and optional side trips/activities (US$380 if you take them all. Departures are approximately monthly except in April, August and December.

Flight Centres

This company is the main Nairobi-based company offering long-distance safaris. Flight Centres offer a choice of 14 long-distance safaris and they're all consistently cheaper than what anyone else has on offer.

Flight Centres offer two gorilla safaris. The shorter two-week trip starts and ends in Nairobi and goes via Uganda taking in three national parks en route in addition to the gorillas. It costs US$400 plus US$330 food kitty. The longer three-week safari does a loop through Tanzania on the return leg and takes in five national parks in addition to the gorillas before terminating in Mombasa. It costs US$650 plus US$475 food kitty. Both of these prices include everything except visa costs and a sleeping bag.

For Ethiopia, there's a choice of safaris with the longer ones incorporating Lake Turkana and Marsabit National Park. The four-week trip costs US$650 plus US$150 food kitty; the five-week trip costs US$700 plus US$175 food kitty, and the six-week trip costs US$750 plus US$200 food kitty. All of these prices include the lot except for visa costs and a sleeping bag.

It also offers a 14-day and a 20-day safari of the game parks of Kenya and Tanzania which take in Masai Mara, lakes Naivasha and Nakuru, Thomson's Falls, Serengeti and Ngorongoro and cost US$790 (plus US$150 food kitty) and US$950 (plus US$195 food kitty), respectively, including everything except visa costs and a sleeping bag.

Its safaris to southern Africa are all one-way only and vary from 18 days to 57 days depending on how many countries you want to visit and where you want to end up – Harare, Victoria Falls or Cape Town. The costs range from US$600 plus US$10 food kitty for a three-week trip to US$1250 plus US$500 food kitty for the 57-dayer.

DO-IT-YOURSELF SAFARIS

This is a viable proposition in Kenya if you can get a group together to share the costs of renting a vehicle and camping equipment. The details of renting a suitable vehicle can be found in the Car & 4WD Rental section earlier in this chapter.

Doing it yourself has several advantages over organised safaris. The main one is flexibility – you can go where you want, stop whenever you like and stay as long as you like. You don't have to follow the standard tourist routes. Another is that you can choose your travelling companions. The main disadvantage is the extra effort you have to put in to organise the safari – hiring equipment, buying food and drink, cooking and agreeing among yourselves where you want to go and which route to take. It can also be a worry if none of you have mechanical skills or the necessary tools and the vehicle breaks down. There's also the security of the vehicle and contents to think about if you want to leave it somewhere and go off walking. If you do this then you'll have to pay someone to guard it. Lastly, there's the question of maps, especially if you intend to get right off the beaten track. Reasonably good large-scale maps are available in Kenya but the detailed ones are unavailable without going through a great deal of red tape. This means you could find yourself out in the middle of nowhere with not a clue where you're going and have to backtrack.

If you want to hire camping equipment (anything from a sleeping bag to a folding toilet seat, tent or mosquito net) the best place to go to is Atul's (☎ (02) 225935), Biashara St, Nairobi. Hire charges have to be paid in full before commencement of hire as well as a deposit for each item. The deposits are refunded when hired items are returned in good condition. Identification, such as a passport, is required.

The items for hire are far too numerous to mention here, but there is a list which you can pick up for KSh 30. Advance booking is highly recommended and saves a lot of time. If you'd like a list before going to Kenya, write to PO Box 43202, Nairobi.

As far as costs go, it's probably true to say that organising your own safari is going to cost at least as much and usually more than going on a cheap organised safari, but how much more depends on a lot of factors – mainly the cost of hiring a vehicle, fuel and what sort of food you want to eat along the way. You'll have to work this out yourself.

Nairobi

Mark Knopfler could almost have been singing about Nairobi when he wrote *Telegraph Road*. Until the late 19th century there was nothing there. It was just a watering hole for the Maasai. Then came the Mombasa to Uganda railway, with its 32,000 indentured Indian labourers from Gujarat and the Punjab, along with their British colonial overlords intent on beating the German colonial push for the Ugandan heartland. Being approximately halfway between Mombasa and Uganda and a convenient place to pause before the arduous climb into the highlands, it quickly became tent city.

Much of the area was still a foul-smelling swamp at this time and game roamed freely over the surrounding plains, yet by 1900 it had become a town of substantial buildings and five years later succeeded Mombasa as the capital of the British East Africa protectorate. Since then it has gone from strength to strength and is now the largest city between Cairo and Johannesburg. Yet, in terms of the world's largest cities, Nairobi is still small with a population of about 1.5 million. You can walk from one end of the central business district to the other in 20 minutes. And where else in the world would you be able to see lions, cheetahs, rhinos and giraffes roaming free with the tower blocks of a city as a backdrop?

It's a very cosmopolitan place – lively, interesting, pleasantly landscaped and a good place to get essential business and bureaucratic matters sewn up. This is no Third World capital city though there are some very overcrowded slums on the outskirts and across the Nairobi River from Kirinyaga Rd. The latter are periodically bulldozed away and burnt down by the city council in the interests of hygiene but it takes only days for them to regenerate!

Like most cities, Nairobi has its crowded market and trading areas, its middle class/office workers' suburbs and its spacious mansions and flower-decked gardens for the rich

and powerful. The first is an area full of energy, aspiration and opportunism where manual workers, exhausted matatu drivers, the unemployed, the devious, the down-and-out and the disoriented mingle with budget travellers, whores, shopkeepers, high-school students, food-stall vendors, drowsy security guards and those with life's little illicit goodies for sale. It's called River Rd – though, of course, it spans more than just this road itself. One of the funniest yet most poignant yarns about an area such as this is to be found in a novel by Kenyan author Meja Mwangi called *Going Down River Road* (Heinemann, African Writers Series). I'd recommend this book to anyone and especially travellers passing through Nairobi. Even if you are not staying in this area you should make a point of getting down there one day just to see how the other half lives on the wrong side of Tom Mboya St.

Elsewhere in Nairobi are all the things you won't have seen for months if you've been hacking your way across the Central African Republic and Zaïre from West Africa or making do with the shortages in Zambia and Tanzania. Things like the latest films on big screens, bookshops, restaurants, cafes and bars full of travellers from all over the world, offices where you can get things done with the minimum of fuss, foreign exchange bureaus where you can change travellers' cheques in a matter of minutes and a poste restante where you can sort out your own letters from the pile. There's also excellent photographic shops, express mail and fax services and even e-mail service providers. It's a great place to stay for a week or so but if you stay too long it can get expensive because almost everyone you meet wants to do the same as you did when you first arrived – splurge at the restaurants, drink their fill in the bars and rage until dawn in the discos.

Unfortunately these days Nairobi is also getting a reputation as one of Africa's most lawless cities, and the city authorities seem unable, or unwilling, to tackle the problem. Petty crime is rife, and other more serious crimes are not infrequent.

Orientation

The compact city centre is in the area bounded by Uhuru Highway, Haile Selassie Ave, Tom Mboya St and University Way. The main bus and railway stations are within a few minutes walk of this area, while the main budget travellers' accommodation area is centred around Latema Rd, just east of Tom Mboya St on the fringe of the bustling and somewhat sleazy River Rd area.

To the west of the centre is one of the more enlightened bits of Nairobi town planning – Uhuru Park. It's a much-needed lung for this increasingly crowded city and is a pleasant place in the daytime. At night it becomes a mugger's paradise and should be avoided.

Directly west of Uhuru Park, and still within walking distance of the centre (but *don't* walk at night!), are some of the city's better middle and top-range hotels, the youth hostel, a number of government ministries and the hospitals. Beyond here is the sprawling upper-middle class suburbs of Kilimani, Upper Hill and Hurlingham with their large detached houses and carefully tended gardens surrounded by high fences, and guarded by *askaris* (private security guards) along with prominent signs warning that the premises are patrolled by 'Ultimate Security', 'Total Security', 'Securicor' and the like. These signs are surely one of the most enduring impressions of suburban Nairobi.

North of the centre is the university, the national museum, the International Casino and one of Nairobi's original colonial hotels, the Norfolk. Beyond here is Westlands, almost a self-contained satellite city of Nairobi proper and another of the city's upper-middle class suburbs. North-east of the centre is Parklands, which is home to many of Nairobi's Asian minority and where the Aga Khan Hospital is to be found.

Going east, there are the bustling and predominantly African suburbs of Eastleigh and Pangani along with the country bus station.

Eastleigh, these days, is so full of Somali refugees that it's dubbed 'Little Mogadishu' by the locals. All manner of illicit and nefarious activities go on here though you'll remain blissfully unaware of this unless you actually live there for some time.

South of the city is the industrial area, the sprawling modern suburbs of Embakasi, Nairobi 'B' and 'C' and Nairobi West, Nairobi National Park, Wilson Airport and, even further south and off to the east, Jomo Kenyatta International Airport which is connected to the city by an excellent dual carriageway.

Maps There are many maps of Nairobi available in the bookshops but probably the best is the *City of Nairobi: Map & Guide* (Survey of Kenya) in English, French and German which has a red front cover with partially coloured photographs on the back cover. It covers the suburbs as well as having a detailed map of the central area. If you're going to be staying for a long time, however, the *Nairobi A to Z* (Kenway Publications, KSh 230), by RW Moss, is worth buying.

Information

Tourist Office In a city the size of Nairobi, and in a country which relies so heavily on tourism, it seems inconceivable that there is no tourist office, but there isn't.

What there is are two free booklets which you can pick up at the better class hotels, the Thorn Tree Cafe, car hire companies and the like. Both booklets have a substantial amount of advertising – no surprise in that, but it would help considerably if they made a little more effort to get their facts right and their maps accurate.

The better of these two publications is *Tourist's Kenya* which comes out usually about once a month and attempts to cover everything of interest in 95 fold-out pages. They don't do a bad job and it's well worth getting hold of a copy.

The other freebie is *What's On* which is published monthly and covers not just Kenya but also Tanzania and Uganda. It's glossier but much less informative and is almost bereft of prices. It also contains some terribly written articles which Tourist's Kenya doesn't even attempt. Still, it's better than nothing.

Foreign Consulates See the Kenya Facts for the Visitor chapter for a full list of diplomatic missions in Nairobi.

Money At Jomo Kenyatta International Airport the branch of Barclays Bank is open 24 hours a day, seven days a week. In Nairobi, the bank's branch on the corner of Kenyatta Ave and Wabera St is open Monday to Saturday from 9 am to 4.30 pm.

Changing money at a bank in Nairobi these days, however, is time-consuming and you're liable to be charged commission on travellers' cheques. It's much quicker and more convenient to change at a forex bureau and most of these charge no commission on cheques. They're found on virtually every street in the city centre including Mama Ngina St (Crown), Standard St (Finerate), Kenyatta Ave (Taipan and Chase), Muindi Mbingu St (Nairobi) and Utalii St. Up in Westlands there's only one choice – the Travellers Forex Bureau in the basement of The Mall shopping centre. All of them display the day's rates for European and North American currencies and some will also take Australian and New Zealand currencies. Exchange rates are pretty standard, and are published daily in the business pages of the *Daily Nation*.

American Express (☎ 334722) at Express Travel Kenya, Bruce House, Standard St, is open Monday to Friday from 10 am to 4 pm. It can issue travellers' cheques in the normal manner but cannot cash them.

Post & Communications The GPO is on Haile Selassie Ave. A new post office on Kenyatta Ave has been under construction for several years now and will probably remain in that condition for some time to come. The office on Haile Selassie is open Monday to Friday from 8 am to 5 pm and Saturday from 9 am to noon. The poste restante is well organised and you are allowed to look through as many piles as you

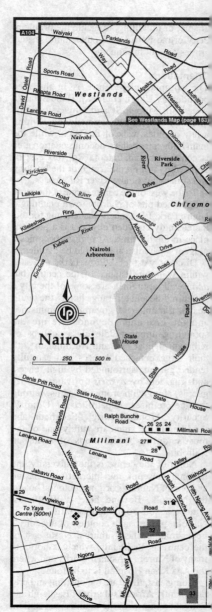

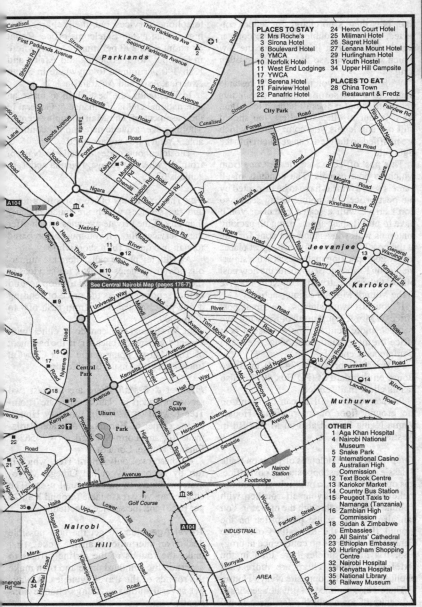

PLACES TO STAY
2 Mrs Roche's
3 Sirona Hotel
6 Boulevard Hotel
9 YMCA
10 Norfolk Hotel
11 West End Lodgings
17 YWCA
19 Serena Hotel
21 Fairview Hotel
22 Panafric Hotel
24 Heron Court Hotel
25 Milimani Hotel
26 Sagret Hotel
27 Lenana Mount Hotel
29 Hurlingham Hotel
31 Youth Hostel
34 Upper Hill Campsite

PLACES TO EAT
28 China Town
    Restaurant & Fredz

OTHER
1 Aga Khan Hospital
4 Nairobi National
   Museum
5 Snake Park
7 International Casino
8 Australian High
   Commission
12 Text Book Centre
13 Kariokor Market
14 Country Bus Station
15 Peugeot Taxis to
    Namanga (Tanzania)
16 Zambian High
    Commission
18 Sudan & Zimbabwe
    Embassies
20 All Saints' Cathedral
23 Ethiopian Embassy
30 Hurlingham Shopping
    Centre
32 Nairobi Hospital
33 Kenyatta Hospital
35 National Library
36 Railway Museum

See Central Nairobi Map (pages 176-7)

like, plus there's no charge for letters collected. The only trouble is that the counter which deals with it is also one of the few which sells stamps, so the queues are often long.

With the huge volume of poste restante mail here it's not surprising that some letters get misfiled but it doesn't happen too often. As a favour to other travellers you should pull out any letters you come across which are misfiled so the clerk can get them into the right pile.

This post office is also the best one from which to post parcels. The contents of all parcels sent overseas have to be inspected by the post office staff before being sealed so don't arrive with a sealed parcel or you'll have to pull it apart again. Bring all packing materials with you as there are none for sale at the post office. One of the cheapest places to buy good packing materials is at the supermarket on Koinange St opposite the new post office. Otherwise, try Biba on Kenyatta Ave at the Muindi Mbingu St intersection.

If you just want stamps, the small post office on Moi Ave just north of Kenyatta Ave is much more central. There's also a post office on the ground floor of the Kenyatta Conference Centre.

American Express (☎ 334722) in Bruce House on Standard St (PO Box 40433) also has its client mail service.

Private couriers, DHL, can be found on the ground floor of International House, Mama Ngina St, and also on Mpaka Rd in Westlands.

Telephone The Extelcoms office is on Haile Selassie Ave, almost opposite the post office. It is open from 8 am to midnight and you can make direct dial calls yourself from here with a phone card or go through the operator. You can also do this at the post office on the ground floor of the Kenyatta Conference Centre and, if there's no conference in progress, it's much quieter here than in the Extelcoms office. There are more card phones on Posta Rd, opposite Nyayo House.

There's also a number of private agencies in the centre of town which offer international telephone services but their charges are higher than at the Extelcoms office. Count on about KSh 290 per minute to anywhere in Europe, North America and Africa and KSh 390 per minute to anywhere in South America, Asia, and Australasia.

In Westlands, the best place to make an international call is at Finance & General in the basement of The Mall shopping centre. There's never a queue here and it's comfortable. Credit cards are accepted.

The telephone code for calls to Nairobi from anywhere in Kenya, Uganda and Tanzania is 02.

Fax The Extelcoms office also offers telex and fax services which are much cheaper than any of the private agencies which offer these services, though you must be prepared to wait in a queue for a short while.

As with telephone calls, there are numerous private agencies offering fax services in the city centre but you need to shop around before sending one as the price of sending a one-page fax can vary from KSh 600 to KSh 1000.

In Westlands you can do it either with Finance & General (cheaper) in the basement of The Mall shopping centre or at CopyCat (more expensive) in the Sarit Centre.

Internet & E-Mail There are at least two service providers in Nairobi. They are Thorn-Tree E-Mail (☎ 229650), Embassy House, on the corner of Harambee Ave and Parliament Rd, and Form-Net Africa (☎ 245630), Finance House, Loita St.

Of these two, only Thorn-Tree, which is run by a company called Omega Microsystems, caters to casual e-mail users. The charges are very reasonable (around KSh 20 per page) and the service excellent.

Travel Agencies To get the best possible deal on an international airline ticket, first make the rounds of the airline offices to ascertain the standard price and then make the rounds of the travel agencies. Always get several quotes as things change constantly.

One of the best agencies to go to (if not the best) is Flight Centres (☎ 210024; fax 334207; e-mail fcswwat@arcc.or.ke), 2nd floor, Lakhamshi House, Biashara St. This company has been doing discounted airline tickets for years and what they don't know probably isn't worth knowing. They also offer a visa service and can advise about safari companies and they also run many of their own.

Also recommended is Let's Go Travel (☎ 340331; fax 336890) which is on Standard St, opposite Bruce House and close to the intersection with Koinange St. This long-established company not only handles all travel requirements, but also puts out a number of very useful lists, including one detailing current accommodation prices around the country.

Bookshops There is a good selection of bookshops in the city centre. The Nation Bookshop is on the corner of Kimathi St and Kenyatta Ave, next door to the New Stanley Hotel, and around the corner on Kenyatta Ave is the Westland Sundries Bookshop – both are excellent.

On Mama Ngina St there's Prestige Books, next to the 20th Century Cinema. There are others in the city centre but they don't carry the same range.

Outside of the immediate city centre there is the Text Book Centre on Kijabe St at the back of the Norfolk Hotel which carries a vast range of books and stationery including everything relevant to Africa. It also has a branch on the ground floor of the Sarit Centre, Westlands.

Libraries The main public library in Nairobi is the Kenya National Library (☎ 227871), Ngong Rd. It's open Monday to Friday from 9.30 am to 6 pm. The other library is the McMillan Memorial Library (☎ 221844), Banda St. It's open Monday to Friday from 9 am to 5 pm and Saturday from 9.30 am to 1 pm.

Cultural Centres All the foreign cultural organisations have libraries which are open to the public and are free of charge except for the American Cultural Center and British Council which are for members only. The French, Japanese and German cultural centres all welcome travellers. The addresses are:

Alliance Française
ICEA building, ground floor, Kenyatta Ave (☎ 340054); open Monday to Friday from 8.30 am to 5.30 pm and on Saturday from 8.30 am to 1 pm
American Cultural Center
National Bank building, Harambee Ave (☎ 334141 ext 343); open Monday, Tuesday and Thursday from 9 am to 5 pm, Wednesday from 9 am to noon and Friday from 9 am to 4 pm
British Council
ICEA building, mezzanine floor, Kenyatta Ave (☎ 334855); open Tuesday to Friday from 10 am to 6 pm and Saturday from 10 am to 1 pm
Goethe Institute
Maendeleo House, on the corner Monrovia and Loita Sts (☎ 224640); open Monday to Friday from 10 am to 5 pm
Italian Cultural Institute
Corner House, 15th floor, Mama Ngina St (☎ 337356 ext 45); open Monday and Tuesday from 8 am to 1 pm and 2 to 6 pm and Wednesday to Friday from 8 am to 2 pm
Japan Information Centre
Postbank House, on the corner of Market and Banda Sts (☎ 340520); open Monday to Friday from 8.30 am to 12.30 pm and 2 to 4 pm
Nairobi Cultural Institute
This centre in Ngong Rd (☎ 569205) has various lectures as well as other functions of local cultural interest.

Camping Equipment If you want to hire camping equipment (anything from a sleeping bag to a folding toilet seat, tent or mosquito net) the best place to go to is Atul's (☎ 225935), Biashara St. It has the lot and is open Monday to Friday from 8.30 am to noon and 2 to 5 pm and on Saturday from 8.30 am to noon and 2.30 to 4 pm. Hire charges have to be paid in full before commencement of hire as well as a deposit for each item. The deposits are refunded when hired items are returned in good condition. The best way to leave a deposit is in the form of countersigned travellers' cheques. Identification, such as a passport, is required.

Photography For passport-size photographs, the cheapest place to go is the machine under the yellow and black sign 'Photo Me', a few doors up Kenyatta Ave from the Nation Bookshop on the corner of Kimathi St. It costs KSh 100 for four prints and takes about three minutes. There's another machine on the corner of Tom Mboya St and Accra Rd. You can also get passport photos from the photography shop in Kimathi House opposite the New Stanley Hotel; they are marginally more expensive.

For camera repairs or equipment rental the best place is Expo Camera Centre (☎ 221797), Jubilee Exchange, Mama Ngina St. They're also very reliable for developing and printing/mounting of both colour print and slide film. Alternatively, try Camera Experts, also on Mama Ngina St, or the Camera Maintenance Centre in the Hilton Arcade.

Laundry There are no launderettes in Nairobi so you either do your own washing or have it done through your hotel. Virtually all hotels offer a laundry service but, if you're on a budget, check prices first – it can turn out surprisingly expensive.

Dry cleaning can be done at one of several places in Nairobi but is not particularly cheap. The most convenient are Diplomat on Kenyatta Ave between Loita and Koinange Sts, and White Rose on Kaunda St between Koinange and Muindi Mbingu Sts.

Medical Services If you need medical treatment try Dr Sheth on the 3rd floor of Bruce House on Standard St. This doctor has his own pathology laboratory if you need blood or stool tests. He charges KSh 800 per consultation plus laboratory fees. There is also a dentist on the same floor.

Otherwise go to outpatients at either Nairobi Hospital (☎ 722160), off Valley Rd, or the Aga Khan Hospital (☎ 740000), Third Parklands Ave, both of which have much the same scale of charges as Dr Sheth. At Nairobi Hospital a consultation costs KSh 660, the treatment is competent and major credit

The striking Jama Mosque is close to Muindi Mbingu Street. The stunning exterior is worth a look, however, entry is not always available to travellers.

cards are accepted. Avoid the Kenyatta National Hospital, because although it's free, treatment here is possibly worse than the ailment, according to local residents. The place is certainly bereft of any semblance of 'bedside manner'.

You can get vaccinations at City Hall Clinic, Mama Ngina St. It is open for jabs from 8.30 am to noon and 2.30 to 4 pm Monday to Friday. The vaccines vary in price with yellow fever and typhoid being the most expensive (KSh 400) and cholera and meningitis the cheapest (KSh 150). If you're concerned about clean needles being used – and you should be! – then bring your own.

If you want a gamma globulin shot (for hepatitis A) go to Dr Sheth (3rd floor, Bruce House, Standard St). The charge is KSh 800.

Emergency In case of emergency you could try the police on ☎ 717777, or simply dial ☎ 999. What response you would get I'm not sure.

For a medical emergency call the Aga Khan Hospital (☎ 740000), as it is reliable and has a 24-hour casualty section.

EARS Medivac (☎ 566683) is one of a number of private companies which provide ambulance service and emergency air evacuation.

Dangers & Annoyances You'll often hear Nairobi referred to as 'Nairobbery' by residents, both Kenyan and expatriate, and you'll certainly read about robberies and muggings, some of them violent, in the newspapers almost daily. This is something you should bear seriously in mind and act in a manner which will minimise your chances of becoming a victim. See the Dangers &

The Kima Killer

Early this century when the railway line was being pushed through from Mombasa to Kampala and beyond, a remarkable incident occurred at Kima, a small siding on the line, about 110 km along the track south-west of Nairobi.

A rogue lion had been terrorising the track gangs and had in fact claimed a few victims. In an attempt to eradicate this menace, a superintendent of Uganda Railways stationed in Mombasa, Charles Ryall, decided to mount a night vigil in a railway carriage specially positioned at the Kima siding. The station staff wanted nothing to do at all with the escapade and had locked themselves firmly in the station buildings.

Ryall left the carriage door open, in the hope that the lion would be lured in, and sat back with rifle at the ready and waited. Inevitably he fell asleep and just as inevitably the lion showed up. The struggle

that ensued caused the sliding door on the compartment to shut and the lion was trapped inside with a firm grip on Ryall's neck. Accompanying Ryall in the carriage were two European merchants who were travelling to Nairobi and had hitched a ride with Ryall, agreeing to the overnight stop in Kima. So petrified were they that one of them ducked into the toilet and bolted the door, while the other watched transfixed as the lion wrested the body out the train window!

A reward was offered by Ryall's mother for the capture of the offending lion but it was only after a trap, baited with a live calf, was devised that the human-eater was snared. It seems there was no reason for the lion to have turned human-eater as it was a healthy beast and there was an abundance of game animals in the vicinity – supposedly it just developed a liking for human flesh.

The railway carriage involved in this incident is today preserved in the Nairobi Railway Museum, while the tombstone of Ryall, which bears the inscription 'He was attacked whilst sleeping and killed by a man-eating lion at Kima', is in the Hill Cemetery, also in Nairobi. ■

Annoyances section in Facts for the Visitor for more information.

Other specific precautions you should take are:

Do not walk from the city centre to any of the hotels on Milimani Rd or to the youth hostel, YMCA or YWCA after dark. Uhuru Park is infamous for its muggers. Take a taxi. That KSh 200 fare could save you everything you've got.

Avoid walking alone at night carrying valuables in any of the streets between Tom Mboya and Kirinyaga (the River Rd area). If that's unavoidable, take with you only as much as you can afford to lose.

National Museum

The Kenya National Museum is on Museum Rd off Museum Hill which itself is off Uhuru Highway, and is well worth a couple of hours.

One of the museum's major exhibits is the Peoples of Kenya portraits display by Joy Adamson (of *Born Free* fame). In the late 1940s she was commissioned by the government to record the traditional cultures of the local people, and went on to paint over 600 images, some of which stand in the museum today. This Ethnography Gallery also houses exhibits on the material culture of the various Kenyan tribal groups.

With so many important fossil sites in Kenya, it's no surprise that the museum has some excellent fossil displays in its Prehistory Gallery, and a stunning re-creation of a prehistoric rock art site.

There's also an extraordinary cast on the floor which clearly records the footprints of three people (actually thought to be *Homo erectus*, probably our direct ancestors) which were laid down as they walked across a bed of volcanic ash nearly four million years ago!

Birders should be well satisfied with the Bird Gallery, as it houses more than 900 stuffed and mounted specimens, including all the ones you're likely to see on any trip to Kenya.

The museum also houses the recently refurbished Gallery of Contemporary East

African Art, which provides a space for local artists to exhibit and sell their work.

Anyone heading for the coast should check out the Lamu Gallery, wehich has a fine display of the coastal Swahili culture, including the distinctive carved wooden doors which adorn traditional coastal houses.

Opening hours are from 9.30 am to 6 pm daily and admission is KSh 200 (KSh 100 for children).

Snake Park

The Snake Park, opposite the museum, has living examples of most of the snake species found in East Africa – some of them are in glass cages, others in open pits. There are also tortoises and crocodiles. Hours and entry charges are the same as for the museum.

National Archives

Right opposite the Hilton Hotel on Moi Ave is the National Archives. It is regarded by many as better than the National Museum and entry is free. It contains more than the usual documents you'd expect to find in such a building, including photographs of Mzee Kenyatta and Moi visiting different countries, and exhibitions of handicrafts and paintings.

Opening hours are from 8 am to 5 pm Monday to Friday.

Railway Museum

The Railway Museum is on Station Rd – follow the railway tracks until you are almost at the bridge under Uhuru Highway or walk across the small piece of vacant land next to the Haile Selassie Ave roundabout on Uhuru Highway.

In addition to the displays of old steam engines and rolling stock, the museum will give you a good idea of Kenya's history since the beginning of the colonial period. There's also a scale model of the venerable MV *Liemba* which plies the waters of Lake Tanganyika between Mpulungu (Zambia) and Bujumbura (Burundi).

Unfortunately this place looks a little sad

these days. The outdoor displays are slowly but surely rotting away, while a number of the interior displays have simply gone. It's a great shame as there is no lack of volunteer groups (local and foreign) who are willing to come and restore the old rolling stock; it seems the Kenya Railways administration just couldn't care less.

The museum is open daily from 8 am to 4.45 pm; entry is KSh 50.

Parliament House

Like to take a look at how democracy works in Kenya? If so, you can get a permit for a seat in the public gallery at parliament house on Parliament Rd or, if parliament is out of session, you can tour the buildings by arrangement with the sergeant-at-arms.

Art Galleries

There's not much in Nairobi in the way of art galleries. At the museum there's the Gallery of Contemporary East African Art, which is worth a look. Of the private galleries, the Gallery Watatu in Lonrho House, Standard St, is the oldest established and has fairly regular exhibitions as well as a permanent display.

Kenyatta Conference Centre

There is a viewing level on the 28th floor of the centre but the revolving restaurant hasn't operated for years. If you'd like to go up there, it costs KSh 100. You're allowed to take photographs from the viewing level. Access is sometimes restricted when there's a conference in progress.

Activities

Clubs & Societies There are lots of specialist clubs and societies in Nairobi, many of which welcome visitors. Most of the foreign cultural organisations have film and lecture evenings (usually free of charge) at least once or twice a week. Give them a ring and see what they have organised or browse through the entertainment sections of the local daily newspapers. In addition to these, some local clubs you may be interested in contacting include:

East African Wildlife Society
  Nairobi Hilton, PO Box 20110, Nairobi (☎ 748170)
  This society is in the forefront of conservation efforts in East Africa and it publishes an interesting bimonthly magazine, *Swara*. Membership costs US$35 which includes subscription to *Swara* (US$70 if you want the magazine sent by airmail rather than surface mail).
Mountain Club of Kenya (MCK)
  PO Box 45741, Nairobi (☎ 501747)
  The club meets every Tuesday at 8 pm at the clubhouse at Wilson Airport. Members frequently organise climbing weekends at various sites around the country. Information on climbing Mt Kenya and Kilimanjaro is available on the same evening.

Sports The following clubs all offer facilities for tennis, squash and cricket, and some also cater for football and hockey. They are all private clubs and membership fees apply.

Impala Club
  Ngong Rd, Nairobi (☎ 568684)
Nairobi Club
  Ngong Rd (☎ 725726)
Nairobi Gymkhana
  Corner of Rwathia and Forest Rds (☎ 742804)
Parklands Sports Club
  Ojijo Rd (☎ 742938)

Swimming Pools Most of the international tourist hotels have swimming pools which can be used by non-guests for a daily fee of around KSh 200. The YMCA on State House Rd also has a large pool with springboard which you can use for KSh 80.

Organised Tours
There's not much in the way of organised tours of Nairobi, simply because there's not a great deal to see. If you are keen, contact Let's Go Travel (☎ 340331) who can organise a two-hour tour for around KSh 1800 per person.

Tours to the sights around Nairobi are easy to find, and take in places such as the Bomas of Kenya, the Karen Blixen Museum and the Nairobi National Park. Anything which includes the national park is going to be expensive as there is the US$20 park entry fee to pay.

Places to Stay – bottom end

Camping The best place to camp in Nairobi is *Upper Hill Campsite* (☎ 720290), Menengai Rd, off Hospital Rd, which is itself off Ngong Rd. It offers camping for KSh 150 per person in green, shady surroundings. If you don't have camping equipment there's dormitory accommodation available for KSh 250 as well as a few private double rooms. The site is enclosed by a high fence and guarded 24 hours a day and is favoured by overland truck companies as well as independent travellers. Facilities include hot showers, a mellow bar, restaurant (open for breakfast, lunch and dinner), fireplace with comfortable chairs, a library, collection of games and a covered workshop for vehicle maintenance. You can also store excess baggage here safely. It's a great place to stay, close to the city (15 minutes walk) and people are very friendly.

You could once say the same of *Mrs Roche's*, on Third Parklands Ave opposite the Aga Khan Hospital, a place which has been making travellers welcome for over 25 years. Unfortunately 'Ma', as she's affectionately known by long-time travellers, appears to have lost the plot these days and spends too much time drinking Tusker lager and not attending to security at the camp. Many travellers have had theft problems recently. It's suggested you be very security conscious if you choose to stay. All this is a great pity as Ma Roche's is situated in a pleasant residential area among trees and flowering shrubs and there are cheap places to eat, drink and shop in the immediate vicinity. Camping costs KSh 100 per night plus KSh 50 for a vehicle with dormitory beds at KSh 200 per person. To get to Mrs Roche's, take a matatu from the junction of Latema Rd and Tom Mboya St right outside the Odeon Cinema. There'll be a sign 'Aga Khan' in the front windscreen. Tell the driver you're heading for Mrs Roche's. It's well known.

Youth Hostel Also worth considering is the *Nairobi Youth Hostel* (☎ 721765), on Ralph Bunche Rd between Valley and Ngong Rds.

It was completely refurbished and extended a few years ago and although it is still a good place to meet other travellers, the prices have risen dramatically and it's not the bargain it once was.

The hostel is very clean, well run, stays open all day and there's always hot showers. The wardens here are very friendly and will lock up gear safely for you for a small charge. On a day-to-day basis there are lockers to keep your gear in when you go out, but you must supply your own lock. The notice board here is also worth a look for travel partners, things to sell, etc. A bed in a 16-bed dorm is KSh 350, in a three or four-bed room it's also KSh 350 while in a twin room it's KSh 400.

Any matatu or bus which goes down either Valley or Ngong Rds will drop you at Ralph Bunche Rd. The No 8 matatu which goes down Ngong Rd is probably the most convenient. You can pick it up either outside the Hilton Hotel or on the corner of Kenyatta Ave and Uhuru Highway. If you're returning to the youth hostel after dark don't be tempted to walk back from the centre of the city. Many people have been robbed. Always take a matatu or taxi (KSh 200).

Hotels – City Centre There is a very good selection of budget hotels in Nairobi and the majority of them, except for two very popular places outside the city centre, are between Tom Mboya St and River Rd so if you find that one is full it's only a short walk to another. Virtually all the hotels in the city centre suffer from pretty chronic water shortages. Often there is only water for a couple of hours a day, so getting a shower at some of these places can be a bit of an ordeal. The area also has a bad reputation for theft and muggings, especially at night. Be careful around here.

Many of the cheaper hotels, such as the Iqbal and the New Kenya Lodge, will store baggage for you, usually for a small daily charge. However, you're advised not to leave anything valuable in your left luggage.

The *New Kenya Lodge* (☎ 222022), on River Rd at the Latema Rd intersection, is a bit of a legend among budget travellers and still one of the cheapest places, though many people feel it's a bit past it these days. There's always an interesting bunch of people from all over the world staying there. Accommodation is basic but clean and there's supposedly hot water in the evenings but you should not count on that. Singles/doubles, which have shared bathroom facilities, cost KSh 200/300.

The same people who own this also have the *New Kenya Lodge Annex* (☎ 338348) just around the corner on Duruma Rd. Prices here are the same as the old place but it lacks the atmosphere of the former. Some of the rooms don't even have windows and security is not what it could be. All the same, it's still quite popular, the staff are friendly and the notice board makes interesting reading.

The nearby *Iqbal Hotel* (☎ 220914), on Latema Rd, has been equally popular for years and is still a pretty good place. There's supposedly hot water available in the morning but you have to be up early to get it. Singles/doubles here cost KSh 200/400 with shared facilities. Baggage is safe and there's a storeroom where you can leave excess gear if you are going away for a while. The Iqbal's notice board is always a good place to look for just about anything.

Also on Latema Rd, the *Sunrise Lodge* is clean, secure and friendly and there's usually hot water in the mornings and evenings. It costs KSh 300/400 for singles/doubles with shared bathroom facilities including a simple breakfast or KSh 240/360 without breakfast. The front two rooms overlooking the street are the largest and have a balcony but they are right next door to the Modern Green Day & Night Bar which rages 24 hours a day, 365 days a year, so if you want a quiet room take one at the back. If you're looking for material for a novel, on the other hand, then take one of the two front rooms.

If the above three places are full there are three others on Dubois Rd, just off Latema Rd. The *Bujumbura Lodge* (☎ 228078) is very basic and a bit rough around the edges, but it's clean and quiet and very secure. The toilets and showers are clean and there is erratic hot water. It's good value at KSh 170/220 for singles/doubles with shared facilities. The *Nyandarua Lodging* and the *New Safe Life Lodging* (☎ 221578) are very similar and cost the same but the single rooms are just glorified closets. Make sure you ask what the check-out time is as it's often very early.

None of the other rock-bottom hotels in this area can seriously be recommended. They're just brothels or somewhere for drunks with a few *shilingi* left to sleep off their hangovers.

Moving up the scale, there are several hotels in the same area which are somewhat more salubrious. One of the cheapest is the *Hotel Gloria* (☎ 228916), on Ronald Ngala St almost at the Tom Mboya St intersection. Rooms here are reasonable value at KSh 600/800 for a single/double. All rooms have bath and hot water, and the price includes breakfast. The only problem here is that most of the rooms cop the noise and car exhaust fumes from the street below and it's quite horrendous.

A couple of doors along from the Gloria is the *Terrace Hotel* (☎ 221636) which has rooms with bath and hot water for KSh 350/450. It doesn't win any prizes for friendliness and some of the rooms are noisy, but overall it's not a bad place.

One of the best places in the budget category is the *Dolat Hotel* (☎ 222797), on Mfangano St, which is very quiet and costs KSh 480/600 for singles/doubles and KSh 960 a triple with own shower (no hot water). The sheets are changed daily, the rooms kept spotless and there's usually 24-hour water. It's a good, secure place with friendly management and quite a few travellers stay here.

Lastly, there's the very quiet and secure *West End Lodgings* (☎ 750524) on Kijabe St, north of the Norfolk Hotel, which is clean and has helpful staff. It's only a few cents more than the Iqbal for a double room, yet is far removed from the noise of Latema Rd.

The 'Y's There is both a *YMCA* (☎ 724066) and *YWCA* (☎ 724699) in Nairobi. The former is on State House Rd and the latter on Mamlaka Rd off Nyerere Rd and both of

✗ NORFOLK

Harry Thuku Rd

University of
Nairobi

★1

6●   Slip   Road

Kirinyaga   Road

Kolonge   Road

Keekorok   Road

Murang'a   Road

Ngariama   Lane

★3

Lane

Street

2

Monrovia

University Way

5○   Mol

7●   River

9▼
10▼

River   Road

Firestation   Lane

11●   Lagos   12●   Road   13●

Jevanjee
Gardens

Street

Monrovia

Street

36▼

35   34

Street   3g▶

Tom

Government   Avenue

8◁

27●

Daddah

37○   Niugu

38

Biashara

Road   Road

32●   Road

Kimathi-

Kigali   Road

Latema   25

26●

Timboroa

28○   Street

Timboroa

Tubman

42

Market Street

41○

Koinange   Street

Mbingu   Street

31

30

Kimathi   Street

29●

67▼
68●
69▼ 70

Lane

Street

43

Banda

44
▼

Avenue

Banda   Street

Wabera   Street

66●

Street

71▼   Street

39

40

Uhuru   Highway

45

56▷
58▷   57●

55

59▷

61▷   62◁   Street

65●

72

Central
Park

Kenyatta

Koinange   Street

Posta Rd

50
Standard   54
Street

51▼

52   ✚

48○   49

46

Kaunda   Street

53

Kaunda   Street

Mama   Way

60▷

63●   Ngina
64●

Hall

City

85

47

Uhuru   Highway

City Square

86

Aga   Khan   Walk

Taifa   Road

Harambee   Avenue

90
■

●87

88

Uhuru

Park

Parliament   Road

89

Harambee   Lane

Tumbo   Avenue

91

93

Parliament   Lane

Haile Selassie Lane

94

Selassie

Procession   Way

Central Nairobi

0   125   250 m

92

Harambee

Country   Road

Haile

Selassie   Avenue

Haile   Station   Road

PLACES TO STAY

2	Nairobi Safari Club
3	Suncourt Hotel
4	Parkside Hotel
7	Meridien Court Hotel
11	Marble Arch Hotel
15	New Kenya Lodge
16	New Safe Life Lodging
18	Hotel Greton
19	Bujumbura Lodge
20	New Kenya Lodge Annex
23	Sirikwa Lodge
25	Oriental Palace Hotel
26	Iqbal Hotel
37	Terminal Hotel & Dove Cage Restaurant
38	Embassy Hotel
39	Grand Regency Hotel
47	Inter-Continental Hotel
55	Sixeighty Hotel
66	New Stanley Hotel, Nation Bookshop & Thorn Tree Cafe
68	Oakwood Hotel
72	Hilton Hotel
74	Ambassadeur Hotel
75	Solace Hotel
77	Dolat Hotel
78	Terrace Hotel
79	Hotel Gloria
81	Princess Hotel
99	Hotel Hermes

PLACES TO EAT

9	Dhaba Restaurant, Nyama Choma Terrace & Bar
10	Supreme, Mayur & Zam Zam Restaurants
14	Bull Cafe
24	Malindi Dishes
28	Nairobi Burgers
30	Minar Restaurant
33	Slush Happy Eater
36	Kenchic Inn, Hoggers Eating Place & Afro Unity Bar
40	Hard Rock Cafe & Kenya Airways (Barclays Plaza)
44	Harvest Cafe
45	Nyama Choma Stalls (NSSF Market)
51	Beneve Coffee House
54	Calypso & Dragon Pearl Restaurants (Bruce House)
56	Great Chung Wah Chinese Restaurant
58	La Scala
60	Cafe Helena & Coffee Bar
61	Trattoria Restaurant
62	Pasara Cafe & Rickshaw Chinese Restaurant
67	Supermac
69	Caprice
70	Jax Restaurant
71	l'ora blu
76	New Bedona Cafe
96	Tamarind Restaurant & American Cultural Center

continued next page

KENYA

OTHER

1	Police
5	Bus Stop (for Westlands)
6	Maasai Market (Tuesday)
8	Moi Ave Post Office
12	Akamba Bus Office
13	Bancko Tours & Travel
17	DPS Peugeots (Share-taxis)
21	Coast Bus, Mawingo, Goldline, Arusha Express
22	Matatus for Embu, Isiolo & Nanyuki
27	Modern Green Day & Night Bar
29	Nakumatt Supermarket
31	McMillan Memorial Library
32	Jama Mosque
34	Flight Centres
35	Atul's (Camping Gear)
41	New Florida Nightclub
42	City Market
43	Air Zimbabwe & Air Tanzania (Chester House)
46	Immigration (Nyayo House)
48	Bus & Matatu Stop (for Hurlingham & Milimani)
49	New GPO (under construction)
50	Let's Go Travel
52	Holy Family Cathedral
53	City Hall
57	Ugandan High Commission
59	Central Rent-a-Car
63	Prestige Books, Dancing Spoons Cafe & Wine Bar/20th Century Cinema
64	Rwandan Embassy, DHL & British Airways
65	Expo Camera Centre
73	National Archives
80	KBS Stagecoach Bus Station
82	Florida 2000 Nightclub
83	Kenya Cinema Plaza & Zanze Bar
84	Zaire Embassy (Electricity House)
85	Law Courts
86	Kenyatta Conference Centre
87	Public Map Office
88	Ministry of Foreign Affairs
89	Office of the President
90	Jomo Kenyatta's Mausoleum
91	Parliament House
92	Tanzanian High Commission
93	Thorn-Tree E-Mail (Embassy House)
94	Main Post Office (GPO)
95	Extelcoms
97	Air India & Indian High Commission (Jeevan Bharati Building)
98	US Embassy

them are popular places to stay. The YMCA offers dorm beds for KSh 310 and mid-range singles/doubles with shared bathroom facilities for KSh 500/800. It also has singles/doubles with attached bathrooms for KSh 800/1200. All these prices include breakfast. Other meals are available for KSh 180 (lunch) and KSh 190 (dinner). Unless you're a member, you must buy temporary membership to stay here which costs KSh 50.

The YWCA offers much the same types of rooms and dorm beds as the YMCA but it's marginally cheaper and takes only couples and single women. It's also more difficult to get into because it's used by many students and young workers on a residential basis due to its even cheaper monthly rates. Like the YMCA, it has its own dining room with all meals available. You also have to pay a temporary membership fee of KSh 50 to stay here.

Places to Stay – middle

City Centre The *Solace Hotel* (☎ 331277) is on the horrendously noisy Tom Mboya St – the matatu drivers here honk and rev their engines to drum up business, and it goes on nonstop from early morning until late at night; it makes a mockery of the hotel's name. Rates are KSh 1320/1650 for small singles/doubles with attached bathrooms, and triples are KSh 1930, all including breakfast. It's somewhat overpriced and the extra money seems to be mainly for a carpet and phone in the room. If you do stay here make sure you get a room away from the street.

The *Sirikwa Lodge* (☎ 333838) on the corner of Munyu and Accra Rds is a good place in the middle bracket, although it's perhaps overpriced these days. For KSh 700/900 you get a clean room with bath, hot water, a phone and breakfast. Accra Rd is somewhat quieter than Tom Mboya St so this place is not a bad bet.

Two other quiet places, both of them on Tsavo Rd between Latema and Accra Rds, are the *Hotel Greton* (☎ 242891) which offers rooms with attached bathrooms, including hot showers, for KSh 800/950 a single/double and KSh 1300 for triples, including breakfast, and the *Grand Holiday Hotel* (☎ 214159) which has singles/doubles with attached bathrooms for KSh 950/1200 and triples for KSh 1800, including breakfast.

Further away from this area, on Tom Mboya St down towards Haile Selassie Ave, is the *Princess Hotel* (☎ 214640). The rooms are somewhat shabby these days, but they have their own bathroom and cost KSh 450/580 including a good breakfast. Like all places on Tom Mboya St, the quietest rooms are at the back, though the street is nowhere near as noisy here as further up near Accra Rd. The hotel has its own bar and restaurant. The food is good and the staff friendly.

Right at the bottom of Moi Ave at the junction with Haile Selassie Ave is the *Hotel Hermes*. The staff here are friendly and pretty laid back and huge singles/doubles with attached bathrooms cost KSh 800/1000 including breakfast.

Across the other side of the city centre, west of Moi Avenue, there's a choice of three reasonably priced hotels which are very popular with travellers. Best value is the recently redecorated *Terminal Hotel* (☎ 228817; fax 220075) on Moktar Daddah St near the junction with Koinange St. It's spotlessly clean; soap, towels and toilet paper are provided and there's hot water around the clock. Security is excellent, the rooms are generally quiet and there's a notice board downstairs. Singles/doubles with attached bathrooms cost KSh 880/1100 and triples KSh 1300. Children sharing with their parents are charged KSh 50 per day. You can also store excess baggage here for KSh 30 per article per day.

Nearby, but a somewhat older place, is the *Embassy Hotel* (☎ 224087; fax 224534) on Biashara St between Koinange and Muindi Mbingu Sts. All the rooms have attached bathrooms, there's hot water, and soap, towels and toilet paper are provided. Small singles here cost KSh 800. Normal singles/doubles are KSh 900/1000 with triples at KSh 1200. Breakfast is not included but is available for KSh 150. The hotel has its own bar and restaurant.

Also nearby is the *Parkside Hotel* (☎ 214154) on Monrovia St which runs alongside Jeevanjee Gardens. The staff here are very friendly and the hotel has its own restaurant. It's a little more expensive than

the previous two but still very good value at KSh 1380/1780 for singles/doubles and KSh 2600 for triples including breakfast. All the rooms have attached bathrooms with hot showers.

Round the block from the Parkside on University Way opposite the junction with Harry Thuku Rd is the *Suncourt Hotel* (☎ 221418; fax 217500). All the rooms here have attached bathrooms and cost KSh 1500/2550 for singles/doubles and KSh 3250 a triple. They also have 'executive' rooms at KSh 2350/3150 for singles/doubles and KSh 3600 for triples. Breakfast is not included but all meals are available in the hotel's restaurant.

Not too far from the Suncourt or the Parkside is the *Meridian Court Hotel* (☎ 333916; fax 333658), Muranga'a Rd off Moi Ave, which has rooms at much the same price. It's a modern building and singles/doubles are KSh 1950/2650 with triples at KSh 2950.

Back into the very heart of town, the *Oakwood Hotel* (☎ 220592; fax 332170), PO Box 40683, Kimathi St, right opposite the New Stanley Hotel, is a good choice. It's a very pleasant place to stay and the 23 rooms, all with attached bathrooms, are quite spacious and definitely comfortable plus they have a TV/video. The rates for residents are KSh 1700/2400 for singles/doubles and KSh 2850 for triples. Nonresident rates for the same thing are US$50/60 and US$75 but this is definitely negotiable and you can pay in Kenyan shillings in any case. Breakfast is included in the rates. The hotel has its own restaurant and a very cosy bar with a balcony overlooking the street below.

Re-entering the Latema Rd/River Rd area again, there are two up-market hotels in this down-market part of town. The cheapest is the relatively new *Oriental Palace Hotel* (☎ 217600; fax 212335) on Taveta Rd which is a huge, quite luxurious place used principally by businessmen. Standard singles/doubles for residents are KSh 2290/2790 or KSh 2790/3260 for deluxe rooms. For nonresidents the rates are US$54/72 for standard singles/doubles and US$72/84 for deluxe rooms. Breakfast is not included. The hotel has a bar and a good Indian restaurant.

Even more expensive is the new *Marble Arch Hotel* (☎ 245720; fax 245724), Lagos Rd, which has 40 spacious rooms all with wall-to-wall carpeting, wood panelling, telephone, TV/video and a bathroom/toilet. It costs KSh 3100/4400 for singles/doubles and KSh 5600 a triple. There's also a suite for KSh 9750. Children between the ages of three and 12 years are charged 75% of the above rates. Breakfast is included in the price of a room. The hotel has its own coffee shop, restaurant, bar and business centre. On the basis of the facilities which this hotel provides it really belongs in the top-end category. The only problem with including it there is its location and that, for a top-end hotel, is a crucial factor. Basically, they got it wrong.

Milimani/Hurlingham Most of the other mid-range hotels are along Milimani, Ralph Bunche and Bishops Rds but there are others scattered around the fringes of the city centre and particularly in Westlands. Many of them are very popular with travellers as well as UN and NGO staffers.

Very popular indeed with travellers and expatriates on contract work is the *Heron Court Hotel* (☎ 720740; fax 721698), Milimani Rd, PO Box 41848. It's a large place, all the rooms have attached bathrooms with hot water, there's a swimming pool, sauna and massage parlour and guarded residents' car park. It's very good value at KSh 750/890 for singles/doubles with soap, towels and toilet paper provided. There are also apartments with a double bedroom, separate lounge with balcony, bathroom and fully equipped kitchen for KSh 900/1050. Breakfast is not included in the room rates. The staff here are friendly and helpful but you're advised not to leave valuables in your room – use the safe at reception. At the front of the hotel is one of Nairobi's most popular bar/restaurants, Buffalo Bill's, which is open daily from early morning until around 11 pm.

Right at the top of Milimani Rd at the Ralph Bunche Rd intersection is the *Sagret Hotel* (☎ 720934), PO Box 18324, which is of a somewhat higher standard than the Heron Court and offers singles/doubles with attached bathrooms for KSh 1925/2950 and triples for KSh 3500 including breakfast. If you stay for a minimum of one week there's a 10% discount on these rates. The hotel has its own bar and restaurant (very popular for nyama choma) and accepts Visa and MasterCard. There's also plenty of parking space.

In between the Sagret and the Heron Court is the *Milimani Hotel* (☎ 720760; fax 722430), PO Box 30715. This is a huge, rambling place popular with expatriates on contract and charges KSh 2700/3780 for singles/doubles with attached bathrooms and KSh 5290 for triples including breakfast for residents. Children between the ages of two and 12 years are charged 50% of the adult rates. There are also more expensive apartments complete with fully equipped kitchens. Facilities at the hotel include a swimming pool, bar, beer garden, restaurant and guarded parking. Meal prices in the restaurant here are KSh 450 (buffet lunch) and KSh 500 (dinner).

Turning left at the Milimani/Ralph Bunche Rds junction and going about 50m, you come to the *Lenana Mount Hotel* (☎ 717044; fax 218809), Ralph Bunche Rd, PO Box 40943. This a fairly small but very pleasant hotel with facilities which include a swimming pool, restaurant and two bars as well as 24-hour room service. It's pretty good value at KSh 2800/4100 including breakfast. Casual meals here cost KSh 150 (breakfast), KSh 200 (lunch) and KSh 230 (dinner).

On Bishops Rd at the back of the Panafric Hotel is the *Fairview Hotel* (☎ 723211; fax 721320), PO Box 40842. Billed as 'the country hotel in the city' (with some justification due to its pleasant garden and quiet location), it offers singles/doubles with shared bath for KSh 2300/3700 or KSh 2800/4400 with private bath. There are also family units and balcony doubles for KSh 4800. All the rooms have a telephone, TV and video service, and prices include breakfast. Other meals average around KSh 400 (set menu) and there's an authentic African buffet every Tuesday and Friday for the same price. The bar has draught Tusker. Guests are entitled to use the swimming pool at the Panafric Hotel.

The long-established *Hurlingham Hotel* (☎ 721920), PO Box 43158, on Argwings Kodhek Rd, west of the Hurlingham shopping centre, is also a popular place to stay. Set in a large garden, it exudes a rustic charm but it's small and often full. Many of the people who stay here return time and time again, so it's best to ring in advance and make sure a room is available. There's a bar and restaurant and it costs KSh 1000/1600 with breakfast. All the rooms have shared facilities.

Parklands A popular place to stay here is the *Sirona Hotel* (☎ 742730), Kolobot Rd, off Forest Rd, on the fringes of Parklands. It's sometimes used by safari companies to accommodate their clients. It's a quiet place and costs KSh 1050/1500 for 'executive' singles/doubles and KSh 1400/1950 for 'VIP' singles/doubles including breakfast. There's a large restaurant and bar area (decorated with some excellent prints of Ernest Watson's paintings – check out 'Night Life at the Studio'), a beer garden, a pool table and ample safe parking. Most major credit cards are accepted.

Places to Stay – top end
In a city the size of Nairobi there are naturally many top-range hotels, some of them in the city centre and others outside this immediate area. If you are planning on staying in one it is worth booking through one of the travel agencies in town, instead of paying the so-called 'rack rates', as an agency can often get you a considerable discount. At the Serena, for example, it's possible to get a discount of nearly 40% by booking through United Touring Company.

City Centre On Muindi Mbingu St, between Standard St and Kenyatta Ave, is the *Sixeighty Hotel* (☎ 332680; fax 332908), PO Box 43436. This is a large hotel and good value at KSh 3375/4230 for standard singles/doubles and KSh 5085 for triples. Deluxe singles/doubles are KSh 4050/5075 with triples at KSh 6100. Breakfast is not included. The hotel has its own terrace bar and restaurant and, although the food in the restaurant is quite good, the terrace bar is nothing special – it's like a wind tunnel. They also put on live bands occasionally, usually at the weekends in the bar.

Better value and with considerably better facilities and a garden setting is the *Boulevard Hotel* (☎ 227567; fax 334071), Harry Thuku Rd, PO Box 42831. It offers rooms with bathroom, balcony, telephone and radio for KSh 3600/4300 for a single/double and KSh 4800 a triple including taxes but excluding breakfast. Facilities include a swimming pool, tennis court, restaurant, barbecue, bar, and beer garden. If you hear stories about the swimming pool being dangerous on account of out-of-control matatus plunging into it off adjacent Chiromo Rd, you can put your mind at rest. That did happen on two occasions in the past but now a fence has been erected which you'd need a tank to get through.

The *Ambassadeur Hotel* (☎ 336803; fax 211472), PO Box 30399, is right in the city centre on Moi Ave and is part of the Sarova Hotels chain. Unfortunately there is no escaping the fact that this place is terribly shabby and run-down, which is a great pity given the excellent location. It has singles/doubles with attached bathrooms for US$40/50 excluding breakfast (US$7 extra). The hotel has a bar and, on the ground floor, a good restaurant with lunch/dinner for around KSh 500.

Also in the centre is the *New Stanley Hotel* (☎ 333233; fax 229388), PO Box 30680, on the corner of Kimathi St and Kenyatta Ave. It was built in 1907 and despite numerous subsequent renovations still has a touch of colonial charm. Singles/doubles (including breakfast and taxes) cost KSh 3850/4600 for residents or US$103/138 for nonresidents. There are also more expensive suites. All the rooms are air-conditioned with colour TV (including cable) and have direct-dial telephones. Facilities include a rooftop swimming pool, two restaurants, a ballroom, bar, health club and shops. At street level, there's the popular Thorn Tree Cafe, though the food here is mediocre and service can be agonisingly slow.

Nairobi's *Hilton Hotel* (☎ 334000; fax 339462), PO Box 30624, on Mama Ngina St near Moi Ave, has all the usual Hilton facilities including a rooftop swimming pool, and the rooms are very well appointed. Singles/doubles here go for US$128/166, while executive rooms with breakfast and complimentary bar are US$225/257, but to all these prices you must add a total of 33% in taxes!

The nearby *Inter-Continental Hotel* (☎ 335550; fax 210675), PO Box 30353, on City Hall Way, is an excellent place since its recent refurbishment. There is of course a swimming pool, as well as business centre, a couple of restaurants and bars, and an airport shuttle bus. Room rates are US$160/200, plus 27% taxes.

Close to the top of the line (though they bill themselves as the *creme de la creme*) you'll find the *Norfolk Hotel* (☎ 335422; fax 336742), PO Box 40064, on Harry Thuku Rd; the *Nairobi Serena Hotel* (☎ 725111; fax 725184), PO Box 46302, the edge of Central Park between Kenyatta Ave and Nyerere Rd, and the *Nairobi Safari Club* (☎ 330621; fax 331201; e-mail nsclub@arcc.or.ke), PO Box 43564, University Way.

The Norfolk is the oldest of Nairobi's hotels – it was built in 1904 – and was *the* place to stay in the old days. It's still extremely popular among those with a taste for nostalgia and the money to spend. All the old world charm has been retained despite facilities having been brought up to international standards. Singles/doubles in the main block cost US$210/220 plus there are suites for US$275 to US$410 and cottages for US$410 to US$570. Residents are charged KSh 6000 for singles or doubles. The prices do not include breakfast which is an extra KSh 350. Other meals are available for KSh 770 each. The Norfolk, which is owned by Lonrho Hotels, has a popular terrace bar (The Lord Delamere) and restaurant.

The Nairobi Serena is a much more recent hotel and imaginatively designed. It's owned by the Serena Lodges group and has singles/doubles for US$165/195 with suites for US$250 to US$430 plus a 10% service charge, 2% training levy and 15% VAT. It has all the facilities you'd expect from a five-star hotel. Even Jimmy Carter stays here. Meals cost US$12 (breakfast), US$18 (lunch) and US$20 (dinner) plus taxes.

The Nairobi Safari Club is a very modern building overlooking Nairobi University and has a very imposing entrance and lobby. All the rooms here are suites and the price includes temporary membership, although this doesn't entitle you to a jolly thing. The ordinary suites are priced at US$195/225 for singles/doubles plus there are presidential suites for US$485 a single or double. Note that these rates include taxes.

Top of the line is the *The Grand Regency Hotel* (☎ 211199; fax 217120), PO Box 57549, Loita St, which is at the centre of a long drawn-out legal battle between the owner, Kamlesh Pattni, and the Central Bank of Kenya. It's the ultimate in luxury (although it is done in dubious taste) and costs KSh 8000 to KSh 12,000 a single and KSh 11,000 to KSh 15,000 a double with suites ranging from KSh 24,500 to KSh 70,000. It's where the politicians bring people when they want to talk about megabuck loans and deals.

Up on the 'border' of Westlands and Parklands is the *Mayfair Court Hotel* (☎ 740920; fax 748823), PO Box 66807, Parklands Rd. This is a large, colonial-style hotel situated in its own beautifully maintained grounds and offers standard singles/doubles at US$110/145 and superior rooms at US$135/170 for singles/doubles including breakfast. Children aged between three and 12 years are charged 50% of the adult rates. There are two swimming pools, a health club, the popular Mischiefs Bar and a free shuttle bus service every hour to the city centre.

Milimani A little outside of the city centre where Kenyatta Ave turns into Valley Rd is the *Panafric Hotel* (☎ 720822; fax 726356), PO Box 30486. Part of the Sarova Hotels

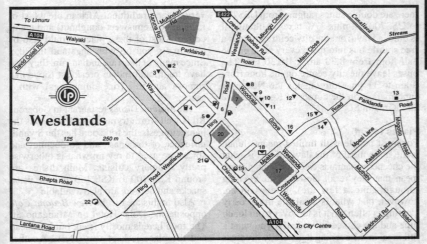

Westlands

chain, it's a large, multistorey modern hotel with all the facilities you'd expect. Rooms here cost KSh 2950/4200 a single/double, plus there are more expensive suites. Prices include breakfast and all taxes.

Westlands Just beyond the main Westlands roundabout off Waiyaki Way is the *Landmark Hotel* (☎ 448713/7; fax 448977), PO Box 14287, which is part of the Block Hotels chain. It's a pleasant place to stay and was recently refurbished. Room rates are US$76/110 for singles/doubles including breakfast. There is also a free shuttle bus for guests between the hotel and the centre of town.

Thika Road A few km out of the centre on the Thika Rd is the swish *Safari Park Hotel* (☎ 802493; fax 802477), PO Box 45038. Set on a 25-hectare site, this hotel features soaring makuti roofs, lots of woodwork, a huge landscaped pool and lush gardens. It's certainly an escape from the city centre, and there's a separate casino complex on the site. Other facilities include a fitness centre, as well as tennis and squash courts. All the rooms have cable TV, mini-bar and four-poster beds, and the cost is US$155/180, or there are double suites ranging from US$210 to US$700, all plus 27% taxes. Although it is quite a way from the city centre, there is a free shuttle bus into town every hour on the half hour from 8.30 am to 10.30 pm. The buses leave the city centre on the hour from 9 am to 11 pm from outside the Nakumatt supermarket on the corner of Kenyatta Ave and Kimathi St.

Places to Eat

For most people with limited means, lunch is the main meal of the day and this is what the cheaper restaurants cater for. That doesn't mean that they're all closed in the evening (though quite a few are). It does mean, however, that what is available in the early evening is often what is left over from lunch time and the choice is limited. If you want a full meal in the evening it generally involves eating from a mid-range (or better) restaurant, or from a barbecue attached to a bar.

Nairobi is replete with restaurants offering cuisines from all over the world – Italian, Spanish, Japanese, Chinese, Korean, Indian, Lebanese, and Thai. There are also steak houses, seafood specialists etc and at many places the prices are surprisingly reasonable. For around KSh 450 per person you can eat well at quite a few of them. For KSh 600 to KSh 750 per person you'd be looking at a banquet and if you spent that much at some of them you'd hardly need to eat anything the next day.

While there is a good selection of restaurants in the city centre, increasing numbers of restaurants are opening up in the suburbs, which makes it difficult if you don't have transport as taxis are expensive. The two main eating centres away from the downtown area are the Westlands shopping centre, about two km north of the centre along Uhuru Highway, and the Yaya Centre, about three km west of the centre on Argwings Kodhek Rd in Hurlingham.

Cheap Cafes & Restaurants There are a lot of very cheap cafes and restaurants in the Latema Rd/River Rd area and at the top end of Tom Mboya St where you can pick up a very cheap, traditional African breakfast of mandazi (a semisweet doughnut) and tea or coffee. Most of these places would also be able to fix you up with eggs and the like. Since many of them are Indian-run, they also have traditional Indian breakfast foods like samosa and idli (rice dumplings) with a sauce.

The *Malindi Dishes* restaurant in Gaberone Rd is well worth trying at least once. As the name suggests, the food here has the Swahili influence of the coast, and so coconut and spices are used to rev up what is otherwise pretty ordinary cuisine. Main dishes are around KSh 100 to KSh 150 and the usual snacks and burgers are also available.

Also in this area is the *New Bedona Cafe* opposite the Dolat Hotel on Mfangano St. The food here is mostly fried, but it's cheap and the place is kept very clean. Another ultra-cheap cafe which is fairly popular is the *Bull Cafe* around the corner from the New Kenya Lodge on Ngariama Lane.

For a good solid meal (mixing western and local cuisine) such as steak and matoke (mashed plantains and maize) or maharagwe (kidney beans), try the *Cafe Helena* on Mama Ngina St opposite the City Hall. It's only open at lunch time and is popular with businesspeople. Meals are priced at around KSh 120 and are excellent value. The *Coffee Bar* next door is similar although more expensive. Another place at this end of town is the *Beneve Coffee House* on the corner of Standard and Koinange Sts. It has a tasty selection of self-service food ranging from stews to curries, fish and chips, sambusa, pasties and a host of other choices. It's good value.

Very popular with the lunch time business crowd is the *Jacaranda Cafe* in the Phoenix House Arcade between Kenyatta Ave and Standard St. A hamburger, chips and salad costs around KSh 150.

An excellent place for submarine sandwiches, cakes and decent coffee is the *Pasara* cafe on Standard St. This self-service place has an open-air patio and an indoor nonsmoking area, and newspapers and magazines are available for reading while you eat. They also do a good breakfast here for KSh 280.

If you're staying at Mrs Roche's up in Parklands, the *Stop 'n' Eat* tin shed just up the road offers ugali (maize meal) and ngombe (beef) at very modest prices.

Kenya is the home of all-you-can-eat lunches at a set price and Nairobi has a wide choice of them, most offering Indian food. One of the best is the *Supreme Restaurant* on River Rd at the roundabout, which offers an excellent Indian (Punjabi) vegetarian thali for KSh 220. It also has superb fruit juices.

Excellent value for breakfast and lunch in the city centre is the *Calypso* in the basement of Bruce House, Standard St. Here you can choose from a limited set menu (including meat and seafood) or the buffet lunch. Count on spending around KSh 250. It's a very popular place to eat at lunch times (despite the sloppy service) so get there early if you don't want to wait for a table. Try the fish pili pili – it's delicious.

Another good place to go for lunch and well-cooked, straightforward food is the *Harvest Cafe* on Kenyatta Ave between Koinange and Loita Sts. It's a very pleasant spot to eat and the service is brisk.

The *Jax Restaurant* on the 1st floor of the Old Mutual building, Kimathi St, is a very popular place for lunch. It offers a wide selection of beautifully prepared hot meals, and has an open-air section. The weekday lunch time buffet features Indian and continental dishes, and is good value at KSh 275. Also good value are the burgers, which come with the ubiquitous chips and salad, from KSh 130. It's open from 8 am to 5 pm Monday to Saturday.

Equally popular at lunch time is the *Dancing Spoons Wine Bar* on the 1st floor of the 20th Century Cinema on Mama Ngina St. It has an excellent range of western-style dishes at very reasonable prices (KSh 150 to KSh 250). Directly above (on the 2nd floor) is the wine bar – if you prefer to sit in here rather than the restaurant section, you can still order meals from downstairs. The entrance to this place is the same as for the cinema.

If you're up in Westlands at lunch time, there are several places where you can find a snack lunch cheaply. They include the *Zee Cafe*, in the basement of The Mall shopping centre; the *Open House Restaurant* on the ground floor under Nirula on Mpaka Rd which offers Indian mini-meals; and the *Westlands Rendezvous* on Woodvale Grove which offers African and European-style meals in its open-air cafe for KSh 120 to KSh 220. The manager of the Rendezvous is very friendly, the food is good and beer is available. It's open up until 8 pm. There's also a popular coffee shop with snacks on the ground floor of the Sarit Centre.

If you don't mind spending a little over the odds, the pizzas in the Landmark Hotel's *New Pizza Garden* are excellent and cost between KSh 175 and KSh 200. It also has a range of other dishes at about the same price, and there's live music on Sunday afternoon. The pizza garden is just over the road from the actual hotel and alongside Waiyaki Way.

Fast Food That well-known English staple, fish and chips, has caught on in a big way in Nairobi and there are scores of places offering it. They're all cheap but the quality varies from greasy and stale to excellent. The number of customers in the shop is one way to separate the good from the mediocre but the best way is to poke your nose inside and to take a look at the chips. If you smell anything stale or the chips are soggy, give the place a miss.

Very popular at lunch time for fish and chips is *Supermac* on Kimathi St (directly opposite the Thorn Tree Cafe) on the mezzanine floor of the shopping centre there. It not only offers some of the best fish and chips in Nairobi, but also serves sausages, salads and fruit juices.

Also recommended for this type of fast food is the *Prestige Restaurant*, in Tsavo Lane off Latema Rd, which offers large servings of sausage, chips and salad for KSh 100. It's popular with local people.

The hamburger is all-conquering in Nairobi too, though, surprisingly, none of the US chains have got a foothold in Kenya yet.

Too much competition from Indian entrepreneurs perhaps? Or perhaps they don't grow the right variety of potatoes in Limuru? What has got a solid foothold is the *Wimpy* chain which has branches on Kenyatta Ave, Tom Mboya St and Mondlane St. These places have the usual range of snacks and meals (burgers, sausages, eggs, fish, chicken, milk shakes etc) costing up to KSh 200. They are open from 7.30 am to 9.30 pm.

Another good cafe for a meal of burgers, fish or chicken with a mountain of chips and salad for around KSh 170 to KSh 190 is *Nairobi Burgers* on Tom Mboya St right opposite the end of Latema Rd. Sweets, soups and ice cream are also served – it's a very popular place.

Also on Tom Mboya St, down near the Princess Hotel, is the *Pipes Restaurant*. This is a US-style, fast food place with all the usual junk-food snacks.

For take-away chicken & chips, you can't beat the amazingly popular *Kenchic Inn*, on the corner of Moktar Daddah and Muindi Mbingu Sts. It sells a phenomenal number of roast chickens every day.

Breakfast The *Growers Cafe* on Tom Mboya St is deservedly popular with both local people and travellers and the prices are reasonable. Food on offer includes eggs (boiled or fried), sausages and other hot foods, fruit salads (with or without yoghurt) and good coffee. Right upstairs is the *Swara Restaurant*, which also does a decent mandazi and tea breakfast, as well as good-value buffet lunches featuring Kenyan food.

If you're staying in the Koinange St area, the *Dove Cage Restaurant* on Moktar Daddah St next to the Terminal Hotel is an excellent little place. A full breakfast with juice and coffee sets you back around KSh 140, and the service is fast and friendly. Very similar is *Calypso* in the basement of Bruce House on Standard St where you can get an English-style breakfast for KSh 120.

For a breakfast splurge, try one of the buffets at a major hotel. The *Illiki Cafe* on the ground floor of the Ambassadeur Hotel on Moi Ave is excellent value. Here you can

tuck in for KSh 390. It offers the works – a variety of juices, milk, yoghurt, cereals, porridge, eggs, bacon, beans, sausages, toast, fruits, cakes – you name it.

Most of the other top-end hotels also do buffet breakfasts, although they are more expensive. The best value is offered by the *New Stanley Hotel* where a continental buffet breakfast costs KSh 450, or a full English breakfast is KSh 650. At the *Hilton* you're looking at about the same while the *Inter-Continental* charges KSh 550/750. If you'd like to breakfast in colonial nostalgia then the *Norfolk Hotel* would have to be the choice. A full continental/English breakfast here costs KSh 700/750.

More Expensive Restaurants The choice here is legion and spans many cuisines. Most of them are mentioned in the *Tourist's Kenya*, though there's no indication of prices.

Most of the more expensive restaurants are licensed and offer beer, wine and spirits but the major exceptions are the Indian vegetarian restaurants which usually offer only fruit juices and tea or coffee. Virtually all these restaurants accept credit cards.

Indian The *Mayur Restaurant* (☎ 331586), above the Supreme Restaurant (see Cheap Cafes & Restaurants) has been famous for superb Indian vegetarian food for years. It's not bad value at KSh 250/280 for a buffet lunch/dinner, but the hushed atmosphere can be a bit daunting.

Also excellent is the *Minar Restaurant* (☎ 229999) in Banda St, which specialises in Mughlai dishes and offers buffet lunches and à la carte dinners. Expect to pay around KSh 500 for a three-course dinner including coffee but excluding alcoholic drinks. The restaurant is licensed, the service friendly and the restaurant is open from noon to 2 pm and 7 to 10.30 pm daily. It also has branches at the Yaya Centre (☎ 561676), Argwings Kodhek Rd, Hurlingham; and at the Sarit Centre (☎ 748340), Westlands. All three of the Minar restaurants have a delicious all-you-can-eat buffet lunch on Sundays with a vast array of dishes (Indian and continental) and desserts all for KSh 425 including tax. These Sunday buffets are superb value so forget about breakfast on Sunday morning. Credit cards are accepted.

The *Zam Zam Restaurant* (☎ 212128), just off Kilome Rd near the top end of River Rd, is a modern place with pleasing decor and good service. The food is good, and remarkably cheap, yet this place remains relatively poorly patronised, perhaps because of its location close to River Rd. Main dishes are all under KSh 250 and the servings are generous.

Another good and relatively cheap place is the *Safeer Restaurant* (☎ 336803) in the Ambassadeur Hotel. Despite appearances, this place is not expensive and two people can eat well here for KSh 600 including a couple of beers. The food is mainly north Indian, and there are complimentary salads, chutney and pickle.

Out at Westlands there are three excellent Indian restaurants. The best of the lot, according to local residents, is the *Haandi* (☎ 448294/5) on the 1st floor of The Mall shopping centre. It's open every day including public holidays from 12.30 to 2.30 pm and 7.30 to 10.30 pm. Judge for yourself. Beautifully conceived and divided into three parts is the *Mauriya Indian Restaurant* on the corner of Mpaka and Muthithi Rds. It's a luxurious place and plainly has no interest in catering to the lunch time crowds as it's only open for dinner from 7.30 pm to 1.30 am daily. This is where you come for a long, languorous dinner with your lover. Credit cards? They'll do nicely, thankyou very much. Lastly, there's the newly opened *Palakhi Indian Restaurant* in New Rehema House at the junction of Rhapta Rd and Ring Road Westlands not far from the Westlands roundabout.

West African The *West African Paradise Restaurant* (☎ 741396) is in Rank Xerox House in Westlands. It offers a wide range of food from a number of West African countries and dishes include poulet yassa (chicken with onions and garlic sauce), jollof (rice with onions), and fufu (maize). It's quite different food and is well worth a try if you haven't been to West Africa. The restaurant is open daily from 9.30 am to 9.30 pm.

Chinese Nairobi has a reasonable selection of Chinese restaurants although none of them are particularly cheap. Probably the cheapest is the *Great Chung Wah*, opposite the Sixeighty Hotel on Muindi Mbingu St. The KSh 250 lunch-time platter is good value and à la carte dishes cost from KSh 200 to KSh 300.

The *Hong Kong Restaurant* (☎ 228612) in College House on Koinange St is very popular at lunch time and the food is good but the decor and furnishings are a bit sparse. The soups here at KSh 150 to KSh 180 make a meal in themselves, but if you have room for more, main dishes cost around KSh 200 to KSh 300.

In Shankardas House, on Moi Ave near the Kenya Cinema complex, is the stylish *Pagoda Restaurant* (☎ 227036). Again, the food here is mainly Szechuan, and you can expect a complete meal to come to around KSh 600 with drinks.

The *Dragon Pearl* (☎ 340451), in Bruce House on Standard St, also has good Chinese food at prices comparable to the other more expensive restaurants. It's open daily for lunch and dinner.

Rated as the best Chinese restaurant in town by some residents is the *Rickshaw Chinese Restaurant* (☎ 223604), in Fedha Towers, Standard St. It has an extensive menu and the food is delicious. Again, you can expect to spend at least KSh 600 per person here.

Also very good if you're staying in the Milimani area is the *China Town Restaurant* on Ralph Bunche Rd adjacent to the Lenana Mount Hotel.

Up in Westlands are another four Chinese restaurants. They all compete with each other in terms of excellence of cuisine and mellow surroundings. Top of the line is probably the *Jiangsu Chinese Restaurant* on the 2nd floor of the Soin shopping arcade. This is a huge place but very classy – so classy, in fact, it's only open for dinner so adjust your wallet accordingly. Round the corner from here is *Nirula* on Mpaka Rd at the junction with Muthithi Rd. It has an open rooftop area as well as a closed section; credit cards are accepted. A stone's throw from here is the *Chinese Corner Restaurant* which is somewhat cheaper but just as good. The *Beijing Restaurant* (☎ 447494), Woodvale Grove, is also very good. It's open from 10.30 am to 2.30 pm and 6 to 10.30 pm and accepts credit cards.

Mongolian The only place you'll find this cuisine is at the *Manchurian Restaurant* (☎ 444263/4), Brick Court, on the corner of Mpaka Rd and Brookvale Grove in Westlands. Here you choose from a range of marinated meats, vegetables, condiments and spices and have your meal cooked in front of you on giant hot plates. A meal costs around KSh 400 (excluding drinks) and you can go back as many times as you like for more of the same or something else so don't pile everything onto the first plate! The secret of putting your own banquet together here is modesty over several dishes. It's open Monday to Saturday from 12.30 pm (lunch) and 7.30 pm (dinner). Credit cards are accepted.

Thai The *Bangkok Restaurant* (☎ 751311), Rank Xerox House, Parklands Rd, Westlands, has been in business now for a number of years and has a good reputation for authentic Thai food. It's open daily from 12.30 to 2.30 pm and 6 to 10.30 pm. Another Thai restaurant has recently opened on the top floor of New Rehema House at the junction of Rhapta Rd and Ring Road Westlands not far from the Westlands roundabout. This is the *Thai Cuisine Restaurant* which is open for lunch and dinner daily. At either place you can eat well for KSh 400 per person.

Italian For Italian food there is the long-running and very popular *Trattoria* (☎ 340855) on the corner of Wabera and Kaunda Sts. It is open daily from 8.30 am to 11.30 pm and both the atmosphere and the food are excellent. There's a wide choice on the menu and à la carte is available at lunch time. In the evening it's all à la carte. A soup, main course, salad, dessert and a carafe or two of house chianti will relieve you of around KSh 600 to KSh 700 per person. As you might expect, the ice cream here is superb.

Probably just as good, but lacking the same reputation (and therefore, prices), is *La Scala*, on Standard St near Muindi Mbingu St. This place specialises in Italian food but also has western dishes such as steaks and burgers. Pizzas and pasta dishes cost KSh 150 to KSh 190, steaks are KSh 260. It's open daily from 7 am to midnight and is very popular with Kenyans looking for a modestly priced decent meal in pleasant surroundings.

Also worth a try is the *Marino Restaurant* (☎ 227150), 1st floor, National Housing Corporation building, Aga Khan Walk, just off Haile Selassie Ave. It has a spacious interior dining area as well as an open-air patio and is open from 9 am to 2 pm and 7 to 10 pm Monday to Saturday; closed on Sunday. There's a wide range of Italian and continental dishes available with main courses priced from KSh 190 to KSh 300.

Also good is the *Capolinea* in The Mall shopping centre at Westlands. This is more of a cafe-style place, and this is reflected in the prices – around KSh 90 to KSh 170 for snacks and sandwiches.

Another excellent place away from the centre is the *La Cucina* (☎ 562871) in the Yaya Centre in Hurlingham. It has everything from pasta to steak, home delivery is available, and there's an attached wine bar. Prices are a bit on the high side, but it's still popular.

The new *l'ora blu* should be open by now. It is a restaurant, wine bar, disco and live-music venue on the corner of Kimathi and Mama Ngina Sts. In its previous incarnation as the Foresta Magnetica it served excellent Italian food and had a fine atmosphere, although it wasn't all that cheap. As the management hasn't changed it should still be worth a look.

Greek & Middle Eastern At the Yaya Centre in Hurlingham there's the *Sugar & Spice (Zorba the Treat)* (☎ 562876) which is a modest place serving a wide variety of snacks. Also here is the *Patra Bakery*, an informal eatery serving Middle Eastern favourites such as felafel (KSh 150) and doner kebabs (KSh 180).

Japanese There's one Japanese restaurant in the city centre, the *Akasaka* (☎ 333948), which you'll find on Standard St opposite Bruce House between Koinange and Muindi Mbingu Sts. It's done out in traditional Japanese style and there's even a tatami room which you can reserve in advance though mostly it's table and chairs. It offers the full range of Japanese cuisine including tempura, teriyaki and sukiyaki as well as soups and appetisers. A full meal costs KSh 400 to KSh 800 per person. It's licensed and open daily from 12.30 to 2 pm for box lunches, and from 6 to 9 pm for dinner.

Korean The only Korean restaurant in Nairobi is the *Restaurant Koreana* in the Yaya Centre, Hurlingham. The food is excellent and authentic but it's expensive. A full meal costs around KSh 800 to KSh 1000 and the restaurant is licensed. It's open from noon to 2.30 pm and 6 to 10.30 pm Monday to Saturday and closed Sunday.

Ethiopian The *Daas* Ethiopian restaurant is in an old house, some distance from the centre off Ngong Rd (signposted) about halfway between Kenyatta Hospital roundabout and the Adams Arcade shopping centre. The décor includes many Ethiopian artefacts and there's often live music in the evenings. Meals are based around excellent unleavened bread and are eaten with the fingers. Expect to pay around KSh 400 to KSh 500 per person for a full meal including drinks.

Seafood The best seafood restaurant in Nairobi is the *Tamarind* (☎ 338959) in the National Bank building on Aga Khan Walk, between Harambee and Haile Selassie Aves.

It offers a wide selection of exotic seafood dishes, and culinary influences range from European to Asian to coastal Swahili. The cuisine is superb as are the surroundings which are decorated in a sumptuous Arabic-Moorish style. Eating here is definitely a major night out as most main courses are priced well over KSh 400 with crab and prawn dishes up to KSh 750. There's also a special vegetarian menu. It's open for lunch Monday to Saturday from 12.30 to 1.45 pm and daily for dinner from 6.30 to 9.45 pm.

Western A good restaurant for plain meat and vegie dishes (eg sausages and mashed potato) is the *Zanze Bar* (☎ 222532) on the top floor of the Kenya Cinema Plaza, Moi Ave, though a range of other dishes are also available. It's open for lunch and dinner daily but is not strictly a restaurant alone – more a combination of bar, wine bar, live music venue and restaurant. You can also play chess, darts and backgammon here. The food is good, reasonably priced (around KSh 250 per person), but you must pay an extra KSh 100 entry in the evenings (free during the day).

The *Hard Rock Cafe* (☎ 220802), on the mezzanine floor, Barclays Plaza, Loita/Market Sts, has become very popular since it opened up a few years ago. It's a much more spacious and interesting place than its sister establishment in Mombasa and the food is good though not particularly cheap at around KSh 250 to KSh 350 for a main course. It's open daily from 9 am to 2 am and there's secure parking available in the building.

Not strictly western (since it does pizzas and Indian dishes, too) but exclusively vegetarian is the *Slush Happy Eater* (☎ 220745), Tubman Rd off Kimathi St. In addition to grilled sandwiches and hot drinks it also offers fresh juices and dessert.

Nyama Choma For steak eaters who haven't seen a decent doorstep since they left Argentina, Australia, Uruguay or the USA and are looking for a gut-busting extravaganza then there's no better place than the *Carnivore* (☎ 501709), out at Langata just past Wilson airport. Whether it's lunch or dinner you take there's always beef, pork, lamb, ham, chicken, sausages and at least three game meats (such as ostrich, eland, hartebeest, crocodile, often wildebeest or zebra). The roasts are barbecued on Maasai spears and the waiters carve off hunks onto your plate until you tell them to stop. Prices include salads, bread, desserts and coffee. Meals here can be surprisingly cheap given the amount you receive and you're looking at KSh 885 for lunch from Monday to Saturday and KSh 985 on Sunday; dinner is priced at KSh 985 daily. This is a very popular tourist restaurant and the car park is usually over-flowing with tourist buses. There's also a disco in the Simba Saloon on Wednesday and usually a live band on Saturday night. To get there take bus No 14, 24 or 124 and tell the conductor where you are going; the restaurant is a one-km signposted walk from where you are dropped off. It's easy to hitch back into the centre when you're ready to go. Otherwise, negotiate for a taxi.

For something a little less extravagant there's the *Nyama Choma Terrace & Bar*, above the Dhaba Restaurant at the top end of Tom Mboya St. This is a decent little place which on weekdays has nyama choma as well as a number of other Kenyan dishes, and it's very cheap. Quite a lot of the press corps come here though it's actually the bar they're most interested in.

Highly rated by residents, particularly Africans, is the nyama choma at the *Sagret Hotel*, Milimani Rd. Any day of the week you pass here, you'll see clouds of delicious-smelling smoke rising from the restaurant. The food is OK, relatively cheap and there's usually a good crowd though service can be slow. It's best to come here with a group of at least four people because you have to choose a hunk of meat from the refrigerated display and there'll be enough meat on each to feed at least four people. Chips or kenyege are available with the roast. Count on around KSh 200 to KSh 300 per person plus drinks. It's open for lunch and dinner everyday.

A definite step down the scale, but worth it for the atmosphere, are the 20 or more wooden shacks of the NSSF Market on the corner of Loita St and Kenyatta Ave. Here you can eat good choma for around KSh 80, and also sample many other Kenyan dishes such as matoke and kenyege. This is a very popular place among the city's office workers, and although foreigners are a rare sight here, you'll be warmly welcomed. Also good are the stalls at the Kariokor Market, across the river east of the city centre.

For authentic, no-frills Nairobi nyama choma the only place to go is the suburb of Kilmichael, some distance from the centre out past Pangani and Eastleigh. It's certainly not for the squeamish as the goats are slaughtered only a few metres away from where you eat and are then barbecued right in front of you, but there's no doubting the freshness of the meat! This is not a place to go to alone, however, as the people here are not used to seeing wazungu and while it's not threatening, it's best to be in the company of a reliable Kenyan. You probably wouldn't find it on your own anyway. African prices apply here so it's cheaper than anywhere else you'll find. Even Smith Hempstone, a former American ambassador to Kenya, once came here, much to the displeasure of the government – Kilmichael isn't exactly ambassadorial territory.

Entertainment

Cinema Nairobi is a good place to take in a few films and at a price substantially lower than what you'd pay back home, but if you don't want scratched films then go to one of the better cinemas such as *Kenya Plaza* on Moi Ave, or *20th Century* on Mama Ngina St. Expect to pay KSh 80 to KSh 100 to see a film. The cheaper ones are on Latema Rd and include the *Odeon* and *Embassy*. The *Cameo* on Kenyatta Ave is also relatively cheap. There are also two good drive-ins if you have the transport: both have snack bars and bars.

Discos There's a good selection of discos in the centre of Nairobi and there are no dress rules, though there's an unspoken assumption that you'll turn up looking half-decent.

Perhaps the most popular disco in the centre of town is the *Florida 2000* on Moi Ave near City Hall Way. The entry fee depends on the night but is between KSh 120 and KSh 180 for men and half that for women and it's open until 6 am. If you want a break from Maria Carey and Black Box, there's a bar and restaurant upstairs which is often just as lively as the mayhem below.

Also very popular is the *New Florida* (known locally as the 'Mad House'), near the corner of Koinange and Banda Sts, which is a mushroom-shaped building above a petrol station! This is a much smaller place than the 2000 though entry charges are the same. It stays open until 6 am and there's a downstairs bar/restaurant where you can find temporary respite from the madness. There are floor shows at about 1 am at both of the Floridas and the dancers are good but it's pretty kitsch.

Another popular disco in the centre is *Visions* on Kimathi St which is open daily except Monday from 9 pm. Less popular but more down-to-earth is the *Hollywood* on Moktar Daddah St between Koinange and Muindi Mbingu Sts where the entry charges are the same as the Floridas.

Further out of town is *Bubbles* at the International Casino, Westlands Rd/Museum Hill, just off Uhuru Highway. This disco is favoured by young people of Asian origin so it's not quite as gutsy as the Floridas.

If you're in the Milimani Rd area, check out *Fredz* next door to the China Town Restaurant on Ralph Bunche Rd. It's open in the evenings from around 6 pm but the disco doesn't fire up until later on. If you get there early there's no cover charge.

There's a live band/disco every Wednesday night at the *Simba Saloon* at the Carnivore in Langata but entry costs KSh 200 per person. There's usually a good crowd and it makes a refreshing change from the more enclosed and crowded space of the discos in town.

Beer in all these places is reasonably priced but other drinks, especially imported liquors, are more expensive. Snacks and meals are available at all of them.

Theatre The *Phoenix Theatre*, Parliament Rd, has a small auditorium which hosts professional productions by the local Nairobi Players drama group, but it's quite expensive. Check with local papers to see what's on.

Live Music In the next block to the Florida 2000 on Moi Ave and on the top floor of the Kenya Cinema Plaza, is the *Zanze Bar*, which has live music most nights. This bar offers a good alternative to the discos, and there's a small cover charge. Drinks are reasonably priced and the toilets have a blackboard on which you can scrawl jokes or obscenities.

Zingara Percussion is a local group which performs every Saturday afternoon at the *Hoggers Eating Place* on Muindi Mbingu St opposite Jeevanjee Gardens.

Much further out of town, right by the roundabout at Dagoretti Corner on Ngong Rd, is the *Bombax Club* which has live bands every Thursday, Friday, Saturday and Sunday night. Unlike many of the other discos and bars mentioned in this section, this one is frequented mainly by local Kenyans with only a sprinkling of wazungu, but the atmosphere is very friendly and convivial. Again, there's a small cover charge. To get there, take a minibus or matatu to Dagoretti Corner from Kenyatta Ave outside Nyayo House, or share a taxi (about KSh 300 to KSh 400).

Jazz For a classy night out try the *Jazz Cafe* at the Yaya Centre in Hurlingham. This is both a restaurant and live music venue, and is well worth a look.

Pubs/Bars The *Thorn Tree Cafe* in the New Stanley Hotel on the corner of Kimathi St and Kenyatta Ave is something of a meeting place for tourists, although the service is generally supercilious and snail-slow. Perhaps this is just a ploy by the management to discourage 'shabby' travellers who might lower the tone of the place. Whatever the case, if you sit down between 11 am and 2 pm and 5 and 7 pm for a drink you'll have to order something to eat as well. The best thing about the Thorn Tree is the notice board where you can leave personal messages (but not advertisements of any kind, such as things for sale, or a request for people to join a safari).

The trouble is, if you pass up the Thorn Tree Cafe, there's not a lot of choice left in terms of bars in the city centre except in the seedy Latema/River Rd area. The *Zanze Bar* is OK during the day but there's a cover charge after 6 pm (presumably to keep out the riffraff). You can forget about the bars at the Hotel Inter-Continental and the Hilton Hotel as they're too expensive (KSh 120 for a bottle of beer) and the *Porterhouse* on Mama Ngina St opposite International House is cosy but essentially the haunt of Asian businessmen. The bar at the *Cameo* cinema on Kenyatta Ave is a bit rough and ready and has a noisy jukebox and the *Afro Unity Bar* on the Muindi Mbingu St side of Jeevanjee Gardens is even more rough and ready, though it does attract students from the nearby Nairobi University and is never dull. One bar which is OK but very quiet is on the 1st floor of the Oakwood Hotel and has a balcony overlooking Kimathi St. It's far from lively but the beers are normal price and cold.

Another rough and ready Nairobi institution is the *Modern Green Day & Night Bar*, on Latema Rd next to the Sunrise Lodge. This place is open 24 hours a day, 365 days a year and the front door has never been closed since 1968. The authorities tried to close it for one day in 1989 during a national census but couldn't find the doors! It used to be a lively place for an educational evening out. These days it seems to have passed its use-by date; late at night, which used to be the liveliest time, it seems that half the patrons are comatose, the other half very nearly so, the juke box lies idle and the atmosphere is, well, downbeat.

Much livelier than the Modern Green is the *Friendship Corner* bar across the road. This tiny place is another 24-hour bar and really kicks on. You'll come across all manner of people here in various stages of inebriation.

Outside of the city centre, the most popular bar among foreigners and expats is *Buffalo Bill's* at the Heron Court Hotel, Milimani Rd. While it's open all day every day until around 11 pm, it only livens up from about 5.30 pm onwards. Meals and snacks are available throughout the day and night plus nyama choma from around 6.30 pm until closing. It's here that you'll meet all of Nairobi's eccentrics, adventurers, entrepreneurs, safari operators, NGO employees, disco queens, hookers and bullshit artistes. Beers cost KSh 70, warm or cold. There's disco music most nights of the week but nowhere to dance.

Further up Milimani Rd at the junction with Ralph Bunche Rd and at the back of the Eagle Star Apartments is the *Candle Bar* (otherwise known as the *Half London*). It's an earthy and quite popular little place illuminated by kerosene lanterns. Beers are cheap (KSh 40).

Even further up Milimani Rd on the right-hand side is the *Salama Hotel Annexe*. This bar and restaurant occupies an old colonial-style house. It's a friendly place and gets very lively most evenings. Beers are cheaper here than at Buffalo Bill's and the music is not as intrusive.

Those looking for more genteel surroundings in which to sip their beer could try the *Ngong Hills Hotel* on Ngong Rd, the beer gardens at the *Boulevard* or *Landmark* hotels, or the *Lord Delamere* bar at the *Norfolk Hotel*.

Up in Westlands there are three other bars which are well worth considering if you have your own wheels or don't mind the taxi fare. *Gypsies*, at the back of Ring Road Westlands opposite Barclays Bank and close to the Landmark Hotel, is a very popular bar, with decent food and good music. It's relatively quiet and there are no hassles and it basically stays open for as long as there are still sufficient people drinking. Friday night is the night to go along to *Mischiefs* at the Mayfair Court Hotel, Parklands Rd, on the 'border' between Westlands and Parklands. It's packed out on this night with a garrulous crowd of mainly wazungu. Mischiefs has an excellent sound system and good bar snacks.

Ngong Races

Every second Sunday for most of the year there's horse racing at the Ngong Racecourse. It's a very genteel day out, and with an entry fee of KSh 50 for the members' enclosure or just KSh 20 in the public enclosure, it's hardly going to break the bank. There's betting with the bookies or the tote, and while the odds you get are hardly going to set the world on fire, it's great fun to have a punt. You can bet as little as KSh 20 so even the most impecunious should be able to afford a flutter.

Local cynics will tell you that all the races, like everything else in the country, are rigged. It may well be true, but it hardly seems to matter. There's a good restaurant on the ground floor of the grandstand and two bars with beer at regular bar prices. If you don't have transport back to town it's easy enough to find a lift if you talk to people in the members' enclosure. Bus or matatu No 24 from the city centre goes right past the racecourse to the Karen shopping centre. ■

Things to Buy

Nairobi is a good place to pick up souvenirs although you do need to shop around. The City Market on Muindi Mbingu St has a good range of items, particularly kiondo baskets, and there's a whole gaggle of stalls in Kigali St behind the Jama Mosque. It's all a bit of a tourist trap and you need to bargain fiercely. There are also hundreds of stalls selling the same sorts of wares along just about every tiny alley which branches off from Biashara St between Muindi Mbingu and Tom Mboya Sts.

Even though they originated in Tanzania (and they're still much cheaper there), makonde woodcarvings are very popular in Nairobi and the shops are full of them. Most of the examples you will see are actually made in Ukambani (the land of the Kamba tribe).

At the cheaper end of the market, it's worth looking at the examples which hawkers bring around to the bars where tourists congregate. Buffalo Bill's at the Heron Court Hotel is one of the best places. The quality of the carving varies a lot, but if you're not in a hurry then you can find some really fine examples at bargain-basement prices. Expect to pay around half to two-thirds of the price first asked.

Another craft item you can find in profusion both at stalls and inside shops are soapstone carvings including chess sets. These originate from the Kisii area of western Kenya but you'll be hard-pressed to find them there. Nakuru is where you'll find them at their cheapest however there's not a lot of price difference between there and Nairobi. The chess sets, of which there are many different designs, are an absolute bargain.

If you're not into bargaining, or want top-quality stuff, there are plenty of 'fixed-price' souvenir shops around although, even at these, they'll usually give you a 'special price' if you are obviously not a Hilton hopper. One of the better shops is on the corner of Kaunda and Wabera Sts, and another on Tubman Rd near the corner of Muindi Mbingu St.

Travellers with more cash at their disposal should think seriously about buying fine art, particularly paintings. There are some superb artists in Kenya and their work is only on the verge of being internationally recognised. It's possible that it will take off in the same way that Australian Aboriginal art did some years ago.

A good place to check out what's happening in this genre is the Gallery Watatu on the 1st floor of Lonhro House, Standard St. There's a permanent display here, much of which is for sale, plus they have regular auctions. Bring your cheque book with you or a credit card. Almost nothing goes for less than KSh 15,000 and for the crème de la crème, you're looking at about KSh 50,000 to KSh 100,000, however the champagne and the vol-au-vents are complimentary. It is also worth checking out the Gallery of East African Contemporary Art which is at the museum.

If you want to get kitted out in the latest designer 'white hunter' safari gear, there are literally dozens of shops selling all the requisite stuff at outrageous prices. But do you really want to look like an absolute nerd that's only ever seen the inside of a luxury tented camp?

The Spinners Web describes itself as a 'consignment handicraft shop' which sells goods made in workshops and by self-help groups around the country. It has some superb items, including hand-knitted jumpers, all sorts of fabrics and the huge Turkana baskets. The shop is on Waiyaki Way, Westlands, near Viking House.

The gift shop of the East African Wildlife Society in the arcade of the Hilton Hotel has a range of souvenirs and interesting knick-knacks, many of them with an animal theme. It's well worth shopping here as the proceeds go towards conserving Kenya's wildlife rather than to conserving the lifestyles of rich Kenyans.

If you're out in the Langata area, there's another couple of places worth investigating. The Ostrich Park has, apart from ostriches, a craft centre with an artisans' workshop, and you can see the items being made. See the Around Nairobi section for details. On Langata South Rd, between Langata Rd and Langata itself, is Utamaduni (☎ 891798). This consists of 18 separate shops which each have one room in a large house. The range of crafts is excellent, the quality good and the prices correspondingly high. On the plus side, an unspecified percentage of the profits goes to Kenya Wildlife Services. It's very much tourist orientated but if you're in the area is worth a look. There's also a good cafe here.

For a much less touristy atmosphere try the Kariokor Market east of the centre on Racecourse Rd in Eastleigh. It's a few minutes ride by bus or taxi. Another place out of the centre is the Undugu crafts shop in Woodvale Grove, Westlands, behind the market. This is a nonprofit organisation which supports community projects in Nairobi.

The Maasai Market is an informal market where Maasai women sell beaded jewellery, gourds, baskets and other Maasai crafts. It only takes place on Tuesdays from around 9 am to mid-afternoon, and has changed location a couple of times in recent years.

Currently it's held at the top end of Moi Ave, on the corner of Slip Rd.

Getting There & Away

Air Airlines with offices in Nairobi include:

Aeroflot
　　Corner House, Mama Ngina St (☎ 220746)
Air France
　　Fedha Towers, Muindi Mbingu (☎ 217512)
Air India
　　Jeevan Bharati House, Harambee Ave (☎ 334788)
Air Madagascar
　　Hilton Hotel (☎ 225286)
Air Malawi
　　Sixeighty Hotel, Muindi Mbingu St (☎ 333683)
Air Mauritius
　　Union Towers, Moi Ave (☎ 229166)
Air Rwanda
　　Mama Ngina St (☎ 332225)
Air Tanzania
　　Chester House, Koinange St (☎ 336224)
Air Zaïre
　　Arrow House, Monrovia St (☎ 222271)
Air Zimbabwe
　　Chester House, Koinange St (☎ 339522)
British Airways
　　International House, 8th floor, Mama Ngina St (☎ 334362)
Cameroon Airlines
　　Rehani House, 9th floor, Koinange St (☎ 224743)
EgyptAir
　　Hilton Arcade (☎ 226821)
El-Al Airlines
　　KCS House, Mama Ngina St (☎ 228123)
Ethiopian Airlines
　　Bruce House, Standard St (☎ 330837)
Gulf Air
　　International House, Mama Ngina St (☎ 214444)
Japan Airlines (JAL)
　　International House, Mama Ngina St (☎ 220591)
Kenya Airways
　　Barclays Plaza, 5th floor, Loita St (☎ 229291)
KLM
　　Fedha Towers, Muindi Mbingu St (☎ 332673)
Lignes Aerienne (Seychelles)
　　Rehema House (☎ 340481)
Lufthansa
　　AM Bank House, University Way (☎ 335819)
Olympic Airways
　　AM Bank House, University Way (☎ 219532)
Pakistan International Airlines (PIA)
　　ICEA building, Kenyatta Ave (☎ 333900)
Royal Swazi
　　Re-Insurance Plaza, mezzanine floor, Taifa Rd (☎ 339351)
South African Airways
　　Lonrho House, Standard St (☎ 229663)

Sudan Airlines
UTC building, General Kago St (☎ 225129)
Virag
Lonrho House, 6th floor, Standard St (☎ 220961)
Uganda Airlines
Uganda House, Kenyatta Ave (☎ 221354)

Kenya Airways is the main domestic carrier and operates from Nairobi's Jomo Kenyatta International airport. There are 12 flights weekly to Kisumu (USS$44 one way), five flights weekly to Malindi (US$83 one way) and 59 flights weekly to Mombasa (US$83 one way). Fares can be paid either in US dollars or in local currency.

Make sure you reconfirm flights 48 hours before departure.

In addition to Kenya Airways, the privately-owned Air Kenya Aviation (☎ 501601), Wilson airport, connects Nairobi with a number of centres:

destination	fare	frequency
Amboseli	US$70/125	daily
Lamu	US$118/236	daily
Malindi	KSh4680/9630	twice weekly
Masai Mara	US$87/150	twice daily
Mombasa	KSh 4680/9360	nine weekly
Nanyuki	US$105/180	daily
Samburu	US$70/115	daily

Note: All fares are one way/return.

The check-in times for all the above flights is half an hour before departure and the baggage allowance is 15 kg. All the flights are nonsmoking.

Bus In Nairobi most long-distance bus offices are along Accra Rd near the River Rd junction. For Mombasa there are numerous companies (such as Coast Bus, Crossline, Akamba, Mawingo, Malindi Bus, Takrim, and Tawfiq) doing the run, both by day and night. They all cost KSh 300 and the trip takes around seven to eight hours with a meal break on the way.

Akamba is the biggest private bus company in the country and has an extensive network. It's not the cheapest, but is probably the safest and most reliable company.

The office is conveniently located on Lagos Rd, just off Latema Rd and very close to Tom Mboya St. Apart from the Mombasa service (KSh 420), it also has daily connections to Isiolo, Nyeri, Meru (KSh 200), Kakamega (KSh 420), Kitale (KSh 400), Chogoria, Embu and Kisumu. If you're heading for Uganda there are three daily Akamba buses direct to Kampala. See the Kenya Getting There & Away chapter for details.

The government KBS Stagecoach company is another large, reliable operator and runs coaches to the major cities and towns from its depot just off Ronald Ngala St not far from the country bus station. To the major destinations – Kisumu, Malaba, Eldoret, Kitale – it uses double-decker buses. The Stagecoach fares are on a par with Akamba's fares; the buses are well maintained and the drivers somewhere approaching sane.

For all other destinations, buses leave from the main country bus station just off Landies Rd, about 15 minutes walk southeast of the budget hotel area around Latema Rd. It's a huge but reasonably well-organised place, and all the buses have their destinations displayed in the window so it's just a matter of wandering around and finding the one you want. There is at least one daily departure and often more to virtually every main town in the country, and the buses leave when full. For more details see Getting There & Away for each place.

Shuttle Minibus A good option for travel to or from Mombasa, but also more expensive than the large buses, are the shuttle services run by two companies – Sav-Line and The Connection. They both offer air-con, 18-seater minibuses for KSh 900 per person one way which will drop you off anywhere in the two city centres. Bookings for Sav-Line should be made at Savage Camping Tours (☎ 228236), Diamond Trust House, Moi Ave, Nairobi. Bookings with The Connection can be made at Inside Africa Safaris (☎ 223304), Wabera St, Nairobi, and at Tamana Holidays (☎ 315208), Moi Ave, Mombasa.

Share-Taxi The share-taxi is a good alternative to that dangerous and heart-stopping mode of transport – the matatu. Although you're still likely to be whisked along at breakneck speed, at least it will be in a vehicle that is not carrying twice its rated capacity and has at least a sporting chance of stopping in a hurry if the need arises. Share-taxis are usually Peugeot 505 station wagons which take seven passengers and leave when full. They are much quicker than the matatus as they go from point to point without stopping, and of course are more expensive. Like matatus, most of the share-taxi companies have their offices around the Accra and River Rds area.

DPS (☎ 210866) on Dubois Rd is typical of these companies and has daily Peugeots to Kisumu (KSh 500, four hours), Busia (KSh 700), Nakuru (KSh 200, two hours), Malaba on the Ugandan border (KSh 500), Kitale (KSh 500), and Kericho (KSh 350). On any of these services you can pay an extra KSh 20 for the front seat. These departures are only in the mornings so you need to be at the office by around 7 am, and it's a good idea to book one day in advance.

Tanzania Taxis for the Tanzanian border at Namanga leave from the top side of the service station on the corner of Ronald Ngala St and River Rd. Most people prefer to take either a bus direct from Nairobi to Arusha, or a shuttle minibus. See the Kenya Getting There & Away chapter for details.

Train The booking office at Nairobi railway station (☎ 335160) is open from 8 am to 7 pm daily.

Nairobi railway station also has a left-luggage office which is open daily from 8 am to noon and 1 to 6.30 pm. It costs KSh 50 per item per day.

Mombasa Trains run from Nairobi to Mombasa every day in both directions at 7 pm and the journey takes about 13 hours. The fares for nonresidents are KSh 2750 in 1st class and KSh 1930 in 2nd class. These prices include dinner, breakfast and bedding whether

you want them or not – there's no discount if you don't want them. This is a popular run so in the high season book your tickets as far in advance as possible, although you shouldn't have any trouble two or three days beforehand.

Kisumu The Nairobi to Kisumu trains depart daily at 6 pm arriving at Kisumu at 7.10 am the next day. In the opposite direction they depart daily at 6 pm arriving at Nairobi at 6.20 am the next day. The fares are KSh 1925 in 1st class and KSh 1320 in 2nd class. This is also a popular route and the train is often heavily booked. If that's the case you may have to rely on the extra coach which is added on the day of departure if demand warrants.

Uganda From Nairobi to the Ugandan border at Malaba there are trains on Friday and Saturday at 3 pm arriving at 8.45 am the next day. In the opposite direction they depart Malaba on Saturday and Sunday at 4 pm and arrive at 9 am the next day. The fares are KSh 2639 in 1st class and KSh 1820 in 2nd class, and again, the fares include meals and bedding. En route to Malaba these trains go through Naivasha, Nakuru (KSh 740/910), Eldoret (KSh 1930/1320) and Bungoma.

There's also a direct Nairobi to Kampala train once a week. See the Kenya Getting There & Away chapter for details.

Car & Motorcycle All the major companies, and many smaller ones, have offices in the city centre, and the bigger ones such as Avis and Hertz have desks at the airport. A comprehensive description of car hire, and a list of companies, can be found in the Kenya Getting Around chapter.

Hitching For Mombasa, take bus No 13, 34 or 109 as far as the airport turn-off and hitch from there. For Nakuru and Kisumu, take bus No 23 from the Hilton to the end of its route and hitch from there. Otherwise start from the junction of Chiromo Rd and Waiyaki Way (the extension of Uhuru Highway) in Westlands.

For Nanyuki and Nyeri take bus No 45 or 145 from the central bus station up Thika Rd to the entrance of Kenyatta National University and hitch from there. Make sure you get off the bus at the college entrance and not the exit. It's very difficult to hitch from the latter. Otherwise, start from the roundabout where Thika Rd meets Forest and Muranga'a Rds.

Getting Around

The Airport The Jomo Kenyatta International airport is 15 km out of town off the road to Mombasa. The cheapest way of getting into town is on the city bus No 34 *but* (and this is a big but) you must keep your wits about you! The number of people who have been ripped off on this bus doesn't bear thinking about. The usual story is that an 'instant crowd' forms, you are jostled and before you know it your bag or money pouch has been slashed or ripped off. It's not much of an introduction to Kenya, so take a taxi. There is generally no problem catching the No 34 city bus *to* the airport because, by then, you'll be familiar with Nairobi. The fare is KSh 20 and the trip takes about 45 minutes, more in peak periods.

The best way to or from the airport is by taxi, and this is really the only option if you have a dawn or late-night flight. The standard fare is KSh 900 from the airport to the city centre. To share a taxi to the airport, check out the notice boards at the Iqbal and the New Kenya Lodge or ask around fellow travellers. As your bargaining position is better in the city, taxis to the airport shouldn't cost more than KSh 750 during the day; late night or early morning you may pay more. Discount Travel Services (☎ 219156; fax 225299) offers an airport shuttle service for KSh 500 per person, with pick-up or drop-off anywhere in the city centre. Book in advance.

To Wilson airport (for light aircraft services to Malindi, Lamu etc) you can take bus or matatu Nos 15, 31, 34, 125 and 126 from Moi Ave opposite the US Embassy. The fare is KSh 15. A taxi from the centre of town will cost you KSh 300 to KSh 400 depending on the driver. The entrance to the airport is easy to miss; get off at the BP station.

Bus Buses are the cheapest way of getting around Nairobi, but hopefully you won't need to use them much. Forget about them in rush hours if you have a backpack – you'll never get on and if by some Herculean feat you manage to do that, you'll never get off!

Useful buses include No 34 to the airport (catch it from the northern side of Kenyatta Ave, or Moi Ave opposite the US Embassy); No 46 from outside the new post office on Kenyatta Ave for the Yaya Centre in Hurlingham (KSh 9), or No 23 from Moi Ave at Jeevanjee Gardens for Westlands (KSh 8).

Matatu Matatus are also packed during peak hours, but are not bad at other times, the main disadvantage being that the drivers are crazy. Matatus are frequent and only slightly more expensive than the buses; you need to be super-vigilant though because they're a pickpocket's paradise. Never take your hand off your valuables and have small change handy for the fare. Matatus follow the same routes as buses, and can be caught in the same places.

Taxi Other than the fleet of London cabs (which belong to the son of the most prominent politician in the country), Nairobi taxis rate as some of the most dilapidated and generally unroadworthy buckets of bolts that ever graced a city street. Taxis cannot usually be hailed on the street (because they don't cruise for passengers) but you can find them parked on just about every second street corner in the city centre. They also hang out at the railway station and outside most of the main hotels. At night, you'll find them outside bars and the nightclubs.

The cabs are not metered but the fares charged are remarkably standard and few cabbies attempt to overcharge, though they're reluctant to give change if it's KSh 20 or less. KSh 200 gets you just about anywhere within the city centre. The same is true from Ralph Bunche Rd or Milimani Rd to the main post office though they may

---

Creative Parking

Though the wildlife parks may be Kenya's premier tourist attraction, it's worth strolling around Kenya's other park – Nairobi's kerbsides – to observe the imaginative and often unbelievable way in which drivers utilise every inch of space to park their frequently scratched and battered vehicles. It's virtually impossible to find a spot to park in central Nairobi any day during business hours except Sunday so if there's the slightest possibility of parking another vehicle between two others in any way whatsoever then someone is going to do it! This is often at 90° to the adjoining cars with no thought about what happens to either the front or back ends. Neither pavements nor parking meters are any impediment to these people or the danger of having either end wiped out by either harassed pedestrians or kamikaze KBS bus drivers. If there's simply not an inch to spare that's just too bad and double parking becomes the order of the day. How you get a car out of this miasma is your problem – not that of the people who've boxed you in.

Parking wardens there certainly are, as well as fines for 'illegal' parking but the deterrent effect of them is minimal and, in any case, always negotiable to a degree.

The best areas to view this spectacle are between Kenyatta Ave and University Way and anywhere between Tom Mboya St and the Nairobi River. ∎

---

sometimes ask for a bit more as it involves backtracking down the other side of Haile Selassie Ave. From the city centre to anywhere in Westlands is around KSh 300 (for locals it's KSh 200). To the Carnivore restaurant from the city centre it is KSh 550.

Bicycle By all means ride a bicycle in Nairobi – if you have a suit of armour, a crash helmet and a constitution of iron. Personally, we wouldn't contemplate it. If you're not run over you'll certainly be run off the road on numerous occasions. No-one is going to give you any room or consideration at any time. Basically, it's dangerous.

Around Nairobi

In addition to the attractions listed below, there is also Nairobi National Park, easily the most accessible in the country. (See the Kenya National Parks & Reserves chapter.)

THE BOMAS OF KENYA

The Bomas of Kenya (☎ 891801) is a cultural centre at Langata – a short way past the entrance to the national park, on the right-hand side as you head out from Nairobi. Here you can see traditional dances and hear songs from the country's 16 ethnic groups amid authentically re-created sur-

roundings, though the dances are all done by one group of professionals rather than representatives of the tribes themselves. There is a daily performance at 2.30 pm (3.30 pm at weekends). Entry costs KSh 300 for adults and KSh 150 for children. There's the usual clutter of souvenir shops around the site.

If you are not on a tour, bus or matatu No 15, 125 or 126 from outside Development House, Moi Ave, will get you there in about half an hour. Get off at Magadi Rd, from where it's about a one-km walk (signposted).

OSTRICH PARK

The Ostrich Park (☎ 891051) is about one km further along Langata Rd, well signposted right opposite the turn-off for Langata itself. This makes a good family excursion, where you can feed ostriches, see artisans at work making handicrafts, and there's also a good kids' playground.

The park is open daily and entry is KSh 200 (KSh 100 for children).

LANGATA GIRAFFE CENTRE

The Langata Giraffe Centre is on Gogo Falls Rd about one km from the Hardy Estate shopping centre in Langata, about 18 km from central Nairobi. Here you can observe and hand-feed Rothschild giraffes from a raised circular wooden structure which also houses a display of information about giraffes. Although the centre is mainly aimed

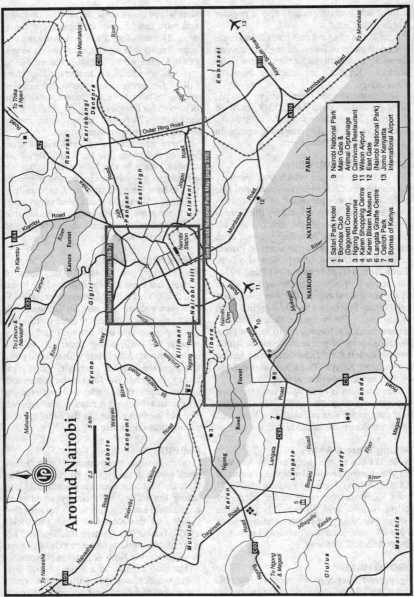

Around Nairobi

1 Safari Park Hotel
2 Bombax Club
   (Dagoretti Corner)
3 Ngong Racecourse
4 Karen Shopping Centre
5 Karen Blixen Museum
6 Langata Giraffe Centre
7 Ostrich Park
8 Bomas of Kenya
9 Nairobi National Park
   Main Gate &
   Animal Orphanage
10 Carnivore Restaurant
11 Wilson Airport
12 East Gate
   (Nairobi National Park)
13 Jomo Kenyatta
   International Airport

at local schoolchildren, it is also a popular tourist drawcard.

Across the road but still part of the centre is a small patch of forest through which you can make a one-km, self-guided forest walk. Booklets (KSh 20) are available from the ticket office.

The centre is open from 9 am to 5.30 pm daily. Admission costs KSh 250 (KSh 70 for children). To get there from the centre take matatu No 24 to the shopping centre in Langata and walk from there.

KAREN BLIXEN MUSEUM

This is the farmhouse which was formerly the residence of Karen Blixen, author of *Out of Africa*, and was presented to the Kenyan government at independence by the Danish government along with the adjacent agricultural college. As you're probably aware from the film of the same name starring Robert Redford and Meryl Streep, this is where Karen Blixen lived between 1914 and 1931. She arrived in Kenya at the age of 29 to marry her second cousin, the Swedish Baron von Blixen-Finecke, who had bought a farm in the area. The marriage failed and she became bankrupt forcing her to sell the farm amidst a series of personal tragedies which eventually left her life in shreds and forced her to leave Kenya. The house was bought by the Danish government in 1959.

The museum is open daily from 9.30 am to 6 pm and entry costs KSh 200. It's right next door to the Karen College on Karen Rd about two km from Langata Rd.

Getting There & Away

A No 111 bus or matatu from Moi Ave will get you there in about 40 minutes at a cost of KSh 30. Alternatively, take public bus No 27 from Kenyatta Ave or from the corner of Ralph Bunche and Ngong Rds to Karen village (the shopping centre) and change to a No 24 matatu there. A taxi will cost you about KSh 850 one way.

NGONG HILLS

Ngong and Karen, to the west of Nairobi, along with Limuru, to the north, were the sites where many white settlers set up farms and built their houses in the early colonial days. The transformation they wrought was quite remarkable so that, even today, as you catch a glimpse of a half-timbered house through woodland or landscaped gardens full of flowering trees, you could imagine yourself to be in the Home Counties of England or some other European location. And, yes, the eucalypts which you see growing everywhere were an Australian import.

There are some excellent views over Nairobi and down into the Rift Valley from various points in the Ngong Hills, but it's unwise to go wandering around alone as people have been mugged here, especially at weekends. What you really need to get a feel for these areas is your own car or, alternatively, that of a resident who is willing to drive you around the place.

Places to Stay & Eat

There's nowhere to stay in this area of Nairobi but there is an excellent place to eat and drink. This is the *Horseman* (☎ 882033) at Karen shopping centre on Langata Rd. Here you have a choice of three restaurants (two open-air and one indoors) and a very popular bar (with draught beer) all set in a leafy compound complete with its own pond and croaking frogs. It's straight out of rural Surrey, England. The food in the restaurants (one of which offers barbecued game meats) is excellent though it is relatively expensive. The bar is often packed in the evenings and usually stays open late.

LIMURU

Limuru possibly has even more of a 'European' feel than the Ngong Hills, except that there are vast coffee and tea plantations blanketing the rolling hills cut by swathes of conifer and eucalypt forest. It's up here that you'll find the *Kentmere Club* (☎ (0154) 41053; fax 40692), Limuru Rd, Tigoni. This is the quintessential white settlers' club – even more so than the Norfolk Hotel in Nairobi.

The club consists of a series of low, intimate, wooden cottages with shingle roofs bathrooms and open fires connected to each other by quaint walkways and bridges. The main block is built in the same style and houses a restaurant and a superb re-creation of an English country pub with low ceilings, exposed beams and log-burning fireplaces. If you'd like to rent a cottage the cost is KSh 2050/3000 for singles/doubles with breakfast. Half-board rates are KSh 2700/4300. It's a very peaceful place, and the restaurant is excellent.

About 10 km beyond the Kentmere Club, and well signposted, is the *Waterfalls Inn* (☎ (0154) 40672) with its picnic site, waterfall, viewing point and restaurant. Admission costs KSh 300 per car (with up to five passengers) on weekends, KSh 150 on weekdays. Although mainly used by day-tripping picnickers, the extensive grounds can also be used for camping (KSh 250 per person). It's a very relaxing place during the week, although you really need your own transport as there are no public transport routes close by. Pony and horse riding is also available at KSh 60.

Another thing you can do in the area is to visit a tea farm. If you've never done this before then it's worth a day out. Visits are organised by Mitchell's *Kiambethu Tea Farm* (☎ (0154) 40756) at Tigoni, about 35 km north-east of Nairobi. Here you'll be shown the whole process of tea production as well as taken on an accompanied walk into the forest to see the colobus monkeys. Visits of the tea farm take place every day starting at 11 am and finish at 2.30 pm. The cost is KSh 1000 which includes tea and biscuits when you get there and lunch at the end of the tour which includes beer, wine, sherry and home-made ice cream. Groups are preferred and visits are by prior arrangement only. A tour from Nairobi costs US$55 per person, including transport and lunch. Contact Let's Go Travel (☎ 340331) in Nairobi.

Getting There & Away
KBS public bus No 116 will take you fairly close to the farm. If you have your own transport, take Limuru Rd (C62) past City Park and turn left at Muthaiga roundabout. Seven km further on you reach Ruaka village

where you turn right by the signpost for Nazareth Hospital and onto D407 Limuru Rd (otherwise known as Banana Rd). This takes you past the Kentmere Club, and the signposted turn-off to the Waterfall Inn.

THIKA
Despite its fame due to the popular *Flame Trees of Thika* novel, the town itself comes as something of a disappointment – there's not even many flame trees in evidence! It's appeal lies in the fact that it makes a great escape from the madness of urban Nairobi just 38 km down the road. If you want to get the feel for a small Kenyan agricultural service town, yet still be in commuting range of Nairobi, it could be just the place.

The town's only 'attraction' as such is **Chania Falls**, one km from the centre of town and on the edge of the busy Nairobi–Nyeri road (which thankfully bypasses Thika). The falls are quite small but there's a good view of them from the up-market Blue Post Hotel, which is a pleasant place to stop for a beer.

Places to Stay & Eat
If you decide to stay, there's a good choice of accommodation, particularly in the mid-range area as it seems Thika is also a popular weekend conference venue.

There's a number of similar boarding & lodgings. The *3 in 1* is typical, and costs KSh 150/250 for singles/doubles with shared facilities. It's passably clean and not too noisy. Another possibility is the *Sky Motel*.

Possibly the best value rooms in town are at the *12th December Hotel* (☎ (0151) 22140) near the post office. Large doubles cost KSh 500, and singles KSh 400, all including breakfast, though in a double room two people only get one breakfast!

Also worth a look is the *Sagret Hotel* (☎ (0151) 21786) where the rooms are a little smaller but all have private bath and balcony, and the price includes breakfast. Small vehicles can be parked securely in the hotel courtyard; larger vehicles remain on the street. The cost for rooms here is KSh 600/900.

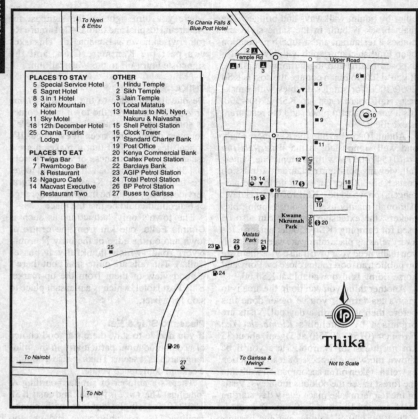

To Nyeri & Embu

To Chania Falls & Blue Post Hotel

Temple Rd

Upper Road

PLACES TO STAY
5 Special Service Hotel
6 Sagret Hotel
8 3 in 1 Hotel
9 Kairo Mountain Hotel
11 Sky Motel
18 12th December Hotel
25 Chania Tourist Lodge

PLACES TO EAT
4 Twiga Bar
7 Rwambogo Bar & Restaurant
12 Ngaguro Café
14 Macvast Executive Restaurant Two

OTHER
1 Hindu Temple
2 Sikh Temple
3 Jain Temple
10 Local Matatus
13 Matatus to Nbi, Nyeri, Nakuru & Naivasha
15 Shell Petrol Station
16 Clock Tower
17 Standard Charter Bank
19 Post Office
20 Kenya Commercial Bank
21 Caltex Petrol Station
22 Barclays Bank
23 AGIP Petrol Station
24 Total Petrol Station
26 BP Petrol Station
27 Buses to Garissa

Uhuru

Kwame Nkrumah Park

Matatu Park

Matatu Park

Road

To Nairobi

To Nbi

To Garissa & Mwingi

Not to Scale

Thika

Further up the range is the *Chania Tourist Lodge* (☎ (0151) 22547), though it is poor value compared with the Sagret. Rooms here are somewhat overpriced at KSh 750/900.

The *Blue Post Hotel* (☎ (0151) 22241) is a reasonable up-market place set uncomfortably close to the very busy highway. Nevertheless, it's a pleasant place and probably worth the KSh 850/1200 charged for the rooms. The hotel has the best restaurant in Thika.

All the mid-range hotels have their own restaurants. For a good meal in a regular restaurant try the amazingly named *Macvast Executive Restaurant Two*! Here the waiters are all done up with pink pinstriped shirts and bow ties, but the prices are low and the menu extensive.

Getting There & Away
Matatus leave from a number of places around Thika. The main matatu stand, used mostly by local matatus, is near the Sagret Hotel. Most long-distance matatus – to Nairobi, Nakuru, Naivasha, Nyeri and Embu – leave from behind Barclays Bank. The trip to Nairobi only takes 45 minutes and costs KSh 30.

The Coast

> This cannot be less than natural beauty, the endless sand, the reefs, the lot, are completely unmatched in the world.
>
> **Ernest Hemingway**

The coast of Kenya is one of the country's main attractions. It offers a combination of historical sites, trading ports with a strong Arab-Muslim influence, superb beaches and diving opportunities – an area not to be missed.

Mombasa is the coast capital, if you like, and is the first port of call for most people after leaving Nairobi. It is an old trading port with a history going back at least to the 12th century, and the old city here shows heavy influence of the town's previous rulers – the mosques and the Portuguese fort in particular. It has a steamy humid climate but is a pleasant place nonetheless. Unfortunately, many people are in such a rush to get to the beach that they really only transit Mombasa, which is a pity as the city, particularly the old part, is well worth exploring.

To the north it's much the same story, with Malindi being the big coastal resort centre, but there's a couple of interesting attractions here as well – the historical site of Gedi just a short bus ride to the south, and the excellent diving on the coral reef in the offshore Malindi and Watamu marine national parks.

Head further north and you come to the island of Lamu – a beautiful Arab-influenced town which has been something of a travellers' mecca for years and still draws visitors by the thousands. Despite this it retains the very distinctive personality which attracted people to it in the first place – an easy-going unhurried pace, traditional architecture, and a unique culture which owes a great deal to its Muslim roots.

The people of the coast are the Swahili, and it's here that Kiswahili (Swahili) – the lingua franca of the modern nation – evolved as a means of communication between the local inhabitants and the Arab traders who first began plying their dhows up and down this coast sometime before the 7th century. Other influences also shaped the language and there is a smattering of not only Arabic but also Portuguese, Hindi and English words.

History

The first traders here appear to have been Arabs from the Persian Gulf who sailed south along the coast during the north-east monsoon, sailing home north with the south-west monsoon. By the 12th century some substantial settlements had developed, mainly on islands such as Lamu, Manda, Pemba and Zanzibar, as these provided greater security than the coast itself. The main export trade in this early part was in ivory, tortoiseshell and leopard skins, while items such as glass beads from India and porcelain from as far afield as China were finding their way here.

From the 12th to the 15th centuries settlements grew and a dynasty was established at Kilwa (in present-day Tanzania). By the end of this period Mombasa, Malindi and Paté (in the Lamu archipelago) were all substantial towns. The inhabitants were largely Arab but there were also significant numbers of African labourers. Intermarriage was common and, culturally, the settlements were more closely connected with the Islamic Persian Gulf than they were with inland Kenya. Although all these city-states had this common heritage and cultural link, they were all virtually independent and were often vying with one another for power.

So preoccupied were they with their own internal struggles that the coastal centres were quite unprepared for the arrival of the Portuguese in 1498. Before long they were paying tribute to the Portuguese and by 1506 the Portuguese had sacked and gained control of the entire coast. In the century which followed, the Portuguese had raided

KENYA

Mombasa on two further occasions and built the beautiful defensive Fort Jesus in that city.

Trade was the main interest of the Portuguese and they concentrated their activities in that area. They did not exercise direct control over the administration of the coastal cities – just kept them in line and dependent.

Not all the locals were happy with this arrangement and trouble started for the Portuguese with local uprisings in the 17th century. They were mainly inspired by the disaffected Sheikh Yusuf of Mombasa, who spent most of his time in conflict with the Portuguese, and in fact occupied Fort Jesus in Mombasa after murdering the Portuguese commandant there in 1631. With the help of the sultans of Oman, the Portuguese were defeated and Fort Jesus occupied by 1698.

The Omani dynasties flourished and Mombasa and Paté became the pre-eminent spots on the coast, although both were defeated by Lamu in 1810. The internecine struggles of the various Omani factions led to Zanzibar coming into ascendancy, which in turn led the rulers of Mombasa to seek British assistance. The British, however, were reluctant to intervene and jeopardise their alliance with Seyyid Said, the Omani ruler, as their route to India passed close to Muscat. Before long the whole coast was under the control of the Omani ruler.

It was in this period of Omani rule that the slave trade flourished. Up until this time it had been carried out only on a small scale, but soon the newly established clove plantations on Zanzibar required labourers, and from there slaves were shipped to the Persian Gulf and beyond. It was also this increase in economic activity that brought the first Indian and European traders into the area. Trade agreements were made with the Americans (1833), the British (1839) and the French (1844), and exports to India also flourished – ivory, cloves, hides and coconut oil were all important. This increase in trade led Seyyid Said to transfer his capital from Muscat to Zanzibar in 1840, and decreased his reliance on the slave trade for revenue. He was thus able to sign a treaty banning the export of slaves to the Middle East.

Despite the fact that the British East Africa Company took over administration of the interior of the country, a 10-mile-wide (16-km-wide) coastal strip was recognised as the sultan's patch and it was leased from him in 1887, first for a 50-year period and then permanently. In 1920 the coastal strip became the British protectorate, the rest of the country having become a fully fledged British colony.

Mombasa

Mombasa is the largest port on the coast of East Africa. It has a population of nearly half a million of which about 70% are African, the rest being mainly Asian with a small minority of Europeans. Its docks not only serve Kenya, but also Uganda, Rwanda, Burundi and eastern Zaïre. The bulk of the town sprawls over Mombasa Island which is connected to the mainland by an artificial causeway which carries the rail and road links. In recent years Mombasa has spread onto the mainland both north and south of the island.

Large Mombasa may be but, like Dar es Salaam in Tanzania to the south, it has retained its low-level traditional character and there are few high-rise buildings except in the very centre of the city. The Old Town between the massive, Portuguese-built Fort Jesus and the old dhow careening dock remains much the same as it was in the mid-19th century, asphalt streets and craft shops apart. It's a hot and steamy town, as you might expect being so close to the equator, but an interesting place to visit.

History

Mombasa's history goes back to at least the 12th century when it was described by Arab chroniclers as being a small town and the residence of the King of the Zenj – Arabic for black Africans. It later became an important settlement for the Shirazis and remained so until the arrival of the Portuguese in the early 16th century. Determined to destroy the

Arab monopoly over maritime trade in the Indian Ocean, especially with regard to spices, the Portuguese, under Dom Francisco de Almeida, attacked Mombasa with a fleet of 23 ships in 1505. After 1½ days it was all over and the town was burnt to the ground. So great was the quantity of loot that much of it had to be left behind, for fear of overloading the ships, when the fleet sailed for India.

The town was quickly rebuilt and it wasn't long before it regained its commanding position over trade in the area, but peace didn't last long. In 1528, another Portuguese fleet under Nuña da Cunha arrived on the East African coast too late to catch the southwestern monsoon which would take them to India, so they were forced to look around for temporary quarters. Naturally, Mombasa was in no mood to welcome them but, unfortunately, Mombasa was at that time engaged in bitter disputes with the kings of Malindi, Pemba and Zanzibar. An alliance was patched together and the Portuguese were again able to take Mombasa, but sickness and constant skirmishing over many months eventually decided the outcome. The city was again burnt to the ground and the Portuguese sailed for India.

The Portuguese finally made a bid for permanency in 1593 with the construction of Fort Jesus, but in 1631 they were massacred to the last person in an uprising by the townspeople. The following year a Portuguese fleet was sent from Goa and Muscat to avenge the killings but was unable to retake the town. By this time, however, the Mombasan ruler had decided that further resistance was useless and, having reduced the town to rubble and cut down all the fruit trees and palms, he withdrew to the mainland. It was reoccupied without a fight by the Portuguese the following year. Portuguese hegemony in the Indian Ocean was on the wane by this time, not only because of corruption and nepotism within Portuguese ranks, but because of Dutch, French and English activity in India and South-East Asia.

The 17th century also saw the rise of

KENYA

Oman as a naval power and it was the Omanis who, in 1698, were the next to drive the Portuguese from Mombasa after a 33-month siege in which all the defenders were slaughtered. Even this disaster wasn't enough to convince the Portuguese that their days were over and Mombasa was reoccupied. However, the end finally came in 1729 following an invasion by an Arab fleet, a general uprising of the population in which Portuguese settlers were slaughtered, and an abortive counteroffensive which involved the entire military resources of the viceroyalty of Goa.

In 1832 the Sultan of Oman moved his capital from Muscat to Zanzibar and from then until Kenya's independence in 1963 the red flag of Zanzibar fluttered over Fort Jesus. Meanwhile, the British became active along the East African coast. In their attempts to suppress the slave trade, they interfered increasingly in the affairs of Zanzibar until, in 1895, the British East Africa protectorate was set up with Mombasa as the capital (until it was moved to Nairobi) and the Sultan of Oman's possessions were administered as a part of it. When independence came, the Sultan's coastal possessions were attached to the new republic.

During the protectorate years the British confirmed Mombasa's status as East Africa's most important port by constructing a railway from Mombasa to Uganda. It was completed in 1901 using indentured labourers from Gujarat and Punjab in India – hence the origin of Kenya's (and Uganda's and Tanzania's) Asian population.

Orientation

The heart of Mombasa is Digo Rd/Nyerere Ave off which three main roads – Moi Ave, Haile Selassie Rd and Jomo Kenyatta Ave – branch north-west and a fourth – Nkrumah Rd – branches south-east towards the Old Town. The railway station is approximately in the centre of the island at the end of Haile Selassie Rd whereas most of the bus companies have their terminals along Kenyatta Ave.

Maps The best map you can buy of Mombasa is the Survey of Kenya's *Mombasa Island & Environs*, last published in 1977. Many of the street names have changed, but little else.

Information

Tourist Office The regional tourist office (☎ 311231) is just past the famous tusks on Moi Ave and is open Monday to Friday from 9 am to noon and 2 to 4.30 pm, and on Saturdays from 9 am to noon. It stocks very few leaflets but the staff are friendly and helpful and will ring up places free of charge to check on tariffs, visa requirements or whatever, but they do tend to be geared to big spenders – mainly those who want to stay at a beach resort hotel – as opposed to budget travellers.

It's worth picking up a copy of the free monthly *Kenya Coast Tourist Guide* which is available from major hotels, travel agencies and car hire companies. It contains listings of virtually all the hotels, restaurants, discos, water-sports outfits and bus companies in Mombasa and along the coast as well as feature articles about particular places. Beware of what is said about any place in these articles since the glowing praise is clearly focused on securing their continued advertising.

Embassies As Mombasa is an important port and tourism town, a number of countries maintain diplomatic offices here. See the Embassies section in the Kenya Facts for the Visitor chapter for details.

Money The branch of Barclays Bank on Moi Ave, 250m west of the Digo Rd/Moi Ave junction, is open Monday to Friday from 9 am to 3 pm (4.30 pm for forex transactions) and on the first and last Saturday of the month from 9 to 11 am. There are also a number of foreign exchange bureaus (forex) which include Pwani Forex Bureau on Digo Rd opposite the main market and the Fort Jesus Forex Bureau right in front of the entrance to the fort. They're both open Monday to Saturday from 8 am to 5 pm. The exchange rates are generally slightly lower

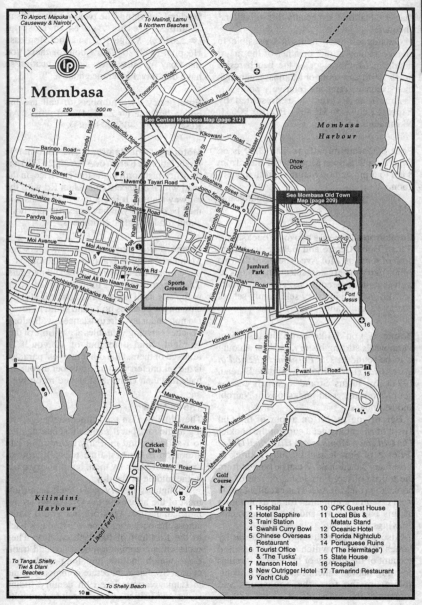

Mombasa

0   250   500 m

See Central Mombasa Map (page 212)

Mombasa Harbour

Dhow Dock

See Mombasa Old Town Map (page 209)

To Airport, Mapuka
Causeway & Nairobi

To Malindi, Lamu
& Northern Beaches

Jomo Kenyatta Avenue
Tononoka Road
Kisauni Road
Tom Mboya Avenue
Mwabundu Road
Gatundu Road
Baringo Road
Mvuleka Rd
Maza Road
Miji Kenda Street
Mwembe Tayari Road
Haile Selasse Road
Machakos Street
Pandya Road
Moi Avenue
Moi Avenue
Sautiya Kenya Rd
Chief Ali Bin Naam Road
Archbishop Makarios Road
Khan Rd
Baluu
Shibu Rd
Kikowani   Road
Kademye St
Blashera Street
Jomo Kenyatta Ave
Msanifu   Kombo St
Digo Road
Makadara Rd
Abdel Nasser Road
Nkrumah   Road
Nyerere   Avenue
Sports Grounds
Jumhuri Park
Fort Jesus

Mnazi Moja Road
Mbaraki Road
Nyerere   Avenue
Mbuyuni Road
Kimathi   Avenue
Kaunda Avenue
Kayanda Road
Pwani   Road
Vanga ~ Road
Mathenge Road
Kaunda~
Avenue
Prince Andrew Road
Mwembe Road
Mama Ngina Drive
Cricket Club
Oceanic Road
Golf Course
Mama Ngina Drive

*Kilindini
Harbour*

Likoni Ferry

To Tanga, Shelly,
Tiwi & Diani
Beaches

To Shelly Beach

1	Hospital	
2	Hotel Sapphire	
3	Train Station	
4	Swahili Curry Bowl	
5	Chinese Overseas	
	Restaurant	
6	Tourist Office	
	& 'The Tusks'	
7	Manson Hotel	
8	New Outrigger Hotel	
9	Yacht Club	
10	CPK Guest House	
11	Local Bus &	
	Matatu Stand	
12	Oceanic Hotel	
13	Florida Nightclub	
14	Portuguese Ruins	
	('The Hermitage')	
15	State House	
16	Hospital	
17	Tamarind Restaurant	

than in Nairobi, especially for travellers' cheques.

Outside of these hours it's possible to change money at one or other of the major hotels in Mombasa or at the beach resort hotels north and south of Mombasa, although their exchange rates are relatively poor.

American Express is represented by Express Kenya (☎ 312461), PO Box 90631, Nkrumah Rd.

Post & Communications The GPO is on Digo Rd and is open Monday to Friday from 8 am to 6 pm and on Saturday from 9 am to noon.

The telephone area code for Mombasa is 011.

Bookshops There are two main bookshops: Bahati Book Centre and Bahari Bookshop, both of them on Moi Ave. These are the two which carry the greatest selection of stock as well as stationery requisites. There are others on Nkrumah Rd but they sell mainly school textbooks and stationery.

Books If you'd like more details about Mombasa's stirring history, the best account is to be found in *The Portuguese Period in East Africa* (East African Literature Bureau, 1971), by Justus Strandes, which can be bought in most good bookshops in Nairobi and Mombasa.

Before you set off on a tour of the Old Town of Mombasa get a copy of the booklet *The Old Town Mombasa: A Historical Guide* (Friends of Fort Jesus), by Judy Aldrick & Rosemary Macdonald. It can be bought from the tourist office, Fort Jesus, or one of the bookshops on Moi Ave. This excellent guide is an essential companion for an exploration of this part of town and has photographs, drawings and a map.

Also well worth buying is *Fort Jesus* by James Kirkman, which gives a detailed account of the history of the Fort, as well as pointing out the salient features. It is available from the fort, the bookshops and sometimes the tourist office.

Medical Services The two best hospitals in Mombasa are the Aga Khan Hospital (☎ 226182), Vanga Rd, and the Mombasa Hospital (☎ 312099). At both of these you must pay for all services and medication so have that travel insurance handy.

Emergency Two numbers to call are the police hot line (☎ 222121) and Africa Air Rescue (☎ 312405, 24 hours).

Motoring Organisations The Automobile Association of Kenya or AAA (☎ 26778) has its office just north of the tourist office on the road which connects Aga Khan Rd with the railway station. It has a few road maps and may be of use if you have specific questions about road or traffic conditions.

Dangers & Annoyances A few years ago Mombasa acquired a bad reputation as a place for snatch-and-run thieves and muggers. That era now appears to have passed as far as the city itself is concerned but it is still the case on the beaches north and south of town. Do not, under any circumstances, walk along beaches carrying valuables at any time of day or night. Nine times out of 10 you'll be relieved of them. One other thieves' paradise is the Likoni ferry where a number of tourists have had their cameras snatched recently.

The Old Town

The Old Town isn't as immediately interesting as the fort, but it's still a fascinating area to wander around in. Early morning or late afternoon is the best time to walk around; there's more activity then, but it's very quiet in the middle of the day.

Though its history goes back centuries, most of the houses in the Old Town are no more than 100 years old but you'll come across the occasional one which dates back to the first half of the 19th century. They represent a combination of styles and traditions which include the long-established coastal Swahili architecture commonly found in Lamu, various late-19th century Indian styles and British colonial architecture with

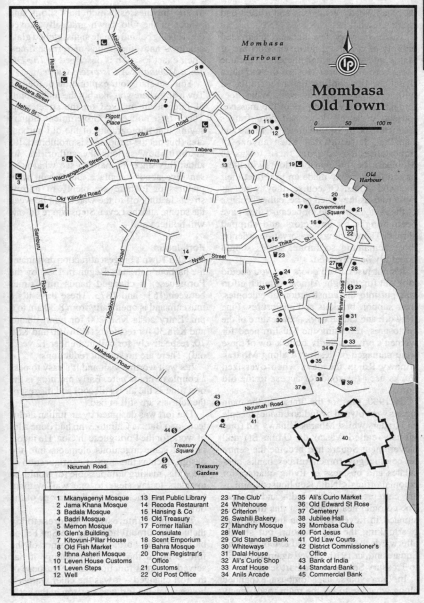

Mombasa Harbour

Mombasa
Old Town

0   50   100 m

Old
Harbour

Mombasa Harbour

Pigott Place

Biashara Street

Nehru St

Kuze Road

Mzizima Road

Kitui Road

Tabere

Mwea

Wachangamwe Street

Old Kilindini Road

Samburu Road

Kibokoni Road

Makadara Road

Nkrumah Road

Nkrumah Road

Treasury Square

Treasury Gardens

Government Square

Thika St

Nyeri Street

Ndia Kuu

Mbarak Hinawy Road

1 Mkanyagenyi Mosque	13 First Public Library	23 'The Club'	35 Ali's Curio Market
2 Jama Khana Mosque	14 Recoda Restaurant	24 Whitehouse	36 Old Edward St Rose
3 Badala Mosque	15 Hansing & Co	25 Criterion	Cemetery
4 Badri Mosque	16 Old Treasury	26 Swahili Bakery	37 Old Edward St Rose
5 Memon Mosque	17 Former Italian	27 Mandhry Mosque	38 Jubilee Hall
6 Glen's Building	Consulate	28 Well	39 Mombasa Club
7 Kitovuni-Pillar House	18 Scent Emporium	29 Old Standard Bank	40 Fort Jesus
8 Old Fish Market	19 Bahra Mosque	30 Whiteways	41 Old Law Courts
9 Ithna Asheri Mosque	20 Dhow Registrar's	31 Dalal House	42 District Commissioner's
10 Leven House Customs	Office	32 Ali's Curio Shop	Office
11 Leven Steps	21 Customs	33 Arcaf House	43 Bank of India
12 Well	22 Old Post Office	34 Anils Arcade	44 Standard Bank
			45 Commercial Bank

its broad, shady verandahs and glazed and shuttered windows.

There are very few houses constructed entirely of coral rag, however. Most are of wattle and daub though they may include coral here and there. Most of the old palm thatch or tile roofing has been replaced with corrugated iron as well. What does remain are many examples of the massive, intricately carved doors and door frames characteristic of Swahili houses in Lamu and Zanzibar. It seems that when anyone of importance moved from these towns to Mombasa they brought their doors with them or had them newly made up to reflect their financial status. Of course, they're not as numerous as they used to be, either because of the ravages of time, or because they have been bought by collectors and shipped abroad. There is now a preservation order on those remaining so further losses should hopefully be prevented.

It's not just carved doors that you should look out for, though. Almost as much effort was put into the construction of balconies, their support brackets and enclosures. Fine fretwork and lattice work are a feature of the enclosures, reflecting the Muslim need for women's privacy. Sadly, quite a few of these were damaged or destroyed along Mbarak Hinawy Rd in the days when oversized trucks used the road for access to the old port.

By 1900, most of the houses in the main streets were owned by Indian businesspeople and traders whilst Mbarak Hinawy Rd (previously called Vasco da Gama St) and Government Square had become the centre for colonial government offices, banks, consulates and business or living quarters for colonial officials. Ndia Kuu housed immigrant entrepreneurs from India and Europe. The colonial headquarters at this time were situated in Leven House on the waterfront overlooking the old harbour, but shortly afterwards they were moved to Government Square and, in 1910, moved again up the hill to Treasury Square above Fort Jesus.

In later years, as Mombasa expanded along what are today the main roads, many

of the businesses which had shops and offices in the Old Town gradually moved out, leaving behind ornate signs, etched glass windows and other relics of former times. Their exact location is described in *The Old Town Mombasa: A Historical Guide*.

You can start your exploration of the Old Town anywhere you like but the main points of interest are marked on the street map. There is a notice in Government Square saying that photography of the old harbour area (but not the buildings) is prohibited. It's doubtful how serious the authorities are about this since it's hard to see what is so sensitive about the place, but if you want pictures of it there are plenty of narrow streets leading off to the waterfront between the square and the Leven Steps where no-one will bother you.

Fort Jesus

The Old Town's biggest attraction dominates the harbour entrance. Begun in 1593 by the Portuguese, it changed hands nine times between 1631 and 1875. These days it's a museum and is open daily from 8.30 am to 6 pm. Entry costs KSh 200 for nonresidents and KSh 30 for residents (KSh 100 and KSh 10, respectively, for children under 12 years old). There are no student reductions.

It's well worth a visit and it's easy to pass a couple of hours here. Early morning is the best time as the air is still cool and the rest of the tourists are still in bed.

The fort was designed by an Italian architect, Joao Batista Cairato, who had done a lot of work for the Portuguese in Goa. He incorporated some ingenious elements into the design, such as the angular configuration of the walls, making it impossible for would-be invaders to lay siege to one wall without being sitting ducks for soldiers in one of the other walls.

The most interesting features today include the **Omani house** in the San Felipe bastion in the north-western corner of the fort. Built in the late 18th century it has served different functions as the purpose of the fort changed – it was the chief warder's house when the fort was a prison in the early

20th century. The view of the Old Town from the roof here is excellent.

The **museum** along the southern wall is built over what was the barracks rooms for the garrison. The exhibits are mostly ceramics but include other interesting odds and ends which have either been donated from private collections or dug up from various sites along the coast. The origins of many of the pieces are a reflection of the variety of cultures which has influenced the coastal culture – Chinese, Indian, Portuguese and Persian. Also displayed in the museum are finds from the Portuguese frigate *Santo António de Tanná* which sank off the fort during the siege in 1697.

The **western wall** of the fort is probably the most interesting and includes an Omani audience hall (now covered by a second storey but still complete with official inscriptions – and unofficial graffiti) and the Passage of the Arches – a passage cut through the coral giving access to the outer part of the fort, although it was later blocked off.

Harbour Cruises

Those looking for a luxury dhow cruise around the harbour should book a trip with Tamarind Dhow (☎ 229520) by calling direct or through Southern Cross Safaris, A La Carte Centre, Ratna Square (☎ 471948). This is a superb way of seeing the harbour, the Old Town and Fort Jesus from the water to the accompaniment of a gourmet meal, cocktails and a live band. You can even dance if you can still move after the meal! The food is excellent and prepared by chefs from the restaurant of the same name. The dhow itself is a motorised, ocean-going boat with an upper and main deck. The cruise, which starts from the jetty below the Tamarind Restaurant, takes you first down the harbour to Fort Jesus and then back up the harbour under Nyali Bridge, where it anchors for about an hour before returning to the jetty. There are two trips a day: the lunch-time cruise at 12.30 pm (two hours, cold seafood buffet, US$22) and the evening cruise at 6.30 pm (four hours, hot seafood or steak dinner, complimentary cocktail, US$65).

Prices include transport to and from your hotel.

A different type of dhow trip can be done with Kenya Marineland (☎ 485248) which is situated at Mtwapa Creek, some way up the coast going north. To join this trip you will be picked up from your hotel and taken to Kenya Marineland. After a tour of the Marineland you set sail for the open sea, weather permitting, and then return to Mtwapa Creek for lunch at the waterside restaurant. After lunch you set sail again up Mtwapa Creek finally returning to Kenya Marineland. On the return journey you will be entertained by acrobats, fire-eaters and limbo dancers. The trip lasts approximately four hours and costs KSh 1250 per person including transfer to and from your hotel, a barbecue lunch and entrance fees to the Marineland park, aquarium and snake farm.

There's also another outfit called Jahazi Marine Ltd (☎ 472213) which offers nighttime dhow cruises on Monday and Thursday for US$65. The price includes a sundowner cruise, with a cocktail, past Mombasa Old Town and the fort, a barbecue at Bamburi Nature Park, a torch-lit safari through the park, a visit to the casino and the Bora Bora Nightclub and transfers to and from your hotel.

Places to Stay

There's a lot of choice for budget travellers and for those who want something slightly better, both in the centre of the city and on the mainland to the north and south. Accommodation up and down the coast from Mombasa Island itself is dealt with later in this chapter.

Places to Stay – bottom end

One of the cheapest places to stay and just about habitable is the *Cozy Guest House* (☎ 313064), on Haile Selassie Rd, though we have had reports that women get hassled here. Singles/doubles cost KSh 260/400 with shared facilities. All the rooms have fans but due to chronic water problems the toilets can stink. The guesthouse will most likely be full if you get there late in the day.

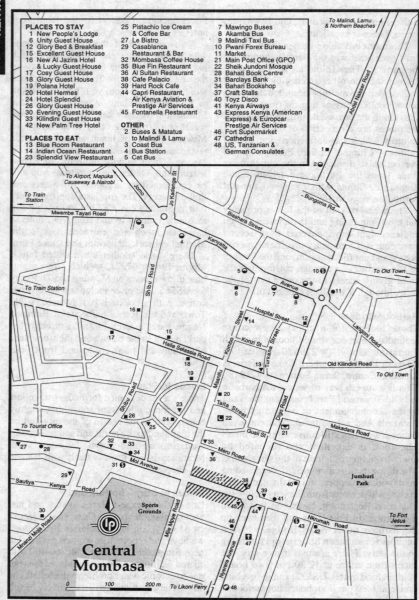

PLACES TO STAY
1 New People's Lodge
6 Unity Guest House
12 Glory Bed & Breakfast
15 Excellent Guest House
16 New Al Jazira Hotel
    & Lucky Guest House
17 Cosy Guest House
18 Glory Guest House
19 Polana Hotel
20 Hotel Hermes
24 Hotel Splendid
26 Glory Guest House
30 Evening Guest House
33 Kilindini Guest House
42 New Palm Tree Hotel

PLACES TO EAT
13 Blue Room Restaurant
14 Indian Ocean Restaurant
23 Splendid View Restaurant

25 Pistachio Ice Cream
    & Coffee Bar
27 Le Bistro
29 Casablanca
    Restaurant & Bar
32 Mombasa Coffee House
35 Blue Fin Restaurant
36 Al Sultan Restaurant
38 Cafe Palacio
39 Hard Rock Cafe
44 Capri Restaurant,
    Air Kenya Aviation &
    Prestige Air Services
45 Fontanella Restaurant

OTHER
2 Buses & Matatus
   to Malindi & Lamu
3 Coast Bus
4 Bus Station
5 Cat Bus

7 Mawingo Buses
8 Akamba Bus
9 Malindi Taxi Bus
10 Pwani Forex Bureau
11 Market
21 Main Post Office (GPO)
22 Sheik Jundoni Mosque
28 Bahati Book Centre
34 Bahari Bookshop
37 Craft Stalls
40 Toyz Disco
41 Kenya Airways
43 Express Kenya (American
    Express) & Europcar
    Prestige Air Services
46 Fort Supermarket
47 Cathedral
48 US, Tanzanian &
    German Consulates

Central Mombasa

Close by on Shibu Rd are the *New Al Jazira Hotel* and the *Lucky Guest House* (☎ 220895) which have singles/doubles with shared bath (no fans) for KSh 150/300. If you choose the Lucky then don't be too surprised if you have to wake up the staff on arrival. The entire lot of them were fast asleep when we arrived one day at 11 am.

Right in the centre of town on Digo Rd at the junction with Hospital Rd is the newly opened *Glory Bed & Breakfast* (☎ 314557) which has clean singles/doubles for KSh 400/500 with shared bathroom facilities. The price includes breakfast. Don't confuse this hotel with the two branches of the Glory Guest House, which are more expensive, or with the Glory Hotel Annexe at the back of the Casablanca, off Mnazi Moja Rd, which is basically a brothel. The name 'Glory' has proliferated around Mombasa in the last few years like mushrooms after rain.

Also good value in this range and convenient for the city centre is the *Evening Guest House* (☎ 221380), Mnazi Moja Rd, which has simple but very clean rooms at KSh 310 a single with shared bathroom facilities and KSh 410/500 for singles/doubles with attached bathroom. All the rooms have a fan and the hotel has its own restaurant. Reception is in the courtyard through the restaurant.

Around the corner from the Evening Guest House is the *Glory Hotel Annexe*. The rooms here are acceptable and include clean bedding, a fan and a washbasin, and the communal showers and toilets are scrubbed out regularly but it's basically a brothel. The price for a room varies but assume KSh 500 a double.

Another budget hotel at the northern end of the city centre, and one which has been popular for years, is the *New People's Lodge* (☎ 312831), on Abdel Nasser Rd right next to where the buses leave for Malindi and Lamu. Some travellers rate this place very highly and it certainly compares very well in price with the others but it is a little tatty and the rooms which face onto the main road are very noisy. The air also stinks of diesel fumes because bus drivers always rev their engines for up to an hour before they actually leave.

The management is friendly, and gear left in the rooms is safe. Rooms cost KSh 103/287 a single/double with shared showers and toilets, and KSh 235/414 a single/double with private facilities. There are also three, four and five-bed rooms with shared facilities. All the rooms have fans, the sheets are clean and the water in the showers is generally lukewarm. It's a large place and is rarely full. There's also a good, cheap restaurant downstairs.

Not far from the tourist office and similar in price to the other budget hotels is the quiet *Kilindini Guest House* off Shibu Rd.

Unless you just want a doss-house or are simply desperate then give the *Hydro Hotel*, Digo Rd at the Kenyatta Ave junction, the *Down Town Lodge*, Hospital Rd, the *Visitor's Inn*, corner of Haile Selassie and Shibu Rds, and the *Mvita Hotel*, corner of Hospital and Turkana Sts, a miss. The Mvita, in particular, has been allowed to decay into an appalling state of repair but, more importantly, it has become a hang-out for thieves who will not only break into your room but set you up for a mugging once you go outside. The management will not lift a finger to help you if this happens and the police are even less cooperative.

Places to Stay – middle

At the very bottom end of this category, but really good value and with a friendly manager, is the *Excellent Guest House* (☎ 311744) on Haile Selassie Rd. It offers bed and breakfast in rooms with bathrooms, mosquito nets, towel, soap, toilet paper and fans for KSh 700/900 for singles/doubles. All the rooms have a balcony and they're very well maintained.

Slightly more expensive is the *Hotel Splendid* (☎ 220967) on Msanifu Kombo St, a large place which is rarely full. It's a bit of a dive and far from splendid but it's relatively clean and has singles/doubles with attached bathrooms for KSh 800/950. The prices include breakfast. It's an old place and there's a popular rooftop restaurant which gets sea breezes in the evenings.

Better value and more modern but in a

somewhat less congenial part of town is the *Unity Guest House* (☎ 221298) just off Msanifu Kombo St. Singles with shared bathroom facilities cost KSh 400 and doubles/triples with own bathroom cost KSh 700/1125. There are also doubles with attached bathrooms, with air-con for KSh 1500. Prices include breakfast. It's a Muslim hotel so there's no bar and alcoholic drinks are prohibited.

Another well-maintained hotel in this category is the *Hotel Hermes* (☎ 313599) on Msanifu Kombo St near the Sheik Jundoni Mosque. The rooms are pleasant and most of them overlook the street but, because it's such good value for money, it's often full. Doubles (no singles) with attached bathrooms and air-con cost KSh 900 including breakfast.

Slightly further afield is the *Glory Guest House* (☎ 313204) on Shibu Rd. The rooms are a bit on the small side but are spotlessly clean and well maintained. Singles/doubles with attached bathrooms with fan cost KSh 600/800 plus there are singles/doubles with air-con for KSh800/1000. They also have a few singles/doubles with shared bathroom facilities for KSh 400/700. Breakfast is included in the price. There is a branch of this hotel on Haile Selassie Rd which offers bed and breakfast for KSh 400/700 with shared bathroom facilities and KSh 500/800 for singles/doubles with attached bathrooms. The standards at the two hotels are much the same.

Top value in this range is the *New Palm Tree Hotel* (☎ 312169), on Nkrumah Rd. All the rooms here are on the 1st and 2nd floor surrounding a spacious courtyard furnished with tables and chairs. A comfortable, spotlessly clean room with attached bathroom and fan costs KSh 897/1170 a single/double including breakfast. The staff are friendly and helpful, you can leave gear safely in the rooms and the hotel has its own bar (cheap, cold beers) and restaurant (tasty food at a reasonable price). It's popular with travellers.

Places to Stay – top end

One of the cheaper top-end hotels is the modern *Manson Hotel* (☎ 222356), on Kisumu Rd. It has 84 rooms with attached bathrooms which cost KSh 900/1200 a single/double without air-con and KSh 1300/1500 with air-con. Prices include breakfast. The hotel has a restaurant (exclusively vegetarian food) but no bar.

Similar in price and also some distance from the centre but close to the railway station, is the new *Hotel Sapphire* (☎ 491657) on Mwembe Tayari Rd. All the rooms have attached bathroomswith air-con and cost KSh 1800/2500 for singles/doubles, KSh 3300 for triples, all including breakfast. Facilities include the Mehfil Restaurant which serves Mughlai and continental dishes.

Much more centrally situated in the heart of the city is the brand new *Polana Hotel* (☎ 222168), Maungano Rd, close to the junction of Haile Selassie Rd and Msanifu Kombo St. It's a huge modern hotel with 140 rooms all of them fully air-con with bath, shower, mini-bar, TV (including CNN) and international direct-dial telephones. Singles/doubles including breakfast cost KSh 1930/2910. Facilities include a restaurant, bar, laundry service and in-house parking.

Superbly located overlooking the Indian Ocean and with a range of amenities which include Indian, Chinese and Italian restaurants, a swimming pool, casino and an open-air bar in a garden setting, is the relatively modern *Oceanic Hotel* (☎ 311191) off Oceanic Rd, not far from the Likoni ferry. Air-con rooms with attached bathrooms in this five-storey hotel cost KSh 1500/1800 a single/double and triples KSh 2100 including breakfast. All the rooms face the sea and most major credit cards are accepted. Considering the price, it's good value and the staff are friendly and helpful. Nonresidents can use the pool for KSh 100 per day.

Top of the range is the *New Outrigger Hotel* (☎ 220822), set in landscaped gardens leading down to Kilindini Harbour on the western side of Mombasa Island. All the rooms have attached bathrooms, with air-con and a balcony facing the harbour. Singles/doubles cost KSh 2300/3300 including breakfast. The hotel is under Belgian management, the cuisine is French and there's a swimming pool.

Places to Eat

Mombasa has a good range of restaurants. If you are putting your own food together, or want to stock up with goodies to take down the coast, the Fort supermarket on Nyerere Ave is well stocked as is Nakumatt on Digo Rd. A wide variety of fruit and vegetables are available in the central market on Digo Rd next to the Hydro Hotel.

Places to Eat – cheap

If you are just looking for fish or chicken with chips try the *Blue Fin Restaurant*, on the corner of Meru Rd and Msanifu Kombo St. There's very little variety but it's not a bad place. There's a better choice at the *Blue Room Restaurant* on Haile Selassie Rd. which is a serve-yourself, fast-food joint offering a whole range of western and Indian staples such as sausages, samosas, pakoras, chips and the like at KSh 30 per piece, as well as burgers from around KSh 100, and pizzas from KSh 150 to KSh 250 depending on toppings. It's very clean, the food is fresh and there's no waiting. It's recommended for an inexpensive breakfast, lunch or late afternoon snack.

Slightly cheaper snacks of the same variety can be found at the *Indian Ocean Restaurant* on Msanifu Kombo St but it also offers lunch-time and evening specials of Swahili and Indian food for around KSh 150 (up to KSh 250 if you want prawns, for example). This restaurant is highly recommended and is open daily from 7 am until 8.30 pm. Specials are chalked up on a blackboard outside the restaurant.

If you're staying at either the Cosy Guest House or the New Al Jazira Hotel, the *Kencoast Cafe* opposite has delicious local dishes at really cheap prices. Service is very friendly.

Recommended for breakfast and snacks is the *Sky Bar & Restaurant* on Moi Ave not far from the tusks. You can eat a main meal here (chicken and chips, for instance) for around KSh 125. Similar is the *Franco Restaurant* just beyond the tusks opposite the tourist office which is open seven days a week and offers buffet lunches and fruit juices at a very reasonable price.

The *Mombasa Coffee House* on Moi Ave is a good place for fresh coffee and snacks, and you can also buy coffee beans here.

Indian Food Since many of the restaurants in Mombasa are Indian-owned you can find excellent curries and thalis and at lunch time (from 12.30 to around 3 pm) there is often a cheap, substantial set meal available.

One such place is the popular *New Chetna Restaurant*, on Haile Selassie Rd directly under the Cozy Guest House. The food here is south Indian vegetarian (with dishes such as masala dosa and idli) and sweets. An all-you-can-eat set vegetarian lunch costs KSh 150.

Excellent tandoori specialities can be found at the very popular *Splendid View Restaurant*, Maungano Rd, which is opposite, but not part of, the Hotel Splendid. Food on offer includes chicken, lamb, fruit juices and lassis and you can eat well here for around KSh 150. There are tables outside and inside. The restaurant is open Monday to Saturday from 11.30 am to 2 pm and 4 to 11.30 pm, and on Sunday from 4.30 to 11.30 pm. It's very popular with local Asians so you know it must be good.

Swahili Food For coastal Swahili dishes made with coconut and coconut milk, the *Swahili Curry Bowl*, on Tangana Rd off Moi Ave, is recommended. Prices are reasonable. It's also one of *the* places for coffee and ice cream. Don't bother trekking out here on a Sunday as it's closed then.

Another excellent place, and one you should try at least once, is the *Recoda Restaurant* on Nyeri St in the Old Town. It's a hugely popular place among the locals and the tables are set up along the footpath. The atmosphere is great and the waiters are keen to explain what is available that day – usually dishes such as beans in coconut, grilled fish, meat, superb chapatis and salad. You may well find yourself coming back here each

KENYA

night. This is a Muslim restaurant so there are no alcoholic drinks and it's closed all day until after sunset during Ramadan.

Places to Eat – more expensive

Going up in price, the rooftop restaurant in the *Hotel Splendid* catches the breeze in the evenings and has surprisingly moderate prices (from KSh 100 for a main meal), though the food is only mediocre. Don't come here with any ideas of having a quick meal, as the service is far from lightning fast.

The new Hotel Sapphire also has the *Mehfil Restaurant* which serves Mughlai and continental dishes as does the *Al Sultan Restaurant* on Meru Rd close to the junction with Msanifu Kombo Rd but the latter is closed for the entire month of Ramadan.

The *Pistachio Ice Cream & Coffee Bar* is a small cafe near the Hotel Splendid. Not only does it have excellent ice cream, but the fruit shakes are great. The buffet lunch or dinner for KSh 150 is not bad value although the selection is limited. À la carte dishes such as spaghetti are also served. It's open daily from 9 am to 10 pm.

For Chinese food you could try the *Chinese Overseas Restaurant* (☎ 221585) on Moi Ave, just north of the tusks on the left-hand side. Main dishes are priced around KSh 250 to KSh 300.

The *Fontanella Restaurant* is in a shady courtyard on the corner of Digo Rd and Moi Ave. The extensive menu runs the whole gamut from fish and chips through steaks to lobster thermidor but it's quite expensive with main dishes ranging from KSh 250 to KSh 350. Consider it something of a splurge unless you're just here for a quiet beer or snack.

For a modest splurge, head for *Le Bistro* (☎ 229470), on Moi Avenue, close to the tusks. This restaurant and cocktail bar is owned and run by the same Swiss Germans who own the Pistacchio and it's open daily from breakfast to late at night. Both the atmosphere and the food, which includes pizza, pasta, steak and seafood, are excellent. Expect to pay around KSh 100 for a starter and from KSh 210 to KSh 300 for a main

dish though there are considerably cheaper snacks such as toasted sandwiches and hamburgers as well as lunch-time specials chalked up on the board outside. Beers are cold and reasonably priced plus there's a fairly extensive wine menu (a bottle of chianti, for instance, costs around KSh 800).

Tasty continental-style food as well as a number of tandoori specialities can be found at the new *Casablanca Restaurant & Bar*, Mnazi Moja Rd, for around KSh 250. It's very popular with westerners and Africans alike and consists of a double-storey, makuti-roofed, open-air bar/restaurant which is open all day until very late. It has an excellent music system, TVs and a disco each evening. It attracts much the same clientele as Buffalo Bill's in Nairobi but the food is streets ahead and there's no hassle plus the beers *are* cold – not lukewarm.

The *Cafe Palacio* (☎ 226149) at the junction of Moi Ave and Digo Rd attempts to be Mombasa's answer to McDonald's and Kentucky Fried Chicken but in this it fails miserably. The chicken is certainly very tender and well cooked but far from hot, the fish is tired and tasteless and the chips are cold and soggy. Worst of all are the so-called 'fruit juices' which are just watered-down synthetic cordial. We didn't try any of the seven varieties of pizza or the doner kebabs – maybe they're better – but you'll reel at the bill which will be around KSh 250 to KSh 300 for what is essentially a very mediocre meal.

Those keen to dine in an atmosphere as far removed from Kenya as anyone could imagine, and to choose from a range of dishes named after famous musicians, should try the *Hard Rock Cafe* (☎ 222221) Nkrumah Rd, next door to Kenya Airways. It's all somewhat contrived and it's nowhere near as well designed as the Nairobi Hard Rock but it's popular with package tourists and local yuppies. Before you go for a meal here you need to be absolutely certain that a constant bombardment of heavy rap music will be conducive to the digestive process. A main course plus a drink will set you back around KSh 400 to KSh 500.

Mombasa's best restaurant by far – at least as far as the island itself is concerned – is the *Capri Restaurant* (☎ 311156), in Ambalal House, Nkrumah Rd, opposite Kenya Airways. Originally set up by a Swiss man and still with a European head chef, the food is superb with a range of continental and seafood dishes as well as a well-stocked cellar of European wines. Nowhere in the island itself compares. It's open daily for lunch and dinner but closed on Sunday and public holidays. Expect to pay around KSh 500 to KSh 600 for a full meal without wine or beer. Attached to this restaurant is the *Hunters' Bar* which is a good place for an ice-cold beer in air-con surroundings as well as somewhat cheaper meals (around KSh 250 to KSh 300 for a main dish) encompassing a range of daily specials. The Hunters' is very popular at lunch times with local office workers. Wildlife conservationists should be aware that the walls of the bar are festooned with hunting trophies from a bygone era and the guy who shot them certainly wasn't a greenie. Even so, the atmosphere is very mellow and the staff are cheerful.

Down on the ground floor of the same building is a branch of the restaurant called the *Arcade Cafe* (open from 8.30 am to 5.30 pm) which serves coffee, fruit juices, milk shakes, pizza, hot dogs, meat pies, sandwiches and ice cream.

Head and shoulders above all the rest is the *Tamarind Restaurant* (☎ 471747) on the foreshore across from the Old Dhow Harbour in Nyali. This is a beautifully conceived, part open-air restaurant in Swahili style and festooned with bougainvillea. The food is superb, the service impeccable and the restaurant is open for lunch and dinner every day. Prices reflect the calibre of the place but it's well worth the splurge. You won't find better seafood anywhere in Kenya. Expect to pay at least KSh 1000 per head and considerably more if you take wine with your meal. Even a beer costs KSh 115 here. It's very popular in the evenings with discerning people who have money to spend.

Entertainment

The best nightclub/disco is the *New Florida Casino & Nightclub* on Mama Ngina Drive. Built right on the seashore and enclosing its own swimming pool, it's owned by the same people who run the Florida clubs in Nairobi. The atmosphere is much the same but here there are three open-air bars as well as an enclosed dancing area. Entry costs KSh 150 for men and KSh 70 for women (slightly more on Friday and Saturday nights) or KSh 50 per person on Sunday afternoon until 8 pm.

If you're looking for a slightly quieter night without the endless booming rap music of the Florida then give *Toyz*, on Baluchi St off Nkrumah Rd, a spin. Entry costs KSh 100 per person, the main part is air-con and there's an upstairs, open-air area where you can get away from the noise. Beers are advertised as costing KSh 60 but, as the night grinds on, they miraculously transform into KSh 70 so keep an eye on your bill.

Things to Buy

While Mombasa isn't the craft entrepôt you might expect it to be, it's still not too bad. The trouble is that there are a lot of tourists and sailors who pass through this port with lots of dollars to shed in a hurry. Bargains, therefore, can take a long time to negotiate. The main craft stall area is along Moi Ave from the roundabout with Nyerere Ave to Msanifu Kombo St. Many specialist craft shops have sprung up in recent years in the Old Town close to Fort Jesus, especially along Mbarak Hinawy Rd and Ndia Kuu.

Along Moi Ave it's mainly makonde woodcarvings, soapstone chess sets and animal or human figurines, basketwork, drums and other musical instruments, and paintings.

Biashara St, which runs west of the Digo Rd intersection, is the centre for fabrics and kangas or kikoi, those colourful, beautifully patterned, wraparound skirts complete with Swahili proverbs, which most East African women (who aren't Hindus) wear even if they wear it under a buibui (black wraparound skirt). You may need to bargain a little over the price (but not too much). What you get is generally what you pay for and, as a rule, they cost around KSh 300 a pair (they are not sold singly). Assuming you are willing to bargain, the price you pay for one will reflect the quality of the cloth. Buy them in Mombasa if possible. You can sometimes get them as cheaply in Nairobi but elsewhere prices escalate rapidly.

Getting There & Away
Air Kenya Airways flies between Nairobi and Mombasa in either direction at least five times daily. Most of these flights are nonstop but some go via Malindi. The fare from Nairobi to either Mombasa or Malindi is KSh 4680 one way. If you're relying on these flights to get back to Nairobi to connect with an international flight, then make absolutely sure you have a confirmed booking or, preferably, go back a day before.

International destinations served from Mombasa are Zanzibar and Kilimanjaro (for Arusha and Moshi). See the Kenya Getting There & Away chapter for details.

Three companies with lighter twin-prop planes operate flights from Mombasa to Malindi and Lamu. They are Air Kenya Aviation (☎ Mombasa 229777), Eagle Aviation Ltd (☎ Mombasa 316054) and Prestige Air Services Ltd (☎ Mombasa 21443). Both Air Kenya and Prestige Air Services have offices on the ground floor of Ambalal House, Nkrumah Rd. Each company has two flights per day in either direction between Mombasa and Lamu (US$85) via Malindi (US$28). The baggage allowance is 15 kg per person on Air Kenya and 10 kg on the other two companies' flights. Most of the time you won't be hassled if your baggage weighs over this amount but, even if you are, excess charges are minimal (KSh 35 per kg).

Air Kenya Aviation also flies south from Mombasa to Ukunda (for Diani Beach) twice a week (US$25).

Bus & Matatu In Mombasa bus offices are mainly along Jomo Kenyatta Ave except for Malindi Bus which is on Abdel Nasser Rd. For buses and matatus to the south of Mombasa you first need to get off the island via the Likoni ferry (see Boat in the later Getting Around section).

Nairobi For Nairobi, there are many departures daily in either direction (mostly in the early morning and late evening) by, among others, Coast, Crossline, Mawingo, Takrim, Tawfiq, Taita, Malindi and Akamba. The fare is KSh 300 and the trip takes from seven to eight hours including a meal break about halfway. Most of these companies have at least four departures daily, usually two in the early morning and two at night, while Malindi Bus has six departures daily at 8.30, 9 and 9.30 am, and 8, 9 and 10 pm.

Safer and more comfortable but more expensive are the shuttle services in either direction run by two companies. They are Sav-Line and The Connection. They both offer air-con, 18-seater minibuses for KSh 900 per person one way which will drop you off anywhere in the two city centres. Bookings for Sav-Line should be made at Savage Camping Tours (☎ 228236), Diamond Trust House, Moi Ave, Nairobi. Bookings with The Connection can be made at Inside Africa Safaris (☎ 223304), Wabera St, Nairobi, and at Tamana Holidays (☎ 315208), Moi Ave, Mombasa.

Malindi To Malindi there are also many departures daily in either direction from early morning until late afternoon by several bus companies and matatus. Buses take up to 2½ hours; matatus about two hours. In Mombasa they all depart from outside the New People's Hotel, Abdel Nasser Rd. See the Malindi section for more details.

It's possible to go straight through from Mombasa to Lamu but most travellers stop en route at Malindi.

Tanzania For Tanga, Dar es Salaam and Morogoro in Tanzania, Hood Bus/Cat Bus has departures three times a week. See the Kenya Getting There & Away chapter for details.

Share-Taxi Shared taxis from Mombasa to Malindi are expensive these days. Assume

KSh 4000 for the car shared between four people. You may occasionally get one for KSh 3500 if you speak Swahili. If you're alone, you can fly for the same amount.

Train Trains to or from Nairobi operate in either direction at 7 pm, arriving the next day at 8.30 am. The fares are KSh 2750 in 1st class and KSh 1930 in 2nd class. Fares include dinner, breakfast and bedding (whether you want them or not). You should make a reservation as far in advance as possible as demand sometimes exceeds supply. The booking office at the station in Mombasa is open daily from 8 am to noon, and 2 to 6.30 pm.

The left-luggage service at the railway station costs KSh 12 per item per day. It's open from 8 am to noon and 2 to 6.30 pm Monday to Saturday, and from 7.30 to 10 am and 2 to 6.30 pm on Sunday.

Boat Depending on the season, it's possible to get a ride on a dhow to Pemba, Zanzibar or Dar es Salaam in Tanzania, but departures are very infrequent; the ferry is much more reliable. See the Kenya Getting There & Away chapter for details.

Getting Around

The Airport Kenya Airways operates a shuttle bus from its Nkrumah Rd office at 10.20 am, and 2.20 and 5.40 pm. There's a regular public bus which goes to the airport and costs a few shillings. Any 'Port Reitz' matatu will take you past the airport turn-off (ask to be dropped off) from where it's about a 15-minute walk. The standard taxi fare is KSh 700 although the initial price starts at KSh 1000.

Taxi Even for short distances, taxi drivers will attempt to charge you whatever they think they can get out of you so you must bargain but, if you're going to spend a lot of time in Mombasa, get down to the New Florida Nightclub outside of which is a board detailing what you should be paying for specific journeys. Otherwise, assume KSh 200 from the railway station to the city centre and

KSh 700 between the city centre and the airport. A 'taxi' can be anything from a well-maintained London cab to a beaten-up old wreck you can't even open the door of and which the police will stop at every opportunity demanding *kitu kidogo* ('a little something').

Car & Motorcycle All the major hire companies and many of the smaller outfits have branch offices in Mombasa. Most of them (such as Avis, Payless and Glory) are on Moi Ave. Europcar is on Nkrumah Rd. Details of hire charges and conditions can be found under Rental Agencies in the Kenya Getting Around chapter.

Boat The Likoni ferry connects Mombasa Island with the southern mainland and runs at frequent intervals throughout the night and day. There's a crossing every 20 minutes on average between 5 am and 12.30 am; less frequently between 12.30 and 5 am. It's free to pedestrians; KSh 17 for a car. To get to the ferry from the centre of town take a Likoni matatu from outside the GPO on Digo Rd.

South of Mombasa

The real attractions of the coast south of Mombasa are the beaches, and although it is basically all resort hotels, there are a few options for the budget traveller – at Tiwi and Diani beaches.

All the beaches are white coral sand and are protected by a coral reef so there is no danger from sharks when you go swimming. Tiwi is probably the best beach since it's less developed though, like Shelly, it suffers from large amounts of floating seaweed, depending on the season. Diani doesn't have this to anywhere near the same extent but in some places much of the sand has been washed away leaving just a coral bed.

SHELLY BEACH
Shelly Beach is the closest beach to Mombasa and as such, is not a bad place to swim if you just want to day-trip from

Mombasa, though, at times, it's like pea soup because of the seaweed problem. There is no budget accommodation available here so forget it for a long stay unless you have plenty of money.

Places to Stay

The cheapest place to stay, but some distance from the beach, is the *CPK Guest House* (☎ (011) 451619) not far from the Likoni ferry. It's a pleasant place, and costs KSh 350 per person with breakfast.

One of the few places to stay on the beach itself (other than renting a holiday let) is the *Shelly Beach Hotel* (☎ (011) 451001), about three km from the Likoni ferry. As far as resort hotels go it's not a bad place, and seems to be popular with British tour groups. Most people seem to prefer swimming in the pool rather than in the sea just a few metres away. Half-board rates are KSh 1400/2000 for singles/doubles, more with air-con. In the off season it should be possible to get a reduction on these rates.

Further south are *Savannah Cottages* (☎ (011) 23456) which have air-con holiday lets with fully equipped kitchens, bathrooms, lounge and dining areas, and double bedrooms with twin-bunk beds.

Getting There & Away

From the Likoni ferry, take the first turn to the left after the bus stand. From here it's a 30-minute walk and there are occasional matatus and enough traffic to make hitching possible. The Shelly Beach Hotel has its own transport into town, but you pay extra for this.

TIWI BEACH

Next along the coast is Tiwi Beach, also about two or three km off the main coast road, along either one of two gravel tracks (only one of which is signposted 'Tiwi') which wind their way through the coastal scrub. This is the best beach to head for if you're on a budget and/or have your own camping gear. It's also the least developed, though there's not much in the way of beachfront which isn't already spoken for.

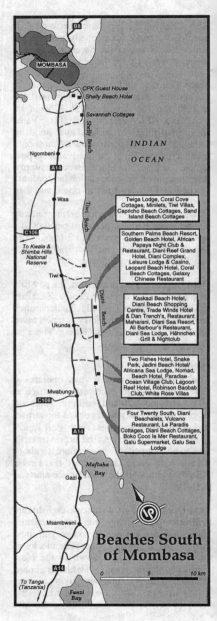

Twiga Lodge, Coral Cove Cottages, Minilets, Tiwi Villas, Capricho Beach Cottages, Sand Island Beach Cottages

Southern Palms Beach Resort, Golden Beach Hotel, African Papaya Night Club & Restaurant, Diani Reef Grand Hotel, Diani Complex, Leisure Lodge & Casino, Leopard Beach Hotel, Coral Beach Cottages, Galaxy Chinese Restaurant

Kaskazi Beach Hotel, Diani Beach Shopping Centre, Trade Winds Hotel & Dan Trench's, Restaurant Maharani, Diani Sea Resort, Ali Barbour's Restaurant, Diani Sea Lodge, Hähnchen Grill & Nightclub

Two Fishes Hotel, Snake Park, Jadini Beach Hotel/ Africana Sea Lodge, Nomad, Beach Hotel, Paradise Ocean Village Club, Lagoon Reef Hotel, Robinson Baobab Club, White Rose Villas

Four Twenty South, Diani Beachalets, Vulcano Restaurant, Le Paradis Cottages, Diani Beach Cottages, Boko Coco le Mer Restaurant, Galu Supermarket, Galu Sea Lodge

Beaches South of Mombasa

0   5   10 km

The good thing here is that the hotels are low key, consisting mainly of individual cottages with a central bar and restaurant appealing to independent travellers. It's a totally different world from the package tourist ghetto of Diani Beach. You'll find the prices also reflect this difference.

The thing which you must do at this beach is book in advance if you intend to stay during the high season (January, April to early July, August to early September and Christmas/New Year), otherwise you may well find them full, although with the current downturn in tourism that is becoming less likely. Even so, it's wise to book ahead for the self-catering lodges at *any* time of year.

The last thing you need to know is that you'll have to bring all your own food and drink if you're staying at a self-catering lodge, though you could, of course, arrange to eat at a lodge which has a restaurant and bar.

From north to south, the hotels are: Sand Island Beach Cottages, Capricho Beach Cottages, Maweni Beach Cottages, Tiwi Villas, Coral Cove Cottages, Twiga Lodge, Minilets and Tiwi Beachalets. Most of these are signposted on the main road.

Activities

Next to the Twiga Lodge is a small outfit called Tiwi Divers, which offers good snorkelling and diving expeditions. Snorkelling is KSh 500 and lasts about two hours. If you just want to snorkel out from the beach, gear can be hired for around KSh 250 per day.

Places to Stay & Eat

Cheapest of the lot (but only by a small margin) is the very popular *Twiga Lodge* (☎ (0127) 51267). It is certainly *the* place to camp along the coast as you can pitch your tent just a few metres from the water plus there's plenty of shade. Camping costs KSh 120 per person, and includes access to good showers and toilets. Single/double rooms go for KSh 500/1000 with breakfast plus there are cottages accommodating four people for KSh 1000 (plus KSh 250 for each extra bed if there are more than four people). There's a restaurant, bar and shop. It's a good place

to stay as there's usually an interesting mix of people here.

Right next door to the Twiga Lodge are the *Coral Cove Cottages* (☎ (0127) 51062). The cottages here are similar in price to those at Twiga Lodge and range from having no facilities to being fully self-contained (complete with cooking equipment). It's a very pleasant place to stay and popular with young expatriate workers.

South of Twiga Lodge are the *Minilets* (☎ (0127) 51059), a collection of small, cottages with attached bathrooms, connected to the beach by a series of paved walkways. Singles/doubles are good value at KSh 600/800, and there's a bar and restaurant. This is a popular place among foreign workers living in Nairobi.

Going further north, *Tiwi Villas* (☎ (0127) 51265) is an attractive complex, on top of a small cliff, with a swimming pool, bar and restaurant. A double cottage here costs KSh 900, and one which sleeps four people KSh 1500.

Further up the coast, the *Capricho Beach Cottages* (☎ (0127) 51231) are a collection of one, two and three-bedroom cottages with lounge/dining room, bathroom, verandah and a full range of cooking equipment. You must provide your own bed linen and mosquito nets, though these can be hired with advance notice. A two-person cottage ranges from KSh 1345 in the off season to KSh 1450 in the high season. A cottage sleeping six people ranges from KSh 2460 to KSh 3000. The complex has its own swimming pool.

Beyond here, the *Sand Island Beach Cottages* (☎ (0127) 51233) is another group of self-catering cottages similar to those at Capricho which range in price between KSh 1345 and KSh 1440 for two people, up to KSh 2457 and KSh 3475 for six people, depending on the season. Bed linen and mosquito nets must be brought with you unless arranged in advance.

Getting There & Away

The buses and matatus drop you at the start of the gravel access road, from where it's a three-km (45-minute) walk. This road is notorious for muggings so, unless you're part of a group (in which case you can assume you're safe), wait for a lift. There are no buses or matatus but quite a few cars so you shouldn't have to wait long. Taxis also run between the beach and highway.

DIANI BEACH

Diani is a package-tourist hotel/resort complex. If you're an independent traveller looking for a patch of authentic Kenyan coast and a mellow atmosphere, chances are you'll hate it here. The promotional literature looks very alluring and the architecture can be very imaginative but the clientele is dreadful. Lobotomised European wage slaves on day release wouldn't be too far from the truth.

At least, that's the story as far as the tarmac stretches at the back of this beachfront development. Further south, it does change and you get back into something resembling the Kenyan coast before the 'developers' decided to recreate the Costa Lotta. It's in this area that you'll find Dan Trench's, the only budget accommodation on this part of the coast.

As at Tiwi beach, it's a good idea to make advance booking for any of the cheaper places at Diani during the high season otherwise you'll find them full, though some sort of accommodation can usually be found at any time at Dan Trench's.

Information

The village of Ukunda on the main Mombasa to Tanzania highway is the turn-off point for Diani Beach. It's here you'll find the nearest post office plus a number of basic lodging houses. From here a tarmac road runs about two km down to a T-junction with the beach road which runs several km in either direction north and south. Along this beach road is everything which Diani has to offer.

Dangers & Annoyances

Do not walk along the road from Ukunda to the beach road. It's notorious for muggings. Avoiding walking is no problem as there are plenty of matatus (and KBS buses) running

backwards and forwards all day on their way to or from Likoni. Similarly, don't walk along the beach from Diani to Tiwi. The place where you cross the creek that divides the two is known locally as Machete Point, and many travellers have been done over here. If you do decide to walk, make sure it is at low tide, as the creek crossing is quite deep at high tide and you'll need to swim across.

Places to Stay – bottom end

The only cheap place is *Dan Trench's* (PO Box 8, Ukunda), behind the Trade Winds Hotel. It's not signposted, but if you turn off when you see the sign for the Trade Winds, it's on the right before you get to the Trade Winds entrance gate. This place is well set up for budget travellers and there's a range of accommodation options. Camping costs KSh 150 per person per night (no tents for hire), and there are single/double rooms at KSh 250 per person per night. There's also a few apartments with kitchen, bathroom, lounge and verandah at KSh 600 per day. It's a mellow place, and there are no security problems. If you're staying here you can use the beach and bar at the Trade Winds Hotel.

Places to Stay – middle

The only places in this category, and even these are not cheap, are the lodges and cottages south of the tarmac on the beach road.

At the southern end, after two km of pot-holed dirt road, is the *Galu Sea Lodge*, a pleasant two-storey building with a swimming pool. Next, heading north, you come to the Galu supermarket then the Boko Boko Coco le Mer Restaurant followed by the *Diani Beach Cottages* (☎ (0127) 3471) at US$55/75 for singles/doubles with half board. All major credit cards are accepted.

Next up are *Le Paradis Cottages*, the Vulcano Restaurant and *Diani Beachalets* (☎ (0127) 2180). At the latter, there's a range of rooms, with attached bathrooms, ranging from KSh 1050 in the high season (KSh 750 in the low season) for one bedroom, up to KSh 1600 in the high season (KSh 1250 in the low season) for four bedrooms, all plus 17% tax.

Further north still, at the beginning of the tarmac, is the popular *Four Twenty South* (☎ (0127) 2065). Here there are a number of different cottages which cost from KSh 1200 a double in the high season (KSh 850 in the low season) plus KSh 300 for each extra person. Bookings can be made through Let's Go Travel in Nairobi.

Unless indicated, all the above places to stay are self-catering and kitchen facilities are provided.

Beyond this point you're looking at major expense and the sort of ennui that only major resort complexes can offer.

Places to Stay – top end
The other hotels along this beach cost megabucks and are basically for those who have got money to burn. They range in price from US$40/50 a single/double to US$55/75 in the low season to *double* and *triple* that in the high season with full board.

With the downturn in tourism at the coast, those who are staying here have usually paid a fraction of these prices as part of an all-inclusive package from Europe. If you just want to stay for a night or two, ring around, as you should be able to get a significant discount.

All the resorts offer much the same – air-con rooms, swimming pool, bars, restaurant, usually a disco, and some have water sports equipment for hire. The better ones (and there are quite a few) have been designed with the environment and local architectural styles in mind; others are not so special.

From north to south along the strip the hotels are as follows (prices are for singles/doubles unless otherwise stated):

Southern Palms Beach Resort – KSh 2500/3500 with half board (low season); KSh 3500/5000 in the high season (☎ (0127) 3721)

Golden Beach Hotel – US$60/90 with half board (low season); US$120/160 in the high season (☎ (0127) 2625)

Indian Ocean Beach Club – US$74/148 with half board (low season); US$147/227 in the high season

Diani Reef Grand Hotel – US$103/144 with half board (low season); US$146/220 in the high season. There are also more expensive deluxe rooms (☎ (0127) 51215).

Leisure Lodge & Casino – US$100/130 with full board (low season); US$140/152 in the high season. There are also more expensive suites (☎ (0127) 2011).

Leopard Beach Hotel – US$60/90 with full board (low season); US$120/180 in the high season. There are also more expensive suites and cottages (☎ (0127) 2111).

Kaskazi Beach Hotel – US$100/140 for singles/doubles including breakfast (low season); US$120/150 in the high season (☎ (0127) 3725)

Trade Winds Hotel – US$50/100 with full board (low season); US$100/130 (high season)

Diani Sea Lodge – US$120/160 with full board in the high season (☎ (0127) 2115)

Two Fishes Hotel – US$57/98 with half board (low season); US$112/144 in the high season (☎ (0127) 2101)

Jadini Beach Hotel/Africana Sea Lodge – US$50/85 with half board (low season); US$87/120 in the high season (☎ (0127) 2269)

Nomad Beach Hotel – US$60/90 for a one-bedroom banda including breakfast; US$111/150 for a three-bed banda/cottage; US$130/170 for a four-bed banda/cottage (☎ (0127) 2155)

Safari Beach Hotel – US$57/95 with half board (low season); US$97/135 in the high season (☎ (0127) 2357)

Lagoon Reef Hotel – US$55/90 with half board (low season); US$124/170 in the high season (☎ (0127) 2627)

The Trade Winds Hotel and the Golden Beach Hotel are part of the African Tours & Hotels group. Bookings can be made through them at PO Box 30471, Nairobi (☎ (02) 336858).

The Lagoon Reef Hotel is part of the Reef Hotels group. Bookings can be made through Mombasa (☎ (011) 471771).

The Safari Beach Hotel, Jadini Beach Hotel and the Africana Sea Lodge are all part of the Alliance Hotels group (☎ (02) 332825).

The Indian Ocean Beach Club belongs to Block Hotels (☎ (02) 540780) in Nairobi.

Places to Eat
Diani beach is well supplied with shopping centres so you needn't bring everything with you from Ukunda village if you are catering

for yourself, though the fruit and vegetables are naturally more expensive on the beach road than they are in Ukunda.

One of the largest complexes is the Diani Beach shopping centre, not far from the Trade Winds Hotel. It has a supermarket, bank, doctor's surgery, boutiques and a branch of Glory Car Hire. Further north there is Quinnsworth supermarket and, further north again, is the Diani Complex which has a supermarket, a branch of the Kenya Commercial Bank, a boutique and an Indian restaurant. Way down south beyond the tarmac and not far from the Galu Sea Lodge, is the Galu supermarket which is OK for basics but carries only a limited range of goods.

If you're staying at the southern end of the beach off the tarmac, there's the *Vulcano Restaurant da Lina* which is an excellent place to eat, though a bit of a splurge. It's open every night from 7 pm until late and offers a range of classic Italian dishes as well as seafood (lobster, prawns, crabs, calamari and fish).

Back on the tarmac about halfway towards the T-junction are a cluster of restaurants and nightclubs. Here you'll find the *Hähnchen Grill & Nightclub* (which, as the name suggests, is a German restaurant), *Temura's Restaurant* and the *Restaurant Maharani*. The latter is an Indian restaurant and is open daily from 7 to 11 pm as well as for lunch on Saturday and Sunday from 12.30 to 3 pm. In the same area but down a track on the opposite side of the road is *Ali Barbour's* which is an expensive seafood restaurant set in a coral cave between the Trade Winds Hotel and the Diani Sea Lodge.

North of the T-junction are the *Galaxy Chinese Restaurant* (which is next to the Quinnsworth supermarket) and the *Shan-e-Punjab* Indian restaurant in the Diani Complex. Beyond here, not far from the Diani Reef Grand Hotel, is the *African Papaya Nightclub & Restaurant*.

Apart from the above, many of the beach hotels offer buffet lunches and dinners at weekends which are open for non-guests. Make enquiries as to which currently offer the best deals and/or food. Most are priced in the KSh 500 to KSh 800 range.

Entertainment

Apart from the discos in the hotels (which you may have difficulty getting into if you're not a guest), there are at least four discos independent of the hotels. Because the clientele is more mixed in these discos they're more lively and worth checking out.

Opposite the Two Fishes Hotel is the *Bush Baby Nightclub*, an open-air restaurant and nightclub which is not a bad place for a bop. Not too far from here is the nightclub at the Hähnchen Grill (see Places to Eat). Almost next door to this is the *Shakatak Disco*. It's probably the best of the lot and entry is free although drinks are expensive.

Lastly, way up near the northern end of the tarmac, is the *African Papaya Nightclub & Restaurant* (see the earlier Places to Eat section).

Getting There & Away

Diani is the most accessible beach if you are dependent on public transport. From the Likoni ferry there are KBS buses (No 32) every 20 minutes or so from early morning until around 7 pm. The fare is minimal and the trip takes about 30 minutes.

Plenty of matatus make the trip from Likoni to Diani. They do the journey slightly faster and cost a little more.

When the buses and matatus get to Diani they first head north along the Diani beach road then turn around and go to the southern end of the bitumen where they turn again and head for Likoni. Just tell the driver where you want to get off.

SHIMONI & WASINI ISLAND

Shimoni is right out at the end of a small peninsula 76 km south of Likoni, and not far from the Tanzanian border. There's not a great deal here apart from the Shimoni Reef Lodge, but it's the headquarters of the Kisite Marine National Park.

Wasini Island itself is just off the coast of the Shimoni Peninsula. It's well wooded and unspoilt and is the perfect place to relax and experience a Swahili culture virtually untouched by the 20th century and tourism. There are no cars, roads or running water and the only electricity comes from generators.

On a wander around you can come across Muslim ruins, local women weaving mats, men preparing for fishing by mending nets and making fish traps, huge old baobab trees and the extensive 'coral gardens' with its odd-shaped stands of old coral that you can walk through (except at certain times of year when the sea floods it).

Kisite Marine National Park
To visit this park, which is offshore to the south-east of Wasini Island, you'll need to go by boat. See the park headquarters in Shimoni to make arrangements. Entry to the park costs US$6 for nonresidents and KSh 100 for residents. Boats to take you there cost KSh 300 per person (less than 12 people) or KSh 150 per person (12 or more people). If the sea is rough, the boats don't sail so keep an eye on the weather and tides.

Snorkelling & Diving
In addition to the boats which can be hired from the Kisite park headquarters in Shimoni, Masood Abdullah (who runs the Mpunguti Restaurant on Wasini Island) can arrange trips to the marine park. He has his own dhow as well as masks and snorkels.

Kisite Dhow Tours in Diani, which operates out of the Jadini Beach Hotel (☎ (0127) 2269) offers full-day tours from Shimoni jetty for US$65 from Diani. This includes transport, snorkelling in the marine park and a seafood lunch. You would be hard pressed to organise it for much less on your own.

Diving safaris off Pemba channel (spectacular!) and dhow trips to Kisite Marine National Park can also be arranged from the Shimoni Reef Hotel, but they are expensive.

Places to Stay & Eat
The only place to stay at Shimoni is the Shimoni Reef Lodge (☎ (011) 471771 in Mombasa; 9 in Shimoni), which is beautifully situated on a bluff overlooking the channel to Wasini Island. The facilities are excellent and it's a very mellow place to stay. The price for singles/doubles with half board is US$55/90 in the low season, US$124/166 in the high season.

Across the channel on Wasini Island, the only accommodation is at the Mpunguti Restaurant, run by Mr Masood Adullah. You can camp here if you have your own gear for KSh 100 per person per night or rent a very clean and pleasant room for KSh 800/1200 (half board). Cooking facilities are available for those who prefer self-catering (fish, coconuts, maize flour and rice are for sale in Shimoni and on Wasini, but very little else).

Masood is a very affable character and well organised, and the traditional Swahili food he turns out is delicious. Alcoholic drinks must be brought with you from the mainland – there are none available on the island.

The only other accommodation in the area is the Pemba Channel Fishing Club, which charges US$110/180 for full board, however it does not take children under eight years old.

Getting There & Away
There are a couple of direct buses and matatus daily between Shimoni and Likoni. Hitching is also a possibility.

From Likoni there are taxis available to Shimoni, or you can take one of the few KBS buses which do the trip daily. You could also take a matatu towards Lunga Lunga and get off at the Shimoni turn-off, but you'd then have to hitch the 14 km from the main road to Shimoni. It's not that difficult – even the locals do it.

Once at Shimoni (unless you intend to stay at the Shimoni Reef Lodge) you'll have to negotiate a dhow ride across the channel. The price for this depends to a degree on who you meet on arrival, how many there are of you and how affluent you look. If you assume KSh 600 for the boat (round trip) you won't be too far wrong.

The same people who run the dhows will also take you to the reefs for snorkelling for much the same price but you'll have to negotiate a price for the hire of snorkelling gear.

North of Mombasa

MOMBASA TO KILIFI

Like the coast south of Mombasa, the north coast has been well developed almost two-thirds of the way up to Kilifi with resort complexes which take up much of the beach frontage. Most of them cater to package tourists on two to three-week holidays from Europe but there is scope for individual initiative here and there, though only the Jauss Farm at Vipingo and the 'youth hostel' at Kikambala genuinely fall into the budget accommodation bracket.

As with Shelly and much of Tiwi beaches south of Mombasa, the northern beaches are plagued with seaweed which clogs them and makes swimming an often unpleasant experience. Only at the expensive resort hotels are people employed to minimise this inconvenience by raking it into piles and either burning it or burying it. Elsewhere you literally have to jump into the soup.

Going north from Mombasa the names of the beaches are Nyali, Bamburi, Shanzu, Kikambala and Vipingo.

Mamba Crocodile Village

Mamba Village (☎ (011) 472709) is north of Mombasa on the mainland opposite Nyali Golf Club in the Nyali Estate. It's a crocodile farm set among streams, waterfalls and wooden bridges. If you've never seen a crocodile farm with reptiles ranging from the newly born to the full grown, here's your chance; if you have, give it a miss. This is a typical collection of concrete and wire-mesh cages with thousands of young crocodiles up to five years old, and a few token, fully grown adults to pull in the punters. You pay through the nose to see them, too, even though the owners of the farms are probably making megabucks selling skins to Gucci and the like. Entry costs KSh 400 for nonresidents and KSh 150 for residents

(for children its KSh 280 and KSh 60, respectively).

Bamburi Quarry Nature Trail

Further up the coast, this nature trail (☎ (011) 485729) has been created on reclaimed and reforested areas damaged by cement production activities which ceased in 1971. Once the forest was established, the area was restocked with plants and animals in an attempt to create a mini replica of the wildlife parks of Kenya. At present, animal species represented include eland, oryx, waterbuck, buffalo, wart hog, bush pig, various monkeys and many different varieties of birds. There's also what the owners claim to be an 'orphan' hippo which was introduced as a baby from Naivasha and which has remained bottle-fed ever since. A likely story!

The complex also includes a fish farm, crocodile farm, reptile pit and plant nursery. The centre is open daily from 2 to 5.30 pm. Feeding time is at 4 pm. To get there take a public bus to Bamburi Quarry Nature Trail stop (signposted) on the main Mombasa to Malindi road.

Places to Stay – bottom end

There are very few cheap places to stay on the beaches north of Mombasa. Even places way back from the beach with nothing special going for them can be remarkably expensive.

One of the few genuine cheapies is the *Kanamai Conference Centre* (☎ (0125) 32046) at Kikambala Beach which was previously a youth hostel but is no longer affiliated. Dormitory beds are KSh 200 in either two, six or 10-bed rooms, while one-bedroom cottages are KSh 880, two-bedroom KSh 1700, and three-bedroom KSh 2640. All the cottages have bathrooms. Meals are available for KSh 130 for breakfast, KSh 200 for lunch and KSh 250 for dinner – expensive for what is basically ugali and chicken stew. The trouble with this place is getting there. First you have to take a matatu to Majengo on the Mombasa to Kilifi road (from near the New People's Hotel in Mombasa). Get off when you see a yellow

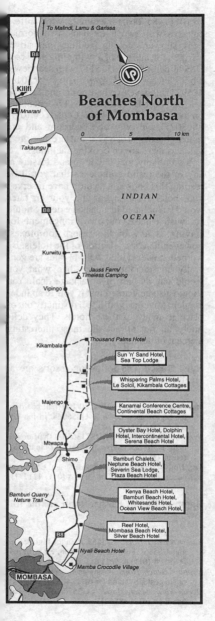

Beaches North of Mombasa

To Malindi, Lamu & Garissa

B8

Kilifi

Mnarani

Takaungu

0   5   10 km

INDIAN

OCEAN

B8

Kurwitu

Jauss Farm/
Timeless Camping

Vipingo

Thousand Palms Hotel

Kikambala

Sun 'n' Sand Hotel,
Sea Top Lodge

Whispering Palms Hotel,
Le Solcil, Kikambala Cottages

Majengo

Kanamai Conference Centre,
Continental Beach Cottages

Oyster Bay Hotel, Dolphin
Hotel, Intercontinental Hotel,
Serena Beach Hotel

Mtwapa

Shimo

Bamburi Chalets,
Neptune Beach Hotel,
Severin Sea Lodge,
Plaza Beach Hotel

Kenya Beach Hotel,
Bamburi Beach Hotel,
Whitesands Hotel,
Ocean View Beach Hotel,

Bamburi Quarry
Nature Trail

Reef Hotel,
Mombasa Beach Hotel,
Silver Beach Hotel

B8

Nyali Beach Hotel

Mamba Crocodile Village

MOMBASA

sign saying 'Kanamai Conference Centre'.
Go down the dirt track by this sign for about
300m and then turn left at the fork. Continue
for about three km and you'll find it on the
left-hand side by the beach. It's a long, hot
walk and lifts are few and far between. With
a backpack it's a major effort.

Close by, a little further to the north along
the track which runs parallel to the beach, are
the *Continental Beach Cottages* (☎ (0125)
32077) which are good value at KSh 1070
per person in the high season (KSh 1200 with
breakfast), dropping to KSh 770 in the low
season. Accommodation is in one and two-
bedroom cottages each with lounge, kitchen,
bathroom and air-con. It's rarely full and
there's a good swimming pool, bar and restaurant and a pleasant beach. Cheap meals
(omelette and chips and curries) are available
for around KSh 170. As with the Conference
Centre, the only problem about this place is
getting there; taxis are expensive.

Right next door to the Continental is
Kikambala Cottages (☎ (0125) 32032), a
very basic place with no pool or restaurant.
However, the cottages are comfortable
enough, and cheap at KSh 1950 with two
bedrooms, bathroom, lounge, and kitchen
with fridge. As there are no shops or cheap
restaurants nearby you need to be fairly self-
sufficient here .

If you're staying at either of the above
places and want a change of scene or a cold
beer, the Whispering Palms Hotel is about 15
minutes walk north along the beach. Breakfasts here cost KSh 330 and you can use the
swimming pool for KSh 200 per day.

A little further north, just behind the Sun
'n' Sand Hotel and about three km off the
main coast road, is the *Sea Top Lodge*
(☎ (0125) 32184), a small hotel which seems
to be a bar first and a hotel second. The cost
is KSh 550 for a small but clean double
room. There are a few small dukas nearby
and the beach is a short walk away. With a
little discretion you could probably use the
facilities at the Sun 'n' Sand.

Further up the coast at Vipingo, about 40
km north of Mombasa, there is *Timeless
Camping* (☎ (0125) 32218) on the Jauss

family farm. It consists of a camp site, budget chalets, and two bungalows. The camp site is equipped with showers and toilets and costs KSh 100 per person per night. The budget chalets are fairly basic twin rooms with clean beds and mattresses, and toilets and showers have to be shared with those occupying the camp site. The cost for these is KSh 330 per person. The bungalows are fully equipped and cost KSh 3200 for the four-bed one, and KSh 4300 for the large bungalow which sleeps 10 people. Unfortunately, this place is pretty run-down these days. If arriving by public transport, get off at Vipingo village and ring from there; someone will come and collect you. If you have your own transport, you'll have to ask the way because there's no signpost. Don't walk in the area unaccompanied as there have been mugging incidents in the past.

Places to Stay – top end

Virtually all the other hotels along this stretch of the East African coast before you arrive at Kilifi are resort complexes and cater largely for package tourists from Europe. Most of them are so self-contained that many of those staying there hardly ever see anything of Africa other than Mombasa airport, the inside of minibuses, the hotel itself and black Kenyan waiters. As at the hotels south of Mombasa and at Malindi, many cater almost exclusively for one specific European nationality whether they be British, German or Italian (French people don't feature prominently in East African tourism). There's precious little intermingling.

All the hotels compete furiously with each other to provide the utmost in creature comforts, mellow surroundings, day trips and sports facilities and there's little to choose between them though it's generally true to say that the further you get from Mombasa, the cheaper and less ritzy they become.

Down at Nyali Beach – the closest to Mombasa – even places which don't face the sea and are in no way hotel resorts, and which you might imagine should be fairly cheap given the facilities they offer, can be surprisingly expensive. *Bamburi Chalets*

(π (011) 485706), for example, which offers cottages with two bunk beds, two normal beds, shower, cooking facilities, gas stove, refrigerator, and use of a swimming pool cost US$78 per night or US$117 with sea views. The *Cowrie Shell Apartments* (π (011) 485971) all have two bedrooms and face the sea, and cost US$58 to US$117 depending on the season. The *Baharini Chalets* (π (011) 486302) have only one bedroom and are much cheaper at US$23, but are not great value as there are no cooking facilities.

It's unlikely that if you intend to stay at any of the resort complexes that you'll be reading this book since you'd have reserved your hotel via an agent and your air fares would be included in a package deal. Should you wish to make your own arrangements for staying at any of the resort complexes, however, here's a selection of the hotels. Be warned, however, that walk-in rates are generally considerably higher than what you would pay as part of a package deal. You should also be warned that if you're an independent traveller, you'll feel distinctly out of place in many of these hotels. They definitely do not attract the most interesting element of humanity.

Nyali Beach The following resorts are at Nyali Beach:

Mombasa Beach Hotel – US$120/160 (half board) in the high season down to US$60/90 in the low season (π (011) 471861)

Nyali Beach Hotel – from US$136/209 (half board) in the high season down to US$62/124 in the low season (π (011) 471551)

Reef Hotel – US$88/132 (half board); add US$10 per person per day for full board (π (011) 471771)

Bamburi Beach Further north are the following hotels:

Bamburi Beach Hotel – US$55/70 in the high season and US$35/55 in the low season, all with half board (π (011) 485611)

Neptune Beach Hotel – singles/doubles with half board cost US$50/64 ($\pi$ (011) 485701)

Ocean View Beach Hotel – US$70/109 with half board ($\pi$ (011) 485601)

Plaza Beach Hotel – US$44/60 with half board (☎ (011) 485321)

Severin Sea Lodge – singles/doubles with half board from US$97/140 and twin suites for US$338 (☎ (011) 4855001)

Travellers' Beach Hotel – US$66/90 with half board (☎ (011) 485121)

Whitesands Hotel – US$70/105 (half board); suites US$215 to US$480 (☎ (011) 485926)

Shanzu Beach At Shanzu Beach are the following resorts:

Dolphin Hotel – US$58/104 with full board (☎ (011) 485801)

Mombasa Intercontinental Resort US$70/140 with breakfast; double suites US$270 to US$445 (☎ (011) 485811)

Oyster Bay Hotel – from US$42/57 with half board (☎ (011) 485061)

Serena Beach Hotel – in the high season singles/doubles with breakfast cost US$150/200; suites US$250 and US$400. In the low season, singles/doubles are US$65/130 with suites at US$150 and US$300. Shoulder season prices are in-between the two. All prices are subject to a service charge (10%), training levy (2%) and VAT (15%) (☎ (011) 485721).

Kikambala Beach Finally, Kikambala Beach offers the following:

Whispering Palms Hotel – singles/doubles with full board cost US$94/122 (low season), and US$120/165 in the high season (☎ (0125) 32004)

Sun 'n' Sand Beach Hotel – US$52/104 in the low season (half board); US$110/130 in the high season; children are charged 50% of the adult rate (☎ (0125) 32133)

Takaungu Right up at the top end of this long line of beaches close to Kilifi is the village of Takaungu. It's supposedly the oldest slave port on the Kenyan coast to Zanzibar is the oldest. It's worth a visit if you have the time. The local people are very superstitious and no-one goes down to the beach at night except the fishers. If you can speak Swahili you'll hear many weird stories going around which date back to the time of slavery. It's an interesting place right off the beaten track where you won't meet many other travellers.

Rooms can be rented in private houses in Takaungu for around KSh 200 per night. Ask at the teashops.

For those with slightly less limited resources there's *Takaungu House* (☎ (02) 502491), a luxury house which is privately owned and run. There are just three bedrooms, but other features include a swimming pool, beach frontage, snorkelling, water-skiing and deep-sea fishing on request. The charge for full board is KSh 6400 per person.

KILIFI

Other than Mtwapa Creek, just north of Mombasa, Kilifi is the first major break in the coastline between Mombasa and Malindi. It has been a backwater for many years, ignored by developers yet coveted by discerning white Kenyans, artists, writers and adventurers from various parts of the world who have gradually bought up most of the land overlooking the wide creek and the ocean and built, in many cases, some quite stunning and imaginative houses. They form a sort of society within a society and keep largely to themselves. Without an introduction, it's unlikely you'll meet them though sailing a yacht into the creek would probably secure you an invitation! Kilifi Creek is a popular anchorage spot for yachties in this part of the world and you can meet them in the evening at the Seahorse Inn off to the left of the main road on the northern side of the creek.

So why stop off in Kilifi? The answer to this is mainly for the contrast it offers to Mombasa and Malindi, and for the Mnarani ruins on a bluff overlooking the creek on the Mombasa side. Very few travellers ever see these ruins yet they're well preserved and just as interesting as those at Gedi though not as extensive. The beach, too, on either side of the creek is very pleasant and doesn't suffer from the seaweed problem which plagues the beaches further south. The only problem is access, which is mostly through private property, though you can walk along it from the old ferry landing at low tide.

The present district centre of Kilifi is on the northern bank of the creek.

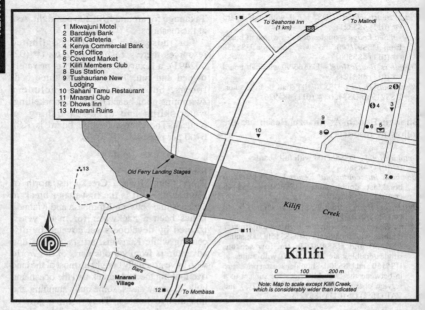

1 Mkwajuni Motel
2 Barclays Bank
3 Kilifi Cafeteria
4 Kenya Commercial Bank
5 Post Office
6 Covered Market
7 Kilifi Members Club
8 Bus Station
9 Tushauriane New
   Lodging
10 Sahani Tamu Restaurant
11 Mnarani Club
12 Dhows Inn
13 Mnarani Ruins

To Seahorse Inn (1 km)
To Malindi

Old Ferry Landing Stages

Kilifi Creek

Kilifi

0   100   200 m
Note: Map to scale except Kilifi Creek,
which is considerably wider than indicated

Bars
Bars
Mnarani
Village
To Mombasa

Information

Kilifi consists of the small village of Mnarani (or Manarani) on the southern bank of the creek and Kilifi itself on the northern bank. It's a small town which you can walk around within minutes.

There's a good variety of shops (including a small bookshop), a lively open-air market and an enclosed fruit and vegetable market, a post office, a number of basic hotels and two banks. Barclays Bank is open Monday to Friday from 9 am to 3 pm and on Saturday from 9 to 11 am. The Kenya Commercial Bank keeps the same hours.

Mnarani

Mnarani, on the southern bank of Kilifi Creek overlooking the ferry landing, was once one of the string of Swahili city-states which dotted the East African coast. Excavations carried out in 1954 showed that the site was occupied from the end of the 14th century to around the first half of the 17th century after which it was destroyed by marauding Galla tribespeople.

The principal ruins here include the Great Mosque with its finely carved inscription around the mihrab (the niche in a mosque showing the direction of Mecca), a group of tombs to the north (including one pillar tomb), a small mosque dating from the 16th century, and also parts of the town wall and a gate. There's also a large and quite forbiddingly deep well whose shaft must go down at least as far as the low-tide level of the creek.

Mnarani was associated with **Kioni**, at the mouth of Kilifi Creek on the same side, and with **Kitoka**, about 3.5 km south of here on the northern bank of Takaungu Creek. A carved stone with an interlaced ornament, probably from a mihrab, was found at Kioni on the cliff above the creek and is presently in the Fort Jesus museum at Mombasa. The ruins at Kitoka include a mosque similar to the small mosque at Mnarani along with a few houses. All these settlements were subject to Mombasa.

The Mnarani ruins are just above the old southern ferry landing stage and the path to them (about 300m long) is prominently signposted on the main road. Entry costs KSh 200 for nonresidents and KSh 30 for residents (KSh 100 and KSh 10 for children) but there's often no-one there to collect the fee.

Places to Stay – bottom end

There are a number of cheap hardboard-cubicle doss-houses scattered around town but you'd have to be desperate to stay there as they're basically bars which make provision for 'short-time' customers.

About the only place where you'll find a half-decent bed is the *Tushauriane New Lodging* (☎ (0125) 22486) near the bus station. This is a recently constructed hotel, several storeys high, which offers good, clean, simple rooms with mosquito nets and shared bathroom facilities for KSh 150/300 a single/double.

The *Kingenda Guest House* close to the central market and the Kenya Commercial Bank, which you'll see advertised in several places around town, has no rooms despite claims to the contrary. It's just a bar and restaurant.

Places to Stay – middle

The best place in this range is the *Dhows Inn* (☎ (0125) 22028) on the main road south of Kilifi Creek opposite the entrance to the Mnarani Club. It's a fairly small place with a number of double rooms surrounding a well-kept garden. There's a lively and quite popular bar and restaurant. A room here with mosquito nets and bath costs KSh 550 per person including breakfast. If arriving by bus or matatu, get the driver to drop you right outside, rather than in Kilifi itself in which case you'll have the long walk across the bridge.

On the northern side of the bridge, just off the main road, is the *Mkwajuni Motel* (☎ (0125) 22472). Set in a spacious garden, the rooms are small but very clean and neat, each with a small patio and table and chairs.

The motel is only about 10 minutes walk into town. Single/double rooms cost KSh 600/850 including breakfast.

Places to Stay – top end

The large resort complex at Kilifi is the somewhat exclusive *Mnarani Club* on the southern side of Kilifi Creek and quite close to the Dhows Inn. It's one of the African Safari Club hotels and they do not encourage casual bookings so these must be made through Mombasa (☎ (011) 485520). The hotel caters largely to package tourists from Germany and Switzerland and it's these people who keep the craft-shop owners of Mnarani village smiling.

Despite its size, the Mnarani Club is hardly visible from the main road or even from a boat on the creek since it's constructed of local materials (including some enormous makuti roofs) and surrounded by beautifully landscaped gardens full of flowering trees and bougainvillea.

The other top-range hotel is the *Seahorse Inn* (☎ (0125) 22813), about 1.5 km off to the left of the main Mombasa–Malindi road on the northern side of the creek. It's a very pleasant place with individual bandas set in a coconut grove right on the banks of Kilifi Creek which, at this point, is a couple of km wide. To stay here will set you back KSh 2600/4300 for full board. Like the Mnarani Club, the Seahorse Inn is run by the African Safari Club, so the same applies with bookings.

If you're thinking of visiting either of these two hotels for the day it will cost you KSh 1500 (KSh 750 for children) including lunch, afternoon tea, all non-alcoholic drinks and use of the pool and all other sports facilities. African Safari Club members who are not guests pay a reduced fee of KSh 750 (KSh 375 for children).

Places to Eat

A cheap and very popular place to eat both for lunch and dinner is the *Tana Hotel* at the bus station. Standard Indo-African fare is on offer, and you can eat well here for around KSh 130 to KSh 180. It's closed all day until after sunset during Ramadan. Another popular place, especially at lunch time, is the *Kilifi Cafeteria* though prices here are somewhat higher.

Across on the southern side of the creek, you can eat at the *Dhows Inn* which has a limited menu of meat and seafood dishes. The only trouble with eating here is that food takes forever to arrive and the quality is variable: sometimes it's good, sometimes it's almost inedible. The average price of a main course is around KSh 200.

For a splurge, go for lunch at the *Mnarani Club* or the *Seahorse Inn* but note the entry fee for non-guests (see previous section). Normally, casual visitors are not allowed in during the evening but this is probably negotiable – for a fee – with the manager.

Even more up-market is the very agreeable *Sahani Tamu Restaurant* on the northern side of the creek, opposite the Mnarani Club. The food here is mainly Italian and seafood and is very well prepared and presented. Main dishes such as spaghetti are in the KSh 200 to KSh 250 range, steaks are around KSh 350, and seafood dishes from KSh 500 to KSh 750. It's well worth the expense and makes a very pleasant evening out. The restaurant is open daily, except Tuesday, from 11 am to 2 pm and 6 to 10 pm.

Entertainment

For a spit-and-sawdust evening on Tusker or White Cap you can't beat the bars in Mnarani village of which there are several, but the amount of action depends largely on how many tourists brave the 200m or so of dirt road between the Mnarani Club and the village. Don't expect cold beers at any of these bars.

The bar at the *Dhows Inn* on the other hand is usually pretty lively and you can be assured of cold beer.

The *Mnarani Club* has a nightly floor show – usually of tribal dancing – followed by a live African band which plays until late. This is, however, a club hotel and it's unlikely they will let you in during the evening, although this is negotiable, for a fee. Look smart if you want to avoid a hassle or even a rejection.

For a far more informal evening pay a visit to the *Kilifi Members Club* on the northern side of the creek.

Getting There & Away

All the buses and matatus which ply between Mombasa and Malindi stop at Kilifi but getting on a bus at Kilifi to go to either Mombasa or Malindi can be problematical since they're often full. Matatus are a much better bet but, like the buses, can be very crowded.

WATAMU

About 24 km south of Malindi, Watamu is a smaller beach resort development with its own marine national park – part of the Marine National Reserve which stretches south from Malindi. The coral reef here is even more spectacular than at Malindi since it has been much less exploited and poached by shell hunters. In addition, underwater visibility is not affected by silt brought down into the sea by the Galana River.

The coast at Watamu is broken up into three separate coves divided by craggy and eroded headlands and there are a number of similarly eroded islands just offshore. The coral sand is a dazzling white and although there is some shade from coconut palms, you'll probably have to retreat to the cooler confines of a hotel bar or restaurant in the middle of the day. The most southerly cove is fronted entirely by beach resorts and exclusive private houses. The central cove also has a number of resorts, though they are not as extensive. The northern cove and part of the headland is covered by the rambling Watamu Beach Hotel at the back of which is the actual village of Watamu.

Before tourist development got underway here, Watamu was a mellow little fishing village of makuti-roofed cottages nestled beneath coconut palms and it still retains much of that atmosphere despite the intrusion of souvenir shops, bars and restaurants catering for the tourist hordes. In fact the contrasts are quite bizarre – it's one of the few places where you'll see package tourists in designer beach attire wandering down the dusty streets of an African village. A lot of development has taken place on the outskirts of the village and is clearly destined to continue. For independent travellers a visit to Watamu is probably not worth it, not only because of the very limited amount of reasonably priced accommodation, but also because most of the beach frontage is taken up by the resort hotels which makes access problematical. That's a pity, because it is a beautiful spot.

Information
There are branches of both Barclays Bank and the Kenya Commercial Bank in the village of Watamu. Barclays is open Monday to Friday from 9 am to 4.30 pm, and KCB is open Monday to Friday from 9 am to 1 pm and 3 to 5 pm, and on Saturday from 9 to 11 am.

Post & Communications There is a post office close to the junction of the coast road and the road to Gedi.

There's also a branch of Phone Home (☎ 32302) at the junction of the coast road and the road leading into Watamu village. This is a private company offering phone and fax services at fixed rates (more expensive than going through the post office in Malindi but less expensive than going through a hotel switchboard).

Watamu's telephone code is 0122.

Watamu Marine National Park
The actual coral reef lies between one and two km offshore and to get to it you'll have to hire a glass-bottomed boat. These can be arranged directly with the owners at the park entrance for KSh 2500 for two people including park fees or for KSh 3000 for a party of up to eight people excluding park fees. You can also arrange these boats through any of the large hotels though they will, of course, charge a commission for their services.

Entry to the park itself costs US$5 for nonresidents and KSh 100 for residents.

There are also boat trips to a group of **caves** at the entrance to **Mida Creek** which are home to a school of giant rock cod many of which are up to two metres long. Diving

equipment is usually necessary to get down to their level since, most of the time, they remain stationary on the bottom.

Places to Stay – bottom end
Budget accommodation has always been something of a problem in Watamu. There are a couple of cheap lodges in the village but they can't seriously be recommended. The *Blue Lodge* charges KSh 350 for a scruffy, stuffy and gloomy double room illuminated by the feeblest of globes – only for the desperate. The other alternative, *Sam's Lodge*, is no better, though it is marginally cheaper at KSh 300 for a double. Neither place has fans or mosquito nets – which are absolutely essential on the coast.

Another possibility in the village is a private house known as the *Maasai House*. It has only one double room with shared facilities and another room with an attached bathroom, both of which cost more than the above two lodges. There's a kitchen, big verandah, a garden with a well, and a housekeeper who will cook meals at a reasonable charge. It's a good place to meet the Samburu performers from the Watamu Beach Hotel.

Of the regular lodges, the best value is the family-run *Villa Veronica/Mwikali Lodge* (☎ 32083), opposite the Hotel Dante Bar & Restaurant. This is a very friendly and secure place which offers clean rooms with double bed, fan, mosquito nets, shower and toilet for KSh 600 and KSh 800 for a room with two double beds including breakfast. The only drawback to this place is that it's tucked into a hollow so you miss out on sea breezes.

The *Hotel Dante* itself is about the cheapest habitable place, and doubles with attached bathrooms (no singles) go for KSh 500 including breakfast. The rooms have fans and mosquito nets and there's a bar and restaurant but the swimming pool is empty.

The only other place that fits this price bracket is *Watamu Cottages* (☎ 32211), on the main access road to the village and about 15 minutes hot walk. These are a good deal at KSh 750 for a double, with bathroom, and including breakfast but are often full. The rooms are set in a pleasant garden which also has a swimming pool.

It may occasionally be possible to get a cheap room at the *Seventh Day Adventist Youth Camp* if there's no group there but don't count on it. You can also camp here if you have your own tent. The facilities are minimal though there is a gas cooker which you can use.

Places to Stay – middle

The best deal in this range is *Peponi Cottages* (☎ 32434). It consists of a small complex of two-storey, makuti-roofed units which are quite pleasant, if a little small. Each has mosquito netting on the windows, and a balcony runs the length of the buildings. There's also a small pool. The Italian owner is very pleasant and *sympatico* but, because it's small, it's often full. A double, with bathroom, costs KSh 1000 excluding breakfast.

On the main road leaving the village is the *Watamu Paradise Restaurant & Cottages* (☎ 32062) which has a number of cottages, mostly doubles though there are some triples. Depending on the standard, a double, with attached bathroom, without breakfast costs from KSh 1000 or KSh 1400 including breakfast. Doubles with shared facilities cost KSh 800 excluding breakfast and KSh 1200 including breakfast. All the rooms have a fan and mosquito nets. It's a very pleasant place to stay and there's a small swimming pool, bar, restaurant and a disco.

Down in the centre of Watamu village is the *Ascot Residence Hotel* (the telephone is out of order), PO Box 14, which is a sprawling walled complex containing numerous makuti-roofed cottages, a bar and restaurant and a huge swimming pool. It gives the appearance of being a top-end hotel but the prices don't reflect this. All the rooms have a fan, mosquito net, private verandah and have attached bathrooms. Doubles without breakfast cost from KSh 1000 or from KSh 1200 with breakfast. It's good value and the surroundings are very pleasant.

Also highly recommended is *Mrs Simpson's Guest House* (☎ 32023), PO Box 33, Watamu. Barbara Simpson has lived in Kenya

PLACES TO STAY
1 Watamu Beach House
2 Sam's Lodge
3 Blue Lodge
6 Ascot Residence Hotel
10 Barracuda Inn
10 Hotel Dante Bar & Restaurant
11 Villa Veronica
13 Peponi Cottages
14 Watamu Paradise Restaurant & Cottages
16 Aquarius Watamu Hotel
17 Seventh Day Adventist Youth Camp
18 Watamu Cottages
19 Ocean Sports Hotel
20 Hemingways Hotel
21 Turtle Bay Beach Club

OTHER
4 Kenya Commercial Bank
5 Bicycle Hire
7 Barclays Bank
8 Happy Night Disco
12 Come Back Club
15 Phone Home (Telephone Service)

Watamu Village

To Gedi & Malindi

To Blue Bay Village (100m)

Watamu

INDIAN OCEAN

0   250   500 m

To Marine National Park Entrance & Temple Point Club

for more than 70 years and has plenty of fascinating and amusing tales to entertain her guests with. The atmosphere is very homely and meals, cooked by Samson, are excellent. She has three double rooms with attached bathrooms for KSh 1600 per person for full board and including any laundry that you want doing. She can also organise snorkelling trips much cheaper than any of the resort hotels and she has a car available. The guesthouse is some 30 minutes walk from Turtle Bay towards Temple Point. Otherwise, ask the matatu driver to drop you at Plot 28.

Places to Stay – top end

Top-end hotels take up much of the beach frontage along each of the three coves. As at Malindi, they're mostly resort-type hotels which cater to package tourists' every need and are quite specific as to the European nationality which they appeal to – German, British or Italian – although that doesn't exclude others.

At the northern end and next to Watamu village is the rambling *Watamu Beach Hotel* (☎ 32001), where most of the German tourists stay. It's one of the many hotels operated by the African Safari Club, a German-based organisation, and casual bookings are not encouraged – they don't even know at the reception desk what the tariff is! If you want to stay, bookings can be made at the African Safari Club office in Mombasa (☎ (011) 485520). It's unlikely you'll stay here unless you've booked. African Safari Club members can use the facilities here for KSh 750 per day (KSh 375 for children). Nonmembers' rates for the same are KSh 1500 (KSh 750 for children) which includes lunch, afternoon tea and all nonalcoholic drinks.

At the northern end of the central cove is the *Barracuda Inn* (☎ 617074). This is an Italian-owned place which also discourages casual bookings. They will, however, let you stay if there's a vacancy. It's a huge place with numerous, double-storeyed cottages, all of them have attached bathrooms with air-con. Non-resident rates for singles/doubles are the equivalent of US$70/100 with half board and US$80/120 with full

board. Resident rates are KSh 2600/4500 with half board and KSh 2800/5000 with full board. Non-guests can use the hotel facilities (pool, tennis courts and billiard table) for a negotiable fee (KSh 100 to KSh 200). There's an enormous bar and restaurant area under a soaring makuti roof.

Just beyond the Barracuda on the same entrance road is the *Aquarius Watamu Hotel* (☎ 32069), PO Box 96, Watamu. This is a new Italian-owned hotel with all the amenities of a resort complex. Prices depend on the season and range from KSh 1300 to KSh 3300 per person for bed and breakfast.

The southern cove sports four hotels, all of them of the resort variety. Closest to Watamu village is the *Blue Bay Village* (☎ 32626), which caters mostly to Italians. Full-board doubles vary from the equivalent of US$68 to US$115 including all taxes and service charges, depending on the type of room you take (standard, deluxe or superior). Single-room supplements vary between the equivalent of US$26 and US$30. Children aged between three and 12 years are charged at the equivalent of US$25 less. Half board rates are the equivalent of US$10 less than full-board rates.

Next along is *Ocean Sports* (☎ 32008), where the clientele is mainly British. It's much smaller than the other places and the facilities are fairly modest. It does, however, have excellent diving equipment and will take experienced divers out for a dive on the reef. Singles/doubles for nonresidents cost the equivalent of UK£46/60 and for residents KSh 3100/3900 with half board. Children between the ages of six and 12 years cost US$11 and KSh 1000, respectively. Most of the clientele are middle-aged and have children with them.

Hemingways (☎ 32256), which is next to Ocean Sports, is a much larger place and, again, caters largely to a British clientele. The rates here for nonresidents start at the equivalent of UK£86/115 a single/double including breakfast in the high season down to UK£45/60 in the low season but it depends what type of room you take. Suites go as high as UK£175 in the high season down to

UK£100 in the low season. Rack rates for residents start at KSh 6210/8280 up to KSh 8100/10,800 for singles/doubles including breakfast in the high season. Children up to the age of five years are free but from five to 12 years are entitled to a 10% discount. The prices include free transport to and from Malindi airport (by prior arrangement) and free snorkelling trips in the marine national park, excluding national park fees.

At the far end of the cove is the *Turtle Bay Beach Club* (☎ 32622) which caters to a mixture of nationalities – mainly British, Italian and German. Like the Watamu Beach Hotel, it's a huge, rambling place with all the usual facilities and water-sports equipment but it's definitely a club and you won't even get past the front gate unless you're a member so, if you're a casual visitor, forget it.

Right at the entrance to the marine park is the lavish *Temple Point Club* (☎ 32057) which caters to young Italians. This is a relatively new place complete with soaring makuti roofs but you can forget about it unless you're a member. They definitely do not encourage casual bookings.

Places to Eat

Budget eating facilities are at a premium in Watamu though it is possible to get simple meals at one or other of the local bars in the village – the *Ujamaa Restaurant*, attached to the bar of the same name, is one possibility. *Friend's Corner* is a small duka on the road between the Come Back Club and Villa Veronica. It has about the best cheap food in town, although the variety is limited.

The *Hotel Dante* is probably the best of the non-resort restaurants. The service is slow but there's warm beer and a juke box to distract you while you're waiting. Almost opposite is the *Come Back Club Restaurant*, but the food is not up to much and it's hard to think of a good reason to come back, except perhaps to dance in the disco which operates some nights.

For better meals at a reasonable price (for Watamu) head for the *Watamu Paradise Restaurant & Cottages* where you can get seafood and European-style meals for between KSh 250 and KSh 400 (more for crab or lobster). There's also a bar with cold beers, and a disco most nights.

That's about the limit if you're an independent traveller but, if you have money to throw away, you could always take one of the buffet lunches at the resort hotels (where available). The price of these for non-guests, including use of facilities, falls into a very similar bracket to those charged at the Watamu Beach Hotel (see earlier) except on Sunday at either Ocean Sports or Hemingways where you can get an excellent buffet lunch for KSh 900 (KSh 450 for children). In the low season they're cheaper though the buffets are somewhat more modest.

Entertainment

For a disco not attached to a hotel there is the makuti-roofed *Happy Night Disco* next to the Hotel Dante. It operates nightly and entry costs KSh 50.

Getting There & Away

Matatus leave from the bus station in Malindi throughout the day. They cost KSh 25 to Watamu and take about 30 minutes. Most of these first go down to the Turtle Bay Beach Club after which they turn around and go to Watamu village. On the return journey they generally go direct from Watamu village to Malindi without first going down to the Turtle Bay Beach Club.

Getting Around

Bicycles can be hired for KSh 250 per day from Subira Bicycle Hire opposite the Ascot Residence Hotel.

Taxis can be found outside the Watamu Beach Hotel.

GEDI

Some four km from Watamu, just off the main Malindi–Mombasa road, are the famous Gedi ruins, one of the principal historical monuments on the coast. Though the ruins are extensive, this Arab-Swahili town is something of a mystery since it's not mentioned in any of the Portuguese or Arab chronicles of the time.

Excavations, which have uncovered such things as Ming Chinese porcelain and glass and glazed earthenware from Persia, have indicated the 13th century as the time of its foundation, however it was inexplicably abandoned in the 17th or 18th century, possibly because the sea receded and left the town high and dry, or because of marauding Galla tribespeople from the north. The forest took over and the site was not rediscovered until the 1920s. Even if you have only a passing interest in archaeology it's worth a visit.

Entry costs KSh 200 for nonresidents and KSh 30 for residents (less for students and children) and the site is open daily from 7 am to 6 pm. A good guidebook with map is for sale at the entrance for KSh 30.

The site is quite large and surrounded by two walls, the inner one of which was possibly built to enclose a smaller area after the city was temporarily abandoned in the 15th to 16th centuries.

In places it actually incorporates earlier houses into its structure. The site is lush and green with numerous baobab trees. Monkeys chatter in the tree tops, lizards rustle in the undergrowth and large, colourful butterflies flutter among the ruins.

The buildings were constructed of coral rag, coral lime and earth and some have pictures incised into the plaster finish of their walls, though many of these have deteriorated in recent years. The toilet facilities in the houses are particularly impressive, generally in a double-cubicle style with a squat toilet in one and a wash stand in the other where a bowl would have been used. Fancier versions even have double washbasins with a bidet between them.

The other notable feature of the site is the great number of wells, many of them remarkably deep.

Most of the interesting excavated buildings are concentrated in a dense cluster near the entrance gate. There are several others scattered around the site within the inner wall and even between the inner and outer walls. Outside the site, by the car park, there's a small museum with some items found on the site. Other items are exhibited in Fort Jesus in Mombasa.

The Tombs

On your right as you enter the site is the Dated Tomb, so-called because the Muslim date corresponding to 1399 has been deciphered. This tomb has provided a reference point for dating other buildings within the complex. Next to it is the Tomb of the Fluted Pillar which is characteristic of such pillar designs found up and down the East African coast. There's another good example of this kind of pillar in Lamu.

The Great Mosque

The Great Mosque originally dates from the mid-15th century but was rebuilt a century later, possibly as a result of damage sustained at the time of Gedi's first abandonment. The mosque is of typical East African design with a mihrab facing towards Mecca. You can see where porcelain bowls were once mounted in the walls flanking the mihrab.

The Palace

Behind the mosque are the ruins of the extensive palace which is entered through an arched door. Once through the doorway, you enter a reception court and then a large audience hall while to the left of this are numerous smaller rooms. Look for the many 'bathrooms' and the room flanking the audience hall with its square niches in the walls intended for lamps. Behind that room is another one with no doorway at all which would probably have been used to store valuables. Entry was by ladder through a small hatch high up in the wall. Beyond this is a kitchen area with a small but very deep well.

The Palace also has a particularly fine pillar tomb, while to the right is the Annexe with four individual apartments, each with its own courtyard.

The Houses

In all, 14 houses have been excavated at Gedi, 10 of which are in a compact group beside the Great Mosque and the Palace. They're named after particular features of

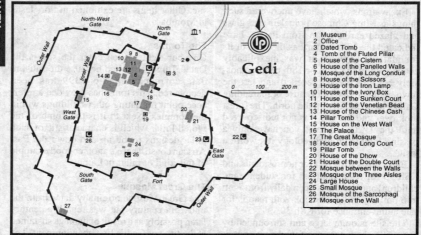

Gedi

1 Museum
2 Office
3 Dated Tomb
4 Tomb of the Fluted Pillar
5 House of the Cistern
6 House of the Panelled Walls
7 Mosque of the Long Conduit
8 House of the Scissors
9 House of the Iron Lamp
10 House of the Ivory Box
11 House of the Sunken Court
12 House of the Venetian Bead
13 House of the Chinese Cash
14 Pillar Tomb
15 House on the West Wall
16 The Palace
17 The Great Mosque
18 House of the Long Court
19 Pillar Tomb
20 House of the Dhow
21 House of the Double Court
22 Mosque between the Walls
23 Mosque of the Three Aisles
24 Large House
25 Small Mosque
26 Mosque of the Sarcophagi
27 Mosque on the Wall

their design or after objects found in them by archaeologists. They include the House of the Cowries, House of the Cistern and House of the Porcelain Bowl.

Other Buildings

Follow the signposted path from the Tomb of the Fluted Pillar to the House of the Dhow and House of the Double Court with a nearby tomb. There are pictures in the wall plaster in these houses.

A path follows close to the inner city wall from the houses to the Mosque of the Three Aisles where you will also find the largest well in Gedi. Beside it is the inner wall of the East Gate from where a path leads to the Mosque Between the Walls; a path cuts back to the car park from here.

Alternatively, from the East Gate you can follow another path right around the inner circuit of the inner wall or divert to the Mosque on the Wall at the southern extremity of the outer wall. The House on the West Wall actually comprises several adjoining houses of typical design while at the northern end of the town there is the more complex North Gate.

Just outside the North Gate is a 'traditional' **Giriama tribal village**, and here the package

tourists are entertained with 'traditional' Giriama dances. Unfortunately it's *very* contrived and the dancing girls' costumes look something like a cross between a Hawaiian skirt and a tennis outfit.

Butterfly Farm

This is situated just before the entrance to the Gedi ruins and is well worth a visit. Entry costs KSh 50.

Getting There & Away

Take the same matatu as you would to go to Watamu but get off at Gedi village where the matatu turns off from the main Malindi–Mombasa road. From there it's about a one-km signposted walk to the ruins along a *murram* road.

It's also possible to get a taxi to take you on a round trip from Malindi for about KSh 1000 with an hour or more to look around the site. This could be worth it if your time is limited and there's a small group to share costs.

MALINDI

Malindi was an important Swahili settlement as far back as the 14th century and often rivalled Mombasa and Paté for control of this part of the East African coast. It was also one of the very few places where the early Portuguese mariners found a sympathetic welcome, and today you can still see the cross which Vasco da Gama erected as a navigational aid.

These days, on account of its beaches, it has experienced a tourist boom similar to that north and south of Mombasa, and resort hotels are strung out all the way along the coast. It still retains a recognisable African centre where commerce, business and everyday activities, which aren't necessarily connected with the tourist trade, continue. Outside this relatively small centre, Italian and, to a lesser extent, German entrepreneurs have transformed Malindi into tinsel and glitter suitable only for high rollers and those with money to burn.

There are now air-con piano bars, karaoke bars, a casino, glitzy shopping centres, discos and all the associated infrastructure necessary to keep package tourists fully distracted 24 hours a day and as distanced from the real Africa as their budgets will possibly allow. It's the perfect example of overkill. However, with the downturn in Kenya's tourist intake, the developers have taken a severe hiding.

Quite a lot of businesses have folded recently: even the Italian consulate has closed. Nevertheless, a meal, other than spaghetti or pizza, will still cost you two to three times as much as you would pay for the same thing in Mombasa or Lamu. Seafood, in particular, is outrageously priced. Still, if you want to pretend you're on the Italian riviera, here it is.

The beach is still there though it isn't anything special and it does have the drawback of suffering from the brown silt which flows out of the Galana River at the northern end of the bay during the rainy seasons. This can make the sea very muddy all the way down to the Vasco da Gama cross hiowever generally not below that, so if you want to avoid this go to Silversands Bay or even further south closer to the marine national park.

Information
Tourist Office There is a tourist office next door to Kenya Airways on the Lamu road. The staff are helpful but have little useful information and very few leaflets.

Money Barclays Bank is open Monday to Friday from 9 am to 4.30 pm, and on Saturday from 9 to 11 am. The Standard Chartered Bank and the Trust Bank have much the same hours except that the Trust Bank is open half an hour later on Saturday morning.

Immigration There is an office next to the Juma Mosque and pillar tombs on the waterfront (see map for location).

Post & Communications The post office is open for international telephone calls from 7 am to 7 pm Monday to Friday and 8 am to 2.30 pm on Saturday. There is also a card phone here but, as usual, the supply of cards is erratic. There's also a branch of Phone Home (☎ 31589) in the Malindi Complex on Lamu Rd which caters for international telephone and fax services.

Malindi's telephone code is 0123.

Warning Don't walk back to your hotel along the beach at night. In past years many people have been mugged at knife-point, although these days the beach appears to be safer. Go back along the main road (which has street lighting) or take a taxi. You also need to exercise caution if returning to Silversands camp site late at night.

Town Buildings
Malindi has a pedigree going back to the 12th century and was one of the ports visited by the Chinese junks of Cheng Ho between 1417 and 1419, before the Chinese emperor prohibited further overseas voyages. It was one of the few places on the coast to offer a friendly welcome to the early Portuguese mariners and to this day the pillar erected by Vasco da Gama as a navigational aid still stands on the promontory at the southern end of the bay. The cross which surmounts this pillar is of Lisbon stone (and it is therefore

KENYA

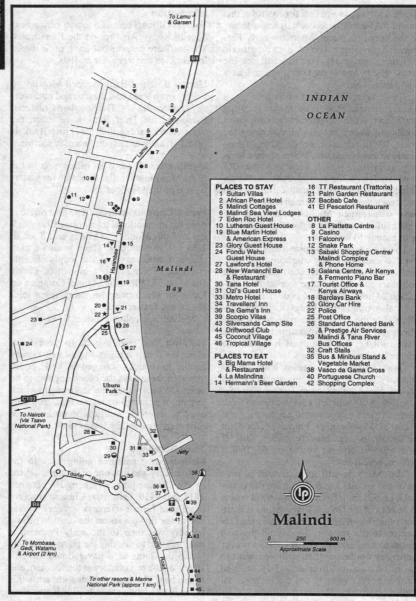

PLACES TO STAY
1 Sultan Villas
2 African Pearl Hotel
5 Malindi Cottages
6 Malindi Sea View Lodges
7 Eden Roc Hotel
10 Lutheran Guest House
19 Blue Marlin Hotel
    & American Express
23 Glory Guest House
24 Fondu Wehu
    Guest House
27 Lawford's Hotel
28 New Wananchi Bar
    & Restaurant
30 Tana Hotel
31 Ozi's Guest House
33 Metro Hotel
34 Travellers' Inn
36 Da Gama's Inn
39 Scorpio Villas
43 Silversands Camp Site
44 Driftwood Club
45 Coconut Village
46 Tropical Village

PLACES TO EAT
3 Big Mama Hotel
   & Restaurant
4 La Malindina
14 Hermann's Beer Garden

16 TT Restaurant (Trattoria)
21 Palm Garden Restaurant
37 Baobab Cafe
41 El Pescatori Restaurant

OTHER
8 La Piattetta Centre
9 Casino
11 Falconry
12 Snake Park
13 Sabaki Shopping Centre/
    Malindi Complex
    & Phone Home
15 Galana Centre, Air Kenya
    & Fermento Piano Bar
17 Tourist Office &
    Kenya Airways
18 Barclays Bank
20 Glory Car Hire
22 Police
25 Post Office
26 Standard Chartered Bank
    & Prestige Air Services
29 Malindi & Tana River
    Bus Offices
32 Craft Stalls
35 Bus & Minibus Stand &
    Vegetable Market
38 Vasco da Gama Cross
40 Portuguese Church
42 Shopping Complex

INDIAN
OCEAN

Malindi
Bay

To Lamu
& Garsen

To Nairobi
(via Tsavo
National Park)

Uhuru
Park

Jetty

To Mombasa,
Gedi, Watamu
& Airport (2 km)

To other resorts & Marine
National Park (approx 1 km)

Malindi

0   250   500 m
Approximate Scale

original) but the supporting pillar is of local coral.

There's also the so-called Portuguese church which Vasco da Gama is reputed to have erected and where two of his crew were buried – at least, that is what the curator will tell you. Maybe he's right but the graves of the sailors are certainly not the originals. Vasco da Gama was not carrying cement on his voyage around Africa! What is more plausible is that this church is the one which St Francis Xavier visited on his way to India. The rest of the compound is taken up by the graves of Catholic missionaries from the late 19th and 20th centuries. The site is run by the Kenya Museums authority so you're supposed to pay an entry fee but the curator is happy with KSh 50 as a contribution towards upkeep.

Not far to the north are a number of pillar tombs and the remains of a mosque and a palace. Other than this, however, little remains of the old town. The nearest substantial ruins from pre-Portuguese days are at Gedi, south of Malindi.

Malindi Marine National Park
The most popular excursion from Malindi is to the Malindi Marine national Park several km south of town past Silversands. Here you can rent a glass-bottomed boat to take you out to the coral reef. Masks and snorkels are provided though they're usually pretty well used and the quality is not what it might be. Fins can be rented for around KSh 100 from the kiosk on the beach inside the marine park gate.

The variety and colours of the coral and the fish are simply amazing and you'll be surprised how close you can get to the fish without alarming them. On the other hand, the area is getting a little overused and there's been a lot of damage to the coral – the boat people actually anchor on the coral itself. Shell collectors have also degraded the area. During the rainy season visibility is severely reduced by the silt in the water which gets washed in from the Galana River.

You can arrange these trips in Malindi – people come around the hotels to ask if you are interested in going. The usual price is around KSh 600 per person which includes a taxi to take you to and from your hotel, hire of the boat and the park entry fee (US$5 for nonresidents and KSh 100 for residents). You may be able to get it for less if you bargain hard but you won't be able to knock too much off this price. The marine park is open daily from 7 am to 7 pm, but the boats only go out at low tide.

Snake Park
Yes, Malindi has the inevitable snake park. It's behind the Sabaki shopping centre/ Malindi Complex on the Lamu road and is open from 9 am to 6 pm daily. Entry is KSh 200 for nonresidents and KSh 100 for residents. Children are half price.

Falconry
The falconry has a number of caged birds of prey, as well as a huge tortoise which roams the grounds, and a chimp on a rope – fine if you like that sort of thing. The opening hours are 9 am to 5.30 pm and the entry fees are the same as for the snake park.

Scuba Diving
If you'd like to go scuba diving you can do this from the Driftwood Club at Silversands Bay. A dive costs the equivalent of US$40 plus the marine park entry fee of US$5 for nonresidents and KSh 100 for residents. There is also a diving school here for those who wish to learn, but it's not cheap at around the equivalent of US$450 for a course.

Deep Sea Fishing
Kenya is famous for the game-fishing opportunities off the coast. The Malindi Sea Fishing Club can organise trips at a cost of around the equivalent of US$470 per boat for four people including all equipment. Most of the resort hotels can also arrange these trips. It's not a good idea to arrange these trips from street touts, as some boats have no safety equipment, navigational aids or radios on board. ■

Places to Stay – bottom end

There are a number of cheap, basic lodges in the centre of town, but they're usually fairly noisy at night and you don't get the benefit of sea breezes or instant access to the beach. Best of the bunch is the *Tana Hotel* (☎ 20657) which has rooms with attached bathrooms, fan and mosquito nets for KSh 400/500 a single/double. There's no bar or restaurant here.

Also reasonable is the *Tana Ocean View Annexe* which has doubles with attached bathrooms for KSh 600 and singles with shared facilities for KSh 300. Much more basic is the *New Wananchi Bar & Restaurant* which costs KSh 150/180 for singles/doubles with shared facilities.

Most travellers prefer to stay in one of the hotels closer to the beach. The best in this area is probably *Ozi's Guest House* (☎ 20218) which is on the foreshore road. It's kept spotlessly clean, and safe lockers are available. The rooms, which all have fans and mosquito nets, cost KSh 350/600 for singles/doubles and KSh 850 for triples with breakfast. Bathrooms and toilets are shared between four rooms. The only problem here is that rooms on one side face the mosque, while those on the other side overlook the Malindi Bus depot – either way you'll be woken early.

Another popular place is the *Silversands Camp Site* (☎ 20412) two km south of town along the coast road. It costs KSh 90 per person to camp here (KSh 50 for children) and there are good toilets, saltwater showers, and freshwater taps but very little shade. Mattresses can be hired for KSh 20 per day. There's also a laundry service. There are also three types of tented banda for rent, the price for which depends on whether you stay two nights or less or three nights or more. The *Mzuri Huts* have attached bathroom and cost KSh 450 for one night or KSh 1290 for three nights for a double.

The *White Huts* have two single beds, mosquito nets, screened windows, electric lights and lockable doors but shared showers and toilets for KSh 330 for one night or KSh 930 for three nights a double. The *Green Huts*, of which there are three, are actually tents under a makuti roof and cost KSh 270 for one night or KSh 780 for three nights a double. The tents have mosquito nets, private bathroom facilities and electric lights. There is no single-occupancy tariff, and prices are negotiable if you plan to stay for a while. Bicycles can be rented for KSh 160 per day or KSh 30 by the hour. There's a cafe on the site which does simple meals at a reasonable price but if you want to do your own cooking then you'll have to buy fruit and vegetables from the main market in town and anything else from the Oasis Complex a little further down the road to the south where there's a super-market.

Also popular in the past has been the *Travellers' Inn*, on the beachfront road just south of the main part of town. It's hard to see the attraction of this place as the rooms are basic and somewhat gloomy, but it is kept clean and the owner is very friendly. Rooms with a fan and shared bathroom facilities cost KSh 350 for a double including breakfast (no singles) but there are no mosquito nets.

Da Gama's Inn (☎ 30295) is a relatively new place just south of the Travellers' Inn, though you wouldn't know this judging from the state of the place. Quite a few travellers stay here and the owner, James, is friendly and helpful and the restaurant is good. The cost of rooms is entirely negotiable but is on a par with the Travellers' Inn and includes breakfast. The rooms have fans but not necessarily mosquito nets.

Forget about the once-popular *Metro Hotel*, also on the sea-front, unless you're desperate and want to be bitten alive by mosquitoes. It has very basic singles/doubles for KSh 150/250 and triples for KSh 300.

Back up in town away from the beach-front, by far the best place is the *Fondo Wehu Guest House* (☎ 30017) in the western part of town. It's about 15 minutes walk from the bus station and well signposted both from Kenyatta and Lamu Rds. The place is run by an English woman and her Kenyan husband and is a very popular place to stay. Dorm beds in the airy upstairs dorm cost KSh 200, and comfortable singles/doubles will cost

KSh 350/500. The price includes an excellent breakfast and free laundry service. Tasty snacks are also available. Fondo will probably greet you on arrival.

Close by is the *Miami Guest House* (☎ 31029) which is a larger place with a rooftop restaurant which offers singles/doubles with attached bathrooms for KSh 450/750 and doubles with shared bathroom facilities for KSh 650. This is a Muslim hotel so alcoholic drinks are prohibited. Like Fondo Wehu, it's well signposted.

Excellent value is the *Lutheran Guest House* (☎ 21098) off the Lamu road at the back of the Malindi Complex and next to the Snake Park. It's a popular place to stay and deservedly so. The rooms are set around a quiet garden courtyard – very reminiscent of an Indonesian *losmen* – and are clean and well maintained as well as having a fan and mosquito nets. Rooms with shared bathroom facilities cost KSh 350/600 for singles/doubles and KSh 430/750 for singles/doubles with attached bathrooms, including breakfast. There are also two fully furnished cottages each having two bedrooms, a bathroom and a living room for KSh 900 per night or KSh 3500 per week but breakfast is not included. Alcoholic drinks are not permitted on the premises.

Places to Stay – middle

There are few places to stay in this price range and tariffs vary according to the season. *Malindi Cottages* (☎ 20304), out on the Lamu road, close to the Eden Roc Hotel, is one of the best. It consists of several fully furnished cottages surrounding a swimming pool. Each cottage has two bedrooms, a sitting room, kitchen, bathroom and verandah. Facilities include a refrigerator, gas cooker, cooking utensils, mosquito nets and fans. Each cottage sleeps up to five adults and costs KSh 1500 per night. There are also so-called single cottages with a double bed for KSh 600 per night.

Just beyond the Eden Roc Hotel on the Lamu road are *Malindi Sea View Cottages* (☎ 20439) which consists of a number of makuti-roofed cottages, some of them divided in half to form two double rooms each with its own shower and toilet. The beds are enormous and have a full mosquito net plus there's a fan in each room but the water pressure in the showers is often very low. The prices here are KSh 1400 per person per night including breakfast negotiable down to KSh 1200 per night. The hotel has it's own swimming pool and there's a bar of sorts but the waiter can be hard to find.

Beyond the Sea View Cottages are two more hotels, both of a similar standard. The first is the *African Pearl Hotel* (☎ 20449) which is good value at KSh 1300/1600 for singles/doubles including breakfast. Kenyan residents pay KSh 1100/1400, respectively. The hotel has its own (dirty) pool, bar and restaurant. Next is *Sultan Villas* which is very similar in standard to African Pearl and offers singles/doubles at KSh 1200/1800 including breakfast. The hotel has its own (clean) pool.

Places to Stay – top end

Malindi's top-range hotels are strung out along the beachfront both north and south of the town centre. Some of them are very imaginatively designed and consist of clusters of makuti-roofed cottages in beautifully landscaped gardens full of flowering trees. Others are fairly standard beach hotels. All of them have swimming pools and other sporting facilities and many have a disco. They cater mostly, but not exclusively, to package tourists from Europe on two to three-week holidays and they all seem to pitch their business at a specific nationality – British, German or Italian. Very little intermingling seems to take place and you can definitely feel you've come to the wrong spot in some hotels if you don't belong to the dominant nationality. It's a common trait with package tourism anywhere in the world.

Most of the hotels impose a supplement over the Christmas and New Year periods which can be quite considerable (KSh 1000 and more is fairly typical), so bear this in mind if you intend to stay at this time of the year.

If being by the beach is important, it's also

worth bearing in mind that the hotels north of town do not have a beach frontage as there is a wide swathe of sand dunes here; those to the south of town are right on the beachfront.

Right in the town itself are *Lawford's Hotel* and the *Blue Marlin Hotel*, which are owned by a German company, Kenya-Hotels GmbH, though bookings can be made by ringing the hotels direct on ☎ 20440. Half board at either is KSh 3150/4200 for singles/doubles for nonresidents and KSh 2700/3600, respectively, for residents. Higher prices prevail in the high season.

North of town on the Lamu road is the *Eden Roc Hotel* (☎ 20480, fax 21225), one of the few hotels which seems to have a mixed clientele. It's also one of the few places with tennis courts, though these are not open to non-guests. The hotel is one of the older resorts in Malindi, and certainly not much imagination has gone into its design. The rates for nonresidents including breakfast are KSh 1804/2406 for singles/doubles in the bungalows, KSh 2060/2740 in the deluxe rooms and KSh 2943/3924 in the private suites. Resident rates for the same thing are KSh 1465/1954, KSh 1650/2200 and KSh 1854/2472, respectively.

South of town, the top-range hotels stretch all the way from the path leading to the Vasco da Gama monument down to Casuarina Beach and the Malindi Marine national Park.

First is *Scorpio Villas* (☎ 20194) which has 40 rooms in 17 cottages spread over some 1.5 hectares of beautiful tropical gardens, with three swimming pools and just 50m from Silversands Beach. All the cottages are fully furnished in Lamu style and come complete with your own house steward. There's an excellent restaurant and bar within the complex. It's Italian-owned and Italians form the bulk of the clientele. Bed and breakfast rates per person per night sharing a double room are from KSh 1700 and full-board rates from KSh 2300.

Further down the beach beyond the Silversands Camp Site is the *Driftwood Club* (☎ 20155, fax 30712). This was one of the first beach resorts to be built at Malindi and it's different from the other hotels as it's used more by individual travellers rather than package groups. Although it gets more of a mixture of nationalities, the clientele is mainly British and white Kenyan. The club offers a variety of rooms from KSh 800/1300 for singles/doubles with fan and shared bathrooms to KSh 2900/3700 with air-con and private bathroom. There are also two luxury cottages each consisting of two air-con bedrooms, two bathrooms, living room and verandah which will sleep up to four people for KSh 10,800. Children between the ages of three and 11 years sharing with parents are charged KSh 500. All prices include breakfast. Full-board rates are also available. The bar, restaurant and other facilities are open to non-guests on payment of a temporary membership fee of KSh 100 per day or KSh 350 per week, so there's often an interesting mix of budget travellers hanging out by the pool.

Next down the beach is *Coconut Village* (☎ 20928, fax 30103), where the clientele is mainly Italian. Double rooms with full board cost KSh 2500 per person per night for nonresidents and KSh 2100 for residents, depending on the time of year (and there are no less than six 'seasons'!). Half-board rates are KSh 2250 and KSh 1900 per person per night for nonresidents and residents, respectively. Children under two years old are free of charge and those under 12 pay 50% of the above rates. All prices include taxes and service charges. The hotel has a popular open-air, makuti-roofed discotheque which overlooks the beach. It operates once weekly on Wednesday night and entry for non-guests costs KSh 300.

Ignoring the *Malindi Beach Club*, which is a private club, next up is the *Tropical Village* and the *African Dream Village* (☎ 20442, fax 20119), both of which are owned by the same people. The clientele is mainly Italian. High-season rates including breakfast are KSh 2000/3500 for singles/doubles and low-season rates are KSh 900/1800. Shoulder-season rates fall between these two sets of prices. Full and half-board rates are also available. These two resort complexes are among the most imaginatively conceived of all the hotels in Malindi with huge soaring makuti-roofed areas for their bars and restaurants.

Further down the coast road is the *White Elephant Sea Lodge* (☎ 20223), which caters mainly to British tourists, but is presently undergoing renovations.

Turning left off the coast road towards the marine national park entrance are the *Dorado Cottages* (☎ 30104, fax 21459). Non-resident rates here in the low season for bed and breakfast are KSh 1800 per person per night. In the high season they are KSh 2450. Resident rates for the same thing are KSh 1550 and KSh 2100 per person per night, respectively. Full and half-board rates are also available. The clientele is mainly Italian.

Next along this road is *Jambo Village* (☎/fax 21245) which caters to a young crowd of various nationalities. Non-resident rates for bed and breakfast are KSh 2000/3800 for singles/doubles and for residents KSh 1800/3400.

Last up is the new *Stephanie Sea House* (☎ 20720, fax 20613) overlooking the marine national park, which is Italian-owned and caters mainly to Italians though not exclusively. This is probably one of the best places to stay and has an excellent beach completely free of seaweed as well as a crystal-clear sea uncontaminated with silt. There are five different 'seasons' and rates vary between the equivalent of US\$25 per person per night through to US\$35 to US\$50 in the low, shoulder and high seasons for bed and breakfast. Transfers can be arranged to and from both Mombasa and Malindi airports for a fairly modest fee.

Places to Eat – cheap

There's not a lot of choice in this range unless you're keen on pizza or spaghetti. Cheap African-style meals can be found in the restaurants at the hotels in the centre of town. The *New Safari Hotel*, for instance, is a very popular place with the locals at lunch time but it's closed all day during the month of Ramadan.

Slightly more expensive but excellent value is the *Palm Garden* on Lamu road

opposite the petrol station. Food here is very tasty, and the place is usually packed with escapees from the resorts. The menu is mainly seafoods and curries. The front part of the restaurant serves snacks and light meals, while the makuti-roofed back section (entered from the side street) does full meals. Meals in the snack area include burgers and chips for around KSh 180, wiener schnitzel (KSh 250), steaks (KSh 220) and curries (KSh 200 to KSh 250).

Similar, and also good value, is the *TT Restaurant* (otherwise known as *Trattoria*) a little further up the Lamu road on the opposite side. It offers much the same meals as the Palm Garden and also has relatively cheap, cold beers.

Continuing up the Lamu road and in the centre of the Malindi Complex (signposted) is the *Golden Shell Restaurant* which offers a range of seafood and curry dishes at very reasonable prices varying between KSh 200 and KSh 300.

At the opposite end of town, it's possible to get fish and chips for around KSh 200 at the *Baobab Restaurant* on Vasco da Gama Rd but not all items on the menu are so reasonably priced. Some items go up as high as KSh 800 and I've seen so-called 'lunch-time specials' priced as high as KSh 750. What they do have here, however, are the cheapest, cold beers in town at KSh 45.

Not far from the Baobab is *El Pescatori Pizzeria & Grill Bar* which is worth checking out for lunch and dinner if you like pizza (from KSh 180) or spaghetti (from KSh 150). The rest of the menu, especially seafood, is just as highly priced as anywhere else in town.

Ozi's Guest House is also worth considering for reasonably priced curries (around KSh 150 to KSh 200) though they do have more expensive seafood dishes such as prawns, crab and lobster.

Places to Eat – more expensive

For a splurge, it's worth trying the *Driftwood Club* where you have to pay KSh 100 for temporary membership. This membership enables you to use their swimming pool, hot showers, bar and restaurant. The prices are quite reasonable – lunch for KSh 450, dinner for KSh 550, good snacks (such as smoked sailfish and prawn sandwiches) from KSh 100, and à la carte seafood main dishes for KSh 200 to KSh 450. The Sunday curry lunch buffet is a bargain at KSh 250. It's very convenient if you are staying at the Silversands Camp Site.

I Love Pizza in front of the fishing jetty and close to the Metro Hotel is a popular place for a splurge. As you might expect, it serves Italian food (pizza and pasta for around KSh 250) and also more expensive meals such as chicken casserole and seafood dishes from KSh 450. It's open from noon to midnight daily.

In the northern part of town, near the disco and casino, are a couple of places which also cater primarily to the resort crowds. At *Hermann's Beer Garden* you are able to eat German and other continental dishes for KSh 300 and more. It's hardly the place you want for a quiet meal as the music is generally quite loud.

Right next door at the Stardust Club is the open-air *Putipu Restaurant,* where the emphasis is very much on Italian food. Main dishes are in the KSh 400 to KSh 750 range, while pizzas cost between KSh 220 and KSh 280.

Further north, off the Lamu road, you can also splurge at one of three places, all of them very close to each other. They are *Big Mama Hotel & Restaurant* (ex-*Eddie's* for which there's still a sign), *Ul-Nil's Poolside Bar & Restaurant* and *La Malindina*. They're all similarly priced so plan on spending at least KSh 600 to KSh 800 per person without drinks.

For superb gelati ice cream, the *Gelateria Bar* in the Sabaki shopping centre has a range of flavours, but it's not cheap. There's a similar place on the opposite side of the road next to the Italian restaurant which offers barbecued game meats.

Good coffee and cakes can be found at the *Karen Blixen Cafe* in the Galana Centre, Lamu Rd, which has tables and chairs in the courtyard.

Entertainment

Discos Because Malindi is a holiday resort there are a number of bars and discos to visit in the evening, some of which rock away until dawn. The most famous of them is the *Stardust Club* which generally doesn't get started until 11 pm and costs KSh 200 for women and KSh 300 for men (more on Saturday nights). Similar is *Club 28* next door to the Eden Roc Hotel.

There's also a disco at least once a week – usually on Wednesday – at *Coconut Village* past the Driftwood Club and, if you get there early enough, you won't have to pay the entry charge. It's a pleasant place to dance away the evening and you won't drown in perspiration as it's open-air under makuti roofs right on the beach. The bar is incredible and is worth a visit just to see it. It's built around a living tree with one of the branches as the bar top!

Bars The liveliest tourist bar is the makuti-roofed *Hermann's Beer Garden*, where the music is loud, the lighting subdued and the girls ever present.

Also fairly popular is the *Fermento Piano Bar* on the top floor of the shopping centre diagonally opposite the Sabaki Centre. This is a ritzy, air-con bar specialising in cocktails, though they also sell beers. Up until around 10 pm they show music videos; after that it's either live music or dreadful Italian karaoke. If it's the latter, you may decide that it's time to drift across the road to the Stardust Club.

The *Malindi Fishing Club*, right next to the Metro Hotel, may also be worth checking out if you're staying in the area. It's a very attractive, traditionally constructed building with a makuti roof. There's a bar and snacks are available. The clientele, mainly British, are friendly, beers are some of the cheapest in town, the only snag being the daily membership charge of KSh 50.

The *Malindi Golf & Country Club*, a couple of km north of town, is open to all comers on payment of a temporary membership fee. Apart from golf, there is tennis, a bar/restaurant, and a library.

If you want to do some serious gambling or simply have a flutter on the one-arm bandits (pokies, to the Aussies) along with the hordes of like-minded addicts then there's the *Casino* on the Lamu road. It has all the usual international games and you can bet as little as KSh 50 on most games. Entry is free and drinks are reasonably priced. It's open daily from noon until 5 am.

Things to Buy

There's a collection of at least 30 craft shops (tin shacks) on the beachfront near the mosque. Prices are reasonable, though you must, of course, bargain, and the quality is also reasonable. Crafts on offer include makonde carvings, wooden animal carvings, soapstone and wooden chess sets, basketware and the like. If you have unwanted or excess gear (T-shirts, jeans, cameras) you can often do a part-exchange deal with these people.

Getting There & Away

Air Three companies each operate two flights a day between Malindi and Mombasa (US$28) and between Malindi and Lamu (US$65). They are Air Kenya Aviation (☎ 30808), Galana Centre; Eagle Aviation Ltd (☎ 21258), next door to Express Kenya/American Express; and Prestige Air Services Ltd (☎ 20861), next door to the Standard Chartered Bank. All these offices are on Lamu Rd.

Kenya Airways (☎ 20237) also flies from Malindi to Nairobi and Mombasa twice daily. If you're relying on these flights to get back to Mombasa or Nairobi to connect with an international flight then make absolutely sure you have a confirmed booking or, preferably, go back a day before.

Bus & Matatu Three bus companies operate between Mombasa and Malindi on a daily basis. They are Malindi Bus, Tana Express and the Faza Express. The first two have offices in Mombasa and Malindi but Faza Express only has offices in Mombasa and Lamu. There are several departures daily in

either direction which take about 2½ hours and cost KSh 60.

There are also matatus which do this run taking about two hours and cost a little more. There's no need to book in advance from Mombasa if you turn up early enough in the morning. In Mombasa the buses leave from outside the New People's Hotel from early morning until mid-afternoon. Matatus leave from the same place all day until late afternoon and go when full.

Both the buses and matatus *fly* up and down this coast road as though they were being pursued by a marauding army of *shifta* (bandits) in high-speed Land Cruisers, and they pack in as many punters as they possibly can. I counted 138 people on one such bus and that didn't include the driver and his mate!

Geoff Crowther

Between Malindi and Lamu there's only one bus line these days and that is the Faza Express. The reason for this is that the other lines have withdrawn their services because of the appalling state of the road and the danger of being held up by armed shifta – this despite the fact that the buses travel with an armed soldier on board. If you do decide to go by bus, you should be aware of the fact that there is a possibility that your bus may be held up by shifta toting AK47s in which case you'll be robbed or, at worst, robbed and shot. Make enquiries locally as to the current situation before setting off on this route.

There are two Faza Express buses to Lamu daily from Malindi which cost KSh 300 and leave from outside the New Safari Hotel in the centre of town at 8.30 am. There's no booking office so just turn up. These buses originate in Mombasa so they're usually pretty full on arrival and a writhing mass of flesh and bones on departure. It's a lousy eight-hour journey, if you're lucky; 11 hours if you're unlucky. Think seriously about flying if you can afford it.

Share-Taxi It's possible to find Peugeot 504 station wagons which do the journey between Malindi and Mombasa, but difficult in the opposite direction. They leave when full (seven passengers) and cost around KSh

400 per person (negotiable). You'll find them at the bus station in Malindi but only in the mornings. Commissioning a normal taxi to take you between Mombasa and Malindi or vice versa will cost you about KSh 4000.

Train You can make advance reservations for Kenyan Railways at most of the large hotels in Malindi and at travel agencies, but you'll be charged KSh 200 for the service. All they do for this is make a telephone call to Mombasa railway station. You can do it yourself (☎ (011) 312220) for a fraction of the cost. See the Mombasa Getting There & Away section for information on train fares and timetables.

Getting Around

You can rent bicycles from the Silversands Camp Site, from Ozi's Guest House and from some of the mid-range and lower top-end hotels. Charges are KSh 30 per hour or KSh 160 per day. This is probably the best way to get around town unless you prefer to walk.

Taxis are mainly concentrated along the Lamu Rd between the post office and the Sabaki Centre. Fares are basically the first figure which comes into the taxi driver's head so you need to negotiate but even a very short journey won't cost you much less than KSh 100. The fare to the airport is KSh 300 from anywhere along Lamu Rd and around KSh 200 from the town centre.

On the main street near the Blue Marlin Hotel, Glory Car Hire (☎ 20065), Hertz (☎ 20069), Avis, and Europcar all have offices. Payless Car Hire (☎ 311643) is up the gravel lane beside the Palm Garden Restaurant. It's advisable to book a car in advance if you want to be sure of getting the class and type of vehicle you want as the choice is limited and demand is high.

GARSEN

This is another nondescript town between Garissa and Lamu, on the one hand, and Malindi and Lamu on the other. There's absolutely no reason to stay here if you're on the only remaining bus line between Malindi and Lamu (the Faza Express) but, if you're hitching between Garissa and Lamu (there are no longer any buses between the two), it may be necessary. There are several basic hotels to choose from. The best is the *3-in-1 Lodging & Restaurant* which is fairly clean and has its own restaurant.

Lamu

In the early 1970s Lamu acquired a reputation as the Kathmandu of Africa – a place of fantasy and other-worldliness wrapped in a cloak of medieval romance. It drew all self-respecting seekers of the miraculous, the globetrotters, and that much maligned bunch of people called hippies. The attraction was obvious. Both Kathmandu and Lamu were remote, unique and fascinating self-contained societies which had somehow escaped the depredation of the 20th century with their culture, their centuries-old way of life and their architecture intact.

Though Kathmandu is now overrun with well-heeled tourists and the hippies have retired to their rural communes or into business as purveyors of the world's handicrafts, Lamu remains much the same as it has always been – to a degree.

With an almost exclusively Muslim population, it is Kenya's oldest living town and has changed little in appearance or character over the centuries. Access is still by diesel-powered launch from the mainland (though there's an airstrip on Manda Island) and the only motor-powered vehicle on the island, other than the occasional tractor, is that owned by the district commissioner. The streets are far too narrow and winding to accommodate anything other than pedestrians or donkeys. Men still wear the full length white robes known as *khanzus* and the *kofia* caps, and women cover themselves with the black wraparound buibui as they do in other Islamic cultures, although here it's a liberalised version which often hugs their bodies, falls short of the ankles and dispenses completely with the veil worn in front of the face.

There are probably more dhows to be seen here than anywhere else along the East African coast and local festivals still take place with complete disregard for camera-toting tourists. The beach at Shela is still magnificent and uncluttered and nothing happens in a hurry. It's one of the most relaxing places you'll ever have the pleasure to visit.

At least, that was the story until the mid-1980s. Since then a number of pressures have been threatening to undermine the fabric of this unique Swahili settlement. The most important of these during the late 1980s and early 1990s was tourism. In those days, during the high season, several hundred tourists would visit Lamu every day, either by air or overland by bus and launch. In the low season, the influx was considerably less but the perceived degradation of Lamu's social fabric attributed to tourism at the time prompted local newspapers to run scare stories under headlines such as, 'Lamu Under Siege'. They did have a point but the days of shock-horror seem to have passed and, with the downturn in Kenya's tourist industry over the last few years, the inflow of tourists, particularly budget travellers, has decreased to such a degree that many of the cheaper hotels have permanently closed their doors.

The other major pressure is population increase. It's expected that the town's current population of around 15,000 will increase to 30,000 by the end of the century. To accommodate and provide services for all those extra people is going to take some very sensitive planning. Even today, it's a well-known fact that Lamu schoolchildren fare worst in the national secondary school certificate examinations compared with the rest of the country. Redressing that deficiency is not going to be an easy task. While it may be true that tourism distorts economic patterns and centuries-old cultural values and can even destroy them, Lamu urgently needs an injection of cash for preservation, restoration, creation of employment, schools and for a cleanup – particularly of the open drainage system. Tourism could be the source of that cash but the boom days are over – at least until the tourist industry picks up again.

What can be done about stabilising the population is another story entirely and a sensitive issue in a traditional Muslim culture. Yet, as the population expands and the demand for water and electricity increases, it's clear that Lamu faces a crisis at some point in the future. Water supplies on the island are very limited and the electricity generating station is running at well below 50% capacity with the bulk of the plant lying idle awaiting repair. When it will be repaired is anyone's guess.

History

The 20th century may have brought Lamu a measure of peace and tranquillity but it has not always been that way. The town was only of minor importance in the string of Swahili settlements which stretched from Somalia to Mozambique. Although it was a thriving port by the early 1500s, it surrendered without a fight to the early Portuguese mariners and was generally politically dependent on the more important sultanate of Paté which, at the time, was the most important island port in the archipelago. Until the late 1700s it did manage to avoid the frequent wars between the sultanates of Paté, Mombasa and Malindi following the decline of Portuguese influence in the area.

After that there followed many years of internecine strife between the various island city-states of Lamu, Paté, Faza and Siyu, which only ended in 1813 when Lamu defeated the forces of Paté in a battle at Shela. Shortly afterwards, Lamu became subject to the sultanate of Zanzibar which nominally controlled the whole of the coastal strip from Kilwa to the Somali border (under a British protectorate from 1890) until Kenya became independent in 1963.

Lamu had a slave-based economy (in common with the other Swahili coastal city-states) until the turn of the 20th century when the British forced the Sultan of Zanzibar to

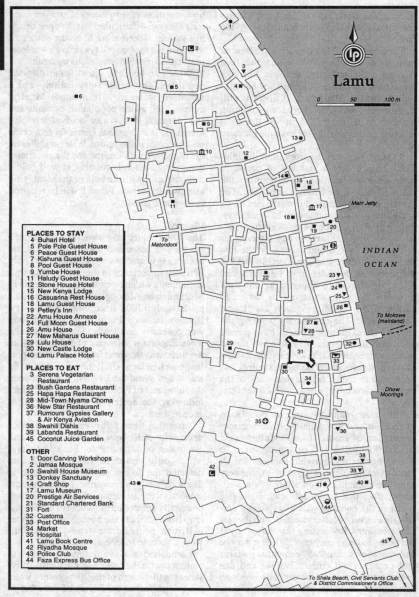

Lamu

0   50   100 m

To Matondoni

Main Jetty

INDIAN OCEAN

To Mokowe (mainland)

Dhow Moorings

To Shela Beach, Civil Servants Club & District Commissioner's Office

PLACES TO STAY
4 Buhari Hotel
5 Pole Pole Guest House
6 Peace Guest House
7 Kishuna Guest House
8 Pool Guest House
9 Yumbe House
11 Haludy Guest House
12 Stone House Hotel
15 New Kenya Lodge
16 Casuarina Rest House
18 Lamu Guest House
19 Petley's Inn
22 Amu House Annexe
24 Full Moon Guest House
26 Amu House
27 New Maharus Guest House
29 Lulu House
30 New Castle Lodge
40 Lamu Palace Hotel

PLACES TO EAT
3 Serena Vegetarian Restaurant
23 Bush Gardens Restaurant
25 Hapa Hapa Restaurant
28 Mid-Town Nyama Choma
36 New Star Restaurant
37 Rumours Gypsies Gallery & Air Kenya Aviation
38 Swahili Dishis
39 Labanda Restaurant
45 Coconut Juice Garden

OTHER
1 Door Carving Workshops
2 Jamaa Mosque
10 Swahili House Museum
13 Donkey Sanctuary
14 Craft Shop
17 Lamu Museum
20 Prestige Air Services
21 Standard Chartered Bank
31 Fort
32 Customs
33 Post Office
34 Market
35 Hospital
41 Lamu Book Centre
42 Riyadha Mosque
43 Police Club
44 Faza Express Bus Office

sign an anti-slavery agreement and subsequently intercepted dhows carrying slaves north from that island. All that cheap labour fuelled a period of economic growth for Lamu and traders grew rich by exporting ivory, cowries, tortoiseshell, mangrove poles, oil seeds and grains, and importing oriental linen, silks, spices and porcelain.

With the abolition of slavery in 1907, the economy of the island rapidly went into decline and stayed that way until very recently when increased receipts from tourism gave it a new lease of life. That decline, and its strong sense of tradition, is what has preserved the Lamu you see today. No other Swahili town, other than Zanzibar, can offer you such a cultural feast and an uncorrupted traditional style of architecture – if you can ignore the TV aerials.

Information

Tourist Office There's a seasonal tourist information counter on the waterfront near the jetty, but it's of limited use.

Money The Standard Chartered Bank and the Kenya Commercial Bank, both on the harbour front, are the only banks in Lamu. They're both open Monday to Friday from 9 am to 3 pm, and Saturday from 9 to 11 am. It's possible that the Standard Chartered Bank may have closed by now.

Post & Communications Lamu's telephone code is 01221.

Books There are some excellent books about Lamu and the Swahili civilisation. The best general account is *The Portuguese Period in East Africa* by Justus Strandes. This is a translation of a book originally published in German in 1899 with up-to-date notes and appendices detailing recent archaeological findings, some of which contradict Strandes' opinions. It's very readable.

Lamu: A Study of the Swahili Town, by Usam Ghaidan, is a very detailed study of Lamu by an Iraqi who was formerly a lecturer in architecture at the University of Nairobi and has since devoted his time to research into the Swahili architecture of the north Kenyan coast. You can find both of the above books in most good bookshops in Nairobi or Mombasa and the latter at the museum in Lamu.

If you're going to stay long in Lamu the leaflet-map *Lamu: Map & Guide to the Archipelago, the Island & the Town* is worth buying at the museum bookshop.

Bookshops Apart from the museum, the Lamu Book Centre, close to Rumours Coffee Shop, has a small but reasonable selection of English-language novels and other books. It's also the only place where you can buy local newspapers, and international news magazines such as *Time* and *Newsweek*. It's open from 6.30 am to 12.30 pm and 2.30 to 9 pm.

Town Buildings

Lamu town dates back to at least the late 14th century when the Pwani Mosque was built. Most buildings date from the 18th century, but the lower parts and basements are often considerably older. The streets are narrow, cool and quiet and there are many small courtyards and intimate spaces enclosed by high walls. Traditionally, buildings were constructed entirely out of local materials – faced coral-rag blocks for the walls, wooden floors supported by mangrove poles, makuti roofs and intricately carved shutters for windows. This is changing gradually with the increasing use of imported materials and is one of the factors of great concern to conservationists.

One of the most outstanding features of the houses here, as in old Zanzibar, is the intricately carved doors and lintels which have kept generations of carpenters busy. Sadly, many of them have disappeared in recent years but the skill has not been lost. Walk down to the far end of the harbour front in the opposite direction to Shela and you'll see them being made.

Only a few of the mosques have minarets and even these are small affairs. This, combined with the fact that there's little outward decoration and few doors and windows

KENYA

opening onto the street, makes them hard to distinguish from domestic buildings.

Both in Lamu and in Shela, private developers have recently been allowed to build ugly, modern hotels despite local pressure, but fortunately there is only one in each place. There has been quite an increase in the number of hotels and guesthouses, but as most of them have used existing buildings the fabric and atmosphere of the old town has, by and large, been retained.

Lamu Museum

A couple of hours spent in the Lamu Museum, on the waterfront next to Petley's Inn, is an excellent introduction to the culture and history of Lamu. It's one of the most interesting small museums in Kenya. There's a reconstruction of a traditional Swahili house, charts, maps, ethnological displays, models of the various types of dhow and two examples of the remarkable and ornately carved ivory *siwa* – a wind instrument peculiar to the coastal region which is often used as a fanfare at weddings. There's a good slide show available at the museum – ask to see it. Entry costs KSh 200 (KSh 100 for children) for nonresidents and KSh 30 (KSh 10 for children) for residents and the museum is open daily from 8 am to 6 pm.

The museum has a good bookshop specialising in books on Lamu and the Swahili culture.

Swahili House Museum

If the museum stokes your interest in Swahili culture then you should also visit this museum tucked away off to the side of Yumbe House (a hotel). It's a beautifully restored traditional house with furniture and other house wares as well as a pleasant courtyard. Entry charges and opening hours are the same as the main museum.

Lamu Fort

The building of this massive structure was begun by the Sultan of Paté in 1810 and completed in 1823. From 1910 right up to 1984 it was used as a prison. It has recently undergone complete restoration and now houses an impressive walk-through aquarium and natural history museum, as well as the island's library. Entry fees and opening times are the same as for the museum.

Donkey Sanctuary

One of the most unexpected sights on Lamu is the Donkey Sanctuary which is run by the International Donkey Protection Trust of Sidmouth, Devon, UK. Injured, sick or worn-out donkeys are brought here to find rest and protection. As in most societies where they're used as beasts of burden, donkeys are regularly abused or get injured so it's good to see something positive being done for their welfare. The sanctuary is right on the waterfront. Although the free clinic has been going since 1985, land for the sanctuary wasn't purchased until 4 July 1987, a day that is celebrated by the sanctuary's manager as Donkey Independence Day (it also just happens to coincide with America's Independence Day!).

The Beach

There's no beach on the Lamu town waterfront itself. What there is here is a muddy, garbage-strewn mess in urgent need of a major cleanup. For a white-sand beach and crystal-clear water you need to go to Shela, a 40-minute walk or 10-minute trip by dhow from Lamu. The beach starts at Peponi Hotel, circles around the headland and continues all the way along the Indian Ocean side of the island. The best part of the beach if you want waves is well past Peponi Hotel – there's no surf at Peponi because you're still in the channel between Lamu and Manda islands. It's possible to hire windsurfing equipment at Peponi for use in the channel.

Matondoni Village
You'll see many dhows anchored along the waterfront at Lamu and at Shela in the harbour at the southern end of town but if you want to see them being built or repaired the best place to do this is at the village of Matondoni.

To get there you have a choice of walking (about two hours), hiring a donkey, or hiring a dhow. If you choose the dhow it will cost KSh 500 per person (minimum five passengers) but it usually includes a barbecue fish lunch.

Walking there is a little more problematical until you find the track at the back of town and that is easier said than done as there are tracks leading every which way. Head first for the football pitch and then follow the telephone wires which go to Matondoni. Sounds easy doesn't it? It isn't, so you'll have to stop and ask directions from local people until you're sure you're on the right track.

Set off early if you are walking. It gets very hot later in the day. There's a small cafe in Matondoni village where you can get fish and rice for around KSh 80 as well as fruit juice. There are no guesthouses in the village but a bed or floor space can usually be arranged in a private house if you ask around. An impromptu group of travellers generally collects later in the afternoon so you can all share a dhow ride back to Lamu.

Kipongani Village
This is also worth a visit. Here local people make straw mats, baskets and hats. It's a friendly place, and tea and snacks can be arranged plus there's a beautiful empty beach nearby with waves.

Shela Village
Shela village, a 40-minute walk from Lamu, is a pleasant little village well worth a wander around. The ancestors of the people here came from Takwa when that settlement was abandoned in the late 17th century and they still speak a dialect of Swahili which is distinct from that of Lamu. Many have migrated to Malindi in recent years. Don't miss the famous mosque with its characteristic minaret at the back of Peponi Hotel. Many of the houses in this village have been bought up and restored by foreigners in the last few years, but while it has a surprising air of affluence, the languorous atmosphere remains unspoiled. Quite a few travellers prefer to stay in Shela rather than in Lamu town itself. It's certainly more convenient for the beach if that's your main interest.

To get to Shela, follow the harbour-front road till it ends and then follow the shore line. You will pass the new hospital built by the Saudi Arabian government and a ginning factory before you have to follow the shore line. If the tide is out, you can walk along the beach most of the way. When it's in, you may well have to do a considerable amount of wading up to your thighs and deeper. If that doesn't appeal, there is a track all the way from Lamu to Shela but there are many turn-offs so stay with the ones which run closest to the shore (you may find yourself in a few cul-de-sacs doing this as a number of turn-offs to the left run to private houses and end there). A popular alternative to walking there is to take one of the frequent motorised dhows which shuttle back and forth between Lamu and Shela. This costs KSh 50 per person assuming there are a minimum of two people.

Dhow Trips
Taking a dhow trip is almost obligatory, and it is a very relaxing way to pass a day. You'll constantly be approached while walking along the waterfront by people wanting to take you out for a trip. The cost is around KSh 300 per person for four or more people, KSh 400 for less than four people. Five is a comfortable number as the boats are not that

big. The price includes fishing and snorkelling, although both are largely fruitless exercises as it's virtually impossible to catch fish during the day, and the best snorkelling is a couple of hours away. A barbecue fish lunch on the beach at Manda is provided, supposedly with the fish you have caught but usually with fish provided by the captain. Make sure you take a hat and some sunblock as there is rarely any shade on the dhows, despite assurances to the contrary.

See the Islands Around Lamu section later in this chapter for details about longer dhow trips.

Places to Stay – bottom end

Lamu has been catering for budget travellers for some two decades and, up to two years ago, there were more budget hotels than you could point a stick at. That situation has now radically changed with the downturn in the tourist industry and many have put up the shutters so there's now only a limited choice. All the same, don't believe a word anyone tells you about there being running water 24 hours a day at any of these places. There often isn't. Water is not an abundant commodity on Lamu and restrictions are in force most of the year. It's usually only available early in the morning and early in the evening which, in most cases, means bucket showers only and somewhat smelly toilets.

Prices are remarkably consistent because of the competition for clientele though you obviously get what you pay for both in terms of facilities and position. A dormitory bed or space on the floor of a rooftop costs around KSh 100, a single room between KSh 150 and 250, and a double room KSh 300 to KSh 500. Almost all of these would involve sharing bathroom facilities but some of the higher priced doubles would have their own bathroom. Prices rise in the high season (August to September and around Christmas/New Year) by a factor of up to 50%; at other times there's plenty of scope for negotiation, particularly if you plan to stay for more than just a day or two. Instant discounts are offered to anyone who plans to stay three or more days. If a lodge is full when you

arrive but you like it a lot and want to be first in line for a room, they'll usually let you sleep on the roof or elsewhere until the following morning.

Where you stay initially will probably depend largely on what sort of room you are offered, what's available and who meets you getting off the ferry from the mainland.

If you plan on staying in Lamu for a while it's worth making enquiries about renting a house, so long as there's a group of you to share the cost. On a daily basis it won't be much cheaper (if at all) than staying at a lodge but on a monthly basis you're looking at a considerable saving. You can share them with as many people as you feel comfortable with or have space for and prices usually include a house steward. Some of the simpler houses can be very cheap indeed and include a refrigerator and cooking facilities. They're available in Lamu town itself but also at Shela and between Lamu and Shela. Some of them can be excellent value and very spacious. You need to ask around and see what is available. It's possible to find some remarkably luxurious places, especially around Shela.

Lamu Town Right on the waterfront is the *Full Moon Guest House* which is a friendly place with an excellent 1st-floor balcony overlooking the water. It costs KSh 250 per room (single or double) in the low season and KSh 500 in the high season, all with shared facilities.

In a similar category is the *New Kenya Lodge*, behind the Kenya Commercial Bank. It's fairly clean and has mosquito nets and cold bucket showers. The rooms cost KSh 250 to KSh 350.

Very good value, clean and simple, is the *Lamu Guest House* at the back of the Lamu Museum. There's a choice of different rooms here but the best are probably those on the top floor. Doubles with attached bathrooms with fan cost KSh 550 and KSh 650 and triples with the same facilities are KSh 750. There are also some doubles with attached bathrooms, but no fan for KSh 400.

Next to the fort is the *New Castle Lodge* which overlooks the main square and picks up sea breezes since it's fairly high up. It used to be very popular with backpackers but these days it's only just habitable. Singles/doubles with shared bathroom facilities cost KSh 150/300. The rooms have mosquito nets and fans. Give the nearby *Bahati Lodging* a wide berth. It's the pits and you wouldn't even stable pigs in there.

Way out the back of town through a maze of sandy alleyways about 15 minutes walk from the waterfront (assuming you don't get lost) is the *Peace Guest House* (☎ 3020) which is very clean, provides mosquito nets and charges KSh 170 (KSh 200) for a bed in a four-bed dormitory including breakfast, and KSh 500 (KSh 600 in the high season) for spacious, doubles with attached bathrooms, with fan. If you're staying more than three nights they'll offer you a discount of approximately 20%. You can also camp here for KSh 80 per tent including the use of kitchen facilities and a fridge. This is a very spacious place surrounded by gardens and flowering trees and has been popular for years though it is quite a way from the centre of town. It's signposted most of the way from the waterfront but you can still get lost in the last 300m.

Closer to the centre of town and back from the waterfront but one of the tallest buildings in Lamu is the *Pole Pole Guest House* which has 15 doubles with attached bathrooms, with fan, some of them with mosquito nets, for KSh 300 excluding breakfast. There's a spacious, makuti-roofed area on top of the hotel from which there are great views over the town and the waterfront.

At the top end of this range is the *Kishuna Guest House* at the back side of town. It's just a modern concrete block devoid of character but it's very clean and offers singles/doubles with attached bathroom for KSh 400/700 including breakfast. All the rooms have a fan and mosquito nets and you have a choice in the double rooms of twin beds or a double bed.

Shela Quite a few travellers, especially beach lovers, prefer to stay at Shela village rather than in Lamu itself. There is no real budget accommodation here unless you can negotiate a room with a local family or rent a whole house and share the cost with a bunch of other people.

If you're going to stay here for a while – and it seems most of the people who stay here do – then it's best to ask around for a house to rent and have a group together to share the cost. Many of the houses here are owned by expatriate foreigners (especially Italians) who have poured vast amounts of money into them but only live here for part of the year. Most of them have been very sensitively upgraded and some are stunning. Quite a lot of them can be rented out so ask around in the restaurants.

Places to Stay – middle

Lamu Town Good value in this range is the *Casuarina Rest House* (☎ 3123) which was formerly the police headquarters. It offers large, airy rooms with good views and is clean and well maintained but often full. It costs KSh 1000 to KSh 1500 a double depending on how long you intend to stay, but like all places it's negotiable to an extent, and prices are much lower in the off season. There's access to a large, flat, roof area.

More expensive but excellent value is the new *Stone House Hotel* (☎ 33544/33149) which has beautiful sea-facing doubles with attached bathrooms for KSh 1850 and others which don't face the sea for KSh 1700. Singles with attached bathrooms are KSh 1450 and singles with shared bathroom facilities are KSh 1300. All prices include breakfast. The hotel has its own superb rooftop restaurant (no alcoholic drinks) with excellent views over the town and waterfront.

Very similar in style and quality is *Lulu House* (☎ 33539) in the maze of streets behind the fort which is relatively new and costs KSh 750/1500 for singles/doubles with attached bathroom, including breakfast. The rooms are very pleasant, the staff friendly and there's a roof area, a table-tennis room and a safe to leave valuables.

Close to the main square is the *New Maharus Guest House* (☎ 33001). There's nothing 'new' about the place and some of the rooms are positively antediluvian plus it totally lacks character but it's relatively cheap at KSh 700/1000 for singles/doubles and KSh 1300 for triples in '1st Class' rooms, KSh 500/700 for singles/doubles and KSh 900 for triples in '2nd class' rooms and KSh 300/400 in '3rd class' rooms in the high season. In the low season you can take KSh 100 to KSh300 off these prices depending on the class of room. Prices include breakfast and the rooms in 1st and 2nd class have attached bathrooms. Third class rooms come with shared bathroom facilities. It's not great value.

One of the most beautiful places in this range is *Yumbe House* (☎ 33101; fax 33300), close to the Swahili House Museum. It's a four-storey traditional house surrounding a central courtyard which has been superbly and sensitively converted into a hotel with airy terraces and makuti roofs. All rooms have attached bathrooms (towels, soap and toilet paper are provided), spotlessly clean, and there are mosquito nets and fan. It's excellent value at KSh 960/1830 for singles/doubles and KSh 2560 a triple including breakfast in the low season and KSh 1020/2130 for singles/doubles and KSh 3050 for triples including breakfast in the high season.

Right on the waterfront is *Amu House* (☎/fax 33420). This hotel is a beautifully restored 16th-century house decorated with plaster carvings and furnished with local antiques. All the bedrooms have attached bathrooms and equipped with fans and some have private verandahs but they all have antique beds with mosquito nets. The hotel also has its own restaurant offering breakfast and dinner specialising in Swahili-style seafood. It's a great place to stay and costs KSh 1500/2000 for singles/doubles including breakfast. If you make a reservation in advance and arrive by air, they'll meet you at Manda airport.

Another good place in this range is the *Pool Guest House*, so-called because it has a small swimming pool, though this is invariably empty. It's a mellow maze of a place surrounding a shady courtyard and the rooms

vary quite a bit, some having waterfront views and sea breezes. All have attached bathrooms with two beds, mosquito nets, a fan and are excellent value at KSh 700 without breakfast in the low season (more in the high season). There's also a rooftop area with good views over town. The staff are friendly and helpful.

The *Buhari Hotel* (☎ 33172) is a fairly new place with a very pleasant rooftop area, but variable rooms. The downstairs rooms are small and gloomy, but the upstairs rooms, particularly those at the front, are very good and cost KSh 800 for a room with a double bed and KSh 1500 for a room with two double beds including breakfast. All rooms have attached bathrooms and have mosquito nets.

Also worth considering is the *Haludy Guest House*. Rooms with attached bathrooms in this spacious and airy place cost KSh 1200 to KSh 1700 in the high season, dropping to KSh 650 to KSh 900 in the low season. There's a fridge and cooking facilities for those who want to put their own meals together. The only problem with this place is finding someone to rent you a room.

Shela The only mid-range places in Shela are whole villas which, as previously described, are available for longer term rental (a couple of weeks or more). Typical is the *White Rock Pool House*, right on the foreshore close to Peponi Hotel, which sleeps up to 10 people and costs the equivalent of US$100 a day in the low season and US$120 in the high season. It comes complete with a house steward, cook and cleaners.

Places to Stay – top end
Lamu Town The best top-range hotel in Lamu itself is the historic *Petley's Inn* (☎ 33107; fax 33378) right on the harbour front next to the Lamu Museum. It was originally set up in the late 19th century by Percy Petley – a somewhat eccentric English colonist who ran plantations on the mainland at Witu until he retired to Lamu – thus making it one of the oldest hotels in Kenya. Unfortunately, it was gutted by fire in August 1993 during which many irreplaceable mementos

were lost forever. Instead of crying into his rum and coke, however, the manager saw this as an opportunity to completely revamp the hotel's layout, facilities and services. This has been done with an admirable sense of good taste – all the traditional features have been restored, including makuti roofs and woven blinds. It's a great place to stay. The bed and breakfast rates for sea-facing rooms with a balcony are KSh 2400/3000 for singles/doubles and KSh 3750 for triples. Standard rooms including breakfast cost KSh 2000/2750 for singles/doubles and KSh 3300 for triples. Facilities include a swimming pool, a bar on the ground floor and an excellent rooftop bar/restaurant (open to non-guests) which catches the sea breezes. There's a sensible seafood and meat menu which changes every day depending on what's fresh, the food is excellently cooked and prices are reasonable.

Also on the waterfront is what some people consider to be Lamu's latest blot on the landscape. Intrusive and large by Lamu standards it certainly is but *some* effort has been put into creating a recognisably Lamu façade. This is the Swiss-managed *Lamu Palace Hotel* (☎ 33272; fax 33104). All the rooms have attached bathrooms and have air-con and cost the equivalent of US$50/80 for singles/doubles and US$100 for triples including breakfast in the high season and the equivalent of US$35/55 for singles/doubles and US$70 for triples including breakfast in the low season. These rates include boat transfer to and from Manda island airstrip. There's also a bar (the Chege Bar) which, like the restaurant, is open to non-guests.

Shela At the far end of Shela village and right on the beach is *Peponi Hotel* (☎ 33421/3; fax 33029) which is *the* place to stay if you want a top-range hotel at Shela. It consists of whitewashed cottages with their own verandahs facing the channel between Lamu and Manda islands and is reckoned to be one of the best hotels in the country, both in terms of its position, its facilities and the quality of the cuisine. The rates for bed and breakfast

in the standard rooms are the equivalent of US$130/170 for singles/doubles and in the superior rooms they are US$150/200. Full-board rates are US$150/220 in the standard rooms and US$180/270 in the superior rooms. Advance booking is essential. Motorised dhow transport between Manda airstrip and Peponi Hotel costs KSh 100 one way or KSh 500 by speedboat.

Peponi Hotel is a waters-ports centre and there are number of activities and equipment available both to guests and non-guests which include water-skiing (KSh 4000 per hour), windsurfing (KSh 500 to KSh 700 depending on the level of your skill), snorkelling (KSh 100 per day for the equipment alone), and scuba diving for certified divers between November and March (KSh 2350 for a single dive or KSh 4700 for two dives at two sites including lunch). It also offers full-moon dhow cruises for KSh 3500 (minimum eight people) including drinks, wine and a lobster dinner. Other facilities open to non-guests are the bar and the lunchtime barbecue area which serves very tasty fish and meat dishes at a reasonable price. The hotel is closed during May and June.

Also on the channel is *Kijani House* (☎ 33235; fax 33237), which has beautifully furnished rooms each with their own verandah arranged around a lush and colourful garden. Facilities include two swimming pools, and like Peponis, it is also closed in May and June. The cost here is the equivalent of US$70/90 for singles/doubles including breakfast in the standard rooms and US$85/120 in the superior rooms. Full-board rates are US$90/160 and US$105/190, respectively. Children between the ages of three and 12 are approximately half price. Boat transfers to and from Manda airstrip are free.

Immediately at the back of Peponi Hotel is the *Pwani Guest House* (☎ 33540), a small place with only three double rooms but very pleasant indeed. The spacious rooms all have two double beds as well as a child's cot and cost KSh 2000 a double including breakfast in the low season and KSh 2500 in the high season. All the rooms have attached bathrooms, hot water and mosquito nets plus there's a beautiful rooftop lounge area overlooking the channel.

In the centre of Shela village is the *Island Hotel* (☎ 33290; fax 245458; (02) 229880 in Nairobi), a superb traditional Lamu-style house with the romantic rooftop Barracuda Restaurant and only five minutes walk from the waterfront. The hotel has 14 rooms, including three family rooms, all of which have attached bathrooms. The rates are the same year-round and singles/doubles with bed and breakfast cost the equivalent of US$47/66 with triples at US$89. Full-board rates are US$65, US$103 and US$145, respectively. Children between the ages of three and 12 sharing their parents' room are charged US$11 for bed and breakfast and US$24 with full board. The room rates are inclusive of boat transfers to and from Manda island airstrip. The very good restaurant here is open to non-guests and prices are very reasonable. Swahili cuisine is the speciality. Starters are priced at KSh 100 to KSh 160 with main dishes at between KSh 240 (fish) and KSh 460 (crab) but it's not licensed to sell alcoholic drinks.

A good deal cheaper, and the place to stay if you want to do your own catering, is the *Shela Rest House* (☎ 33091) not far from the Island Hotel. It too has open makuti-roofed areas and sea views. Two-bedroom apartments with kitchen and fridge cost the equivalent of US$39 for three people and US$52 for four. It's a friendly place and the management can arrange for a cook to prepare your meals if you want a rest from doing it yourself.

Also reasonably priced is the *Shella Beach House* (☎ /fax 33420) which is owned by the same people who run Amu House in Lamu town. There are two rooftop bedrooms here and another one on the ground floor as well as a makuti-roofed sitting area and another one for dining. It costs KSh 1100/1500 for singles/doubles including breakfast.

Lastly there's the ugly three-storey blot on the foreshore that should never have got past the planning stage – the *Shela Beach Hotel*. This place sticks out like the proverbial dogs' balls but, fortunately – or unfortunately, seeing as it's still standing – construction has ceased and it's anyone's guess when it will be completed. It would be far better if it were demolished.

At the opposite (south-west) end of Lamu island is **Kipungani** where there's another top-end hotel called *Sea Breezes*. It's owned by Prestige Hotels and charges much the same as Petley's Inn.

Places to Eat – cheap

It's important to know that *all* of the cheap places to eat and many of the more expensive restaurants are closed all day until after sunset during the month of Ramadan. This leaves you with only three choices for breakfast (if your hotel doesn't provide this) and lunch. They are Petley's Inn, the Lamu Palace Hotel and Peponi Hotel.

One of the cheapest places to eat in Lamu is the *New Star Restaurant.* You certainly won't beat the prices and some people recommend it highly, but service can be slow (depending on what you order and the time of day). Fish and chips or rice costs KSh 150 to KSh 180.

Cheaper still is the very basic *Swahili Dishis* (sic) just off the waterfront. This tiny place caters purely for the locals and serves no-frills African food at rock-bottom prices. Another local eatery is the *Mid-Town Nyama Choma* cafe on the main square by the fort. There are no prizes here for culinary excellence, but for a cheap meat meal it's the place to go.

For consistently good food at a reasonable price there are a handful of very popular restaurants. The menus at all are pretty standard, with fish, seafood, steaks and curries. All do excellent juices and shakes. Despite the excellent seafood available, the seafood meals in Lamu are really quite basic.

Close by the dhow moorings is the *Labanda Restaurant* which, apart from the standard dishes, also does poulet yassa, a delicious Senegalese chicken dish for KSh 280. It also serves some vegetarian dishes, which are hard to find on Lamu.

For exclusively vegetarian fare head for the *Serena Vegetarian Restaurant*. This restaurant has been popular for years though under various names such as Coral Rock and Yoghurt Inn – there's still a sign at the front saying Yoghurt Inn. It has a good range of vegetarian dishes as well as banana pancakes, lassi and fruit juices. Expect to pay around KSh 150 to KSh 200 for main dishes. It's open daily but often closed on Tuesday during the low season.

Somewhat more expensive but extremely popular is the *Bush Gardens* on the waterfront, next door to the Hapa Hapa Restaurant. It's run by the very personable and energetic 'Bush Baby' who personally supervises the cooking which sometimes makes for slow service but guarantees you an excellent meal. Fish dishes (barracuda, tuna, snapper or shark) cost KSh 200, crab KSh 450, prawns KSh 350 and lobster KSh 750, all served with chips or coconut rice and salad. Fruit juices are also available. It's arguably the best seafood restaurant in Lamu.

Next door is the *Hapa Hapa Restaurant* which is also very good, and offers a similar range of dishes, including seafood and possibly the best fruit juices and milk shakes in town. Prices are similar to those at Bush Gardens, and it's also a very popular place, especially at breakfast time.

Juice lovers should pay at least one visit to the *Coconut Juice Garden* on the waterfront beyond the Lamu Palace Hotel heading for Shela. It serves excellent, cheap fruit juices and coconut milk.

Many travellers come across a man popularly called Ali Hippy who, for several years, has been offering travellers meals at his house. The meal usually includes lobster, crab, fish, coconut rice and vegetable stew and the whole family entertains you while you eat. Some people come away quite satisfied (it's definitely an unusual evening out) but the majority these days feel it's somewhat contrived, and indeed it's not unusual for the whole evening to be cancelled with no explanations – or refunds – given. Expect to pay around KSh 200. A number of other local families have begun to imitate Ali so don't be surprised if you're approached on the street with a similar proposal.

At Shela, the *Stop Over Restaurant* right on the beach is a popular place to eat or drink and prices are very reasonable though they only offer simple meals. Similar, and offering a slightly wider range, is the *Bahari Restaurant* on the foreshore between Kijani House and Peponi Hotel.

Places to Eat – more expensive

For an up-market snack or coffee, *Rumours* in the same building as Gypsies Gallery, on the street parallel to the waterfront, is worth a try. It's open from 8.45 am to 8.45 pm and is European-owned. It doesn't close during Ramadan.

The rooftop restaurant at *Petley's Inn* is a great place to eat and is surprisingly inexpensive considering the quality of the food. It's also open to non-guests. The menu is changed daily depending on what is fresh. The cheapest dishes are spaghetti, seafood curry and burgers (KSh 250). More expensive dishes include fish and steaks (KSh 300), prawns (KSh 350) and lobster (KSh 550). This is also one of the very few places where you can have a beer (KSh 60) or other alcoholic drink with your meal. It's open year-round for breakfast, lunch and dinner including during Ramadan.

For a splurge meal the range is strictly limited. The restaurant at the *Lamu Palace Hotel* is far from cheap and the food is quite patchy – some nights it's excellent, other times it's mediocre which is surprising seeing as the Swiss owner/manager used to run the Castle Hotel in Mombasa. There's also a bar here. The restaurant is open during Ramadan.

The rooftop restaurant at the *New Mahrus Hotel* touts itself as a classy restaurant but the food is only average and the hygiene suspect. Basically, you can forget about it.

For a modest splurge at Shela the *Barbecue Grill* at Peponi Hotel offers delicious food and is open to non-guests. There's a choice of both barbecued fish and meat and a superb range of salads and sauces.

For a romantic night out with excellent food go for dinner at the rooftop *Barracuda Restaurant* at the Island Hotel in Shela. It's open to non-guests and prices are reasonable. Starters go for KSh 100 to KSh 160 and main dishes range from KSh 240 (fish) to KSh 460 (crab). Lobster is more expensive.

Entertainment

Bars There are a number of places where you can get a beer in Lamu itself but only three of them have cold beers. One of them is the makuti-roofed terrace bar at *Petley's Inn* which is a very pleasant place to relax and catch the sea breeze. It's the most popular watering hole on the island and is open to non-guests. On the ground floor of the hotel there's an 'African' bar which serves warm beer at cheap prices.

The other place with cold beer is the bar at the *Lamu Palace Hotel* on the waterfront. It's also a good place to catch the breezes, and as you're on ground level it's interesting to watch the passing parade of pedestrians.

The *Police Club* by the police station serves warm beer. It's open in the evenings until fairly late and you don't have to be in the police force to get in.

There's another bar at the *Civil Servants' Club* which has a disco on some Friday and Saturday nights. Keep an eye out for advertising posters around the town. Entry costs KSh 100 and it's a good night out.

Out at Shela, *Peponi Hotel* is a mandatory watering hole and the beer here is always ice-cold. The bar is on the verandah overlooking the channel and beach. It's open all day until late at night and there's always a lively and friendly bunch of characters swapping stories, jokes and anecdotes.

Getting There & Away

Air Three companies each operate twice-daily flights from Lamu to Mombasa (US$85) and Malindi (US$65). They are Air Kenya Aviation (☎ 33445), Baraka House, next door to Rumours Cafe, Eagle Aviation (☎ 33313) and Prestige Air Services Ltd (☎ 33055). The last two have their booking offices on the waterfront in Lamu close to Petley's Inn.

The airport at Lamu is on Manda Island and the ferry across the channel to Lamu

costs KSh 50. You will probably be met by registered guides at the airport who will offer to carry your bags to the hotel of your choice for a small consideration (say, KSh 100).

Air Kenya Aviation (☎ 33445; (02) 501421 in Nairobi) operates daily flights in either direction between Lamu and Nairobi's Wilson airport (US$112).

Bus There's only one bus company which operates between Malindi and Lamu and vice versa and that is Faza Express. It has offices in Mombasa and Lamu but not in Malindi. The pick-up point in Malindi is at the New Safari Hotel in the centre of town. The fare between Malindi and Lamu is KSh 300 and between Mombasa and Lamu it's KSh 350. The journey between Malindi and Lamu takes about eight hours if you're lucky; 11 hours if you're unlucky. Two buses leave in either direction daily at 8.30 am from Malindi and 7 am from Lamu. The buses to and from Lamu arrive and depart from the ferry jetty on the mainland not far from Mokowe. Between here and Lamu you take a motorised ferry which costs KSh 50 per person and takes about 20 minutes (this means you have to get up early if travelling from Lamu to Malindi/Mombasa). The Faza Express office in Lamu is open daily from 8.30 am to 12.30 pm, 2.30 to 4.30 pm and 7 to 8.30 pm. Early booking is advisable as demand is heavy.

Refer to the Malindi section for details of the possible dangers of travelling by bus between Malindi and Lamu. Better still, think seriously about flying if you can afford it.

Dhow Other than trips around the Lamu archipelago, you *may* be able to find a dhow sailing to Mombasa but it's unlikely and you'll need to get permission first from the district commissioner. The journey takes two days on average and prices are negotiable.

Getting Around

Boat There are frequent ferries between Lamu and the bus terminal on the mainland (near Mokowe). The fare is KSh 50. Ferries between the airstrip on Manda Island and

Lamu also cost KSh 50. Between Lamu village and Shela there are plenty of motorised dhows in either direction throughout the day until around sunset which cost KSh 50 per person or KSh 200 for the boat. They'll take up to 10 people at a time. Expect to have to wade back to shore at the Lamu end but not at the Shela end.

There are also regular ferries between Lamu and Paté Island – see the following section for details.

Islands Around Lamu

A popular activity while you're in Lamu is to take a dhow trip to one of the neighbouring islands. You need a small group (six to eight people) to share costs if you're going to do this but it's very easy to put a group like that together in Lamu. Just ask around in the restaurants or the budget hotels.

Since taking tourists around the archipelago is one of the easiest ways of making money for dhow owners in Lamu, there's a lot of competition and you'll be asked constantly by different people if you want to go on a trip. Negotiation over the price and what is included is essential both to avoid misunderstandings and being overcharged. The price of day trips is usually settled quickly because a lot of travellers will have been on them and the cost will be well known.

Dhow trips are usually superb whoever you go with so it's unfair to recommend any particular dhow or captain but, if you're going on a long trip – say, three days – then it's a very good idea to check out both the dhow and the crew before committing yourself. Don't hand over any money until the day of departure except, perhaps, a small advance (say KSh 500 per person) for food. Also, on long trips, it's probably best to organise your own beer, soft drinks and bottled water supplies. Beer, incidentally, isn't easy to organise as there's no longer a Kenya Breweries depot in Lamu. Enquire at Petley's Inn or the police canteen. Lastly, remember that the person who touts for your business is often not the captain of the boat but an intermediary who takes a commission for finding you.

Dhows without an outboard motor are naturally entirely dependent on wind to get them anywhere, though poling – or even pushing – the boat is fairly common along narrow creeks and channels. If you have to pole the boat or you get becalmed out in the channels between the islands, there's no point in remonstrating with the captain. He's not God and there's nothing he can do about it, yet it's surprising how many people imagine otherwise. With that in mind, never go on a long trip if you have a deadline to meet. A three-day trip can occasionally turn into a five-day one, although this is unusual.

Likewise, dhows are dependent on the tides. You can't sail up creeks if the tide is out and there's not enough depth of water to float the boat. This will be the main factor determining departure and return times.

To give you some idea of what a longer dhow trip involves, see the boxed story on pages 264-5 which gives a description of a dhow trip Geoff Crowther took with five others. It was written a few years ago but it's still current.

MANDA ISLAND

This is the easiest of the islands to get to since it's just across the channel from Lamu and almost everyone takes a half-day trip to the Takwa ruins at the head of the creek which almost bisects the island. The average cost of a dhow to this place is around KSh 1000 shared by however many people you can put together. Sometimes (but not always) this includes a barbecued fresh-fish lunch so settle this issue before you leave.

The extensive Takwa ruins are what remains of an old Swahili city which flourished between the 15th and 17th centuries and which attained a peak population of some 2500. It was abandoned for reasons unknown when the townspeople moved to Shela. The ruins consist of the remains of about 100 limestone and coral houses, all aligned towards Mecca as well as a mosque and tomb dating from 1683 (1094 by the

Islamic calendar). The settlement is surrounded by the remains of a wall and huge baobab trees dot the site. It's maintained by the National Museums of Kenya and entry costs KSh 200 (KSh 30 for residents).

Just off the north-east coast of Manda is **Manda Toto Island** which offers some of the best snorkelling possibilities in the archipelago. The reefs here are excellent and there are also good beaches. The only way to get here is by dhow and you need a full day to get there and back. There's no accommodation on Manda Toto itself.

Places to Stay

The only place to stay here is the *camp site* adjacent to the ruins but very few people stay here because the facilities are minimal.

Getting There & Away

The trip across to Manda takes about 1½ hours and can only be done at high tide as it's reached by a long mangrove-fringed inlet which is too shallow at low tide. You may well have to wade up the final stretch, so wear shorts. Since you have to catch the outgoing tide, your time at the site will probably not be more than an hour.

It's possible to walk to the Takwa ruins from either the airstrip or the village of Ras Kitau but it's quite a long way and the paths are not too clear.

PATÉ ISLAND

There are a number of historical sites on Paté Island including Paté the town, Siyu, Mtangawanda and Faza. All are still inhabited – mainly by fishers and mangrove-pole cutters – but very little effort has been put into preserving or clearing the remains of the once powerful Swahili city-states and that's not likely to happen until tourist receipts warrant the expense. Indeed, the only foreigners who come to this island are those on dhow trips and the occasional archaeologist so you can expect to be a novelty and treated

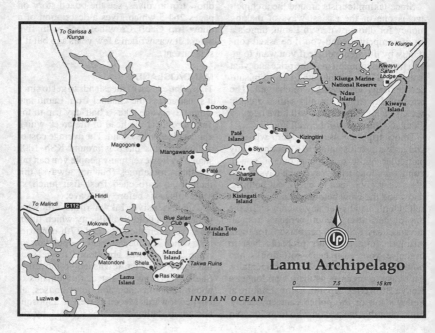

Lamu Archipelago

with friendly curiosity especially by the local children.

Accommodation and food on the island is easy to arrange with local families. The cost is negotiable but very reasonable. There are no guesthouses as such except at Faza but there are generally one or two simple restaurants which offer basic meals like bean or meat stews and tea.

Mosquitoes are a real pest and you're going to need insect repellent. Mosquito coils are for sale in the island's shops.

History

The origins of Paté are disputed. There are claims that it was founded in the 8th century by immigrants from Arabia, but recent excavations have produced nothing earlier than the 13th century when another group of Arabs, the Nabahani, arrived and gradually came to exert considerable influence over the other semiautonomous settlements along the coast.

By the time the Portuguese arrived in the early 16th century, Paté's fortunes were on the decline but were given a shot in the arm by the European mariners' interest in the silk cloth for which the town was famous and the introduction by the Portuguese of gunpowder. A number of Portuguese merchants reputedly settled here but their welcome was relatively short-lived, and by the mid-17th century their descendants had withdrawn to Mombasa following a series of uprisings by the Patéans against taxes imposed by the Portuguese authorities.

For the next half century or so, Paté regained some of its former importance and successfully fought off attempts by the Omani Arabs to take it over. Paté's harbour, however, had long been silting up and the city-state was eventually forced into using that of Lamu. The dependency created frequent tensions, particularly as Paté claimed sovereignty over Lamu, and the two were frequently at war. The final crunch came in 1812 when a Patéan army was soundly defeated at Shela. Thereafter, Paté faded into insignificance and lost all importance after the ruling family was driven out by Seyyid

Majid in 1865 and was forced to set up the short-lived sultanate of Witu on the mainland.

Today, Paté resembles a down-at-heel Lamu. The narrow, winding streets and the high-walled houses are there but the streets are earthen and the coral-rag walls are unplastered. Its one redeeming feature is the Nabahani ruins which are just outside of town. These are quite extensive and include walls, tombs, mosques and houses. They're worth exploring but they've never been seriously excavated or cleared so it can be difficult to get around because of the tangle of vegetation. In addition to that, local farmers plant their tobacco crops among the ruins and have demolished substantial sections of the walls.

Getting There & Away

There is a motor launch which usually leaves Lamu for Mtangawanda (about two hours) and Faza (about four hours) three times a week on Monday, Wednesday and Friday (Tuesday, Thursday and Saturday in the opposite direction). The fare is KSh 150.

From Mtangawanda it's about an hour's walk to Paté town along a narrow footpath through thick bush and across tidal flats but you're unlikely to get lost as the path is easy to follow and you'll probably be walking it with local people who get off the launch.

The launch doesn't always call at Mtangawanda on the return trip from Faza to Lamu, so it's best to walk across to Faza and take it from there, paying a visit to Siyu on the way.

SIYU
History

Founded in the 15th century, Siyu was famous not for commerce or military opportunism but as a centre of Islamic scholarship and crafts. In its heyday (between the 17th and 19th centuries) it boasted some 30,000 inhabitants and was the largest settlement on the island though, today, less than 4000 people live here and there are few signs of its former cultural and religious influence.

Though one of the last upholders of coastal independence, Siyu's demise came in

A Dhow Trip to Kiwayu

After discussions with three different intermediaries in Lamu about trips to Kiwayu we made our choice and arranged to meet outside the Kisiwani Lodge at 6 am the next day. The price was fixed at US$120 for a three-day trip, or around US$6 per person per day including food. Meanwhile we purchased beers and soft drinks from the Kenya Breweries depot and dropped them off at the Kisiwani (the crews will generally do this for you but it will cost more).

Next morning the dhow finally turned up at 7.30 along with a crew of four and we set off in the direction of the channel between Manda Island and the mainland. Since the wind wasn't in the right direction, the dhow had to tack all the way to the channel by which time it was low tide. There was sufficient water in the channel to just keep the boat afloat – but the wind had dropped completely. There was no alternative but to pole and push the dhow all the way to the end of the channel and naturally we all lent a hand. It took hours.

Once out in the open sea again, the wind picked up and we were able to get close to Paté Island but again the wind dropped and the clouds burst. It looked very much like we and all our gear were about to get a soaking so it was with considerable relief that we discovered the crew had brought along an enormous sheet of plastic.

After the storm, the wind picked up again and we reached Mtangawanda by about 3.30 pm where we got off the boat and had a late lunch cooked by the crew. Despite only having one charcoal burner, they did an excellent job of this and the food was delicious.

We set off again about 4.30 pm and headed for Faza with a stiff side wind which enabled us to make good progress for the next two hours. After that it died completely and darkness fell. By 10 pm, it was obvious we were going nowhere that night so the anchor was dropped and a meal prepared (by torchlight!). By now we were all getting to know each other very well and there was a good rapport between crew and passengers. The tranquillity and beauty of a becalmed night at sea added immensely to this. After the meal, we all bedded down as best we could for a night of 14th-century discomfort.

By first light we discovered that seepage through the hull of the boat had brought the water level to well above the toe-boards so it was all hands on deck and bail out with anything to hand. Shortly after this, the wind picked up and we sped our way across the channel between Paté Island and Kiwayu, arriving at about 11 am off the tip of the island. At this point, all the passengers and one of the crew got off the dhow and went snorkelling among the reefs on the eastern side. The dhow, meanwhile, sailed on to Kiwayu village.

We caught up with the dhow again around 3 pm after walking along the beach and climbing over the ridge. Lunch was prepared by the crew (again delicious) and we settled down to an afternoon and evening of relaxation – sunbathing, fishing and exploring the village. Those with tents camped on the beach and the others took a banda at the camp site.

1847 when it was occupied by the Sultan of Zanzibar's troops. The huge fort outside town dates from this period and is one of the largest buildings on the island. It's well worth a visit, as unlike many other Swahili relics, it has undergone considerable renovation.

The modern village displays little of Siyu's former glory and consists essentially of a sprawl of simple mud-walled and makuti-roofed houses.

Getting There & Away

The mangrove-lined channel leading up to Siyu is too shallow and silted up to allow the passage of anything but the smallest boats and so can't be reached directly from the sea by dhow or motor launch. The only feasible access is on foot either from Paté or Faza.

From Paté it's about eight km to Siyu along an earth track through the bush. The first part is tricky since there are turn-offs which are easy to miss so it's a good idea to take a guide with you as far as the tidal inlet. From here on it's easy as the path bears left and then continues straight through to Siyu. This last leg should take you about one hour.

FAZA
History

Faza has had a chequered history. It was destroyed by Paté in the 13th century and rebuilt in the 16th century only to be

Next morning brought heavy rain but by 11 am we were on our way back to Lamu with a strong tailwind and making excellent progress. Just off Faza, however, the wind died again and the captain (rightly) predicted there'd be no more that day so it was Faza for the night at his family's house. But it wasn't that simple getting off the boat! The tide was out and we couldn't sail up the creek to the town. It didn't look like a particularly feasible idea from the relative 'comfort' of the boat but, after some persuasion, we all jumped overboard with our packs on our heads and headed for the shore in thigh-deep water. There were no mishaps but a lot of jokes and laughter. Half an hour later we reached Faza.

The dhow was brought up at high tide and we were given three bedrooms to share at the family house. That evening a superb meal was prepared for us by the captain's family which we ate in the company of what must have been a good proportion of the town's younger children, all fascinated by this strange collection of wazungu that had turned up in town. Though we did offer, the family refused to take any money for the meal and the accommodation.

After the meal, the captain gave us his prediction about the winds next day – pretty pessimistic – and advised us to take the motor launch back to Lamu. The food was at an end, the last beers had been consumed with the meal that night and so, in the end, we all opted for the motor launch rather than another possible two days and a night back to Lamu. He did, on the other hand, firmly offer to take any or all of us back to Lamu on the dhow at no further cost if that's what we preferred.

All things considered, an excellent trip, superb value, great company, quite an adventure and I'd do it again.

Geoff Crowther

destroyed again by the Portuguese in 1586 as a result of its collaboration with the Turkish fleet of Amir Ali Bey. It was subsequently re-established and switched its allegiances to the Portuguese during their attempts to subdue Paté in the 17th century but declined into insignificance during the 18th and 19th centuries. These days it has regained some of its former importance after being chosen as the district headquarters for Paté Island which includes part of the Kenya mainland to the north.

Orientation

The modern town is quite extensive and includes a post office, telephone exchange, the district headquarters, a simple restaurant, two general stores and two guesthouses.

Things to See & Do

Faza has very little to offer in the way of interesting ruins. About the only thing there is in the town itself are the remains of the **Kunjanja Mosque** right on the creek front next to the district headquarters where the ferries anchor. Even so, most of it is just a roofless pile of rubble though there's a beautifully carved mihrab and some fine Arabic inscriptions above the doorway. Outside town is the tomb of Amir Hamad, commander of the Sultan of Zanzibar's forces, who was killed here in 1844 whilst campaigning against Siyu and Paté.

KENYA

It's an interesting place to wander around and easy to strike up conversations with just about anyone – men, women or children. Most of the houses here are mud-walled or coral-rag with makuti roofs though concrete and corrugated iron make an occasional appearance.

Places to Stay & Eat

The two guesthouses – *Lamu House* and *Shela House* – are essentially family residences but they're more than willing to turn over one or more bedrooms for your use and cook you a delicious evening meal if you need somewhere to stay. The price is negotiable and the families are very friendly.

The simple restaurant mentioned earlier offers bean stews, tea and mandazi for just a few cents and is a popular meeting place for the men of the town.

Getting There & Away

The inlet leading up to Faza from the main channel is deep enough at high tide to allow the passage of dhows and motor launches (though at low tide you'll have to walk in over the mud and sandbanks from the main channel).

There's a regular motor launch which connects Lamu with Faza via Mtangawanda three times a week on Monday, Wednesday and Friday (Tuesday, Thursday and Saturday in the opposite direction). The fare is KSh 150 and the journey takes four hours. From Faza to Lamu, the launch leaves at about 6 am but you need to be down by the district headquarters about half an hour before that as you have to be ferried out to the launch in small boats.

Getting to Siyu from Faza involves a two-hour walk through shambas and thick bush along an earth track. The first hour's walk as far as the disused airstrip is no problem, and there are generally people you can ask for directions if you're unsure. The second half is more confusing and you may need a guide so it might be best in the long run to take a guide with you all the way from Faza.

KIWAYU ISLAND

Kiwayu Island is at the far north-east of the Lamu archipelago and is included in the Kiunga Marine National Reserve. It acquired a reputation some years ago as an exclusive hideaway for rock stars and various other members of the glitterati, both local and foreign. It's unlikely you'll be rubbing shoulders with these people.

The main reason for coming here is to explore the coral reefs off the eastern side of the island which the tourist literature rates as some of the best along the Kenyan coast. That may be true but it's somewhat overrated (Watamu and Manda Toto island are better) yet the dhow trip there is definitely a highlight of a trip to Lamu and comes highly recommended.

The village on the western side of the island where the dhows drop anchor is quite small but it does have a general store with a few basics.

Places to Stay & Eat

Virtually the only place to stay here at a reasonable price is the *Kiwayu Camping Site* run by a man named Kasim. There used to be several very pleasant bandas to stay in here but, although they still exist, they've been allowed to fall into decay so don't expect anything special. The cost varies depending on which one you take but the 'tree house' is KSh 600 per night (sleeps three). Clean sheets, pillows and mattresses are provided as well as a kerosene lantern and mosquito coil. There are basic toilet and salt-water shower facilities. Campers can erect their tents here for KSh 150 including use of showers and toilets. You'll pay the same charge even if you camp on the beach below the site since this is also apparently owned by Kasim. There's a covered dining and cooking area for the use of both campers and banda dwellers.

Further up the coast across from Kiwayu on the mainland is the luxury lodge, *Munira Safari Camp*, which costs the equivalent of US$80 per person per night with full board or US$50 per person per night for Kenyan residents. There's a speed launch which goes

The Rift Valley

In Kenya the Rift Valley comes down through Lake Turkana, the Cherangani Hills, lakes Baringo, Bogoria, Nakuru and Naivasha, and then exits south through the plains to Tanzania. Together these areas make up some of Kenya's most interesting places to visit. Lake Turkana (see the Northern Kenya chapter) is a huge lake in the semidesert north, home to nomadic pastoralists and a world away from the tourist minibuses and fancy hotels of the south. The Cherangani Hills (see the Western Kenya chapter) provide some excellent walking opportunities and brilliant scenery – and hair-raising roads. More accessible are the central lakes which attract literally hundreds of bird and mammal species – they're a naturalist's dream and a visit to at least one of them is a must.

Volcanic activity is usually an accompaniment to rift valleys, and Kenya has several extinct volcanoes, the most prominent of which are Mts Longonot, Kenya and Kulal. Longonot is the most accessible, easiest to climb and certainly the most dominant feature of the landscape as you enter the Rift Valley from Nairobi. Mt Kenya, at 5200m, is a challenging climb, although Point Lenana, at 4985m, can be reached without specialist equipment. Kulal is more forbidding, unpredictable and harder to get to, being in the vicinity of Lake Turkana. Further south are the vast plains which are the home of the Maasai – and also home to a profusion of wildlife that you're not likely to come across anywhere else in the world. This is an area not to be missed.

What is known as the Rift Valley in Kenya is in fact part of the Afro-Arabian rift system which stretches some 6000 km from the Dead Sea in the Middle East, south through the Red Sea, Ethiopia, Kenya, Tanzania and Malawi to Mozambique. There's a western branch of the system which forms the string of lakes in the centre of the African continent: Albert and Edward, which make up part

of the Uganda-Zaïre border; Kivu on the Zaïre-Rwanda border; and Tanganyika on the Tanzania-Zaïre border. This western arm joins up with the main system at the northern tip of Lake Malawi.

Soda Lakes

Because the shoulders of the rift (see the Rift Valley diagram on page 98) slope directly away from the valley, the drainage system in

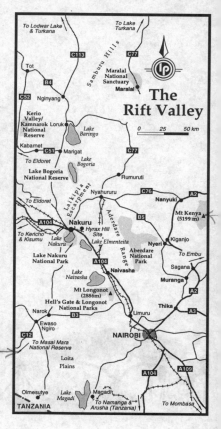

from Lamu which takes less than an hour, or flights by Air Kenya Aviation from Lamu which take 10 to 15 minutes.

Getting There & Away

The only ways of getting to Kiwayu is by dhow, speedboat or air and, for most people, this would be part of a longer trip from Lamu by dhow with stopovers elsewhere.

If there's sufficient wind, the return trip to Kiwayu from Lamu takes three days and two nights.

the valley is generally poor. This has resulted in the shallow lakes found along the valley floor in Kenya, some of which have no outlet. Due to high evaporation, the waters have become extremely concentrated and the high alkalinity from the area's volcanic deposits makes the perfect environment for microscopic blue-green algae and diatoms, which in turn provide food for tiny crustaceans and insect larvae. These in turn are eaten by certain species of soda-resistant fish.

The water of these soda lakes (Bogoria, Nakuru and Magadi in Kenya, and Lake Natron in Tanzania) may feel a little strange to the touch (it's soapy) and often doesn't smell too pleasant (though this is mostly due to bird droppings). However, the abundant algae, insect larvae, crustaceans and fish make these lakes a paradise to many species of water bird and they flock here in their millions.

Foremost among the birds is the deep-pink lesser flamingo (*Phoenicopterus minor*), which feeds on the blue-green algae, and the pale-pink greater flamingo (*Phoenicopterus ruber*), which feeds on the tiny crustaceans and insect larvae. Also numerous are various species of duck, pelican, cormorant and stork. The highest concentrations of these birds are found where food is most abundant and this varies from year to year and lake to lake. Lake Nakuru, for instance, sometimes almost dries up, forcing the birds to migrate to other soda lakes.

Another curious feature of the uplifting of the valley shoulders is the effect this has had on existing drainage patterns, although this of course happened in the last couple of million years. In Uganda, the uplifting caused the White Nile to form a pond (Lake Nyoga) after it left Lake Victoria, and to flow up what was previously a tributary and into the northern end of Lake Albert via a circuitous route. Prior to the uplift, the river had flowed direct from Lake Victoria into the southern end of Lake Albert.

Viewpoints

The best places to view the escarpments of the Rift Valley are from the viewpoints which are signposted along the Nairobi to Naivasha road, just past Limuru. Here the road descends into the valley and the views are stunning. Mt Longonot is directly in front while the plains of the Maasai sweep away to the south. Predictably, there are souvenir stalls at the viewpoints, but there are few bargains to be found because of the number of tourists who stop here.

The old road to Naivasha also descends into the rift in this area, and it's the route to take if you are heading for Mt Longonot or Masai Mara, as the new road runs direct to Naivasha. It's also the road used by heavy vehicles and is often in a diabolical state of disrepair. This road was originally built by Italian POWs in WWII, and there is a chapel at the bottom of the scarp.

Getting There & Around

Lakes Naivasha, Nakuru, Elmenteita and, to a lesser extent, Baringo are readily accessible to independent travellers without their own vehicle. There are plenty of buses and matatus and a rail link between Nairobi, Naivasha and Nakuru, and less frequent buses and matatus between Nakuru and Marigat/Kampi ya Samaki (for Lake Baringo). The other lakes, however, are more remote and there's no public transport. Hitching is very difficult and can be impossible. There's also the problem that lakes Nakuru and Bogoria are both in national parks/reserves, which you are not allowed to walk in – you must tour them in a vehicle. For details about these parks, and also the Rift Valley's Mt Longonot and Hell's Gate parks, see the Kenya National Parks & Reserves chapter.

Renting a vehicle may be expensive for budget travellers, but it would certainly work out cheaper for four people to hire a vehicle to visit Naivasha, Nakuru, Bogoria and Baringo than for them all to pay individually for safari-company tours. A one day tour of Lake Nakuru starting from Nairobi goes for around US$60 per person. A two day tour of lakes Nakuru, Bogoria and Baringo costs about US$180 per person. A car hired for several days and shared between four people would cost less than the total cost of a two day tour for four people.

KENYA

NAIVASHA

There's very little of interest in the town of Naivasha itself. It's just a small service centre for the surrounding agricultural district. Most travellers just pass through here on the way to or from Mt Longonot, Lake Naivasha, Hell's Gate National Park and Nakuru. The main road skirts the town so if you're going directly from Nairobi to Nakuru you don't actually pass through Naivasha. It's a good place to stock up with supplies if you're planning a sojourn by the lake as there are very limited stocks in the dukas dotted along the lakeshore road.

The area around Naivasha was one of the first settled by wazungu, and the Delamere Estates, originally owned by Lord Delamere, surround the town and stretch away to the west towards Nakuru. Many of the plots around Naivasha are still European-owned, which is hardly surprising given that this was one of the stamping grounds of the Happy Valley set of the 1930s.

The town basically consists of two main roads and a handful of other streets, and everything is within walking distance.

Information

There are branches of Barclays Bank and the Kenya Commercial Bank on Moi Ave which are open during normal banking hours.

Places to Stay – bottom end

If you need to stay overnight in Naivasha there's a good range of budget hotels. The *Naivasha Super Lodge* has no doubles but the single beds are large enough for a couple; at KSh 150 these are not bad value.

For something a little less cosy try the *Olenkipai Boarding & Lodging* or the *Heshima Bar Boarding & Lodging*, both of which are adequate. The Heshima charges KSh 150/300 for a twin room with common bath.

Good value if you're alone is the *Othaya Annexe Hotel*, in Station Lane, which is clean and has singles (no doubles) for KSh 200 with common bath. The hotel has its own bar and restaurant.

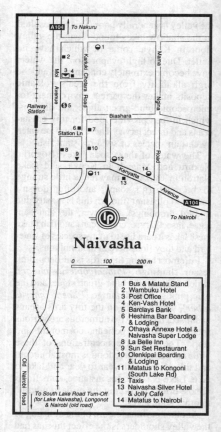

Naivasha

0   100   200 m

1 Bus & Matatu Stand
2 Wambuku Hotel
3 Post Office
4 Ken-Vash Hotel
5 Barclays Bank
6 Heshima Bar Boarding & Lodging
7 Othaya Annexe Hotel & Naivasha Super Lodge
8 La Belle Inn
9 Sun Set Restaurant
10 Olenkipai Boarding & Lodging
11 Matatus to Kongoni (South Lake Rd)
12 Taxis
13 Naivasha Silver Hotel & Jolly Café
14 Matatus to Nairobi

There are plenty of other cheap places along Kariuki Chotara Rd.

Places to Stay – middle

For more salubrious lodgings the *Naivasha Silver Hotel* (☎ (0311) 20640) on Kenyatta Ave has rooms with hot water for KSh 300/400 a single/double. There's an upstairs bar and restaurant.

Places to Stay – top end

The best accommodation in town is the rustic *La Belle Inn* (☎ (0311) 20116) on Moi Ave, which is a popular rendezvous for local residents and a watering hole and meal stop for safari companies. The staff are friendly and rates are good value at KSh 1100/1500 for singles/doubles with shared bathroom facilities, or KSh 1500/1900 with private bath. Prices include breakfast. There's a guarded car park, and all credit cards are accepted.

The huge new *Ken-Vash Hotel* (☎ (0311) 30049), behind the post office, seems a little out of place in small-town Naivasha. The rooms are small, definitely nothing special, and for KSh 800/1200 including breakfast it's hard to see who they are going to get to fill this place.

Places to Eat

If you appreciate good food, there's essentially only one place to eat in Naivasha, *La Belle Inn*. The food is very reasonably priced and the outdoor terrace is a great place to have a beer or a meal despite the occasional clouds of dust raised by trucks on their way further west. It's open daily (all day) except Tuesday.

The *Jolly Cafe* next to the Silver Hotel on Kenyatta Ave is slightly less extravagant and has passable food. For good old no-frills African stodge try the Sun Set Restaurant on the corner of Kenyatta Ave and Kariuki Chotara Rd.

Getting There & Away

Bus & Matatu The main bus and matatu station is on Kariuki Chotara Rd. There are frequent buses and matatus to Nairobi (KSh 90), Nakuru (KSh 90), Nyahururu (KSh 120) and all points further west. Note that matatus to Nairobi leave from the matatu stand on Kenyatta Ave.

Train Travel from Naivasha to Nairobi by train is inconvenient as most of the trains pass through in the early hours of the morning. The trains to Kisumu and Malaba pass through in the late afternoon or evening. Unless you are prepared to travel 3rd class, make a booking in Nairobi before catching the train in Naivasha.

Hitching It's useless trying to hitch out of Naivasha town to Nairobi without first getting onto the main road. The accepted point for hitching, and where the main road passes closest to the town, is about 500m east of the bus station. It's about one km to the main road in either the Nakuru or Nairobi direction.

LAKE NAIVASHA

Naivasha is one of the Rift Valley's freshwater lakes and its ecology is quite different from that of the soda lakes. It's home to an incredible variety of bird species and a focus of conservation efforts in Kenya. Not everyone supports these efforts, however, and the ecology of the lake has been interfered with on a number of occasions, the most notable introductions being sport fish, commercial fish (such as Nile perch), the North American red swamp crayfish, the South American coypu (an aquatic rodent, also called a nutria, which escaped from a fur farm) and various aquatic plants including salvinia, which is a menace on Lake Kariba in southern Africa.

The lake has ebbed and flowed over the years, as half-submerged fencing posts indicate. Early in the 1890s it dried up almost completely but then it rose a phenomenal 15m and inundated a far larger area than it presently occupies. It currently covers about 170 sq km.

Since it's a freshwater lake which can be used for irrigation purposes, the surrounding countryside is a major production area of flowers, fresh fruit and vegetables as well as beef cattle for domestic consumption and export. There's even a vineyard on the eastern shore. The flower market has become a major industry in the Naivasha area, as all the shade houses indicate. It's incredible, but flowers picked here in the very early morning can be at the daily flower auctions in Holland the same day, and sell for little more than half the price of those produced in Europe!

Between 1937 and 1950 Lake Naivasha was Nairobi's airport! Imperial Airways and then BOAC flew Empire and Solent flying boats here on the four day journey from

Southampton. Passengers came ashore at the Lake Naivasha Hotel (now the Lake Naivasha Country Club), where buses would be waiting to shuttle them to Nairobi. The lake also featured strongly with the decadent Happy Valley settler crowd in the 30s.

For a full account of the history of European activity in the area, get hold of a copy of *Naivasha & the Lake Hotel* by Jan Hemsing, available from the Lake Naivasha Country Club.

Things to See & Do

On the western side of Lake Naivasha, past the village of Kongoni, there is a **crater lake** with lush vegetation at the bottom of a beautiful but small volcanic crater. If you have transport it's worth visiting. The crater is part of the Crater Lake Game Sanctuary, and entry costs KSh 100.

South of the lake is the Hell's Gate National Park which is well worth exploring and one of the few national parks in which you're allowed to walk (see the National Parks & Reserves chapter). On the eastern side of the lake is **Crescent Island**, a bird sanctuary which you can visit by boat (see Getting Around later in this section).

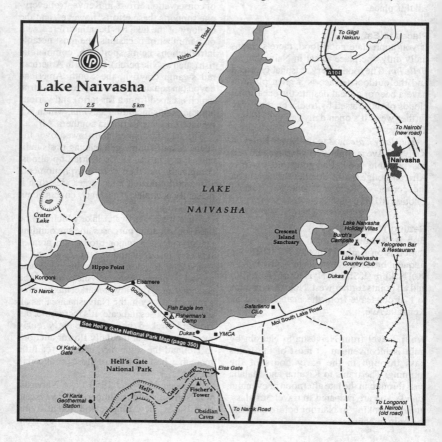

Lake Naivasha

The mansion known as Oserian (or the Djinn Palace) which features in the book (and the dreadful movie) *White Mischief* is on the southern shore of the lake. It's privately owned and is not open to the public.

Elsamere

Almost opposite Hippo Point, a couple of km past Fisherman's Camp, is Elsamere, the former home of the late Joy Adamson of *Born Free* fame. She bought the house in 1967 with the view that she and her husband, George, might retire there. She did much of her writing from Elsamere right up until her murder in 1980. It seems George never spent much time there. It is now a conservation centre and open to the public daily from 3 to 6 pm. The entrance fee of KSh 250 includes afternoon tea on the lawn, a visit to the memorial room and a film-viewing of *The Joy Adamson Story*.

The only other way to visit is to stay here (see Places to Stay) or book in for a meal – lunch costs KSh 500, dinner KSh 600. Bookings can be made through the Elsamere Conservation Centre (☎ (0311) 21055; fax 21074), Moi South Lake Rd, PO Box 1497, Naivasha.

Places to Stay – bottom end

There are several budget accommodation possibilities on the lakeshore. The most popular is *Fisherman's Camp* (☎ (0311) 30088) on the southern shore. You can camp here for KSh 150 per person with your own tent, or there are tents for hire at KSh 200 per night. There are also fully self-contained *bandas* (round, concrete or mud-brick huts with makuti roofs) with four beds in each for KSh 500 per person, or a dorm at KSh 350 with bedding. They also have what is known as the *Top Camp* (up the hill across the other side of the road). Here they have a range of bandas, or you can camp. Firewood is for sale at both camps plus, at the main camp, there's a basic bar and restaurant. You can also rent boats between 8 am and 5 pm (see Getting Around). It's a very pleasant site with grass and shady acacia trees. Make sure you camp well away from overland trucks

unless you want to party all night, though finding a quiet spot isn't a problem as it's a huge site.

Another choice is the *YMCA* (☎ (0311) 30396), three km back towards Naivasha town close to the turn-off for Hell's Gate National Park. Although it's difficult to get down to the lakeshore from the YMCA, it's still a good camp site, especially if you intend to walk into Hell's Gate. Camping costs KSh 150 per person per night plus there are a number of somewhat spartan and rundown bandas for KSh 200 per person (children half-price). Firewood and bedding can be provided for a small charge. It gets busy here with school groups during school holidays. Bring all your own food and drink with you (the nearest dukas are about one km down the road towards Elsamere).

A third possibility is *Burch's Campsite* (☎ (0311) 21010) about one km beyond the Yelogreen Bar & Restaurant towards Fisherman's Camp. There's a range of accommodation options here, as well as a store selling basic provisions, including home-grown apples. Pitching your tent in the shady camp site costs KSh 150 per person, or there are basic but adequate twin-bed rondavels (bed and mattress only, no other bedding supplied) for KSh 450, or bigger, four-bed rondavels with attached bath for KSh 900 for a double, plus KSh 300 for each extra person. This includes bedding, cooking equipment and use of a gas stove. Campers and those in the basic rondavels have access to hot showers and a communal cooking area.

Lastly, you can also camp at the Safariland Club (see Places to Stay – top end), which is not a bad option as you have access to the hotel's other amenities. The cost is KSh 200 per person.

Places to Stay – middle

Right next door to the Fisherman's Camp is the *Fish Eagle Inn* (☎ (0311) 30306). This new place has a number of very cramped rooms around a spacious lawn. Quite how they justify the outrageous price of KSh 850 *per person* I'm not quite sure. The dormitory even costs KSh 520! You can also camp here (KSh 200), but you can't get your vehicle down to the camp site, and there's little shade.

Places to Stay – top end

The *Safariland Club* (☎ (0311) 21013; fax 21216), is a top-end hotel with all the facilities you might expect. A single/double room with half board in the high season (December to March and July to August) costs US$83/121 (US$52/72 low season). There are also one-bedroom cottages for US$161 (US$112) and two-bedroom cottages for US$322 (US$224). The club accepts all the usual credit cards, and facilities include boat hire (US$27 per hour for four people, or US$9 per person to Crescent Island), horse riding, lawn tennis and table tennis. Nonresidents can use the swimming pool for KSh 250 per day.

Very similar is the *Lake Naivasha Country Club* (☎ (0311) 21004; fax 21161) and since it's part of the Block Hotels chain, bookings should be made through Nairobi (☎ (02) 540780; fax 543810). This hotel has a beautiful, expansive garden with access to the lake, a good kids' playground and a pool. They also have some interconnecting rooms, making it a good option for families. Singles/doubles with half board in the high season cost US$118/181 (US$51/102 low season) plus there are two-bedroom cottages for US$451 (US$254). Boat trips cost KSh 1000 per hour; to Crescent Island, which is just a short hop from here, the trip is KSh 800 return, and they will leave you on the island and pick you up later in the day – with a picnic lunch it's an excellent day excursion.

Virtually next door to the Country Club is the very pleasant *Lake Naivasha Holiday Villas* (☎ (02) 224998; fax 230962 in Nairobi). This smaller place consists of a number of very nice, spacious rooms at KSh 1400/2800 in the low season, KSh 4000/5000 in the high season for half board. The only drawback here is that there is no lake frontage.

Lastly there's the *Elsamere Conservation Centre* (☎ (0311) 21055; fax 21074), beyond Fisherman's Camp. Here you can get a room in the grounds of Joy Adamson's former house with full board (the only choice) for KSh 3200 per person per night. Children under seven years of age are not allowed to stay since it's basically a research centre. It's a very pleasant place to stay and the staff are very friendly.

Places to Eat

If you're not eating at any of the above hotels or camp sites, there's the *Yelogreen Bar & Restaurant* near the eastern end of Moi South Lake Rd. It's a pleasant place for a cold beer, and the food is good and reasonably priced. However, you'll probably want your own transport to get here as it's more than one km from the nearest lake accommodation.

Getting There & Away

The usual access to Lake Naivasha is along Moi South Lake Rd. This also goes past the turn-off to Hell's Gate National Park (both the Elsa and Ol Karia gate entrances). There are fairly frequent matatus between Naivasha town and Kongoni on the western side of the lake. It's 17 km from the turn-off on the old Naivasha to Nairobi road to Fisherman's Camp and costs KSh 30.

Getting Around

Motorboats for game-viewing on Crescent Island can be hired from the Safariland Club and the Lake Naivasha Country Club.

Much cheaper rowing and motorised boats can be hired from Fisherman's Camp, but it's a long way from there to Crescent Island. Rowing boats (four people maximum) cost KSh 200 per hour, and small motorboats KSh 1000 per hour.

For land exploration, bicycles can be hired from Fisherman's Camp for KSh 250 per day.

LAKE ELMENTEITA

Like Lake Nakuru, Elmenteita is a shallow, soda lake with a similar ecology. Flamingos live here too, but in nowhere near the same numbers as at Nakuru. Elmenteita is not a national park, so you can walk around it and there are no entry fees. However, there are few tracks and, as most of the shoreline is privately owned, there's a lot of fencing.

The easiest way to get there is to take a matatu along the Naivasha to Nakuru road and get off at one of the signposted viewpoints on the escarpment above the lake. You can either walk down from there or hitch a ride.

Places to Stay

The beautiful *Lake Elmenteita Lodge* (☎ (0367) 5040) has excellent views over the lake, and costs US$40/80 in the low season, or US$110/140 in the high season. Game drives can be arranged, and horse riding is offered at the trifling charge of US$18 per person per hour.

KARIANDUSI PREHISTORIC SITE

The Kariandusi site is signposted off to the right of the main road on the way from Naivasha to Nakuru. There's not much to see as the only excavation was carried out by Louis Leakey in the 1920s, although the small museum is worth a look.

NAKURU

Kenya's fourth largest town is the centre of a rich farming area about halfway between Nairobi and Kisumu on the main road and railway line to Uganda. It's here that the railway forks, one branch going to Kisumu on Lake Victoria and the other to Malaba on the Ugandan border and on to Kampala.

It's a pleasant town with a population of around 80,000 but is of interest mainly to those who work and farm in the area. The big draw for travellers is the nearby Lake Nakuru National Park with its usually prolific bird life; information about the park is detailed in the Kenya National Parks & Reserves chapter. The Menengai Crater and Hyrax Hill Prehistoric Site in the immediate area are both worth a visit (see later in this chapter).

Information

Nakuru has one foreign exchange bureau – it's on George Morara Rd (the highway) next

to Marshalls (Peugeot dealers), a short walk west of the town centre.

Places to Stay – bottom end

The *Amigos Guest House* on Gusil Rd is a very friendly place to stay and the best value in this range. The rooms and bathroom facilities are passably clean, towels are provided and there's hot water. Singles/doubles with shared facilities cost KSh 250/300. Don't confuse this place with the other Amigos at the junction of Kenyatta Ave and Bondoni Rd. The other one isn't anywhere near as good and can be very noisy because of the upstairs bar.

Right in the centre of town is the *Shik Parkview Hotel* (☎ (037) 212345), on the corner of Kenyatta Ave and Bondoni Rd. It's a large place, but whoever designed it surely made a basic mistake since, although the single rooms have a private bathroom, the doubles do not! The beds are comfortable but what other furniture you get varies. Singles/doubles cost KSh 230/400 with common bath and breakfast; singles with private bathroom cost KSh 300. The rooms overlooking Kenyatta Ave are noisy. The best thing about this place is its proximity to the bus and railway stations.

You could also check out the *Shiriksho High Life Hotel* on Mosque Rd, which is conveniently close to the bus and matatu station but is not a great bargain. It's similar in price to the Shik Parkview, but none of the rooms have private bathroom.

Places to Stay – middle

Going up in price, an excellent choice is the *Mukoh Hotel* (☎ (037) 213516), on the corner of Mosque and Gusil Rds, which is clean and comfortable and has good views of the lake from the rooftop. Singles/doubles cost KSh 300/450 with private bath. Soap and towels are provided and there is erratic hot water. The hotel has its own bar and restaurant, and the management is very friendly.

Not far from the Mukoh and similar in quality is the *Carnation Hotel* (☎ (037) 43522) which has singles/doubles priced at

KENYA

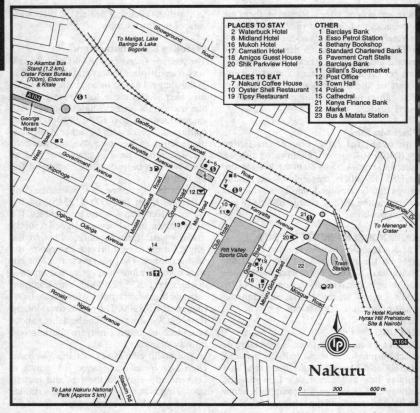

PLACES TO STAY
2 Waterbuck Hotel
8 Midland Hotel
16 Mukoh Hotel
17 Carnation Hotel
18 Amigos Guest House
20 Shik Parkview Hotel

PLACES TO EAT
7 Nakuru Coffee House
10 Oyster Shell Restaurant
19 Tipsy Restaurant

OTHER
1 Barclays Bank
3 Esso Petrol Station
4 Bethany Bookshop
5 Standard Chartered Bank
6 Pavement Craft Stalls
9 Barclays Bank
11 Gillani's Supermarket
12 Post Office
13 Town Hall
14 Police
15 Cathedral
21 Kenya Finance Bank
22 Market
23 Bus & Matatu Station

Nakuru

0   300   600 m

KSh 360/700 including breakfast. There's hot water in the bathrooms and the hotel has its own restaurant.

Places to Stay – top end

There's a choice of two top-end places in Nakuru. The *Midland Hotel* (☎ (037) 212155; fax 44517) on Geoffrey Kamati Rd is a rambling old place with rooms and attached bathroom with hot water for KSh 2000/2500 including breakfast. It has three bars (including the Long Bar) and two restaurants (one outdoor and one indoor).

Somewhat cheaper, and very pleasant, is the *Waterbuck Hotel* (☎ (037) 215672) on the corner of Government Ave and West Rd, which offers rooms with attached bathroom and balcony for KSh 1200/1300. The price includes a good breakfast. This is the low season price; expect to pay more at other times. The hotel has its own bar, restaurant and barbecue bar, and the staff are very friendly. Vehicles can be parked safely in the hotel compound, which is guarded 24 hours a day.

Further away from the centre of town on the road to Nairobi, and close to the turn-off for Hyrax Hill, is the modern *Hotel Kunste*

☎ (037) 212140) which is a conference centre/hotel. Rates for its rooms with an attached bathroom are KSh 600/900 for a single/double including breakfast. Lunch or dinner costs KSh 250.

Further out, several km down the road towards Nairobi, is the *Stem Hotel* (☎ (037) 85432) which has rooms for KSh 1200 a double with half board. It's really only of interest to those with their own transport.

Places to Eat

For price and quality, the best place to eat is the *Tipsy Restaurant* on Gusil Rd. It's very popular with local people, especially at lunch time. Dishes include Indian curries, western food and lake fish. The food is very tasty and very reasonably priced – around KSh 90 to KSh 130 for main dishes.

The restaurant on the ground floor of the *Mukoh Hotel* is a good place for breakfast and also serves good meals and snacks. For just a coffee and a snack try the *Nakuru Coffee House* on the corner of Moi Rd and Kenyatta Ave. You can also buy roasted coffee beans there.

The open-air bar at the *Midland Hotel*, which offers barbecued chicken and a Sunday curry buffet (chicken or beef), is a popular place to eat, especially at lunch time. It's very reasonably priced at around KSh 170 to KSh 250 for main courses. The outside bar of the *Waterbuck Hotel* is also very similar.

Going up somewhat in price, one of the town's best restaurants is the *Oyster Shell Restaurant* (☎ (037) 40946), upstairs on Kenyatta Ave near the Club Rd corner. The menu is extensive and includes western, Indian, Mughlai and Indonesian dishes. It's open daily for lunch and dinner and is very reasonably priced; main dishes range between KSh 150 and KSh 250.

Entertainment

Apart from the bars mentioned earlier, there is one disco in Nakuru – the *XTC* above the Oyster Shell Restaurant. It's quieter than the discos in Nairobi, but it has excellent equipment and a good mixture of music. There is

no cover charge. Beers sell for normal bar prices.

Getting There & Away

Bus & Matatu The bus and matatu station is right in the thick of things at the eastern edge of town, near the railway station. It's a pretty chaotic place though generally it doesn't take too long to locate the bus, matatu or Peugeot you want. There are regular matatu/Peugeot departures for Naivasha (KSh 90), Nairobi (KSh 150/200), Nyahururu (KSh 80/100), Nyeri (KSh 150/180), Eldoret (KSh 150/200), Kericho (KSh 120/150), Kisii (KSh 220/250) and Kisumu (KSh 200/250).

Akamba buses also service Nairobi and points west. The only problem is that the Akamba depot is about one km west of town, at the Agip station on the main road out.

Other buses go to Eldoret (KSh 130), Nairobi (KSh 130) and Baringo (KSh 80), among other places.

Train As is the case with Naivasha, trains often come through in the middle of the night so you're better off going by road, as the buses and matatus arrive in the daytime only. The daily Kisumu and Nairobi trains come through at 11.30 pm and 1 am respectively, while the Malaba trains are on Friday and Saturday at 8 pm.

For Kampala, the weekly train from Nairobi comes through at 3 pm on Tuesday. The fare is KSh 3240/2590 in 1st/2nd class.

As for travel to Naivasha, you need to make an advance reservation in Nairobi if you're heading west and want 1st or 2nd class.

MENENGAI CRATER

Rising up on the northern side of Nakuru is the Menengai Crater, an extinct 2490m-high volcano. The crater itself descends to a maximum depth of 483m below the rim. You can drive right up to the edge, where there's one of those totally trivial signs telling you that you're five million km from some city halfway across the world.

To walk up to the crater takes a solid couple of hours, and it really is *up*, but still a very pleasant walk. The views back over Lake Nakuru are excellent, as are the views north to Lake Bogoria once you reach the top. About three-quarters of the way along there is a small group of dukas where you can get basic meals, soft drinks and, of course, the amber fluid. There's a map showing the crater's location on page 356.

LAKE BOGORIA

The two completely dissimilar lakes of Bogoria and Baringo are north of Nakuru off the B4 highway to Marigat and Lodwar. Lake Bogoria is a shallow soda lake and Lake Baringo a deeper freshwater lake. The B4 road is a superb, sealed highway the whole way to Kampi ya Samaki on the western shore of Lake Baringo.

Lake Bogoria covers an area of 30 sq km and has a maximum depth of nine metres. As with the other soda lakes in Kenya, Bogoria has no outlet and so the intense evaporation has led to high levels of salts and minerals. The result is that the lake supports no fish at all, but is ideal for blue-green algae, which is the staple food of the flamingos. For more information about Lake Bogoria see the Kenya National Parks & Reserves chapter.

LAKE BARINGO

Some 15 km north of the town of Marigat you come to the village of **Kampi ya Samaki** which is the centre for exploring Lake Baringo. This lake, like Naivasha, is freshwater and, until fairly recently, used to cover around 170 sq km with a maximum depth of just 12m. Over the last few years, however, with the damming of the rivers which feed it for irrigation purposes, coupled with a drought, the level of the lake has shrunk so

---

Hyrax Hill Prehistoric Site

Just outside Nakuru on the Nairobi road, this prehistoric site is open daily from 9 am to 6 pm and admission is KSh 200. The small booklet, *Visitor's Guide to the Hyrax Hill Site*, is available from the museum there. For its location see the Lake Nakuru National Park map on page 356.

Archaeological excavations were first conducted here in 1937 although the significance of the site had been suspected by Louis Leakey since 1926. Further excavations have been conducted periodically, right up into the 1980s.

The finds at the site indicate three settlements were made here, the earliest possibly 3000 years ago, the most recent only 200 to 300 years ago. From the museum at the northern end you can take a short stroll around the site, starting with the North-East Village where 13 enclosures, or pits, were excavated. Only Pit D, investigated in 1965, is still open; the others have grown over. The North-East Village is believed to be about 400 years old, dated by comparison with the nearby Lanet site. A great number of pottery fragments were found at the site, some of which have been pieced together into complete jars and are displayed in the museum.

From the village the trail climbs to the scant remains of the stone-walled hill fort near the top of Hyrax Hill, which gave the site its name. You can continue up to the peak, from which there is a fine view of the flamingo-lined Lake Nakuru.

Descending from the hill on the other side you come to the Iron Age settlement where the position of Hut B and Hut C is clearly visible. Just north of these huts, a series of burial pits containing 19 skeletons was found. Since they were mostly male, and a number of them had been decapitated, it's possible they were killed in some sort of fighting. Unfortunately, souvenir seekers have stolen the bones that were displayed.

Virtually underneath the Iron Age site, a Neolithic site was discovered. The Iron Age burial pits actually topped a Neolithic burial mound, and a second Neolithic burial mound was found nearby. This mound is fenced off as a display. Between the burial mound and the Nairobi road are more Iron Age pits, excavated in 1974. The large collection of items found in these pits included a real puzzle – six Indian coins, one of them 500 years old, two of them dating from 1918 and 1919!

Finally, following the path back to the museum, there's a *bau* board in a large rock. This popular game is played throughout East Africa.

You are free to walk around the site yourself but a guide is useful. He'll expect a small tip at the end. ∎

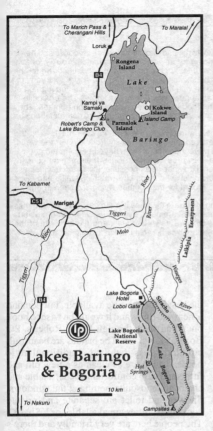

To Marich Pass &
Cherangani Hills

To Maralal

Loruk

B4

Rongena
Island

L a k e

Kampi ya
Samaki

Ol Kokwe
Island

Island Camp

Robert's Camp &
Lake Baringo Club

Parmalok
Island

B a r i n g o

To Kabamet

C51

Marigat

Tiggeri

River

River

Molo

Laikipia Escarpment

Tiggeri

B4

Lake Bogoria
Hotel

Loboi Gate

River

Wuseges

Siracho Escarpment

Lake Bogoria
National
Reserve

**Lakes Baringo
& Bogoria**

Hot
Springs

Lake Bogoria

0   5   10 km

To Nakuru

Campsites

Despite all this, Lake Baringo, with its islands (two of them inhabited) and encircling mountains, is still a spectacular sight and a very mellow place to visit. Boating trips are a popular activity and there's even a so-called 'Devil's Island' which local people will tell you is haunted. They don't mind taking you there during the day but at night they won't go near the place and say you can see flames and hear people screaming even though no-one lives on the island.

Activities

Other than bird walks, the most popular activity is boat rides on the lake and visits to the islands. Although these can be arranged at either Lake Baringo Club (expensive) or Robert's Camp (considerably cheaper), you can also make your own arrangements at the Fish Factory, a five minute walk from Robert's Camp – follow the path heading north along the fence line of Robert's. Here you will find what are basically out-of-work fishers many of whom still have their own fibreglass boats, powered by outboard motors. The prices for boat rides are pretty similar to those at Robert's Camp but it depends who you meet. Ask around for Joshua Lechiwgei, a friendly young Maasai, who has trained two fish eagles on the island of Ol Kokwe to come out to his boat and take out of the water the fish Joshua brings with him from the lake shore.

One-hour boat trips from Lake Baringo Club (see Places to Stay) cost KSh 800 per person (minimum two people), bird walks KSh 500 per person including transport, horse rides KSh 800 per hour and camel rides KSh 350 per half hour. The club also offers trips to Lake Bogoria for KSh 3000 per person (minimum two people), including park fees and transport, and to a nearby Njemps village for KSh 400 per person (minimum two people). The Njemps are a local tribe who live in villages around the lake shore and practice a mixture of pastoralism and fishing. The club has an arrangement with the headman of the village you visit so you're allowed to walk around freely and

alarmingly that the shoreline is now several hundred metres from where it used to be. And that isn't all. Soil erosion is so bad on the western perimeter of the lake that the seasonal *luggas* (creeks) which flow into the lake whenever there's a downpour bring down massive amounts of mud and silt so that the lake water is almost always muddy. It's also been over-fished to such an extent that the tilapia which are caught these days are rarely more than 15 cm long. This has virtually put the fishers out of business and brought to a halt the construction of a new fish-processing factory.

Baringo Wildlife

The lake supports many different species of aquatic animal and bird life as well as crocodile and herds of hippo which invade the grassy shore every evening to browse on the vegetation. You'll probably hear their characteristic grunt as you walk back to your tent or banda after dark or settle down for the night. They might even decide to crop the grass right next to your tent. If they do, stay where you are. They're not aggressive animals (they don't need to be with their bulk and jaws!) but if you frighten or annoy them they might go for you. And, despite all appearances, they can *move*! The crocodile is relatively small and so, so far, there have been no recorded incidents of them attacking humans. They prefer goats, of which there are vast flocks around this area contributing seriously to deforestation and soil erosion.

Crocodile and hippo apart, Lake Baringo's main attraction is the bird life and the lake is the bird-watching centre of Kenya. People come here to engage in this activity from all over the world. Kenya has over 1200 different species of bird and more than 450 of them have been sighted at Lake Baringo. Some bird-watchers are so keen they're known as 'twitchers' since their primary concern seems to be to rack up sightings of as many different bird species as possible. It's a serious business and Lake Baringo Club even has a 'resident ornithologist' who leads bird-watching walks and gives advice to guests. A few years ago she set a world record for the number of species seen in one 24 hour period – over 300!

There's a constant twittering, chirping and cooing of birds in the trees around the lake, in the rushes on the lake and even on the steep face of the nearby escarpment. Even if you've had no previous interest in bird-watching, it's hard to resist setting off on a dawn bird walk and the highlight of the morning is likely to be a sighting of hornbills or the magnificent eagles which live almost exclusively on rock hyrax. ■

take photographs; you'll probably be hassled to buy some of the villagers handicrafts.

The facilities at the club are open to non-residents on payment of KSh 100 per person per day temporary membership on weekdays and KSh 150 on weekends, although this fee is waived if you're eating either lunch or dinner (KSh 850) there. Use of the swimming pool costs KSh 150 per person per day on top of the daily membership fee. If you arrive at the club by vehicle you probably won't be asked for the fee. At 7 pm each evening there's a slide show and commentary featuring some of the more common birds sighted in the area.

Places to Stay – bottom end

There's a great place to stay just before the village called *Robert's Camp* (☎ Kampi ya Samaki 3 through the operator) where you can camp for KSh 200 per person per night (KSh 100 for children under 12 years old). Bundles of firewood cost KSh 50. Facilities include clean showers and toilets. There are also three double bandas available for KSh 600 per person plus 15% tax. The bandas are

the best if there is one available, but demand is heavy at times and it would be wise to book one in advance through Mrs E Roberts, PO Box 1051, Nakuru. The bandas are beautiful, circular, grass-thatched, traditional-style houses which are as clean as a new pin and furnished with comfortable beds, a table and chairs and mosquito netting at the windows. Shower and toilet are separate and private cooking facilities are available for KSh 400. The people here are very friendly and there's a huge land tortoise which ambles around the grounds and appears to be used to the attention it receives. Other facilities include a store with an excellent selection of groceries, meat (fresh and processed) and dairy products, and a bar which is open daily from 8 am to noon and 1 to 8 pm. The bar will stay open later than 8 pm at a cost of KSh 20 per extra hour. You can also organise boat trips from here for KSh 1100 per hour for the boat (up to seven people).

If you're camping here then you need to exercise some common sense regarding the hippos. Although hippos may graze within just a metre of your tent at night, you should stay at least 20m away from them when you can, especially if they have young ones. Don't frighten them in any way with headlights, torches (flashlights) or loud noises and don't use flash photography. No-one's ever been hurt by a hippo in over 10 years but they are wild animals and should be treated with respect.

If Robert's Camp bandas are full or you have no camping equipment then there's a choice of several basic lodges in Kampi ya Samaki. The best of these is the *Bahari Lodge* where all the drivers of safari vehicles stay. It's very clean and each room has two single beds with clean sheets and a blanket and (usually) a mosquito net. The cost is just KSh 100 per bed. Shower and toilet are shared. There's a bar/restaurant offering cheap, tasty meals and *cold* beers (KSh 40) – yes, they have a fridge. The *Hippo Lodge* at the entrance to the village is similarly priced but somewhat grubby.

Places to Stay – top end

Right next door to Robert's Camp is the *Lake Baringo Club*, one of the Block Hotels chain (☎ (02) 540780; fax 543810 in Nairobi). Singles/doubles with full board are US$39/78 in the low season and US$83/128 in the high season (July and August). Children under 12 years sharing a room with adults stay for free, and pay only for meals (50% of adult meal prices). The rooms here are very pleasant, the cuisine excellent and the staff very friendly. Facilities at the club include a swimming pool, dart boards, table-tennis table, badminton court, a library and a whole range of local excursions including boat trips and bird-watching trips accompanied by an expert.

While the Lake Baringo Club is an excellent place to stay, so too is the *Island Camp Baringo*, which is a luxury tented lodge sited on the extreme southern tip of Ol Kokwa Island in the lake. It's a beautifully conceived place, with a labyrinth of stone walls and steps set among flowering trees, and is the perfect hideaway. There are 25 double tents each with their own shower and toilet, and all of them have superb views over the lake.

Facilities at Island Camp include two bars, a swimming pool and watersports equipment. Full board costs US$141/187 for singles/doubles in the high season and US$69/138 in the low season inclusive of return boat transfer. Children between the ages of two and 12 years pay US$44 and KSh 985, respectively. For guests with their own vehicles, guarded parking is available in the village between the main street and the lakeshore. The locals can all point you in the right direction. The boats leave from a jetty at the far northern end of Kampi ya Samaki village. Bookings can be made either direct through Island Camp (☎ (071) 374069) or through Let's Go Travel (☎ (02) 340331; fax 336890) in Nairobi.

Places to Eat

If you're camping at Robert's Camp and doing your own cooking you need not bring your own food or equipment with you as all this is available at the camp itself. The shop at the site has an excellent range of fresh and packaged foods (see Places to Stay). The only things that are in short supply are fresh vegetables and fruit though there's a very limited supply available in Kampi ya Samaki. Marigat has a much better choice of these things.

Those who want to splurge can eat at the *Lake Baringo Club*. As you might expect, the meals here are excellent but it will cost you KSh 850 for either lunch or dinner. Beers at the club are very expensive at KSh 120 for a large Tusker. The club is also the only place where you can buy petrol and diesel between Marigat and Maralal.

Getting There & Away

There are three buses (KSh 80) per day in either direction between Kampi ya Samaki and Nakuru as well as a number of matatus (KSh 100) and Nissan minibuses (KSh 120). The journey takes between 1½ and two hours. From Kampi ya Samaki, two of the buses leave around 7 am. There's no regular schedule for the matatus and Nissans. If you have difficulty finding direct transport from Kampi ya Samaki to Nakuru at any time of day, first take something to Marigat (KSh 20) and then arrange transport from there. From Marigat there are more frequent connections to Nakuru.

It's an interesting journey between Nakuru and Baringo since the country remains relatively lush and green until you pass the equator, where it almost immediately becomes drier and dustier and continues to get more barren and forbidding the further north you go. As you get near Marigat there are spectacular mountains, ridges and escarpments.

A gravel track connects Loruk at the top end of the lake with the Nyahururu to Maralal road. It's in good shape if you have your own transport. There's no public transport along this road and hitching is extremely difficult.

LAKE MAGADI

Lake Magadi is the most southerly of the Rift Valley lakes in Kenya and is very rarely visited by tourists because of its remoteness. Like most of the Rift Valley lakes, it is a soda lake and supports many flamingos and other water birds. It also has a soda extraction factory, hence the railway line there. Some years ago it was the site of a major rescue operation of young flamingos when drought threatened hundreds of thousands of them because of soda encrustation on their feathers – this doesn't affect the adults.

Magadi is quite different from the lakes to the north as it is in a semidesert area. Temperatures hover around the 38°C mark during the day and much of the lake is a semisolid sludge of water and soda salts. There is a series of hot springs around the periphery of the lake.

The town of Magadi is purely a company town, owned and built by the multinational, ICI.

Olorgasailie Prehistoric Site

Important archaeological finds were made at this site by Louis and Mary Leakey in the 1940s. Hand axes and stone tools thought to have been made by *Homo erectus* around half a million years ago were unearthed. While casts of some are on display in the Nairobi museum, most have been left in place, protected from the elements by shade roofs.

Places to Stay

At Olorgasailie there are three twin-bed bandas for rent at KSh 500. You need to bring all your own food, but water is available.

Getting There & Away

There is a rail link to the lakeshore which branches off from the main Nairobi to Mombasa line but there are no passenger services along it. There's also a minor road from Nairobi (the C58), along which two buses run daily. The first leaves Nairobi country bus station around 10 am, the other around 5 pm; return trips are at 6 am and 3 pm. Both buses pass the junction which leads to the archaeological site, about two km from the main road.

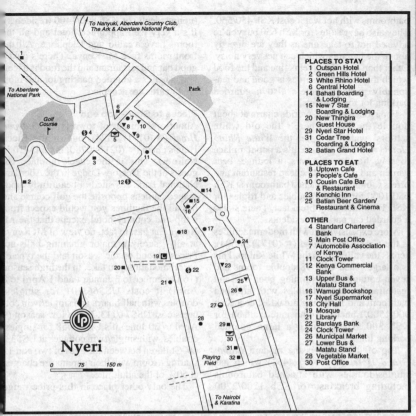

To Nanyuki, Aberdare Country Club,
The Ark & Aberdare National Park

To Aberdare
National Park

Park

Golf
Course

Nyeri

0   75   150 m

To Nairobi
& Karatina

On the other hand, there are two excellent budget hotels to choose from. The first one is the *Nyeri Star Hotel* (☎ (0171) 4213), close to the lower bus and matatu stand. This offers singles/doubles with attached bathroom for KSh 250/400 with towel and soap provided and there's hot showers. It's a friendly place, secure and has a popular bar and restaurant. Despite it's proximity to the bus station you can't hear the noise and it's rarely full as it's a large place.

The second place is the *New Thingira Guest House* (☎ (0171) 4769), just down the hill off the main road from Karatina. This is also very good value at KSh 300/450 for singles/doubles with attached bathrooms. Breakfast is available for KSh 70. There's also a ground floor bar and restaurant.

Another one you could try if the above are full (unlikely) is the *Josmica Boarding & Lodging* on the top side of the lower bus station. Some of the rooms here have attached bathrooms.

Places to Stay – middle

One of the best in this range is the modern *Central Hotel* (☎ (0171) 4233) at the top end of town. Singles/doubles with their own

KENYA

bathrooms with hot water cost KSh 450/550. They also have suites for KSh 650 but you're advised not to take one as they are directly above the bar area which can get very noisy. Other than that, the hotel is fine and the food which the restaurant serves is good and reasonably priced. There's also a guarded parking lot for residents.

For a touch of olde-worlde charm at about double the price, there's the old white settlers' watering hole, the *White Rhino Hotel* (☎ (0171) 30934). It's a popular place to stay, has several bars, a lounge, beer garden and a relatively cheap restaurant and offers rooms with attached bathroom at KSh 650/1000 for singles/doubles and triples for KSh 1300 including breakfast. There's also a guarded car park for residents.

More expensive but with modern facilities is the *Green Hills Hotel* (☎ (0171) 30604), across the valley from the White Rhino. This is a large place with 98 double rooms and seven cottages, a swimming pool, bar and restaurant. Singles/doubles with attached bathroom and including breakfast cost KSh 900/1500. Lunch and dinner are available for KSh 300. There's also a large guarded parking lot.

Top of the range is the modern *Batian Grand Hotel* (☎ (0171) 4451) which has singles/doubles with attached bathrooms including breakfast for KSh 1200/2200

(nonresidents) or KSh 800/1400 (residents). It's a very well appointed hotel and all the rooms have a radio and telephone. All the front rooms face Mt Kenya. There's also a good bar and restaurant and the food is excellent. There's a guarded parking lot and most credit cards are accepted.

Places to Stay – top end

About one km out of town is the *Outspan Hotel* (☎ (0171) 2424), one of the Block Hotels chain (☎ (02) 540780; fax 543810 in Nairobi). This is the check-in place for guests of the Treetops Lodge in the Aberdare National Park. It's sited in beautifully landscaped gardens opposite the golf course and has all the facilities you would expect from a top-end country hotel except that the Mt Kenya Bar has, in fact, no view of Mt Kenya at all – surely a major planning balls-up. Prices depend on the season and the type of accommodation you take. In the high season (16 December to 3 January and 1 April to 8 April) it costs US$66/101 for singles/ doubles with half board, and single/twin cottages cost US$74/113. In the low season (9 April to 30 June) it's US$29/58 for singles/ doubles, with single/twin cottages at US$33/ 66. Children between the ages of two and 12 sharing a room with their parents are charged at 50% of the adult rate.

The only other place in this price range

Baden Powell Museum

Nyeri is famous as the former home of Lord Baden Powell, the founder of the worldwide Scouts Movement. It was here in the cottage called Paxto, in the grounds of the Outspan Hotel, that he lived until his death and it's here that he was buried. The cottage was later occupied by Jim Corbett – 'destroyer of man-eating tigers in central India during the 1920s and 1930s', according to the plaque in front of the cottage. These days it's a museum packed with scouting memorabilia which bus loads of boy scouts and girl guides from all over the world tramp through every day. Just about everyone who visits leaves a memento so the place is awash with troop colours. Baden Powell's gravestone is in the garden at the front. Entry is free to members of the movement and KSh 50 to anyone else (how the curator tells the difference is anyone's guess).

It's ironic that a white colonist should be honoured in this manner in Nyeri yet one of Kenya's foremost independence fighters, General Dedan Kimathi, lies in an unmarked grave at the other end of town. Kimathi was captured by the British colonial authorities towards the end of the Mau Mau Rebellion and hanged in Kamiti prison – or so the western history books say. That, however, is not what is taught in Kenyan schools. They are taught that he was buried alive. That's hard to believe but who knows the truth? All the same, where's the headstone? ■

s the *Aberdare Country Club*, at Mweiga about 12 km north of Nyeri, which is part of the Lonrho Hotels Kenya group (☎ (02) 216940; fax 216796 in Nairobi). Like the Kentmere Club at Limuru and the Norfolk Hotel in Nairobi, this was once one of the quintessential white planters' watering holes and social foci except that these days it caters for the international leisure set and those with the money to burn on a night or two at The Ark. Full board (including temporary membership) costs US$120/156 for singles/doubles in the high season and US$74/123 in the low season. Children aged from two to 12 years sharing a room with their parents are charged US$44 at any time of year. All the rooms and cottages have excellent views of the plains below and across to Mt Kenya and the club is surrounded by its own, private 500 hectare wildlife sanctuary. Facilities at the club include a swimming pool, tennis courts, golf course, horse riding, game rides, walking safaris and trout fishing.

Places to Eat

The most reliable places for a meal are the *White Rhino Hotel* and the *Central Hotel* where you can eat well and relatively cheaply. Expect to pay around KSh 150 to KSh 200 for a main meal.

The very popular *Uptown Cafe* is worth a visit if you want cheap, tasty no-frills food. It offers a good range of food such as burgers, various curries and steaks. Two other cheap places for meals, snacks and coffee are the *People's Cafe* near the main post office and the *Cousin Cafe Bar & Restaurant*.

For fast food of the McDonald's-clone variety, try the *Kenchic Inn*, one of the many branches of this chain in Kenya. A quarter fried chicken with chips here costs KSh 120.

Getting There & Away

From the upper bus stand there are regular buses to Nyahururu, Nakuru, Thika, Nairobi (KSh 100) and Nanyuki, and less frequently to places further afield such as Meru and Eldoret. The buses to Nairobi may involve a change at Karatina so check before buying a ticket.

Nissan minibuses are more comfortable and faster between Nyeri and Nairobi and normally cost KSh 120 but can be up to KSh 160 if demand is high. A Peugeot share-taxi to Nairobi costs KSh 180. A Nissan minibus to Nanyuki costs KSh 80. To Nakuru, a Nissan minibus costs KSh 150 and a Peugeot taxi KSh 170.

NYAHURURU (THOMSON'S FALLS)

Nyahururu, or 'T Falls' as virtually everyone calls it, was one of the last white settler towns to be established in the colonial era and didn't really take off until the arrival of the railway spur from Gilgil (on the main Nairobi to Kisumu line) in 1929. The railway still operates but these days carries only freight. Nyahururu is one of the highest towns in Kenya (at 2360m) and the climate is cool and invigorating. The surrounding undulating plateau is intensively cultivated with maize, beans and sweet potatoes, and is well forested, mainly with conifers. The most interesting approach to the town is probably along the excellent road from Nakuru which snakes up and down through farmlands and forests and offers some spectacular views over the Aberdares.

The falls, on the outskirts of town, are named after Joseph Thomson who was the first European to walk from Mombasa to Lake Victoria in the early 1880s. They're a popular stopover for safari companies en route to Maralal and points further north and are well worth a visit. Formed by the waters of the Ewaso Narok River, the falls plummet over 72m into a ravine and the resulting spray bathes the dense forest below in a perpetual mist. A series of stone steps leads down to the bottom of the ravine and is the only safe access. Don't attempt to go down any other way as the rocks on the side of the ravine are often very loose. Up above the falls and partially overlooking them (though the view is obscured by a row of ugly souvenir shacks) is the old colonial watering hole, Thomson's Falls Lodge, which has retained much of its quaint atmosphere and is still the most interesting place to stay. The hotel

KENYA

grounds are a popular place for a Sunday picnic with local families.

Nyahururu has an inexplicably large population of street kids who hang around the bus station and will hassle you for small change. Have some handy if you don't want to be followed all the way up the street; they're very persistent.

Places to Stay – bottom end

The best place to stay if you have camping gear is the camp site at *Thomson's Falls Lodge*. It's very pleasant and costs KSh 300 per person per night with as much firewood as you need and hot showers included.

For those without camping equipment, there are several budget hotels in town. Good value is the *Good Shepherd's Lodge*, which offers rooms with attached bathrooms with towel and soap provided for KSh 140 a single (no doubles). It's very clean and there's a restaurant next door.

For solo male travellers the best bet is probably the quiet *Nyandarua County Council Guest House*, behind the post office and provincial headquarters. It only has single rooms (sharing not permitted), but they all have attached bathrooms with soap, towel and toilet paper provided. The cost is KSh 150 and there is a restaurant and TV room. The staff are very friendly.

Going up in price, the *Stadium Lodging* (☎ (0365) 22002) is quite good value at KSh 200/300 for singles/doubles with attached bathrooms with hot water. It's clean, there's a table and chair in each room and security is excellent.

Right opposite the bus stand is the *Cyrus Lodge* which has singles/doubles with attached bathrooms for KSh 120/170. The hotel has its own bar and restaurant.

The modern, five storey *Nyaki Hotel* (☎ (0365) 22313) is set back from the main road in the centre of town. It's very clean and quiet and costs KSh 200/750 for singles/doubles with attached bathrooms with

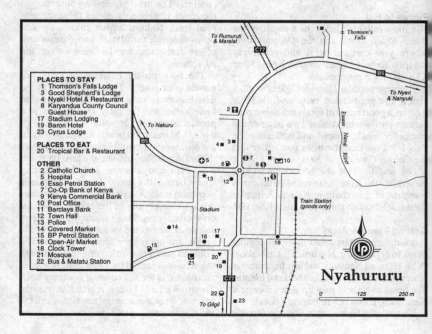

PLACES TO STAY
1 Thomson's Falls Lodge
3 Good Shepherd's Lodge
4 Nyaki Hotel & Restaurant
8 Karyandua County Council Guest House
17 Stadium Lodging
19 Baron Hotel
23 Cyrus Lodge

PLACES TO EAT
20 Tropical Bar & Restaurant

OTHER
2 Catholic Church
5 Hospital
6 Esso Petrol Station
7 Co-Op Bank of Kenya
9 Kenya Commercial Bank
10 Post Office
11 Barclays Bank
12 Town Hall
13 Police
14 Covered Market
15 BP Petrol Station
16 Open-Air Market
18 Clock Tower
21 Mosque
22 Bus & Matatu Station

To Rumuruti & Maralal

Thomson's Falls

To Nyeri & Nanyuki

To Nakuru

Euaso Narok River

Stadium

Train Station (goods only)

To Gilgil

Nyahururu

0   125   250 m

towels and soap provided, but the price does not include breakfast. The hotel has its own bar and restaurant.

There's also the *New Nyahururu Guest House* which offers rooms with attached bathrooms for KSh 150 per person.

Places to Stay – middle

The place to stay in this category if you have the money is *Thomson's Falls Lodge* (☎ (0365) 22006; fax 32170), overlooking the falls. Though it's no longer frequented by white planters, it exudes nostalgia and olde-worlde charm with its polished wooden floorboards and log fires. Accommodation is available either in the main building with its bar, lounge and dining room, or in separate cottages scattered over the well-maintained lawns. Rooms here have attached bathrooms with hot water and your own log fire, and cost KSh 1600/2000 for singles/doubles, with triples at KSh 2800 including breakfast.

If you prefer modernity and a place in the centre then the *Baron Hotel* (☎ (0365) 32751) is the choice. It's clean and well organised and rooms with attached bathrooms with hot water go for KSh 350/600 a single/double, with suites at KSh 900, all including breakfast. The hotel has its own bar and restaurant and the food is good with a choice of three dishes each day – fish, meat or chicken. Prices are very reasonable.

Also in this category is the new *Kawa Falls Hotel* (☎ (0365) 32295), on the way out of town towards Gilgil. There are 83 rooms, all of them with attached bathrooms, but the hotel likes to think it's something special so it has both resident and nonresident rates which is ridiculous in a place like Nyahururu. Rates are KSh 550/900 for singles/doubles and KSh 1200/1500 for suites, all including breakfast. Clearly, there's room for negotiation here. You can't fill an 83 room hotel in Nyahururu at that price in a big hurry.

Places to Eat

Most of the budget hotels and many of the bars have a restaurant where you can get standard African food. Meals at the *Baron Hotel* are also excellent value.

For local colour and a barbecued meal, try the *Tropical Bar & Restaurant* around the corner from the Baron Hotel.

For a minor splurge – or if you're staying there – eat at *Thomson's Falls Lodge*. Breakfast, lunch and dinner are available, but you need to give advance warning if you intend to take your meal in the main dining room. A full English-style breakfast costs KSh 200. Three-course lunches or dinners with dessert and tea or coffee cost KSh 500. There's also an open-air grill which operates at lunch time and offers a variety of dishes, including soups and various types of nyama choma (barbecued meat). A meat dish will cost you about KSh 250. The lodge has the most interesting and one of the liveliest bars in town with deep, comfortable armchairs and blazing log fires. All facilities are open to nonresidents, including campers.

For those who want to prepare their own meals, there's an excellent choice of fruit, vegetables and meat in the covered market.

Entertainment

The *Baron Hotel* has a discotheque every Friday and Saturday night.

Getting There & Away

There are plenty of buses and matatus throughout the day until late afternoon in either direction between Nyahururu and Nakuru (KSh 100) and Nyeri (1½ hours, KSh 150). Other destinations served by regular matatus and buses include Nairobi (about two hours, KSh 200), Nanyuki (KSh 150) and Naivasha (1½ hours, KSh 150).

There's also at least one minibus per day in either direction between Maralal and Nyahururu which leaves early in the morning and costs KSh 200 to KSh 250 depending on the bus. Get there early if you want a seat. For the rest of the day, hitching is feasible but not easy. The road is surfaced as far as Rumuruti after which it's gravel or *murram* (dirt). Parts of this gravel road are in bad shape but it improves considerably the nearer you get to Maralal.

Around Mt Kenya

Mt Kenya is circled by an excellent tarmac road along which are the area's main towns – Naro Moru, Nanyuki, Meru and Embu, and Isiolo at the extreme north-eastern end. For details on climbing the mountain, see the Kenya National Parks & Reserves chapter.

NARO MORU

The village of Naro Moru, on the western side of the mountain, consists of little more than a string of small shops and houses, a couple of very basic hotels, a market, agricultural warehouses and the famous Naro Moru River Lodge, but it's the most popular starting point for climbing Mt Kenya. There's a post office here but no banks (the nearest are at Nanyuki and Nyeri).

The other important thing to bear in mind is that the Naro Moru River Lodge has an exclusive franchise on the mountain huts along the Naro Moru route, including those at the meteorological (Met) station, so you have to go to this lodge to make bookings. It's all been carefully calculated to sew up

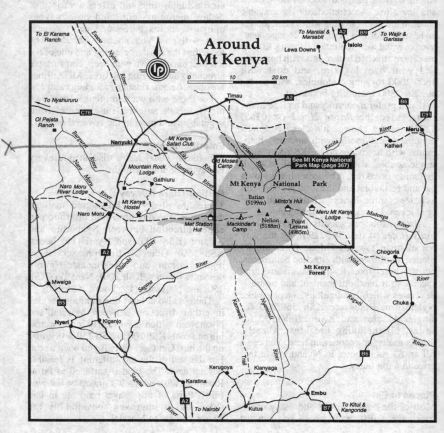

Around Mt Kenya

0   10   20 km

See Mt Kenya National Park Map (page 367)

the market on this route but that doesn't prevent you from climbing independently as long as you're willing to camp and carry the appropriate equipment.

Places to Stay

There are a number of basic hotels in Naro Moru village but very few travellers who are intent on climbing the mountain stay here. Most stay at the Naro Moru River Lodge (just outside the village), at the Mt Kenya Hostel or the Mountain Stop Motel (both about halfway between Naro Moru and the Met Station) or at the Mountain Rock Hotel (halfway between Naro Moru and Nanyuki). Still, if you want to stay in the village, you can do that. There are four hotels: the *Naro Moru 82 Lodge; Naro Moru Hotel 86; Wananchi Tours Lodge* and the *Mountain View Hotel*. They're all much the same and you can get a bed for KSh 150 to KSh 200 but the best of the lot is the Mountain View Hotel.

The village apart, and if you're an independent traveller and intent on scaling the summit, think seriously about walking 12 km and staying at the *Mt Kenya Hostel & Campsite* on the way to the start of the Naro Moru trail. The original hostel burnt down several years ago but Joseph and James have since done a prodigious amount of work and rebuilt it so that it now has several well-appointed bedrooms, a kitchen, lounge and bathrooms. It's a great place to stay and very friendly, plus you can pick up information about the mountain since there are always people staying here who have either just come down or are about to go up. You can camp here for KSh 150 per person or take a bed for KSh 200 (there are 30 in total). They also have a fully equipped store of mountain gear for hire as well as a 4WD vehicle to take you to the park entrance/Met Station for KSh 2500 shared between up to nine people. You can hire guides, porters and cooks here, too (KSh 290 per day for guides and cooks and KSh 270 per day for porters). All meals are available here with advance notice.

Just outside the entrance to the hostel is the *Mountain Stop Motel* which has camping

for KSh 150 per person and 10 bandas (doubles) for KSh 250 per banda. Toilets and showers (hot water) are shared. There's a large bar/lounge area with a fireplace under a makuti roof, a barbecue and a separate small bar which is popular with local people. Meals are available on request. The owner, Solomon Wanjohi, is enthusiastic and helpful.

In the village itself, is the *Naro Moru River Lodge* (☎ (0176) 62622; fax 62212), which is about 1.5 km off to the left down a gravel track from the main Nairobi to Nanyuki road. It's essentially a top-range hotel set in landscaped gardens alongside the Naro Moru River, but it does have a well-equipped camp site with hot showers and toilets for US$4 per person per night and firewood at US$2 per load. Also at the camp site are dormitory bunkhouses where a bed costs US$6. Campers are entitled to use all the hotel facilities.

Those seeking a degree of luxury either before or after climbing the mountain have the option of 'standard' or 'superior' rooms with attached rooms or self-service cottages. In the low season (11 April to 30 June and 16 September to 15 December) the rooms cost US$30/55 a single/double in standard and US$40/65 in superior with half board. In the high season (16 December to 10 April and 1 July to 15 September), the rooms cost US$72/94 a single/double in standard and US$82/114 in superior. The self-service cottages vary in price depending on which one you take, and range between US$45 and US$105 per night. Between 22 December and 5 January there's a surcharge of US$20 per person per day.

Facilities at the hotel include a swimming pool, two bars, restaurant, secure parking and fishing opportunities.

The main reason for coming to this lodge if you're an independent traveller is that it's here you must book and pay for any of the mountain huts which you want to stay at along the Naro Moru route. Those at the Met Station cost US$8 and the ones at Mackinder's Camp US$11. Members of the Mountain Club of Kenya are entitled to a

25% discount on these prices and the accommodation charges at the lodge.

The other reason for coming to this lodge if you don't have a tent, cooking equipment or appropriate clothing is that it runs a comprehensive hire service which is open daily from 7 am to 1 pm and 2 to 8 pm. The charges are similar to those at Atul's in Nairobi and are detailed in the National Parks & Reserves chapter. The River Lodge can arrange transport to the park entry gates on either the Naro Moru or Sirimon trails. The charge is US$60 one way to the Naro Moru gate and US$90 one way to the Sirimon gate shared between up to six people.

There's also an excess baggage store which costs KSh 20 per piece per day. You can use this service whether you are a guest or not.

Seven km north of Naro Moru on the Nanyuki road is the *Mountain Rock Hotel* (☎ (02) 210051; fax 210051 in Nairobi), tucked away in wooded surroundings less than one km from the main road. This is the place to head for if you're intent on taking either the Sirimon or Burguret routes up Mt Kenya. It offers pleasant cottages each with hot showers and fireplaces for US$26/29 a single/double. 'Superior' rooms are also available and these cost US$32/39. There's also a well-equipped camp site with hot and cold water, toilets, cooking facilities, electricity and ample firewood for US$5 per person per night. All prices include taxes and service charges. Facilities at the hotel include a spacious dining room, two bars (one open-air), lounge, nyama choma barbecue and a beer garden. Patrick, who runs this hotel, is a very friendly and reliable person.

Horse riding (US$13 per hour), trout fishing (US$6.50 per hour including fishing rod and licence) and bird-watching are some of the activities which the lodge caters for, plus there are traditional dances performed when demand warrants it (US$5 per person with a minimum of six people).

The main reason for coming here, however, is to take one of the hotel's guided treks to the summit of Mt Kenya via the Naro Moru, Burguret or Sirimon routes. There is a whole range of these to choose from depending on where you want to go and how long you wish to take. The full range of possibilities is outlined in the section on climbing Mt Kenya in the Kenya National Parks & Reserves chapter.

Places to Eat

There are no restaurants worth a mention at Naro Moru so you'll either have to cook your own food or eat at the *Naro Moru River Lodge*. There's very little choice of food available at the shops in Naro Moru so bring your own or, if you have transport, go to Nanyuki to buy it.

Getting There & Away

There are plenty of buses, Nissan minibuses and Peugeot share-taxis from Nairobi and Nyeri to Nanyuki and Isiolo which will drop you off in Naro Moru. The fare from Nairobi to Naro Moru is around KSh 200 (more for a Peugeot) and the journey takes about 2½ hours. From Nyeri to Naro Moru the fare is KSh 50 and the journey takes a little over half an hour.

The Naro Moru River Lodge also operates a shuttle bus between the lodge and Nairobi assuming there's sufficient demand – minimum two people – and you must book 24 hours in advance. The fares are KSh 3000 per person one way and KSh 4000 return. In Nairobi you have to book the bus on the 1st floor of College House (☎ (02) 337501), University Way. In Naro Moru, book at the lodge itself.

The lodge also does transfers to Nanyuki airstrip for KSh 600 per person one way and KSh 900 return, and to the meteorological station for US$78, the park gate for US$39 or the trailhead on the Sirimon route for US$137.

NANYUKI

Nanyuki is a typical small country town about halfway along the northern section of the Mt Kenya ring road and a popular base from which to trek up the mountain via either the Burguret or Sirimon routes. It was founded by white settlers in 1907 in the days when game roamed freely and in large numbers over the surrounding grassy plains. The game has almost disappeared – shot by the settlers for meat and to protect their crops from damage by foragers – but the descendants of the settlers remain and the town has also become a Kenyan airforce base as well as a British army base for the joint manoeuvres conducted by the two armies each year. It's a fairly pleasant town and still has a faint ring of the colonial era to it. All the usual facilities are here, including banks, a post office and a good range of well-stocked stores.

Places to Stay – bottom end

The cheapest place is the *Nanyuki Youth Hostel* (☎ (0176) 2112) at the Emmanuel Parish Centre, Market Rd, but it's pretty basic, even dismal. The showers have only cold water. There are also some simple lodges, including the *Silent Guest House* and the *Juba Boarding & Lodging*.

More expensive but a popular place to stay is the *Josaki Hotel* (☎ (0176) 2181) which

has large, clean, singles/doubles with attached bathrooms with hot water for KSh 400/600 including breakfast. There's a bar and restaurant on the 1st floor which has cold beer for KSh 45. Secure parking is available.

Also popular, but not as good, is the *Sirimon Guest House* (☎ (0176) 32344) fronting the central park. It has singles/ doubles with attached bathrooms in the main hotel for KSh 170/320 or KSh 200/400 in the annexe.

Similar in price to the Sirimon is the *Jambo House Hotel* (☎ (0176) 22751), which is opposite the Josaki, and offers singles/doubles with attached bathrooms without breakfast for KSh 140/250 and triples for KSh 380. The hotel has its own bar and restaurant.

Also in this range is the *Nyako Boarding & Lodging*, but it's very difficult to find anyone to show you a room and, in any case, it's right next door to the matatu stand which makes it very noisy.

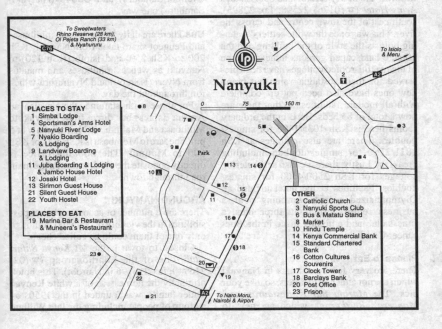

Nanyuki

0   75   150 m

To Sweetwaters Rhino Reserve (28 km), Ol Pejeta Ranch (33 km) & Nyahururu

C76

To Isiolo & Meru

A2

To Naro Moru, Nairobi & Airport

A2

Park

PLACES TO STAY
1 Simba Lodge
4 Sportsman's Arms Hotel
5 Nanyuki River Lodge
7 Nyakio Boarding & Lodging
9 Landview Boarding & Lodging
11 Juba Boarding & Lodging & Jambo House Hotel
12 Josaki Hotel
13 Sirimon Guest House
21 Silent Guest House
22 Youth Hostel

PLACES TO EAT
19 Marina Bar & Restaurant & Muneera's Restaurant

OTHER
2 Catholic Church
3 Nanyuki Sports Club
6 Bus & Matatu Stand
8 Market
10 Hindu Temple
14 Kenya Commercial Bank
15 Standard Chartered Bank
16 Cotton Cultures Souvenirs
17 Clock Tower
18 Barclays Bank
20 Post Office
23 Prison

Places to Stay – middle

A short distance from the centre of town off the Isiolo road is the *Simba Lodge*, not far from the Catholic church. Rooms with attached bathrooms in this comfortable and quiet hotel cost KSh 500/900 including breakfast. Soap and towel are provided and the hotel has its own cosy restaurant and bar. Vehicles can be parked in the hotel compound and are guarded by an askari. Credit cards are not accepted.

More convenient for the centre of town and tucked in alongside the Nanyuki River is the *Nanyuki River Lodge* (☎ (0176) 32523). This is quite a large place and offers singles/doubles with attached bathrooms including breakfast at KSh 550/850. There's a bar and restaurant where you can also eat lunch and dinner for KSh 200 (four courses). There's adequate guarded parking and a disco on Saturday nights (KSh 100 for men and KSh 50 for women).

Top of the line and a very pleasant place to stay is the newly refurbished *Sportsman's Arms Hotel* (☎ (0176) 22598; fax 22895), south-east of the town centre and across the river. This was once the white settlers' watering hole as the style of the building and the 10-acre landscaped gardens indicate. Some of the makuti-roofed cottages have been preserved for their nostalgia value but brand new ones have also been put up, complete with all modern facilities, so that there are now a total of 85 beds. B&B in the ordinary rooms here is KSh 1035/1495 for singles/doubles. There are also cottages at KSh 1811/2760 for singles/doubles including breakfast. Lastly, there are also self-catering cottages for KSh 2500/4500 for singles/doubles. Facilities at the hotel include an Olympic-sized heated swimming pool, a business centre, restaurant, three bars, a fitness club and a nightly disco in the Buccaneer Club.

Places to Eat

There are very few restaurants in Nanyuki which are not attached to hotels, so take your pick. The *Marina Bar & Restaurant* and *Muneera's Restaurant*, which are next to each other on the main road, are reasonable places to eat and the Marina is an expats' watering hole. For something more sophisticated, go for a meal at the *Sportsman's Arms*. It serves the best food in town.

Things to Buy

There are a number of souvenir stalls and shops set up around town, catering mostly to the British army. The Cotton Culture store on the main street has some interesting items, including beautiful woollen jumpers hand-knitted by a local women's cooperative.

Getting There & Away

Air Air Kenya Aviation (☎ (02) 501421; Wilson airport, Nairobi), flies daily from Nairobi to Nanyuki and Samburu and then back again to Nairobi via Nanyuki. It departs Nairobi at 9.15 am, Nanyuki at 10.10 am, Samburu at 10.50 am, Nanyuki at 11.30 am and arrives back in Nairobi at 12.15 pm. The fares are US$70 (Nairobi-Nanyuki), US$105 (Nairobi-Samburu) and US$40 (Nanyuki-Samburu) one way.

Bus There are daily buses, Nissan minibuses and Peugeot share-taxis from Nairobi (KSh 200 to KSh 250) and Isiolo (KSh 120) to Nanyuki as well as minibuses and matatus from Nyeri (KSh 60) and Nyahururu which run throughout the day.

For those with stamina, there's also an Arusha Express bus direct from Nanyuki to Mombasa and Malindi via Nairobi daily at 5 pm. The fare to Mombasa is KSh 500, or KSh 600 to Malindi. The booking office is directly opposite the clock tower on the main road through town.

AROUND NANYUKI

There are a number of accommodation possibilities in the vicinity of Nanyuki, although only one of them could be called cheap.

Closest to town is the *Mt Kenya Safari Club*, one of the Lonrho group (☎ (02) 216940; fax 216796 in Nairobi). This hotel, originally the homestead of a white Kenyan settler family, was founded in the 1950s by a group of people including the late William

Holden, and is now one of the most exclusive in the country. The views up to Mt Kenya are excellent, and facilities include golf, tennis, croquet, snooker, swimming (heated pool), fishing and bowls.

The tariff for all this luxury starts at US$239/310 with full board in a standard room, going up to US$579 for a presidential suite, plus there are more expensive cottages and villas. Children aged from two to 12 years sharing with their parents are charged US$48. The turn-off for the hotel is a couple of km from Nanyuki along the Naro Moru road, and from there it's nine km along a dirt road which becomes treacherous in the wet.

More luxury options exist on the *Ol Pejeta Ranch* (☎ (02) 216940 in Nairobi), west of Nanyuki along the Nyahururu road. This 9000 hectare ranch has been converted into a private rhino sanctuary and is accessible only to those who can afford the accommodation. The Ol Pejeta homestead, also belonging to the Lonrho group, was the former vacation getaway of the now bankrupt international financier Adnan Kashoggi. As he was not one to spare any expense, the hotel is lavishly decorated, and still features Kashoggi's four-metre-wide bed! Full-board rates are US$78/130 in the low season (April to June, and November to mid-December) and US$163/208 the rest of the year. More expensive suites are also available. Children under 16 years are *personae non gratae* here.

Also on the Ol Pejeta Ranch is the *Sweetwaters Tented Camp*, where a number of luxury permanent tents (though they are tents in name only) have been constructed beside a water hole (floodlit at night). The dining room, bar and reception are inside the quaint, original farmhouse. With the water hole as a focus, game-viewing is the main activity and there's a choice of day and night game drives in 4WD vehicles, walking safaris and camel safaris. Full-board accommodation is US$64/120 in the low season, and US$141/187 in the high season. Children aged from two to 12 years are charged US$44. Bookings should be made through Lonrho in Nairobi (☎ (02) 216940; fax 216796).

Yet another option, and a much more affordable one, is the *El Karama Ranch* (☎ (02) 340331; fax 336890 in Nairobi), 42 km north-west of Nanyuki on the Ewaso Nyiro River. Billed as a 'self-service camp', El Karama is a family-run ranch with a number of bandas for guests. The accommodation is basic but comfortable and each banda is supplied with beds, mattresses, table and chairs, wash basin, bucket, shower, fireplace and firewood. Long-drop toilets are situated close to the bandas. Prices are very reasonable at KSh 400 per person per night (KSh 200 for children between the ages of two and 12 years). You should bring along everything you need, including food, though you can rent bedding (KSh 80), cooking utensils (KSh 80) and kerosene lamps (KSh 80). Meals are not available. Activities here include wildlife walks (KSh 50 per person) starting daily at 7 am and 4 pm and horse riding (KSh 500 per person). During the rainy seasons (April, May and November) you preferably need a 4WD vehicle to get here. Let's Go Travel in Nairobi can provide you with a map of how to get here, and is also the booking agent.

ISIOLO

Isiolo, where the tarmac ends, is the frontier town for north-eastern Kenya – a vast area of both forested and barren mountains, deserts, scrub, Lake Turkana and home to the Samburu, Rendille, Boran and Turkana peoples. It's a lively town with a good market and all the usual facilities including petrol stations, a bank, a post office and a good choice of hotels and restaurants. There are also bus connections to places north, east and south of Isiolo.

The resident population of Isiolo is largely Somali in origin as a result of the resettlement of Somali ex-soldiers following WWI. It ought, in addition, to be famous for the number of formidable speed bumps which force traffic to a snail's pace on the way into town from the south. There are no less than 21 of these and more still at the northern edge of town!

Information

Isiolo is the last place going north which has a bank (Barclays) until you get to either Maralal or Marsabit. There are no banks on the way to or at Lake Turkana (assuming you bypass Maralal).

Likewise, there are no petrol stations north of here until you reach Maralal or Marsabit except at the Samburu Lodge (in Samburu National Park). This doesn't mean that petrol or diesel is totally unobtainable since you can buy it in Baragoi (with ease) and possibly at Christian mission stations elsewhere (with difficulty or not at all if they're low on stock) but you will pay well over the odds for it due to transport costs and irregularity of supply. Stock up in Isiolo.

Travellers about to go to the national parks north of here or to Lake Turkana, and who intend to do their own cooking, should stock up on food and drink in Isiolo as there's very little available beyond here except at Maralal, Marsabit and (less so) Wamba. There's a very good market in Isiolo adjacent to the mosque for fresh fruit, vegetables and meat. The general stores, too, have a good range of canned food and other items.

Places to Stay – bottom end

There are a number of fairly basic lodging houses available for those tight on funds. These include the *Maendeleo Hotel, Farmers Boarding & Lodging, Savannah Inn, Frontier Lodge, Coffee Tree Hotel* and the *National Hotel*, all offering rooms with shared bathroom facilities (cold water only) from KSh 180/250 a single/double. The downstairs area of the Frontier Lodge is taken up by a lively bar which sometimes hosts live bands.

The best place to stay, however, is the *Jamhuri Guest House* which is excellent value and has been popular with travellers for a number of years. The rooms are very clean and pleasant, mosquito nets are provided and the communal showers have hot water in the mornings. Rooms cost KSh 200/260 a single/double. Belongings left in the rooms are quite safe. Next door to it and similar in price and quality is the *Silent Inn*.

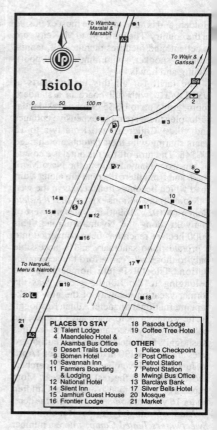

Isiolo

0   50   100 m

PLACES TO STAY
3 Talent Lodge
4 Maendeleo Hotel &
   Akamba Bus Office
6 Desert Trails Lodge
9 Bomen Hotel
10 Savannah Inn
11 Farmers Boarding
   & Lodging
12 National Hotel
14 Silent Inn
15 Jamhuri Guest House
16 Frontier Lodge
18 Pasoda Lodge
19 Coffee Tree Hotel

OTHER
1 Police Checkpoint
2 Post Office
5 Petrol Station
7 Petrol Station
8 Mwingi Bus Office
13 Barclays Bank
17 Silver Bells Hotel
20 Mosque
21 Market

Another possibility is the *Talent Lodge*, near the post office. It offers rooms with shared bath for KSh 150/200 a single/double. There is supposedly hot water all day in the showers but this is wishful thinking. The centre of the hotel and the terrace overlooking the street are taken up by a bar so it's not as quiet as the Jamhuri Guest House.

Going up in price, there is the *Pasoda Lodge* which is clean and quiet and offers doubles with bath for KSh 350. There are no singles. The hotel has its own restaurant and bar. At the top of the budget category is the *Desert Trails Lodge*, clearly visible behind the BP station on the main street. The design of this place is perhaps a little claustrophobic given all the wide open spaces close by, but it does mean the security is good. Rooms are good value at KSh 250/450 with a bathroom shared between two rooms.

Places to Stay – middle

There's only one mid-range hotel in Isiolo and that is the *Bomen Hotel* (☎ (0165) 2225). This three storey hotel has a total of 40 spacious rooms, tastefully decorated and furnished. Rates are KSh 900/1300 for singles/doubles with shower (hot water) and toilet, and prices include breakfast, taxes and service charges. The hotel has its own bar and restaurant which serves excellent food at very reasonable prices. Guarded parking is available in the hotel compound. This is an excellent place to stay if you want to visit the nearby reserves of Samburu or Buffalo Springs but can't afford the charges at the lodges inside the parks or don't want to camp.

Places to Eat

Most of the simple boarding houses also have restaurants where you can eat typical African-style meals for less than KSh 150. The *Frontier Lodge* has a good cafe, the restaurant at the *Pasoda Lodge* is one of the better ones, and the *Silver Bells Hotel* does excellent chicken curry.

For a minor splurge, go for lunch or dinner at the *Bomen Hotel*.

Things to Buy

A good proportion of the young men who hang around on the main street of Isiolo are salespeople for the brass, copper and aluminium/steel bracelets which you'll already have come across elsewhere except that the craft here is particularly fine. If you're one of those people who like decking out your forearms with as many of these bracelets as you can, then this is the place to buy them. They're much cheaper here than anywhere else though haggling is, of course, obligatory. The same people also sell daggers in leather scabbards but the craftsmanship in these is generally unremarkable.

If you're simply walking around Isiolo then these salespeople will hardly ever bother you but if you're driving around and especially if you're filling up with petrol at a station then expect a real hassle. Their wares will be thrust in front of your face from both sides and you'll be hard-pressed to drive away.

Getting There & Away

Akamba operates three buses daily to Nairobi at 7.30 and 9 am and 8 pm. The journey takes about seven hours and costs KSh 280. The buses travel via Nanyuki, Naro Moru and Thika, and it's not a bad idea to book one day in advance. If you'd prefer the more comfortable Nissan minibuses, the fare is KSh 330. Peugeot share-taxis cost KSh 380.

Mwingi Buses operates buses to Marsabit (KSh 350) supposedly a couple of times a week, but this is very flexible. It also operates less frequent buses to Moyale on the Ethiopian border (KSh 350 from Marsabit). For either of these services it's just a matter of enquiring at the office several times to try and pin down a departure time or day. There's no alternative except to simply hang around and wait, negotiate a ride on a truck (relatively easy and usually somewhat less than the bus fare) or walk out to the police checkpoint north of town where the tarmac ends and hitch a ride with tourists (not so easy). The Mwingi office is an anonymous shopfront at the rear of the Bomen Hotel; just look for the derelict buses out the front.

Mwingi also operates buses to Maralal a few times a week (depending on demand) which cost KSh 300. Again, the departure times are uncertain.

For Moyale there are regular convoys, and it's easy enough to hitch a ride on a truck. The journey takes two days, so stock up with provisions. The cost is KSh 100 to KSh 600, depending on the driver. If there has been any rain the road turns to mud and becomes impassable.

There's no scheduled transport to Wajir and Mandera, north-east of Isiolo, and besides, this area is the domain of the *shifta*

(Somali bandits, usually armed) and only those people with a specific reason (or a suicide wish) should contemplate travelling there. Every morning at 8 am a convoy of vehicles headed for Wajir, Mandera or Garissa leaves the police checkpost. They are mostly trucks and many will take passengers for a fee. If you are heading for Garissa a stop is made overnight in the beautiful little village of **Mado Gashi**. Here the *New Mount Kenya Lodge* is good value at KSh 200 for a large double room.

AROUND ISIOLO
Lewa Downs
Lewa Downs is a privately owned ranch of some 16,000 hectares which has been turned into a rhino and wildlife sanctuary, although ranching activities are still maintained. The entire area is enclosed by a solar-powered electric fence to keep out stock from neighbouring properties.

Black rhinos from other parts of the

Giraffes are a protected species in Kenya and are numerous; see them at Lewa Downs.

country have been relocated here and are now breeding. The ranch also has a small group of the more placid white rhino, and these are a big attraction, especially since those in Meru National Park were slaughtered a few years ago. Other wildlife abounds, and visitors can expect to see elephant, giraffe, eland, oryx, buffalo, leopard and lion.

The Craig family runs the *Wilderness Trails Lodge* on the ranch, and this is a small, superbly sited stone and makuti thatch set-up with stunning views across to Isiolo and the northern plains. It's a top-end place, so you can expect to part with about US$260 per person per day for full board, but the level of service is excellent and the setting perfect. The lodge is closed during April and May, and from 1 November to 15 December. Bookings must be made in advance through Chris Flatt in Nairobi (☎ (02) 502491; fax 502739).

MERU
Up at the north-eastern end of the ring road around the southern side of Mt Kenya, Meru is an important town which services the intensively cultivated and forested highlands in this part of Central province. It's quite a climb up to Meru from either Isiolo or Embu and, in the rainy season, you'll find yourself in the clouds up here along with dense forest which frequently reaches right down to the roadside. When the weather is clear there are superb views for miles over the surrounding lowlands. Views of the peaks of Mt Kenya, on the other hand, are hard to come by due mostly to the forest cover.

Although there's a small centre of sorts, Meru is essentially just a built-up area along the main road and, as far as travellers' interests go, there's precious little reason to stay the night there. It's certainly much too far away from any of the route heads leading to the peaks of Mt Kenya to be a suitable base to take off from. The nearest of these begins at Chogoria, about halfway between Meru and Embu.

Meru's main claim to fame is the quality of its *miraa*. These are the bundles of leafy

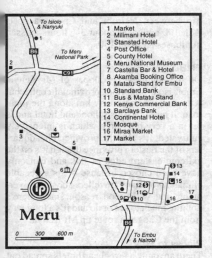

Meru

1	Market
2	Milimani Hotel
3	Stansted Hotel
4	Post Office
5	County Hotel
6	Meru National Museum
7	Castella Bar & Hotel
8	Akamba Booking Office
9	Matatu Stand for Embu
10	Standard Bank
11	Bus & Matatu Stand
12	Kenya Commercial Bank
13	Barclays Bank
14	Continental Hotel
15	Mosque
16	Miraa Market
17	Market

0   300   600 m

twigs and shoots which you'll see people all over Kenya (and particularly Somalia and Ethiopia) chewing for its stimulant and appetite-suppressant properties. While it still grows wild here, much of it is now cultivated and it's become a major source of (legal) income for the cultivators and harvesters who supply both the internal market and also export it to neighbouring countries. No doubt the marijuana growers are green with envy!

For more information about the Meru people see the Tribal Groups & Cultures section which starts on page 106.

Meru National Museum

This small museum just off the main road is worth visiting if you're staying here or passing through. It has the usual display detailing the progress of evolution, along with exhibits of stuffed birds, animals and mounted insects, but there's also a small and informative section concerning the agricultural and initiation practices of the Meru people and their clothing and weapons. Out at the back of the building are a number of appallingly small and sordid cages containing obviously neurotic and pathetically bored specimens of baboon, vervet monkeys and a caracal cat which someone ought to liberate immediately as an act of sheer pity if not humaneness. There's also a reptile pit with a notice advising visitors that 'Trespassers will be bitten'.

The museum is open daily from 9.30 am to 6 pm except on Sunday and holidays when it's open from 11 am to 6 pm and 1 to 6 pm respectively. Entry costs KSh 50.

Places to Stay

Two of the cheapest places to stay in Meru are the *Castella Bar & Hotel* and the *Continental Hotel* in the town 'centre'. They're basic and neither is particularly special. The Castella has a noisy bar downstairs, and a curious sign at reception warns that 'Combing of the hair in the room is not allowed'. Somewhat better value is the *Stansted Hotel* (☎ (0164) 20360) on the main road past the post office. It is clean, quiet and offers rooms with attached bathrooms at KSh 200 per person including breakfast. The hotel has its own bar and restaurant.

Also good value is the *Milimani Hotel*, further up the hill from the Stansted. It offers good, rooms with attached bathrooms with hot water for KSh 400/550 a single/double. Vehicles can be parked safely in the hotel compound and at weekends there's a disco. If you don't have transport, this hotel is probably too far from the centre – it's about two km uphill.

The best mid-range hotel is probably the *County Hotel*, again on the main road and close to the turn-off for the museum. It's clean, comfortable, has its own restaurant and lively bar, and secure parking. Rooms with attached bathrooms cost KSh 1200/1750 a single/double with breakfast.

Those with their own transport might like to check out the *Rocky Hill Inn*, about eight km out of town to the north, which is essentially a barbecue and bar but has basic chalets for rent, or the *Forest Lodge*, even further out, which has a swimming pool and pretensions to being a sort of country club with expensive chalets.

Places to Eat

For a good, cheap meal of curried fish or chicken try the *Copper Coin* restaurant near the bus stand. Another good bet is the snack bar at the *County Hotel*. A la carte meals cost from around KSh 200 or there's a three course set meal which is great value at KSh 180. The food is unexciting, but it's filling and you can have a beer with your meal. The hotel also has a more up-market restaurant.

Getting There & Away

Meru is served by Akamba buses to and from Nairobi (KSh 240) with departures from Meru at 7.30 and 9 am, and 8 pm. The buses travel via Chogoria, Embu and Thika. The buses can be booked in advance, and the office is in the town centre, just off the main road.

From the matatu park there are regular departures for Isiolo, Embu and Nairobi. Nissan minibuses to Nairobi cost KSh 200.

CHOGORIA

The only reason to come to this small town on the lower eastern slopes of Mt Kenya is that it is the access point for one of the most scenic routes up the mountain – the Chogoria route. Guides and porters can be engaged through the Chogoria Guides Club, which is based at the Transit Motel.

Places to Stay & Eat

The choices here are limited. The *Transit Motel* (☎ 96 in Chogoria) is about half an hour's walk up from Chogoria, and has cheap and clean singles/doubles. Camping is also possible for KSh 100 per person. The other alternative is the *Forest Station*, at the barrier across the track about five km up the route from Chogoria. The 15 cabins here are fully equipped with kitchens, fireplaces, hot showers and three beds.

The *Lenana Restaurant*, just inside the gates of the hospital, is a good place for cheap, substantial meals.

Getting There & Away

The Akamba buses running between Nairobi and Meru pass through Chogoria, or there are regular matatus to Embu and Meru. The bus trip between Nairobi and Chogoria costs KSh 100 and takes about 3½ hours. Nissan minibuses are KSh 130.

EMBU

On the south-eastern slopes of Mt Kenya, Embu is an important provincial centre but is spread out over many km along the main road. It has a famous school and hotel and is set in a very hilly area which is intensively cultivated. It's also the provincial headquarters of the Eastern province though it's on the extreme eastern edge of this and can only have been chosen because of its agreeable climate. Not many travellers stay here overnight, and with good reason since there's nothing much to see or do and it's a long way from the Chogoria route up Mt Kenya.

Places to Stay

There are quite a few cheap hotels spread out along the main road but most of them are very basic and can't be recommended. Behind a row of shops almost opposite the bus and matatu park is the *Eden Guest House*. While hardly paradise, it offers clean, quiet rooms with shared facilities for KSh 180/280.

The *Al-Aswad Hotel*, just a little further up the road, has no single rooms, but the doubles are quite good value at KSh 350. The hotel also has a good restaurant where you can eat for just KSh 120. The *Kubukubu Lodge*, further down the hill from the Eden Guest House, is another reasonable choice.

The *Valley View Hotel* (☎ (0161) 20147), also in this range, has rooms with attached bathrooms with hot water for KSh 400/675 with breakfast. It's clean and tidy and soap and towel are provided, plus the staff are friendly and helpful. The hotel has its own bar and restaurant, and it's much quieter than the hotels around the bus stand.

If you'd like to splurge then consider a night at the *Izaak Walton Inn* (☎ (0161) 20128), about two km up the main road towards Meru from the town centre. It is right out of the colonial era and set in extensive lawns and gardens with a good restaurant and cosy bar – both with log-burning fireplaces. Rates are KSh 1200/1500

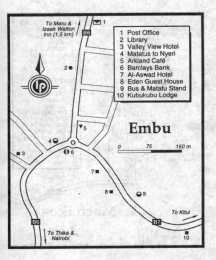

Map legend for Embu:
1 Post Office
2 Library
3 Valley View Hotel
4 Matatus to Nyeri
5 Arkland Café
6 Barclays Bank
7 Al-Aswad Hotel
8 Eden Guest House
9 Bus & Matatu Stand
10 Kubukubu Lodge

To Meru & Izaak Walton Inn (1.5 km)

Embu

0   75   150 m

To Kitui

To Thika & Nairobi

for singles/doubles including breakfast, with suites and triples at KSh 2200. The staff are friendly and helpful and it's definitely *the* place to stay if you have the money. Even if you don't stay here it's worth turning up for a beer or a meal.

Places to Eat

The *Arkland Cafe* near the main roundabout in the centre of town, is a good place for a meal or snack at lunch time. If you want the full treatment, head for the restaurant at the Izaak Walton.

Getting There & Away

There are daily Akamba buses between Nairobi and Embu and this is the safest way to travel between the two places. The fare is KSh 120 and the booking office is on the top side of the bus and matatu stand.

Matatus also offer the same service but they are invariably overcrowded, often dangerously so, and the drivers really drive like maniacs. The fare to Nairobi on the matatus varies between KSh 100 and KSh 130 and they terminate on Accra Rd (if you're fortunate enough to get that far).

The alternative to a bus or matatu is a Peugeot share-taxi, although, if anything, these are more dangerous because they travel faster. The fare is KSh 150 to KSh 200 depending on the driver and the time of day.

The matatus to Meru are not quite the same hair-raising and dangerous prospect since there's not the same pressure on the drivers, but they're no joy ride either. Take the Akamba bus or a Peugeot taxi in preference.

The Akamba Country

The land of the Akamba people (Ukambani) lies to the south-east of Nairobi and encompasses a broad swathe of wooded hill country east of the Athi River through Machakos (the main town) all the way down onto the semi-arid plains around Kitui. It's a pleasant area and people here are very friendly but very few travellers get out this way. Most of the foreigners you see here work for NGOs or Christian missionary groups. There's not a great deal to do or see in this part of Kenya, but the hills around Machakos offer excellent walking opportunities and superb views down onto the plains to the east. For more details about the Akamba, see the Tribal Groups & Cultures section on page 106.

MACHAKOS

A decade or so before Nairobi was even established, Machakos was the site chosen by the Imperial British East Africa company as an upcountry trading post on account of the Akamba's reputation as middlemen between the Swahili of the coast and the Maasai and Kikuyu to the west and north.

It's a small town hemmed in on two sides between wooded hills and steep valleys and has a very laid-back feeling to it – though you wouldn't guess that judging by the number of buses and matatus which ply between here and Nairobi daily. Clearly, a lot of business must be being transacted as the goods for sale in the open market demonstrate but, basically, it's a place to come for a few days of recreation and rest from the urban madness of Nairobi.

KENYA

Places to Stay – bottom end

One of the cheapest places to stay is the *Songa Guest House*, round the corner from the KAFOCA Club. It's clean and friendly and has singles/doubles with attached bathrooms for KSh 200/300.

The *Medium Lodge Boarding & Lodging* close to the market is also OK and has quite a few rooms for about the same price, but you wouldn't want to stay there on Saturday nights as the rooms sit above a large bar and disco area and would be very noisy. Not just that, but during the day it's almost impossible to find anyone to open up a room for you. The *T Ten Hotel* on the road in from Nairobi is similar to the above but a little more down-at-heel, though it does have its own restaurant and bar.

Better is the *Ikuuni Hotel* (☎ (0145) 21166) which is very friendly and has rooms circling a central courtyard. All the sheets are washed and ironed (!) daily and it costs KSh 350/400 for singles/doubles with shared bathroom facilities (clean). The hotel has its own bar and restaurant out the front.

Places to Stay – middle

The only place to stay in this range – and it's superb value – is the *KAFOCA Club* which has singles/doubles with shared bathroom facilities for KSh 350/450 as well as singles with attached bathrooms for KSh 800. Everything is spotlessly clean, the staff are very friendly and there's a bar, beer garden, restaurant and guarded parking.

Places to Stay – top end

The best hotel in town is the *Garden Hotel* (☎ (0145) 30037) which is a huge place with its own restaurant, bar and beer garden and a range of room prices depending on what you take. Standard singles/doubles with attached bathrooms cost KSh 1700/3110 including breakfast, plus there are suites for KSh 3230/4370 for singles/doubles including breakfast. There's a live band in the bar most nights of the week. A lot of people use this place for seminars and conferences so

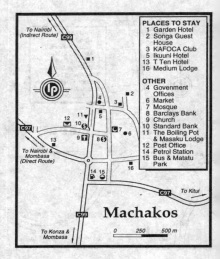

don't be surprised if the place is humming with activity when you arrive. There's draught beer in the beer garden and the food is good.

Places to Eat

Other than the restaurants at the above hotels, there's not much choice. Quite a few of the hotels on the road adjacent to the open-air market and around the bus/matatu stand do standard African fare, but otherwise the most popular place to eat is *The Boiling Pot/Masaku Lodge* which features an upstairs bar/restaurant with a verandah overlooking the street. It's a very popular place to eat.

Getting There & Away

The best way to get here is to take a Nissan minibus from the country bus station on Landhies Rd in Nairobi to Machakos. The fare is KSh 100 and the journey takes about one hour. There are also ordinary buses for KSh 80. Quite a few of the Nissans continue on to Kitui. The fare to Kitui from Nairobi is KSh 150. Ordinary buses cost KSh 100.

Western Kenya

Western Kenya is an area with many attractions, but is often overlooked by travellers, and you won't find a single safari minibus out this way either. For this reason alone it's worth spending a bit of time exploring here, just to get the feel of Kenya without the tourists.

The countryside is, for the most part, beautiful rolling hills, often covered with the bright green bushes of vast tea plantations. Further west you have Lake Victoria and the regional capital of Kisumu on its shore, and from here there are plenty of possibilities. Just a short distance to the north lies the Kakamega Forest with its lush vegetation and abundant wildlife. Further north still, close to the regional town of Kitale, are the national parks of Mt Elgon (well worth exploring) and Saiwa Swamp, where the only way of getting around is on foot and the attraction is the rare sitatunga or marshbuck deer. (See the Kenya National Parks & Reserves chapter for details.)

If you have your sights set on more distant horizons, head west for Busia or Malaba and Uganda, or south to Isebania and across the border into Tanzania.

This western part of the country is the home of Kenya's Luo people. Numbering around two million they make up the third largest ethnic group in the country. Marginalised politically, they are nevertheless a friendly people. (See the Tribal Groups & Cultures section starting at page 106 for more information.)

Getting Around

This is the most densely populated part of the country, so the road system is good and there are hundreds of matatus of varying shapes and sizes plying the routes. Accidents are unnervingly common, but they usually seem to involve the very small matatus, which are usually dangerously overloaded. The small-truck sized matatus are a lot safer as they generally travel more slowly and can carry loads with greater ease.

One annoying factor of matatu travel in this region is the way the destination changes suddenly depending on the number of passengers. So if your matatu is supposedly going from, say, Kakamega to Kitale and it gets to Webuye and everyone gets out, it's a fairly safe bet that you will have to as well. When this happens, and you have paid the fare to the final destination, the driver will find you a seat in another vehicle and fix things with its driver. You will get there in the end, but it may take longer than you think.

Lake Victoria

With an area approaching 70,000 sq km, Lake Victoria is obviously the major geographical feature in this part of the continent. Unlike the lakes further west, Victoria is not part of the Rift Valley system, and so is wide and shallow (only 100m deep) compared with, say, Lake Tanganyika which is nearly 1500m deep.

Lake Victoria touches on three countries – Uganda, Tanzania and Kenya – and it's possible to take a boat between Kenya (Kisumu) and Tanzania (Mwanza), and Uganda (Port Bell) and Tanzania (Mwanza), but not between Kenya and Uganda. The only possibility for lake excursions within Kenya is the ferry which runs from Kisumu to Kenyan ports further south.

Bilharzia is prevalent in Lake Victoria so don't swim in the water or walk in the grass along its shores – this is the hide-out of the snails which are the host for the parasitic flukes which invade your body. (See the Health section in the Regional Facts for the Visitor chapter for more information.) Admittedly, you face only a very small risk of contracting bilharzia if you spend only a short time here.

KENYA

KISUMU

Although it hardly feels like it, Kisumu is Kenya's third largest town. It has a very easy going, almost decaying, atmosphere. Kisumu was a busy port from early this century right up until the East African Community split up in 1977, but it seems that from this point on the town has just been marking time. With the recent increase in cooperation between the former partners in the community, however, Kisumu's fortunes may once again be on the rise. Already it is a major transhipment point for petroleum products: a recently completed pipeline brings the raw fuel from Mombasa, and it is then refined and separated into the various individual products and shipped by truck to Uganda, Rwanda, Burundi and eastern Zaïre. The resumption of the international ferry route to Mwanza in Tanzania is another positive sign, although the sinking of the MV *Bukoba* in 1996, with the loss of at least 600 lives, won't do anything for the confidence of potential passengers.

Despite its relative isolation, Kisumu is the ideal place to head for from the east of the country as the travel connections are excellent, especially by rail. There's also enough to

Western Kenya

0   25   50 km

do in the town itself to make it an interesting place to stop for a few days.

If you've arrived from the higher country further east the first thing that you will notice is the heat and humidity. Kisumu is always a good few degrees hotter than, say, Nairobi and the steamy conditions only add to the general torporific air.

Orientation

Kisumu is sited on the gently sloping shore of Lake Victoria. Although it's a fairly sprawling town, everything you are likely to need is in walking distance. The main drag is Oginga Odinga Rd and along it are almost all the shops, the banks and the post office.

The railway station and ferry jetty are about a five minute walk from Oginga Odinga Rd, while the noisy bus and matatu station is behind the market on Jomo Kenyatta Highway, about a 10 minute walk from the centre.

Most of the cheap hotels are in the area between Oginga Odinga Rd and Otiena Oyoo St. The mid-range and top-end hotels are mostly to be found along Jomo Kenyatta Highway. The best access to the lake itself is at Dunga, a small village about three km south of town along Nzola Rd.

Information

The post office is in the centre of town on Oginga Odinga Rd. It's open Monday to Friday from 8 am to 5 pm, Saturday from 9 am to noon. If you need to make international calls there is a cardphone outside and you can call direct. Phonecards are sold at the post office.

The British Council, also on Oginga Odinga Rd, has newspapers and magazines and quite a good library. It's open from 9.30 am to 1 pm and 2 to 5 pm Monday to Friday, and 8.30 am to 12.45 pm on Saturday.

Immigration is on the 1st floor, Reinsurance Plaza (behind Deacons department store), on the corner of Oginga Odinga Rd and Jomo Kenyatta Highway. The officials here are friendly and helpful.

The best bookshop in town is the well-stocked Sarit Bookshop on Oginga Odinga Rd, diagonally opposite the post office.

Markets

Kisumu's main market is one of the most animated in the country, and certainly one of the largest. Whether you're after a bag of potatoes or are just curious, it's worth a stroll around.

If you're in town on a Sunday don't miss the Kibuye Market, a huge outdoor affair which draws people from all around the district. You can buy anything here, from second-hand clothes to furniture and food. It is held on Jomo Kenyatta Highway, about one km north of the main intersection with Nairobi Rd. Share-taxis from the intersection cost KSh 5.

Kisumu Museum

It comes as something of a surprise to find this excellent museum here – it's among the best in the country and is well worth a visit. The museum is on Nairobi Rd, within easy walking distance of the centre, and is open daily from 8.30 am to 6 pm; entry is KSh 200.

The displays are well presented and wide-ranging. There's a very good collection of everyday items from the various peoples of the area, including agricultural implements, bird and insect traps (including a white-ant trap!), food utensils, clothing, furniture, weapons, musical instruments and a fairly motley collection of stuffed birds and animals, including an amazing centrepiece of a lion riding on a wildebeest.

Outside there is a traditional Luo homestead consisting of the husband's mud and thatch house, and separate houses for each wife. There's usually a man near the homestead who will show you around for a few shillings and point out the salient features. Also outside are the inevitable crocodile and tortoise enclosures, which are small and a bit depressing. ■

KENYA

Hippo Point

Hippo Point is at Dunga, about three km south of town, and the cafe on the point is a good place to head for. There are usually no hippos in evidence but it's a pleasant spot all the same. Known as Dunga Refreshments, the cafe is well signposted once you get out of town along Nzola Rd. This place also has the only camp site in Kisumu (see Places to Stay). If you want to get out on the lake there are a number of young boys hanging around who will oblige – for a reasonable fee.

Places to Stay – bottom end

Camping Campers should head for *Dunga Refreshments* (☎ (035) 42529) at Hippo Point, right on the shores of Lake Victoria, three km south of town. It takes nearly an hour to walk there, or you can take a taxi for KSh 250. It's a well-run place with good facilities but there's little shade. Camping here costs KSh 100 per person plus there's also a dormitory block which costs KSh 250 per bed with shared facilities. It's a relaxing place to stay and highly recommended. The complex includes a very pleasant restaurant with reasonably priced meals. It caters for vegetarians, and fruit juices and cold beers are available. The restaurant is open weekdays (closed Monday) from 10 am to 3 pm and 5 to 8 pm, and on weekends from 10 am to 9 pm.

Hotels One of the cheapest options for accommodation is the *YWCA* (☎ (035) 43192) on the corner of Omolo Agar and Nairobi Rds. It has dorm beds (three people per room) for KSh 150 with shared facilities, and also has double rooms with attached bathrooms which vary from KSh 250 to KSh 350 per person. The Y takes both men and women and there's a canteen where you can get basic meals.

A good budget option is the *Razbi Guest House* (☎ (035) 44771), upstairs on the corner of Oginga Odinga Rd and Kendu Lane. It's very secure (there's a locked grille at the top of the stairs), the rooms are clean and a towel and soap are provided. The rates

are KSh 150/200 for singles/doubles with shared cold-water bath.

Two streets south-east of Ogada St is Apindi St, where you'll find the basic *Mirukas Lodge* with OK rooms at KSh 120/200 – they don't come any cheaper than this.

Back on Oginga Odinga Rd, the *Mona Lisa Guest House* (behind the restaurant of the same name) has singles/doubles with attached bathrooms for KSh 200/300. This is probably the best value in Kisumu, and there's hot water supposedly 24 hours a day.

Places to Stay – middle

The *Black & Black Boarding & Lodging*, in the centre of town, has singles/doubles for KSh 340/560, all including breakfast. Bathrooms are shared by three rooms and there is hot water.

Close by is the very pleasant *New Victoria Hotel* (☎ (035) 21067), on the corner of Kendu Lane and Gor Mahia Rd. It's good value, especially if you get one of the front rooms with a balcony and views of Lake Victoria. The singles, at KSh 450, are probably overpriced; the doubles, at KSh 750, are about right. All rates include breakfast. The hotel also has a good restaurant and a popular TV lounge.

Closer to the lake, but without the views, is the *Western Lodge* (☎ (035) 42586) which only has single, rooms with attached bathrooms at KSh 400.

Just off Jomo Kenyatta Highway, close to the Imperial Hotel, is the *Hotel Inca* (☎ (035) 40158) which is also good value. It's a large place and offers well-furnished, very clean, rooms with fan and attached bathroom with hot water for KSh 500/850. There's a bar and restaurant and the staff are friendly.

Places to Stay – top end

The best hotel in this range is the charming *Hotel Royale* (☎ (035) 21079) on Jomo Kenyatta Highway. It's an old hotel with a gleaming white façade, open-air terrace bar and polished wooden floorboards. If you have the money, and can get one of the rooms

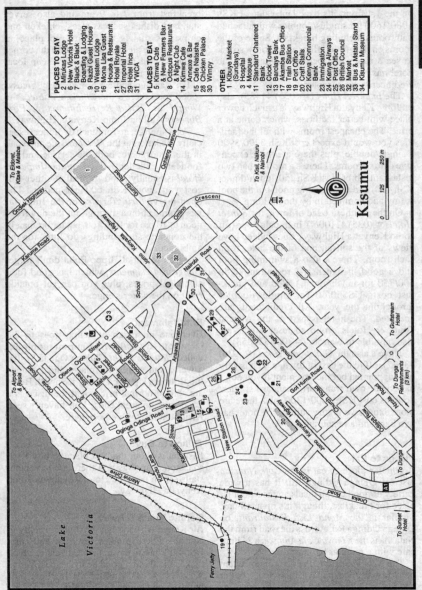

PLACES TO STAY
2 Mirukas Lodge
6 New Victoria Hotel
7 Black & Black
     Boarding & Lodging
9 Razbi Guest House
10 Western Lodge
16 Mona Lisa Guest
     House & Restaurant
21 Hotel Royale
27 Imperial Hotel
29 Hotel Inca
31 YWCA

PLACES TO EAT
5 Kimwa Cafe
     & New Farmers Bar
8 Octopus Restaurant
     & Night Club
14 Kimwa Cafe
15 Annexe & Bar
     Cafe Natasha
28 Chicken Palace
30 Wimpy

OTHER
1 Kibuye Market
     (Sundays)
3 Hospital
4 Mosque
11 Standard Chartered
     Bank
12 Clock Tower
13 Barclays Bank
17 Akamba Bus Office
18 Train Station
19 Port Office
20 Craft Stalls
22 Kenya Commercial
     Bank
23 Immigration
24 Kenya Airways
25 Post Office
26 British Council
32 Market
33 Bus & Matatu Stand
34 Kisumu Museum

Kisumu

0   125   250 m

Lake
Victoria

on the 1st floor, it's excellent value at KSh 1080/1600 for singles/doubles with attached bathrooms including breakfast. Some of the rooms on the ground floor are gloomy, so ask to see a room first before booking in. The hotel has its own very good restaurant, and credit cards are accepted.

The *Imperial Hotel* (☎ (035) 41485), also on Jomo Kenyatta Highway, is a much newer place with better facilities, which come at a price. The cheapest rooms with all the facilities you would expect cost KSh 3290/3900 a single/double, plus there are more expensive deluxe rooms. There's a rooftop bar, two restaurants (breakfast KSh 250, lunch/dinner KSh 400) and a swimming pool, but the pool is tiny and hemmed in by the building.

On the southern edge of town, the *Sunset Hotel* (☎ (035) 41100/4), in Impala Lane (off Jomo Kenyatta Highway), does indeed have views of the sunset, and of the lake, from each room. There's also a swimming pool and a good, if expensive, restaurant (KSh 500/750 for lunch/dinner). Bed and breakfast costs US$50/60 for singles/doubles throughout the year. All credit cards are accepted. The hotel is part of the African Tours & Hotels group so reservations are also possible in Nairobi (☎ (02) 336858).

There's also the *Gulfstream Hotel* (☎ (035) 43927), off to the east of town, which is very well appointed but inconvenient if you don't have your own transport. Standard singles/doubles cost KSh 1000/1200, plus there are more expensive luxury suites. The hotel has two bars and a restaurant.

Places to Eat

A popular place to eat is the *Cafe Natasha* just off Oginga Odinga Rd. It has a wide variety of good cheap meals and is a popular place for breakfast, though it's open all day. Similar is the *Mona Lisa Restaurant*, on Oginga Odinga Rd. Across the road from the Natasha is the *Kimwa Cafe Annexe*, a 24 hour cafe with a popular bar upstairs.

The *New Victoria Hotel* does an excellent breakfast of juice, papaya, eggs, toast, butter and tea or coffee for KSh 100. It's open for breakfast from 7 to 9 am and also serves standard dishes such as steak, chicken and chips. As this is a Muslim-run place, it doesn't serve alcohol. Just around the corner is the *Kimwa Cafe*, which has cheap local dishes such as matoke and irio.

For stand-up-and-eat or take-away greasy-spoon food there's the *Chicken Palace*, the *Wimpy* or *Rafiq Refreshments & Fast Burgers* – all on Jomo Kenyatta Highway.

For a splurge, go for lunch or dinner (especially the latter) at the *Hotel Royale* and soak in the atmosphere; both the service and the food are excellent. Food at the *Imperial Hotel* is equally good. A meal at either will cost you about KSh 600 per person. The open-air *Victoria Terrace* at the Imperial has nyama choma throughout the day from noon to 10 pm for KSh 160, but unfortunately the concrete surroundings do little for the ambience.

If you're out at Hippo Point don't forget *Dunga Refreshments*, which has good food at budget prices, plus you can eat outside right on the water's edge.

Entertainment

Everyone in search of action goes to the excellent disco/bar/restaurant complex called *Octopus Night Club* on Ogada St. It's a weird and wonderful place, and includes the Bottoms Up disco (entry KSh 90). Beers are sold at normal prices and the disco is a good rage on weekends. You haven't seen Kisumu until you've been here.

Things to Buy

Kisumu is about the best place to buy Kisii soapstone carvings and there are pavement stalls set up near the Hotel Royale on Jomo Kenyatta Highway.

Getting There & Away

Air Kenya Airways has 12 flights weekly to Nairobi. The trip takes one hour and costs US$44. You can pay in local currency, which makes the flight a good deal cheaper. Kenya Airways (☎ (035) 44055) is in the Alpha building on Oginga Odinga Rd.

Bus & Matatu Buses, matatus and Peugeots leave from the large bus station just north of the market.

The best buses for Nairobi are the double-decker KBS buses, which leave from the northern edge of the bus station. The fare is KSh 350 and the journey takes six hours. Akamba has its own depot in the centre of town and has departures for Nairobi at 10 am and 8.30 pm, also for KSh 350. There's also the deluxe Akamba Royal service to Nairobi daily at 10.30 am and 10.30 pm for KSh 600.

There are plenty of Nissan matatus to Nairobi (KSh 300), Busia (KSh 120), Eldoret (KSh 150), Kakamega (KSh 100) and Kisii (KSh 140). There are very few direct services to Kitale; take a vehicle to Kakamega and change there.

Peugeot share-taxis go to Nairobi (KSh 500), Nakuru (KSh 450), Kakamega (KSh 100) and Busia (KSh 100).

Uganda Akamba has a daily direct bus to Kampala at noon; the fare is KSh 600.

Train There are trains to Nairobi daily at 6 pm, arriving at 7 am the next day. Fares to Nairobi are KSh 1930/1320 in 1st/2nd class. It's advisable to book in advance. The booking office at the station is open daily from 8 am to noon and 2 to 4 pm.

There's also a daily 3rd class passenger train to Butere at 9 am, about 50 km northwest of Kisumu. It's strictly for the dedicated.

Car For car rental see Lake Travels (☎ (035) 42204) in the Reinsurance Plaza, corner of Jomo Kenyatta Highway and Oginga Odinga Rd. Avoid Mara Mbose Tours & Travels.

Boat Lake ferries ply between Kisumu and the small Kenyan ports to the south, as well as to Mwanza in Tanzania.

Kenyan Ports The MV *Alestes* plies the route to Homa Bay, departing on Tuesday at 9.30 am, arriving in Homa Bay at 2.30 pm. The fare is KSh 84/41 in 2nd/3rd class. It leaves Homa Bay at midnight on Saturday, returning to Kisumu late on Sunday night.

For the rest of the week it operates between Homa Bay and Mfangano Island.

Tanzania There is a weekly service between Kisumu and Mwanza. Although this was operated by the now-defunct MV *Bukoba*, the service should have now resumed with the MV *Victoria*. The vessel departs Kisumu at 6 pm on Friday, arriving at Mwanza around 10 am the following day. From Mwanza it sails for Kisumu on Thursday at 6 pm, arriving in Kisumu the following morning. The fare is KSh 1200/ 950/600 in 1st/2nd/3rd class, although 3rd class is not recommended as it is just seating space, not a berth. Advance bookings can be made at the port office on weekdays from 8 am to noon and 2 to 4 pm.

AROUND LAKE VICTORIA
Kendu Bay
This small lakeside village has little to offer apart from a somewhat strange volcanic lake a couple of km from town. There's basic accommodation in the town, and the ferry jetty is about one km away.

Homa Bay
This is a very nondescript yet surprisingly busy town on a small bay in Lake Victoria. Most of the action involves transporting agricultural products from the area to Kisumu. Nearby is the intriguing volcano-shaped **Mt Homa** and the small **Ruma National Park**.

Places to Stay & Eat There are several budget hotels along the main road from the ferry, but none are anything to rave about. The best is probably *Asego Stores*, up behind the main road. The sign just announces Bed & Breakfast (although the breakfast doesn't seem to exist). Doubles here cost KSh 200. Next door is the *Nyanza Lodge*, which costs the same but is not as good.

If, on the other hand, you have money to spare, there's the very pleasant *Homa Bay Hotel* (☎ (0385) 22070), set in its own grounds on the shore of the lake. It's part of the Msafiri Inns group so you can book in Nairobi (☎ (02) 330820; fax 227815). A good room here facing the lake costs KSh 1750/2250, and meals are reasonably priced. It's a mellow place to relax if you want to get away from it all for a few days.

Getting There & Away There are frequent matatus to Kisii (KSh 100), Kisumu (three hours, KSh 90) and Rusinga (KSh 40).

From Wednesday to Saturday the MV *Alestes* operates a daily service to Mfangano Island. On Saturday at around midnight it sails for Kisumu.

Rusinga Island

Mbita is the town on Rusinga Island which is connected by a causeway to the mainland. The only remarkable thing about the island is the mausoleum of Tom Mboya on the northern side of the island – he was born here in 1930 and was shot dead by police in 1969 during political unrest. (See the History section in the Kenya Facts about the Country chapter for more details.)

There are matatus to Homa Bay, as well as ferry services to Kisumu, Mfangano Island and Homa Bay.

Places to Stay & Eat There's one small lodge in Mbita, which is cheap, clean and friendly. The *Viking Hoteli* is a great little local eatery serving fish fresh from the lake.

On the northern side of the island is the exclusive *Rusinga Island Fishing Club*. As the name suggests, this place is for those whose primary concern is hooking things out of the water on the end of a bit of nylon, but the bird life is also prolific. Accommodation is in individual thatched huts, each with a fine lake view. For bookings contact Nairobi (☎ (02) 447267).

Mfangano Island

There's little to see here and very little in the way of facilities. The small fishing community is about as far off the beaten track as you can get in Kenya.

There is one cheap hotel, and the island is connected to the mainland by ferry (see Homa Bay, Getting There & Away). On other days you can catch a local boat from Mbita (at the causeway for Rusinga Island).

Places to Stay While there are no hotels on Mfangano, it should be possible to arrange accommodation with the local inhabitants. Failing that, the only possibility is the up-market *Mfangano Island Camp* on the northern side of the island, where accommodation costs US$125 per person for full board. This is primarily a fishing resort, and fishing trips are available at US$100 per day. For bookings contact Mutiara Ltd in Nairobi on ☎ (02) 331871.

On the tiny island of Takawira nearby, there's a similar lodge, the *Takawira Island Resort*. For bookings contact Kisumu (☎ (035) 43141; fax 44644).

Western Highlands

The western highlands make up the agricultural heartland of Kenya, and separate Kisumu and Lake Victoria from the rest of the country. In the south around Kisii and Kericho lie vast tea plantations, while further north around Kitale and Eldoret it's all fertile farming land.

The towns of the highlands are really just small agricultural service towns, much the same as you'd find in similar areas in Australia or the USA – and they're about as interesting. For visitors, the attractions of the area lie outside these towns – the tea plantations around Kericho, Kakamega Forest near Kakamega, Mt Elgon and Saiwa Swamp national parks (both near Kitale), and the Cherangani Hills which lie north-east of Kitale and Eldoret. See the Kenya National Parks & Reserves chapter for details.

KISII

As you might expect, this is where Kisii soapstone comes from but it's not on sale here at all, the simple reason being that Kisii sees very few tourists and those that do come this way tend to just keep moving. You can,

KENYA

however, visit the quarries if you like. Not much happens in Kisii, and even the locals will tell you that it's 'a remote place'. But the people are friendly and as so few tourists come here, you'll be regarded with curiosity.

Kisii is the main centre of the region known as the **Gusii Highlands**, home of the Gusii people. The Gusii, numbering around one million, are a Bantu-speaking people in the middle of a non-Bantu area; the Maasai to the south, Luo to the west and north and Kipsigis to the east all speak unrelated languages. (See the Tribal Groups & Cultures section on page 106 for more information.)

The town centre is compact and, as usual, the market is the liveliest place in the town during the day.

While you're here, it's worth making the four-hour round trip to the top of nearby **Manga Ridge** from which the views, especially over Lake Victoria, are magnificent. You can also see Kisumu in the distance and the tea plantations of Kericho behind you.

Places to Stay – bottom end

The best value budget place is the *Sabrina Lodge*, just around the corner from the Tabaka matatu stand. It's a very friendly place and has rooms with shared facilities for KSh 200/300 a single/double, and security is good. The hotel also has a bar and restaurant.

Somewhat more expensive, and not as good, is the *Safe Lodge* (☎ (0381) 202950), which has friendly staff but small and gloomy rooms. It costs KSh 200/300 for singles/doubles with hot-water bath. Soap and towels are provided, and breakfast is included in the price. The single rooms have double beds so a couple could get away with a single. It also has a rough and ready bar which can be noisy in the late afternoons when people come in for a drink after work.

On the Kisumu road out of town are two other budget hotels, the *Kianbu Lodge* and the *Highway Lodge*, right next door to each other. Both offer singles/doubles with attached bathrooms for KSh 250/400. There's a bar and restaurant upstairs at the Kianbu.

Places to Stay – middle

The modern high-rise building on the north-eastern side of the market is the *Sakawa Towers Hotel* (☎ (0381) 21218). Rooms with attached bathrooms, with balcony (some with good views) and hot water in the mornings cost KSh 450/600 including breakfast.

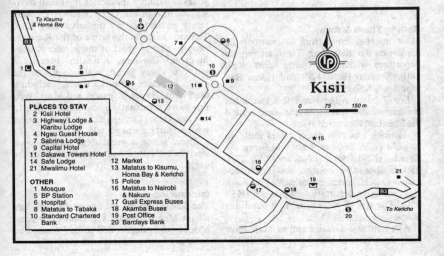

PLACES TO STAY
2 Kisii Hotel
3 Highway Lodge &
   Kianbu Lodge
4 Ngau Guest House
7 Sabrina Lodge
9 Capital Hotel
11 Sakawa Towers Hotel
14 Safe Lodge
21 Mwalimu Hotel

OTHER
1 Mosque
5 BP Station
6 Hospital
8 Matatus to Tabaka
10 Standard Chartered
   Bank
12 Market
13 Matatus to Kisumu,
   Homa Bay & Kericho
15 Police
16 Matatus to Nairobi
   & Nakuru
17 Gusii Express Buses
18 Akamba Buses
19 Post Office
20 Barclays Bank

To Kisumu & Homa Bay

B3

Kisii

0   75   150 m

To Kericho

The staff are friendly and it's a clean place to stay. Towels are provided and there's a bar and restaurant on the 1st floor.

At the eastern end of town is the modern *Mwalimu Hotel* (☎ (0381) 20933) in its own compound. Singles/doubles with attached bathrooms cost KSh 420/620 including breakfast. The hotel has a popular bar, terrace, beer garden and restaurant. There's also guarded parking.

The most pleasant place to stay is the *Kisii Hotel* (☎ (0381) 30134) which is set in its own large gardens (complete with turkeys) on the western side of town. It's a single storey building with a popular bar and restaurant and has singles/doubles with attached bathrooms for KSh 420/600 including breakfast.

Places to Eat

There's not a lot of choice when it comes to eating. One good place is the tiny restaurant inside the *Sabrina Lodge*. It doesn't look all that flash, but it serves good honest local food at sensible prices, and you can have a cold beer with your meal.

For something a bit more sophisticated, head for the *Kisii Hotel* or the *Mwalimu Hotel*.

Getting There & Away

Most matatus leave from in front of the market on the main drag. There are regular departures to Kisumu (three hours, KSh 140), Kericho (KSh 120) and Homa Bay (one hour, KSh 60).

For Tabaka, Migori and the Tanzanian border, matatus leave from the stand behind the Standard Chartered Bank.

Akamba has two direct buses daily to Nairobi (KSh 360) at 9 am and 9 pm via Kericho (KSh 100) and Nakuru (KSh 200). Tickets should be booked one day in advance. Gusii Express Buses, across the road, also has daily departures for Nairobi (KSh 250). The trip to Nairobi takes around 8½ hours.

Akamba and Gusii Express both have daily departures to Homa Bay (KSh 100).

TABAKA

This is the village where the soapstone is quarried and carved, and on arrival it's easy enough to locate someone who can show you one of the workshops. It's basically just a cottage industry and there are few people who actually work the stone for a living – to most people it's just a handy way to supplement the meagre income made from agriculture.

To get there, take one of the fairly infrequent matatus from Kisii.

KERICHO

Tea – it's everywhere! This is the heart of western Kenya's tea plantation area and the rolling hills are a uniform bright green. Kericho's climate is perfect for growing tea, mainly because of the afternoon showers which fall every day of the year. Yes, Kericho is a wet place, but the showers are generally only brief and, apart from benefiting the tea bushes, they also make the area green and pleasant.

The town takes its name from the Maasai chief, Ole Kericho, who was killed by the Gusii in the 18th century in a battle over land – the Maasai had been in the area for years and didn't appreciate the Gusii moving in, though the Gusii themselves were being pushed out by the advancing Luo. The area today is the home of the Kipsigis people, who are part of the greater Kalenjin group. The name 'Kalenjin' (literally 'I tell you') was given in the 1950s to the group of Nandi-speaking tribes, including the Pokot, Nandi, Kipsigis and Marakwet. For more information about the Kalenjin see the Tribal Groups & Cultures section which starts on page 106.

There's not a great deal to the town itself but it's not a bad place to stop for the night.

Information

The post office and the two main banks are all on Moi Highway. The banks are open Monday to Friday from 8 am to 1 pm and on Saturday from 8.30 to 11 am.

Tea Plantations

The closest plantation to town is behind the Tea Hotel, itself once owned by the Brooke Bond company. If you walk through the hotel grounds behind what was the service station and out through the back gate, the path leads through the tea bushes to the hotel workers' huts. If you're lucky there may be picking in progress.

It may be possible to organise a tour of a plantation and processing plant through the Tea Hotel.

Places to Stay – bottom end

Campers should head for the *Kericho Garden Lodge* (☎ (0361) 20878), where you can camp in the pleasant grounds for around KSh 100 per person per night. The rooms here are reasonable value at KSh 240/330 with attached bath. With breakfast the price jumps to KSh 300/450.

Cheaper accommodation is not all that flash. At the *Njekimi Lodging* on John

Kericho Rd you can get a basic single/double with common bath for KSh 200/250.

A better bet is probably the *Fairview Tas Hotel*, which is pretty rough and ready, and has small rooms at KSh 150/250.

Places to Stay – middle

In the centre of town there's the reasonably modern *Mwalimu Hotel* (☎ (0361) 30039) which has a popular bar and restaurant. Singles/doubles with private bath cost KSh 400/520 including breakfast.

Places to Stay – top end

The cheapest of the top-range hotels is the *Mid-West Hotel* (☎ (0361) 20611) which has standard singles/doubles with private bath for KSh 875/1150, and more expensive deluxe rooms and suites. Prices include a substantial breakfast and all taxes. The hotel has its own bar and restaurant.

At the top of the line is the grand old *Tea Hotel* (☎ (0361) 30004; fax 20576), which

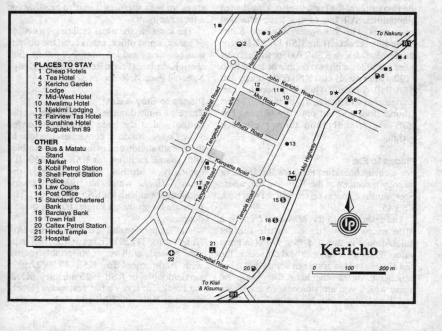

PLACES TO STAY
1 Cheap Hotels
4 Tea Hotel
5 Kericho Garden Lodge
7 Mid-West Hotel
10 Mwalimu Hotel
11 Njekimi Lodging
12 Fairview Tas Hotel
16 Sunshine Hotel
17 Sugutek Inn 89

OTHER
2 Bus & Matatu Stand
3 Market
6 Kobil Petrol Station
8 Shell Petrol Station
9 Police
13 Law Courts
14 Post Office
15 Standard Chartered Bank
18 Barclays Bank
19 Town Hall
20 Caltex Petrol Station
21 Hindu Temple
22 Hospital

Kericho

0   100   200 m

To Nakuru

To Kisii & Kisumu

Picking Tea

Kenya is the world's third largest producer of tea, and it accounts for about 20 to 30% of the country's export income. Tea picking is obviously one of the main jobs in the Kericho area. A top tea picker can pick up to 100 kg per day, and they are paid at the rate of KSh 0.80 per kg. The bushes are picked every 17 days, and the same picker picks the same patches of the plantations each time. If you look closely at one of the fields of bushes you can see how one stalk of a bush is left to grow here and there; these are the markers by which workers identify their patch. The bushes are cut right back to about 50 cm high in January to March every four years, and after 90 days are ready for picking again. ■

was originally built by the Brooke Bond company in the 1950s for its managers. It's set in its own well-tended grounds and exudes an atmosphere of days gone by. The rooms are spacious in the extreme, especially the two suites at the back overlooking the tea plantations. All the rooms have attached bathrooms with hot-water showers. Rates (including breakfast) are KSh 1725/2100 for singles/doubles, or KSh 2700 for triples, plus there are suites with two double beds for KSh 3190. Other meals cost KSh 650 (lunch) and KSh 750 (dinner). There's a popular bar/lounge area which sprawls over much of the ground floor and out onto the terrace. The staff are friendly and there's guarded parking.

Places to Eat

For a cheap breakfast head for the 1st floor balcony restaurant at the *Fairview Tas*, where eggs, sausage, toast and tea will set you back KSh 45.

The restaurant in the *Mwalimu Hotel* is a little more sophisticated, while the set lunch/dinner in the *Mid-West Hotel* is good value. The buffet lunches and dinners at the *Tea Hotel* are also good but somewhat more expensive. On the other hand, there is a grand piano which you are welcome to use if you feel like playing some Mozart or Elton John.

Getting There & Away

The matatu station is fairly well organised, with matatus on the upper level and mini-buses and buses on the lower level.

As is the case throughout the west, there is plenty of transport in any direction. Nissan minibuses leave regularly for Kisumu (KSh 100), Kisii (KSh 100) and Nairobi (KSh 270). There are also Peugeots to Eldoret (KSh 180), Kitale (KSh 250), Nairobi (KSh 350), Kisii (KSh 120) and Kisumu (KSh 120).

If you are hitching, the turn-off to Kisumu is about two km south of town along the Kisii road, so you need to get there first, either on foot or by matatu.

KAKAMEGA

The town of Kakamega is on the A1 route, 50 km north of Kisumu and 115 km south of Kitale. About the only reason to stay here is if you are heading for the Kakamega Forest Reserve and arrive too late in the day to walk or get a vehicle. It's also the last place to stock up with supplies if you're heading for a forest sojourn.

The town has the usual facilities – a couple of banks, a post office, market and the ubiquitous boardings and lodgings. For information about Kakamega Forest Reserve see the Kenya National Parks & Reserves chapter.

Places to Stay & Eat

There's a limited range of hotels here. At the bottom end of the scale is the *New Garden View Lodge*, which is conveniently close to the matatu station and offers singles/doubles with shared facilities for KSh 150/250. It's basically a brothel. Much better is the *Franca Hotel*, which has two-bed rooms with hot-water bath for KSh 300 a room. The beds are larger than a single, but not quite a double.

At the opposite end of the scale is the *Golf Hotel* (☎ (0331) 20125; fax 30155), set in its own grounds with very comfortable rooms, with bathrooms, for KSh 1750/2250 a single/double, or KSh 2925 a triple, including breakfast. It has a bar, restaurant (lunch/dinner is KSh 400/500) and barbecue area.

It's also a great place to relax with a cold beer even if you're not staying here.

Getting There & Away

The matatu station is at the Total station on the northern edge of town. There are buses and matatus to Kisumu (KSh 100), Webuye, Kitale (two hours, KSh 110), Nairobi and Busia. Hitching is not too difficult.

ELDORET

There is little to see or do in Eldoret but it may make a convenient stop for the night in your peregrinations around the western highlands, particularly if you are heading to or from the Cherangani Hills which lie to the north of Eldoret.

The town has benefited hugely from the university here, leading to a lot of new development. Eldoret has also been at the centre of some controversy recently, as the government has built a munitions factory in the area, and a brand-new international airport! Theories abound as to why Eldoret might need such an airport, one of them being that the western part of the country would secede if Moi lost the 1997 election. At this stage, both events seem unlikely.

Information

The post office is on the main street, Uganda Rd, and is open Monday to Friday from 8 am to 5 pm and Saturday from 9 am to noon. Also on the main street are branches of Barclays and Standard Chartered banks.

For car rental, check out the Eldoret Travel Agency (☎ (0321) 33351) on Kenyatta St.

Dorinyo Lessos Creameries Cheese Factory

Perhaps the main attraction here is the local cheese factory, where you can buy any of 20 locally made cheeses at very reasonable prices. Here they produce everything from Stilton to Gruyère and cheddar, all priced at around KSh 360 per kg. You can taste as many as you like, and there is a minimum purchase of 250 gm. They also make about a dozen different ice-cream flavours, and

you can buy these in dinky little buckets for KSh 12.50.

The factory is close to the centre of town, at the end of a very grubby lane which is the home of engineering workshops and car wreckers.

Places to Stay – bottom end

For cheap accommodation the best bet is the *Mahindi Hotel* (☎ (0321) 31520), which is close to the bus and matatu station and is good value at KSh 200 a single with shared bath or KSh 300/400 for singles/doubles with private bath. The hotel has a restaurant, and the noise from the hopefully named Silent Night Bar downstairs can sometimes be distracting. Very similar and also close to the bus station is the *New Miyako Hotel* (☎ (0321) 62757) which charges KSh 200 a single with shared bathroom facilities and KSh 250/400 for singles/doubles with attached bathrooms. There's hot water in the showers and the hotel has an upstairs bar.

Also in this same area is the *Sosani View Hotel* which offers singles/doubles with hot-water bath for KSh 300/400. The hotel has its own bar and restaurant.

One option for campers is the *Naiberi River Campsite*, some 22 km south-east of town on the C54 road to Kaptagat. It's a beautiful spot right on the Naiberi River, and is very popular with overland trucks. This is an utterly eccentric rabbit warren of a place, with two bars (one with waterfall) which stay open until the last person falls over, and meals are available. Solo females might find the comments in the visitors' book enlightening. As well as camping (KSh 150) there is a dormitory (KSh 250) and a few very comfortable double cabins with private bathrooms at KSh 1200. Getting there by local transport is a pain, but the owner, Raj Shah, works in Eldoret during the day, so if you ring before 5 pm on weekdays he can give you a lift out to the site. The contact number for Raj is ☎ (0321) 32644.

Places to Stay – middle

A popular place to stay in this range, and one of the cheapest, is the *New Lincoln Hotel*

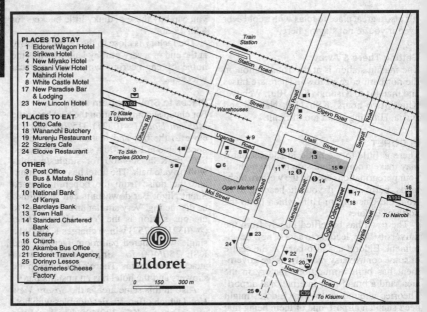

PLACES TO STAY
1 Eldoret Wagon Hotel
2 Sirikwa Hotel
4 New Miyako Hotel
5 Sosani View Hotel
7 Mahindi Hotel
8 White Castle Motel
17 New Paradise Bar & Lodging
23 New Lincoln Hotel

PLACES TO EAT
11 Otto Cafe
18 Wananchi Butchery
19 Murenju Restaurant
22 Sizzlers Cafe
24 Elcove Restaurant

OTHER
3 Post Office
6 Bus & Matatu Stand
9 Police
10 National Bank of Kenya
12 Barclays Bank
13 Town Hall
14 Standard Chartered Bank
15 Library
16 Church
20 Akamba Bus Office
21 Eldoret Travel Agency
25 Dorinyo Lessos Creameries Cheese Factory

Eldoret

0   150   300 m

To Kitale & Uganda
To Sikh Temples (200m)
To Nairobi
To Kisumu
Train Station
Station Road
64 Street
Warehouses
Uganda Road
Utalii Street
Oloo Road
Elgeyo Road
Sergoit Road
Kenyatta Street
Oginga Odinga Street
Nyala Street
Mol Street
Open Market
Nandi Road
Dhama Rd
A104

(☎ (0321) 22093), which is quiet and has guarded parking. Rooms with attached bathrooms are good value at KSh 500/700 including breakfast. The staff are friendly, there's hot water in the showers and the hotel has its own bar and restaurant.

More expensive and somewhat characterless is the *White Castle Motel* (☎ (0321) 33095) on Uganda Rd, which offers bed and breakfast for KSh 900/1400 a single/double. There's a bar and restaurant on the ground floor.

The pick of the hotels in this range is the *Eldoret Wagon Hotel* (☎ (0321) 62270) on Oloo Rd. This hotel was built years ago in the colonial era and was once a watering hole for white settlers. It still exudes a certain charm but the open verandah where you used to be able to sit and drink a cold beer has been entirely enclosed. The bar memorabilia, however, is still intact. Singles/doubles with attached bathrooms including breakfast cost KSh 1000/1500. Credit cards are accepted.

The bar keeps 'English' hours: 11 am to 2 pm and 5 to 11 pm.

Places to Stay – top end
The only top-end hotel here is the modern *Sirikwa Hotel* (☎ (0321) 63433; fax 61018), which has rooms for KSh 3500/4300 a single/double including breakfast. All major credit cards are accepted and the hotel has the only swimming pool in Eldoret. Meals in the restaurant here cost KSh 300 (lunch) and KSh 500 (dinner).

Places to Eat
A popular lunch-time spot is *Otto Cafe* on Uganda Rd. It offers good, cheap western-style meals such as steak, chicken, sausages, eggs, chips and other snacks.

For a slightly more up-market meal or snack try the popular *Sizzlers Cafe* on Kenyatta St, near the Eldoret Travel Agency. Here you'll find a whole range of burgers, curries, steaks and sandwiches.

For nyama choma there are a couple of lively places. The *Wananchi Butchery* on Oginga Odinga St will hack you off a half kg and barbecue it for KSh 85. Slightly more salubrious is the *Murenju Restaurant* further down the same street, which has a nyama choma bar out the back.

The *Elcove Restaurant*, on Oloo Rd opposite the New Lincoln Hotel, is also good. For a splurge, eat at either the *Eldoret Wagon* or *Sirikwa* hotels.

Getting There & Away
Bus & Matatu The bus and matatu station is in the centre of town, just off Uganda Rd. For some strange reason *mzungu* males wandering around here all get called 'Mr John' by the locals. Just who John is/was remains a mystery for the moment.

Matatus/Peugeots depart throughout the day for Kisumu (KSh 150/180), Nakuru (KSh 150/200), Nairobi (KSh 300/400), Kericho (KSh 130/180) and Kitale (KSh 90/100). There are also buses on all these routes.

Akamba buses leave from the company's office/depot on Oginga Odinga St. Executive services to Nairobi (KSh 320) leave at 10.30 am and 9 pm, and there are daily Royal services to Nairobi at 1 pm (KSh 700) and Kampala (KSh 1800) at 11 am.

Train There are services three times a week to Nairobi (KSh 2340/1840 in 1st/2nd class) – on Saturday and Sunday at 9.35 pm, arriving the next day at 9.30 am, and on Thursday at 8.35 am. Trains to the Ugandan border at Malaba (KSh 1260/1030) depart on Saturday and Sunday at 2.40 am, and the train to Kampala (KSh 2250/1710) comes through at 9.45 pm on Tuesday.

CHERANGANI HILLS
The beautiful Cherangani Hills are part of the rift valley system and extend for about 60 km from the north-east of Eldoret. They form the western wall of the spectacular **Elgeyo Escarpment**. You could easily spend weeks exploring here, and never come across another mzungu.

The area is best explored on foot as the roads are rough and some of those which scale the Elgeyo Escarpment are incredibly steep. In wet conditions the roads in this area become treacherous. For serious exploration you'd need copies of the relevant Survey of Kenya maps to the area, which are almost impossible to get (see the Maps section in the Kenya Facts for the Visitor chapter). Otherwise contact Jane or Julia Barnley of Sirikwa Safaris, PO Box 332, Kitale, who can organise ornithological tours of the hills along with a guide at a very reasonable price. Jane and Julia also run an excellent guest house and camp site 23 km north of Kitale (see the Kitale section for details).

The hills are dotted with small towns and although none of them have any recognised accommodation, it should be possible to arrange something with the local people (ask the village chief or ask in the bars). If you have a tent it's just a matter of finding a good spot and asking permission.

From Eldoret it should be possible to hitch, or find a matatu, as far as Kapsowar, 70 km to the north-east in the Kerio Valley and right in the heart of the hills. Coming from the north there is a road which starts from Sigor at the Marich Pass and finds its way to Kapsowar via Tot and the impossibly steep escarpment road, but don't expect much in the way of transport along it.

The hills are the home of the Marakwet or Markweta people (part of the greater Kalenjin grouping) who migrated here from the north. The area was secure, and the streams were ideal for agriculture as the rainfall was low. To this end they have made good use of, and extended, the water distribution channels which were already in existence when the Marakwet first migrated to the area. The channels distribute the water to all the small *shambas* in the hills.

For further details on these hills, see the Marich Pass section in the Northern Kenya chapter.

KABARNET
Kabarnet is a shabby little town which has a

KENYA

spectacular location in the Tugen Hills on the eastern edge of the Kerio Valley. It is the chief town of the Baringo district and boasts a post office, cinema and supermarket.

Places to Stay

The unmarked *lodge* in front of the market has good double rooms with attached bathrooms for KSh 170. You'll have to ask for directions.

Otherwise there's the *Mombasa Hotel* with double rooms with bucket shower at KSh 200. The video room here is a popular place (KSh 10 to see a movie!).

KITALE

Kitale is another in the string of agricultural service towns which dot the western highlands. It does have an interesting museum but its main function for travellers is as a base for explorations further afield – Mt Elgon, Saiwa Swamp National Park – and a take-off point for the trip up to the western side of

Lake Turkana. The Nationa Parks chapter has more details about these places. As such Kitale is a pleasant enough town and can make an enjoyable stopover for a couple of days.

Information

The post office is on Post Office Rd (surprise, surprise) and is open the usual hours. It's possible to make international calls but, as there's no cardphone, these have to be made through the operator in Nairobi, and this takes time. Kitale has the usual banks and a busy market.

Kitale Museum

The museum has a variety of indoor exhibits, including good ethnographic displays of the Turkana people. The outdoor exhibits include traditional homesteads of a number of different tribal groups, the inevitable tortoise enclosure and an interesting biogas display.

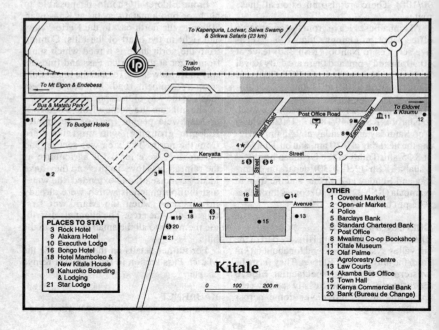

Kitale

PLACES TO STAY
3 Rock Hotel
9 Alakara Hotel
10 Executive Lodge
16 Bongo Hotel
18 Hotel Mamboleo &
   New Kitale House
19 Kahuroko Boarding
   & Lodging
21 Star Lodge

OTHER
1 Covered Market
2 Open-air Market
4 Police
5 Barclays Bank
6 Standard Chartered Bank
7 Post Office
8 Mwalimu Co-op Bookshop
11 Kitale Museum
12 Olaf Palme
   Agroforestry Centre
13 Law Courts
14 Akamba Bus Office
15 Town Hall
17 Kenya Commercial Bank
20 Bank (Bureau de Change)

0   100   200 m

Probably the most interesting feature is the small **nature trail** which leads through some virgin forest at the back of the museum. There are numbered points along the way; the small guidebook available from the craft shop in the museum explains the points of interest.

The museum is open daily from 8 am to 6 pm; entry is KSh 200.

Agroforestry Project

Next to the museum along the highway is the Olaf Palme Agroforestry Centre. It's a Swedish-funded program aimed at educating the local people about protection and rehabilitation of the environment. The project includes a small demonstration farm and agroforestry plot, and an information centre. It's open daily and entrance is free.

Places to Stay – bottom end

Best of the usual bunch of cheapies/brothels is the *New Kitale House*, which offers singles with clean sheets and shared bath for just KSh 150. Next door is the *Hotel Mamboleo* (☎ (0325) 20172), which is also not bad though the rooms are somewhat gloomy. Singles/doubles with attached bathrooms cost KSh 200/300, plus there's hot-water showers.

Up the scale somewhat is the *Executive Lodge* (☎ (0325) 30689), on Kenyatta St, which has singles with common bath at KSh 350 and doubles with attached bathrooms at KSh 650.

If you want to camp, the only place in the area is *Sirikwa Safaris*, 23 km north of Kitale on the Kapenguria road. It's run by Jane and Julia Barnley at their farmhouse and is a beautiful place to stay. Jane and Julia are very friendly and know the western highlands like the back of their hand, plus they're great conversationalists. Stay here and feel right at home! You won't regret the little effort it takes to get here. Camping with your own tent costs KSh 300 per person including the use of firewood, hot-water showers, flush toilets and electricity. If you don't have your own tent, that's no problem as there are also very comfortable 'permanent' furnished tents for KSh 900/1200, plus taxes (35%). To

find Sirikwa Safaris, look for the sign on the right-hand side one km after the small village of Kesagen. Kapenguria matatus from Kitale go right by Sirikwa (KSh 40), and the drivers all know it.

Places to Stay – middle

The most popular place to stay in this range is the *Bongo Hotel* (☎ (0325) 20593) on Moi Ave, with singles/doubles with shared bath for KSh 300/500, or KSh 550/700 with private bath, all including an excellent breakfast. There's hot water in the showers, clean sheets, and towel, soap and toilet paper are provided.

Also good value is the *Alakara Hotel* (☎ (0325) 20395) on Kenyatta St, offering spacious singles/doubles with shared bath for KSh 400/600. Rooms with private bath cost KSh 600/900. Prices include breakfast. Facilities include a good bar/restaurant, a car park and a residents' video room. The staff are friendly and helpful.

Outside of town, Sirikwa Safaris is the place to head for (see Places to Stay – bottom end for directions). Apart from tents there are two very comfortable rooms with double beds for KSh 1800/2700 a single/double plus tax (35%) and including breakfast. Half-board and full-board rates are also available. Children are half-price and babies stay free of charge. It's a very quiet and homely place and Jane and Julia are the perfect hosts. For advance bookings write to PO Box 332, Kitale.

Places to Eat

The *Executive Restaurant*, at the lodge of the same name, is a very popular lunch-time spot. The menu is extensive and the food good and reasonably priced.

The *Suncourt Cafe* has a nice terrace with views of the surrounding hills. It is behind the town hall, and has good cheap food.

The *Bongo Hotel*, on the corner of Moi Ave and Bank St, has a slightly more up-market restaurant which is a good place for an evening meal. It also serves alcohol. Right next door is the lively Bongo Bar and there's also a take-away food section.

Even better, though slightly more expensive, are the meals at the *Alakara Hotel* on Kenyatta St. You can either eat in the restaurant section or have meals brought to you in the popular bar.

Getting There & Away

The bus and matatu park is fairly chaotic – it's just a matter of wandering around and finding a vehicle going your way. Competition for passengers is usually keen and you'll soon be spotted and pointed in the right direction.

For Lodwar and Kalekol in the Turkana district, there is usually one minibus per day for KSh 350; you'll just have to ask around. The Nissan matatus are more reliable and leave about five times daily (five hours, KSh 400).

On the Nairobi route there is a variety of transport – bus, matatu, Peugeot – so it's a matter of finding which suits you. Akamba runs daily buses to Nairobi at 9 am and 9 pm (seven hours, KSh 400). There's also the Eldoret Express which runs a number of times daily and costs KSh 350. The bus companies have their offices mainly around the bus station area; the exception is Akamba which has its office on Moi Ave.

Matatus/Peugeots also run to Nairobi (KSh 400/500), Eldoret (KSh 90/120) and Nakuru (KSh 240/320). There are also matatus to Kisii (KSh 180) and Kakamega (KSh 110), and Peugeots to Nyeri (KSh 580) and Nyahururu (KSh 600).

For the village of Endebess (the nearest place to Mt Elgon National Park), Nissan matatus cost KSh 60. (See the Kenya National Parks & Reserves chapter for more details on getting to this national park.)

Northern Kenya

This vast area, covering thousands of sq km to the borders with Sudan, Ethiopia and Somalia, is an explorer's paradise hardly touched by the 20th century. The tribes which live here – the Samburu, Turkana, Rendille, Boran, Gabra, Merille and El-Molo – are some of the most fascinating people in the world. Like the Maasai, most of them have little contact with the modern world, preferring their own centuries-old traditional lifestyles and customs which bind members of a tribe together and ensure that each individual has a part to play. Many have strong warrior traditions and, in the past, it was the balance of power between the tribes which defined their respective areas.

As late as 1980 there was a clash between the Samburu and the Turkana over grazing land near South Horr which required army intervention. Since most of the tribes are nomadic pastoralists these sort of conflicts have a long history. Nevertheless, the settlement of disputes between the tribes is based on compensation rather than retribution so wholesale violence is a rare occurrence.

Change has been slowly happening to these people as a result of missionary activity (there is an incredible number of different Christian missions, schools and aid agencies, many of them in very remote areas), their employment as rangers and anti-poaching patrollers in national parks and game reserves, the construction of dams and roads, and the tourist trade. You may well be surprised, for example, to see a young man dressed smartly in Western-style clothes doing some business in a small town and then later on the same day meet him again out in the bush dressed in traditional regalia. It might even turn out that he's a college student in Nairobi for much of the year. Pride in their heritage is one thing these people are very unlikely to lose. For more information see Tribal Groups & Cultures on page 106.

Not only are the people another world away from Nairobi and the more developed areas of the country but the landscapes are tremendous with an incredible diversity.

Geography

Much of northern Kenya is scrub desert dissected by *luggas* (dry river beds which burst into a brief but violent life whenever there is a cloud burst) and peppered with acacia thorn trees which are often festooned with weaver birds' nests. But there are also extinct and dormant volcanoes; barren, shattered lava beds; canyons through which cool, clear streams flow; oases of lush vegetation hemmed in by craggy mountains and huge islands of forested mountains surrounded by sand deserts. And, of course, the legendary 'Jade Sea' (Lake Turkana) – Kenya's largest lake and, as a result of the Leakeys' archaeological digs, regarded by many as the birthplace of humanity.

A long narrow body of water, Lake Turkana stretches south from the Ethiopian border for some 250 km, yet is never more than 50 km wide. While it looks fairly placid most of the time, it is notorious for the vicious squalls which whip up seemingly out of nowhere and are largely responsible for fatalities among the local Turkana and El-Molo people who live along the lake shores.

The lake was first reached by Europeans in the late 19th century in the form of two Austrian explorers, von Hehnel and Teleki, who named it Lake Rudolf; it wasn't until the early 1970s that the name was changed to Turkana. The fossil hominid skulls discovered here by the Leakeys in the 1960s are thought to be around 2½ million years old. At that time it is believed that the lake was far more extensive than it is today and supported a richer plant and animal life. Around 10,000 years ago the water level was high enough for the lake to be one of the sources of the Nile, which accounts for the presence of the huge Nile perch still found in the lake.

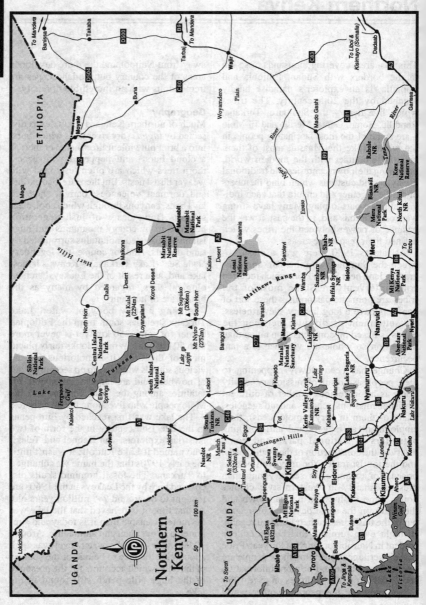

Climate

The contrasts are incredible in this part of Kenya and the climate mirrors this. By noon on the plains the temperature can reach 50°C without a breath of wind to relieve the sweat pouring from your brow. Mirages shimmer in the distance on all sides. Nothing moves. Yet in the evening, the calm can suddenly be shattered as a violent thunderstorm tears through the place taking all before it. And, just as suddenly, it can all be over leaving you with clear, star-studded skies. It's adventure country *par excellence*.

National Parks & Reserves

There are several national parks and game sanctuaries in the area, three of them along the Ewaso Nyiro River just north of Isiolo (Samburu, Buffalo Springs and Shaba). Further north are the national reserves of Maralal, Losai and Marsabit, and right up near the Ethiopian border, on the eastern shores of Lake Turkana, is the Sibiloi National Park. For further information see the Kenya National Parks & Reserves chapter.

The national parks and game reserves of Marsabit, Maralal, Samburu, Buffalo Springs, Shaba and Meru on the eastern side of the lake, and Saiwa Swamp on the western side,

are all accessible by a combination of public transport and hitching, but that won't guarantee you access to the actual parks and game reserves. Think seriously instead about going on an organised safari or getting a small group together and renting a 4WD vehicle. See the Safari section of the Kenya Getting Around chapter for details of companies which offer safaris to Samburu, Buffalo Springs, Shaba and Marsabit game reserves and national parks.

Getting There & Around

Bus & Matatu There is regular public transport on the west side of Lake Turkana as far as Kalekol. On the east side of the lake you are pretty much on your own.

Car & 4WD For most travellers who want freedom of movement and to see a lot of places it comes down to hiring a vehicle or going on an organised safari. If you're taking your own vehicle remember to bring a high-rise jack, sand ladders, a shovel, a long, strong rope or chain (that you can hitch up to camels or other vehicles) plus enough fuel and water. The only regular petrol pumps you will find are at Isiolo, Maralal and Marsabit. Elsewhere there's usually nothing except missions, which will reluctantly sell you limited amounts of fuel for up to three times the price in Nairobi. You can't blame them – they have to transport it in barrels in the back of their Land Rovers or pay for someone else to do it in a truck. A 4WD vehicle is obligatory and, except for Samburu National Game Reserve and Buffalo Springs National Reserve, you'd be extremely foolhardy to attempt such a journey in anything else.

Hitching Apart from four routes (Kitale to Lodwar; Nyahururu to Baragoi via Rumuruti and Maralal, Isiolo to Moyale via Marsabit; and Isiolo to Maralal, there is no public transport in this area of Kenya). You can certainly hitch as far as Maralal or Marsabit (from Nyahururu or Isiolo) on the eastern side of Lake Turkana, and to Lodwar (from Kitale) on the western side, but that's about

---

Life In The Wild

A remote region like this with such diverse geographical and climatic features naturally supports varied fauna. Two species you will see a lot of here (but not elsewhere) are Grevy's zebra, with their much denser pattern of stripes and saucer-like ears, and the reticulated giraffe. Herds of domestic camel are commonplace in the area and often miraculously emerge from a mirage, along with their owner, when you are bogged down to the axles in soft sand or mud in the middle of the desert. A rope is all you need, although it's a seller's market of course. Lake Turkana also supports the largest population of Nile crocodiles in Kenya. They feed mainly on the lake fish but will quite happily dine on incautious humans swimming there. The giant eland finds sanctuary in the forested hills around Marsabit. ∎

the limit of reliable hitching possibilities. There is *very* little traffic on any other routes though travellers regularly report that hitching to Loyangalani is possible, although it does take time.

The mission stations/schools invariably have their own Land Rovers (and some have their own light aircraft) but they usually only go in to regional centres once a week or once a fortnight. Although most will try to help you out if you're stuck, you cannot be guaranteed a lift. The vehicle might be full of people who need urgent medical assistance or (on the return journey) full of supplies.

Hitching is possible, of course, but you must have no deadlines to meet and you must be the sort of person who is quite happy to wait around for days for a ride. In some ways, this could be a very interesting way of getting around and you'd certainly meet a lot of local people.

You could, of course, buy a camel and do a John Hillaby but this isn't something to approach lightly. It is, however, a distinct possibility especially if you are part of a small group. You'd have the adventure of your life!

Safaris There are no organised safaris which go to the west of Lake Turkana. All of them go to the east side of the lake and most of them last from seven to 10 days, though there are others which last 14 days, and they all seem to follow much the same route. Other options include camel and donkey safaris.

See the Safaris section in the Kenya Getting Around chapter for a full run-down of the options.

West of Turkana

From Kitale the road north winds through fertile highlands, passing the turn-off for the tiny Saiwa Swamp National Park (well worth a visit; see the Kenya National Parks & Reserves chapter) before reaching Kapenguria, the town most famous for being the place where Jomo Kenyatta and five associates were held and tried in 1953 for their alleged part in the Mau Mau Rebellion.

The road then snakes its way up along a forested ridge and through the narrow northern gorges of the Cherangani Hills, emerging on to the desert plains through the Marich Pass. The change in scenery is dramatic and there are some fantastic views of the plains. The only town in this part of the hills is **Ortum**, just off the road. If you want to stop and explore the area, there is basic accommodation in the town but the best place to stay is the Marich Pass Field Studies Centre further north (see the following Marich Pass section).

Shortly after Marich Pass is a turn-off to the left (west) to the **Turkwel Gorge**. It's here that you'll find the huge hydroelectric project which was built to supply electricity to a large area of the densely populated highlands – the northern areas still have to rely on generators.

After km of endless plains and dry creek beds the town of **Lokichar** is little more than a collection of dismal *dukas* by the side of the road. The heat here is oppressive and the settlement seems to be gripped by a permanent torpor. The one redeeming feature of the place is that it is possible to buy basketware and other Turkana trinkets cheaper than you'll find them further north.

MARICH PASS AREA
The main reason for visiting this area is to stay at the Marich Pass Field Studies Centre (see Places to Stay & Eat) and use this as a base for a number of excursions in the area.

Those with their own vehicles should bring sufficient supplies of petrol as there are no service stations between Kapenguria and Lodwar. If you intend walking in the vicinity then you need·to be adequately prepared for a variety of weather conditions.

A few km to the north-west, **Mt Sekerr** (3326m) can be climbed comfortably in a three-day, round trip via the agricultural plots of the Pokot tribe, passing through forest and open moors. The views from the top are magnificent in clear weather.

To the south are the **Cherangani Hills**, which offer some of the best hill walks anywhere in Kenya ranging from half-day excursions to week-long safaris by vehicle and on foot. Possibilities include a half-day walk along the old road perched high on the eastern side of the Marich Pass to a local Pokot trading centre; a hard day's slog up the dome of Koh which soars some 1524m above the adjacent plains; a safari of several days duration along the verdant Weiwei Valley to Tamkal and then up to Lelan Forest and the main peaks of the Cherangani.

The **Elgeyo Escarpment** rises to more than 1830m in places above the Kerio Valley and offers spectacular views and waterfalls. It's only 1½ hours away from the field studies centre along a road that passes through several local market centres and intensively farmed garden plots.

The **South Turkana National Reserve** in dry and rugged hills north-east of the field studies centre is the domain of Turkana herders and rarely visited by outsiders. The 50-km drive to get there traverses grazing lands of the pastoral Pokot.

Lastly, the **Turkwel Gorge** hydroelectric station is only 30 km away along a fine tarmac road. Much of the gorge, with its towering rock walls, has not been affected by the construction, while the dam itself (the highest of its type in Africa) is spectacular.

Places to Stay & Eat

The best place to stay in this area is the *Marich Pass Field Studies Centre*, PO Box 454, Kapenguria West, Pokot. It's essentially a residential facility for groups doing field courses in geography, botany, zoology, ecology, geology and rural development, but it's also open to independent travellers who want to spend a day or a month in a little-known corner of Kenya. Just turn up, there's usually plenty of space available.

The centre occupies a beautiful site alongside the Weiwei River and is surrounded by dense bush and woodland. The bird life here is prolific, monkeys and baboons are 'in

residence', while wart hog, buffalo, antelope and elephant are regular visitors. Facilities include a secure camp site (KSh 200 per person per night) with drinking water, toilets, showers and firewood, as well as dorm beds for KSh 250 and simple but comfortable *bandas* for KSh 400 (two people) and KSh 700 (three people).

English-speaking Pokot and Turkana guides are available on request. There's also a restaurant where you can get reasonably priced meals, which should ideally be ordered in advance since the very friendly manager often has to walk into the nearest village to buy the food. You can, of course, bring your own food with you and cook it at the centre. There's little available in the villages of this area.

Getting There & Away

To reach the field studies centre, take the main Kitale to Lodwar road and watch out for the centre's signpost, two km north of the Sigor to Tot road junction (signposted), at Marich Pass. The centre is about one km down a clearly marked track.

There are three approaches to Marich Pass. The first and easiest is through Kitale and Kapenguria and then a further 67 km down a tarmac road (described as 'possibly Kenya's most spectacular tarmac road'). There are daily bus services from Nairobi to Kapenguria, and matatus (KSh 70 in a Nissan) from Kitale to Kapenguria. There are also a few daily matatus which cover the stretch from Kitale to Lokichar via Marich Pass.

The second approach is through Iten, either from Eldoret or via Kabarnet using the scenic road across the upper Kerio Valley from Kabarnet. The all-weather Cherangani Highway can be picked up from Iten to cross the main pass of the Cherangani Hills and join up with the Kitale to Lodwar road near Kapenguria.

The roughest of the three approaches is the road from Lake Baringo through the Kito Pass and across the Kerio Valley to Tot, but its main advantage is that it gives you the chance to visit the hot waterfalls at **Kapedo**.

From Tot, the track skirts the northern face of the Cherangani Hills and may be impassable after heavy rain.

LODWAR

The hot and dusty administrative town of Lodwar is the only town of any significance in the north-west. With a bitumen road connecting it with the highlands it is no longer the isolated outpost of the Northern Frontier District, as the area was known during colonial days, but is certainly lagging a few steps behind the rest of the country.

Lodwar is also the base for any excursions to the lake from the western side and you will probably find it convenient to stay here for a night at least. There's little to do in the town itself but it has an outback atmosphere which is not altogether unpleasant and just watching the garrulous locals is entertainment in itself. The Turkana have found that tourists are a good touch when it comes to selling trinkets and they approach with alarming audacity and don't conceal their disgust when you don't want to buy. They are also remarkably persistent. The small market is a good place to watch women weaving the baskets.

Information

The town has a post office and a branch of the Kenya Commercial Bank.

Places to Stay – bottom end

Lodwar is one place where it's worth spending a bit more on accommodation – mainly to get a room with a fan. The rooms in the cheaper places are all hellishly hot and, as the mosquitoes are fierce, you need to cover up or burn coils if you don't have a net.

Probably the best of the cheapies is the *Mombasa Hotel*. The friendly Muslim owners charge KSh 200/300 for singles/doubles. The singles are cooler (it's all relative though) as they have high ceilings. If you have a mosquito net you can sleep in the courtyard.

The *Marira Boarding & Lodging* is a small place which offers single/double rooms at KSh 250/350.

Another good option, and the only one for campers, is the *Nawoitorong Guest House* (☎ (0393) 21208). The turn-off is signposted one km south of Lodwar on the main road, and from there it's a further two km. This place was built entirely out of local materials and is run by a local women's group. Camping costs KSh 100, and meals are available. There's also one banda, which can accommodate up to six people, which costs KSh 300/400 for a single/double including breakfast.

Places to Stay – middle

The *Turkwel Hotel* (☎ (0393) 21201) is the town's social focus and also has the best accommodation. Single rooms with fan and shared bath go for KSh 300, while singles/doubles with fan and bath cost KSh 350/450. There are also a few spacious cottages which are very pleasant and cost KSh 650 for two, including breakfast.

Places to Eat

The restaurant at the *Mombasa Hotel* does reasonable local food. The *Marira Boarding & Lodging* has little variety but its chips are excellent and freshly cooked to order. For something a bit more sophisticated the *Turkwel Hotel* restaurant does standard Western fare such as steak, chips etc. Breakfast here consists of a couple of eggs and a sausage, and non-guests are not served until all the hotel guests have finished. The bar here is also a popular place.

Getting There & Away

There is one daily minibus from Kitale to Lodwar which generally leaves around 10 am, but sometimes it doesn't don't run at all. The Nissan matatus are more reliable and there are usually five per day which leave when full. The trip takes around seven hours and costs KSh 400.

Matatus also run from Lodwar to Kalekol near the lake if demand warrants, but you can't count on them. The trip takes one hour. If you want to hitch to Kalekol the place where the locals wait is under the tree about 200m north of the Kobil station. To give an indication of how long you can expect to wait, there is a chai (tea) stall here which also sells mandazis.

KALEKOL
Most visitors to the area head on from Lodwar to Kalekol, a fairly dismal little town a few km from the lake shore. The main building in this one-street town is the fish-processing factory built with Scandinavian money and expertise and, although not that old is currently not operating. There is also an Italian-sponsored plant closer to the lake shore.

Places to Stay & Eat
The main problem with a visit here is lack of accommodation options. Two basic budget places have closed down in recent years, leaving only the *Safari Hotel* which has a reasonable restaurant.

Getting There & Away
Irregular matatus do the run to Kitale.

To get out to the lake it's a hot 1½-hour walk. Local people will point you in the right direction, or just walk to the Italian fishing project and cut across the lake bed from there.

FERGUSON'S GULF
This is the most accessible part of the lake shore and although it's not particularly attractive, the sense of achievement in just getting there usually compensates. The water has receded greatly over the last decade or so, mainly due to water use in Ethiopia, so you have to walk a long way over the lake bed to actually get to the water. The birdlife along the shore is prolific. There are also hippos and crocodiles, so seek local advice before having a refreshing dip.

There's a small fishing village of grass huts on the far side of the defunct Turkana Fishing Lodge and that's about the limit of development.

In the middle of the lake is the **Central Island National Park**, a barren yet scenic volcanic island, but unless you're on an organised trip there is no way of getting to it

from here. Talk to the fishers and they *might* take you out but make sure their craft is sound – the danger posed by the lake's squalls is not to be taken lightly.

Places to Stay
If you don't mind really roughing it, the local villagers will put you up for a small fee, otherwise you'll have to come here just for a day trip from Kalekol.

The *Lake Turkana Fishing Lodge* closed some years ago, supposedly just for renovations, but it's doubtful it will reopen in the foreseeable future. It is supposedly on an island but the level of the lake has fallen so far in recent years that it's now possible to drive to the lodge. It takes around 1½ very hot hours to walk out there from Kalekol – follow the track to the Italian fishing project then head across the lake bed from there. There are children with canoes who will

Look for herons at Ferguson's Gulf, where they may be seen wading in shallow waters.

paddle you across the 20m or so of channel. By car you just follow the main road through Kalekol and it takes a circuitous route to the far side of the lodge. Although the water once used to lap at the edge of the bar terrace, it is now more than 100m away across a blinding expanse of sand.

ELIYE SPRINGS

This is a far more attractive place than Ferguson's Gulf but is inaccessible without a 4WD. The small village here has an army post, a couple of dozen grass huts, and a lodge which is of marginal status to say the least. The springs however do provide moisture enough for a curious variety of palm tree (the doum palm) to grow here which gives the place a very misplaced tropical island feel. This particular variety of palm tree has an unusually shaped fruit which the locals eat.

If you do make it here you will be greeted by a number of Turkana girls and young women selling trinkets at absurdly cheap prices. With an average of just a few vehicles a week, it's a real buyer's market. Items you might find for sale might include fossilised hippo teeth and fish backbones threaded into necklaces!

Places to Stay & Eat

The camp site at the lodge here is very pretty, with doum palms and views of the lake. The *Eliye Springs Lodge* itself has seen better days and is in fact something of an on-again, off-again set-up. You're best to make enquiries in Lodwar before relying on this place being open.

Getting There & Away

The turn-off for Eliye Springs is signposted about halfway along the road from Lodwar to Kalekol. There are a few patches of heavy sand so a 4WD is advisable, although you'd probably get through in a conventional vehicle. As there are so few vehicles, hitching is not an option and it's 35 long, hot km if you plan to walk it.

LOKICHOKIO

This frontier town is the last on the Pan African Highway before the Sudan border. The road is sealed all the way here and is in excellent condition but you can't get beyond Lokichokio without a police permit. Even if this was forthcoming, the area is not safe to visit as long as the civil war in southern Sudan continues.

Places to Stay

There's a hotel of sorts here with a couple of mud huts out the back, and there's a bar in town. On the other hand, if you get this far, you'll probably find yourself staying with aid/famine relief workers who take care of the refugee camps around here.

East of Turkana

There are two main routes here. The first is the A2 highway from Nairobi to Marsabit, via Isiolo and Laisamis, and north from there to Moyale on the Ethiopian border. The other is from Nairobi to Maralal, via Gilgil, Nyahururu and Rumuruti or via Nakuru and Lake Baringo, and north from there to Loyangalani on Lake Turkana, via Maralal, Baragoi and South Horr. It's also possible to cross from Isiolo to Maralal. From Loyangalani you can make a loop all the way round the top of the Chalbi Desert to Marsabit via North Horr and Maikona.

Getting There & Around

Bus & Matatu Mwingi buses run from Isiolo to Marsabit but there is no real schedule so you could be stuck in either place for a few days. The fare is KSh 350. There's no alternative except to simply hang around and wait or either negotiate a ride on a truck (relatively easy and usually somewhat less than the bus fare) or walk out to the police checkpoint north of Isiolo town where the tarmac ends and hitch a ride with tourists (not so easy). A convoy system is in operation in order to deter *shiftas* (bandits) from stopping and robbing trucks, buses and cars.

Mwingi also operates regular buses from Isiolo to Wamba where you can change onto another bus or matatu for Maralal. The cost from Isiolo to Wamba is KSh 100 and the journey takes about one hour. From Wamba to Maralal the buses cost KSh 150 and the matatus KSh 200, and the journey takes about 3½ hours.

North of Maralal, the only public transport is a matatu which plies between Maralal and Baragoi once daily if demand warrants it.

Car & 4WD None of the roads in this region are surfaced and the main A2 route is corrugated *murram* which will shake the guts out of both you and your vehicle depending on your speed.

The road connecting Isiolo with Maralal (which branches off the A2 north of Archer's Post) is similarly corrugated but otherwise in good shape. The road from Lake Baringo to Maralal and from Maralal to Loyangalani, however, is surprisingly smooth, though there are bad patches here and there including a diabolical section of several km from the plateau down to Lake Turkana.

There's also a minor cross route between Isiolo and Baragoi which bypasses Maralal and goes via Wamba and Parsaloi (though you don't actually go through Wamba itself).

This road leaves the Archer's Post-Maralal road about 20 km north-west of Archer's Post and joins the Maralal to Loyangalani road about 15 km south of Baragoi. Though a minor route, this road is very smooth most of the way with the occasional rough patch. Its main drawback is the steep-sided luggas, none of which are bridged. In the dry season you won't have any problems with a 4WD (impossible with a 2WD) but you can forget about it in the wet season.

The worst of these luggas is just outside Wamba – there's a way around it by taking the Maralal road from Wamba and turning first right along a dirt road once you've crossed an obvious bridge. You'll probably only use it if you want to visit the Mathews Range and the Ndoto Mountains.

Forget about the Maralal to Parsaloi road

marked on the Survey of Kenya maps. It's all washed out and you won't even make it in 4WD.

WAMBA

Wamba is a small, essentially one-street town off the Isiolo to Maralal road north of Samburu National Game Reserve and a sort of provincial headquarters for the surrounding area. There's precious little here for the traveller and its only claim to fame is that it was from here that John Hillaby organised his camel trek to Lake Turkana which resulted in his book, *Journey to the Jade Sea*.

It has quite a few well-stocked dukas, a butchery, a hospital, schools and a large police station but no bank and no electricity despite its proximity to Isiolo.

Places to Stay & Eat

There's only one lodge in the village and that is the *Saudia Lodge* which is at the back of the main street off to the right-hand side coming into town (signposted). You get a pleasant, clean room here (mosquito nets, soap, towel and toilet paper are provided) for just KSh 250/325 a single/double. Bathroom facilities are communal. A wholesome breakfast can be provided for you if you order it in advance.

There's a lively bar on the main street, on the right-hand side as you enter the main part of town, where you can drink your fill though there's no refrigeration. You can't miss it – just listen for the cassette player blaring away!

MARALAL

Maralal is high up in the hills above the Lerochi Plateau (essentially a continuation of the central highlands), north of Nyahururu and Nanyuki and north-west of Isiolo, and connected to all these towns by gravel roads. Surrounding it is the Maralal National Sanctuary which is home to zebra, impala, eland, buffalo, hyena and wart hog, all of which you can see from the road leading into Maralal from the south or at the Maralal Safari Lodge which has the only permanent water hole in the area.

It's an attractive area of grassy undulating plains and coniferous forests which was coveted by white settlers in the colonial era. However, the settler's designs for taking it over were scotched by the colonial authorities due to anticipated violent opposition from the Samburu for whom it holds a special significance.

The town itself, while a regional headquarters, retains a decidedly frontier atmosphere. There's a sense of excitement blowing in the wind that frequently sweeps the plains and whips up the dust in this somewhat ramshackle, but very lively, township with its wide streets and wild-west-type verandahs.

It's also the preferred route and overnight centre for the safari companies which take people up to Lake Turkana. People here are very friendly and it's a great place to buy Samburu handicrafts.

There's a post office (with telephones), petrol stations, mechanics, the only bank north of Isiolo other than in Marsabit, shops with a good range of stock, hotels, bars, one of the best camp sites in Kenya, a surprising number of butchers' shops and regular bus transport to Isiolo. There are also matatus to

Baragoi which leave from the Shell station. If you are not travelling with a safari company you may well consider spending a few days here. It's a bizarre but captivating place.

Information
Money The Kenya Commercial Bank is open during normal banking hours. This is the last bank going north, apart from those in Marsabit, so stock up on cash. Changing cash or travellers' cheques is fast and efficient here. Outside of banking hours, try Yare Safaris Club.

Post & Communications The post office is open normal hours and the staff are very helpful should you want to make national or international calls.

Fuel There are two petrol stations (Shell and Total) in the centre of town where you can be assured of getting what you need at regular prices. However, north of here you will only find petrol at Baragoi and Loyangalani, and if there is some petrol there you will find it is always at a much higher price.

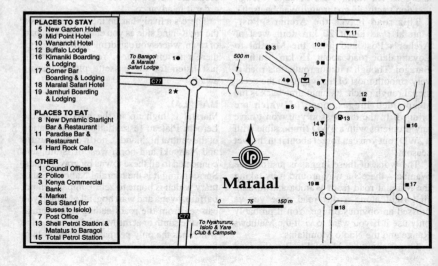

PLACES TO STAY
5 New Garden Hotel
9 Mid Point Hotel
10 Wananchi Hotel
12 Buffalo Lodge
16 Kimaniki Boarding & Lodging
17 Corner Bar Boarding & Lodging
18 Maralal Safari Hotel
19 Jamhuri Boarding & Lodging

PLACES TO EAT
8 New Dynamic Starlight Bar & Restaurant
11 Paradise Bar & Restaurant
14 Hard Rock Cafe

OTHER
1 Council Offices
2 Police
3 Kenya Commercial Bank
4 Market
6 Bus Stand (for Buses to Isiolo)
7 Post Office
13 Shell Petrol Station & Matatus to Baragoi
15 Total Petrol Station

To Baragoi & Maralal Safari Lodge

500 m

Maralal

0   75   150 m

To Nyahururu, Isiolo & Yare Club & Campsite

Safaris

Regular camel safaris, and Lake Turkana safaris by truck depart from Yare Safaris' Yare Club & Campsite (see the Other Safaris section in the Kenya Getting Around chapter and earlier on in this chapter for details).

Places to Stay – bottom end

The best place to stay here, and one which is very popular with travellers is *Yare Club & Campsite*, three km south of town on the Isiolo/Nyahururu road, and signposted. Here you have a choice of camping or renting a self-contained banda. It's been thoughtfully constructed with local materials and the facilities include a well-stocked bar/lounge, games room, and self-service restaurant serving local dishes. There's also guarded parking (not that you need it around here). The camp site has its own showers (cold water only) and toilets. Camping costs KSh 200 per person per night.

The bandas have private bathrooms and are clean, comfortable and provide excellent value at KSh 820/1100 for singles/doubles

and KSh 1485 a triple including breakfast. Kenyan residents pay KSh 640/830 and KSh 1045, respectively. Soap and towels are provided and a bucket of hot water is available in the morning at no extra cost.

Advance booking is absolutely essential for any sort of accommodation here during the week of the camel derby (last week of October). For bookings, contact Yare Safaris (☎/fax (02) 214099), 1st floor, Union Towers, Mama Ngina St, PO Box 63006, Nairobi, or ☎/fax (0368) 2295, Maralal.

In Maralal itself the most popular place to stay is the *Buffalo Lodge* (☎ (0368) 2228) which is a fairly modern structure offering rooms with clean sheets, towels and hot water in the mornings for KSh 375 a single or double. It's a lively place and there's a bar/video room at the back. Sammy, the barman here, is a real live wire and very friendly. This place may be changing hands soon because, very sadly, Kamau, the owner died recently, however it probably won't change too much.

Cheaper, and excellent value, is the

Maralal International Camel Derby

Inaugurated by Yare Safaris in 1990, this annual event takes place on the Saturday of the third week of October. It's a great time to be here and the three races which are held (amateurs, semi-professional, and professional) are open to everyone. It attracts riders and spectators from the four corners of the earth, there's substantial prize money to be won (over US$5000), the media is there in force, you can make excellent contacts which will stand you in good stead for the rest of your trip, it's good fun, and, last but not least, it's one hell of a binge!

The races start and finish at Yare Safari's Club & Campsite, a few km south of town on the road to Nyahururu/Isiolo, and there's no chance of missing it as the road will be festooned with flags and bunting and choked with activity. Entry fees up until 15 October for the various categories are US$30 (KSh 300 for residents) in the amateur competition; US$50 (KSh 500 for residents) in the semi-professional and US$100 (KSh 500 for residents) on the professional races. Thereafter, entries are accepted up until the start of the race at a premium of 50%. Applications for entry should be made to either the Maralal International Camel Derby (MICD) Secretariat, PO Box 47874, Nairobi, or Yare Safaris, PO Box 63006, Nairobi. Camels with saddle and/or handler can be hired locally for US$125 (KSh 5000 for residents). The amateur class requires you to use a handler but the semi-professional and professional classes are not allowed to use them. If you need a handler, it will cost extra.

A substantial amount of the money made on these events goes towards the provision of medical facilities for the Samburu people.

And just in case you're thinking this is a good laugh for the humans but a lousy deal for the animals, International Camel Races Association rules apply so the camels are checked daily by a vet and monitored by a KSPCA officer. Any rider beating an animal unnecessarily is disqualified.

Get yourself up there! This is one of the major events on the Kenyan calendar and the social event after the races at Yare Safaris Lodge is unbelievable and goes on all night. For transport from Nairobi to Maralal, contact Yare Safaris, Payless Car Hire, Safari Camp Services or the Mountain Rock Lodge. ■

Kimaniki Boarding & Lodging which is a two-storey wooden building offering good rooms for KSh 100/150 a single/double. Clean sheets are provided as well as hot showers (if requested) and vehicles can be parked safely in the hotel compound. There's also the *Mid Point Hotel* (☎ (0368) 2221), which offers good lodging for single people at the same price plus there's hot water in the mornings.

Also good is the *Silence Hotel*, with 24-hour hot water and mosquito nets. Double rooms cost KSh 150.

Other possibilities include the *Corner Bar Boarding & Lodging, Jamhuri Boarding & Lodging, Maralal Safari Hotel, New Garden Hotel* and *Wananchi Hotel* – all rather basic.

Places to Stay – top end
The only top-range hotel in Maralal is the *Maralal Safari Lodge* (☎ (0368) 2060 in Maralal; (02) 211124 in Nairobi), PO Box 70, Maralal and PO Box 45155, Nairobi. It consists of a main building housing a restaurant, bar and souvenir shop, and a series of cottages. It costs US$120/150 for singles/doubles with full board. Extra beds are US$60. Half-board rates are also available but amount to only a small reduction per person on the full-board rates so it's hardly worth it. Meals are available to non-guests for KSh 250 (breakfast) and KSh 500 (lunch or dinner). There's a watering hole, which attracts a varied selection of game, right in front of the bar's verandah so you can watch the animals while sipping a cold beer. Facilities include a golf course and swimming pool – certainly the only ones for some km in any direction! – both of which are open to the public. The lodge is about three km away from the centre of Maralal, off the road to Baragoi (signposted).

Places to Eat & Entertainment
The best place to eat here is the *Hard Rock Cafe* opposite the Shell station. The food is good and the staff are friendly and eager to please. As a result, it's the most popular place in town. The Buffalo Lodge can also come up with a very tasty and filling meal.

The liveliest bar – and one where you can get good, tasty, cheap food – is the improbably named *New Dynamic Starlight Bar & Restaurant* which, nevertheless, does live up to its name. The inside rooms are painted with the most bizarre and florid representations of African flora and fauna. Unfortunately, there's no refrigeration so the beers are warm but the company makes up for it, and some of the characters who come in here have walked straight out of a Breugel canvas.

The Buffalo Lodge is equally popular and has two good bars but the one out at the back, although the best, is essentially a video lounge. The front bar is where the real drinkers come and it gets very lively here in the early afternoon. It's also where the 'Elastic Boys' come – local young entrepreneurs who sell handicrafts and can act as guides if you'd like to do some walking around the area. The Buffalo Lodge usually has a disco on Friday and Saturday nights.

Getting There & Away
There are Nissan minibuses which ply between Maralal and Nyahururu via Rumuruti on a daily basis, usually in the mornings. They cost KSh 200 to KSh 250 depending on the time of day and take four to five hours.

Between Maralal and Isiolo there are no direct buses or matatus. To get between the two towns you must first take a bus or matatu to Wamba and then change there. The cost between Maralal and Wamba is KSh 150 by bus and KSh 200 by matatu, and the journey takes about 3½ hours. Between Wamba and Isiolo there are many matatus and regular buses every day. The cost is KSh 100 and the journey takes about one hour.

The only other public transport out of Maralal is north to Baragoi by Land Rover. There's usually one each day or two – it depends on demand. The cost varies but, on average, it is KSh 300 and the journey takes about three hours. You need to make enquiries about this Land Rover in advance and, preferably, meet the driver. No-one ever seems to know when they're leaving.

All the buses and matatus leave from the dirt patch opposite the Shell station.

MATHEWS RANGE

North of Wamba, off the link road between Wamba and Baragoi via Parsaloi is the Mathews Range. Much of this area is thickly forested and supports rhino, elephant, lion, buffalo as well as many other animal species. The highest peak here rises to 2285m.

The whole area is very undeveloped and populated by Samburu tribespeople but the government is in the process of making it into a game sanctuary especially for the rhino. Some of the tribespeople are already employed to protect the rhino from poachers, and there's a game warden's centre.

A few km from this centre (where you have to report to on the way in to the sanctuary, though there are no charges as yet) is a camp site with no facilities other than river water and firewood. At one time it was a well set-up research centre, as the derelict huts indicate. It's a superb site and a genuine African bush experience. You are miles from the nearest village and elephant are quite likely to trundle through your camp in the middle of the night – lions too. During the day, traditionally dressed Samburu warriors will probably visit you to see if you need a guide (which you will if you want to see game or climb to the top of the range). Agree on a reasonable price beforehand, and remember you'll also have to pay for the one who stays behind to guard your vehicle.

Also, don't forget that the rules of hospitality will oblige you to provide them with a beer, soft drink or cup of tea, a few cigarettes and perhaps a snack when you get back to camp. They're extremely friendly people. One or two will be able to speak English (the nearest school is in Wamba) but most can converse in Swahili as well as Samburu.

Another accommodation possibility is the *Kitich Camp* (☎ (0176) 22053), on the banks of the Ngeng River, off the Wamba to Parsaloi road, about 40 km from Wamba. It's mainly set up as a luxury tented camp with all the facilities, and it costs KSh 3000 per person with full board. Children are half price. It's also possible to camp for KSh 200 per person, but the facilities for independent campers are minimal. You can also make bookings for this camp through Let's Go Travel (☎ (02) 340331) in Nairobi.

Getting There & Away

Getting to the camp site in the Mathews Range is not at all easy, even with 4WD. There are many different tracks going all over the place and you are going to have to stop many times to ask the way. Perhaps the best approach is from the Wamba to Parsaloi road. Just before Wamba you will get to a T-junction. Instead of going into Wamba, continue north and take the first obvious main track off to the right, several km after the junction. If there are tyre tracks in the sand – follow them. There are two missions down this track and both have vehicles. You will be able to ask the way at either one of them.

One of the mission stations is right next to a large river course which generally has some water flowing through it and which you have to ford. If you get lost, ask a local tribesman to come along and guide you but remember that you will have to drive him back to his *manyatta* after you have found the place. No-one in their right mind walks around in the bush after dark except if they are in large groups – the buffalo and elephant make it too dangerous. It might sound like a *tour de force* getting to this place but it's well worth it!

PARSALOI

Further north, Parsaloi (sometimes spelt Barsaloi) is a small scattered settlement with a few very basic shops but no petrol station. It has a large Catholic Mission which may or may not offer to accommodate you or allow you to camp. There are no lodges. The EC recently funded the construction of quite a large school.

There are two very rugged and steep-sided luggas at this point on the road, one on either side of the village, and you'll definitely need 4WD to negotiate them.

BARAGOI

Next up the road towards Loyangalani is Baragoi, a more substantial settlement full of tribespeople, a couple of very basic lodges, a new and better appointed hotel, and a few shops. There's also a derelict petrol station, but petrol can usually be bought here from a barrel – the local people will show you where to find it. If you're white, you'll probably be the only one in town and therefore an object of considerable curiosity. Quite a few people speak English around here. The town seems to get rain when everywhere else is dry so the surroundings are quite green.

Be careful not to take photographs in the town as it's supposedly forbidden and the local police are keen to enforce the rule and are not at all pleasant about it.

Places to Stay & Eat

If you ask at any of the restaurants in town they'll usually come up with accommodation, but it will be very basic – just a bed in a bare room with no toilet facilities. Some will also allow you to camp in their back yards.

If you have camping equipment, the best place to stay is the camp site at the water-pumping station about four km to the north of town. To get there, take the road north towards South Horr. After a while you'll go through a small gully and then, a little further on, across a usually dry river bed. Take the next track on the right-hand side and follow this for about one km. It will bring you to a concrete house and a fairly open patch of ground. This is the camp site and there's always someone around. Facilities include toilets and showers and your tent will be guarded by Samburu moran. It costs KSh 200 per person per night. Trips can be arranged to nearby manyattas for a small fee and you'll be allowed to take photographs.

There's a large hotel in town which costs KSh 350/650 for a clean single/double with shared bathroom. It's the first building you come to when arriving in Baragoi from the south.

For food in the town itself, the best is the *Wid-Wid Inn* run by Mrs Fatuma. It's on the top side of the main street and you'll know you've got the right place because all the staff wear garishly pink pinafores! She'll cook you up an absolutely delicious meat stew and chapatis for dinner as well as pancakes, omelettes and tea for breakfast. Prices are very reasonable.

There are also two bars in the town but only one of them – the *Sam Celia Joy Bar*, at the end of the main street going north – usually has beers. The other, on the back street, usually only has *konyagi* (local firewater) and other spirits.

SOUTH HORR

The next village is South Horr which is set in a beautiful lush canyon between the craggy peaks of Mt Nyiro (2752m) and Mt Porale (1990m) and Mt Supuko (2066m). It's a lively little place with a huge Catholic Mission, you'll find the missionaries won't sell you petrol.

Places to Stay & Eat

There are two small and very basic hotels on the main street – the *Mt Nyiro Hotel* and the *Good Tourist Hotel* – where you can find accommodation of sorts as well as a reasonably tasty meal of meat stew, mandazi and tea for around KSh 100 per person. The hotels will generally need up to two hours notice if you want to eat, but tea is usually immediately available. The price of accommodation is entirely negotiable.

For campers, the camp site which most people stay at is the Forestry HQ, off to the left as you enter town coming from the south (signposted). There's a river which runs past the site but, otherwise, it's completely undeveloped and there are no facilities but it costs just KSh 10 per person.

Other than this, there's Dick Hedges' (of Safari Camp Services, Nairobi) camp site some 15 km north of South Horr (the signpost reads 'Camping' but it's easy to miss) on the right-hand side as you head north. It's a pleasant site and facilities include showers and toilets. There's also plenty of firewood. The charge is KSh 150 per person per night.

Guards can be arranged to watch your tent if you want to eat in town.

South Horr also sports a very lively bar – the *Serima Bar* – on the main road heading north out of town. It's only open in the evening and seems to have a plentiful supply of beer, though there is no refrigeration.

LAKE TURKANA (THE JADE SEA)

Further north, the lushness of the Horr Valley gradually peters out until, finally, you reach the totally barren, shattered lava beds at the southern end of Lake Turkana. Top the ridge here and there it is in front of you – the Jade Sea. It's a breathtaking sight – vast and yet apparently totally barren. You'll see nothing living here except a few brave, stunted thorn trees. When you reach the lake shore, you'll know why – it's a soda lake and, at this end, highly saline. The northern end of the lake isn't anywhere near as saline because it's fed by the Omo River from Ethiopia (is that where the name of the washing powder came from!?). At this point, most people abandon whatever vehicle they're in and plunge into the lake. If you do this, watch out for crocodiles. They're quite partial to a meal of red meat as a change from Nile perch.

LOYANGALANI

A little further up the lake shore and you are in Loyangalani – Turkana 'city'. There is an airstrip, post office, fishing station, luxury lodge, two camp sites, a Catholic Mission (which may reluctantly sell petrol at up to three times the price in Nairobi) and all of it surrounded by the yurt-like, stick and doum-palm dwellings of the Turkana tribespeople. Taking photographs of people or their houses here will attract 'fees'.

If you're an independent traveller and want to visit the village where the El-Molo tribe live ask the safari-truck drivers at the camp sites if they have room for you and agree on a price. Organised safaris to this part of Kenya usually include a trip to the El-Molo village. They're one of the smallest tribes in Africa and quite different from the Turkana, though it seems their days are numbered as a distinct tribe. Tourism has

also wrought inevitable changes in their lifestyle and you may feel that the whole thing has been thoroughly commercialised. You'll also pay handsomely for taking photographs.

Trips to **Mt Kulal** and **Mt Porr** can be arranged at the Oasis Lodge but they're expensive. The Mt Kulal trip is a part-drive, part-walking trip up to the forest there, and Mt Porr is a well-known fossicking spot. A better thing to do would be to get in touch with Francis Langachar who is a very friendly young Turkana man and ask him to organise something similar for you. He speaks fluent English, and his father accompanied John Hillaby on his trek to Lake Turkana, recounted in *Journey to the Jade Sea*. If you do this trip by yourself in your own 4WD then allow two days and stay overnight. You can not do it in one day there and back from Loyangalani.

Places to Stay & Eat

Of the two camp sites, it's hard to favour one over the other, though only one has a restaurant and bar. Both are staffed by friendly people and theft doesn't appear to be a problem at either of them. The first you come to is *El-Molo Camp* (☎ (02) 724384), PO Box 34710, Nairobi. It has excellent facilities including good showers and toilets, a swimming pool (KSh 200 for day use), a large dining hall and bar (with cold beer at KSh 601) and electricity up to 9.30 pm at night (kerosene lanterns after that). Camping costs KSh 100 per person per night. There are also 20 self-contained bandas for rent which cost KSh 2000. Meals can be ordered at short notice in the dining room, whether you are staying on the site or not, but they take a long time to arrive: 1½ hours is normal. The food, on the other hand, is very good.

The other camp site adjacent to El-Molo is *Sunset Strip Camp,* which is run by Safari Camp Services in Nairobi. It costs KSh 100 per person per night. Facilities include showers and toilets and covered dining areas, but you cannot buy food and drink here and there's no electricity or swimming

Skull 1470

In the early 1970s, palaeontologist Richard Leakey made a significant fossil find on the shores of Lake Turkana. It was the discovery of a fossilised skull, which came to be known somewhat prosaically as 1470 (its Kenya Museum index number).

The almost complete, but fragmented, skull was thought to be from an early hominid. It was hoped that it would back up earlier fossil discoveries made by the Leakey Family in the Olduvai Gorge in Tanzania in the 1960s which suggested that the direct human ancestral line went back further than the 1½ million years that most people thought at the time.

The pieces of the skull were painstakingly fitted together – a demanding task in itself which kept two people fully occupied for over six weeks. The completed jigsaw confirmed what they had suspected: here was an evolutionary sophisticated hominid, named *Homo habilis*, which was a direct ancestor of *Homo sapiens*. It was 2½ million years old.

Since then *homo* fossil finds have been made which push the date back even further, but at the time the 1470 was a very important person! ∎

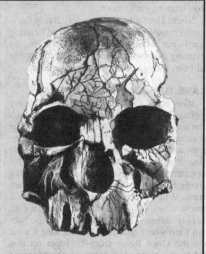

pool. It's also dusty when the wind blows, which in this part of the world is most of the time.

Neither camp site has firewood so you will have to bring your own from further south.

Whichever place you camp at, beware of sudden storms which can descend from Mt Kulal. If there is a storm, stay with your tent otherwise it may not be there when you get back because of the wind, and neither will anything else.

Other than the camp sites there is the luxury *Oasis Lodge* (☎ (02) 751190; PO Box 34464, Nairobi) which has 25 double bungalows with private bathrooms and electricity (own generator) at US$100 per person with full board. It's a beautiful place with two spring-fed swimming pools, and ice-cold beer and meals are available. The only trouble is that if you are not staying there but you want to use the facilities (bar and swimming pools), it's going to cost you a KSh 600 entrance fee, and there are times when you won't even be allowed in.

For places to eat other than the El-Molo Camp, there are a couple of basic tea houses on the main street of Loyangalani and, if you ask around, you'll meet villagers who will cook up a meal of Nile perch for you in their homes.

Getting There & Away

There is no scheduled transport of any sort in or out of Loyangalani, so you need to be completely independent.

For the rich and/or famous, the Oasis Lodge can arrange a light plane to the local airstrip.

Going north or north-east from here involves crossing the Chalbi Desert towards North Horr. It's fine in the dry season but can be treacherous after rain.

You also need to stop at every village you come across and ask for directions otherwise it's very easy to go off on the wrong track and not even realise it until an hour or two later. Don't just assume that tyre tracks in the sand will lead you in the right direction, they won't necessarily.

NORTH HORR

North of Loyangalani the road loops over the lava beds to North Horr. There is a short cut across the desert through the village of Gus.

There are no lodges here and no petrol available but the people at the Catholic Mission are very friendly and may offer you somewhere to stay for the night if you are stuck. It's staffed by German and Dutch people.

MAIKONA

Next down the line is Maikona where there is a large village with basic shops (but no lodges) and a very friendly Catholic Mission and school, staffed by Italian people, where you will undoubtedly be offered a place to stay for the night. Please leave a donation before you go if you stay here. The mission usually has electricity and the Father goes into Marsabit once a fortnight in his Land Rover.

MARSABIT

South of Maikona is Marsabit, where you are back in relative civilisation. Here there are three petrol stations, a bank, post office, dry cleaners, shops, bars and lodges, buses and an airport. The main attraction here though is the Marsabit National Park & Reserve centred around Mt Marsabit (1702m).

The hills here are thickly forested and in stark contrast to the desert on all sides. Mist often envelopes them in the early morning and mosses hang from tree branches. The views from the telecommunications tower on the summit above town are magnificent in all directions. In fact, they're probably as spectacular as any of the views from Mt Kenya or Kilimanjaro.

The whole area is peppered with extinct volcanoes and volcanic craters (called *gofs*), some of which have a lake on the floor of the crater.

For information on Marsabit National Park & Reserve see the Kenya National Parks & Reserves chapter.

Places to Stay & Eat

If you have no camping equipment there's a good choice of lodges available in the town of Marsabit. One of the best is the *Marsabit Highway Hotel* which costs KSh 250 for a double with shower and toilet. It's a large place and very clean. The hotel has its own bar/restaurant which is open from 11 am to 2 pm and 5 pm to midnight. There is a disco on Friday and Saturday nights.

The cheapest place, though not such good value, is the *Hotel Al-Jazeera* which costs KSh 150 per person with communal showers. There's a bar and restaurant at the front.

For something vaguely mid-range, try the *Badassa Hotel*.

The best place for tea, mandazi and snacks is the *Bismillah Tea House* in front of the Catholic Technical School.

Marsabit Tribespeople

One of the most memorable sights in Marsabit is the tribespeople thronging the streets and roads into town. Most noticeable are the Rendille, dressed in skins with elaborate braided hairstyles and fantastic multicoloured beaded necklaces and bracelets. These people graze camels and, like the Samburu and Maasai, show little interest in adopting a more sedentary lifestyle, preferring to roam the deserts and only visiting the towns when necessary for trade. They are the major non-Muslim people in what is otherwise a largely Muslim area.

The other major tribes are the Boran and the Gabra, both pastoralists who graze cattle rather than camels. They're allied to the Galla peoples of Ethiopia from where they originated several hundred years ago. Many have abandoned their former transient life style and settled down to more sedentary activities. In the process, many have adopted Islam and the modes of dress of the Somalis with whom they trade and who have also migrated into the area. There are also quite a few Ethiopians in town as a result of that country's tragic and turbulent recent past. ■

Getting There & Away

Mwingi buses run from Marsabit south to Isiolo. They supposedly run a couple of times a week depending on demand and breakdowns – be prepared for a wait. The cost is KSh 350 and the trip takes six hours. If, for any reason, Mwingi buses are not running then you'll have to arrange a lift with a truck. Lifts on a truck are a standard US$10 (Marsabit to Isiolo).

All vehicles, including buses travelling between Marsabit and Isiolo or Marsabit and Moyale, must travel in convoy to minimise the danger of attack from shiftas.

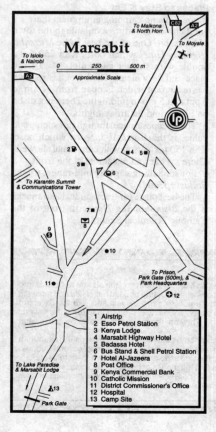

Marsabit

To Maikona & North Horr

To Isiolo & Nairobi

To Moyale

0   250   500 m
Approximate Scale

To Karantin Summit & Communications Tower

To Prison, Park Gate (500m), & Park Headquarters

To Lake Paradise & Marsabit Lodge

Park Gate

1 Airstrip
2 Esso Petrol Station
3 Kenya Lodge
4 Marsabit Highway Hotel
5 Badassa Hotel
6 Bus Stand & Shell Petrol Station
7 Hotel Al-Jazeera
8 Post Office
9 Kenya Commercial Bank
10 Catholic Mission
11 District Commissioner's Office
12 Hospital
13 Camp Site

MOYALE

Straddling the Kenyan-Ethiopian border, Moyale lies some 250 km north of Marsabit across the Dida Galgalu Desert. It's a small town of sandy streets with bars, a post office, police station, several shops selling a reasonable selection of commodities, and a small market area. Unlike Marsabit, however, where most of the roofs these days are of corrugated iron, there are still a large number of traditionally built houses here. They have sturdy pole frames supporting mud and stick roofs which can be up to half a metre thick thus ensuring that the interiors stay cool even when the outside temperature is 30°C and more. There is a bank in Moyale which is open during normal banking hours.

The Ethiopian side of the town is somewhat larger and the facilities are much better, with sealed roads, electricity, a number of bars and small restaurants, a hotel, and a lively market area.

Places to Stay & Eat

There are only three places to stay on the Kenyan side of Moyale and they're all pretty basic but the best of the bunch is the *Hotel Medina* which costs KSh 100/160 a single/double. It's clean but, like the other hotels, there's no running water. The *Barissah Hotel*, which also has the town's only bar, is nowhere near as good but it does offer reasonable food, the usual fare being meat stew and chapatis.

If the above two are full, head for the *Bismillahi Boarding & Lodging* across from the Barissah and up behind the derelict Esso station. It's a family-run place and you'll find yourself sharing the same roof as the family. A bed here costs KSh 100 and facilities are absolutely minimal.

On the Ethiopian side of Moyale, a good place to stay is the *Hotel Awasha* near the checkpoint, which costs Birr 14 for a single room with running water and shower. The bank is nearby where you can change money legally – travellers' cheques are no problem but they may refuse to change cash. Another hotel recommended in the past is the *Bekele Molla Hotel* which is government owned and about two km from the border. It has a very lively bar, especially in the evenings, and the rooms are clean and they have private bathrooms.

For somewhere to eat closer to the border, try the *Negussie Hotel*, which is up on the hill to the left after you have crossed the border. It offers the standard Ethiopian fare of wat (a fierce hot sauce) and injera (bread made of millet flour), and there's also a bar here.

Kenyan shillings are acceptable when paying for meals and drinks.

Getting There & Away

Trucks between Isiolo and Moyale take two days and cost KSh 600 to KSh 1000. See the Isiolo section in the Central Highlands chapter for details.

There are buses going north from the Ethiopian side of Moyale but they start early at around the break of dawn. See the Ethiopia information in the Land section of Getting There & Away.

A word of warning: When it's 1997 in Kenya, it's 1987 in Ethiopia, and when it's noon in Kenya, it's 6 am in Ethiopia (because, in Ethiopia, the day starts at 6 am, not midnight). This is very important when you're catching a bus otherwise you'll find yourself six hours out of kilter.

CROSSING TO ETHIOPIA

The border between the two countries is open, though you'll still need an Ethiopian visa to enter. After first clearing Kenyan immigration and customs you will arrive at the Ethiopian customs post where they will ask how much money (cash and travellers' cheques) you are bringing with you. This will be entered into your passport alongside your visa stamp. If you intend to use the street market for changing money inside the country (there's a 10% difference between the bank and street rates) then you'll have to declare less than you actually have. After customs, there's a two-km walk into town where you have to go to immigration for an entry stamp. It's a good idea to find a hotel along the way so you don't have to carry all your gear with you.

The North-East

Like the north of Kenya, the north-east up to the border with Somalia covers a vast area of desert and semidesert with very few centres of population and limited public transport possibilities. The main towns are Garissa and Wajir. Most of the area is relatively flat, yet it's through here that one of Kenya's major rivers, the Tana, flows. The river enters the ocean about halfway between Malindi and Lamu and is the territory of the Orma, Pokomo and Bajun tribes. Straddling this river just north of Garsen is the Tana River Primate Sanctuary which is included on a few safari companies' itineraries but otherwise difficult to get to.

The reserve was set up to protect the red colobus and the crested mangabey monkey both of which are endangered species. The other main river, the Ewaso Nyiro which flows through Samburu and Buffalo Springs National Reserves, eventually peters out into the Lorian Swamp, never quite reaching the ocean.

Few travellers come this way except those looking for trouble or a dangerous adventure. The area north and east of Garissa is now the domain of gun-toting shiftas from Somalia, so, if you come here, it helps if you speak Somali. When the UN/American troops went into Somalia in late 1992 to help in the distribution of food aid, many of those with guns sought shelter in Kenya where they could rustle cattle and create havoc with relative impunity. They're still doing it even though the UN has pulled out. It's not a safe area to venture into even if you're with one of the aid agencies. Although the Somali border is still open, the country itself is pretty much a no-go area for the average traveller.

Other than a visit to Meru National Park (see the Kenya National Parks & Reserves chapter), which would be worth it if security could be guaranteed, and the Tana River area, the north-east isn't a particularly interesting region even for desert fans. However, Wajir, with its mostly Somali population,

Beau Geste fort and market, would definitely have the edge over Garissa, itself quite a nondescript town hardly worth stopping for.

GARISSA
The only reason to come to Garissa is if you are taking the back route to Lamu direct from Nairobi via Garsen. There's nothing much to see or do here and the heat and humidity are unrelenting. However there is a bank (open normal hours), petrol stations, bars and a fair choice of places to stay. The only trouble with going via Garissa is getting there. As on the Malindi-Lamu run, most of the bus companies which used to service the town have pulled out because of the danger of shifta and the state of the road.

Places to Stay & Eat
Perhaps the best place to stay for the night is the *Safari Hotel* which offers relatively cheap, clean rooms with running water and reasonable food in the attached restaurant.

The *Garissa Government Guest House*, a short distance out of town, is somewhat more expensive for rooms with bathroom and breakfast, but is worth the extra money. If both are full then there's also the more basic *Nile Lodging* or the *Kenya Hotel & Lodging*. to check out.

Getting There & Away
Garissa Express operates a bus from the KBS depot Eastleigh, Nairobi, to Garissa on Monday, Wednesday, Friday and Sunday at 8 am. The depot is a 10-minute matatu ride from Ronald Ngala St (route No 9). The fare is KSh 350 and the journey takes about eight hours. It's a rough journey once you're off the tarmac so be prepared for discomfort.

LIBOI
Liboi, right on the Kenya-Somalia border, is a staging post in the *qat* (miraa) trade to Somalia. It has also become a major refugee centre following the civil war and famine in Somalia. It has only one place to stay, the *Cairo Hotel*, though depending on who you get a lift with (there are no buses) you might find accommodation in an NGO compound.

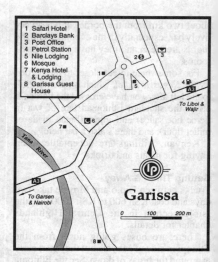

1 Safari Hotel
2 Barclays Bank
3 Post Office
4 Petrol Station
5 Nile Lodging
6 Mosque
7 Kenya Hotel & Lodging
8 Garissa Guest House

To Liboi & Wajir

Tana River

To Garsen & Nairobi

Garissa

0   100   200 m

On the other hand, why you would come here unless you're into disaster tourism, a dangerous adventure, or work for an NGO, is anybody's guess. Basically no-one in their right mind attempts to enter Somalia overland any longer. Those who must go there fly from either Nairobi or Mombasa to either Kismayu or Mogadishu. As this edition was being researched, there was still no discernible central government in Somalia and fighting between the various factions had broken out yet again. Despite all this, Somalis must have their *qat* so there must be some intrepid characters to risk their lives coming through overland.

GARSEN
This is another nondescript town near Lamu There's absolutely no reason to stay here if you're on the only remaining bus line between Malindi and Lamu (the Faza Express) but, if you're hitching between Garissa and Lamu (there are no longer any buses between the two), it may be necessary. There are several basic hotels to choose from. The best is the *3-in-1 Lodging & Restaurant* which is fairly clean and has its own restaurant.

National Parks & Reserves

Kenya's national parks and reserves rate among the best in Africa. Obviously the tremendous variety of birds and mammals is the main attraction, and the more popular parks such as Masai Mara Game Reserve and Amboseli National Park see huge numbers of visitors – from the budget campers to the hundreds-of-dollars-a-day Hilton hoppers. In the peak season (from January to February) on a game drive, you can observe at close

quarters the daily habits of the prolific Nissan Urvan. Other smaller parks, such as Saiwa Swamp National Park, near Kitale in the country's western highlands, would be lucky to see a handful of visitors a day at any time of year.

In addition to the protection of wildlife, some parks have been created to preserve the landscape itself, and these too can be exciting and rewarding places to visit – places

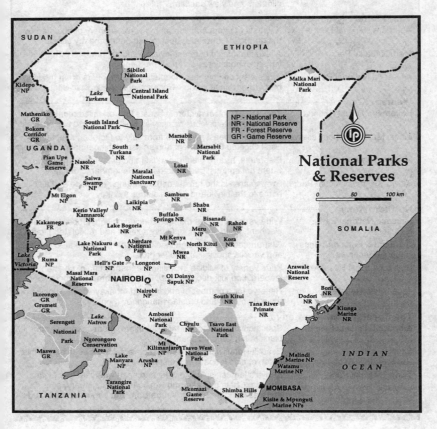

KENYA

REGION	FEATURES
Nairobi	
Nairobi National Park	Gazelle, oryx, lion, zebra, giraffe, buffalo, cheetah and leopard abound; great chance to spot a rhino.
The Rift Valley	
Hell's Gate National Park	Zebra, Thomson's gazelle, antelope, baboon, the occasional cheetah and leopard, ostriches and lammergeyer.
Lake Bogoria National Park	Thomson's gazelle, greater kudu and klipspringer; flamingos abound at the lakes southern end; hot springs and geysers.
Lake Nakuru National Park	'The world's greatest ornithological spectacle' is home to flamingos and pelicans; also waterbuck and black rhino.
Longonot National Park	The dormant volcano Longonot (2886m) offers much for hill climbers and view seekers.
The Central Highlands	
Aberdare National Park	A variety of fauna and flora and diverse scenery punctuated by the dramatic Gura Falls; best visited during the dry season.
Meru National Park	A luxuriant jungle of forest, swamp and tall grasses with a wide variety of herbivores and their predators.
Mt Kenya National Park	Africa's second highest mountain (5199m) offers great trekking; best visited January to late February or late August to September.
Western Kenya	
Kakamega Forest Reserve	This virgin tropical rainforest boasts the red-tailed monkey and black-and-white colobus monkey as well as over 330 bird species.
Masai Mara National Reserve	Annual wildebeest migration from July to October; spectacular Esoit Olooloo Escarpment and an astonishing amount of game.
Mt Elgon National Park	Elephants, bizarre giant groundsel and giant lobelia plants and Suam hot springs; best visited from December to January.
Saiwa Swamp National Park	Swamp area is the habitat of the sitatunga antelope and also home to the black-and-white colobus monkey.
Northern Kenya	
Marsabit National Park & Reserve	Wide variety of larger mammals including lion, leopard, cheetah, elephant, rhino, wart hog, Grevy's zebra and reticulated giraffe.
Samburu & Buffalo Springs National Reserves	Guaranteed close-up sightings of elephants, reticulated giraffe and various species of smaller gazelle.
Shaba National Reserve	Wide variety of wildlife including elephant, buffalo, cheetah, leopard, lion, dik-dik, wart hog, Grevy's zebra and crocodile.
Tana River Primate National Reserve	Reserve for a number of endangered monkey species, including the red colobus and crested mangabey monkeys.
The Coast & Southern Kenya	
Amboseli National Park	Spectacular backdrop of Mt Kilimanjaro; great chance to spot black rhino; large elephant herds.
Shimba Hills National Reserve	Beautiful forest setting; the rare sable antelope is seen only in this reserve; also leopard and elephant.
Tsavo National Park	Kenya's largest, split into west and east; west features Mzima Springs, Chaimu Crater and Ngulia Rhino Sanctuary; east features Kanderi Swamp, Aruba Dam and large elephant herds.

such as Mt Kenya, Mt Elgon, Hell's Gate, Mt Longonot and the Kakamega Forest are all worth investigating.

Marine life is also in abundance and the marine national parks of Malindi and Watamu off the central coast both offer excellent diving possibilities. Shimoni and Wasini islands in the extreme south offer even better opportunities but are much less accessible and developed.

What probably helps to make Kenyan parks such a draw card for the budget traveller is that the competition among safari companies for the traveller's dollar is so fierce that a safari of at least a few days is within the reach of the vast majority of travellers. For those at the other end of the scale the competition is equally brisk and there are lodges and tented camps within the major parks which have superb facilities and are a real experience – if you can afford them.

Information

Entry Fees Entry fees to national parks are controlled by the Kenya Wildlife Services, while national reserves, such as Masai Mara, are administered by the local council.

Kenya Wildlife Services recently introduced a differential pricing structure for the various national parks which, it is hoped, will encourage visitation to less popular parks and take some of the strain off the major parks. The fees cover visitors for a 24-hour period, so if you enter a park at 3 pm, you have until 3 pm the following day before having to leave or pay again.

The parks now come into one of four categories, and you are charged accordingly.

The entry fee to Masai Mara Game Reserve is the same as for the Category A parks.

Books & Maps If you are driving your own vehicle it's a good idea to equip yourself with maps of the parks before you set out. The best are all published by the Survey of Kenya and obtainable either from the Public Map Office or bookshops in Nairobi. The ones you will need are SK 87 *Amboseli National Park*, SK 86 *Masai Mara Game Reserve*, SK 82 *Tsavo East National Park*, and SK 78 *Tsavo West National Park*.

Macmillan also publishes some pretty decent maps to a number of parks, including Masai Mara, Amboseli and Tsavo.

If you're interested in walking in the national parks of Mt Kenya, Mt Elgon and Aberdare, Lonely Planet's *Trekking in East Africa* has details.

Accommodation

Camping out in the bush is, of course, the authentic way of experiencing an African safari. There's nothing quite like having just a sheet of canvas between you and what you would normally see only on the residents' side of a zoo. Full-on contact with the bush along with its potential dangers and rewards is surely what you are looking for. Anything more luxurious than this is going to dilute the experience and remove the immediacy of it all.

There are some beautifully conceived and constructed game lodges and, if you have the

Park Entry Prices

Category	Parks	Nonresident Adults/children	Resident Adults/children
A	Aberdares, Amboseli, Lake Nakuru	US$27/10	KSh 250/50
B	Tsavo East & West	US$23/8	KSh 200/50
C	Nairobi, Shimba Hills, Meru	US$20/5	KSh 150/50
D	All other parks	US$15/5	KSh 100/50
Others	Marine Parks	US$5/2	KSh 100/50
	Mountaineering	US$10/5	KSh 100/50

KENYA

Animal Spotting

When you visit Kenya's parks and reserves, you'll be spending a lot of time craning necks and keeping watchful eyes out for the animals and birds you've come so far to see. There are a few telltale signs to note, as well as a few things you can do, to maximise your chances. Most of them are just common sense, but it's amazing the number of people who go belting around noisily expecting everything to come to them.

- Drive slowly and, wherever possible, quietly, keeping eyes trained not only on the ground ahead but also to the side and in the branches above.
- Go in search in the early morning or the late afternoon. In the more popular parks, such as Amboseli and Masai Mara, the animals are actually changing their normal hunting habits to fit in with the tourists, so at midday, when most people are safely back in their lodges stuffing their faces, the carnivores are out hunting in the hope that they may be able to do the same thing – in peace.
- Vultures circling are not necessarily an indication of a kill below, but if they are gathering in trees and seem to be waiting you can reasonably assume they are waiting their turn for a go at the carcass.
- In wooded country, agitated and noisy monkeys or baboons are often a sign that there's a big cat (probably a leopard) around.

money, it's worth spending a night or two at one or another of them, though it's probably true to say they are mainly for those who prefer to keep the bush at arm's length and a glass of ice-cold beer within arm's reach.

Certainly the way in which some game lodges attract wildlife to their door is somewhat contrived. Hanging up shanks of meat in a tree which a 'resident' leopard comes to feed off 10 minutes later – despite the spotlights – is hardly the essence of Africa. It's only fair to add, however, that not all game lodges go in for this sort of circus.

The Parks & Reserves

Kenya's national parks and reserves are listed in this chapter in alphabetical order.

ABERDARE NATIONAL PARK

This park essentially encloses the moorland and high forest of the 60-km-long Kinangop plateau along with an eastern salient reaching down to the lower slopes in the vicinity of Nyeri. Only rarely does this park feature in the itineraries of safari companies and it's even less visited by individual travellers. There are various reasons for this. The main one is perhaps the weather. As on Mt Kenya, rain can be expected at any time and when it arrives, it's heavy. Roads turn into mud slides and 4WD is absolutely essential. The park is often closed during the wet season as a result.

Another drawback (though the wild game would no doubt describe it as a plus) is the difficulty of seeing animals because of the dense forest. This is not savanna like Amboseli and Masai Mara so you have to take your time and stay a few nights, which brings us to the third drawback – finding a place to stay. Though there are three camp sites within the park, facilities are minimal and you're going to need a good tent and warm sleeping gear. Add to this the fact that there's no public transport whatsoever, hitching is virtually impossible and that, as elsewhere, walking isn't permitted without special permission. That essentially puts the Aberdares

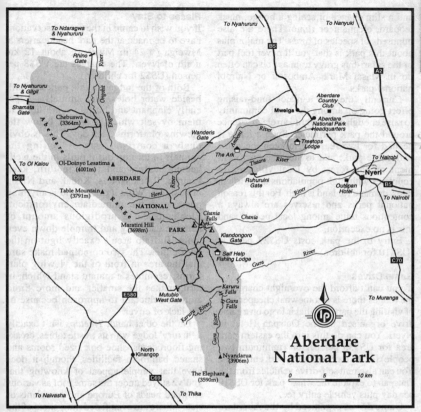

Aberdare National Park

out of reach of anyone without their own transport. And, lastly, unless you're camping, the only other accommodation possibilities are two very expensive lodges, The Ark and Treetops, which you are not allowed to drive to in your own vehicle. You must make advance reservations for both and be driven there in the lodges' transport.

In the dry season it may be possible to walk over the high moorland between the four main peaks if the weather is favourable but you can't do this without permission from the officials at the park headquarters at Mweiga, north of Nyeri (☎ (0171) 55024).

They will provide an armed ranger (obligatory) to guide you. If this is what you want to do then it might be best to first contact the Kenya Mountain Club in Nairobi before setting out, as they may be planning such a trip.

These sorts of difficulties and/or the expense involved put off most independent travellers but if you're determined to go then the rewards can well justify the effort.

The park does offer a variety of fauna, flora and scenery which you won't find elsewhere except, perhaps, on Mt Kenya. There are also the dramatic **Gura Falls** which drop a full 300m, thick forest, alpine moorland

and a slim chance of seeing a bongo, black leopard, elephant or rhino. There are also hundreds of species of birds. The major plus about this park is that you'll never feel part of the safari-bus gravy train as you can often do in Masai Mara, Amboseli or Nairobi national parks.

Currently there is a major fund-raising effort going on among the local community to raise enough cash to build an electric fence around the park perimeter. Such a fence is needed for two reasons: to keep the game within the park; and to stop the encroachment on the forest by local villagers. In countries with high populations and growth rates, demand for land is high. For this reason national parks and reserves are always a contentious issue among local people, and this is no exception.

Entry to the park costs US$27 per day (US$10 for children).

Game Drives

If you can't afford the overnight charges at the lodges there is a somewhat cheaper way of visiting the park and that is to go on a game drive organised by the Outspan Hotel in Nyeri. You can do this into the eastern park area for US$35 per person (minimum two people) for the day excluding park entry fees. You can also rent self-drive vehicles from the Outspan to explore the whole park for US$10 per day plus vehicle entry fee.

Game drives organised by the Aberdare Country Club are yet another option, although these aren't particularly cheap either. A game drive in the salient costs US$138 for the whole vehicle for half a day, or US$264 for a full day shared between however many there are of you. A surcharge of 20% is made if you're not staying at either the Country Club or The Ark. The Country Club also offers a half-day walking safari in its own private 500-hectare wildlife sanctuary for US$46 per person including brunch (plus 20% surcharge if you are not a guest). The sanctuary abounds with Thompson's and Grant's gazelle, zebra and giraffe and you may even catch sight of a leopard.

Places to Stay

If you wish to camp in the park, reservations have to be made at the park headquarters at Mweiga (☎ 24 in Mweiga), about 12 km north of Nyeri. The charges are US$8 per person (US$2 for children).

Both of the lodges in this park are built beside water holes, and animals – especially elephant and buffalo – are lured to them by salt which is spread below the viewing platforms each day. This is obviously a contrived way of getting the animals to turn up but it pulls in the well-heeled punters and they, in turn, keep Lonrho, Block Hotels, Kodak and Nikon in business. What it doesn't do is anything positive to the immediate environment. Elephants eat a prodigious amount of herbage each day and trample down even more. Buffalo aren't exactly light on the hoof either. The two combined make sure that the area in front of the viewing platforms resembles a matatu stand which, in turn, makes the smaller and more timid animals reluctant to approach because of the lack of cover.

On the other hand, *Treetops* isn't exactly a 'luxury' lodge with its trestle tables, creaking floorboards, shoe-box sized rooms and shared bathroom facilities, though it does have that yuppie appeal of knowing that you've stayed under the same roof as various crowned heads of Europe and presidents of state – there are even faded mug-shots of the *nomenclatura* on the walls.

Full board (including transfer from Nyeri but excluding park entry fees) at Treetops depends on the time of year you stay there. In the high season (16 December to 3 January and 1 April to 8 April) it costs US$124/248 for singles/doubles whereas in the low season (9 April to 30 June) it costs US$62/124 for the same thing. During the rest of the year, the prices are in-between the two. Kenyan residents are entitled to substantial discounts on the above prices. Children under seven years old are not admitted and those over seven years old are charged at full adult rates. You must book in advance through Block Hotels (☎ (02) 540780; fax 543810) in

Nairobi. Having booked, you then turn up at the Outspan Hotel in Nyeri by 12.30 pm for transfer to the park.

The Ark is somewhat better appointed than Treetops and is further into the park but it costs much more. Full board here, including transfer from Mweiga but excluding park entry fees, costs US$270/321 for singles/doubles in the high seasons and US$147/173 in the low seasons. As at Treetops, children under seven years old are not admitted and those over seven years pay the full adult rate. You must book in advance through Lonrho Hotels Kenya (☎ (02) 216940; fax 216796) in Nairobi. Having booked you must turn up at the Aberdare Country Club at Mweiga, 12 km north of Nyeri, on the appointed day and you'll be driven to the lodge.

AMBOSELI NATIONAL PARK

Amboseli is the next most popular park after Masai Mara, mainly because of the spectacular backdrop of Africa's highest peak, Mt Kilimanjaro, which broods on the southern boundary of the park.

At 392 sq km Amboseli is not a large park, and it certainly doesn't have the profusion of game which you find in Masai Mara but the game here is easy to spot. The western section of the park is the dry bed of Lake Amboseli, and although it is occasionally flooded in the wet season, for the majority of the time it is a dry, dusty, shimmering expanse.

Probably the best reason for visiting Amboseli is that you stand the best chance of spotting a black rhino. Amboseli also has huge herds of elephant, and to see a herd of them making their way sedately across the grassy plains, with Kilimanjaro in the background, may be a real African cliche but is an experience which certainly leaves a lasting impression.

Other animals which you are likely to see here include buffalo, lion, gazelle, cheetah, wildebeest, hyena, jackal, wart hog, Masai giraffe, zebra and baboon.

Amboseli more than any other park has suffered greatly from the number of minibuses which drive through each day. It has a much drier climate than Masai Mara and so

for much of the year is a real dust bowl. If you are driving through the park, stick to the defined tracks, and hopefully others will follow suit.

Most visitors approach Amboseli through **Namanga**, the main border post between Kenya and Tanzania. If you're stuck, there's accommodation at the *Namanga Hotel* among others. The petrol station is a good place to ask around for lifts.

Outside the town's petrol station there are a couple of shops selling Maasai crafts. The first prices asked are totally ridiculous, so bargain fiercely.

Entry to the park costs US$27 per person (US$10 children) per day.

Activities
Microlight Flights For an aerial view of the mountain and the plains, take a microlight flight from the Kilimanjaro Buffalo Lodge, east of the park (see Places to Stay). Flights are made on demand, and cost KSh 3500 per person.

Places to Stay – bottom end
Once again the only budget option is a *camp site*. This one is right on the southern boundary of the park. The only facilities are a couple of long-drop toilets, and a kiosk where you can buy warm beer and sodas and pay the camping fees (US$8 per person). The water supply here is extremely unreliable so bring some water with you. Elephants are a real problem in this camp site at night and practically everyone who has stayed here has an elephant story to relate – there are some hilarious (and not so hilarious) ones doing the rounds. At night make sure all food is locked away inside your vehicle. *Don't* keep food in your tent as elephants have a habit of investigating, as do baboons during the day when you're out on a game drive.

Places to Stay – top end
There are a number of options within the park, and also outside the park to the east, on the road to Tsavo. These latter places provide a good alternative to those within the park,

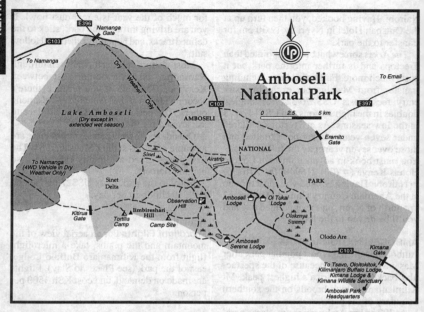

Amboseli National Park

---

as you don't have to pay the daily park entry fees.

In the Park The two lodges in the centre of the park are strategically situated for views of Kilimanjaro. The *Amboseli Lodge* is run by the Kilimanjaro Safari Club in Nairobi (☎ (02) 227136; fax 219982). The lodge consists of a number of comfortable cottages dotted around an expansive lawn and garden, with sweeping views of Kilimanjaro (weather permitting, of course). Facilities include a swimming pool, and airy central building with dining room and bar. Rooms cost US$70 per person for full board during the low season. High-season rates are US$168/210.

Close by is the new *Ol Tukai Lodge*, belonging to Block Hotels (☎ (02) 540780; fax 540821). This brand new lodge has a beautiful central building with polished floors and lots of timber. Like the Amboseli Lodge, the guest cottages are spread around

a lawn, and two of them have wheelchair access. This is a very comfortable hotel, complete with swimming pool. Rooms cost US$107/165 in the high season.

Close to the southern perimeter of the park is the *Amboseli Serena Lodge* (☎ (02) 711077; fax 725184 in Nairobi), a sensitively designed and constructed lodge which blends in well with the landscape. The nearby Enkongo Narok Swamp ensures constant bird and animal activity. Room charges are US$55/110 with full board during the low season, rising to US$128/166 in the high season.

Also on the southern edge of the park, at the western end, is the secluded *Tortilis Camp* (☎ (0154) 22551; fax 22553), beautifully situated with views across the plains to Kilimanjaro, which looms very large from here. The open-air, makuti-roofed lounge and dining areas are in an elevated position to make the most of the views, while the permanent tents, each with verandah, makuti shelter and wood-panelled bathroom, are nestled in among a stand of *Acacia tortilis* trees. The whole place has been designed to be eco-friendly, making use of solar power for water heating, and ensuring that no wood is used for fires. The food is excellent, and reflects the Kenyan owners' Italian background. As this place is actually on the national park boundary, they can offer activities such as guided nature walks, which are not possible within the park. There is no access to the camp from outside the national park. Accommodation rates are US$100/200 for full board in the low season, rising to US$170/264 in the high season. This price includes taxes.

Outside the Park Some 30 or so km east of the park, and close to the Kimana Wildlife Sanctuary (see next section) is the *Kilimanjaro Buffalo Lodge*, operated by the Kilimanjaro Safari Club in Nairobi (☎ (02) 227136; fax 219982). Although showing its age somewhat, this lodge is still a good prospect, and it's likely that the rooms will have been renovated by now. There are excellent views of the mountain, and the Hemingway Bar gives good views back towards the Chyulu Hills. Room rates are US$70/140 in the low season, up to US$160/ 200 in the high season. There's a swimming pool, and a demonstration of Maasai dance every evening.

Close by, and on the road which connects Emali on the Nairobi–Mombasa road with Oloitokitok on the Tanzanian border, is the *Kimana Lodge*, also owned by the Kilimanjaro Safari Club. The lodge has little in the way of views, although most evenings a leopard comes up to a bait out the front. Rates are US$50/100 in the low season, US$152/190 in the high.

Very close to the settlement of Oloitokitok, and accessible by matatu from Emali, is *Kibo Slope Cottages* (☎ (0302) 22091; fax 22427). The rates here are US$20/35 for bed and breakfast, dropping to KSh 600/1000 in the low season.

Getting There & Away

Air Air Kenya Aviation has daily flights between Wilson airport (Nairobi) and Amboseli. These depart from Nairobi at 7.30 am and Amboseli at 8.15 am; the trip takes about an hour and costs US$70 one way. The return flight leaves Amboseli at 8.30 am.

Car & 4WD The usual approach to Amboseli is through Namanga, 165 km south of Nairobi on the A104, and the last fuel stop before the park. The road is in excellent condition from Nairobi to Namanga, however, the 75-km dirt road from Namanga to the Namanga Gate is fiercely corrugated at times if the grader hasn't been over it for a while. The whole trip from Nairobi takes around four hours.

It's also possible to enter Amboseli from the east via Tsavo. This road is not in bad condition, but there have been bandit attacks in the past, so all vehicles must travel in a convoy, accompanied by armed policemen. The convoys leave the Kimana Gate of Amboseli at 8.30 and 10.30 am, and 2.30 pm. Most of the vehicles are tourist minibuses, and as the drivers belt along at great speed, the 'convoy' gets so spread out that any protection which might be offered by the police (who travel in the front and rear vehicle) is negligible. Fortunately, incidents are very rare (just one in the last five years). The trip to Chyulu Gate and Kilaguni Lodge in Tsavo East takes about three hours.

AROUND AMBOSELI
Kimana Wildlife Sanctuary

About 30 km east of Amboseli, close to the road which connects Amboseli to Tsavo, is this 40-hectare wildlife sanctuary. It is owned and run by the local Maasai people, and is an important project in giving them some control over their own land. Any communities living on the fringes of the national parks tend to get a pretty rough deal, not only because valuable land is set aside for wild animals, but also that these wild animals then come and encroach upon the land outside the park, often in a destructive manner. The Maasai here decided that a tourism venture was the best way to make the best of things, and so with the help of USAID and the Kenya Wildlife Service, the sanctuary was established, and opened in 1996. While it is still in its early stages, and the rangers are still learning their craft, they are very enthusiastic and helpful, and it's well worth a visit – projects like this which empower the local people are all too rare.

There are graded tracks through the sanctuary, and wildlife viewing is probably as good – if not better – than within Amboseli itself. There's also a hippo pool.

Entry to the sanctuary cost US$10 per person, plus KSh 100 per vehicle.

Places to Stay There are three guarded *camp sites* within the sanctuary, where you can camp for KSh 150.

HELL'S GATE NATIONAL PARK

This park is one of only two lowland parks in the country which you can walk through without a ranger/guide (the other is Saiwa Swamp near Kitale). The looming cliffs and the Hell's Gate gorge itself are spectacular, and are home to a wide variety of bird and animal life. On a walk through the park it is possible to see zebra, Thomson's gazelle, antelope, baboon and even the occasional cheetah or leopard. Ostriches and the rare lammergeyer are also sighted on occasion.

The usual access point is through the main **Elsa Gate**, two km from Moi South Lake Rd. From here the road takes you past **Fischer's Tower**, a 25m-high column of volcanic rock named after Gustav Fischer, a German explorer who reached here in 1883. He had been commissioned by the Hamburg Geographical Society to find a route from Mombasa to Lake Victoria but this was about as far as he got, largely because he was unable to get on good terms with hostile Maasai.

The road then continues through the steep-sided gorge and emerges at the **Ol Karia Geothermal Station** – a power project which utilises one of the hottest sources in the world. You can see the plumes of steam rising into the air from many of the viewpoints in the park. South-east of here, you'll see Central Tower, another column of volcanic rock similar to Fischer's Tower but much larger. From the geothermal plant the track heads back to the lake shore via the Ol Karia Gate, and emerges in the vicinity of Oserian farm (now a large supplier of cut flowers, fruit and vegetables to the European market) and Elsamere.

The entire walk from the lake road turn-off via Elsa Gate and Ol Karia Gate to the lake shore is 22 km. The distance between the two

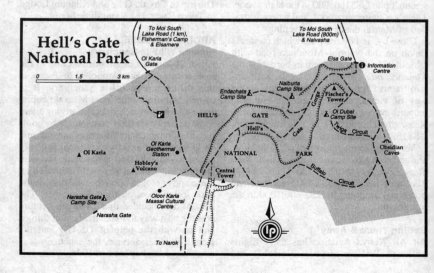

Hell's Gate National Park

gates via the lake road is nine km. If you intend walking the whole way through the park, allow a full day, and take along some drinking water and something to eat. The only drinking water available in the park is at the camp sites.

Entry to the park costs US$15 (US$5 for children), and camping costs US$6 per person.

If you don't want to walk through the park it may be possible to arrange a trip by car if you ask around at Fisherman's Camp.

KAKAMEGA FOREST RESERVE
The Kakamega Forest Reserve is a superb slab of virgin tropical rainforest in the heart of an intensively cultivated agricultural area. It is home to a huge variety of birds and animals and is well worth the minimal effort required to get to it.

The Forest Department maintains a beautiful four-room rest house in the south of the reserve at Isecheno, as well as a large nursery for propagating trees and shrubs used for ceremonial occasions around the country and for planting in the area. The workers are very friendly and it's no problem to get

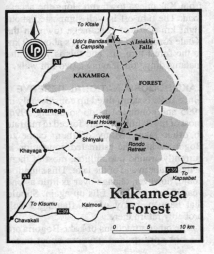

Kakamega Forest

shown around. In the northern part of the reserve at Buyangu the Kenya Wildlife Services maintains a camp site and bandas.

For the visitor the choice is which area to visit – the Buyangu (northern) area is the more easily accessible by public transport and only involves a walk of two km; to Isecheno you may have to walk a lot further.

The forest itself comprises a number of habitats, but is generally very dense and is the home of a number of primate species, such as the red-tailed monkey, black and white colobus monkey and the blue monkey; and more than 330 species of birds have been recorded.

Information
As this is not a national park, there are no entry fees. The Kenya Indigenous Forest Conservation Program (KIFCON) publishes an excellent little guide to the forest (KSh 400), and this is available from the East African Wildlife Society Gift Shop in the Hilton Hotel Arcade in Nairobi.

Walking Trails
The best way to appreciate the forest here is to walk, and there are two trail systems which radiate out from the two forest stations. The trails are signposted and marked with coloured flashes at main junctions, so getting lost is not a major problem. To enhance your appreciation of the forest, it's not a bad idea to hire a guide. Staff at either of the forest stations should be able to arrange for somebody to accompany you.

The trails vary in length from one to seven km, the longest being the Isiukhu Trail up to the insignificant Isiukhu Falls.

Places to Stay & Eat
Isecheno The *Forest Rest House* is a superb place to put your feet up for a few days. It's an elevated wooden building with a verandah which looks directly on to the seemingly impenetrable Kakamega Forest. There are only four double rooms but they all have a bathroom and toilet. Blankets are supplied but you need to have your own sleeping bag

or sheet. The rooms cost KSh 100 per person plus you can also camp for KSh 50. If the rest house is full when you arrive, and you have your own sleeping gear, it is usually possible to sleep on the verandah for next to nothing. If you want to be sure of a room, book in advance through the Forest Ranger, PO Box 88, Kakamega.

The only problem here is food. Basically you need to bring your own and preferably something to cook it on, although it is possible to cook on a fire. There's a small kiosk which sells beer, tea and soft drinks (sodas) and also cooks basic meals at lunch time. Evening meals are cooked on request (beans or corn and rice is about the limit), but you need to make sure they know you are coming as the kiosk closes at 6.30 pm. You can get basic meals and supplies from a small group of dukas about two km back towards Shinyalu.

Three km further along the road from Isecheno is the *Rondo Retreat*, a former sawmiller's residence built in the 1920s. It is owned by the church group and offers very comfortable top-end accommodation either in the main house or in bungalows with their own bathrooms. The charges are KSh 2500 per person for room only, or KSh 4400 for full board. Advance bookings can be made during business hours (☎ (0331) 41345, 30268).

Buyangu The KWS operates the *Udo's Bandas & Campsite*, named after Udo Savalli, a well-known ornithologist. There are seven bandas here each with two beds, a communal cooking and dining shelter, pit toilets and basic showers. While you need to bring your own food, it should be possible to find someone to cook it for you if need be. The bandas are a bargain at KSh 250 per person, and this is also the charge for camping. Advance booking can be made through the District Warden, KWS, PO Box 879, Kakamega (☎ (0331) 20425).

Getting There & Away
Isecheno The Forest Rest House lies about 12 km east of the A1 Kisumu–Kitale road, about 30 km north of Kisumu. Access is possible either from Kakamega village on the main road when coming from the north, or from Khayaga also on the main road when coming from the south. From both places dirt roads lead east to the small market village of Shinyalu, from where it's a further five km to the rest house, signposted to the left. There are matatus from Kakamega to Shinyalu, and even the occasional one from Khayaga to Shinyalu.

If you want to walk – and it is beautiful walking country – it's about seven km from Khayaga to Shinyalu, or about 10 km from Kakamega to Shinyalu. These roads become extremely treacherous after rain and you may prefer to walk when you see how the vehicles slip all over the road. There's very little traffic along either of the roads but you may get a lift with the occasional tractor or Forest Department vehicle. Whatever means you employ to get there, allow half a day from Kitale or Kisumu. From the turn-off to the rest house the dirt road continues on to Kapsabet, so you could also come from that direction but it is a long walk if you can't get a lift.

Buyangu It's somewhat easier to reach the northern part of the reserve as local matatus from Kakamega town run along the access road. The turn-off is well signposted about eight km north of Kakamega town on the Kitale road, and from there it's about 10 km to the forest turn-off, and this is where the matatus drop you, leaving a two-km walk.

LAKE BOGORIA NATIONAL RESERVE
Since Lake Nakuru dried up considerably in 1995 and continued to do so during 1996, most of the flamingos were forced to migrate to other lakes. Many of them came to Bogoria where the estimated population is currently around one million, most of them at the southern end of the lake. This situation could, however, change over as little as one year if Lake Nakuru fills up again. Should that happen, many of the flamingos will probably return there.

The other attractions of Lake Bogoria are the **hot springs** and **geysers** about three-quarters of the way along the lake going south. They're not comparable with those at Rotorua in New Zealand but if you've never seen geysers before then this is the place. The springs are boiling hot so don't put your bare foot or hand into them unless you want to nurse scalds for the next week.

The land to the west of the lake is a hot and relatively barren wilderness of rocks and scrub, and animals are few and far between though you'll almost always catch sight of small herds of Thomson's gazelle and you may be lucky to see a greater kudu, impala or klipspringer. The eastern side of the lake is dominated by the sheer face of the north-eastern extremities of the Aberdares.

Lake Bogoria is a very peaceful place not much visited by tourists so you'll probably have the park to yourself – though this may change if the flamingos stay on. As Bogoria is a national park there's an entry fee of US$15 per person (US$5 for children and students) plus KSh 200 per vehicle.

Places to Stay

There are two camp sites at the southern end of the lake – *Acacia* and *Riverside* – but there are no facilities and the lake water is totally unpalatable. Bring all water and food with you if you are intending to stay at either site. Otherwise, the camp sites are shady and very pleasant though the road to them deteriorates rapidly beyond the hot springs. Camping charges are the usual US$8 per person for nonresidents or KSh 150 for residents. Children and students pay US$2 and KSh 50, respectively.

If you don't want to camp there's an excellent cheap place to stay right outside the northern entry gate (the Loboi gate). This is the new *Papyrus Inn* (☎ 1 Loboi through the operator) which offers bed and breakfast at KSh 400/600 for singles/doubles with shared bathroom facilities. For large groups these prices are negotiable and there's a special student rate of KSh 200 per bed. It's well run and the staff are very friendly, plus there's a restaurant and bar.

Two km before the same entry gate is the huge *Lake Bogoria Hotel* (☎ (037) 42696).

This top-end place is very pleasant and set in well-tended gardens, but few people seem to stay here. Rooms cost the equivalent of US$105/130 a single/double with half board and US$120/160 with full board. There's a swimming pool and the place is open to nonresidents for lunch (KSh 380) and dinner (KSh 420).

The only other feasible place to stay in this area is at the *Marigat Inn* in Marigat town. It's signposted on the main road but to get to it you have to walk or drive about 1.5 km through the town and turn left after the mosque just where the tarmac ends. You'll find it behind a row of small shops. It's a pleasant place with friendly staff and the rooms are arranged around a shady court-yard. Singles with shared bathroom facilities cost KSh 250 and doubles/triples with attached bathrooms are KSh 400/600. The hotel has its own bar and restaurant.

Getting There & Away

There are two entrance gates to Lake Bogoria – one from the south (Mogotio) and another from the north (Loboi). You'll see the sign-post for the Mogotio gate on the B4 about 38 km past Nakuru heading north but, if you take it, you'll probably regret it! Most of this road is good smooth dust or gravel but there is about five km of it leading down to the southern park entrance which will certainly rip apart any tyres and destroy any vehicle driven at more than a few km/h. Without 4WD you'd be wasting your time. These razor-sharp lava beds don't end once you reach the park gate but continue for at least as far on the other side. In addition, signpost-ing along the route from the turn-off is almost nonexistent.

A far better entry to the park is from the Loboi gate just a few km before you reach Marigat on the B4. It's also signposted. From the turn-off, it's 20 km to the actual park entry gate along a good, sealed road.

Whichever gate you use, you're going to need your own vehicle since hitching is well-nigh impossible. Very few people visit Bogoria and those who do are usually in tourist minibuses which won't pick you up

Rhino Rescue

Many of Africa's animals are threatened by the loss of their habitat due to human overpopulation or by poachers, and it's the poor rhino which is in the greatest danger. The rhino's horn, its trademark, causes the problem – plenty of people covet it and this only serves to push the price up as it becomes increasingly rare.

The stark statistics are horrific. In 1970, it is estimated that Kenya had about 20,000 black rhinos. By 1985, that number had dwindled to just 425, and rhinos were so few and so scattered that it was becoming increasingly difficult for a lady rhino to meet a compatible gentleman rhino, with the object of creating baby rhinos. With this huge fall in numbers, the price of rhino horns on the black market had soared from US$35 per kg to over US$30,000 per kg – and is still rising. Elsewhere in Africa, the fall in rhino numbers has been equally dramatic.

Rhino horn is a popular ingredient in many Chinese traditional medicines and we have all heard of the supposed effects of rhino horn on the libido. But the major market for rhino horn is the Yemen, where Djambia daggers with rhino horn handles are worth over US$15,000. These fantastic prices are inspiring ruthless tactics from poachers who tote modern weapons and are as likely to shoot as run when confronted by rangers. In 1990, their brazenness reached new heights when they shot not only Kenya's only five white rhinos (in Meru National Park) but first shot the armed guards in order to do so.

The only solution is felt to be the creation of small parks where rhinos can be carefully watched and protected. Funded by Rhino Rescue, an organisation set up in 1986 specifically to save the rhinos, the Nakuru National Park was selected as the first manageable rhino sanctuary. The park is now protected by a 74 km electric fence with guard posts at 15-km intervals. The construction involved over 11,000 fence posts and 880 km of high-tensile wire. An initial group of 19 rhinos was established and there are plans to increase this number, possibly to as many as 60.

Additional sanctuaries are planned but saving the rhino isn't going to come cheap. Donations can be sent to Rhino Rescue, PO Box 1, Saxmundham, Suffolk, IP17 3JT, UK. ■

unless you're booked with them. It *may* be possible to walk into the park since there are no large predators living here (with the possible exception of the occasional leopard) but don't count on it. Officially, you're supposed to tour the park in a vehicle.

If you're driving your own vehicle, there's an Esso petrol station on the main road at Marigat.

LAKE NAKURU NATIONAL PARK

Created in 1961, the park has since been considerably increased in size and now covers an area of some 200 sq km. Like most of the other rift valley lakes, it is a shallow soda lake. Some years ago the level of the lake rose and this resulted in a mass migration of the flamingos to other rift valley lakes, principally Bogoria, Magadi and Natron. What had been dubbed 'the world's greatest ornithological spectacle' suddenly wasn't anywhere near as spectacular. Since then the level of the lake has been decreasing steadily, and has now reached the point where it is almost dry during the dry season, and the flamingos have once again sought happy hunting grounds – mainly Lake Bogoria. While the situation does change from year to year, it seems that Lake Nakuru is no longer the ornithologists' paradise it once was. Hopefully the situation will change.

The lake is very shallow and the level fluctuates by up to four metres annually. When the water is low the soda crystallises out along the shoreline as a blinding white band of powder which is going to severely test your skills as a photographer. Lake Nakuru last dried up in the late 1950s and, at that time, soda dust storms and dust devils whipped up by high winds made life unbearable for people in the town and surrounding area. In the dry season you'll see these dust devils (like tiny tornadoes) whipping soda up into the air as they course along the shoreline.

Since the park also has areas of grassland, bush, forest and rocky cliffs there are many other animals to be seen apart from birds. One species you'll see plenty of are wart hogs with their amusing way of running with their tails erect. Right by the water you'll come across waterbuck and buffalo, while further into the bush are Thomson's gazelle and reedbuck – there's even the occasional leopard. Around the cliffs you may catch sight of hyrax and birds of prey. There's even a small herd of hippo which generally lives along the northern shore of the lake.

The park is also surrounded by a high electric fence, which keeps in a number of black rhino which were introduced some years ago.

The national park entrance is about six km from the centre of Nakuru. Entry costs US$27 per person (US$10 for children) plus KSh 200 per vehicle. As in most national parks, you must be in a vehicle. Walking is not permitted so you will either have to hitch a ride with other tourists, rent your own vehicle or go on a tour. You can, however, get out of your vehicle on the lake shore and at certain viewpoints.

Warning Don't drive too close to the water's edge, the mud is very soft! Take your cue from the tracks of other vehicles.

Places to Stay – bottom end

There is a good camp site, known as the *Backpackers' Camp Site* just inside the park gate. Fresh water is available and there are a couple of pit toilets, but you need to bring all your own food. Make sure tents are securely zipped up when you're away from them otherwise the vervet monkeys or baboons will steal everything inside them. If you are backpacking and trying to hitch a ride, the rangers at the gate will let you camp here without paying the park entry until you are successful. Camping here costs US$15 per person (US$2 for children).

A km or so further into the park is the *Njoro Camp Site* and this is the one to head for if you have a vehicle. It's a beautiful grassy site under acacia trees and there's firewood, water on tap and the usual pit toilets. The charge here is also US$15 per person.

If you have no camping equipment there's the very basic *Florida Day & Night Club* about half a km before the entrance gate.

KENYA

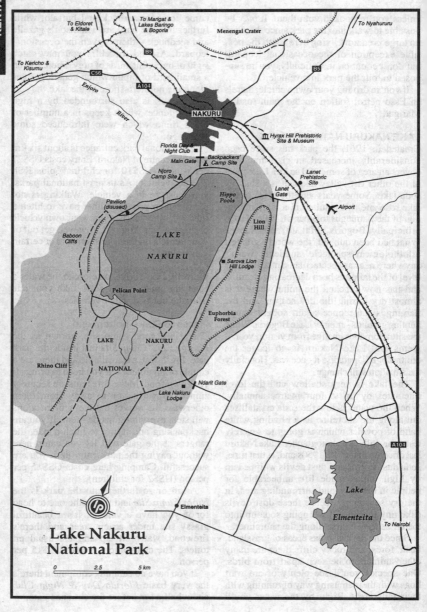

To Eldoret & Kitale

To Marigat & Lakes Baringo & Bogoria

To Nyahururu

Menengai Crater

To Kericho & Kisumu

B5

C56

A104

Enjoro River

Njoro River

NAKURU

B5

Hyrax Hill Prehistoric Site & Museum

Florida Day & Night Club

Main Gate

Backpackers' Camp Site

Njoro Camp Site

Lanet Prehistoric Site

Lanet Gate

Airport

Pavilion (disused)

Hippo Pools

Lion Hill

Baboon Cliffs

LAKE NAKURU

Sarova Lion Hill Lodge

Pelican Point

Euphorbia Forest

Rhino Cliff

LAKE NAKURU NATIONAL PARK

Ndarit Gate

Lake Nakuru Lodge

A104

Lake Elmenteita

Elmenteita

To Nairobi

Lake Nakuru National Park

0   2.5   5 km

Places to Stay – top end

The first place you come to down the eastern access road of the park is Sarova Hotels' *Sarova Lion Hill Lodge* (☎ (02) 333248; fax 211472). It has all the usual facilities including a swimming pool and open-air bar/restaurant area. High-season prices with full board are US$135/165 for singles/doubles. In the low season, prices drop to US$55/110. There are also more expensive suites. It's a well thought-out site but there are only occasional views of the lake through the thorn trees.

Almost three km beyond the southern end of the lake is the *Lake Nakuru Lodge* (☎ (02) 224998; fax 230962). Like the Sarova Lion Hill, it has all the usual facilities and consists of a series of shingle-roofed cottages. Low season prices for full board are US$50/100; in the high season it's US$135/160. Children aged three to 12 are charged 50%.

Bear in mind that if you are staying at either of these lodges you must also add the US$27 per day park entry fee.

Actually outside the park, between Nakuru town and the national park, is the *Sundowner Lodge* (☎ (02) 226778; fax 230962), which may be more convenient if you have your own transport. Rooms here cost KSh 800/1500 for bed and breakfast.

Getting There & Away

If you don't have your own vehicle, the only way into the park from Nakuru is by taxi (unless you can persuade a tourist with a car to take you in). A taxi costs around KSh 1000 for three hours, though you'll have to bargain hard for this. Alternatively, contact Birds Paradise Tours (☎ (037) 211143), upstairs behind the Bethany Bookshop on Kenyatta Ave. They organise two-hour trips to the lake for KSh 1000 per person, plus park entry fees.

If you're driving, there's access from three points: the main gate; Lanet, just a few km along the Nairobi road; and Ndarit Gate near the southern end of Lake Nakuru.

LONGONOT NATIONAL PARK

Hill climbers and view seekers should not miss the opportunity of climbing to the rim of dormant Longonot (2886m), a fairly young volcano which still retains the typical shape of these mountains, although it's far from being a perfect conical shape.

As this is a national park there is an entrance fee of US$15. The scramble up to the rim takes about 45 minutes from the parking area, and to do the circuit of the rim a further 2½ to three hours is needed. If you're feeling game there's a track leading down inside the crater to the bottom, though it's worth hiring a local guide before you set off.

Places to Stay

There's no accommodation in the park or immediate vicinity, but it is possible to camp at the ranger station at the foot of the mountain. If you are just on a day trip you can leave your gear at the Longonot railway station or the police station.

Getting There & Away

If you don't have your own transport it's a long walk from Longonot railway station just off the old road to Naivasha. It's about seven km to the trail head, and even if you have your own car it's wise to pay someone to keep an eye on it, or leave it at the Longonot railway station.

MARSABIT NATIONAL PARK & RESERVE

The Marsabit National Park & Reserve is home to a wide variety of the larger mammals including lion, leopard, cheetah, elephant, rhino, buffalo, wart hog, Grevy's zebra, the reticulated giraffe, hyena, Grant's gazelle, oryx, dik-dik and greater kudu among others. Because the area is thickly forested, however, you won't see too much game unless you spend quite some time here and, preferably, camp at **Lake Paradise**. The lake, which occupies much of the crater floor of Gof Sokorte Guda, is appropriately named. It's an enchanting place and right out in the bush. Entry to the park, which is open from 6 am to 7.15 pm, costs US$15 per person (US$5 for students and children) plus KSh 200 for a vehicle (less than six seats) or KSh 500 (six to 12 seats).

The Survey of Kenya's map, *Marsabit*

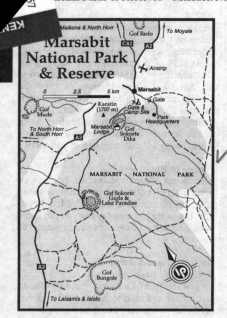

Marsabit National Park & Reserve

National Park & Reserve (SK 84) is worth buying if you are touring this park.

Places to Stay & Eat

Few camp sites in Kenya would rival the one at Lake Paradise. There are no facilities (except lake water and firewood) so bring everything with you. A ranger has to be present when you camp here so it costs more than an ordinary site (US$10 per person for non-residents or KSh 200 per person for residents and only one group at a time is allowed to camp here) but you can arrange all this at the park entrance gate. There's also another good camp site next to the entrance gate (water and plenty of firewood) but the so-called showers are a joke. You could die of thirst waiting for enough water to wet the back of your ears here. Camping at this site costs US$8 per person.

There's also the *Marsabit Lodge* (☎ (0183) 2044), a luxury safari lodge overlooking a lake in another gof, Sokorte Dika. This costs

US$94/120 for a single/double with full board in the high season with triples at US$140. In the low season, the full-board rates are US$54/70 for singles/doubles and KSh 80 for triples. Bookings should be made with Msafiri Inns (☎ (02) 229751; fax 227815) in Nairobi.

For information on getting there and away see the Marsabit section in the Northern Kenya chapter.

MASAI MARA NATIONAL RESERVE

The Mara (as it's often abbreviated to) is the most popular game park in Kenya. Virtually every person who visits Kenya goes to Masai Mara, and with good reason as this is the Kenyan section of the wildly evocative Serengeti Plains and the wildlife abounds. This is also traditionally the land of the Maasai, but these people have been displaced in favour of the animals.

The Mara is a 320-sq-km slab of open grassland dotted with the distinctive flat-topped acacia trees tucked away in the south-west corner of the country. It is watered by the tree-lined Mara River and its tributary the Talek River. The western border of the park is the spectacular Esoit Oloololo (Siria) Escarpment and it's at this edge of the park that the concentrations of game are the highest. It must also be said that it's the most difficult area of the park to get around in as the swampy ground becomes impassable after heavy rain. Conversely, the concentrations of tourist and minibuses are highest at the eastern end of the park around the Oloolaimutiek Gate and Talek Gate as it's these areas which are the most accessible by road from Nairobi.

Fauna

Wherever you go in the Mara, however, the one certain thing is that you'll see an astonishing amount of game, often in the one place at the one time. Of the big cats, lion are found in large prides everywhere and it's not at all uncommon to see them hunting. Cheetah and leopard are harder to spot but are still fairly common. Elephant, buffalo, zebra and hippo also exist in large numbers within the

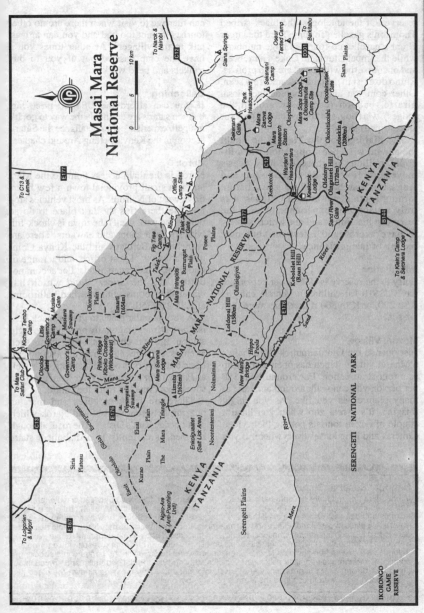

Masai Mara
National Reserve

KENYA

reserve. Of the antelopes, the black-striped Thomson's gazelle (Tommys) and the larger Grant's gazelle are found in huge numbers, while the impala, topi and Coke's hartebeest and of course the wildebeest are also profuse. Rhino do exist in the park but are rarely seen. Other common animals include the Masai giraffe, baboon (especially around the lodges), wart hog, spotted hyena and grey (or side-striped) jackal.

The highlight of the Mara is no doubt the annual wildebeest migration when literally millions of these ungainly beasts move north from the Serengeti in July and August in search of the lush grass, before turning south again around October. It is truly a staggering experience to be in the reserve at that time – and one which is likely to have a profound effect on your own feeling of insignificance.

Information

Entry to the reserve is US$27 per person per day (US$10 for children). Vehicle entry is KSh 200, or KSh 500 if there are more than six seats.

Maasai Village

Just outside the Oloolaimutiek Gate there's a Maasai village which has opened itself up as a tourist attraction. For around KSh 350 per person you can walk around and take as many pictures as you like. As you might imagine, it's a real zoo when you have a couple of dozen tourists poking their video cameras and long lenses everywhere. If you

can manage to visit when there are no other tourists it's not too bad and you can at least talk to the villagers. At other times you'll have the crap hassled out of you to buy trinkets and bead work.

Ballooning

If you can afford the US$360 price tag, balloon safaris are definitely the way to go. It's a superb experience. For details see the Safaris section in the Kenya Getting Around chapter.

Narok

Narok is the main access point to the Mara and is a small provincial town a few hours drive west of Nairobi. As most vehicles stop to refuel here (it's the last place to do so before the park itself) the town is chock-full with souvenir shops and hawkers. There are branches of Barclays and the Kenya Commercial banks, a post office, and a range of budget and mid-range hotels. For accommodation, try the *Spear Hotel* which has reasonable rooms with attached bathrooms at KSh 250/350.

A very popular place to grab a snack here is *Kim's Dishes* diagonally opposite the Agip station. It offers cheap fast-food items such as chips, sausages etc. There are also several basic but busy bars on the main street as well as *Pussy's Bar* across the river from the main street about one km from the centre.

There are frequent buses and matatus buzzing between Nairobi and Narok which park outside Kim's Dishes. The road, although bitumen, is currently in a diabolical state,

---

National Reserve Status

Masai Mara doesn't have national park status. The fundamental difference between a national park and a national reserve is that in a national reserve people (in this case the Maasai) can graze their animals and can also shoot animals if they are attacked. In a national park, however, the entire area is set aside exclusively for the wildlife and the natural environment. Where it also differs from a national park is that it is administered by the local council – in this case, Narok – rather than by Kenya Wildlife Services. Unfortunately the Narok council seems unwilling to reinvest in the park, despite the enormous revenues it receives from the gate takings. Consequently the tracks within the park are in a shocking condition, and there is very little policing of vehicles straying from the defined trails, and so you find minibuses driving over the grasslands at will, with informal tracks crisscrossing all over the place. If this situation is allowed to continue the Mara is going to become seriously degraded. ■

although in 1996 the contract was awarded for its resurfacing, so things should be better.

Places to Stay – bottom end

There is no budget accommodation within the reserve, so it's camp or pay high prices at the lodges and tented camps. It's possible to camp just outside the park at any of the gates for KSh 150 per person. There are no facilities but you can usually get water from the rangers.

The Maasai run the *Oloolaimutiek Campsite* between the gate of the same name and the Mara Sopa Lodge at the eastern extremity of the park. This place is very popular with the budget safari outfits and is usually pretty lively. For KSh 200 per person the Maasai provide firewood and an askari at night. The water supply here is very limited and if you need any water you'll have to buy it from the Maasai. The staff canteen of the nearby Mara Sopa Lodge is usually a lively place and you can get cheap meals and warm beer.

There are official camp sites within the reserve along the Talek River by the Talek Gate on the north-eastern border of the park, and just outside the reserve on the banks of the Mara River near the Oloololo Gate. The only problem with using these sites is that they are none too secure – baboons and thieves can both take their toll on your gear. The cost at the sites is a hefty US$15 per person.

Places to Stay – top end

The lodges and tented camps are all pitched at the top end of the market and should all be booked in advance. There's been a wild proliferation of these places over the years, and you now have the choice of a dozen or more.

Prices for accommodation with full board vary between about US$50 and US$250 per person per night. The lodges generally consist of separate bandas with their own bathrooms, while the tented camps are often almost identical, the difference being that the 'rooms' have canvas walls protected from the elements by an open-sided makuti-roofed structure. It's certainly stretching things to call them tents but it seems to satisfy the desire for a token of authenticity among those with money to burn.

The *Mara Sopa Lodge* (☎ (02) 336088) by Oloolaimutiek Gate is a fairly modern place and has a commanding view. It's been attractively designed and built. The rates for singles/doubles with full board are US$78/120 in the low season, rising to US$162/216 in the high season.

The *Keekorok Lodge* is one of the Block Hotels (☎ (02) 540780; fax 543810) and is an older but well-maintained lodge on a grassy plain. Singles/doubles with full board cost US$47/94 in the low season, US$119/183 in the high season. Keekorok is one of the two lodges which operates balloon flights.

The *Mara Sarova Lodge* is part of the Sarova Hotels chain (☎ (02) 333248; fax 211472) and is not far from the Sekenani Gate and has the works, including a swimming pool. The room rates here with full board are US$55/110 a single/double in the low season, US$150/185 in the high season.

Along the northern banks of the Talek River are the *Fig Tree Camp* (☎ (02) 221439; fax 332170), and the *Mara Intrepids Club* (☎ (02) 338084; fax 217278). The Fig Tree Camp is attractively designed, has a swimming pool, and is approached across a wooden bridge from the car park on the opposite bank. It's a tented camp and has singles/doubles for US$125/170 with full board in the high season, US$50/100 in the low season. This is the other lodge from which you can take a balloon safari. It's wise to book them in advance at the Nairobi office though you can also do this at the camp. Game drives are available for US$35, game walks cost US$15, or you can take a horse safari for US$30. The Mara Intrepids Club has 30 tents and is considerably more expensive at US$223/304 for singles/doubles with full board but the price does include game drives. Low season prices of US$100/160 are a relative bargain. The views over the river from the bar are excellent, as are the sunset views over the plains.

In the centre of the reserve is the *Mara Serena Lodge* (☎ (02) 711077; fax 718103; e-mail 62578620@eln.attmail.com) on a site overlooking the Mara River. It blends in beautifully with the surrounding countryside and was built to resemble a modern Maasai village. Singles/doubles with full board cost US$120/160, dropping to US$50/100 in the low season.

More expensive again is the *Mara Safari Club* (☎ (02) 216940; fax 216796), part of the Lonrho chain of hotels. It is actually outside the reserve, so you don't pay the high park entry fees for just staying here. The camp is built on a bend in the Mara River, and the main building is cantilevered right out over the bank. Singles/doubles with full board cost US$275/372 in the high season and US$198/263 in the low season, and all prices include three game drives per day.

In the northern section of the park is another group of tented camps including the *Governor's Camp* (☎ (02) 331871; fax 726427) and *Little Governor's Camp* (owned by the same people). These are both beautiful little places where service is very personalised and excellent. Singles/doubles with full board plus game drives at either place costs US$260/390.

In this same area, and just outside the northern boundary, is the *Kichwa Tembo Camp* (☎ (02) 750298; fax 746826), which has spectacular savanna views. Rates are US$140/190 in the high season, dropping to US$60/120 in the low season.

Other accommodation outside the park north of Oloololo Gate includes the *Mara River Camp* (☎ (02) 331191) at US$60/104 in the low season, US$125/175 in the high season, including game drives and walks.

About 15 km from Sekenani Gate is another tented lodge, *Siana Springs* (☎ (02) 750298; fax 746826). The 'cottages' are dotted around a beautiful green clearing with shady trees, sweeping lawns and flowers. There's an open bar and dining room and a roaring log fire at night. Although it's not actually in the reserve there's a lot of game around the camp itself. There is a baited hide nearby and you have a good chance of seeing leopards. Dawn walks and night-time spotlight game drives are also organised from the

camp. The cost is US$140/190 in the low season, rising to US$205/280.

Also on the north-eastern boundary of the reserve is the *Sekenani Camp* (☎ (02) 333285; fax 228875). This is a small place, with just 15 tents, and is well placed to make the most of the views. The cost is US$58/116 in the low season, and US$167/225 in the high season, for full board including game drives.

The *Oseur Tented Camp* (☎ (02) 545648; fax 545649) is another in this area, and costs US$120/170 in the low season, rising to US$196/280 in the high season.

Even if you can't afford to stay in one of these camps, they are usually great places to drop in for a cleansing ale and perhaps a snack although, not surprisingly, prices are relatively high.

The Mara Sarova Camp, Keekorok Lodge and Mara Serena Lodge all sell petrol and will usually part with it to non-guests, though prices are higher than in Narok or Nairobi.

Getting There & Away

Air Air Kenya Aviation has twice-daily flights between Nairobi's Wilson airport and Masai Mara, departing from Nairobi at 10 am and 3 pm, and from the Mara at 11 am and 4 pm. The one-way fare is US$87, but if you are not on a package and being met by your hosts, to these you have to add the cost of chartering a vehicle in the park to collect you from the airstrip.

Car & 4WD The Mara is not a place you come to without transport. There is no public transport to or within the park, and even if there was there's certainly no way you could do a game drive in a matatu. If you are patient and persistent you should be able to hitch a ride with other tourists, in the high season at least, but get yourself to Narok first.

From Narok onwards the bitumen runs out and public transport dries up. It's almost 100 km from here to any of the park gates.

It's also possible to approach the reserve from Kisii and the west along reasonably well-maintained dirt roads. You can get closer to the park by public transport but there are far fewer tourist vehicles to hitch a ride with. Matatus run as far as Kilgoris directly south of Kisii, or Suna on the main A1 route close to Isebania on the Tanzanian border.

MERU NATIONAL PARK

On the lowland plains east of the town of Meru, the Meru National Park is a complete contrast to the more northerly reserves of Samburu, Buffalo Springs and Shaba where open bush is the norm. In Meru, abundant rainfall and numerous permanent streams flowing down from the Mt Kenya massif support a luxuriant jungle of forest, swamp and tall grasses which, in turn, provide fodder and shelter to a wide variety of herbivores and their predators. As in other parks, such as Marsabit, where the vegetation is dense, the wildlife is not so easily sighted so you need to spend a few days here if you're to fully appreciate what the park has to offer.

Unfortunately this area was one of the worst hit by poachers and shifta, and so there is not the abundance of wildlife that you find in other parks. With some difficulty, elephant, lion and cheetah can all be seen. Buffalo and giraffe are more common, and eland and oryx are the main antelope to be seen. Monkeys, crocodiles and a plethora of bird species are common in the dense vegetation alongside the watercourses.

Meru National Park was also the home of Kenya's only herd of white rhinos which were imported from the Umfolozi Game Reserve in South Africa. Jealously guarded 24 hours a day by rangers to protect them from poachers, these huge animals were quite unlike their more cantankerous cousins, the black rhino, in being remarkably docile and willing to allow their keepers to herd them around the camp sites and park headquarters area during the day and pen them up at night. Sadly, that's all gone now. Heavily armed poachers shot the lot of them and, for good measure, killed their keepers too.

The park is also famous for being Joy and George Adamson's former base where they raised orphaned lion and leopard cubs until they were old enough to be returned to the wild. Both paid for their efforts with their lives – Joy many years ago when she was murdered in Meru park by poachers, and George in 1989 when he too met the same fate along with two of his assistants in the nearby Kora National Reserve.

Security in the park has been beefed up since George Adamson was murdered but there is still a small risk of encountering poachers and bandits here so you need to bear this in mind, especially if you're driving your own vehicle. It's true to say, however, that the chances of running into bandits is just as great in Masai Mara or Tsavo as it is in Meru. The one major plus about Meru National Park is that you're unlikely to come across another safari vehicle anywhere in the park except at the lodges.

The tracks through the park are well maintained and signposted though it's a good idea to have a copy of the Survey of Kenya's *Meru National Park* map with you.

Entry to the park costs US$20 (US$10 for students and US$5 for children) plus KSh 150 for a vehicle (less than six seats) and KSh 500 (six to 10 seats). Camping is the standard US$80.

Places to Stay

There are several public camp sites in the park, but the one at junction 12 is the only one operating. There's running water and an askari in attendance.

The only functioning lodge is the *Meru Mulika Lodge* (☎ (0164) 20000) which has all the usual facilities of a luxury lodge including a swimming pool and where singles/doubles with full board cost US$94/120 with triples at US$140, except from 1 April to 30 June when it drops to US$54/70 with triples at US$80. Bookings should be made through Msafiri Inns (☎ (02) 229751; fax 227815) in Nairobi.

Getting There & Away

Getting to Meru National Park by public transport is a problem. There are no buses or matatus which will take you either to the lodges or the camp sites and park headquarters. Likewise, attempting to hitchhike is basically a waste of time as so few vehicles

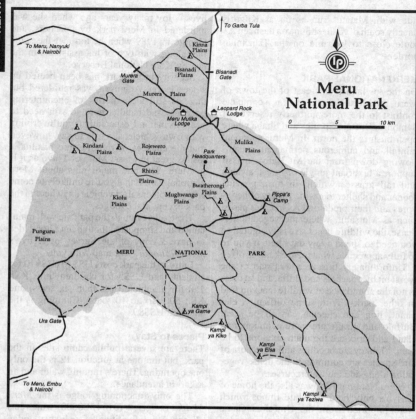

Meru National Park

To Garba Tula

Kinna Plains

To Meru, Nanyuki & Nairobi

Bisanadi Plains

Bisanadi Gate

Murera Gate

Murera Plains

Meru Mulika Lodge

Leopard Rock Lodge

Kindani Plains

Rojewero Plains

Park Headquarters

Mulika Plains

Rhino Plains

Bwatherongi Plains

Kiolu Plains

Mughwango Plains

Pippa's Camp

Punguru Plains

MERU   NATIONAL   PARK

Ura Gate

Kampi ya Game

Kampi ya Kiko

Kampi ya Elsa

To Meru, Embu & Nairobi

Kampi ya Teziwa

0   5   10 km

come into the park and those that do are mainly tour groups so they won't pick you up. Quite a few safari companies include Meru National Park on their itineraries but they are all liable to cancel visits at short notice if there has been any trouble with shiftas in the park.

MT ELGON NATIONAL PARK

Mt Elgon sits astride the Kenya-Uganda border and, while it offers similar trekking possibilities to Mt Kenya, its location makes it a far less popular goal. The lower altitude also means that conditions are not so cold,

although rain can be more frequent here than on Mt Kenya.

The mountain is an extinct volcano and the national park extends from the lower slopes right up to the border. The highest peak is Wagagai (4321m) which is actually on the far side of the crater in Uganda. The highest peak on the Kenyan side is Koitoboss. The Mt Elgon range is the fourth-highest in East Africa after Mt Kilimanjaro Mt Kenya and the Ruwenzoris. There are warm springs in the crater itself, the floor of which is around 3500m above sea level.

The mountain's biggest attraction is the

The African elephant is the world's largest living land mammal.

elephants, renowned the world over for their predilection for salt, the major source of which is in the caves on the mountain slopes. The elephants are such keen excavators that some have gone so far as to claim that the elephants are totally responsible for the caves! Sadly, the numbers of these saline-loving creatures has declined over the years, mainly due to incursions by poachers from the Ugandan side. There are three caves open to visitors – Kitum, Chepnyali and Mackingeny. Kitum is the one which you are most likely to see elephants in, while Mackingeny is the most spectacular. Obviously a good torch (flashlight) is essential if you want to explore the caves.

Kitum Cave has been associated with the fatal Ebola virus, following the deaths of two people who visited the cave. However, other people have safely visited the cave since. Research about Ebola is inconclusive, but there may be some risk of contracting it in Kitum Cave so the cave is probably best avoided at this point.

A less obvious attraction is the range of vegetation found on the mountain. Starting with rainforest at the base, the vegetation changes as you ascend to bamboo jungle and finally alpine moorland with the bizarre giant groundsel and giant lobelia plants. The lower forests are the habitat of the impressive black-and-white colobus monkey along with many other species of birds and animals. Those most commonly sighted include buffalo, bushbuck, giant forest hog and Sykes monkey.

Elgon can be a wet place at any time of the year, but the driest months seem to be December, January and February. As well as waterproof gear you are going to need warm clothes as it gets cold up here at night.

Access to the 170-sq-km national park is now permitted without a vehicle. Entry costs US$10 per person per day. A ranger will escort you to the camp site (which is one km inside the park) and on any walks you may want to do on the lower forested slopes – such as to the caves – for which a small fee may be payable.

Walks

If you want to walk on the mountains, the most popular route is from **Kimilili**, a small village 36 km south of Kitale on the main A1 road to Webuye and Kisumu. There's basic accommodation here, and matatus run the 12 km to **Kapsakwany**, from where it's a five km walk to Kaberua Forest Station. There's a Department of Forestry office and a Kenya Wildlife Services office at Kaberua. From there it's a further 20 km to the now abandoned Chepkitale Forest Station, and another seven km past this station to a tumbledown mountain hut. You will need a tent and all your own gear for camping.

At the time of writing, the Kimili route was closed to hikers and trekkers, due to an outbreak of cross-border cattle-rustling and general banditry in the area. It was also because the Mt Elgon park authorities are trying to encourage hikers inside the park, rather than outside it. This is expected to change in 1997 and hikers should be allowed in again. For the latest situation phone the Kenyan Wildlife Services headquarters in Nairobi or Mt Elgon National Park (ask for the assistant warden, or chief tourism officer).

From the hut it takes around four hours to reach the lake known as Lower Elgon Tarn, and from here it's a further one-hour walk up a faintly marked trail (occasional cairns and white blazes) to Lower Elgon peak.

The pass at the foot of Koitoboss peak and the **Suam hot springs** are several hours of tough walking around the crater rim to the right (north-east) and once here you are in the national park. The options are to return the same way, or via the third route, known as the Masara route, which goes to the small village of **Masara** on the northern slopes of the mountain, a trek of about 25 km.

As park authorities are now trying to promote walks, hikes and treks in the park, those without vehicles may be allowed to trek from the park entrance, Chorlim Gate, to Koitoboss Peak (requiring one or two overnight camps on the way), or may even be able to arrange a lift part way in a park patrol vehicle.

Places to Stay

There are no lodges in the park itself but there is a beautiful camp site with good facilities close to the Chorlim Gate which you'll be allowed to walk to. You will need to bring all your own food, camping and cooking equipment with you as there's none for hire and there is only one small shop (called the canteen) which sells beer and a few basics for the park staff and their familes.

About one km before the Chorlim Gate is the *Mt Elgon Lodge* (PO Box 7 Enderbess, Kitale), one of the Msafiri Inns chain of hotels (☎ (02) 330820; fax 227815). Comfortable rooms with full board cost KSh 2750/4250 a single/double. The hotel has a bar and restaurant.

Getting There & Away

To get to the village of Enderbess (the nearest place to Mt Elgon National Park), there are normal matatus for KSh 40 or Nissan matatus for KSh 60 from Kitale. Part of this road is good tarmac but there are also some horrific sections with huge potholes. The turn-off for Mt Elgon National Park (Chorlim Gate) is several km before Enderbess on the left-hand side (clearly signposted). If you're hitching, you'll need to get to the turn-off but it's still a long way into the park from there and

there's very little transport. Rangers' vehicles and support trucks do come along the road at least once a day but you could be waiting half the day. Although the road into the park is a good gravel road, in the wet season the only way in is to have your own 4WD.

MT KENYA NATIONAL PARK

Although a distinctly separate massif from the Aberdares, Mt Kenya also forms part of the central highlands. Africa's second-highest mountain at 5199m, its gleaming and eroded snow-covered peaks can be seen for miles until the late-morning clouds obscure the view. Its lower slopes, like those of the Aberdares, are intensively cultivated by the Kikuyu and the closely related Embu and Meru peoples, along with the descendants of the white settlers who grow mainly wheat on the grassy and largely treeless plains on the northern side.

So vast is this mountain that it's not hard to understand why the Kikuyu deified it, why their houses are built with the doors facing the peak and why it was probably never scaled until the arrival of European explorers. It's the seat of *Ghai*, the Kikuyu god. And Ghai is still very much alive despite the fact that it's every traveller's dream to get to the top and take home with them a memory which money cannot buy. You *must* climb to the top of this mountain. It's a superb experience. But take it steady otherwise Ghai will teach you a lesson.

Mt Kenya's highest peaks, Batian and Nelion, can only be reached by mountaineers with technical skills. However, Point Lenana, the third-highest peak, can be reached by trekkers and this is the usual goal for most people. As you might imagine, there are superb views over the surrounding country from Point Lenana and other high points around the main peaks, though the summit is often clothed in mist from late morning until late afternoon.

Safety

It's not surprising that trekking on this mountain is high on many travellers' priority list. However, because Mt Kenya is so easy to

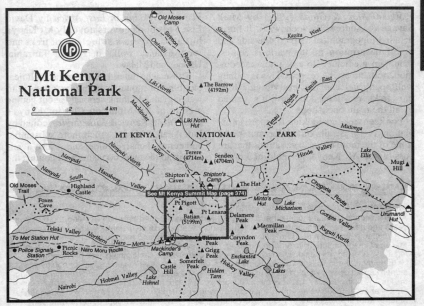

Mt Kenya National Park

0   2   4 km

MT KENYA   NATIONAL   PARK

Old Moses Camp
Sirimon
Kazita West
Ontulili
Liki North
Mackinder
The Barrow (4192m)
Liki North Hut
Timau Route
Kazita East
Mutonga
Namyuki
Namyuki North
Valley
Terere (4714m)
Sendeo (4704m)
Hinde Valley
Lake Ellis
Mugi Hill
Namyuki South
Hausberg Valley
Shipton's Caves
Shipton's Camp
The Hat
Chogoria Route
Old Moses Trail
Highland Castle
See Mt Kenya Summit Map (page 374)
Pt Pigott
Minto's Hut
Lake Michaelson
Gorges Valley
Urumandi Hut
Foxes Cave
Teleki Valley
Northern Naro – Moru
Batian (5199m)
Pt Lenana
Delamere Peak
Macmillan Peak
Ruguti North
To Met Station Hut
Tilman Peak
Corydon Peak
Police Signals Station
Picnic Rocks
Naro Moru Route
Mackinder's Camp
Grigg Peak
Enchanted Lake
Carr Lakes
Castle Hill
Somerfelt Peak
Hidden Tarn
Hobley Valley
Hohnel Valley
Lake Hohnel
Nairobi

reach, and because Point Lenana is not technically difficult, this can create its own set of problems. Many people do the ascent much too quickly and end up suffering from headaches, nausea and other (sometimes more serious) effects of altitude sickness (see the Health section in the regional Facts for the Visitor chapter for more details). Another problem can be the weather; even though they end up seeing the glaciers on the summits, many visitors go up the mountain without proper gear and completely unprepared for the cold and wet conditions often encountered.

This situation is made worse by some tour companies (and some guidebooks) billing the trek to Point Lenana as an easy hike. It's not unknown for ill-prepared independent trekkers to get hopelessly lost on Mt Kenya, sometimes with fatal results. Most years there are reports of people simply disappearing on the mountain.

So, when planning your trek up Mt Kenya,

it is important to realise that this is no small mountain: Point Lenana is just under 5000m – not much lower than the Everest Base Camp in Nepal. If you spend at least three nights on the ascent before going to the summit of Lenana, you stand a much better chance of enjoying yourself, and with proper clothes and equipment, you stand a much better chance of surviving too.

If you're not a regular mountain walker, and don't know how to use a map and compass, going up and down anything other than the Naro Moru or Sirimon routes, without a competent companion or a local guide, is simply asking for trouble. A guide is not compulsory but a very good idea.

The best times to go, as far as fair weather is concerned, is from mid-January to late February or from late August to September.

Books & Maps

Before you leave Nairobi we strongly recommend that you buy a copy of *Mt Kenya*

1:50,000 Map & Guide (1993) by Mark Savage & Andrew Wielochowski. It has a detailed topographical map on one side and a full description of the various routes, mountain medicine, flora & fauna, accommodation, etc on the reverse. This is money well spent and contains everything which most trekkers will need to know. It's stocked by all the main bookshops.

For keen trekkers looking for more information, or for details on wilder routes and some of the more esoteric variations that are possible on Mt Kenya, get hold of Lonely Planet's *Trekking in East Africa* by David Else. This book covers not only Mt Kenya but also covers a selection of treks and long-distance walks in Kenya, Tanzania, Uganda and Malawi.

Those who intend to do some technical climbing or mountaineering (as opposed to walking) should think seriously about getting a copy of the Mountain Club of Kenya's *Guide to Mt Kenya & Kilimanjaro*, edited by Iain Allan. This is a much more substantial and comprehensive guide, and is also available in all the main bookshops, or contact the

Mt Kenya – Geology, Flora & Fauna

Africa's second-highest mountain at 5199m, Mt Kenya was formed between 2½ and three million years ago as a result of successive eruptions of the volcano. Its base diameter is about 120 km, and it is probable that when first formed it was over 6000m in height and had a summit crater much like that on Kilimanjaro. Intensive erosion, however, principally by glacial ice, has worn away the cone and left a series of jagged peaks, U-shaped valleys and depressions containing glacial lakes, or tarns.

In many of these valleys you will come across terminal moraines (curved ridges of boulders and stones carried down by the glaciers) whose position – some as low as 3000m – indicates that during the Ice Ages the glaciers must have been far more extensive than they are today. They began retreating rapidly about 150,000 years ago as the climate changed and the process is still going on today. Since records were first kept back in 1893, seven of the glaciers have already disappeared leaving only the current 11, yet even these are getting quite thin. It's estimated that if the present trend continues, there might be no permanent ice left on the mountain in 25 years.

The volcanic soil and the many rivers which radiate out from the central cone have created a very fertile environment, especially on the southern and eastern sides which receive the most rain. Human agricultural activity currently extends up to around 1900m in what used to be rainforest, yet which today is still well wooded in many parts. Above this zone – except where logging takes place – stretches the untouched rainforest, characterised by an abundance of different species, particularly the giant camphors, along with vines, ferns, orchids and other epiphytes. This forest zone is not quite so dense on the northern and eastern sides, since the climate here is drier and the predominant tree species are conifers. Vines, likewise, are absent here.

The forest supports a rich variety of wildlife and it's quite common to come across elephant, buffalo and various species of monkey on the forest tracks. Rhino, numerous varieties of antelope, giant forest hog, and lion also live here but are usually only seen in the clearings around lodges.

On the southern and western slopes the forest gradually merges into a belt of dense bamboo which often grows to 12m or more. This eventually gives way to more open woodland consisting of hagena and hypericum trees along with an undergrowth of flowering shrubs and herbs.

Further up still is a belt of giant heather which forms dense clumps up to four metres high interspersed with tall grasses. Open moorland forms the next zone and can often be very colourful because of the profusion of small flowering plants which thrive there. The only large plants to be found in this region – and then only in the drier, sandier parts such as the valley sides and the ridges – are those bizarre specimens of the plant kingdom, the giant lobelias and senecios. This moorland zone stretches right up to the snow line at between 4500m and 4700m though the vegetation gets more and more sparse the higher you go. Beyond the snow line, the only plants you will find are mosses and lichens.

The open woodland and moorland support various species of antelope, such as the duiker and eland, as well as zebra, but the most common mammal is the rock hyrax. Leopard also live in this region and have occasionally been observed as high as 4500m! The larger birds you'll undoubtedly see up here include the verreaux eagle (which preys on hyrax), auger buzzard and the lammergeier (or bearded vulture). Smaller birds include the scarlet-tufted malachite sunbird, which feeds on nectar and small flies, and the friendly cliff chat which often appears in search of scraps. ■

Mountain Club of Kenya, PO Box 45741, Nairobi.

Clothing & Equipment

The summits of Mt Kenya are covered in glaciers and snow, and the temperature at night often drops to below -10°C so you are going to need a good sleeping bag. A closed-cell foam mat is also advisable if you are going to sleep on the ground as it provides the necessary insulation under your body and is far more comfortable than sleeping without one. A good set of warm clothes is equally important and that should include some sort of headgear and gloves. As it can rain at any time of year – and heavily – you will also need waterproof clothing. A decent pair of boots is an advantage but not strictly necessary. A pair of joggers is quite adequate most of the time though it's a good idea to have a pair of thongs, sandals or canvas tennis shoes to wear in the evening if your main shoes get wet. The one thing you will be very glad you brought with you is a pair of sunglasses. When the sun hits those snow-beds and glaciers on the summits, your eyes will hurt unless they're protected.

Remember that it's not a good idea to sleep in clothes which you have worn during the day because the sweat which your day clothes absorb from your skin keep them moist at night and therefore reduce their heat-retention capabilities.

If you don't intend to stay in the huts along the way you'll need a tent and associated equipment.

Unless you intend to eat only canned and dried food along the way (not recommended) then you'll also need a stove, basic cooking equipment and eating utensils and a water container with a capacity of at least two litres per person as well as water-purifying tablets for use on the lower levels of the mountain. Stove fuel in the form of petrol and kerosene (paraffin) is fairly easily found in towns, and methylated spirits is available in Nairobi, as are gas cartridges although the supply of these is not guaranteed. Except in an emergency, using wood gathered from the vicinity of camp sites to light open fires is prohibited within the confines of the national park and for good reason. In any case, there's no wood available once you get beyond the tree line. If you intend to engage porters then you'll also have to supply each of them with a rucksack to carry your gear and theirs.

Equipment Hire All the gear you need for the trek can be hired in Nairobi at Atul's (☎ (02) 225935), Biashara St, PO Box 43202, which is open Monday to Friday from 9 am to noon and 2 to 5 pm and on Saturday from 9 am to noon and 2.30 to 4 pm or from the Natural Action Mountain Centre (☎ (02) 740214), PO Box 12516. Atul's also sells some second-hand and locally made trekking and camping equipment. Examples of the sort of daily hire charges and deposits which you'll have to pay at Atul's are indicated on the equipment hire table.

These rates apply for the first 10 days of hire; longer term rentals are quite a bit cheaper. Rates at the Naro Moru River Lodge are consistently higher than those at Atul's.

Natural Action claims to be the only specialist outdoor shop on the African continent

Equipment Hire Price List

Item	Hire Cost (KSh)	Deposit (KSh)
sleeping bag	70 to 220	1300 to 3000
air mattress	80 to 150	600 to 1200
air-mattress pump	40	800
dome tent		
(two-person)	320 to 620	3000 to 4000
(three-person)	420	4000 to 5000
gas stove	110 to 170	1000 to 2000
kerosene stove	75	600
water container		
(one litre)	10	40
(10 litre)	25	60
mess kit	10	300
cooking pot	15 to 60	120 to 500
gas lamp	100 to 160	2000
kerosene lamp	30	400
rucksack	150 to 300	2000 to 4000
woollen socks	40	300
woollen gloves	40	300
rain poncho	70	800
rain pants	60	800
climbing boots	90	1000

(outside South Africa) and also has a good range of equipment. The guys who run the shop are off-duty guides from Mt Kenya and are helpful with information and advice. Advance booking of gear (from Atul's) is a good idea if you want to be absolutely sure, but is not normally necessary except in the case of boots – an ill-fitting pair will make the trip a misery.

Rental gear is also available at the Naro Moru River Lodge (☎ (0176) 22018), PO Box 18, Naro Moru, and is mostly in good condition and well maintained, although it cannot be booked in advance. Both places carry plenty of stock. The Mountain Rock Hotel near Naro Moru also has equipment for hire, but the range is less extensive.

Food

In an attempt to cut down on baggage, quite a few people forgo taking a stove and cooking equipment and exist entirely on canned and dried foods. You can certainly do it so long as you keep up your fluid intake but it's not a good idea. That cup of hot soup in the evening and pot of tea or coffee in the morning can make all the difference between enjoying the trek and hating it or, at least, feeling irritable.

There are, however, a few things to bear in mind about cooking at high altitudes. The major consideration is that the boiling point of water is considerably reduced. At 4500m, for example, water boils at 85°C. This is too low to sufficiently cook rice or lentils (pasta is better) and you won't be able to brew a good cup of tea from it either (instant coffee is the answer). Cooking times are also considerably increased as a result (with consequent increased use of fuel).

The best range of suitable foods for the mountain is, of course, to be found in the supermarkets of Nairobi. If you're going straight to the mountain from Nairobi by bus or share-taxi, it's no problem to bring all your supplies from there. The best supermarkets in Nairobi are the Nakumatt and Uchumi chains.

Otherwise there's a good range of food in the towns around the mountain (Nyeri, Nanyuki, Embu and Meru) although precious little at Naro Moru. Remember when you're buying dehydrated foods to buy the pre-cooked variety to cut down on cooking time – two-minute noodles are the answer here. Fresh fruit and vegetables are available in all reasonably sized towns and villages.

Take plenty of citrus fruits and/or citrus drinks with you as well as chocolate, sweets or dried fruit to keep your blood sugar levels high on the trek.

One last thing – and this is important to avoid severe headaches caused by dehydration – is to drink at least three litres of fluid per day. It may also help to avoid altitude sickness.

Park Fees

Entry fees to the national park are US$10 per day (US$5 if you have an international student card, and US$5 for children). If you take a guide and/or porters then you'll have to pay their entry fees too, and these are KSh 150 per person per night. Camping fees are an additional US$8 per person.

Guides, Cooks & Porters

The charges for guides, porters and cooks vary according to the route taken but as a general guide assume KSh 450 per day for a senior guide, KSh 300 for an ordinary guide, KSh 350 per day for a cook and KSh 250 per day for a porter excluding all park entry fees (KSh 150 per person per day) and tips at the end of the trek. If you assume KSh 500 per trip for guides and cooks and KSh 250 per trip for porters as a tip you won't be too far off the mark.

Porters will carry up to 18 kg for a three-day trip or 16 kg for a longer trip, excluding the weight of their own food and equipment. If you want them to carry more then you'll have to negotiate a price for the extra weight. A normal day's work is regarded as one stage of the journey – from the Met Station to Mackinder's Camp on the Naro Moru route or from the Chogoria road head to Minto's Hut on the Chogoria route, for example. If you want to go further than this then you'll have to pay them two days wages even if they don't do anything the following day.

One important thing you must remember regarding guides and porters is that, if you ascend the mountain along one route and descend along a different one, you will be responsible for arranging and paying for their transport back to where they started from. It would be a good idea to sort this out before you set off and agree on a price for return transport plus any additional wages, food and hotel costs along the way. If, for instance, you ascend via the Naro Moru or Sirimon routes and descend via the Chogoria route then, depending on what time you arrive in Chogoria village, the guide and porters may have to stay the night at a hotel before returning and they'll be entitled to another day's wages as well.

Guides, porters and cooks can be engaged at the Naro Moru River Lodge, the Mountain Rock Lodge, the Mt Kenya Hostel and the Mountain Stop Motel on the northern side of the mountain. You can also find them at the Naro Moru entry gate but this isn't as reliable so it's better to contact the Naro Moru Porters & Guides Association (☎ (0176) 6205), PO Naro Moru, in advance.

On the southern side they can be booked through one of the hotels in Chogoria village or at the Chogoria Forest Station or in advance through Mr Nabae, PO Box 449, Chogoria. If you book through Mr Nabae there's a booking fee of KSh 40 for each guide, cook or porter. You can also book them at the Meru Mt Kenya Lodge but, in this case, you'll have to pay for them to be transported to the lodge (KSh 1500) or the road head (KSh 1750). Don't assume you can engage guides and porters at the Chogoria Gate. You might be lucky but you might not. Better still, contact the Chogoria Porters (☎ 88 in Chogoria), PO Box 96, Chogoria, who are based at the Transit Hotel in the village.

Everyone likes to think they're super-fit and capable of scaling this mountain without a worry. If you are – no problem. Most people are not and even fewer are acclimatised to heights of 4000m and more. Even British Army squaddies sometimes have to be rescued on account of altitude sickness and it's unlikely your training regime matches theirs. That being so, think seriously about whether you want to enjoy this climb or flunk out on the last leg to the summit. Having someone carry your heavy gear up this mountain is like the difference between a matatu and a Mercedes Benz. The difference in enjoyment is immeasurable. In other words, think seriously about taking on a guide and porters. It will enhance your appreciation of this mountain a hundred fold and at the wages (and even tips) which they charge, it's a bargain.

Accommodation

There are quite a lot of huts on the mountain but not all of them are available to the general public. Several are owned by the Mountain Club of Kenya (MCK). A few of these huts are reserved exclusively for use by members, others can be used by the public, although these are all basic and most are in very bad condition.

There are also some larger bunkhouses with more facilities on the mountain. These are owned by lodges outside the park and are mainly for people going on treks organised by these lodges, but they can also be used by independent trekkers. Beds in the large bunkhouses have to be booked and paid for, but there is no reservation system.

On the Naro Moru route, the bunkhouses are at the meteorological station (always called the Met Station), and Teleki Lodge (more usually called Mackinder's Camp), and both can be booked through the Naro Moru River Lodge, or Let's Go Travel in Nairobi. The Met Station costs US$8 per bed and Mackinder's costs US$11 per bed.

On the Sirimon route, the bunkhouses are at Old Moses Camp and Shipton's Camp, and both can be booked through the Mountain Rock Hotel. They cost US$8 and US$9, respectively, if you pay at the Mountain Rock but otherwise KSh 600 and KSh 800 if you pay on arrival. Make sure you get a receipt otherwise, when you leave the park, the rangers will assume you've been camping and will charge you US$8 per night.

On the Chogoria route, there are 12 comfortable bandas at the *Meru Mt Kenya Lodge*, near the park gate, each containing a lounge/dining area with fireplace, bedroom with two single beds and a small extra bed, and a bathroom with shower (hot water) and toilet. Electricity (at an additional charge) is provided by generator in the evenings until 11 pm and in the early mornings. Cooking is on single ring electric cookers and primus stoves. All crockery, cutlery, cooking utensils and bed linen are provided. There's also a central lounge/dining area with a kitchen and toilets. The bandas cost KSh 625 per person per day (KSh 105 for children between the ages of two and 15 years). Electricity costs KSh 10 per day. Reservations are not always necessary but probably best and can be made through Let's Go Travel (☎ (02) 340331) in Nairobi.

The small MCK huts can be booked and paid for in Nairobi at the MCK clubhouse, at Let's Go Travel or at the Naro Moru River Lodge. They cost around US$3, but are generally in such bad condition that very few trekkers use them. If you are going independently and not planning to use the bunkhouses, it's much better to camp than to use these MCK huts.

You don't have to worry about any of these hut bookings if you're going on an organised climb because all this will be taken care of.

Officially you can camp anywhere on the mountain but it is usual to camp near one of the huts or bunkhouses as there is often a water supply nearby.

Getting to the Trekking Routes

There are at least seven different routes up the mountain, but only the three main routes are covered here – Naro Moru, Sirimon and Chogoria. The other routes are much harder to follow and there's a real chance you can get lost without decent maps and the ability to read them, and if you have no experience with a compass.

If you intend to do the trek independently then public transport (bus or matatu) along the Mt Kenya ring road is the first step towards getting to the mountain. For the Naro Moru route it's Naro Moru village where there's a prominent signpost on the right-hand side just outside the village on the way to Nanyuki. For the Sirimon route, first go to Nanyuki and then take another matatu about 13 km up the main road towards Isiolo where the route is signposted off to the right. For the Chogoria route all matatus and buses between Embu and Meru stop at Chogoria village, just off the main road. From where the buses or matatus drop you it's quite a walk to any of the park entry gates but it's possible to find private (though relatively expensive) transport from the main roads to the park entry gates. See the individual routes for details.

If you have your own transport, you can get up to the Naro Moru and Sirimon national park entry gates in 2WD but you will not get up to the Chogoria park entry gate in anything other than 4WD. Likewise, you'll probably make it up to the road head (Old Moses Camp) on the Sirimon route in 2WD but you certainly won't make it up to the Met Station on the Naro Moru route or the road head on the Chogoria route in 2WD. There are times, too, when you won't even make it to the Met Station or the park entry gate on the Chogoria route in a small Suzuki 4WD after rain. The road from Chogoria village to the park entry gate is diabolical and the top section of the 'road' through the bamboo forest is totally impassable in wet weather even for 4WDs fitted with snow chains.

Mt Kenya Routes

The normal weather pattern is for clear mornings with the mist closing in from 10 am, though this sometimes clears again in the early evening. This means that if you want to make the most of the trek you should set off early every morning and, for the final assault on Point Lenana (the highest point that can be reached by trekkers), you need to make an early start if you want to see the sunrise from the top.

Naro Moru Route

This is the most straightforward and popular of the routes. It's also the least scenic, although it's still a spectacular and very enjoyable trail. You should allow a minimum of four days for the trek up and down this route, or three if you have transport between Naro Moru and the meteorological station, although doing it this quickly if you're not acclimatised is asking for altitude sickness.

Naro Moru to the Met Station Your starting point here is the village of Naro Moru. The first part of the route takes you along a relatively good gravel road through farmlands for some 12 km (all the junctions are signposted) to the start of the forest where there's a wooden bridge across a small river. A further five km brings you to the park entry gate at 2400m. Having paid your fees, you continue on another eight km to the road head and Met Station Hut (3000m) where you stay for the night.

If your time is limited you can cut out this part of the trek by taking the Naro Moru River Lodge's Land Rover or the Mt Kenya Hostel's 4WD all the way to the meteorological station but remember that this is an expensive way of getting there unless you're sharing the cost with a full complement of other climbers. Hitching is also possible but the chances of a lift *up* the mountain are limited – it's easier to get a ride on the way down.

Met Station to Mackinder's Camp On the second day you set off up the Teleki Valley along a well-marked path past the police signals station and up to the edge of the forest at around 3200m. From here you scale the so-called Vertical Bog and up onto a ridge from where you can see Mackinder's Camp. The route divides into two here and you have the choice of taking the higher path, which gives the best views but is often wet, or the lower path which crosses the Naro Moru River and continues gently up to Mackinder's Camp (4160m). This part of the trek should take around 4½ hours. Here you can stay the night (bunkhouse or camping). The stone cabins at Mackinder's are quite comfortable with two large dorms. The bunk beds have mattresses, there are toilets, and drinking water is available. The caretaker here checks your bunkhouse booking receipts.

Mackinder's Camp to Point Lenana On the third day you can either rest at Mackinder's Camp (to help acclimatise) or aim for Point Lenana. From Mackinder's to Point Lenana takes about four to five hours, so it's usual to leave around 2 am (you'll need a torch or flashlight) to reach the summit of Lenana in time for sunrise. From the bunkhouse, continue up the valley past the ranger station to a fork in the path. Keep right, and go across a swampy area, followed by a moraine and then up a very long scree slope – this is a long, hard slog. You reach Austrian Hut about three to four hours from Mackinder's. This is about one hour below the summit of Lenana, so it's a good place to rest before the final push for the summit. This section of the trek, from Austrian Hut up to Point Lenana, takes you up a steep ridge and then across the edge of a snow-covered glacier. In good weather the going is fairly straightforward, but in bad weather you should not attempt to reach the summit unless you are experienced in trekking in mountain conditions, or have a guide. Plenty of inexperienced trekkers have come to grief on this section, falling off icy cliffs or even disappearing into crevasses.

To avoid the long slog in the dark, it is also possible to walk from Mackinder's to the Austrian Hut on the third day, stay there, then go for the summit of Lenana on the morning of the fourth day. However, conditions at Austrian Hut are very basic, so you need to be well equipped.

Those who are camping and not staying at either Mackinder's Camp or the Austrian Hut have a third choice of where to spend the night. This is the so-called American Camp, which you get to by branching off left along a minor track just before the swampy area and above the ranger station. It's an excellent camp site on a grassy meadow.

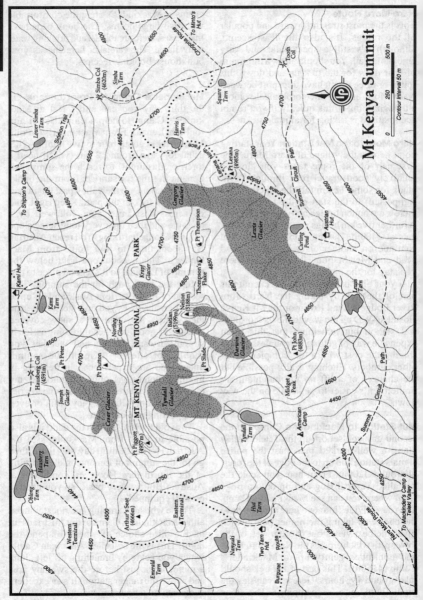

Mt Kenya Summit

Return Routes From Point Lenana most people return to the Met Station back down the same route. Assuming you get to Point Lenana early in the day, you can reach the Met Station on the same day.

Alternatively, you can return to Austrian Hut then walk north and north-west around the base of the main peaks to reach the top of either the Sirimon or Chogoria routes, and go down one of those routes. This is on the Summit Circuit path (described briefly in the Sirimon Route section), which is reckoned to be one of the most exciting trekking routes in East Africa. Completely circling the mountain, you cross several major cols, and get great views of the peaks and glaciers from all angles. The Summit Circuit path can also be demanding and potentially dangerous. Many people have got lost on this trail and you should not attempt it unless you have plenty of time, proper equipment, and a map and compass that you know how to use.

Sirimon Route

This is the least used of the three main routes but the driest and one of the most scenic. It is also the longest approach to Point Lenana but, once you reach the Mackinder Valley, it's plain sailing all the way to Shipton's Camp and there's beautiful alpine vegetation the whole way. You should allow a minimum of four days to undertake this trek.

Probably the best way to climb the mountain along this route is to first head for the Mountain Rock Hotel between Naro Moru and Nanyuki. Here you stay for the night, book the mountain lodges – Old Moses Camp and Shipton's Camp – and arrange transport the next day to the park entry gate.

If that's not in your budget then take transport from Nairobi to Nanyuki, stay the night there and then take one of the frequent Nissan minibuses going to Timau on the main road towards Isiolo and tell the driver you want to be dropped off at the start of the Sirimon trail (signposted). It's about 13 km north of Nanyuki. If you go over a fairly large river (the Sirimon River), you've gone too far.

Turn-Off to Old Moses Camp On the first day you walk from the main road to the park entrance gate (about 10 km) and on from there to the road head at 3150m (a further nine km). The going is straightforward to this point. At the road head there's a good camp site and the Old Moses Camp bunkhouse. This bunkhouse is well maintained, clean, and the bunks are provided with mattresses but you need your own cooking equipment and food. There's also plenty of water for washing and cooking and toilets on site.

Old Moses Camp to Shipton's Camp On the second day you leave Old Moses Camp, aiming uphill on a gradually deteriorating track. After about one hour you reach a fork – the left branch goes to the Liki North Hut, although this route is not used much. Take the right branch, which leads to a path over two ridges into the Mackinder Valley. Look out for red and white marker posts. When you get to the top of the last ridge you'll be presented with breathtaking views of the snow-covered peaks and others, to the north, of the Aberdares. It's even possible to see the Mt Kenya Safari Club way down below. From here, the path leads down the east side of the valley, eventually crossing the Liki North Stream and passing Shipton's Caves (in an obvious cliff on the left side of the path) before reaching Shipton's Camp bunkhouse and camp site, directly below the peaks of Batian and Point Lenana. From the road head at Old Moses Camp to Shipton's Camp takes about seven hours. Shipton's Camp is a good place to spend two nights and have a rest day to help acclimatise. However, if you're feeling OK, one night here is sufficient. The bunkhouse is well maintained, clean and the bunks have mattresses. There are toilets on site and a clean stream which goes directly past the bunkhouse.

Shipton's Camp to Point Lenana There are various ways you can approach Point Lenana from Shipton's Camp.

Via the North Face This is the shortest route, which means you can go from Shipton's up to Lenana then down to a high camp or hut on one of the other routes in one day. However, the option is very difficult, and impassable after snow. There are no tracks and it should only be tackled by experienced trekkers, or by groups with competent local guides. It's basically straight uphill, and very steep, so if it's the one you take, go easy! You reach Harris Tarn, then aim for the summit of Lenana up the North Face. It takes 31/2 to five hours to reach the summit this way.

Once you get to the top, you have a choice of descending back the same way you came (two to four hours back to Shipton's), or descend part of the way, then branch off down the Chogoria route. If you choose the Chogoria route you're looking at a strenuous descent over an enormous scree bed which will take you the best part of two hours followed by another one to 1½ hours down to Minto's Hut. Your other option is descending to Austrian hut, where you join the Summit Circuit path, and then dropping down to the Naro Maru route (about three to four hours to Mackinder's Camp).

Via American Camp This option requires an extra day. From Shipton's Camp on the third day you can follow the Summit Circuit path west of the main peaks. Go straight up the valley side from Shipton's, keeping the main peaks to your left, to reach Kami Hut (which is in very bad condition) and then continue up a long scree slope to reach the Hausberg Col. From here you drop down into the next valley to reach Hausberg Tarn and Oblong Tarn. Follow the path between the tarns, then go up again to the col between the summit of Arthur's Seat and the Western Terminal. Aim south from here, passing Nanyuki Tarn to your right, to reach Two Tarn Hut, from where you drop down to American Camp at the head of the Teleki Valley. You can camp here or go down to the nearby Mackinder's Camp bunkhouse. From Shipton's Camp to American Camp by this route takes about four to five hours. On the fourth day you can reach Point Lenana (as described in the Naro Moru Route section).

Via Austrian Hut Your other choice from Shipton's is to go east of the main peaks. This option also requires an extra day. Head up the steep-sided valley to Simba Col, or go up the large scree slopes to Harris Tarn. From both of these points you can reach Simba Tarn, then Square Tarn. From Square Tarn you aim south, through Tooth Col (next to a large, jagged pinnacle) and then gradually up to reach Austrian Hut. From Shipton's Camp to Austrian Hut by this route takes about six hours. On the fourth day you can reach Point Lenana (as described in the Naro Moru Route section). If you are going east of the main peaks and don't feel like going for the summit of Lenana, from Simba Col you can join the Chogoria route and drop down to Minto's Hut.

Chogoria Route
This route, from the eastern side of the mountain, is undoubtedly the most beautiful of the access routes to the summit and certainly one of the easiest as far as gradients go. This is a good route if you've got a tent and some trekking experience. From Minto's Hut there are breathtaking views of the head of the Gorges Valley and the glaciers beyond.

To get started on this route, take an Akamba bus from Nairobi direct to Chogoria village, or one first to Embu and then a matatu to Chogoria. Unless you get to Chogoria village early in the day, you will probably have to spend the night in Chogoria before setting off up the mountain, as the first day's hike is a long slog. It's about 30 km from the village to the park entry gate up the forest track with nowhere to stay en route.

Chogoria to Park Entry Gate The first day is spent walking up to the park entry gate at 2990m through superb rainforest and on into the bamboo zone. You have the choice here of staying at the Meru Mt Kenya Lodge, near the park entry gate, or continuing on a further three km to the small MCK's Urumandi Hut. At the road head itself (3200m), six km from the park entry gate, there's also an excellent camp site but there are no facilities whatsoever except water (from the adjacent river).

It's possible to hitch all the way to the park entry gate from Chogoria as at least one official vehicle does the run most days between the village and the Meru Mt Kenya Lodge, though there's no set timetable. There may also be people staying at the lodge who can help out with lifts. Alternatively, if you want guaranteed transport, this can be arranged at one of the hotels in Chogoria village for around KSh 1500 per person. Natural Action (see the earlier Equipment Hire section for details) also has a base and transport here.

Park Entry Gate to Minto's Hut The second day is spent walking from either the Meru Mt Kenya Lodge, the Urumandi Hut or the road head camp site to Minto's Hut with spectacular views all the way. The route is well defined and first crosses a stream then climbs to a ridge which it follows all the way to Minto's Hut. You need to bring water with you as there are no sources en route. From the road head to Minto's Hut should take you about 4½ to five hours. Minto's Hut is in a disgusting state and you wouldn't keep pigs in there but that's hardly the point because the guides and porters will have taken over the place long before you get there. The only realistic option here is to camp in the field next to the tarn – which is also your source of water. It's a good site and there may still be a few small sheets of corrugated iron to shield your stove from the wind (there were in 1996). There's also a long-drop toilet adjacent to the hut. Take time out here to peer over the precipice of the gorge. It's spectacular!

Minto's Hut to Austrian Hut On the third day you continue to the head of the Gorges Valley, a steep climb eventually across scree slopes, aiming south-west to reach Square Tarn. The last section of this leg of the route is very steep.

From the tarn the route becomes the Summit Circuit path, continuing south through Tooth Col (to the east of Point Lenana), after which it descends briefly and then goes up across a scree slope to the right to reach Austrian Hut.

The route is marked with cairns in some places but it is still easy to get lost, especially in mist or snow. The section between Tooth Col and Austrian Hut is where most trekkers get lost. It is essential to realise that there is another huge valley (called Hobley Valley) in-between the Gorges and Teleki valleys. The route goes *around* the head of the Hobley, not down into it. From Minto's to Austrian Hut should take about four hours.

Austrian Hut to Point Lenana From Austrian Hut you can scale Point Lenana (allow another one to two hours) the same day or stay there for the night and make the ascent the following morning, as described in the Naro Moru section.

Return Routes From Point Lenana you can retrace the route back down to Minto's Hut which should take about three to four hours after which it's a further four to five hours back down to the Meru Mt Kenya Lodge. Alternatively, from Austrian Hut you can descend to Mackinder's Camp, and then return via the Naro Moru route.

Organised Treks
If your time is limited or you'd prefer someone else to make all the arrangements for a trek on Mt Kenya, there are several possibilities.

The Mountain Rock Lodge (☎ (0176) 62625), or Mountain Rock Tours & Adventure Safaris (☎ (02) 210051; fax 333448), PO Box 40270, Jubilee Insurance House, Wabera St, Nairobi, are the real specialists in Mt Kenya climbs, though not exclusively. They offer a two-tier pricing structure: a 'Standard' (budget) package for those who are willing to be flexible but want to keep costs down, and an 'Executive' package for those who don't want to share facilities, guides and porters with other climbers. The cost of one of their organised climbs, whether it be 'Standard' or 'Executive' depends very much on how many are in your group. It's cheapest with eight or more people rising to about double this amount if there's only one of you.

There's a whole range of options to choose from starting with quick two-day treks all the way through to seven-day treks. A three-day trek up and back down the Sirimon route, costs US$316 to US$174 (one to eight people, respectively). An alternative which takes the same time is to ascend along the Sirimon route and descend via the Naro Moru route. This is slightly more expensive at US$346 to US$190. Four-day treks up and back down the Sirimon route cost US$398 to US$236. An alternative which takes the same amount of time is to ascend via the Sirimon route and descend via the Chogoria route. This costs US$480 to US$320.

Their longest trek is a seven-day package which takes in the Sirimon route as well as the Summit Circuit path and costs US$572 to US$403.

The above prices are for 'Standard' treks; 'Executive' packages are somewhat more expensive. If you're a student or a Kenyan resident there are substantial discounts on these prices because of the reductions available on park entry and camping fees. All prices include park entry and camping fees, food, hut accommodation, a guide, cook and porters and transfer to the Mountain Rock Hotel before and after a climb. Some packages also include transfer to and from Nairobi and one or two nights at the hotel. Write, ring or fax for a copy of their brochure before you set off.

The Naro Moru River Lodge (☎ (0176) 22018), PO Box 18, Naro Moru, also does a range of trips, all of which include a guide/ cook, porters, all meals, park entry fees, camping fees, and transport to and from the road heads. Their prices are similar to those of the Mountain Rock Hotel but the normal route up the mountain from here is via the Naro Moru route. Write or ring for their brochure before you set off. If you take one of their treks, you're entitled to a special half-board deal at the hotel.

There are several safari companies in Nairobi which offer Mt Kenya treks, but most of these companies just sell the treks operated by Naro Moru and Mountain Rock lodges, charging you an extra commission in the process. However, some companies are running their own treks, and these include:

Kenya Hiking & Cycling
Arrow House, Koinange St, PO Box 39439, Nairobi (☎ (02) 218336)
This company's Mt Kenya trek goes up the Sirimon route and down the Naro Moru in five days, staying at bunkhouses. The cost is US$520 including transport to and from Nairobi.

Natural Action Ltd
PO Box 12516, Nairobi (☎ /fax (02) 763927)
This is a specialist, high quality trekking outfit, favouring remote routes. A standard five-day Mt Kenya trek goes up the Chogoria route and down the Naro Moru, following more unusual paths for some of the way. The cost is around US$754 per person, including park fees, transport to/from Nairobi, and hotel accommodation after the trek.

Bike Treks
PO Box 14237, Nairobi (☎ (02) 446371; fax 44237)
This company offers a range of possibilities from three days/two nights Naro Moru route for US$300, four days/three nights Sirimon/Naro Moru routes for US$400, and seven days/six nights Sirimon/Chogoria routes for US$560. The prices include transfer to and from Nairobi, park entry and camping fees, guide, cook and porters, food and tents. It excludes rucksacks, clothing and boots and tips.

Executive Wilderness Programmes
PO Box 15014, Nairobi (☎ (02) 884068; fax 882723)
This company specialises in mountain trekking all over East Africa including Mt Kenya, Kilimanjaro, Mt Elgon, Mt Kulal, the Chyulu Hills and the Ruwenzori.

NAIROBI NATIONAL PARK

This park is the most accessible of all Kenya's game parks, being only a few km from the city centre. You should set aside a morning or an afternoon to see it. As in all the game parks, you must visit it in a vehicle; walking is prohibited. This means you will either have to arrange a lift at the entrance gate with other tourists, go on a tour, or hire a car.

Nairobi National Park is the oldest park in the country, having been created in 1946. For a park so close to the city centre you can see an amazing variety of animals – with a backdrop of jumbo jets coming in to land at Jomo Kenyatta International airport which is adjacent to the park. Gazelle, oryx, lion, zebra, giraffe, buffalo, cheetah and leopard are all seen regularly. Elephants are not to be found in this park as the habitat is not suitable.

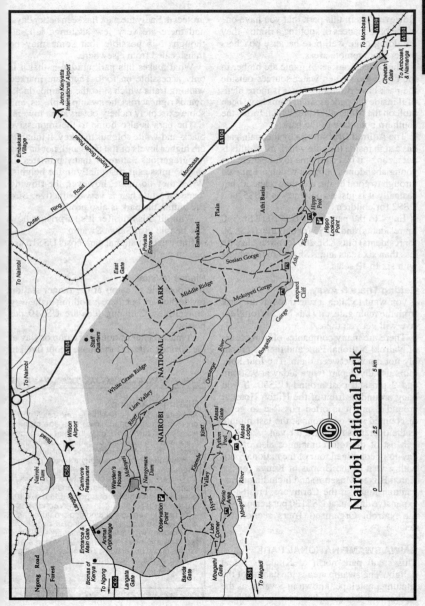

Nairobi National Park

However, it's in this park that you have one of the best chances of spotting a rhino – they are doing quite well here because poachers prefer more remote areas.

The concentrations of game are higher in the dry season when water sources outside the park have dried up. Water is more plentiful inside the park as small dams have been built on the Mbagathi River which forms the southern boundary of the park.

The **Animal Orphanage** by the main gate has a sign inside the gate which reads 'this is not a zoo' – it is. From time to time there are young abandoned animals which are nursed through to good health and then released, but basically it is just a zoo; entry is US$5, and US$2 for children.

Entry to the park costs US$20 (KSh 150 for residents) and US$5 for children (KSh 50 for residents) plus KSh 200 for a vehicle with less than six seats and KSh 500 for a vehicle with six to 12 seats.

Getting There & Away
If you want to hitch a ride through the park from the main gate, city bus No 24 from Moi Ave will get you there.

There are many companies offering tours of Nairobi National Park and there's probably not much between them. The four-hour tours usually depart twice a day at 9.30 am and 2 pm and cost around US$50. If you hang around in front of the Hilton Hotel at around 2 pm it is often possible to get a discounted seat on a tour at the last minute as the operators try to fill the van.

Most of the tour companies also offer a day-long combined tour of the national park with a visit to the Bomas of Kenya (or the Karen Blixen Museum) and including a gargantuan lunch at the Carnivore, but it's an expensive day out at US$130 per person (see the Nairobi Organised Tours section for details).

SAIWA SWAMP NATIONAL PARK
This small park north of Kitale is a real delight. The swamp area is the habitat of the sitatunga antelope, known in Swahili as the *nzohe*, and this park has been set aside to

protect it. Sadly the park has seen better days, and there are very few sitatunga left, although it is possible that some may be translocated from elsewhere.

What makes this park unique is that it is only accessible on foot. There are marked walking trails which skirt the swamp, duckboards right across the swamp in places, and some extremely rickety observation towers.

The park is also home to the impressive black-and-white colobus monkey. It inhabits the higher levels of the trees and, not having the gregarious nature of many primates, is easy to miss as it sits quietly in the heights. When they do move, however, the flowing 'cape' of white hair is very distinctive. Bird life within the park is also prolific.

With all this on offer it's surprising how few people visit Saiwa Swamp.

Entry to the national park costs US$15 per person per day.

Places to Stay
It is possible to camp at the ranger station inside the park but there is nothing in the way of facilities. Camping fees are US$10 per person.

A much better option is to camp or stay at the *Sirikwa Safaris* farmhouse about five km

---

Sitatunga Antelope

The sitatunga is fairly elusive and really the only way to spot one is to sit atop one of the observation towers armed with a pair of binoculars and a hefty dose of patience. As is the case in most of the parks, the best time for animal-spotting is in the early morning or late afternoon.

This shy antelope is not unlike a bushbuck in appearance, although larger, and has elongated hooves which are supposed to make it easier for it to get around in swampy conditions – it's hard to see how, but no doubt nature has it all worked out. The colouring is basically grey-brown, with more red noticeable in the females, and both sexes have white spots or stripes on the upper body. The males have long twisted horns which grow up to a metre in length. ■

further north along the Kapenguria road from the Saiwa Swamp turn-off. For the cost of camping or staying in a room here see the Kitale section. The owners can also arrange a field guide who is well versed in the bird life of the park for KSh 300 (half day) or KSh 600 (full day) as well as transport to the park entrance.

Getting There & Away

Saiwa Swamp National Park lies five km east of the main A1 road, 18 km north of Kitale. Any of the matatus running between Kitale and Kapenguria will let you off at the signposted turn-off, from where you'll probably have to walk to the park as there is little traffic along the dirt road.

SAMBURU, BUFFALO SPRINGS & SHABA NATIONAL RESERVES

Just north of Isiolo are three national reserves, Samburu, Buffalo Springs and Shaba, all of them along the banks of the Ewaso Nyiro River and covering an area of some 300 sq km. They are mainly scrub desert and open savanna plain, broken here and there by small rugged hills. The river, however, which is permanent, supports a wide variety of game and you may see elephant, buffalo, cheetah, leopard and lion as well as dik-dik, wart hog, Grevy's zebra and the reticulated giraffe. Crocodiles can also be seen on certain sandy stretches of the riverbank.

You are guaranteed close-up sightings of elephants, reticulated giraffe and various species of smaller gazelle in both Samburu and Buffalo Springs but other game is remarkably thin on the ground, particularly on the route into Samburu from Archer's Post. The rhino were wiped out years ago by poachers.

If you are driving around these parks in your own vehicle it's useful to have a copy of the Survey of Kenya map, *Samburu & Buffalo Springs Game Reserves* (SK 85).

The roads inside Buffalo Springs and Samburu are well maintained and it's easy to get around, even in 2WD, though you might need a 4WD on some of the minor tracks.

Entry to each of the three parks or game reserves costs US$27 per person (US$10 for students and children) plus KSh 200 per vehicle per day (less than six seats) or KSh 500 per day (six to 12 seats). Even though they're continuous, if you drive from Buffalo Springs to Samburu (or vice versa) in one day then you'll have to pay two lots of park entry fees. However, if it's very late in the afternoon when you cross the boundary, the guards will generally postdate your ticket for the following day.

These parks are much less touristed than Amboseli or Masai Mara so, once you're out of the immediate vicinity of the lodges and camp sites, you'll frequently have the place to yourself.

Places to Stay

Buffalo Springs In Buffalo Springs National Reserve there are four *public camp sites* close to the Gare Mara entrance gate (the nearest to Isiolo and accessible from the main Isiolo–Marsabit road). However, none of them are particularly safe as far as robberies go so stick with a group and make sure your tent is guarded when you're out on game drives or pack it up and take it with you. There's also a *special camp site* further west. Camping costs US$2.50 per person per night.

For those with adequate finances, there's the *Buffalo Springs Tented Lodge* (☎ (0165) 2234) up at the north-eastern end of the reserve just south of the Ewaso Nyiro River. The lodge consists of 30 tents shielded from the sun by makuti roofs and each with its own bathroom. There are also eight cottages which sleep two to four people. The lodge has a swimming pool and a bar/restaurant overlooking a natural spring where you can sit and observe the wildlife. In the high season, tents or cottages cost US$120/160 for singles/doubles with full board. In the low season the prices are US$50/90. The price includes a game drive. Advance bookings can be made through African Tours & Hotels Ltd (☎ (02) 223285; fax 218109), PO Box 30471, Nairobi. The best access to the lodge is either from the Gare Mara Gate or the Buffalo Springs Gate just south of Archer's Post.

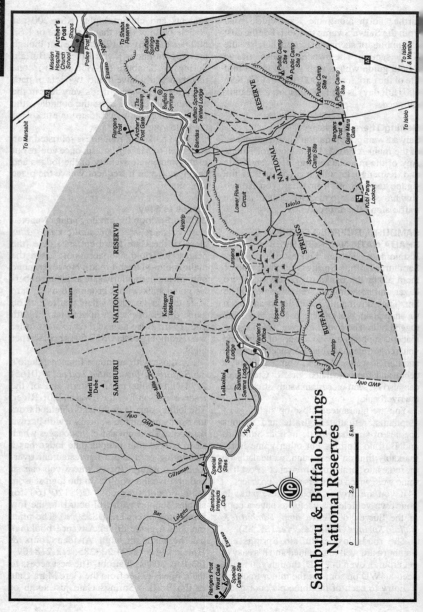

Samburu & Buffalo Springs National Reserves

Samburu In Samburu National Reserve, the most convenient places to stay are the *public camp sites* close to the Samburu Lodge and close to the wooden bridge which connects the western extremity of Buffalo Springs to Samburu across the Ewaso Nyiro River. The sites themselves are fairly pleasant and adjacent to the river but the facilities are minimal and the 'toilets' are nothing short of pigsties. If you don't want to cook for yourself the only advantage is that they're very close to the lodge with its restaurant and bar. There are also two *special camp sites* which are further west. Camping costs US$2.50 per person per night.

For those with money, there's a choice of four top-range lodges/tented camps. The most popular is perhaps the *Samburu Lodge* which is part of the Block Hotels chain (☎ (02) 540780; fax 543810), PO Box 40075, Block House, Lusaka Rd, Nairobi. It's built right alongside the river and consists of a main building (stone and makuti roof) which houses the restaurant, bar and reception area, and a series of cottages with their own bathrooms strung out along the riverbank. The tariff depends on the season. In the high season it's US$100/153 with half-board for singles/doubles, whereas in the low season it's US$39/78 with half board for singles/doubles. Rates in the two shoulder seasons are intermediate. Kenyan residents pay KSh

3185/4730 with half board for singles/doubles. The lodge is the only place in the two parks where petrol can be bought. Game drives through the park can be organised at the lodge.

Further east and also alongside the river is *Larsens* which is a luxury tented camp also owned by the Block Hotels chain. The rates depend on the season. In the high season (16 December to 3 January and 1 April to 8 April) half board costs US$142/219 in a tent and US$165/255 for a suite, whereas in the low season (9 April to 30 June) the corresponding rates are US$57/114 and US$67/134. All these rates include two game drives. Children under seven years old are not allowed at Larsens and those over this age are charged the full adult rate.

The *Samburu Intrepids Club* (☎ (02) 335208; fax 217278 in Nairobi), further upstream on the northern side of the river, is another luxury tented lodge and more like a beach resort in many ways. A night here costs US$121/183 with full board.

The *Samburu Serena Lodge* charges US$110/150 for singles/doubles with full board in the high seasons and US$50/100 with full board in the low season (9 April to 30 June). These prices are subject to 10% service charge, 2% training levy and 15% VAT. For bookings contact Serena Lodges & Hotels (☎ (02) 711077; fax 718103), PO Box 48690, Nairobi.

You can take any of the park access gates to get to these lodges but remember that if you drive through Buffalo Springs and into Samburu on the same day then you'll be up for two lots of park entry fees. You can avoid this by entering through the Archer's Post Gate.

Shaba The spectacular *Shaba Sarova Lodge* in Shaba National Game Reserve has single/double rooms with full board for US$55/110 in the low season, rising to US$130/165 for high season. Bookings should be made through Sarova Hotels (☎ (02) 333248; fax 211742), PO Box 30680, New Stanley Hotel, Kenyatta Ave, Nairobi. For those with lots of money to spend but little time at their

---

Night Show

The supposed 'highlights' of any evening here are the appearance of a leopard across the other side of the river and the crocodiles which crawl up onto a sandy bank adjacent to the bar. The leopard, which is lured by a hunk of meat strung up from a tree by two very blasé employees just before dusk, is extremely contrived but Kodak make a fortune supplying film to fools who think they can get anything but a picture of midnight in the bush with an Instamatic from about 100m. The crocodile 'show' is equally contrived but at least it takes place right in front of you even if pieces of dead meat in the sand don't encourage dynamism. ∎

disposal, there's a weekend package (Saturday and Sunday) available which costs KSh 18,100 per person and includes a return flight from Nairobi to Shaba (twin-engine light aircraft), full-board accommodation at the lodge, three game drives, park fees, and transfers from the airports at both ends.

For campers there's a beautiful *camp site* about 20 minutes drive away. There's abundant firewood here but you need to bring water from the lodge.

SHIMBA HILLS NATIONAL RESERVE

This national reserve is in the hills behind the coast south of Mombasa, directly inland from Diani Beach. The forest setting is beautiful but the game is not prolific. There is a baited water hole at the Shimba Hills Lodge, and so it's possible you'll see leopards and plenty of elephants but not much else. Other animals which frequent the reserve include the rare sable antelope – a tall and compact animal with beautifully curved horns on both the male and female. The adult bull is a dark brown on the upper body and white below, while the female is a lighter brown. The animals are, unfortunately, often killed by poachers for meat, and this is the only reserve where they are found.

Entry to the reserve costs US$20 (US$5 for children) for nonresidents.

Places to Stay

The camp site has a superb location on the edge of the range with views right down to Diani Beach. It's about three km from the main gate, which itself is about three km from the village of Kwale. Camping charges are KSh 200 per person.

The only alternative to camping is Block Hotels' *Shimba Hills Lodge* (☎ (02) 540780 in Nairobi) where singles/doubles with half board cost US$44/88 in the low season (9 April to 30 June) and US$71/142 in the high season. Note that children under seven years old are not admitted to this lodge, and that children over seven pay full rates. The water hole here is baited to attract a few animals and is floodlit at night.

Getting There & Away

There are KBS buses to Kwale, from where it shouldn't be too difficult to hitch to the park entrance. Once there, however, you may have a long wait for a vehicle back. The road from Kwale to Kinango, the next inland town, actually passes through the northern part of the park and there's a chance of seeing animals from the KBS buses. The No 34 bus runs from Likoni to Kwale.

TANA RIVER PRIMATE NATIONAL RESERVE

Well south of Garissa and not too far north of Garsen is the Tana River Primate National Reserve which, as its name suggests, is a reserve for a number of endangered monkey species. It's possible to get close to the sanctuary by public transport but there's still a lot of walking involved and the facilities have long fallen into disrepair so you need to take everything with you. Very few safari companies include the reserve on their itineraries. Check with Let's Go Travel (☎ (02) 340331) to see if they still provide for a visit to this sanctuary on one of its safaris.

TSAVO NATIONAL PARK

At just over 20,000 sq km, Tsavo is the largest national park in Kenya, and for administrative purposes it has been split into Tsavo West National Park, with an area of 8500 sq km, and Tsavo East National Park, which covers 11,000 sq km.

The northern area of Tsavo West, west of the Nairobi–Mombasa A109 road, is the most developed and has some excellent scenery. It is particularly beautiful at the end of the wet season when things are green; at other times of the year it tends to get very dusty in Tsavo. Tsavo East consists of vast rolling plains with scrubby vegetation. Almost the entire area north of the Galana River (and this constitutes the bulk of the park) is off limits to the general public. This is due to the ongoing campaign against poachers, who still find the relative remoteness of Tsavo a good prospect. Happily it seems the authorities are winning the battle, but in the meantime the rhino population has been

Lamu's architecture has a distinct Arab influence (top). Donkeys and pedestrians are the main traffic in the town's narrow, winding streets (middle). The waters off this unique Swahili settlement are dotted with wooden dhows, and they're totally at the mercy of the wind (bottom).

DEBRA TAN

HUGH FINLAY

GEOFF CROWTHER

HUGH FINLAY

Lake Turkana is home to the El Molo people (top) who derive an income from fishing and tourism. It is also home to the Turkana tribe who make their living from fishing and mustering cattle (middle photos). The lushness of Eliye Springs at Lake Turkana (bottom) belies the barren land surrounding it.

absolutely decimated – from around 8000 in 1970 to less than 200 today.

By Kenyan standards, Tsavo sees relatively few visitors, which means for those that do visit there is none of the congestion found in other parks and reserves.

Information

Entry to the park is US$23 per person per day. Note that the two parks are administered separately, and to visit both parks you'll need to pay separate entrance fees.

All track junctions in Tsavo West have a numbered and signposted cairn, which in theory makes navigation fairly simple. In practice, however, the cairns are not all there (especially in the little-visited southern reaches of the park), and those which are there don't always give comprehensive directions. It's also difficult to find a map which marks these numbered intersections and therefore gives you some clue as to where you are. The Macmillan map is about the best. To their credit, the Kenya Wildlife Services are in the process of redoing all these cairns, and, once completed, navigation with a reliable map will be easy.

Don't attempt this park without 4WD if you intend to get off the main routes. You can certainly get to Kilaguni Lodge and Ngulia Lodge on the main service road from Mtito Andei in a 2WD but you'll get into strife and possibly get hopelessly stuck on the minor tracks. You will not make it to the above lodges in a 2WD if you enter through the Tsavo Gate further south unless you're a rally driver and/or willing to risk damaging the car. There are some diabolical sections on this access road; the lava flows along here will rip the underside of any normal car apart.

Fuel is available at Kilaguni and Ngulia lodges in Tsavo West.

Tsavo West National Park

The focus here is the watering holes by the Kilaguni and Ngulia lodges. The one at Kilaguni is the better of the two and attracts huge varieties of animals and birds, particularly during the dry season when water may be scarce elsewhere.

The **Mzima Springs** are not far from Kilaguni Lodge and the pools here are favourite haunts of both the hippo and crocodile. The much vaunted underwater viewing chamber was designed to give you a view of the hippos' submarine activities, but the hippos have retreated to the far end of the pool. There are, however, plenty of fish to be observed. The springs are the source of the bulk of Mombasa's fresh water and there is a direct pipeline from here to the coast.

Also in the area of the lodges is the spectacular **Shetani lava flow** and **caves**. Both are worth investigating, though for the caves you'll need to exercise caution and carry a torch (flashlight). The black lava flow is very spectacular and is actually outside the Chyulu Gate on the track which leads to Amboseli.

The **Chaimu Crater** just south of Kilaguni Lodge can also be climbed. It's worth remembering while walking on any of these nature trails that the park animals are far from tame, and while there's little danger, you do need to keep your eyes on what's happening around you. These nature trails are also the only places where you are permitted to get out of the vehicle.

Another attraction in Tsavo West is the **Ngulia Rhino Sanctuary**, at the base of Ngulia Hills, not far from the Ngulia Lodge. Here 70 sq km has been surrounded by a metre-high electric fence, and 30 black rhinos now live here in relative security. There are tracks within the enclosed area and there's a good chance of seeing one of these elusive creatures.

Places to Stay – bottom end Tsavo West has a number of basic camp sites, namely at each of the three main gates (Tsavo, Mtito Andei and Chyulu). The fees to use these are KSh 150 per person.

The self-service accommodation at the *Ngulia Safari Camp* and the *Kitani Safari Camp* is, by park standards, quite cheap at KSh 500 per person (minimum charge of KSh 2000 per banda) in the fully equipped bandas but you must bring all your own food

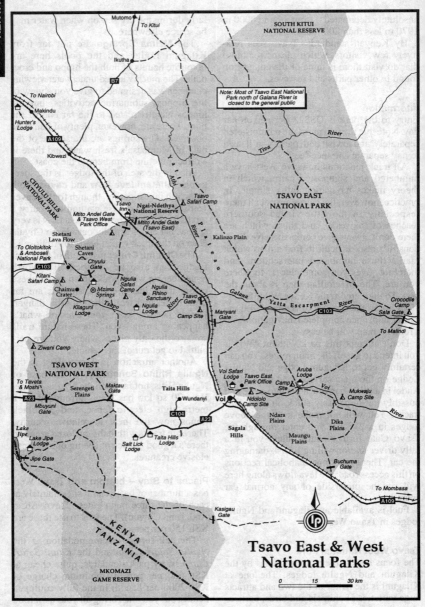

Note: Most of Tsavo East National Park north of Galana River is closed to the general public

Tsavo East & West National Parks

0   15   30 km

and drink with you or eat at one of the lodges. The Kitani Camp is in the north-western part of the park, and while it's not the best location, is well set up. The Ngulia camp is perched on the edge of the Ngulia Hills, and with its elevation has some fine views. Both camps consist of one-bedroom bandas with bedding, towels, mosquito nets, bathroom, a fully equipped kitchen, and kerosene lanterns. Take with you toilet paper, washing-up liquid, soap, matches, drinking water and an ice box. For reservations at either camp, contact Let's Go Travel (☎ (02) 340331; fax 336890 in Nairobi).

Places to Stay – top end The *Ngulia Lodge* is part of the African Tours & Hotels group (☎ (02) 336858; fax 218109). It's not the most attractive of lodges but it is comfortable and the views are excellent. Singles/doubles with full board cost US$120/150 in the high season and US$60/120 in the low season. The water hole here is small but there's a leopard which visits each evening to pick up

Kilaguni Lodge

The lodge is beautifully situated looking out over the rolling hills. The large water hole, floodlit at night, is right in front of the lodge and you can sit in the bar or restaurant, or on the verandah in front of your room, and watch the wildlife. You can even lie in bed with your binoculars to hand – every room faces a water hole. All this luxury, including a swimming pool and lush garden, doesn't come cheap, but where else do you need a pair of binoculars and a field guide at hand while you eat?

We arrive in time for lunch and watch the comings and goings at the water hole. To the left there are impala and a couple of waterbuck; back from the water there's a small group of ostrich, and off to the right there's a herd of oryx. Marabou storks lounge around in the foreground while right in front of the restaurant are groups of smaller birds and mongoose. There's so much activity it's hard to concentrate on lunch – and this is just after the wet season when the game are less concentrated at the water holes!

The scene is only spoilt by the idiots who persist, in spite of numerous posted warnings, in throwing bread out to the animals. This has already taught some of the storks (notoriously efficient scavengers) to line up in front of the restaurant wall. It would be all too easy to turn this wonderful scene into a cheap zoo with animals begging for hand-outs. This is the same Africa of Ethiopia and Mozambique and there's something obscene about dumb tourists hurling whole bread rolls just for amusement and a better shot with the Instamatic.

After lunch we watch from the verandah of our room – some zebra and two more ostriches appear but all the storks have left and gradually the animals wander off as the afternoon wears on. By 4.30 pm there's only the solitary waterbuck left; even the ostriches finally troop off in a stately line.

Down at the northern end of the lodge grounds is a tree full of weaver-bird nests with twittering hordes of these bright yellow birds furiously at work. Some of their nests, mainly older ones, have fallen out of the tree, and on close examination they are amazingly intricate and neatly woven; coconut-sized with a funnel-like entrance underneath. Right in front of our room a small squad of mongoose appears, cavorts around for a few minutes, then wanders away. By 5 pm it's baboon time again and the tribe wanders down to the water hole again for their evening visit. A few of them come up to our room to hassle us but soon give up. Rock hyrax scamper around, one even coming right into our room, and the mongoose come and go. Gradually the impala reappear.

Dinner time, unhappily, is the one blot on the perfect experience. Once again there are the idiotic food hurlers at work and a hyena trots up and waits expectantly for hand-outs, joined by a slender mongoose-like genet. With much shouting, loud conversation and cameras flashing madly there's a distinct theatre-restaurant feel to the whole meal and we're glad to get back to the quiet of our rooms.

The baboons leave soon after dark and by bedtime it's basically the impala and zebra. I get up several times in the night to check what's up but, apart from bats swooping around, the scene seems static until dawn. The impala keep watch all night long.

At dawn the zebra wander off, the oryx reappear, the whole baboon tribe wanders back and immediately start carousing merrily. A couple of pairs of impala bucks square off for a morning duel and the whole cycle starts again.

Although we didn't see elephants or lions we still enjoyed every minute of it. Now if only they could put those 'don't feed the animals signs' on every table...

Tony Wheeler

meat strung up on a dead tree outside the patio. Elephants are also regular evening visitors to the lodge's waterhole.

The *Kilaguni Lodge* is owned by the same hotel group and costs exactly the same, and the main attraction here is also the water hole which attracts a wide variety of game. It's a more attractive lodge than the Ngulia and there are extensive views of the Chyulu Hills out to the north-west. See the separate boxed story.

In a fairly isolated spot on the western boundary of the park and almost on the Tanzanian border, the *Lake Jipe Lodge* (☎ (02) 227623; fax 218376) is one of the cheaper places but it's a long way from anywhere else. Once again, the views are excellent; this time it's the Pare Mountains just across the border in Tanzania. As well as game drives, it's also possible to take a dhow ride on nearby Lake Jipe for KSh 750 per person. Accommodation costs US$100/160 for full board.

Also tucked away is *Ziwani*, a permanent tented camp on the bank of the Tsavo River and just outside the boundaries of the national park.

If you don't have the money to stay at one of the lodges in the park but don't want to camp or go to the trouble of organising your own food, etc for one of the self-catering camps, then you have options though they involve staying just outside the park boundaries at Mtito Andei on the main Nairobi to Mombasa road.

Right opposite the Mtito Andei Gate is the *Tsavo Inn* (☎ (014) 30217) which is fairly pleasant but otherwise unremarkable. Singles/doubles with breakfast cost KSh 2080/2600, but there seems little reason to stay.

Mtito Andei also has plenty of cheap and basic 'boardings & lodgings' if you need them.

Better is the *Hunter's Lodge* (☎ (0302) 22469) at Kiboko, 85 km from Mtito Andei on the main Nairobi to Mombasa road. The lodge's outdoor *Tilapia Springs Restaurant* is a popular lunch stop for tour groups, and the food is priced accordingly. Room rates are KSh 990/1670 including tax. Breakfast costs KSh 320, lunch or dinner KSh 415.

Getting There & Away The main access to Tsavo West is through the Mtito Andei Gate on the Mombasa–Nairobi road near the northern end of the park. The park headquarters is here and there's a camp site. From the gate it's 31 km to the Kilaguni Lodge.

A further 48 km along the main road away from Nairobi is the Tsavo Gate, where there's another camp site. This gate is 75 km from the Kilaguni area, so if you're hitching the Mtito Andei Gate is much closer and far busier. It's also worth taking into consideration the diabolical state of certain sections of the road between the Tsavo Gate and the lodges.

From Voi there is access past the Hilton-owned Taita Hills and Salt Lick lodges via the Maktau Gate. This road cuts clear across the park, exiting at the Mbuyuni Gate, to Taveta from where it's possible to cross into Tanzania and the town of Moshi at the foot of Kilimanjaro.

There's also a road running west from the Chyulu Gate which connects Tsavo West with Amboseli. This is a popular route with groups from Mombasa, but because of problems with bandits, all vehicles must travel in convoy, and an armed policeman rides in the first and last vehicles. However, within minutes of setting off the safari bus drivers have bolted at a million miles an hour and the convoy is spread out over many km. The convoys leave daily from the Chyulu Gate at 8.30 and 10.30 am, and at 2.30 pm. The trip to Amboseli takes a couple of hours.

Tsavo East National Park

The southern third of this park is open to the public and the rolling scrub-covered hills are home to large herds of elephants, usually covered in red dust.

The **Kanderi Swamp**, not far into the park from the main Voi Gate and park headquarters, is home to a profusion of wildlife and there's a camp site here. Further into the park, 30 km from the gate, is the main attraction in this part of the park, the **Aruba Dam** built across the Voi River. Here too you'll encounter a wide variety of game without the usual hordes of tourists – very few people visit Tsavo East.

Places to Stay – bottom end There are camp sites at the Voi Gate, Kanderi Swamp (*Ndololo Campsite*), Aruba Lodge and the *Mukwaju Campsite* on the Voi River 50 km in from the main gate.

Places to Stay – top end The *Voi Safari Lodge* (clearly signposted in the town of Voi) is part of the African Tours & Hotels group (☎ (02) 336858; fax 218109) and is five km inside the park from the Voi Gate. As you might imagine, things are a good deal more peaceful here than at the lodges in Tsavo West. Singles/doubles with full board cost US$150/200 in the high season. In the low season they are US$60/120.

The nicest place to stay is the *Tsavo Safari Camp*, run by the Kilimanjaro Safari Club (☎ (02) 338888; fax 219982), in a beautifully shady spot on the banks of the Athi River. Vehicles are left on the west bank of the river (guarded parking), and guests are shuttled across in rubber rafts. The camp is very peaceful and is a great place to chill out for a few days. There's a swimming pool, and game drives can be arranged for the energetic. Access to the lodge, which lies 27 km off the main Nairobi–Mombasa road, is from Mtito Andei; the turn-off is well signposted, one km out of town towards Mombasa. To stay in the well set-up permanent tents costs US$50/100 for full board in the low season, rising to US$152/190 in the high season.

Getting There & Away The main access point and the park headquarters is Voi Gate near Voi off the Nairobi–Mombasa road. Further north near the Tsavo Gate entrance of Tsavo West is the Manyani Gate. The murram (dirt) road from here cuts straight across to the Galana River and follows the river clear across the park, exiting at Sala Gate on the eastern side, a distance of 100 km. From Sala Gate it's a further 110 km to Malindi.

AROUND TSAVO
Taita Hills

The Taita Hills to the west of the main Nairobi–Mombasa road cover a vast area and are scenically spectacular. They have the status of a game reserve despite the fact that the main Voi–Taveta road and railway line pass through it on the southern side. Game is prolific in this area and you can even see plenty of it along the road to Taveta. There are also two up-market Hilton lodges on the south-western side – the Taita Hills Lodge and the Salt Lick Lodge.

Places to Stay The *Taita Hills Lodge* and the *Salt Lick Lodge*, are both owned by the Hilton Hotel in Nairobi (☎ (02) 334000; fax 339462), and the charge is US$193/225 in the low season; US$236/268 in the high season.

Getting There & Away There are matatus from Voi to Wundanyi (in the heart of the Taita Hills) for KSh 60, and both trains (five hours) and matatus (2½ hours) from Voi to Taveta for KSh 150. The trains and matatus from Voi to Taveta will get you close to the lodges but, if you can afford to stay there, you'll probably be in your own vehicle anyway.

Voi

The town of Voi was once described by a Peace Corps volunteer who worked there as, 'an attractive spaghetti western-like setting surrounded by hills that are good for hiking and catching expansive views of the surrounding plains'. That's close to the truth but it's not Maralal and a lot of development is going on. Nevertheless, it's a pleasant, small town and worth considering as a base for exploring the Taita Hills and Tsavo National Park or even as an overnight stop between Mombasa and Nairobi.

The cheapest place to stay with decent facilities is *Johari's Guest House* (☎ (0147) 2079) where singles/doubles go for KSh 200/350 with shared bath. They also show videos here each evening starting at 7.30 pm.

The *Voi Restpoint Hotel* (☎ (0147) 2079)

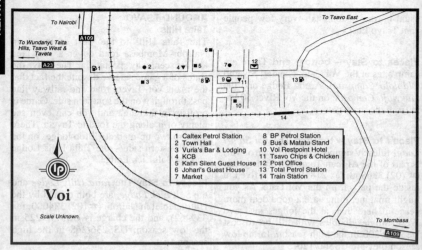

1 Caltex Petrol Station
2 Town Hall
3 Vuria's Bar & Lodging
4 KCB
5 Kahn Silent Guest House
6 Johari's Guest House
7 Market
8 BP Petrol Station
9 Bus & Matatu Stand
10 Voi Restpoint Hotel
11 Tsavo Chips & Chicken
12 Post Office
13 Total Petrol Station
14 Train Station

Voi

Scale Unknown

is the only budget hotel with rooms with attached bathrooms including fan and telephone. Singles/doubles with breakfast cost KSh 350/500. There are three restaurants in the hotel, including one on the rooftop.

Slightly more expensive is the *Kahn Silent Guest House* (☎ (0147) 2058), on Moi Hospital Rd opposite the Kenya Commercial Bank. It has singles/doubles for KSh 250/ 350.

Up in price is *Vuria's Bar & Lodging*, opposite the town hall, which offers rooms with attached bathrooms for KSh 300/400 including breakfast.

All the guesthouses have reasonable restaurants plus there's *Tsavo Chips & Chicken* at the matatu stand. The *Bird's Cafe* next to the bus and matatu stand is also worth a try.

Out on the main Nairobi–Mombasa road at the roundabout is the Caltex petrol station which has a whole complex of shops, fast-food outlets and a bar. The food here is OK and very reasonably priced, plus beers in the bar are ice-cold.

Getting There & Away There are plenty of buses and matatus to both Nairobi (five hours) and Mombasa (two hours). They also run regularly to Taveta, on the Tanzanian border.

There is also a weekly (Saturday) train which connects Voi with Moshi in Tanzania. The journey takes five hours, and the train returns the same day. See the Kenya Getting There & Away chapter for full details.

Uganda

Introduction

Uganda's long string of tragedies since independence in 1962 has featured in the western media to such an extent that most people probably still regard the country as dangerously unstable and to be avoided.

The reality is very different. Stability has returned to most parts of the country. Kampala has virtually returned to normal and is now the modern, bustling capital of Uganda with the fastest growing economy in Africa – the change has been astounding.

Before independence Uganda was a prosperous and cohesive country. Its great beauty led Winston Churchill to refer to it as the 'Pearl of Africa', but by early 1986 Uganda lay shattered and bankrupt, broken by tribal animosity, nepotism, politicians who had gone mad on power, and military tyranny.

Yet despite the killings and disappearances, the brutality, fear and destruction of the past, Ugandans appear to have weathered the storm remarkably well. You will not meet a sullen, bitter or cowed people. Rather, though hard to believe, they are a smiling and friendly people with an openness absent in other places.

For the traveller, all this means that Uganda is a safe and friendly country to visit.

The natural attractions are among the best in the region, and as tourism is still being re-established, you don't get the crowds found elsewhere.

It's a beautiful country with a great deal to offer, and sooner or later the tourist hordes will 'discover' it – make sure you get there before they do.

Facts about the Country

HISTORY
Early Settlement

Until the 19th century, there was very little penetration of Uganda from outside. Despite the fertility of the land and its capacity to grow surplus crops, there were virtually no trading links with the East African coast. Some indigenous kingdoms came into being from the 14th century onwards, among them Buganda, Bunyoro, Toro, Ankole and Busoga, with Bunyoro initially being the most powerful.

Over the following centuries, the Buganda people eventually created the dominant kingdom. They make up about 20% of Uganda's population and were once ruled by a *kabaka* (king).

During the reign of Kabaka Muteesa I in the mid-19th century, contacts were established with Arab traders who began to travel inland from Zanzibar in search of ivory and slaves. They brought with them Islam, and some of the practices of this religion were adopted by the Bugandan court. The first European visitor to Buganda was the explorer John Hanning Speke, who spent several months at the royal capital in 1862. He was followed by Henry Morton Stanley in 1875. Muteesa told Stanley he wanted to have teachers of European learning and religion sent out to live in his country, and this resulted in the arrival, in 1877, of the first Anglican missionaries. They were not quite what the kabaka had in mind, however, as they would only teach him about Christianity, not the practical skills of construction, manufacture and warfare he had hoped to learn. Muteesa died in 1884 and was succeeded by his teenage son, Mwanga.

While Muteesa had allowed his Muslim and Christian guests to compete with each other for converts as long as they never became powerful enough to threaten his authority, the situation changed radically in the early years of his successor. By that time, converts to the two religions had become

UGANDA

Area: 236,580 sq km
Population: 21.3 million
Population Growth Rate: 2.5%
Capital: Kampala
Head of State: President Yoweri Museveni
Official Language: English
Currency: Ugandan shilling
Exchange Rate: USh 1070 = US$1
Per Capita GNP: US$220
Inflation: 5%
Time: UTC + 3

more numerous and were less willing to obey the kabaka on matters which conflicted with their new religious beliefs. Mwanga responded to their growing disobedience by having 32 burned to death in 1886. The Catholic victims of this purge were later canonised by the Vatican and are known today as the Ugandan Martyrs.

Two years later, a number of Mwanga's leading Christian and Muslim chiefs, believing the kabaka was about to have them drowned in Lake Victoria, combined forces and overthrew Mwanga, placing one of his

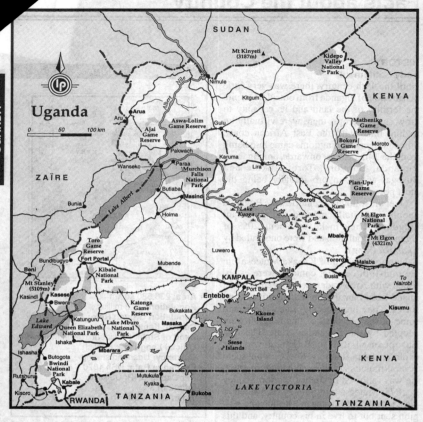

brothers on the throne. However, they were unable to agree among themselves on how the kingdom should be ruled, and fighting broke out, leading to the defeat and exile of the Christian faction. These Christians eventually joined forces with the exiled Mwanga and waged a war against the Muslims, which they won. Mwanga was restored to the throne in 1889.

It was at this time that the European 'scramble for Africa' was reaching its height. The British were the first to reach Buganda, in 1890, arriving with a small military force under the command of Captain Lugard, who established a base on Kampala hill near the royal capital. Fighting was still going on between the Muslim and Christian factions when Lugard arrived and there was also a rivalry developing between the Protestant and Catholic chiefs.

The Protestant chiefs regarded the British as their natural allies so, when it became clear that the kabaka was siding with the Catholics, they turned to Lugard for help. The ensuing power struggle led to a declaration of British control over Buganda and the stripping away of most of the kabaka's powers. In 1897, Mwanga fled the capital and took up arms against the British with the help of his Catholic supporters and the Bunyoro king, Kabarega. The rebellion failed, however, and Mwanga was eventually captured and sent into exile in the Seychelles, where he died in 1903.

The British placed Mwanga's infant son, Daudi Chwa, on the throne and appointed three powerful chiefs, two Protestant and one Catholic, as regents until the new kabaka reached his majority in 1918.

The Colonial Era
After the 1890 Treaty of Berlin, which defined the various European countries' spheres of influence in Africa, Uganda, Kenya and the islands of Zanzibar and Pemba were declared British protectorates in 1894. Although the colonial administrators adopted a policy of indirect rule, giving the traditional kingdoms a considerable degree of autonomy, major changes took place in Buganda during this period. Cotton and coffee were introduced as cash crops, the railway between Kampala and Mombasa was completed and the concept of private ownership of land was introduced. This last measure resulted in the kabaka and a few thousand Bugandan chiefs being granted huge estates, on the basis of which they made their fortunes.

After the protectorate had been declared, the British tended to favour the recruitment of Buganda for the civil service. Other tribespeople, unable to acquire responsible jobs in the colonial administration or to make inroads into the Buganda-dominated commercial sector, were forced to seek other ways of joining the mainstream. The Acholi and Lango, for example, chose the army and became the tribal majority in the military. Thus were planted the seeds for the intertribal conflicts which were to tear Uganda apart following independence.

The Bugandan kabaka, Daudi Chwa, died in 1939 and was succeeded by his 15-year-old son, Muteesa II, who was educated at English-language boarding schools and later at Cambridge University. In 1953, however, a conflict developed between Muteesa II and the British governor over changes to the Ugandan constitution. Muteesa II was deposed and sent into exile in England. The action gave rise to a storm of protest in Buganda, and the British were eventually forced to back down and return the kabaka to his throne.

Independence
Unlike Kenya and, to a lesser extent, Tanzania, Uganda never experienced a large influx of European settlers and the associated expropriation of land. Instead, tribespeople were encouraged to grow cash crops for export through their own cooperative groups. As a result, nationalist organisations sprouted much later than those in neighbouring countries, and when they did, it was on a tribal basis. So exclusive were some of these that when independence began to be discussed, the Buganda even considered secession. By the mid-1950s, however, a Lango schoolteacher, Dr Milton Obote, managed to put together a loose coalition headed by the Uganda People's Congress, which led Uganda to independence in 1962 on the promise that the Buganda would have autonomy. The kabaka was the new nation's president and Milton Obote was its prime minister.

It wasn't a particularly propitious time for Uganda to come to grips with independence. Civil wars were raging in neighbouring southern Sudan, Zaïre and Rwanda, and refugees streamed into Uganda, adding to its problems. Also, it soon became obvious that Obote had no intention of sharing power with the kabaka. It meant that a confrontation was inevitable.

Obote moved fast, arresting several cabinet ministers and ordering his army chief of staff, Idi Amin, to storm the kabaka's palace. The raid resulted in the flight of the kabaka and his exile in London, where he died in 1969. Following this coup, Obote had himself made president, the Bugandan monarchy was abolished, along with those of the kingdoms of Bunyoro, Ankole, Toro and Busoga, and Idi Amin's star was on the rise.

UGANDA

The Amin Years

Events started to go seriously wrong after that. Obote had his attorney general, Godfrey Binaisa (a Bugandan), rewrite the constitution to consolidate virtually all powers in the presidency. He then began to nationalise foreign assets.

In 1969, a scandal surfaced over US$5 million in funds and weapons allocated to the Ministry of Defence that could not be accounted for. An explanation was demanded from Amin. When it wasn't forthcoming, his deputy, Colonel Okoya, and some junior officers demanded his resignation. Shortly afterwards Okoya and his wife were shot dead in their Gulu home and rumours began to circulate about Amin's imminent arrest. It never came. Instead, when Obote left for Singapore in January 1971 to attend the Commonwealth Heads of Government Meeting (CHOGM), Amin staged a coup. The British, who had probably suffered most from Obote's nationalisation program, were among the first to recognise the new regime. Obote went into exile in Tanzania.

So began Uganda's first reign of terror. All political activities were quickly suspended and the army was empowered to shoot on sight anyone suspected of opposition to the regime. Over the next eight years an estimated 300,000 Ugandans lost their lives, often in horrifying ways: bludgeoned to death with sledgehammers and iron bars or tortured to death in prisons and police stations all over the country. Nile Mansions, next to the Conference Centre in Kampala, became particularly notorious. The screams of those who were being tortured or beaten to death there could often be heard around the clock for days on end. Prime targets of Amin's death squads were the Acholi and Lango, who were decimated in waves of massacres. Whole villages were wiped out. Next Amin turned on the professional classes; university professors and lecturers, doctors, cabinet ministers, lawyers, businesspeople and even military officers who might have posed a threat to Amin were dragged from their offices and shot or simply never seen again.

Next in line was the 70,000-strong Asian community. In 1972 they were given 90 days to leave the country with virtually nothing but the clothes they wore. Amin and his cronies grabbed the US$1000 million booty they were forced to leave behind and quickly squandered it on new toys for the army and frivolous luxury items. Amin then turned on the British and nationalised, without compensation, US$500 million worth of investments in tea plantations and other industries. Again the booty was squandered.

Meanwhile, the economy collapsed, industrial activity ground to a halt, hospitals and rural health clinics closed, roads cracked and became riddled with potholes, cities became garbage dumps and utilities fell apart. The prolific wildlife was machine-gunned by soldiers for meat, ivory and skins, and the tourist industry evaporated. The stream of refugees across the border became a flood.

Faced with chaos and an inflation rate which hit 1000%, Amin was forced to delegate more and more powers to the provincial governors, who became virtual warlords in their areas. Towards the end, the treasury was so bereft of funds that it was unable to pay the soldiers. At the same time, international condemnation of the sordid regime was strengthening daily as more and more news of massacres, torture and summary executions leaked out of the country.

About the only source of support for Amin at this time was Libya, under the increasingly idiosyncratic leadership of Colonel Gaddafi. Libya bailed out the Ugandan economy, supposedly in the name of Islamic brotherhood (Amin had conveniently become a Muslim by this stage), and began an intensive drive to equip the Ugandan forces with sophisticated weapons.

The rot had spread too far, however, and was way past the point where it could be arrested by a few million dollars in Libyan largesse. Faced with a restless army in which intertribal fighting had broken out, Amin was forced to seek a diversion. He chose a war with Tanzania, ostensibly to teach that country a lesson for supporting anti-Amin dissidents. It was his last major act of insanity and in it lay his downfall.

Post-Amin Chaos

On 30 October 1978 the Ugandan army rolled across north-western Tanzania virtually unopposed and annexed more than 1200 sq km of territory. Meanwhile, the air force bombed the Lake Victoria ports of Bukoba and Musoma. President Julius Nyerere ordered a full-scale counterattack, but it took months to mobilise his ill-equipped and poorly trained forces. By the following spring, however, he had managed to scrape together a 50,000-strong people's militia composed mainly of illiterate youngsters from the bush. This militia joined with the many exiled Ugandan liberation groups (united only in their determination to rid Uganda of Amin). The two armies met. East Africa's supposedly best equipped and best trained army threw down its weapons and fled and the Tanzanians pushed on into the heart of Uganda. Kampala fell without a fight, and by the end of April, organised resistance had effectively ceased. Amin fled to Libya, where he remained until Gaddafi threw him out following a shoot-out with Libyan soldiers. He now lives in Jeddah on a Saudi Arabian pension.

The Tanzanian action was criticised, somewhat half-heartedly, by the Organisation for African Unity (OAU), but it's probably true to say that most African countries breathed a sigh of relief to see the madman finally thrown out. All the same, Tanzania was forced to foot the entire war bill, estimated at US$500 million. This was a crushing blow for an already desperately poor country. No other country has ever made a contribution.

The rejoicing in Uganda was short-lived. The 12,000 or so Tanzanian soldiers who remained in the country, supposedly to assist with reconstruction and to maintain law and order, turned on the Ugandans as soon as their pay wasn't forthcoming. They took what they wanted from shops at gunpoint, hijacked trucks arriving from Kenya with international relief aid and slaughtered more wildlife.

Once again the country slid into chaos and gangs of armed bandits roamed the cities, killing and looting. Food supplies ran out and hospitals could no longer function. Nevertheless, thousands of exiled Ugandans began to answer the new president's call to return home and help with reconstruction.

Usefu Lule, a modest and unambitious man, was installed as president with Nyerere's blessing, but when he began speaking out against Nyerere, he was replaced by Godfrey Binaisa, sparking riots supporting Lule in Kampala. Meanwhile, Obote bided his time in Dar es Salaam.

Binaisa quickly came under pressure to set a date for a general election and a return to civilian rule. Although this was done, he found himself at odds with other powerful members of the provisional government on ideological, constitutional and personal grounds – particularly over his insistence that the pre-Amin political parties not be allowed to contest the election.

The strongest criticism came from two senior members of the army, Tito Okello and David Ojok, both Obote supporters. Fearing a coup, Binaisa attempted to dismiss Ojok, who refused to step down and instead placed Binaisa under house arrest. The government was taken over by a military commission, which set the election for later that year. Obote returned from exile to an enthusiastic welcome in many parts of the country and swept to victory in an election which was blatantly rigged. Binaisa went into exile in the USA.

The honeymoon with Obote proved to be relatively short. Like Amin, Obote favoured certain tribes. Large numbers of civil servants and army and police commanders belonging to the tribes of the south were replaced with Obote supporters belonging to the tribes of the north. The State Research Bureau, a euphemism for the secret police, was re-established and the prisons began to fill once more. Obote was about to complete the destruction that Amin initiated. More and more reports of atrocities and killings leaked out of the country. Mass graves were unearthed that were unrelated to the Amin era. The press was muzzled and western journalists were expelled. It was obvious that Obote was once again attempting to achieve absolute power. Intertribal tension was on the rise, and in mid-1985 Obote was overthrown in a coup staged by the army under the leadership of Tito Okello.

The NRA Takeover

Okello was not the only opponent of Obote. Shortly after Obote became president for the second time, a guerrilla army opposed to his tribally biased government was formed in western Uganda. It was led by Yoweri Museveni, who had lived in exile in Tanzania during Amin's reign and who had served as defence minister during the chaotic administrations of 1979 and 1980.

From a group of 27 grew a guerrilla force of about 20,000, many of them orphaned teenagers. In the early days, few gave the guerrillas, known as the National Resistance Army (NRA), much of a chance. Government troops made frequently murderous swoops across the Luwero Triangle (Museveni's original base), and artillery supplied by North Korea pounded areas where the guerrillas were thought to be hiding. Few people outside Uganda even knew of the existence of the NRA, due to Obote's success in muzzling the press and expelling journalists. At times it seemed that Museveni might give up the battle – he spent several months in London at one point – but his dedicated young lieutenants kept fighting.

The NRA was not a bunch of drunken thugs like Amin's and Obote's armies. New recruits were indoctrinated in the bush by political commissars and taught that they had to be the servants of the people, not their oppressors. Discipline was tough. Anyone who got badly out of line was executed. Museveni was determined that the army would never again disgrace Uganda. Also, a central thrust of the NRA was to win the hearts and minds of the people, who learnt to identify totally with the persecuted Bugandans in the infamous Triangle.

By the time Obote was ousted and Okello had taken over, the NRA controlled a large slice of western Uganda and was a power to be reckoned with. Recognising this, Okello attempted to arrange a truce so that the leaders from both sides could negotiate on sharing power. However, peace talks in Nairobi failed. Wisely, Museveni didn't trust a man who had been one of Obote's closest military aides for more than 15 years. Neither did he trust Okello's prime minister, Paulo Mwanga, who was formerly Obote's vice president and minister of defence. Also, Okello's army was notorious for its lack of discipline and brutality. Units of Amin's former army had even returned from exile in Zaïre and Sudan and joined with Okello.

What Museveni wanted was a clean sweep of the administration, the army and the police. He wanted corruption stamped out and those who had been involved in atrocities during the Amin and Obote regimes brought to trial. These demands were, of course, anathema to Okello, who was up to his neck in corruption and responsible for many atrocities.

The fighting continued in earnest, and by late January 1986 it was obvious that Okello's days were numbered. The surrender of 1600 government soldiers holed up in their barracks in the southern town of Mbarara, which was controlled by the NRA, brought the NRA to the outskirts of Kampala itself. With the morale of the government troops at a low ebb, in February the NRA launched an all-out offensive to take the capital. Okello's troops fled, almost without a fight, though not before looting whatever remained and carting it away in commandeered buses. It was a typical parting gesture, as was the gratuitous shooting-up of many Kampala high-rise offices.

During the following weeks, Okello's rabble were pursued and finally pushed north over the border into Sudan. The civil war was over, apart from a few mopping-up operations in the extreme north-west and in Karamoja Province. The long nightmare had finally ended.

Rebuilding

Despite Museveni's Marxist leanings (he had studied political science at Dar es Salaam University in the early 1970s and trained with the anti-Portuguese guerrillas in Mozambique), he has proved to be pragmatic since taking control. Despite the radical stand of many of his officers on certain issues, he appointed several arch-conservatives to his cabinet and made an effort to reassure the country's influential Catholic community.

In the late 1980s, peace agreements were negotiated with most of the guerrilla factions who had fought for Okello or Obote and were still active in the north and north-east. Under an amnesty offered to the rebels, by 1988 as many as 40,000 had surrendered, and many were given jobs in the NRA. In the north-west of the country, almost 300,000 Ugandans returned home from across the Sudanese border.

With the peace came optimism – services were restored, factories which had lain idle for years were again productive, agriculture was back on line, the main roads resurfaced and the national parks' infrastructure restored and revitalised. On the political front, all political parties were banned.

There was, however, still one thorn in Museveni's side: the refugee problem from neighbouring Rwanda. Western Uganda was saddled with some 250,000 Tutsi refugees who had fled Rwanda's intermittent tribal conflicts, and feeding and housing them was a severe drain on Ugandan resources. On several occasions Museveni tried hard to persuade Rwanda's President Habyarimana to set up a repatriation scheme, but to no avail. It seems Museveni's patience finally snapped, and in late 1990, Rwanda was invaded by a 5000-strong guerrilla force from western Uganda which included NRA units and weaponry.

The evidence supports the contention that Museveni knew of preparations for the invasion, though he denies it. In any event, the rebels were thrown back across the border by the Rwandan army, assisted by troops from Belgium, France and Zaïre, and the ensuing witch-hunt of Tutsi inside Rwanda added to the number of refugees inside western Uganda. But the rebels were back in force shortly afterwards and by early 1993 were in control of around one-third of Rwanda, and finally came to power following the bloodbath of 1994.

The 1990s

The stability and rebuilding which came with Museveni's coming to power in 1986 has been followed in the 1990s with economic prosperity and unprecedented growth. Uganda now has the fastest growing economy in Africa, and has become a favourite among investors.

One of the keys to the success of the last few years was the decision to invite back the Asians who had been so unceremoniously evicted under Amin. As in Kenya, the Asians had a virtual monopoly on business and commerce. Without these people the economy was going nowhere fast, and it was clear to the pragmatic Museveni that Uganda needed them. They were, not surprisingly, very hesitant about returning, but assurances were given and kept, and property was and is still being given back to returned Asians or their descendants.

In 1993 a new draft constitution was adopted by the National Resistance Council (NRC). One surprising recommendation in the draft was that the country should adopt a system of 'no-party' politics for at least another five years, basically extending Museveni's National Resistance Movement (NRM) mandate for that period. Under the draft constitution, a Constituent Assembly was formed, and in 1994 elections for the assembly showed overwhelming support for the government. The only 'problem' area for the government was the north, where voters generally favoured anti-NRM candidates.

Also in 1993 the Bugandan monarchy was restored, but with no political power. This gave rise to concern among the Buganda that the existence of their tribal kingdom in the future would be threatened, and in protest against the NRM government they joined forces with the two main opposition parties, former president Obote's Ugandan Peoples Congress (UPC) and the Democratic Party (DP), led by foreign affairs minister Dr Paulo Ssemogerere. In 1994 the Constituent Assembly voted to limit the kabaka's role to a purely ceremonial and traditional one.

Democratic 'no-party' elections were called for May 1996. Despite strong opposition from supporters of political parties, the elections went ahead, the main candidates being Museveni and Ssemogerere, who had resigned as foreign minister in order to campaign. For all intents, it was still a party political election, between Museveni's NRM (officially a 'movement' and not a political party), and Ssemogerere, being supported by the former Democratic Party in alliance with the immensely unpopular (among the Buganda) UPC. Museveni won a resounding victory, capturing almost 75% of the vote. The only area where Ssemogerere had any real support was the anti-NRM north.

It is in fact the north which is the last major issue which Museveni has yet to deal with. Anti-government rebels of various factions – mainly the bizarre, Sudanese-allied Lords Resistance Army, led by Joseph Kony, and the West Nile Bank Front, which is led by Idi Amin's former minister, Colonel Juma Oris – are still a problem in the area. Violent incidents occur on a fairly regular basis and travel in the north and west is not as secure as it might be.

The 1996 elections can be seen as Uganda's final step on the road to complete rehabilitation and rebuilding. With the elections out of the way, the country is set to boom. Many potential investors had things on hold, just in case the elections didn't go smoothly and the country slid back into chaos. Tourism too is a sector with a bright future.

What is the greatest pity is that Uganda still has a huge image problem; to most of the world it seems Uganda is synonymous with two things – Idi Amin and HIV/AIDS. Nevertheless, the future for Uganda and its people is brighter now than it has been for many, many years.

GEOGRAPHY

Uganda has an area of 236,580 sq km, of which about 25% is fertile arable land capable of providing a surplus of food. Lake Victoria and the Victoria Nile, which flows through much of the country, together create one of the best watered areas of Africa.

The land varies from semidesert in the north-east to the lush and fertile shores of the lake, the Ruwenzori Mountains in the west and the beautiful, mountainous south-west.

The tropical heat is tempered by the altitude, which averages over 1000m.

CLIMATE

As most of Uganda is fairly flat, with mountains only in the extreme east (Mt Elgon), extreme west (the Ruwenzoris) and close to the Rwanda border, the bulk of the country enjoys the same tropical climate, with temperatures averaging about 26°C during the day and 16°C at night. The hottest months are from December to February, when the daytime range is 27 to 29°C.

The rainy seasons in the south are from April to May and October to November, the wettest month being April. In the north, the wet season is from April to October and the dry season is from November to March. During the wet seasons, the average rainfall is 175 mm per month. Humidity is generally low outside the wet seasons.

ECOLOGY & ENVIRONMENT

With its relatively low population density and scarcity of wildlife (the latter courtesy of the decimation which occurred during the bad old days), Uganda lacks many of the environmental pressures faced by most other countries in the region. The absence of any notable numbers of tourists in the last 20 years means that the national parks and wilderness areas are generally in good shape, and conditions are ideal for the native animals to re-establish themselves.

Uganda is therefore ideally placed to ensure that the environment remains in good condition. Programs are already in place for the responsible management of the national parks, and US Peace Corps volunteers can be

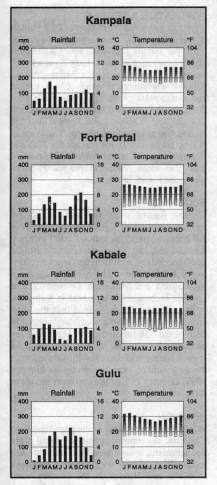

Kampala

Rainfall / Temperature charts

Fort Portal

Rainfall / Temperature charts

Kabale

Rainfall / Temperature charts

Gulu

Rainfall / Temperature charts

UGANDA

Ecology Threat
There is a potential threat to the ecology of Lake Victoria and the livelihood of the people who live by its shores, with the rapidly growing problem of water hyacinth (*Eichhornia crassipes*). This aquatic noxious weed, originally from South America, floats in large 'islands' on the lake surface. It grows so prolifically that it chokes waterways and is so dense that it stops light penetrating the lake surface, making it impossible for fish to live beneath it. Visitors to the Owen Falls Dam at Jinja can get a graphic idea of how rampant the weed is – the area below the dam is choked almost solid and local people have great difficulty in manoeuvring their canoes through it. For further information see the boxed story on page 656. ■

The governing 245-member Constituent Assembly has elected members, who, although standing as individuals, are affiliated with various political organisations (formerly parties), including the National Resistance Movement (NRM), the Uganda Patriotic Movement (UPM), Democratic Party, Uganda People's Congress and the Conservative Party.

At the base of the NRM political administration are the local councils (formerly Resistance Committees) – a village-based administration tool which is responsible for village matters – members of which can, in theory, be elected and pass through the system all the way to the Constituent Assembly. Apart from being a way to channel new faces into the political system, the councils provide the NRM with a direct line to disseminate policy information to the people and have improved security at a local level.

ECONOMY
Before Amin's coup, Uganda was approaching self-sufficiency in food and had a small but vital industrial sector and profitable copper mines. Boosting export income were the thriving coffee, sugar and tourist industries. Under Amin the country reverted almost completely to a subsistence economy. The managerial and technical elite was either expelled, killed or exiled and the country's

found in most parks undertaking conservation projects, such as building boardwalks and constructing walking paths.

GOVERNMENT & POLITICS
Uganda is a republic and a member of the Commonwealth. The president is head of state, the government and the armed forces.

UGANDA

infrastructure was virtually destroyed. Some cash crops made a tentative recovery under Obote, but Museveni's government inherited major problems.

In 1987 there was a massive devaluation, a new currency was issued, an International Monetary Fund (IMF) restructuring deal was accepted and the government made a real attempt to tackle its economic problems. Despite this, inflation was running at more than 100% within a year and another massive devaluation followed.

Uganda's problems stem from its almost total reliance on coffee, which accounts for 98% of exports, plus the fact that 60% of foreign earnings is used to pay off the large overseas debt.

The remainder of the exchange reserves are spent on items aimed at bringing about improvements in the long term. Short-term benefits are few and poverty is widespread.

One of the more interesting aspects of the Ugandan economy is the barter system, whereby the country makes deals with foreign trading partners, exchanging goods (usually coffee) for much-needed imports. So far it has struck deals with Algeria, Cuba, the Czech and Slovak republics, Germany, Italy, Libya, North Korea, Rwanda, Somalia, Sudan and (the former) Yugoslavia.

Despite the obvious problems, the Ugandan economy is finally taking off again, and with growth of 10% in 1995, is now the fastest growing in Africa.

Agriculture is the single most important component of the Ugandan economy. It accounts for 70% of gross domestic product (GDP) and employs 90% of the workforce. Coffee, sugar, cotton and tea are the main export crops. Crops grown for local consumption include maize, millet, cassava, sweet potato, beans and cereals.

The manufacturing sector's share of GDP has shrunk from 12% in 1970 to around 5% now. Manufactured goods include textiles, soap, cement and steel products. Foreign aid is used mostly to supply vital imported fuel, to purchase spare parts to get factories back to full production, and for other measures to repair the economic infrastructure.

POPULATION & PEOPLE

Uganda's estimated population of 21.3 million is increasing at the alarming rate of close to 2.5% per annum. It is made up of a complex and diverse range of tribes. Lake Kyoga forms the northern boundary for the Bantu-speaking peoples, who dominate much of east, central and southern Africa and, in Uganda, include the Buganda and several other tribes. In the north live the Lango (near Lake Kyoga) and the Acholi (towards the Sudan border), who speak Nilotic languages. To the east are the Teso and Karamojong, who are related to the Maasai and who also speak Nilotic languages. Pygmies live in the forests of the west.

EDUCATION

Current figures show that out of the 3.5 million children of school-going age, only 1.7 million attend the around 8000 primary schools, and 250,000 students attend around 1000 secondary, technical and teacher-training schools. The main higher education institutions are Makerere University and Uganda Technical College, both in Kampala.

In 1996 Museveni pledged that the government would set up a secondary school in each of the 838 subdistricts of Uganda. Free primary education for the first four children in each family was due to be introduced with the new school year beginning in January 1997. Literacy in Uganda currently stands at 48%.

RELIGION

While about two-thirds of the population are Christian, the remaining one-third still practise animism, with a small percentage who follow Islam. There were sizeable numbers of Sikhs and Hindus in the country until Asians were expelled in 1972, although many are now returning following a presidential invitation.

LANGUAGE

The official language is English, which most people can speak. The other major languages are Luganda and Swahili, though the latter isn't spoken much east of Kampala or in the capital.

Facts for the Visitor

PLANNING

When to Go

The best time for a visit to Uganda is January and February, as the weather at this time of year is generally dry. From June to September is also good as the weather is still dry.

Maps

The best available map of Uganda is the Macmillan 1:1,350,000 *Uganda Traveller's Map*, which is available in book shops in Kampala (USh 7000). It also has insets of the Murchison Falls and Queen Elizabeth national parks, and a street map of Kampala.

HIGHLIGHTS

Without a doubt the main highlight of a trip to Uganda is tracking the mountain gorillas in the south-western rainforests. However, this is not all Uganda has to offer: the national parks of Murchison Falls and Queen Elizabeth are both worth a visit for their natural attractions. Another big attraction is the chimpanzees at Kibale National Park near Fort Portal.

For those who want a more physical adventure, nothing surpasses the mountain trekking in the Ruwenzoris, the legendary 'mountains of the moon', on the western border with Zaïre, or on Mt Elgon on the Kenyan border in the east.

While Uganda's natural beauty is stunning, the local people are among the friendliest and most open you'll find anywhere in Africa. It's easy to spout this old cliched remark, but in Uganda it really is true.

As tourism is still recovering from the bad old days, you won't find Uganda crawling with tourists – in fact it's the opposite – and although increasing numbers of people are rediscovering the 'Pearl of Africa' it's still largely devoid of rubbernecks – the country received only 175,000 visitors in 1995.

TOURIST OFFICES

The Ministry of Tourism, Wildlife & Antiq-uities operates a good tourist office (☎ (041) 242196; fax 242188) in Kampala. It's in the IPS building on the corner of Parliament Ave and Kimathi St.

VISAS & DOCUMENTS

Visas

Some visitors to Uganda require visas, although there are many exceptions: nationals of Canada, Denmark, Finland, France, Germany, Israel, Japan, Norway, Sweden and most Commonwealth countries (except India, New Zealand and Nigeria) do not require visas.

Visa costs vary depending on what your nationality is: the maximum is US$25 for a three-month, single-entry visa. Two photos are required and the visas are issued in 24 hours; in Nairobi you can get them the same day.

Visas are available at the border on entry for the usual fee, though you probably won't need a photo. They may give you less than three months but the visa is renewable in the normal way.

See Embassies below for information on obtaining visas in Uganda for neighbouring African countries.

Visa Extensions For visa extensions pay a visit to immigration, which is on the lower level of the Crested Crane Towers in Kampala, the ugly landmark building on Nile Ave in the city centre.

Getting Other Visas in Uganda Kampala is not a bad place for picking up visas to other countries as there are usually no queues at the various embassies. See Foreign Embassies in Uganda below for the addresses of the various embassies.

Burundi

Don't plan on getting a visa for Burundi in Uganda, as these are only issued to Ugandans and Ugandan residents.

UGANDA

HIGHLIGHTS

	REGION	COMMENTS
Natural Beauty Spots		
Murchison Falls		
Spectacular falls on the Victoria Nile River; experience this mighty river first hand with a boat ride to the base.	Northern Uganda	An amazing sight when viewed up close – the water crashes through the narrow gap in the river with a breathtaking force.
Ssese Islands		
Mellow islands; the place to kick back for a few days.	South-Western Uganda	A refreshing and interestingly different aspect of Uganda, these islands remain largely unspoiled and provide the perfect place to put your feet up and take it easy.
Activities		
Nile River		
Exhilarating white-water rafting on Africa's most famous river.	South-Eastern Uganda	The Victoria Nile near Jinja is a class five, making it more challenging than the popular Zambezi at Victoria Falls in Zimbabwe.
National Parks & Reserves		
Kibale National Park		
Fascinating primate reserve within lush surroundings; chimp-spotting walks.	South-Western Uganda	Said to have the highest density of primates in the world including an estimated 500 chimpanzees.
Bwindi National Park		
Trek to see mountain gorillas deep in the hidden surroundings of natural rainforest.	South-Western Uganda	Encompasses one of the last remaining habitats of mountain gorilla and is home to half of the world's surviving mountain gorillas with an estimated 320 individuals. Experience the thrill of being close to these enormously powerful but gentle creatures.
Ruwenzori Mountains		
Superb trekking on the 'Mountains of the Moon'.	South-Western Uganda	The astonishingly beautiful mist-covered Ruwenzoris are overlooked by the majority of travellers, yet they are at least the equal of Kilimanjaro and Mt Kenya.
Urban Centres		
Kampala		
A city on the up; well worth a few days.	Kampala	A modern, bustling capital with the fastest growing economy in Africa. The recovery from civil strife has been astounding.

Kenya

If you apply before noon, the visa can usually be issued the same day. The cost is US$30 and two photos are required.

Rwanda

Visas cost USh 20,000 (same for all nationalities), require two photos and are issued in 24 hours, or the same day if you apply early in the morning. They are also available at the border.

Sudan

Visa applications are only accepted on Monday and Thursday. A one-month tourist visa costs US$10 (shillings are not accepted) and requires two photos, a letter of introduction from your embassy and an onward ticket. Visas can take anything up to a month to issue, as all applications have to be referred to Khartoum. The border between Uganda and Sudan is effectively closed due to the civil war in southern Sudan.

Tanzania

Visas are valid for three months, take 24 hours to issue and require two photos. Costs vary according to your nationality: French USh 25,000; German USh 10,000; UK and USA USh 50,000; others are around USh 10,000 to USh 20,000.

Zaïre

A single/multiple-entry visa will cost you USh 45,000/70,000 for one month, the cost is USh 80,000/105,000 for two months and its USh 115,000/135,000 for three months. Two photos are required, and the visa is issued in 24 hours.

Other Documents

Driving Licence If you have an international driving licence, bring it, although you really only need your local licence from home.

EMBASSIES
Ugandan Embassies Abroad

There are Ugandan embassies in the following places:

Belgium

Ave de Tervuren 317, 450 Brussels (☎ (02) 762-5825; fax 763-0438)

Canada

231 Cobourg St, Ottawa, Ontario KIN 8J2 (☎ (613) 233-7797; fax 232-6689)

Denmark

Sofievej 15, DK 2900, Hellerup (☎ 3962-0966)

Egypt

9 Midan El Messaha, Dokki, Cairo (☎ (091) 348-5975; fax 348-5980)

Ethiopia

Africa Ave H-18, K-36, N-31, Addis Ababa (☎ (01) 513531; fax 514355)

France

13 Ave Raymond Poincare, 75116 Paris (☎ 01 47 27 46 80; fax 01 47 55 12 21)

Germany

Duerenstrasse 44, 53173

Italy

Via Ennio Quirino Visconti 8, 00193 Rome (☎ & fax (06) 322-5220)

Japan

39-15 Oyama-chi, Shibuya-ku, Tokyo 151 (☎ (03) 3465-4552; fax 3465-4970)

Kenya

Uganda House, Baring Arcade, 4th floor, Kenyatta Ave, Nairobi (☎ (02) 330801; fax 330970)

Rwanda

Ave de la Paix, Kigali (☎ 76495; fax 73551)

South Africa

Trafalgar Court, Aprt 35B, 634 Park St, Arcadia 0083, Pretoria (☎ (012) 344-4100; fax 343-2809)

Sudan

House No 9, Sq 42, New Extension, Khartoum (☎ (011) 78409)

Tanzania

Extelecoms Building, 7th floor, Samora Ave, Dar es Salaam (☎ (051) 31004; fax 46256)

UK

Uganda House, 58/59 Trafalgar Sq, London WC2N 5DX (☎ (0181) 839-5783; fax 839-8925)

USA

5909 16th St NW, Washington DC 20011-2896 (☎ (202) 726-0416; fax 726-1727)

Zaïre

17 Ave Tombalbaye/Ave de Travailure, Kinshasa (☎ 22740)

BP 877, Goma (☎ 366)

Foreign Embassies in Uganda

The telephone area code for Kampala is 041.

Burundi

7 Bandali Rise, Bugolobi (☎ 221697). Open Monday to Friday from 8.30 am to 12.30 pm and 3 to 5.30 pm.

France

9 Parliament Ave (☎ 242120; fax 241252)

Italy

11 Lourdel Rd, Nakasero (☎ 241786; fax 250448)

Kenya

Nakasero Rd (☎ 258235; fax 267369). Open Monday to Friday from 8.30 am to 12.30 pm and 2 to 4.30 pm.

Netherlands

Kisozi Complex, Nakasero Lane (☎ 231859)

Rwanda

Plot 2, Nakaima Rd (next door to the Uganda

Museum) (☎ 244045). Open Monday to Friday from 8.30 am to 12.30 pm and 2.30 to 5 pm.

South Africa
Plot 9, Malcolm X Ave, Kololo (☎ & fax 259156)

Sudan
Plot 21, Nakasero Rd (☎ 243518). Open Monday to Friday from 9 am to noon.

Tanzania
6 Kagera Rd (☎ 256272). Open Monday to Friday from 9 am to 4 pm.

UK
10 Parliament Ave (☎ 257301)

USA
Rear of UK High Commission Building, 10 Parliament Ave (☎ 25791)

Zaïre
20 Philip Rd, Kololo (☎ 233777)

MONEY
Costs
Since the elimination of the black market and the introduction of foreign exchange bureaus, Uganda is now one of the more expensive countries in the region. Obviously, there are many ways of keeping costs to a minimum, but if you demand a reasonable level of comfort and facilities, you'll find your Ugandan notes diminishing at what can be an alarming rate.

A budget hotel will cost you around USh 5000 to USh 10,000 for a double room, usually with a shared bathroom. Transport is cheap, as is food at a no-frills restaurant, but a splurge at a good restaurant will cost you around USh 15,000-plus. National park entry fees are set at USh 15,000 per person per day, while camping costs USh 10,000 per person. Foreign residents of Uganda pay somewhat less, and local Ugandans pay less again.

The cost of seeing the gorillas in Bwindi National Park is the local equivalent of US$150, at Mgahinga it's US$120.

Currency
The Ugandan shilling (USh) is a stable currency and floats against the US dollar. It is also fully convertible (ie you can buy Ugandan shillings with US dollars or US dollars with Ugandan shillings) at banks and foreign exchange bureaus.

Notes in circulation are USh 10,000, USh 5000, USh 1000, USh 500, USh 200, USh 100, USh 50, USh 20 and USh 10. There are no coins.

Currency Exchange

USA	US$1	=	USh 1032
UK	UK£1	=	USh 1691
France	FFr1	=	USh 185
Germany	DM1	=	USh 625
Australia	A$1	=	USh 788

Changing Money
The Ugandan shilling trades at whatever it's worth against the US dollar/UK pound and there's very little fluctuation from day to day. There is no black market. As a result, it doesn't really matter too much where you change your money, though the foreign exchange bureaus generally offer a slightly better rate than the banks. The trouble is that there are not foreign exchange bureaus in every town and, where one doesn't exist, the banks take advantage of this by giving lousy rates. Likewise, hotels give lousy rates.

You will find foreign exchange bureaus at both the Malaba and Busia border posts (Uganda-Kenya border), Jinja, Kabale, Kampala (where there are scores of them), Kasese, Masaka, Mbarara and Fort Portal. They don't exist in Tororo, Mbale and Kisoro, so if you're going there, plan ahead.

POST & COMMUNICATIONS
Post
The cost of sending a postcard or aerogram is USh 500; for a letter it's USh 550 per 10 gm. There is an efficient poste restante service at the GPO in Kampala.

Telephone
Telephone connections, both domestic and international, are pretty good these days – you'll even see people with cellular phones in Kampala.

In all towns of any size you'll come across card phones (yellow phone boxes) outside the post office. These phones can be used for national and international calls, and cards are available from the post office.

From public phone boxes international

calls are charged at the rate of USh 7500 per minute (!), and the highest denomination phone card is USh 15,000 – clearly you're not meant to talk for long!

In Kampala there's a much cheaper option, the private operator called Starcom, which has an office and card phones (green boxes) around town. Their charge is USh 2500 for one minute. See the Kampala section for details.

Telephone Area Codes The telephone area codes for the major towns in Uganda include:

Entebbe	042
Fort Portal	0493
Jinja	043
Kabale	0486
Kampala	041
Kasese	0483
Masaka	0485
Masindi	0465
Mbale	045
Mbarara	0485
Tororo	045

Fax & E-Mail
Fax charges are relatively cheap, at USh 1500 per page when sending from the GPO in Kampala; with Starcom it's USh 2500.

Starcom also has e-mail facilities, but at present these are only available to account-holders on a monthly basis; there is no casual use.

BOOKS
There are not many books which relate specifically to Uganda, but the following may be of interest.

Uganda Since Independence by Phares Mutibwa and *Uganda – Landmarks in Rebuilding a Nation* (various authors) are both fairly dry accounts of the country's recent history.

Uganda – From the Pages of Drum is an interesting compilation of articles which appeared in the now defunct *Drum* magazine. These chronicle the rise of Idi Amin, the atrocities he committed and Museveni's

bush war and coming to power. It is complete with photos and forms a powerful record of what the country went through.

Fong & the Indians, by Paul Theroux, is set in a fictional East African country which bears a remarkable likeness to Uganda. It is set in pre-civil war days and is at times both funny and bizarre as it details the life of a Chinese immigrant and his dealings with the Asians who control commerce in the country.

The Man With the Key Has Gone! by Ian Clarke is a recent account of the time spent in the Luwero Triangle district by a British doctor and his family.

NEWSPAPERS & MAGAZINES
The pavements in Kampala are awash with printed matter. The daily *New Vision* is the government-owned newspaper. Unlike its equivalent in Tanzania, it's a good read, with plenty of African coverage, though less of other world events.

Much better for gutsy, analytical journalism is the weekly *The Monitor*, which contains feature articles as well as better coverage of international news. It should keep you busy most of the day.

The Kenyan daily, *Nation*, is available in the late morning as far west as Jinja. International magazines like *Time, Newsweek, New African* and *South* are also readily available, but dailies are harder to find (try the shops at the Sheraton in Kampala).

RADIO & TV
The government-run TV station is Uganda Television. In Kampala there's also a commercial station, Sanyu TV.

Radio Uganda broadcasts in English and other languages on AM frequencies.

Kampala has two commercial FM stations: the phenomenally popular Capital FM (91.3 MHz), and Radio Sanyu (88.2 MHz). Both play western pop music.

PHOTOGRAPHY
Colour print film is widely available in Kampala, less so elsewhere, at prices similar to what you pay in Kenya. Expect to pay

around USh 3000 for a 36-exposure colour print film. Slide film is much harder to find – it's safer to bring your own. The Star Photo Studio (☎ (041) 232047), Wilson Rd, Kampala, is a good place to find film. It has both print and slide film at prices better than you can find elsewhere (Fujicolor USh 3000, Fujichrome 36 USh 8000).

Although there are no official restrictions on photography, there is a certain amount of paranoia about photos being taken of anything which could be interpreted as spying (military and civilian infrastructure) or of poverty or deprivation. Most of the time, there are no problems, but it's probably best to ask permission before taking photos of people. Usually people will be more than happy to be photographed, but respect their feelings if they aren't.

HEALTH

You must take precautions against malaria. Bilharzia is also a serious risk in all of Uganda's lakes and rivers. Avoid swimming and walking barefoot, especially where there are lots of reeds (the snails which are the intermediate host for the bilharzia parasite live in areas such as these).

HIV/AIDS continues to be a huge problem in Uganda. A government campaign focuses on preventing infection through fidelity and abstinence, in addition to the use of condoms. Blood is screened in main medical centres and the incidence of cases arising from contaminated blood is declining. (For more information, see the Health section in the Regional Facts for the Visitor chapter.)

Acute Mountain Sickness (AMS) is a potentially fatal condition that can occur when climbing or trekking over 3000m. If you're planning to do any high-altitude trekking in Uganda, see the Health section in the Regional Facts for the Visitor chapter.

DANGERS & ANNOYANCES

Even now, more than 10 years on from Museveni's rise to power, Uganda still has a lingering image as a dangerous and unstable country to visit. This is a great shame, as it is currently the most stable and least corrupt country in the region, and also one of the safest; in Kenya, for instance, there is a far higher incidence of mugging and petty theft – things that are almost unheard of in Kampala.

Having said that, there are still some places where your safety cannot be guaranteed, but these are limited to the area north of the Arua to Soroti road. If you want to visit this part of the country (and there's very little reason to do so), make enquiries before setting off.

PUBLIC HOLIDAYS

The following holidays are observed in Uganda:

January
    New Year's Day (1st)
    NRM Anniversary Day (26th)
March
    Women's Day (8th)
March/April
    Good Friday
    Easter Monday
May
    Labour Day (1st)
June
    Martyrs' Day (3rd)
    Heroes Day (9th)
October
    Independence Day (9th)
December
    Christmas Day (25th)
    Boxing Day (26th)

ACTIVITIES
White-Water Rafting

While well established in other African countries, this activity is very much in its infancy here, having only started in mid-1996. Trips are on the Nile River near Jinja and the ride is said to rival the Zambezi in Zimbabwe.

The trips are operated by a New Zealand outfit, Adrift, cost US$95 for a day trip, including transport to and from Kampala, and can be booked in Kampala.

Trekking

Uganda has always had a strong attraction

among the dedicated trekking fraternity, mainly for the opportunities presented by the Ruwenzori Mountains in the west and Mt Elgon in the east. Both are national parks in pristine condition; see the Uganda National Parks & Reserves chapter for more detailed information.

Gorilla Tracking

This is one of the major reasons travellers come to Uganda. It's possible to track the mountain gorillas in Bwindi (US$150) and Mgahinga (US$120) national parks in the south-west, although bookings should be made in Kampala first. See the Kampala and National Parks & Reserves chapters for full details.

ACCOMMODATION
Camping

There are enough opportunities for camping in Uganda that it's worth considering carrying a tent. There are a few private camp sites, but most are found in the national parks, and the facilities are basic. The cost of camping in national parks is USh 10,000 per person per day, although you must add to this the cost of entering a national park (USh 15,000 per person per day).

Hotels

Hotels range from the fleapit to the five star, although at this stage the former far outnumber the latter. As tourism and commerce picks up, so does the construction of new hotels and lodges. Currently, up-market hotels are limited to Kampala; elsewhere the best you'll find is no more than about three-star quality.

The same applies to the lodges in the national parks – this is not Kenya. Again, things are gradually improving, but be prepared to rough it.

At the other end of the scale, you can count on all small towns having at least one basic lodge. These are cheap but you need a fairly strong constitution.

FOOD

Local food is much the same as what you find in Kenya, except that here *ugali* is called *posho* (maize meal), and is far less popular than *matoke* (mashed plantains).

Fast food is not well entrenched, so once away from the relatively cosmopolitan Kampala, you'll have the choice of good, cheap local food, or expensive western food from the more expensive hotels and lodges.

Vegetarians will find themselves reasonably well catered for, although as most local dishes are meat-based there is little choice – posho and matoke and the occasional Indian dishes are about the limit.

DRINKS
Nonalcoholic Drinks

Sodas are everywhere, the most popular being Fanta, Pepsi and Coke (ho hum). Prices range in price from USh 150 to about USh 300.

Alcohol

Like all East Africans, Ugandans love their beer, and mercifully, unlike their counterparts in Kenya, they don't have a fetish for drinking the stuff warm – if a town has electricity you can be sure it will have a fridge, and this will have beer in it!

Uganda Breweries and Nile Breweries are the two local companies, and they produce similar unexciting but quite drinkable lagers. You'll also find South African Castle beer in cans, as a third brewer was recently given the licence to import it.

Bottled local beer costs from USh 1000 to USh 2000 a bottle, depending on where you're drinking.

Waragi is the local millet-based alcohol and is relatively safe, although it can knock you around and give you a mean hangover.

ENTERTAINMENT

Nightlife in Uganda is fairly low-key. In Kampala there are a few nightclubs and discos, some of which have live music. There's not even a cinema here yet.

Away from the capital things are much quieter. You'll always be able to find somewhere to have a drink in the evening, but there's very little action.

UGANDA

Getting There & Away

Possible access routes into Uganda are by air, land and lake. By land there are rail and bus connections; by lake the only boat connection is between Uganda and Tanzania – Port Bell (Kampala) and Mwanza – across Lake Victoria. There are no passenger-boat connections between Uganda and Kenya.

AIR

Few travellers enter Uganda by air because most of the discounted air fares available in Europe and North America use Nairobi as the gateway to East Africa. Unlike Nairobi, you will not find discounted fares available in Kampala, so if you fly out of Entebbe (Kampala's international airport), it will be more expensive.

Kenya

If you intend flying from Entebbe to Nairobi, book at least a few days in advance, as flights are sometimes heavily subscribed. Flights cost US$136 one way and take between one and 1¾ hours, depending on the type of aircraft. Flights are operated by Kenya Airways and Uganda Airlines.

Rwanda

There are flights four times weekly between Entebbe and Kigali with Uganda Airlines.

Tanzania

In theory, there are weekly connections between Kampala and Dar es Salaam (US$206 one way) with Air Tanzania (via Kilimanjaro) and Uganda Airlines (via Nairobi).

LAND
Kenya

The two main border posts which most overland travellers use are Malaba and Busia, with Malaba being by far the more commonly used. You would probably use Busia only if you were coming from Kisumu and

wanted to go directly to Jinja or Kampala, bypassing Tororo.

Bus Akamba operates three direct buses between Kampala and Nairobi daily which cost USh 18,000 (KSh 900), depart at 7 am and 7 pm, and take around 12 to 14 hours. Its office in Kampala is on Dewinton St; in Nairobi it's on Lagos Rd. Akamba also has its daily Royal service, which is real luxury with large seats similar to 1st class in an aircraft. There are only three in each row! Tickets cost USh 42,000 (KSh 2100), and the price includes a meal at the halfway point (Eldoret).

Mawingo operates daily buses at 3 pm. These are marginally cheaper than Akamba (USh 16,000 from Kampala), but are more crowded and take up to 15 hours. The depot in Kampala is right by the old taxi park. Tawfiq also operates daily buses, and is the cheapest at USh 12,000.

Doing the journey in stages, there are frequent taxis until the late afternoon between Kampala (USh 5000, three hours) or Jinja (USh 5000, two hours) and Malaba. There are also frequent taxis in either direction between Tororo and Malaba (Uganda) which cost USh 250 and take less than one hour. The road is in excellent condition, although it does mean that the drivers can get up to terrifying speeds. Luckily, there's not much traffic on this road except close to Kampala.

The Ugandan and Kenyan border posts are about one km from each other at Malaba and you can walk or take a *boda-boda* (bicycle taxi).

On the Kenyan side there are daily buses with different companies between Malaba and Nairobi which depart at around 7.30 pm arriving at about 5.30 am the next day. The fare is KSh 450 with Akamba. If you prefer to travel by day there are plenty of *matatus* between Malaba and Bungoma which take about 45 minutes. If you stay in Bungoma overnight there are plenty of cheap hotels to choose from. From Bungoma there are several daily buses to Nairobi which leave at about 8 am and arrive about 5 pm the same day.

Taking a vehicle through this border crossing is fairly straightforward and doesn't take more than an hour or so.

The other entry point into Kenya from Uganda is via Busia, which is further south. There are frequent taxis between Jinja and Busia and matatus between Busia and Kisumu. Akamba has direct buses on this route which connect Kisumu and Kampala. The buses leave Kisumu daily at noon, and cost KSh 600.

Train The recent increase in East African cooperation has led to the reintroduction of a classic rail journey, between Nairobi and Kampala. This is an excellent way to travel between the two capitals, and the border crossing is a breeze as the immigration officials come through the train and you don't even have to leave your compartment. The Kenyan Railways train is hauled by Kenyan locomotives and staffed by Kenyan crew on the Kenyan side; Ugandan locos and crew take over on the Ugandan side. The spirit of cooperation is not total, however: the picture of Moi, the Kenyan president, in the buffet car remains up the whole way and Museveni doesn't get a look in!

Departure from Nairobi is at noon on Tuesday, arriving in Kampala on Wednesday at 9.30 am. The fare is KSh 4400/3520 in 1st/2nd class, which includes bedding and meals. From Kampala the departure is 4 pm on Wednesday, arriving in Nairobi at 2.40 pm on Thursday, and the fare is USh 57,850/35,300 in 1st/2nd class. The train is often subject to delays of anything up to six hours.

There are also trains from Nairobi to the border at Malaba via Nakuru and Eldoret on Friday and Saturday at 3 pm, arriving at Malaba the next day at 8 am. The fares are KSh 2630/1820 in 1st/2nd class including meals and bedding. In the opposite direction they leave Malaba on Saturday and Sunday at 4 pm, arriving in Nairobi the following morning.

Rwanda

There are two main crossing points: Kabale to Kigali via Katuna (Gatuna), and Kisoro to Ruhengeri via Cyanika.

Kabale to Kigali From Kabale to Kigali there are many minibuses daily which cost USh 7000 and take about two hours (not including immigration formalities and army roadblocks). These are only supposed to take 14 passengers but sometimes they squeeze in a few more. Expect a delay at the border while time-wasting immigration officials examine your passport minutely and ask a lot of silly questions. It takes about 45 minutes to get through the two border posts.

There are two military checkpoints between the border and Kigali where your baggage will be searched.

Going in the opposite direction from Kigali to Kabale, the last minibus leaves Kigali at 1 pm and may dump you at the border even if you've paid to go to Kabale. That's not a problem as the touts at the border will organise onward transport to Kabale for you. This, naturally, will cost extra.

There are also Ugandan buses which do the run between Kigali and Kabale in either direction once a day, leaving Kigali at 6.30 am and Kabale at 7 am, taking around two hours. The cost is the same as the minibuses.

For those in a hurry to get between Kigali and Kampala, there's a daily bus in either direction which leaves Kampala at 7 am and Kigali at 6.30 am. These buses are operated by Jaguar or Happy Trails (in Kampala), cost USh 15,000 or US$15 and take about 10 hours.

Kisoro to Ruhengeri From Kisoro to Ruhengeri via Cyanika there's very little transport and the road is in a very poor state. There's also the danger of being ambushed by rebels. Things should improve as the dust settles in Rwanda but, in the meantime, it's suggested you avoid this route.

Tanzania

The route into Uganda goes through the Kagera salient on the west side of Lake Victoria between Bukoba and Masaka, via Kyaka. Road conditions have improved considerably over the last few years, so it's possible to do the journey from Masaka to Bukoba in one day. There are taxis from Masaka to Kyotera (USh 1200, 45 minutes) plus several daily pick-ups from there to the border at Mutukula (USh 1500, one hour), which go when full. The border crossings are easy and there are moneychangers on the Tanzanian side, though they give a lousy rate. The border posts are right next to each other. There's also a basic place to stay and eat on the Tanzanian side.

From the border, a daily bus goes to Bukoba early in the morning (TSh 3000, about six hours) over variable roads. If the bus has departed before you arrive at the border, your only option is to hitch (not easy, as there's little traffic) or stay overnight. South of the border, there's a checkpoint in Bunazi, where you're obliged to stop and have your passport checked.

There's also a bus between Bukoba and Mutukula which departs from Bukoba daily (except Sunday) at 11.15 am, costs TSh 1200 and takes about four hours. In the opposite direction, it leaves Mutukula for Bukoba at 5 pm.

Zaïre

The two main crossing points are west from Kisoro to Rutshuru via Bunagana, and northwest from Kasese to Beni via Katwe and Kasindi. The Ishasha crossing between Kasese and Rutshuru is also open. There are several buses daily with Safe Journey between Kasese and Kampala (USh 8000). Following the massive upheavals in eastern Zaïre in late 1996 it is likely that the situation at these crossings will have changed, although the crossings themselves should still be open.

There are less-used border posts further north, between Mahagi and Pakwach and between Aru and Arua. If you're thinking of crossing between Aru and Arua, you'd be wise to make enquiries about security before setting off – rebels are active in this area, although incidents are few.

Kisoro to Rutshuru The most popular crossing is that between Kisoro and Rutshuru, a distance of about 35 km. This gives you direct access to Djomba, one of Zaïre's principal gorilla sanctuaries, although whether this is still an option, in light of the recent turmoil in eastern Zaïre, is unclear. The best bet for information is to check with other travellers in Kampala or Kabale.

If it is still possible to visit the gorillas, come here with a visa. Otherwise, you can buy a temporary three-day visa to visit the gorillas at Djomba (just over the border) for US$50, but you have to leave your passport at the Zaïre border post until you return. You also have to buy a new Ugandan visa to re-enter Uganda (unless you have a multiple-entry visa).

There's reasonable accommodation in Kisoro and basic accommodation on the Zaïre side of the border.

There is a daily bus between Kampala and Kisoro (USh 11,000).

Kasese to Rutshuru The Ishasha border is another possibility. As there's a Friday market at Ishasha, this is probably the best day to go because trucks from Rutshuru to Ishasha leave early in the morning (about 5.30 am) and return in the evening. There's also a Saturday market at Isharo (about halfway between Rutshuru and Ishasha), so there are trucks from Rutshuru early on Saturday mornings.

On the Ugandan side, the Ishasha River Camp is 17 km from Ishasha inside the Queen Elizabeth National Park. You'll have to wait for a lift, as walking in this part of the park is prohibited due to the lions. There are no supplies (apart from Primus beer from Zaïre), though the rangers will cook something up if you're desperate. Camping costs USh 10,000 and *bandas* (circular, grass-thatched traditional-style houses) are USh 15,000.

From Ishasha, the road to Katunguru is pretty good (2WD with care), although in the wet season it can be closed for days. The alternative route is the road through Kihihi and Rukungiri to Ishaka on the Kasese to Mbarara road. There is a steady trickle of traffic along this route, so hitching from Ishaka shouldn't be too much of a problem, and there's even the occasional taxi.

Kasese to Beni The route from Beni to Kasese via Kasindi, Mpondwe and Katwe involves hitching unless you can find a taxi. Depending on the day you go, this could involve a considerable wait (hours rather than days), whichever of the two routes you use from the Ugandan border to Kasese.

Kasindi has a couple of hotels, a bar and a restaurant of sorts. It's three km from Kasindi to the border post at Bwera. You'll probably have to walk.

In Bwera, the *Modern Lodge Hotel* is a clean and very friendly concrete place. Rooms cost around US$2 per night, and coffee and omelettes are available across the road. Pick-ups leave at about 7 am for the trip to Kasese.

BOAT
Tanzania

There's a regular lake service between Port Bell (Kampala) and Mwanza (Tanzania) which departs from Port Bell on Monday and Thursday at 6 pm and arrives in Mwanza the following day at 10 am.

In the opposite direction, it leaves Mwanza on Sunday and Wednesday at 3 pm and arrives in Port Bell the following day at 7 am. It's a good trip and costs US$35/25/20 in 1st/2nd/3rd class, plus a US$5 passenger tax. From Mwanza the fares are TSh 7500/6000/4500 plus US$20 port tax.

Tickets should be booked at 2 pm on the day of departure at the Port Bell port gate (☎ (041) 221336). This is going to involve you in a taxi trip, unless you want to hang around all day until the ferry leaves.

This is assuming that ferry services have resumed following the sinking of the MV *Bukoba* in 1996 with the loss of 600-plus lives (the boat had a registered capacity of 430).

Getting Around

AIR

Uganda Airlines is the only carrier, but there are no scheduled internal flights.

BUS

Normal buses connect the major towns on a daily basis. They're cheaper than taxis, but travel just as fast. They are much slower overall, however, because they stop a great deal to pick up and set down passengers.

EMS Post Buses

In addition to the normal private buses there are also the EMS Post minibuses. These travel from Kampala to all the major centres three times a week. The cost is less than what you'd pay on a normal bus or taxi, and they are safe and stop much less frequently. Bookings can be made in advance; do this the day before at the town post office.

The outward journeys from Kampala are at 7 am on Monday, Wednesday and Friday; the return journeys are on Tuesday, Thursday and Saturday. See the Getting Around section in the Kampala chapter for details on routes and fares.

TAXI (MINIBUS)

Uganda is the land of share minibuses (known as taxis), and there's never any shortage of them. Fares are fixed and vehicles leave when full. Unlike Kenya, where the concept of 'full' has no meaning, travel by taxi in Uganda is relatively civilised, even though many drivers are speed maniacs who go much too fast to leave any leeway for emergencies. Luckily, traffic density on Ugandan roads is much lower than on Kenyan roads, so accidents are much less frequent.

TRAIN

There are two main railway lines in Uganda. The first starts at Tororo and runs west all the way to Kasese via Jinja and Kampala. The other line runs from Tororo north-west to Pakwach via Mbale, Soroti, Lira and Gulu. However, services between Tororo and Gulu have been suspended.

Travelling by train these days is an endurance test – the rolling stock and tracks are all in poor condition, which means that travel is slow and uncomfortable, and subject to long delays. There are also only 3rd-class carriages available on Ugandan trains, so if you're looking for discomfort, this is the way to go.

Between Kampala and Kasese there is one train per week on Friday at 3 pm which supposedly arrives in Kasese at noon the following day and costs USh 4500.

Between Kampala and Tororo, there are trains on Friday at 9 am, arriving the following morning. The fare is USh 2500.

CAR & 4WD

There's an excellent system of sealed roads between most major centres of population in the southern part of the country, and work is well in hand on the roads to Gulu and Fort Portal.

Between Fort Portal and Kasese there are several potholed sections where you need to be careful. The road between Kabale and Kisoro is gravel but is well graded and in excellent condition. In the north, minor roads are usually badly potholed and, after heavy rain, become impassable in anything other than a 4WD.

What is totally missing in Uganda is road signs. There are hardly any, even outside major towns. Unless you know where you're going, it's possible to get hopelessly lost.

Carrying a map is one suggestion, but you'll also need a compass, since there are no decent large-scale maps. Getting out of the vehicle and talking to local people is obviously the best idea, but sometimes, they don't know the way either!

What is good in Uganda is road safety. All the main roads you're likely to use are sealed and traffic volume is minimal – the main danger being excessive speed.

Fuel Costs

Fuel is horrifically expensive. Petrol is USh 1110 per litre; diesel only a few shillings cheaper.

Rental

Unlike Kenya, vehicle hire in Uganda is in its infancy and there are few options. Avis is currently the only major operator here, and its office is in the Airline building, Kimathi Ave, Kampala (☎ (041) 257280; fax 257277). It also has an office at Entebbe airport (☎ (042) 20516, ext 3225). Its all-inclusive rates (insurance, VAT and 100 free km) for a small car/4WD are US$132/212 for two days, US$623/1061 for a week; extra km are charged at US$0.30/0.50. Simple daily hire charges are US$40/70 per day plus US$20/25 for insurance plus US$0.30/0.50 per km. Drivers can be hired for US$10 per day.

A cheaper option is to rent a vehicle from one of the smaller local operators. A good company is Nile Safaris (☎ (041) 259983; fax 245092), Farmers House (next to the UK High Commission), Parliament Ave, Kampala. Its rates are very reasonable and include a driver. For a small car/4WD including 100 km you're looking at USh 45,000/75,000 per day, with extra km charged at USh 300/350.

Also worth trying is City Cars (☎ (041) 232335) at Baumann House, Parliament Ave. They have Suzuki 4WDs for rent, and also have camping gear available.

HITCHING

Without your own transport, hitching is virtually obligatory in some situations, such as getting into national parks to which there's no public transport. Most of the lifts you will get will be on trucks, usually on top of the load at the back, which can be a very pleasant way to travel, though sun protection is a must. Free lifts on trucks are the exception rather than the rule, so ask before you get on.

Other sources for lifts are game wardens and rangers who work in the parks, international aid workers, missionaries, businesspeople and the occasional diplomat, but you may have to wait a long time in some places before anyone comes along. See the introductory Getting Around chapter for more information on hitching in East Africa.

BOAT
Lake Victoria Ferries

There are very limited opportunities for travel by boat on Lake Victoria, the only options being the various methods of getting to the Ssese Islands from Bukakata (east of Masaka) and Kasenyi (a 30-minute taxi ride from Kampala). See the Ssese Islands section for details.

LOCAL TRANSPORT

Kampala has a local share-taxi network, as well as 'special hire' taxis for private trips. Elsewhere you'll have to rely on bicycle taxis (known locally as *boda-boda*, as they originally only used to shuttle people between border (boda) posts) or, in some places such as Fort Portal, on motorcycle taxis.

SAFARIS
Organised Vehicle Safaris

As tourism in Uganda slowly gains momentum, so do the number of safari operators and the options open to punters.

Currently there are quite a few reliable companies which offer safaris to the national parks and other places of interest, including trips to the gorillas of Bwindi and Mgahinga in the extreme south-west of the country. National parks which are covered by these companies include Murchison Falls, Queen Elizabeth, Kibale, Bwindi, Mgahinga, Lake Mburo and Semliki Valley (hot springs, Pygmies).

Other places of interest covered include Lake Bunyonyi (Kabale) and the Source of the Nile (Jinja). None of them goes to Kidepo Valley National Park or to Mt Elgon.

Costs Unlike Kenya, where budget travellers are well catered for with no-frills camping safaris, Ugandan companies rely heavily on lodge and hotel accommodation while on safari, so they're proportionally much more expensive. Even where camping is involved, it's usually the luxury tented camp variety and thus no cheaper.

Since none of the Ugandan companies offers genuine budget camping safaris such as those in Kenya, it's worth considering going with a Kenyan company which covers Uganda (and usually the gorillas of Zaïre or Rwanda). Check out the Organised Safaris section of Kenya's Getting Around chapter.

Costs vary from one company to another, but are consistently high, and depend considerably on how many people are in the group – the more there are of you, the less you pay individually. As an example, the per person cost of a three-day safari to Murchison Falls National Park can vary from US$990 (one person) to US$435 (four people).

In general, if you budget for US$150 to US$250 per day you won't be too far off the mark. This should include all transport, three meals a day, accommodation (including all camping equipment where appropriate) and park entry fees (though some companies exclude park entry fees).

Note that with these prices, it is assumed that you're willing to share accommodation with one other person. If you're not, there will be an additional 'single person supplement' which will bump up the cost by quite a margin.

Departure Frequency Most companies have weekly departures (some more frequent) for all the safaris they offer. Even where departures are not so frequent, there are usually departures two or three times per month. As in Kenya, any safari company will lay on a trip almost immediately if you have a group of at least three (sometimes four) people.

Choosing a Company Among the companies which can be recommended are the following. Note that these have been listed alphabetically and are not in any order of preference or reliability:

African Pearl Safaris

Lower Ground Floor, Embassy House, Kampala (☎ (041) 233566; fax 235770). This company offers three/four-day gorilla-tracking safaris to Bwindi National Park, staying at their very comfortable Buhoma Homestead right at the park headquarters, for US$581/662; five-day safaris which also include Queen Elizabeth National Park for US$929; and three-day Murchison Falls trips for US$454. As usual, these prices assume a minimum of four people, and are inclusive of national park entry fees and gorilla-tracking permits (where needed).

Blacklines Tours

2 Colville St, PO Box 6968, Kampala (☎ (041) 255520). Like African Pearl, this company offers a three-day safari of Queen Elizabeth National Park (US$300), a three-day safari of Murchison Falls National Park and a 12-day 'Circuit of the Kingdoms' which takes in Lake Mburo National Park, Lake Bunyonyi (Kabale), Queen Elizabeth National Park and Murchison Falls National Park. There are weekly departures to all of these.

Gametrackers

Raja Chambers, Parliament Ave, PO Box 7703, Kampala (☎ (041) 258993; fax 244575). This is an offshoot of the well-known Kenyan company. Currently it offers four-day gorilla-tracking trips to Bwindi or Mgahinga national parks for US$610; six-day trips to Queen Elizabeth and Kibale national parks and the Semliki Valley for US$905; and five-day gorilla-tracking safaris into eastern Zaïre for US$570. All prices assume a minimum of four passengers; you can subtract about 20% if there are six passengers.

Hot Ice Ltd

Uganda Travel Bureau, Kimathi Ave, PO Box 151, Kampala (☎ (041) 266598; fax 266741). This company has been operating for years and is very well set up. It maintains radio contact with its safaris so, if anything goes wrong, something can be done quickly. Hot Ice's short trips include a three-day Queen Elizabeth National Park safari for US$874 and a three-day Murchison Falls National Park safari for US$839. Longer safaris include a six-day trip through Queen Elizabeth National Park to see the gorillas in eastern Zaïre for US$1543; a five-night trip to track the gorillas at Bwindi National Park, stopping overnight at Lake Mburo each way for US$1583; and a five-night 'Highlights of Southern Uganda' which takes in Lake Mburo, Queen Elizabeth, Fort Portal and Kibale National Park, for US$1563. All trips need a minimum of two people to operate.

Nile Safaris Ltd

Farmers House, Parliament Ave, PO Box 12135, Kampala (☎ (041) 244331; fax 245967). Nile's three-day safaris to Murchison Falls National Park, and to Lake Mburo and Queen Elizabeth

DAWN DELANEY

DAWN DELANEY

From a gathering of villagers to a banana seller in Kampala's Nakasero Market, Ugandans have a reputation for being East Africa's friendliest people.

HUGH FINLAY

DAWN DELANEY

HUGH FINLAY

Uganda's earthy contrasts: colourful passenger boats on Lake Albert, Kampala's Nakasero Market and village life in the mountainous south-west.

national parks, cost US$435 and US$525 respectively. A three-day gorilla-tracking safari to Bwindi costs US$600, while a six-day safari to Lake Mburo, Queen Elizabeth and Bwindi national parks is US$1175. Prices are all-inclusive and assume there are four passengers.

This is not an exhaustive list of safari companies but most of the others are top-range. They include Belex Tours & Travel Ltd (☎ (041) 244590), Speedbird Tours & Travel Ltd (☎ (041) 234669; fax 234252) and Abercrombie & Kent (☎ (041) 259181).

Do-It-Yourself Safaris

The possibilities of doing this without your own transport are limited in Uganda, as there's so little traffic into the national parks.

That doesn't mean you can't do it – travellers do – but it involves a fair amount of hitching and waiting around for a ride, or the hire of a vehicle and driver.

Climbing the Ruwenzoris is much easier in this respect, as it's all very well organised and caters to walkers. All you have to do is get yourself to Kasese and contact the Ruwenzori Mountaineering Services office there. They'll get you fixed up and arrange everything. See the Ruwenzori Mountains section in the Uganda National Parks & Reserves chapter for details.

Climbing Mt Elgon isn't so easy to arrange, as there's not much in the way of infrastructure. See the Mt Elgon section in the Uganda National Parks & Reserves chapter for details.

Kampala

The Ugandan capital, Kampala, suffered a great deal during the years of civil strife following Idi Amin's defeat at the hands of the Tanzanian army in 1979. The turmoil only ended with the victory of Yoweri Museveni's NRA in early 1986.

Unless you've had previous experience of upheavals like these, it's hard to believe the amount of gratuitous destruction and looting that went on: office blocks and government offices had the bulk of their windows shattered; the buildings were riddled with rifle fire; plumbing and electrical fittings and telephone receivers were ripped from walls; buses were shot at and abandoned; and stores were looted of everything, down to the last bottle of aspirin or the last odd shoes.

In the decade since Museveni's victory, the city has gone from a looted shell to a thriving, modern city befitting the capital of one of the most rapidly developing countries in Africa – the electricity works, water comes out of the taps, damaged buildings have been restored and many new ones built, and the shops and markets are once again well stocked. These days Kampala even has casinos, nightclubs and decent restaurants. The fact that many Asians have returned has certainly given business and commerce in Kampala a major boost.

The best thing about Kampala, though (and this is in stark contrast to Nairobi), is that it's quite safe to walk around at any time of the day or night in virtually any part of the city. You won't get mugged here – the city is green and attractive, and the people are very friendly – it's a great place.

Orientation

Kampala is said to be built on seven hills, though you'll probably spend most of your time on just one of them – Nakasero, in the city centre. The top half of this hill is a type of garden city, with wide, quiet avenues lined with flowering trees and large, detached houses behind imposing fences and hedges. Here you'll find many of the embassies, international aid organisations, top-class hotels, rich people's houses, the high court and government buildings.

Between Nakasero and the lower part of the city is Kampala's main thoroughfare – Kampala Rd (which turns into Jinja Rd at one end and Bombo Rd at the other). On this road are the main banks, the post and telecommunications office, the railway station and a few hotels and restaurants.

Below Kampala Rd, towards the bottom of the valley, are heaps of shops and small businesses, budget hotels and restaurants,

---

Kampala's Lottery Madness

You don't have to be in Kampala long to notice that lotteries are all the rage. In the past couple of years Premier Lotteries has become wildly successful in Kampala, and every week in the newspapers there are pictures of the lucky ones receiving the keys to new cars, or facsimile cheques for thousands – or even millions – of shillings.

All over the city centre, but especially around the bus and taxi parks, the dozens of touts under their colourful sun umbrellas try to outdo each other, luring the punters into parting with USh 1000 (US$1) for a chance to win big.

It's easy to see which touts are the most successful. Those at the bottom of the scale have a stall which consists of nothing more than a cardboard box strung around their neck, or a sheet of cardboard on the ground. Those on the next level sport a microphone, car battery and loudspeaker, and often operate from a derelict car body; while those with the most business actually have a car that goes! ■

the market, the immense temples of the Asian Hindu community, and the bus station and taxi parks. It's a completely different world to that on the top side of Kampala Rd. Here there are congested streets thronged with people, battered old cars and minibuses, lottery ticket sellers, impromptu street markets and pavement stalls offering everything from rubber stamps to radio repairs. There are hawkers, newspaper sellers, hustlers, and one of the most mind-boggling and seemingly chaotic taxi parks you're ever likely to see.

To the east, across the golf course, is Kololo, which is a fairly exclusive residential area. A number of embassies are situated here, as are a few hotels and the Uganda Museum. To the west is Namirembe, on top of which stands the Anglican cathedral.

To the south of the city centre, across the railway tracks, lies Tank Hill, where there are a number of mid-range hotels, good restaurants and that famous Kampala landmark, the Half London bar, to which everyone in search of good live music goes.

Information

Tourist Office The tourist office (☎ 242196; fax 242188) is in the IPS building, near the UK High Commission on Parliament Ave. The staff here are very well informed and have all sorts of information at their fingertips, although nothing much in the way of printed information.

The office is open weekdays from 8 am to 1 pm and 2 to 5 pm, and on Saturday from 8.30 am to 12.30 pm.

National Parks Office The Uganda Wildlife Authority office (☎ 530574; fax 530159), which is where you make bookings to see the gorillas in Bwindi and Mgahinga, is inconveniently located a few km from the city centre, just off Kira Rd at 31 Kamjokya St, Kamjokya. To get there take a Kamjokya ('kamwocha') taxi (USh 300) from the old taxi park, and get off when you see a row of small market shops below the road on the left; the office is signposted to the right – taxi drivers usually know it.

In addition to information on the gorillas, the office also has useful handouts on all the national parks. It is open from 8 am to 1 pm and 2 to 5 pm weekdays, and 9 am to noon on Saturday.

Money Kampala Rd and the streets parallel to it going up the hill is where you'll find all the banks and many foreign exchange bureaus. These exchange bureaus generally stay open longer than the banks, and offer competitive rates with no commission. Daily rates at the main bureaus are listed in the daily *New Vision*.

At the Sheraton is Express Uganda (☎ 236767; fax 236769; PO Box 353), the American Express agent, offering the usual range of Amex facilities, including a clients' mail service.

Post & Communications The GPO is on the corner of Kampala and Speke Rds. It's open Monday to Friday from 8 am to 6 pm, and on Saturday from 8 am to 2 pm. The poste restante is well organised and as the volume of mail here is low things don't go astray.

The post office also houses the international telephone exchange, and there are public phones where you can ring and fax overseas. Phone cards are sold at the post office, and there are many card phones (yellow phone boxes) around town.

For overseas and long-distance phone calls it's much cheaper (one-third the price) to use Starcom Communications on Entebbe Rd, just down from Kampala Rd. Here you can also make direct phone-card calls and send faxes cheaply. Starcom has a number of phone boxes around town (green boxes), but only the ones at the Sheraton and the popular Backpackers are set up for international calls. The Starcom office is open from 7.30 am to 9 pm Monday to Saturday, and 11 am to 4 pm on Sunday.

The telephone area code for Kampala is 041.

Travel Agencies One agent which is reliable is Afri Tours & Travel Ltd (☎ 232306; fax 232307), Lumumba Rd on Nakasero Hill.

UGANDA

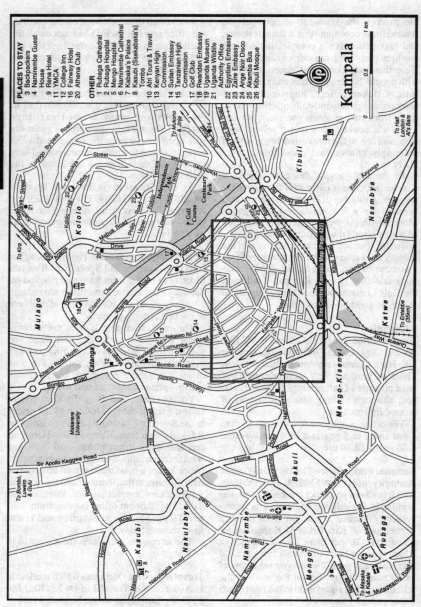

Kampala

PLACES TO STAY
3   Backpackers
4   Namirembe Guest House
9   Rena Hotel
11 YMCA
12 College Inn
16 Fairway Hotel
20 Athena Club

OTHER
1   Rubaga Cathedral
2   Rubaga Hospital
5   Mengo Hospital
6   Namirembe Cathedral
8   Kasubi (Seekabaka's) Tombs
10 Afri Tours & Travel
13 Kenyan High Commission
14 Sudan Embassy
15 Tanzanian High Commission
17 Golf Club
18 Rwandan Embassy
19 Uganda Museum
21 Uganda Wildlife Authority Office
22 Egyptian Embassy
23 Zaire Embassy
24 Ange Noir Disco
25 Akamba Bus
26 Kibuli Mosque

See Central Kampala Map (Page 422)

Book Shops For English-language publications, one of the best places is the Aristoc Booklex shop on the corner of Kampala Rd and Colville St. Also worth a look is the Uganda Bookshop around the corner on Colville St.

Cultural Centres Alliance Française is on the 1st floor of the National Theatre near the parliament buildings.

The British Council (members only) is in the IPS building on Parliament Ave.

Medical & Emergency Services One private practitioner who has been recommended is Dr Gibbons, who has his practice in the UK High Commission on Parliament Ave. A consultation costs around USh 30,000. Another option is the Mengo Hospital (☎ 270222).

For emergency police assistance dial ☎ 999.

Things to See

Uganda Museum The Uganda Museum on Kira Rd is open Monday to Saturday from 10 am to 6 pm and on Sunday from 3 to 6 pm. Entry costs USh 1500 (USh 500 for children). It has good ethnological exhibits covering hunting, agriculture, war, religion and *juju*, as well as archaeological and natural history displays. Perhaps its most interesting feature is a collection of traditional musical instruments, which you're allowed to play.

A booklet for sale here, *Kasubi Tombs*, describes the history of the Buganda and the royal palace enclosure on the hill above Makerere University.

There's also an office of the East African Wildlife Society at the museum, open from 10 am to noon on Monday, Wednesday and Friday.

To get there catch a Kamjokya taxi from the old taxi park (USh 200).

Kasubi Tombs Also well worth a look are the Kasubi Tombs (also known as the Ssekabaka's Tombs), on Kasubi Hill just off Masiro Rd, which were first built in 1881.

Here you will find the huge traditional reed and bark cloth buildings of the *kabakas* (kings) of the Buganda people. The group of buildings contains the tombs of Muteesa I, his son Mwanga, Sir Daudi Chwa II, and his son Edward Muteesa II, the last of the kabakas. He died in London in 1969, three years after being deposed by Obote.

The kabaka's palace is also here, but is closed to the public. The palace and tombs are taken care of by the Ganda clans.

The Kasubi Tombs are open every day, including Sunday and holidays, from 8 am to 6 pm; the entry fee is USh 2000. Remove your shoes before entering the main building. You can get to the tombs by taxi, either from the old taxi park in the city centre (ask for Hoima Rd) or from the junction of Bombo and Makerere Hill Rds. The taxis you want are the ones which terminate at the market at the junction of Hoima and Masiro Rds. The tombs are a few hundred metres walk up the hill from here (signposted).

Religious Buildings Also worth a visit are the four main religious buildings in Kampala: the gleaming white Kibuli Mosque dominating Kibuli Hill on the other side of the railway station from Nakasero Hill; the huge Roman Catholic Rubaga Cathedral on Rubaga Hill; the Namirembe Anglican Cathedral (where the congregation is called to worship by the beating of drums); and the enormous Hindu temple in the city centre.

Botanical Gardens & Zoo At Entebbe, outside Kampala, the botanical gardens are worth visiting if you have half a day available. Laid out in 1898 by A Whyte, the first curator, they're along the lakeside between the sailing club and the centre of Entebbe. Even if you're not particularly interested in botany, there are some interesting, unusual trees and shrubs and the gardens are fairly well maintained.

The Uganda Wildlife Education Centre is close by. Formerly just a small zoo, it is being revamped with a grant from USAID, although things are moving very slowly and

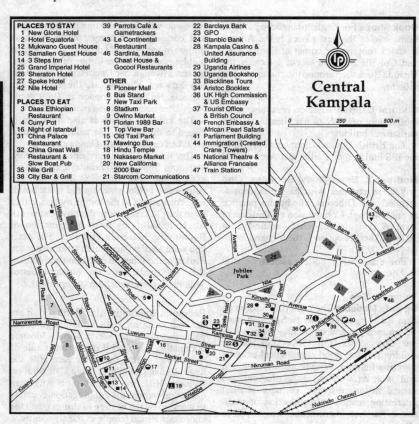

Central Kampala

PLACES TO STAY
1 New Gloria Hotel
2 Hotel Equatoria
12 Mukwano Guest House
13 Samalien Guest House
14 3 Steps Inn
25 Grand Imperial Hotel
26 Sheraton Hotel
27 Speke Hotel
42 Nile Hotel

PLACES TO EAT
3 Daas Ethiopian
    Restaurant
4 Curry Pot
16 Night of Istanbul
31 China Palace
    Restaurant
32 China Great Wall
    Restaurant &
    Slow Boat Pub
35 Nile Grill
38 City Bar & Grill

39 Parrots Cafe &
    Gametrackers
43 Le Continental
    Restaurant
46 Sardinia, Masala
    Chaat House &
    Gocool Restaurants

OTHER
5 Pioneer Mall
6 Bus Stand
7 New Taxi Park
8 Stadium
9 Owino Market
10 Florian 1989 Bar
11 Top View Bar
15 Old Taxi Park
17 Mawingo Bus
18 Hindu Temple
19 Nakasero Market
20 New California
    2000 Bar
21 Starcom Communications

22 Barclays Bank
23 GPO
24 Stanbic Bank
28 Kampala Casino &
    United Assurance
    Building
29 Uganda Airlines
30 Uganda Bookshop
33 Blacklines Tours
34 Aristoc Booklex
36 UK High Commission
    & US Embassy
37 Tourist Office
    & British Council
40 French Embassy &
    African Pearl Safaris
41 Parliament Building
44 Immigration (Crested
    Crane Towers)
45 National Theatre &
    Alliance Francaise
47 Train Station

it's not really worth the trek out here. Entry costs USh 500.

There are frequent taxis to Entebbe from the old taxi park in Kampala (USh 1000, 35 to 40 minutes). Ask where to get off as it's before the end of the line; from here you can take a motorcycle taxi for a few hundred shillings.

Activities

White-Water Rafting Day trips on the Victoria Nile near Jinja are operated by Adrift, and the river is supposedly a Class 5, making it more challenging than the more popular

Zambezi at Victoria Falls in Zimbabwe. This cost is US$95 including transport from Kampala and lunch. Bookings can be made either through Adrift (☎ (075) 707668; fax (041) 241245; e-mail adrift@starcom.co.ug) or the Backpackers (☎ 258469; fax 272012; e-mail ptcu@starcome.co.ug).

Places to Stay

Accommodation in Kampala is not cheap if you want anything with a modicum of comfort and a bathroom. There's not a great deal of choice for the budget traveller although things are gradually improving.

Places to Stay – bottom end

Camping Campers have a choice of three places in Kampala (the YMCA, the Athina Club and the Backpackers) and one expensive option in Entebbe (the Imperial Botanical Beach Hotel). See later in Places to Stay for details on all these places.

Hostels The *YMCA* (☎ 230804) is on Buganda Rd, about 15 minutes walk from the city centre. You can camp here for USh 1500 but you won't get much privacy, as the site is on a playing field which fronts onto busy Kampala Rd (Bombo Rd). In the building itself, you can sleep on the floor on a mattress for USh 2000. It's a popular place to stay, though somewhat inconvenient as you must pack up and be out by 8 am each day, as it's used as a school on weekdays. The showers are erratic and the toilets could do with a good scrub, but otherwise it's OK. There's also a canteen here, which is open from 7 am to 8 pm.

Another popular place is the *Backpackers* (☎ 258469; fax 272012; e-mail ptcu@starcom.co.ug), about a 10-minute taxi ride out of the centre at Kalema Rd, Lunguja, not far from the landmark Namirembe Cathedral. This place is run by an Australian guy who is setting up a permaculture resource centre and demonstration plot on the site. It's a quiet, relaxed place, popular with travellers and overland truck drivers. Camping costs USh 2300 per person, or there are basic rooms for USh 4600 in a dorm, or USh 11,500 for a double. There are no cooking facilities, but meals are available and there are a couple of basic restaurants and a bar nearby. There's also a Starcom card phone which is set up for international direct dialling. To get there, take a Natete taxi from the new taxi park (USh 300); there's a sign on a light pole in the middle of the park – you can just ask for the Backpackers.

Hotels The budget hotels are all in the busy part of town near the taxi parks and bus station. There's not a great deal of choice. Far and away the best place is the friendly little *Mukwano Guest House* (☎ 232248) on Nakivubo Place, right opposite the amazingly busy Owino Market. This place is cleaned daily, sheets are also changed daily and there's hot water in the showers. Dorm beds are USh 6000 (four-bed) or USh 7000 (three or two-bed), or there are a couple of singles at USh 11,500. There are great views over the market from the rooftop.

Just a few doors along is the *Samalien Guest House* (☎ 245737), which is clean and OK, although the welcome is not exactly overpowering. It's also somewhat overpriced at USh 15,000/19,000 for single/double rooms with attached bathroom. This place has a good little restaurant out the back which also sells cold beers.

Further along again, towards Entebbe Rd, is the *3 Steps Inn* (☎ 24539), another basic but decent guesthouse, with double rooms only at USh 15,800 with shared bathroom.

Also on Nakivubo Place is the *Kadepro Tourist Guest House* (☎ 255040), which is OK but as all rooms face the road it's noisy. A bed in the cramped dorm is USh 7000, or there are singles/doubles with breakfast at USh 12,000/16,000. All rooms have shared facilities.

At the top of this range, and next to the Namirembe Cathedral, is the *Namirembe Guest House* (☎ 272071). It's set in spacious grounds in a quiet suburb and has a range of rooms. Singles/doubles with shared bathroom cost USh 14,400/19,200 in the old wing; rooms with attached bathroom in the new wing are USh 16,800/21,000. It's a pleasant place to stay. Meals are available for USh 4600 (breakfast), USh 5750 (lunch) and USh 6900 (dinner).

Places to Stay – middle

There's very little choice in this range. Reasonably good value in the city centre, at least by Kampala standards, is the *New Gloria Hotel* (☎ 257790), on William St. It's a small place which has recently been renovated, and has a cafe. Rooms with attached bathroom cost USh 25,000/45,000.

West of the city centre, the *Rena Hotel* (☎ 272336) on Namirembe Rd is good value, at USh 17,500/25,000 for a single/double with shared bathroom or USh 25,000/36,000 with private bathroom. All prices include breakfast, and the hotel has its own bar and restaurant.

Far better, but a 15-minute walk from the centre, is the *College Inn* (☎ 531994), just off the large roundabout at the top of Bombo Rd. Here you can get a single/double with attached bathroom, including breakfast, for USh 30,000/50,000. The staff are friendly and the food in the restaurant is good.

Places to Stay – top end

Although most of the accommodation in this price bracket is quoted in hard currency (US dollars), you can pay your bill in local or foreign currency.

Very popular is the *Speke Hotel* (☎ 259221; fax 235345) on Nile Ave. It has plenty of character and atmosphere. Most of the rooms have attached bathrooms and are spacious, and the majority have a TV and balcony. It's good value at US$50/70, including breakfast. The terrace bar is a popular meeting place, and there's a snack bar/coffee shop and a good Indian restaurant.

The *Fairway Hotel* (☎ 259571; fax 234160) on Kafu Rd, near the golf course, is another option. It's recently been refurbished, and rooms cost US$75/95 including tax. The hotel has two open-air restaurants – one Indian, the other nyama choma.

North-east of here, on Kololo Hill, is the *Athina Club* (☎ 241428) on Windsor Crescent. This is a reasonable place to stay, with lots of atmosphere, and is run by Greek Cypriots (the Cypriot High Commission is also here). Some overland safari companies use the Athina for camping (which costs USh 3000 per person per night) but it's not the best of sites and is really only for vehicle-based camping. Singles/doubles with attached bathroom (with hot water) and full board cost US$60/75. Nonresidents can also eat here for USh 11,000 (lunch or dinner).

On Tank Hill, to the south-east, is a reasonable place but forget about staying here unless you have your own transport, as it's near the top of the hill and some considerable distance from a taxi route. The views,

however, are excellent. The *Hotel Diplomate* (☎ 267625; fax 267690) has an excellent range of rooms from US$66/78 including breakfast and taxes. The staff are very friendly, there's a bar, a restaurant and even a video bank.

In the centre of town are two recently opened places, both of which were shot-up hulks from the bad old days. The *Hotel Equatoria* (☎ 250780; fax 250146) has quite decent air-con rooms, most with a small balcony with views. There's also a small swimming pool and two restaurants. The cost is US$79/89, or US$89/94 with air-con, both including breakfast.

The very plush *Grand Imperial Hotel* (☎ 250681; fax 250605) is smaller and more intimate than the Sheraton (see below), and has very good facilities, including a very small swimming pool, a bar, a cafe and restaurant. At US$125/145 it's hardly cheap, but good value for this end of the market.

At the very top end of this scale are two large hotels on Nakasero Hill. The *Sheraton Hotel* (☎ 244590; fax 256696), on Ternan Ave just above the Speke Hotel, is situated in Jubilee Park (which is open to the public in daylight hours but closes at 7 pm). It has all the facilities you'd expect of a Sheraton hotel, including swimming pool, several restaurants and bars, and a shopping precinct. There's live music in the enclosed bar every night and in the open-air bar on Sunday afternoon and evening (no charge for entry; non-guests welcome). Singles/doubles with breakfast cost US$171/195, US$10 more for a room with a view, all plus 20% tax.

Cheaper than the Sheraton is the *Nile Hotel* (☎ 235900; fax 259130), adjacent to the Uganda International Conference Centre on Nile Ave. It has all the usual facilities, including a pool, and offers singles/doubles for US$110/120 including breakfast; taxes are extra. It's often fully booked when there is a conference in progress.

Entebbe Even though Entebbe is 35 km from Kampala, it's essentially a suburb of the capital and is also where the international airport is situated. There's good top-end accommodation here close to the edge of the lake.

The cheaper of the two places to stay here is the *Imperial Botanical Beach Hotel* (☎ 20800; fax 20832), right on the shores of Lake Victoria. You can camp on a fine grassy site here for a mere US$20 per person! Alternatively, there are pleasant rondavels with double beds and attached bathrooms at US$73/90 plus taxes. Beers and soft drinks are available, as well as meals and snacks.

At the top end of the market is the well-appointed *Windsor Lake Victoria Hotel* (☎ 20645; fax 20404), which has singles/doubles for US$95/120, including breakfast, plus 20% taxes. There's a swimming pool, bars and restaurants. It's a very popular place among the well heeled for a meal and drinks on the weekend.

Places to Eat – cheap

If you're staying at the YMCA (as a number of travellers do), there are a couple of cheap local restaurants by the roundabout, such as the *Ploughmans Cafe*, or you can eat at the YMCA's own canteen. There's also the *College Inn*, which has good meals of roast chicken or steak and chips at very reasonable prices.

Very close to the Nakasero Market in the centre of town is the small *Night of Istanbul*. Main courses are heavily Indian-influenced and cost USh 4000 to USh 5000, and there are also good doner kebabs for USh 4500 and felafels for USh 2000. It's a good place which stays open until quite late.

If you're staying in the taxi park area of town, the choice is limited. Best is the tiny *City Restaurant*, in the small group of shops on the southern side of the old taxi park. Here you can get a good egg and tea breakfast for USh 1000, and other basic meals for around USh 2000. There are a couple of other places in this group of shops, including *Fresh Corner*, a take-away fast-food place.

For a cheap Indian meal try the *Masala Chaat House* on Dewinton Rd, opposite the National Theatre. This is a popular little place which serves vegetarian thali meals for USh 3200, and other vegetarian and non-vegetarian dishes. Just a few doors down is the *Gocool Restaurant*, another Indian place with main dishes for USh 2500 to USh 3200, and Gujarati thali meals for USh 4800.

Another popular Indian restaurant is the *Curry Pot*, on Kampala Rd. It offers good curries and stews for USh 3000 to USh 5000.

Surprisingly, one of the best deals in town is to be found at the *Kampala Casino* on Kimathi Ave. On Thursday evenings they put on a Ugandan buffet, and at USh 6500 this is great value. If you haven't tried local food this is a good opportunity, and there's live music while you eat. You do, of course, need to be reasonably smartly dressed to get in here.

Places to Eat – more expensive

A popular city centre meeting place on Kampala Rd is the *Nile Grill*. It's not the cheapest place to go but is popular with expatriate aid workers and well-to-do locals. Outside there are tables with umbrellas. The food is expensive and not that great, but if you're hanging out for a steak or roast chicken, it's one place to head for. Many people come here for just a coffee or a beer. It's open Monday to Saturday from 9 am to 10 pm and on Sunday from 9 am to 9 pm. There's occasionally live music here on Saturday night.

For Chinese food, there are a couple of places to go. Well regarded is the *China Palace Restaurant*, on the 1st floor of the high-rise office building on Pilkington St (signposted, though inadequately, on the ground floor). Main dishes cost from USh 3000 to USh 5000. It's open Tuesday to Sunday for lunch and dinner.

Also reasonable is the long-running *China Great Wall* on Kampala Rd, up from and on the opposite side of the road to the Nile Grill. It's open daily from noon to 11 pm. Right next door is the *Slow Boat Pub*.

The *Sardinia* on Dewinton St is also well regarded for a decent meal. It serves a range of grills for around USh 8000 and puts on a Saturday lunch-time Chinese menu.

On the lower part of Kampala Rd, towards the railway station, is the smart *City Bar &*

UGANDA

Grill. This is a very popular lunch-time hangout, and serves excellent tandoori and other Indian dishes, as well as western meals such as steak. Prices are in the USh 5000 to USh 7500 range, and there's also a full-sized snooker table and bar.

Another good lunch-time place is the small, open-air *Parrots Cafe* (☎ 251895) on Parliament Ave near the UK High Commission. It's reasonably priced at USh 5000 to USh 7000, and it does home delivery.

For Greek food, the best place to go is the *Athina Club*, on Windsor Crescent in Kololo. It's run by Greek Cypriots, so you know the food is authentic. You're looking at USh 11,000 for a set meal including a glass of wine. It's open for both lunch and dinner.

Another excellent place serving French and Zaïrese dishes is *Le Continental* near the UNDP headquarters on the north side of Nakasero Hill. Dishes are meat-oriented but are very nicely done, and good value at USh 5000 to USh 7000.

For African cuisine of a different type try the *Daas Ethiopian Restaurant* up at the top end of Kampala Rd. The downstairs bar and TV seem to be the main attraction here, but the food, served in the upstairs restaurant, is pretty good. Dishes will cost you USh 4500 to USh 6000.

If you want to get out of the city centre, try the *Gallery Cafe*, which is two km along Masaka Rd from Entebbe Rd, not far from Natete. The gallery itself is worth a look (see Things to Buy later for more on the gallery, and directions), and you can sit on the front verandah and enjoy a pleasant lunch chosen from a small eclectic menu. Dishes will cost you USh 5000.

Despite its somewhat formidable reputation as an expensive place, the Sheraton Hotel offers reasonable western-style food for around USh 7000 to USh 9000 at its *Victoria Restaurant*. Also reasonable are the buffet meals at the Lion Bar (separate from the main building but in the same grounds). The all-you-can-eat buffet meals are particularly good value. You might also want to check out the buffet breakfast at the Sheraton – for USh 14,000, you can tuck into a mind-boggling array of food as often as you like. You won't need lunch when you've finished.

Further afield, a very popular place with excellent food is the *Half London* on Gaba Rd (sometimes spelt Ggaba). It offers a range of grills and western-style food and the service is good, but it's not just a restaurant. The bar is one of *the* places to go in the evenings among young people, both black and white. You're looking at around USh 8000 for a meal.

Closer to town and just off Gaba Rd is the cluster of bars and restaurants at Kabalagala. These places are mostly open-air, and are only really popular in the evenings. The *Fasika* serves excellent Ethiopian food, with main courses around USh 5000. Other places here include the *Ethiopian Village* and the *7th Happiness Chinese Restaurant*.

Entertainment

Nightlife in Kampala is not bad these days, although the city still lacks a cinema.

Bars There are plenty of good African bars around town. One good cheap place is the *Florian 1989 Bar* on Nakivubo Place, down near the new taxi park. This is a great place in the evening as tables and chairs are set up on the broad footpath. It's a very popular place among travellers staying in this area.

Another popular local bar here is the open-air *Top View Bar*, which has a live band every night. As the name suggests, it's on the rooftop.

Pioneer Mall, on the corner of Kampala Rd and Ben Kiwanuka St, is Kampala's latest trendy hangout. The open-air bar here is very popular with the young crowd, and the music is not bad.

Discos & Nightclubs One of the cheapest and most informal nightclubs, where there's always a good crowd, is the *New California 2000 Bar*, on Luwum St. There's usually live music here, and a small entry fee is charged.

Perhaps the most popular disco is the *Ange Noir* (pronounced locally as 'Angenoa'), which is just off Jinja Rd east of the two main roundabouts leaving the city centre and one street behind. Everyone knows it but it's not signposted on the main road. It's open nightly from 9 pm to 5 am and entry costs between USh 2000 and USh 4000, depending on the night. On Wednesday and Thursday nights women pay only USh 1000.

The *Half London* (on Gaba Rd below Tank Hill) is also a very popular place for live music any night of the week but especially from Thursday to Sunday. It's partially open-air, partially enclosed, the crowd is multiracial, the bar is friendly and boisterous and the beers are normal price. Get here early at weekends if you want a table or the luxury of parking anywhere within 500m of the joint. During the day until early in the evening you can get taxis here (USh 300) from the old taxi park (just ask for Half London); later in the evening you'll need to take a special hire taxi.

Right next door to the Half London is *Al's Bar*, another partially open-air place which is very popular. This is a lively place playing a good range of loud western music, and is open until well into the night.

Theatre & Dance If you're interested in traditional dance and music, check out the Ndere Troupe. It's composed of members of the many ethnic groups in Uganda and has gained international acclaim in Europe and North America. The troupe performs fairly regularly in Kampala; contact the booking office at the National Theatre to see if any performances are coming up. The National Theatre hosts a range of productions; call in for details.

Casino The Kampala Casino on Kimathi Ave is open daily from 2 pm until late. There's the usual range of gaming tables, good meals (see Places to Eat), live music, and free beer if you're playing on the tables. No shorts or scruffy gear is allowed here.

Things to Buy
With such a fledgling tourism industry, Kampala doesn't have a huge range of shops selling crafts and other items of interest.

Right behind the National Theatre is the Uganda Arts & Crafts Village, which con-

sists of a number of stalls selling handicrafts such as caneware, wood carvings and small trinkets from around the country at quite reasonable prices. It is open Monday to Saturday from 9 am to 7 pm, and on Sunday from 10 am to 4 pm.

The Pioneer Mall shopping centre on Kampala Rd has a number of fairly swish boutique-type clothes shops, with prices to match.

On Bombo Rd, not far from the YMCA, is Uganda Crafts, a nonprofit shop selling a wide variety of crafts, including goods made from leather, wood and cane, and there's a good little open-air cafe.

The Gallery Cafe, out on the Masaka Rd, two km from Entebbe Rd, is probably the best source of contemporary crafts (ceramics, fabrics, sculpture) and paintings. It's also a great lunch spot (see Places to Eat). To get there by public transport, take a Natete taxi from the old taxi park, and get off just after it passes the large Uganda Railways locomotives workshop on the left; the gallery is on the right.

Getting There & Away
Air The following airlines run scheduled flights to Entebbe:

Air France
    Diamond Trust building (☎ 233495)
Air Tanzania
    United Assurance building, Kimathi Ave
British Airways
    Kampala Rd (☎ 257414)
Egypt Air
    Metropole House, Entebbe Rd (☎ 233960)
Ethiopian Airlines
    United Assurance building, Kimathi Ave
    (☎ 254796)
Kenya Airways
    United Assurance building, Kimathi Ave
    (☎ 256506)
Sabena
    Sheraton Hotel (☎ 234201)
Uganda Airlines
    Colville St (☎ 232990)

Bus The main bus stand is on the corner of Allen Rd and Luwum St, below Kampala Rd. It's a busy place with daily buses to every main town in the country. Most buses leave in the morning, so make enquiries the day before to get there early for a decent seat.

To Butogota (for Bwindi National Park), there is one departure daily at 6 am with Silverline; the trip takes most of the day and costs USh 10,000. There are daily buses to Kabale (many companies, six hours, USh 8000) via Masaka and Mbarara; Kasese (Safe Journey, three daily, eight hours, USh 8000); Masindi (daily, three hours, USh 5000); and Fort Portal (two daily, six hours, USh 7000).

EMS Post minibuses depart at 7 am from the GPO on Monday, Wednesday and Friday for Kabale (USh 6500) via Masaka (USh 2500) and Mbarara (USh 4000); Soroti (USh 6000) via Mbale (USh 4500); Masindi (USh 4000); Hoima (USh 5500); and Fort Portal (USh 7000) via Mbarara and Kasese (USh 6000). These are an excellent way to travel, and bookings should be made at the GPO a day or so in advance.

Nairobi & Kigali For daily buses to Nairobi, Mawingo has its office just on the uphill side (Burton St) of the new taxi park, while Akamba has its office on Dewinton Rd on the eastern edge of the city centre.

Direct buses to Kigali (Rwanda) depart daily from the bus station. See the Uganda Getting There & Away chapter for details.

Taxi Kampala has two taxi parks. Although on first appearance these places seem utterly chaotic, they are in fact highly organised and taxis for a particular destination always leave from the same place within each park. Both parks serve destinations both within Kampala and around the country. The old taxi park, on the triangle formed by Burton, Luwum and South Sts, is the bigger of the two and serves all parts of the city and country to the east; the new taxi park services destinations to the west and north.

As with buses, there are taxis to all major parts of the country, including Jinja (one hour, USh 1000), Mbale (three hours, USh 6000), Malaba (two hours, USh 3000), Masindi (three hours, USh 6000), Fort Portal

(six hours, USh 8000), Kabale (six hours, USh 9000), Masaka (two hours, USh 3000) and Mbarara (four hours, USh 7000).

Train The train schedules from Kampala should be taken with a large pinch of salt. Delays and cancellations are the order of the day and passenger services have been severely curtailed.

Trains to Tororo depart on Friday at 9 am and arrive the following morning (USh 2500). To Kasese, the trains depart on Friday at 3 pm and arrive the following day about noon (USh 4500). There is only 3rd class available on these trains and they are particularly slow and uncomfortable. Go by road.

Nairobi The weekly train to Nairobi leaves on Wednesday afternoon, arriving in Nairobi the following afternoon. Bookings should be made a day or two in advance at Kampala railway station. See the Uganda Getting There & Away chapter for full details.

Ferry From Kampala's Port Bell, there used to be ferries to the Ssese Islands (Kalangala) twice a week, but these have been suspended indefinitely. The best way to the islands now is from Masaka, although you can still catch fishing boats from Kasenyi (near Entebbe). Unfortunately these are small, leave in the afternoon and so travel in the dark, and are generally none too safe. See the Ssese Islands in the South-Western Uganda chapter for more details.

Mwanza The twice-weekly ferries which connect Port Bell with Mwanza (Tanzania) leave Port Bell on Monday and Thursday at 6 pm. Tickets should be bought by 2 pm on the day of departure from the port gate at Port Bell. Taxis to Port Bell leave from the old taxi park in Kampala. See the Uganda Getting There & Away chapter for full details.

Getting Around
The Airport The international airport is at Entebbe, 35 km from Kampala. There are public taxis between Kampala (old taxi park) and Entebbe town (USh 1000), and then you

can catch another taxi from there to the airport (three km, USh 500). A special hire taxi from Kampala to Entebbe airport costs about USh 25,000.

Taxi The ubiquitous white minibus taxis leave from the two taxi parks and fan out all over the city. They are cheap, quick and leave every few minutes to most destinations in the city. To find the taxi you want, simply ask around at the taxi parks – people are generally very helpful.

Special Hire In Kampala itself, there are plenty of 'special hire' taxis, but they're difficult to identify since there's no standardised colour and they have no signs.

Good places to find them in the centre are outside the railway station, at the upper end of Colville St and outside the Pioneer Mall on Kampala Rd. A standard short-distance fare is around USh 2500. Negotiate a price for longer distances, including waiting time if that's what you want.

South-Eastern Uganda

TORORO

In the very eastern part of Uganda, not far from the border with Kenya, is Tororo. It must have looked particularly beautiful once, with its flowering trees, and it obviously had a substantial Asian community, as the two large Hindu temples suggest. These days, however, there's little of interest and the town wears a cloak of dereliction. Its only redeeming feature is the intriguing, forest-covered volcanic plug that rises up abruptly from an otherwise flat plain at the back of the town. The views from the top are well worth the climb.

For travellers, Tororo is a place to stop and rest en route to Mbale, Mt Elgon and points further north and north-west, although the accommodation options are much better in Mbale.

Information

There are no foreign exchange bureaus in Tororo and it's difficult to change money after banking hours, even if you have cash. Bring sufficient local currency with you.

Places to Stay & Eat

The only cheap place worth considering is the *Tororo Christian Guest House*, diagonally opposite the Total petrol station on Mbale Rd. It's clean enough and the people who run it are friendly. It costs USh 4500/6000 for singles/doubles with shared toilet.

The clean and friendly *Coop Hotel* is the next best and charges USh 6000/7500 for singles/doubles with shared bathrooms. Bucket showers are available and the toilets are kept clean enough. (Trivia lovers will be thrilled to know that the cisterns are genuine

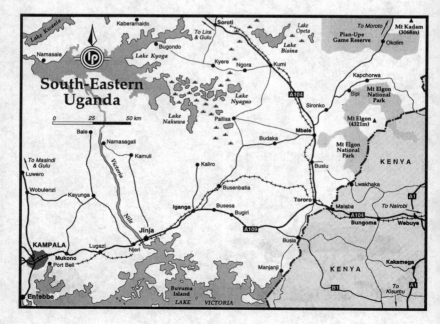

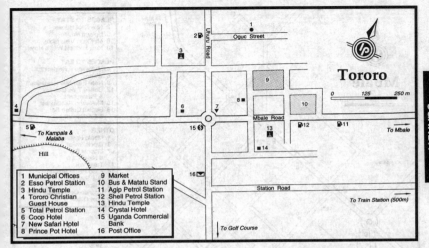

Key to map:

1 Municipal Offices
2 Esso Petrol Station
3 Hindu Temple
4 Tororo Christian
   Guest House
5 Total Petrol Station
6 Coop Hotel
7 New Safari Hotel
8 Prince Pot Hotel
9 Market
10 Bus & Matatu Stand
11 Agip Petrol Station
12 Shell Petrol Station
13 Hindu Temple
14 Crystal Hotel
15 Uganda Commercial
   Bank
16 Post Office

UGANDA

cast-iron Shanks 'Made in England'.) The hotel has its own bar and restaurant.

The best hotel in town, and the only one with rooms with private bathroom, is the *Crystal Hotel*, which has clean doubles (no singles) for USh 10,000. There's a bar and restaurant. If you're not eating at your hotel, try the *New Safari Hotel*, on the corner of Mbale and Uhuru Rds.

Getting There & Away

Taxi A taxi to Kampala costs USh 6000 and takes about 3½ hours. The short ride to Malaba, on the Kenyan border, costs USh 1000, or to Mbale it's USh 1500.

Train Tororo is a railway town, although now that the through train between Kenya and Uganda is running again, most train travellers give Tororo nothing more than a passing glance and perhaps a wave out the window.

The line running north from here to Mbale, Soroti and Gulu no longer takes passenger trains due to security problems in the north. Even when the trains are running they are tediously slow and have 3rd class only.

MBALE

In stark contrast to Tororo, Mbale is a thriving provincial city with plenty of activity and well-maintained facilities. It also enjoys a superb setting at the base of Mt Elgon, and makes an excellent base for expeditions to the mountain on the Ugandan side. It's also the base from which to visit Sipi Falls, the country's most beautiful waterfall and the one you will frequently see featured on posters promoting Uganda.

Information

There are no foreign exchange bureaus in Mbale, so bring sufficient local currency with you.

For information on Mt Elgon, visit the Uganda Wildlife Authority office near the Mt Elgon Hotel. It is open every day from 8 am to 5 pm, and the staff here can help organise your trip.

Places to Stay – bottom end

Cheap accommodation is hard to find. Pick of the very meagre bunch is the *Nile Rest House*, which charges USh 3000/4000 for single/double rooms with attached bathrooms, but don't expect too much.

UGANDA

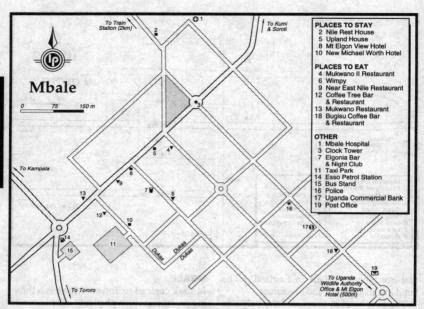

Mbale

0   75   150 m

To Train
Station (2km)

To Kumi
& Soroti

To Kampala

To Tororo

To Uganda
Wildlife Authority
Office & Mt Elgon
Hotel (500m)

Dukas

Dukas

PLACES TO STAY
2 Nile Rest House
5 Upland House
8 Mt Elgon View Hotel
10 New Michael Worth Hotel

PLACES TO EAT
4 Mukwano II Restaurant
6 Wimpy
9 Near East Nile Restaurant
12 Coffee Tree Bar
 & Restaurant
13 Mukwano Restaurant
18 Bugisu Coffee Bar
 & Restaurant

OTHER
1 Mbale Hospital
3 Clock Tower
7 Elgonia Bar
 & Night Club
11 Taxi Park
14 Esso Petrol Station
15 Bus Stand
16 Police
17 Uganda Commercial Bank
19 Post Office

Somewhat more salubrious is the *Upland House*, right in the centre of town. Spartan but reasonably clean rooms go for USh 6000/11,000, and there's hot water in the communal bathroom.

Also habitable is the *Mt Elgon View Hotel*, which has clean and bright doubles (no singles) for USh 10,000 with a bathroom that is shared.

Best of all in this range is the recently refurbished *New Michael Worth Hotel*, which offers singles/doubles with attached bathroom for USh 8000/11,000, most with a small balcony overlooking the street. It's kept very clean, and there's hot water in the showers and friendly staff. The hotel has its own bar and restaurant on the ground floor.

Places to Stay – top end
The only hotel in this category is the *Mt Elgon Hotel* (☎ (045) 33454). It has seen better days but it's still comfortable and the rooms are very spacious. Doubles with

attached bathroom cost USh 35,000 including breakfast and taxes. It's in a very quiet area of Mbale, surrounded by its own grounds, with guarded parking out the front. The bar here is a very popular social spot in the evenings with guests, local project workers and businesspeople. The staff are friendly and helpful.

Places to Eat
Most of the cheap hotels have their own simple restaurants, or you can get cheap local food at the *Mukwano* or *Mukwano Part 2 Restaurant*. Another popular place is the *Near East Nile Restaurant*, which serves local food and greasy spoon.

For snacks and coffee, try the *Bugisu Coffee Bar & Restaurant* opposite the post office. It's popular with office workers at lunch time. There's also a *Wimpy*, which offers the usual fare.

Slightly more expensive, but good value, the *Coffee Tree Bar & Restaurant* offers meals from USh 1800 to USh 2000. There's a choice of Ugandan dishes and western-style meals. The open-air terrace bar which overlooks the street is a popular place for a cold beer or two in the afternoon and early evening.

Entertainment

The nearest thing you'll get to a nightclub in Mbale is the disco held at the *Coffee Tree* on Saturday night.

Elgonia Bar & Night Club is basically a place where people come to talk. The best thing about it is the deep, upholstered lounge suites.

Getting There & Away

There are frequent matatu taxis to Tororo (USh 1500), Jinja (USh 5000) and Kampala (USh 6000), as well as to Soroti. To smaller nearby places, such as Budadiri (USh 1000; for Mt Elgon), they are much less frequent. The matatu taxi park is small but fairly chaotic – just ask around. Next to it is the bus stand, where you can find buses to Jinja and Kampala and the occasional one to Soroti. Destinations are posted in the front window.

For travel around town, there are plenty of boda-boda. The trip to the Mt Elgon Hotel or National Parks office is USh 200.

SIPI FALLS

Sipi Falls is a truly beautiful sight, and it's well worth making the effort to get there. The falls are situated about 55 km north of Mbale, in the foothills of Mt Elgon and not far from the town of Kapchorwe. The cheapest way to get there is to take a matatu taxi from Mbale to Kapchorwe and get off close to the falls. However, these matatu are not very frequent, so it may be more convenient to hire a taxi for the day.

If you'd like to stay here for the night, there's the *Sipi Falls Rest House* at USh 5000 per person per night, or you can camp for USh 3000. Perhaps a better option is the *Elgon Maasai House* in Sipi village, which offers singles for USh 5000 and also has food available.

JINJA

Jinja lies on the shores of Lake Victoria and is a major marketing centre for southern Uganda. It's an interesting little place with many old Asian-style buildings, reflecting the days when the town had a sizeable Asian community. The town was virtually owned by Asians, and since many of them have started to return Jinja is once again becoming prosperous. There are a lot of spacious mansions in various states of repair, surrounded by expansive lawns overlooking the lake along Nile Crescent adjacent to the golf club and the agricultural showground. The town didn't suffer as badly as many others during the last civil war and so does not wear the same air of dereliction. According to local residents, Okello's retreating troops were told in no uncertain terms that they wouldn't be welcome.

Jinja is close to the Owen Falls Dam, a hydro-electric station which supplies Uganda with the bulk of its electricity. The Chinese are currently installing more turbines at the hydro station, which should hugely increase its output. The main Kampala to Jinja road runs across the top of the dam, and the railway line crosses on a bridge close by. Just below the golf course is the 'Source of the Nile', formerly Ripon Falls.

Information

The foreign exchange bureaus are along Main St and there's a Barclays Bank at the end of this road, near the town hall.

Things to See

Source du Nil The Source du Nil (Source of the Nile) is billed as one of Jinja's premier attractions, and tourists are bussed in to see it from Kampala, but there's actually very little to see. Before the building of the Owen Falls Dam, this was the site of Ripon Falls, where the Nile left Lake Victoria on its way to the Mediterranean. The actual falls were inundated by the waters of the dam but you can still make out from the turbulence where they used to be. A walkway and observation deck has been constructed down to the edge of the falls, with the inevitable brass plaque

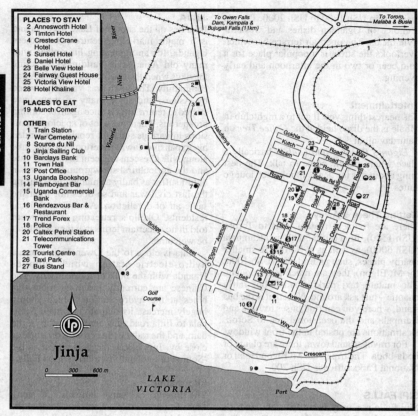

PLACES TO STAY
2 Annesworth Hotel
3 Timton Hotel
4 Crested Crane Hotel
5 Sunset Hotel
6 Daniel Hotel
23 Belle View Hotel
24 Fairway Guest House
25 Victoria View Hotel
28 Hotel Khaline

PLACES TO EAT
19 Munch Corner

OTHER
1 Train Station
7 War Cemetery
8 Source du Nil
9 Jinja Sailing Club
10 Barclays Bank
11 Town Hall
12 Post Office
13 Uganda Bookshop
14 Flamboyant Bar
15 Uganda Commercial Bank
16 Rendezvous Bar & Restaurant
17 Trend Forex
18 Police
20 Caltex Petrol Station
21 Telecommunications Tower
22 Tourist Centre
26 Taxi Park
27 Bus Stand

Jinja

0   300   600 m

LAKE VICTORIA

commemorating Speke and Grant's discovery of the source of the Nile in 1862.

Access to the source is off Bridge St, and there's a toll gate where you pay your USh 1000 entry fee. If you're not with a tour group, it's a pleasant walk from the centre of town, or you can take a bicycle taxi.

Bujugali Falls Ripon Falls may have been inundated and the Owen Falls dammed but the Bujugali Falls, some 11 km from Jinja, still survive. If you have the time and the transport, it's worth visiting them. There's a well laid-out picnic area and good signposts.

To get there, take Nalufenya Rd out of the centre down to the roundabout on the main Kampala to Tororo road and go straight across. About 10 km further on, you'll see a prominent signpost on the left-hand side for the falls. They're about one km from here.

Jinja Sailing Club Although it seems that many years have gone by since any sailing took place, the Sailing Club is well maintained and has green lawns which run to the edge of the lake. The shade *bandas* give welcome relief from the sun, and cold beer and soft drinks are sold, as are basic meals.

UGANDA

Gandhi in Uganda?

It comes as something of a surprise to find a statue commemorating Mahatma Gandhi (or more precisely, the scattering of his ashes) at a Hindu temple near Jinja.

It seems that on Gandhi's death in 1948, his ashes were divided up and sent to many locations around the world to be scattered – and some ended up in the Nile River here in Uganda. (There were also some which ended up in a bank vault in India and were only released in 1997 following a lengthy custody dispute!) ■

On Friday and Saturday nights, when the disco starts up, it's the town's focal point.

The club is 200m past the port. You can walk (about 20 minutes) or take a bicycle taxi.

Places to Stay – bottom end

Campers should head for the Timton Hotel (see below), where you can pitch your tent in the garden for USh 3000 per person. If you're on foot it's a bit of a haul from the taxi park, although there are plenty of cycle taxis (USh 300).

One of the cheapest places to stay is the *Fairway Guest House* (☎ (043) 21784), Kutch Rd, close to the matatu taxi park. It's basic, with no hot water, but is otherwise OK and provides clean sheets. Singles/doubles with attached bathroom cost USh 6500/7500 including breakfast.

A few doors away is the *Victoria View Hotel* (☎ (043) 21363), though the name is pure wishful thinking. Nevertheless, it's clean and pleasant, with singles/doubles with attached bathroom for USh 8000, including breakfast. The door locks are purely cosmetic but the place seems safe enough. The hotel has its own restaurant.

Places to Stay – middle

At the bottom of this range and close to the centre of town on Kutch Rd is the comfortable *Belle View Hotel*. It's away from the noisy matatu taxi park and good value at USh 10,000/13,000 for singles/doubles with bath and breakfast. The hotel also has a reasonable restaurant, bar and TV lounge.

Up in price, the *Annesworth Hotel* (☎ (043) 20086) on Nalufenya Rd is a pleasant hotel set in its own grounds, but it's a considerable way from the centre of town. It offers singles/doubles with attached bathroom, including breakfast, for USh 20,000/25,000.

Very close by is the Ministry of Tourism's *Crested Crane Hotel* (☎ (043) 21513). It's not a bad place, with a large garden. Rooms cost USh 25,500/31,000 including breakfast. There's also a bar and TV lounge here.

Still in this area is the *Timton Hotel*, a small, modern place with just a few rooms and a very nice garden. The upstairs rooms are good value at USh 25,000 for a double including breakfast.

More expensive but with views of the lake are two popular hotels on Kiira Rd. The cheaper of the two is the *Daniel Hotel* (☎ (043) 20971), which is popular with Asians and expatriates. It costs USh 25,000/35,000 for singles/doubles with attached bathroom, including breakfast. There's a bar and restaurant, a video bank and guarded parking.

Close by is the *Sunset Hotel* (☎ (043) 20115), a larger place with a spacious bar, beer garden and terrace restaurant. It's comfortable and reasonable value at USh 28,750/39,000 for singles/doubles with attached bathroom, including breakfast. Credit cards are not accepted but there is a foreign exchange bureau here. Even if you can't afford to stay, it's worth having a drink in the gardens, especially on Sunday afternoon, when African dancers perform.

Places to Eat

For a cheap local meal of beans, rice and vegetables, go to the market opposite the Victoria View Hotel. It closes at 9.30 pm.

There's not much other choice in the budget range. The best eatery in town is the restaurant at the *Belle View Hotel*, where you can get a good lunch or dinner for around USh 2500. The beers are cold too. The *Victoria View Hotel* serves basic meals for lunch and omelettes and bread for breakfast.

Also popular is the *Rendezvous Bar & Restaurant*, on Main St, but chicken and chips is about the limit.

It comes as something of a surprise to find an Indian restaurant, complete with screeching Hindi film-score music, in sleepy Jinja. The *Munch Corner* does reasonable masala dosas for USh 2500, vegetarian curries for USh 2000 and non-vegetarian for USh 3500. It also serves that old Indian favourite – pizza (USh 3000).

The restaurants at the *Sunset Hotel* and the *Daniel Hotel* are also good but, if you're not staying there, are somewhat inconveniently

located away from the centre of town. The Sunday afternoon buffet at the Sunset is popular with expats and Asians. It costs USh 9000, and it's easy to while away the afternoon here.

Getting There & Away

Bus & Taxi The trip from Kampala to Jinja by matatu taxi costs USh 1000 and takes about one hour on a very good road. By ordinary bus, the fare is marginally less but the journey takes more than two hours.

There are also regular taxi departures for Malaba (USh 5000), Mbale (USh 5000) and Tororo (USh 4500).

Train Jinja is on the Tororo-Kampala main railway line. A local train runs in each direction weekly, but it's horrifically slow. The railway station is about one km out of town on the Tororo road.

Ferry Ugandan Railways ferries operate to Mwanza in Tanzania but they don't take passengers. To get to Mwanza, you'll have to take the ferry from Port Bell (see Getting There & Away in the Kampala chapter for details).

South-Western Uganda

FORT PORTAL

Fort Portal, a green, pleasant and quiet town at the north-eastern end of the Ruwenzori Mountains, is the centre of a verdant tea-growing area and the provincial headquarters for Kabarole District. The town is also the base from which to explore the Semliki Valley (hot springs and Pygmy villages), the Kibale National Park and the crater lakes in the area. It's an area of Uganda well worth exploring, so set aside a week or so to make the most of it.

Information

Kabarole Tours (☎ (0493) 22182; fax 22636), signposted behind the Esso petrol station, is an excellent tour agency and information bureau on all the area's places of interest. The staff are very friendly and helpful, and tour prices are very reasonable,

as long as you have a group to share the cost. See the following section for details of the tours offered.

For changing money, the Moons foreign exchange (forex) bureau is across the road from the Wooden Hotel but it's very unreliable and seems to be closed more than it's open.

Organised Tours

Unless you're intent on doing it the hard way, the best place to arrange transport and tours to the places of interest around Fort Portal is through Kabarole Tours. The office is open daily from 8 am to 6 pm. Kabarole has departures to the Semliki Valley (full day, USh 60,000 shared between up to four people, plus USh 15,000 per person national parks fee); to Kibale Forest (half day, USh 40,000

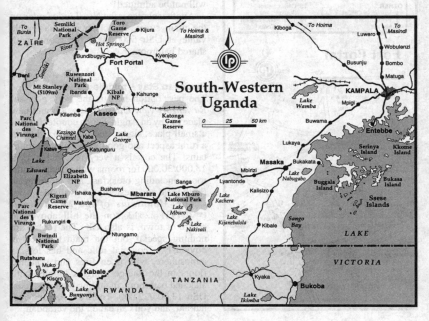

437

for up to four people plus USh 15,000 per person park entry fee and USh 7000 for a guide); to Lake Nkuruba (full day, USh 55,000 up to four people); a cultural tour which also visits a local village, as well as lakes and caves (full day, USh 70,000 for a minimum of four passengers); and a combined walking/driving tour to hot springs towards Kasese (full day, USh 35,000 per person, minimum of two people). Kabarole can also organise bicycle day trips in the area, which cost USh 5000 and include a map and suggested itinerary and treks to the northern Ruwenzoris (three days, USh

PLACES TO STAY	4 Shell Petrol
9 Kyaka Lodge	Station
20 Wooden Hotel	5 Taxis to Kamwenge
22 New Linda Lodge	& Rwaihamba
	6 Bank
PLACES TO EAT	7 Bank
13 Mawenu Growers	8 Uganda Bookshop
Restaurant	10 Cinema
14 RA Bistro	11 Bus Stand
15 Tree Shades Restaurant	12 Taxi Park
& Glue Pot Bar	16 Esso Petrol Station
	17 Kabarole Tours
OTHER	18 Caltex Petrol
1 Municipal Offices	Station
2 Post Office	19 Total Petrol Station
3 Market	21 Moons Forex

Fort Portal

35,000 plus USh 30,000 national park entry fees; or two days with overnight accommodation in Bundibugyo, USh 34,000 plus USh 15,000 park entry fee). Kabarole Tours is a reliable operation and is recommended.

Places to Stay – bottom end
One of the cheapest places to stay is the *Kyaka Lodge* on Kuhadika Rd. Here you can get a simple room with shared bathroom for USh 3000/4000, but it's not a very attractive proposition.

Much better is the *Wooden Hotel* (☎ (0493) 22560) on Lugard Rd. Very clean, comfortable rooms with shared bathroom cost USh 5000/8000 for singles/doubles. With attached bath it's USh 8000/10,000, and bucket hot water is delivered to your room. The hotel has a bar/restaurant whose décor could have been inspired by a visit to a New Orleans brothel. A sign at the entrance to the bar warns that patrons wearing caps or slippers will not be admitted!

Another choice is the *New Linda Lodge* on the main street. It's clean and reasonable value at USh 6000/8000 for rooms with shared bathroom.

Places to Stay – middle
The best option here is the very pleasant *Ruwenzori View Guest House*, a brand new place run by an Anglo-Dutch couple. It's just a small place, signposted off Toro Rd, with a rural aspect and good views of the mountains. The cost is a very reasonable USh 18,000/30,000 for rooms with attached bathroom, including breakfast, and other meals (both local and western) are available.

The *Mountains of the Moon Hotel* (☎ (0493) 22513), on the hill above the centre of town, is also OK. The rooms are nothing special, but the main building is obviously a colonial relic and has lots of atmosphere, with open fires and polished floors in the lounge. Singles/doubles with attached bathroom, including breakfast, cost USh 13,000/22,000. There's a bar and restaurant, and you can eat on the verandah.

Places to Eat

There's good, reasonably priced food at the *Wooden Hotel* (if you can see what you're eating). It's also worth checking out the *Tree Shades Restaurant* opposite the Esso petrol station. Good, solid local meals are served here for around USh 1500 to USh 2500.

The best food in town, however, is to be found at the *RA Bistro*, on Rukidi III St, which serves western-style food. It isn't that cheap, at USh 3500 to USh 4000 for a main course, but it's excellent, with good service and friendly staff. Have a good night out and eat here.

Entertainment

There are not many riveting places to go for a drink in Fort Portal. Most of the bars have turned into dreary video parlours where no-one talks to each other. On weekends there's live music in the bar at the *Wooden Hotel*, and this goes on until late.

Getting There & Away

The taxi park is on Kahinju Rd, near the junction with Lugard Rd. As elsewhere, there's no schedule so you just hang around until they're full, but there are fairly frequent departures to Hoima (USh 5000), Kasese (USh 2500) and Kampala (USh 8000).

From the bus stand at the bottom end of Babitha Rd things are a little more predictable. There's a daily bus to Kabale (USh 8000, via Kasese) at around 6 am, and departures for Kampala (USh 7000) leave at 7 and 10 am.

Local taxis (pick-ups) to Kamwenge (for Kibale Forest) and Rwaihamba (for Lake Nkuruba) leave from the intersection near where the main road crosses the river. There's not a lot of traffic, but there are usually a few taxis each day. Monday and Thursday are market days in Rwaihamba and so there's plenty then.

AROUND FORT PORTAL
Kibale National Park

Fort Portal is a good access point for this national park, famous for its chimpanzees, which is 30 km to the south-east. See the Uganda National Parks & Reserves chapter for more information.

Lake Nkuruba

Lake Nkuruba, 25 km south of Fort Portal, is a stunning crater lake, which is believed to be bilharzia free. There are also good walking opportunities from the camp here, including a one-hour trek to Lake Nyabikere, from where you can continue to Rweteera and Kibale Forest.

Places to Stay The *community camp site* at the lake is quite basic, but the welcome is warm and the setting ideal for a few days of rest and relaxation. It costs USh 2000 to pitch a tent, and there is one for hire at USh 1000. You can also just come on a day trip from Fort Portal and pay USh 1000 to use the facilities, which include a cooking shelter and bush shower. Cheap vegetarian meals are available (order in advance), or you can get limited supplies from the trading centre of Rwaihamba, only one km away.

Getting There & Away Taxis from Fort Portal to Kasenda or Rwaihamba pass Lake Nkuruba (USh 800), which is signposted on the left just before Rwaihamba. There's not much traffic, but at least three vehicles a day do the trip, except on Monday and Thursday (market days in Rwaihamba) when there's plenty of traffic.

Semliki Valley

Many visitors to Fort Portal make a day trip (at least) to the Semliki Valley and to **Bundibugyo** on the other side of the Ruwenzoris.

The main attractions are the hot springs near Sempaya in the **Semliki National Park** and the Pygmy villages near the village of Ntandi in the forest of the Semliki Valley, a few km before Bundibugyo. However, the best part of this trip is the magnificent views over the rainforest and savannah of the Semliki Valley and into Zaïre.

Unfortunately the Pygmy villagers have gone the way of those in eastern Zaïre and are now horribly commercialised, their culture moribund, and in all it's a depressing proposition. Still, the tourists roll in day by day, allowing themselves to be harassed and fleeced. Meanwhile, another unique culture hits the dust. If you insist on going, the 'official' charge for a visit to their village is USh 1500 per person, but you'll be lucky to get away with paying less than three times that amount and the pressure to buy rubbish is enervating.

The other 'attraction' is the hot springs. At least you won't get hassled here but the place is very much a let-down. This is not Bogoria National Park (Kenya) and it's worlds away from the geysers of Rotorua (New Zealand) and Iceland. There is a walking trail around the springs.

Places to Stay Near the toll station, there's a simple hotel where you can stay the night for USh 3000 a double. You can also stay at one of the two bandas run by Morence Mpora (☎ (0493) 22245) at Kichwamba/Nyankuku, on the way to Bundibugyo. Morence has been offering accommodation for years now in an effort to help finance the orphanage he runs. Just ask the taxi driver to drop you in the right place – it's near the Kichwamba Technical College.

At the Semliki National Park headquarters at Ntandi there's a basic site where you can camp for USh 1000 per person. Also in this area is the *Semliki Safari Camp*, an up-market camp with permanent tents at USh 30,000 including breakfast, or you can set up your own tent for USh 5000.

If you find yourself in Bundibugyo (the local administrative centre) and need to stay the night, there's the *Moonlight Hotel* which costs USh 5000 per person, or the *Union Guest House*.

Getting There & Away The best way to get to the Semliki Valley is to go on one of Kabarole Tours' full-day excursions (USh 60,000 shared between up to four people). Alternatively, hire a car and driver for the day. This will cost much the same. There are occasional taxis between Fort Portal and Bundibugyo, but as they're obviously not going to hang around while you visit the sights, you'll be left stranded. Hitching is a waste of time.

KASESE

Kasese is the western railhead of Uganda and the base from which to organise a trip into the Ruwenzori Mountains or to Queen Elizabeth National Park. There's no other reason to visit, however – it's a very small, hot, quiet town in a relatively infertile and lightly populated area, and it wears an air of permanent torpor, although it was once important to the economy because of the nearby copper mines at Kilembe (copper was Uganda's third most important export during the 1970s), though these are now closed.

Information

There's a foreign exchange bureau on the ground floor of the Saad Hotel block but it's not always open.

Ruwenzori Mountaineering Services, or RMS (☎ (0483) 44115), PO Box 33, Kasese, has an information and booking office on Alexandra Rd. It is open daily. This is where you make arrangements for climbing the Ruwenzoris. For further details, see the relevant section in the Uganda National Parks & Reserves chapter.

Things to See

Kasese has no attractions, but if you have half a day to kill, hire a bicycle and cycle the 13 km up to the copper mine at Kilembe for an interesting diversion. It is a long gradual uphill climb, which makes for hard work on the way there but is great fun on the way back! You can sometimes get a tour of the surface remnants (crushers, concentrators and separators etc) free of charge but you're not allowed underground. The manager of your hotel should be able to arrange bicycle hire. You can call off for a cold beer en route at the Margherita Hotel, 4.5 km from Kasese.

Places to Stay – bottom end

The *Rumukiya Inn* is a fairly new place and it claims to 'maximumly serve'. As with most hotels in Kasese, the rooms are set around a little courtyard, and cost USh

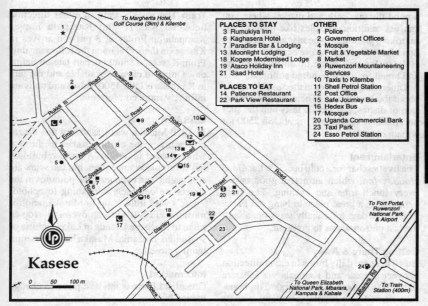

Kasese

0   50   100 m

PLACES TO STAY
3 Rumukiya Inn
6 Kaghasera Hotel
7 Paradise Bar & Lodging
13 Moonlight Lodging
18 Kogere Modernised Lodge
19 Ataco Holiday Inn
21 Saad Hotel

PLACES TO EAT
14 Patience Restaurant
22 Park View Restaurant

OTHER
1 Police
2 Government Offices
4 Mosque
5 Fruit & Vegetable Market
8 Market
9 Ruwenzori Mountaineering Services
10 Taxis to Kilembe
11 Shell Petrol Station
12 Post Office
15 Safe Journey Bus
16 Hedex Bus
17 Mosque
20 Uganda Commercial Bank
23 Taxi Park
24 Esso Petrol Station

To Margherita Hotel, Golf Course (3km) & Kilembe

To Fort Portal, Ruwenzori National Park & Airport

To Queen Elizabeth National Park, Mbarara, Kampala & Kabale

To Train Station (400m)

4000/6000 with shared bathroom, or there's one double room with attached bathroom for USh 8000.

Also good, and very similar to the Rumukiya, is the *Kogere Modernised Lodge* on Stanley St. Rooms at this little place all have shared bathrooms, and cost USh 4000/5000.

There are a number of other cheapies around town, including the *Moonlight*, *Paradise* and *Kaghasera*, but they are not up to much.

The welcome at the *Ataco Holiday Inn* is less than overwhelming; it's a pity the same can't be said for the stench from the toilets. Gloomy rooms cost USh 6000/8000.

Places to Stay – middle

The *Saad Hotel* (☎ (0483) 44139) on Ruwenzori Rd is a popular place, and just about everyone who climbs the Ruwenzoris stays here for rest and recreation both before and after the climb, though there is no bar (the owners are Muslim). The staff are very friendly and the rooms are pleasant and rea-

sonably clean. It has double rooms (with two single beds) with private bathroom only, but they allow three people to share a room. For two people, it costs USh 15,000 and for three it's USh 25,000. The hotel has its own restaurant and upstairs TV/video lounge.

Places to Stay – top end

The *Margherita Hotel* (☎ (0483) 44015), 4.5 km out of town on the road up to Kilembe, has singles/doubles including breakfast for USh 36,000/54,000. The hotel is on a beautiful site looking out towards the Ruwenzoris on one side and the golf course on the other, surrounded by flowering trees. A film of the trek from the Margherita to Stanley peaks in the Ruwenzoris is shown daily, if you want to know what you're up for. The restaurant here serves reasonable food at USh 7000 for main courses.

Places to Eat

There are several inexpensive restaurants

around the taxi park and market where you can get traditional staples like meat stews, matoke (plantains), beans and rice. For breakfast the *grocery store* next to the Ataco Holiday Inn will rustle up an omelette, tea and bread for a few hundred shillings.

Otherwise, the meals at the *Saad Hotel* are about the best option. There's a good selection of dishes, the food is tasty and the staff are friendly. You're looking at USh 2500 for a main course.

Entertainment
The liveliest bar for a cold beer is at the *Ataco Holiday Inn*, which attracts a good crowd every lunch time and evening. The front verandah is a great place to hang out in the heat of the day. It basically stays open until the last person wants to go home.

Getting There & Away
Bus There are daily buses in either direction between Kasese and Kampala via Mbarara (USh 8000, about eight hours). The hopefully named Safe Journey company, with its offices on Margherita Rd, has departures at 6, 8 and 11 am.

There's also a daily bus in either direction between Fort Portal and Kabale via Kasese and Mbarara. It starts from Fort Portal at 6 am, arriving in Kasese at around 8 am. It then continues on to Kabale, taking about 7½ hours. The fare from Kasese to Kabale is USh 7500. The last part of the journey south crosses a mountain pass from which, weather permitting, you'll be rewarded with spectacular views to the west of the volcanoes along the Uganda-Rwanda border.

Taxi There are frequent taxis to Fort Portal (one hour, USh 2500) and Mbarara (USh 4000).

Getting to Queen Elizabeth National Park by taxi is pretty straightforward. Catch a Mbarara taxi and ask for the national park entrance, which is signposted on the left just before the trading centre of Katunguru. From here you'll have to hitch into the park, but you may have to wait a couple of hours for a lift.

Train The weekly train in either direction between Kasese and Kampala leaves Kampala on Friday at 3 pm and arrives in Kasese (in theory) at noon the following day. From Kasese, it should depart late on Saturday. Only 3rd class is available and the fare to Kampala is USh 4500. Buses and taxis are infinitely more comfortable.

MASAKA
In 1979 Masaka was trashed by the Tanzanian army in the closing stages of the war which ousted Idi Amin. A lot of rebuilding has taken place since then, but the scars are still visible and even now the potholes in the streets are definitely something to behold! There's very little to do in Masaka, and for most travellers it's just an overnight stop en route to the Ssese Islands in Lake Victoria or south into Tanzania. Masaka has a museum, but it's closed.

Information
Greenland forex is the best place to change money here.

Places to Stay & Eat
There's very little choice of hotels in Masaka (most were destroyed in the war). The *Victoria End Guest House* costs USh 6000 for a single and is good. The *Elgin Inn* restaurant here has good meals for USh 1500.

About four km from town, and just off the road to the Tanzanian border, is the *Masaka Backpackers* (☎ (0485) 21288). Here you can camp for USh 2500, take a bed in a dorm for USh 3500, or a room for USh 5000. To get there from Masaka, take a Kirimya taxi, get off at Kasanvu and follow the signs from there.

In the mid-range, there's a choice of two hotels, both of which are very pleasant. The cheaper of the two is the *Hotel La Nova* (☎ (0485) 21520), which is popular with aid workers. All the rooms have attached bathrooms and cost USh 20,000/23,000 including breakfast. The staff are very pleasant and there's a bar, restaurant and guarded parking.

Somewhat more expensive is the *Laston Hotel* (☎ (0485) 20309), which has a wide

UGANDA

range of doubles (no singles) with attached bathrooms for USh 25,000. This is a very well-managed hotel, spotlessly clean and with friendly staff. There are several open-air terraces and balconies where you can eat and drink, as well as an indoor bar and restaurant. Meals here are good value and cost, on average, around USh 6000.

Getting There & Away
Buses and taxis run frequently to Kampala (USh 2500) and Mbarara (USh 2500) and less frequently to Kabale.

Bukakata (from where boats leave for the Ssese Islands) is 36 km east of Masaka along a *murram* (dirt) road, which is in reasonable shape except for a rough 10-km stretch close to Masaka. There are infrequent and very crowded taxis between the turn-off at Nyendo (about three km on the Kampala side of Masaka) and Bukakata (USh 1000).

Getting to Bukakata in your own transport can be an exercise in frustration, as there are no signposts whatsoever and the only people who seem to know the way are other drivers. Basically, you head downhill (east) out of Masaka centre, cross over the river bridge and then turn first right (where there's a sign for the Church of Uganda Holiday & Conference Centre). From here you go straight across the first junction and then turn left at the next T-junction.

Masaka is also the starting point for crossing into Tanzania via the Kagera salient to Bukoba. See the Uganda Getting There & Away chapter for details.

SSESE ISLANDS
This group of 84 islands lies off the north-western shores of Lake Victoria, east of Masaka and south of Entebbe. The islands are connected to the mainland by ferries from Bukakata to Luku and fishing boats from Port Bell to Kalangala.

The islands offer an interesting and refreshingly different facet of Uganda which is worth exploring, but don't come here looking for 'action' – this is rest and recreation time. Unlike the mainland, these islands escaped the ravages of the civil wars and so remain largely unspoiled. The people, known as the Basese, form a distinct tribal group, with their own language, culture and folklore. They are primarily fishers, and farmers of coffee, sweet potato, cassava, yams and bananas. As you might expect, fish forms a major part of their diet.

Most islanders are members of one or other of the various Christian sects. A minority are Muslims. Communities are tightly knit and there are no dangers associated with wandering around the islands on foot. In fact, this is the best way to see them.

The main islands of Buggala, Bufumira, Bukasa, Bubeke and Kkome are hilly and, where not cultivated, are forested with a wide variety of trees. Animals you're likely to come across include various species of monkey, hippo, crocodile and many different types of bird, but there are no large predators (other than crocodiles).

Many spots afford beautiful views over the lake and across to the other islands.

PLACES TO STAY	
2	Laston Hotel
21	Hotel La Nova

OTHER	
1	Masaka Sports Club
3	Bank of Uganda
4	Esso Petrol Station
5	Agip Petrol Station
6	Bus Stand
7	Peugeot Taxis
8	Taxi Park
9	Taxi Park
10	Post Office
11	Uganda Commercial Bank
12	Shell Petrol Station
13	Immigration
14	Greenland Forex
15	Police
16	Hindu Temple
17	Museum
18	Mosque
19	Market
20	High School

Masaka

You'll have no problems persuading the fishers to take you out on their boats. Swimming is also possible off most of the islands, as long as you observe the usual precaution about avoiding reedy areas (where the snails which carry the bilharzia parasite live).

All up, you're looking at a very mellow and peaceful time on these islands. There is a plentiful variety of food and, although they are becoming increasingly popular, the islands are far from overrun with visitors.

Information

The main town on the islands is Kalangala on Buggala island. It's the administrative centre, with a post office (telephone connections to Kampala) and a branch of the Uganda Commercial Bank.

Places to Stay & Eat

Buggala Island The most popular place on the island these days is the *Hornbill Camp Site*, about 15 minutes walk from Kalangala. Camping costs USh 1500, and filling meals are USh 1500. The people who run this place are very friendly, and it's a fun place to stay.

Another option is *PTA Andronico's Malanga Safari Lodge* (☎ Kalangala (0481)

255646), owned by Mr PT Andronico Ssemakula, a schoolteacher who speaks fluent English. A bed here in rather scruffy rooms costs USh 3000 and meals cost USh 2000. Camping is possible (USh 1500) although there's not much space. Beers and soft drinks are also available and you can rent bicycles.

Panorama Camping Safaris is another camp site and lodge in Kalangala. It has been well set up, with camping in sites among the rainforest at USh 2000, and a number of bandas at USh 15,000. Excellent meals are available (around USh 3000) and the service is good and very friendly. To find it, walk down to the lake opposite the post office, and it is the place with red-roofed stone huts.

In Liku, about 500m from where the ferry from Bukakata docks, is the *Scorpion Lodge*, a pleasant place with rooms at USh 3000/7000, or you can camp for USh 1500. It also does decent meals (around USh 1800) and you can arrange bike hire here.

Other Islands There are also several lodges and guesthouses in the other main towns on the islands. On Bukasa island, ask for *Agne's House*. It is a very friendly place, but dark

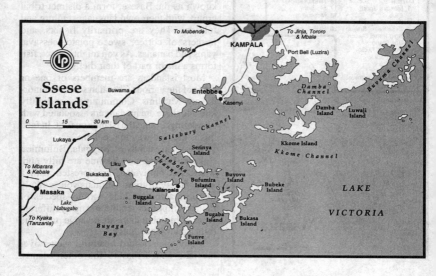

and rundown. It is reasonably cheap, though, at USh 5000 per person for bed, breakfast and dinner. Camping is allowed in the garden. There is also a community *guesthouse* and *camp site*, run by Father Christopher.

Getting There & Away

Boats (fishing boats and outboard canoes) go to the islands from the mainland departure points of Bukakata (35 km east of Masaka) and Kasenyi (a 30-minute taxi ride from Kampala).

See the Masaka section for details of transport to Bukakata. Once in Bukakata there are outboard canoes which ferry people across to Liku (USh 1000), from where pick-ups make the trip to Kalangala (USh 1000). Vehicles can safely be left at the police station in Bukakata for a small fee.

For fishing boats to Buggala and Bukasa from Kampala, take a taxi to Kasenyi. There is no pier here so you have to pay someone to ferry you out to the boat on their shoulders! The boat for Bukasa leaves around 3 pm daily except Sunday, costs USh 3000 and arrives around 6 pm. Boats for Kalangala (Buggala) also leave in the late afternoon and

so arrive in the dark, often as late as 11 pm, and cost USh 5000. As these boats travel in the dark and have little in the way of safety equipment, it may be preferable to take the short ride from Bukakata.

MBARARA

The main town between Masaka and Kabale, Mbarara suffered a great deal during the war to oust Idi Amin but now bears few scars of those times. It's a very spread out town, but pleasant, with a good range of facilities and is a good place to stay overnight between central and western Uganda.

The Nile Bank forex is the best place to change money.

Places to Stay – bottom end

A reasonable, cheap place to stay is the *Super Tip Top Lodge, Bar & Restaurant*, which has singles/doubles with shared bathroom for USh 4000/6000. Bucket hot showers are available. Similar is the *Hotel Plaza*, which has singles/doubles with shared bathroom for USh 4500/7000.

Places to Stay – middle

A good place to stay in this range is the

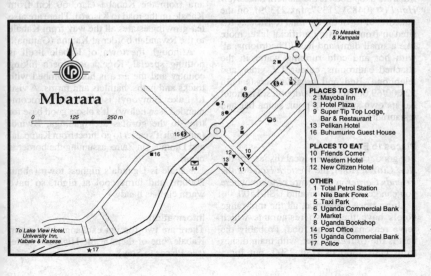

Mbarara

0   125   250 m

To Masaka & Kampala

To Lake View Hotel, University Inn, Kabale & Kasese

PLACES TO STAY
2 Mayoba Inn
3 Hotel Plaza
9 Super Tip Top Lodge, Bar & Restaurant
13 Pelikan Hotel
16 Buhumuriro Guest House

PLACES TO EAT
10 Friends Corner
11 Western Hotel
12 New Citizen Hotel

OTHER
1 Total Petrol Station
4 Nile Bank Forex
5 Taxi Park
6 Uganda Commercial Bank
7 Market
8 Uganda Bookshop
14 Post Office
15 Uganda Commercial Bank
17 Police

UGANDA

Mayoba Inn, on the main road. It has singles/doubles with shared bathroom for USh 8000/10,000, slightly more for rooms with attached bathroom. The hotel has its own bar and restaurant.

If you'd prefer to be off the main road, try the homely *Buhumuriro Guest House* (☎ (0485) 21145), which is quiet and surrounded by its own gardens. It offers doubles (no singles) for USh 11,000 with shared bathroom. There's a bar, and meals are also available.

Up in price but close to the centre of town is the *Pelikan Hotel* (☎ (0485) 21100), which is quiet, has friendly staff and costs USh 10,000/18,000 for singles/doubles with attached bathroom. There's a bar and restaurant and credit cards are accepted.

Also good value is the *University Inn* (☎ (0485) 20334), set in its own grounds at the other end of town. It's a friendly place and rarely full, and offers doubles (no singles) with attached bathroom, including breakfast, for USh 18,000. There's a bar and restaurant.

Places to Stay – top end

Mbarara's top hotel is the modern *Lake View Hotel* (☎ (0485) 21397; fax 21399), on the outskirts of town off the road to Kasese. It's sited in front of a tiny artificial lake (more like a small dam) and has 70 bedrooms, all with hot and cold running water in the attached bathrooms, colour TV, video and telephone. Bed and breakfast costs USh 52,000/69,000 for singles/doubles. The hotel has its own swimming pool, sauna bar and restaurant.

Places to Eat

For good, cheap, filling local dishes, try the *New Citizen Hotel*, the *Western Hotel* or the *Friends Corner* in the centre of town, where you can get meals for around USh 1500.

Up in price somewhat, all the mid-range hotels have their own restaurants which serve reasonably good food. Probably the best is the *University Inn*, with main dishes from USh 1500 to USh 2500, but for a splurge, try the *Mariza Restaurant* at the Lake View Hotel.

Getting There & Away

There are frequent buses and taxis from Mbarara to Kampala (four hours, USh 7000), Masaka (USh 2500), Kabale (USh 4000, two hours) and Kasese (USh 4000). There are also EMS Post minibuses to Kampala which operate on Tuesday, Thursday and Saturday (USh 4000).

For the Queen Elizabeth National Park, catch a Kasese-bound taxi and ask to get off at Katunguru (USh 3000), from where you'll need to hitch into the park.

KABALE

Kabale is in the Kigeza area, which tourist brochures are fond of dubbing the 'Switzerland of Africa', though I've never seen volcanoes in Switzerland. Nevertheless, this south-western corner of Uganda is certainly very beautiful, with its intensively cultivated and terraced hills, forests and lakes. It offers breathtaking views of the Virunga chain of volcanoes from the summits of various passes (such as the one just before you drop down into Kabale on the road from Mbarara, and from the Kanaba Gap, 60 km from Kabale on the road to Kisoro). There are also tea-growing estates all the way from Kabale to the Rwandan border at Katuna (Gatuna).

Although the town of Kabale itself is nothing special, Kigeza is superb hiking country and the area is honeycombed with tracks and paths, hamlets and farms. A visit to Lake Bunyonyi is particularly recommended (see below). It's also a good base for trips to the gorillas at Mgahinga, Bwindi (although it's easier to go direct from Kampala) and Djomba (in Zaïre, assuming the border is open).

Kabale is Uganda's highest town (about 2000m) and turns cool at night, so have warm clothes handy.

Information

There are two foreign exchange bureaus in Kabale, one of them at the Highland Hotel (see Places to Stay).

The Uganda Wildlife Authority maintains an office in the main street, but as they cannot actually book gorilla trips here, and are not in direct contact with either Bwindi or Mgahinga, there's very little the staff can do for you.

Places to Stay – bottom end

If you are camping, there is a free site close to the White Horse Inn but it has no facilities.

One cheap place to stay is *St Paul's Training Centre & Hostel*, where double rooms cost USh 4500. It's a clean place, the staff are friendly and simple meals are available.

There are also two very popular budget hotels here. The first is the *Visitours Hotel* (☎ (0486) 22239), which is divided into units of three rooms which share a bathroom, a toilet and a small lounge. It's very clean, and towels are provided. Singles/doubles cost USh 2500/5000. The hotel has a restaurant and there's an attractive upstairs verandah overlooking the street.

The other good option, but somewhat more expensive, is the *Skyblue Hotel* (☎ (0486) 22154), which also has very clean rooms with towel and soap provided and

bucket hot water on request. It costs USh 6000/8000 for singles/doubles with shared bathroom.

Places to Stay – middle

The most popular place to stay in this range is the *Highlands Hotel* (☎ (0486) 22125). The staff here are very friendly and helpful, but some rooms are better than others. It costs USh 12,000 for a double room with a shared bathroom, or USh 23,000 with attached bathroom (no singles), breakfast included. Towel and soap are provided and there's hot water in the showers if the plumbing is intact (otherwise, bucket hot water is provided). The big plus about this hotel is the excellent food offered in the restaurant and the very popular bar with its log fire. It's a great place to meet people.

Much better in terms of facilities which work is the airy *Victoria Inn* (☎ (0486) 22134), which offers very comfortable rooms with attached bathroom for USh 12,000/20,000 a single/double, with soap and towel provided. A light breakfast (tea and bread) is included. The hotel has its own bar and restaurant and the staff are friendly.

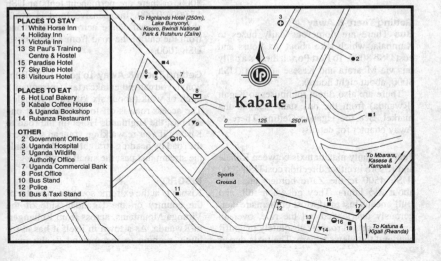

PLACES TO STAY
1 White Horse Inn
10 Holiday Inn
11 Victoria Inn
13 St Paul's Training
    Centre & Hostel
15 Paradise Hotel
17 Sky Blue Hotel
18 Visitours Hotel

PLACES TO EAT
6 Hot Loaf Bakery
9 Kabale Coffee House
   & Uganda Bookshop
14 Rubanza Restaurant

OTHER
2 Government Offices
3 Uganda Hospital
5 Uganda Wildlife
   Authority Office
7 Uganda Commercial Bank
8 Post Office
10 Bus Stand
12 Police
16 Bus & Taxi Stand

To Highlands Hotel (250m),
Lake Bunyonyi,
Kisoro, Bwindi National
Park & Rutshuru (Zaïre)

Kabale

0   125   250 m

Sports
Ground

To Mbarara,
Kasese &
Kampala

To Katuna &
Kigali (Rwanda)

Places to Stay – top end

Kabale's best hotel is the *White Horse Inn* (☎ (0486) 22020; fax 23717), up on the hill overlooking the town. It's a very attractive place and offers doubles (no singles) for USh 45,000 including breakfast. The hotel has a bar and restaurant.

Places to Eat

You can find a good cheap breakfast (omelette, bread and tea or coffee) at the *Visitours Hotel* or the *Skyblue Motel*. Both places also serve good local food for lunch and dinner. The *Rubanza Restaurant* is worth checking out for lunches and dinners.

The best value, however, is the restaurant at the *Highlands Hotel*. It costs around USh 1500 to USh 2500 for a main course but it's well worth it, assuming they have what you want to eat (fish is frequently not available). You have the choice here of eating in the enclosed restaurant or in the partially open-air bar area with a log fire to warm your cockles.

For a real splurge, but not necessarily better food, go for a meal at the *White Horse Inn*, which has a pleasant garden setting. Expect to pay around USh 5000 to USh 6000 for a main course.

Getting There & Away

Bus There are numerous daily buses to Kampala, which take about six hours and cost USh 8000. To Fort Portal, there's a daily bus via Mbarara and Kasese at 7 am (USh 8000, about eight hours).

There are also direct minibuses to Kigali (Rwanda) from the bus stand next to the market. See the Uganda Getting There & Away chapter for details.

Taxi The daily matatu taxis between Kabale and Kisoro in either direction cost USh 4000 (USh 4500 to the Zaïre border) and take about 2½ hours. They go when full, and 'full' means just that! Most of them are dangerously overloaded but the ride, over an excellent gravel road, is absolutely magnificent and the views superb. The taxis depart

from the Shell petrol station next to the Visitours Hotel.

There are also regular departures for Kampala (USh 9000) which go via Mbarara (USh 4000).

For Bwindi National Park there are a couple of vehicles to Butogota daily, and for these you'll pay as much as USh 10,000, although locals pay only half that. It's a slow but highly scenic journey, and you'll have to stay overnight in Butogota before going on to the park.

AROUND KABALE
Lake Bunyonyi

A *must* in this area is a trip to Lake Bunyonyi, a famous beauty spot over the ridge to the north-west of Kabale. It's a large and irregularly shaped lake with a number of islands, and the surrounding hillsides, as elsewhere in this region, are intensively cultivated. Many of the villagers have boats and you shouldn't have any difficulty arranging a trip on the lake.

Places to Stay On Bushara island in the lake there's the *Bushara Island Camp* (☎ (0486) 22447), a community project set up with foreign help. You can camp here for USh 3000, or there are permanent tents at USh 15,000/20,000. Inexpensive food is available. A dugout canoe across to the island from the end of the road from Kabale costs USh 1000.

Getting There & Away To get to Lake Bunyonyi, you can either take a taxi (infrequent), hitch or walk (about six km from Kabale). The access road is off to the left about one km past the Highlands Hotel on the road to Kisoro. If you're walking, you can short cut the road by heading straight uphill alongside the stream just past the small dams.

KISORO

Kisoro is at the extreme south-western tip of the country on the Ugandan side of the Virunga Mountains, across from Ruhengeri in Rwanda. As a town in itself it has absolutely nothing to recommend it; the main draw for travellers is as a base from which to visit the gorillas in Mgahinga National Park to the south or the gorillas at Djomba just over the border to the west in Zaïre.

Information

The Uganda Wildlife Authority office is on the main road in the centre of town, and it's here you should make enquiries about seeing the gorillas at Mgahinga and arrange for transport to take you there. The office is open daily from 8 am to 12.30 pm and 2 to 5 pm.

There is no foreign exchange bureau in Kisoro, so bring sufficient local currency with you, including enough to pay for food and guide tips for the trip to see the gorillas at Djomba if you intend to go there. The Zaïreans in this area prefer payment in Ugandan shillings rather than zaires. There's no bank at the border.

Places to Stay

If you have camping equipment and are intending to visit the Djomba gorillas in Zaïre and return to Uganda, go to the border at Bunagana and camp free outside the Ugandan immigration post. The people here are very friendly and will keep an eye on your tent while you're away at Djomba. Bring food with you. Drinks (beer and soft drinks) are available at the border – local youths will arrange all this for you.

About 1.5 km from Kisoro on the road to Zaïre is the *Rugigana Tourist Valley Campsite*, where you can camp for USh 1500 or take a basic room for USh 2000 per person.

In Kisoro itself, the best place to stay is the *Mubano Hotel*, which has twin-bed doubles for USh 6000 with attached bathroom, or with a double bed and sitting room for USh 8000. It's reasonably clean, the staff are friendly and there's a bar and restaurant, although no electricity or running water.

A cheaper bet is the new *Vivunya Hotel* with rooms at USh 6000 with common bath and good cheap food. *Avoid Dave's Safe Modern Hotel* – it's neither.

Somewhat more expensive is the *Travellers' Rest*, although it is hardly the Ritz. It offers no-frills double rooms (two beds) with attached bathroom and bucket hot water. Reasonably priced meals here are tasty and good value but take some time to arrive, as the cooking facilities are limited.

Places to Eat

For a cheap local meal, go to the *Virunga Restaurant* on the main street. Other than this, the only places to eat are the *Mubano Hotel* and the *Travellers' Rest*. Both offer much the same kind of food at similar prices.

Getting There & Away

Between Kabale and Kisoro there are frequent daily matatus, which depart when full and cost USh 4000 (see the Kabale section earlier for more details). These matatus continue on from Kisoro a further nine km to the border at Bunagana (USh 500).

There's a direct bus between Kampala and Kisoro daily, leaving Kampala at 7 am and costing USh 11,000. It passes through Kabale around noon if you want to pick it up there (USh 4000).

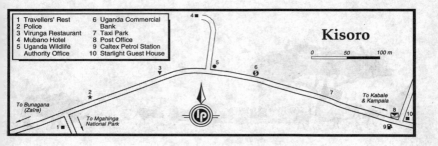

1 Travellers' Rest	6	Uganda Commercial Bank
2 Police	7	Taxi Park
3 Virunga Restaurant	8	Post Office
4 Mubano Hotel	9	Caltex Petrol Station
5 Uganda Wildlife Authority Office	10	Starlight Guest House

Kisoro

0   50   100 m

To Bunagana (Zaïre)

To Mgahinga National Park

To Kabale & Kampala

If you intend to head further into Zaïre after seeing the gorillas at Djomba, the only public transport to Rutshuru is on Friday. The rest of the time you'll have to hitch, and there's very little traffic.

For information on getting to the Mgahinga National Park, see the Uganda National Parks & Reserves chapter.

The Rwandan border south of Kisoro at Cyanika is open, but the road is in an appalling state and there have been some security problems along here in recent times. It's better to go via Katuna (Gatuna) from Kabale. See the Uganda Getting There & Away chapter for full details of the routes into Rwanda and Zaïre.

Northern Uganda

For all practical purposes the northern part of Uganda is virtually a separate country from the south. Politically it has been isolated from the south, and it is one of the few black marks in Museveni's otherwise excel-lent record that he has failed to reconcile the north and deal with the rebels.

From a tourist point of view the main (indeed, only) focus of interest is in the west, where the Murchison Falls National Park (see the Uganda National Parks & Reserves chapter) and Lake Albert area are well worth exploring.

GULU

Gulu is the largest Ugandan town in the north of the country and is on the railway line between Tororo and Pakwach. Thirty km north of Gulu at Patiko is Baker's Fort, built by the British in the 1870s as a base from which to suppress the slave trade.

Places to Stay & Eat

A good, cheap place and excellent value is

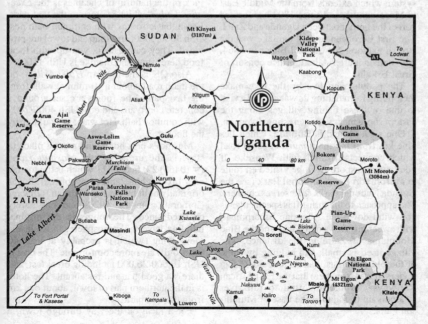

the *Church of Uganda Guest House*. Also excellent value is the *Uganda Red Cross Society*, which has a couple of cheap rooms where travellers can stay. Other places recommended in the past include the *New Gulu Restaurant* in Pakwach Rd and the *Luxxor Lodge* opposite the truck park.

The top hotel is the *Acholi Inn*. It has standard singles/doubles with attached bathroom for US$25/35.

Getting There & Away
Buses and taxis go between Kampala and Gulu. The road is good bitumen most of the way and the buses absolutely fly along here, doing the trip in around four hours. Gulu is on the railway line which connects Pakwach with Tororo in the south-east, but passenger services were suspended some years ago due to security problems.

LAKE ALBERT
Lake Albert is part of the Great Rift Valley system which extends from the Middle East to Mozambique, and since 1894 has formed part of the border between Uganda and Zaïre. The first European to spot the lake was the British explorer Sir Samuel Baker in 1864, who named it after Albert, prince consort of Great Britain.

The people who live by the lake make their living from fishing its waters, and a visit to one of these fishing villages along the eastern shore makes an interesting diversion.

One such village is **Butiaba**, which lies nine km from the main *murram* (dirt) road which connects Masindi with Wanseko. If you have transport it can be visited en route to **Murchison Falls National Park** (see the Uganda National Parks & Reserves chapter). The approach to the turn-off is spectacular as you wind down the Albertine Escarpment, with sweeping views of the lake and the Blue Mountains of Zaïre in the distance. The village itself is small, and judging by some of the old buildings, had its share of Asian traders. It was from here that the East African Railways Corporation used to run river steamers up to Fajao at the base of Murchison Falls.

The best time to visit is in the late morning when the fishing catch is brought ashore from the small fishing boats – huge Nile perch weighing in excess of 30 kg are quite commonplace.

While there is no formal accommodation in the village, you could probably find someone willing to put you up for a day or two, but be sure not to misuse local hospitality.

MASINDI
Masindi is a small, easy-going provincial headquarters, and is the last town of any substance if you're heading for Murchison Falls. It's a good place to stock up on provisions – and fuel, as it's the last you'll find until returning here.

The town boasts a post office (with card phones), a branch of the Uganda Commercial Bank and a regional administration building.

Places to Stay & Eat
Pick of the handful of cheapies is the *Executive Lodge*, which is close to the taxi park. Large, basic rooms with common bath cost USh 3000/6000, and soap and towel are provided. They can also fix you up with local food here (stew and matoke is USh 1500).

Also OK is the modern *Hotel Aribas*, on the main road, about a 10-minute walk from the taxi park. The rooms are set around a concrete courtyard and cost USh 4000/7000 with common bath. Hot water is available by the bucket.

Masindi's best hotel, and a great place to stay, is the creaking old *Masindi Hotel* (☎ (0465) 23; fax 20411 which is the town's only fax machine, at the post office). It was originally built by the East African Railways Corporation in the 1920s and has barely changed since. The rooms in the original building have the atmosphere; those in the 'new' wing (which is probably at least 40 years old!) are more comfortable. The cost is USh 16,000/26,000 including breakfast, and there's a good bar and restaurant. The hotel is in the northern part of town, about one km from the taxi park.

For a meal on the way through town, a

popular spot is the *Travellers' Corner Restaurant* near the post office, which caters to western tastes and has prices to match – main courses are around USh 3000 to USh 4500.

Getting There & Away

Taxis between Kampala and Masindi travel throughout the day. The trip takes about three hours and costs USh 6000. There are also irregular departures to Wanseko (USh 4000), Bulisa (USh 3000), Hoima (one hour, USh 2500) and Butiaba (usually one daily in the morning).

Buses between Kampala and Wanseko pass through Masindi. These currently run on a daily basis (at night), but this may decrease if the Gulu to Arua road becomes popular once again. The fare to Kampala is USh 5000.

For hitching to Paraa, check at the Game Department office near the post office to see if any national parks vehicles are around; you may be able to get a ride with them. Otherwise, check out the Travellers' Corner Restaurant and the Masindi Hotel for hitching opportunities.

National Parks & Reserves

Uganda's national parks are right up there with the best parks and reserves found elsewhere in East Africa, and while they may not be as stacked full of game, neither are they as full of other visitors, making them very pleasant and relaxing places to visit. They also offer quite different experiences: viewing the mountain gorillas in Bwindi, the chimps in Kibale and the Nile's Murchison Falls are all highlights not to be missed.

While the low visitor numbers is a great bonus, it's also a disadvantage in that the infrastructure in the parks is less developed – the luxury lodges and tented camps found elsewhere are few and far between here. Also, the organised safari options, especially for budget travellers, are much more limited. Despite this, many of the parks are relatively easy to visit, and the rewards are ample for those who make the effort to get there.

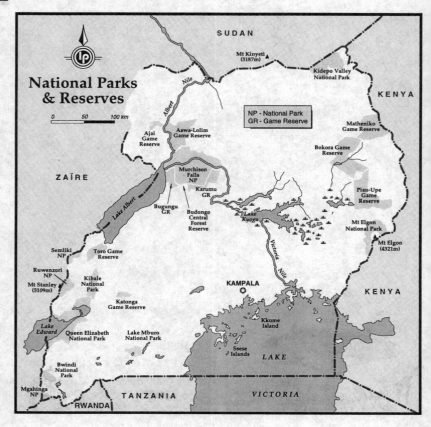

National Parks & Reserves

0   50   100 km

NP - National Park
GR - Game Reserve

SUDAN

Mt Kinyeti (3187m)

Kidepo Valley National Park

KENYA

Matheniko Game Reserve

Bokora Game Reserve

Ajai Game Reserve

Aswa-Lolim Game Reserve

Murchison Falls NP

Karumu GR

Pian-Upe Game Reserve

ZAÏRE

Bugungu GR

Budongo Central Forest Reserve

Lake Kyoga

Mt Elgon National Park

Mt Elgon (4321m)

Semliki NP

Toro Game Reserve

Ruwenzori NP

Mt Stanley (5109m)

Kibale National Park

Katonga Game Reserve

KAMPALA

KENYA

Lake Edward

Queen Elizabeth National Park

Lake Mburo National Park

Kkome Island

Ssese Islands

LAKE VICTORIA

Bwindi National Park

Mgahinga NP

RWANDA   TANZANIA   VICTORIA

REGION	FEATURES
South-Eastern Uganda	
Mt Elgon National Park	Views from the higher reaches across wide plains are some of the most spectacular in Uganda; there's also unique montane vegetation such as giant groundsels and giant lobelias.
South-Western Uganda	
Bwindi National Park	Encompasses one of the last remaining habitats of mountain gorillas in the world; one of Africa's richest areas for flora and fauna.
Kibale National Park	Believed to have the highest density of primates in the world including about 500 chimpanzees and Uganda's third largest elephant population.
Lake Mburo National Park	Houses some rarer animals such as sitatunga, eland and roan antelope. There's also zebra, buffalo and hippo.
Mgahinga National Park	Habitat of some of the rarest creatures on earth – the mountain gorilla deep in lush tropical rainforest.
Queen Elizabeth National Park	See hundreds of hippos and perhaps a rare shoebill stork, go chimpanzee viewing or enjoy a walking safari of Kyambura Gorge.
Ruwenzori National Park	For the well-prepared, these mist-covered mountains probably offer the best trekking in East Africa.
Northern Uganda	
Budongo Central Forest Reserve	A superb place for viewing chimpanzees; dense virgin tropical forest with massive mahogany trees and a wealth of bird life.
Kidepo Valley National Park	Engulfed by rugged, dry mountains and rich in ostrich, cheetah and giraffe.
Murchison Falls National Park	Take a boat ride up the Victoria Nile to the breathtaking Murchison Falls, spotting crocodile, hippo, elephant and thousands of birds.

BUDONGO CENTRAL FOREST RESERVE

The Budongo Forest is right on the road to Murchison Falls, just to the south of the park, and is a great place to stop and have a guided walk through the dense virgin tropical forest, the main attraction being the numerous primates, including chimpanzee, which you have a good chance of sighting. Also of interest are the prolific bird life and the huge mahogany trees which dominate the forest in this area.

Two areas have been put aside for chimpanzee habituation and viewing. **Kaniyo Pabidi** is on the main Masindi to Paraa road, 29 km north of Masindi and actually inside the southern boundary of Murchison Falls National Park. **Busingiro** is 40 km west of Masindi on the road which connects Masindi with Murchison via Lake Albert.

At both places guided walks take place every day at 7.30 am (USh 6000) and 2 pm (USh 4000), and there's an additional USh 4000 entry fee. There are no minimum numbers and the walks last anything from an hour to three hours, depending on what your group wants. Walkers are accompanied by a guide and an armed guard, and these guys are usually very knowledgeable about the forest and the wildlife.

It's also possible to camp at both places. The sites are basic, with pit toilets and showers, and the fee is USh 3000 per person.

Busingiro is on the route used by buses and taxis heading for Wanseko; however Kaniyo Pabidi is not served by regular public transport.

BWINDI NATIONAL PARK

Bwindi is one of Uganda's most recently created national parks, and is in the southwest of the country, very close to the Zaïre border. Formerly known as the Impenetrable Forest, the park, which covers 331 sq km, encompasses one of the last remaining habitats of the mountain gorilla, and is where half of the surviving mountain gorillas in the world live – an estimated 320 individuals. Because of the unrest in Rwanda and eastern Zaïre, Bwindi has become the main place in East Africa for seeing the mountain gorillas.

A major conservation effort has been going on here for a number of years to protect the gorillas' habitat. As a result, encroachment on the montane forest by cultivators has been stopped, poaching has ceased and the gorilla families have been gradually habituated to human contact.

Gorillas are not the only animals to have benefited from this project. The park contains elephant (around 20 animals), at least 10 species of primate, including chimpanzee, colobus monkey and baboon, duiker and bushbuck and the rare giant forest hog, as well as a host of bird and insect species. It is one of the richest areas in Africa for flora and fauna.

The park headquarters is at Buhoma, on the northern edge of the park, and it's here that the gorilla visits start from and where you'll find the only accommodation.

Entry to the park is USh 15,000 per person per day. There are no vehicle entry charges as vehicles cannot proceed beyond the park headquarters. Be aware that this area is a rainforest, and so not surprisingly it rains a hell of a lot – be prepared.

Activities

Tracking the Gorillas The gorillas in Bwindi are fairly well habituated to human contact, and sometimes you don't have to walk more than 10 minutes from the park headquarters at Buhoma to find them. There are two families here which have been habituated – the Mubare group (12 gorillas) and the Katendegyere group (six gorillas).

Group numbers for gorilla tracking are limited to six people in each, and unfortunately demand far exceeds supply. The big safari companies often block-book places months in advance, meaning that for the individual and casual visitor, it can be difficult to get a confirmed place. However, one place on each group is set aside as a 'standby' place, so that if you just rock up at the park headquarters and are prepared to wait for a day or so you can usually get on. All bookings must be made through the Uganda Wildlife Authority office in Kampala (PO Box 3530, Kampala; ☎ (041) 530574; fax 530159), and staff will often tell you that there are no vacancies for months. Be persistent, and if necessary, turn up at the park and try to get on stand-by.

Once you finally get on a tracking group, the chances of finding the gorillas are excellent – they have even been known to hang around very close to the camp site! The time you actually spend with the gorillas once you find them is limited to one hour.

Gorilla-tracking permits cost US$150 (in addition to the park entry fee), payable in hard or local currency. The trips leave at 8.30 am each day, and you have to report to park headquarters 30 minutes prior to that. Note that children under 15 years old are not permitted to track the gorillas, and anyone with a cold or other illness is likewise excluded.

A full refund is given to anyone who withdraws due to ill health.

Forest Walks The park headquarters at Buhoma has a beautiful setting, and there are three walks in the area which are well worth doing. Two of them are in the park, and the third outside, so for this one there is no entry fee payable. For the walks inside the park, the cost is USh 30,000 (in addition to the park entry fee) and all walkers are accompanied by a ranger.

The **Waterfall Trail** takes you to a 33m waterfall on the Munyaga River. It's a fairly strenuous walk which takes around three hours for the round trip.

The **Muzabijiro Loop Trail** gives excellent views south to the Virunga volcanoes and the western Rift Valley in Zaïre, weather permitting. It also takes around three hours.

Lastly there's the **Munyaga River Trail**, an easy half-hour walk in the vicinity of the park headquarters and actually outside the park.

Places to Stay & Eat

Buhoma There are a couple of options at Buhoma. Cheapest of these is the *Buhoma Community Campground*, which is right by the park headquarters. It has a beautiful setting and you can camp here for USh 3000. There are also four-bed bandas, which cost USh 6000 per person or USh 22,000 for the whole banda. These are very basic, but sheets and blankets are supplied and there's hot water by the bucket.

Right across the track from the camping ground is the *H&P Canteen*, where you can get filling local meals for USh 3500 for dinner and USh 2000 for breakfast, although they must be ordered in advance. Primus beer from Zaïre is also available (USh 2000).

Also in this area is the *Buhoma Homestead*, a private set-up owned and run by African Pearl Safaris (☎ (041) 233566; fax 235770) in Kampala. This is a very pleasant and well-run place, and the communal evening candlelit meal is very convivial. Most of the people who stay here are African Pearl Safari clients, but others can also stay

for US$65 for full board. Advance bookings are essential.

Butogota There is also accommodation at Butogota, the nearest trading centre to Buhoma and the closest you can get to the park by public transport. Without your own transport it's too far from the park to use as a base for gorilla tracking, but many travellers spend a night here en route from Kabale or Kampala before walking the 17 km to Buhoma the next day, and visiting the gorillas the day after that. There's also an immigration office here and a border crossing nearby, so there's no reason why you couldn't cross to Rutshuru in Zaïre, although traffic is light.

The only place in town is the *Butogota Travellers Inn*, a modest place with clean rooms at USh 4000/6000. This is where the bus to and from Kampala terminates.

Getting There & Away

There is a direct Silverline bus daily in each direction between Kampala and Butogota, which goes via Kisizi. It leaves Kampala at around 6 am, arriving in Butogota around 6 pm; the fare is USh 10,000.

The other alternative is the irregular pickups and taxis which connect Kabale and Butogota. If you can find one, the fare is USh 10,000, although locals pay much less. If there is nothing from Kabale to Butogota, take a Kihihi taxi as far as Kanyantorogo, from where you can pick up the bus as it comes through from Kampala.

By private vehicle the better route is via Kabale as you stay on the bitumen a lot longer. The turn-off to Bwindi/Buhoma is signposted off the road to Kisoro, and the trip from Kabale takes around three hours. It's a very scenic road through mountainous rainforest.

From Butogota to Buhoma it's 17 km and there is no scheduled transport, so you'll have to walk although you may get lucky and score a ride. Otherwise you can hire a pick-up (USh 20,000 to USh 30,000) or a motorcycle (USh 15,000) to take you.

KIBALE NATIONAL PARK

This national park some 30 km south-east of Fort Portal is home to chimpanzee, baboon, red and white colobus monkey, and larger mammals such as bushbuck, sitatunga, duiker, civet, buffalo and elephant. It's said to have the highest density of primates in the world, including an estimated 500 chimpanzees, and Uganda's third-largest population of elephants.

The star attraction is the **chimpanzees**, five groups of which have been partially habituated to human contact. Nevertheless, you have only a 25% chance of seeing them on any particular day, though you'll almost certainly hear them as they scamper off into the bush on your approach. If you want to be sure of sighting them, plan on spending a few days here.

Activities

Guided Walks The park headquarters is at Kanyanchu, signposted on the left-hand side about six km before you reach the trading centre of Bigodi coming from Fort Portal. It's from here that guided walks can be arranged along well-marked tracks (about a three-km round trip) in search of the chimps. There are daily walks from 7 to 11 am (the best time to go) and from 3 to 6 pm, costing USh 7000 per person, plus USh 15,000 park entry fee. The price includes a guide. The group size is limited to six people but any number of groups can set off, as long as they go off in different directions. Even if you don't see the chimps, you will see the colobus monkeys and the incredible number of butterflies and birds which live in this forest. The vegetation is equally lush.

Reception at the headquarters closes daily at 6 pm sharp.

Places to Stay

You can camp at the headquarters for USh 10,000 per person per night. Facilities include water, firewood, a toilet and shower block. There are only soft drinks for sale at the headquarters, so you must bring all your own food or (if you have transport) drive to Bigodi village and eat there.

If you don't want to camp at park headquarters, there are a few alternatives. Charles Lubega runs the *Safari Hotel*, which is in Nkingo village, about 45 minutes walk from the park headquarters towards Bigodi village. Here there are singles/doubles for USh 3000/6000, or you can camp for USh 2000. You can also get excellent, tasty meals if you order in advance.

The *Crater Valley Beach Resort* is on the right just past Rweteera trading centre. You can camp here in your own tent for USh 3000 per person, or stay in bandas at USh 25,000 per person including meals.

Right in Bigodi itself is *Mucusu*, at the back of the village, run by David Nyamuganya and his wife. It's a very cosy and friendly place which costs USh 3000/6000 for singles/ doubles including breakfast. Excellent, tasty food is available if ordered in advance. The communal bathroom facilities are clean and bucket hot water is available.

Getting There & Away

Taxis to Kamwenge from Fort Portal pass the reserve headquarters (USh 600) and continue via Bigodi (USh 1200). Alternatively, you can charter a minibus from Kabarole Tours in Fort Portal to take you to Bigodi (USh 25,000 one way shared between up to seven people). You can also arrange to have them collect you and take you back to Fort Portal, for the same price. The gravel road between Fort Portal and Bigodi is in excellent condition, apart from one or two rough patches.

KIDEPO VALLEY NATIONAL PARK

Surrounded by mountains and notable for ostrich, cheetah and giraffe, this park covers an area of 1440 sq km in the extreme north-east of Uganda, along the border with Sudan. Make enquiries in Kampala about safety before heading off in this direction, although there seem to be no problems at present.

Entry to the park costs USh 15,000 per day, plus a further USh 5000 per trip for a locally registered vehicle (USh 20,000 with foreign registration).

Places to Stay

At the *Apoka Rest Camp* there's accommodation in the *Student Hostel* huts for USh 22,000, or you can camp for USh 10,000.

There's also the *Apoka Lodge* (PO Box 7404, Kampala), an up-market set-up which costs US$220 per person for half board.

Getting There & Away

It is possible to drive from Kampala via Tororo and Moroto, but check with police regarding safety along this road before setting out.

The only other option is to charter a light plane from Kampala – check with the tourist office in Kampala.

LAKE MBURO NATIONAL PARK

Between Mbarara and Masaka and covering an area of 260 sq km, this national park is mainly savannah with scattered acacia trees. There are five lakes, the largest of which is Lake Mburo. Created in 1982, the park features some of the rarer animals, such as impala, eland, roan antelope, reedbuck, klipspringer and topi, as well as zebra, buffalo and hippo.

Adjacent to the park are the ranches of the Bahima tribe, who herd the famed long-horned Ankole cattle which are a common sight. This is one of the parks you're allowed to walk through (accompanied by a ranger), or you can go on game drives. Canoes, either paddled (USh 8000) or outboard-driven (USh 26,000), are available on Lake Mburo.

Entry to the park costs USh 10,000 per person per day, plus USh 5000 for a small vehicle.

Places to Stay

There are three camp sites in the park (USh 10,000 per person per night), or you can stay at the park headquarters at the *Rwonyo Rest Camp*, which has three double, two single and one four-bed banda with bedding, mosquito nets and bathroom facilities. They cost USh 20,000 per person. Meals are also available here or you can cater for yourself. Fresh fish is sold each morning by fishers from the lake. There's no electricity or refrigeration but kero lanterns, pit latrines and warm bucket showers are available.

A slightly more up-market option is the *Kachira Camp*, run by Hot Ice Safaris (☎ (041) 236777; fax 254240) in Kampala. This is a permanent tented camp, and the cost is US$98 per person per night. Bookings should be made in advance.

Getting There & Away

The park is on the main Masaka to Mbarara road. Coming from Masaka, the turn-off is signposted 13 km after Layantonde, or 50 km before Mbarara. It's possible to hitch lifts in the irregular but accommodating park vehicles from the main road. If you're taking your own vehicle, 4WD is recommended.

MGAHINGA NATIONAL PARK

Mgahinga National Park is tucked away in the far south-western corner of the country. It covers just 34 sq km and the tropical rainforest is another mountain gorilla habitat. The park is contiguous with the Parc Nacional des Volcans in Rwanda, and the Parc National des Virungas in Zaïre. The three together form the Virunga Conservation Area, which covers 420 sq km, and is home to an estimated half of the world's mountain gorilla population of around 640 animals (the other half are found in Bwindi National Park).

As at Bwindi, it is possible to track gorillas here, but access is less convenient and the gorilla groups also have a tendency to duck across the mountains into Rwanda or Zaïre. As a result, fewer people visit the gorillas here, instead opting for the more reliable choices of Bwindi or Djomba, across the border in Zaïre (the latter choice is dependent upon the border crossing being open).

> **WARNING**
> There have been isolated security problems in this area in recent times, due to its proximity to the Zaïre and Rwandan borders. Check with the Uganda Wildlife Authority office in either Kabala or Kampala before planning a visit to this park. ∎

UGANDA

The park headquarters is 12 km from Kisoro at Ntebeko Camp, and entry is USh 15,000 per person per day for the first two days, extra days no charge.

Activities

Tracking the Gorillas A gorilla-tracking group of six people heads out each morning from the park headquarters at 8.30 am. Reservations for the trips are best made at the Uganda Wildlife Authority head office in Kampala (PO Box 3530; ☎ 530574; fax 530159), and the cost is US$120, payable in local currency at the park office in Kisoro. You need to check in at the booking office in Kisoro (by the Mubano Hotel) by 5 pm on the day before your trip and pay your fee. It's here that you can find out whether the gorillas are actually in the park. Unlike the gorilla tracking at Bwindi, there are no stand-by places available at Mgahinga, but it is generally much easier to get a confirmed booking.

Trekking Two of the three volcanoes in the park (Mt Muhabura at 4127m and Mt Gahinga at 3437m) can be climbed for USh 10,000 per person 'rescue fee' plus USh 12,000 per group for a ranger/guide. There's also a 13-km nature trail (USh 6000 per group plus USh 6000 per person) which gives you a chance to spot some of the 185 species of bird found in the park.

Caving The Garana Cave is about two km from the park headquarters and visits cost USh 6000 per group plus USh 6000 per person. Bring a torch (flashlight), or rent one for USh 2000.

Places to Stay & Eat

There is basic *camping* (USh 5000) at the park headquarters but you need to be fully equipped as only water and firewood is available. Also at the main gate is the *Arnajambere Iwacu Community Campground* which costs USh 3000 in your own tent or USh 5000 in a basic banda. Limited food is available.

The only other options are 12 km away in Kisoro (see the South-Western Uganda chapter).

Getting There & Away

There is no transport along the rough 12-km track between Kisoro and the park headquarters; without your own vehicle you'll have to walk (a couple of hours) or hope for a lift (very little traffic). Local pick-ups from Kisoro cost USh 20,000, or you can occasionally get lifts with national parks vehicles for USh 15,000.

MT ELGON NATIONAL PARK

This is one of the most recently created of Uganda's national parks and encompasses the upper regions of Mt Elgon up to the Kenyan border.

The mountain (Wagagai is the highest peak at 4321m) is said to have one of the largest surface areas of any extinct volcano in the world and is peppered with cliffs, caves, gorges and waterfalls. The views from the higher reaches across the wide plains are some of the most spectacular in Uganda. The upper slopes are clothed in tropical montane forest, while above this lies a vast tract of alpine moorland which extends over the caldera, the collapsed crater which covers some 40 sq km at the top of the mountain. **Sipi Falls**, north of Mbale in the foothills of the mountain (see the South-Eastern Uganda chapter), has to be the most beautiful and romantic waterfall in the country, regardless of what you might think about Murchison Falls. Don't miss it, even if you don't trek up the mountain.

The best time to climb the mountain is from December to March, but the seasons are unpredictable and it can rain at any time.

The Uganda Wildlife Authority office in Mbale can help with any information you might need about trekking on the mountain, as can the park headquarters at Budadiri, which has an information centre.

Entry to the park is USh 15,000 for one day, USh 30,000 for two to five days, with additional days at USh 5000. You can pay park fees at the Budadiri office, as well as

UGANDA

arrange guides and porters find information accommodation, routes etc.

Trekking

Tourism on Mt Elgon is still in its infancy, so you need to be resourceful, patient, self-sufficient and not expect well-worn paths such as those you find on Mt Kenya and Kilimanjaro. You obviously need your own camping and cooking equipment, your own food, appropriate clothing and a guide. Don't attempt the trek without a guide – you'll get lost. So far, there are three established camp sites along the Sasa River Trail, the usual route to the summit.

Give yourself a minimum of three days to do this trek and five if you want to reach Jackson's Point, Wagagai and Suam Gorge. Guides and porters can be found at the *Wagagai Hotel* (☎ Budadiri 4) in Budadiri, 30 km north-east of Mbale, where you can also camp (USh 4000) or stay in singles/doubles at USh 5000/7000 per night. The usual rates for guides/porters are USh 8000/7000 per day, with USh 2000 payable in advance and the remainder at the end of the trek.

From Budadiri, which, for the present, can be considered the trailhead, a road leads to Bugitimwa, then it's about three hours walk to the forest. Almost as soon as you enter the forest, you reach Mudangi cliffs, which are scaled by means of 'ladders' (piles of branches). From the top, the trail is less steep and the path well defined. Half an hour's walk up this path is the bamboo forest and a further half hour's walk across the other side of the Sasa River brings you to the first camp site. Getting across the river involves boulder-hopping or wading knee-deep in fast-flowing water, depending on the season.

The camp site is marked by a well-used fireplace and there are enclosed toilets and a rubbish pit. If it's still early in the day when you reach here, you have the option of continuing another two hours further up the trail to stay at the next camp site, some 300m to the left of the trail near the Environmental Task Force hut.

The next part of the trail goes up to the top of the forest and into the heathland, where there's another possible camp site close to a small cave (about three hours beyond the first camp site). The moorland is studded with giant senecio (groundsel) and you'll often see duikers bounding through the long grass and Lammergeier vultures overhead.

A further three hours walk brings you to a split in the path just before the caldera, the left fork leading directly into the caldera and the hot springs at the head of the Suam Gorge, the right fork going to Jackson's Summit via Jackson's Pool. The latter path crosses a permanent stream, and is a possible camp site if you wish to stay up here.

Jackson's Summit and Wagagai can be reached in one day, allowing for a comfortable return to the second camp site in good light. The return journey from the second camp site to the road head can be done in five to six hours.

If you're heading over the border into Kenya via Suam Gorge (not strictly legal), you can stay at *Kabyoyon Farm*, about eight km off the main road, but you need to bring your own food if you turn up unexpectedly.

Getting There & Away

There are regular, if infrequent, taxis to Budadiri from Mbale. Between Mbale and Kampala, there are frequent matatu taxis (USh 6000).

MURCHISON FALLS NATIONAL PARK

The largest park in Uganda is Murchison Falls National Park, through which the Victoria Nile flows on its way to Lake Albert.

Murchison Falls National Park used to contain some of the largest concentrations of game in Uganda. Unfortunately, poachers and retreating troops, both armed with automatic weapons, wiped out practically all game, except the more numerous (or less sought after) herd species. There are now no lions and only a few rhinos, but you will see good numbers of elephant, Ugandan kob, buffalo, hippo and crocodile.

Game drives usually take place north of the Nile, in the area between Paraa and Lake Albert. The problem here is the ferry across

UGANDA

When a Disaster Isn't

Although it seems like sacrilege to say it, the decimation of the wildlife that took place in Murchison was in fact a good thing from an ecological viewpoint. Prior to the war, the park was carrying many more animals – particularly elephants, when herds of more than 500 were commonly seen – than was sustainable. The elephants alone, which numbered over 14,000, chomped their way through 1.4 million *tonnes* of vegetation each year! Add to this the 26,000 buffalo, plus herds of hartebeest, kob and hippo, and the scale of the problem can be appreciated.

The wiping out of most of the large animals has given the environment here a breather, and while it was obviously a major disaster from a wildlife point of view, it means that the park is now in excellent condition and the animals are once again on the increase. The concentrations of game are still low, however, so don't come to Murchison expecting animals everywhere. Aerial surveys in 1995 put the estimates at 200 elephant, 1000 buffalo and around 10,000 hartebeest and kob. ■

---

the river, which only carries a few vehicles at a time and is prone to break down. See the Getting Around section below for details of its schedule.

Entry to the park is USh 15,000 per person per day; vehicle entry is USh 5000 for Uganda-registered vehicles and USh 20,000 for foreign vehicles; this is per trip not per day.

Murchison Falls

Despite the lack of game, it's still worth visiting Murchison, if only for a visit to the Murchison Falls, which involves a boat ride up the Victoria Nile to their base – it's a superb trip. En route you'll see crocodile and hippo, thousands of birds and, usually, elephant. The falls were once described as the most spectacular thing to happen to the Nile along its 6700-km length. They were named by Sir Samuel Baker after a president of the Royal Geographic Society.

You can also visit the falls by vehicle. A rough track (2WD with care) leads off from the main access track 24 km south of Paraa, and from here it's about a half-hour drive. The falls are quite a sight when viewed up close – the river here is only a few metres wide and the water crashes through the gap with amazing force. There's an old ranger station here, which is now staffed by local people who sell sodas and will guide you around for a small fee. There's also a picnic area (shade bandas) and camp site (long-drop toilet).

Activities

The three-hour launch trip from Paraa up to the base of the falls operates on demand at 9 am and 3 pm daily. It's certainly a highlight of the park. The cost is USh 10,000 per person if there's 10 or more people; if less than 10, then the minimum charge is USh 100,000 for the whole boat. On weekends there's a good chance of finding other people to share the cost with; on weekdays you may have to cough up the entire USh 100,000 if you want to go.

Places to Stay & Eat

Paraa Paraa is on the southern bank of the river and is the park headquarters. As well as a small African village, there's also the *Paraa Rest Camp*, where you can camp (USh 10,000) on a grassy site with limited views of the river, or in basic but comfortable mud and thatch bandas at USh 24,000 per person. There's not much in the way of facilities here, but basic meals are provided on request (USh 3000).

The *Paraa Lodge* across the river was bombed, burnt and looted years ago, but has recently been completely refurbished by Sarova Hotels (☎ (02) 333233; fax 211472 in Nairobi) and is once again open for business. It has a superb location with views up the river towards the falls. Prices are around US$50/75 for singles/doubles.

Elsewhere in the Park The *camp site* at the head of the falls has a very nice position right

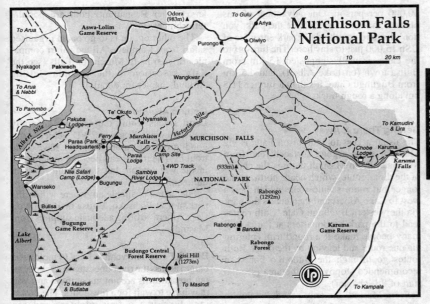

UGANDA

on the river, although you'll definitely need 4WD to get to the best sites on the river's edge. You'll also need to be self-sufficient as there are no supplies of any sort, and the only facilities are a long-drop toilet. Camping here costs USh 10,000.

Just off the main track, right by the turn-off to the falls, is the *Sambiya River Lodge* (☎ (041) 232306; fax 232307 in Kampala), a brand new and very comfortable lodge in a secluded spot. Accommodation is in individual twin-bed units, and the cost is US$140/240 for full board. It's a very nice place and, unlike Paraa, this area is completely free of mosquitoes.

North of the river are two more old lodges – the *Pakuba Lodge*, very close to the Albert Nile in the western part of the park, and the *Chobe Lodge*, on the Victoria Nile in the far east of the park and accessible from the Masindi to Gulu road. Both places were being renovated at the time of writing, and should be open by now. Enquire at park headquarters at Paraa, or at the tourist office in Kampala.

There are also national parks bandas at Rabongo Forest, in the remote southern part of the park. These cost the same as those at Paraa.

Outside the Park Probably the best place to stay actually lies outside the park's western boundary, between the Bugungu Gate and Lake Albert. The *Nile Safari Camp* (☎ (041) 258273; fax 231687 in Kampala) has an unrivalled position high up on the south bank of the Victoria Nile with sweeping views over the water. Accommodation is in comfortable individual, permanent tents, each with their own bathroom, balcony and chairs with river view. There's also a bar and dining area. It's all tastefully done, but comfort doesn't come cheap at US$160/240 for half board. There's also a well-appointed camp site where you can stick up a tent for USh

10,000 per person. One advantage of this place is that as it lies outside the park, you don't have to pay the daily park entry fee of USh 15,000 just to stay here. The turn-off to the camp is well signposted 15 km from Bulisa town (on Lake Albert), and 4.5 km from Bugungu Gate; it's then a further 11.5 km along a rough track.

Getting There & Away

The usual access to Murchison Falls is via Masindi, along a good surfaced road from Kampala. From Masindi there is the choice of the direct route, which heads north, or the longer but more scenic route which heads west to Lake Albert and then enters the park via the western Bugungu Gate. Both routes lead to the park headquarters at Paraa, and many people make it a round trip, entering via one route and leaving by the other. Both routes go through the Budongo Forest, a recommended stopover in the area (see the start of this chapter).

From Masindi the only scheduled public transport is irregular buses and taxis to Wanseko, on Lake Albert close to where the Victoria Nile joins it and the Albert Nile leaves it. These run on a daily basis, and are currently popular as local people from the Arua region in the north-west are at present travelling to Kampala via the lake rather than via Gulu, because of security problems along the Arua to Gulu road.

For the same reason, there are taxis going from Masindi through Paraa and on to Pakwach, and as long as this continues you can get a taxi from Masindi to Paraa, but they are very crowded.

Without your own vehicle the only other alternative is to hitch. The best chance is with the parks vehicles which come in to Masindi a few times a week and may have room to take a passenger back. Enquire at the Game Department office opposite the post office. On weekends there's a good chance of getting a lift with other tourists, as Murchison is becoming an increasingly popular weekend getaway for Kampala residents. Hang around at the Masindi Hotel or Travel-

lers Corner Restaurant; both are popular refreshment stops.

The other option is to go on an organised safari from Kampala. All the safari companies offer trips to Murchison Falls (see the Safaris section in the Uganda Getting Around chapter for details).

Getting Around

Land Tracks within the park are generally well maintained, and a 2WD vehicle with good ground clearance should have little trouble. The tracks can become treacherous in the wet season, but they seem to drain quite quickly.

Fuel is not available anywhere within the park, nor at Wanseko, Bulisa or Butiaba on Lake Albert, so bring adequate supplies from Masindi.

Boat & Ferry The vehicle ferry (a motorised barge) across the river operates to a schedule, but breakdowns are not uncommon and you may have to wait for a few hours. The crossings take just a few minutes, and are scheduled at 7, 9 and 11 am, noon, and 2, 4 and 6.30 pm. The fare is a hefty USh 18,000 each way for passenger vehicles (more for trucks) and USh 1500 for passengers.

If the ferry is not due to run for a while, you can take a speedboat across at any time, and this costs USh 4600 return per person.

All ferry and speedboat fees are payable at the park headquarters, at the top of the south bank about 200m from the ferry landing.

QUEEN ELIZABETH NATIONAL PARK

This park covers almost 2000 sq km and is bordered to the north by the Ruwenzori Mountains and to the west by Lake Edward.

The Queen Elizabeth National Park was once a magnificent place to visit, with its great herds of elephant, buffalo, kob, waterbuck, hippo and topi. But like the Murchison Falls National Park, most of the game was wiped out by the retreating troops of Amin and Okello and by the Tanzanian army which occupied the country after Amin's demise. They all did their ivory and trophy-hunting best. Although the animals are slowly recovering, there's still very little game in the park, apart from gazelle, buffalo, hippo, a couple of small herds of elephant, and the occasional lion. But it's worth a visit just to see the hippo and the birds, and there are also opportunities for walking and chimpanzee viewing.

Most of the tourism activity is based around **Mweya**, in the north of the park. A much less visited area of the park is that around **Ishasha**, in the southern part of the park on the border with Zaïre. The lions in this area are famous for their habit of climbing trees, and the setting is superb. The track between Katunguru and Ishasha cuts right through the park and is in reasonable condition, but remains impassable for much of the wet season. This makes a convenient way to combine a visit to Bwindi with Queen Elizabeth National Park.

The Maramagambo Forest in the southeastern section of the park has recently been opened for limited tourism, and now sports a small tourism centre, camp site and up-market lodge.

Entry to the park costs USh 15,000 per day. The price for a car is USh 5000.

Queen Elizabeth National Park

0   10   20 km

1 Ishasha Camp
2 Ishasha Gate
3 Mweya Safari Lodge
4 Kabatoro Gate
5 Katunguru Gate

Activities

Kazinga Channel Launch Trip Almost every visitor takes a launch trip up the Kazinga Channel to see the thousands of hippos and the pelicans. If you're lucky you will also catch sight of one of the elephant herds and very occasionally see a lion or leopard. The two-hour trip costs USh 90,000 shared by up to 10 people or USh 9000 per person if there are more than 10 of you. There are trips at 9 (the best time) and 11 am, and at 3 and 5 pm. Bookings can be made at Mweya Safari Lodge, and the trips leave from just below the lodge

Chimp Island Sanctuary For a real close-up view of chimpanzees take the daily launch trip from Mweya to this small island sanctuary (9 am and 2.30 pm, USh 15,000), where orphan chimps have been relocated from Entebbe zoo before being released into the wild.

Kyambura Gorge Walking Safari In the eastern corner of the park is the beautiful Kyambura (Chambura) Gorge, and a concessionaire operates walking safaris from its Fig Tree Camp at 7.30 am daily. The gorge is home to a variety of primates, including chimpanzee, and these are often seen on the walking safaris, which last from three to five hours and cost USh 40,000 per person; children under 15 years are not permitted. Bookings can be made at the Mweya Safari Lodge or Fig Tree Camp.

Game Drives There is a small network of trails around the Mweya Safari Lodge and the northern gate. North of the road to Katwe there are some stunning craters, which also lie within the park. Baboon Cliffs is a viewpoint which gives excellent views over the surrounding area.

Forest Walks In the south-eastern section of the park, guided forest walks are available in the Maramagambo Forest. These last from 2½ to 4½ hours, and are great if you enjoy bird-spotting.

Places to Stay & Eat

Mweya The places to stay are on the Mweya Peninsula close to the Mweya Safari Lodge. The cheapest way to stay is to camp at the *Students' Camp*, which costs USh 1000 per person per night. It's a reasonable site but has no shade. Hippos wander through the site at night. If you don't have a tent, you can get a dormitory bed with shared bathroom for USh 1000. The *Tembo Canteen* is where the safari drivers hang out, and decent meals are served here for USh 3000, but you need to order in advance.

A good deal more expensive is the *Ecology Institute*, where you can get a clean and comfortable double room with shared bathroom for USh 20,000 per person.

Top of the line is the *Mweya Safari Lodge* (☎ (041) 235915; fax 235563 in Kampala), which has a stunning position on the raised peninsula, with excellent views over Lake Edward to Katwe and Zaïre and in the other direction along the Kazinga Channel. Sitting on the terrace with a cold drink at sunset is perfect. The lodge has recently changed hands and is due for a US$4 million refurbishment, so may have changed dramatically by now – or be in the process of changing. Before the refit it was very comfortable, with single/double rooms for US$60/82 with attached bathroom, including breakfast. During the week the place is almost deserted but it gets busy on weekends. Good lunches and dinners are available here at reasonable prices (USh 12,000 for the excellent buffet dinner) and the restaurant is open to all. Watch out for the mongoose which come scampering across the lawns in the late afternoon; at night, hippos browse across the lawns, so watch what you're walking into!

Ishasha In the southern part of the park there are bandas at the Ishasha ranger station, which cost USh 15,000 per person, or you can camp for USh 10,000.

Maramagambo Forest The camp site here is set right at the foot of the Kichwamba Escarpment, and as yet sees few visitors. Access is possible direct from the highway.

Getting There & Away

The main Katunguru Gate is on the Mbarara to Kasese road near the small trading centre of Katunguru, where the road crosses the Kazinga Channel. From here it's six km along a track which follows the channel to Mweya, where most of the park activity is based. There are regular taxis to Kasese (USh 1000, one hour) and Mbarara (USh 3000, two hours). Any vehicle travelling from Kampala to Kasese passes through Katunguru. Hitching out of the park from Mweya is easy – just stand by the barrier at the Mweya Safari Lodge and ask the driver for a lift. Better still, make arrangements the night before at the lodge.

For Maramagambo Forest, get off the bus or taxi at the trading centre of Ndekye, south of Katunguru, from where a 10-km path leads through small villages to Maramagambo (also known locally as Nyamusingiri). Ask locals for directions.

The road from Katunguru to Ishasha and Zaïre cuts through the park and, although you don't need to pay any park entry fees to travel along this road, you'll be fined USh 100,000 if you're caught venturing off it and into the park. This road passes Ishasha Gate and leads to the trading centre of Ishasha, from where you can cross into Zaïre, or head south for Butogota and Bwindi National Park – it takes around five hours to drive from Bwindi to Mweya.

RUWENZORI NATIONAL PARK

The legendary, mist-covered Ruwenzori Mountains on Uganda's western border with Zaïre are almost as popular with travellers as Kilimanjaro and Mt Kenya but definitely harder to climb. They have a well-deserved reputation for being very wet at times. This was best summed up by a comment on the wall of Bujuku hut: 'Jesus came here to learn how to walk on water. After five days, anyone could do it'. Be prepared and take warm, waterproof clothing.

The mountain range, which is not volcanic, stretches for about 100 km. At its centre are several mountains which are permanently snow and glacier-covered: Mt Speke (Vittoro

Emmanuele is its highest peak at 4890m); Mt Baker (Edward is its highest peak at 4843m); Mt Gessi (Iolanda, 4715m); Mt Emin (4791m); and Mt Luigi di Savoia (4627m). The three highest peaks in the range are Margherita (5109m), Alexandria (5083m) and Albert (5087m), all on Mt Stanley.

Trekking

Five days is the absolute minimum for a trek through the range, but seven or eight days is better, with one or two days at the top huts. The best times to trek are from late December.to the end of February, and mid-June to mid-August, when there's less rain. Even at these times, the higher reaches are often enveloped in mist, though this generally clears for a short time each day.

With heavy USAID investment, many improvements have been made to the tracks as well as the huts. There are new bridges over the larger rivers, the huts now have essentials such as kitchens, walls and roofs (which they lacked not long ago) plus there's a wooden pathway over the bog. All this has been done to lessen the impact of walkers on the fragile environment.

If you want to reach one of the main summits you need to have some mountaineering experience. The routes to the peaks on Mts Stanley and Baker all cross snow and glaciers, and require the use of ice-axe, ropes and crampons, plus a competent guide. In the right conditions, the summit of Mt Speke is an easier proposition but still requires some mountain experience.

Books & Maps Before attempting a trek in the Ruwenzori Range, it's strongly recommended that you obtain a copy of *Ruwenzori – Map & Guide* by Andrew Wielochowski. This is an excellent large-scale contour map of the mountains, with all the main trails, huts and camp sites marked (as well as other features).

On the reverse side are detailed descriptions of the various possible treks as well as sections on history, flora and fauna, weather and climate, necessary equipment, useful contacts, costs and advice in the event of an accident. It's for sale in most Kampala book shops.

Food & Equipment Preparations for a trek are made in Kasese, where you'll find a good selection of foodstuffs and equipment as well as the office of the Ruwenzori Mountaineering Services (☎ (0483) 44115), Alexandra Rd, PO Box 33, Kasese. It's through the RMS office that you make bookings to climb the mountain, organise guides and porters, and arrange transport to the trailhead at Ibanda/Nyakalengija, off the Kasese to Fort Portal road.

The RMS organises everything you'll need to get up there and back again, and they control all the facilities on the mountain. You'll save nothing by attempting to do it all yourself, since a guide and porter are compulsory for anything other than a short day walk and there's nowhere to hire equipment in Kasese (other than at the RMS – see below). The whole scene is sewn up these days, but that doesn't mean that there's no flexibility.

No special equipment is required for this trek if you don't go onto the ice or snow, but whatever you bring, make sure it's warm and waterproof, that you have a change of dry clothing packed in plastic bags and that you have a decent pair of boots. Joggers are definitely not recommended – your feet will get soaked walking through the bogs, making you cold and miserable all day.

Since night temperatures often drop below zero, you'll need a good sleeping bag, an insulating sleeping mat and suitable warm clothing. This should include a warm hat (up to 30% of body heat is lost through your head).

Another essential item is a waterproof jacket, as it's almost impossible to stay dry in these mountains. Waterproof trousers (or at least a waterproof covering) are advisable. All your extra clothing, sleeping bag and perishable food should be wrapped in strong plastic bags to protect them from water. A small day pack is useful if porters are going to be carrying the bulk of your equipment.

Don't forget insect repellent, maximum protection sunscreen, sunglasses, a torch (flashlight), water bottle, first-aid kit, cutlery and a cup.

As far as your own food is concerned, be warned that the variety of food available in the two 'supermarkets' and the market in Kasese is very limited. This is not Kampala. If there's anything you particularly want to eat on the trek or you have any special requirements, bring these items with you. Don't assume you can buy them in Kasese. You'll need a camp cooker of some description as fires are banned. Kerosene and methylated spirits are available in Kasese.

Equipment Hire The RMS has the following equipment for hire in Kasese:

Item	Cost (USh per trek)
crampons	5000
rope	10,000
ice-axe	5000
trekking boots	5000
rubber boots	5000
sleeping bag	10,000
closed cell mat	5000
raincoat	5000
gaiters	5000

Guides, Porters & Fees There are standard fees for everything you need. Park entry fees are USh 15,000 for one day, USh 30,000 for two to five days, with extra days at USh 5000, plus a one-off USh 10,000 rescue fee. There's also a USh 10,000 per day service fee which includes use of the RMS huts; you can reduce the fee by USh 5000 per day by using your own tent, but this is discouraged.

To this you must add the cost of porters (USh 4000 per stage) and guides (USh 4700) plus food for these people (USh 1800 each per day), transport to and from the trailhead (USh 10,000 return) and fuel (USh 10,000 per day). See the table for a list of the standard all-inclusive packages offered by RMS. A porter can carry 22 kg, which comprises 10 kg of his own gear and 12 kg of the trekker's.

Note that guides' and porters' fees are per *stage* not per day. The stages are: Ibanda/Nyakalengija to Nyabitaba; Nyabitaba to John Mate; John Mate to Bujuku; Bujuku to Kitandara (or Bujuku to Irene Lakes, or to Speke Peak or to Margherita); Elena Hut to Margherita; Kitandara to Guy Yeoman (or Kitandara to Baker or to Lugigi); Guy Yeoman to Nyabitaba; and Nyabitaba to Ibanda/ Nyakalengija. If you walk more than one stage in the day, you have to pay for two stages.

Remember that if you want a good trip, befriend your guide and porters. These people are drawn from the Bakonjo, a hardy but friendly mountain people, most of whom have Biblical names. They'll be staying in rock shelters overnight while you stay in the huts or in your own tent, so be generous with small handouts and give a decent tip at the end of the journey.

Altitude Sickness Be aware of the dangers of Acute Mountain Sickness (AMS). In extreme cases it can be fatal. High-altitude sickness usually becomes noticeable above 3000m and is a sign of your body adjusting to lower oxygen levels. Mild symptoms include headaches, mild nausea and a slight loss of coordination. Symptoms of severe altitude sickness include abnormal speech and behaviour, severe nausea and headaches, a marked loss of coordination and persistent coughing spasms. When any combination of these severe symptoms occurs, the afflicted person should immediately descend 300 to 1000m. When trekking, such a descent may even have to take place at night.

There are no known indicators as to who might suffer from altitude sickness (fitness, age and previous high-altitude experience all

UGANDA

RMS Trekking Packages

Trek	Duration	Cost per person (USh)		
		1 person	2 to 3 people	4 to 6 people
Nyabitaba (solo)	1 day	31,200	23,700	21,900
Nyabitaba (porter & guide)	1 day	64,600	52,000	46,000
John Mate Camp	3 days	147,000	102,300	91,100
Bujuku (3rd Camp)	5 days	203,200	134,400	117,200
Circuit	7 days	246,700	162,200	141,100

All rates include everything except your own food.

seem to be irrelevant), and the only cure is an immediate descent to lower altitudes.

The Trails Ibanda/Nyakalengija is the starting point for a trek in the Ruwenzoris. There are two basic trails up the mountain starting from here which will take you between the peaks of Mt Baker and Mt Stanley. They both have the same approach as far as Nyabitaba Hut on the first day. After that you can either go clockwise or anticlockwise between the peaks.

The following is the clockwise route (the anticlockwise route is the reverse of the following and takes the same amount of time):

Day 1 Nyakalengija to the Nyabitaba Hut (2650m), the first stage, is a fairly easy walk taking four to five hours.

Day 2 From Nyabitaba Hut, you can either take the old route to the Guy Yeoman Hut (3450m, five to six hours) or the new but safer route (seven hours). Along the new route, you also have the choice of staying at Kuruguta Hut/camp site (2940m). The route takes you through tropical vegetation, over two minor streams, across the Mahoma River and finally up the side of a steep valley to the ridge on which the hut is situated.

Day 3 From the Guy Yeoman Hut, you pass through a bog to the Kabamba rock shelter (3450m) and waterfall, then via the Bujongolo rock shelter and the Freshfield Pass (4215m) to the Kitandara Hut (3990m). This takes about seven hours. The hut is picturesquely situated on the shore of the lake of the same name.

Day 4 This is possibly the most interesting part of the trek. After leaving the twin Kitandara lakes, you climb over boulders at the foot of Mt Baker on the one side and the

glaciers of Savoia and Elena on the other. From here you cross Scott Elliot Pass (4372m) and proceed down to Bujuku Hut (3900m). The walk takes about four hours. If you intend to scale Mt Stanley, on the other hand, you head for Elena Hut (4547m), in which case both you and your guide and porters will need appropriate equipment to deal with ice and snow.

Day 5 Assuming you don't scale Mt Stanley, the trek from Bujuku Hut is all downhill to the John Mate Hut (3350m). The walk takes about five hours. En route you pass the Bigo Hut (3400m), where you have the option of taking a difficult track north leading to Mt Gessi, Mt Emin and the Lac de la Lune via a series of bogs. There are also three bogs between the Bujuku Hut and the John Mate Hut, but it's here you'll come across stands of giant heather, groundsel and bamboo. Should you decide to spend the night at Bigo Hut, it sleeps up to 12 people and there is room for tents.

Day 6 From the John Mate Hut, it's downhill again along a rough track to Nyabitaba (about five hours).

Day 7 The final stage is the return to Nyakalengija and onward travel to Kasese.

There are quite a few other minor trails, both up the mountain and across the top into Zaïre and down to Mutwanga (the Uganda-Zaïre border essentially crosses the peaks), although crossing the frontier this way is illegal.

Organised Treks If it's your time rather than your money that is limited, you can have all the necessary arrangements made for you by a safari company.

Rwanda

Rwanda

Rwanda has become indelibly etched into the consciousness of the late 20th century as the focus of one of the world's most horrific attempts at genocide. What happened here in 1994 was beyond belief.

Following the shooting down of an aircraft carrying the president (and also the president of neighbouring Burundi), half a nation went on the rampage.

Within just three to four months, up to one million people were dead, hacked to death with *pangas* (machetes), shot through the head or otherwise butchered with anything to hand.

In addition, up to two million people fled their homes and lived as refugees in the border regions of neighbouring countries.

Before the outrages in 1994, many travellers used to come to Rwanda to visit the beautiful Parc Nacional des Volcans in the north, where the borders of Rwanda, Uganda and Zaïre meet.

The thickly forested slopes are one of the last remaining sanctuaries of the mountain gorilla. This endangered species, too, suffered in the civil war, losing quite a few of its dwindling numbers. However, you can now once again visit two of the family groups, and travellers are starting to trickle back.

RWANDA

Area: 26,338 sq km
Population: 7.9 million
Population Growth Rate: 2.7%
Capital: Kigali
Head of State: President Pasteur Bizimungu
Official Languages: French, Kinyarwanda
Currency: Rwandan franc
Exchange Rate: RFr 301 = US$1
Per Capita GNP: US$210
Inflation: 12%
Time: UTC + 2

Facts about the Country

HISTORY
Early Settlement
As in neighbouring Burundi, the original inhabitants of Rwanda, the Twa Pygmies, were gradually displaced from 1000 AD onwards by migrating Hutu tribespeople who, in turn, came to be dominated by the Watutsi from the 15th century. The Watutsi used the same methods here for securing

472

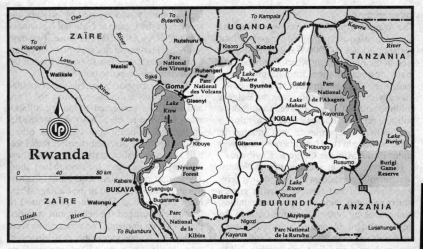

domination over the Hutu as they did in Burundi – the introduction of a feudal land system and a lord-peasant relationship with regard to services and the ownership of cattle, which represented wealth. There the similarities with Burundi end. The authority of the Rwandan *mwami* (king) was far greater than that of his opposite number in Burundi, and the system of feudal overlordship which developed in Rwanda was unsurpassed outside Ethiopia.

Not only was the Rwandan mwami an absolute ruler in every sense of the word, with the power to exact forced Hutu labour and to allocate land to peasants or to evict them, but the Watutsi overlordship was reinforced by ceremonial and religious observances. Military organisation, likewise, was the sole preserve of the Watutsi. Rwanda, however, was more intensively farmed than Burundi, and in the process of growing food on all available land, the Hutu eventually denuded the hills of trees. The consequent erosion, lack of fuel and competition with the Watutsi pastoralists for land frequently threatened the Hutu with famine. Indeed, in the 20th century alone, there have been no less than six famines.

Faced with such a narrow margin of secu-

rity, something was bound to give sooner or later among the Hutu, who account for 89% of the country's population. However, the process was interrupted by the colonial period.

The Colonial Era

The Germans took the country in 1890 and held it until 1916, when their garrisons surrendered to the Belgian forces during WWI. At the end of the war, Rwanda and Burundi were mandated to the Belgians by the League of Nations. From then until independence, the power and privileges of the Watutsi were increased, as the Belgians found it convenient to rule indirectly through the mwami and his princes. They were not only trained to run the bureaucracy but had a monopoly on the educational system operated by the Catholic missionaries.

The condition of the Hutu peasantry deteriorated and led, in 1957, to a series of urgent demands for radical reform. Power and privilege are rarely given up voluntarily in Africa, however, and in 1959, following the death of Mwami Matara III, a ruthless Watutsi clan seized power and murdered Hutu leaders.

RWANDA

Independence

The Watutsi grab for power was a serious miscalculation and provoked a massive Hutu uprising. About 100,000 Watutsi were butchered in the bloodletting which followed, and many thousands fled into neighbouring countries. The new mwami fled into exile. Faced with carnage on this scale, the Belgian colonial authorities were forced to introduce political reforms, but they were all a little too late. When independence was granted in 1962, it brought the Hutu majority to power under Prime Minister Gregoire Kayibanda.

However, certain sections of the Watutsi were unwilling to accept the loss of their privileged position and formed guerrilla groups which mounted raids on Hutu communities, thus provoking further Hutu reprisals. In the fresh round of bloodshed which followed, thousands more Watutsi were killed and tens of thousands of their fellow tribespeople fled to Uganda and Burundi.

Although intertribal tensions eased for many years after that, there was a resurgence of anti-Tutsi feeling in 1972 when tens of thousands of Hutu tribespeople were massacred in Burundi.

The slaughter reignited the old hatreds in Rwanda at that time and prompted the army commander, Major General Juvenal Habyarimana, to oust Kayibanda. He ruled the country until killed (some say assassinated) in a mysterious plane crash at Kigali airport in 1994. During his tenure of office he managed to keep the country on a relatively even keel, despite depressed prices for tea and coffee (the country's major exports) and an influx in 1988 of 50,000 refugees from the ethnic conflict in Burundi. He also managed to stay clear of applying for IMF loans and the austerity measures which are a usual precondition.

Then, in October 1990, the whole intertribal issue was savagely reopened. On the first day of the month, Rwanda was invaded by some 5000 well-armed rebels of the Rwandan Patriotic Front (RPF), a Tutsi-dominated military front, from their bases in western Uganda. They were led by Paul Kagame, a former security chief of the Ugandan army, and assisted by officers and soldiers of the Ugandan National Resistance Army (NRA). All hell broke loose. Two days later, at Habyarimana's request, France, Belgium and Zaïre flew in troops to help the Rwandan army repulse the rebels.

With this support assured, the Rwandan army went on a rampage against the Tutsi and any Hutu 'suspected' of having collaborated with the rebels. Thousands were shot or hacked to death and countless others indiscriminately arrested, herded into football stadia or police stations and left there without food or water for days. Many died. Those that could, fled to Uganda. Zaïrese troops, likewise, joined in the carnage. President Museveni of Uganda was accused of having encouraged the rebels and supplied them with equipment. The accusations were denied but it's inconceivable that Museveni was totally unaware of the preparations which were going on, and it was also common knowledge that Uganda was keen to see the repatriation of the 250,000 Tutsi refugees in western Uganda.

The setback for the RPF was only temporary, however. They invaded again in 1991, this time better armed and prepared. The government forces were thrown back over a large area of northern Rwanda, and by early 1992, the RPF was within 25 km of Kigali, at which point a cease-fire was cobbled together and the warring parties brought to the negotiating table in Arusha (Tanzania).

The negotiations stalled several weeks later and hostilities were renewed. At this point, French troops were flown in, ostensibly to protect foreign nationals in Kigali, but they were accused by the RPF of assisting the Rwandan army. The accusations were denied but TV footage of their activities didn't quite confirm their denials. Meanwhile, with morale in the Rwandan army at a low ebb, the RPF launched an all-out offensive. Habyarimana attempted to contain this by calling a conference of regional presidents to which the RPF was invited. Power sharing was part of the agenda. Habyarimana came away from this conference in April 1994 with somewhat less than he would have liked (and Museveni of Uganda was less than supportive) but just as his light jet was about to land at Kigali airport on the way home it was shot down by a surface-to-air missile. Both he and his colleague, the president of Burundi, died in the crash. It will probably never be known who fired the missile (there are several theories) but this event unleashed one of the 20th century's worst explosions of bloodletting.

The Genocide

Habyarimana's Hutu political and military supporters decided at that point to activate what amounted to a 'final solution' to the Tutsi 'problem' by exterminating them. It was clearly all pre-planned and the principal player among those in favour of this course of action was the army commander, Col Theoneste Bagosora, who had been in charge of training the Hutu Interahamwe militias in Kigali before the shoot-down. One of his first acts was to direct the army to kill the 'moderate' Hutu prime minister, Agathe Uwilingiyimana, and a company of Belgian UN peacekeepers. The killing of the UN peacekeepers prompted Belgium to withdraw all of its troops – precisely what Bagosora had calculated – and the way was then open for the genocide to begin in earnest.

Rwandan army and Interahamwe death squads ranged at will over the countryside killing, looting and burning, and roadblocks were set up in every town and city. Every day thousands of Tutsi and any Hutu suspected of sympathising with them or their plight were butchered on the spot. The streets of Kigali were littered with dismembered corpses and the stench of rotting flesh was everywhere. Those who attempted to take refuge in religious missions or churches did so in vain and, in some cases, it was the nuns themselves who betrayed the fugitives to the death squads. Any mission which refused the death squads access was simply blown apart. But perhaps the most shocking part of the tragedy was the enthusiasm with which ordinary Hutu – men, women and even children as young as 10 years old – joined in the carnage.

It's probably true to say that a large number of Hutu who took part in the massacre were caught up in a tide of blind hatred, fear and peer pressure, but there's no doubt whatsoever that it was inspired, controlled and promoted by the Rwandan army and Interahamwe under the direction of their political and military leaders. Yet it also proved to be their nemesis. While up to a million people were being butchered – mainly Tutsi but also many so-called 'moderate' Hutu – the RPF pressed on with its campaign and with increasing speed pushed the Rwandan army and the Interahamwe militias out of the country into Zaïre and Burundi. The massacre finally ended with the RPF in firm control of the country but with some two million of the country's population huddled in refugee camps over the border in Zaïre, Burundi and Tanzania.

The Aftermath

Of course, that is far from the end of the story. Within a year of the RPF victory, a legal commission was set up in Arusha to try those accused of involvement in the genocide; Rwandan prisons are overflowing with suspects (including women and youths). The legal commission has just begun handing down its first sentences as this book goes to press. However, the problem is that many of the main perpetrators of the genocide – the Interahamwe and former senior army officers – fled into exile out of the reach of the long arm of the RPF.

Some went to Kenya where they enjoy the protection of President Moi who refuses to hand them over. This has created severe tensions between Kenya and Rwanda and led to the breaking of diplomatic relations. Others, including Col Theoneste Bagosora, the alleged architect of the genocide, and Ferdinand Nahimana, the director of the notorious Radio Milles Collines which actively encouraged Hutu to butcher Tutsi, fled to Cameroon where they enjoyed the protection of that country's security boss, John Fochive. However when Fochive was sacked by the newly elected president of Cameroon, Paul Biya, the Rwandan exiles were arrested.

RWANDA

RWANDA

They have yet to be handed over since no extradition treaty exists between Cameroon and Rwanda.

Of more importance though were the activities of the Interahamwe and former army personnel in the refugee camps of Zaïre and Tanzania. Determined to continue their fight against the RPF, they cynically manipulated the situation in the camps to their advantage by spreading the fear among the refugees that if they returned home they would be killed. When Zaïre and Tanzania began to demand the repatriation of the refugees, the grip of the Interahamwe on the camps was so complete that few dared move. Even when the UN made a valiant effort to persuade the refugees to return home, they succeeded only in scratching the surface and then gave up.

However, what concerned the RPF most, was that the Interahamwe used the refugee camps as staging posts for raids into Rwanda, with the complicity of the Zaïrese army. Zaïre was warned by Rwanda that if these raids did not stop then the consequences would be dire. The raids continued and the patience of the RPF finally snapped. They mounted a lightning two-day campaign into Zaïre and targeted one of the main refugee camps north of Goma. Tens of thousands fled further west into the bush along with the Interahamwe but many others took the opportunity to return home to Rwanda.

Several months after this, events in Eastern Zaïre totally changed the picture. In October 1996, a new guerilla movement known as the Alliance of Democratic Forces for the Liberation of Congo/Zaïre, led by Laurent Kabila, suddenly emerged. Composed largely of Banyamulenge (ethnic Tutsi born in Zaïre who had been dispossessed and disenfranchised by the Zaïrese government), they swept through eastern Zaïre and, by December, were in control of every town and city in the region.

The Zaïrese army retreated in disarray west towards Kisangani, looting and pillaging as they went. They were joined by their allies, the Interahamwe and former Rwandan army personnel.

The grip of the Interahamwe on the refugee camps had been broken. Hundreds of thousands of refugees began streaming back into Rwanda, not only from Zaïre but also from Tanzania. Most of the camps in Zaïre are now almost empty and Rwanda is faced with the massive task of resettling some two million refugees. How things will go remains to be seen and whether the Interahamwe threat returns will depend very much on the fortunes of the rebels in eastern Zaïre.

Rebuilding

Rwanda does seem to be slowly getting back onto its feet. You can walk around in safety again without having to climb over dismembered bodies in the streets and deal with panga-wielding thugs. All the same, not everyone is happy with the RPF government.

A number of prominent Hutu, including the former interior minister, Seth Sendashonga, have resigned from the government citing financial irregularities on the part of the Ministry of Defence, controlled by Paul Kagame, Rwanda's strongman and head of the RPF.

Other ministers, including the prime minister, Faustin Twagiramungu, the justice minister, Alphonse-Marie Nkubito, the information minister, Jean Nkuliyingoma and the transport & communications minister, Imaculee Kayumba, were subsequently sacked for being critical of the army following the RPF's massacre of refugees at the Kibeho refugee camp in 1996.

This was certainly a tragic blunder on behalf of the RPF and did nothing to encourage refugees outside the country to feel secure about returning.

It's unlikely, however, that the new opposition party, the Resistance Forces for Democracy, formed by Sendashonga and Twagiramungu, will make much headway. Many of its members supported the RPF in the days before it took over and certainly have no truck with either the old regime or the Interahamwe. It's also not surprising that the RPF is still very wary of criticism. As recently as March 1995, it was well known that Bagosora took delivery of a consignment of South African arms (supplied by private dealers there using the Seychelles as a conduit) and that Habyarimana's widow, Agathe, and her brother-in-law went to China in October 1994 to secure arms valued at US$5 million (China refused to ban arms sales to the ousted regime despite pleas by the RPF government). France and Zaïre have also violated the arms embargo.

The RPF may well have a friendly and supportive ally in Uganda but Zaïre is another kettle of fish. The authorities there have done virtually nothing to prevent the training of ex-Hutu army soldiers in the Lake Kivu area and have allowed Hutu militias to launch cross-border raids into both Rwanda and Burundi from the refugee camps in the Uvira region. What is potentially more dangerous is a repetition of what happened in Rwanda in Burundi. Intertribal tension there has reached a crisis point with some 150,000 people having been killed in clashes over the last two years. If it were to explode, the whole region would, once again, be sucked into the vortex.

GEOGRAPHY

Rwanda is one of the world's most densely populated countries. To feed the people, almost every available piece of land is under cultivation, except for the Akagera (along the border with Tanzania) and the higher slopes of the volcanoes. Since most of the country is mountainous, this involves a good deal of terracing. The banded hillsides are similar to those in Nepal or the Philippines. Tea plantations take up considerable areas of land. In terms of statistics, Rwanda's mountainous terrain occupies 26,338 sq km. Land use is about 35% arable, 20% pasture and 11% forest.

CLIMATE

The average day temperature is 30°C with a possible maximum of 34°C, except in the highlands, where the day range is 12 to 15°C. There are four discernible seasons: the long rains from mid-March to mid-May, the long dry from mid-May to mid-October, the short rains from mid-October to mid-December and the short dry from mid-December to mid-March.

It rains more frequently and heavily in the north-east, where volcanoes are covered by rainforest. The summit of Karisimbi (4507m), the highest of these volcanoes, is often covered with sleet or snow.

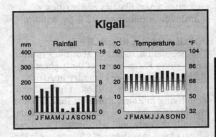

GOVERNMENT & POLITICS

The head of state of the Rwandan Patriotic Front (RPF) government is President Pasteur Bizimungu but the real power in Rwanda is wielded by the Vice President and Defence Minister, Paul Kagame, who is also head of the RPF.

There is a Constituent Assembly composed of both Tutsi and Hutu members and while it enjoys certain powers in formulating policy and acting on that, the army retains overriding influence. There are good reasons for that, the main one being the continuing threat of invasion by forces of the ousted regime which are still flush with cash looted from the central bank before their flight from Kigali.

ECONOMY

The economy is agriculturally based, with coffee by far the largest export, accounting for about 75% of export income. Tungsten, tin, pyrethrum and tea are also important, although the tin industry is presently in limbo following the forced liquidation of the state mining company after the collapse of the International Tin Agreement in 1985.

The country is a major recipient of international aid, particularly from the People's Republic of China, Belgium and Germany.

Agriculture is the main employer and export earner, contributing about 40% of GDP. The principal food crops include plantain, sweet potato, beans, cassava, sorghum and maize.

The manufacturing sector accounts for nearly 20% of GDP. Local produce includes cigarettes, soap, plastics and textiles.

Inflation is running at 12% per annum.

POPULATION & PEOPLE

The population stands at about 8.9 million which gives Rwanda one of the highest population densities of any country in Africa.

Most of the one million refugees who were living in Zaïre, Burundi, Tanzania and elsewhere have now returned to Rwanda, virtually the only ones who haven't are those who had any involvement whatsoever in the genocide of 1994.

RELIGION

About 65% of the population are Christians of various sects, a further 25% follow tribal religions and the remaining 10% are Muslims.

LANGUAGE

The national language is Kinyarwanda. The official languages are Kinyarwanda and French. Kinyarwanda is the medium of school instruction at primary level, and French is used at secondary level (only 8% of the population reach secondary level). Little English is spoken but Swahili is useful in some areas.

Facts for the Visitor

PLANNING

For details about planning your trip, and what to bring, see the Planning section in the Regional Facts for the Visitor chapter.

HIGHLIGHTS

It's hard to talk about 'highlights' in Rwanda after the recent genocide. Yet the butchery took place in a country which is scenically beautiful. There are thickly forested volcanic mountains along the entire border with Uganda and Zaïre, to the north, which are the home of the endangered mountain gorillas. Many of these family groups had previously been habituated to human contact and thousands of overseas visitors had the unique experience of spending some time in their presence. Incredibly, they're still there, despite the artillery battles which engulfed the mountains, but their numbers have, regrettably, been depleted. With relative peace having been re-established, you can now visit these remarkable animals once again. This is *the* highlight of a visit to Rwanda.

Trekking the volcanoes is, for the intrepid, an equal buzz but requires a high degree of resilience. They're a tough climb and discomfort is the name of the game. Unfortunately, access is currently prohibited.

The Parc National de l'Akagera used to be awash with wildlife of every description but civil wars and bad management have resulted in serious depletion. Hopefully, the new government will see the value of maintaining an environment conducive to the restoration of the wildlife in this part of Africa.

TOURIST OFFICES

The tourist office, ORTPN (☎ 76514), in Kigali is open Monday to Friday from 8 am to 5 pm. Its main function is to take bookings for the gorillas. There is very little printed information or maps, though it does have a list of current prices for the mid-range and top-end hotels around the country.

VISAS & DOCUMENTS
Visas

Visas are required by everyone except French and German nationals. Avoid applying for your visa outside East Africa, as this often involves a lot of red tape. They cost about US$30 in most countries, require two photos, allow a one-month stay and generally take 24 hours to issue, though you can sometimes get them the same day if you get your application in first thing in the morning. When applying for a visa, you do not have to show an onward ticket or 'sufficient funds', though the form you sign does say you have to spend a minimum of US$20 per day.

When applying for a visa, request a double-entry or multiple-entry visa, especially if you intend to re-enter Rwanda from Zaïre. There's no extra cost and it gives you flexibility. The main reason for this is that one of the routes between Bukavu (Zaïre) and Bujumbura (Burundi) is via Rwanda, and for this you will need a Rwandan visa, even though only one-third of the road is through Rwanda and you have no intention of getting off the bus, truck or car. As Rwandan transit visas (valid for 12 hours) cost about US$10, you might as well apply for a multiple-entry tourist visa in the first place. There are alternatives to this route, so a Rwandan visa is not absolutely essential.

Most travellers, however, get their visa on arrival at the border. The 15-day transit visa costs US$20 and takes 10 minutes.

Those driving their own vehicles are required to buy a permit at the border which costs US$76.

Visa Extensions Both tourist and transit visas can be extended in the capital, Kigali, at MININTER (Ministère de l'Intérieur) (☎ 85856) in the Kacyiru district, about seven km north-east of the city centre. Extensions take one to two days, cost RFr 4000 and you can get up to three months. Visas cannot be extended in Ruhengeri even though there's an immigration office there.

Getting Other Visas in Rwanda If you want to get visas to neighbouring countries while you're in Rwanda, take note of the following (see Foreign Embassies below for the addresses):

Burundi
    Visas are issued only to Rwandan residents, so don't waste your time. Visas are available at the border but you're strongly advised not to travel through northern Burundi as this area of the

country is not under the control of the central government.
Kenya
    Visas cost US$30 or the equivalent in local currency, require two photographs and are issued the same day if you apply before 11.30 am. No onward tickets or minimum funds are asked for. If the Rwandan embassy in Nairobi is closed then this embassy will probably also be closed.
Tanzania
    Visas require two photos and generally take 48 hours to issue. The cost depends on your nationality (see the Tanzania Facts for the Visitor chapter for details).
Uganda
    Visas cost US$20 or US$25 (depending on your nationality), require two photos and are issued in 24 hours.
Zaïre
    Visa costs are the same as elsewhere (see the Zaïre chapter for details), require three photographs and are issued in 24 hours. A letter of recommendation from your own embassy is generally not needed nor is an onward ticket, but these regulations change from time to time.

EMBASSIES
Rwandan Embassies Abroad
There are Rwandan embassies in Brussels (Belgium), Ottawa (Canada), Cairo (Egypt), Addis Ababa (Ethiopia), Paris (France), Bonn (Germany), Abidjan (Ivory Coast), Tokyo (Japan), London (UK) and Washington DC (USA).

In East Africa, visas can be obtained from the following Rwandan embassies:

Burundi
    24 Ave du Zaïre, Bujumbura (☎ 26865)
Kenya
    12th Floor, International House, Mama Ngina St, Nairobi (☎ (02) 334341; fax 336365)
Tanzania
    32 Ali Mwinyi Rd, Dar es Salaam (☎ (051) 46502)
Uganda
    Plot 2, Nakaima Rd, Kampala (☎ (041) 244045)

There are no Rwandan consulates at either Bukavu or Goma in eastern Zaïre, so it's advisable to get your visa in Kinshasa (or elsewhere) if you're coming from the west.

On the other hand, 15-day Rwandan transit visas are available at the border for US$20.

Foreign Embassies in Rwanda

Kigali, the capital of Rwanda, is a small city, and most foreign embassies are within easy walking distance of the centre.

Belgium
Ave de la Paix (☎ 75551)
Burundi
Rue de Ntaruka off Ave de Rusumo (☎ 73465)
France
Rue Député Kayuku (☎ 75225)
Kenya
Rue Kadyiro, near the Hôtel Umubano, Kacyiru (☎ 82774; fax 86234). Open Monday to Friday from 8.30 am till noon and 2 to 4.30 pm.
Tanzania
Ave Paul VI near Ave de Rusumo (☎ 76074). Open Monday to Friday from 9 am to 2 pm.
Uganda
Ave de la Paix (☎ 76495; fax 73551)
UK
Avenue Paul VI (☎ 75219 or 84098)
USA
Ave des Milles Collines (☎ 75327)
Zaïre
Rue Député Kamuzinzi off Ave de Rusumo (☎ 75327)

MONEY
Costs

Rwanda is a relatively expensive country because of the large number of expatriates and NGOs here. Being landlocked, a lot of export earnings are spent importing food, drink and transport requirements for the expatriates. As a budget traveller, you will be hard-pressed even if you stay in mission hostels. It's difficult to exist on a Kenyan, Tanzanian or Ugandan budget, and student cards are only useful to get into the national parks at a discount.

Transport (by minibus) and food in roadside restaurants cost much the same as in the rest of East Africa, so long as you don't want meat with your meal. Meat will just about double the price. Anything on which culinary expertise has been lavished will be expensive.

Currency

The unit of currency is the Rwandan franc (RFr). It's divided into 100 centimes, but it's unlikely you'll come across these.

Currency Exchange

USA   US$1   =   RFr 301 (cash)

Foreign exchange bureau rates and street transaction rates are US$1 = RFr 315 for large bills and RFr 300 for small bills but they only take cash – no travellers' cheques.

Changing Money

The banking sector is gradually returning to normal after virtually all the banks were shot-up, looted and trashed during the genocide. There are now five banks open in Kigali: Banque de Kigali (open Monday to Friday from 8.30 to 11 am and 2 to 4 pm and on Saturday from 8.30 to 11 am); Banque á la Confiance d'Or (open Monday to Friday from 8 am to 4 pm and on Saturday from 8 to 11 am); Banque National de Rwanda (open Monday to Friday from 8.30 to 11.45 am); Banque Commerciale de Rwanda (open Monday to Friday from 8 am to 1.30 pm); and the Banque de Commerce de Developement et de l'Industrie.

There are also banks open again in Butare and Ruhengeri (Banque de Kigali) but one has yet to reopen in Gisenyi. This will obviously change in the near future.

In addition to the banks, there are several foreign exchange bureaus in Kigali, mainly around the post office.

Another option is to change cash on the street or in shops, and there doesn't appear to be any danger associated with this, but it's safer to do so at a foreign exchange bureau, where available.

Credit cards are generally accepted only in relatively expensive hotels and restaurants in places such as Kigali and Gisenyi. You cannot make cash withdrawals against a Visa card at any bank in Rwanda, but some banks will give you cash against a MasterCard, though only in Rwandan francs and less a commission.

POST & COMMUNICATIONS
Postal Rates
Overseas postal rates are RFr 105 for an air-mail letter to Europe/North America and RFr 120 for Australasia/Japan.

Receiving Mail
There is a poste restante facility at the post office in Kigali. See the Kigali section for details.

Telephone & Fax
International calls are relatively expensive at RFr 900 per minute to most countries including the UK and Australia. Fax charges are the same. There are no telephone area codes in Rwanda.

BOOKS
For an in-depth appraisal of the Rwandan tragedy read *The Rwanda Crisis – History of a Genocide* by Gérard Prunier, written in English by a French historian; and *Rwanda & Genocide* by Alain Destexhe, a Belgian senator and former Secretary General of Médecins sans Frontières.

Gorillas in the Mist is an account of Dian Fossey's time spent among the gorillas of the Parc Nacional des Volcans.

NEWSPAPERS & MAGAZINES
The local press has yet to recover from the civil war and there's nothing currently available. You can get imported newspapers, mainly from Uganda, such as *New Vision*. They can be purchased at top end hotels.

RADIO
There are two AM and five FM radio stations, which generally broadcast in either Kinyarwanda or French. There are also programs in Swahili and English.

PHOTOGRAPHY
Bring plenty of film with you, as it is very expensive here and the choice is extremely limited – usually only 64 ASA and 100 ASA colour negative film and then only in places like Kigali and Gisenyi. Slide film is almost impossible to obtain. If you buy film, check the expiry dates carefully.

To take photos of the gorillas in the Parc Nacional des Volcans, you will need high-speed film. It's often very dark in the jungle where they live, so normal film will produce very disappointing results when developed. Use 800 ASA or 1600 ASA fast film, which in East Africa can only be found in Kenya (and it's difficult to find even there).

TIME
Rwanda time is GMT/UTC plus two hours.

ELECTRICITY
The electricity supply is 220V AC.

WEIGHTS & MEASURES
Rwanda uses the metric system.

HEALTH
As with most African countries, you should take precautions against malaria while in Rwanda, but mosquitoes generally are not a problem.

Expatriate residents suggest that you should take special care in Rwanda to avoid illness and/or treatment which could require a blood transfusion. A study of prostitutes in this country a few years ago indicated that about 80% carry the HIV virus. If you think you'll need any injections while you're there, take your own disposable syringes.

There are certain parts of Lake Kivu where it is very dangerous to swim, as volcanic gases are released continuously from the lake bed and, in the absence of wind, tend to collect on the surface of the lake. Quite a few people have been asphyxiated as a result. Make enquiries or watch where the local people swim and you'll probably be safe.

Bilharzia is also a risk in Lake Kivu. Stay away from shore areas where there is a lot of reedy vegetation. Also keep away from slow-moving rivers. (See the Health section in the introductory Facts for the Visitor chapter for more information.)

It's advisable not to drink tap water. Purify all water used for drinking, except that obtained from mountain streams and springs above any human habitation. Soft drinks, fruit and beer are available in even the smallest places.

Other than the necessary precautions mentioned here, you'll find Rwanda a fairly healthy place to visit, especially as much of the country is considerably higher than Tanzania, Uganda and Zaïre. Cholera vaccination certificates are compulsory for entry or exit by air. If entering overland, the check is cursory but officials sometimes ask about it.

DANGERS & ANNOYANCES

Night-time curfews exist in many places around the country and local soldiers have orders to shoot on sight. So far, no tourists have been shot but you're advised not to take risks. This is especially true in Kigali. Take a taxi after dark.

Out in the countryside, do not walk along anything other than a well-used track; you may step on a landmine.

Never take photographs of anything connected with the government or the military (post offices, banks, bridges, border posts, barracks, prisons, dams etc). Your film and maybe your equipment will be confiscated.

The most common annoyance is the roadblocks on all of the main roads. You must stop at these and your baggage will be searched along with whatever vehicle you are in. The soldiers will also want to check your passport.

BUSINESS HOURS

Normal business hours are 8 am to 12.30 pm and 2.30 to 5.30 pm.

Many shops and offices tend to be closed between 1 and 5 July.

PUBLIC HOLIDAYS

January
    New Year's Day (1st)
    Democracy Day (28th)
March-April
    Good Friday
    Easter Monday
May
    Labour Day (1st)
    Ascension Thursday
    Whit Monday

July
    National Day (1st)
    Peace & National Unity Day (5th)
August
    Harvest Festival (1st)
    Assumption (15th)
September
    Culture Day (8th)
    Kamarampaka Day (25th)
October
    Armed Forces Day (26th)
November
    All Saints' Day (1st)
December
    Christmas Day (25th)

ACCOMMODATION
Camping

Camping in the Parc Nacional des Volcans is prohibited due to rebel activity and, for the same reason, the RPF will not allow you to camp free anywhere else in the countryside.

Hostels

If you don't mind dormitory accommodation at the mission hostels, you're looking at between US$2.50 and US$3.50 per night without food. A private double room at the hostels will cost from US$7 to US$12.50 per night.

Mission hostels seem to attract an exceptionally conscientious type of person who takes the old adage 'cleanliness is next to godliness' fairly seriously. You might not get hot water but your bed and room will be spotless. The one catch with mission hostels is that they're often full, particularly on weekends or in places where there is only one mission hostel in town. Also, the door is usually closed at 10 pm (or earlier).

Hotels

Hotels, as opposed to mission hostels, are considerably more expensive and rarely worth the extra amount, especially at the bottom end, where they are often none too clean. There are exceptions, but not many. The top-range hotels are much the same as their counterparts elsewhere in Africa. The difference in Rwanda is that many of them are semi-permanently full of expatriates working for various NGOs and the UN agencies, so advance booking by telephone is a very good idea.

FOOD & DRINK

African fare in Rwanda is very similar to that in Kenya and prices are reasonable. (See the Food section in Kenya Facts for the Visitor.) You'll find *tilapia*, which is Nile perch, and *wat* and *injera* are a staple Ethiopian dish. There's also a wide variety of continental food available and some of it is excellently prepared and presented but it is considerably more expensive than local fare. Soft drinks and beer are available everywhere as is the local firewater, *konyagi*, but wines (both South African and European) are generally only available in the more expensive restaurants and hotels.

Getting There & Away

You can enter Rwanda by air or road; there are no railways. Lake ferries are suspended at present.

AIR

International airlines flying into Rwanda are Aeroflot, Air Burundi, Air France, Air Tanzania, Air Zaïre, Cameroon Airlines, Ethiopian Airlines, Kenya Airways, Sabena and Uganda Airlines.

Air tickets bought in Rwanda for international flights are expensive and compare poorly with what is on offer in Nairobi. You can pay for them in local currency which makes it a bit cheaper as they work on an exchange rate of RFr 323 to the US dollar.

Kenya

Kenya Airways flies from Nairobi to Kigali and vice versa twice a week, on Tuesday and Friday. The fare is US$196 one way or US$255 return on a 21-day excursion ticket.

Tanzania

Air Tanzania flies from Kigali to Mwanza via Entebbe once a week on Wednesday and the fare is US$359 one way. There are connections from Mwanza to Dar es Salaam.

Uganda

Uganda Airlines flies from Entebbe to Kigali and vice versa four times a week and the fare is US$120 one way.

LAND

Rwanda shares borders with Zaïre, Uganda, Tanzania and Burundi.

> **WARNING**
> At the time of writing, it is dangerous to cross the Rwanda border into Burundi as the northern part of Burundi is out of the control of the central government. We do not recommend it, however the information below is provided in the event that the situation changes. ∎

Burundi

Kigali to Bujumbura The main crossing point between Rwanda and Burundi is via Kayanza, on the Kigali to Bujumbura road via Butare. The road is sealed all the way. There are share-taxis which do the trip daily leaving at 8 am, cost RFr 4000 and take five hours.

Cyangugu to Bujumbura To get to Bujumbura take a minibus from Kamembe (near Cyangugu), cross over to Bukavu in Zaïre and then take a minibus from there to Bujumbura. These buses go partly via Rwanda and partly via Zaïre before terminating in Uvira. From there, you'll need to take another minibus or taxi across the Zaïre/Burundi border to Bujumbura. It's a good, sealed road but you *may* need a Rwandan transit visa or, better still, a re-entry visa, and you will definitely need a dual or multiple-entry Zaïrese visa. See the Bukavu section in the Zaïre chapter for details of these minibuses.

Tanzania

First take a bus from Mwanza to Ngara.

There are two types of buses along this route: minibuses operated by Samma Bus Co in Mwanza which depart once a week on Tuesday, take about 12 hours and cost TSh 6000; and normal size Isuzu buses operated by Tanganyika Bus Service in Mwanza which depart on Tuesday and Friday at 4 am, arriving the same day, and which cost TSh 6000. It's a good road part of the way but there are some very rough sections. From Ngara, you hitch a ride with a petrol truck (which might take you all the way to Kigali) or take a pick-up across the border to Rusumo (the first Rwandan town) and then a minibus from there to Kigali (once a day on average). Rusumo to Kigali costs RFr 1400 and takes about three hours.

Uganda

There are two main crossing points: Kabale to Kigali via Katuna/Gatuna, and Kisoro to Ruhengeri via Cyanika.

Kabale to Kigali From Kabale to Kigali there are many minibuses daily which cost USh 7000 and take about two hours. From Kigali to Kabale, the last minibus leaves Kigali at 1 pm. Normal Ugandan buses leave both Kigali and Kabale daily, at 6.30 and 7 am respectively (USh 7000). Several private Kambala-based buses operate daily between Kigali and Kampala (USh 15,000 or US$15, 10 hours). For more information on this crossing, see the relevant section in the Uganda Getting There & Away chapter.

Kisoro to Ruhengeri This route via Cyanika is poorly serviced by transport and prone to ambush by rebels. Currently it's suggested you avoid this route.

Zaïre

The two main crossing points from Rwanda to Zaïre are between Goma and Gisenyi (at the northern end of Lake Kivu) and between Bukavu and Cyangugu (at the southern end of Lake Kivu). These borders are open between 6 am and 6 pm (for non-Africans). For Africans, they are open from 6 am until midnight.

Goma to Gisenyi The two crossing points are the Poids Lourds crossing (a rough road) along the main road north of the ritzy part of Gisenyi, and a sealed road along the lake shore. It's only two to three km either way. From Goma, it's a couple of km to either post.

The easier of the two routes is along the lake shore, but from the border, you'll have to take a taxi or a taxi-motor into Gisenyi. There are minibuses from the Poids Lourds post into Gisenyi.

There are regular minibuses between Kigali and Gisenyi (RFr 1000).

Bukavu to Cyangugu From Bukavu, it's a three-km walk or a taxi ride to the Ruzizi border post. It is an easy border crossing in that you can walk between the two posts.

On the Rwandan side, Cyangugu is the actual border post but Kamembe is the town and transport centre. From the border, minibuses make the 15-minute ride to Kamembe.

There are regular minibuses between Kamembe and Kigali via Butare.

Getting Around

AIR

Internal flights with Air Rwanda from Kigali to Gisenyi and Kamembe (close to Cyangugu) are currently suspended.

BUS

Rwanda has an excellent road system, mainly due to massive injections of foreign aid. The only unsealed roads now are those to Kibuye, on the shore of Lake Kivu, and the road between Ruhengeri and Cyanika.

You'll find plenty of well-maintained, modern minibuses serving all the main routes. Between dawn and about 3 pm, at the bus stand in any town, you can almost always find one going your way. Destinations are displayed in the front window and the fares are fixed (ask other passengers if you're not sure).

Minibuses leave when full, and this means when all the seats are occupied (unlike in Kenya and Tanzania, where most of the time they won't leave until you can't breathe for the people sitting on your lap and jamming the aisle). You should not be charged for baggage. Many minibuses have decent sound systems, so you might hear some good African music which isn't ear-splitting.

There are also modern government buses (many of them bearing the Japan-Rwanda assistance program logo) on quite a few routes. These are cheaper than minibuses but take longer and are far less frequent.

Whichever form of transport you take you must be prepared for military checkpoints. These vary in number depending on where you're going but at each you'll be required to get off the vehicle and allow the soldiers to examine your luggage. Other than the time it takes, there's no hassle.

CAR

Car hire isn't well established in Rwanda, so you'll have difficulty finding something. They're basically only available in Kigali and Ruhengeri. Enquire at Airmasters in Kigali, which has cars for US$50 per day, or at the ORTPN tourist office which can usually put you in touch with a Range Rover (eight seats) for around US$100 per day. All hire cars come with a driver.

HITCHING

Hitching around Rwanda is relatively easy because of the prodigious number of NGO vehicles on the roads. Most of these people will give you a lift so you may find you hardly need to bother with the minibus system. Drivers will rarely ask you to pay for a lift. They're more interested in talking to you about your experiences in Africa. You may find a list of vehicle licence plates useful, as they indicate the province of origin of the vehicle (though that doesn't mean they are going there):

AB	Kigali
BB	Gitarama
CB	Butare
DB	Gikongoro
EB	Cyangugu
FB	Kibuye
GB	Gisenyi
HB	Ruhengeri
IB	Byumba
JB	Kibungo

If you're looking for lifts on trucks from Kigali to Uganda, Kenya, Burundi or Zaïre, go to MAGERWA (short for Magasins Généraux de Rwanda) in the Gikondo suburb, about three km from the centre of Kigali. Take your pick from the scores of trucks at the customs clearance depot. To get there, head down the Blvd de l'OUA and turn right when you see the sign. It's sometimes possible to find a free lift all the way to Mombasa, but usually it's a matter of negotiating a fare with the driver. Remember, travellers who decide to hitch should understand that they are taking a small but potentially serious risk.

BOAT

Before the latest civil war, there used to be ferries on Lake Kivu which connected the Rwandan ports of Cyangugu, Kirambo, Kibuye and Gisenyi but these are all suspended at present.

LOCAL TRANSPORT
Taxi-Motor

Most towns are compact enough to get around on foot, but where you need transport, the taxi-motor is a good bet. It's just a motorcycle and you ride on the back. The driver can usually sling your pack across the petrol tank and they generally drive pretty safely, though of course there's no helmet for the passenger.

ORGANISED TOURS

Organised tours are individually customised and are expensive. Check tour and safari prices in Kigali at Rwanda Travel Service (☎ 2210), Hôtel des Diplomates (☎ 75111), 45 Blvd de la Révolution; the Umubano Tours Agency (☎ 2176), BP 1160; and Agence Solliard (☎ 5660), 2 Ave de la République.

Kigali

The tourist organisation used to describe Rwanda as the 'Land of Eternal Spring'. Kigali, the capital, still lives up to this description to a large extent. Built on a ridge and extending down into the valley floors on either side, it's a small but attractive city with an incredible variety of flowering trees and shrubs. From various points on the ridge, there are superb views over the intensively cultivated and terraced countryside. The mountains and hills seem to stretch forever and the abundant rainfall keeps them a lush green.

Unfortunately, there was a tremendous amount of damage done to the city during the latest civil war and many buildings lie in partial or total ruin, though a lot of rehabilitation work has been done and continues to be done. All the same, the scars are everywhere to be seen. At least the banks and the post office are back in normal operation, as is the transport system.

The one big problem with Kigali is finding accommodation. The city is full of NGOs, various UN organisations, aid organisations and journalists. Some of these have their own compounds where accommodation is provided for their own personnel but others use the major hotels, leaving very little for anyone else. The situation is very similar in the budget category on account of the massive displacement of people from their homes during the civil war. Many of those who have returned have nowhere else to stay but the budget hotels and the missions which offer accommodation. In addition, many of the missions were trashed and so can no longer offer you a bed. You'll have to take things as you find them and be very flexible.

On the other hand, law and order has largely been re-established though there's precious little nightlife because people are afraid of the RPF soldiers patrolling the streets. It's probably best to stay indoors at night if you want to avoid hassles, though this is changing rapidly.

Information

Tourist Office The national tourist office, Office Rwandais du Tourisme et des Parcs Nationaux (ORTPN) (☎ 76514), BP 905, is on the Place de l'Indépendence, opposite the post office (PTT). It's open Monday to Friday from 8 am to 5 pm. The office has a few leaflets (in French and English) about the mountain gorillas, but little else. Reservations must be made here to see the mountain gorillas in the Parc Nacional des Volcans. You may have trouble here if you can't speak French.

The cost for a gorilla visit is US$126 per person (US$95 for students), which includes a gorilla permit, the park entry fee as well as two guides and two armed guards per group.

Money There are five banks in Kigali. See Money in the earlier Facts for the Visitor section.

Post & Communications The poste restante is quite well organised and staff will let you look through the logbook of letters, so it's unlikely that you'll miss anything sent to you for collection, including parcels. There's a small charge for each letter collected. The post office is open Monday to Friday from 8.30 am to 12.30 pm and 1.30 to 4.30 pm. The telephone office is also here and is open the same hours except that it is also open on Saturday.

The cheapest place to make an international telephone call is *L'Oasis* snack bar, which is open daily from 7.30 am to 9 pm and charges the equivalent of US$2 per minute (as against US$3 per minute at the main exchange). There are no telephone area codes in Rwanda.

Book Shops There are a few book shops in Kigali, selling mainly French-language publications. The best is probably Librairie Caritas on Ave du Commerce.

Camping Goods The so-called disposable Campingaz cartridges can be bought at the Rwanda Petrolgaz shop below the market, or at the Janmohammed Store on Rue du

RWANDA

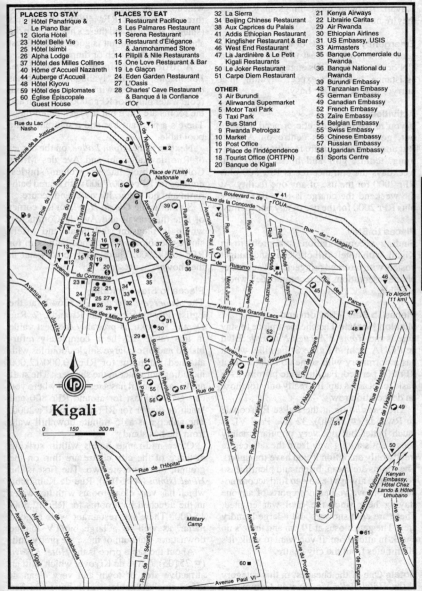

PLACES TO STAY
2   Hôtel Panafrique &
    Le Piano Bar
12 Gloria Hotel
23 Hôtel Belle Vie
25 Hôtel Isimbi
26 Alpha Lodge
37 Hôtel des Milles Collines
43 Hôme d'Accueil Nazareth
44 Auberge d'Accueil
48 Hôtel Kiyovu
59 Hôtel des Diplomates
60 Église Épiscopale
    Guest House

PLACES TO EAT
1   Restaurant Pacifique
8   Les Palmares Restaurant
11 Serena Restaurant
13 Restaurant d'Élégance
    & Janmohammed Store
14 Pilipili & Nile Restaurants
15 One Love Restaurant & Bar
24 Eden Garden Restaurant
27 L'Oasis
28 Charles' Cave Restaurant
    & Banque á la Confiance
    d'Or

32 La Sierra
34 Beijing Chinese Restaurant
40 Aux Caprices du Palais
41 Addis Ethiopian Restaurant
42 Kingfisher Restaurant & Bar
46 West End Restaurant
47 La Jardinière & Le Petit
    Kigali Restaurants
50 Le Joker Restaurant
51 Carpe Diem Restaurant

OTHER
3   Air Burundi
4   Alirwanda Supermarket
5   Motor Taxi Park
6   Taxi Park
7   Bus Stand
9   Rwanda Petrolgaz
10 Market
16 Post Office
17 Place de l'Indépendance
18 Tourist Office (ORTPN)
20 Banque de Kigali

21 Kenya Airways
22 Librairie Caritas
29 Air Rwanda
30 Ethiopian Airlines
31 US Embassy, USIS
33 Airmasters
35 Banque Commerciale du
    Rwanda
36 Banque National du
    Rwanda
39 Burundi Embassy
43 Tanzanian Embassy
45 German Embassy
49 Canadian Embassy
52 French Embassy
53 Zaïre Embassy
54 Belgian Embassy
55 Swiss Embassy
56 Chinese Embassy
57 Russian Embassy
58 Ugandan Embassy
61 Sports Centre

Kigali

0   150   300 m

To Airport
(11 km)

To
Kenyan
Embassy,
Hôtel Chez
Lando & Hôtel
Umubano

Travail. As with most things in Rwanda, they're not cheap.

Emergency In the case of a medical emergency, it's probably best to visit either the UN or one of the NGOs engaged in medical assistance, but don't expect anything in a hurry; these people are busy.

Activities

If you're feeling energetic or need a workout, go to the sports centre on Ave du Rugunga where there are facilities for swimming, tennis, golf and horse riding. On weekdays the entrance fee is RFr 500 plus RFr 2000 for the use of any one facility. At the weekend the charge is RFr 1000 entry plus RFr 2000 for the use of any one facility.

Places to Stay

Finding accommodation is a problem in Kigali, with hotels full of NGOs and budget hostels with returned refugees. Advance telephone reservations are recommended where possible.

Places to Stay – bottom end

Mission Hostels The cheapest place to stay here is the *Hôme d'Accueil Nazareth*, Blvd de l'OUA, behind Église St Famille, which has a dormitory with some 15 bunk beds at RFr 200 per bed. Facilities are primitive – a basic toilet and a tap. It's really only for those on desperation row.

The *guesthouse* at the Église Épiscopale au Rwanda (☎ 76340), 32 Ave Paul VI, is much better but not very popular, mainly because it's a long way from the city centre (really only an option if you have transport). The rooms are clean, bright and plentiful, so you should always be able to find accommodation, but we've had no reports of anyone staying here since the civil war erupted. There are cold showers and a large laundry area. The gate closes at 10 pm and there's no check-in after 9 pm. If you want to walk, it's 30 minutes from the city centre.

Hotels One of the cheapest in this category is the *Hôtel Belle Vie*, Ave du Commerce,

which has one single room at RFr 3000 and three doubles at RFr 4000. The toilets (shared) are clean and there's hot water in the shower. The restaurant is good for breakfast but not open for lunch or dinner.

A little higher in price is the *Hôtel Panafrique*, Blvd de Nyabugogo, which has doubles (no singles) with attached bathroom (cold water only) for RFr 5000. It's clean and the rooms are large but it's seen better days. There's a pleasant bar and restaurant and a pool table.

Next up is the *Alpha Lodge*, on the corner of Rue de Kalisimbi and Ave des Milles Collines, which has very clean singles/doubles for RFr 4000/7000 with shared bathroom and hot water. It's quiet and secure.

Similar is the *Gloria Hôtel*, on the corner of Rue du Travail and Ave du Commerce, which is pleasant and clean and offers singles/doubles with attached bathroom for RFr 4000/6000. There's only cold water in the showers at present.

Places to Stay – middle

The *Auberge d'Accueil* (☎ 73640) at the Église Presbytérienne au Rwanda, 2 Rue Député Kayuku, is probably the best value in this range. It's been completely refurbished and offers large singles/doubles with attached bathroom for RFr 10,000/12,000 including hot water in the showers. The staff are friendly and it has a restaurant where you can get breakfast for around RFr 800 and lunch or dinner for RFr 1500 to RFr 2000. The auberge is a 15-minute downhill walk from the bus stand.

Other mid-range hotels within striking distance of the city centre are thin on the ground, but there are two. The first is the *Hôtel Isimbi* (☎ 75109), Rue de Kalisimbi, which has very clean rooms with hot water in the attached bathrooms for RFr 12,500/15,000. There's a restaurant with a good menu, as well as a large bar/TV lounge downstairs, but both of these are pretty dull.

About the same price is the *Hôtel Kiyovu* (☎ 75106), 6 Ave de Kiyovu, which is in an attractive area of town and very clean. It offers singles/doubles which have attached bathrooms (hot water) for US$40/60. The restaurant here offers a good selection of continental dishes for RFr 2000 to RFr 2500, plus there's a bar/TV lounge.

Places to Stay – top end

One of the cheapest in this range is the *Hôtel Chez Lando* (☎ 84328), but it's a long way out in the Remera suburb and not an option for those without their own transport. Rooms here with attached bathroom (hot water) are US$60/90. The hotel has its own restaurant, bar and nightclub.

Closer to town but still a long way out in the Kacyiru suburb is the *Hôtel Umubano* (☎ 85814). This is quite a bit more expensive at RFr 25,000/35,000. The hotel has a swimming pool and a good restaurant with meals for around RFr 3500.

In the town centre, probably the best value is the *Hôtel des Diplomates* (☎ 75111/2), 43 Blvd de la Révolution, a large but pleasant hotel with a good restaurant (RFr 2500 to RFr 3000 for a meal) and its own nightclub. It costs RFr 24,000/31,000 with breakfast included.

Top of the range is the *Hôtel des Milles Collines* (☎ 76530), 1 Ave de la République, which has singles/doubles for US$140/160 including breakfast. This has all the facilities you would expect of a hotel at this price including a swimming pool and restaurant (around RFr 5000 for a meal). Use of the hotel swimming pool costs RFr 1500 for non-guests.

Places to Eat – cheap

There are five good places to get a cheap feed in the centre of Kigali. One of the cheapest is *Les Palmares*, Rue du Travail, which has kebabs for RFr 150 up until 11 pm as well as cheap Primus beer (RFr 250). Likewise, the *Restaurant Pacifique*, Blvd de Nyabugogo, offers good African fare for RFr 500 up until 9 pm. For a good African buffet lunch, the *Pilipili*, Rue de Kalisimbi, is a good bet at RFr 600 to RFr 1000 and is open from 7.30 am until around 8 pm.

Also a good bet is the *Serena Restaurant*, Ave du Commerce, opposite the market, which offers African dishes for RFr 600 to RFr 800 and is open from 7 am to 4 pm. Further afield is the *Carpe Diem Restaurant*, Ave de Kiyovu, which serves a mixture of African and French dishes. Kebabs are RFr 600 and steaks RFr 1500. The restaurant is open from 9 am to 5 pm daily.

For snacks, you probably can't beat *L'Oasis*, Ave de la Paix, which has good pies for RFr 300 as well as ice cream and fruit juices. It's open between 7.30 am and 9 pm. Similar is *Le Glaçon*, Rue de Kalisimbi, which is basically an ice cream parlour but also offers snacks and milkshakes and is open from 8 am to 8 pm.

Travellers who want to cater for themselves or who are planning a safari can find most of the things they need at *Alirwanda Supermarket* on Ave du Commerce, close to the bus stand.

Places to Eat – more expensive

A good selection of French/Italian dishes, including steaks, chicken and spaghetti, can be found at the *Hotel Panafrique*, Blvd de Nyabugogo, for around RFr 1500. It's a pleasant place to eat and is open daily until 11 pm.

For a very good African buffet as well as some continental dishes priced between RFr 1200 and RFr 2500, try the *West End Restaurant*, Rue de l'Akagera, which is open between noon and 10 pm.

The *Eden Garden*, Rue de Kalisimbi, has been a great place to eat for many years with its bamboo décor and informal ambience. It's open daily from 7 am to 10 pm and offers very good French steaks, chicken and tilapia with french fries and salad for an average price of around RFr 1800.

Lacking the ambience of the Eden somewhat and with an enclosed dining area is the *Restaurant d'Élégance*, Rue du Travail, which does reasonable African dishes for around RFr 1500. It's open daily from 7 am to 11 pm.

Up slightly in price but an excellent choice for something different is the *Addis Ethiopian Restaurant*, Blvd de l'OUA, which serves excellent goat and chicken dishes along with wat and injera for RFr 1500 to RFr 2000. It's open from 10 am to 10 pm and also has a pleasant terrace bar.

Those in search of European/North American dishes at any time of day should check out *Le Piano Bar*, Blvd de Nyabugogo, next to the Hôtel Panafrique. This is a very lively and popular place where you can meet local people and expatriates and either eat or drink. It's open for food between 8 am and midnight but doesn't close until 1 am. Steaks cost RFr 1000 to RFr 2000, hamburgers RFr 800 to RFr 1500 and chicken RFr 1500 to RFr 4000. It's suggested you eat early before the crowds arrive in the evening. Cold local beers cost RFr 300 and imported beers are around RFr 600.

Moving up in this category, *Charles' Cave*, Ave de la Paix, does good French cuisine as well as a number of Indian dishes for RFr 2500 daily, except for Sunday, from 9 am to 2 pm and 5.30 to 9.30 pm. Similar, and a pleasant place to eat, is *La Jardinière* which has good French and Italian food for around RFr 3000. It's open daily, except Monday, from noon to 2 pm and 6 to 9.30 pm. Next door and with a very similar menu but with the addition of a number of Lebanese items is *Le Petit Kigali*. Like the Jardinière, it has a pleasant ambience.

Top of the line in terms of French cuisine are the *Kingfisher*, Rue du Mont Juru, which has dishes for RFr 4000 and is open daily, except Tuesday, from 11 am to 2 pm and 5 to 11 pm; and *Aux Caprices du Palais*, Rue de Ntaruka, which is excellent but considerably more expensive – US$30 to US$40 per head without wine. It's open daily, except Sunday, from noon to 2 pm and 6 to 10 pm.

Moving away from French cuisine, there's a choice of Indian and Chinese food. One of the best Indian restaurants but with a limited menu is *La Sierra*, which offers a buffet lunch for RFr 3000 and dinner for RFr 3500. It's open daily, except Sunday, from noon to 2 pm and 7 to 9.30 pm. It's a popular place to eat and also for afternoon drinks. For good Greek food head for the *Hellenique*, but be warned: it's quite a way from the centre, will

cost you a minimum of RFr 4000 and the portions are small.

The Chinese food at the *Beijing Chinese Restaurant*, Blvd de la Révolution, isn't too bad but it's expensive and the quality doesn't really justify its prices – RFr 3000 plus rice etc. It's open daily from noon to 3 pm and 6 to 11 pm.

In a similar bracket is *Le Joker*, quite a walk from the centre at the junction of Rue de l'Akagera and Ave de Kiyovu, which serves oriental dishes as well as steaks for around RFr 3000. It's open daily, except Tuesday, from noon to 3 pm and 6 to 11 pm.

Entertainment

Discos Perhaps the best of these and one which is very popular as well as being conveniently in the city centre is *Le Piano Bar*. Apart from being a restaurant during the day, it kicks off every night from 8 pm until around 1 am with a live band and gets very lively from 10 pm onwards. There's a RFr 1000 cover charge and a good selection of cold imported beers (RFr 500 to RFr 700). It's a mixed crowd of both local people and expatriates.

Also in the centre is the disco at the *Hôtel des Diplomates* which has a RFr 1500 cover charge. It kicks off every night and attracts a small, but pleasant, mixed crowd. The music is more African than western. Beers cost around RFr 600.

Very popular, but a long way from the centre in the Kimikurure district, is *Cadillac*, a large, partly open-air venue which plays a mixture of high-life, soukous and western rock and roll on Wednesday, Friday and Saturday from 5 pm. There's a cover charge of RFr 1000 and the beer is expensive (RFr 1000 for Primus) but it is *cold*.

Even further out of town in the Remera district is *Chez Lardo*, which is popular at weekends among those who have their own transport.

Bars Apart from the discos, which many people use as bars as opposed to dance venues, there's the *Nile Restaurant*, Rue de Kalisimbi, next to the Pilipili Restaurant. This has a popular terrace bar where people gather for a drink and to people-watch. The beers are cheap – around RFr 350. The terrace bar at the *Kingfisher* serves much the same purpose.

You should also check out the mellow, open-sided reggae bar on the top floor of *One Love Restaurant & Bar*, Rue de Kalisimbi, which is run by a bunch of Rastas. It's open daily from 9 am to 10 pm and beers cost RFr 300 to RFr 400.

Getting There & Away
Air Airline offices in Kigali include Air Rwanda (☎ 73793), Air France (☎ 75566), Ethiopian Airlines (☎ 75045), Kenya Airways (☎ 73999), Sabena (☎ 75290) and Aeroflot (☎ 73646).

Bus Minibuses run from the main bus stand to towns all over Rwanda, including Butare (RFr 800, about two hours), Gitarama (about RFr 1600, about 1½ hours), Katuna (RFr 1500, about two hours), Kibuye (RFr 800), Ruhengeri (RFr 1800, about 2½hours), Rusumu (RFr 1400, about three hours), and Gisenyi (RFr 1000, about 3½ hours). These minibuses leave every day, all day, when full except at weekends when they tend to dry up between 2 and 3 pm. All you have to do is turn up and tell someone where you're going. See the respective town entries for further details. At the time of writing there were no minibuses to Cyangugu as travel was too dangerous.

Getting Around
The Airport The international airport is at Kanombe, 12 km from the city centre. A taxi costs RFr 3000, but you can get there more cheaply by taking a direct minibus from the bus stand (RFr 200).

Taxi A taxi fare within the city centre costs, on average, RFr 1000, more if you're going out to the suburbs.

Western Rwanda

GISENYI
Gisenyi is a resort town for rich Rwandans and expatriate workers and residents. Their beautifully landscaped villas, plush hotels and clubs take up virtually all the Lake Kivu frontage and are quite a contrast to the African township on the hillside above.

For those with the money, there's a wide variety of water sports available, plus night-clubs and restaurants. For those without, there are magnificent views over Lake Kivu and, looking north-west, the 3470m-high volcano of Nyiragongo. Swimming and sun-bathing on the sandy beach are also free. It's a pleasant town to stay in but is, as you might expect, expensive, especially if you want some action.

Information
Visas & Embassies There is no Zaïrese consulate here, so you must obtain your visa elsewhere if you intend going to Zaïre. The nearest embassy is in Kigali.

Money As we go to press, there is no bank open yet in Gisenyi so, if you are carrying only travellers' cheques, you've got big problems. Those with cash can change at a shop about 150m east of the ERP petrol station which has a kind of foreign exchange bureau in operation. The rates are slightly down on those offered in Kigali.

Places to Stay – bottom end
There are a few small hotels up in the African part of town but they're hard to find (no signs) and the standard of accommodation is low. Most travellers used to stay at the Mission Presbytérienne's *Centre d'Accueil* (☎ 40522), about 100m from the market and bus stand, but the place was trashed during the civil war and the beds are wrecked. All the same, it's apparently still open for business and you can get a dorm 'bed' for RFr 500 or a single room for RFr 1000. There are

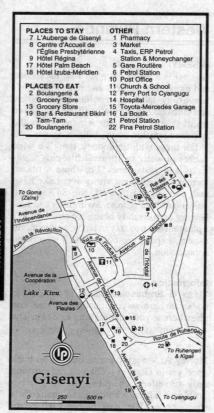

PLACES TO STAY	OTHER
7 L'Auberge de Gisenyi	1 Pharmacy
8 Centre d'Accueil de	3 Market
l'Église Presbytérienne	4 Taxis, ERP Petrol
9 Hôtel Régina	Station & Moneychanger
17 Hôtel Palm Beach	5 Gare Routière
18 Hôtel Izuba-Méridien	6 Petrol Station
	10 Post Office
PLACES TO EAT	11 Church & School
2 Boulangerie &	12 Ferry Port to Cyangugu
Grocery Store	14 Hospital
13 Grocery Store	15 Toyota-Mercedes Garage
19 Bar & Restaurant Bikini	16 La Boutik
Tam-Tam	21 Petrol Station
20 Boulangerie	22 Fina Petrol Station

RWANDA

To Goma (Zaïre)

Avenue de l'Indépendance

Ave de la Révolution

Avenue de l'Umuganda

Rue des Poissons

Avenue du Marché

Rue de l'Hôtel

Rue de l'Industrie

Avenue de l'Indépendance

Avenue de la Coopération

Lake Kivu

Avenue des Fleures

Route de Ruhengeri

To Ruhengeri & Kigali

Gisenyi

0   250   500 m

To Cyangugu

Avenue de la Production

no other decent cheap places to stay in Gisenyi.

Places to Stay – middle

All of the other acceptable hotels are near the lake front. The best are the *Hôtel Palm Beach* (☎ 61304) and the *Hôtel Régina* (telephone currently out of order), both on Ave de la Coopération, the palm-shaded lake-shore drive. The Régina has singles with attached bathroom for RFr 6500. The Hôtel Palm Beach costs RFr 10,000/15,000 for a single/double with attached bathroom (hot water in the showers). The staff at either of

these hotels are likely to treat backpackers with a considerable degree of disdain (as are the clientele).

Places to Stay – top end

The *Hôtel Izuba-Méridien* (☎ 61319) is roughly the equivalent of the Hôtel des Diplomates in Kigali and costs RFr 15,000/19,000 for a single/double excluding breakfast. Meals here are RFr 2000 (breakfast) and RFr 4000 (lunch or dinner). It's a very pleasant place to stay and right on the lake shore.

Places to Eat

Several simple restaurants on the main road in the African part of town serve cheap meals (usually matoke, rice, beans and a little meat), but the standard isn't up to much.

More expensive but still reasonably priced is the curiously named *Bikini Tam-Tam Bar & Restaurant*, on the beach on Ave de la Production. A main course here costs about RFr 1000.

For self-caterers, there's a wide variety of fruit and vegetables available at the main market.

Entertainment

The only place you'll find any action at present is the *Bikini Tam-Tam Bar*, which rocks on every night.

Getting There & Away

Air There are no flights into or out of Gisenyi at present.

Bus A bus from Ruhengeri to Gisenyi takes about 1½ hours (RFr 1400). It's a beautiful journey through upland forest and villages and there are panoramic views of Lake Kivu as you descend into Gisenyi. Minibuses between Kigali and Gisenyi take around 3½ hours and cost RFr 1000. There are two border posts into Zaïre (see the Getting There & Away section earlier in this chapter for details).

Boat All ferries across Lake Kivu to other Rwandan ports are currently suspended.

KIBUYE

A small town about halfway along Lake Kivu, Kibuye has an excellent beach and water sports facilities. It's a pleasant place to relax for a few days. If coming here by road from Gisenyi, try not to miss **Les Chutes de Ndaba**, a waterfall at Ndaba. It's more than 100m high.

Places to Stay

The missions which used to offer budget accommodation here were destroyed during the civil war. That leaves the *Guest House Kibuye* (☎ 68191) on the lakeside as the only place to stay. It's expensive (RFr 5900/8000/9500 for singles/doubles/triples), but you can camp in the grounds for free. The guesthouse has a good outdoor bar, with cold beers at the usual price, and a diving board which anyone can use.

Places to Eat

Two cheap places, the *Restaurant Nouveauté* and *Restaurant Moderne*, are at the eastern end of town. They have the same menu (goat stew, beans, rice, potatoes, omelettes) and you can eat well for RFr 500 to RFr 800. They also offer cold beers and soft drinks.

Getting There & Away

From Kigali, the road is partly sealed and minibuses cost RFr 800.

CYANGUGU

At the southern end of Lake Kivu and close to Bukavu (Zaïre), Cyangugu is an attractively positioned town on the lake shore and the Zaïre border. Kamembe, a few km from the border, is the main town and transport centre and an important centre for the processing of tea and cotton. Nearby is the Rugege Forest, home for elephant, buffalo, leopard, chimpanzee and many other mammals and birds.

The **waterfalls** of the Rusizi River and the **hot springs** of Nyakabuye are here.

Places to Stay & Eat

A convenient place to stay if you're heading for Zaïre (or coming from there) is the *Hôme St François* at the border. It's friendly, spotlessly clean and offers reasonably priced singles, doubles and triples. The only problem is that couples may be separated. The meals are excellent and very good value. Similar is the *Mission Pentecoste* which has great views over the lake. Both cost around US$4 per person.

The only other accommodation option is the expensive *Hôtel du Lac* opposite the St François mission.

Good Rwandan food is available for RFr 300 to RFr 600 at both the *Black & White* and *La Jeunesse* around the market in Kamembe. More expensive is the *Restaurant La Saveur*, but service here is very slow.

Getting There & Away

Bus There are minibuses between Cyangugu and Kamembe, and share-taxis from Kamembe to Butare (a total of four hours). This road is incredibly spectacular in parts and passes through the superb Nyungwe rainforest.

From Kamembe, there are minibuses to Kigali via Butare.

Boat Ferry services connecting Cyangugu with Kibuye and Gisenyi across Lake Kivu are currently suspended.

RUHENGERI

Most travellers come to Ruhengeri when they are on their way to the Parc Nacional des Volcans, which is where the Rwandan mountain gorillas live.

It's a small town with two army barracks, a very busy hospital and some magnificent views of the volcanoes to the north and west – Karisimbi, Visoke, Mikeno, Muside, Sabinyo, Gahinga and Muhabura.

Forget any ideas you may have about climbing the hill near the post office, as it's a military area and access is prohibited.

Information

Money The only bank open at present is the Banque de Kigali near the Hôtel Muhabura.

RWANDA

It's open Monday to Saturday from 8.30 to 11.30 am. Commission rates for travellers' cheques are about the same as in Kigali.

Post The temporary new post office (PTT) is housed in the prefecture until a new one is built. It's open Monday to Friday from 8 am to noon and 2 to 4 pm.

Telephone The telephone exchange is situated in the building opposite the old post office. Rates are the same as those in Kigali.

Places to Stay – bottom end

The only place to consider seriously is the *Centre d'Accueil d'Eglise Episcopale*, on the north-west corner of Rue du Pyrethre and Ave du 5 Juillet. It's clean and has dormitory beds for RFr 800 (six bunk beds in two rooms) and singles/doubles for RFr 1500/2500. The communal showers have hot water and the toilets are clean. There's a restaurant with meals for RFr 500 but you need to order food in advance.

In contrast, the *Hôme d'Accueil*, on Ave du 5 Juillet in the town centre, has eight small rooms and, although it charges the same for singles/doubles and you get your own bathroom, there's no hot water. Other than that, it's OK.

Somewhat cheaper is the *Omukikane Inn*, near the minibus park on Ave du 5 Juillet, which has singles with shared bathroom for RFr 1000 and doubles with attached bathroom for RFr 2000. It's clean and secure but has only cold water in the showers.

There's also the *Ruhengeri Rest House* on Rue Muhabura which is fairly clean but has only single rooms at RFr 1500 with own toilet and sink but shared cold bucket showers.

The *Restaurant La Renaissance*, on Rue Muhabura, is about to complete a number of rooms with attached bathrooms which

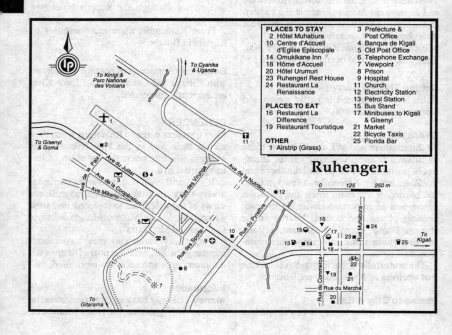

PLACES TO STAY
2 Hôtel Muhabura
10 Centre d'Accueil d'Eglise Episcopale
14 Omukikane Inn
18 Hôme d'Accueil
20 Hôtel Urumuri
23 Ruhengeri Rest House
24 Restaurant La Renaissance

PLACES TO EAT
16 Restaurant La Difference
19 Restaurant Touristique

OTHER
1 Airstrip (Grass)
3 Prefecture & Post Office
4 Banque de Kigali
5 Old Post Office
6 Telephone Exchange
7 Viewpoint
8 Prison
9 Hospital
11 Church
12 Electricity Station
13 Petrol Station
15 Bus Stand
17 Minibuses to Kigali & Gisenyi
21 Market
22 Bicycle Taxis
25 Florida Bar

Ruhengeri

To Cyanika & Uganda

To Kinigi & Parc National des Volcans

To Gisenyi & Goma

To Kigali

To Gitarama

Ave du Juillet
Ave de la Paix
Ave de la Coopération
Ave Mikeno
Ave des Viranga
Ave de la Nutrition
Rue du Pyrethre
Rue des Sports
Rue Muhabura
Rue du Commerce
Rue du Marché

0   125   250 m

should be open by the time you read this. They will cost RFr 1500/2500 for singles/ doubles.

Places to Stay – middle

The cheapest in this range is the *Hôtel Urumuri* (☎ 46229), close to the market, which has no singles but is very clean and pleasant and offers doubles with attached bathroom (hot water) for RFr 3000.

Ruhengeri's best hotel is the *Hôtel Muhabura* (☎ 46296), Ave du 5 Juillet, which offers large, clean, airy rooms with attached bathroom and hot water for RFr 3850/4950 a single/double. Only one blanket is provided so you may need a sleeping bag in the winter months. The food here is quite reasonably priced – two large brochettes with chips for RFr 800 – plus they have cold Primus beer for RFr 300. There's one waiter who speaks a little English if you cannot speak French.

Places to Eat

The *Centre d'Accueil* offers excellent dinners (stewed meat, beans, cabbage, sautéed potatoes) for RFr 500, but the breakfasts aren't such good value at RFr 200 (tea, bread, margarine, jam). Cold beers are available at the usual price.

Cheapest of the African eateries is the *Restaurant La Difference* on Ave de la Nutrition (a suitable location!) which offers cheap kebabs for RFr 100 along with other items until 9 pm each day.

The *Hôtel Urumuri*, down a small side street off Rue du Marché, has an outdoor area where you can get good meals of chicken or spaghetti (RFr 500 to RFr 800) from 7 am until evening – if they don't run out. They also have very cold beers.

Up in price somewhat is the *Restaurant La Renaissance* which has great kebabs, chicken and steak for RFr 700 to RFr 900 and is open from noon to 10 pm.

For a splurge, it's well worth going to the *Restaurant Touristique*, Rue du Commerce, where the food is excellent. The four-course set menu is RFr 2000. It has a pleasant ambience and is open daily from 7 am to 6 pm.

If you are putting your own meal together, there's a good variety of meat, fish, fruit and vegetables at the market in the town centre.

Entertainment

Ruhengeri is a quiet place in the evenings and you won't find anywhere open after around 10 pm. However, if you want to meet some local people after dinner, try either the *Restaurant La Renaissance* or the *Florida Bar*, both of which are open until 9 or 10 pm and have Primus beer at RFr 300.

Getting There & Away

Bus From Kigali, minibuses take about 2½ hours and cost RFr 1800. The road ascends and descends magnificently over the intensively cultivated mountains. From Cyanika, on the Rwanda-Uganda border, minibuses to Ruhengeri cost RFr 300 if you can find one but that's very unlikely at present because of the danger of rebel ambushes. From Gisenyi, on the Rwanda-Zaïre border, they cost RFr 1400 for the two-hour trip.

Getting Around

There are no taxis in Ruhengeri but there are 'taxi bicycles' if you don't want to walk. A typical fare from the bus stand to the Hôtel Muhabura would be RFr 300.

Bicycles are for hire near the market, but at RFr 800 per day, they're not that cheap.

Southern Rwanda

BUTARE

Butare is the intellectual centre of Rwanda, and it's here that you'll find the National University, the National Institute of Scientific Research (folklore dance displays) and the excellent National Museum.

In the surrounding area are several craft centres, such as **Gihindamuyaga** (10 km) and **Gishamvu** (12 km). If you're thinking of buying anything at these places, look first at the quality and prices of what's for sale at the two top-range hotels in town, the Hôtel Ibis and Hôtel Faucon.

Those interested in trees should visit the Arboretum de Ruhande.

National Museum

This huge museum was opened in 1989 and is probably the best museum in East Africa. It's certainly the most amazing building in the country. A gift from Belgium to commemorate 25 years of independence, it's well worth a visit for its ethnological and archaeological displays. The museum is open on Monday from 2.30 to 4.30 pm, Tuesday to Friday from 9 to 11.30 am and 2.30 to 4.30 pm, Saturday from 2 to 5 pm, and Sunday from 9 am till noon and 2 to 5 pm. Entry is RFr 200, or RFr 100 if you have a student card. It's about 15 minutes walk north of the centre, past the minibus stand.

Places to Stay – bottom end

Many travellers used to stay at the Procure de Butare, a very attractive building surrounded by flower gardens, but it no longer has accommodation. That leaves you with those places to stay along the street near the market. The clean and friendly, *Weekend Hôtel* has singles/doubles for RFr 1200/ 2000. Better value is the *International Hôtel* across the road. It has double rooms with good beds, a bath and hot water for RFr 2000.

Places to Stay – middle

The only place in this category is the fairly new *Hôtel des Beaux-Arts* (☎ 30584), about 300m on the left of Ave du Commerce just past Rue Rwamamba. It has two types of rooms. The cheaper rooms (Nos 1 to 9) cost RFr 3000/4000 for singles/doubles and the better appointed rooms (Nos 5 and 10A) cost RFr 4000/5500 for singles/doubles. All the rooms have attached bathroom, two beds, a table and chair and mosquito netting over the windows. None is air-conditioned. Children under six years of age sharing a room with their parents are RFr 500. A full meal here costs RFr 900 to RFr 1800.

Places to Stay – top end

The only choice here is the *Hôtel Ibis* (☎ 30335). It charges RFr 9300/11,000 for singles/doubles with attached bathroom, including breakfast. It also has a good terrace bar which serves drinks and snacks. The restaurant here serves good, French-style food for RFr 2000 per meal but the service is very slow.

Places to Eat

The *Restaurant Chez Nous* near the market has good local food. Next door to the International Hôtel and in a pleasant setting, the *Jacaranda Restaurant* has a very good three-course set menu for RFr 800.

Two travellers recommended the *Chic-Choc*, on Rue Santé, two blocks from the Procure de Butare, as 'the best restaurant in Africa'. That sounds like an extravagant claim, but they described it as '...very new and quaint with excellent service, sympathetic table settings, lots of plants and a menu

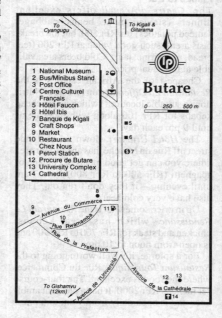

1 National Museum
2 Bus/Minibus Stand
3 Post Office
4 Centre Culturel
   Français
5 Hôtel Faucon
6 Hôtel Ibis
7 Banque de Kigali
8 Craft Shops
9 Market
10 Restaurant
   Chez Nous
11 Petrol Station
12 Procure de Butare
13 University Complex
14 Cathedral

Butare

To Cyangugu
To Kigali & Gitarama

0   250   500 m

Avenue du Commerce
Rue Rwamamba
Rue de la Prefecture
Avenue de l'Université
Avenue de la Cathédrale
To Gishamvu (12km)

to suit most budgets'. Dishes range from RFr 400 to RFr 1200 with a three-course menu for RFr 1400 (rabbit) or RFr 1600 (beef). It also does breakfasts for RFr 300 to RFr 500 (continental and American). Beers are normally priced.

Getting There & Away

The bus stand is just a patch of dirt about one km north of the town centre, by the stadium. Arriving minibuses often drop you in the centre of town, but when leaving, you have to get yourself to the bus stand. Taxi-motors abound, so this is not a problem.

To Kigali, matatu minibuses cost RFr 800 and take about two hours. To Kamembe (close to Cyangugu), it's RFr 1000 and departs around 10 am daily. The road is spectacular in parts and passes through the Nyungwe Forest, which contains some amazing virgin rainforest between Uwinka and Kiutabe.

There are also minibuses to the Burundi border but there's not much point going there at present as the north of Burundi is out of the control of the central government, and is therefore dangerous.

National Parks

PARC NACIONAL DES VOLCANS

This area along the border with Zaïre and Uganda has to be one of the most beautiful sights in Africa. There is a chain of no less than seven volcanoes, one of them (Karisimbi) more than 4500m high.

But it's not just the mountains which attract travellers. On the bamboo and rainforest-covered slopes is one of the last remaining sanctuaries of the mountain gorilla (Gorilla beringei). These animals were studied in depth by George Schaller and, more recently, by Dian Fossey.

Fossey spent the best part of 13 years living at a remote camp high up on the slopes of Visoke in order to study the gorillas and to habituate them to human contact. She'd probably still be there now had she not been murdered in December 1985, most likely by poachers with whom she had made herself very unpopular. Without her tenacious efforts to have poaching stamped out, however, there possibly wouldn't be any gorillas left in Rwanda.

It remains to be seen what will happen to the four known groups which survive but, during the early part of the latest civil war, these mountains were the focus of intense fighting which included artillery duels. This was hardly conducive to good gorilla-human relationships and it was reported that at least seven of the gorillas had met their end – probably at the hand of soldiers greedy for 'trophies'.

It isn't just poaching or dumb-headed soldiers, however, which threaten the gorillas. Also clawing away at their existence is local pressure for grazing and agricultural land, and the European Community's pyrethrum project – daisy-like flowers processed into a natural insecticide. This project was responsible in 1969 for reducing the size of the park by more than 8900 hectares – almost half its area! The park now covers only 0.5% of the total land area of Rwanda.

Fossey's account of her years with the gorillas and her battle with the poachers and government officials, Gorillas in the Mist, makes fascinating reading. Pick up a copy before coming here. Her story has also been made into a film of the same name, and following its success, the tourism industry in the country boomed for a while, until fighting between the government and the RPF put the area out of bounds to tourists. Things have cooled down since then and the park is again safe to visit.

Visiting the Gorillas

As with visiting the gorillas in Zaïre and Uganda, many travellers rate a visit to these beautiful creatures as one of the highlights of their trip to Africa. It isn't, however, a joy ride. The guides can generally find the gorillas within one to four hours of starting out, but this often involves a lot of strenuous effort scrambling through dense vegetation up steep, muddy hillsides sometimes to more than 3000m. It also rains a lot in this area. If

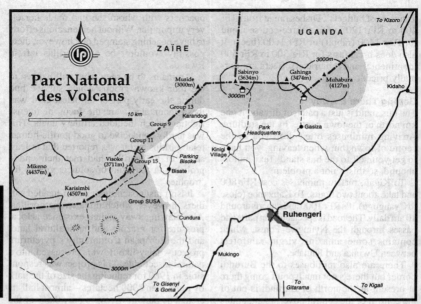

Parc National
des Volcans

0   5   10 km

RWANDA

you don't have the right footwear and clothing, you're in for a hard time.

An encounter with a silverback male gorilla
at close quarters can also be a hair-raising
experience if you've only ever seen large wild
animals in the safety of a zoo. Despite their size,
however, they're remarkably nonaggressive
animals, entirely vegetarian, and are usually
quite safe to be around. For most people, it's a
magical encounter.

There are two gorilla groups you can visit,
including the SUSA group, which has 29
members. Numbers of people allowed to
visit either of the groups varies, but is no
more than eight people at any one time, and
may be less.

Reservations To see any group, you must
make advance reservations at the tourist office
in Kigali, Office Rwandais du Tourisme et des
Parcs Nationaux (☎ 76514), BP 905. These
used to be hard to get in the days before the
genocide but there's no longer any pressure so

you're virtually guaranteed a booking on any
day you care to name. BUT, do not turn up
in Ruhengeri without a booking – you will
not be entertained.

Children under 15 years of age cannot
visit the gorillas.

Having made a booking in Kigali and paid
your fees, you must then go to the prefecture
(opposite the Hotel Muhabura) in Ruhengeri
and speak with Mr Augustine Nzanurabano
who will arrange for you to go and see the
gorillas the following morning. You will also
have to arrange a vehicle to take you to the
point at which you start climbing up to where
the gorillas are situated. This is no problem
but it will cost you around US$70 shared
between however many there are in your
group. You must report back to the prefecture
before 8 am the next morning and from there
you will be accompanied by the guards and
guides to the take-off points. When you've
seen the gorillas these people will also
accompany you back to the prefecture.

Visits to the gorillas are restricted to one hour and flashes and video cameras are banned unless you are prepared to pay US$6000 for a video permit!

Park Fees Fees are US$126 per person (US$95 for students) for a gorilla visit (including compulsory guides and guards), payable in hard currency. Resident foreigners can pay the equivalent in local currency. Porters are also available but you pay extra for this service. The guides, guards and any porters will expect a tip at the end.

WARNING

Other than to visit the gorillas, climbing the volcanoes is prohibited at present. There are good reasons for this, the main two being the inability of the government to guarantee your safety from armed rebels and the very real possibility of stepping on a landmine. The government is justifiably concerned about the adverse publicity which a maimed or dead tourist would attract in the western media.

Perhaps, one day, the mines will be cleared and you'll be allowed to climb the mountains again so, just in case this becomes possible, we're including a description of the possible climbs. ■

Trekking the Volcanoes

There are several possibilities for trekking up to the summits of one or more of the volcanoes in the park. The treks range from several hours to two days or more. For all these, a guide is compulsory (at the usual fee) but porters are optional.

The ascents take you through some remarkable changes of vegetation, ranging from thick forests of bamboo, giant lobelia or hagenia on to alpine meadows. If the weather is favourable, you'll be rewarded with some spectacular views over the mountain chain. It is forbidden to cut down trees or otherwise damage vegetation in the park and you can only make fires in the designated camping areas. The following treks are among the more popular:

Visoke (3711m) The return trip takes six to seven hours from Parking Bisoke. The ascent takes you up the very steep south-western flanks of the volcano to the summit, where you can see the crater lake. The descent follows a rough track on the north-western side, from where there are magnificent views over the Parc National des Virunga (Zaïre) and Lake Ngezi.

Lake Ngezi (About 3000m) The return trip takes three to four hours from Parking Bisoke. This is one of the easiest of the treks, and if you get there at the right time of the day, you may see a variety of animals coming to drink.

Karisimbi (4507m) The return trip takes two days. The track follows the saddle between Visoke and Karisimbi and then ascends the north-western flank of the latter. Some five hours after beginning the trek, you arrive at a metal hut, which is where you stay for the night (the hut keys are available at Parking Bisoke). The rocky and sometimes snow-covered summit is a further two to four hours walk through alpine vegetation. You descend the mountain the following day. To do this trek, you need plenty of warm clothing and a very good sleeping bag. It gets very cold, especially at the metal hut, which is on a bleak shoulder of the mountain at about 3660m. The wind whips through, frequently with fog, so you don't get much warmth from the sun.

Sabinyo (3634m) The return trip takes five to six hours from the park headquarters at Kinigi. The track ascends the south-eastern face of the volcano, ending up with a rough scramble over steep lava beds along a very narrow path. There's a metal hut just before the start of the lava beds.

Gahinga & Muhabura (3474m and 4127m) The return trip takes two days from Gasiza. The summit of the first volcano is reached after a climb of about four hours along a track which passes through a swampy saddle between the two mountains. There is a metal

RWANDA

hut here, which offers a modicum of shelter, but it's in a bad state of repair. The trip to the summit of Muhabura takes about four hours from the saddle.

Getting There & Away
The access point for the national park is Ruhengeri. Minibuses between Kigali and Ruhengeri take 2½ hours and cost RFr 1800.

PARC NATIONAL DE L'AKAGERA
Created in 1934 and covering an area of 2500 sq km, Akagera is one of the least visited but most interesting wildlife parks in Africa.

One reason for this is its three distinct environments. Large areas of the park are covered with treeless savannah, but there is an immense swampy area about 95 km long and between two and 20 km wide along the border with Tanzania. This contains six lakes and numerous islands, some of which are covered with savannah, others are covered with forest.

There is a chain of low mountains (ranging from 1618m to 1825m high) which stretches through much of the length of the park. The vegetation here is variable, ranging from short grasses on the summits to wooded savannah and dense thickets of xerophilious (adapted to a dry habitat) forest on the flanks of the park.

There's an extraordinary variety of animals to be seen here and they're often much easier to find than in other wildlife parks. In just a two to three-day trip, you can usually come across topi, impala, roan antelope, giant eland, bushbuck, oribi, various types of duiker, buffalo, wart hog, red river hog, baboon, vervet monkey, lion, leopard, hyena, zebra, hippo, crocodile and, at night, hare, palm civet, genet, galagos (bushbabies) and giant crested porcupine. There are also herds of elephant.

Unfortunately, this park, like the Virunga Mountains, was a major focus of the 1994 civil war and the northern portion is still out of bounds because of uncleared landmines (that is, north of Plage Hippos). The southern section of the park is still open but camping anywhere in the park is still prohibited.

The best time to visit, in terms of access, is during the dry season (mid-May to mid-September). November and April are the wettest months.

Tsetse flies can be particularly troublesome in the north and east, but you could be bothered by the odd one anywhere in the park, so bring a fly swat and/or a good insect repellent.

Hiring a guide is a waste of money. You won't find any more animals with a guide than you will without. All you need is a map of the park, your eyes and a pair of binoculars. Park maps, for sale at the tourist office in Kigali, are remarkably accurate despite the way they appear – you can't buy these at the park. A wildlife handbook is also a useful thing to have.

Take all your own food, drinking and washing water, and fuel. It's best to assume you won't be able to get these in the park. Sometimes fuel is available at the hotels but they're very reluctant to sell it.

Park entry fees are RFr 3500 per person (RFr 1200 for students and children between the ages of seven and 18 years), plus RFr 1600 for a car, RFr 2200 for a jeep or RFr 2400 for a minibus or truck. A guide costs RFr 500 per day and a fishing licence costs RFr 1500 per day. You need to pay your park entry fees before you get there, either at a travel agent or at the tourist office in Kigali.

Places to Stay
Camping is not allowed inside the park. There are two lodges in the park, but the *Gabiro Guest House* was trashed during the civil war and is closed. It's unlikely to open again in the near future.

The only place which is currently open is the *Hôtel Akagera*, which is very expensive. It sits on the top of a hill and commands excellent views. A boat trip on the lake is recommended, as it's cheap and there are plenty of birds to be seen.

Getting There & Away
The only problem with getting to Akagera is that you need to have your own transport or to join an organised safari. Safaris do not, as

in Kenya and Tanzania, cater to budget travellers. Check out car hire and safari prices in Kigali at Rwanda Travel Service (☎ 72210), Hôtel des Diplomates (☎ 75111), 43 Blvd de la Révolution; Umubano Tours Agency (☎ 72176), BP 1160; and Agence Solliard (☎ 75660), 2 Ave de la République.

The only feasible entry into the park at present is via Nyamiyaga, about 16 km from the sealed road going through Kayonza. This road will take you through to the Hôtel Akagera.

NYUNGWE FOREST CONSERVATION PROJECT

Despite not being a national park, the Nyungwe Forest ranks among Rwanda's foremost attractions. One of the largest protected montane rainforests in Africa, it covers 970 sq km and offers superb scenery overlooking the forest and Lake Kivu as well as views to the north of the distant volcanoes of the Virunga.

The conservation project began in 1988 and is sponsored by the American Peace Corps, the New York Zoological Society and the Rwandan government. The project aims to promote tourism in an ecologically sound way while also studying the ecology of the forest and educating local people about its value.

The main attraction is the guided tours to view large groups of black-and-white colobus monkeys (up to 300 per group). The lush, green valleys also offer outstanding hiking across 20 km of well-maintained trails passing through enormous stands of hardwoods, under waterfalls and through a large marsh. There are about 270 species of tree, 50 species of mammal, 275 species of bird and an astonishing variety of orchids and butterflies.

The guided tours depart from the project headquarters at Uwinka three times daily, at 8 and 11 am and 2 pm. An information centre is also at the headquarters. The tours cost RFr 1000 per person and you should expect to walk for about an hour. Sturdy shoes, binoculars and rain gear are advisable.

Another guided tour (RFr 1000 per person) goes to the Kamiranzovu Marsh, where the area's six remaining elephants reside in the forest.

In addition to the tours, there are six other trails, ranging from one to nine km in length, along which you're free to hike without a guide.

Entry fees to Nyungwe Forest are the same as those at the Parc National de l'Akagera.

WARNING

Landmines have been found in Nyungwe Forest so we do not recommend that you go there. It is not known when they will be cleared. Please bear this in mind if you intend to go there. ■

Places to Stay

There are nine camp sites at the Uwinka headquarters but you must bring everything you need – tent, sleeping bag, cooking equipment, water, food and warm clothes (the nights are cool at 2400m). There is nothing here other than toilets, charcoal and wood. Camping fees are RFr 500 per person per night.

The nearest towns for provisions are Cyangugu and Butare. Plans are being made to connect the existing trails with other camp sites to enable those who prefer backpacking to take two to three-day treks in the forest. Uwinka sits on a ridge overlooking the forest and offers impressive views in all directions. There's also a camp site at Karamba, which is about 14 km towards Cyangugu from Uwinka.

Getting There & Away

The Nyungwe Forest lies between Butare and Cyangugu. From Kigali, head south to Butare and then west towards Cyangugu. Minibuses leave from Kigali and Butare to Kamembe throughout the day, and from there you can catch a minibus to Cyangugu. The Uwinka headquarters is just past the

RWANDA

90-km post and is marked by a board on which a black-and-white colobus monkey is painted. The trip from Kigali takes between four and six hours.

From Cyangugu, take a minibus towards Butare and get off at Uwinka, which is just past the 54-km post. The journey takes about one hour.

Burundi

Facts about the Country

HISTORY
Early Settlement

Burundi

BURUNDI

Area: 27,835 sq km
Population: 6.4 million
Population Growth Rate: 3%
Capital: Bujumbura
Head of State: President Pierre Buyoya
Official Languages: Kirundi, French
Currency: Burundi franc
Exchange Rate: BFr 320 = US$1
Per Capita GNP: US$225
Inflation: 10%
Time: UTC + 2

Burundi is a small and beautiful mountainous country. Sandwiched between Tanzania, Rwanda and Zaïre, there are magnificent views over Lake Tanganyika.

Burundi has had a stormy history of tribal wars and factional struggles between the ruling families. This has been further complicated in recent times by colonisation, first by the Germans and later by the Belgians. Since independence in 1962, intertribal tensions have boiled over on numerous occasions leading to the deaths of tens of thousands of people. That is happening all over again right now and, by the time you read this, Burundi may have exploded into much the same genocidal tragedy as engulfed Rwanda in 1994. The situation looks very bleak.

Burundi is one of the most densely populated countries in the world, with 180 people per sq km. Despite this, there are very few urban centres. The only towns of any size are the capital, Bujumbura, and Gitega. Most people live in family compounds known as *rugos*.

Facts about the Country

HISTORY
Early Settlement
The original inhabitants of the area were the Twa Pygmies, who now comprise only 1% of the population. They were gradually displaced from about 1000 AD onwards by Hutu, mostly farmers of Bantu stock, who now make up 85% of the population.

In the 16th and 17th centuries, the country

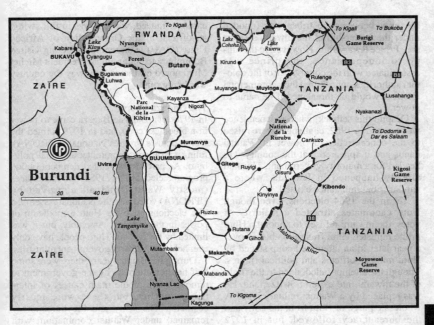

experienced another wave of migration. This time it was the tall, pastoralist Watutsi from Ethiopia and Uganda, who now make up 14% of the population. The Watutsi gradually subjugated the Hutu into a type of feudal system, similar to that which operated in medieval Europe. The Watutsi became a loosely organised aristocracy with a *mwami*, or king, at the top of each social pyramid. Under this system the Hutu relinquished their land and mortgaged their services to the nobility in return for cattle – the symbol of wealth and status in Burundi.

The Colonial Era

At the end of the 19th century, Burundi and Rwanda were colonised by Germany. However, the country was so thinly garrisoned that the Belgians were easily able to oust the German forces during WWI. After the war, the League of Nations mandated Burundi (then known as Urundi) and Rwanda to Belgium.

Taking advantage of the feudal structure, the Belgians ruled indirectly through the Watutsi chiefs and princes, granting them wide-ranging powers to recruit labour and raise taxes. The Watutsi were not averse to abusing these powers whenever it suited them. After all, they considered themselves to be a superior, intelligent people, born to rule, while the Hutu were merely hard-working but dumb peasants. The Christian missionaries encouraged this view by concentrating on educating the Watutsi and virtually ignoring the Hutu. As the missions had been granted a monopoly on education, this policy remained unchallenged.

The establishment of coffee plantations and the resulting concentration of wealth in the hands of the Watutsi urban elite further exacerbated tensions between the two tribal groups.

Independence

In the 1950s, a nationalist organisation based

on unity between the tribes was founded under the leadership of the mwami's eldest son, Prince Rwagasore. However, in the run-up to independence, the prince was assassinated with the connivance of the colonial authorities, who feared their commercial interests would be threatened if he came to power.

Despite this setback, when independence was granted in 1962, challenges were raised to the concentration of power in Watutsi hands and it appeared that the country was headed for a majority government. This had already happened in Rwanda, where a similar tribal imbalance existed.

Yet in the 1964 elections, even though Hutu candidates attracted a majority of votes, the mwami refused to appoint a Hutu prime minister. Hutu frustration boiled over a year later in an attempted coup staged by Hutu military officers and political figures. Though the attempt failed, it led to the flight of the mwami into exile in Switzerland. He was replaced by a Watutsi military junta. A wholesale purge of Hutu from the army and the bureaucracy followed, but in 1972 another large-scale revolt saw more than 1000 Watutsi killed.

The military junta responded to this challenge with what amounted to selective genocide. Any Hutu with wealth, a formal education or a government job was rooted out and murdered, often in the most horrifying way. Certainly few bullets were used, and convoys of army trucks full of the mutilated bodies of Hutu rumbled through the streets of Bujumbura for days on end, initially even in broad daylight. Many Hutu were taken from their homes at night, while others received summonses to police stations.

It is hard to believe how subservient the Hutu had become to their Watutsi overlords. Even the most uninformed peasant was aware of what was occurring. After three months, 200,000 Hutu had been killed and 100,000 had fled to Tanzania, Rwanda and Zaïre.

Neither the Christian missions inside the country nor the international community outside raised any protest against this carnage. Indeed, while it was in full swing, an official of the Organization of African Unity (OAU) is on record as having visited Bujumbura to congratulate President Michel Micombero on the orderly way the country was being run!

The Bagaza Years

In 1976 Jean-Baptiste Bagaza came to power in a bloodless coup, and in 1979 formed the Union pour le Progrès National (UPRONA), ruling with a central committee and small politburo. As part of a so-called democratisation program, elections in 1982 saw candidates (mostly Watutsi and all approved by UPRONA) voted into the National Assembly. The elections gave the Hutu a modicum of power in the National Assembly, but it was limited by the fact that Hutu people have only ever held about 25% of government ministries.

During the Bagaza years, there were some half-hearted attempts by the government to remove some of the main causes of intertribal conflict, but these were mostly cosmetic. The army and the bureaucracy remained under Watutsi domination, with the Hutu confined to menial jobs, agriculture and cattle raising. The government even vetoed international aid when it suspected that this might be used to educate or enrich the Hutu, and thus sow seeds of discontent.

In 1985 the government tried to lessen the influence of the Catholic Church, which it believed was sympathetic to the Hutu majority. Its fears of a church-organised Hutu revolt were heightened by the fact that in Rwanda, Hutus were in power. Priests were put on trial and some missionaries were expelled from the country.

Bagaza was toppled in September 1987 in a bloodless coup led by his cousin Major Pierre Buyoya. The new regime did a reasonable job of mending fences between the government and the Catholic Church/international aid agencies. It also attempted to address the causes of intertribal tensions yet again by gradually bringing Hutu representatives back into positions of power in the government. However, there was a renewed outbreak of intertribal violence in the north of the country in August 1988. As in previous clashes of this nature, the violence was unbelievable. Depending on whose figures you do believe, somewhere between 4000 and 24,000 people were massacred and thousands more fled into neighbouring Rwanda.

The 1990s
Then, in 1992, Buyoya bowed to international pressure and announced that multi-party elections would be held the following year. For a time, it seemed that sense and reason might prevail over the endless cycle of bloodletting. However, it was not to be.

Although peaceful elections were duly held in June 1993, which brought a Hutu-dominated government to power headed by Melchior Ndadaye (also a Hutu), a dissident army faction, led by Colonel Sylvestre Ningaba, staged a bloody coup in late October the same year, assassinated the president along with several prominent ministers and went on the rampage. The coup failed when army generals disowned the plotters but, in the chaos which followed the assassination, thousands of people were massacred in intertribal fighting and an estimated 400,000 refugees fled across the border into Rwanda. Surviving members of the government, who had holed up in the French embassy in Bujumbura, were able to reassert some degree of control several days later with the help of French soldiers and troops loyal to the government. Yet it was not until February the following year that things had cooled down sufficiently for Cyprien Ntaryamira to be sworn in as the new president. Ntaryamira, a Hutu, was chosen as part of a compromise deal worked out between the government and the opposition. Part of the deal was the allocation of 40% of government posts to the opposition. Once again, the future looked bright, but it was an illusory new dawn.

Recent Events
On 6 April 1994, the new president was killed along with President Habyarimana of Rwanda when the plane in which they were travelling together was shot down as it was about to land at Rwanda's Kigali airport. While this was the spark which ignited the genocide in Rwanda, Burundi remained relatively calm and Sylvestre Ntibantunganya was immediately appointed as the interim president.

Unfortunately, it was just another window-dressing stand-off. Neither Hutu militias nor the Tutsi-dominated army passed up the opportunity to go on the offensive. No war was actually declared but at least 100,000 people were killed in clashes between mid-1994 and mid-1996, most of them in counter-reprisals. The Burundian army retained nominal control of the capital, Bujumbura, and much of the centre and south of the country, but they quickly lost control of the northern part to the Hutu militias. It was, essentially, a stalemate and something had to give, but what did eventually give does not bode well for the country's future.

On 25 July 1996, Buyoya, the former president, carried out a successful coup and took over as the country's president with the support of the army. It's too early to say what will happen but it doesn't look good.

GEOGRAPHY
Burundi occupies a mountainous 27,835 sq km. The capital, Bujumbura, is on the north-eastern tip of Lake Tanganyika.

CLIMATE
Burundi has a variable climate. The lower land around Lake Tanganyika is hot and humid, with temperatures around 30°C. In the more mountainous north, the average temperature is around 20°C. The rainy

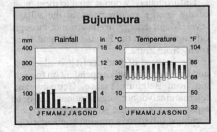

season lasts from October to May, with a brief dry spell in December and January.

GOVERNMENT & POLITICS

Following multi-party elections in June 1993, the Burundi Democratic Front (FRODEBU) came to power with some 71% of the vote compared to some 26% garnered by the previous ruling party, UPRONA. This gave the Hutu a majority of deputies in the National Assembly (65 out of a total of 81). The president, Sylvestre Ntibantunganya, a Hutu, was ousted in the July 1996 coup led by Pierre Buyoya, a Tutsi. International sanctions have been placed on Burundi to force Buyoya to step down or stage elections.

ECONOMY

Burundi's economy is predominantly agricultural, with coffee, the main commercial crop, accounting for 65% of export income. Recently attempts have been made to encourage development of the non-coffee sector in an effort to diversify the economy. Consequently, the production of tea has increased greatly in the past few years.

Agriculture accounts for more than 50% of GDP and employs about 85% of the workforce. Apart from coffee and tea, cash crops include cotton, palm oil and tobacco. Subsistence crops (which occupy most of the cultivated land) include cassava, bananas, sweet potatoes, maize and sorghum.

The manufacturing sector, based in Bujumbura, accounts for 15% of GDP, with output including cigarettes, glass, textiles, cement, oxygen and processed coffee.

Unfortunately, wood is used to meet most of the energy requirements at the village level. Major energy needs are met through oil imports from the Persian Gulf and electricity from Zaïre.

The balance of trade deficit is alarming and Burundi is heavily dependent on foreign aid from Belgium, France, Germany and international donor organisations. Its debt repayments consume some 44% of export earnings. Inflation is running at about 10%.

POPULATION & PEOPLE

The population of 6.4 million is about 14% Watutsi and 85% Hutu.

RELIGION

The majority of the population are Christians of various sects. Muslims are a significant minority.

LANGUAGE

The official languages are Kirundi and French, and Swahili is also useful. Hardly anyone speaks English.

Facts for the Visitor

PLANNING

For details about planning your trip, and what to bring, see the Planning section in the Regional Facts for the Visitor chapter.

HIGHLIGHTS

Burundi is one of those strange places in the world which doesn't appear to have any obvious highlights. There are no mountain gorillas, no volcanoes, no national parks worth the mention, in fact, nothing other than its location alongside the eastern boundary of Lake Tanganyika. Most travellers simply pass through here en route to Tanzania or Zaïre, but those who have stayed here for a long time attest to the warmth of its people and to the richness of its culture. Economic and social life appear to be almost totally controlled by European Francophone expatriates to the detriment of local Africans, and inter-ethnic violence appears to be a way of life.

VISAS & DOCUMENTS

Visas

Visas are required by all visitors to Burundi. Transit visas cost US$10 and a one-month tourist visa costs US$20. You will need two photos and can generally get your visa the same day, if you apply early enough.

There's no extra charge for requesting a multiple-entry visa, so if there's any chance you could need this, get it now rather than later.

For some reason, certain Burundi embassies (Nairobi in Kenya and Kigali in Rwanda are two) will not issue visas, telling you to get them at the border. They are still available at the embassy in Kampala (Uganda) and at the consulates in Kigoma (Tanzania) and Bukavu (Zaïre).

Tourist visas can be extended at the immigration office in Bujumbura. These cost BFr 1000 per month and take 24 hours to issue. Apply early in the morning, as it's very busy in the afternoon.

Getting Other Visas in Burundi If you need visas for neighbouring countries, these are the conditions:

Rwanda
A one-month multiple-entry visa costs US$20, requires two photos and is issued in 24 hours.
Tanzania
Visas require two photographs and are issued in 24 hours. Costs vary according to your nationality (see the Tanzania Facts for the Visitor chapter for details).
Zaïre
Visa costs are the same as in other countries (see the Zaïre chapter for details), three photos are required and the visa is issued in 24 hours.

EMBASSIES
Burundi Embassies
In the region, there are Burundi embassies in:

Kenya
Development House, Moi Ave, PO Box 44439, Nairobi (☎ (02) 218458; fax 219005)
Rwanda
Rue de Ntaruka off Ave de Rusumo, Kigali (☎ (07) 73465)
Tanzania
Plot 1007, Lugalo Rd, Dar es Salaam (☎ (051) 46307)
Also in Kigoma
Uganda
7 Bandali Rise, Bugolobi, Kampala (☎ (041) 221697)
Zaïre
SINELAC building, top floor, 184 Ave du Président Mobutu, Bukavu
Also in Kinshasa

Elsewhere in Africa there are Burundi embassies in: Addis Ababa (Ethiopia), Algiers (Algeria), Cairo (Egypt) and Tripoli (Libya).

Outside Africa, there are Burundi embassies in Beijing (People's Republic of China), Bonn (Germany), Brussels (Belgium), Bucharest (Romania), Geneva (Switzerland), Moscow (Russia), Ottawa (Canada), Paris (France) and Washington DC (USA).

Foreign Embassies in Burundi
Embassies in Bujumbura for neighbouring African countries include:

Rwanda
24 Ave du Zaïre (☎ 26865). Open Monday to Friday from 8 am to 4 pm and on Saturday until 11.30 am.
Tanzania
Ave de l'ONU. Open Monday to Friday from 8 am till noon and 2 to 5 pm.
Zaïre
Ave du Zaïre, Bujumbura. Open from 8.30 am till noon.

MONEY
Costs
Burundi can be an expensive place to stay if you want to be near the town centre in Bujumbura, but there are reasonably cheap places in the suburbs. Besides Bujumbura town centre, meals can usually be found at a fair price and transport costs are about the same as in Rwanda.

Currency
The unit of currency, the Burundi franc (BFr), is divided into 100 centimes, which you're highly unlikely to come across. Notes in circulation are BFr 5000, BFr 1000, BFr 500, BFr 100, BFr 50 and BFr 10. The only coins are BFr 5 and BFr 1.

Currency Exchange
The exchange value of the Burundi franc fluctuates according to the international currency market, particularly the value of the US dollar and the French franc, and devaluations are not uncommon.

| USA | US$1 | = | BFr 320 |
| France | 1FFr | = | BFr 60 |

BURUNDI

Changing Money

Commission rates for changing travellers' cheques are bad news at most banks – some charge up to 7%! The Banque de la République du Burundi is the best place to change, as it charges only a very small commission and may even change small amounts of dollar travellers' cheques to cash dollars. Banking hours are Monday to Friday from 8 to 11.30 am. Outside these hours, you can change travellers' cheques at one of the large hotels in Bujumbura (eg Novotel, Chaussée du Peuple Burundi). Their rates are fractionally below those offered by the banks, though they charge no commission.

There's a relatively open street market in Bujumbura. Dealers generally hang around the front of the main post office. Rates obviously vary according to the official exchange rate and the amount you want to change (large bills are preferred). For currencies other than the US dollar, you're better off at the bank.

Tanzanian shillings can also be bought here, which is handy if you're heading for Kigoma, but the rate is not that good. The nearest Tanzanian banks are in Kigoma.

If you take your own food on the Lake Tanganyika steamer (and don't intend to buy drinks), there's no need for shillings, but you'll need some for the Nyanza Lac and Gombe Stream route. If you're not providing your own food or are taking the steamer all the way to Mpulungu, you'll need shillings, as it's a Tanzanian boat and meals and drinks must be paid for in Tanzanian shillings.

At the border post between Uvira (Zaïre) and Bujumbura, you'll run into a lot of moneychangers. Their rates are quite reasonable, so long as you know the current street rates for the Burundi franc.

Currency declaration forms are not issued on arrival.

POST & COMMUNICATIONS
Post

The postal service is reasonably efficient, but the poste restante service at the main post office (PTT) in Bujumbura is poorly organised. Make sure you check not only the pile for your surname but also those for any other possible combinations or spellings. It's open Monday to Friday from 8 am till noon and 2 to 4 pm, and on Saturday to 11 am.

Telephone

Rates for international telephone calls are extremely high; however, connections from the main post office in Bujumbura take no more than a few minutes. There are no area codes in Burundi.

NEWSPAPERS

The main newspaper is the French-language daily, *Le Rénouveau du Burundi*. It's under strict government control.

RADIO

Local radio stations broadcast in Kirundi, French and Swahili. There are occasional broadcasts in English on the local FM station (98.10 MHz). This station also plays some pretty decent African music.

TIME

The time in Burundi is GMT/UTC plus two hours.

ELECTRICITY

Power supply is 220V AC.

HEALTH

As with most African countries, you should take precautions against malaria in Burundi. There is a good beach (with expensive hotels and restaurants) at the northern end of Lake Tanganyika, between Bujumbura and the Burundi-Zaïre border. It may be safe to swim there, but it's probably best avoided. You should definitely avoid bathing in this lake wherever there is reedy vegetation, due to the risk of contracting bilharzia. Also see Health in the Regional Facts for the Visitor chapter.

PUBLIC HOLIDAYS

January
New Year's Day (1st)
March/April
Good Friday
Easter Sunday

May
Labour Day (1st)
Ascension
July
National Day (1st)
August
Feast of the Assumption (15th)
September
National Holiday (18th)
October
National Holiday (13th)
November
All Saints' Day (1st)
December
Christmas Day (25th)

Getting There & Away

You can enter Burundi by air, road or lake ferry. There are no railways.

AIR

International airlines servicing Burundi are Aeroflot, Air Burundi, Air France, Air Rwanda, Air Tanzania, Cameroon Air, Ethiopian Airlines, Kenya Airways and Sabena.

If you're heading for Tanzania and are thinking of flying internally from Kigoma to Dar es Salaam, it's worth making a reservation at the Air Tanzania office in Bujumbura. You don't have to pay for the ticket until you get to Kigoma but Air Tanzania staff will give you written confirmation of your flight reservation.

LAND
Rwanda

There is a choice of two routes. Which one you take will depend on whether you want to go from Kigali direct to Butare and on to Bujumbura, or via Cyangugu (Lake Kivu).

Butare to Bujumbura Although this is the most direct route to Bujumbura, you are seriously warned not to take it as the northern section of Burundi is out of the control of the central government and it's a dangerous area to be in.

Cyangugu to Bujumbura The safest way between these two places is to cross the border to Bukavu from Cyangugu and take a minibus from there to Uvira and then a taxi from there to the Zaïre/Burundi border and another taxi from there into Bujumbura. This road goes back into Rwanda part of the way (but not through Cyangugu) before re-entering Zaïre so you'll need a multiple-entry Rwandan visa and a multiple-entry Zaïrese visa. Rwandan transit visas are available at the border if you don't have a multiple-entry visa. See the Bukavu section in the Eastern Zaïre chapter for details.

Zaïre

There are two possible routes between Burundi and Zaïre but you're seriously advised to avoid the route which passes through north-western Burundi via Bugarama as it's dangerous (there's fighting going on).

Bukavu to Bujumbura via Uvira This is the longer and less comfortable route. First read about travel between Bukavu and Uvira in the Eastern Zaïre chapter, as this route has two options, one through Rwanda and the other direct to Uvira.

BOAT
Tanzania & Zambia

The two routes available both use Lake Tanganyika at different points. A direct route is to/from Kigoma on the venerable MV *Liemba*. However, a more interesting route is via Nyanza Lac and Gombe Stream National Park, the chimpanzee sanctuary across the border in Tanzania.

Ferry The MV *Liemba* connects Tanzania with Burundi and Zambia. It used to operate in conjunction with a sister ship, the MV *Mwongozo*, but this boat now only services ports on the Tanzanian part of the lake (see the Tanzania Getting Around chapter).

The services for the MV *Liemba* can be delayed for up to 24 hours at either end, depending on how much cargo there is to load or unload. Departures are frequently cancelled according to the security situation in Bujumbura. Engine trouble can also delay it at any point, though usually not for more than a few hours.

Officially, the MV *Liemba* departs once a week from Bujumbura, on Monday at about 6 pm, and arrives in Kigoma (Tanzania) on Tuesday at 8 am. It leaves Kigoma at about 4 pm on Wednesday and arrives in Mpulungu (Zambia) on Friday at 8 am. It calls at many small Tanzanian ports en route between Kigoma and Mpulungu, but rarely for more than half an hour. In the opposite direction it departs Mpulungu on Friday at 6 pm and arrives in Kigoma on Sunday at 10 am. It leaves Kigoma on Sunday at 6 pm and arrives in Bujumbura on Monday at 8 am. The fares from Bujumbura are:

Port	1st class	2nd class	3rd class
Kigoma	US$19	US$15	US$12
Mpulungu	US$78	US$62	US$48

In addition, port fees of BFr 500 are payable upon boarding in Bujumbura. Tickets for the ferry can be bought from SONACO, Rue des Usines (off Ave du Port), Bujumbura, on Monday morning from 8 am.

Tickets bought in Mpulungu for the trip north to Kigoma or Bujumbura and tickets bought in Bujumbura for the trip south to any of the ports en route must be paid for in US dollars.

To save money when going all the way from Bujumbura to Mpulungu, buy a ticket to Kigoma, then once the boat docks, get off, immediately make a reservation for a 1st or 2nd-class cabin and change money into Tanzanian shillings. Pay for your ticket the following morning at 8 am using the shillings you changed. This will save you approximately US$33 in total (assuming you take 1st class) because the fares from Kigoma to Mpulungu are much cheaper than the equivalent US dollar fares all the way from Bujumbura to Mpulungu. The fares from Kigoma are:

Port	1st class	2nd class	3rd class
Bujumbura	TSh 4900	TSh 4320	TSh 3430
Mpulungu	TSh 13,715	TSh 11,605	TSh 9090

When travelling from Bujumbura direct to Mpulungu, you have to stay overnight on the boat for the 36 hours or so that it docks in Kigoma, though you are allowed into town during the day even if you don't have a Tanzanian visa (where required). Passports have to be left with immigration in the meantime.

Third class consists of bench seats either in a covered area towards the back of the boat or in another very poorly ventilated area with bench seats in the bowels of the vessel. The best plan is to grab some deck space. The 2nd-class cabins are incredibly hot, stuffy and claustrophobic. They have four bunks and are very poorly ventilated. If you want a cabin, go the whole hog and take a 1st-class one. These have two bunks, are on a higher deck, have a window and fan and are clean and reasonably cool. Bedding is available for a small fee.

Third class is not usually crowded between Bujumbura and Kigoma, so this is a reasonable budget option, especially as it's only overnight. It's no problem to sleep out on the deck – the best spot is above the 1st-class deck, though you need to be discreet, as it's supposedly off limits to other passengers. On the lower decks, you need to keep your gear safe, as some petty pilfering does sometimes occur. If you're travelling 3rd class between Bujumbura and Kigoma and want to upgrade to a cabin for the Kigoma-Mpulungu leg, make sure you do this as soon as the boat docks in Kigoma. Third class is not recommended between Kigoma and Mpulungu, as it's usually very crowded.

Meals and drinks are available on board and must be paid for in Tanzanian shillings, so bring enough to cover this. Three-course meals of soup, chicken and rice followed by dessert are not bad value and breakfast is reasonable, too. You can buy cold Safari lager (Tanzanian) at TSh 600 or Primus (Zaïrese) at TSh 900.

Coming from Bujumbura, the MV *Liemba* arrives at Kigoma at about 5 am, but you can't get off until 8 am, when customs and immigration officials arrive. Instead of packing your bags and hanging around, it's a good idea to have breakfast.

Lake Taxi & Matatu The alternative to the MV *Liemba* is to travel partly by matatu and partly by lake taxi between Bujumbura and Kigoma, via the Tanzanian border village of Kagunga and the Gombe Stream National Park. The national park is primarily a chimpanzee sanctuary and is well worth a visit, but it does cost US$100 entry fee plus US$20 for accommodation. If you can't afford this, then simply stay on the lake taxi, which will take you all the way to Kigoma.

From Bujumbura, matatus go daily to Nyanza Lac (BFr 1400). You must go through immigration here; the office is about one km from the town centre towards the lake. After that you take a matatu (BFr 200) to the Burundi border post. From this post to the Tanzanian border post at Kagunga, it's a two-km walk along a narrow track. From Kagunga, there are lake taxis to Kigoma (actually to Kalalangabo, about three km north of Kigoma), which cost TSh 1000, leave some time before dawn and take most of the day. The taxis call at Gombe Stream (about halfway), where you can get off if you like. The fare to Gombe Stream is TSh 500, as is the fare from there to Kigoma.

The lake taxis are small wooden boats, often overcrowded not only with people but with their produce, and they offer no creature comforts whatsoever. They're good fun when the weather is fine, though if there's a squall on the lake, you may be in for a rough time. If you have a choice, try to get a boat with a cover, as it gets stinking hot out on the lake in the middle of the day. These boats do not operate on Sunday.

Getting Around

AIR

Air Burundi, the national airline, does not have regular internal flights.

BUS

As in Rwanda, most of the major routes are sealed. Most of the vehicles available are modern, Japanese minibuses. They are not overcrowded and are cheaper than share-taxis. However, they are not that frequent since the troubles started in 1994 because some three-quarters of the owners, who were Rwandans, have decamped and gone back to Kigali. Destinations are displayed in the front window and vehicles depart when full. You can usually find one heading in your direction any day between early morning and early afternoon at the *gare routière* (bus stand) in any town or city.

Government OTRACO buses serve the area around Bujumbura.

Bujumbura

Sprawling up the mountainside on the north-eastern tip of Lake Tanganyika, Bujumbura overlooks the vast wall of mountains in Zaïre on the other side of the lake. The Burundi capital is a mixture of grandiose colonial town planning (wide boulevards and imposing public buildings) and dusty crowded suburbs like those which surround many African cities. It's also one of the most important ports on Lake Tanganyika.

Like Kigali in Rwanda, Bujumbura has a sizeable expatriate population of international aid organisation workers, medicos, missionaries and businesspeople. Even Colonel Gaddafi has made his mark here, in the form of the large and beautifully conceived Islamic Cultural Centre and mosque, which must have cost a small fortune. There is also a pleasant botanical surprise: like many places along Lake Tanganyika, Bujumbura sports coconut palms – most unusual at well over 1000 km from the sea! While not a lot of English is spoken, there is more English spoken here than in most parts of Rwanda or eastern Zaïre.

Bujumbura has a slightly sleazy atmosphere and is certainly not the friendliest place in the world. You are advised not to walk along Ave de la Plage between the Cercle Nautique and the port, even during the day, as there have been reports of muggings. Rue des Swahilis, in the same area, should also be avoided for the same reason. You're also advised to avoid the Buyenzi and Mbwiza areas of town as there's a constant vendetta between the army and Hutu militias in those areas. Gunfire and corpses on the street are a constant reminder that this is a society whose people are at war with each other. You should also avoid Kamenge further up the hill. Army personnel will want to know why you're there and will assume you are up to no good. Possession of a camera will guarantee you a hard time.

Information

Tourist Office This is on Blvd de l'UPRONA but the information available is limited. The office has a wide range of handicrafts for sale, but they're not cheap. They also sell maps of Burundi/Bujumbura (BFr 2000) but the country map is less than useless. The office is open Monday to Saturday from 7.30 am till noon and on Monday to Thursday from 2 to 5.30 pm.

Foreign Embassies African countries with diplomatic representation in Bujumbura include Rwanda, Tanzania and Zaïre – see Facts for the Visitor earlier in this chapter.

Other countries with embassies here include Belgium, Denmark, France, the Netherlands, Germany and the USA.

Post & Communications The main post office is in the city centre, on the corner of Blvd Lumumba and Ave du Commerce. The international telephone service is housed in the same building. Both are open Monday to Friday from 8 am till noon and 2 to 4 pm, and on Saturday to 11 am.

Cultural Centres The American Cultural Center on Chaussée Prince Rwagasore screens video news from the USA from Monday to Friday at 5.15 pm. Its library is open Monday to Friday from 2 to 8 pm and on Tuesday and Thursday from 9 am till noon. Alliance Francaise is across the road and has similar services and facilities.

The Islamic Cultural Centre and mosque is a beautiful building near the main square.

Paid for by the Libyan government, it is well worth visiting. Sometimes there are public performances by dance troupes, drummers and singers.

Things to See & Do

Bujumbura's two museums and its reptile park are within a block of each other on the Ave du 13 Octobre, which leads down to the Cercle Nautique on the lake front.

Musée Vivant This is a reconstructed traditional Burundian village with basket, pottery, drum and photographic displays. Occasionally there are traditional drum shows. Entry costs BFr 200 (BFr 50 for students) and the museum is open daily from 9 am till noon and 2.30 to 5 pm, except Monday.

Parc des Reptiles Adjacent to the Musée Vivant, this park (☎ 25374) exhibits just what you might expect. Entry costs BFr 500 but the park is only open on Saturday from 2 to 4 pm, or by appointment during the rest of the week.

Musée de Géologie du Burundi Opposite the reptile park, the geology museum is dusty and rundown but has a good collection of fossils. Entry is free. The museum is open on weekdays from 7 am till noon and 2 to 5 pm.

Swimming Pool To use the pool at the Novotel will cost BFr 1000, whereas the public pool at the stadium costs BFr 300.

Places to Stay – bottom end

It can be difficult to find a reasonably priced place to stay in Bujumbura. The main reason for this is the continual clashes between the army and those opposed to the government or, on a more basic level, intertribal clashes between the Tutsi and Hutu. It's a dangerous place to be. Gunfire and violent house searches are common occurrences, especially at night. As a result, most of the budget hotels have been closed for several years now. This is particularly true of the suburb of Mbwiza, about 10 minutes walk northwest of the city centre where many of them

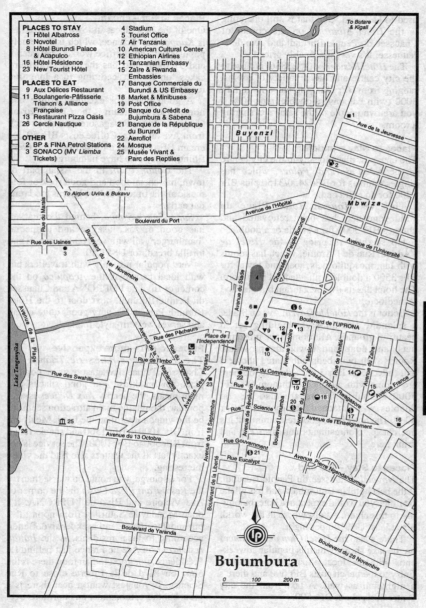

PLACES TO STAY
1 Hôtel Albatross
6 Novotel
8 Hôtel Burundi Palace & Acapulco
16 Hôtel Résidence
23 New Tourist Hôtel

PLACES TO EAT
9 Aux Délices Restaurant
11 Boulangerie-Pâtisserie Trianon & Alliance Française
13 Restaurant Pizza Oasis
26 Cercle Nautique

OTHER
2 BP & FINA Petrol Stations
3 SONACO (MV Liemba Tickets)
4 Stadium
5 Tourist Office
7 Air Tanzania
10 American Cultural Center
12 Ethiopian Airlines
14 Tanzanian Embassy
15 Zaïre & Rwanda Embassies
17 Banque Commerciale du Burundi & US Embassy
18 Market & Minibuses
19 Post Office
20 Banque du Crédit de Bujumbura & Sabena
21 Banque de la République du Burundi
22 Aeroflot
24 Mosque
25 Musée Vivant & Parc des Reptiles

To Butare & Kigali

Ave de la Jeunesse

Buyenzi

Mbwiza

Avenue de l'Hôpital

Avenue de l'Université

Chaussée du Peuple Burundi

Boulevard du Port

To Airport, Uvira & Bakavu

Rue du Marais

Rue des Usines

Boulevard du 1er Novembre

Avenue du Stade

Boulevard de l'UPRONA

Avenue de la Plage

Lake Tanganyika

Rue des Pêcheurs

Avenue de la Tanganyika

Rue des Paysans

Place de l'Independance

Rue de l'Imbo

Rue des Swahilis

Avenue des Nahararuga

Rue Nahararuga

Avenue du Commerce

Avenue Victoire

Mission

Chaussée Prince Rwagasore

Rue de l'Amitié

Avenue du Zaïre

Avenue France

Rue Industrie

Rue Science

Boulevard Lumumba

Avenue du Marché

Avenue de l'Enseignement

Avenue de Révolution

Avenue du 18 Septembre

Avenue du 13 Octobre

Rue Gouvernment

Rue Eucalypt

Boulevard de la Liberté

Avenue Pierre Ngendandumwe

Boulevard de Yaranda

Boulevard du 28 Novembre

BURUNDI

Bujumbura

0   100   200 m

used to be found. One that is still operating is the *Hôtel Albatross* on the corner of Chaussée du Peuple Burundi and Ave de la Jeunesse. It's very reasonably priced.

The *Hôtel Résidence* (☎ 23886) is close to the city centre and has a variety of rooms, ranging from BFr 2800 (no balcony) to BFr 3000 (with balcony) a double, plus 50% if you are two people of the same sex sharing a room.

Places to Stay – middle

The cheapest place to stay in the city centre is the *Hôtel Burundi Palace*, which has singles/doubles for BFr 2450/3150 plus BFr 1200 for an extra bed.

The *New Tourist Hôtel*, Place de l'Indépendence, has been renovated and charges BFr 3000 for a single or a double.

Up slightly in price is the *Hôtel de l'Amitié*, Rue de l'Amitié, which has rooms with fan, mosquito nets, soap and towel for BFr 3500 a double with attached bathroom. The hotel has its own restaurant but the food is mediocre.

Better is the *Hôtel le Doyen*, Ave du Stade, a splendid colonial-style building set in beautiful grounds. All rooms have mosquito nets, and soap and towel are provided. Rooms with twin beds but shared showers and toilets cost BFr 3000 a double, or there are rooms with attached bathroom for BFr 5000 a double. There are also air-con doubles with attached bathroom for BFr 8000. The hotel has a good restaurant but it's not cheap. Nonresidents can also eat and drink here.

Places to Stay – top end

The *Novotel*, Chaussée du Peuple Burundi, is the best hotel in Bujumbura and has all the facilities you would expect in a hotel belonging to this chain. As elsewhere in the world, it's at least US$100 per night.

There's also the *Hôtel Club des Vacances* on the lake shore, which is popular at weekends with the local expatriate population. Entry to the beach costs BFr 500 and there's a nightclub as well. A taxi from the city centre costs about BFr 500.

Places to Eat – cheap

One of the best places in town for breakfast is *Kappa*, Rue Science, which is extremely popular with local office workers between 8 and 9 am. It also has the best strawberry cakes 'on earth', according to a longtime resident.

A good place for excellent coffee and home-made ice cream is the *Café Polar* on Chaussée Prince Rwagasore, one block back from Ave du Zaïre. Coffee costs BFr 50, ice cream BFr 100 and a tortilla BFr 250 (very filling). They also have hamburgers.

The *Cotton Club*, in the Asian part of town, has cheap food and good rock or folk music all the time. Don't be late, as food runs out early.

Super-Snack-Sympa, behind the market, has good pizzas, lasagne and a special 'hamburger', all with vegetables, cream and tortilla bread, for US$1.50.

Very popular not only with travellers but with local people is the *Acapulco* on the corner of Blvd de l'UPRONA and Chaussée du Peuple Burundi, next door to the Hôtel Burundi Palace. It's very good, quite cheap and serves western-style food.

Places to Eat – more expensive

The *Boulangerie-Pâtisserie Trianon* on Chaussée Prince Rwagasore is a popular place for breakfast. For good snacks and main meals, the nearby *Aux Délices* is also popular, though the main attraction seems to be the video rather than the food. Meals are from BFr 1000 to BFr 1500 and snacks range from BFr 500 to BFr 1000. The service is not exactly fast as the waiters also find the video interesting.

For a splurge, you could do worse than try the *Restaurant Pizza Oasis* on the corner of Ave Victoire and Blvd de l'UPRONA. It's open Monday to Saturday from noon till 2 pm and 7 to 10 pm, and is expensive. Better, according to local residents, is the *Italian restaurant* on Ave de France just behind Le Présidence. For good Indian food there is the *Sitar* on Blvd de la Liberté close to Rue Science. If you just want a beer there is a great bar there, too, under an enormous tree.

Quite expensive is the *Cercle Nautique* on the lake front at the end of Ave du 13 Octobre. Some visitors rate the snacks at this place as good value: residents describe them as 'disgusting'. All the same, it's a great place to sip a cold beer even if you don't want to eat and you might even be entertained by the occasional hippo. The Cercle is open daily, except Tuesday, from 5 pm and on Sunday from 11 am.

Entertainment
Most nightclubs are by the lake shore in the vicinity of the Hôtel Club des Vacances. The best ones are the *Black & White* (frequently closed as the owner is Rwandan and often in Kigali), the *Bamboo* and the *Cadillac*. There's great dancing at all of them. A taxi from the city centre costs about BFr 500; it's not safe to walk. Close to town in the Asian quarter (west of Blvd de la Liberté) is *Mimosa*, next to the movie theatre on Ave des Paysans, which has a great garden. Close by is *Le Container* – which is exactly what it is.

Getting There & Away
Air At the time of writing, there were no international flights to or from Burundi because of the sanctions imposed against the Buyoya regime. Air France (☎ 26310) has its main office on Blvd Lumumba and a branch office in the Novotel. The Air Tanzania office is also in the city centre on Place de l'Indépendence. The Sabena office is on Blvd Lumumba near the corner of Ave de la Croix Rouge. Other airlines, such as Kenya Airways, are represented by the travel agent on Ave du Commerce. The international airport is 11 km from the city.

Car If you're thinking of hiring a car, ask for Freddy, whose sister is one of the receptionists at the Hôtel le Doyen (see Places to Stay). He has a convertible Suzuki Samurai which he rents out for around BFr 10,000 per day – less if you hire it for more than a few days.

AROUND BUJUMBURA
By far the best and safest beach is at **Resha**, where there are no crocodiles, hippos or the risk of catching bilharzia. It's usually deserted and the sand is almost white and very clean. Resha is one hour from Bujumbura by car but there are also buses available. The one hotel here offers circular thatched *huts* with attached bathroom and electricity until 10 pm. The huts cost BFr 5000 and mosquito nets are provided. The hotel also has a restaurant, but the service is slow and the food is not exactly cheap.

Around the Country

GITEGA
Gitega is the second-largest town in Burundi and is home to the **National Museum**. Although small, the museum is well worth a visit and is very educational. Entry is free. There might be a folklore performance – ask if the *tambourinaires* are playing. They usually play at Gishola, about 10 km away, on the last Sunday of every month.

A good day trip from Gitega is to the **Chutes de la Kagera**, near Rutana. They're spectacular in the wet season (October to January) but there's no public transport there, so you'll have to hitch.

Places to Stay & Eat
The *Mission Catholique* has a huge guesthouse and is probably the best place to enquire for budget accommodation. You should be able to get a bed here for BFr 500 to BFr 1000.

A good place to eat is the *Foyer Culturel*, which does good, cheap food but has slow service. For a small splurge, the *Pakistani restaurant* in the town centre is excellent value for money. The *Zanzibar* is a good place for a cold beer.

KAYANZA
Kayanza is on the road north to Kigali, near the Rwandan border. It has a good market on Monday, Wednesday and Saturday.

The missions won't take guests, so stay at the *Auberge de Kayanza*, which costs BFr 1500 a double.

BURUNDI

Matatus from Bujumbura cost BFr 600 and take about two hours.

KILEMBA

The principal attraction here is the **Kibabi Hot Springs**, 16 km from town. There are several pools of differing temperature, the main one hovering around 100°C. A little further uphill is a waterfall, and another deep pool where it's safe to swim.

Most people stay at the *Swedish Pentecostal Mission*, which has a very good guesthouse. A bed in the dormitory costs BFr 500. Private rooms with a shower and toilet and the use of a fully equipped kitchen cost BFr 1000 per person.

SOURCE DU NIL

This is supposedly the southernmost source of the Nile, though Ugandans dispute this. It is no more than a trickle – not exactly a riveting sight. You can stay at the *Mission Catholique* in Rutana, seven km away.

Eastern Zaïre

Area: 2 345 510 sq km
Population: 36 million
Population Density (per sq km): 15.5
Capital: Kinshasa

Facts about the Country

HISTORY

Eastern Zaïre

ZAÏRE

Area: 2,345,410 sq km
Population: 43.9 million
Population Growth Rate: 3.3%
Capital: Kinshasa
Head of State: President Mobutu Sese Seko
Official Language: French
Currency: New Zaïre (NZ)
Exchange Rate: NZ 144,000 = US$1 (official); NZ 200,000 to NZ 250,000 = US$1 (black market)
Per Capita GNP: US$185
Inflation: 4000%
Time: UTC +1 (west), UTC +2 (east)

This section covers a narrow strip of eastern Zaïre from the northern tip of Lake Tanganyika to Lake Albert, along the borders with Burundi, Rwanda and Uganda. It is included in this book because it is an integral part of the mountainous area that forms the western wall of the Rift Valley. It is also considerably easier to get to/from East Africa than from the west coast, which entails a journey through the jungles of the Congo Basin.

A full history of Zaïre would not be appropriate, since only a small part of Kivu Province is covered and many of the historical events which have taken place in the western parts of Zaïre have no connection with events on the eastern borders.

Eastern Zaïre has some magnificent countryside and many things to see and do, such as mountain treks, and visits to gorilla and chimpanzee sanctuaries and Pygmy settlements, the unfortunate thing being that the whole area is currently a no-go zone.

Facts about the Country

HISTORY
Eastern Zaïre shares much of its history with neighbouring Uganda, Rwanda and Burundi but precious little with that of the rest of the country to the west and south-west. Its inclusion in present-day Zaïre is purely a legacy of colonialism and therein lies the anatomy of the current crisis engulfing the region.

Because of the altitude and the fertile soil in eastern Zaïre, the Belgian colonialists developed many coffee plantations early in the 20th century in what is otherwise known as the Great Lakes region. They also built up the lake resort towns of Bukavu and Goma and several mountain retreats further north.

With the Belgian colonialists gone (but not the businessmen) it was Mobutu, president of Zaïre since 1965, and his cronies, who maintained summer palaces here, partly to ensure that their presence was felt in this far-flung corner of the country. Even so, that has not prevented insurrections and attempts at secession at various times since the time of independence.

Mobutu, however, was not alone in wanting to maintain a presence in this region. In few other areas of East Africa would you encounter so much Christian missionary activity. The number of different sects hard at work saving souls was, until recently, little short of amazing. The whole range of Catholic and Protestant sects were involved, as were the ubiquitous Seventh Day Adventists, Mormons and Jehovah's Witnesses. It was probably a good thing that they chose to work this area so intensively, as their schools and hospitals provided many people with their only educational and medical facilities. Few funds were available for these sorts of facilities from the central government and, because Mobutu's regime was – and still is – so incredibly corrupt, the funds for maintenance and development shrank with every succeeding year.

In the early years following independence in 1960, there was very little direct control of North and South Kivu provinces by the central government in Kinshasa and, consequently, local governors enjoyed virtual autonomy.

The attempted secession by the southern province of Shaba (formerly Katanga) under Moise Tshombe, and the subsequent intervention by the United Nations is well known. These events prompted the overthrow and murder of Zaïre's first prime minister, Patrice Lumumba, and his replacement by Joseph Kasavubu with assistance from

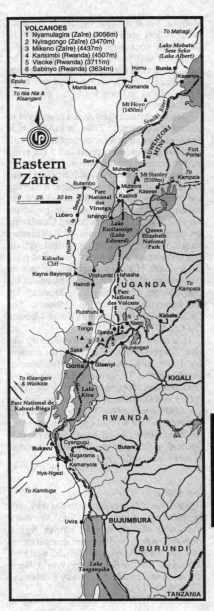

VOLCANOES
1 Nyamulagira (Zaïre) (3056m)
2 Nyiragongo (Zaïre) (3470m)
3 Mikeno (Zaïre) (4437m)
4 Karisimbi (Rwanda) (4507m)
5 Visoke (Rwanda) (3711m)
6 Sabinyo (Rwanda) (3634m)

Eastern Zaïre

EASTERN ZAÏRE

Mobutu, the army commander at the time. What is less well known is that after the Katangan secession had been crushed, Kasavubu was faced with armed revolt by the governors of the eastern Kivu provinces. His failure to crush the rebellion and bring the governors to book led to his overthrow by Mobutu in 1965.

Mobutu certainly restored a high level of centralised control to Zaïre, but the costs in terms of wasted resources, repression, jailings, executions, corruption and a decaying infrastructure were enormous.

In order to entrench his hold on power in this vast and diverse country, Mobutu, a cunning and ruthless politician, perfected a cult of personality which few other African presidents have even come close to matching. Combining the sophisticated techniques of 20th-century communication with traditional tribal symbolism, he successfully projected himself as god's gift to Zaïre. His photograph was to be seen everywhere, often accompanied by one of the many slogans underlining his indispensability and benevolence, such as 'Mobutu: The Unifier', 'Mobutu: The Pacifier' and 'Mobutu: The Guide'.

Trite and vacuous as all this obviously was given his propensity for bleeding the country dry financially, he had powerful international backers. These were the days of the Cold War and Mobutu was seen by the USA, France and Belgium as a bulwark against the spread of Communism. They were more than prepared to turn a blind eye to his excesses and the country's spiralling debt and provide him with arms so long as he continued to toe an anti-Communist line.

The 1990s

Mobutu was able to continue in this way until the break-up of the USSR and America's increasing obsession with human rights. Mobutu, by then, had become an embarrassment and his backers quickly abandoned him. Likewise, the IMF and the World Bank refused to reschedule the country's debts and pulled out in 1993.

Remarkably, Mobutu managed to hang on to power despite the chaos engulfing the country. While the army mutinied, looted, raped and trashed cities and the politicians in Kinshasa came to blows over the introduction of multiparty politics, Mobutu continued to pull the strings in glorious isolation from his palace hideaway at Gdabolite on the northern border with Central African Republic (CAR). During all these upheavals, he somehow found plenty of time to go on long – and legendary – shopping trips to Europe with his wife until the French government, perhaps out of embarrassment, banned him – though only temporarily.

The reckoning finally came in 1996 when he was forced to go to Switzerland for prostate cancer therapy. During the three months he was away, an alliance of rebel forces took control of a 500 km swathe of eastern Zaïre stretching from Bunia to Uvira and vowed to press on to Kinshasa with the stated object of toppling Mobutu. The rebels were composed largely of ethnic Tutsi whose tribe had been in eastern Zaïre for the past 150 years.

Mobutu has vowed to retake the rebelheld territory but that will be difficult without access to any of the airstrips along the eastern border. He also has to contend with rebellious, undisciplined and ill-equipped troops whose morale is at a low ebb. And, although the Organisation of African Unity and the United Nations have both hosted talk-fests on the crisis, neither have indicated any willingness to commit peace-keeping forces to the region. This is not that surprising given the complexity of the situation but a blood bath and the possible dismemberment of Zaïre are almost inevitable.

GEOGRAPHY

Geographically this area is quite different from the rest of Zaïre. It is a land of huge volcanoes and vast, deep lakes. Some of the volcanoes, such as those at the northern end of Lake Kivu, have erupted in the last decade and Nyiragongo is still smoking, but the rest are currently dormant. Others, where the borders of Zaïre, Rwanda and Uganda meet, haven't erupted in living memory and their

How the 1996 Insurrection Started

The roots of the insurrection go back to pre-colonial times when a Tutsi clan, known as the Banyarwanda, quarrelled with their Mwami (king) and migrated from Rwanda to the Uvira region where they were gradually assimilated into the local community.

Another wave of Tutsi migrants, who became known as the Banyamulenge, arrived from Rwanda in 1959 after the Hutu revolution and settled in both North and South Kivu provinces. Neither group had any intention of returning to Rwanda and considered themselves Zaïrese citizens – and were treated as such – until a new nationality law came into force in 1972 which gave the Banyarwanda, but not the Banyamulenge, citizenship. This was all reversed in 1981 when another nationality law was enacted depriving both groups of Zaïrese citizenship and prohibiting them from acquiring land and property. The stage was firmly set for a conflict between the ethnic Tutsi and other tribes, who were supported by the Zaïrese army. By 1993, some 7000 people had been killed and 250,000 rendered homeless in various clashes. Even so, worse calamities were to follow.

In 1994, around two million Hutu fled Rwanda into Zaïre following the genocide there and the victory of the Tutsi-led Rwandan Patriotic Front (RPF). The refugees found themselves virtually held hostage in camps controlled by the *Interahamwe*, Hutu extremists who had perpetrated the genocide. The extremists were joined in 1995 by Hutu militias from eastern Zaïre and together, with the encouragement of the Zaïrese army Chief of Staff, began an 'ethnic cleansing' of Tutsi from eastern Zaïre as well as mounting cross-border raids into Rwanda.

It was a serious miscalculation on behalf of the Interahamwe and the Zaïrese army command. In late October 1996, the Rwandan RPF army attacked four refugee camps in northern Kivu precipitating the return of Hutu refugees to Rwanda (and from elsewhere) as well as forcing the retreat of the Interahamwe and the Zaïrese army further west towards Kisangani. The initiative was soon taken up by the Banyamulenge who joined the Alliance of Democratic Forces for the Liberation of Congo-Zaïre (ADFL) led by Laurent Kabila. Though not a specifically Tutsi force, the ADFL drew its principal support from the Banyamulenge who had not only a political but a very real practical axe to grind, having been essentially dispossessed and threatened with annihilation.

By early December the rebels were in control of the entire eastern border region from Aru (on the Ugandan border) down to Uvira at the northern end of Lake Tanganyika and were also hell-bent on capturing Kisangani.

It is widely acknowledged that the ADFL rebels were supported by both Rwanda and Uganda – claims which both governments deny – but it's on record that, in late October 1996, President Bizimungu of Rwanda announced that his country had a moral duty to stop the genocide of the Banyamulenge and the vice-president, Paul Kagame, warned Zaïre that if the cross-border raids of the Interahamwe did not stop then Rwanda would exercise the right of hot pursuit.

The Zaïrese government in Kinshasa interpreted the Rwandan statements as a virtual declaration of war and of an intention by Rwanda of creating a Greater Rwanda to encompass parts of North and South Kivu provinces. That remains to be seen but, as the Zaïrese army and their Interahamwe allies fled west in complete disarray and indiscipline, they fed fear and loathing into every city and village they passed through by raping, looting and killing. No town or city was spared and most of them are in virtual ruins. So much for a 'hearts and minds' campaign. The rebels were generally welcomed but there is resentment in some parts against at what is perceived to be a Tutsi takeover. ∎

upper slopes are among the last remaining sanctuaries for the rare mountain gorilla.

The Ruwenzori Mountains along the border with Uganda are the highest in the region and the only ones with permanent snow cover on the peaks, but they are atypical since they are not volcanic. It's a wild and beautiful area of Africa despite the recent tragedies.

CLIMATE

Eastern Zaïre enjoys a Mediterranean-like climate. This is one reason, apart from the magnificent views and water sports, why those with sufficient money (including the president) have made Goma and Bukavu, on Lake Kivu, into resort towns. The seasons are similar to those in Rwanda and Burundi. The main rainy season is from mid-March to mid-May and the dry season is from mid-May to mid-September. The short rains last from mid-September to mid-December and the short dry season from mid-December to mid-March.

GOVERNMENT & POLITICS

Executive power is held by the president, who has a seven-year mandate and the right to appoint a prime minister of his choice, though this is disputed and has led to serious riots and the virtual collapse of central government. The legislative council (parliament) consists of 210 deputies elected for a five-year term by universal suffrage. Opposition parties have been legalised and are vocal but it's all window-dressing and Mobutu continues to dictate through the Mouvement Populaire de la Révolution (MPR). In practice, both the government and law and order have collapsed and the country is in chaos. Nothing will be resolved until Mobutu either steps down or is deposed.

ECONOMY

Zaïre is potentially a rich country, with a huge array of natural resources. Unfortunately the years of colonial mismanagement and exploitation, followed by civil war, corruption and inefficiency, have prevented this potential being fulfilled. The country's vast size (Zaïre is the third-largest country in Africa) and its dilapidated transport infrastructure have exacerbated the problems. Subsistence agriculture is the basis of most people's existence.

Copper, cobalt, oil, diamonds (Zaïre is the world's largest producer of industrial diamonds) and coffee account for the bulk of Zaïre's export income but production of all these has rapidly declined in the 1990s.

The agricultural sector contributes about 30% of GDP. Of that, 50% is subsistence farming, employing about 70% of the workforce. The main subsistence crops include cassava, maize and rice. With the terrible infrastructure, supplies are basically limited to urban areas. Zaïre was once self-sufficient in foodstuffs but now imports more than 125,000 tonnes of grain alone each year. Cash crops include coffee, cocoa, rubber, tea, palm oil, cotton, sugar and tobacco.

Essentially, Zaïre is bankrupt. The World Bank, owed US$45 million, pulled out in 1993 declaring Zaïre insolvent. Likewise, the IMF, owed US$315 million, pulled out in 1994. These events were reflected in the currency market where hyper-inflation rendered the country's currency worthless. At Z 2,500,000 to US$1 in 1994, no-one wanted to deal in Zaïres: virtually all transactions were being done in convertible foreign currency. As a suitable vignette, the Bank of Zaïre flooded the country with freshly minted bundles of Z 50 and Z 100 notes in April 1994 which circulated unopened in their plastic wrappings since, individually, they were worth less than toilet paper. Nothing has improved since then.

POPULATION & PEOPLE

Zaïre's population of about 44 million is divided between more than 200 tribes, several of which extend into neighbouring countries. Eastern Zaïre is one of the few areas in Africa where there are significant numbers of Twa People (the Pygmies). The forest-dwelling Twa have resisted attempts to integrate them into the wider economy, and many continue their nomadic, hunting and gathering existence. Tourist curiosity, on the other hand, has sadly commercialised many of these people.

RELIGION

Those who have an acknowledged religion are mainly Christian though there is a small minority of Muslims. Many of the tribes in the bush are animist.

LANGUAGE

The official language is French, but Swahili is widely spoken in Kivu Province. Most army personnel speak Lingala but this isn't widely known outside the army. Very little English is spoken. The following is a list of words and phrases in Lingala:

Greetings & Civilities

hello	*mbote*
What's new?	*Sangonini?*
nothing new	*sangote*
OK/thanks	*malam*

Useful Words & Phrases

go	*nake*
depart	*kokende*
Where?	*Wapi?*
Where are...?	*Okeyi wapi..,?*
Why?	*ponanini?*
very far	*musika*
tomorrow	*lobi*
house	*ndako*
home	*mboka*
strong	*makasi*
a lot	*mingi*
new	*sango*
dog	*mbwa*

Food & Drink

to eat	*kolia*
to drink	*komela*
things to eat	*biloko yakolia*
water	*mai*
manioc	*songo*
bananas	*makemba*
rice	*loso*
beans	*madeso*
salted fish	*makaibo*
fresh fish	*mbisi*
meat	*nyama*
peanuts	*injunga karanga*
market	*nazondo*

Facts for the Visitor

PLANNING
For details about planning your trip, and what to bring, see the Planning section in the Regional Facts for the Visitor chapter.

VISAS & DOCUMENTS
Visas are required by all visitors to Zaïre, and Zaïrese visas are some of the most expensive in the world. Transit visas (three days) cost US$45. A one-month, single-entry tourist visa costs from US$75 (US$120 for multiple entry), a two-month, single-entry visa costs US$135 (US$180 multiple entry), a three-month, single-entry visa costs US$200 (US$225 multiple entry) and a six-month, single-entry visa costs US$270 (US$360 multiple entry). Visas take 24 hours to issue.

All visa applications must be accompanied by a letter of introduction from your own embassy, except in Bangui (CAR) and Harare (Zimbabwe). You may also be asked for an onward ticket and vaccination certificates (cholera and yellow fever) but this isn't normal.

You don't need a visa if you simply wish to hop over the border from Kisoro (Uganda) to visit the gorillas at Djomba and return the following day. In that case, you pay US$50 to immigration at the border, leave your passport with them and collect it the following day. It's a scam to make money but it's cheaper than buying a normal one-month, single-entry tourist visa.

EMBASSIES
Zaïre Embassies Abroad
In Africa, visas can be obtained from Zaïrese embassies in, among other places, Abidjan (Ivory Coast), Accra (Ghana), Bangui (CAR), Brazzaville (Congo), Bujumbura (Burundi), Dakar (Senegal), Dar es Salaam and Kigoma (Tanzania), Harare (Zimbabwe), Kampala (Uganda), Kigali (Rwanda), Lagos (Nigeria), Lusaka (Zambia), Nairobi (Kenya) and Yaoundé (Cameroon).

Outside Africa, there are Zaïrese embassies in Brussels (Belgium), Berlin and Bonn (Germany), London (UK), Madrid (Spain), Paris (France), Rome (Italy) and Washington DC (USA).

Burundi
The embassy is on Ave du Zaïre in Bujumbura. Visas cost the same as in other countries, require three photographs and are issued in 24 hours. The embassy is open from 8.30 am to noon only.

Kenya
The embassy is at Electricity House, Harambee Ave, Nairobi (☎ (02) 229771). Four photographs and a letter of introduction from your own embassy are required and the visa is issued in 24 hours. Staff are pleasant and the embassy is open Monday to Friday from 8.30 am till 12.45 pm and 2 to 5 pm.

Rwanda
The embassy is on Rue Député Kamuzinzi off Ave de Rusumo in Kigali (☎ 75327). There are

three photographs required for any visa, which is issued in 24 hours. A letter of recommendation from your own embassy is generally not needed, nor is an onward ticket. There are no Zaïrese consulates in either Gisenyi or Cyangugu.

Tanzania

The embassy is on Malik Rd near the junction with United Nations Rd in Dar es Salaam (☎ (051) 660000. You will need three photos and a letter of introduction from your own embassy. Visas take 24 hours to issue and the embassy is open Monday to Friday from 8 am to 3 pm.

Uganda

The embassy is at 20 Philip Rd, Kololo (☎ (041) 2337777. It's open Monday to Friday from 8 am to 3 pm, though visa applications are only accepted before noon. You need a letter of introduction from your own embassy and three photos, and the visa is issued in 24 hours.

Foreign Embassies in Eastern Zaïre

Burundi

The consulate in Bukavu is in the SINELAC building, top floor, 184 Ave du Président Mobutu. It's open Monday to Friday from 7.30 am to noon and 2.30 to 5 pm.

Rwanda

There are no Rwandan consulates at either Bukavu or Goma in eastern Zaïre but Rwandan transit visas are available at the border for US$10. These can be converted into normal tourist visas in Kigali at the immigration office.

Kenya, Tanzania & Uganda

There are no consulates for these countries in eastern Zaïre (the embassies are in the capital Kinshasa in the west). The nearest embassies are in Kigali (Rwanda) and Bujumbura (Burundi).

MONEY
Currency

The unit of currency is the Nouveau Zaïre (NZ).

Currency Exchange

USA   US$1   =   NZ 144,000

The Zaïrese financial system is in total chaos and the inflation rate is astronomical (around 4000%). By the time you read this, it could be double the above exchange rate. What this means to travellers in eastern Zaïre is that you pay for everything in US dollars or Ugandan shillings. Zaïres are still acceptable but no-one wants them. They're toilet paper.

Even a cone of peanuts requires a fist-full of nouveau zaïres.

The easiest way to keep a grip on reality, given the financial chaos, is to assume that a bottle of Primus beer (the national brew) has always been worth about US$1, regardless of the exchange rate. So simply measure all your costs against bottles of Primus. It makes life a lot easier.

Changing Money

You can forget about banks in Zaïre. No-one with hard currency and any common sense goes anywhere near them. Bring US dollars and change them either on the street or in a hotel or restaurant – or anywhere else where change is offered. Most of the time you won't even have to bother because you will be able to pay your bills in US dollars or Ugandan shillings.

POST & COMMUNICATIONS

Forget about the post offices here. If, and when, your letter ever arrives is entirely in the hands of the gods. Should a letter arrive for you, by some miraculous feat, and even reach poste restante, there's a small charge for each letter collected. Have a US$1 bill handy – it saves messing around with nouveau zaïres and may actually ensure that you get the letter.

Likewise, forget about telephones, faxes and telegrams. You might as well be on the moon.

PHOTOGRAPHY

Bring all your film requirements to Zaïre. You will not find them anywhere.

If you encounter officials (police, immigration and customs) or army personnel, many of whom haven't been paid for years, you may be required to buy a 'photography permit' either on entry or elsewhere in the country. This is nothing more than an unbridled act of creativity on their part but don't argue about it. Basically, you pay or you waste half the day messing around. You might even get your visa cancelled and your camera confiscated. Just pay. These guys are desperados and they don't mess around.

Warning

Don't take photographs of anything vaguely connected with the military or of government buildings, banks, bridges, border posts, post offices or ports. If anyone sees you, the chances are you'll have your film confiscated and you'll have to pay a 'fine'.

TIME

Eastern Zaïre is GMT/UTC plus two hours.

ELECTRICITY

What electricity!? It's 240V AC *when* it's available but don't count on it. Bring candles with you.

HEALTH

Take precautions against malaria, it's even more important if you stay in Zaïre a long time. I've met very few American Peace Corps volunteers in Zaïre who haven't had at least one bout of malaria, despite the fact they were taking prophylactics.

Tap water is not safe to drink, so purify it first.

Another condition you might pick up, especially if you only wear thongs, is jiggers (tropical fleas which burrow under your skin). Get them pulled out at a clinic. They're easy to remove if you know what you're doing.

If you are trekking the Ruwenzoris you may suffer altitude sickness. See Health in the Regional Facts for the Visitor chapter for details.

PUBLIC HOLIDAYS

Eastern Zaïre is not a holiday zone but if anything ever returns to normal then the following holidays *may* apply:

January
   New Year's Day (1st)
   Day of the Martyrs for Independence (4th)
May
   Labour Day (1st)
   MPR Day (20th)
June
   Zaïre Day (24th)
   Independence (30th)

August
   Parents' Day (1st)
   National Holiday(14th)
October
   President's Birthday (14th)
   National Holiday(27th)
November
   Armed Forces Day (17th)
   Anniversary of the New Regime (24th)
December
   Christmas Day (25th)

Getting There & Away

AIR

The national airline, Air Zaïre, is virtually defunct except when the president, or his wife, wants to go to Europe for shopping or prostate cancer therapy. In any case, it no longer flies into Goma or Bukavu since the rebels took those cities.

The UN and various other NGOs *may* still be flying into Goma from Nairobi (Wilson) so if you want a lift (paid for or otherwise), ask around in the Dam Busters Club (a bar) at Wilson airport. You'll quickly find out if anyone is flying there.

LAND

Before attempting any of the following land routes into Zaïre, make enquiries locally about whether they're feasible and whether you'll be allowed entry into Zaïre. At the time of going to press it was not safe to cross the Rwanda and burundi borders into Zaïre.

Burundi

There are two routes to Zaïre from Burundi.

Bujumbura to Bukavu via Cyangugu (Rwanda) This route goes from Bujumbura via the Burundi-Rwanda border at Bugarama to Cyangugu in Rwanda, from where it's just a short hop across the Zaïre border into Bukavu. However, you're seriously advised not to use this route at present as much of northern Burundi is controlled by Hutu rebels fighting the central government and your security cannot be guaranteed.

Bujumbura to Bukavu via Uvira (Zaïre)
The second route goes from Bujumbura to Bukavu via Uvira (in Zaïre, just across the border from Bujumbura). This route has two variations: the first (and less comfortable) is the direct road between Uvira and Bukavu (see the Bukavu section).

The second, also from Uvira to Bukavu, goes mostly through Rwanda to make use of the greatly superior Rwandan roads. To take this route you'll need a Rwandan visa, and a multiple-entry Zaïrese visa to re-enter Zaïre. In the past, border formalities have sometimes been dispensed with so that officially, you never left Zaïre. This was because the amount of time you spent in Rwanda was minimal and you had no intention of staying in that country. This doesn't seem to happen any more, so make sure that you have the necessary visa stamps.

Rwanda
The two main crossing points between Rwanda and Zaïre are between Gisenyi and Goma and between Cyangugu and Bukavu.

Gisenyi to Goma There are two border crossing points between Gisenyi and Goma – the Poids Lourds crossing (a rough road) along the main road north of the ritzy part of Gisenyi, and a sealed road along the lake shore. It's between two and three km either way.

Once you're through the Zaïre border post, it's a couple of km into Goma.

Cyangugu to Bukavu Cyangugu is the actual border post here, but Kamembe is the town and transport centre and is where you'll be dropped off if arriving from elsewhere in Rwanda. From here, there are minibuses for the 15-minute ride to the border at Cyangugu. It's an easy border crossing and you can walk between the two posts. From the Zaïre side, it's three km into Bukavu.

Uganda
The two main crossing points are from Kisoro to Rutshuru via Bunagana (in the extreme south-western part of Uganda) and

north-west from Kasese to Beni via Katwe, Bwera and Kasindi. The Ishasha crossing between Kasese and Rutshuru is another possibility. There are more border posts further north, between Mahagi and Pakwach and between Aru and Arua.

Kisoro to Rutshuru The most reliable and, until recent times, frequently used crossing is between Kisoro and Rutshuru via Bunagana, a distance of about 30 km. This was the crossing used by travellers who wanted to hop across the border into Zaïre for two days, see the gorillas at Djomba and return to Uganda the following day. Thousands of people used to do this every year until the rebels took over eastern Zaïre. It may no longer be possible so make enquiries beforehand in Kabale or Kisoro.

There are crowded matatus/pick-ups from Kisoro to the border (nine km). The two border posts are right next to each other. From the Zaïre side there are occasional minibuses and pick-ups to Rutshuru.

If you just want to see the gorillas at Djomba and return to Uganda the following day, you don't need a Zaïrese visa. You simply give the Zaïrese immigration officials US$50, leave your passport with them and walk to Djomba. After seeing the gorillas, you walk back to the border, collect your passport and re-enter Uganda (a visa, where necessary, costs US$20, unless you already have a multiple-entry visa). Again, this unofficially may well have changed, so seek local advice before travelling.

Kasese to Rutshuru The Ishasha border between Katunguru and Rutshuru is less reliable. There's a steady trickle of traffic along this route, so hitching is feasible, and there's even the occasional taxi.

Kasese to Beni The route from Kasese to Beni via Katwe, Mpondwe and Kasindi involves hitching, unless you can find a taxi. Again, depending on the day you go, this could involve a considerable wait (though hours rather than days) going west. If you want to take this route, it would be a good idea to make enquiries in Kasese before you set off.

Central Zaïre

Kisangani to Goma & Bukavu The traditional main route between eastern Zaïre and Kisangani, on the Zaïre River, is from Komanda on the Beni to Bunia road, travelling via Mambasa, Epulu, Nia Nia and Bafwasende.

There are some diabolical stretches of road en route but it's generally passable, even in the wet season. You're looking at hitching truck rides along this route however you should make it to Kisangani in under three days.

The alternative is between Kisangani and Bukavu via Lubutu and Walikale. About half of this route is along a new highway which was destined to be completed by 1993 but came to a halt because of the fighting. There's regular transport along this route and journey times are obviously much faster than on the traditional route.

Both of these routes are definitely out of the question at present as they cross the firing line between the rebels and the Zaïrese government troops.

BOAT

Tanzania

SNCZ used to operate boats from Kalemie to both Uvira and Kigoma. For information on these boats in Kigoma, see the stationmaster at the railway station.

Getting Around

AIR

A number of private airline companies used to operate small planes between various places in eastern Zaïre but it's unlikely they will still be doing this given the current situation. The main routes were between Goma and Bukavu and between Bukavu and Kisangani and the companies which serviced them were Virunga Air Charters (VAC) and

Scibé-Airlift. Both had offices in Goma and Bukavu.

LAND

Before attempting any of the land routes in eastern Zaïre, make enquiries locally about the degree of danger involved. Many of the routes may simply be out of the question at present.

There are very few regular buses of any description, and most of the time you will have to hitch lifts on trucks. Free lifts are the exception, unless you meet the occasional Somali or Kenyan driver. Usually you will have to pay for lifts, with the price often reflecting the difficulty of the journey rather than the distance but being more or less 'fixed'.

This doesn't mean you'll be quoted the price local people pay straight away. Negotiation is the name of the game.

There's generally a truck park in every town where drivers will congregate, and it's here that you will find a lift. In small places, the truck park is usually found around the petrol station.

There's little point in quoting hitching costs on trucks, since these will change and, to some extent, will depend on your bargaining ability. To get the best price, don't be in a hurry and ask around before you have to leave.

BOAT

In theory, there are three boats which ply between Goma and Bukavu on Lake Kivu, but much of the time, at least two of them will be out of service. If they're running, it's a pleasant trip with incomparable views of the Virunga volcanoes across the lake. None of the boats call at Rwandan ports.

The boats are the *Karisimbi*, the *Vedette* and the *Mulamba*. The first two are government owned and operated. The *Vedette* is purely a passenger boat, while the *Karisimbi* takes freight, including motorcycles. Both are crowded and you'll find they are not particularly comfortable.

EASTERN ZAÏRE

Eastern Zaïre from North to South

BUNIA

This large town in the hills above Lake Albert is one of the starting points for the trip west to Kisangani via Komanda, Mambasa and Nia Nia.

If you get this far, it's worth making a side trip to the fishing village of **Tshoma**, on the lake, via the border-post town of Kasenye. It's a lively village with bars open 24 hours a day to accommodate the fishers' unsocial hours. The hospitality is excellent and the fresh fish very cheap, but unfortunately, it's not safe to swim in the lake because of the risk of contracting bilharzia.

Places to Stay & Eat

The *Hôtel Semliki* and the *Hôtel Ituri*, both close to each other, are good mid-range hotels and serve food at reasonable prices. Further down the hill in the *cité* are plenty of other cheapies.

Going up in price, the *Hôtel Rubi*, on the main street, is one of the best. Also recommended is the *Butembo II* which also serves very good food.

Getting There & Away

There used to be a few buses each week between Goma and Bunia but, as elsewhere in this region, you'll find transport is extremely variable.

KOMANDA

Komanda has a small market and a bakery. The *Hôtel LL*, about 50m from the monument on the Bunia road, offers spacious, clean rooms. Nearby, several small restaurants serve cheap meat and rice.

Trucks between Epulu and Komanda take eight hours along a very good road.

BENI

Beni is the starting point for trekking the Ruwenzori Mountains from the Zaïre side. Several of the hotels offer excess baggage

---

> **WARNING**
> When this edition of *East Africa* was being researched, eastern Zaïre had become a war zone and, consequently, a very dangerous place to be. As a result, we weren't able to do first-hand research. Since then things have gone from bad to worse. As the Zaïrese army was pushed out of one town and city after another by the rebels, its troops went on the rampage, looting and pillaging. Many towns are virtually in ruins. If the Zaïrese army ever does launch a counter-offensive (which it has pledged to do) there will be even more destruction. What this means in practical terms is that many, if not the majority, of the hotels, restaurants and facilities which used to exist will no longer be there at all or will be derelict. In the absence of first-hand research, it's impossible to say which are still standing (and functioning) and which are not.
>
> Consequently, what we have done with this section of the chapter is to list the places and facilities which used to exist before the civil war began but without details which cannot be verified. In the meantime, if, and when, things ever return to normal in this part of Zaïre and travellers begin to return there, remember that, for the local people, life must go on so there will always be *somewhere*, however basic, to rest your head, as well as food and transport. ■

---

storage facilities, though you can also leave gear at the park warden's office in Mutsora.

Places to Stay

One of the cheapest places is the *Hôtel Walaba*, about 100m down the Kasindi road from the roundabout. It's a good place to meet other travellers. You can leave baggage safely here while you climb the Ruwenzori. They don't mind if you cook your own food, though they also have a cheap restaurant.

Another popular place is the *Hôtel Jumbo*, which offers good rooms with bucket showers but has no electricity. To get there, go down the main street to the roundabout, then walk west about 30m; the hotel is on the left. Also good value is the *Hôtel Basmie*.

There's also the *Hôtel Sina Makosa* and the *Hôtel Majestic*, by the roundabout.

For a mid-range hotel, try the *Hôtel Busia Beni* or the *Hôtel Isale*.

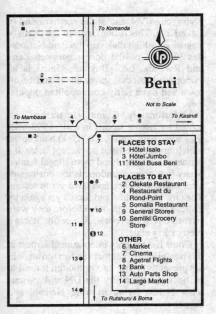

PLACES TO STAY
1 Hôtel Isale
3 Hôtel Jumbo
11 Hôtel Busa Beni

PLACES TO EAT
2 Olekate Restaurant
4 Restaurant du Rond-Point
5 Somalia Restaurant
9 General Stores
10 Semliki Grocery Store

OTHER
6 Market
7 Cinema
8 Agetraf Flights
12 Bank
13 Auto Parts Shop
14 Large Market

main road, offers doubles without shower or toilet but does have a good restaurant.

Somewhat more expensive is the *Hôtel Ambiance*. It's very pleasant, with electricity, running water, showers and facilities for washing clothes.

The *Oasis Hôtel* is a deteriorating colonial place displaying a delightful air of neglected elegance. Excellent meals are available here and there's a bar and disco. Similar is the *Hôtel Kyavagnendi* at 55 Ave Bukavu.

Other travellers have recommended staying at one or other of the three missions close to town.

Getting There & Away

There are buses to Goma; the journey takes at least 10 hours. Trucks leave from outside a group of shops on the left towards the southern end of the main street.

Between Butembo and Beni, there are pick-ups and minibuses. The trip takes about five hours. To get to Komanda takes about 14 hours.

KAYNA-BAYONGA

This town is a truck stop on the road between Goma and Butembo, particularly if you're heading south, since drivers are not allowed to travel through the Parc National des Virunga at night. As far as views are concerned, this is to your advantage, as you would otherwise miss seeing the **Kabasha Escarpment**.

Places to Stay

Although there are a few small places in the town centre, most truck drivers (and thus travellers looking for a lift) stay at the *Hôtel Italie*, about three km north of town. It has clean, concrete toilets and bucket showers (cold water). There's no electricity but kerosene lamps are provided, and there's food too.

Getting There & Away

Buses from Butembo to Goma pass through here four times a week – if there are no breakdowns.

Trucks leave for Goma early in the

Getting There & Away

There are pick-ups and minibuses between Beni and Butembo. In Beni, both the minibuses and trucks leave from the petrol station, which is down the Komanda road from the roundabout. Pick-ups to Komanda take about six hours. Trucks to Mutwanga are also available.

For lifts out of Beni, ask at the CAPACO depot about trucks to Goma. The journey often takes about 24 hours.

BUTEMBO

With a population of 100,000, Butembo is a large town about halfway between Goma and Bunia. It has a good market and excellent views of the surrounding countryside.

Places to Stay

Most of the cheapies are near the market. The *Logement Apollo II* is a reasonable place to stay and has bucket showers. The *Semliki Hôtel*, at the northern end of town on the morning either from the Hôtel Italie or from the market.

RUTSHURU

Rutshuru is perhaps the most convenient departure point for a visit to the mountain gorillas in the Parc National des Virunga, where they are found on the slopes of Muside and Sabinyo volcanoes (which Zaïre shares with Rwanda and Uganda). First make your way to Djomba. The turn-off for Rutshuru is actually about two km south of Rutshuru and is clearly signposted.

Places to Stay & Eat

Probably the best place to stay in Rutshuru is the *Catholic Mission Guest House*, about four km outside town. It's a friendly place and showers and meals are available. You may be able to camp in the mission grounds free of charge.

A cheaper option is the unnamed *lodging house* about 50m north of the police station on the opposite side of the road. It has basic rooms, bucket showers and an earth toilet.

The *Hôtel Gremafu*, close to the truck park, is very clean but has no electricity or running water. Bucket showers and candles are provided. There's a bar, and meals of meat, chips and salad are available at a reasonable price if you order an hour in advance. It's just beyond the truck park (on the main street) at the northern end of town and off to the right.

Getting There & Away

There is a daily bus to and from Goma which takes about two hours. You can also hitch with a truck for about the same price, though, in this case, it's advisable to make an early start (say 5 am), as breakdowns and/or punctures often prolong the journey. To get to Butembo in a pick-up takes about 11 hours.

It's also possible to hitch to the Ugandan border and head for Kisoro. There's a basic hotel at the border. (See the Uganda Getting There & Away chapter.)

GOMA

Goma sits at the foot of the brooding Nyiragongo Volcano at the northern end of Lake Kivu. This is not far from the chain of volcanoes which make up the Parc National des Virunga, on the border between Zaïre and Rwanda. Like Bukavu, Goma is an important business, government and resort town and has a fairly cosmopolitan population.

Unfortunately, Goma was trashed and looted by rioting troops in early 1993 after they were paid with Z 5,000,000 banknotes, which traders refused to accept after the prime minister declared them illegal tender. Many foreigners abandoned their businesses after this experience and have yet to return. The city was trashed and looted yet again by Zaïrese troops in late 1996 before they were pushed out by the rebels. As a result, it's in a pretty sorry state.

Goma has the only international airport in this part of Zaïre (not that any foreign airlines are presently flying into it, though it used to be heavily utilised by the UN and various other NGOs flying in from Nairobi and Entebbe).

Information

Tourist Office The small tourist office one block north of Ave Mobutu and not far from the post office is the place to book a visit to the gorillas in the Parc National des Virunga. It's also possible to book at Rwindi, at the radio shack, but you may have to wait a week for confirmation. It's just as easy to take pot luck, go direct to Djomba and book a gorilla visit at the park headquarters for the following day.

Places to Stay – bottom end

The best value for money in this category is the mission hostels. The *Mission Catholique* is an anonymous yellow building about 300m from the post office along Ave du Rond Point. It's exceptionally clean and quiet and is totally secure. The rooms are very small and have a washbasin. Breakfast is available.

Next door is the *Centre d'Accueil Protestante*, which is a good deal less austere than its Catholic neighbour but is more expensive. On the other hand, the rooms are much larger and the price includes breakfast and hot showers.

The budget hotels in this town are generally characterised by their advanced state of decrepitude and uncleanliness. Places which fit into this category are the *Chambres Aspro*, the *Macho kwa Macho* and the *Hôtel Haut-Zaïre*.

Much better is the *Hôtel Couboki*, at the bottom of the football field. It's not particularly clean but the toilets are passable and there are good communal shower and laundry facilities.

A much better bet than all these places is the *Hôtel Lumumba*, not far from the post office at the main traffic roundabout. Another recommended place is the *Hôtel Amani*, north of the football field on Ave du 20 Mai. It offers single rooms which can sleep two people and the staff are very friendly.

Places to Stay – middle

One of the cheapest in this range is the *Hôtel Jambo*, behind the Banque du Peuple (which itself fronts onto the main roundabout).

Much more expensive is the *Hôtel Rif*,

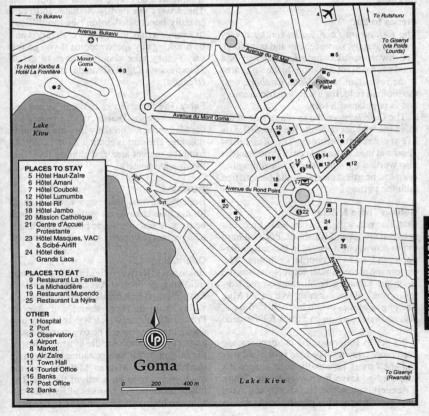

PLACES TO STAY
5 Hôtel Haut-Zaïre
6 Hôtel Amani
7 Hôtel Couboki
12 Hôtel Lumumba
13 Hôtel Rif
18 Hôtel Jambo
20 Mission Catholique
21 Centre d'Accueil Protestante
23 Hôtel Masques, VAC & Scibé-Airlift
24 Hôtel des Grands Lacs

PLACES TO EAT
9 Restaurant La Famille
15 La Michaudière
19 Restaurant Mupendo
25 Restaurant La Nyira

OTHER
1 Hospital
2 Port
3 Observatory
4 Airport
8 Market
10 Air Zaïre
11 Town Hall
14 Tourist Office
16 Banks
17 Post Office
22 Banks

Goma

To Bukavu
Avenue Bukavu
To Hotel Karibu & Hôtel La Frontière
Mount Goma
Lake Kivu
To Rutshuru
To Gisenyi (via Poids Lourds)
Avenue du 20 Mai
Football Field
Avenue du Mont Goma
Avenue Kasenga
Ave du Port
Avenue du Rond Point
Avenue Mobutu
Lake Kivu
To Gisenyi (Rwanda)
0 200 400 m

EASTERN ZAÏRE

near the post office, which offers doubles with bathrooms including hot water.

Places to Stay – top end

There are four top-end hotels in Goma but only two of them are in the town centre. You're very unlikely to find accommodation in any of them as they're usually full of semi-permanent NGO officials who are involved with the refugees. These are the *Hôtel Masques and the Hôtel des Grands Lacs*. The other two are the *Hôtel La Frontière* and the *Hôtel Karibu*. The first is off Ave Bukavu beyond the port and the other is way out, off the road to Bukavu on the lakeside.

Places to Eat

The *Restaurant La Famille*, run by a very friendly family, serves cheap and tasty food. The owner speaks some English and is a good source of information. In the same area is the restaurant in the *Hôtel Couboki*, near the football field. It's a simple African eatery and is popular with locals.

The *Café Tora*, on the southern side of the main roundabout opposite the post office, is highly recommended. The *Restaurant Yeneka* at the Centre d'Accueil Protestante is also worth a try – the food is unexciting but even the heartiest eaters should be satisfied with the portions.

Getting There & Away

Bus There is a daily bus in both directions between Goma and Rutshuru. It's a bit hard to pin down, but it leaves in the early afternoon and takes a couple of hours. The customary place to wait for it is outside the Boutique Lavao, a small shop on the Rutshuru road, 500m north of Ave du 20 Mai. The journey takes two to 2½ hours. You can also hitch this section on a truck for the same price.

To get to Butembo, the connections are even more tenuous. The road is in a bad way and the bus is in equally poor shape. It's supposed to leave from outside the Centre d'Accueil Protestante. Buy tickets and make enquiries there as to where the bus is and its

current state of disassembly – running repairs are carried out all the time. The trip takes at least 10 hours.

Minibus There are daily minibuses to Bukavu from near the Hôtel Rif. Buy your ticket the day before from the office with the corrugated-iron front in the first building back from the main road which skirts the back of the post office. The so-called road is diabolical – a single-lane dirt track full of large potholes – and the trip is exhausting.

Hitching Often there are Kenyan trucks outside the coffee depot on Ave Mobutu, waiting to load coffee to haul to Mombasa. The drivers are mostly Somalis and are a friendly bunch. It shouldn't be too difficult to arrange a ride, though you certainly won't be breaking any speed records if you go this way – they take about 10 days to get to Mombasa via Kigali (Rwanda) and Kampala (Uganda).

Ferry The three ferries between Goma and Bukavu were the *Vedette*, the *Karisimbi* and the *Mulamba*; it's unlikely they are currently running. The port is about a 20-minute walk from the market area and slightly less from the mission hostels.

BUKAVU

Built over several lush tongues of land which jut out into Lake Kivu, and sprawling back up the steep mountainside behind, Bukavu is a large (and previously very attractive) city.

Orientation

Bukavu is effectively divided into two parts, following the lines of Ave des Martyrs de la Révolution, which heads south straight up a valley from the lake shore, and Ave du Président Mobutu, which winds its way east above the lake shore. The two parts are separated by the grassy saddle of a hill. Most of the budget hotels and restaurants, the main market (Marché Maman Mobutu) and the truck parks are in the south of the city. The business centre, government offices, consulates, the huge cathedral and the ritzier parts

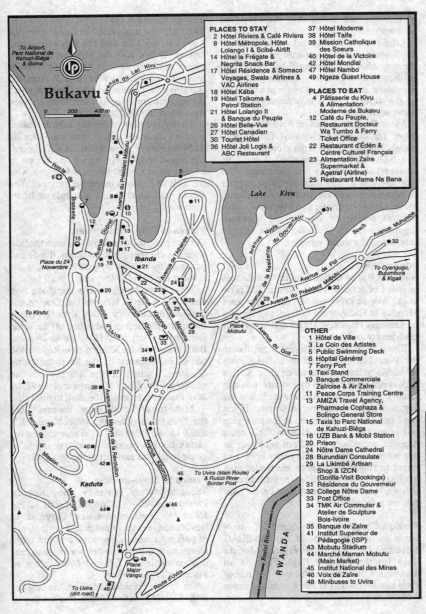

Bukavu

To Airport,
Parc National de
Kahuzi-Biéga
& Goma

0   200   400 m

Route de la Brasserie

Avenue du Lac Kivu

Avenue du Président Mobutu

Place du 24
Novembre

Avenue Dipret

Ibanda

To Kindu

Lake Kivu

Avenue de l'Athénée

Avenue Kasongo

Avenue Kindu

Avenue Maniema

Avenue Nyoia
du Gouverneur

Avenue de la Résidence du Gouverneur

Avenue de Fizi

Avenue du Président Mobutu

Beach

Avenue Muhumba

To Cyangugu,
Bujumbura
& Kigali

Place
Mobutu

Avenue du Golf

Avenue des Martyrs de la Révolution

Avenue de la Mission

Kaduta

Avenue Mahenge

To Uvira (Main Route)
& Rusizi River
Border Post

Avenue Kasongo

Place Major
Vangu

To Uvira
(dirt road)

Route d'Uvira

Rusizi River

RWANDA

PLACES TO STAY

2 Hôtel Riviera & Café Riviera
8 Hôtel Métropole, Hôtel Lolango I & Scibé-Airlift
14 Hôtel la Frégate & Negrita Snack Bar
17 Hôtel Résidence & Somaco Voyages, Swala Airlines & VAC Airlines
18 Hôtel Kéba
19 Hôtel Tsikoma & Petrol Station
21 Hôtel Lolango II & Banque du Peuple
26 Hôtel Belle-Vue
27 Hôtel Canadien
30 Tourist Hôtel
36 Hôtel Joli Logis & ABC Restaurant
37 Hôtel Moderne
38 Hôtel Taifa
39 Mission Catholique des Soeurs
40 Hôtel de la Victoire
42 Hôtel Mondial
47 Hôtel Nambo
49 Ngeza Guest House

PLACES TO EAT

4 Pâtisserie du Kivu & Alimentation Moderne de Bukavu
12 Café du Peuple, Restaurant Docteur Wa Tumbo & Ferry Ticket Office
22 Restaurant d'Éden & Centre Culturel Français
23 Alimentation Zaïre Supermarket & Agetraf (Airline)
25 Restaurant Mama Na Bana

OTHER

1 Hôtel de Ville
3 Le Coin des Artistes
5 Public Swimming Deck
6 Hôpital Général
7 Ferry Port
9 Taxi Stand
10 Banque Commerciale Zaïroise & Air Zaïre
11 Peace Corps Training Centre
13 AMIZA Travel Agency, Pharmacie Cophaza & Bolingo General Store
15 Taxis to Parc National de Kahuzi-Biéga
16 UZB Bank & Mobil Station
20 Prison
24 Nôtre Dame Cathedral
28 Burundian Consulate
29 La Likimbé Artisan Shop & IZCN (Gorilla-Visit Bookings)
31 Résidence du Gouverneur
32 College Nôtre Dame
33 Post Office
34 TMK Air Commuter & Atelier de Sculpture Bois-Ivoire
35 Banque de Zaïre
41 Institut Superieur de Pédagogie (ISP)
43 Mobutu Stadium
44 Marché Maman Mobutu (Main Market)
45 Institut National des Mines
46 Voix de Zaïre
48 Minibuses to Uvira

EASTERN ZAÏRE

of the city are along Ave du Président Mobutu.

Like Goma, Bukavu suffered heavily in 1993 when rioting troops trashed and looted the city after discovering the Z 5,000,000 banknotes in which they'd been paid were worthless. It was trashed again in mid-1996 by the same troops as they retreated before the rebel forces.

More English is spoken here than in the other francophone cities of the region, mainly because of the large presence of UN and NGO staff who were, until recently, stationed at the nearby refugee camps. The city also has a more than adequate number of mosquitoes, so have a net or coils on hand. Make sure your cholera and typhoid vaccinations are up to date: these diseases regularly used to break out in the refugee camps and the threat remains.

Information

National Parks Office The Institut Zaïrois pour la Conservation de la Nature (IZCN) is at 185 Ave du Président Mobutu and is open Monday to Friday from 8.30 am to 3 pm and on Saturday from 8.30 am till noon. The staff are friendly and helpful.

If you want to visit the plains gorillas in the Parc National de Kahuzi-Biéga, it's advisable to book at this office first. As this park is not often visited by tourists, you can usually get on a group tour for the following day, though this cannot be guaranteed. If you can't get a booking, turn up at the park gate and hope there's a cancellation. This often happens, especially as it's not necessary to pay when booking. People often book and forget to cancel. Weekends are busier than weekdays. Your US$125 fee (payable in cash or travellers' cheques) is collected at the park gate on your arrival.

Foreign Consulates The Burundi Consulate is on the top floor of the SINELAC building, 184 Ave du Président Mobutu (look for the Burundi flag). There is no Rwandan Consulate in Bukavu, but transit visas can be bought at the Rwandan border for US$20.

Things to See & Do

The only real attractions in Bukavu are the views of the lake and the city's beautiful setting. If this was the Mediterranean, the place would be full of millionaires' mansions. Take a walk past the Hôtel Riviera and out along the peninsula to the Cercle Sportif. Along here are many old villas which must have been splendid in their day.

For a good view of the city, take the minor road which heads uphill from the Place du 24 Novembre. Follow it past the girls' boarding school and keep going for another km or so. The entire city is laid out before you, with the hills of Rwanda in the background. The whole walk should take a couple of hours each way.

Places to Stay – bottom end

For camping, the *Cercle Sportif* is on the lake shore. A cheaper place to camp, if you can persuade them to allow you to do so, is the lawn of the *Hotel Métropole*.

Most of the budget hotels are along Ave des Martyrs de la Révolution. One of the cheapest hotels is the *Hôtel Taifa*. Its bar is one of the liveliest in town. Just off the same street is the very tatty *Hôtel de la Victoire*. Back in the Ave des Martyrs de la Révolution one of the cheapest of the lot is the *Hôtel Moderne*. Further up the hill towards the market are the *Hôtel Mu-ungu* and the *Hôtel Mundial*, both a similar standard to the Taifa.

At the top of the hill, where the minibuses for Uvira leave, is the cosy *Hôtel Nambo*. It's really too far from the city centre for convenience but is a good place to stay if you're going to take an early morning bus to Uvira.

Places to Stay – middle

These hotels are generally along Ave du Président Mobutu. One exception is the *Hôtel Joli Logis*, on Ave des Martyrs de la Révolution. Set in a garden and with plenty of parking space, it's popular and has large rooms with a bath and hot water. Also recommended is the *Tsikoma Hotel*, close to Place du 24 Novembre.

On Ave du Président Mobutu, the best bet is the *Hôtel Canadien*. About one km east of the city centre, almost opposite the Burundi Consulate, it's a friendly place and some English is spoken.

Up the scale a bit is the *Hôtel Métropole*, very conveniently situated in the city centre. Almost next door is the *Hôtel Lolango I*. The *Hôtel Lolango II*, further up Ave du Président Mobutu, is owned by the same people and has similar prices. The beds here are large and there are good views.

Places to Stay – top end

The *Hôtel Résidence* is in the city centre, on Ave du Président Mobutu. Rooms have all the facilities you'd expect.

The *Hôtel Riviera* has a cramped location on the edge of the lake, at the bottom end of town. It's a comfortable hotel and the service is good.

Places to Eat

There's a good choice of cheap, African eateries in Bukavu. One of the simplest, and perhaps the most atmospheric in the entire region, is the colourfully named *Restaurant Docteur Wa Tumbo*, near the Place du 24 Novembre. It's practically a hole in the wall, with no electricity and only bench seating for 10 people at a squeeze. The owner is very amenable and the food, though extremely basic, is filling and cheap. The view out the back door isn't bad either!

Just up from the market, on the corner of Ave du Président Mobutu, brochette stalls set up in the evening, and a couple of brochettes with bread are a cheap filler. Similar African fare is available from the many local restaurants by the main market on Ave des Martyrs de la Révolution.

Getting There & Away

Air A number of private airline companies used to operate small planes between various places in eastern Zaïre but it's unlikely they are still flying due to the civil war. Two such companies were Scibé-Airlift (which had an office next to the Hôtel Lolango I) and VAC (which had an office in the Hôtel Résidence).

Minibus Minibuses going north usually start

from the Place du 24 Novembre but often do at least one run up the Ave des Martyrs de la Révolution to collect passengers before setting off. If you're heading for the Parc National de Kahuzi-Biéga, hitch or catch a minibus heading for Miti.

Minibuses to Uvira (via Rwanda) leave when full from the Place Major Vangu (at the very top of the Ave des Martyrs de la Révolution, opposite the Hôtel Nambo). The trip takes about four hours.

Most travellers who simply want to get from Bukavu to Goma take the Lake Kivu ferry, since it's quicker, cheaper and smoother than going by road. However, there is one minibus daily between the two towns. The trip can take as little as eight hours or as long as 24 hours, depending on the state of the road and whether you have breakdowns.

Hitching The main truck parks are around the Marché Maman Mobutu and around Place Major Vangu.

You can also pick up trucks going north from the BRALIMA brewery, about two km from the Place du 24 Novembre along the Goma road.

Ferry Three ferries used to operate between Bukavu and Goma on Lake Kivu: the *Vedette*, the *Karisimbi* and the *Mulamba* (see the Getting Around section at the beginning of this chapter).

The *Vedette* and *Karisimbi* docked at the port, just off Place du 24 Novembre. The *Mulamba* does the beer run, so it docks at the BRALIMA brewery, two km along the Goma road.

Getting Around

There are plenty of dilapidated yellow taxis. Drivers generally hike up the prices when they see a foreigner, so bargain hard.

UVIRA

Uvira is on the north-western tip of Lake Tanganyika, facing Bujumbura, the capital of Burundi, across the lake. It's not a particularly attractive or interesting place.

The actual port area, **Kalundu**, is four km

EASTERN ZAÏRE

south of Uvira. You'll be very lucky to find a boat going south and the road south is not safe.

Places to Stay

One of the cheapest places is the *Hôtel Babyo 'La Patience'*, on Ave Bas-Zaïre near the mosque. If it's full, try the *Pole Pole*. There's no running water but it has a bar and good brochettes for sale. Another good place which is clean and quiet is the *Hôtel Rafiki*.

Getting There & Away

Minibus & Truck There are two possible routes between Uvira and Bukavu. The first goes entirely through Zaïrese territory and involves finding a lift on a truck (there are usually several daily). The route takes a mountain road on the western side of the Rusizi River via Kamanyola and Nya-Ngezi through stunning countryside. There are minibuses between Uvira and Kamanyola if you can't find a truck.

The second route goes most of the way through Rwanda, to take advantage of the excellent Rwandan road system, and there are plenty of minibuses. The trip takes three to four hours. If you use this route, you'll need a Rwandan transit or tourist visa, and a multiple-entry visa to get back into Zaïre, though in the past, this rule has not always been enforced; officially you never left Zaïre. Rwandan transit visas are available at the border.

Taxi Taxis to the Zaïre border post take 10 minutes. It's about one km from the Zaïre post to the Burundi post, and bicycle taxis are available if you don't want to walk. From the Burundi post, there are taxis into Bujumbura.

National Parks

PARC NATIONAL DE KAHUZI-BIÉGA

Lying between Bukavu and Goma, this park was created in 1970 with an initial area of 600 sq km but was expanded to 6000 sq km in 1975. It was primarily created to preserve the habitat of the eastern lowland (plains) gorilla *(Gorilla gorilla graueri)*, which was once found all the way from the right bank of the Zaïre River to the mountains on the borders with Uganda and Rwanda. Now this gorilla is an endangered species, as is the mountain gorilla which lives on the slopes of the volcanoes on the borders between Zaïre, Rwanda and Uganda.

Many other animals also live in this park. These include chimpanzee, many other species of monkey, elephant, buffalo, antelope, leopard, genet, serval and mongoose. The bird life is prolific.

The altitude varies between 900m and 3308m (Mt Kahuzi) and the average annual rainfall is fairly heavy (1900 mm), with the largest falls in April and November. The dry season runs through the months of June, July and August. Most areas of the park have a temperate climate with a fairly constant average temperature of 15°C.

Because of the heavy rainfall and the varying altitude, there's a wide variety of vegetation, ranging from dense rainforests at the lower levels, through bamboo forests between 2400m and 2600m, to heath and

---

WARNING

It may not be possible or even safe to visit any of the national parks mentioned below at present due to the civil war. All of the Kenyan and Ugandan-based safari companies which used to offer trips to the gorilla and chimpanzee sanctuaries in Zaïre have switched their operations back to the Parc Nacional des Volcans in Rwanda. You must keep your eye on the political situation and make enquiries locally before setting off.

Another danger to be aware of concerns climbing the Ruwenzori from the Zaïre side. The foothills of these mountains are home to the training camps of the Lord's Resistance Army who are opposed to the Ugandan government. A ridiculous, unprincipled and hopeless bunch of fools they may be, but they're dangerous and well armed. There's a distinct possibility you could be shot or kidnapped. This threat may disappear in the near future if the Ugandan armed forces take advantage of the civil war in eastern Zaïre and wipe them out. ■

alpine meadows on the summits of the highest mountains. Many animals tend to live in the denser parts of the forest and so are often difficult to see.

Visiting the Gorillas

There are several groups of gorillas, though you will usually see only one of the groups which has become accustomed to humans. In 1990 there were 27 gorillas in the family group. It's usually possible to get within a metre or two of the silverbacks and large females.

The gorillas can be visited any day of the year, including public holidays. Children under 15 years of age are not allowed to visit. Ideally you should make a reservation at the IZCN national park office in Bukavu (Institut Zaïrois pour la Conservation de la Nature, 185 Ave du Président Mobutu), but often, if you just turn up at Station Tshivanga (the park entrance and departure point) by 8 am, there's no problem. As most people use

Bukavu as a base, it's easy to make a booking, in which case there is no need to be at the gate until 9 am. The visit ends back at the gate at about 1 pm.

The cost is US$125, payable in hard currency (cash or travellers' cheques) at the park entrance on the day of your visit. Payment in zaïres is not accepted. The ticket you get is valid for seven days, but though you could stay in the park for seven days, it is only good for one trip to see the gorillas.

The fee includes a guide, trackers (who chop the vegetation to make a track) and a gun-toting guard (who scares off elephants). They all expect a tip at the end – so would I if I had to chop my way through thick jungle with a bunch of tourists every day!

The average tip is US$2, given to each of them back at the gate.

You must have appropriate footwear and clothing, preferably a pair of stout boots and waterproof clothes – this is not a picnic. It's often very muddy and hard-going up steep

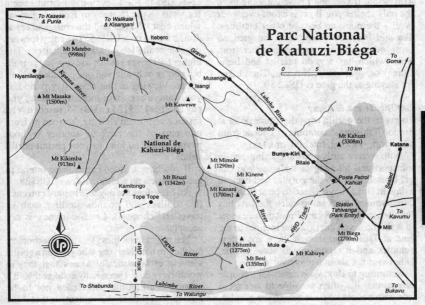

slopes. You need to be careful about what you grab hold of to pull yourself up, as many vines and other plants carry thorns or will sting. A pair of gloves is a good idea. It can rain even in the dry season.

The guides can generally locate a group of gorillas within two hours, though it can take up to five hours or as little as five minutes (unusual). If you don't see any the first day, your fee covers you for another attempt the next day. No refunds are possible if you can't return the next day.

To photograph the gorillas, you need the fastest film you can get – ASA 1600 is the best or ASA 800 at the very least. Anything less and you'll be very disappointed when you get home. When you finally find a group of gorillas, the trackers start hacking away at the bush to give you a better view. Depending on how much time it's taken to locate the gorillas, you spend about an hour with them.

Places to Stay
It's possible to stay at the park gate at Tshivanga. If you don't have camping gear, the only shelter you'll get is a roof over your head – there are no beds or other facilities. Tea and beer are available at the gate, so bring other supplies with you, either from Miti (which has a good market and basic stores) or, preferably, Bukavu. The charge for staying at the gate is US$2.50.

Getting There & Away
To get to the gorilla trips departure point at Station Tshivanga, combine or choose from a bus trip, walking, hitching or a taxi.

With a very early start and using public transport and hitching or walking, you can get from Bukavu to the gorillas and back in a day. In Bukavu, you need to be at Place du 24 Novembre by 6 am to catch the first bus (or hitch) to Miti (18 km). From there, expect to walk the seven km (gradual incline) to the gate at Tshivanga, though there are a few vehicles and it's possible to score a ride. Otherwise it's about a two-hour walk.

Returning to Bukavu is easier for a couple of reasons: it's often possible to arrange a ride with people who are seeing the gorillas,

and if you can't get a ride from the gate, at least it's a downhill walk back to Miti. If you are worried about getting to the gate in time, take two days and spend the night before the visit at the gate.

A taxi is feasible if there's a group.

PARC NATIONAL DES VIRUNGA
This park covers a sizeable area of the Zaïre-Uganda and Zaïre-Rwanda borders, stretching all the way from Goma almost to Lake Albert via Lake Edward. Much of it is contiguous with national parks in Uganda and Rwanda.

Created in 1925, the Virunga was Zaïre's first national park. It covers an area of 8000 sq km. For administrative purposes the park has been divided into four sections. From the south these are: Nyiragongo, Nyamulgira and Karisimbi; Rwindi and Vitshumbi; Ishango; and the Ruwenzoris. Entry to any part of the Parc National des Virunga (except if you're passing straight through on transport between Rutshuru and Kayna-Bayonga) costs US$45 for a seven-day permit except for visits to the Djomba or Bukima gorillas which cost US$125 and the chimpanzees at Tongo which cost US$65. The entry fees are payable at the local park headquarters. The higher fees cover you for a seven-day permit, but you're only allowed one gorilla or chimpanzee viewing in that seven-day period. If you want to see them more than once, you pay another US$125 or US$65, respectively, for each additional viewing. You can go from one part of the park to another without paying twice, so long as your permit is still valid.

If you have a video camera and intend to use it, there's an additional fee of US$25.

All these fees are payable in hard currency (US dollars and pounds sterling cash or travellers' cheques). Local currency is not acceptable.

You might think these fees are extortionate, but they're not. Everyone who goes on a gorilla viewing enthusiastically agrees that they're worth every cent. I personally endorse that. It's a once-in-a-lifetime experience not to be missed. You should also remember that if the trackers and rangers (who are local people) couldn't make a reasonable living out of taking visitors to see the gorillas, and the national parks organisation didn't have money to maintain the sanctuaries and their facilities, the gorillas would probably have been wiped out by now. Your US$125 gives them a sporting chance at survival.

The gorilla sanctuaries at Djomba and Bukima are managed by the IZCN. If you want to be absolutely sure of getting on a gorilla-viewing group, book at the tourist office in Goma. The office is open daily between 9 and 11 am and sometimes later, but it's not easy to find (see the Goma section for details). If you don't book, you can still see the gorillas if there is room (group size is limited to eight people). Usually there is room, but make sure you get a reservation at the park headquarters on the afternoon prior to your visit – otherwise you'll have to join the fray first thing in the morning when the park office opens. Be warned that if an over-land safari truck arrives and you haven't got a reservation, you may have to wait several days before they fit you in.

Djomba

Djomba is on the slopes of Muside and Sabinyo volcanoes. To see the gorillas, you must be at the departure point by 8 am to pay the fee and be allocated to a group. The fee includes a compulsory guide and an armed ranger, both of whom will expect a tip from each person at the end (US$2 is about average but many people tip more, since this is, after all, one of life's unique experiences).

There are two families of gorillas here, known as the Marcel family (23 animals) and the Oscar family (11 animals). The guides can usually find their allotted group of gorillas within an hour or two, sometimes less.

Note that other than gorilla viewing fees, which must be paid in hard currency, everything at Djomba has to be paid for in hard

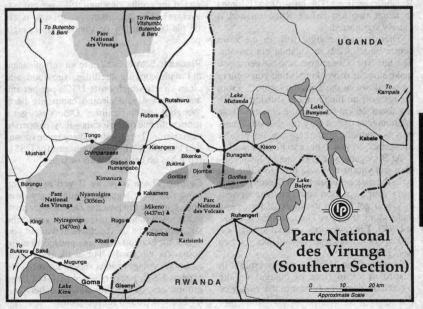

Parc National des Virunga (Southern Section)

0   10   20 km
Approximate Scale

EASTERN ZAÏRE

currency or in Ugandan shillings. No-one accepts zaïres.

Places to Stay & Eat There's an excellent hut at the park headquarters, containing two dormitories with four beds in each (good value at US$2 per bed). Clean sheets are provided and there's an earth toilet outside. There's also ample camping space with a tap and earth toilet. Camping costs US$1 per tent (if the money is collected – often it's not). If you're not cooking your own food, you can buy very tasty home-cooked meals at the park headquarters.

There's also the possibility of staying at the *Catholic Mission* in Bunagana or at the *American Baptist Mission* at Rwanguba, five km uphill from Bunagana, but neither is very welcoming towards travellers, and you'd have to make a very early start to get to the park headquarters by 8 am.

Getting There & Away To get to Djomba from Goma, first go to Rutshuru (see the Rutshuru section). The turn-off for Djomba is about two km before Rutshuru and is clearly signposted.

There's another right fork in the town centre which leads to Uganda via Ishasha. The bus from Goma goes into the centre, so make sure the driver knows that you want to be put down at the Djomba turn-off. From the turn-off on the Goma to Rutshuru road, it's about 26 km to the Zaïre border village of Bunagana over a very rough road. Transport is sporadic and there are no regular minibuses, so you'll have to hitch or walk.

At Bunagana, you'll be met by local children and youths who will offer to guide you up to the park headquarters at Djomba and/or carry your bags. Don't pass up their services or you'll get lost in the maze of farms and paths along the way. The usual tip is US$2 to US$3. The seven-km, gradual uphill walk to the park headquarters should take you two to 2½ hours.

Coming from Uganda, stay overnight in Kisoro or camp (free of charge) on the Ugandan side of the border in the village of Bunagana. Next day, cross the border into Zaïre. You need a Zaïrese visa to do this *unless* you are only going to visit the Djomba gorillas and then return to Uganda afterwards. In this case, immigration will charge you US$50, retain your passport and allow you to go to Djomba. When you return, you get your passport back. This is cheaper than buying a tourist visa (US$75 for one-month, single-entry). Re-entry into Uganda costs US$20 or US$25, depending on your nationality, unless you already have a multiple-entry visa.

Bukima

After booking in Goma, get to the Station de Rumangabo on the Rutshuru road, 45 km from Goma (about a two-hour drive). A guide will take you up the mountain (about a four-hour walk), where you stay overnight. The next morning there's a two-hour walk to find one or other of the three families of habituated mountain gorillas (*Gorilla gorilla beringei*), after which you return the same day to Rumangabo – a long day. The guides will expect a tip at the end of the gorilla viewing (US$2 per guide is average). The maximum group size is six people but this may be stretched up to eight people.

Places to Stay & Eat There's a very pleasant hut with cooking facilities, firewood and clean sheets which costs US$2 per person, and there's also a cleared camp site here, though it has no facilities. Otherwise, get a room with one of the locals – they're open to negotiation. There's also a very basic mountain hut (*gîte*), which you can use for US$1, but it has no beds, curtains or water.

Getting There & Away If you're coming from Kisoro in Uganda, a guide may meet you about one km past the Zaïre border post, at the restaurant, and offer to take you to the hut. He knows a short cut which will get you to the hut in two hours (as opposed to eight hours via the road). The walk is through mountain villages and is very interesting. He expects US$5 per person for this, but large groups can barter this down to between US$10 and US$20 for the group.

Tongo Chimpanzee Sanctuary

Tongo is Zaïre's first chimpanzee sanctuary. It's a pity there are not more as poachers are decimating these primates elsewhere in the country.

Viewing starts at 6 am, but as it can often take up to four or five hours before the group is located, expect a strenuous walk. There are also colobus monkeys and baboons to be seen, as well as a wide variety of bird life. Butterflies are everywhere.

Places to Stay & Eat Besides a camp site with toilets, shower and kitchen (US$1 per person per night), there's also the *Sokomutu Lodge*, with very clean rooms, electricity and hot water. The lodge is on a beautiful site above the village of Tongo, looking out towards the Virunga Mountains. Accommodation must be paid for in hard currency.

Getting There & Away Take transport from Goma to Rutshuru but get off at Kalangera village, about 10 km south of Rutshuru. From there, a 17-km dirt track leads you to Tongo. Market day in Tongo is Friday, so this is the best day to get a lift along this road. Otherwise, it's a pleasant four-hour walk.

Porters congregate at the turn-off for Tongo and will carry your pack to Tongo for US$1 to US$2 (though they start off asking a considerably higher price).

Nyiragongo

This volcano (3470m), which broods over Goma, used to be a spectacular sight when it was erupting but is now merely smoking. It's still worth trekking to the top for the views. Since it only takes five hours up and three hours down, it can be done in one day if you set off very early. However, a one-day trip isn't recommended because the summit is only clear of mist or cloud in the early morning and again, briefly, in the late afternoon; it's better to make it a two-day event.

The starting point is at **Kibati**, about 15 km north of Goma on the Rutshuru road. Here you find the Camp des Guides, a long, white, unmarked building set back above the road at the foot of the volcano. Either hitch or walk to this place.

The US$45 entry fee is paid at the camp and includes the services of a guide (who will expect a tip at the end). Porters can also be hired at Kibati. The trouble with porters and guides is that they'll set off with neither food nor bedding, so you'll have to provide this if you want to make the climb a two-day event. Bring all your food and drink from Goma, as there's nothing for sale at Kibati. Firewood is also in short supply.

Places to Stay It's possible to stay at the *Camp des Guides* the day before you go up the mountain but there's no regular accommodation. Many travellers buy the head guide a bottle of beer and end up sleeping on his floor. Otherwise, you can camp at the free camp site about two km south of the Camp des Guides.

Nyamulgira

You will need at least three days to climb Nyamulgira volcano (3056m), but you shouldn't have to pay the park entry fee again if you haven't used all your original seven days. As with Nyiragongo, you'll have to tip the guides extra. Bring all your food requirements and a tent, as there's nowhere to stay at the Nyamulgira base camp.

The trip starts at Kibati (as for Nyiragongo) and the first part involves a 45-km walk (two days) to the base camp through beautiful countryside. The next stage is a six-hour climb through an incredibly varied landscape ranging from old and recent lava flows (some of them with lava pools) to dense upland jungles. You may be lucky enough to catch sight of elephant, chimpanzee, buffalo and antelope, but you'll see and hear hundreds of different birds.

The first night on the mountain is spent at a decaying but rambling hut (for which you pay extra), though it is possible to return to the base camp the same day if you set off early enough. Camping is an alternative. The guides generally cook their own food.

The next day you set off for the crater rim. It takes about one hour to reach the tree line and then another hour to get to the crater rim across recent lava flows (slippery when wet). The views from the summit are magnificent. You descend the mountain the same day.

Rwindi & Vitshumbi

The main attraction in this part of the park is the game – lion, elephant, hippo, giraffe, antelope, hyena, buffalo and many others. The Queen Elizabeth National Park in neighbouring Uganda (which is contiguous with the Parc National des Virunga) used to be much the same but was sadly depleted of wildlife during that country's civil wars. You cannot hire vehicles to tour this part of the Virunga.

The lodge at Rwindi is somewhat expensive. If you can't afford to stay at the lodge, enquire about rooms in the drivers' quarters; you may be lucky and get a cheap room. There's also a small guesthouse in the nearby village but they're not that keen on taking tourists.

While you're in this area, you should pay a visit to the fishing village of Vitshumbi, at the southern end of Lake Edward. A visit to the fishing village of Kiavinyonge at the northern end of the lake, near Kasindi, is also interesting.

Ishango

This is similar to the Rwindi/Vitshumbi part of the park except that there are no elephants. Ishango is just a park camping area with a small airstrip and a derelict lodge, which you can use free of charge. Camping is preferable but you'll be charged for this. There are no fences, so it's advisable to be careful at night. Campers have encountered hyenas and leopards that have come too close for comfort.

Those who know the area well say that it's possible to swim in either Lake Edward or in the Semliki River, which flows into it. While there's apparently no danger of bilharzia (but don't count on it), they do give a strong warning about hippos. If you decide to swim, watch closely for 10 to 15 minutes to make sure there are no hippos anywhere near you. One traveller who ignored the warnings had a buttock bitten off. The wildlife and, partic-

ularly, the bird life is prolific where the Semliki flows into the lake.

To get to Ishango, first travel to Kasindi either from Beni (Zaïre) or Kasese (Uganda). It's possible to hitch, as there are usually a fair number of trucks on the road between the two places. Wait at the turn-off in Kasindi for a lift into the park. If you get stuck at the turn-off, it's three km to the park entrance. You can generally rent a bedroom in one of the park buildings, but you will have to pay the park entrance fee again if your seven-day permit expires. There is a way around this if you don't want to go to Ishango: tell them you are going to Kiavinyonge, which is 10 km beyond Ishango and is not strictly in the national park. No-one else pays to get there, as the only road in is through Kasindi and Ishango. The trip involves a ferry crossing over a river literally swarming with hippos.

Kiavinyonge

This large fishing village has a spectacular setting at the foot of a mountain range leading down to the northern end of Lake Edward. Herds of hippo wallow close to the beach and large marabou birds are everywhere. At about 6 am, the village becomes a hive of activity as fishing boats land their catches on the sandy beach in front of the restaurant and houses. The men look after the nets and the women sort the fish, which are then smoked during the day. Few tourists visit, so you're in for a treat.

Places to Stay & Eat The *Logement Spécial*, at the west end of the village, has cheap rooms. There's a *restaurant* on the lake shore which sells coffee, tea, bread and hot corned beef (of all things!) but the best thing to buy are fish and rice – it won't be found fresher anywhere else.

Getting There & Away To leave Kiavinyonge, enquire about trucks taking fish to Butembo. These leave at around 8 am and take about four hours. It's an incredible journey up over the mountains on a dirt road with many hairpin bends (not the normal Kasindi to Butembo road).

DAWN DELANEY

DAWN DELANEY

ROGER JONES

East Africa's beauty spots include Lake Kivu (top) and the mist-covered Ruwenzoris (left). It can be an adventure just getting to them (right).

DAWN DELANEY

ROGER JONES

A couple of life's great moments: coming face-to-face with a silverback gorilla in Rwanda and watching a bull elephant's ritual dust bath at Tanzania's Ngorongoro Crater.

Ruwenzori

This is the most northerly part of the Parc National des Virunga, and its major appeal for travellers is the climb up the Ruwenzori Mountains. It is also possible to climb from the Ugandan side, since the border between the two countries passes along the summits. Don't underestimate the difficulties of this trek from either side. It's much tougher than trekking up Kilimanjaro. True, some people do make it in joggers and normal clothes but they suffer for it. Anywhere above Hut Three (about 4200m) you can almost freeze to death without adequate clothing and a warm sleeping bag. Snow is not unusual at or above this point. Prepare for it properly and it will be one of the most memorable trips in your life.

Before even considering doing this trek, obtain the appropriate footwear, clothing and sleeping bag. Don't forget a woollen hat and gloves. Pots and pans are very useful and will repay their cost several times over, especially if you're trying to economise on weight by taking dried soups. You need to take *all* your own food, including enough to feed the guide and any porters hired. A stove is a good idea but is not absolutely essential.

The guide and porters are very partial to cigarettes at the end of the day. If you run out, they can become unpleasant. Leave your 'clean and healthy living' fetishes at home; these people are not trekking for fun. Sure, they're being paid, but it's not a king's ransom. Before setting off, make sure that all parties agree on what are your and their responsibilities, who pays for what, where exactly you are going and how many days the trip will take. Be firm, but remember that other trekkers will follow, so try to keep them happy. If they end up wanting to string you up from the nearest tree, I don't want to be on the trek which follows yours. Five days or more is a long time to be with people who want to battle with you at every turn.

The best selection of food is at Beni, but there are also some fairly well-stocked shops and a reasonable market (meat, fruit, vegetables, beer, soft drinks etc) in Mutwanga.

The actual trek starts when you get to the park headquarters in Mutsora, about four km from Mutwanga. Both of these places are about halfway between Beni and Kasindi on the road to Uganda.

Park Fees These are paid at the park headquarters in Mutsora, which is also where you arrange guides and porters. Fees are US$45 (park entry), US$5 (camera), US$2 (guide per day), US$2 (guide's porter per day), US$2 (other porters per day) and US$2 (hut fees per person per day). These fees must be paid in hard currency. The guide's and porters' fees supposedly include food but it's best to assume they don't, so bring enough food for them too. In addition, both the guide and porters will expect a good tip at the end of the trek.

Guides & Maps Before attempting to climb the Ruwenzoris, it's a very good idea to get hold of a copy of *Ruwenzori – Map & Guide* by Andrew Wielochowski. Published in 1989, it has an excellent large-scale contour map with the Ruwenzoris on one side and information on geology, flora and fauna, walking routes, hire of guides and porters, costs, equipment, useful contacts and weather on the other side. It's available from Nairobi bookshops or from 32 Seamill Park Crescent, Worthing BN11 2PN, UK (☎ (0903) 37565).

It may still be possible to get hold of a copy of Osmaston & Pasteur's *Guide to the Ruwenzori*, last published in 1972. The only places I know of where you can buy this book are West Col Productions, 1 Meadow Close, Goring-on-Thames, Reading, Berks, UK, and Stanfords Map Centre, Long Acre, Covent Garden, London WC2, UK.

Places to Stay & Eat A large, clean, well-furnished room at the park headquarters costs US$3/5 for singles/doubles. Camping costs US$1 per person per night, plus a vehicle charge if you have one. Most budget travellers, however, go to Mutwanga, about four km away. Here you will find an abandoned hotel, variously called the Hôtel Ruwenzori or the Hotel Engles, where you can stay (no furniture) or camp for free, but please leave a tip with the caretaker.

All three huts on the normal route have

been refurbished, so they're weatherproof and as clean as the last occupants left them. They have fireplaces and beds but no mattresses. Hut 1 accommodate 24 people, and huts 2 and 3 accommodate 12 people each.

There's also a fourth hut (Moraine, at 4312m), on the edge of the moraine, but you'll be charged extra for this and you have to sign an indemnity releasing the national parks from any responsibility for whatever might happen to you – part of the route is across bare rock with only a rope to hold on to. Properly equipped climbers can also make the ascent of the peaks of Mt Stanley.

The Trek The standard trek takes five days. The trip is: Mutsora (1700m) to Kalongi Hut (2042m), about five hours; Kalongi to Mahungu Hut (3333m), about 5½ hours; Mahungu to Kyondo Hut (4303m), about 4½ hours; Kyondo to the summit and back to Kalongi, about seven hours; and Kalongi to Mutsora, about four hours.

Variations to this route and scheduling are possible; arrange these before setting off.

Getting There & Away There are trucks from close to the Hôtel Lualaba in Beni to the turn-off to Mutsora and Mutwanga. From there you walk, though it is possible to get a lift all the way to Mutwanga. It's about 13 km from the turn-off on the Beni to Kasindi road to either Mutsora or Mutwanga.

Mt Hoyo

Mt Hoyo is about 13 km off the Beni to Bunia road, close to Komanda. Its drawcards are the waterfall known as the **Chutes de Vénus**, the **grottos** (small caves) and the **Pygmy villages** nearby. It also used to be possible to climb Mt Hoyo (a two-day trek) but the track is now overgrown and there's no longer a hut at the top. This shouldn't deter those who are determined; guides can be found at the hotel.

The waterfall and grottos are managed as an extension of the Parc National des Virunga, so you must pay for a seven-day permit, which includes the services of a compulsory guide. The guide may tell you that you have to pay him direct but this isn't true; you must pay at the Auberge. The tour of the waterfall and grottos lasts about two hours and takes you to three different cavern systems (illuminated with a kerosene lantern) and finally down to the base of the waterfall.

The Pygmy villages have seen too many tourists and are very commercialised. You'll be hassled to death and will have to pay for every photograph you take. If you have the time, spend a few days here and gradually build up a relationship with the Pygmies by trading with them or buying food from them before visiting their village.

A better place to visit the Pygmies is at **Loya**, at the first bridge over the Loya River south of the Mt Hoyo turn-off. There is a small car park south of the bridge (with a very small sign on the roadside). Park there and someone will soon appear. A trip to their village can then be arranged by *pirogue* (a dug-out canoe). So far, these people are much less commercialised and don't give you the hard sell.

If you come here on the Eka Massambe bus from Butembo (Monday and Thursday from Butembo, about seven hours), it will drop you at the Mt Hoyo turn-off at about 5 pm, so you have to make the 13-km walk to the hotel at night. It's possible to hire porters for this three-hour walk. Seven km down the road is a fruit plantation which has pineapples, papayas, avocados and bananas for sale. Buy some while you have the chance because food at the hotel is very expensive.

The hotel, *Auberge de Mont Hoyo*, is not cheap for a room with three beds, and you will literally have to beg for electricity. It's possible to camp cheaply, the cost for which includes use of a toilet and showers. Otherwise, there's a small room adjoining the toilet and bathroom which you can rent fairly cheaply (it sleeps up to four people on the floor). Meals are very expensive. Some food can be bought from Pygmies who come up to the hotel.

Tanzania

Tanzania, with its magnificent wildlife reserves, is East Africa at its best. Famous parks such as the Serengeti or the wonderful crater of Ngorongoro offer some of the best safari opportunities on the continent. While these two may be the best known of the country's numerous parks and reserves, many others deserve a visit. These range from the tiny Gombe Stream National Park chimpanzee sanctuary near the Burundi border to the huge and virtually untouched Selous Game Reserve in the south-east.

Parks and wildlife are not all Tanzania has to offer. In the north near the Kenyan border is snowcapped Mt Kilimanjaro, the highest mountain in Africa. Scaling this 5895m peak is the goal of many visitors.

Offshore in the Indian Ocean are several islands, including exotic Zanzibar, with its labyrinthine old Stone Town, ruined palaces and Persian baths, massive fort and its many other reminders of the Omani period – and that's not to mention its beaches and coral reefs.

TANZANIA

Facts about the Country

HISTORY
Early Settlement
Not a great deal is known about the early history of the Tanzanian interior except that by 1800 AD, the Maasai, who in previous centuries had grazed their cattle in the Lake Turkana region of Kenya, had migrated down the Rift Valley as far as Dodoma. Their advance was only stopped by the Gogo, who occupied an area west of the Rift Valley, and the Hehe to the south of Dodoma. Because of their reputation as a warrior tribe, the Maasai were feared by the neighbouring Bantu tribes and avoided by the Arab traders, so the northern part of Tanzania was almost free from the depredations of the slave trade and the civil wars which destroyed so many villages and settlements in other areas of the country.

Arab Traders & Slavers
Though the coastal area had long been the scene of maritime rivalry, first between the Portuguese and Arab traders and later between the various European powers, it was Arab traders and slavers who first penetrated the interior as far as Lake Tanganyika in the middle of the 18th century. Their main depots were at Ujiji on the shores of Lake Tanganyika and at Tabora on the central plain. Their captives, generally acquired by commerce rather than force, were taken first to Bagamoyo and then to Zanzibar, where they were either put to work on plantations or shipped to the Arabian Peninsula for sale as domestic servants.

It was, nevertheless, a sordid trade which devastated the tribes of the interior. The young and the strong were abducted, children and old people were left to die, and the few who resisted were eliminated. Mothers unable to carry both their babies and their ivory load were dispatched with a spear or machete. It's estimated that by the late 19th century, over 1.5 million people had been

TANZANIA

Area: 945,087 sq km
Population: 28.8 million
Population Growth Rate: 3.1%
Capital: Dodoma (official)
Dar es Salaam (seat of government)
Head of State: President Benjamin William Mkapa
Official Languages: Swahili, English
Currency: Tanzanian shilling
Exchange Rate: TSh 565 = US$1
Per Capita GNP: US$180
Inflation: 40%
Time: UTC + 3

transported to the coast and that 10 times that number had died along the caravan routes.

Zanzibar had been ruled for decades from Oman at the mouth of the Persian Gulf. By the first half of the 1800s, it had become so important as a slaving and spice entrepôt that the Omani sultan Seyyid Said moved his capital there from Muscat in 1832. Though cloves had only been introduced to Zanzibar from the Moluccas in 1818, by the end of Seyyid Said's reign Zanzibar was producing 75% of the world's supply.

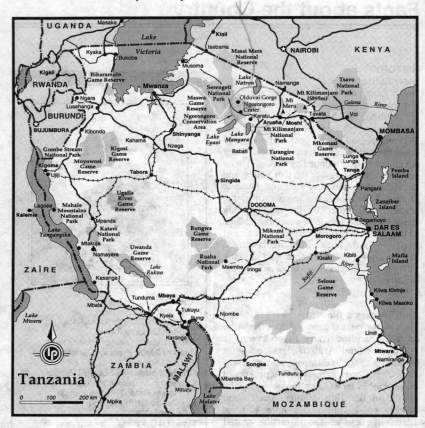

Tanzania

British Influence

Britain's interest in this area stemmed from the beginning of the 19th century, when a treaty had been signed with Seyyid Said's predecessor to forestall possible Napoleonic French threats to British possessions in India. The British were only too pleased that a friendly Oriental power should extend its dominion down the East African coast rather than leave it open to the French. When Seyyid Said moved to Zanzibar, the British set up their first consulate there.

At that time, Britain was actively trying to suppress the slave trade, and various treaties limiting the trade were signed with the Omani sultans. But it wasn't until 1873, under the threat of a naval bombardment, that Sultan Barghash (Seyyid Said's successor) signed a decree outlawing the slave trade. Though the decree abolished the seaborne trade, slavery continued on the mainland for many years, as it was an integral part of the search for ivory. Indeed, slavery probably intensified the slaughter of elephants, since ivory was now one of the few exportable commodities which held its value, despite transport costs to the coast. Slaves were the means of transport.

TANZANIA

European explorers began arriving around the middle of the 19th century, the most famous being Stanley and Livingstone. Stanley's famous phrase, 'Dr Livingstone, I presume', stems from their meeting at Ujiji on Lake Tanganyika. Other notable explorers in this region included Burton and Speke, who were sent to Lake Tanganyika in 1858 by the Royal Geographical Society.

The German Colonial Era

A little later, the German explorer Carl Peters set about persuading unsuspecting and generally illiterate chiefs to sign so-called 'treaties of friendship'. On the strength of these, the German East Africa Company was set up to exploit and colonise what was to become Tanganyika. Though much of the coastal area was held by the Sultan of Zanzibar, German gunboats were used to ensure his compliance. The company's sphere of influence was soon declared a protectorate of the German state, after an agreement signed with Britain gave the Germans Tanganyika, Rwanda and Burundi while the British took Kenya and Uganda.

Like the British in Kenya, the Germans set about building railways and roads to open their colony to commerce; building hospitals and schools; and encouraging the influx of Christian missionaries. However, unlike Kenya's fertile and climatically pleasant highlands, eminently suitable for European farmers to colonise, much of Tanganyika was unsuitable for agriculture. Also, in large areas of central and southern Tanganyika, the tsetse fly made cattle grazing or dairying impossible. Most farming occurred along the coast and around Mt Kilimanjaro and Mt Meru. A few descendants of the original German settlers still live in these areas.

The detachment of the sultan's coastal mainland possessions didn't go down too well with his subjects, and Bagamoyo, Pangani and Tanga rose in revolt. These revolts were crushed, as were other anti-German revolts in 1889. The most serious revolt against German rule, however, was the Maji Maji uprising between 1905 and 1906, triggered by resentment over a cotton

scheme. Believing themselves invincible when anointed by 'holy water' (*maji* is Swahili for water) but inadequately equipped, some 75,000 to 120,000 Africans lost their lives before the revolt fizzled out in the face of superior German weaponry.

The German occupation continued until the end of WWI, after which the League of Nations mandated Tanganyika to the British and Rwanda and Burundi to the Belgians, but not before a long and hard campaign had been fought. The famous German cruiser *Königsberg* harassed and sank British ships along the East African coast, including the *Pegasus* in Zanzibar harbour, before it was forced to take refuge in the Rufiji delta, where the British finally located it using aerial reconnaissance and sank it. Inland, the fighting was equally protracted. While steamers exchanged fire on Lake Victoria, the British were forced to transport gunboats all the way from South Africa to Lake Tanganyika to counter the German naval threat on that lake. On land, General Paul von Lettow-Vorbeck led the British forces a withering cat-and-mouse game throughout the war, including beating them soundly at Tanga and holding them at bay in the south. The armistice in East Africa was only declared two weeks after the same was declared in Europe and with von Lettow-Vorbeck still unbeaten.

The British Period

Because of the tsetse flies that made much of central and southern Tanzania unsuitable for agriculture and stock raising, the British tended to neglect development of Tanganyika in favour of the more lucrative and fertile options available in Kenya and Uganda. Nevertheless, political consciousness gradually coalesced in the form of farmers' unions and cooperatives through which popular demands were expressed. By the early 1950s, there were over 400 such cooperatives, which, shortly after, amalgamated with the Tanganyika Africa Association (TAA), based in Dar es Salaam.

Independence

By 1953, Julius Nyerere was leader of the

TAA, and quickly transformed it into an effective political organisation by amalgamating it with other political groups into the Tanganyika African National Union (TANU), which had as its slogan 'Uhuru na Umoja' (Freedom and Unity). The British would have preferred to see a 'multiracial' constitution adopted by the nationalists so as to protect the European and Asian minorities, but this was opposed by Nyerere. Sensibly, the last British governor, Sir Richard Turnbull, ditched the idea and Tanganyika attained independence in 1961 with Nyerere as the country's first president.

It was a smooth, bloodless transition and TANU was fortunate in having no tribal conflicts, dominant tribe or linguistic divisions which could have torn it apart.

The island of Zanzibar had quite a different experience in its push for independence. It had been a British protectorate since 1890, and had a 16-km-wide strip of the entire Kenyan coastline which was considered to belong to the sultan. The main push for independence came from the Afro-Shirazi Party (ASP), which was formed in 1957. It was opposed by two minority parties, the Zanzibar & Pemba People's Party and the Arab Sultanate-oriented Nationalist Party, which were favoured by the British administration. The British actively intervened on behalf of the two minority parties, denying the ASP power in three pre-independence elections so that, at independence in 1963, it was the two minority parties which formed the first government.

But it didn't last long. Angered by continued victimisation, the ASP, led by Abeid Amaan Karume and supported by TANU on the mainland, initiated a bloody revolution which quickly resulted in the toppling of the sultan and the massacre or expulsion of the bulk of the island's Arab population. The sultan was replaced by a revolutionary council formed by the ASP. A short time later, Zanzibar and the other offshore island of Pemba merged with mainland Tanganyika to form the United Republic of Tanzania. Later, in 1977, in order to promote unity and collective leadership, TANU and ASP

merged to form the Chama Cha Mapinduzi (CCM), which still rules today.

Socialist Tanzania

Nyerere inherited a country which had been largely ignored by the British colonial authorities, since it had few exploitable resources and only one major export crop, sisal. Education had been neglected too, so that at independence, there were only 120 university graduates in the whole country.

It was an inauspicious beginning, and the problems it created eventually led to the Arusha Declaration of 1967. Based on the Chinese communist model, the cornerstone of this policy was the Ujamaa village – a collective agricultural venture run along traditional African lines. The villages were intended to be socialist organisations, created by the people and governed by those who lived and worked in them. Self-reliance was the key word in the hundreds of villages that were set up. Basic goods and tools were to be held in common and shared among members, while each individual was obligated to work on the land.

Nyerere's proposals for education were seen as an essential part of this scheme and were designed to foster constructive attitudes to cooperative endeavour, to stress the concept of social equality and responsibility, and to counter the tendency towards intellectual arrogance among the educated.

At the same time, the economy was nationalised, as was a great deal of rented property. Taxes were increased in an attempt to redistribute individual wealth. Nyerere also sought to ensure that those in political power did not develop into an exploitative class, by banning government ministers and party officials from holding shares or directorships in companies or from receiving more than one salary. They were also prohibited from owning rented properties. Nevertheless, corruption remained widespread.

In the early days of the Ujamaa movement, progressive farmers were encouraged to expand in the hope that other peasants would follow their example. This enriched those who were the recipients of state funds but resulted in little improvement in rural poverty. The approach was therefore abandoned in favour of direct state control and peasants were resettled into planned villages with the object of modernising and monetising the agricultural sector of the economy. The settlements were to be well provided with potable water, clinics, schools, fertilisers, high-yielding seeds and, where possible, irrigation. This new approach also failed, since the finance for this sort of venture was well beyond the country's resources, and there was a lot of hostility and resentment among the peasants towards what they regarded as compulsory resettlement without any consultation or influence over the decision-making process.

Following the second failure, a third scheme was adopted. This was based on persuading the peasants to amalgamate their smallholdings into large, communally owned farms, using economic incentives and shifting the emphasis to self-reliance. In this way, the benefits reaped by the members of Ujamaa settlements would be a direct reflection of the dedication of those who lived there. The scheme had its critics but was relatively successful and prompted the government to adopt a policy of compulsory 'villagisation' of the entire rural population.

Despite lip service to his policies, there was little development aid from the west, so Nyerere turned to the People's Republic of China as a foreign partner. Part of the aid package involved China building the TAZARA railway from Dar es Salaam to Kapiri Mposhi in the copper belt of Zambia, at a cost of some US$400 million. For a while it was the showpiece of eastern and southern Africa and considerably reduced Zambia's dependence on the Zimbabwean (at that time Rhodesian) and South African railway systems. OPEC's oil price hike at the beginning of the 1970s, however, led to a financial crisis and Tanzania was no longer able to afford any more than essential maintenance of the railway. There were also serious fuel shortages. As a result, the railway no longer functioned anywhere near as well as it did when first built, though things have recently been improving.

Tanzania's experiment in radical socialism and self-reliance might have been a courageous path to follow in the heady days following independence, and during the 1970s when not only Tanzania but many other African countries were feeling the oil price pinch. However, only romantics would argue with the assessment that it failed. The transport system fell into ruin, agricultural production became stagnant, the industrial sector limped along at well under 50% capacity, and virtually all economic incentives were eliminated. Obviously, numerous factors contributed to Tanzania's woes, and many of them were beyond its control, not least the fact that Tanzania is one of the world's poorest countries – at least, that was true of the mainland, for Zanzibar was one of the most prosperous countries in Africa at the time of independence.

Part of the trouble was that Nyerere had no intention of changing and he tolerated no dissent. In 1979, Tanzanian jails held more political prisoners than South Africa's, though over 6000 were freed late that year and a further 4400 the following year. Even though Nyerere is no longer president, his influence lingers on. Ali Mwinyi (president of Tanzania from 1986 to 1995) successfully distanced himself from Nyerere and his policies, but the pace of change remained slow, and corruption, especially in the ports, continued apace.

Tanzania's other major drain on its economy during the Nyerere years was its support for the African liberation movements in Angola, Mozambique, Zimbabwe and South Africa. It paid dearly for this but what cut it to the bone was Nyerere's offer of sanctuary to Ugandan political exiles, particularly Milton Obote, during Idi Amin's regime in Uganda.

In October 1978, Idi Amin sent his army into northern Tanzania and occupied the Kagera salient, and also sent in his air force to bomb the Lake Victoria ports of Bukoba and Musoma. It was done, so he said, to teach Tanzania a lesson for supporting exiled groups hostile to his regime, but it's more likely that it was a diversionary movement

TANZANIA

to head off a mutiny among his restless troops.

As Tanzania had hardly any army worth mentioning, it took several months to scrape together a people's militia of 50,000 men and get them to the front. They were ill-equipped and poorly trained but they utterly routed the Ugandans – supposedly Africa's best trained and best equipped army at the time. The Ugandans threw down their weapons and fled and the Tanzanians pushed on into Uganda. A 12,000-strong Tanzanian contingent stayed in the country for some time to maintain law and order and to ensure that Nyerere could exert a significant influence over the choice of Amin's successor. The war cost Tanzania around US$500 million, and it received not a single contribution from any source.

Multiparty Politics

With the fall of communism in Europe at the beginning of the 1990s, the writing on the wall became clear for Tanzania. Aid donors, particularly the Scandinavian countries, were no longer prepared to bail out the economy in the face of widespread corruption which just about matched the amount of aid which was flowing into the country. Demands were made for a cleanup and the replacement of ministers held responsible. When this failed to eventuate, aid was abruptly withheld by all four Scandinavian countries. Other donors promptly followed suit and the country was plunged into a financial crisis. Heads rolled (metaphorically speaking) and opponents of the CCM hegemony became more vocal in their demand for multiparty elections. The US government, the IMF and the World Bank were quickly drawn into the fray, and by the time the dust had settled, several ministers had been sacked, the currency, previously pegged at a totally unrealistic level vis-a-vis the 'hard' currencies, had been floated, opposition parties had been legalised and a date set for multiparty elections.

The elections were duly held in October 1995 but described by some as a complete shambles. It was, nevertheless, true that the ruling CCM won comparatively easily on the mainland (four million votes to 1.8 million) under the leadership of Benjamin Mkapa, but the result on Zanzibar was a virtual stalemate where the CCM lost every one of its 21 seats on Pemba island, giving the incumbent president, Salmin Amour, only 50.2% of the vote as opposed to the 49.8% of his sole rival, Seif Shariff Hamad, of the CUF. Of the nearly 333,900 who had voted on the islands, over 4900 had spoilt their ballot papers – enough to change the result. Even Nyerere intervened in the ensuing uproar, telling the Electoral Commission Chairman, Zuir Mzee, that he could not afford to have a CUF victory even though he (Mzee) had initially declared Hamad the victor. Amour was reinstated as president of Zanzibar but the conflict burns on.

Benjamin Mkapa was declared the new president of the union. Meanwhile the donor nations prevaricated about whether to hand over the promised US$1 billion in aid but eventually concluded, however reluctantly, that the election result reflected the voters' wishes and came up with the cash. Nevertheless, the elections reactivated tribal allegiances particularly among the Chagga (Mt Kilimanjaro region) despite all the years of Ujamaa.

It's very unlikely that Tanzania will dissolve into the tribal conflicts which have plagued Kenya over the last five years so there's no cause for alarm, but the near stalemate on the islands is unlikely to go away so easily.

GEOGRAPHY

A land of plains, lakes and mountains with a narrow coastal belt, Tanzania is East Africa's largest country. The bulk of its 945,087 sq km is a highland plateau, some of it desert or semidesert and the rest savannah and scattered bush. Much of the plateau is relatively uninhabited because the tsetse fly prevents stock raising. The highest mountains – Meru (4556m) and Kilimanjaro (Africa's highest at 5895m) – are in the north-east, along the border with Kenya.

Along the coast is a narrow low-lying strip and offshore are the islands of Zanzibar,

Pemba and Mafia. More than 53,000 sq km of the country is covered by inland lakes, most of them in the Rift Valley.

CLIMATE

Tanzania's widely varying geography accounts for its variety of climatic conditions. Much of the country is a high plateau, where the altitude considerably tempers what would otherwise be a tropical climate. In many places, it can be quite cool at night; on the Makonde Plateau, in the south, it's decidedly cold at night.

The coastal strip along the Indian Ocean and the offshore islands of Pemba, Zanzibar and Mafia have a hot, humid, tropical climate, tempered by sea breezes. The high mountains are in the north-east, along the Kenyan border, and this area enjoys an almost temperate climate for most of the year.

The long rainy season is from April to May, when it rains virtually every day. The short rains fall during November and December, though it frequently rains in January, too.

GOVERNMENT & POLITICS

Executive power rests with the president and the ruling Chama Cha Mapinduzi (CCM or 'Party of the Revolution'). The national assembly consists of 297 members, the majority of which are CCM and the minority CUF members. The president and the national assembly are elected for five-year terms. Both the prime minister of Tanzania and the president of Zanzibar are vice presidents of the Republic of Tanzania.

ECONOMY

Tanzania, or Tanganyika as it once partly was, was always the poor cousin of the British colonial Kenya-Uganda-Tanganyika trio. Although it did not have the problem of a large influx of European settlers, Tanzania was still a seriously underdeveloped country at the time of independence. Things have not improved – the economy is still overwhelmingly agricultural and, overall, has been marked mostly by mismanagement and decline.

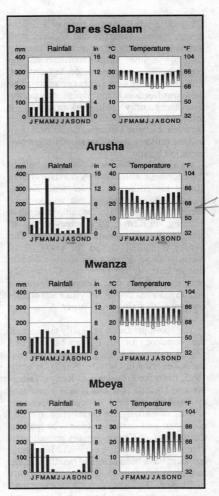

Sisal, a fibre plant used for cordage, is the leading export. Other cash crops are cloves (80% of world supply), coffee, cotton, coconuts, tea, cashew nuts and timber. Diamonds, gold, tin and mica are mined.

Perhaps Tanzania's economy wouldn't have got into such a difficult state if the East African Economic Community had been

TANZANIA

allowed to work. At the time of independence, Kenya, Tanzania and Uganda were linked in an economic union which shared a common airline, telecommunications and postal facilities, transportation and customs. Their currencies were freely convertible and there was freedom of movement. Any person from one country could work in another. It fell apart in 1977 due to political differences between socialist Tanzania, capitalist Kenya and the military chaos that stood for government in Uganda.

As a result of Kenya grabbing the bulk of the economic community's assets, Nyerere closed his country's border with Kenya. Though one idea behind this was to force tourists to fly directly to Tanzania rather than entering via Kenya, all it achieved was an alarming loss of tourism for Tanzania. The border remained closed for years. Until recently, about the only remaining evidence that an East African Economic Community once existed was that Kenyans, Ugandans and Tanzanians could still visit each other's country with a simple ID paper. A passport was not required.

The stand-off faded gradually throughout the presidency of Ali Hassan Mwinyi and gained momentum once Yoweri Museveni had taken over in Uganda. Finally, in early 1995, the three presidents of Kenya, Tanzania and Uganda met and signed a protocol establishing the East African Cooperation which, essentially, re-established the old economic and customs union – at least in theory. Moi, of Kenya, initially prevaricated (due mainly to a falling out with Museveni), but there have been practical benefits. Trade has been liberalised, border restrictions minimised, the Lake Victoria steamers and railway connections between Kenya and Uganda and Tanzania restored. There's still a long way to go before it becomes a reality but at least a start has been made. Decades of mistrust and accusations don't exactly engender instant cordial relations.

POPULATION & PEOPLE
The population of Tanzania is about 29 million. There are more than 100 tribal groups, the majority of which are of Bantu origin. The Arab influence on Zanzibar and Pemba islands is evident in the people, who are a mix of Shirazis (from Persia), Arabs, Comorians (from the Comoros Islands) and Bantu from the mainland, though the latter predominate. People of Asian descent are a significant minority especially in the towns and cities. Europeans (either by descent or expatriate) are a smaller minority.

The major non-Bantu people are the Maasai (Nilotic speakers) who inhabit the north-eastern section of Tanzania. These days the Maasai occupy only a fraction of their former grazing grounds and have been forced to share it with some of Tanzania's most famous national parks and game reserves. Although some of the southern clans have built permanent villages and planted crops, their northern cousins have retained their pastoral habits and are the least affected by, or interested in, the mainstream of modern Tanzania.

Most of the other tribes of this country have more or less given up their traditional customs under the pressure of Nyerere's drive to create a unified nation which cuts across tribal divisions.

EDUCATION
Tanzania may be a poor country but virtually every child goes to school for eight years. Facilities in the rural areas are primitive, less so in the urban areas, but literacy is high. Instruction is in Swahili; English is the second language. What happens after primary school is very much dependent on family fortunes, and university education is only a distant possibility.

SOCIETY & CONDUCT
One of the first impressions you might gain from this country is the modesty of its people. If you behave in a similar fashion, you'll make plenty of friends and they'll be your friend forever. This isn't San Francisco, New York, London, Bangkok or Sydney. Leave all that at home. You can be as eccentric as you like (they might even like that!) but don't be arrogant. Give your mouth a rest

TANZANIA

and listen – and learn some Swahili in the process. It's received with warmth and a smile. You'll never have a problem in this society if you make a friend. And, while you're doing this, cast a glance at the way they dress. Like their attitude, it's modest. Take a leaf from their book and do the same – especially in strongly Muslim cultures like Zanzibar and Pemba. You have no right to outrage these people. You're just a visitor. Respect their customs.

Too many travellers ignore this aspect of conduct and dress and that's the sort of thing which breeds resentment. Don't contribute to it. Dress modestly and be polite. They'll reciprocate in kind. *Tafadhali* ('please') goes a long way in Tanzania. It might not cut the ice in Kenya where *Weh!* ('Hey, you!') is, all too often, the way to address a person, but it certainly greases the wheels of social interaction in Tanzania.

Please think about this. Others will come after you.

RELIGION

The two main religions are Christianity (31%) and Islam (42%), with Hindus accounting for around 25%. The majority of Muslims are concentrated along the coast and in the islands. Islam has been around ever since Arab traders arrived here in the 12th century. Not until the 19th century did Christianity make any impact, and then it was mainly among the tribes of the interior. The principal Christian sects are Catholic, Lutheran, Anglican, Presbyterian and Orthodox.

On the other hand, there are still many tribes who follow neither of the majority religions and instead worship the ancient spirit of their choice. Principal among them are the Maasai, who place their faith in the god Engai and his Messiah, Kindong'oi, from whom their priests are descended. Worship is conducted under special fig trees or at Ol Doinyo Lengai, 'the mountain of god'. This volcanic mountain is north-east of Ngorongoro Crater.

In Tanzania, as in many African countries, religion plays an important part in the availability of educational and medical facilities, as is obvious from the number of schools, clinics and hospitals attached to mosques and churches. It's claimed, however, that no religious bias exists in the country's political and civil administration.

LANGUAGE

Swahili (KiSwahili) and English are the official languages; English is widely spoken and is the principal language of commerce. There are also many local African languages, reflecting the tribal diversity of the country. Outside the cities and towns, far fewer local people speak English than you would find in comparable areas in Kenya. It's said that the Swahili spoken in Zanzibar is of a much purer form than that which you find in Kenya (at least, that's their story – but the Kenyans agree), and quite a few travellers come here to learn it, since the Institute of KiSwahili & Foreign Languages is on the island.

Facts for the Visitor

HIGHLIGHTS

Top of the list for Tanzania has to be a trek up Mt Kilimanjaro, the highest mountain in Africa. Few travellers get this far without an attempt on the snowcapped summit of Mawenzi – though not everyone makes it!

The other drawcards are the world-famous national parks/reserves of Ngorongoro Crater and the Serengeti. These vast parks with their prolific wildlife and annual wildebeest migration need no introduction, and will etch themselves onto your memory and stay with you for the rest of your life.

From endless blue-hued vistas and wildlife beyond imagination, you can immerse yourself in the romantic, narrow streets of East Africa's most substantial and famous Swahili city-state – Zanzibar, the spice capital of Africa and the place through which many of the European explorers passed on their way into the interior in the 19th century. It's all still there, mostly intact, including the palaces of the sultans, and lateen-sailed dhows still drift silently along the waterfront in the setting sun.

And, when you've finished your romantic reveries, you can pull on a modern wet suit and tanks and go scuba diving off the coral reefs which ring this island or even those further north of Pemba island.

Then you can head north-west to the Gombe Stream National Park and meet the chimpanzees and, later, sail down Lake Tanganyika on the historic steamer MV *Liemba*, built by the Germans in 1914. It's still going strong despite being scuttled during WWI and later raised and put back in service.

Further afield there's the vast, untouched wilderness of the Selous Game Reserve and, in the very south, the Makonde Plateau where the carving of the same name originated.

TOURIST OFFICES
Local Tourist Offices

The Tanzania Tourist Corporation (TTC) has offices in Dar es Salaam (☎ (051) 2485), Maktaba St, PO Box 2485, and Zanzibar (☎ (054) 32344), Livingstone House, PO Box 216.

The TTC can make bookings for you at any of the large hotels and national park lodges under their control.

Tourist Offices Abroad

The TTC has offices in the following countries:

Germany
: Kaiserstrasse 13, 6000 Frankfurt Main 1 (☎ (069) 280154)

Italy
: Palazzo Africa, Largo Africa 1, Milano (☎ (02) 432870)

Sweden
: Oxtorgsgatan 2-4, PO Box 7627, 102 94 Stockholm (☎ (08) 216700)

UK
: 43 Hertford St, London W1 (☎ (0171) 499 8951)

USA
: 201 East 42nd St, New York, NY 10017 (☎ (212) 986 7124)

VISAS & DOCUMENTS

Visas are required by all visitors to Tanzania, except nationals of most Commonwealth countries (Canada and the UK excepted), Scandinavian countries, the Republic of Ireland, Rwanda, Romania and Sudan. For these nationalities, a free visitor's pass, valid for one to three months, is obtainable at the point of entry (you'll be asked how long you want to stay – three months is no problem).

The cost of a visa depends on your nationality: US$55 for British nationals, US$45 for Americans, US$26 for Japanese, US$16 for Germans, and US$10 for others, usually valid for three months.

Visa Extensions

Extensions to a visitor's pass or a visa can be made at an immigration office in any of the major towns and cities. You'll be allowed up to a further three months. If there's no

HIGHLIGHTS

	REGION	COMMENTS
Natural Beauty Spots		
Zanzibar A traveller's magnet – Coastal Swahili par excellence, Old Stone Town, ex-sultans' palaces, museums, east coast beaches, spice tours, the best coral reefs on the East African coast, scuba diving and wood carving.	The Coast	This place has an irresistable charm and mystique. But be warned – once you arrive you may not want to leave.
Makonde Plateau Home of the original Makonde carvings, coffee plantations and virtually free of tourists.	Southern Tanzania	Rarely visited by travellers and getting there involves a series of bus rides and overnight stays but this superb part of the country is unlikely to disappoint.
National Parks & Reserves		
Mt Kilimanjaro Africa's highest mountain; soak up the splendour of the snow-capped peaks.	North-Eastern Tanzania	One of Africa's most awesome sights. Realise the dream of scaling the summit, watching the dawn break and gazing out over the vast African plains.
Mt Meru Snow-capped and packed with wildlife.	North-Eastern Tanzania	Amazing wildlife viewing nestled within a mixture of lush forest and bare rock engulfed by a spectacular crater.
Serengeti National Park Where wildebeest migrate across vast plains and landscape in search of precious grassland.	North-Eastern Tanzania	Nowhere else on earth will you see wildebeest, gazelle, zebra and antelope in such enormous, mind boggling numbers. Gently rolling savannah plains makes spotting wildlife easy.
Ngorongoro Crater One of the world's largest calderas containing prolific wildlife.	North-Eastern Tanzania	The views from the crater rim are positively majestic and the wildlife plentiful. The crater floor has been compared to Noah's Ark and the Garden of Eden.
Selous Game Reserve Vast expanses of wilderness virtually untouched by humans.	Southern Tanzania	Probably the world's largest game reserve – marvel at what may be the highest concentration of elephant, buffalo, crocodile, hippo and hunting dog on earth.
Gombe Stream National Park Nestled snugly on the shores of Lake Tanganyika is Jane Goodall's remarkable chimpanzee sanctuary.	Central & North-Western Tanzania	Mingle with the adorable chimps at this tiny but popular national park.

TANZANIA

immigration office where you are then go to a police station and make enquiries there.

Zanzibar and Pemba jealously cling to their semiautonomous status in the Union of Tanganyika and Zanzibar so, on arrival there, you will have to go through immigration again. You'll be asked how long you wish to stay. Up to one month is no problem, but get this right because if you overstay they'll attempt to 'fine' you when you want to leave.

Getting Other Visas in Tanzania

The following visas can be picked up in Tanzania:

Burundi
Visas cost US$20 (or the equivalent in local currency), require two photos and are issued in 24 hours. At the consulate in Kigoma, visas cost US$20, require two photographs and are issued while you wait.

Francophone Countries
Dar es Salaam is a good place to stock up on francophone country visas (Central African Republic, Chad etc). As there are very few of these embassies in the capital you must get them all from the French Embassy.

Kenya
Visas cost US$30 (or equivalent in local currency), require two photographs and take 24 hours to be issued.

Rwanda
Visas cost US$20 (or equivalent in local currency), require two photographs and take 24 hours to be issued. They're valid for a stay of one month.

Uganda
Visas cost US$20 or US$25, depending on your nationality, require two photographs and are issued in 24 hours.

Zaïre
A single/multiple-entry visa costs US$75/120 for one month, US$135/180 for two months and US$200/225 for three months. Three photographs and a letter of recommendation are required from your own embassy. Visas are issued in 24 hours.

Travel Permits

If you bring a vehicle across a border into Tanzania you will have to buy a 90-day road permit for TSh 1000.

EMBASSIES
Tanzanian Embassies Abroad

Tanzania maintains the following embassies in the region:

Burundi
Ave de l'ONU, Bujumbura
Kenya
Continental House, corner of Uhuru Highway and Harambee Ave, Nairobi; PO Box 47790. Open 8.30 am to noon (☎ (02) 331056; fax 218269).
Palli House, Nyerere Ave, Mombasa. Open weekdays from 8.30 am to 12.30 pm and 2.30 to 5 pm (☎ (011) 229595; fax 227077).
Rwanda
Ave Paul VI near Ave de Rusumo, Kigali (☎ 76074)
Uganda
6 Kagera Rd, Kampala (☎ (041) 256272)

There are also Tanzanian embassies in Addis Ababa (Ethiopia), Bonn (Germany), Brussels (Belgium), Cairo (Egypt), Conakry (Guinea), Geneva (Switzerland), The Hague (Netherlands), Harare (Zimbabwe), Khartoum (Sudan), Kinshasa (Zaïre), Lagos (Nigeria), London (UK), Lusaka (Zambia), New Delhi (India), New York (USA), Ottawa (Canada), Paris (France), Rome (Italy), Stockholm (Sweden), Tokyo (Japan) and Washington DC (USA).

Foreign Embassies in Tanzania

Foreign embassies in Dar es Salaam include:

Belgium
7th Floor, NIC Investment House, Samora Ave (☎ 46968). Open Monday to Friday from 8 am to 2 pm.
Burundi
Plot 1007, Lugalo Rd (☎ 46307). Open Monday to Friday from 8 am to 3 pm.
Canada
38 Mirambo St, Garden Ave (☎ 46000). Open Monday to Friday from 7.30 am to 3 pm.
Denmark
Ghana Ave (☎ 46319). Open Monday to Friday from 8 am to 1 pm.
Egypt
24 Garden Ave (☎ 32158). Open Monday to Friday from 8.30 am to 2.30 pm.
France
Corner of Bagamoyo and Kulimani Rds (☎ 66021). Open Monday, Tuesday, Wednesday

and Friday from 8.30 am to 2 pm and Thursday from 8 am to 4 pm.

Germany
10th Floor, NIC building, Samora Ave (☎ 46334). Open Monday to Friday from 8 am to noon.

India
11th Floor, NIC building, Samora Ave (☎ 33754). The consular section is at 28 Samora Ave (☎ 20295). Open Monday to Thursday from 8 am to 3.30 pm and on Friday from 8 am to 6 pm.

Italy
316 Lugalo Rd (☎ 46352). Open Monday and Tuesday from 7.30 am to 1 pm and 3.30 to 6 pm, Wednesday and Friday from 7.30 am to 1 pm, and Thursday from 7.30 am to 1 pm and 3.30 to 7 pm.

Japan
Plot 1018, Ali Mwinyi Rd (☎ 46356). Open Monday to Friday from 8.30 am to 3.30 pm.

Kenya
14th Floor, NIC building, Samora Ave (☎ 46362; fax 46519). Open Monday to Friday from 8 am to 3 pm (visa applications accepted from 9 am).

Madagascar
143 Malik Rd (☎ 29442). Open Monday to Friday from 8 am to 2 pm and on Saturday from 8 am till noon.

Malawi
6th Floor, NIC building, Samora Ave (☎ 46673). Open Monday to Friday from 8 am till noon and 2 to 5 pm.

Mozambique
25 Garden Ave (☎ 33062). Open Monday to Friday from 8.30 am to 4 pm.

Netherlands
2nd Floor, New ATC building, corner of Garden Ave and Ohio St (☎ 46391). Open Monday to Friday from 8 am to 3 pm.

Pakistan
149 Malik Rd (☎ 27972). Open Monday to Thursday from 7.30 am to 3.30 pm, on Friday from 7.30 to 11.30 am, and also on Saturday from 8 am to 1 pm.

Rwanda
32 Ali Mwinyi Rd (☎ 46502). Open Monday to Friday from 8 am to 12.30 pm and 2 to 5 pm.

South Africa
c/o Oysterbay Hotel, Touré Drive, Oyster Bay (☎ 68062)

Sudan
64 Ali Mwinyi Rd (☎ 46509). Open Monday to Friday from 8.30 am to 3.30 pm.

Uganda
7th Floor, Extelecoms building, Samora Ave (☎ 31004; fax 46256). Open Monday to Friday from 8 am to 3.45 pm.

UK
Hifiadhi House, Samora Ave (☎ 29601). Open Monday to Friday from 7.30 am to 2.20 pm.

USA
36 Laibon Rd (☎ 66010). Open Monday to Friday from 7.30 am to 4 pm.

Zaïre
438 Malik Rd (☎ 66000). Open Monday to Friday from 8 am to 3 pm.

Zambia
5/9 Sokoine Drive at Ohio St (☎ 46383). Open Monday to Friday from 8 am to noon and 2 to 4.30 pm.

Zimbabwe
6th Floor, NIC building, Samora Ave (☎ 46259). Open Monday to Friday from 8.30 am to 1 pm and 2 to 4 pm.

The nearest Australian, Eritrean and New Zealand high commissions are in Nairobi.

MONEY
Currency
The unit of currency is the Tanzanian shilling (TSh). There are bills of TSh 5000, 2000, 1000, 500, 200 and 100, and coins of TSh 100, 50, 20, 10 and five shillings.

Currency Exchange

US$1	=	TSh 565 (cash)
US$1	=	TSh 520 (travellers' cheques)
UK£1	=	TSh 840 (cash)
UK£1	=	TSh 810 (travellers' cheques)

Despite the liberalisation of the currency, there is still an official exchange rate, which is US$1 = TSh 345. This will only affect you if you use international credit cards, in which case you'll be billed at the official exchange rate – not the foreign exchange (forex) rate, except in the case of American Express which will bill you at the forex rate *if* the card is used for payment of a bill of A$1000 or over. If it's less than that, they bill you at the official rate of exchange. Disregarding that one severely limiting proviso, it obviously makes sense not to use credit cards in Tanzania unless you have no alternative.

The export of Tanzanian shillings is officially limited to TSh 200; import is officially prohibited. However, no-one cares about this any more.

Changing Money
Forex Bureaus There are forex bureaus in most towns and cities where you can change

cash or travellers' cheques at the prevailing free market exchange rate. You can do the same at the Commercial Bank of Tanzania. The day's rates are prominently displayed at both places and there's no messing about. A transaction takes a couple of minutes. There is no black market for hard currency so, if anyone offers you substantially more than the forex or bank rates, forget it. You're being set up for a robbery.

If you need to change money where there are no forex bureaus, the banks will only change at the official rate. Why? Because you have no choice! There are forex bureaus at Namanga, Arusha, Moshi, Dar es Salaam, Zanzibar, Mwanza and various other places, but none in Morogoro or Bukoba, for instance. The forex bureau at Dar es Salaam airport offers rates comparable to those in the city centre, so you can change here with confidence.

The introduction of forex bureaus meant you could not only trade hard currency for local currency but could also buy hard currency with local currency, albeit at a premium. In theory, that's true. If you want to buy US dollars with Tanzanian shillings, then they'll cost you US$1 = TSh 573 – if they have them and if they want to sell them. If you want to do this, however, then you'll generally be asked for a bank receipt to prove that you changed your money into Tanzanian shillings legally. Otherwise, there's no problem. Check the US dollars you're given carefully – there's a fair amount of counterfeit US currency doing the rounds.

Beware of commission rates when changing money. They're usually either nil or 1% but in some places (eg Tanga) they can be up to US$5 per cheque.

Border Change

If you're coming from Zambia on the TAZARA train and have useful amounts of Zambian *kwacha* with you, change them at the border with the moneychangers who board the train. Railway staff will not accept them and it's very unlikely any of the passengers will change them for you either. ∎

Kenyan currency is considered to be a more-or-less 'hard' currency in Tanzania. The current rate is KSh 1 = TSh 10.

Hard Currency Payments Despite the introduction of forex bureaus in Tanzania, there are a lot of things which must be paid for in hard cash or travellers' cheques. This includes national park entry and camping fees, most mid-range and top-end hotels, airline tickets and even the hydrofoil between Zanzibar and Dar es Salaam. The rest (cheap hotels, meals, transport etc) are payable in local shillings.

The problem here is that if you're paying in travellers' cheques and the amount of the cheque doesn't match the bill, you'll be given change in local currency at the prevailing forex rate of exchange. If you pay in cash US dollars but your banknote doesn't match the charge you have to pay, you have a sporting chance of getting the change in US dollars cash – but don't count on it. Have lots of small US dollar bills handy to counter this. It's not usually a hassle at the national park gates, since they generally have plenty of change in hard cash.

Credit Cards Diners Club, American Express and, to a lesser extent, Visa and MasterCard credit cards are generally acceptable in the more expensive restaurants and major hotels, as well as a few other places, but you'll be billed at the official bank rate. Another disadvantage to using a credit card for paying bills is that most establishments will charge you a 'commission' for using a card which varies from 5% to 15%.

What you can *not* do with any credit card in Tanzania is get a cash advance against the card even at a bank. Don't even try; it's an utter waste of time.

POST & COMMUNICATIONS
Sending & Receiving Mail
The poste restante is well organised in the capital and the main towns and you should have no problems with expected letters not turning up. The same is true for telegrams. There's a small charge for collecting letters.

Telephone

Never rely on the telephone system in Tanzania. The equipment is as old as the hills and it's touch and go whether you'll get through – and that includes calls to neighbouring Kenya and Uganda. There are days when you get straight through and days when it's all but impossible. One of the most notorious lines is that between Arusha and Nairobi.

There's only one exception to the above and that is Extelecoms House, on Samora Ave in Dar es Salaam, which has an efficient and reliable international exchange. You can usually get a connection in just a couple of minutes, but it's expensive. Expect to pay around US$10 *per minute*! Reverse-charge (collect) calls cannot be made from here.

You can also make overseas and local calls through a hotel switchboard, but they'll add on a commission of at least 25%.

Note that calls to Kenya and Uganda are classified as long-distance calls, not international ones.

The telephone area codes for some of the main towns in Tanzania are as follows:

Arusha	057
Bukoba	066
Dar es Salaam	051
Dodoma	061
Iringa	064
Morogoro	056
Moshi	055
Mwanza	068
Tabora	062
Zanzibar	054

Fax & E-mail

Virtually all of the safari companies and most of the upper-middle and top-end hotels have fax machines, and sending a fax *to* them from outside the country is usually no problem. If you want to send a fax from Tanzania to somewhere else then you'll have to negotiate a price with someone or an organisation which owns a machine. The cost of this will be much the same as the price of a telephone call plus a commission of at least 25%. It's cheaper in Dar es Salaam to do this at Extelecoms House on Samora Ave where it will cost you only the time it takes to put the fax through.

E-mail hasn't caught on yet in Tanzania and there are no local providers but this will change rapidly as most businesses are now computerised. However, it will remain of limited use until the antediluvian telephone system is replaced or upgraded.

BOOKS

The *Tourist Guide to Tanzania*, by Gratian Luhikula, is probably the best local guide available and is good value at TSh 3200. The descriptive passages provide excellent background information on all places of interest, but accommodation and transport are inadequately covered. The maps, too, are of limited use. It's available in book shops in Dar es Salaam.

Also worth buying, if you're going to Zanzibar and/or Pemba is the *Guide to Zanzibar* by David Else which contains detailed sections on places to stay, things to do, historical sites in Stone Town and around the island, flora and fauna, marine wildlife, history, plus a section on Pemba. Also good is *A Tale of Two Islands – Zanzibar*, by the Commission for Tourism. It covers all the places to see and the places to stay quite adequately and includes prices. The maps are not too bad.

There's also a recently published series of well-produced and illustrated booklets which cover most of Tanzania's principal national parks. Published by the Tanzania National Parks Authority in cooperation with the African Wildlife Foundation, they cost about US$5 each and are excellent safari companions. The series includes *Arusha National Park, Kilimanjaro National Park, Tarangire National Park, Ngorongoro Conservation Area, Mikumi National Park, Selous Game Reserve* and *Gombe Stream National Park*, among others.

Another good booklet is *Ngorongoro's Geological History* published by the Ngorongoro Conservation Area Authority. It's available from book shops and hotel stores.

TANZANIA

NEWSPAPERS & MAGAZINES

Apart from Dar es Salaam and Arusha where international magazines and periodicals are available as well as the Kenyan daily, *The Nation*, and weekly, *The East African*, prepare yourself for a media black hole in Tanzania.

Just about the only newspaper that's available outside these cities is the government's official English-language newspaper, the *Daily News*, a dreadful rag and essentially a 'what the president did today' type of publication. Foreign news coverage is minimal.

RADIO & TV

You can forget about these unless you speak fluent Swahili or you're staying at an upper-middle range or top-end hotel, some of which have cable TV.

PHOTOGRAPHY

Bring all your photographic requirements with you, as very little is available outside Dar es Salaam, Arusha and Zanzibar. Even in these places, the choice is very limited and prices are high. Slide film is a rarity – colour negative and B&W film are what's mostly available. If you're desperate for film, the large hotels are probably your best bet. You'll be extremely lucky to find film at any of the national park lodges.

Developing facilities are even more of a rarity and you're seriously advised to get your film developed back home or take it to Nairobi and get it done there.

Don't expect to find any camera-rental or repair shops anywhere in Tanzania.

Don't take photographs of anything connected with the government or the military (government offices, post offices, banks, railway stations, bridges, airports, barracks etc). If you do, you may well be arrested and your film confiscated. If you're on the TAZARA train from Dar es Salaam to Kapiri Mposhi (Zambia) and want to take photographs of game as you go through the Selous Game Reserve, get permission first from military personnel if possible or, failing that, from railway officials. You might think that what you are doing is completely innocuous but they may well think otherwise.

ELECTRICITY

Mains power is 230V, 50 cycles, AC, but surges up to 310V and troughs of as low as 150V are common. If you're using electronic equipment (computers, fax machines etc) bear this in mind otherwise you could wreck your machine. Power cuts are fairly frequent but generally don't last more than an hour or two.

Power sockets come in all shapes and sizes – 15-amp three-pin round, 13-amp three-pin round, 13-amp three-pin square, 13-amp three-pin angled, and two-pin angled. You never know what you're going to find so, if you intend to use electrical equipment, make sure you have a full range of adaptors. Most of these can be bought in Tanzania very cheaply.

HEALTH

Make sure you have a valid vaccination certificate for yellow fever before arriving in Tanzania. You won't be asked for it at land borders and you probably won't be asked for it if you arrive by air through either Kilimanjaro or Dar es Salaam airports, but it's essential for Zanzibar and Pemba. Officially, you are prohibited from entering Zanzibar or Pemba without a valid certificate, and these will be checked on the dockside at Dar es Salaam before boarding any of the boats to Zanzibar or on arrival by air. In practice, it's just about negotiable but you're in for a major hassle.

As in most African countries, you must take precautions against malaria. Most of the lakes and rivers of Tanzania carry a risk of bilharzia if you bathe in them or walk along the shores without footwear, especially where the vegetation is very reedy. Tsetse flies are distributed over large areas of the central plateau, though they're only a real nuisance in a few places (insect repellent and a fly whisk are useful). Tarangire National Park is infested with them – keep the windows shut on game drives!

HIV/AIDS is a serious risk, though not as prevalent as in Uganda. Take precautions.

See the Health section in the Regional Facts for the Visitor chapter for a full rundown on travel health in East Africa.

DANGERS & ANNOYANCES

There are very few of these in Tanzania – it's a very law-abiding country. Thieves and muggers hardly exist on the streets, although there are two exceptions – bus terminals and railway stations. Watch your bags at these places and don't allow your attention to be distracted.

PUBLIC HOLIDAYS

The following public holidays are observed in Tanzania:

January
    New Year's Day (1st)
    Zanzibar Revolution Day (12th)
February
    CCM Foundation Day (5th)
April
    Union Day (26th)
May
    Labour Day (1st)
July
    Peasants' Day (7th)
December
    Independence Day (9th)
    Christmas Day (25th)
    Boxing Day (26th)

Variable public holidays are Good Friday, Easter Monday, Eid al-Fitr (end of Ramadan) and Eid al-Hajj.

ACTIVITIES
Safaris

Perhaps the main reason most travellers come to Tanzania is to visit world-famous national parks such as Serengeti and Ngorongoro Crater. There are many others, too, which are just as spectacular and where you will see the same range of wildlife. See the Tanzania Getting Around and the National Parks chapters for a close look at all the possibilities.

Mountain Trekking

Equally popular with travellers is an attempt on the summit of Mt Kilimanjaro, Africa's highest mountain. It's a five to six-day trek and you need to be reasonably fit to accomplish it. Full details of what is involved can be found in the Mt Kilimanjaro and Mt Meru sections in the Tanzania National Parks chapter.

Snorkelling & Scuba Diving

Tanzania's Indian Ocean coast and, particularly, the islands of Zanzibar, Pemba and Mafia are ringed with spectacular coral reefs and offer some of the best diving possibilities in the world. Charges for this are very reasonable in comparison with many other places in the world. Full details can be found under the Zanzibar and Mafia Island sections in The Coast chapter.

ACCOMMODATION
Camping

Except in the national parks where there are established camp sites, camping possibilities are limited in Tanzania. There are established sites in Arusha, Moshi, various places on Zanzibar island and north of Dar es Salaam. You can, of course, camp just about anywhere you like, with permission, but there won't be any facilities.

Hotels

Hotels range from fleapits and brothels to grandiose establishments like the Sheraton. The choice is yours and there's usually plenty to choose from but it's best not to leave your arrival time until late in the afternoon or early evening, as you may find your preferred choice full. It's perhaps a little glib to suggest you make a reservation in advance by phone since, half the time, the phones don't work, but it's worth a try if you want to stay in a particular place.

A room with attached bathroom in a reasonable hotel costs around US$10 to US$15 a double in the countryside and about double that in Dar es Salaam, Arusha, Moshi, Mwanza and Zanzibar. Paying US$30 to US$40 a double will generally guarantee you a air-con room with private bathroom, hot water in the showers, and towels, soap and toilet paper provided. If you intend to stay more than just a few days then it's worth enquiring about a discount.

Many of the higher-priced hotels still price their rooms in US dollars and they may insist on payment in US dollar cheques or cash but it doesn't really matter in these days of forex bureaus. The lower-priced hotels will accept local currency at the prevailing forex exchange rate.

FOOD
Local Food
There's precious little difference between local food in Kenya and Tanzania except that potatoes are generally substituted with *matoke* (boiled plantain) or, on the coast, rice. As in Kenya, *nyama choma* (barbecued meat) has taken over in a big way especially in the restaurants with attached bars.

On the coast and in Zanzibar and Pemba, there is a wide range of traditional Swahili dishes based on seafood cooked in coconut, with or without spices.

There are, of course, Chinese restaurants as well as quite a lot of Indian restaurants which offer excellent value, especially at lunch time.

DRINKS
Nonalcoholic Drinks
Soft drinks ('sodas') are available everywhere and they're usually cold. The most common fresh fruit juices are passion fruit, orange and sugar cane. The fresh juices are really cheap so you needn't even think twice about ordering another. Bottled sodas cost about half the price of a cheap beer (say, TSh 200).

Alcoholic Drinks
Here you have a choice of beer or spirits (local and imported). The national brew is Safari Lager. This used to be so variable in quality that you never knew whether you'd double up with stomach cramps or get drunk first. Things have improved considerably since then – possibly because of competition.

Tanzania opened up the market to foreign beers some time back, so now you can get Kenyan Tusker Lager (known locally as *Tusker ndovu kubwa*), South African Castle, German Becks, Heineken, Tuborg and even Australian XXXX and Fosters. They're generally a little more expensive than Safari

---

Drinking Anecdotes (or 'The Safari Lager Trail')
If you frequent one bar long enough – and a few days is sufficient – then you'll acquire a nickname. 'Geoff' was too hard to remember. 'Mzee kipara na mandevu' (Respected elder with the bald head and beard) was easier. It gave me an instantly recognisable face which everyone related to. Even the bills were made out to that Swahili name.

For your part, you must learn the name of the barperson. This way you get instant service; they may even remember the brew you drink and keep a few bottles cold for you.

Tanzania relaxed its import restrictions a few years ago so there's now a choice of beers from Kenya, South Africa, Northern Europe and even Australia. Yes, you can even buy Heineken and Castlemaine XXXX.

But you must remember that Kenya's Tusker collection must be ordered *specifically*! 'Lete Tusker baridi tafadhali' (Give me a cold Tusker please), is OK in Kenya but will not make the grade in Tanzania. You must specify the exact brew. So, if it's a large Tusker Lager you want, you must ask for, 'Lete Tusker ndovu kubwa baridi tafadhali' (Give me a large, cold, Tusker elephant please). The elephant comes from the label on the bottle. Otherwise, you could very well get a small bottle of Tusker Export.

Another thing to remember when buying take-aways (from a bar, supermarket etc) is that you must bring empties with you, otherwise you pay extra for the bottles. This adds considerably to the cost.

Geoff Crowther

Lager but not by any great margin. The price of a bottle of beer at the very cheapest places is around TSh 450. In a more salubrious place you'll be looking at a cost of around TSh 600.

The local liquor is *konyagi* which tastes like a very rough Bacardi. It's very cheap but you probably won't be able to drink it without a Pepsi (Coke isn't much in evidence). Be careful with this stuff – it creeps up on you!

Imported liquors are available but you don't want to know about the price of those.

ENTERTAINMENT

There are cinemas in most urban centres but they screen rubbish and old, scratched copies to boot.

Want to rage? No worries, as there are discos in Dar es Salaam, Arusha, Mwanza or Zanzibar and, to a lesser degree, in Moshi or Morogoro. Dar es Salaam offers the best with Zanzibar a poor second.

Quite a few hotels in Tanzania put on live music, mostly at weekends. The best places to catch this are in Arusha and Dar es Salaam. Most of the bands are from Zaïre.

Getting There & Away

AIR

Kenya

Dar es Salaam to Nairobi One of the cheapest regular options to fly between Tanzania and Kenya are the flights between Dar es Salaam and Nairobi (US$139 one way) though you must add the US$20 departure tax to this price. There's usually one flight per day in either direction on each sector by one or the other airline. The flights are usually easy to get on given a day or two advance booking.

Zanzibar to Mombasa Another very popular flight is the three-times weekly service between Mombasa and Zanzibar by Kenya Airways and Air Tanzania, which costs US$69 one way plus US$20 airport departure tax. In the high season flights need to be booked as far in advance as possible as there's heavy demand for seats.

Eagle Aviation also flies this route twice a week.

Other Routes Eagle Aviation flies three times a week between Mombasa and Kilimanjaro (for Arusha and Moshi). Precision Air Services (☎ 210014 Nairobi) flies between Nairobi and Kilimanjaro (US$127) and between Mombasa and Kilimanjaro (US$127) twice a week.

Air Victoria (☎ 602491) and Western Airways (☎ 503743), both with offices at Wilson Airport, between them fly from Mwanza to Nairobi (US$175 and US$150 respectively) five times a week.

Rwanda

Air Rwanda flies twice a week in either direction between Kigali and Mwanza on Monday and Friday.

LAND

Kenya

Bus There are several land connections between Kenya and Tanzania:

Mombasa to Dar es Salaam Hood Bus/Cat Bus has departures from Mombasa to Dar es Salaam (KSh 400, TSh 4000) via Tanga on Monday, Tuesday and Friday at 9 am. In the opposite direction, buses depart Dar es Salaam for Mombasa on Tuesday, Wednesday and Friday at 9 am. Officially, the journey from Mombasa to Tanga takes about eight hours and to Dar es Salaam about 12½ hours but, in practice, it can take as long as four hours to clear all 50 or so passengers through both border posts at Horohoro/Lunga Lunga so the journey time may be that much longer. The bus office in Dar es Salaam is on Msimbazi St, close to the Kariakoo Market and the Caltex station. In Mombasa, it's on Kenyatta Ave. The road between Dar es Salaam and Tanga is surfaced and in good condition but from there to the border it's diabolical. From the border to Mombasa you're back on a good tarmac road.

No-one but a masochist would do this journey the hard way by taking a bus first to Tanga followed by another one from there to the border and yet another from there to Mombasa. For a start, there's a six-km walk between the two border posts and hitching is well-nigh impossible. Once on the Kenyan side, however, there are frequent matatus for the one-hour journey to Mombasa. Doing it this way could take you the best part of two days.

Nairobi to Dar es Salaam Direct buses between Nairobi and Dar operate roughly every second day from each city. In Dar the buses, operated by Tawfiq, leave from the bus station on the corner of Morogoro Rd and Libya St.

The journey takes 10 to 12 hours and costs TSh 10,000.

Nairobi to Arusha & Moshi Between Nairobi and Arusha there's a choice of normal buses and minibus shuttles. All of them go through the border posts without a change.

The minibus shuttles between Nairobi and Arusha vary slightly in price but all take the same amount of time (four hours). One of the cheapest is Riverside Shuttle (☎ (057) 8323) which has its office next to the Chinese Restaurant on Sokoine Rd in Arusha. It departs Nairobi daily at 8.30 am from opposite the Norfolk Hotel on Harry Thuku Rd, and, in the opposite direction, from Arusha at 2 pm. The fare is TSh 7000 or KSh 1000 and the shuttle will drop you at any down-town hotel at either end on request. At the Nairobi end, they will also drop you at Jomo Kenyatta International airport on request.

Slightly more expensive is the Davanu Shuttle (☎ (057) 4311 Arusha and (02) 222002 Nairobi) which has its office at Windsor House, 4th Floor, University Way, Nairobi, and at the Adventure Centre, Goliondoi Rd, Arusha. It departs Nairobi for Arusha daily at 8.30 am and 2 pm and Arusha for Nairobi daily at 8 am and 2 pm. The fare is TSh 8000 or KSh 1000. As with Riverside, Davanu will drop you at any down-town hotel at either end on request. Be careful with both companies regarding fares as they will initially attempt to charge you the equivalent of US$25 (Riverside) and US$30 (Davanu) if you're a nonresident.

Much cheaper is Arusha Express, which operates full-sized buses and has its office in amongst the cluster of bus companies down Accra Rd in Nairobi. In Arusha, the office is at the bus station. It operates a daily service leaving Nairobi at 8.30 am and costs KSh 400 or TSh 3000 and takes about four hours. It returns to Nairobi the same day at around 2 pm.

Getting through customs and immigration on all the above buses is straightforward.

It's also easy, but less convenient, to do this journey in stages, and since the Kenyan and Tanzanian border posts are next to each other at Namanga, there's no long walk involved. There are frequent matatus and shared taxis from Arusha to Namanga every day. These go when full and cost TSh 700 to TSh 1300 (negotiable). The taxis normally take about 1½ hours, though there are a number of kamikaze drivers who are totally crazy and will get you there in just one hour. From the Kenyan side of the border, there are frequent matatus and share-taxis which go when full. Both have their depot outside the petrol station on Ronald Ngala St, close to the junction with River Rd in Nairobi.

Voi to Moshi The crossing between Voi and Moshi via Taveta is also reliable as far as transport goes (buses, matatus and shared taxis), as long as you go on a Wednesday or Saturday, which are the market days in Taveta. A matatu between Voi and Taveta (along a bumpy road) takes 2½ hours and costs KSh 200. From Taveta to Holili (the Tanzanian border), however, it's a three-km walk, but there are also *boda-boda* (bicycle taxis) for TSh 300. From Holili there are plenty of matatus and share-taxis to Moshi. A matatu from Holili to Moshi will cost you TSh 400 and take about 45 minutes.

Kisii to Musoma/Mwanza There are no direct buses between Kenya and Tanzania through the Isebania border and doing it in stages is a pain in the arse. The road between Mwanza and Musoma is terrible and between there and the border it's diabolical. Once over the border, it's plain sailing on tarmac roads but you'll need a night's sleep at Kisii before continuing. There's very little traffic on the road between the Isebania border and Musoma so give yourself plenty of time and don't count on lifts with overland companies, the UN or other NGOs. Ideally, you need your own vehicle.

Serengeti to Masai Mara If you look at any detailed map of the Serengeti National Park and Masai Mara National Reserve, you'll see that there's a border crossing between Bologonja and Sand River, and so you would assume it's possible to cross here. It is if you're crossing *from* Kenya *to* Tanzania, assuming you have the appropriate vehicle documentation (insurance and temporary entry permit). But officially, it isn't possible

TANZANIA

to cross in the opposite direction because you must pay the park entry fee to Masai Mara and you must pay it in Kenyan shillings, which you ought not to have since, under Kenyan currency regulations, you're not allowed to export them. And the nearest place where you *might* be able to change money is at Keekorok Lodge, 10 km away. In practice, the border guards/park officials are very helpful, so if you just happen to have a sufficient stash of Kenyan shillings to pay the park entry fees, then you shouldn't encounter problems. There is, of course, no public transport along this route.

Train Through service to Tanzania has recently recommenced, with a once-weekly connection between Voi and Moshi. From Voi the departure is on Saturday at 5 am, arriving in Moshi at 11.30 am. The return trip leaves Moshi at 2 pm, arriving in Voi at 7.10 pm. The fare from Voi to Taveta is KSh 330/175 in 1st/2nd class; Voi to Moshi is KSh 475/255.

Rwanda

Bus To get from Rwanda into Tanzania you first need to take a matatu from Kigali to Kibungu (RFr 700) followed by a share-taxi from there to the border at Rusumo (RFr 400). From the Tanzanian side of the border there are pick-ups to Ngara from where there are several buses daily to Mwanza for TSh 6000. Except for a short stretch of good tarmac, the road on the Tanzanian side is diabolical so expect a rough journey. This route is the same one used by petrol trucks supplying Kigali and Bujumbura so hitching the entire way is also possible.

Alternatively, organise a lift all the way from Kigali. Take a Gikondo matatu from the Place de l'Unité Nationale in Kigali, go about three km down the Blvd de l'OUA to the STIR truck park and ask around there. Many trucks leave daily from here at about 9 am, heading for Tanzania. Most of the drivers are Somalis, and if you strike up a rapport with them, you may well get a free lift all the way to a major city in Tanzania. If

not, you're looking at about US$20 from Kigali to Mwanza.

A third possibility is a flight from Ngara to Mwanza. Ngara has the nearest airstrip to the Rwandan refugee camps on the Tanzanian border so it's used frequently by UN and NGO personnel. If you ask around, you may well find a flight going to Mwanza or even Dar es Salaam or Nairobi. Some of these lifts will be free (given that there are spare seats) but, normally, you would have to pay for them. It all depends who you meet.

Uganda

Bus The route into Uganda goes through the Kagera salient on the west side of Lake Victoria between Bukoba and Masaka, via Kyaka. This is the route which the overland safari companies take. Road conditions have improved considerably over the last few years, so it's possible to do the journey from Masaka to Bukoba in one day. There are taxis from Masaka to Kyotera (USh 1200, 45 minutes) plus several daily pick-ups from there to the border at Mutukula (USh 1500, one hour), which go when full.

The border crossings are easy-going and there are moneychangers on the Tanzanian side, though they give a lousy rate. The border posts are right next to each other.

From the border, a daily Land Rover goes to Bukoba (TSh 3000, about four hours) over appalling roads. If the Land Rover has departed before you arrive at the border, your only option is to hitch – not easy, as there's little traffic. There's a checkpoint in Kyaka, where you're obliged to stop and have your passport checked.

There's also a bus between Bukoba and Mutukula which departs from Bukoba daily (except Sunday) at 11.15 am, costs TSh 1200 and takes about four hours. In the opposite direction, it leaves Mutukula for Bukoba at 5 pm.

BOAT
Burundi & Zambia

Ferry The main ferry on Lake Tanganyika is the historic MV *Liemba*, which connects Tanzania with Burundi and Zambia. This ferry operates a weekly service connecting Bujumbura (Burundi), Kigoma (Tanzania) and Mpulungu (Zambia); a great way to go.

The MV *Liemba* is a legend among travellers and must be one of the oldest steamers in the world still operating on a regular basis. Built by the Germans in 1914 and assembled on the lake shore after being transported in pieces on the railway from Dar es Salaam, it first saw service as the *Graf von Goetzn*. Not long afterwards, following Germany's defeat in WW I, it was greased and scuttled to prevent the British getting their hands on it. In 1922 the British colonial authorities paid the princely sum of UK£4000 for it. Two years later they raised it from the bottom of the lake, had it reconditioned and put back into service as the MV *Liemba*. The fact that it's still going after all these years is a credit to its maintenance engineers.

The schedule for the MV *Liemba* is more or less regular, but the ferry can be delayed for up to 24 hours at either end, depending on how much cargo there is to load or unload. Engine trouble can also delay it at any point, though not usually for more than a few hours.

Officially, the MV *Liemba* departs from Bujumbura on Monday at about 6 pm and arrives in Kigoma (Tanzania) on Tuesday at 8 am. It leaves Kigoma at about 4 pm on Wednesday and arrives in Mpulungu (Zambia) on Friday at 8 am. It calls at many small Tanzanian ports en route between Kigoma and Mpulungu, but rarely for more than half an hour except at Kasanga where it anchors overnight. In the reverse direction, the ferry departs Mpulungu at 6 pm on Friday and arrives in Kigoma on Sunday at 10 am. It leaves Kigoma at 6 pm on Sunday and then arrives in Bujumbura on Monday at 8 am.

The fares from Bujumbura (in US$) are:

Port	1st class	2nd class	3rd class
Kigoma	19	15	12
Mpulungu	78	62	48

The fares from Kigoma (in Tanzanian shillings) are:

Port	1st class	2nd class	3rd class
Bujumbura	4900	4320	3430
Kasanga	12,885	10,785	8485
Mpulungu	13,715	11,605	9090

In addition, port fees of BFr 500 are payable upon boarding in Bujumbura. Tickets for the ferry can be bought from SONACO, Rue des Usines off Ave du Port, Bujumbura, on Monday morning from 8 am.

Tickets bought in Mpulungu for the trip north to Kigoma or Bujumbura and tickets bought in Bujumbura for the trip south to any of the ports en route must be paid for in US dollars. Local currency is not acceptable. Tickets bought at any of the Tanzanian ports can be paid for in Tanzanian shillings.

To save money when going all the way from Bujumbura to Mpulungu, first buy a ticket to Kigoma, then once the boat docks, get off and immediately make a reservation for a 1st or 2nd-class cabin. Then change money into Tanzanian shillings and pay for your ticket the following morning at 8 am using the shillings you changed. This will save you approximately US$33 (1st class) or US$24 (2nd class) in total.

When travelling from Bujumbura direct to Mpulungu, you have to stay on the boat for the 36 hours or so that it docks in Kigoma, though you are allowed into town during the day even if you don't have a Tanzanian visa (where required). Passports have to be left with immigration in the meantime.

Third class consists of bench seats either in a covered area towards the back of the boat or in another very poorly ventilated area with bench seats in the bowels of the vessel. The best plan is to grab some deck space. The 2nd-class cabins are incredibly hot, stuffy and claustrophobic. They have four bunks and are very poorly ventilated. If you want a cabin, go the whole hog and take 1st class. These have two bunks, are on a higher deck, have a window and fan, and are clean and reasonably cool. Bedding is available for a small fee.

Third class is not usually crowded between Bujumbura and Kigoma, so this is a reasonable budget possibility, especially as it's only overnight. It's no problem to sleep out on the deck – the best spot is above the 1st-class deck, though you need to be discreet as it's supposedly off limits to passengers. On the lower decks you need to keep your gear safe, as some petty pilfering does sometimes occur. If you're travelling 3rd class between Bujumbura and Kigoma and want to upgrade to a cabin for the Kigoma to Mpulungu leg, make sure you do this as soon as the boat docks in Kigoma. Third class is not recommended between Kigoma and Mpulungu, as it's usually very crowded.

Meals and drinks are available on board and must be paid for in Tanzanian shillings. Bring enough shillings to cover this. Three-course meals of soup, chicken and rice followed by dessert are not bad value at TSh 800 for lunch, TSh 1000 for dinner and TSh 600 for breakfast. Cold Safari lager (Tanzanian) is for sale at TSh 500, and Primus (Zaïrese) costs TSh 900.

Coming from Bujumbura, the MV *Liemba* arrives at Kigoma at about 5 am, but you can't get off until 8 am when customs and immigration officials arrive. So, instead of packing your bags and hanging around, it's a good idea to have breakfast.

A part-lake steamer, part-road route via Kasanga on Lake Tanganyika is also becoming increasingly popular if you're heading from Bujumbura or Kigoma to Malawi but don't want to go via Zambia. It will also save you up to US$35. Instead of going all the way to Mpulungu, get off the steamer at Kasanga and, from there, hitch a ride to Sumbawanga (about TSh 2500). From Sumbawanga there are daily 'express' buses to Mbeya via Tunduma for TSh 4000 which take about six hours. The road is sealed from Tunduma to Mbeya. From Mbeya you then take the normal route to Karonga in Malawi via Tukuyu.

In addition to the MV *Liemba*, there is another lake steamer, the MV *Mwongoza*, which plies between Kigoma and Mpulungu via all the usual Tanzanian lake ports. It departs Kigoma on Monday at 4 pm and arrives in Mpulungu on Wednesday at 8 am.

In the reverse direction, it departs Mpulungu on Wednesday at 6 pm and arrives in Kigoma on Friday at 10 am. The fares are the same as for the MV *Liemba*.

Lake Taxi & Matatu The alternative to the MV *Liemba* is to travel partly by taxi and partly by lake taxi between Bujumbura and Kigoma via the Tanzanian border village of Kagunga and the Gombe Stream National Park. The national park is primarily a chimpanzee sanctuary and is well worth a visit, but it does cost US$100 entry fee plus US$20 for accommodation. If you can't afford this, simply stay on the lake taxi, which will take you all the way to Kigoma.

From Bujumbura, taxis go daily to Nyanza Lac (BFr 1400). You must go through immigration here – the office is about one km from the town centre towards the lake. After that, take a taxi (BFr 200) to the Burundi border post. From this post to the Tanzanian border post at Kagunga, it's a two-km walk along a narrow track. From Kagunga, there are lake taxis to Kigoma (actually to Kalalangabo, about three km north of Kigoma), which cost TSh 1000, leave before dawn and take most of the day. The taxis call at Gombe Stream (about halfway), where you can get off if you like. The fare to Gombe Stream is TSh 500, as is the fare from there to Kigoma.

The lake taxis are small, wooden boats, often overcrowded not only with people but with their produce, and they offer no creature comforts whatsoever. They're good fun when the weather is fine, but if there's a squall on the lake, you may be in for a rough time. If you have a choice, try to get a boat with a cover, as it gets stinking hot out on the lake in the middle of the day. These boats do not operate on Sundays.

Kenya

It's possible to go by dhow between Mombasa, Pemba and Zanzibar but sailings are very infrequent these days. What is much more reliable is the ferry, MS *Sepideh*, operated by Zanzibar Sea Ferries Ltd (☎ Zanzibar (054) 33725, Dar es Salaam (051) 38025, Pemba 56210 and

Mombasa (011) 311486), which connects Mombasa with Tanga, Pemba, Zanzibar and Dar es Salaam. The schedule varies according to the season but it's usually twice a week in either direction. The fares are US$65 Mombasa-Dar es Salaam, US$50 Mombasa-Zanzibar, US$45 Tanga-Zanzibar, US$40 Mombasa-Tanga or Mombasa-Pemba, US$30 Tanga-Pemba or Pemba-Zanzibar and US$25 Zanzibar-Dar es Salaam.

There used to be a steamer service which connected Kisumu (Kenya) with Mwanza (Tanzania) on Lake Victoria on a once-weekly basis but the ship which serviced this route (the MV *Bukoba*) sank in May 1996. It's likely that the schedules of the other two boats – the MV *Victoria* and the MV *Serengeti* – will have been altered so that the two ports are connected again but you'll have to make enquiries. Even when the two ports were connected, cancellations were frequent.

Uganda

There's a regular lake service between Port Bell (Kampala) and Mwanza (Tanzania) which departs from Port Bell on Monday and Thursday at 6 pm and arrives in Mwanza the following day at 10 am. In the opposite direction, they leave Mwanza on Sunday and Wednesday at 3 pm and arrive in Port Bell the following day at 7 am. It's a good trip and costs US$35/25/20 in 1st/2nd/3rd class, plus

a US$5 passenger tax. From Mwanza the fares are TSh 7500/6000/4500 plus US$20 port tax.

Tickets should be booked at 2 pm on the day of departure at the Port Bell port gate (☎ (041) 221336). This is going to involve you in a taxi trip, unless you want to hang around all day until the ferry leaves.

This is assuming that ferry services have resumed following the sinking of the MV *Bukoba* in 1996 with the loss of 600-plus lives (the boat had a registered capacity of 430).

Zaïre

SNCZ operates boats from Kalemie to both Uvira and Kigoma, usually once a week. The boat to Uvira generally leaves on Tuesday. For information on these boats in Kigoma, see the stationmaster at the railway station. Tickets can only be bought the day before departure, early in the morning.

There also used to be another privately owned boat, called the *Lwenge*, owned by a man called Fizi. He had a business in Kalemie called PGC, which was almost opposite the Hôtel de la Gare. His boats used to run once weekly (usually on Thursday) from Kalemie to Uvira and take around 36 hours but we haven't heard of anyone who has taken this boat in recent years so it's possible the service has been discontinued. Make enquiries at the Hôtel de la Gare.

Getting Around

AIR

Air Tanzania, the national carrier, serves most of the major internal routes but its 'fleet' consists of just one jet and several F27 propeller planes. In the past, Air Tanzania was effectively 'Air Maybe' but that's all changed since it forged a managerial deal with British Airways. As a result, it's now pretty reliable and delays are the exception rather than the rule. The sectors which it covers are Dar es Salaam-Nairobi (US$139 one way), Dar es Salaam-Kilimanjaro (US$123 one way), Dar es Salaam-Kigoma (US$220 one way), Dar es Salaam-Mwanza (US$187 one way), Dar es Salaam-Zanzibar (US$43 one way), Dar es Salaam-Mombasa (US$69 one way), and Zanzibar-Mombasa (US$54 one way). There are daily departures in either direction on most of these sectors but the schedule changes quite frequently.

Advance booking is a good idea, though it's unlikely you won't get a seat a day or so before a flight. Everything is computerised and you'll find that all Air Tanzania offices accept credit cards (including American Express).

Several private airlines operate light aircraft (six to eight-seaters) not only on the main routes but also on many of the minor routes including those to the national parks and game reserves of Serengeti, Selous, Ruaha and Rubondo island.

In addition to servicing domestic routes, these small airlines also service sectors such as Mwanza-Nairobi, Kilimanjaro-Mombasa and Zanzibar-Mombasa. They include Air Zanzibar, Zan Air, Precision Air, Air Victoria, Western Airways and Highland Aviation. Their head offices are either in Zanzibar, Arusha or Mwanza. The schedules and fares of their flights can be found under the respective city and town sections as well as the national parks.

Domestic airport departure tax is TSh 1000. For sectors which take you to neighbouring countries it is US$20.

BUS & DALLA DALLA

Tanzania's economy is definitely on the mend but there's still very little spare cash for road or rail maintenance. So expect the worst, and when it's better than that, be grateful. Except for certain sections – Namanga to Arusha, Arusha to Tarangire, Arusha to Dar es Salaam via Moshi, Moshi to Himo and Marangu, and Dar es Salaam to Morogoro – the roads vary from poor to atrocious. At one time many roads were sealed, but the tarmac has since broken up and large potholes have formed, making them worse than poorly maintained gravel roads. It's not particularly dangerous, especially during daylight hours, because no-one can travel at high speed.

On the main long-haul routes, there's generally a choice between luxury and ordinary buses. It's worth taking the luxury buses where there's a choice, as they're only marginally more expensive than the ordinary ones, are far more comfortable and get to their destination faster. Ordinary buses pick up and put down more frequently, so take longer.

Advance booking on long hauls is definitely advisable. Don't expect to turn up an hour or so before departure and be able to buy tickets. A day in advance is usually sufficient.

On short hauls the choice is between ordinary buses and *dalla dalla* (the Tanzanian equivalent of a Kenyan matatu), and for those who want to get somewhere fast and have the money, share-taxis. Ordinary buses and dalla dalla leave when full and the fare is fixed. A few Tanzanian towns (Moshi, Arusha and Mwanza) have central bus and dalla dalla stations, so it's easy to find the bus you want. Other places, Dar es Salaam being the prime example, don't have a central bus stand and buses depart from several locations, some of which are not at all obvious.

Beware of pickpockets and thieves at bus stations. There are usually scores of them and they're all waiting for you! Don't let your attention wander, even for a moment. Arusha is notorious for them, with Moshi a close second.

If you have the option, it's always better to travel 1st or 2nd class on a train for long hauls than to go by bus. Take a look at the haggard faces of travellers who stumble off the ordinary buses between the Rwandan border and Mwanza, Mwanza and Arusha, and Mbeya and Dar es Salaam and you won't need any further convincing!

Finding a place to put your pack on a bus can sometimes present problems. The racks above the seats are generally too small to accommodate rucksacks but there's usually room up front near the driver. On long hauls, don't allow your bag to be put on the roof if there's any possibility of passengers being up there with it. There won't be much left in it by the time you arrive at your destination. The safest thing to do is insist that it go under your seat or in the aisle where you can keep your eye on it.

TRAIN

Apart from Arusha, Tanzania's major population centres are connected by railway. The Central Line linking Dar es Salaam with Kigoma via Morogoro, Kilosa, Dodoma and Tabora was built by the German colonial authorities between 1905 and 1914. Later it was extended from Tabora to Mwanza by the British. The other arm of this line links Dar es Salaam with Moshi and Tanga via Korogwe. There's a branch off this line which links Moshi with Voi (in Kenya) via Himo and Taveta.

The other major line is the TAZARA railway linking Dar es Salaam with Kapiri Mposhi, in the heartland of the Zambian copper belt, via Mbeya and Tunduma/Nakonde. It is Zambia's most important link with the sea and passes through some of the most remote country in Africa, including part of the Selous Game Reserve. Built by the People's Republic of China in the 1960s, the line involved the construction of 147 stations, more than 300 bridges and 23 tunnels – the most ambitious project ever undertaken by the Chinese outside their own territory.

Unfortunately, maintenance hasn't matched the energy with which the Chinese first constructed the railway, so schedules can be erratic, though there are usually three trains in either direction each week.

As with bus travel, keep an eye on your gear at all times, particularly in 3rd class. Even in 1st and 2nd class, make sure that the window is jammed shut at night. There is usually a piece of wood provided for this, as the window locks don't work. It's common practice for thieves to jump in through the window at night when the train stops at stations.

Classes

There are three classes on Tanzanian trains: 1st class (two-bunk compartments), 2nd class (usually six-bunk compartments) and 3rd class (wooden benches only).

Second class on the Dar es Salaam to Moshi and Dar es Salaam to Tanga trains is seats only. You'd have to be desperate to go any distance in 3rd class – it's very uncomfortable, very crowded and there are thieves to contend with. It's definitely not recommended. Second class is several quantum levels above 3rd class in terms of space and comfort (though the fans may not work) and is an acceptable way to travel long distances.

The difference between 1st and 2nd class is that there are two people to a compartment instead of six. Men and women can only travel together in 1st or 2nd class if they book the whole compartment.

Some trains (Dar es Salaam to Kigoma, Mwanza, Moshi and Tanga) have restaurant cars which serve good meals (TSh 800 for dinner, TSh 600 for breakfast), soft drinks and beer. Bed rolls are available in 1st and 2nd class at a cost of TSh 500, regardless of how long the journey is. These can be a good investment on the long runs from Dar es Salaam to Mwanza or Kigoma.

Reservations

Buying a ticket can be a daylight nightmare, especially in Dar es Salaam and Moshi. It's chaos at the stations and nowhere will you find any schedules. The only information that's usually posted is a list of fares (often out of date). Even when you try to book a ticket several days in advance, you may well be told that 1st and 2nd class are sold out. The Central Line station in Dar es Salaam is notorious for this. The claim is usually pure, unadulterated rubbish, but it helps to secure 'presents' for ticket clerks. If you are told this, see the station master and beg, scrape and plead for his assistance. It may take some time but you'll get those supposedly 'booked' tickets in the end. The claim is generally true, on the other hand, on the day of departure.

Schedules & Fares
Central Line trains from Dar es Salaam to Kigoma and Mwanza depart at 6 pm on Monday, Wednesday, Friday and Sunday. In the opposite direction, there are departures from both Kigoma and Mwanza for Dar es Salaam at the same time and on the same days. The journey normally takes about 36 hours but can take 40.

Central Line trains from Dar es Salaam to Moshi and Tanga depart at 4 pm on Sunday and Friday. In the opposite direction, there are departures from both Moshi and Tanga for Dar es Salaam at the same time and on the same days. The journey to Moshi takes 15 to 18 hours and to Tanga about 16 hours. The service to Tanga was (temporarily?) suspended in early 1996 but the reasons for this were not at all clear – nothing ever is at the Central Line station – but, by the time you read this, it will probably have been restored.

The fares (in Tanzanian shillings) for express trains from Dar es Salaam are listed below. The fares for ordinary trains are only marginally cheaper (less than 10%) but as the journey time is longer the express trains are the way to go.

Class:	1st	2nd (sleeping)	2nd (sitting)	3rd
Moshi	11,585	8285	5680	3540
Tanga	8945	6120	4155	2630
Mwanza	23,450	16,470	11,430	6975
Kigoma	23,000	16,710	11,600	7075

The schedule for the TAZARA trains can be found in the Zambia section of the earlier Tanzania Getting There & Away chapter.

CAR & 4WD
Driving in Tanzania is a trade-off between speed and potholes. Traffic density is low outside the main towns, so collisions are rare. Wiping yourself out on a large pothole is another matter. Keep your speed down. The gravel roads in the national parks of the north-east (Serengeti, Ngorongoro, Lake Manyara, Tarangire and Arusha) are usually pretty good, as are the sealed roads leading to them, but there are some very rough stretches between Lake Manyara and the entrance to Ngorongoro. You could make it in a 2WD vehicle in the dry season but certainly not in the wet season.

Rental
Self-drive car rental is still in its infancy in Tanzania except in Zanzibar where the wheels are well oiled. On the mainland it's an expensive option since there are very few companies offering this service – basically, only the large, international outfits like Hertz, Avis, Europcar, etc – but things are changing slowly. Even so, at the present time, you can only find self-drive car rentals in Dar es Salaam, Arusha and Zanzibar. You certainly won't find them anywhere else.

The cheapest of the companies is Evergreen (☎ Dar es Salaam 21839; fax 44677), PO Box 1476, Nkrumah St, Dar es Salaam. It rents a range of vehicles but the cheapest (a Toyota Corona) goes for US$40 per day or US$245 per week including insurance with 100 km free per day plus US$0.30 per extra km. The smallest of their 4WD vehicles (a Suzuki Samurai) costs US$42 per day or US$259 per week including insurance with 100 km free per day plus US$0.45 per extra km. Drivers must be 21 years of age or over and have a driving licence from their country of origin. The company accepts all credit cards.

Next up is Avis (☎ Dar es Salaam 30505; fax 37426), which also has a range of cars, the cheapest (a Hyundai Accent) costing

White-washed huts are a hallmark of Tanzania. You'll see them everywhere, from this village near Arusha (top) to Changuu (Prison) island (bottom).

If you tire of exotic Zanzibar's labyrinthine old Stone Town, ruined palaces, Persian baths and fort, there's always the superb beaches, dhow trips and magnificent coral reefs.

US$50 per day or US$315 per week including insurance and 100 km free per day or unlimited km on rentals of three days or more. The smallest of their 4WD vehicles (an Asia Rocsta diesel) costs US$70 per day or US$455 per week including insurance and the same km limits. Collision damage waiver (US$3000 without cover) costs an extra US$15 per day and theft protection waiver a further US$5 per day.

The most expensive is Hertz (☎ Dar es Salaam 25753; fax 44568, or Arusha 8455), PO Box 20517, Dar es Salaam. Hertz charges US$81 per day or US$62 per day on a two to seven-day rental with unlimited km on their cheapest cars (a medium saloon) but excluding collision damage waiver (US$15 per day) and theft protection waiver (US$6 per day). Their cheapest 4WD vehicles cost US$98 per day or US$72 per day on a two to seven-day rental with unlimited km plus the same extras for collision damage and theft protection waivers. Drivers must be aged 25 years or older. The company accepts all major credit cards.

Self-drive car hire rates on Zanzibar are about the same as Evergreen's (US$40 to US$50 per day all-inclusive) but there are no agencies. All arrangements on this island have to be made on a personal basis. See the Zanzibar section for more details.

BOAT
Lake Ferries
Lake Victoria There are two Tanzanian ferries, the MV *Victoria* and the MV *Serengeti*, servicing the lake ports of Mwanza and Bukoba and there used to be a third, the MV *Bukoba*, which connected Mwanza with Port Bell (Uganda) and Kisumu (Kenya) but it sank in May 1996 killing some 600 people so there's no longer any service on those two routes. It's possible that the schedules of the remaining two boats will have been altered to fill this gap but you'll have to make enquiries in Mwanza. The schedules and fares of the boats which ply between Mwanza and Bukoba are to be found in the Mwanza section.

Lake Malawi Two ferries operate on the Tanzanian part of Lake Malawi, sailing between Itungi and Mbamba Bay via a number of other small ports. The MV *Songea* departs from Itungi at 7 am on Monday and Friday, arriving at Mbamba Bay the same day at 11 pm. In the opposite direction, it leaves Mbamba Bay at midnight on Tuesday and Saturday and arrives in Itungi at 4 pm the same day.

The other ferry, the MV *Mbeya*, runs south from Itungi on Wednesday but only goes as far as Njambi.

Offshore Islands & South Coast See the Dar es Salaam and Zanzibar chapters for details of services to the islands off the Tanzanian coast.

To the mainland ports south of Dar es Salaam as far as Mtwara, near the Mozambique border, there is the FB *Canadian Spirit*, operated by Adecon Marine Inc (☎ 20856; fax 33972), PO Box 63027, Dar es Salaam. The office is on Sokoine Drive in amongst all the other shipping companies which service the Dar es Salaam to Zanzibar route and it's open Monday to Friday from 7.30 to 10.30 am and 2.30 to 6.30 pm. The schedule and fares for this boat can be found in the Dar es Salaam section.

Dhows
Dhows have sailed the coastal waters of East Africa and across to Arabia and India for centuries. Though now greatly reduced in number, they can still be found if you're looking for a slow and uncomfortable but romantic way of getting across to the islands or up to Mombasa.

Most of the dhows are motorised but it's still possible to find the smaller ones which rely entirely on their sail. Dependent on the wind and tides, they sail only when these variables are favourable; otherwise, too much tacking becomes necessary. This may mean that they sail at night which, on a full moon, is pure magic. There's nothing to disturb the silence but the lapping of the sea against the sides of the boat. Remember they are open boats without bunks or luxuries.

TANZANIA

You simply bed down wherever there is space and where you won't get in the way of the crew. Fares are negotiable but are often more than you would pay on a modern vessel for the same journey.

The larger, motorised dhows used to be a standard form of public transport connecting Dar es Salaam to Zanzibar. They've been superseded by modern ferries, catamarans and hydrofoils, but still operate between Zanzibar and Pemba and between Tanga and Pemba. They usually run on a daily basis, but you need to negotiate with the captains personally regarding departure times and fares. It may also involve getting written permission from the district commissioner. See the Zanzibar, Pemba and Tanga sections for more details.

Safaris

ORGANISED VEHICLE SAFARIS

Going on an organised safari is the way most travellers visit Tanzania's national parks.

Safaris to Arusha National Park, Tarangire National Park, Lake Manyara National Park, Ngorongoro Conservation Area and Serengeti National Park are best arranged in Arusha, where there are plenty of companies to choose from. Kilimanjaro National Park is the exception here, with treks best arranged in Moshi (see the relevant section). Visits to Sadani Game Reserve, Mikumi National Park, Ruaha National Park and Selous Game Reserve are best arranged in Dar es Salaam, while those to Gombe Stream and Mahale Mountains national parks are best arranged from Kigoma. Getting to Rubondo Island National Park (in Lake Victoria) is only feasible by light aircraft from Mwanza.

As in Kenya, most of the safari companies offer a choice of camping safaris (the cheaper option) and lodge safaris (the more expensive option). If you haven't been to Kenya and haven't read the Safaris section in the Getting Around chapter for that

country, do it now. There's no point in repeating all the same general points here.

But, specifically, there are a few things you should bear in mind about safari companies in Arusha. This place is awash with 'briefcase' companies and 'flycatchers' – bullshit artists on the make and touts, respectively. If you're a backpacker, then you're a prime target for an ear-full of bullshit the moment you get off the bus. You must be very firms with these guys otherwise you'll regret it. You'll end up in a rust box that's going nowhere with pumpkin soup every night and a driver who doesn't know a lion from a leopard and couldn't care less anyway. As for 'briefcase' companies, the Arusha International Conference Centre (AICC) is riddled with them. A desk and a telephone (and, sometimes, not even that) is all you need to set up shop. Never mind about vehicles, experienced drivers and cooks, an operating licence or anything of that nature. The point is to separate you from your money and not be around when the shit hits the fan. These fly-by-night merchants know perfectly well that tourists only have a limited amount of time and very little leverage when it comes to a dishonoured contract or a settlement of grievances.

Most of the reliable companies which have been in business for years belong to TATO (Tanzanian Association of Tour Operators) and the organisation has a code of ethics which its members must adhere to if they want to retain their membership. That being so, you *may* be able to get *some* redress in the event of a genuine complaint, but don't count on it. TATO, like its Kenyan equivalent, KATO, is something of a paper tiger in that it cannot legally enforce anything at all.

The other organisation to which many small operators belong is ATTO (Association of Tanzanian Travel Operators), PO Box 999, Room 234, Ngorongoro Wing, AICC, Arusha (☎ (057) 6269; fax 8264). This organisation is similar in many ways to TATO and also has a code of ethics which it expects its members to adhere to but it's essentially a political lobbying group which looks after the interests of safari companies operating on a low capital base. On the other hand, it does take an interest in the reputation of the safari business in Tanzania and may be worth contacting if you have genuine complaints. It can also advise on which safari companies are reliable and those which are not.

Routes

From Arusha Arusha is the safari capital of Tanzania, and there's a plethora of companies which offer a range of possibilities to suit all tastes and pockets. Cost and reliability vary widely, and to a large extent, you get what you pay for.

The safaris available vary from just one day to 15 days. A one-day safari takes you to Arusha National Park and a two-day safari to Tarangire National Park. Most travellers, however, prefer longer safaris – four to seven days on average. You need a minimum of three days and two nights to tour Lake Manyara and Ngorongoro Crater, four days and three nights to tour Lake Manyara, Ngorongoro Crater and Serengeti, and six days and five nights to tour Lake Manyara, Ngorongoro Crater, Serengeti and Tarangire. These are absolute minimum tour lengths. If you can afford to stay longer, do so. You'll see a lot more and you won't come back feeling that half the driving time was taken up just getting to and from Arusha. A longer tour will also enable you to make more economical use of park entry fees. If you leave one park within 24 hours and enter another (between Ngorongoro Crater and Serengeti, for instance), you'll be up for two lots of park entry fees (US$40 per person) instead of one (US$20 per person).

If you want to have a good look at Lake Manyara, Ngorongoro Crater and Serengeti, plan on a five to six-day safari. On a 10-day safari, you could take in all the places mentioned plus Lake Natron and Arusha National Park, but not many companies offer safaris of that length.

The national parks aside, the safari business in Arusha has undergone something of an ecological transformation in the last few years. There's now a wide range of walking safaris available which are based outside the national parks but which take you to areas of outstanding natural beauty and in which you will also see many of the same animals encountered in the national parks. Most of these safaris take you through Maasailand north and north-east of Arusha. On these, most of the distance is covered on foot but you'll be met by support vehicles at various points. See under Other Safaris further on in this section.

From Dar es Salaam Safaris to Mikumi typically last two to three days, to Mikumi and Ruaha five days, and to Selous five days, though weekend visits are also an option on the latter. Safaris which take in all three parks last for around nine days.

The possibilities of camping in these parks are much more limited than in the northern parks. On most safaris, you'll stay in lodges or permanent tented camps.

From Mwanza Mwanza is the base for visits to the Western Corridor of Serengeti National Park and to Rubondo Island National Park but there's basically only one safari outfit in town so your options are limited.

From Kigoma Most travellers prefer to visit Gombe Stream and/or Mahale Mountains national parks independently rather than go through a safari company, though there is one company in Kigoma which can arrange this. Some companies in Dar es Salaam can also arrange this, but it's generally part of a much longer trip and these are expensive.

Costs

The cost of a safari depends on two main factors: whether you camp for the night or stay in a lodge or permanent tented camp, and how many people are on the safari.

The two factors are closely linked, but a camping safari is obviously much cheaper than one which uses lodges for overnight accommodation. The exact cost depends partly on how long you want to go for and partly on where you want to go. In general, it's true to say that the longer you go for and the more people there are in your group, the less, proportionally, it will cost you per day. The rock-bottom outfits in Arusha quote around US$75 per person per day, assuming a minimum of five people on the trip, US$80 with four people and US$95 with three people. This includes park entry and camping fees, camping equipment, transport and meals. It's hard to see how they can do this, considering that park entry and camping fees represent US$40 of that alone, but one or two of them do it and do it reliably; many others do not. A more realistic figure is US$85 per person per day, assuming a minimum of four people, or US$110 per person per day, assuming a minimum of two people.

While it's all right to use the above figures as a benchmark, it's not that simple, as the prices quoted by various companies differ by quite a margin but it's probably true to say that if you pay a little over the odds, you'll get a better vehicle and better food and the tents won't be in urgent need of retirement. The price you pay should include park entry and camping fees, food (three meals per day), transport and camping equipment. You would also expect two game drives per day (usually one in the early morning and another in the late afternoon) when you're in a national park. Most reliable companies will supply you with an itinerary so you know what to expect. If you contact a company which doesn't supply you with this then think seriously about going with a different company.

The prices for safaris which involve staying in lodges or luxury tented camps are considerably higher, being in the US$130 to US$160 per person per day range assuming a minimum of four people. With only two people the daily rate per person rises to around US$160 to US$175 all-inclusive. As with camping safaris, you would expect two game drives per day when you're in a national park.

All this means that, whatever sort of safari you want to go on, there's no substitute for legwork. Collect as many leaflets as you can, decide where you want to go, compare prices, work out what's included and what isn't, and then make your choice.

One last thing to remember is that prices are based on the assumption that you will share accommodation (a tent or room) with one other person. If you don't want to do this, you'll have to pay what's called a 'single room supplement'. This can be up to 50% above the daily per person rate.

Tipping

Regardless of whether you go on a camping safari or a lodge safari, the driver/guide and the cook(s) will expect a reasonable tip at the end of the journey. Be generous. You may think you've paid a lot of money for your safari but most of it will have gone to the national parks, the lodges and the safari company. The wages of the driver and cooks will have been minimal. Remember that others will come after you and there's nothing worse than a driver/guide and/or cooks who couldn't care less and who feel exploited.

Departure Frequency

This varies a lot from company to company but the larger outfits generally have guaranteed departures at regular intervals for the most popular parks, assuming there are at least two clients. Virtually any company will get you on the road either the same or the next day if you have a group together and if they have a vehicle and driver on hand.

Choosing a Company

The same general comments about safari companies outlined in the Kenya chapter apply to Tanzanian companies, though it tends to be easier to make a choice in Tanzania because Arusha is a much smaller place than Nairobi and in Dar es Salaam there are far fewer companies. In Mwanza there's only one.

Arusha The majority of safari companies here have offices in the Arusha International Conference Centre (AICC). Others are along India St, Boma Rd, Sokoine Rd, Goliondoi Rd and Seth Benjamin Rd. Check out a number of companies before deciding on a particular one.

For camping safaris try the following (listed in alphabetical order, not under any order of preference):

Easy Travel & Tours Ltd

2nd Floor, Clock Tower Centre, Joel Maeda Rd, PO Box 1912, Arusha (☎ /fax (057) 7322)

In addition to offering treks of Mt Kilimanjaro and Mt Meru, Easy Travel offers camping safaris as well as lodge safaris of the northern national parks. A six-days/five-nights safari of Tarangire, Lake Manyara, Ngorongoro and Serengeti is priced at US$535 per person (five people) and US$630 (three people) but they have a whole range of options from two days/one night to seven days/six nights.

Equatorial Safaris Ltd

India St and Room 460/1, Serengeti Wing, AICC, PO Box 2156, Arusha (☎ (057) 7006, fax 2617)

Equatorial is a reliable company undertaking all the usual safaris to Tarangire, Lake Manyara, Ngorongoro and Serengeti. Camping safaris cost US$85 per person per day all-inclusive.

Fauna Wise Use Safaris

Room 147, Kilimanjaro Wing, AICC, PO Box 15, Arusha (☎ (057) 3181, ext 1619; fax 7065)

This somewhat strangely named company caters for both big game hunting and photographic safaris. The company offers camping safaris to the northern national parks for an average of US$70 per person per day (assuming a minimum of five people) and also Kilimanjaro treks along the Marangu route (US$420, five days) and the Machame route (US$750, six days).

Hoopoe Adventure Tours

India St, PO Box 2047, Arusha (☎ (057) 7011; fax 8226)

This is a well-established company with an excellent reputation, top-notch vehicles and equipment, and keen, committed staff. Apart from offering both the Kilimanjaro and Mt Meru treks, they offer a range of options on the Lake Manyara, Ngorongoro, Serengeti and Tarangire circuit. For a short five-day safari to Lake Manyara, Ngorongoro, Serengeti and Tarangire safari they charge US$724 per person (five people) or US$855 per person (two people). On the longer seven days of the same circuit the price is US$1184 per person (five people) or US$1205 (two people).

Kibo Express Guide & Safaris

YMCA, India St, PO Box 934, Arusha (☎ (057) 7460; fax 8220)

This is a small but reliable company which caters for the Kilimanjaro trek along the Marangu route (US$500) plus camping (average US$90 per person per day), lodge (US$150 per person per day) and walking safaris (US$120 per person per day).

Nyika Treks & Safaris Ltd

Room 405, Serengeti Wing, AICC, PO Box 13077, Arusha (☎ (057) 8886; fax 4030)

There's also a branch at the Tourist Centre Inn on Pangani St near the Uhuru Monument. This is another small company which offers the standard northern national parks circuit at average per-day prices. We've had good reports from travellers about this company. It quotes an average daily rate per person of US$95 for camping safaris, Kilimanjaro treks and walking safaris.

Peacock Tours & Safaris

Room 21, 3rd Floor, Regional CCM Building, PO Box 10123, Arusha (☎ (057) 7884; fax 8256)

Apart from offering treks of Mt Kilimanjaro, this company offers camping safaris of Lake Manyara, Ngorongoro, Serengeti and Tarangire ranging from two to seven days for US$80 to US$90 per person per day, depending on numbers. It's a reliable company and the staff are eager to please.

Pelican Safaris

Joel Maeda Rd, PO Box 6148, Arusha (☎ (057) 8181)

This company offers all the usual safaris, ranging from day trips to Arusha and Tarangire National parks to seven-day Tarangire, Lake Manyara, Ngorongoro and Serengeti trips. It quotes an overall US$130 per person per day.

Roy Safaris Ltd

Opposite Sokoine/Goliondoi Rd junction, PO Box 50, Arusha (☎ (057) 8010; fax 8892)

In addition to offering the Mt Kilimanjaro trek via the Marangu route and the Mt Meru trek, Roy covers all of the northern national parks and is arguably the cheapest reliable safari company in Arusha. This is where quite a few of the more expensive companies send people in search of a rock-bottom safari with no frills. Their basic, all-inclusive per person rates range from US$75 (five people) per day to US$95 (three people). A five-days safari to Lake Manyara, Ngorongoro and Serengeti costs from US$405 (six people) to US$560 (three people). A seven-days safari to the same parks but also including Tarangire costs from US$620 per person (six people) to US$785 (three people).

Shidolya Tours & Safaris

Room 333/334, Serengeti Wing, AICC, PO Box 1436, Arusha (☎ (057) 8506; fax 8242)

This company is one of the smaller but reliable outfits. It offers all-inclusive camping safaris for US$75 per person per day assuming a minimum of four people. The company has good 4WD Nissan vans. It's been operating successfully for years and is keen on maintaining standards.

Sunny Safaris Ltd
 Col Middleton Rd, PO Box 7267, Arusha
 (☎ (057) 7145; fax 8094)
 Sunny, opposite the Golden Rose Hotel, is a
 well-established safari company with excellent
 4WD vehicles and very enthusiastic staff. In
 addition to catering for the Mt Meru trek, they
 cover all the northern national parks for a price
 per person per day of US$75 (four to five people)
 or US$115 (two people). This company comes
 highly recommended. They can also offer you
 Kilimanjaro along the Marangu route for
 US$475 (five days) or US$550 (six days) starting
 and finishing in Arusha as well as the Mt Meru
 trek. Sunny gets consistently good reports from
 everyone who has used their services. All major
 credit cards are accepted.

Tropical Tours Ltd
 Adventure Centre, Goliondoi Rd and Joel Haeder
 Rd, PO Box 727, Arusha (☎ (057) 8353; 8907)
 This company specialises mainly in walking and
 camping safaris off the beaten track and in this
 they're the leaders in Arusha. It's a deliberately
 small but very enthusiastic outfit committed to
 eco-tourism and the involvement of local people.
 All the same, they do offer the 'standard' Lake
 Manyara, Ngorongoro and Tarangire circuit
 lasting four days which costs US$440 (four
 people) or US$600 (two people). Similar is their
 seven days of the Serengeti and Ngorongoro
 except that on this safari there is some walking
 involved and includes visits to Lake Natron, the
 semi-active volcano of Oldonyo Lengai and to a
 Maasai village at Sonjo. The price of this safari
 is US$770 (four people) or US$1050 (two
 people). If you'd prefer a greater complement of
 walking then see later under Other Safaris for a
 description of what they offer in northern
 Maasailand and around Longido (between
 Arusha and Namanga). Tropical Tours also offer
 treks of Mt Meru and Kilimanjaro – see the
 relevant sections.

Wild Spirit Safari
 India St, PO Box 2288, Arusha
 (☎ /fax (057) 4215)
 A relative newcomer to the safari scene, Wild
 Spirit offers a number of unusual options which
 include cycling and walking safaris but they also
 cover Lake Manyara, Ngorongoro and Serengeti,
 combined with a visit to Lake Natron and a trek
 to the top of Oldonyo Lengai, the Maasai sacred
 mountain and a semi-active volcano. This safari
 takes seven days and costs from US$60 per
 person per day (six people) to US$85 (three
 people). Wild Spirit also cater for Mt Kilimanjaro
 treks up the Marangu, Machame, Umbwe,
 Mweka and Shira routes.

This is by no means a comprehensive list of
companies which offer camping safaris.
There are plenty more on just about every
floor of the AICC building. You could easily
spend a whole day checking out the various
offices.

Virtually all the companies which offer
camping safaris can also arrange a lodge
safari. In addition to those listed above, the
following companies are also worth trying:

Bobby Tours & Safaris
 Goliondoi Rd, PO Box 2169, Arusha
 (☎ /fax (057) 8176)
Bushtrekker Safaris
 PO Box 3173, Arusha (☎ (057) 3727; fax 8085)
Pelican Safaris
 Joel Maeda Rd, PO Box 6148, Arusha
 (☎ (057) 8181)
Ranger Safaris
 Room 333, Ngorongoro Wing, AICC, PO Box 9,
 Arusha (☎ (057) 3074)
Savannah Tours Ltd
 PO Box 3063, Arusha (☎ (057) 8455)
Simba Safaris
 Joel Maeda Rd, PO Box 1207, Arusha
 (☎ (057) 3509; fax 8207)
Takims Tours & Safaris
 Room 421, Ngorongoro Wing, AICC, PO Box
 6023, Arusha (☎ (057) 8026)
United Touring Company
 Corner Sokoine and Goliondoi Rds, PO Box
 2211, Arusha (☎ (057) 8844/5; fax 8222)
Wildersun Safaris & Tours
 Joel Maeda Rd, PO Box 930, Arusha
 (☎ (057) 8848; fax 8223)

WARNING
On the basis of reading through many readers'
letters and talking to various tour operators in
Arusha, it's suggested you treat with caution
any of the following companies:
 AA Tours, Africa Shoestring Safaris (ASS), Ali
Baba Tours, Amango Tours & Services, Angoni
Tours & Safaris, Arumeru Tours & Safaris, Blue
Sky Safaris, Great Mammals Safaris, Kili Trek-
king Safaris, Kilimanjaro Travel, Ostrich Tours &
Safaris, Paradise Safaris, Prince Kili Safaris, Star
Tours and Top Tours. Some of these are just
'briefcase' companies; others have come in for a
lot of negative comment. The tourist office in
Arusha also maintains a 'blacklist' of companies
which have been the cause of problems in the
past, so it's worth checking this out as well. ∎

TANZANIA

Again, this is by no means a comprehensive list of companies offering lodge safaris. There are many more in the AICC building and elsewhere.

Mwanza There's only one safari company in Mwanza and that is Kijereshi Tented Camp Ltd, Hotel Tilapia, Capri Point Rd, PO Box 190, Mwanza (☎ (068) 4067; fax 50142). Their agents in Arusha are Mamba Safaris Ltd, PO Box 1212 (☎ (057) 2127). This company offers only lodge safaris of Serengeti, Ngorongoro and Lake Manyara, some of which start and finish in Mwanza, while others start in Mwanza and finish in Arusha. A night or two at their luxury tented camp in the Western Corridor of the Serengeti is an integral part of all their safaris. Their range of six-day safaris start at US$875 per person (four people) and US$1150 (two people). Kijereshi also cater for Ekerewe Island and Rubondo Island National Park, both in Lake Victoria.

Dar es Salaam There are far fewer safari companies in Dar es Salaam, and they are scattered throughout the city centre. They cater mainly for safaris to Mikumi, Ruaha and Selous, and there are guaranteed departures, at least once a week, to all these parks. On the other hand, if you have a group together, most will lay on a safari any time you're ready.

Check out the following companies, which offer lodge-based safaris:

Bushtrekker Safaris
PO Box 5350, Dar es Salaam (☎ 36811)
Also very reliable, this company goes to all three parks on a regular basis.

Coastal Travels Ltd
Ali Mwinyi Rd, PO Box 3052, Dar es Salaam (☎ (051) 37479, fax 46045)
This is a well-established company which not only makes airline, hotel and lodge bookings but also specialises in safaris to Mikumi and Selous. It offers a two-day Mikumi trip which costs US$250 per person with full board at the lodge but excludes park entry fees. Extra days cost US$100 per person per day. A chartered flight, game drives, boat trips and walking safaris are all extra. Coastal can also arrange safaris to Ruaha

National Park along with chartered flight bookings. See the Selous Game Reserve and Ruaha National Park sections under National Parks for further details.

Gogo Safaris Ltd
Mkwepu St, PO Box 70647, Dar es Salaam (☎ (051) 32533; fax 46739)
This company can also offer a two-day Mikumi trip for US$240 per person with full board at the lodge but excluding park entry fees.

Impala Tours & Safaris
Zanaki St, PO Box 4783, Dar es Salaam (☎ (051) 25779)
This company specialises in safaris to Selous, and owns and runs the Impala Safari Camp in the game reserve. It can organise everything for you.

Savannah Tours Ltd
Kilimanjaro Hotel, PO Box 20517, Dar es Salaam (☎ (051) 35437; fax 113748)
This company, which is also the Hertz franchisee, specialises in the southern circuit – Selous, Ruaha and Mikumi – and comes highly recommended. It has a modern fleet of safari vehicles.

Takims Tours & Safaris
Jamhuri St, PO Box 20350, Dar es Salaam (☎ (051) 25691)
This reliable, long-established company goes to all the parks within reach of Dar es Salaam and has regular departures.

OTHER SAFARIS

With the expansion of the safari business in Arusha in recent years, more and more companies are beginning to offer unusual safaris which don't just involve driving around the game parks in vehicles but demand more input from you – basically, eco-tourism safaris. These include walking safaris (usually outside the national parks), camel safaris and cycling safaris.

Note Details of trekking Mt Kilimanjaro and Mt Meru along with costs and safari companies offering organised treks can be found in the relevant sections under the National Parks chapter. For trekking Mt Hanang, Tanzania's third-highest mountain, see below.

Walking Safaris

Other than Camels Only (see next section), the best outfit for these north of Arusha is Tropical Tours, The Adventure Centre, Goliondoi Rd, PO Box 727, Arusha (☎ (057)

8353; fax 8907), and Joel Haeder Rd (near the Clock Tower), Arusha (☎ (057) 2417). This company is fully committed to environmentally responsible tourism and has a wealth of experience in treks north-east and north of Arusha. They offer several walking safaris involving varying amounts of walking, and supported here and there by supply vehicles. Prices range from US$220 per person (minimum two people) for three days, and places covered include north Maasailand east of Ngorongoro and Serengeti, Mt Longido (2650m), not far from Namanga, and the Monduli Mountains rainforest, some 40 km north-west of Arusha.

Another possibility is to go walking with Japhet and Victor, a friendly local duo, who are based at Sunny Safaris, Col Middleton Rd, Arusha (☎ (057) 7145; fax 8094). They offer a full-day guided walk through the foothills of Mt Meru taking in a visit to a Maasai boma. The trip leaves every day at 8.30 am and returns to town around 4 pm. It costs just US$12, assuming a minimum of four participants, and includes a packed lunch. The same two people can also organise longer walking safaris – two to five days – which take you through Ngorongoro to Lake Eyasi where you can visit the Bushmen and Tatoga tribes.

Further afield, to the south-west of Arusha at Babati on the main Arusha-Dodoma road, are several other possibilities for walking safaris as well as trekking Mt Hanang (3417m). These are offered by Kahembe's Enterprises (☎ Babati 88; fax (057) 8801), PO Box 366, Babati. This is the only outfit which offers safaris of this nature in this part of Tanzania. For trekkers, there's a choice of a three-day 'tough route' up Mt Hanang for US$240 or a four-day 'easy route' for US$300 all-inclusive.

For those with more time and a desire to experience Tanzanian village life in-depth there are three walking safaris ranging from seven days to 16 days at US$60 per person per day, including trekking Mt Hanang. These safaris are memorable, hands-on adventures, but they do, obviously, require a flexible approach to life.

Camel Safaris

As in the Samburu and Pokot lands of northern Kenya, the Maasai lands of north-eastern Tanzania have been hosting camel safaris for several years now. This is a beautiful way to see the country at a leisurely pace. It gives you the opportunity to become fully involved in the daily lives of the local Maasai people who walk with you, do the camel handling and the cooking and other camp chores. The company running these trips is called Camels Only (The Adventure Centre, Goliondoi Rd, PO Box 12530, Arusha, ☎ (057) 7111; fax 8997) and their tented headquarters is situated in the northern foothills of Mt Meru, about 85 km from Namanga and 56 km from Arusha, well off the main road to the Kenyan border. There are three options, from a one-day safari (US$50 excluding transfers from/to Arusha but including lunch) to a 14-day adventure (US$3000 inclusive of vehicle transfers, full-board accommodation and national park fees).

Cycling Safaris

About the only outfit which offers a cycling safari is Wild Spirit Safari Ltd, India St, PO Box 288, Arusha (☎ /fax (057) 4215). On this six-day camping safari you spend 5½ days cycling to the foothills of Mt Kilimanjaro and then round the north-eastern side of Kilimanjaro, ending up in Moshi. The cost is from US$100 per person per day (five or more people) to US$210 (two people) and includes bikes, food, a guide and cook, camping equipment and vehicle transfers to Arusha. In case of problems, a car is available at any time throughout the safari.

Balloon Safaris

There are daily balloon safaris over the Serengeti which last about two hours and cost US$300 per person, including a full champagne breakfast after the flight. Demand for places is high, so advance booking is highly recommended. You can do this before you get to the Serengeti through Serengeti Balloon Safaris Ltd, Adventure Centre, Goliondoi Rd, PO Box 12116, Arusha (☎ (057) 8578; fax 8997). Otherwise, book them at either the

Seronera Lodge or the Serengeti Sopa Lodge when you're in the park itself.

DO-IT-YOURSELF SAFARIS

Tanzania is not Kenya as far as this goes because of the difficulties of hiring self-drive vehicles. Essentially, it's not worth it without your own vehicle, and if you bring a foreign registered vehicle into Tanzania, the park entry fees for the vehicle alone will be US$30 per 24 hours, as opposed to just TSh 1000 for a locally registered vehicle. Also, if you intend to stay at lodges, you won't be entitled to the discounts which agents can get for group bookings, so you'll be up for the full cost (the agents' commission for booking lodges is usually 10%).

Dar es Salaam

Dar es Salaam, the 'Haven of Peace', started out as a humble fishing village in the mid-19th century when the Sultan of Zanzibar decided to turn the inland creek (now the harbour) into a safe port and trading centre. It became the capital in 1891, when the German colonial authorities transferred their seat of government from Bagamoyo, whose port was unsuitable for steamships.

Since then the city has continued to grow and now has a population of about 1.5 million. Although quite a few high-rise buildings have appeared in the centre and at various places in the suburbs, Dar es Salaam remains substantially a low-rise city of red-tiled roofs, with its colonial character largely intact. The harbour is still fringed with palms and mangroves, and Arab dhows mingle with huge ocean-going vessels.

Like most large African cities, there are substantial contrasts between the various parts of the city. However, you won't find here the glaring disparity in living standards between the slums and the more salubrious suburbs that you would in Nairobi. The busy, dusty streets and concrete buildings around the Kariakoo Market and clock tower are certainly a world away from the wide, tree-lined boulevards of the government and diplomatic quarters to the north, but there's no way you would describe them as slums.

From being a relatively unrewarding place for nightlife in the mid to late 1980s, Dar es Salaam has considerably livened up, particularly if you're willing to head towards Oyster Bay.

Information

Tourist Office The Tanzania Tourist Corporation (TTC) office (☎ 27671) is on Maktaba St, near the junction with Samora Ave and opposite the New Africa Hotel. It's open Monday to Friday from 9 am to 5 pm and Saturday from 9 am till noon. The office has a limited range of glossy leaflets about the national parks and other places of interest, a notice board with out-of-date railway and lake ferry timetables and fares, a (not too good) map of the city and, sometimes, a 1:2,000,000 scale map of Tanzania, though they're often out of stock of the latter.

The TTC can also make reservations at any of the larger hotels in Tanzania and at most of the beach hotels and national park lodges (payment in foreign currency only) but they can't help you with budget accommodation. It's better to book national park lodges through a travel agency, as they may offer special deals.

Money Banking hours are Monday to Friday from 8.30 am to 3 pm and Saturdays from 8.30 to 11.30 am. The best rates offered by the banks are to be found at the National Bureau de Change on Samora Ave diagonally opposite Extelecoms House. This bank actually offers better rates than most of the foreign exchange bureaus.

In addition to the banks, there are many foreign exchange (forex) bureaus scattered around the centre of Dar. They are generally open between 8 am and 5 pm from Monday to Saturday and some are open on Sunday mornings. The Falcon Bureau de Change generally offers the lowest rates but is open for longer hours.

American Express is represented by Rickshaw Travels Ltd (☎ 29125; fax 29125), Ali Mwinyi Rd, PO Box 1889, Dar es Salaam. It offers the full range of Amex travel services and can issue US dollars travellers' cheques against an American Express card and a personal cheque. It's open Monday to Friday from 8 am to 5 pm and on Saturday from 8.30 am to 12.30 pm.

Post & Communications The main post office is on Maktaba St and it's here that you will find the poste restante. There's a small charge for letters collected. The post office

1 Pink Coconut Disco
2 Burundian Embassy
3 Palm Beach Hotel
4 Etienne's Hotel
5 Rwandan Embassy
6 Upanga Mishkaki House
7 Diamond Jubilee Hall
8 Barbeque House
9 Casino & California
   Dreaming Disco
10 Zanzibar Shipping
   Corporation (CCM
   Youth Building)
11 Oriental Restaurant
12 Kariakoo Market
13 National Museum
14 State House
15 Supreme Restaurant

Selander Bridge

To Beach Resorts & Bagamoyo

Dar es Salaam

0   250   500 m

United Nations Rd

Lugalo Road

Malik Road

Kiba Sila Road

Nyangato

Undali St

Mewen St

Ocean Road

INDIAN

OCEAN

See Central Dar es Salaam Map (page 589)

Mazengo Road

Maume Road

Alykhan

Mapora Street

Ohio Street

Ali Mwinyi Road

Golf Course

UWT Street

Ghana Avenue

Kibo St

Shaaban Robert Street

Mirambo Street

Botanical Gardens

Lithuli Road

13

Kisutu Street

Mtendeni St

Street

Morogoro Road

Garden Avenue

Panda Rd

Samora Avenue

Sokoine Drive

14

Libya Street

Jamhuri

Gandhi

Indira

Mosque St

India Street

Mkwepu St

Kaluta Street

Zanaki St

Bridge St

Makaba Street

Lumumba Street

Mnazi Mmoja

Aggrey St

Market St

Uhuru St

Algeria St

Lindi St

Sokoine Drive

Nkrumah

Train Station

Mapogoni Street

Kivukoni Front

Ocean Road

HARBOUR

To Airport & Tazara
Train Station

Ferry

Main Quay

TANZANIA

is open Monday to Friday from 8 am to 1 pm and 2 to 4.30 pm and on Saturday and Sunday from 9 am to noon.

International telephone calls are most reliably made from the Extelecoms office on the ground floor of Extelecoms House (the entrance is on Bridge St). It generally only takes a few minutes to make a connection here. This is the cheapest place to make an international call – six minutes to Australia costs TSh 8500, less to either Europe or North America.

Connections through hotel switchboards are less reliable plus you'll be charged commission which can be as high as 40%.

To call Kenya or Uganda, the cheapest way is to buy a phone card (TSh 3000 and TSh 5000) from the Extelecoms office and use the card phone outside the entrance.

The telephone area code for Dar es Salaam is 051.

Book Shops Unless you're particularly fond of heavy Marxist tomes and anticolonial rhetoric, there are no good book stores in Dar es Salaam. The ones that exist stock only a very limited selection of the paperback Heinemann African Writers Series.

For a much better selection, try any of the second-hand street stalls along Samora Ave, Maktaba St and outside Tancot House, opposite Luther House. Most of these also sell international news magazines such as *Time, Newsweek, New African, South* etc.

Street Name Changes Two of Dar's main streets were renamed in 1995 but everyone still knows them by their old name. They are:

Upanga Rd (old) = Ali Mwinyi Rd (new)
UWT St (old) = Bibi Titi Mohammed St (new)

National Museum

The National Museum is next to the Botanical Gardens, between Samora Ave and Sokoine Drive. It houses important archaeological collections, especially the fossil discoveries of Zinjanthropus (Nutcracker Man), and has sections on the Shirazi civilisation of Kilwa, the Zanzibar slave trade and the German and British colonial periods. There are also displays of handicrafts, witchcraft paraphernalia and traditional dancing instruments. Entry costs TSh 200 for residents, TSh 800 for nonresidents, and it's open daily from 9.30 am to 6 pm.

Village Museum

Another museum definitely worth visiting is the Village Museum, about 10 km from the city centre along the Bagamoyo road. This is an actual village consisting of a collection of authentically constructed dwellings from various parts of Tanzania, which display several distinct architectural styles. Open daily from 9 am to 7 pm, there's a small charge for entry plus another charge to take photographs. Traditional dances are performed on Saturday and Sunday between 4 and 8 pm.

Mwenge

Three km further down the Bagamoyo road at Mpakani Rd is Mwenge, a *makonde* (ebony-carving) community. It's an excellent place to pick up superb pieces of this traditional art form at rock-bottom prices. If you're heading this way by public transport, watch carefully, as it's not obvious from the Bagamoyo road.

Another good place to find makonde carvings, though at slightly higher prices, is the beer garden in front of the Palm Beach Hotel on Ali Mwinyi Rd. Every evening, vendors do the rounds of the tables with examples of the craft.

Art Centre

Local oil, water and chalk paintings can be seen at the Nyumba ya Sanaa building at the junction of Ohio St, Ali Mwinyi Rd and Bibi Titi Mohammed St, overlooking the Gymkhana Club. You can see the artists at work, and there are also makonde carvers and batik designers.

Kariakoo Market

Between Mkunguni and Tandamuti Sts, this market has a colourful and exotic atmosphere

PLACES TO STAY

3 Sheraton
  Dar es Salaam
9 Mawenzi Hotel
10 YMCA
14 YWCA
18 Embassy Hotel
23 Kilimanjaro Hotel
25 Luther House
27 New Africa Hotel
28 Motel Agip
39 Motel Afrique
47 Traffic Lights Motel
48 Holiday Hotel
49 Safari Inn
50 Jambo Inn
51 Peacock Hotel
52 Delux Inn
54 Hotel Tamarine &
  Hotel Internationale
57 Hotel Continental

58 Kibodya Hotel

PLACES TO EAT

15 Garden Plaza
  Restaurant
16 Azam
24 Hotel & Tourism
  Training Institute
32 Salamander Cafe
33 The Alcove
37 Sno-Cream Parlour
38 Rendezvous
40 Open House
  Restaurant
42 Chic King
43 Amrapali Restaurant
44 Night of Istanbul
45 The Cedars

OTHER

1 Gymkhana Club

2 Nyumba ya Sanaa
4 Air India
5 KLM, Ethiopian Airlines,
  Rosie Forex Bureau
  & Irish Embassy
6 Kenya Airways &
  Lufthansa
7 Rickshaw Travels &
  American Express
8 Coastal Travels
11 Immigration
12 Botanical Gardens
16 Mozambican Embassy
17 Main Post Office
19 Air Tanzania
20 Aeroflot
21 Belgian, German, Finnish,
  Indian, Kenyan, Malawian
  & Zimbabwean Embassies &
  High Commissions
22 Zambian High Commission

26 Lutheran Church
29 UK High Commission
30 Tourist Office (TTC)
31 Public Buses to
  Airport & TAZARA
  Train Station
34 Extelecoms House &
  Ugandan Embassy
35 Ticket Office for
  Boats to Zanzibar,
  Mafia & Mtwara
36 Roman Catholic Cathedral
41 Impala Tours
46 Buses to Moshi & Arusha
53 Clock Tower
55 Buses to Iringa & Mbeya
56 Buses to Tanga
59 Train Station
60 Malindi Dock (Ticket
  Office for Dhows
  to Zanzibar)

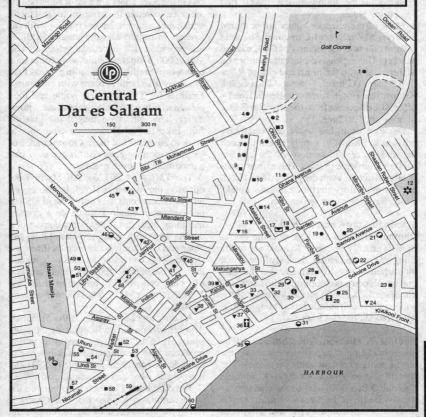

Central Dar es Salaam

0   150   300 m

Golf Course

HARBOUR

TANZANIA

– fruit, fish, spices, flowers, vegetables etc – but very few handicrafts for sale.

Places to Stay

Finding a place to stay in Dar es Salaam can be difficult. The later you arrive, the harder it gets. It's not that there aren't a lot of hotels – there are – but they always seem to be full, and this applies as much to the expensive places as to the budget hotels. So, whatever else you do on arrival in Dar es Salaam, *don't* pass up a vacant room. Take the room and then look for something else if you're not happy with it. You can always make a booking for the following day if you find something better.

Most of the cheaper hotels are scattered between Maktaba and Lumumba Sts, with several others in the vicinity of the Kariakoo Market. The expensive places are either on Maktaba St or to the north and east of it.

All the TTC hotels – New Africa Hotel, Kilimanjaro Hotel, Kunduchi Beach Hotel – offer 50% discounts from the day after Easter Sunday until 30 June.

Dar es Salaam has water and electricity problems. Basically, supply doesn't match demand, so certain sections of the city are shut off from time to time. This affects practically all hotels, even the New Africa Hotel, but not the Kilimanjaro or Embassy hotels, which have their own generators.

Places to Stay – bottom end

Camping There is nowhere to camp in Dar itself. The only option is to head out to the Rungwe Oceanic Hotel, the last of the beach hotels heading north from Dar and the only one which permits camping. This is some 27 km north of Dar and you can get most of the way on the beach shuttle bus although you'll have to walk the last km or so.

Hostels & Mission Guesthouses Three places stand head and shoulders above the rest as being excellent value for money. The first is *Luther House* (☎ 46687), Sokoine Drive, PO Box 389, next to the characteristically German Lutheran church at the junction of Sokoine Drive and Kivukoni

Front. A double with communal bathroom facilities costs US$15 and a single with private bathroom costs US$20. Breakfast is extra. It's clean and secure, mosquito nets are provided and there's hot water. As you might expect, it's a very popular place to stay. So popular in fact that it's likely to be booked out at least a week in advance, so to be sure of a room, write in advance requesting a booking and, preferably, enclosing a deposit.

Equally popular is the very clean and secure *YWCA* on Maktaba St, PO Box 2083, next to the main post office, which takes couples as well as women. The entrance is on Ghana Ave. There are a lot of rules (shorts are not allowed in the canteen, for instance), which are enforced, but everything works as a result. Mosquito nets and laundry facilities are provided. It's excellent value, at TSh 4000/6000 a single/double with communal bathroom facilities, including breakfast. There are also family rooms with communal facilities for TSh 5000. Be polite and look clean and tidy when asking about accommodation here, otherwise they'll tell you it's full. Like Luther House, it's advisable to book in advance, but there's more chance of getting a room here, as visitors can only stay a maximum of seven nights.

The *YMCA* (☎ 26726), Ali Mwinyi Rd opposite the Mawenzi Hotel, is also excellent value and costs the equivalent of US$10 per person in either a single or a double, including breakfast. The rooms consist of a double bed with mosquito net, table and chair and a balcony. Bathroom facilities are shared. You can also get lunch here and there's a bar of sorts. It's very secure and you can park cars in the compound. Like the YWCA, the YMCA takes both men and women.

Also worth checking out is the *Salvation Army Hostel* on Kilwa Rd, outside the town centre. It costs US$5 per person including breakfast, and accommodation is in separate bungalows. Meals are available (US$3) and there's also a bar and swimming pool.

The *Mzimbazi Centre* is also outside the town centre, on Kigogo Rd. The Centre is run by the archdiocese of Dar es Salaam and has pleasant gardens. Rooms cost US$4/6.50, the shared facilities are very clean and mosquito nets are provided. Couples have to stay in the two-bedroom flats (US$8 and with private bathroom), and you can camp in the gardens. The centre has a bar and a canteen selling basic meals.

Hotels Two of the cheapest hotels are the *Holiday Hotel*, Jamhuri St, and the *Traffic Lights Motel* (☎ 23438), corner of Jamhuri St and Morogoro Rd, both of which have singles/doubles for TSh 3600/4100 with shared bathroom facilities. They also have doubles with private bathroom for TSh 4600. All the rooms are pretty basic.

Going up in price a little, one of the best places to stay, and one which has become very popular with travellers, is the *Safari Inn* (☎ 38101; fax 46333), Band St, PO Box 21113, off Libya St behind the Jambo Inn. It's very clean and friendly and has a reasonably useful notice board. It's excellent value at TSh 5000/8000 for singles/doubles with private bathroom and breakfast. There are also a number of air-con rooms, which go for TSh 10,000 a double including breakfast. Checkout time is 11 am. There used to be a sign saying 'Women of moral turpitude not allowed', but it's been replaced with one saying 'No alcohol permitted'. Perhaps they decided that it was alcohol that was the font of all iniquity?

The *Jambo Inn* (☎ 30568) on Libya St is also reasonable value at TSh 5000/8000 for singles/doubles with private bathroom and fan, and suites for TSh 9000. The room rates include a continental breakfast. The hotel has its own restaurant, which specialises in Indian nonvegetarian food. There's a laundry service and checkout time is 11 am.

Further afield, in the vicinity of the clock tower, are several other cheapies, which include the *Hotel Tamarine* (☎ 20233) on Lindi St which offers doubles with private bathroom and fan for TSh 4000. On the opposite side of the road is the *Hotel Internationale* (☎ 22785) which has similarly priced doubles. Both are essentially 'knocking shops'. Much better, but more expensive,

is the *Kibodya Hotel* (☎ 31312) on Nkrumah St, which has doubles (no singles) with bathroom for TSh 8000. Breakfast is extra. The Kibodya is a popular place to stay and is often booked out three days in advance.

Places to Stay – middle

City Centre Worth a try in this category is the *Hotel Continental* (☎ 33418), Nkrumah St. There are no singles, and doubles with private bathroom cost TSh 17,500 including a continental breakfast. The hotel has its own bar and restaurant which is open 24 hours a day.

Similar in standard is the *Motel Afrique* (☎ 46557), corner Kaluta and Bridge Sts, which has singles with shared bathroom for TSh 5000 to TSh 8500 and doubles with private bathroom and air-con for TSh 14,500 to TSh 16,500. The room rates include breakfast. The hotel has a bar and restaurant on the 4th floor.

The *Hotel Skyways* (☎ 27061), corner Sokoine Drive and Ohio St, also used to be a popular place to stay in this range but is currently closed for renovations.

Not far from the main post office is the *Mawenzi Hotel* (☎ 27761; fax 46561), PO Box 3222, on the corner of Ali Mwinyi Rd and Maktaba St, opposite the YMCA. This hotel is excellent value, very clean and the staff are friendly. It has singles/doubles at US$35/50 and triples for US$45. They also have deluxe rooms for US$50. All prices include breakfast but they're of the Gulag variety. All rooms have private bathroom, air-con and telephone, room service is available and the hotel has its own bar and restaurant. Only rarely is this hotel full, even in the late afternoon.

Top of the range in this category is the brand-new *Peacock Hotel* (☎ 35075; fax 44215), PO Box 70270, Bibi Titi Mohammed St, which offers singles/doubles with private bathroom and air-con for US$50/55 including a continental breakfast. If you want a TV in your room (with CNN) it costs US$5 extra. They also have executive doubles at US$65 and triples for US$75. The hotel has its own very salubrious bar and restaurant and the staff are friendly and helpful.

Upanga North of the city centre (a 15 to 20-minute walk or TSh 3000 taxi ride), you can't beat the Greek-owned *Palm Beach Hotel* (☎ 22931), Ali Mwinyi Rd, near the junction with Ocean Rd. The hotel is efficiently run, secure and hassle-free, has friendly staff and is as clean as a whistle. There are a variety of rooms, all with air-con and telephone, at US$30/35 a single/double with shared bath and US$35/40 a single/double with private bath. Children between the ages of two and 12 years are charged 50% of adult rates. Prices include breakfast (extra charge for eggs) and the hotel has a laundry service. The restaurant has an indoor area (basically seafood and meats), and a beer garden barbecue area where you can eat al fresco.

Not far from the Palm Beach Hotel is *Etienne's Hotel* (☎ 20293) on Ocean Rd. It has a kind of engaging leafy degeneracy about it with hints of a down-at-heel rural English pub, and comes complete with one of the world's most indolent bartenders. It's tropical languor *par excellence*. Fans groan lazily above your head, the springs on the lounge seats succumbed to posterior pressure long ago, the lights are dim and people talk in conspiratorial tones. There's a beer garden and meals are available. There are no singles, and doubles with shared bathroom cost approximately the same as at the Palm Beach Hotel.

Places to Stay – top end

There are only five top-end hotels in the city centre, three of which are privately owned while the others are operated by the TTC. All accept credit cards.

Of the privately owned, marginally the cheapest is the *Embassy Hotel* (☎ 30006; fax 44991), PO Box 3152, 24 Garden Ave, which has 150 rooms, all with private bathroom, air-con, a telephone and 24-hour room service. On the lower two floors these cost US$71/80 for singles/doubles, while on the upper two floors they cost US$80/90 for singles/doubles, with suites at US$120. All rates include a continental breakfast. There's a swimming pool, two bars, grill, restaurant and all the usual services.

Slightly more expensive is the *Motel Agip* (☎ 23511; fax 39833), PO Box 529, Pamba Rd, at the back of the New Africa Hotel. Singles/doubles with private bathroom and air-con cost US$90/95, including a continental breakfast. Extra beds are US$37. The hotel has its own bar and two restaurants.

The first of the TTC hotels is the *New Africa Hotel* on Maktaba St. A well-known landmark, it's been undergoing renovation and extensions for some years. By the time it reopens, it will probably have much the same pricing structure as the Kilimanjaro Hotel.

Also TTC-owned, the *Kilimanjaro Hotel* (☎ 21281; fax 46762), PO Box 9574, Kivukoni Front, has singles/doubles with a full breakfast for US$95/110 plus 5% service charges. All the rooms are well appointed and fully air-con plus there's an Olympic-size swimming pool, ample parking, two restaurants, a cocktail bar, shopping arcade and a bureau de change.

Top of the range is the brand-new *Sheraton Dar es Salaam* (☎ 44111; fax 44847), PO Box 791, Ohio St, adjacent to the golf course/Gymkhana Club. This place is awash with polished marble and, once inside, you can pretend the rest of Dar es Salaam doesn't exist. It's all air-con, there's a swimming pool, health centre, two restaurants, two bars, a shopping arcade (including a branch of Rickshaw Travels/American Express, and British Airways), a 24-hour business centre and room service. Every room has a colour TV. Singles/doubles are from US$182/192 plus 25% government taxes and service charges. Room rates do not include breakfast.

Places to Eat – cheap

There are many small restaurants in the city centre where you can buy a cheap traditional African meal or Indian food (usually the latter). Some of these places are attached to hotels.

Very popular, especially for lunch, is the *Salamander Cafe*, Samora Ave at Mkwepu St, where you can eat either inside or outside on the verandah. An average lunch costs about TSh 1500. They have seafood, spaghetti, hot dogs, hamburgers and chicken as well as prawns (TSh 4000), and the service is brisk. Right opposite is the *Burger Bite*, a McDonald's clone, with prices similar to those at the Salamander.

Other good cheapies include the *Pop-In*, the restaurant at the *Jambo Inn* (lunch-time specials such as mutton biriyani and pilau or chicken for TSh 1500), and the *Nawaz Restaurant*, Msinhiri St, between Mosque St and Morogoro Rd, which has cheap rice and meat dishes.

Possibly better than all the above at lunch time, however, is the *Hotel & Tourism Training Institute* (previously known as Forodhani's) on Kivukoni Front. This is where hospitality-trade college students do their practical training. There's a set menu every day which costs just TSh 1500 and, as you might imagine, the students are doing their best to impress. The menu is excellent value and is served between 12.30 and 2 pm. Everyone is obsequiously friendly and there's a very popular attached bar which is always packed out, though it does close at 6 pm. Beers are cheap, too, and *cold*!

For vegetarian restaurants, *Pandya's Vegetarian Restaurant*, Kaluta and Bridge Sts, is highly rated. Here you can get an all-you-can-eat lunch or dinner for around TSh 3000. Similar but possibly better is *Amrapali's* on the north side of the junction between Libya, Mtendeni and Zanaki Sts. Try the vegetable curries, samosas and bhajis. The service here is instant. Neither Pandya's nor Amrapali's sells alcohol.

Also very good for vegetarian Indian food is the *Supreme Restaurant*, Nkrumah St. This place has been operating for years and has a well-deserved good reputation. It's open Monday to Saturday from 8.30 to 11 am (snacks), 12.30 to 2.30 pm (lunch), 4.30 to 6 pm (snacks) and 7.30 to 10 pm (dinner). On Sunday it's open from 7.30 to 10.30 am (snacks) and noon to 2 pm (lunch). The

Royal Restaurant, Jamhuri St, between Mosque and Kitumbini Sts, also does vegetable curries and the like.

For even cheaper stand-up-and-eat or take-away snacks, try one of the cafes near the junction of Mkwepu and Makunganya Sts.

Meat-eaters have a choice of three inexpensive places just north of the city centre off Ali Mwinyi Rd. First up is *Barbecue House*, which offers Indian food in clean surroundings. The house speciality is tandoori chicken but their samosas, kachoris and bhajis are also good. Alcoholic drinks are not served but you can bring your own. Close by is *Upanga Mishkaki House*, Alykhan Rd next to Skylark Video. It serves basic chicken dishes, mishkaki, chips and samosas. You can either eat in or take-away. A little further afield on Malik Rd is the *Diamond Jubilee Hall* where there's another Indian restaurant inside the main gate. The menu is dominated by chicken. It's open weekday evenings from 7 pm and also for Sunday lunch. Like the other two, there are no alcoholic drinks available.

Back in the centre of town, ice-cream freaks should make at least one visit to the *Sno-Cream Parlour*, Mansfield St, near the junction with Bridge St. Mansfield St is between Samora Ave and Sokoine Drive. This place has the best ice cream in Tanzania and is well on the way to becoming a legend among travellers. You should see the number of Indian families who come here on Sundays! Also very good is *Azam* at the junction of India and Jamhuri Sts. Lastly, for fruit juices, peanut brittle and gooey cakes, go to *Siefee's Juice Shop*, Samora Ave. It also has good samosas. Other travellers recommend the *Cold Drink House* for cheap fruit juices – it can be found opposite the Open House restaurant.

Places to Eat – more expensive

Dar es Salaam is a far cry from Nairobi so the choice is limited.

For a not-too-expensive splurge, the *DSM Chinese Restaurant* in the basement of the NIC building, Samora Ave at Mirambo St, is excellent value and has been a popular place for a small spree for years, especially if you want a break from Indian or western food.

For a good Indian meal, try the *Shalimar Restaurant* on Mansfield St, next door to the Sno-Cream. They have a good selection of North Indian and Mughlai dishes here. The *Rendezvous* on Samora Ave is a steakhouse, and popular with local people as well as being good value. Meals cost TSh 2000 to TSh 3000. The restaurant is closed on Mondays, but open for lunch until 3.30 pm and for dinner during the rest of the week.

Meals at the *Hotel Agip* have been described by a few Italian travellers as being 'as good as a 1st-class restaurant in Rome with better service and at a fraction of the cost'. Nevertheless, it is very middle-class and the food is quite expensive. More reasonably priced food can be found at the *Garden Plaza Restaurant* on Maktaba St opposite the main post office. It serves a variety of European dishes and you can sit inside or out on the terrace.

Out of the city centre, it's worth heading for the very popular outdoor barbecue at the *Palm Beach Hotel*, Ali Mwinyi Rd, especially if you're thinking of doing some serious drinking afterwards (they never run out of beer, even if you're not eating). Barbecued chicken or doner kebab with chips and salad costs around TSh 1500. The indoor restaurant offers somewhat more expensive, standard European dishes but the food is only average. It's an excellent place to make useful contacts. Nearby *Etienne's Hotel*, Ocean Rd, also offers lunch and dinner, is recommended by Peace Corps volunteers and is also popular with local people. It's somewhat cheaper than the Palm Beach.

The *Night of Istanbul*, on the corner of Bibi Titi Mohammed and Zanaki Sts, used to be Dar's only Turkish/Lebanese restaurant but it closed down a few years ago for renovations and, judging from the pace at which these are going, it could be some time before it reopens. If it is open by the time you read this, give it a go, as in the past the food was very good. In the meantime, you're in luck if you want Lebanese food because just round the corner from the Istanbul is *The Cedars* on Bibi Titi Mohammed St, which offers fast, tasty, distinctive food with plenty of pita bread and salad. The felafel and hummus are particularly recommended. There's even a pool table in the back room if you fancy a game after your meal.

For a totally different cuisine, try the *Oriental Restaurant* on Lumumba St near the junction with Morogoro Rd. This is a Korean restaurant where you can barbecue the meat at your own table. The menu is limited but the kimchi is excellent. You have the choice of eating al fresco or indoors.

For a real splurge, there's a choice of four restaurants. One of the most popular is *The Alcove*, Samora Ave, which offers Indian and Chinese dishes in air-con comfort and soft lighting. The food would rate a mention in any international restaurant guide. Average prices for a main course are TSh 3000 to TSh 4000, though if you also have a starter and a dessert your bill will be considerably higher. Only imported beers are available, and these are (naturally) more expensive than Safari Lager or Tusker. The Alcove is open for lunch and dinner. Get there early or reserve a table if you don't want to stand around.

Similar but with a more intimate atmosphere than The Alcove is *Open House* on Zanaki St, which is owned by the same people. The Indian food is some of the best in Dar but the Chinese menu has a definite Indian bias (it's hot and spicy). They also serve decent pizza. Only imported beers are available.

More expensive still is the *Pearl Club Restaurant*, overlooking the Gymkhana Club on the roundabout where Ali Mwinyi Rd, Ohio St and Bibi Titi Mohammed St meet. It's very up-market, with starched linen tablecloths and an extensive wine list, and you have the choice of eating al fresco on the covered balcony or inside with air-con. Main dishes range from TSh 4000 (fish, pepper steak etc) up to TSh 8000 (lobster). Prawns are TSh 5000, with salads and soups between TSh 1500 and TSh 1800. There's usually a live band playing at weekends.

Most people have at least one meal at the

rooftop restaurant in the *Kilimanjaro Hotel*. The views over the harbour at night are superb and the food is usually good, though the quality is not consistent. It's popular with businesspeople, local expatriates and well-heeled tourists. Prices are roughly the same as those at The Alcove.

There's one more place well worth considering if you have transport and that is the *Euro Bar*, some seven km north of town close to the beach. It has a superb continental/seafood menu and the food is the best in Tanzania. Prices are in the TSh 4000 to TSh 7000 range. As its name suggests, there's also a bar here which is very popular with expatriates any night of the week. The only trouble with this place is finding it, especially after dark! Basically, you take the Old Bagamoyo Rd (off New Bagamoyo Rd) and keep going until you pass over a rickety wooden bridge. After that, it's the second turning on the right. It's well lit and there are always a number of cars parked there, so it is easily recognisable.

Entertainment

Cinemas Films are shown at the British Council (☎ 22716), Samora Ave, on Monday and Wednesday and at the Goethe Institut (☎ 22227), IPS building, Maktaba St, on Friday. They're open to all and there's no entry fee. The US Information Service (☎ 26611), Samora Ave, offers much the same thing.

Discos Far and away the most popular disco in Dar es Salaam is *Club Bilicanas*, at the back of the former Mbowe Hotel on Mkwepu St. This is one of the best discos in East Africa. It's obviously had mega-dollars poured into it, has been imaginatively designed and has all the lighting and other effects you'd expect from a world-class disco. Drink prices are reasonable and the place is fully air-con. It's open every night until around 4 am and entry costs TSh 2000 for a single person or TSh 3000 for a couple, except on Friday and Saturday nights, when the price is TSh 2500 and TSh 3000 per person, respectively.

Also right in the centre is the delightfully sleazy *Margot's* on Bridge St, adjacent to the Extelecoms building. It's a disco-video bar and perfect for that last 'one for the road' late at night.

Halfway up Ali Mwinyi Rd is the brand-new *California Dreaming Disco*.

Right at the end of Ali Mwinyi Rd at Selander Bridge is the *Pink Coconut* (frequently nicknamed the Pink Parrot) which is popular with school and university students.

Another disco, which is open nightly, is at the *Oyster Bay Hotel*, though you'll definitely need a taxi (TSh 3000) to get there from the centre. This is an open-air disco with live bands. Entry costs TSh 2000 per person. It used to be very popular but is often almost empty these days. The clientele has obviously deserted it in favour of Bilicanas. The problem with coming here without your own transport is that the taxi drivers have you over a barrel when you want to leave.

Popular with local people but quite a long way out of the centre in the Kinondoni district is *Tazara*, which plays mainly Zaïrese music.

There are also regular discos at the *Kilimanjaro Hotel* and at the beach resort hotels but they're relatively tame affairs and the drinks are more expensive.

Live Music There's not much work for musicians in Dar es Salaam except at expensive restaurants and one or two discos so don't come here with big expectations. One place where you can find live music, and which is worth making the effort to get to, is the *Vijana Social Hall* in the Kinondoni district. There's a live band here every Sunday which kicks off at around 4 pm.

Bars There are very few gripping bars in Dar es Salaam but three of the liveliest are the *Hotel & Tourism Training Institute* (formerly Forodhani's) on Kivukoni Front, the *Palm Beach Hotel*, Ali Mwinyi Rd at Selander Bridge, and *Etienne's Hotel* on Ocean Rd. Note that the Tourism & Training Institute bar closes at 6 pm. The mezzanine bar at the *Embassy Hotel*, Garden Ave, varies according to who is staying there but you can usually expect a friendly and garrulous crowd of resident expatriates and Tanzanians every evening from around 5 pm onwards. You need to be fairly well dressed to get in here, otherwise you'll feel very much out of place.

Other than the Euro Bar (mentioned earlier), another major expatriate hangout is *Smokies* in Oyster Bay close to the International Upper School. You'll need a taxi to get there and you need to book a return trip because there are no taxis running from this place.

Getting There & Away

Air Dar es Salaam is the major international arrival point for flights from overseas. See the earlier Getting There & Away and Getting Around chapters for Tanzania for details of international and domestic flights – except those connecting Zanzibar with Kenya, which can be found in the Zanzibar section.

Airlines with offices in Dar es Salaam are:

Aeroflot
    Eminaz Mansion, Samora Ave (☎ 34602)
Air France
    Peugeot House, corner of Ali Mwinyi Rd and Bibi Titi Mohammed St (☎ 20356). Air France announced in March 1996 that it was pulling out of Tanzania so this office may now be closed.
Air India
    Corner of Ali Mwinyi Rd and Bibi Titi Mohammed St (☎ 23525)
Air Tanzania
    ATC House, Ohio St (☎ 38300)
British Airways
    Coronation House, Samora Ave (☎ 560250). There's also a branch at the Sheraton Dar es Salaam, Ohio St.
EgyptAir
    Matasalamat Mansion, Samora Ave (☎ 23425)
Ethiopian Airlines
    TDFL building, Ohio St (☎ 24174)
Kenya Airways
    Peugeot House, Ali Mwinyi Rd (☎ 25352)
KLM
    TDFL building, Ohio St (☎ 37519)
Lufthansa
    Peugeot House, Ali Mwinyi Rd (☎ 38843)
Sabena
    AMI building, Samora Ave (☎ 30109)
Swissair
    Luther House, Sokoine Drive (☎ 34068)

Bus As there's no central bus station in Dar es Salaam, buses to various parts of the country leave from a variety of places within the city.

Buses for Bagamoyo, Mwanza, Morogoro and Dodoma leave throughout the day until about 3 pm from outside the Kariakoo Market on Msimbazi St. They depart when full. The fare to Bagamoyo is TSh 400 one way and the journey takes between two and three hours.

Heading for Moshi, Arusha and Mtwara buses depart from the bus station on the corner of Morogoro Rd and Libya St. Buses depart daily between 6 am and noon for Moshi and Arusha and cost TSh 6500 (luxury), TSh 5800 (semi-luxury, Arusha) and TSh 5500 (semi-luxury, Moshi). Fresh ya Shamba, Mkewma, Osaka Royal Class and Dar Express have the best buses. They take about seven hours between Dar and Moshi and a further hour to Arusha. The road is excellent all the way from Dar to Arusha.

Buses to Tanga, Iringa and Mbeya depart from various offices on the south side of Mnazi Mmoja park along Bibi Titi Mohammed St between Uhuru and Nkrumah Sts. The buses to Tanga take between seven and eight hours and those to Mbeya take about 20 hours. See the individual town entries for details of fares and schedules. In the same place you'll also find a Metro-International bus which departs once a week on Tuesday and goes direct from Dar es Salaam to Lilongwe (Malawi). For details see the Tanzania Getting There & Away chapter.

Train For information about the TAZARA line between Dar es Salaam and Kapiri Mposhi (Zambia), see the earlier Tanzania Getting There & Away chapter. For details of the Central Line railway between Dar es Salaam and Kigoma, Mwanza, Tanga and Moshi, see the Tanzania Getting Around chapter.

Boat There are boats to Zanzibar and other points on the coast.

Zanzibar There's a choice of four different

boats: a hydrofoil, a catamaran and two ordinary ferry boats. It's all very well organised and there are daily departures on most.

The one thing you *must* have before you're allowed to board *any* boat to Zanzibar is a yellow fever vaccination certificate. This requirement has officially been abolished but this hasn't, apparently, percolated down to the port staff, so make sure you have one in order to avoid unpleasantness.

Whichever form of transport you take, there's a US$5 port charge in addition to the boat fare.

All the ferry companies have their offices alongside the dock on Sokoine Drive opposite the Roman Catholic cathedral. Departure times vary but are chalked up on blackboards outside the ticket offices. You'll be besieged by young men offering 'help' (for a tip) on arrival but you don't need it. Everything is perfectly obvious.

The cheapest ferry boats are the MV *Muungano*, operated by Azam Marine & Co (☎ 26699 in Dar es Salaam, (054) 31262 in Zanzibar) and the *MV Noora*, operated by the Africa Shipping Corporation (☎ Dar es Salaam 33414, or Zanzibar (054) 33031). The MV *Muungano* departs daily at 11.15 am and arrives at Zanzibar at 2.30 pm. The fare is US$10. The MV *Noora* departs daily at 12.30 pm and arrives at Zanzibar two hours later. In the opposite direction it departs Zanzibar daily at 10 pm and takes five hours to Dar but you stay on the boat until dawn. The fare costs US$10 VIP class, TSh 4500 1st class and TSh 3700 2nd class.

Next up is the *Zanzibar Sea Ferries* which plies between Dar and Tanga via Zanzibar and Pemba and costs US$15 (Dar-Zanzibar). It departs Dar on Monday, Tuesday, Wednesday and Thursday at 10 pm and takes five hours but you stay on the boat until dawn off Zanzibar. Quite a few travellers use this boat as you can sleep on board overnight and have the advantage of getting into Zanzibar very early (and, therefore, have the pick of the budget hotels).

Faster, but somewhat more expensive, is the *Kondor 5*, also operated by Azam Marine, which departs Dar daily at 8.15 am

and 1 pm and arrives at Zanzibar 1½ hours later. In the opposite direction, the *Kondor 5* departs Zanzibar for Dar es Salaam at 10.30 am and 3 pm. The fare is US$20. The same company also operates the *Serengeti* but the schedule for this boat is irregular. It's slower – 2¾ hours – but costs the same.

The fastest and most expensive boat is the hydrofoil *Sea Express* operated by Sea Express Services Ltd. This departs daily from Dar at 7.30, 8 and 10 am, noon and 2.30 and 4.30 pm and takes just 45 minutes. In the opposite direction, the *Sea Express* departs Zanzibar for Dar es Salaam at 7 and 10 am, noon and 2.30, 4.30 and 4.45 pm. The fare is US$35 1st class and US$30 2nd class. The only difference between 1st and 2nd class is a little extra legroom.

Mafia Island, Kilwa & Mtwara The only ferry connecting Dar es Salaam with places south towards Mozambique is the FB *Canadian Spirit* operated by Adecon Marine Inc (☎ 20856; fax 33972 in Dar es Salaam). It departs Dar es Salaam every week on Wednesday at 9 am, arrives at Mafia island seven hours later and Mtwara 18 hours later. In the opposite direction, it departs Mtwara on Friday at 5 pm. The fares from Dar to Mtwara are TSh 12,000/8000/6000 in 1st/2nd/3rd class, plus TSh 300 port taxes. Fares to Mafia island are TSh 8000/6000/5000 in 1st/2nd/3rd class. Adecon Marine's office is at the southern end of the Zanzibar ferries offices on Sokoine Drive and it's open Monday to Saturday from 7.30 to 10.30 am and 2.30 to 6.30 pm.

Depending on passenger and freight demand, this ferry sometimes also calls at Kilwa and Lindi. If it's going to do that, this will be indicated on the blackboard at the company's office.

Getting Around
The Airport Dar es Salaam airport is 13 km from the city centre. Bus No 67 connects the two but, if you get on at the airport, make sure that it is going right into the city centre – some don't. From Dar, the buses leave from Kariakoo Market (Shule ya Uhuru).

A shuttle bus between the centre of Dar es Salaam and the airport is operated by Takims Tours & Safaris. It leaves for the airport from the New Africa Hotel, Maktaba St, at 8 and 10 am. In the opposite direction, shuttle buses from the airport to Dar es Salaam connect with incoming flights between 9 am and 6 pm and will take you direct to your hotel. The fare is TSh 600 (TSh 400 for children).

A taxi to or from the airport costs TSh 5000 (but first quotes are often higher). You can share this with up to four people.

Bus Local buses are operated by both government (UDA buses) and private firms (Dala Dala). Neither type is numbered. Instead, buses have their first and last stop indicated in the front window. The bus to the TAZARA railway station is marked 'Posta Vigunguti'. Fares are fixed and are only a few shillings, but all buses are very crowded. It would be almost impossible to get onto them with a rucksack, let alone get off at your destination. The main terminals are:

'Old Posta' on Sokoine Drive opposite the Lutheran Church (for Temeke, Mbagala, Mtoni, Ubongo and Buguruni)

'Stesheni' near the clock tower (for Mwenge and Massasani)

'New Posta' opposite the main post office on Maktaba St (for Kinondoni, Temeke and Mwenge)

Taxi Taxis have no meters and charge a standard TSh 2000 per journey inside the immediate city centre. Slightly outside this area, they'll charge TSh 2000 to TSh 3000, to Oyster Bay TSh 3000 to TSh 4000, depending on the time of day. To the TAZARA railway station, they should cost you around TSh 3000.

Around Dar es Salaam

THE NORTHERN BEACHES

Oyster Bay is the nearest beach, six km north of the city centre and on the fringes of where the affluent and the foreign ambassadors have their residences. As you might expect, it's a particularly beautiful stretch of tropical coastline fringed with coconut palms, but keeping it that way has become a bone of contention between local environmental groups and the city council.

There are other beaches a little further up the coast from here, but the major resort area is 25 to 27 km north of the city, east of the Bagamoyo road. Strung out along the coast here, from south to north, are the Kunduchi Beach Hotel, Silversands, the Rungwe Oceanic Hotel and the Bahari Beach Hotel. It's an idyllic mixture of sea, sand, sun and landscaped tropical extravagance. The only drawback is the copious amount of seaweed, which makes swimming at high tide very unpleasant. When the tide goes out, however, the seaweed tends to stay on the beach, thus providing clear sea in which to enjoy yourself. There are also several wooded islands with good beaches offshore, to which the beach hotels run boats.

If you stay at any of these beach resorts, don't walk from one to the other either along the beach or along the connecting roads unless you're with a large group. Many people have been robbed, some violently. Always take a taxi or get a lift.

Boat trips to offshore islands such as **Mbudya**, where you can swim, snorkel or sunbathe, are available from the Kunduchi Beach Hotel, the Rungwe Oceanic Hotel and the Bahari Beach Hotel. There are usually several trips per day from Monday to Saturday and more on Sundays and public holidays. You need a minimum of four people, unless you're willing to pay a surcharge. You can also go sailing from these places or rent a catamaran but it won't be a cheap day out.

Places to Stay

The *Oyster Bay Hotel* (☎ (051) 68062), Touré Drive, PO Box 2261, Dar es Salaam, about six km from the city centre, is the first of the beach hotels north of Dar es Salaam. All rooms face the sea and have private bathroom and air-con. Bed and breakfast costs US$90/110 for singles/doubles, and there are suites for US$150 and US$170. Credit cards are not accepted. The hotel has its own bar, restaurant and disco.

Of the other hotels further up the coast, the TTC *Kunduchi Beach Hotel* (☎ (051) 47621) is quite pleasant (although the tourist office in town will tell you otherwise) and all rooms face the ocean. Singles/doubles with private bathroom and a continental breakfast cost US$36/45, including taxes but excluding 5% service charges. Temporary daily entry for nonresidents costs TSh 500, plus a further TSh 200 to use the swimming pool, but you don't pay this if you arrive on the State Transport Corporation shuttle bus, since they assume you're going to stay there or go further up the coast to one of the other hotels.

Next up the coast is the *Rungwe Oceanic Hotel* (☎ (051) 47021), which is favoured by overland truck companies because it's the only beach hotel where camping is permitted. This makes it the only one within reach of the budget traveller. Camping costs TSh 500 per person per night, but the site is somewhat run-down and water is rarely available. It's possible to leave a vehicle here for a small nightly charge while you go to Zanzibar.

Top of the range is the *Bahari Beach Hotel* (☎ (051) 47101), a stunningly beautiful construction in coral rag and makuti, and very thoughtfully landscaped with flowering trees and coconut palms. Apart from the reception and dining areas, the Bahari consists of a series of two-storey chalets, each with four bedrooms, private showers, individual balconies and air-con. There's a swimming pool and a very popular weekend disco. Doubles (no singles) with a continental breakfast cost US$90 and triples cost US$110 in the high season, including taxes. If you want a fridge in your room this costs an extra TSh 2500. Temporary daily entry costs TSh 500 on weekdays and Saturdays and TSh 800 on Sundays, when there's live music. Bookings should be made through Bushtrekker Safaris (☎ (051) 31957; telex 41178), PO Box 5350, Dar es Salaam.

Places to Eat

It's more than likely that you'll eat at the hotel where you're staying, but if you're just a day guest, you can also eat lunch and dinner at any of the hotels. The cost for either meal is about US$12 (payable in shillings). Those relying on the State Transport Corporation shuttle bus from Dar es Salaam to the hotels only have the option of lunch, since the last bus back to Dar es Salaam leaves at about 6 pm. If you're staying for dinner, you'll need your own transport back.

Getting There & Away

It is possible to get to the Kunduchi beach resorts using local buses from the centre of Dar es Salaam, but these will drop you in the village, from where it's quite a walk to the hotels. Also, there's a good chance of being robbed. It's much safer and more convenient to take the State Transport Corporation shuttle bus from the New Africa Hotel in Dar es Salaam, which leaves the hotel at 9 am, 2 and 5 pm Monday to Friday; 9 am, 1 and 5 pm on Saturday; and 9 and 11 am and 1 and 5 pm on Sunday and public holidays. In the opposite direction, ask at your hotel for the return times, and don't worry if the bus doesn't arrive on time – it's often half an hour late. The fare costs TSh 600 (TSh 400 for children).

THE SOUTHERN BEACHES

Some 28 km south of Dar es Salaam, there's the *Ras Kutani Beach Resort*, a relatively new place which is built of local materials to blend with the environment, but with the full range of creature comforts. It is owned by the Selous Safari Company (☎ (051) 28485), PO Box 1192, Dar es Salaam, and consists of 25 units with private bathroom built around a beautiful freshwater lagoon. The units cost US$120 per person per night with full board and including taxes but excluding service charges (5%). There's a 50% supplement on the above rates during July and August, October and January and December. Bookings can be made through Coastal Travels Ltd (☎ (051) 37479; fax 46045 in Dar es Salaam).

Getting There & Away
The only way to get to Ras Kutani is by taxi or to arrange for the hotel to provide transport. This is negotiable and could be free depending on how many nights you intend to stay.

The Coast

BAGAMOYO

The name of this coastal town 75 km north of Dar se Salaam derives from the word *bwagamoyo*, meaning 'lay down your heart'. It's a reminder that this was once the terminus of the slave trade caravan route from Lake Tanganyika. This was the point of no return, where the captives were loaded onto dhows and shipped to Zanzibar for sale to Arab buyers.

Bagamoyo later became the headquarters of the German colonial administration, and many of the buildings which they constructed remain, though in a dilapidated state of repair. However, its history goes back to the 14th century, when the East African coast was being settled by Arabs and Shirazis from the Persian Gulf. The ruins they left at Kaole, just outside Bagamoyo, are similar to those at Gedi and around the Lamu archipelago further north in Kenya.

Warning

Be careful about walking on the beach if you are carrying valuables, as there have been incidents of robbery in the past.

Things to See & Do

The tourist literature would have you believe that Bagamoyo is a mini version of Zanzibar or Mombasa, with a historical centre of narrow, winding alleys, tiny mosques, cafes and whitewashed German colonial buildings. There's certainly a small section of town down by the waterfront which corresponds to such a description, but it has all seen better days and the most lasting impression is one of near-terminal decay. Restoration is being carried out on the customs house at the beach but the other colonial buildings show only benign and mildewy neglect. All in all, it's debatable whether what remains is worth a four to six-hour return bus trip.

Museum The Catholic Mission north of town maintains a museum, with relics of the slave trade and displays about the early European explorers Burton, Speke and Stanley. The chapel where Livingstone's body was laid before being taken to Zanzibar en route to Westminster Abbey is also here. Don't walk to this museum alone, as there's a good chance you'll be mugged.

Kaole Visiting the 14th-century ruins at Kaole involves a one-hour walk along the beach going south past Kaole village into the mangrove swamps. When the beach apparently ends, go inland and look for the stone pillars. The guardian, Mr Kajeri, has a hut nearby and is well informed about the ruins.

Entry costs TSh 400 (less if you don't want a receipt). Don't bring any valuables along this beach and make a determined effort to look poor; otherwise, robbery is a near certainty.

Art College At Chuo ya Sanaa, 300m south of the Badeco Beach Hotel, you can watch students practise music and dance. There's a festival here each year in the last week of September.

Places to Stay & Eat

There are three hotels in the centre of Bagamoyo but they're very basic and essentially used only by prostitutes and their clients. They include the *Alpha* and the *Habib*. Much better is the *Azania Guesthouse*, five minutes walk from the new market/bus stand. It's quiet, the rooms, toilets and showers are very clean, the fans function and there's always water. It costs TSh 1200 per person but it is a 15-minute walk from the beach.

Most travellers head out to the *Badeco Beach Hotel*. This was taken over by a German expatriate a few years ago and offers pleasant doubles with good beds and mosquito nets for TSh 5000 per person.

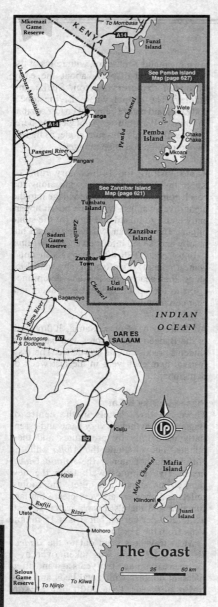

Breakfast is included and for lunch and dinner there is a quite extensive menu. The water doesn't run every day, especially in the dry season, but the verandah restaurant has great views.

Other beach hotels include the *Mwambao* and the *Travellers' Lodge*; the latter costs TSh 2500 per person. More expensive is the *Bagamoyo Beach Resort* (also known as the *Gogo Beach Resort*; ☎ 83 Bagamoyo or ☎ (051) 67843 Dar es Salaam), which offers singles/doubles with private bathroom and breakfast for US$30/40 including taxes. You can also camp here and there's a swimming pool.

If you're catering for yourself, you can buy lobster and other seafood from the fishers near the old German customs building. They land their catches here in the late morning and late afternoon.

Getting There & Away
Buses depart from Dar es Salaam throughout the day until about 3 pm from Msimbazi St, opposite the Agip station. They leave when full, are very crowded, cost TSh 800 one way and take two to three hours.

PANGANI
Pangani is a small village north of Bagamoyo and some 50 km south of Tanga. It's on a beautiful stretch of coast, with many reefs and islands offshore. From Pangani you can organise fishing trips to the reefs and snorkelling at the two islands of **Mawe Mdogo** and **Mwamba Mawe**.

There's also a small marine park on the island of **Maziwi** and boat trips are possible to see the wildlife up the Pangani River.

Places to Stay & Eat
The *YMCA* is more than six km north of Pangani, so it's really only suitable for those with their own transport or a penchant for walking more than 1½ hours to the nearest restaurant. It costs TSh 250 per person; breakfast costs TSh 250 and dinner is TSh 400. It's basic but mellow, and though there are no locks on the doors, gear appears to be safe.

A more convenient place is the *Panga-deco*, at the beach end of the main street on the high-water mark, about 50m through the coconut palms. The rooms are clean but mosquito nets are not provided and you may not be too impressed with the sky-blue décor. There's no running water, so bucket showers are the order of the day. It costs TSh 1500 a double and food is available on request. There's also a good bar.

There are two other guesthouses: the *River Inn* is on the road running alongside the river, about halfway from the boat yard to the ferry stage, and the *Udo* is on the same road but nearer the ferry.

The most expensive place to stay is the *Pangani Lodge* (☎ (0811) 440044; fax 440045), which is a semi-luxury lodge offering air-con singles/doubles for US$35/50 including breakfast. The lodge has its own private beach, bar and restaurant (good food), and offers deep-sea fishing trips from mid-September onwards with professional crews and full tackle.

Entertainment

Pangani is a Muslim town and has only one public bar, which is noisy despite an average clientele of only six people per night.

Getting There & Away

Buses go to and from Tanga three times daily and depart between 8 am and noon. If you have your own vehicle, the best access to Pangani is from the main Dar to Tanga road turning off at Muheza.

Trips by motorboat (from the frozen-fish factory) are expensive – around TSh 5000 for two hours.

TANGA

Strolling around Tanga, amid its sleepy, semi-colonial atmosphere, you'd hardly be aware that this is Tanzania's second-largest seaport. However, it's a surprisingly large town which sprawls well into the hinterland. It was founded by the Germans in the late 19th century and is a centre for the export of sisal. Not many travellers come here, apart from those looking for a dhow to Pemba island or heading north to Mombasa.

Tanga briefly hit the headlines in early 1990 when, after a tip-off, police uncovered hundreds of elephant tusks buried in the sand in gunny sacks on a tiny offshore island. Those involved were obviously intent on smuggling them out of the country one dark night but there were no reports of subsequent arrests. Sound like a familiar tale?

The telephone area code for Tanga is 053.

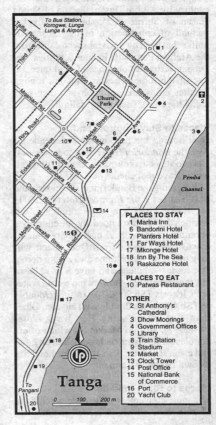

PLACES TO STAY
1 Marina Inn
6 Bandorini Hotel
7 Planters Hotel
11 Far Ways Hotel
17 Mkonge Hotel
18 Inn By The Sea
19 Raskazone Hotel

PLACES TO EAT
10 Patwas Restaurant

OTHER
2 St Anthony's Cathedral
3 Dhow Moorings
4 Government Offices
5 Library
8 Train Station
9 Stadium
12 Market
13 Clock Tower
14 Post Office
15 National Bank of Commerce
16 Port
20 Yacht Club

Tanga

0   100   200 m

TANZANIA

Amboni Caves

This area is predominantly a limestone district, and the Amboni Caves, off the road to Lunga Lunga, are not too far from town.

Tongoni Ruins

The Tongoni Ruins are 20 km south of Tanga on the Pangani road. There's a large ruined mosque and more than 40 tombs, the largest concentration of such tombs on the East African coast.

According to accounts which came into the hands of the Portuguese when they first arrived at Kilwa in 1505, both Kilwa and Tongoni were founded at the end of the 10th century by Ali bin Hasan, the son of Sultan Hasan of Shiraz in Persia. Certainly the method of construction of the mosque is unlike that used by the Arabs who came from the Arabian Peninsula in later centuries. Yet Persian script has only been found once, on one of the tombstones at Tongoni, though Persian coins are common at other sites along the coast, such as at Malindi.

Places to Stay – bottom end

Overlooking the harbour on Independence Ave, the *Bandorini Hotel* used to be the best place to stay but is currently closed, although it may have reopened.

Assuming the Bandorini is still closed, the next best bet is the *Planters Hotel* (☎ 2041) on Market St. It's a huge, rambling, old wooden hotel surrounded by an enormous verandah and with a bar and restaurant downstairs. Aussies from Queensland will love this place – it's home away from home. The rooms are clean and have a hand basin but the communal showers have cold water only. It costs TSh 2000/3000 a single/double or TSh 4000 for a double with air-con. Other than this, there's the *Far Ways Hotel* (☎ 46097), also on Market St, which offers doubles with private bathroom, balcony, fan and clean sheets for TSh 3000. The hotel has its own bar and restaurant.

Places to Stay – middle

The most convenient mid-range hotel is the *Marina Inn*, which is a well-maintained, modern place offering air-con doubles for around TSh 5000, including breakfast. There are no singles. The hotel has it's own bar and restaurant.

Going west from the town centre along Hospital Rd are three other mid-range hotels: the *Mkonge Hotel*, *Inn by the Sea* and *Raskazone Hotel*. Those who have stayed at the Raskazone recommend it highly.

More expensive is the *Baobab Hotel* (☎ 40638), but it's about five km from the centre and inconvenient without your own transport.

Places to Eat

A good place to eat is the *Patwas Restaurant*, opposite the market in the town centre. This very clean and friendly Asian-run restaurant offers excellent curries for lunch and dinner, with snacks and tea in-between, but is not particularly cheap. An alternative is the *Baht*, a take-away snack bar on Second Ave, between the two railway crossings. Here you can get an excellent selection of vegetarian bhajis, samosas and sweets.

The *Marine Restaurant* on Market St is very popular with local people for lunch. Meals are cheap but the food is only average.

For a minor splurge, you can eat at the *Planters Hotel*. The service is a bit on the slow side but the food is worth the wait. Fish, chips and salad or curried prawns with rice cost TSh 1500.

Also check out the *Food Palace* on Sokoine Ave next to the junction with Customs Rd. They do Asian and European dishes with main courses around TSh 1700.

The *Yacht Club* is the focus of the lives of resident foreigners, though alcohol is the main motivation for coming here and the conversation is pretty uninspiring as a rule. Still, the club is a good place to track down people who are driving to Dar es Salaam, Mombasa and other places.

Getting There & Away

Bus There are usually one or two buses daily from Dar es Salaam to Tanga. The trip takes seven to eight hours and costs TSh 3200.

There are also a number of operators

running buses between Tanga and Mombasa. The journey takes about five hours over roads which have improved somewhat recently. Fares are TSh 3000 for minicoaches which leave Tanga at around 11 am or TSh 2500 for a night bus which leaves at around 10 pm.

For the Tanzanian border post of Horohoro, try to catch one of the infrequent buses from the bus station – otherwise, you'll have to hitch, though there's very little traffic. See the Tanzania Getting There & Away chapter.

Train Service on the Korogwe-Tanga line was (temporarily?) suspended in early 1996 and enquiries at Dar es Salaam Central Line railway station elicited no explanation. It's possible the service will be restored and, if it is, the old schedule will probably apply. This involved departures at 4 pm on Monday, Wednesday and Friday in either direction between Tanga and Dar es Salaam. Despite the suspension of the service, however, the fares were available: TSh 8945 (1st class), TSh 6120 (2nd class), TSh 4155 (2nd-class sitting) and TSh 2630 (3rd class); the trip takes about 13 hours.

If you want to get from Tanga to Moshi while the service is suspended, you'll first have to get to Korogwe by bus and then take the Dar es Salaam to Moshi train from there.

Boat Dhows operate between Tanga and Pemba but they are irregular. Usually they go two to three times per week. You need to enquire down at the dhow sheds at the port. The fare is around TSh 3000 plus a port tax of US$5 but forget about doing this trip if the weather is rough.

More reliable is the MS *Sepideh* operated by Zanzibar Sea Ferries Ltd (☎ (054) 33725; fax 30987 in Zanzibar; ☎ (051) 38025 in Dar es Salaam; ☎ (054) 56210 in Mkoani (Pemba); and ☎ (011) 311486 in Mombasa). Depending on the season, this ship does the run between Mombasa and Dar es Salaam via Pemba, Tanga and Zanzibar three to four times a week but schedules change constantly with Tanga and Dar es Salaam frequently being dropped so you need to

make enquiries. Fares from Tanga are: US$30 to Pemba, US$40 to Mombasa and US$45 to Zanzibar, plus US$5 port taxes.

Zanzibar

History
The annals of Zanzibar read like a chapter from *The Thousand and One Nights* and doubtless evoke many exotic and erotic images in the minds of travellers. Otherwise known as the Spice Island, Zanzibar has lured travellers to its shores for centuries, some in search of trade, some in search of plunder and still others in search of an idyllic home. The Sumerians, Assyrians, Egyptians, Phoenicians, Indians, Chinese, Persians, Portuguese, Omani Arabs, Dutch and English have all been here at one time or other. Some, notably the Shirazi Persians and the Omani Arabs, stayed to settle and rule.

It was early in the 19th century under the Omani Arabs that the island enjoyed its most recent heyday, following the introduction of the clove tree in 1818. Not long afterwards, the sultan's court was transferred from Muscat, near the entrance to the Persian Gulf, to Zanzibar. By the middle of the century, Zanzibar had become the world's largest producer of cloves and the largest slaving entrepôt on the east coast. Nearly 50,000 slaves, drawn from as far away as Lake Tanganyika, passed through its market every year.

As a result, Zanzibar became the most important town on the East African coast. All other centres were subject to it and virtually all trade passed through it. However, this changed with the establishment of the European protectorates towards the end of the 19th century and the construction of the Mombasa-Kampala railway. The Omani sultans continued to rule under a British protectorate until 1963, when independence was granted, but were overthrown the following year in a bloody revolution instigated by the Afro-Shirazi Party. This occurred prior to the union with mainland Tanganyika.

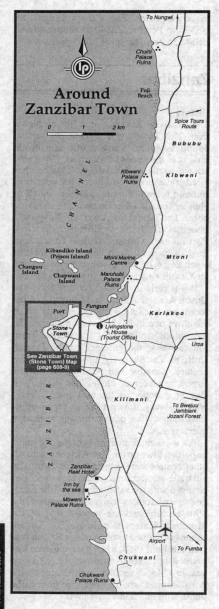

Around Zanzibar Town

0   1   2 km

To Nungwi

Chuini Palace Ruins

Fuji Beach

Spice Tours Route

Bububu

Kibweni Palace Ruins

Kibweni

C H A N N E L

Kibandiko Island (Prison Island)

Mtoni Marine Centre

Mtoni

Changuu Island

Chapwani Island

Maruhubi Palace Ruins

Funguni

Port

Kariakoo

Stone Town

Livingstone House (Tourist Office)

Uroa

See Zanzibar Town (Stone Town) Map (page 608-9)

Z A N Z I B A R

Kilimani

To Bwejuu Jambiani Jozani Forest

Zanzibar Reef Hotel

Inn by the sea

Mbweni Palace Ruins

Airport

To Fumba

Chukwani

Chukwani Palace Ruins

The many centuries of occupation and influence by all these various peoples has left its mark, and the old Stone Town of Zanzibar is one of the most fascinating places on the east coast. Much larger than Lamu or the old town of Mombasa, it's a fascinating labyrinth of narrow, winding streets lined with whitewashed, coral-rag houses, many with overhanging balconies and magnificently carved brass-studded doors. Regrettably, many of these doors have disappeared in recent years.

There are endless quaint little shops, bazaars, mosques, courtyards and squares, a fortress, two former sultans' palaces, two huge cathedrals, former colonial mansions, a Persian-style public bathhouse and a bizarre collection of foreign consulates.

Outside town there are more ruined palaces, other Shirazi remains, the famous Persian baths and that other perennial attraction – magnificent, palm-fringed beaches with warm, clear water, ideal for swimming, snorkelling and scuba diving.

Orientation
Guidebooks & Maps David Else, who writes a number of camping and mountain trekking guides to Kenya, has brought out a *Guide to Zanzibar & Pemba* which has plenty of information in it but is utterly spoiled by poor production and totally lacking in colour photographs except for the cover.

The best map of Zanzibar and the Stone Town (other than the one available from the tourist office) is that produced by MACO, PO Box 322, Zanzibar. This is a superb, full-colour map with the entire island on one side and the Stone Town on the other. At about TSh 2000 it's excellent value. You can find it at the dive shops and various other places.

Information
Tourist Office The Tanzania Tourist Corporation (☎ 32344), PO Box 216, has an office in Livingstone House on the main road out of town going north. It has an excellent map of Zanzibar town (1:10,000) and one of the

island (1:200,000). The town map (TSh 800) is worth buying for exploring the alleys of the old town. They also sell the booklet *A Tale of Two Islands – Zanzibar*, in English and French. It's basically a guidebook to the islands of Zanzibar and Pemba which lists hotels, restaurants, places to see, tour operators and beaches and gives a rundown on history, geography and transport connections. It's overpriced (TSh 6000) but might be useful if you're staying a long time.

Bookings for government-owned Zanzibar beach chalets must also be made at the tourist office.

Foreign Consulates The island has consulates for the Sultanate of Oman, Egypt, India, Mozambique and the People's Republic of China. The first is in the old Stone Town, while the others are on the road to the airport.

Immigration Although Zanzibar is part of the United Republic of Tanzania, it jealously guards its autonomy, and makes this point quite plain by requiring foreign visitors to go through its own immigration and customs on arrival and on leaving. You'll be required to fill in an immigration form and state how long you want to stay. It's best to ask for longer than you intend to stay (otherwise, you'll have to have the permit renewed, which is a hassle if you're not staying in Zanzibar town itself – the immigration office is outside the Stone Town). Don't overstay your permit, as officials get shirty about this and may attempt to fine you.

The customs inspection on arrival is cursory – basically, all they do is chalk your bag without opening it.

Money As on the mainland, Zanzibar has foreign exchange bureaus where you can change travellers' cheques and cash with the minimum of fuss. Otherwise, there's the National Bank of Commerce, which is open Monday to Friday from 8.30 am to 4 pm and on Saturday from 8.30 am to 12.30 pm.

Post & Communications Overseas phone calls can be hard to make and expensive. To call the USA, for example, costs TSh 4000 to TSh 12,000 per minute (you must shop around) with some places having a three-minute minimum.

Other than private phones, you can make international telephone calls from the exchange next to the main post office but be prepared for a long wait for no result. The exchange is open Monday to Saturday from 8 am to 8 pm and on Sunday from 8 am to noon.

The telephone area code for Zanzibar is 054.

Cultural Centres The Institute of KiSwahili & Foreign Languages on Vuga Rd runs four-week courses in KiSwahili for beginners and intermediate-level students and a two-week advanced course. The price is US$60 per week. Alternatively, take classes on an hourly basis at US$6 per hour. Class sizes are between two and five people and lessons are conducted from 8 am to noon five days a week. It's worth booking in advance.

Medical Services According to everyone who's ever had to use it, avoid at all costs the government hospital, the VI Lenin on Kaunda Rd. Instead call Dr Mario Mariani MD at the Zanzibar Medical & Diagnostic Centre, Tiger House (☎ 33113). The centre is in the same building as Kenya Airways. He has a mobile phone which either he or one of his staff will answer 24 hours a day. He comes highly recommended.

Dangers & Annoyances While not strictly falling into this category, there are two things of which you should be aware. The first is driving licences if you hire a self-drive car. To do this, officially you must have an International Driving Licence or a Tanzanian, Zanzibarian, Kenyan, Ugandan or South African driving licence. No-one will ever ask to see any of these when you rent but if you're stopped by the police they will certainly want to see one. It's a scam, of course, to extract money from you (the usual 'fine' is TSh 2000 to TSh 4000). It would be

PLACES TO STAY
4 Bwawani Plaza Hotel
6 Malindi Guest House
7 Warere Guest House
8 Ciné Afrique
12 Narrow Street Hotel
21 Hotel Kiponda
23 Narrow Street Annexe
26 Hotel International
27 Spice Inn
28 Emerson House & Restaurant
30 Riverman Inn
39 Bottoms Up Guest House
40 Hotel Clove
47 Karibuni Inn
48 Coco de Mer Hotel
53 Stone Town Inn
54 Tembo Hotel
56 Zanzibar Serena Inn
66 Blue Ocean Hotel
66 Mazson's Hotel
67 Dhow Palace
69 Baghani House
70 Zanzibar Hotel
72 Africa House Hotel
74 Cave Resort
77 Garden Lodge
79 Florida Inn Guest House
80 The Haven
81 Flamingo Guest House
83 Jambo Guest House
88 Victoria Guest House

PLACES TO EAT
5 New Gulf Restaurant
18 Sea View Indian Restaurant
25 Zee Pizza & Spice Shop
42 Mayur Indian Restaurant
43 Luis' Yogurt Parlour
45 Floating Restaurant
49 Luna Mare Restaurant
51 Fisherman Restaurant
57 Oman International Restaurant
62 Green Garden Restaurant
63 Dolphin Restaurant
65 Sunrise Restaurant
73 Camlurs Restaurant
75 Maharaja Restaurant
78 La Lampara Restaurant
82 Green Garden Restaurant

OTHER
1 Customs & Immigration
2 Boat Company Ticket Offices
3 Boat Company Ticket Offices
9 Zan Air
10 Police
11 Petrol Station
13 Old Dispensary
14 Institute of Marine Science
15 Ijumaa Mosque
16 The Big Tree
17 Indian Ocean Divers
19 Old Customs House
20 Palace Museum
22 Agha Khan Mosque
24 Markets
29 Al Ridha: Motorbikes to Rent
31 Fruit Market
32 Daranjani Market
33 Bus Station
34 Old Slave Market
35 UMCA Cathedral
36 Anglican Mission & Slave Chambers
37 Forex Bureau
38 Persian Baths

41 House of Wonders (Beit-el-Ajaib)
44 Arab Fort
46 The First British Consulate
50 Le Pécheur Pub
52 Tarumbeta Disco
55 Starehe Club
58 Post Office
60 Air Zanzibar
61 St Joseph's Cathedral
64 Forex Bureau
68 Livingstone Bar
71 One Ocean Diving Centre
76 High Court
84 ZAMEDIC: Zanzibar Medical & Diagnostic Centre
85 Kenya Airways Booking Office
86 Institute of KiSwahili & Foreign Languages
87 Air Tanzania: Booking Office
89 State House
90 VL Lenin Hospital
91 National Museum
92 National Museum
93 House of Representatives

Zanzibar Town (Stone Town)

0   1   2 km

TANZANIA

cheaper to buy a Zanzibari licence down at the dock (same day if you get there early).

The other thing is the electricity supply which can drop to as low as 150 volts and surge as high as 380 volts. If you're using electrical equipment it could cost you hundreds of dollars in repair bills.

Old Stone Town

The old Stone Town of Zanzibar is a fascinating place to wander around and get lost in, though you can't really get lost for too long because, sooner or later, you'll end up either on the seafront or on Creek Rd. Nevertheless, every twist and turn of the narrow alleyways will present you with something of interest – be it a school full of children chanting verses from the Koran, a beautiful old mansion with overhanging verandahs, a shady square studded with huge old trees, a collection of quaint little hole-in-the-wall shops selling everything from Panadol to pawpaws, or a gaggle of women in *bui-bui* (veils) sharing a joke and some salacious local gossip.

You'll see a lot of crumbled and crumbling buildings as you walk around the Stone Town, and it's a great pity that so much of the fabric of this historic place has been allowed to fall into disrepair. A determined effort is now being made to restore a lot of the more important buildings, and you'll often come across expatriate aid workers wandering around with clipboards, making notes. Nevertheless, it would be a good idea if the entire Stone Town was declared a World Heritage site and appropriate funds provided to restore it to its former glory. The provision of a garbage service would be a good first step. Tourist receipts have done a lot to encourage the local authorities to halt the decay but priorities are elsewhere and money, as usual, is in short supply.

It's not really possible to suggest any sort of 'itinerary' or route, since it takes at least a week for a newcomer to come to grips with the town's layout, even with a map (though a map does help). Still, it's worth putting in the effort to see some of the town's major features.

TANZANIA

Beit-el-Ajaib (House of Wonders)

One of the most prominent buildings in the old Stone Town is the Beit-el-Ajaib, or House of Wonders, formerly the sultan's palace and one of the largest structures in Zanzibar. Built in 1883 by Sultan Barghash (1870-88), it's an elegant four-storey structure surrounded by wide verandahs. In 1896 it was the target of a British naval bombardment, the object of which was to force Sultan Khalid bin Barghash, who had claimed the throne after the death of Hamid bin Thuwaini, to abdicate in favour of a British nominee. After it was rebuilt, Sultan Hamoud used the upper floor as a residential palace until his death. These days it's the local political headquarters of the CCM (Chama Cha Mapinduzi) but is due to be converted into a museum of history and culture in the near future. Beside it is the more modest palace to which Barghash's successor moved after vacating the Beit-el-Ajaib in 1911.

Beit-al-Sahel (The Palace Museum)

This palace, next to the Beit-el-Ajaib, was begun in 1828 by Seyyid Said bin Sultan, the ruler of Oman and Zanzibar, and served as the residence of the Al-Busaid sultans of Zanzibar until 1964, when the dynasty was overthrown. Since those days, it has been through many changes, especially after the naval bombardment by the British in 1896 when it was partially destroyed. For many years after the revolution, it remained closed to the public but has now been opened as a museum displaying the period of the Zanzibar sultanate.

The ground floor displays details of the formative period of the sultanate from 1828 to 1870, during which commercial treaties were signed between Zanzibar and the USA (1833), Britain (1839), France (1844) and the Hanseatic Republics (1859), and includes memorabilia of Zanzibar's first embassy to New York by Ahmed bin Nu'man in 1840 as well as Princess Salme's exploits.

The 2nd floor exhibits focus on the period of affluence from 1870 to 1896 during which modern amenities such as piped water and electricity were introduced to Zanzibar under Sultan Barghash. The 3rd floor consists of the modest living quarters of the last sultan, Khalifa bin Haroub (1911-60), and his two wives, both of whom clearly had radically different tastes in furniture.

To the north of the palace lies the Makusurani graveyard which is where most of the Al-Busaid sultans are buried.

Entry to the museum costs TSh 2000 and it's open Tuesday to Saturday from 9 am to 6 pm and on Sunday and public holidays from 9 am to 3 pm. It's well worth a visit, not only for the historical memorabilia, but also to clothe some of the myths with a modicum of reality. This was certainly no Mughal Empire or anything approximating the streets paved with gold of Prester John's realm.

Fort

On the other side of Beit-el-Ajaib is the 'Arab' fort, a typically massive, crenellated and bastioned structure. Originally built by the Portuguese in 1700, there's little inside other than a craft gallery. Some restoration was undertaken on the fort walls a few years ago but the southern wall is still obviously used by local people as a rubbish tip. There might be an entry fee, but the last time I visited, the guard was fast asleep on the table. The main drawcard here, though, is the open-air theatre inside the grounds of the fort. Keep an eye open for posters around town advertising events.

The craft gallery has an excellent selection of first-rate batiks, worth a look even if you don't want to buy any.

Old Slave Market & UMCA Cathedral

Another prominent landmark is the Anglican cathedral. Completed in 1877 by the United Mission to Central Africa (UMCA), it was the first Anglican cathedral to be built in East Africa. It stands on the site of the Old Slave Market, alongside Creek Rd, and is still in very good condition. If you want to have a look inside, you may well have to hunt around for the man with the key. Entry costs TSh 300 which includes access to the two slave chambers under the adjacent guest-house.

St Joseph's Cathedral
The towers of this Roman Catholic cathedral, set back from the fort, are easily spotted on arrival at the island by ferry. However, the building is deceptively hard to find in the narrow confines of the adjacent streets. Designed by the French architect Beranger, it was completed in 1896.

Hamamni Persian Baths
Perhaps worth a visit are these baths, built by Sultan Barghash as public baths. They're a protected monument and are locked, but if you show a passing interest, the guardian (who runs a shop a few metres away) will rush up with the key and show you around, then ask you for a 'donation'. There's no water inside any more, so it's not that interesting, especially if you've ever been inside a functional Persian/Turkish bath. They were built between 1870 and 1888 but ceased to be used from 1920.

Mosques
As Zanzibar is a strongly Muslim society, there are quite a few mosques – 50 in all – scattered around the Stone Town. Perhaps the most famous is the **Msikiti wa Balnara** (Malindi Minaret Mosque), originally built in 1831, enlarged in 1841 and extended again by Seyyid Ali bin Said in 1890. Others include the **Agha Khan Mosque** and the **Ijumaa Mosque**, on which renovations and extensions are nearing completion. It's unlikely you'll be able to enter any of these, as they're all functional.

National Museum
The larger of the two buildings which make up the National Museum presents a catalogued history of the island from its early days up until independence. It contains Livingstone memorabilia, artefacts from the days of the Omani sultans and the British colonial period, as well as drums used by the sultans, and a priceless collection of old lithographs, maps and photographs dating mainly from the 19th and early 20th centuries. There are also stamp and coin displays. The smaller building houses a natural history collection specialising in butterflies, fish, small mammals, snakes and shells. There's also a collection of deformed animal foetuses. Outside is a pen housing two giant tortoises. Entry costs TSh 1000.

Livingstone House
Outside the Stone Town, to the north-east along Malawi Rd, this building was the base for the missionary/explorer's last expedition before he died. It's now the main tourist office. If you want to have a look around then speak pleasantly to the staff.

Special Events
The festival of Id al Fitr (the end of Ramadan) lasts about four days, and if you visit the island at this time, don't miss the Zanzibari equivalent of the tug-of-war at Makunduchi in the south of the island. Men from the south challenge those from the north by beating each other silly with banana branches. After that, the women of the town launch into a series of traditional folk songs, and the whole town eats and dances the night away.

Activities
Scuba Diving In the last few years scuba diving has taken off in a big way on Zanzibar – which is not surprising, given the numerous beautiful coral reefs off the main island and its many offshore islets. The water, too, is clear and warm (27 to 30°C) throughout the year with visibility ranging from 10 to 40m.

There's a wide variety of hard and soft corals here including giant fungia, rose coral, huge brain corals and enormous plate acropora, along with hectares of staghorn coral. The other marine life is equally spectacular with schools of bat fish, flashing goldies, a variety of angel fish, lion fish, blue spotted rays and turtles. You may even be lucky enough to encounter whale sharks and hammerheads. There's also a variety of dive sites ranging from leisurely shallow dives to drift dives and 100m drop-offs.

It's the perfect place to dive and if you're not certified or even have no experience at all, there's no problem: take a diving course. These are very reasonably priced at US$200 to US$300 including the charge for PADI registration for a four to five-day course which will certify you to dive anywhere in the world to a maximum depth of 18m. There are also advanced courses, lasting three days and costing US$220, which will qualify you to extend your range to 30m.

All of the dive centres have the full range of top-quality equipment, fully qualified instructors as well as their own motorised boats and you can even rent underwater cameras. Other than actual courses, both centres offer half-day (one dive) and full-day (two dives) trips as well as special night dives and they're open seven days a week.

In no order of preference, the centres are:

One Ocean – The Zanzibar Dive Centre
    PO Box 608, Zanzibar (☎ 33816; fax 30406). This outfit is on the ground floor of the Africa House Hotel on the seafront. They offer two diving trips per day (9.30 am to noon and 2.30 to 5 pm) which cost US$25 including equipment as well as a regular night dive (6 to 8 pm) which costs US$40 including equipment. They also offer a half-day 'fun dive' for those unfamiliar with scuba diving. The cost is US$45.
Indian Ocean Divers
    PO Box 2370, Zanzibar (☎ /fax 33860). This outfit is run by a group of South Africans and is located next to 'The Big Tree' on Mizingani Rd on the waterfront. They offer two diving trips per day (morning and afternoon) at US$20 to US$30. If all you want to do is snorkel then you can go on any of the above trips for US$15 including all gear and the boat ride. Like One Ocean, they also offer a half-day 'Discover Scuba' dive, for US$50. Night dives off Bawe island are offered at US$60, and include a barbecue on the beach after the dive.
    Indian Ocean Divers also has a branch at Paradise Bungalows (in front Baraka Bungalows) at Nungwi – the northernmost tip of Zanzibar island.
CAT-Diving Ltd
    PO Box 3203, Zanzibar (☎ /fax 31040). This is a somewhat more expensive, German-based outfit which operates seven to 13-day dive trips, for

experienced divers only, off the Pemba island coast for US$150 per day all-inclusive.

Sunset Cruises One Ocean – The Zanzibar Dive Centre (see Scuba Diving for details) offers sunset dhow cruises, given sufficient demand, on Tuesday, Thursday and Saturday from 5.30 to 6.45 pm. The price is US$20 and includes snacks and soft drinks.

Places to Stay

All accommodation on the island has to be paid for in foreign currency (preferably US dollars) unless you're a Tanzanian resident. There are no exceptions. Make sure you have sufficient small-denomination travellers' cheques or bills to pay for this and, if you haven't, then get sufficient from a foreign exchange (forex) bureau. Change is given only in local currency.

Places to Stay – bottom end

One of the cheapest places is the small *Flamingo Guest House* (☎ 32850), Mkunazini Rd. It's very friendly but lacks character. Rooms with a fan and mosquito net and shared bathroom facilities cost US$8/14 for singles/doubles including breakfast. Rooms with private bathroom are US$10/20.

About 100m slightly north-east of the Flamingo and off the main street (signposted) is the relatively new *Jambo Guest House* (☎ 33779). Singles/doubles with common bathroom in the low (high) season cost US$8/15 (US$10/20) while those with air-con cost US$10/18 (US$15/25) including breakfast. The guesthouse offers free transport to and from the port and other facilities include local and international telephone and fax services and a laundry service. Alcohol is not allowed on the premises and guests cannot entertain visitors in their rooms at any time.

Close by and even cheaper is the *Haven Guest House* (☎ 33454) which offers bed and breakfast at US$7 per person with shared bathroom facilities. It's very popular with budget travellers.

Just off Vuga Rd, and close to the Omani Consulate, is the quite popular *Victoria Guest House* (☎ 32861), Victoria St. It's a modern place, the staff are friendly, and rooms with private bathroom, fan and including breakfast cost US$10 per person. A notice in reception says 'Unmarried couples will not be entertained', but I've never heard of them demanding to see marriage certificates. What they do ban is alcoholic beverages.

In the same area and great value, as well as being a very pleasant place to stay, is the *Garden Lodge* (☎ 33298) on Kaunda Rd. The staff are very friendly and you can get a bed in a triple room with private bathroom and fan for US$8 per person. They also have doubles with private bathroom for US$18.

In the Arab Fort area are two other cheapies. The better of them in terms of facilities is the *Karibuni Inn* (☎ 33058) which has 12 rooms. It's a well-run place and close to a lot of restaurants and bars as well as the post office. Singles/doubles with fan and shared bathroom facilities cost US$15/20 plus they have doubles with private bathroom for US$25. All prices include breakfast.

Cheaper is the *Bottoms Up Guest House* (☎ 33189), Hurumzi St. Here you can get a clean, comfortable room with fan, carpet and mosquito net from US$6/12 a single/double. Bathroom facilities are shared but all prices include a full breakfast. Try to get room No 7 or 8 which are on the roof. Quite a lot of travellers stay here. There's a popular bar on the ground floor (painted the most lurid red) with taped music.

East of this area close to the UMCA cathedral is another good cheapie, the *Riverman Inn* (☎ 33188), which offers bed and breakfast with shared bathroom facilities for US$10/20 for singles/doubles. It's a quiet place and has a bar. A restaurant was being constructed and may be open by now.

Up in the Malindi area of town, close to the docks and at the back of the Ciné Afrique, is another good cheapie, the *Warere Guest House* (☎ 31187). It's very clean and well kept and offers beds for US$7 per person including breakfast. Bathroom facilities are communal.

My own nomination for best place to stay (with which many travellers would agree) is the *Malindi Guest House* (☎ 30165), Funguni Bazaar, also in the Malindi area. This is a beautiful place with bags of atmosphere, superbly maintained and constantly being repainted. The staff are very friendly. There's a range of rooms, all with shared bathroom facilities, a fan and mosquito nets, and it costs US$10 per person for bed and breakfast. There's hot water in the bathrooms and they're all squeaky clean. Both Visa and MasterCard are accepted and there's *no* commission charged on these (unlike most other hotels in Zanzibar which accept credit cards). This is a very popular place so, if you want to be sure of a room, get there early in the day. There's a curfew of 11 pm unless prior arrangements have been made.

Places to Stay – middle

All of the hotels in this section, except where indicated, accept major credit cards but their use attracts a commission of between 10% and 15%.

For authentic Zanzibari character and atmosphere, the best value in this range is the *Stone Town Inn* (☎ /fax 33658), PO Box 3530, on Shangani St. It's housed in a beautifully and sensitively refurbished traditional coral-rag house and several of the rooms have uninterrupted views of the ocean. Aircon is fitted if you want to use it but fans and mosquito nets are provided if you don't. All the furniture is of traditional design – the beds are double posters! It offers doubles with private bathroom for US$25 per person (negotiable down to US$20 per person) and a single with common bathroom facilities for US$15. The place is friendly, secure and the showers have hot water.

Another beautifully restored traditional house which has been opened as a hotel is the *Hotel Kiponda & Restaurant* (☎ 33052; fax 33020), PO Box 3446, Kiponda St, near the UNICEF office. It's relatively new, spotless and has a superb rooftop restaurant which catches the sea breezes, and the staff couldn't be more friendly. It offers singles/doubles with shared bathroom for US$18/35 and doubles with private bathroom for US$45. All the rooms have a fan, and breakfast is included. The restaurant is open from noon to 3 pm and 7 to 10.30 pm daily except Sunday. There are cold beer and soft drinks available.

Further afield towards Creek Rd is *Narrow Street Hotel* (☎ 32620), in the street of the same name. It's certainly a very well appointed, clean place and the staff are friendly but it leans too heavily in favour of people who are looking for things they should have left at home – TV, video and air-con – but each room does have a fridge. Doubles (no singles) with private bathroom and an Indian breakfast cost US$45/55. There's a 10% discount on all rooms in the low season. The hotel has its own restaurant, with very reasonable prices.

Back in the centre of the Stone Town, the *Spice Inn* (☎ 30728), close to the Agha Khan Mosque, is a popular place to stay. This would have to be the Raffles Hotel of Zanzibar. It's decidedly Somerset Maugham, with its timeless 1st-floor lounge full of easy chairs and local antiques. Some of the rooms are like this too, but you have to choose carefully and book in advance if possible, as some of the cheaper rooms are plain in the extreme and very basic. There are a variety of rooms, the best being those with a verandah overlooking the small square. Prices range from US$20/25 to US$25/50 a single/double with fan and shared bathroom facilities, and air-con doubles with private bathroom from US$30 to US$50. All prices include breakfast, and lunch and dinner are also available.

Great value and with a superb ambience is *Bhagani House* (☎ 33889), between the Dhow Palace Hotel and the Zanzibar Hotel. This is a very tastefully restored traditional Zanzibari house with spacious rooms and attractive furnishings. Rooms with private bathroom and breakfast cost US$35/45 for singles/doubles. Visa card is accepted and there's no commission charged.

Round the corner from Bhagani House is the rambling *Zanzibar Hotel* (☎ 30708/9), PO Box 392, tucked away in the narrow alleys of the Stone Town and only a three-minute walk from the Africa House Hotel. But while it's a gem of Zanzibari architecture, at least in the public areas, the rooms themselves are very plain and utilitarian and the plumbing antediluvian. Rooms cost US$25/40 for singles/doubles without own bathroom, US$30/45 with own bathroom. There are also air-con rooms with private bathroom, which cost US$30/45. Prices include breakfast and all taxes. Credit cards are not accepted.

The same company which owns the Zanzibar Hotel also owns the *Africa House Hotel* (☎ 30708), which used to be the 'British Club' in the days when Zanzibar was a British protectorate. Esoteric reminders of those bygone years are still to be found around the place. It's one of the very few hotels actually on the waterfront and it's a popular place to stay, though like the Zanzibar, it's somewhat overpriced given the standard of accommodation it offers. Prices are exactly the same as at the Zanzibar. The staff are friendly but there are problems with the water supply on the upper floors (though none, apparently, downstairs). The hotel has a restaurant above the bar.

A better place to stay if you're looking for atmosphere is *Emerson House* (☎ 32153), down the street from the Spice Inn. The rooms here have been beautifully decorated by a local artist and are furnished with antiques, but not all of them have private bathroom. Prices range from US$40 to US$70 per room (single or double) including breakfast. Dinner is served on the rooftop, from which there are good views of the town, but it's expensive (around TSh 5000 for a meal, plus the cost of drinks).

Another relatively classy hotel is the new *Coco de Mer Hotel* (☎ 30852), PO Box 2363, on the same street as the Karibuni Hotel. All the rooms have private bathroom with hot and cold showers and cost US$20/30 for singles/doubles including breakfast, but avoid the ground-floor rooms flanking reception if you want any privacy. The hotel has its own bar and restaurant.

In the immediate area is the *Hotel Inter-*

national (☎ 33182; fax 30052), PO Box 3784, a large, multistorey hotel which has singles/doubles for US$48/55 including breakfast. There's a 25 to 30% discount on these prices in the low season. All the rooms have private bathroom, with air-con, TV and fridge. The hotel has its own bar, and a restaurant which serves Indian, Chinese and continental dishes, but the service is very slow. Everything works here but it doesn't quite exude the ambience of the Stone Town.

There's also the *Hotel Clove* (☎ 31785), Hurumzi St, close to the Beit-el-Ajaib. This is very clean and good value but lacks character – it's essentially a concrete box. All the rooms have private bathroom, with air-con and a fridge, and cost US$20/35 a single/double.

Lastly, there's the *Blue Ocean Hotel* (☎ 33566; fax 33566), PO Box 4052, which has singles/doubles with private bathroom for US$20/40 including breakfast. Fans and mosquito nets are provided and all the rooms have private bathroom and air-con. It's a pleasant place and convenient for the Stone Town but those who have stayed here comment that it's somewhat impersonal.

Places to Stay – top end

Stone Town Two hotels stand out in this range above all others. The first is the *Dhow Palace Hotel* (☎ 33012; fax 33008), PO Box 3974, Bhagani St, which is a brand-new hotel where no expense has been spared in restoring a large traditional Zanzibari house. There are 10 superbly furnished, rooms with private bathroom, air-con and a minibar. Singles are all US$50, while doubles cost US$60 to US$80 including breakfast and all taxes. Credit cards are not accepted. Facilities include a restaurant, the Livingstone Pub and Stanley's Wine & Jazz Bar.

Close by on Kenyatta Rd and fronting a small, leafy plazuela is the equally tasteful *Mazsons' Hotel* (☎ 33694; fax 33695), PO Box 3367. Like the Dhow Palace, it's a brand-new hotel with all the facilities you'd expect including air-con, attached bathrooms with hot and cold water, room service, colour TV (with CNN) and free safe deposit boxes. Room rates, including breakfast, are

US$60/80 for singles/doubles and an extra bed is US$10. Most of the rooms have a verandah overlooking the plazuela. The house is one of the oldest in the Shangani area of the Stone Town.

Right on the seafront and next to the old British Consulate is the much larger and relatively new *Tembo Hotel* (☎ 33005; fax 33777), PO Box 3974, Shangani St, opposite the Fisherman Restaurant. All the rooms have private bathroom, air-con, fridge and telephone. Other facilities include a swimming pool and an extensive seafront restaurant. It's a popular place for package tourists so the atmosphere inside may not be quite to your liking if you're travelling independently. Singles/doubles without views cost US$65/70; doubles with views cost US$80. All prices include breakfast and taxes. Credit cards are not accepted.

The new *Zanzibar Serena Inn*, part of the Serena Lodges & Hotels group (☎ Arusha (057) 8175 and Nairobi (02) 711077), should also be open by now. It's on the seafront in Shangani in the old Extelecoms office. Prices will probably be in the range of US$165/200 a single/double.

Outside the Stone Town Closest to the centre of town but totally characterless is the *Bwawani Plaza Hotel* (☎ 30200; fax 32820), PO Box 670, overlooking Funguni Creek. This hotel was built in the era when the new town was being constructed and it exudes heavy Marxist architectural banality, though, to be fair, the new owners have made an effort to mitigate this. All the rooms have private bathroom and air-con and the price includes a full breakfast and all taxes. Ordinary singles/doubles are US$75/95, and seafront singles/doubles are US$90/110. In the low season there's a 10% discount on these prices. The hotel has all the usual facilities, including a swimming pool, tennis and squash courts, restaurant, bar (expensive beers!) and a nightly disco (10 pm to 2 am and open to non-guests).

Off the road going north at Mtoni (three km from the Stone Town) is the *Mtoni Marine Centre* (☎ /fax 32540), PO Box 992, which has a range of double rooms, cottages and suites set among well-maintained gardens which front onto the beach. It's a modest and unpretentious place and the staff are very friendly. Standard, air-con doubles with private bathroom cost US$35. Better-appointed doubles are US$60. They also have suites which cost US$60 and consist of a double and a single bedroom, lounge and a porch with ocean views, and four cottages with two to three air-con bedrooms, living room and porch with ocean views for US$60 to US$90. All prices are inclusive of a continental breakfast but exclude government taxes of 15%. Facilities at the centre include a bar, satellite TV, a billiards table, occasional disco and a restaurant with a strong Italian influence. If you arrive by taxi, the hotel will pay the fare.

Even further north is the *Mawibini Venta Club* (☎ 31163), a self-contained resort complex which specialises in water sports (except diving). The clientele are entirely Italian and even most of the staff don't speak a word of English. Room rates are full board and cost US$60/120 for singles/doubles. The club has all the usual facilities which you'd expect of a hotel at this price.

Going south from the Stone Town, at Mbweni (about four km) is the *Zanzibar Reef Hotel* (☎ 30208; fax 30556), PO Box 2586, an expanse of makuti-roofed cottages and lounge/restaurant/bar areas set among lawns which border the seafront. It's a resort complex very much like many others along the East African coast and attracts a lot of package tourists but it's fairly pleasant and the staff are friendly. Standard rooms without sea views and including half board cost US$125/170 for singles/doubles. Rooms with sea views cost US$140/200 with half board. Bed and breakfast rates are US$10 per person less and full-board rates attract an additional US$12 per person. All the rooms have private bathroom, air-con, TV and telephone. The hotel facilities include two bars, a restaurant, swimming pool, a fitness centre, tennis and squash courts, sauna and a nightclub with live music.

Places to Eat – cheap
Undoubtedly the cheapest place to eat in the evening is in the Jamituri Gardens in front of the fort. The townspeople gather here at that time to socialise and watch the sun go down. Food stalls sell spicy curries, roasted meat (mishkaki) and maize, cassava, smoked octopus, sugar-cane juice and ice cream – all at extremely reasonable prices.

Just about as cheap and very popular, especially with local people, is the cafe at the *Ciné Afrique*, where basic African dishes are available.

Somewhat more expensive but very popular with travellers is the *Dolphin Restaurant*, close to the post office on Kenyatta Rd. The Dolphin has been going for years and offers all the usual seafood dishes plus a few other items.

Those staying at either the Warere Guest House or the Malindi Guest House should try the meals at the *New Gulf Restaurant/ Golden Falcon*, opposite the entrance to the Malindi Guest House.

For breakfast you could try the *1001 Nights Café* at the Palace Museum. It's open daily, except Monday, from 9.30 am to 3.30 pm and 7 to 10 pm.

Travellers looking for something resembling fast food might like to check out the *Chicken Inn*, next door to the Karibuni Inn, or the *Jabco Fast Food International*, on the seafront next door to the Africa House Hotel.

One place you *must* visit, especially if you're a fruit-juice or ice-cream freak, is the *Baobab Bar* not far from St Joseph's Cathedral. It was built, as the name implies, under a baobab tree and designed by someone with imagination. It's excellent.

Places to Eat – more expensive
For a not-too-expensive splurge, there's a choice of four very popular restaurants. The first is the *Fisherman Restaurant*, on Shangani St opposite the Tembo Hotel and run by a French Alsatian man. Set in a traditional Zanzibari house, which makes for an intimate atmosphere, the restaurant offers a full range of excellent seafood at competitive prices. Salads and soups average TSh 600 and main courses average TSh 2500 (fish, calamari etc), with prawns at TSh 4500 and

TANZANIA

lobster from TSh 6000. It's open daily from 9 am to 10 pm. Get there early for lunch or dinner if you want the best choice of tables. Ice-cold imported Löwenbräu and Castle beer is available. They also have a range of European wines. The staff here are very friendly.

The second is *Camlurs Restaurant* on Kenyatta Rd close to the Africa House Hotel. This beautiful little restaurant with a very intimate atmosphere offers Swahili food – meat, seafood and vegetable curries cooked with coconut. The food is excellent and a main dish costs around TSh 2500. It's open Monday to Saturday from 6.30 to 10 pm. The staff here are very friendly and eager to please.

Close by on the same street is the *Maharaja Restaurant* which serves good Indian food and offers a fixed-price lunch for TSh 2500. You can eat in or take-away and it's open daily except Tuesday for lunch and dinner.

The fourth choice is the *Sea View Indian Restaurant* (☎ 32132), on Mizingani Rd overlooking the harbour, on the 1st floor. This restaurant has one of the best locations of any on the island and offers a choice of eating outside on the balcony or inside. A full range of seafood is offered as well as Indian curries. It's a very pleasant place to dine but the service can be slow – so slow at times that the starters occasionally turn up after you've finished the main course! This is partly because the chefs insist on cooking everything in the traditional manner over charcoal and disdain the use of a gas oven, even though they have one. If you plan to eat here in the evening, it's advisable to pop in earlier in the day and choose your menu so that they have time to organise it. Book a table if you want to eat on the balcony.

Another relatively new place which is similar to the Fisherman is the *Oman International Restaurant* close to the Africa House Hotel on Shangani St. Not many travellers seem to come here but the food is excellent (seafood, meat and vegetarian dishes) and there's a delightful 1st-floor balcony where you can eat overlooking the ocean. They also have a good music system and a well-stocked bar. It's open daily from noon for lunch and dinner and there are lunch-time 'specials' which attract a 10% discount off the menu prices.

Also very good, but not so well known, is the *Chit Chat Restaurant* (☎ 33003), 500 Cathedral St, which offers Goan Indian food. It's run by an Indian from Goa, so you know the dishes are authentic and spicy. A very tasty meal costs around TSh 2500 and is excellent value. It's open Tuesday to Sunday from 6 to 11 pm. It's best to make a reservation in advance and find out what's on the menu by ringing Mr Lobow.

Another Indian restaurant well worth a try is the *Mayur Indian Restaurant*, just at the back of the fort next to the Arya Samat Hindu Temple.

For Italian food there's a choice of *Zee Pizza*, Kiponda St, which offers large, tasty pizzas; *Luna Mare*, on Gizenga St, which serves a mixture of Italian, French, Indian and Chinese dishes; and *La Lampara* on Victoria St next to Victoria Guest House. The last two are very popular. Count on paying around TSh 4000 for a meal.

You can also find Italian food at the *Sunrise Restaurant* on Kenyatta Rd opposite the Stone Town forex bureau but its menu is composite, consisting of Italian, Indian, Zanzibari and seafood specialities. There's a choice here of eating inside or al fresco. It only opened recently but appears to be quite popular.

Near the Jambo Guest House is the *Green Garden Restaurant*, which is a very pleasant place to eat in leafy surroundings. It serves Zanzibari food as well as other items but there's a ban on alcohol (it's a Muslim restaurant). It's open all week except Friday for lunch between 12.30 and 3 pm and dinner between 7 and 10 pm.

As far as hotel restaurants go, the *Spice Inn* and the *Hotel International* are definitely worth checking out. The food at both is reasonably priced and well prepared. Also very good is the rooftop restaurant at the *Hotel Kiponda*. Here you can eat in quiet style and catch the sea breeze, plus there are cold beers. Prices are very reasonable. It's open for lunch from noon to 3 pm and for dinner from 7 to 10.30 pm. It's advisable to make an advance reservation if you want a certain dish.

About the top of the range is *Emerson House* where a five-course meal with great views over town will come to around TSh 7000. You need to book in advance here. Comparable in price and quality would be a meal at either the *Dhow Palace Hotel* or *Mazsons' Hotel*.

The *Africa House Hotel* also has a restaurant above the bar but few people eat there as it's not up to the standard of the other hotel restaurants.

Lastly, there's the *Inn by the Sea Resort* (☎ 31755), next to the Mbweni ruins, off the road to the airport and just past the Chinese Consulate. The restaurant is right by the sea and is open for lunch and dinner. It serves chicken and chips for around TSh 2000 and has a fairly popular bar. It's a long way to go (at least four km from town) and you'd have to take a taxi, which would make it relatively expensive unless a group of you were sharing the cost.

Entertainment

Discos The best disco on the island is the *Tarumbeta Club*, part of the Fisherman Restaurant, Stone Town Inn and Le Pêcheur complex. It's open nightly from around 8 pm until early in the morning. Entry costs TSh 900 (free entry for women on Monday and Tuesday). Drinks are reasonably priced.

The *Bwawani Plaza Hotel* also has a nightly disco which kicks off at 10 pm and is open to non-guests. There's a small cover charge but the beers are expensive.

Bars Virtually everyone goes to the *Africa House Hotel* for a cold beer in the late afternoon/early evening. The bar is on the 1st-floor terrace overlooking the ocean and is a favourite spot to watch the sun go down. The beers are reasonably priced and generally cold but, depending on demand, they get

warmer as the evening wears on. They're also prone to run out completely by 9 am. Safari Lager is available as well as imported beers (Stella Artois, Becks, Löwenbräu, South African Castle and even Aussie Castlemaine XXXX). The bar is open throughout the day, from around 10 am to 11 pm. It's *the* place to meet old friends and acquaintances and to make contacts for visits to Changuu island and the beaches on the east coast.

Under the Africa House Hotel to the right of the entrance as you face it is another recently opened bar, the *New Happy Bar & Restaurant*. It's a pleasant place to have a drink and, unlike the bar at Africa House, never runs out of beer. They're also consistently cold.

Also very popular, especially in the evening after dinner, is *Le Pêcheur*, right next door to the Fisherman Restaurant. It's a very lively place with a good notice board and has the best selection of local and imported beers and liquors on the island, plus a reasonable selection of taped music. It's open all day, every day from around 9.30 am, and basically doesn't close until the last customer leaves.

The bar at the *Bottoms Up Guest House* is another option. It, too, is open all day, every day and has a good selection of music. The beer is always cold, though the lurid décor might make you wonder whether you fell into purgatory en route to pleasure.

The *Cave Resort* opposite Camlurs restaurant is the place to go if you want to mix with local people. It's an intimate little place with no frills but if you're in there in the afternoon and there's a power cut (stopping the fans) it gets stiflingly hot. At night it doesn't seem to matter so much.

Another bar to which surprisingly few people go is the *Starehe Club* on Shangani St. It's quite a large place right next to the beach overlooking the harbour. Since it rarely has too many customers, the beers are always ice-cold. It has an occasional disco in the evenings, for which there might be a small cover charge.

Much more salubrious – and somewhat

more expensive – is the *Livingstone Bar* at the Dhow Palace Hotel. It's the place to come if you'd like to get away from the madding crowd and drink in air-con comfort. Also at the same hotel is *Stanley's Wine & Jazz Bar* for a complete change of pace and atmosphere. You'll be expected to be reasonably dressed at either of these bars.

Getting There & Away

Air Air Tanzania operates one flight daily except on Thursday and Sunday in either direction between Dar es Salaam and Zanzibar. The fare is US$43 one way plus TSh 1000 airport tax and the journey takes 25 minutes.

Air Tanzania also flies from Mombasa to Zanzibar on Tuesday, Thursday and Sunday. It flies in the reverse direction on the same days but there's a stopover in Dar es Salaam. The one-way fare between Mombasa and Zanzibar is US$54 plus US$20 departure tax. Kenya Airways shares this route with Air Tanzania and flies between Mombasa and Zanzibar nonstop in either direction on Monday, Wednesday, Friday and Sunday. The fare and departure tax are the same as with Air Tanzania and the journey time is 45 minutes. Early booking for these flights is essential as there's heavy demand for tickets.

Eagle Aviation (☎ Mombasa (011) 434480; Skyland Safaris, Zanzibar, ☎ (054) 31744) also flies Mombasa to Zanzibar in either direction on Thursday and Friday. The departure times are 7 am on both days from Mombasa but 9 am from Zanzibar on Thursday and 5 pm on Friday. The fare is US$55 plus US$20 departure tax and the journey takes one hour.

The Air Tanzania office in Zanzibar is on Vuga Rd and is open Monday to Friday from 8 am to 12.30 pm and 2 to 4.30 pm and on Saturday from 8 am to 12.30 pm. The Kenya Airways office (☎ 32041) is close to Air Tanzania off Vuga Rd in Tiger House.

Also connecting Zanzibar with Dar es Salaam are three private companies, two of them based in Zanzibar and the third in Arusha, which operate six and nine-seater planes. They are:

Air Zanzibar
   307 Kenyatta Rd, Shangani, Zanzibar
   (☎ /fax (054) 32512)
   Pemba (☎ (054) 2398)
   Dar es Salaam (☎ (051) 843033)
Zan Air
   Zanzibar (☎ (054) 33670)
Precision Air
   Maha Travel, Zanzibar (☎ (054)33154)
   Arusha (☎ (057) 6903)
   Emslies Ltd, Moshi (☎ (055) 51742)
   Tan Travel, Dar es Salaam (☎ (051) 24551)

Air Zanzibar has flights to Dar (US$40) and Pemba (US$45). Zan Air flies only on request, but both these companies also occasionally fly from Zanzibar to Arusha, Mombasa and Nairobi. For details about these flights, keep your eye on the notice boards at either the Africa House Hotel or the Fisherman Restaurant.

Precision Air connects Zanzibar with Dar es Salaam (US$55), Moshi and Arusha (US$165).

Boat The majority of budget travellers come to Zanzibar by ferry boat, catamaran or hydrofoil from Dar es Salaam and return the same way. The schedule for these boats can be found in the Getting There & Away section of the Dar es Salaam chapter. The ticket offices for all these boats in Zanzibar are just inside the dock gates.

Motorised dhows have to be booked at the Malindi Sports Club directly opposite Zan Air on the morning before departure. Tickets are sold here. This is also where you book a passage on a dhow to Pemba island – the dhows dock at Mkoani in the south of the island. There are no regular schedules for these.

Sea Express Services Ltd also operates a hydrofoil between Zanzibar and Pemba (Mkoani) in either direction from Monday to Friday, departing Zanzibar at 9.30 am. The fare is US$20 (TSh 5000 for residents).

Dhows and other boats also run between Zanzibar and Mombasa, usually once or twice a week in either direction. To find out the schedule and to book, go to the Institute of Marine Science workshop on Mizingani

Rd – there's a small sign at the gate (which is flanked by the Tanzanian and Zanzibari flags) which says, 'Tickets for Dar, Pemba, Mombasa'. The fare is about US$15 or TSh 7500 and the journey takes about 12 hours but can take quite a bit longer, depending on the currents. We haven't heard of any travellers taking these dhows for a few years now so don't be disappointed if you can't find one.

Getting Around

The Airport Municipal buses run between the airport and town for a few shillings. They're marked 'U'. A taxi will cost TSh 5000.

Car & Motorcycle In stark contrast to the position on the mainland, renting mopeds, motorcycles and self-drive cars on Zanzibar is no problem at all and works out a lot cheaper than hiring taxis if there are a few of you to share the cost. Motorcycles range from around US$30 for one day to US$18 per day for one week or more. Self-drive cars would typically cost US$50 for one day to US$35 per day for a week or more. There are no mileage charges or deposits and the rates include insurance (though what sort of fix you'd be in if you had a smash-up or rolled a vehicle is anyone's guess).

There are a lot of places offering motorbike and vehicle hire, including travel agents and tour agencies, but some of the cheapest deals can be found by asking around in the bar of the Africa House Hotel any evening. If not, ask the barman if Secrete (pronounced as in French) is around. He's a totally trustworthy local young man who will fix you up with a good vehicle the next morning. Otherwise, try Samo Tours (☎ 31776).

Most of the vehicles you will be offered are Suzuki 4WDs and most of them are quite new. Many of them even have a music system so don't forget your tapes. You may be asked to sign an 'agreement' but this is just a formality. You may also be asked to show a driving licence and your passport but you won't have to leave your passport with them as a surety. What they will want from you is full payment for the number of days you want to keep the vehicle when you take delivery. Do *not* pay advance deposits.

It's important to read the warning about driving licences under Dangers & Annoyances in Information earlier in this section if you don't want problems with the traffic police. Solve all this by having an international licence or a Zanzibari licence.

Bicycle There are many places where you can rent these and most budget and many mid-range hotels can point you in the right direction. Two places which have been operating for years are Al Ridha Transport, close to the Empire Cinema off Creek Rd, and Maharouky's Store, on Creek Rd next to the petrol station in Daranjani. The latter is signposted, so you can't miss it. The average rental price is TSh 2000 per day for a gearless bike and TSh 3000 per day for one with gears.

Bicycles can be put on the roofs of local buses if you get tired of pedalling.

Around Zanzibar

RUINS

There are a number of historical sites around the island which are worth visiting.

Mbweni Palace

Just south of Zanzibar town off the airport road are the Mbweni Palace ruins, which might interest you if you have a yen for Arab architecture but which otherwise are totally neglected and largely overgrown.

Mvuleni

Close to the top of the island and north of Mkokotoni are the ruins of Mvuleni, which date from an abortive Portuguese attempt to colonise the island.

Shirazi Mosque

Near Kizimkazi in the south are the ruins of the Shirazi Dimbani Mosque. An inscription around the mihrab is dated 1107 – the oldest inscription found in East Africa. Excavations have indicated the existence of an earlier mosque on the same site. **Kizimkazi** was the island's capital until the 17th century, and there are remnants of a wall which used to surround the settlement.

Maruhubi Palace

The Maruhubi Palace, north of Zanzibar town, was built by Sultan Barghash in 1882 to house his harem but was unfortunately largely destroyed by fire in 1899. The columns which remain once supported a

Zanzibar Island

large upper-floor balcony and an overhead aqueduct.

Other Ruins

The **Persian Baths**, near Kidichi, built by Sultan Seyyid Said for his Persian wife at the highest point on the island (153m), and the **Mangapwani Slave Caves** (used for illegal slave trading after the legal trade was abolished by the British in the late 1800s), about 16 km north of Zanzibar town, are best visited in conjunction with a Spice Tour.

SPICE TOURS

To visit all the above sites separately involves a lot of effort and backtracking. It's much better to take one of the popular Spice Tours. Perhaps the best person to tour with is an elderly Indian man named Mitu, who owns taxis and has been doing these trips for years. It was Mitu who originally put this trip together and he has since trained quite a few others who now operate on their own. Mitu has an office round the corner from the Ciné Afrique (the street on the right-hand side as you face the Ciné Afrique). Try to book a tour the day before or get there at around 8 am.

Also offering excellent value for money are Tembo Tours & Safaris (☎ (054) 30466). Their guides, David and Ahmed, know Zanzibar's history and geography intimately and both speak fluent English. A tour lasts from 9 am to 5 pm, costs TSh 4000 per person and includes lunch at a local restaurant. Contact David any night at the bar at the Africa House Hotel between 6 and 8 pm.

Another bunch which has been recommended is Triple M at the Africa House Hotel but you must make your booking through Suliman, who is a reliable person and an excellent guide, and not through Luis who owns the outfit. Luis is fond of the hard stuff and often forgets he's taken a deposit from you the previous night so you'll be late starting and might even lose your deposit if he can't be found the next morning.

More reliable is Kalungu Island Tours (☎ /fax (054) 32664), PO Box 1107, Mkunazini Rd, which offers both a short Spice Tour (three hours, US$10 per person including lunch) and a longer tour (five hours, US$12 per person including lunch). The longer tour includes a visit to Mangapwani cave and the nearby beach.

The major components of a Spice Tour (other than the palace ruins and Persian baths) are visits to the various spice and fruit plantations in the centre of the island. Along the way you'll be invited to taste all the spices, herbs and fruits which the island produces. Some of these are cloves, black pepper, cardamom, cinnamon, nutmeg, rambutan, iodine plant, breadfruit, jackfruit, five-star fruit, vanilla and lemongrass. Lunch, either at a local restaurant or in the form of a picnic lunch, is included.

To get a tour going, you need four people to share a taxi. A typical tour begins at about 9.30 am, returns by 5 pm and costs TSh 16,000 (shared between four), plus the price of the fruit you eat (minimal). These tours are excellent value and are very popular.

JOZANI FOREST

Some 24 km south-east of Zanzibar town, between Chwaka and Uzi bays, is the Jozani Forest, a nature reserve for the rare red colobus monkey, two antelope species and the Zanzibar duiker and sunni. You'll probably also be told it's the haunt of the Zanzibar leopard but that's just make-believe. To get there, you need to organise your own transport or get a group together and hire a taxi. A trained guide will conduct you around the forest on foot. Put aside about half a day for the tour. Entry to the forest costs US$2.

Organised tours can be booked through either the tourist office, Kalungu Island Tours (see Spice Tours above for the address) or Centre Island Tours (☎ (054) 33845), Hurumzi St. Kalungu charges US$10 per person for this trip plus US$2 entry. Central Island charges US$15 per person but this includes lunch and a visit to Kizimkazi where you are able to go swimming with the dolphins.

OFFSHORE ISLETS

Just offshore from Zanzibar town are several islands ringed with coral reefs. Three of them

– Nyange, Pange and Murogo – are simply sandbanks which partially disappear at high tide, but the other four – Kibandiko, Changuu (Prison island), Bawe and Chumbe (on which there's a lighthouse) are well-forested, idyllic tropical islands with small but superb beaches. There are superb snorkelling and scuba diving opportunities off several of these islands especially Bawe, Pange, Murogo and Nyange. These are where the two dive centres conduct most of their dives.

Changuu Island

The island which everyone seems to visit is Changuu island, also known as Prison island. It's the most famous of the offshore islands and in the 19th century was owned by an Arab who used it, as the sign says, for housing 'recalcitrant slaves'. It was later bought by a Briton who constructed a prison (which apparently was never used, though the ruins remain). Now the island is used by Zanzibar day-trippers as a pleasant day out.

The beach is superb, the sea is crystal clear and there's a whole family of (frequently copulating) giant land tortoises which roam around the main landing spot. It's thought they were brought to the island from Aldabra in the Seychelles around the turn of the century.

The island has a two-storey house with a verandah, a bar and a restaurant, adjacent to which are several basic rooms to rent. Lunch (seafood, chips and salad) costs about the same as on the main island and cold beers are available.

The island is run by the Tanzania Tourist Corporation, which charges an entry fee of US$1, UK£1 or DM 2, payable in *cash* – neither shillings nor UK£1 coins are accepted. If you don't have that spare dollar you'll have to sit on the boat all day unless you can persuade them to give you change in dollars.

Activities here include windsurfing, sailing, scuba diving and snorkelling, but you have to pay for equipment.

It's easy finding transport across from Zanzibar. In Zanzibar town, enquire at Chemha Brothers Tours (☎ (054) 31751), next to the Fisherman Restaurant; Fisherman Tours (☎ (054) 30468), Creek Rd; Kalungu Island Tours (☎ (054) 32664), Mkunazini Rd; or the tourist office. Motorised boats cost on average TSh 6000 shared by up to 10 people. They generally leave at 9 am and return by 4.30 pm (departure and return times are entirely up to you).

Bawe Island

The beach at the northern tip of this island is one of the best places in Zanzibar for snorkelling. There's a restaurant of sorts here but it only serves chips and omelettes, though fish is sometimes available. On landing, you have to pay the English manager of the still nonexistent hotel a TSh 250 landing fee. A boat to Bawe should cost around TSh 7000.

Chumbe Island

A marine national park is being created here, as well as a diving-education centre, but it's not yet open to the public. All the same, it certainly looks very inviting from the ferry which passes the island just before you reach Zanzibar town.

BEACHES

There are some superb beaches, particularly on the east coast of the island, which are as unspoilt as you're likely to find. This is rapidly changing, however, as new guesthouses open their doors each week. All the same, most of the accommodation available is for those who can do without electricity, hot and cold running water, swimming pools and night entertainment. Paradise here is still simple and uncomplicated and the local people have not yet jumped on the tourism gravy train. It's totally relaxing and, unlike many of the beaches on the western side of the island close to Zanzibar town, there are no concerns about being robbed or mugged.

The roads to these places are also pretty rugged in parts, so a fair amount of effort is necessary to get to them, though the bulldozers and graders have been hard at work so things change all the time. There's also been a surge in foreign investment on resort complexes, so if you want to experience the place before it begins to resemble the beaches north and south of Mombasa, get there soon.

The main beaches on the east coast, from the northern tip of the island, are: **Nungwi,** then **Matemwe, Pwani Mchangani, Uroa, Chwaka, Bwejuu, Paje, Jambiani** and **Makunduchi.** Everyone has their favourite but there's actually not too much to choose between them except Nungwi which doesn't suffer from seaweed problems. All are protected by coral reefs offshore and have white coral-sand beaches and, depending on the season, a soup of seaweed to swim in. Don't knock the seaweed – the local people harvest it for export, and you'll see it drying in the sun in all the villages.

Places to Stay & Eat

Since the Zanzibari government ditched its Marxist proclivities and subliminal xenophobia some years back and allowed in foreign entrepreneurs, the hotel situation at the various beaches around the island has improved by leaps and bounds. The government still owns various bungalows at Bwejuu, Chwaka, Jambiani, Makunduchi and Uroa which sleep up to five people and cost US$30 or US$40 depending on facilities. None of them have electricity but kerosene lanterns are provided and you can make your own arrangements with the caretakers to cook for you if you don't want to do this yourself. Bookings for these bungalows must be made at the tourist office (Livingstone House) in Zanzibar before arrival.

As far as private guesthouses go on the east coast, there are plenty to choose from, many with a booking office in Zanzibar town. If you don't have your own transport and don't want to take pot luck on arrival, advance booking is probably not a bad idea, though by doing this, you'll essentially lose any opportunity to strike a cheaper deal. If you simply turn up and your choice of guesthouse isn't full, you can haggle over the price.

Bwejuu The most popular place to stay here

– and the cheapest – is the *Bwejuu Dere Beach Resort* (☎ (054) 31017), which consists of three main buildings and associated bungalows. Many of the rooms face the sea, giving you the benefit of sea breezes. The staff are friendly and the bar/restaurant offers excellent seafood (fish and chips for TSh 1400) plus egg and chicken dishes. The rooms themselves are simple but adequate with fan, mosquito nets, towel and toilet paper. The bathroom facilities (clean) are generally shared, though they do also have rooms with private bathroom. In the low season, a double with private bathroom is US$16 whereas in the high season it is US$20. Rooms with shared bathroom facilities come a few dollars cheaper. Snorkelling gear can be hired for TSh 1500 per day plus they can also arrange bicycle hire for TSh 1000 to 1500 per day depending on the type of bicycle. Cold beers are available in the restaurant.

Close by is the *Palm Beach Inn* (no phone), which is good value at US$10/20 a single/double in the low season and US$15/30 in the high season including breakfast. All rooms have private bathroom and the staff are friendly. There's a large bar and restaurant, done in local style, and meals average TSh 1500, with lobster at around TSh 3500. Security is good and parking is available in the compound at the back.

Not directly on the beach but cheaper than the above, the *Kibuda Family Guest House* offers accommodation for just US$5 per person including breakfast. Bucket showers are available and meals can be arranged. Ask for Jamal in the village.

The beach north of Bwejuu is rapidly being developed but several projects, all of them in an advanced state of development, appear to have come to a complete standstill. There are, however, a few places up and running. About one km north of the Dere Beach Resort is the *Twisted Palm*, which is right on the beach and offers bed and breakfast for US$9 per person. Most of the rooms are doubles with huge double beds and mosquito nets but no fans (there's no electricity). They also have two single rooms. There's a

restaurant upstairs overlooking the sea with lunch for TSh 2500 and dinner for TSh 3000. You must order meals in advance. It's a very quiet place.

Further north along the same road is the *Sunrise Hotel & Restaurant* which offers bed and breakfast in rooms with private bathroom for US$40/50 a single/double. It's a pleasant place with its own bar and restaurant and electricity is available in the evenings by generator.

None of the other places further north along this road are open for business yet, but judging from their style and size, they will probably be expensive. Also, the road deteriorates alarmingly the further you go. Don't attempt it in anything other than a sturdy 4WD.

About four km north of Bwejuu is what's known as the 'lagoon', where there's a superb beach. There are magnificent snorkelling opportunities here, but you must wear shoes or fins, or you'll walk away on crutches. The sea urchins and stone fish are not keen on being squashed by unwary feet. Local youths will guide you there along the beach road.

A little further south down the coast, at the entrance to Bwejuu village, the *Seven Seas Guest House* offers bed and breakfast for about the same price as the Dere Beach Resort but doesn't have anywhere near the same facilities.

Chwaka A good place to stay here is the *Chwaka Bay Beach Hotel* which has rooms with private bathroom at US$20 per person including breakfast. The hotel has its own restaurant and bar. The Zanzibar town agent for this hotel is Bottoms Up Guest House.

Jambiani A few years ago, Jambiani was one of the favourite beaches to head for, so there's a good choice of guesthouses. It's a *long* village, so if you're coming in on the bus, make sure you get off near where you want to stay or you could find yourself walking up to two km. Some of the smaller guesthouses are basically just square boxes with the absolute minimum of facilities, so if you're looking for more than that, take a better place first and then check the others out later.

The best of them in terms of facilities is the *Jambiani Beach Hotel*, which has rooms arranged around a rectangular compound. Bathroom facilities are communal and no mosquito nets are provided but it has a bar and a good restaurant, there's a good selection of tape music and the staff are very friendly. Rooms here cost US$15 per person including breakfast, and meals of fish, squid or octopus cost around TSh 1500.

Right at the end of Jambiani village is the *Gomani Guest House*, which you'll see advertised in Zanzibar town. It's a very pleasant place on a coral outcrop overlooking the sea, so there are plenty of sea breezes. It costs US$10 per person in the high season and US$8 per person in the low season, including breakfast. The guesthouse consists of a number of bungalows with twin beds provided with mosquito nets. There's also a 'family room' with two bedrooms and a verandah. Most of the rooms have private bathroom but there's no electricity. The guesthouse has its own restaurant and beers are usually available but, otherwise, right next door is the *Baharini Restaurant* which offers good seafood meals at reasonable prices.

Also popular is the *Shehe Guest House* (☎ (054) 33188), in the centre of the village, which offers rooms with shared bathroom facilities, two beds, fan and mosquito net for US$8 per person, including breakfast. Other meals can be arranged on request. Book in advance at the office in the Africa House Hotel bar.

Other travellers have recommended the *Lowea Beach Bungalow* which costs US$20 per person including breakfast. Other meals are available for TSh 3000 per person. You can book the bungalow at Serene Tours (☎ /fax (054) 31816), PO Box 326, Zanzibar.

There are several other guesthouses at Jambiani which include the *Horizontal Inn* (very clean, toilets and showers with running water), *East Coast New Mwambao Guest House* (☎ (054) 32789), *East Coast Rising Sun, East Coast Visitors Inn, Starehe* and *Manufaa Guest House*. You're looking at US$10 to US$20 per person in all of these, depending on the season, including breakfast.

Matemwe The only choice here is *Matemwe Bungalows* (☎ 31342), which you can book through its office, opposite the High Court in Zanzibar town. It consists of 12 bungalows, six of them with private bathroom, a bar and a restaurant, and water sports equipment is available. The staff are friendly and the food is good but there's no electricity. The price in the high season is US$45 per person with shared bathroom or US$55 per person with own bathroom, including full board. Boats can be hired but are very expensive (around TSh 35,000 for four hours).

Mnemba Island This is the only island off the east coast and is surrounded by its own coral reef. The island is owned by Archer's Ltd, which has an office (Archer's Aviation) facing the park opposite the old Extelecoms building in Shangani in Zanzibar town. It's an exclusive resort development and has all the facilities you might expect for US$300 per person. It's closed from April to June.

Nungwi At the extreme north end of Zanzibar, Nungwi has few tourists but this is changing rapidly as more and more travellers discover its mellow charm. It arguably has one of the best beaches on the island since there's no seaweed and the tide doesn't go out for miles, but it is only a very small beach. Indian Ocean Divers of Zanzibar town also has a branch here at the Paradise Restaurant & Bungalows – look for the PADI sign.

Just as you enter Nungwi village you'll be stopped by one of the local men and will be required to pay an entry 'fee' of TSh 500 (for the vehicle) which goes towards the village development fund. He even gives you a receipt for this!

The cheaper places to stay are off to the left of the village as you arrive from the south. The first that you come to is *Baraka*

Bungalows which has doubles at US$10 per person and triples with private bathroom at US$12 per person in the low season. Breakfast is included in these prices. It's a friendly place and has a restaurant which serves simple but tasty meals for TSh 1500. Camping is permitted on the adjacent beach and costs TSh 1500 per tent. Bookings for the bungalows can be made with Ocean Tours (☎ (054) 33642) in Zanzibar.

Right next door to the Baraka is the *Paradise Restaurant & Bungalows*. It offers somewhat more basic accommodation at US$8 per person including breakfast with shared bathroom facilities. There's also a restaurant here which offers simple but tasty meals though advance booking is recommended. The restaurant overlooks the ocean where you can watch the sun go down.

If, instead of turning into the Baraka, you continue on the dirt road for another 100m you'll come to the *Amaan Bungalows* (☎ (0811) 327747 or Zanzibar (054) 31086). Here you'll find a cluster of 24 bungalows, six of them with private bathroom. In the low season these cost US$16 a double with shared facilities and US$35 a double with private bathroom. In the high season, the doubles with private bathroom cost US$50. All prices include breakfast. There's a restaurant overlooking the ocean which offers seafood meals for TSh 2500 but these must be ordered in advance.

The more expensive places to stay are off to the right of the village just before you pay your village entrance 'fee'. Head for the lighthouse and then follow the signs. The first you come to off to the left is *Mnarani Beach Cottages* (☎ (054) 33440), PO Box 3361, Zanzibar. This is a brand-new place consisting of a number of detached cottages and a partially complete restaurant/bar structure. All the cottages have private bathrooms with hot water and the price includes breakfast. In the low season they cost US$15/30 a single/double and in the high season they are US$30/60. It's an attractive place but has one major drawback and that is 'location'. While it's right on the shore, there's no beach at this point.

Beyond the Mnarani Cottages, the road deteriorates into a vehicle-crunching nightmare and finally ends at the *Lala Salama Hotel* which, to all intents and purposes, appears to be a building site but is actually a fully functioning hotel. The rooms are somewhat spartan but otherwise very clean and comfortable. All of them have private bathroom. In the low season they cost US$25 per person on the top side and US$35 per person on the bottom side, including breakfast. The corresponding prices in the high season are US$60/70. The hotel has its own generator but it doesn't get turned on until evening so don't expect cold drinks during the day, even if you're prepared to buy them in the first place at TSh 1500 for a can of Castle (three times the normal price!).

Driving from Zanzibar town to Nungwi, there's a choice of two routes. After some 23 km of driving north the tarmac appears to end at Mahonda. If you continue heading directly north at this point, it's a rough road as far as Mkokotoni (13 km) followed by another tarmac road as far as Fukuchani. It's good gravel to Nungwi from there. You can cut out the rough section to Mkokotoni if you turn right where the first section of tarmac ends at Mahonda and head for Kinyasini. From there, it's plain sailing all the way to Nungwi.

Paje Paje is about halfway between Bwejuu and Jambiani beaches. Best value here is the *Paje Ndame Village* which is very popular and offers doubles with private bathroom for US$20 in the low season and US$30 in the high season including breakfast. The hotel has its own restaurant and there's ample safe parking.

Also good value is *Paradise Beach*, somewhat further north towards Bwejuu, which costs US$20 per bungalow with private bathroom and including breakfast. There's a bar and restaurant, which specialises in Japanese and continental dishes. You can book in advance at the Warere Guest House in Zanzibar town.

Simpler guesthouses in Paje include the *Amani Guest House* and the *Ufukwe Guest*

House. They cost US$10 to US$20 per person including breakfast.

Uroa The principal resort hotel here is the *Tamarind Beach Hotel* (☎ (054) 51859; fax 31859), where singles/doubles with private bathroom and breakfast cost US$35/50. Accommodation consists of beach cottages built in local style, plus there's a bar and restaurant. There's also a full range of water sports equipment available (which costs extra). Transport to the resort can be arranged from the docks or the airport on arrival with Fisherman Tours (☎ (054) 30468; fax 32387). Otherwise, bookings can be made at their office on Creek Rd, Daranjani, in Zanzibar town. More expensive is the *Uroa Bay Hotel & Fishing Club* (☎ (054) 33552), which consists of 18 bungalows (36 rooms in total). Rooms have private bathroom and cost US$60 to US$80 per person, including breakfast. There's a bar, restaurant, swimming pool, tennis court, diving centre and water sports equipment (most of it at no extra cost). The food here is excellent but somewhat expensive at TSh 4000 for a buffet lunch. Transport is available from Zanzibar town or from the airport.

Getting There & Around
To get to the east-coast beaches, you'll have to take a local bus, hire a taxi or rent your own motorcycle or vehicle. The bus station is on Creek Rd opposite the market.

Bus No 9 leaves for Jambiani at 10 am and 4 pm (TSh 600, three hours), and also goes to Bwejuu. The return bus from Bwejuu to Zanzibar departs from the village at about 2 am and reaches the market in Zanzibar by 6.30 am. Bus No 10 goes to Makunduchi, No 6 goes to Chwaka (1½ hours) and the No 6 'Special' goes to Uroa.

Taxis to the east coast tend to be quite expensive. Count on around TSh 30,000 to Bwejuu, Paje or Jambiani for a car shared between up to five people. At that price – and bearing in mind that that's one way – you might as well rent a car or, better still, a motorbike so long as you're not intending to stay for a lengthy period of time on the

beach. It's *definitely* worth considering if you're heading to Nungwi because the taxi fares there are considerably more than those to the east-coast beaches. A Suzuki 4WD can be as little as US$35 a day and a motorbike as little as US$18 a day. For more details on car and motorbike hire see the Zanzibar Getting Around section.

Other Islands

PEMBA
While most travellers make it to Zanzibar, very few ever make the journey to Pemba island, north of Zanzibar. It's perhaps not surprising since, in terms of tourism, the island is in its infancy. It's not that there are no historic sites to visit or good beaches, because there are plenty of these, but it's very difficult to get to them because there is little public transport off the island's only main

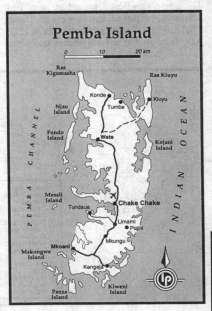

Pemba Island

road. Most of the beaches are small, too, due to the extensive mangrove forests which ring the island. Nevertheless, it's quite a contrast to Zanzibar.

The island is very laid-back, and the people are friendly and interested in where you come from and why you're there. It's the sort of place where you make an effort to get to know people and find out what's going on rather than go to see things in the usual tourist mode.

Cloves are the mainstay of the island's economy, and the crop is three times as large as the crop from Zanzibar. There are 3.5 million clove trees on Pemba, many of which date from the early 19th century, when they were introduced from the Moluccas. Everywhere you go on this island, you'll see the ripe cloves laid out to dry in the sun and you'll smell their distinctive aroma.

Although Pemba was never as important as Zanzibar or other settlements on the Tanzanian coast, it has had some interesting and remarkable associations during its history. The island's earliest ruins are those of Ras Mkumbu, on the peninsula west of Chake Chake, where the Shirazis settled about 1200 AD. This site has several houses and pillar tombs and the remains of a large 14th-century mosque.

At Pujini on the island's east coast, there is a fortified settlement and the remains of a palace destroyed by the Portuguese in 1520.

The trouble with the ruins on Pemba is that most are in poor condition, have never been excavated and are largely overgrown. Perhaps something will be done about them when the government has sufficient money or an international organisation provides the funds.

Pemba's other major attraction is the coral reefs around the island. These are rated by many divers as the best in the world. The problem is getting to them and the expense involved. Very few dive outfits cater for Pemba at an affordable price and none of them are based on Pemba itself. Those based on Zanzibar island will certainly put a Pemba dive trip together for you but you'll need a fat wallet. The main outfit which operates Pemba dives is CAT-Diving Ltd; see Scuba Diving in the Zanzibar Activities section.

Wete

This is the most northern of the island's main towns and has the second most important

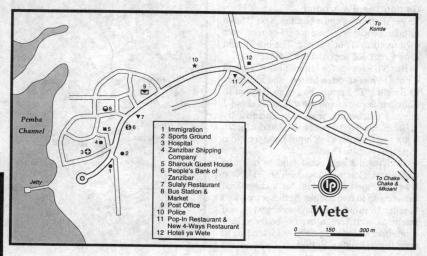

1 Immigration
2 Sports Ground
3 Hospital
4 Zanzibar Shipping Company
5 Sharouk Guest House
6 People's Bank of Zanzibar
7 Sulaly Restaurant
8 Bus Station & Market
9 Post Office
10 Police
11 Pop-In Restaurant & New 4-Ways Restaurant
12 Hoteli ya Wete

Pemba Channel

Jetty

To Konde

To Chake Chake & Mkoani

Wete

0   150   300 m

TANZANIA

port, through which most of the clove crop is exported. It's essentially a one-street town which snakes up the hillside from the docks. A branch of the People's Bank of Zanzibar is on the main road, but it won't change travellers' cheques. You must go to Chake Chake for this.

Places to Stay & Eat There are only two places to stay in Wete. The main one is the *Hoteli ya Wete* (☎ (054) 4301), a government-owned place on the main street at the top end of town. Rooms with private bathroom cost US$15 per person (payable in hard currency) including breakfast. They're clean and well maintained, the staff are very friendly and English is spoken. Lunch and dinner are priced at TSh 1700 each and ice-cold beers are available at normal prices (so long as the nearby police canteen still has a supply of them!).

The other place to stay is the simpler *Sharouk Guest House* (☎ (054) 4386), in the centre of town, where there are five rooms, one with private bathroom. It's clean, friendly and costs US$7 per person including breakfast. The owner is good about finding

dhows to Dar es Salaam, Zanzibar and Tanga.

For a slight change of diet, you could try one of the restaurants in town, though they're all pretty basic. They include the *Sulaly Restaurant, Pop-In Restaurant* and the *New 4-Ways Restaurant*. The latter two are opposite the Hoteli ya Wete.

Chake Chake

This is Pemba's principal town and a lively place to wander around in the early mornings and late afternoons. It has a well-defined but small old centre, complete with bazaar and the remains of a late 18th-century fort, and it sits on top of a ridge overlooking a largely silted-up creek into which dhows occasionally sail when the tides allow. The site of the fort is now occupied by a hospital, and only the eastern corner and tower survive. The overall impression of the town from the ridge is of a mixture of makuti and rusty old tin roofs, but times are changing rapidly here. There's a new hospital, for instance, funded by the European Union, and a huge sports stadium on the outskirts of town. Chake Chake also has the island's only airport,

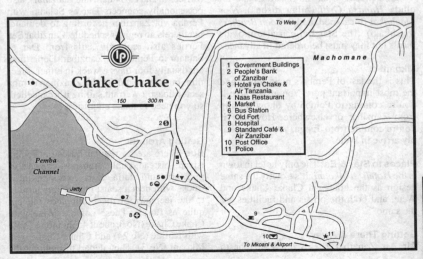

Chake Chake

0   150   300 m

Pemba Channel

Jetty

To Wete

Machomane

1 Government Buildings
2 People's Bank of Zanzibar
3 Hoteli ya Chake & Air Tanzania
4 Naas Restaurant
5 Market
6 Bus Station
7 Old Fort
8 Hospital
9 Standard Café & Air Zanzibar
10 Post Office
11 Police

To Mkoani & Airport

TANZANIA

about seven km from town off the road to Mkoani.

Information The tourist office (☎ (054) 2121) is next door to the Hoteli ya Chake. Unfortunately, they have no literature and only limited information.

The People's Bank of Zanzibar changes travellers' cheques and can provide you with US dollars cash to pay your hotel bill against hard currency travellers' cheques (though they don't particularly like doing this). The staff are friendly and efficient.

On arrival at the airport in Chake Chake, you will have to pass through immigration and customs and have your passport stamped.

Places to Stay & Eat The only place to stay in the centre of town is the *Hoteli ya Chake* (☎ (054) 2069). This is exactly the same design as the hotel in Wete and has the same prices and facilities, including a bar (which is frequently dry except for local spirits). There are also two private guesthouses, the *Guest House Nassir* at Machomane and the *Star Inn* opposite the stadium, but they're both well outside the centre. The Star Inn costs TSh 5000 per person.

Good places to eat in Chake Chake include *Hamisa Grill* (pilau dishes), *New Machakos* (local food) and *Balloon Brothers* (mishkaki). The Star Inn can also provide meals but they must be ordered in advance.

Mkoani

This is the last of Pemba's main towns and the most important port. You arrive here if you're coming to Pemba by dhow or ship from Zanzibar or elsewhere. However, if you're coming from Tanga, you will probably arrive in Wete.

Places to Stay & Eat The only hotel in town is the *Hoteli ya Mkoani*. It's exactly the same design as the hotels in Chake Chake and Wete, and both the prices and facilities are the same.

Getting There & Away

Air Air Zanzibar flies from Zanzibar to Pemba every Wednesday at 7 am and Pemba to Zanzibar on the same day at 8 am. The fare is US$45 and bookings can be made at the office in Zanzibar (☎ (054) 33098) on Kenyatta Rd or in Pemba at the airport office.

Boat Dhows from Tanga sometimes dock at Wete. These dhows are usually not motorised, so sailing times depend on the tides and the winds; nor are they always easy to find. In addition, you might need permission from the district commissioner before you can sail. It can be a rough crossing on a dhow.

Boat connections between Zanzibar and Mkoani are more reliable. The MS *Sepideh*, operated by Spear's Ship Contractors (☎ Zanzibar (054) 38025; ☎ Mkoani (054) 311486), sails every second or third day between Mombasa and Zanzibar via Pemba, Tanga and Shimoni in either direction but the schedule varies so you need to make enquiries. The fares from Pemba are US$30 to either Zanzibar or Tanga and US$40 to Mombasa.

Another possibility is the MV *Steni*, which plies between Mkoani and Tanga once a week on Saturday at 10 am.

The *Serengeti*, operated by Azam Marine (offices in Dar es Salaam and Zanzibar), also occasionally connects Dar es Salaam with Pemba via Zanzibar according to demand, but there's no regular schedule. Zanzibar Sea Ferries also regularly sails from Dar es Salaam to Pemba via Zanzibar. Departures are usually four days a week in either direction, but if demand for the Zanzibar-Pemba sector doesn't warrant sailing it's cancelled, so you need to make enquiries.

Getting Around

Bus There are no regular buses on Pemba island. Instead, public transport consists of pick-ups and dalla dalla (wooden-sided trucks with bench seats, remarkably similar to the jeepneys of the Philippines but not quite as florid). These connect Wete with Chake Chake (No 6, about 45 minutes), Wete with Koride (No 24) and Chake Chake with Mkoani (No 3). They depart throughout the

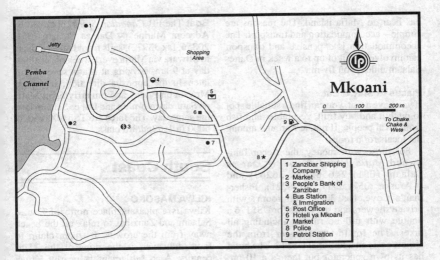

Mkoani

0   100   200 m

To Chake
Chake &
Wete

1 Zanzibar Shipping
   Company
2 Market
3 People's Bank of
   Zanzibar
4 Bus Station
   & Immigration
5 Post Office
6 Hoteli ya Mkoani
7 Market
8 Police
9 Petrol Station

day as soon as they're full. The road is sealed and in excellent condition.

Pick-ups and dalla dalla only go to the airport from Chake Chake and Mkoani when a flight is due as that's the only time there's any business there.

MAFIA

Mafia island lies south of Zanzibar off the mouth of the Rufiji River. It was an important settlement from the 12th to 14th centuries, in the days when the Shirazis ruled much of the East African coastal area. However, by the time the Portuguese arrived at the beginning of the 16th century, it had lost much of its former importance and had become part of the territory ruled by the Sultan of Kilwa. Little remains above ground of the Shirazi settlement, though you may occasionally come across pottery shards and coins on the shore where the sea is eroding the ruins south of Kilindoni.

On the nearby island of Juani are the extensive remains of Kua, a much later town dating from the 18th century but with a history going back to the 14th century. The principal ruins here are those of five mosques. The town was destroyed by raiders

from Madagascar in the early 19th century, and the inhabitants eaten by the invaders!

Mafia island is covered by coconut palms and cashew trees established by Omanis in their Zanzibari heyday, but the soil is poor and the island has never been able to support a large population.

These days Mafia is better known as a resort island for deep-sea fishing and scuba diving. It's a superb place to do this – a 200m-deep trough running along the sea bed about one km off the western shoreline of the island is the habitat of a vast number of different aquatic species. The coral formations are best off the small islands scattered around the main island, the best being the Okuto and Tutia reefs around Juani and Jibondo islands close to Chole Bay.

Mafia is also notable as a favourite breeding ground for giant turtles, which come up onto the white coral sands to lay their eggs. They do this principally on the uninhabited islands of Shungumbili, Burukini and Nyororo. Unfortunately, their numbers have been drastically depleted due to excessive hunting by local fishers, who also dig up and take away their eggs.

You're unlikely to meet any traveller who

has been to Mafia island. The reasons are simple – accommodation and transport. The accommodation is expensive and transport can involve a wait of up to a week in Dar es Salaam unless you fly in.

Places to Stay & Eat

If you have a tent, you can find a suitable spot to pitch it and buy fruit, vegetables and fish from local people. If not, ask around among the locals for a room.

For those with money, the Accor/Tahi-owned *Mafia Island Lodge* (☎ Dar es Salaam (051) 24658; fax 36263; and ☎ Arusha (057) 2711; fax 8221), Fisherman's Cove, has 30 air-con rooms with private showers and sea views for US$176 a double with full board and including all taxes. The round-trip transfer from the airport costs an additional US$12. The hotel has its own generator but there's a 10 pm curfew and water is limited. The lodge mainly attracts those who want to scuba dive or go big game fishing and it has the full range of top-quality equipment as well as highly trained staff and several motor-powered boats equipped with VHF radio.

The other place to stay is *Kinasi Camp* (☎ (051) 46045), PO Box 3052, Dar es Salaam. This is a small luxury lodge for 20 guests, built with natural materials and traditional palm thatching. All the rooms have private bathroom and all overlook Chole Bay and the islets of Jibondo and Juani. The cuisine is based on local seafood and all items on the menu are home-made. The lodge is fully equipped for water sports including scuba diving, snorkelling, big game fishing and sailing. The tariff is much the same as at the Mafia Island Lodge.

Getting There & Around

Air Coastal Travels (☎ (051) 37479; fax 46045), Dar es Salaam, operates regular light planes to Mafia from Dar es Salaam four times a week, some of which are direct; others go via Ras Kutani and Selous Game Reserve. The fare from Dar es Salaam is US$70 and the journey (direct) takes 45 minutes.

Boat The FB *Canadian Spirit*, operated by Adecom Marine (☎ Dar es Salaam (051) 20856; fax 33972), sails from Dar es Salaam to Mtwara via Mafia every week on Wednesday at 9 am, arriving at Mafia seven hours later. In the opposite direction, it departs Mtwara on Friday at 5 pm arriving at Mafia on Saturday morning and Dar es Salaam later the same day. The fares are TSh 8000/6000/5000 in 1st/2nd/3rd class.

South Coast

KILWA MASOKO

Kilwa is a pleasant place north of Dar es Salaam and Zanzibar to relax on the beach away from the crowds. Its main claim to fame, however, is the ruins of the 15th-century Arab settlement at nearby Kilwa Kisiwani. There are also two good beaches here and a coral reef at least as good as those off Zanzibar.

A little further up the coast from Kilwa Masoko is **Kilwa Kivinje**, which is a quiet fishing village with some of the Zanzibar-type doors along with a number of old German colonial buildings.

Kilwa Kisiwani

History Kilwa was one of the most important mercantile towns of East Africa before the arrival of the Portuguese in the Indian Ocean towards the end of the 15th century. On the evidence of archaeological digs it seems Kilwa was occupied in the 10th century AD but it wasn't until the arrival of the Shirazis in the mid to late 12th century that it began to expand.

At the beginning of the 14th century, the Sultanate of Kilwa passed to a new ruling dynasty, the Abu'Muwahib, a Hadhrami family from the southern end of the Arabian Peninsula, who were still ruling at the time of the Portuguese arrival.

A decline in prosperity was followed by a revival in the 15th century when the Great Mosque was reconstructed after an influx of population and funds from Malindi. This was only done, however, at the cost of granting important public offices – those of Qadhi and Amir – to the newcomers. This led to divisions which the Portuguese were able to exploit in their conquest of Kilwa but which later effectively prevented them from setting up a stable subject regime.

Kilwa continued as a trade entrepôt during the 17th century and was where a factor of the Portuguese Captaincy of Mombasa resided. Another period of prosperity was experienced towards the end of the 18th century when it became a source of slaves for the French plantations in the Mascarene islands.

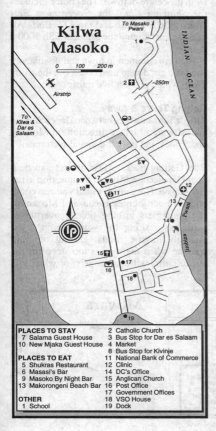

The Monuments Along with Gedi (south of Malindi in Kenya), Kilwa possesses the most important group of public monuments dating from the Swahili period on the coast of East Africa. The earliest of these is the **Great Mosque** which dates back to the 12th century but which collapsed in the early 14th and was not rebuilt until the 15th century. It was restored by the Antiquities Division of Tanzania in the late 1960s. Nearby is another domed mosque similar to those at Takwa and Shanga in the Lamu archipelago which dates from the same time as the reconstruction of the Great Mosque.

About 1.5 km from these two buildings and built on a bluff are the ruins of one of the first **palaces** to be constructed in Kilwa and dating from the early 14th century. It included reception courts, a bathing pool and a large court surrounded by small window-less rooms which acted as storerooms. Excavations indicate it was not occupied for very long. Nearby is another large building, the **Husuni Ndogo**, which consists of a large enclosure surrounded by polygonal columns at 13m intervals. Its purpose has not been identified. A later palace, constructed in the 18th century, is also in the vicinity but the palace stormed by the Portuguese captain, Almeida, has yet to be identified.

Near the 18th-century palace is a large house with an attached mosque which was built in the 15th century and may have been the house of the Amirs who played such an important part in the politics of that period.

Another significant ruin here is the **Fort of Santiago** which was originally built in 1505 by the Portuguese and has a round tower or keep in one corner. It was restored at the turn of the 18th century to serve as the stronghold of the representative of the Zanzibar governor.

Before you come here, make sure you visit the National Museum in Dar es Salaam where there's an excellent display of the ruins of Kilwa Kisiwani.

Places to Stay & Eat

For budget accommodation in Kilwa Masoko, the *Salama Guest House* and the

PLACES TO STAY	2 Catholic Church
7 Salama Guest House	3 Bus Stop for Dar es Salaam
10 New Mjaka Guest House	4 Market
	8 Bus Stop for Kivinje
PLACES TO EAT	11 National Bank of Commerce
5 Shukras Restaurant	12 Clinic
6 Masasi's Bar	14 DC's Office
9 Masoko By Night Bar	15 Anglican Church
13 Makorongeni Beach Bar	16 Post Office
	17 Government Offices
OTHER	18 VSO House
1 School	19 Dock

Kilwa Masoko

To Masako Pwani

INDIAN OCEAN

0   100   200 m

Airstrip

To Kilwa & Dar es Salaam

~250m

Pwani

Jimbizi

TANZANIA

Shukras Guest House are both good bets but the best is the *New Mjaka Guest House*, which also does good food (order in advance).

Good bars include *Masasi's Bar*, the *Masoko By Night Bar* and the *Makorongeni Beach Bar*.

Getting There & Away

From Dar es Salaam, the Nacet bus leaves at 5 am daily from near the Malapa Hotel on Mnazi Moja and takes about 12 hours. Booking a few days in advance is recommended. Otherwise, buses going from Dar es Salaam to Mtwara will drop you off at Nanguruku, a few km north of Kilwa Masoko, from where you can get a lift to Masoko. Remember that the road from Dar es Salaam to Kilwa Masoko is impassable in the wet season.

Locally, there are buses between Kilwa Masoko and Kilwa Kivinje and Nanguruku.

MTWARA

This is Tanzania's southernmost port and almost on the border with Mozambique. It's a sleepy, relatively small and largely uninteresting place which rarely sees a traveller.

If you're looking for a beach to lie on, take a local bus to **Msimbati**, about an hour away, which has a long, deserted sandy beach. There's nowhere to stay but you can camp. Some 19 km north of Mtwara is **Mikindani**, where there are the ruins of an old Arab town which you can wander around.

The only place to change money is the Commercial Bank of Tanzania facing the town hall. No commission is charged on travellers' cheques.

Places to Stay & Eat

There's little choice of reasonable accommodation here. There are plenty of very basic *hotelis* near the bus stand but they *are* very basic. The best of the lot is the *Jagasu Holiday Lodge*, on the main street facing the post office, which charges TSh 2000 a single with shared cold showers.

There's a much better choice of hotels outside of town but you really will need a car to get there as they're about an hour's drive from the centre of town. The choice includes the *Shingani Club*, the *Government Rest House*, the *Fin Club* and the *ATC Club*. All of these cost around the same, at TSh 5000 a double.

Bars are common in town and if what you need is a good rage then check out the *Evergreen* which puts on live music.

Getting There & Away

Air Air Tanzania flies between Dar es Salaam and Mtwara in either direction on Monday and Friday, but only if demand warrants it.

Bus Getting back to Dar by bus can be a major headache and out of the question in the wet season. Not only that, but you can count on a 36-hour journey because of Mozambican smugglers bribing police, overturned vehicles, pushing the vehicle you're on through horrific roads, getting out and walking when the road is too steep for the bus to climb with passengers, or when it is

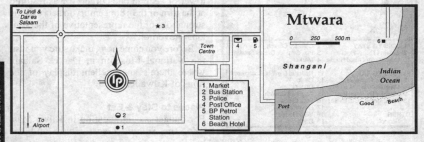

To Lindi &
Dar es
Salaam

★3

Town
Centre

4 5

Mtwara

0   250   500 m

6 ■

Shangani

*Indian
Ocean*

1 Market
2 Bus Station
3 Police
4 Post Office
5 BP Petrol
   Station
6 Beach Hotel

Port

Good   *Beach*

To
Airport

2

1

TANZANIA

just too rugged to risk the bus toppling over. You can also get stuck overnight at the Rufiji River ferry which officially doesn't operate after 6 pm without bribes being paid. It's a rough ride, but, if you want to get back to Dar, get on the first thing that's going. The fare is around TSh 6000. In Dar es Salaam, the buses for Mtwara depart from the Morogoro Road bus stand.

Boat The best way to get to Mtwara (and back again) is to take the FB *Canadian Spirit* from Dar es Salaam. It is operated by Adecon Marine and departs regularly once a week on Wednesday at 9 am from Dar es Salaam and on Friday at 5 pm from Mtwara. The journey takes approximately 18 hours. See the Tanzania Getting Around chapter for further details of this ferry.

North-Eastern Tanzania

ARUSHA

Arusha is one of Tanzania's most attractive towns and was the headquarters of the East African Community in the days when Kenya, Tanzania and Uganda were members of an economic, communications and customs union. It has once again become the headquarters of a revived clone of this attempt at regional cooperation under the name of East African Cooperation, following the signing of a number of protocols by the three heads of state in November 1994 and a further 'summit' meeting in April 1996.

The town sits in lush, green countryside at the foot of Mt Meru (4556m) and enjoys a temperate climate throughout the year. Surrounding it are many coffee, wheat and maize estates tended by the Waarusha and Wameru tribespeople, whom you may see occasionally in the market area of town. For travellers, Arusha is the gateway to Serengeti, Lake Manyara and Tarangire national parks and the Ngorongoro Conservation Area. As such, it's the safari capital of Tanzania. Mt Meru can also be trekked from here.

Arusha is a pleasant town to walk around and take in the sights, and the market area is particularly lively, but the main concern of most travellers will be arranging a safari and taking off for the national parks. You'll find people here very friendly and easy to approach and, if you've just arrived from Nairobi, you'll appreciate the breath of fresh air and lack of hassle. But, as always, be wary of 'flycatchers' (street touts grubbing up business for safari companies, real or imagined).

Orientation

The town is in two parts, separated by a small valley through which the Naura River runs. The upper part, just off the main Moshi to Namanga road, contains the government buildings, post office, immigration, most of the top-range hotels, safari companies, airline offices, curio and craft shops, and the huge Arusha International Conference Centre (AICC). Further down the hill and across the valley are the commercial and industrial areas, the market, small shops, many of the budget hotels and the bus station.

Information

National Parks Office The Tanzania National Parks headquarters (☎ 3471, ext 1104), 6th floor, Kilimanjaro Wing, International Conference Centre, PO Box 3134, usually stocks a few leaflets about the national parks. Otherwise, you probably won't need to come here.

Money There are several foreign exchange (forex) bureaus in Arusha. The best, in terms of exchange rates, is Northern at the bottom of India St, which will change both cash and travellers' cheques as well as give cash advances in local currency against Visa cards. Others will not change travellers' cheques – cash only. Most of the bureaus are open from 9 am to 5 pm. You can also change money quickly and efficiently, and at much the same rates as the forex bureau, at the National Bank of Commerce at the clock tower at the junction of Sokoine and Sinani Rds. It's open Monday to Friday from 8.30 am to 3 pm and on Saturday from 8.30 am to noon.

American Express is represented by Rickshaw Travels Ltd (☎ 576655), PO Box 13959, Sokoine Rd, but they cannot issue American Express travellers' cheques against one of their cards and a personal cheque. You can only do this with their representatives in Dar es Salaam.

Post & Communications The main post office is on Boma Rd opposite the clock tower. It's open Monday to Friday from 8 am to 1 pm and 2 to 4.30 pm and on Saturday and Sunday from 9 am to noon.

The telephone exchange is also on Boma Rd, opposite the New Safari Hotel, and is the best place from which to make calls, both domestic and international – when the lines are working! It's often crowded in the morning but is usually deserted in the evening. It's open Monday to Saturday from 8 am to 10 pm, and from 9 am to 8 pm on Sunday.

The telephone area code for Arusha is 057.

Immigration The immigration office is on Simeon Rd near the Makongoro Rd junction. The people here are reasonably efficient and helpful if you need a visa extension.

Language Courses If you'd like to learn Swahili (or improve your command of the language), contact CoCo (☎ 2527 or ☎ /fax 8875). They're in the AICC building, 4th floor, Room 410, Ngorongoro Wing.

Dangers & Annoyances Arusha is the worst place in Tanzania for 'flycatchers' (street touts) and 'briefcase' safari companies who prey on the gullibility of newly arrived travellers by offering them safaris and Kilimanjaro treks at ridiculously low prices. If you're stupid enough to believe them – or, even worse, give them money in exchange for a bogus receipt – then you need psychiatric treatment. The AICC building, in particular, is full of 'briefcase' safari companies. Leave them well alone. For more about this, see the National Parks chapter.

National Museum

At the top of Boma Rd, this place simply has to be a joke. It consists of one corridor about 20m by five metres with facsimiles of the evolutionary progress of Homo sapiens based on the digs at Olduvai Gorge. You've seen it all before. It's open Monday to Friday from 7.30 am to 5 pm, 7.30 am to 4.30 pm on Saturday. Entry costs TSh 50.

Snake Park

Run by a family of South Africans, the park is some 20 minutes drive from Arusha on the road to Tarangire National Park. Entry costs TSh 500 and there are numerous species of snake, some of them poisonous, as well as crocodiles, monitor lizards and iguanas. It's worth a visit if you've never seen a snake park.

Places to Stay – bottom end

There's a good choice of budget hotels in Arusha, most of them within a few minutes walking distance of the bus station. The greatest concentration is in the streets north of the top side of the stadium (Makongoro Rd) and east of Col Middleton Rd, though there are others around the central market area. The camp sites are all on the outskirts of town and involve a two to three-km walk or taxi ride from the bus station.

The area at the back of the Golden Rose Hotel on Col Middleton Rd is a warren of budget hotels. Every second house is a hotel and/or bar-restaurant. It's here that you'll find the cheapest hotels in town. The most popular are the *Mashele Guest House* (TSh 3000 a double with shared bathroom facilities or TSh 4000 for a double with private bathroom – clean, quiet, mosquito nets); *Levolosi Guest House* (TSh 2500/3000 for singles/doubles with shared facilities); *Monjes Guest House* (TSh 2500/3050 for singles/doubles – clean and quiet); and *Kitundu Guest House* (TSh 2500/3000 for singles/doubles with shared facilities or TSh 5500 for a double with private bathroom – clean with hot showers, bar and restaurant). Others which are just as good include the *K Guest House, Twins Guest House, Loitay Guest House, Annex Mrina Motel* and *Ninja Guest House*.

Across the opposite side of Col Middleton Rd, at the back of Sunny Safaris and along the road running parallel to it, are two more popular places. The first is the *Miami Beach Guest House* (☎ 7531) which has doubles (no singles) for US$10 with shared bathroom facilities, but it can be noisy and dusty because of its proximity to the bus station. The hotel has its own bar and restaurant and hot showers are available. Further up the

TANZANIA

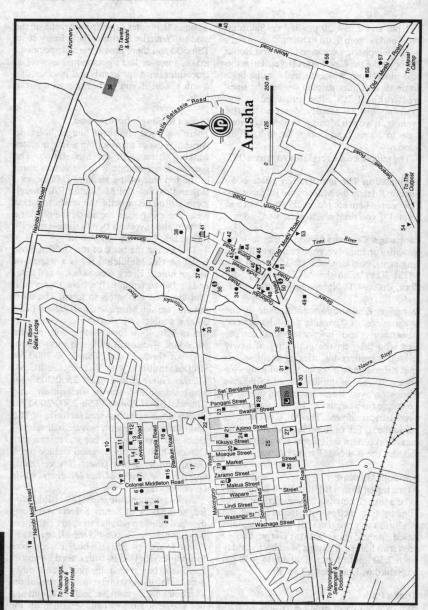

Arusha

PLACES TO STAY

1 Eland Hotel
2 Miami Beach Guest House
3 Hotel AM 1988
4 Midway Hotel
5 William's Inn
7 Golden Rose Hotel
9 Twins Guest House
  & Annex Mrina Motel
10 Mashele Guest House
11 Levolosi Guest House
12 Ninja Guest House
13 Monjes Guest House
14 Kitundu Guest House
15 Hotel Arusha by Night Annexe
16 Stadium Bar & Guest House
19 Amazon Hotel
21 Kilimanjaro Villa
23 Arusha Centre Inn
24 Robannyson Hotel
26 Hotel Pallson's
28 Hotel Arusha by Night
32 Greenland Hotel
35 YMCA & Silver City Bar
39 Novotel Mount Meru
40 Hotel 77
43 New Safari Hotel
44 Hotel Equator
48 Naaz Hotel
49 Arusha Resort Centre
51 New Arusha Hotel
55 Hotel Impala

PLACES TO EAT

8 Taj Restaurant
20 Khan's
27 Pita Pizzeria
31 Chinese Restaurant
47 Mambo The Café
53 Roaster's Garden
54 Mandarin Palace Restaurant

OTHER

6 Sunny Safaris
17 Stadium
18 Bus Station
22 Uhuru Monument
25 Market
29 Mosque
30 Metropole Cinema
33 Police
34 Adventure Centre
36 Central Bank of Tanzania
   & Ngorongoro Conservation Authority
37 Immigration
38 Arusha International Conference Centre
41 National Museum
42 Municipal Council
   Offices
45 Air Tanzania
46 Post Office
50 National Bank of
   Commerce
52 Clock Tower
56 Bushbuck Safaris
57 Club 21 & Casino

same road is the *Midway Hotel* (☎ 2790), which is frequently used by American students and has doubles (no singles) for US$10 with shared bathroom facilities. There's a bar and restaurant at the hotel.

Opposite the main market is the *Robannyson Hotel* on Somali Rd, which offers singles/doubles with shared bathroom facilities for TSh 1600/3000. Hot showers are available, mosquito nets are provided and the hotel has its own restaurant (no bar), but it's not very clean. Similar is *Kilimanjaro Villa* at TSh 2600/3000 for singles/doubles with shared facilities but it suffers from water problems. In the same area is the *Amazon Hotel*, which is better and costs US$10/12 for singles/doubles.

Only marginally more expensive but a very popular place to stay and convenient for the safari companies is the *YMCA/Youth Hostel* on India St. It's fairly clean and well furnished but the toilets won't flush and the showers often don't work. Still, it's an excellent place to meet people, especially if you're trying to get a group together to go on safari. Bed and breakfast costs US$10/13 for singles/doubles with shared toilet facilities (cold water only). The breakfast isn't up to much – boiled egg, dry bread and margarine, plus tea – but the staff are very friendly, your gear is safe and there's a laundry service. Downstairs is the Silver City Bar, but it closes relatively early in the evening so there's no problem about noise. Get here early if you want a room.

For campers, the best place is *Masai Camp* about 2.5 km from the centre of town on the Old Moshi Rd. It's excellent but it does collect quite a few long-haul overland trucks. Camping costs US$3 per person, and there are hot showers, a bar and restaurant, a volleyball court, a children's playground, facilities for

TANZANIA

mechanical repairs and well-landscaped surrounds. The restaurant offers a plethora of dishes ranging from burgers (TSh 1500) and Mexican food (TSh 2500 for chilli con carne) to pizzas (TSh 2000 to TSh 2800) and steak and chips (TSh 3500). Beers are TSh 600 and they're *cold*. It's open all day until late.

The other camp site is *Klub Afriko* (☎ 8878), just off the main road to Moshi about one km beyond the Novotel Mount Meru (signposted). It's much smaller than Masai Camp but very pleasant and has a bar, restaurant and library as well as bucket hot-water showers. It's used mainly by students who come here to study at the School of International Training and you won't encounter long-haul overland trucks here. Camping costs US$3 per person, and security is excellent.

Places to Stay – middle

One of the cheapest of the mid-range hotels is the *Arusha Naaz Hotel* on Sokoine Rd. It's very clean, pleasant, secure and well maintained and costs US$20 for a double with private bathroom – all the rooms have twin beds so there's no rate for single occupancy. The downstairs restaurant is very good and has a range of snacks and full meals at reasonable prices.

The *Hotel Arusha by Night* (☎ 8326) on Swahili St is equally popular and costs the same for a double with private bathroom but there's no hot water or mosquito nets. The hotel has its own bar and restaurant on the ground floor. There's an annexe to the hotel, on the north side of the stadium, called the *Hotel Arusha by Night Annexe*, which is almost as large as the main hotel and costs the same but has no bar or restaurant.

Somewhat out of town along Serengeti Rd, off the Old Moshi Rd, is *The Outpost* (☎ 8405), PO Box 11520. This is a family guesthouse set in shady surroundings and offering bed and breakfast for US$16/20 for singles/doubles. Hot showers are available though most of the rooms do not have a private bathroom. Those who stay here rate the place highly. Inexpensive but very tasty dinners are available.

More expensive, the *Hotel Pallson's* (☎ 3790), Market St, is a relatively new hotel offering bed and breakfast in singles/doubles with private bathroom for US$25/35. There's hot water in the showers and the hotel has its own bar and restaurant.

Up in price, but for no discernible reason, is the *Golden Rose Hotel* (☎ 7959), Col Middleton Rd, close to the bus station, which offers singles/doubles with private bathroom for US$40/50 including a continental breakfast. There's hot water in the showers and the rooms have a balcony, but they're nowhere near as spacious as those at the Hotel Equator and there's no garden. There is, however, a bar and a very good restaurant.

The *Hotel Equator* (☎ 3127), Boma Rd, is by far the best value at the upper end of this range. It offers large, airy rooms with enormous double beds and private bathroom for US$45 a double (no singles) and a balcony overlooking a well-kept garden It's as clean as a whistle, with hot water in the showers and room service, and a continental breakfast included in the price. Downstairs there's a popular bar with a live band five nights a week, as well as a good restaurant. There's guarded parking and a spacious beer garden. The staff are friendly and security is excellent. Visa and MasterCard are accepted. If you have the money, this is *the* place to stay – excellent value.

The *Arusha Resort Centre* (☎ 8033), Sinani Rd, is slightly cheaper at US$40 a double (no single occupancy) but the rooms are considerably smaller than those at the Equator. They also have two-room suites with four beds for US$80. All the rooms have private bathroom and the price includes breakfast. There's a terrace bar in a garden setting, and a restaurant. Credit cards are not accepted.

Another in this category, as far as price goes, is the new *Splendid Hotel*, which offers singles/doubles with private bathroom for US$30/35 including breakfast. It's very clean and pleasant but, basically, in the wrong location. Why build a hotel like this in the back streets off the central market?

Out on the busy ring road are two other

mid-range hotels. Nearer to town is the *Eland Motel* (☎ 7868) which offers bed and breakfast for US$30/40 for singles/doubles. It's a pleasant place with a bar and restaurant with lunch/dinner available for TSh 4500. Credit cards are not accepted.

Further from town towards Namanga is the *Manor Hotel* (☎ 3750) which has doubles (no singles) including full breakfast for US$30 and 'executive' suites for US$40. There's a bar and restaurant with lunch/dinner available at TSh 5000 and a 24-hour room service. Credit cards are not accepted. It's easy to miss this place because, although it's a prominent building, there are no signs whatsoever – not even on the hotel itself.

Places to Stay – top end

Very popular with expatriates living in Arusha is the *Hotel Impala* (☎ 8450), at the junction of Moshi and Old Moshi Rds. It's a relatively new place with well-appointed rooms and offers bed and breakfast for US$40/60. There's a pleasant bar, restaurant and secure parking. It's a good place to stay but inconvenient for town without your own vehicle.

Up the road from the Impala and close to the ring road is the *Hotel 77*. This costs US$45/60 for singles/doubles including breakfast, plus there are more expensive suites. It's a somewhat featureless place consisting of very plain 'cottages', though they are scattered around spacious grounds. There's a bar and restaurant. Like the Impala, it's inconvenient for town without your own vehicle. Credit cards are not accepted.

Back in the very centre of town on Boma Rd is the venerable *New Safari Hotel* (☎ 3261), which costs US$35 a single with shared facilities and US$40/60 for singles/doubles with private bathroom and breakfast. 'New' it is not, but it is a relatively popular place to stay. There's a bar and restaurant, and a delightful beer garden/barbecue with makuti roof shelters which is a good place to meet people. Credit cards are not accepted.

Better because of its extensive grounds is the *New Arusha Hotel* (☎ 8541), on the clock tower roundabout, which has good rooms for US$65/70 for singles/doubles including a full breakfast. There's a bar, restaurant, snack bar, shopping arcade, beer garden, casino and secure parking.

Close to the bus station on the dirt road parallel to Col Middleton Rd is the brand-new *Hotel AM 1988* (☎ 7873), which has singles/doubles for US$40/60 including breakfast. It's a well-designed building with views from most of the rooms but it's in the wrong location and there are no surrounding gardens. It does, however, have cable TV.

At the top of this category is the *Novotel Mount Meru* (☎ 2712), set in landscaped grounds just off the main Arusha to Moshi road. It has all the usual facilities, including a swimming pool, shopping arcade and lounge/bar areas, and has singles/doubles for US$110/138 including breakfast and all taxes. The swimming pool can be used by nonresidents on payment of a temporary membership fee. You can also change money at the hotel but at a lousy rate of exchange.

If you'd like to stay well out of town in a sylvan setting of flowering trees and shrubs, there's the beautiful *Ilboru Safari Lodge* (☎ 7834) about two km north of the ring road. It consists of six double makuti-roofed bandas, each with private bathroom and their own verandah, which cost US$60/72 for singles/doubles including breakfast. The lodge has its own bar and restaurant. It's very quiet here but, of course, inconvenient without your own vehicle.

Even further afield but in equally beautiful surroundings close to Mt Meru National Park, there are two other places. The closest one to Arusha is the *Hotel Restaurant Dik Dik*, PO Box 1499, which is owned and managed by a Swiss team. It consists of nine bungalows with two double rooms in each, and a central amenities area which includes a swimming pool, spacious dining hall and a bar. No expense has been spared setting up this place and it's very comfortable. The rates are US$55/65 for singles/doubles including breakfast.

Further out and overlooking Lake Duluti is the *Mountain Village Lodge* (☎ 2699), PO Box 376. It's imaginatively designed to resemble a traditional African village and consists of 42 thatched bandas arranged in semicircular groups among tropical flowering trees. All the bandas have private bathroom, are furnished with a variety of local crafts and have a private verandah. There's a central amenities area (adapted from an old colonial villa), bar and restaurant. It's a superb place to stay and costs US$63/74 for singles/doubles. Breakfast is extra (US$7) and lunch/dinner costs US$10.

Places to Eat – cheap

Plenty of simple cafes and cheap restaurants in the lower part of town, along Sokoine Rd, offer standard Afro-Indian fare – curries, ugali or matoke (plantains) with meat stew and beans, samosas, biriyani and the like, for about TSh 1500. Bars and discos usually have barbecued food – nyama choma, kebabs and chips or matoke for the same price. Try the *Silver City Bar*, attached to the YMCA, which is cheap and has a nyama choma grill.

The fast-food cafeteria in the *New Arusha Hotel* has McDonald's-type food as well as samosas, but, late in the day, only a fraction of what's on the menu is available. Similar fast food is available from *Chick King* on Goliondoi Rd.

The best place to go for an excellent and very tasty outdoor barbecue dinner is *Khan's* on Mosque St, off Somali Rd and close to the central market. This place is extremely popular and deservedly so. Local people come from miles away for take-aways but you can also eat here. Just rock up and choose whatever you like and then help yourself to the spicy salads and vegetables. Everything is cooked in front of you so you know it's fresh. Expect to pay around TSh 2000. It's only open in the evenings; the rest of the day it's a vehicle spare parts agency!

Also popular but open all day, every day is *Roaster's Garden* on the Old Moshi Rd just over the river bridge beyond the New Arusha Hotel. It's a large place with three bars, a restaurant and a nyama choma grill as well as several open-air, makuti-roofed structures set in spacious gardens. It does a range of dishes such as sausage and chips, omelette and chips (both TSh 1500) and nyama choma (one kg for TSh 2000) but its main function is as a watering hole, especially in the evenings, and there's a disco on Friday, Saturday and Sunday nights which runs till late. They have an excellent range of beers and spirits (both local and imported) at reasonable prices.

The restaurant on the ground floor of the *Naaz Hotel* is worth trying for a better-than-average meal. It's very clean and offers Indian-style food as well as standard snacks.

Places to Eat – more expensive

For an excellent breakfast if you're ravenous head for *Mambo – The Cafe* on Goliondoi Rd. It's more or less opposite the Adventure Centre and offers full breakfasts for TSh 3500 as well as baguettes, cakes, pastries, soups (TSh 1400), toasted sandwiches and salads (TSh 1500). They also do such things as chicken and potato salad and grilled fish fillets and potatoes for around TSh 3500. It's open Monday to Friday from 7.30 am to 4 pm and on Saturday from 10 am to 2 pm.

For a splurge, most travellers go to one of two restaurants: the *Safari Grill* (part of the New Safari Hotel); or the *Chinese Restaurant*, on Sokoine Rd near the bridge between the two halves of town. Probably the more popular is the Safari Grill, which has a good range of fish and meat dishes as well as soups and desserts. The food is well cooked and presented and costs an average of TSh 1000 for soups and TSh 2500 to TSh 3000 for main courses, plus 15% taxes and service charge. It also serves very cold beers (TSh 600). It's open all day, every day for lunch and dinner. There's cheaper barbecued meat (chicken or goat) in the New Safari's beer garden at the back of this restaurant if you prefer to eat al fresco. You can get a good plate of tasty food here for around TSh 1500.

The Chinese Restaurant has a very extensive menu, which includes seafood, though this tends to be expensive (around TSh 4500). Prices are much the same as those at the Safari Grill but the food is very good and it's a popular place to eat. You'll find it open for breakfast, lunch and dinner and menu prices include taxes.

A little further along Sokoine Rd is the *Pita Pizzeria*, on the corner of Azimo St. It's a pleasant place to eat and, as the name suggests, specialises in Italian and Greek food. It offers such items as doner kebab (TSh 3100), beef fillets (TSh 4800), pork chops (TSh 4500), chicken (TSh 4500) and fish (TSh 4200), all with chips or rice and vegetables. It's open daily, except Tuesday, from 11.30 am to 2.30 pm and 7 to 10 pm.

For excellent Indian Mughlai cuisine, go to the *Shamiana Restaurant* at the Hotel Pallson's. Main courses cost around TSh 3000. It's closed on Tuesday. Very good Indian food is also available at the *Taj Restaurant*, on Col Middleton Rd adjacent to the Golden Rose Hotel, at much the same prices.

The restaurant at the *Golden Rose Hotel* is also very good and the menu changes daily. The chef has obviously trained overseas, so watch out for some delicious Eastern European specialities. Average prices for lunch and dinner are TSh 3000.

If you have your own vehicle or don't mind taking a taxi, the *Mandarin Palace Restaurant* (☎ 7844) on Serengeti Rd, off the Old Moshi Rd (signposted), is a great place to eat in a quiet garden setting. The menu is Chinese, with soups for TSh 1200, main courses from TSh 1800 to TSh 4200, sizzlers for TSh 2600 to TSh 4200 and desserts from TSh 800. All prices include tax and service charges. The background music (over an excellent sound system) tends to be European classical.

Entertainment

Two of the liveliest and cheapest bars are the *Silver City Bar*, part of the YMCA, on India St, and *Brahma's* opposite the Adventure Centre on Goliondoi Rd. The former is a meeting place for both travellers and local people so it's easy to strike up a conversation. The latter is a popular African bar – the beer 'garden' at the back is best – so you're likely to be the only mzungu there but that's no problem. Both have barbecue grills. Otherwise, in the afternoons, the beer gardens at

the *New Safari* and *New Arusha* hotels are great places to relax and converse.

The indoor bar at the *Hotel Equator* is probably the best and most lively of all the bars any evening of the week. Everyone looking for action comes here. It kicks off with video films from around 6.30 to 8 pm, after which a live band plays until around 1 am (later at weekends). There's no cover charge. On Sunday afternoons, the band plays in the beer garden (TSh 500).

The only nightly disco is at the *Hotel Arusha by Night*. This goes on until about 3 am and is popular with local people and wazungu. There are no hassles, drinks are the normal price and the sexes are about equally matched in number. There's plenty of dancing space and the lights are low. Entry costs TSh 500. The best nights (according to the notice outside) are on Wednesday and Saturday.

In the basement of the New Safari Hotel is the *Cave Disco*, which is very popular at weekends (nothing during the week), when it rocks all afternoon until very late at night. The tourist literature describes it as 'a sensation'. That's far from accurate, but deafening it certainly is. Entry will cost you TSh 500.

Another great place to rip loose over the weekend is *Roaster's Garden* (see Places to Eat) which has a disco on Friday, Saturday and Sunday nights, firing up at around 10 pm and continuing at top volume until early in the morning.

Things to Buy

There are several very good craft shops along the short street between the clock tower and Goliondoi Rd. These have superb examples of makonde carving at prices lower than in Dar es Salaam. There's also an alley with many craft stalls between India St and Goliondoi Rd. Bargaining is the order of the day at any of these shops.

Getting There & Away

Air Kilimanjaro international airport is halfway between Moshi and Arusha. Air Tanzania flies between Dar es Salaam and

Kilimanjaro in either direction, usually once daily. Book well in advance to be sure of a seat, as demand is high. The fare is US$123 one way and US$246 return. The Air Tanzania office is on Boma Rd diagonally opposite the New Safari Hotel.

Precision Air Services has a regular schedule connecting Arusha with Seronera (US$135), Mwanza (US$145), Bukoba (US$230), Dar es Salaam (US$165) and Zanzibar (US$165). They use the local airstrip (ie not Kilimanjaro international airport). Departures are daily except on Sunday when there's a direct Arusha-Zanzibar flight. You can buy Precision Air tickets directly from their main office (☎ 6903) at the Arusha International Conference Centre, Ngorongoro Wing, Rooms 302/303/304, or from the Adventure Centre on Goliondoi Rd.

KLM and Ethiopian Airlines also service Kilimanjaro airport on their way to and from Dar es Salaam. Their offices are next door to the New Safari Hotel.

Bus
Nairobi Between Arusha and Nairobi there's a choice of normal buses and minibus shuttles. All of them go through the border posts without a change. The cheapest way to go is by normal bus, which costs TSh 3000 or KSh 400 and takes about four hours. See the Tanzania Getting There & Away chapter for full details.

Dar es Salaam There are many buses in either direction between Arusha and Dar es Salaam. Buses depart daily between 6 am and noon and cost TSh 6500 (luxury) and TSh 5800 (semi-luxury). Fresh ya Shamba, Mkewma, Osaka Royal Class and Dar Express have the best buses. They take about eight hours and the road is excellent all the way from Dar to Arusha. It's advisable to book the day before travel. The ordinary buses along this route are cheaper but not worth the hassle as they're forever stopping to put down and pick up passengers and so take considerably longer.

Mwanza There's a choice of buses which go direct through Ngorongoro and the Serengeti National Park, and others which bypass the parks and go via Singida and Shinyanga. Those which go through the parks, despite being much quicker, cost much more because you have to pay two sets of park entry fees in addition to the fare. However, although it's much more expensive to go via Serengeti/Ngorongoro, you're strongly advised to do so as the roads via Singida and Shinyanga are diabolical and there's no way you will get there in the quoted 18 hours.

There are quite a few bus lines doing both of these routes so there's at least one departure daily. Make enquiries and book a seat the day before you want to travel. Going via Serengeti/Ngorongoro the fare is TSh 19,000 (plus US$40 park entry fees, payable in hard currency) and the journey is supposed to take 12 hours but you can count on 18 hours. Going via Singida and Shinyanga, the fare is TSh 9800 and the journey can take anything from 36 to 100 hours.

Tanga For Tanga, enquire at the Hood Ltd booking office at the bus station. They usually have a daily departure.

Moshi There are Nissan minibuses all day, every day until late between Arusha and Moshi, which leave when full. The fare is TSh 700 and the journey takes 1½ hours over a good, sealed road. Share-taxis between the two places cost more and the fare is negotiable but they're more convenient if you have a backpack. They leave from the top side of the bus station.

Getting Around
The Airport The State Transport Corporation operates shuttle buses to the airport to connect with all incoming and outgoing flights. The buses depart from outside the Air Tanzania office and the fare is TSh 1500 each if there are six or more of you, TSh 9000 for only one passenger. The journey takes about half an hour.

A taxi to the airport costs around TSh 20,000.

Taxi Arusha is a small place, so it's easy to

get from one place to another on foot. Taxis charge around TSh 1000 per journey during the day and slightly more at night.

MOSHI

Moshi is the gateway to Kilimanjaro and the end of the Central Line railway from Dar es Salaam but is otherwise not a very interesting place. Rather than stay here, many travellers head straight out to Marangu and arrange a trek up the mountain from there, but this might not always be the best thing to do. The pros and cons are discussed in the National Parks chapter.

Information

Money There are three forex bureaus in Moshi, two of them in the same block as the Moshi Hotel on the Boma Rd side. K's Bureau generally offers the better rate of exchange. None of them charge commission on travellers' cheques.

Post & Communications The main post office is opposite the clock tower and is open Monday to Friday from 8 am to 1 pm and 2 to 4.30 pm and on Saturday and Sunday from 9 am to noon.

International telephone calls can be made from the telecommunications office next door to the post office.

The telephone area code for Moshi is 055.

Immigration The Moshi immigration office can renew your visa or stay permit. It's in Kibo House, close to the clock tower on the road leading to the YMCA. The office is open Monday to Friday from 7.30 am to 3.30 pm.

Dangers & Annoyances Moshi, like Arusha, has its fair share of 'flycatchers' and 'briefcase' safari companies who prey on the gullibility of newly arrived travellers by offering them Kilimanjaro treks at ridiculously low prices. For more about this, see the National Parks chapter.

Places to Stay – bottom end

The cheapest budget hotel in town and excellent value is *Mlay's Residential Hotel* (☎ 51792) at 72 Market St. It's very clean, always has water and also has a restaurant and bar. Doubles with shared bathroom facilities are TSh 2000.

About the same price but considerably more basic is the *Kilimanjaro Hotel*, just down from the clock tower towards the railway station. It offers singles/doubles with private bathroom (cold water only) for TSh 2000/3000 and has a restaurant and bar.

Right in the centre of town around the central market area are a number of other budget hotels. One of the cheapest is the *Hotel Serengeti* which offers singles or doubles with private bathroom for TSh 3500. It's habitable but there's a noisy bar at the front and little privacy.

Much better is the *Motel Silva* (☎ 53122) which offers singles/doubles with shared bathroom facilities for TSh 3600/4000 or TSh 4000/6000 with private bathroom. Breakfast is included. There's a restaurant and bar downstairs and a roof garden.

Equally good value, if not better, is the four-storey *Kindoroko Hotel* (☎ 52988) on Mawenzi Rd near the junction with Chagga St. Singles/doubles with shared facilities cost TSh 3500/4000, or with private bathroom for TSh 4500/5000 including breakfast. The staff are friendly and there are two restaurants and a shady courtyard bar with a makuti roof. The food is very reasonably priced.

Similar in price but not such great value is the *Haria* (☎ 511228), Mawenzi Rd, which has doubles (no singles) for TSh 5000, excluding breakfast which is an extra TSh 600. Some of the rooms have private bathroom. Meals are available for TSh 1400.

The vast majority of travellers stay at the *YMCA* (☎ 52923), on the roundabout some 300m from the clock tower. It's a large, modern building with a gymnasium, swimming pool, dining room and TV lounge/coffee bar. The rooms are spotlessly clean and well furnished and some face Mt Kilimanjaro. It costs the equivalent of US$10/13 for singles/doubles with shared bathroom facilities and US$23 for double bandas with private bathroom and breakfast (fruit, eggs, bread and butter and tea/coffee). There's no hot water in the showers. Lunch (12.30 to 1.45 pm) and dinner (7.30 to 8.45 pm) are good value but must be ordered 20 minutes in advance. Trans Kibo Travels are located here and can arrange treks up Kilimanjaro, plus there's a store which sells toiletries and the like. It's a friendly place and there's a guarded car park.

Back in the town centre, close to the clock tower, is the *Coffee Tree Hotel*, on the 2nd and 3rd floors of the large office block. There's no prominent sign but the entrance

is in the courtyard. Singles with shared facilities cost TSh 2500; singles/doubles with private bathroom go for TSh 3500/5500 including breakfast. There are great views of Kilimanjaro from the restaurant and some of the rooms.

If you don't mind a bit of walking on arrival (about one km) then head for the *Rombo Cottage Hotel* (☎ 52112), off the Himo/Marangu road (signposted). It's well maintained, very clean, has friendly staff and is excellent value. Doubles (no singles) with twin beds, private bathroom, fan and mosquito nets cost the equivalent of US$10.

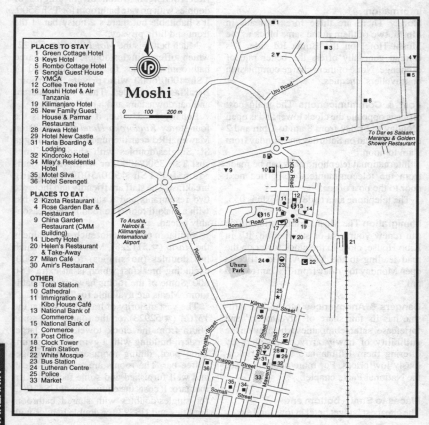

PLACES TO STAY
1 Green Cottage Hotel
3 Keys Hotel
5 Rombo Cottage Hotel
6 Sengia Guest House
7 YMCA
12 Coffee Tree Hotel
16 Moshi Hotel & Air Tanzania
19 Kilimanjaro Hotel
26 New Family Guest House & Parmar Restaurant
28 Arawa Hotel
29 Hotel New Castle
31 Haria Boarding & Lodging
32 Kindoroko Hotel
34 Mlay's Residential Hotel
35 Motel Silva
36 Hotel Serengeti

PLACES TO EAT
2 Kizota Restaurant
4 Rose Garden Bar & Restaurant
9 China Garden Restaurant (CMM Building)
14 Liberty Hotel
20 Helen's Restaurant & Take-Away
27 Milan Café
30 Amir's Restaurant

OTHER
8 Total Station
10 Cathedral
11 Immigration & Kibo House Café
13 National Bank of Commerce
15 National Bank of Commerce
17 Post Office
18 Clock Tower
21 Train Station
22 White Mosque
23 Bus Station
24 Lutheran Centre
25 Police
33 Market

Moshi

0   100   200 m

To Dar es Salaam, Marangu & Golden Shower Restaurant

To Arusha, Nairobi & Kilimanjaro International Airport

Uru Road

Kibo Road

Boma Road

Arusha Road

Uhuru Park

Kilma Street

Kenyatta Street

Market Street

Maweni Road

Chagga Street

Somali Street

There's a quiet bar, a restaurant and safe parking.

For campers, there's a site adjacent to the playing field about two km out of town on the main road to Arusha. Facilities include cold showers. There's also a camp site next to the Golden Shower Restaurant on the road to Marangu, owned by Let's Go.

Places to Stay – middle

There's a very limited choice in this range. The best is probably the *Hotel New Castle* (☎ 53203) on Mawenzi Rd, which usually has plenty of rooms available. Doubles (no singles) with shared facilities cost the equivalent of US$15 while doubles with private bathroom are US$25. Breakfast is included. The hotel has its own rooftop bar and restaurant. If you stay here, you'll no doubt appreciate the management's efforts to maintain tranquillity, as the notices on the stairs indicate: 'We highly appreciate your cooperation in upholding our want for maintaining maximum noiselessness while passing in this last residential floor', and 'For the honour of our residents and all visitors who treasure tranquillity you're urged to maintain calmness for their total comfort and pleasure'.

Good value, but further away from the centre of town, is the *Green Cottage Hotel* (☎ 53198) on Nkomo Ave. This is in a very pleasant area surrounded by trees and has safe parking. It's a small place run by friendly people and costs the equivalent of US$15 a double with shared bathroom facilities and US$20 for doubles with private bathroom. Breakfast is included. There's also one single room available.

Places to Stay – top end

The best value in this range is the new *Keys Hotel* (☎ 52250; fax 50073), PO Box 933, Uru Rd, which is very tastefully designed and in a pleasant area of town. Singles/doubles with private bathroom for nonresidents cost the equivalent of US$30/50 including a continental breakfast. There's a considerable discount for guests who book on one of their Kilimanjaro treks. Most of the

rooms have a TV but that doesn't mean that they always work. The ground floor is entirely taken up by a large restaurant and a bar which is a popular meeting place in the evening for Kilimanjaro trekkers as well as local and expatriate businesspeople. There's also a swimming pool and a guarded parking lot.

More expensive but also somewhat impersonal is the TTC-owned *Moshi Hotel* (☎ 55212). Singles/doubles with shared bathroom facilities for nonresidents cost the equivalent of US$20/30 or with private bathroom for US$50 including breakfast. The hotel has a fairly popular indoor/outdoor bar and a restaurant.

Places to Eat – cheap

Apart from the YMCA and the Swahili menu at the Moshi Hotel, there's a serious lack of good eating places in Moshi. Cheap meals are available at *Chrisburger*, a few doors up the road from the clock tower and towards the YMCA on the left-hand side. It serves excellent egg burgers and fresh orange juice and is open Monday to Friday from 7 am to 4.30 pm and on Saturday from 7 am to 2 pm. The *Parmar Restaurant* is also good for cheap meals. The *Arawa Hotel*, off Mawenzi Rd, is similar.

Helen's Restaurant & Take-Away, on Mawenzi Rd not far from the clock tower, is also good value for cheap snacks, as is *Kibo House*, right opposite the clock tower, which also has good coffee.

Very popular with local office people, especially at lunch time on weekdays, is the *Liberty Hotel* which offers cheap Tanzanian fare, but it hardly functions at the weekend.

The *Rombo Cottage Hotel* (see Places to Stay) is certainly worth visiting for lunch or dinner if you don't mind the walk. The food is very good and prices are competitive. Across from the Rombo Cottage is the popular *Rose Garden Bar & Restaurant*. It's a large place with a number of makuti-roofed pavilions and a main bar/restaurant. They offer a range of Tanzanian and European dishes at reasonable prices.

TANZANIA

Places to Eat – more expensive

For a splurge, you have a choice of three places. Right in the centre of town, the *Moshi Hotel* offers a lunch or dinner menu of soup, main course, dessert and coffee for about TSh 4000 including taxes, but remember that it's much cheaper to order a Tanzanian dish (around TSh 1000) from the à la carte menu in the bar.

It's also worth considering an evening at the *Keys Hotel* if you want to dine in style. Prices are similar to the lunch and dinner menu at the Moshi Hotel but the food is of a higher standard.

For good Chinese food at moderate prices, try the *China Garden Restaurant* at the CCM building on the ring road. It's open daily from noon until midnight.

My favourite, though it's a good 1.5 km out of town on the Himo/Marangu road, is the *Golden Shower Restaurant*. This place has a delightfully intimate atmosphere and offers a choice of dining inside or outside in the garden. It also has a very cosy bar. The food is excellent and tastefully presented and the service is fast. Prices are similar to those at the Moshi Hotel plus there's nyama choma available. Despite the distance from town, this restaurant is surprisingly popular with travellers, especially those who have trekked Kilimanjaro and feel like celebrating.

Getting There & Away

Air Kilimanjaro international airport is halfway between Moshi and Arusha. Air Tanzania flies between Dar es Salaam and Kilimanjaro. The Air Tanzania office is next to the Moshi Hotel. See the Arusha section for flight details.

Precision Air Services has a regular schedule connecting Moshi with Arusha and Moshi with Dar es Salaam and Zanzibar. Tickets can be bought from either Emslies Ltd (☎ 51742) or Huduma Exim Ltd (☎ 53320) in Moshi.

Bus Most of the minibus shuttles which service the Nairobi-Arusha sector also continue on from Arusha to Moshi but the normal buses do not. The principal minibus shuttle is Davanu (☎ 51827 Moshi) which has its office on Kaunda St opposite the Moshi Hotel. It departs daily for Arusha and Nairobi at 11.30 am. See the Tanzania Getting There & Away chapter for full details.

There are many buses daily in either direction between Moshi and Dar es Salaam. All originate in Arusha and only have a certain number of seats allocated for passengers boarding at Moshi so it's advisable to book the day before travel. The fare is TSh 6500 on the luxury buses and TSh 5800 on the semi-luxury buses. Departure times are usually between 6 am and noon and the journey takes around seven hours. All the bus lines have offices at the central bus station in Moshi.

There are frequent daily buses and Nissan vans in either direction between Arusha and Moshi from 5 am to around 6 pm, departing when full. The fare is TSh 700 and the trip takes about 1½ hours along what will soon be a good, sealed road.

Matatus to Marangu (for Mt Kilimanjaro) also leave from the central bus station throughout the day when full and cost TSh 400. The journey takes about 45 minutes.

Train Trains depart from Dar es Salaam for Moshi on Tuesday and Friday at 4 pm. In the opposite direction, they leave Moshi for Dar es Salaam on Thursday and Sunday at 4 pm. The journey takes from 15 to 18 hours and the fares are TSh 11,585 (1st class), TSh 8285/5680 (2nd class sleeping/sitting) and TSh 3540 (3rd class). Bedding is extra and dinner is available in the buffet car. Advance booking is essential for 1st and 2nd class. Buying a ticket at Moshi station is an exercise in tenacity and determination. It's little short of chaos and you'll just have to join the rabble.

There's also a direct train once a week on Saturday from Moshi to Voi (Kenya). See the Tanzania Getting There & Away chapter for details.

Getting Around

The Airport State Transport Corporation shuttle buses to the airport leave from the Air

Tanzania office about two hours before flight arrivals and departures. See the blackboard outside the office for departure times. The fare is TSh 1500 if there are six or more passengers, increasing to TSh 9000 if there's only one passenger. The journey takes around 45 minutes.

A taxi costs TSh 20,000.

Taxi A taxi from one end of town to the other costs around TSh 1600 although the first quote will probably be TSh 2000. For shorter journeys it's a fairly standard TSh 1000. From Moshi to Marangu (for Mt Kilimanjaro) it's TSh 30,000 return shared between four or five people; less if you're only going one way.

MARANGU

This is the most commonly used base for treks up Kilimanjaro. Most people who trek the Marangu route spend the night before the trek here, even though it's only about an hour's drive to Moshi.

Marangu has a post office, a petrol station, a small market and several shops selling a limited range of goods. It's an attractive place with an alpine atmosphere and a boulder-strewn stream which flows through the centre.

At the park entry gate (five km above the town) there is a general store, which stocks items such as candles, flour, beer, soft drinks, whisky, *konyagi*, tinned meat and vegetables, dried soup, biscuits, fresh bread, cooking fat, margarine, chocolate, cigarettes and matches. There are no fresh fruit or vegetables available (limited quantities of these can be bought in Marangu and at various houses between there and the park entry gate).

Places to Stay

The first hotel you encounter on the road into Marangu from Moshi/Himo is the *Marangu Hotel* (☎ (055) 50639; fax 50639), PO Box 40, Moshi. It consists of a collection of cottages set in pleasant, leafy gardens and costs US$50 per person in double rooms with private bathroom (including hot-water showers, breakfast and dinner). Single occupancy of the rooms costs US$70. There are special discounted rates for those who take one of the hotel's fully equipped treks. Credit cards are accepted except for American Express. The hotel is seven km from the park entry gate.

By turning left over the river bridge in Marangu village and continuing on for several hundred metres, you will come to the *Kibo Hotel* (☎ Marangu 4; fax (055) 51308), PO Box 102, Marangu. This hotel has a superb position overlooking the surrounding countryside and has bags of olde-worlde character. Rooms with private bathroom cost US$57/74 for singles/doubles plus 5% tax. Breakfast costs US$4, lunch US$8 and dinner US$10 plus 20% tax and service charges. Campers are welcome and are charged US$6 per night. The Kibo is about 5.5 km from the park entry gate.

On the other side of the village from the Kibo Hotel (turn right just before the river bridge) are two other places to stay. They're both considerably cheaper than the Kibo and both accept payment in local currency. The nearest – about 500m from the village – is the *Babylon Lodge* (☎ Marangu 5), PO Box 227, Marangu, above the road on the left-hand side (signposted). The owner of this lodge is a very friendly guy who has put a lot of effort and money into the place over recent years, so it's excellent value at US$25/40 for singles/doubles including breakfast. All the rooms have private bathroom, there's hot water in the showers and soap and towels are provided. Campers are welcome at US$5 per person per night. The lodge has a bar and restaurant with lunch or dinner for US$6. It's a very popular place to stay.

Much further down the track (about 3.5 km from Marangu village) is the *Ashanti Lodge* (☎ (057) 2745), PO Box 6004, Arusha. This is a relaxing place to stay and has a restaurant which serves breakfast, lunch and dinner. There's a bar, a pleasant garden and a trekking-gear hire service. Campers are welcome. There are also hot showers. To get there from Marangu, either walk or hitch a ride with whatever is going down this gravel road – tractors, pick-ups and trucks, there's not much else.

About halfway between Marangu village and the park entry gate on the left-hand side is the beautiful and brand-new *Capricorn Hotel* (☎ /fax (055) 51309), PO Box 938, Marangu. A double with private bathroom costs US$100 including breakfast but excluding taxes. Credit cards are not accepted.

Up at the park entry gate (five km beyond Marangu), you can either camp for the usual fee, get a bed in the *Youth Hostel* for US$10 per night or stay at the *Kilimanjaro Mountain Lodge* for US$20 per person without breakfast, US$25 per person including breakfast or US$30 per person including breakfast and dinner. Children between the ages of 12 and 18 pay only half rates. Bathroom facilities are shared. The rates include all taxes. There's a bar/canteen at the lodge. You should remember that all these facilities at the park entry gate are actually inside the national park boundary so, in theory, you should have to pay the park entry fee in addition to accommodation costs but, in practice, you don't need to do this.

USAMBARA MOUNTAINS

This area between Moshi and Korogwe and the Kenyan border is a spectacularly beautiful area which you shouldn't miss if you have the chance to visit. The Michelin map marks the road up to Soni and Lushoto as 'scenic', which is a major understatement. Getting up there involves negotiating a series of huge hairpin bends with sheer drops on the outer lane virtually the whole way. Yet despite the steepness, the mountains are cultivated from top to bottom (with the usual maize, bananas, pineapples, beans and tree plantations), so the landscape looks as if it's had a chequered green tablecloth thrown over it.

The Soni and Lushoto areas were favoured by first the Germans and later the British during colonial times, and there are quite a few buildings characteristic of that period scattered through the region.

Away from the main farming areas, large stretches of the mountains are still covered by dense tropical forests, famous for their bird and butterfly life.

This is walking country, especially for those who like to get to the top of mountains without too much effort. There is an endless number of gently graded tracks which zigzag up the mountains, with breathtaking views at every turn. It's almost impossible to get lost as long as you stick to the track. One of the most popular tracks takes you to what's known as the Irente Viewpoint – a slab of rock at the top of a cliff face looking out over the Mombo to Tanga road and the Masai Plain. The walk takes about one hour from Lushoto. However, unless you're very good at orienting yourself, it's unlikely you'll find the way there without local help, so ask someone local to show you the way. The views from the top are simply incredible.

LUSHOTO

Lushoto, the main centre of population in the Usambara Mountains, sits in a valley at about 1200m, though the town is built on several levels, producing a feeling of space. Most of the houses are built from locally manufactured mud bricks and have pitched roofs. The main government buildings are European in style, and indeed Lushoto was once slated to become the capital of German East Africa back in colonial times. These days it's a religious centre of sorts, with a bewildering variety of churches, missions and mosques.

Activities

Walking Tours With advice from the Netherlands Development Organisation, the Usambara farmers have set up a scheme to assist visitors wishing to see the area's beauty spots, visit the tropical forests and gain some insight into the various development projects which are being undertaken. These walking tours are intended to be partially educational and partly recreational. Profits from the scheme are ploughed back into the development projects.

Various tours are available, some from Lushoto and others from Soni. The two guides organising the walks are Jeromy

Mwamboneke and Yassin Madiwa. They are knowledgable, enthusiastic, very friendly and can do anything from a few hours stroll to a five day trek, or anything in between. If you got for a two to five day option, you can camp if you have gear, or they can take you to villages with local guesthouses. For a full-day walk, groups of up to four people pay TSh 6000 to the guide plus TSh 1500 each to the project. Accommodation, if required, is paid direct. Other items like food or transport back to the start after the trek is also paid direct. For groups of five or more, guide rates are negotiable. Jeromy and Yassin can be found in the Green Valley Restaurant in Lushoto most days (unless they're out guiding) and one or both of them is there every evening. Leaflets and bookings can be made there.

Hang-Gliding An interesting pair of guys here are Carter and George. Both are keen hang-gliders and George is involved in training

Lushoto

0   125   250 m

To 'Viewpoint'

To Soni & Mombo

1 Post Office
2 Church
3 Bank
4 Market & Bus Station
5 Green Valley Hotel & Restaurant
6 Shops
7 Christian Bookshop
8 Kilimani Guest House
9 The Lawns Hotel

buzzards and falcons to assist glider pilots in staying airborne indefinitely, the idea being that these birds are far more capable than humans of reading the landscape and finding thermals. Once the pilot has been guided to the thermals, the birds sit on the steering bar until the glider wishes to land! You can often find these two at The Lawns Hotel or the Kilimani Guest House, or at the Green Valley disco on Saturday nights.

Places to Stay
The *Kilimani Guest House* has rooms set around a courtyard, at the centre of which is a bar. Singles/doubles cost TSh 1200/2000. The beds are comfortable, usually with clean linen, and there's a table and chair. The women who run it can't speak two words of English between the four of them, but they're very friendly and helpful and are excellent cooks. However, be wary as travellers have reported being asked to pay for the room several times during their stay, even though they paid on arrival. There's no running water, but a bucket of hot water and a mug will be provided on request.

Somewhat cheaper and just as good is the *Cool Breeze Bar, Restaurant & Guest House* which charges TSh 1500 for a large double room with huge beds, shower and toilet. The restaurant serves mainly meat dishes but they're tasty and good value, plus the staff are friendly.

The *Green Valley Hotel & Restaurant* has a few small rooms behind the restaurant for TSh 2000 per person (but don't stay here on disco nights unless you enjoy sleeping with very loud music). The *Kinuyu Guest House*, just around the corner from the bus station and the Green Valley is small, quiet, clean and friendly and has singles/doubles for TSh 1000/2000. The *Milimani*, in between the Kinuyu and the Kilimani, and about halfway between them in quality. Singles/doubles cost TSh 1200/2000.

Up a grade is the Mandarin Hotel which overlooks the town. It is a vast place which has been under construction for some time, and has clean singles/doubles from TSh 6500/8500 with breakfast.

651

by a resident expatriate, the most ... e place is *The Lawns Hotel*. It's a ... pical colonial-style hotel with a large front lawn mown by two cows, and has a verandah with easy chairs and a well-stocked bar. The comfortable rooms cost TSh 10,000/15,000 for singles/doubles including breakfast. There are no mosquito nets but there is a very cosy open fireplace in the bar of an evening. The service leaves a little to be desired.

Places to Eat
The *Green Valley Restaurant*, in the centre of town, is the best place to eat. The staff are pleasant and the food is very good.

Getting There & Away
To get to Lushoto, take a bus from Mombo on the main Moshi to Korogwe road (TSh 2500 from Moshi, three hours, or TSh 3500 from Arusha, 4½ to five hours). Anyone in Mombo will show you where the bus departs from. The journey from Mombo to Lushoto takes about 1½ hours and costs TSh 500. Buses are usually crowded, but the road is well maintained and sealed all the way, and it's a beautiful journey.

There are direct buses from Lushoto to Dar es Salaam for TSh 3500 (about five hours) as well as direct buses between Lushoto and Tanga.

If you have to stay in Mombo overnight, try the *Usambara Inn*, next to the petrol station on the corner of the road to Lushoto. It's something of a time warp but has a garden, bar and restaurant. Single rooms have a sink, a towel and a large fan and cost TSh 1500.

OLDUVAI GORGE
The Olduvai Gorge made world headlines in 1959 following the discovery by the Leakeys of fossil fragments of the skull of one of the ancestors of Homo sapiens. The fragments were dated back 1.8 million years. The Leakeys were convinced by this and other finds that the fragments represented a third species of early humans, which they dubbed *Homo habilis*. They proposed that the other two, known as *Australopithecus africanus* and *Australopithecus robustus*, had died out and that *Homo habilis* had given rise to modern humankind. The debate raged for two decades and is still not settled.

Meanwhile, in 1979, Mary Leakey made another important discovery in the shape of footprints at Laetoli which she claimed were of a man, woman and child. They were dated back 3.5 million years, and since they were made by creatures which walked upright, this pushed the dawn of the human race much further back than had previously been supposed.

The gorge itself isn't of great interest unless you are archaeologically inclined. However, it has acquired a kind of cult attraction among those who just want to visit the site where the evolution of early humans presumably took place. There is a small museum on the site, which is only a 10 to 15-minute drive from the main road between Ngorongoro Crater and Serengeti. The museum closes at 3 pm and in the rainy season is often not open at all. It's possible to go down into the gorge at certain times of the year if you would like to see the dig sites.

Places to Stay
There is nowhere to stay at Olduvai, but at the western end of the gorge, where the creek which flows through it empties into Lake Ndutu, the *Ndutu Safari Lodge* (☎ (057) 6702), PO Box 6084 in Arusha or PO Box 1501 in Karatu, sits on the borders of the Serengeti National Park. The lodge offers 32 double rooms with private bathroom, six tents with separate toilet and washroom facilities, and an open-air bar and dining area with an excellent view of the lake. Bed and breakfast in the high season is US$66/81 for singles/doubles. Half-board rates are US$79/117. The lodge is open all year and can provide 4WD vehicles for game drives in the area.

TANZANIA

Lake Victoria

MWANZA

Mwanza is Tanzania's most important port on the shore of Lake Victoria and is the terminus of a branch of the Central Line railway from Dar es Salaam. It's a fairly attractive town interspersed with hills strewn with enormous boulders, between which many of the houses on the outskirts of the main area of town nestle. Mwanza's port handles the cotton, tea and coffee grown in the fertile western part of Tanzania. The Wasukuma people, who live in the area, make up the largest tribe in the country.

An attractive town it may be but, when it rains heavily in Mwanza, the centre turns into a muddy lake up to half a metre deep and the road to the airport becomes almost impassable. What drainage system ever existed here became clogged with rubbish years ago. And it's not just the drainage system which is clogged. Many of the lake inlets – including the ferry terminal – also become clogged, although in this case with water hyacinth. This imported weed has become a seemingly intractable problem in many places along the shores of Lake Victoria and Mwanza is where you can see it at its worst.

Information

Money There are three forex bureaus in Mwanza. The best is Zeid, in the New Mwanza Hotel, which is open daily including Sunday from 8 am to 6 pm.

Post & Communications As elsewhere in Tanzania, the telephone system in Mwanza is a major headache. It can take all day to make an outside connection and, after rain, you can forget about it completely.

The telephone area code for Mwanza is 068.

Travel Agencies The best and busiest travel agency is Fourways Travel Service (☎ 40653), PO Box 990, near the Station Rd roundabout. They offer computerised air ticket sales, game lodge bookings and local safaris (Serengeti, Ngorongoro etc), and the staff are very friendly and helpful. They also offer a shuttle bus between the town and the airport for TSh 1000 per person.

Sukuma Museum

About 15 km east of Mwanza on the Musoma road, the Sukuma Museum (sometimes called the Bujora Museum) was originally put together by a Quebecois missionary. Its displays are about the culture and traditions of the Wasukuma tribe. There is an excellent drum collection, and about once a week the museum puts on traditional tribal dances, including the spectacular Bugobogobo, the Sukuma Snake Dance. It's well worth enquiring in town. Entry costs TSh 100 (or TSh 200 if you want to take photographs). To get there, take a local bus from the bus station in Mwanza to Kisessa, from where it's about a one-km walk. It's also possible to camp at the museum or rent a banda.

Boat Hire

Kijereshi Tented Camp has a substantial motor yacht for hire. It doesn't come cheaply but would be an excellent way of exploring the lake if you have the money. Make enquiries through Kijereshi Tented Camp (☎ 41068/2191), PO Box 190, Mwanza.

Places to Stay – bottom end

Camping You can generally camp for free at the *Sukuma Museum*, and if you have no tent, there are two-bed bandas for rent. It's a lovely spot and many travellers stay here. Far more convenient for town is the *New Blue Sky Campsite*, on Capri Point Rd on the lake shore, which costs TSh 1000 per tent. The staff are friendly, there are toilets, cold showers, a bar and a regular disco.

Mwanza

0 125 250 m

Lake Victoria

To Airport

Victoria

Machemba Road

Customs Road

Bantu Road

Post Road

Liberty St

Uhuru Road

Footbridge

Nyerere Road

Temple Rd

Karuka Road

Lumumba Road

Rwagasore Road

Pamba Road

Station Road

Capri Point Road

Lake Victoria

Capri Point

To Shinyanga, Tabora & Dar es Salaam

To Musoma & Sukuma Museum

PLACES TO STAY
- 2 Tumaini Guest House
- 3 Hotel De Luxe
- 4 Kishamapanda Guest House
- 5 Geita Guest House
- 15 Iko Hotel
- 17 Tilapia Hotel
- 18 New Blue Sky Campsite
- 20 Lake Hotel
- 22 Pamba Hostel
- 24 New Mwanza Hotel
- 29 Majukano Hotel
- 34 Annexe Zimbabwe Guest House
- 36 Gardenia Hotel
- 39 Ramada Hotel
- 42 Victoria Guest House
- 43 Nsimbo Hotel

PLACES TO EAT
- 11 Tivoli Restaurant
- 12 Sizzler Restaurant & Air Tanzania
- 23 Fourways Bar & Restaurant
- 27 Jafferies Hotel
- 30 Sitar Restaurant
- 31 YMCA Restaurant
- 35 Chake Chake Restaurant
- 37 Surve Inn
- 38 Nyanguge Hotel
- 41 Skyline Restaurant

OTHER
- 1 Hospital
- 6 Local Dalla Dalla Station
- 7 Clock Tower
- 8 Police
- 9 Lake Ferries Terminal
- 10 Local Ferries
- 13 Post Office
- 14 Tennis Club
- 16 Yacht Club
- 19 Train Station
- 21 Fourways Travel Service & State Transport
- 25 Hindu Temple
- 26 Hindu Temple
- 28 National Bank of Commerce
- 32 Market
- 33 Bus Station
- 40 Kijereshi Forex Bureau

Hotels There's quite a choice of reasonably priced hotels around the bus station and in the centre of town. Closest to the bus station is the *Victoria Guest House*, which costs just TSh 1500 a double with shared bathroom facilities but baggage left in the rooms is not safe – break-ins are not uncommon.

Much better by far is the friendly *Nsimbo Hotel* close by. Doubles with private bathroom cost TSh 3000.

Also not far from the bus station are the *Zimbabwe Guest House* and the *Annexe Zimbabwe Guest House*, but they're both fleapits.

North of the bus station across Nyerere Rd and over a footbridge which spans a small river is the *Majukano Hotel* (☎ 41857). It's excellent value at TSh 3500/4000 for singles/doubles with private bathroom and breakfast. There's also a restaurant and a bar with cheap beers.

In the centre of town, either on or just off Uhuru Rd, there's a choice of four hotels. The most popular and the cheapest is the *Kishamapanda Guest House* which is a huge place but often full. It costs TSh 2000 a single with shared bathroom facilities and TSh 2500/3000 for singles/doubles with private

TANZANIA

bathroom. The *Tumaini Guest House* and the *Geita Guest House*, both on Uhuru Rd, are of a similar standard and price.

Better, but more expensive, is the *Hotel De Luxe* (☎ 40644) which offers singles/doubles with private bathroom for TSh 4000/5000 including breakfast.

Also excellent value is the Tema Hotels' *Pamba Hostel* (☎ 2697) on Pamba Rd, in the centre of town. There are no fans and the bathroom facilities are shared but the rooms are spotlessly clean and cost TSh 3000/4500 a single/double including breakfast. There's a good restaurant here with meals for around TSh 2000. The 1st-floor terrace bar also has a live band most nights of the week and there's no cover charge.

Most of the above hotels provide mosquito nets and most, though not all, have fans.

Places to Stay – middle

The best and most popular in this range is the *Lake Hotel* (☎ 3263), on Station Rd close to the railway station. It has singles/doubles with twin beds, fan, mosquito nets and private bathroom (cold showers) for TSh 6000/7000 including a meagre breakfast. On the other hand, it's secure and clean, and you can get a bucket of hot water in the morning if you request it. There's also a very popular bar here but no restaurant, though there is nyama choma available at lunch time.

If you're looking for a hot shower then the *Ramada Hotel* (☎ 40190) on Rwagasore Rd is the place to head for. This is a modern hotel which offers singles/doubles for TSh 6000/7000 including breakfast. It's a fair walk from the centre but good value.

Places to Stay – top end

The cheapest place to stay in this range is the *Iko Hotel* (☎ 42467) on the upper side of Capri Point Rd. It's a small place with its own bar and restaurant and surrounding compound and offers doubles (no singles) with private bathroom and fan for TSh 10,000 including breakfast. Facilities include guarded parking.

Right in the centre of town and a very popular meeting place is the *New Mwanza Hotel* (☎ 40620), Post St. It offers air-con doubles with private bathroom for US$40. A buffet continental breakfast is included. There's a bar and restaurant downstairs as well as a restaurant and casino upstairs (the upstairs restaurant has occasional live bands). Meals are relatively expensive, the service is slow and change is even slower arriving. Credit cards are not accepted, despite the stickers on the door.

Top of the range is the *Tilapia Hotel* (☎ 50517; fax 50141), Capri Point Rd, where everyone with someone else's money to spend stays. It's a large complex adjacent to the lake and close to the Yacht Club and it costs US$75 a double plus 5% service charges. There's a bar and restaurant, swimming pool, business centre and a regular disco. It's a lively spot if you have the money.

Places to Eat

For tasty, cheap food at around TSh 1500 for a main course there are three restaurants to choose from. They are the *Blue Café* on Post St, the *Pamba Hostel* on Pamba St and *Fourways Bar & Restaurant* at the junction of Pamba St and Station Rd on the roundabout. All are open for breakfast, lunch and dinner, but don't turn up late for dinner as the choice of dishes is very limited.

Going up in price, the *Sitar Restaurant*, a few metres away from the junction of Lumumba Rd and Nyerere Rd, does the best Indian and Chinese food in town and the service is excellent. It has been recommended by many travellers and is open daily from noon to 3 pm and 7 to 11 pm.

Also good for a splurge is *The Sizzler Restaurant* on the other side of the roundabout from the New Mwanza Hotel. It does excellent Indian, Chinese and continental food. It's popular with wazungu, and main dishes are from TSh 2000 to TSh 3400. It's open daily except Thursday from noon to 3 pm and 6.30 to 10.30 pm. They have soft drinks only. If you're hanging out for an excellent pizza then head for the *Kuleana Pizzeria* next door to the New Mwanza Hotel. This place also operates as a bakery.

Top of the range is the *Tilapia Hotel* at Capri Point which offers exquisite Indian cuisine and is also a good place to sit and have a quiet drink. Remember that 15% sales tax will be added to your food bill. Meals at the *New Mwanza Hotel* are also fairly good, but, like the Tilapia, 15% sales tax and 5% service charge will be added to your food bill, making it a relatively expensive place to eat. Service at the New Mwanza is slow.

For ice cream and fruit juices, the best place in town is the *Salma Cone* on Bantu St near the Kishamapanda Guest House.

If you need western supermarket goodies you can find the lot at *Chakula Bora* on Nyerere Rd next to the YMCA Restaurant, but be warned – it's pricey.

Entertainment

The *Delux Disco* fires up every night from Wednesday to Sunday and is very popular among local people. It's open from 11 pm until 5 am and plays mostly Zaïrese music. Entry costs TSh 1000 but is free for women on Thursday nights.

Even livelier and free of charge is the open-air 1st-floor bar at the Pamba Hostel, where a live band plays every night of the week, but closes around midnight.

Another good disco is the *TK Discotheque* at the Tivoli Restaurant on Post St which rocks away until dawn every night. There's also a good bar here on the 1st floor which is open all day. Lastly, there's also a disco at the Tilapia Hotel but drinks are relatively expensive here.

The bar at the Lake Hotel is a popular meeting place both for wazungu and Africans at lunch time and in the evening. Another lively African bar is the one at the top right-hand corner of the bus station on the Rwagasore St side. It's always packed with drinkers (cold beers are TSh 500), they show continuous African music videos and it never seems to close.

Getting There & Away

Air Air connections to and from Mwanza have improved by leaps and bounds over the last few years and there are now connections to Bukoba, Ngara, Arusha and Dar es Salaam (Tanzania), Goma (Zaïre), Bujumbura

---

Water Hyacinth

Over the past 10 years, almost the entire shoreline of Lake Victoria has become clogged with a dense mat of the introduced weed, water hyacinth. In most countries where it grows, it's considered to be a serious pest and all of the countries which border Lake Victoria – Tanzania, Kenya and Uganda – seem to share that view. It certainly makes life very difficult for the people who fish the lake using small boats.

All manner of remedies have been proposed to eradicate it including physical removal (extremely laborious and, at best, only a temporary fix), the release of beetles which eat the plant (environmentally sensitive but a very slow process) and even the spraying of 2-4-5 T, a carcinogenic defoliant (extremely hazardous and totally environmentally insensitive).

All those concerned agree that it should be eradicated where it poses a threat to people's livelihood and to the movement of lake traffic but not everyone agrees about its total eradication.

Those who disagree point out that during the colonial era, before the weed's introduction, local fishers used to harvest bumper catches of the indigenous lake fish until the carnivorous Nile perch was introduced in the 1950s. This species proliferated like wildfire and decimated the indigenous fish. Catches plummeted and the fishing industry almost collapsed, albeit only temporarily.

However, Nile perch can only live in open, fully-oxygenated fresh water. They can not survive in the oxygen-depleted shallows created by thick beds of water hyacinth. The indigenous species of fish, on the other hand, are capable of doing this. As a result, the beds of hyacinth have inadvertently provided a safe haven for these species and their numbers are, once again, on the increase.

It's a complicated situation and one which is unlikely to be resolved in the near future, if only because of the inertia of the governments concerned. ∎

(Burundi), Kigali (Rwanda), Entebbe (Uganda) and Nairobi (Kenya). Bookings for all flights other than Air Tanzania should be made through Fourways Travel Service on Pamba Rd at the roundabout (see Information above). Credit cards are not accepted despite the stickers on the door.

Air Tanzania flies daily to and from Dar (US$187, 1½ hours), either direct or via Kilimanjaro. They also fly to Bujumbura three times a week and Entebbe once a week. The Air Tanzania office (☎ 40413) accepts credit cards.

On the light planes, ACS flies Goma-Mwanza-Dar on Tuesday and in the opposite direction on Wednesday. Precision Air flies from Arusha to Mwanza (US$145) and on to Bukoba (US$65) and back again three times a week. Air Victoria and Western Airways between them fly from Mwanza to Nairobi (US$175 and US$150, respectively) five times a week.

Air Rwanda also has a twice-weekly flight between Kigali and Mwanza.

Bus From Mwanza to Arusha there's a choice of regular buses, some of which go through the Serengeti National Park and Ngorongoro, and others which go via Shinyanga and Singida, but it's important to get the right one. See the Arusha Getting There & Away section for details. Check departure times with Mruma Bus Co at the bus station. Advanced booking is advised.

To Rusumo (on the Rwandan border), there are no direct buses so you must take a bus to Ngara first (several daily) followed by a pick-up from there to the border. The road is diabolical except for a short stretch of good tarmac and the fare is TSh 6000.

To Musoma there's a choice of regular buses (uncomfortable and slow) and nonstop minibuses which cost TSh 2000 and depart daily at 1 and 4 pm from the bus station. The quoted journey time is three hours but you can count on it being substantially more.

Train There are departures for Dar es Salaam and Kigoma at 5 pm on Tuesday, Wednesday, Friday and Sunday. In the opposite direction,

there are departures from both Kigoma and Dar es Salaam for Mwanza at the same time and on the same days. The journey to either normally takes 36 hours but can take 40. Going from Mwanza to Kigoma involves a change at Tabora.

Travelling from Mwanza to Kigoma, there are only 1st and 2nd-class reservations available as far as Tabora. Beyond that point you cannot be guaranteed a reservation in the same class on the connecting train. On the through journey from Mwanza to Dar es Salaam there are no such problems.

The fares from Mwanza (in TSh) are:

Class:	1st	2nd (sleeping)	2nd (sitting)	3rd
To Tabora	12,460	8810	6320	4215
To Dar es Salaam	23,450	16,470	11,430	6975

Boat Just as the international lake ferries had got fully back into operation, the MV *Bukoba* turned turtle and sank, killing some 600 people in May 1996. It's likely the service will have been resumed. See the Tanzania Getting Around chapter for details.

Two ferries, the MV *Victoria* and the MV *Serengeti*, between them service Mwanza and Bukoba. The fares are TSh 7220 (Victoria class), TSh 6115 (1st class), TSh 5205 (2nd class sleeping), TSh 4155 (2nd class sitting) and TSh 2535 (3rd class). Victoria and 1st classes are two-bunk cabins with a hand basin. Second class sleeping is six-bunk cabins without a hand basin. Second class sitting is exactly what it says and 3rd class is basically any patch of lower deck space you can find to stretch out on. Bedding in 1st and 2nd classes is available for TSh 500. Port tax is TSh 1000 between Mwanza and Bukoba. Dinner is available on board (TSh 1500) and there's a bar which serves drinks until late.

The MV *Victoria* leaves Mwanza on Sunday, Tuesday and Thursday at 10 pm, arriving in Bukoba at 6 am the following day. From Bukoba it sails on Monday, Wednesday and Friday at 9 pm, arriving in Mwanza at 6 am the following day.

The MV *Serengeti* sails from Mwanza at

9 pm on Monday, arriving in Bukoba at 7 am the next day. It leaves Bukoba for Mwanza on Tuesday at 9 pm, arriving at 7 am on Wednesday.

BUKOBA

Bukoba is Tanzania's second-largest port on Lake Victoria. It's a fairly popular overnight stop for travellers coming through from or on their way to Uganda or Rwanda. Bukoba is somewhat like Mwanza but smaller and quieter and there's not a great deal to see or do but it's a pleasant place and the people are friendly.

The main part of town is some 2.5 km from the port so you'll need a taxi if you have heavy bags.

Information

There are no forex bureaus in Bukoba, but there's a branch of the National Bank of Commerce on the same road as the post office.

Places to Stay – bottom end

The most popular camp site is in the grounds of the *Lake Hotel* where it costs TSh 2000 per tent. Quite a few overland trucks stop

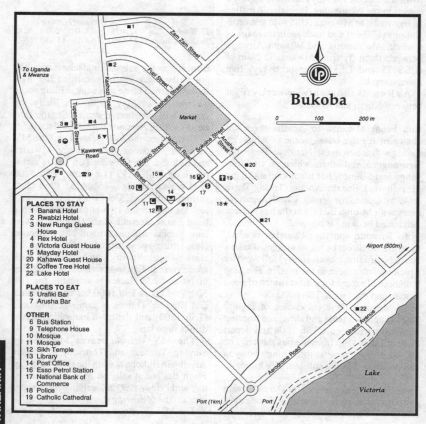

Bukoba

0   100   200 m

PLACES TO STAY
1 Banana Hotel
2 Rwabizi Hotel
3 New Runga Guest House
4 Rex Hotel
8 Victoria Guest House
15 Mayday Hotel
20 Kahawa Guest House
21 Coffee Tree Hotel
22 Lake Hotel

PLACES TO EAT
5 Urafiki Bar
7 Arusha Bar

OTHER
6 Bus Station
9 Telephone House
10 Mosque
11 Mosque
12 Sikh Temple
13 Library
14 Post Office
16 Esso Petrol Station
17 National Bank of Commerce
18 Police
19 Catholic Cathedral

To Uganda & Mwanza

Zam Zam Street
Kashozi Road
Tupengana Street
Kawawa Road
Bushara Street
Fupi Street
Market
Jamhuri Road
Mosque Street
Migevo Street
Sokoine Street
Arusha Street

Airport (500m)

Ghana Avenue
Aerodrome Road

Port (1km)   Port

Lake Victoria

TANZANIA

here. Campers can use the toilet and shower facilities at the hotel.

The cheapest place to stay is the *Nyumba wa Vijana* (youth centre), at the Evangelical Lutheran Church on the road to the hospital– if you ask around someone should give you directions. A dormitory bed costs TSh 500 and you can leave your gear here safely.

For a cheap private room, there are several possibilities around the bus station. Try the *Victoria Guest House, New Runga Guest House* or the *Rex Hotel*. Doubles at all of them with shared bathroom facilities cost TSh 1500.

Up in quality but still at a very reasonable price is the *Kahawa Guest House* (☎ 578), which has doubles with shared facilities for TSh 2000, or doubles with private bathroom for TSh 2800.

The *Mayday Hotel* is similar and has doubles with shared facilities for TSh 1600 or TSh 2500 with private bathroom and breakfast but is often full.

Places to Stay – middle
A good choice of mid-range hotel is the fairly new *Banana Hotel* on Zam Zam St which offers singles/doubles with private bathroom for TSh 4500/5000. The hotel has its own bar and restaurant.

On the other side of town on Jamhuri Rd is the larger *Coffee Tree Hotel* (☎ 20412) which has singles/doubles for TSh 3000/ 4000 with common bath, and suites with two bedrooms and private bathroom for TSh 5000. Breakfast is included in the price and the hotel has its own bar and restaurant.

Close to the lake shore at the end of Jamhuri Rd is the olde-worlde *Lake Hotel* (☎ 20237) set in its own grounds. It's an attractive place with a lot of character though the plumbing system dates back to at least the 1940s or 50s. There is one single and five doubles with shared bathroom facilities at TSh 3000 and TSh 3500 as well as three doubles with private bathroom at TSh 5000. They also have four doubles with private bathroom and hot water for TSh 6500, all including breakfast. The hotel has its own cosy bar with fireplace (used to house the fire extinguisher!), a restaurant (which does tasty meals for TSh 1000) and a beer garden. Credit cards are not accepted.

Getting There & Away
Air Precision Air flies from Bukoba to Mwanza (US$65) and Arusha (US$230) three times a week. Bookings have to be made and flight times confirmed at the airstrip, which is about 500m from the Lake Hotel along Aerodrome Rd.

Bus For details of the route between Bukoba and Masaka (Uganda) via Kyaka, see the Tanzania Getting There & Away chapter.

Boat See the Mwanza section for details of ferries to Mwanza. The lake ferry jetty is about 2.5 km from the town centre and you must go there to make bookings. A taxi costs TSh 2000.

MUSOMA
Musoma is a small port on the eastern shore of Lake Victoria, close to the Kenyan border. It's connected to Bukoba and Mwanza by lake ferry.

Places to Stay & Eat
Most travellers stay at the very clean, cheap and friendly *Mennonite Centre*. The only drawback is that it's a long way from the ferry terminal. If it's too far, try the reasonably priced *Embassy Lodge* in the town centre, or the slightly more expensive *Musambura Guest House* around the corner.

More expensive but excellent value is the *Hotel Orange Tree*, Kawawa St off Iringa St, right by the lake. It offers singles with shared bathroom for TSh 3500 and singles/doubles with private bathroom for TSh 6000/7000 including breakfast. There's an attached restaurant with good meals for around TSh 1500.

Another mid-range hotel is the *Railway Hotel*, about half an hour's walk from the town centre. It's worth coming here for a meal while you're in town, even if you don't stay.

Getting There & Away

To Mwanza there's a choice of either regular buses (uncomfortable and slow) or nonstop minibuses, which cost TSh 2000 and depart twice daily from the bus station. The quoted journey time is three hours but you can fairly definitely count on it being substantially more.

Central & North-Western Tanzania

MOROGORO

Sprawling over a relatively flat valley bottom between two huge verdant walls of mountains, Morogoro is a fairly attractive town, though there's not a great deal to do here unless you're into golf (it has one of Tanzania's most highly rated courses) or trekking to the top of the mountains. It is, however, the nearest town to Mikumi National Park, so you could use it as a base for safaris to the park and thus avoid having to stay at the expensive lodge in the park itself.

There is no foreign exchange bureau in Morogoro, so you'll have to change money at the banks if necessary.

Places to Stay – bottom end

Those on a strict budget should try the *New Plaza Hotel* (very noisy), the *Sanga Guest House* or the *Nighesha Lodging* (both quiet). All three are basic.

More expensive but a quantum leap in comfort is the *Hotel New Tegetero* (☎ (056) 2571), on the main street and very close to the bus station. Good rooms with clean sheets cost TSh 1500 a double (no singles) with shared bathroom facilities or TSh 2000 with private bathroom. The hotel has its own restaurant.

Similar in standard and just a few doors up is the *Hotel Luna*, which has doubles (no singles) with shared bathroom facilities for TSh 1500 or TSh 2000 with private bathroom facilities.

At the opposite end of town but close to the railway station is the *Acropol Hotel*,

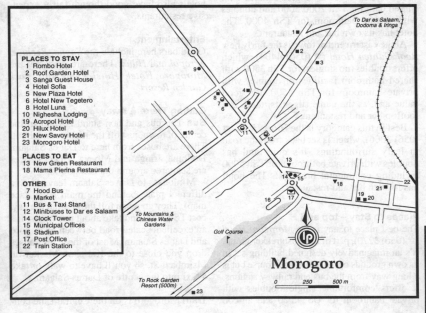

PLACES TO STAY
1 Rombo Hotel
2 Roof Garden Hotel
3 Sanga Guest House
4 Hotel Sofia
5 New Plaza Hotel
6 Hotel New Tegetero
8 Hotel Luna
10 Nighesha Lodging
19 Acropol Hotel
20 Hilux Hotel
21 New Savoy Hotel
23 Morogoro Hotel

PLACES TO EAT
13 New Green Restaurant
18 Mama Pierina Restaurant

OTHER
7 Hood Bus
9 Market
11 Bus & Taxi Stand
12 Minibuses to Dar es Salaam
14 Clock Tower
15 Municipal Offices
16 Stadium
17 Post Office
22 Train Station

To Dar es Salaam, Dodoma & Iringa

To Mountains & Chinese Water Gardens

To Rock Garden Resort (500m)

Golf Course

Morogoro

0   250   500 m

TANZANIA

which offers doubles (no singles) with shared bathroom facilities for TSh 2000 or TSh 2500 with private bathroom. It's an old place, but the staff are very friendly and there's a good bar and restaurant.

Places to Stay – middle

Just outside the railway station is the *New Savoy Hotel* (☎ (056) 2345) on Station Rd, which offers doubles (no singles) with private bathroom for TSh 4000 but there are no fans in the rooms. It's another old place and, considering the facilities, is overpriced but it does have a popular bar and restaurant.

Much better, but more expensive, is *Mama Pierina Restaurant* (☎ (056) 7172), also on Station Rd. This is essentially a family residence for the expatriates who run the restaurant but it does have a few rooms. It offers doubles with continental breakfast for TSh 5000 but there are no fans in the rooms.

Cheaper and centrally located is the *Hotel Sofia* (☎ (056) 4848), which is popular with businesspeople. It has singles/doubles with shared bath for TSh 2000/3000 and doubles with private bathroom for TSh 4000. The hotel has its own bar and restaurant.

At the eastern end of town is the fairly new *Roof Garden Hotel* (☎ (056) 4404), which offers doubles (no singles) for TSh 3500 with shared bathroom facilities or doubles with private bathroom for TSh 4500. It's good value and, as the name suggests, there is a rooftop bar and restaurant.

Best in this category is the *Hilux Hotel* (☎ (056) 3066), which is set back from the road in leafy surroundings. It's quiet and has doubles with private bathroom for TSh 5000 including continental breakfast. The hotel has its own bar and restaurant.

Places to Stay – top end

The best place to stay is the *Morogoro Hotel* (☎ (056) 3270), part of the Bushtrekker group. It's an imaginatively designed building set in its own grounds opposite the golf course but is a long way from the bus and railway stations. It offers comfortable singles/doubles with private bathroom for US$45/50 and air-con

doubles for US$55 including breakfast. The hotel has its own bar and restaurant.

About half a km further up the same road is the *Rock Garden Resort*, which is very pleasant and charges much the same.

Places to Eat

A cheap place to eat here is the *Pop In* near the bus station, which offers main meals (traditional African fare) for TSh 500 to TSh 1000, but the food is only average.

The *New Green Restaurant* near the clock tower is far better. It does excellent food at reasonable prices and is open daily for lunch and dinner.

Much more expensive but with superbly cooked and presented food is the *Mama Pierina Restaurant* on Station Rd. Main dishes are TSh 2000 to TSh 3000. It's the best restaurant in town, service is prompt, and there's a bar and verandah with comfortable armchairs to relax in afterwards. It's open daily for lunch and dinner.

The *Roof Garden, Hilux* and *Morogoro* hotels also have good though fairly expensive restaurants.

Entertainment

Good bars here include the *Sapna, Beehive, Acropol* and *Hilux*. There are discos at the *Morogoro Hotel, Hotel Luna* and *Rock Garden Resort*.

Getting There & Away

Bus The bus and taxi stand is right in the centre of town, just off the main roundabout. There are buses from here to Dar es Salaam, Dodoma, Iringa and Mbeya. Ticket offices are scattered around the compound.

Minibuses to Dar es Salaam leave from a different place behind the main street (see map). They go when full throughout the day, cost TSh 1500 and take about two hours. It's an excellent sealed road between Morogoro and Dar es Salaam. Most of these minibuses drop you close to the Kariakoo Market on Msimbazi St, so you'll have to walk or take a taxi into the centre of Dar es Salaam.

Train Morogoro is on the Central Line connecting Dar es Salaam with Mwanza and Kigoma, you can use the trains to get between the two, though they are much slower than the buses and minibuses and, if you're coming from Dar es Salaam, you won't arrive until well after dark. Fares from Dar es Salaam are TSh 3920 (1st class), TSh 2805 (2nd class), TSh 1925 (2nd class sitting) and TSh 1200 (3rd class). See the Tanzania Getting Around chapter for the schedule.

DODOMA

Dodoma is the CCM party political headquarters and the official capital of Tanzania, though so far none of the embassies and high commissions in Dar es Salaam has moved here. Nor are they likely to do so in the near future. Who would want to live here? It's a wasteland with nothing to do and minimal facilities – a far cry from the other new African capitals of Yamoussoukro (Côte d'Ivoire) and Abuja (Nigeria).

Dodoma is, however, one of the few wine-producing areas of Africa south of Morocco/Algeria and north of South Africa. Bacchanalians shouldn't get too excited though, as Tanzanian viniculture has a long way to go before it will interest those with a taste for anything other than wine vinegar. Not only that, but with the South Africans importing their own products heavily into the country, the Tanzanians will have an uphill battle competing with them.

Places to Stay & Eat

One of the cheapest places is the *Ujiji Guest House*, near the bus station. It has clean showers and toilets, provides mosquito nets and costs TSh 500 a single. Also within walking distance of town is the *Horombo Malazi*, Nyumba wa Wagena, a simple local guesthouse where you can get a cheap double room. The owner is friendly and you'll probably be the only wazungu there. Others recommend the *Morning Star*, at TSh 2000 per person.

The best value, however, is the *Christian Council of Tanzania Guest House* (ask people for the CCT), which has double

rooms with a cold shower, towels and mosquito nets for TSh 2500 including *one* continental breakfast. The canteen serves reasonable meals for about TSh 400 (omelette and chips). If you're staying here and going out in the evening you need to be back by 11 pm.

Somewhat more expensive is the *Jamboree Hotel & Restaurant*, which is friendly, good value and costs TSh 3500 a double including breakfast.

The *Central Province Hotel* (☎ (061) 21177) is also a reasonable place to stay. To get there, leave the front entrance of the railway station and turn right along the road running parallel with the tracks. Continue to the first roundabout and turn right. Walk to the next roundabout and turn right again. The hotel is 50m down the first street on the left.

For a top-end hotel, the *Dodoma Hotel* offers doubles with private bathroom for US$35. Its restaurant serves excellent breakfasts and dinners. The bar is a popular hangout for local people and expatriates.

A very popular place to eat in Dodoma is *Nureens Hotel* which does chicken and chips in the evening. Cheaper meals are available at the *Keshumani Hotel*.

Bars are thin on the ground in this town but the *NK Disco* plays a variety of music and gets going after 11 pm. Entrance is TSh 800 – often free to women. Popular at weekends with expatriates and rich Tanzanians is the *Climax Club*. To get in you must either pay a membership fee or get someone to sign you in. It has a pool, squash courts, sauna and bar. They also do meals but they take forever to arrive.

Getting There & Away

Bus The daily bus to Arusha departs at 9.30 am, costs TSh 3500 and takes about 15 hours. It's operated by Sahib bus service and tickets can be bought from the office opposite the Caltex station. Book a day in advance. The road is diabolical until you get to Tarangire National Park, after which it's a good sealed road.

Train The railway line from Dar es Salaam

to Kigoma/Mwanza runs through Dodoma. See the Tanzania Getting Around chapter for details of the schedule. Fares from Dar es Salaam are TSh 9815 (1st class), TSh 7020 (2nd class), TSh 4815 (2nd class sitting) and TSh 3000 (3rd class).

TABORA

Tabora is a railway junction town where the Central Line branches for Mwanza and Kigoma. You may have to stay the night here if you're changing trains and can't get immediate onward reservations. Tabora is something of a backwater with a population of some 130,000 inhabitants.

The only bank in town is the National Bank of Commerce on School St close to the junction with Market St.

For limited photographic supplies and black and white processing, try Photo Express on Manyema St.

Things to See & Do

If you have time to spare, there is a small museum in one of Livingstone's former homes, just outside town, although the road there is terrible – like most of Tabora's roads.

To the south-west of Tabora is the **Ugalla River Game Reserve**. Tours can be arranged through Africa House in town close to the Hotel Wilca on Boma Rd, or through Mr Alnashir Kassamali (☎ (062) 4062), PO Box 1880, Tabora.

Places to Stay & Eat

The *Moravian Guest House* is probably the best place to stay and is exceptionally cheap. It's pleasant and the staff are friendly.

As far as hotels go, the *Vatican Hotel, Bar & Restaurant*, Market St, the *Golden Eagle Hotel*, at the junction of School and Market Sts, and the *Country Roses Hotel*, on West Boma Rd, are all reasonable places to stay at around TSh 3000 a double.

Up in price, the *Hotel Wilca* (☎ (062) 2397), Boma Rd, offers clean, comfortable doubles with private bathroom for TSh 7500 including breakfast and hot showers. The owners are very friendly and helpful and the restaurant here offers tasty, varied and rea-

sonably priced meals. There's also a bar and a garden area.

Top of the line is the recently reopened *Tabora Hotel* (☎ (062) 4566), at the junction of Boma and Station Rds. Formerly called the Railway Hotel, it was originally built by a German baron as a hunting lodge but has been completely rehabilitated and has been franchised out to private enterprise. It has a great verandah overlooking the gardens and offers large doubles with private bathroom, clean sheets and mosquito nets for TSh 7500. Breakfast of eggs, toast and tea/coffee costs

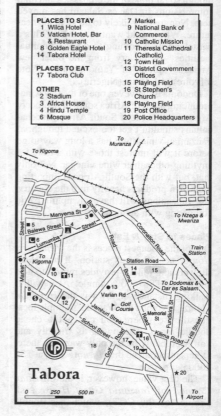

PLACES TO STAY	7 Market
1 Wilca Hotel	9 National Bank of
5 Vatican Hotel, Bar	Commerce
& Restaurant	10 Catholic Mission
8 Golden Eagle Hotel	11 Theresia Cathedral
14 Tabora Hotel	(Catholic)
	12 Town Hall
PLACES TO EAT	13 District Government
17 Tabora Club	Offices
	15 Playing Field
OTHER	16 St Stephen's
2 Stadium	Church
3 Africa House	18 Playing Field
4 Hindu Temple	19 Post Office
6 Mosque	20 Police Headquarters

Tabora

0   250   500 m

TSh 225. Lunch and dinner costs TSh 1700 but you need to order in advance.

Other than what's mentioned above, you can find a meal at *Africa House* on Boma Rd.

For the nearest thing to a supermarket, go to either Mr Sudra's store, off Lumumba St close to the junction with Market St, or Surat store on Jamhuri St close to the junction with Market St.

For entertainment try the *Honey Pot Disco*.

Getting There & Away
Train The railway line north-west of Dar es Salaam splits at Tabora, one line continuing west to Kigoma on Lake Tanganyika, the other heading north to Mwanza on Lake Victoria. See the Getting Around chapter for details of departures. The fares to Dar es Salaam are TSh 12,460 (1st class), TSh 8810 (2nd class), TSh 6320 (2nd class sitting) and TSh 4215 (3rd class).

Getting Around
Most of the taxis are located across from the market at the junction of Lumumba and Market Sts. The best service is operated by Uncle Taxi and the driver's name is Rev Wyne Lubisha. Expect to pay a little more than you would in Dar es Salaam.

KIGOMA
Kigoma is the most important Tanzanian port on Lake Tanganyika and is the terminus of the railway from Dar es Salaam. Many travellers come through here en route to or from Bujumbura (Burundi) or Mpulungu (Zambia) on the Lake Tanganyika steamer MV *Liemba*. It's a small but pleasant town, its one main street lined with huge, shady mango trees. Life ticks over at a slow pace. If you get stuck waiting for the train (a few days is not uncommon) or the boat (a day or two), you'll have to amuse yourself with walks around town and visits to Ujiji. There's very little of interest in the Kigoma township, but it's a good base for visits to Gombe Stream National Park (see the National Parks chapter).

Don't bother trying to climb any of the hills that flank the town in search of a view

– these are military zones and are off limits to mere mortals. The best (accessible) view of the town is from outside the new church, which is just to the left of the main road as you head up the hill towards Muwanga.

Information
Foreign Consulates Kigoma has consulates for Burundi and Zaïre (see the Visas & Documents and Embassies sections in the Tanzania Facts for the Visitor chapter for details).

Immigration It's not necessary to visit immigration in Kigoma if you're heading north to Gombe Stream National Park. All exit formalities are dealt with at Kagunga, the last Tanzanian village before you cross the border into Burundi. If, however, you're taking the lake steamer to either Bujumbura or Mpulungu, you'll have to pass through immigration before boarding the steamer.

Money There are no forex bureaus in Kigoma, so you'll have to change money at a bank.

Places to Stay – bottom end
The best value for money is the *Kigoma Hotel*, on the main street in the middle of town. Its double rooms are huge and excellent value, while the singles are smaller but still good. Singles/doubles with shared bathroom facilities cost TSh 1600/2500. There's a fixed-menu lunch available for TSh 800. The *Lake View Hotel*, a bit further up the hill on the left-hand side, is very similar to the Kigoma but marginally more expensive.

The *Mapinduzi Hotel*, a basic African hotel, charges TSh 1000 for doubles that can accommodate four people without any problem. There are no singles.

All the other hotels are further up the hill and are hardly worth the walk. The *Safari Lodging* is about as far up as you need to go. It charges TSh 1500 a double with shared facilities, but it is opposite the mosque, so you'll be woken early.

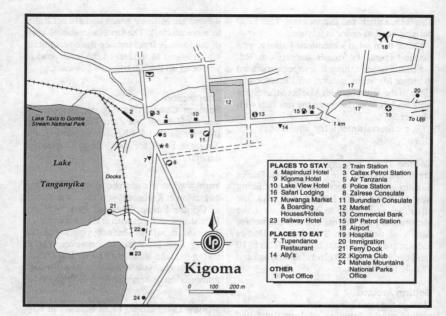

Kigoma

0   100   200 m

PLACES TO STAY
4 Mapinduzi Hotel
9 Kigoma Hotel
10 Lake View Hotel
16 Safari Lodging
17 Muwanga Market
   & Boarding
   Houses/Hotels
23 Railway Hotel

PLACES TO EAT
7 Tupendance
   Restaurant
14 Ally's

OTHER
1 Post Office

2 Train Station
3 Caltex Petrol Station
5 Air Tanzania
6 Police Station
8 Zaïrese Consulate
11 Burundian Consulate
12 Market
13 Commercial Bank
15 BP Petrol Station
18 Airport
19 Hospital
20 Immigration
21 Ferry Dock
22 Kigoma Club
24 Mahale Mountains
   National Parks
   Office

Lake Taxis to Gombe
Stream National Park

Lake
Tanganyika

Docks

To Ujiji

1 km

Places to Stay – middle

Kigoma's only mid-range hotel is the *Railway Hotel*, overlooking the lake, a few hundred metres south of the centre. The position is excellent and the views are good, but you have to pay in hard currency. The rates are US$20 a double with private bathroom and breakfast. There's a bar and a reasonably good restaurant.

Places to Eat

Lunch is the main meal of the day here – you'll find there is far less variety available in the evenings. One of the cheapest is the *Kigoma Hotel*, where you can get a basic meal for TSh 800. The cardamom tea is also excellent. The *Lake View* has similar meals and prices and is the place to go for breakfast – papaya, porridge, two eggs, bread and two cups of tea for TSh 600.

A bit further up the hill is the Muslim-owned *Ally's*. Although the service is slow, this place has the best range of food in Kigoma, especially in the evenings, when there is little available elsewhere. Chips are cooked on request, though these take half an hour or so.

The *Tupendance Restaurant*, near the police station, has excellent ndizi and chicken for lunch, and also has a fan.

For what amounts to a splurge in Kigoma, you could try a meal at the *Railway Hotel*. The food isn't bad but nothing to write home about. Lunch or dinner costs TSh 1500.

Entertainment

The *Kigoma Hotel* has a reasonable bar and warm beer. The music system has seen better days, so the distortion levels are high. The *Railway Hotel* has a disco on Saturday night for TSh 1000 and another on Sunday afternoon for TSh 400.

Getting There & Away

Air Air Tanzania flies Dar es Salaam to

Kigoma twice a week (US$220). The Air Tanzania ticket office accepts credit cards.

If you're coming from Burundi and want to fly to Dar es Salaam from Kigoma, you can make a reservation in advance in Bujumbura at the Air Tanzania office, although you actually pay for the flight in Kigoma.

Train There are departures at 5 pm on Tuesday, Wednesday, Friday and Sunday for Dar es Salaam and Mwanza. The journey to Dar normally takes about 36 hours but can take 40. The fares from Kigoma to Dar es Salaam are TSh 23,000 (1st class), TSh 16,710 (2nd class sleeping), TSh 11,650 (2nd class sitting) and TSh 7075 (3rd class). See the chief booking clerk at the station in Kigoma for 1st-class bookings. The train is often booked out in 1st and 2nd class, but with persistence you can usually get a booking, at least as far as Tabora where a lot of people get off to connect with the train to Mwanza.

Bus & Truck The buses in this area only serve local towns, but it is possible to find trucks to Mwanza if you are prepared to wait a few days. Ask around in the shops on the main street. On the other hand, going by road to Mwanza is a nightmare journey over appalling roads and can take up to six days. Save yourself the nightmare and go by train instead, even if it means waiting a few days until you can secure a ticket.

Ferry For details of the MV *Liemba* services to Mpulungu and Bujumbura, see the Tanzania Getting There & Away chapter.

The 'dock' for lake taxis to the Gombe Stream National Park is about an hour's walk up the railway tracks from the station.

Getting Around

Air Tanzania runs a minibus from their office in town to the airport about 1½ hours before flight departures. There's a small charge.

UJIJI

Down the lake shore from Kigoma, Ujiji is one of Africa's oldest market villages and is a good deal more interesting than Kigoma. This is where the famous words 'Dr Livingstone, I presume' were spoken by the explorer and journalist Henry Morton Stanley. There's the inevitable plaque at the site where this event allegedly occurred, although there is a similar plaque at a site in Burundi! The site is to the right of the main road (when coming from Kigoma), down the side street next to the Bin Tunia Restaurant – just ask for Livingstone and the bus driver will make sure you get off at the right place.

The two mango trees growing in the walled compound at the site are said to have been grafted from the original tree growing there when the two men met. There's also a museum, which houses a few pictorial representations by local artists of Livingstone's time here. The pictures bear captions such as: 'Dr Livingstone sitting under the mango tree in Ujiji thinking about slavery'. Entry costs TSh 200, which seems to go straight into the caretaker's pocket.

About 500m past the compound along the same street are the beach and the local boat-builders. This seems to be a thriving local industry, and there may be as many as a dozen boats in various stages of construction. No power tools are used and construction methods have hardly changed in generations.

Places to Stay

The *Matunda Guest House*, on the main street, is a cosy place to stay and costs TSh 1000 a double with shared facilities.

Getting There & Away

There are frequent buses to Ujiji from outside the railway station in Kigoma. The fare is TSh 200.

Southern Tanzania

IRINGA

Iringa is a bus and train junction about halfway between Dar es Salaam and Mbeya. A town of some 100,000 inhabitants, it's the gateway to **Ruaha National Park** to the west, and the **Isimala Stone Age** site is also nearby.

Have warm clothes handy in Iringa as it sits on a high plateau and gets cold at night. Snow occasionally falls here at certain times of the year.

Places to Stay & Eat

There are plenty of relatively cheap guesthouses in the town centre which include the *Iringa Hotel*, recommended for its open fire and good food, the *Living Lights Hotel*, the *Isimila Hotel* and *The Taj*. All are around TSh 4000 a double.

Going up in price, perhaps the best place to stay is *Huruma Baptist Conference Centre*, just off Mkwawa St and close to the Danish School for the Deaf, about 15 minutes walk from the bus station. It's very clean and costs TSh 6960 a double excluding breakfast. Breakfast may be available but don't count on it. Other meals are not.

Highly recommended is the *MR Hotel* (☎ (064) 2006; fax 2661), which charges TSh 7500/9000 for singles/doubles with private bathroom, including a light breakfast.

For a dirt-cheap meal, try either *Khartoums*, which sells ugali and beans, or the *Samosa Stand* on India St. Slightly more expensive are the *Staff Inn* (around TSh 1000 a meal), the *Iringa Hotel* (TSh 1500), *The Taj*, and *Lulu's Restaurant*, on Benbela St just behind the Railway Hotel and next door to the Iringa Bakery. Lulu's has a varied menu and costs around TSh 3000 for a full meal. There's also the *Hasty Tasty* which does Indian snacks and burgers.

Recommended bars include the *Family Bar*, *TipTop* and the *Stereo Bar*.

KASANGA

Kasanga is the last port in Tanzania going south on Lake Tanganyika. Many travellers going between Lake Tanganyika and Lake Malawi come through Kasanga these days because it's easier to go between Kasanga and Karonga via Mbeya, Tunduma and Sumbawanga than it is to go between Mpulungu and Karonga via Mbala, Nakonde and Chitipa. There's an additional advantage for travellers heading north and that is that fares on the Lake Tanganyika ferries are considerably cheaper if you board at Kasanga rather than Mpulungu – a saving of approximately US$35, assuming you take 1st class. However, if you're coming south from Kigoma, the ferries arrive at Kasanga between midnight and 2 am and it's chaos getting off the ferry into the small boats which you have to take to the shore. At that time of night, too, you won't want to/be able to walk the one km to Muzi where there's a hotel so you'll be stuck with whatever is available (very primitive accommodation) until the morning. There's also no electricity in town.

However, you don't *have* to join this mêlée in the dead of night. It's important to understand that the ferry anchors off Kasanga for the night and doesn't leave until 6 am so the thing to do is to speak with the purser before you arrive and get permission to stay on board overnight. Then, when the midnight mêlée starts, negotiate with one of the boatmen to come and collect you at 5 am. This way you avoid all the drama and can get some sleep on the boat.

If you're *boarding* the boat here, there's no such drama.

Kasanga consists of three villages: Muzi, Lumbo and Kitika, and it is at Lumbo that you embark/disembark on the lake ferries. There's no 'dock' as such so getting to or from the ferry has to be done in a small boat.

If you have a day or two to spare in Kasanga it's worth trekking to the **Kalambo Falls** which are about four hours walk going south. The river mouth on the lake is home to an amazing number of crocodiles. Ask for directions in the Kasanga villages before you set off.

Kasanga is also the site of the ruined German 'Bismark Fort'.

Places to Stay & Eat

The best place to stay here is the *Mwenya Guesthouse* in Muzi village which is a one-km walk along the beach and over a small hill from Lumbo. Here they offer singles/doubles for TSh 600/700 with clean bedding but no mosquito nets or electric lights (kerosene lanterns are provided). Cold showers are available.

There are numerous kiosks and bars which serve simple meals all day until late in the evening for around TSh 350.

If you need any help or information in Kasanga, a good person to contact is Mr Mipata, a general merchant who speaks English and lives in Muzi. His wife runs a very good restaurant there.

Getting There & Away

Assuming you're heading for Malawi, you first have to hitch a ride from Kasanga to Sumbawanga which should cost around TSh 3000 and take about four hours. It's a rough road, especially at the beginning. There are many cheap guesthouses and hotels in Sumbawanga for between TSh 1200 and TSh 2000. From Sumbawanga, there are daily 'express' buses via Tunduma to Mbeya which take six to eight hours and cost TSh 4000. These buses generally leave at around 6 am. The road is sealed between Tunduma and Mbeya.

Travellers heading for Zambia rather than Malawi are given the option of getting off near Tunduma and taking a minibus to the Tanzania/Zambia border.

MBEYA

Mbeya lies in a gap between the verdant Mbeya mountain ranges to the north and the Uporoto Mountains to the south-east. It was founded in 1927 as a supply centre for the gold rush at Lupa (to the north) but is now an important staging centre on the main road

and TAZARA railway between Tanzania and Zambia. Many travellers also stay here overnight en route to Malawi via the Songwe river bridge to Karonga.

The surrounding area is very fertile, with banana, tea, coffee and cocoa plantations, and though few travellers seem to stay more than a night, there are many places of interest in the vicinity.

Kaluwe

For those with just a day to spare, it's worth trekking this 2834m peak in the Mbeya range, which overlooks the town to the north. The views from the top are amazing, though it's probably wise to stay away from the radio mast or people might think you're a spy. To get there, head from the roundabout towards the waterworks but turn left before you reach the gates, along a gravel track (about 150m from the roundabout). You will pass a quarry on the right-hand side after 50m or so and then a few houses below a eucalypt forest. The track then goes to the left of a clearing where maize is grown. From there, follow one of the paths which go to the mountain top. It will take about two hours to get to the top.

Ngozi

This 2621m volcanic peak in the Uporoto Mountains is to the east of the Mbeya to Tukuyu road and is well worth the attention of enthusiastic hikers. Other than the hike up to the summit, which takes you through thick rainforest and out onto alpine heathland, you'll be rewarded on the summit with a view of the Ngozi Crater Lake, some 2.5 km long by 1.5 km wide, surrounded by sheer cliffs dropping 200m down to the lake. Ngozi is approached from a track off the main road, and you'd be advised to engage a local guide. The walk to the summit should take about two hours.

Natural Bridge & Kijungu A little further south and, again, off the Mbeya to Tukuyu road is the Natural Bridge, which spans a small waterfall. Estimated to have been formed some 1800 million years ago by

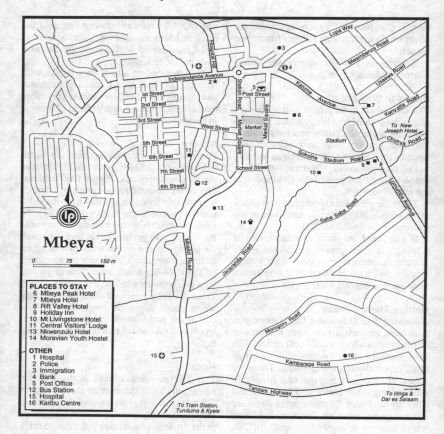

Mbeya

0   75   150 m

PLACES TO STAY
6 Mbeya Peak Hotel
7 Mbeya Hotel
8 Rift Valley Hotel
9 Holiday Inn
10 Mt Livingstone Hotel
11 Central Visitors' Lodge
13 Nkwenzulu Hotel
14 Moravian Youth Hostel

OTHER
1 Hospital
2 Police
3 Immigration
4 Bank
5 Post Office
12 Bus Station
15 Hospital
16 Karibu Centre

water flowing through cooling lava spewed out from the nearby erupting Rungwe Volcano, it is situated eight km from Kiwira Prison College. A further three km up the steep gorge from the Natural Bridge is Kijungu ('cooking pot'), where the entire Kiwira River tumbles into a seething sump in the riverbed. It's an impressive sight, even during the rainy season when the river overflows its banks.

Places to Stay – bottom end

If at all possible, you should arrive early in the day, as places fill up rapidly by late afternoon. One of the most popular places to stay is the *Moravian Youth Hostel* on Jacaranda Rd. It's excellent value, clean and friendly and costs TSh 600 a double, but there are no meals available. A similar place, but a considerable distance from the centre of town, is the *Karibu Centre*, 500m off the Tanzam Highway in Forest Area. It's run by Swiss missionaries and is very clean and friendly, though alcoholic drinks are prohibited on the premises. According to local people, it has the best food in town.

There are many other cheap lodges scattered around town but they're mostly basic.

TANZANIA

One which is good value is the *Nkwenzulu Hotel*, opposite the bus station on Mbalizi Rd, which has doubles with shared bath for TSh 1100 and doubles with private bathroom for TSh 1700. The rooms are spacious but there are only cold showers available. There's a bar, and a restaurant which serves good, cheap food. Also pretty good value is the *Central Visitors' Lodge* on Waseni St.

Further out to the east, near the junction of Sokoine Stadium Rd and Lumumba Ave, the Asian-run *Holiday Inn* is clean and good value, at TSh 1000 a double. Mosquito nets are provided. It's been recently renovated and has a good restaurant.

Places to Stay – middle

Not far from the Holiday Inn, just 100m off Lumumba Ave on Chunya Rd, is the *New Joseph Hotel*, which is highly recommended by local people. It's in the lower mid-range category.

Going up in price, there's the *Mbeya Hotel*, at the junction of Lumumba and Karume (Kaunda) Aves. This is owned by Tanzanian Corporation and is a pleasant, colonial-style hotel with comfortable rooms, clean sheets, mosquito nets and hot showers. Singles/doubles with private bathroom cost US$10/14 (payable in hard currency) including breakfast. There are also cheaper rooms with shared bathroom facilities. The hotel has a bar, and a restaurant which serves good food for TSh 600.

Places to Stay – top end

Top of the line are three hotels which offer amenities and cuisine comparable to other top-end hotels throughout Tanzania. They are the *Mt Livingstone Hotel, Mbeya Peak Hotel* and *Rift Valley Hotel*. You're looking at around US$35 to US$45 a double at any of them. They're all fairly close to the town centre and all have bars and restaurants.

Places to Eat

Most of the good bars and restaurants are in the above-mentioned hotels, though there are others in the town centre, close to the market and bus station.

The Tanzanian Coffee Board has a coffee shop on the corner of the market square, where you can get a good cup of coffee for a few shillings.

Getting There & Away

Bus There are five daily express buses between Mbeya and Dar es Salaam via Iringa and Morogoro (TSh 2500, 20 hours). The road is rough as far as Morogoro, after which it's an excellent sealed road. Zainabs bus company has been recommended as fast and comfortable. Advance booking is essential. The Dar es Salaam to Mbeya road goes through the Mikumi National Park, and there's a lot of game visible during the day, including elephant, giraffe, zebra and gazelle.

For details on the trip from Mbeya to Karonga (Malawi), see the Boat section in the Tanzania Getting There & Away chapter.

Train Trains on the TAZARA railway to Dar es Salaam or Kapiri Mposhi (Zambia) are heavily booked, so make a reservation well in advance. The express trains depart Mbeya at 11 am on Wednesday and Saturday and arrive in Dar es Salaam at 7 am the following day. The ordinary trains depart Mbeya at 4 pm on Tuesday, Friday and Sunday and arrive in Dar es Salaam at 3 pm the following day. Fares between Mbeya and Dar es Salaam are TSh 18,300 (1st class), TSh 12,000 (2nd class) and TSh 7200 (3rd class) on the ordinary train and TSh 19,400 (1st class), TSh 12,700 (2nd class) and TSh 7600 (3rd class) on the express train. Reservations can be made at the railway station, or at the Tanzanian Railways office in town, at the junction of Station Rd and Post St.

KYELA

If it's early in the day and you're on your way to the Malawi border, there's no need to come to Kyela, as the turn-off to the border is about five km back up the road towards Mbeya. From the turn-off, it's seven km to the border, which is open until 6 pm. If it's late, you may have to stay the night in Kyela.

TANZANIA

Places to Stay

The *Ram Hotel*, not far from the bus stand, is excellent value at TSh 600 a double with clean sheets and mosquito nets. The hotel has its own generator (so there are lights after dark) and good food is available. The *Salaam Hotel*, on the main road, has beds for TSh 400 per person, but the showers have cold water only.

THE MAKONDE PLATEAU

Hardly any traveller ever visits the south-eastern part of Tanzania adjacent to the Mozambique border, but this is where the famous makonde carvings originally came from (they've since been copied by artisans all over East Africa). It's also a very beautiful part of the country. Getting there involves a series of bus journeys and overnight stays in the towns en route, but there's no shortage of transport.

The first leg is a bus from Mbeya to Njombe via Makumbako, on the TAZARA railway line. The best place to stay in **Makumbako** is the *Lutheran Guest House*, opposite the railway station. It costs TSh 500 for a basic double room with cold bucket showers and shared toilet.

Njombe is one of the highest and coldest parts of Tanzania, so you'll need plenty of warm clothes. It's a prosperous agricultural area. The best place to stay here is the *Njomba Highland Green Hotel* – go down the hill from the bus station and turn left at the Eidina Hotel. It has luxurious doubles with private bathroom (hot water), two double beds, starched white linen, lounge chairs and soap and towel for TSh 1800. Tasty meals can be ordered in advance and cost TSh 300 (breakfast) and TSh 500 (dinner). The *Eidina Hotel* also offers cheap, tasty food.

Between Njombe and Songea is a new British-built road over a stunningly beautiful mountain area where a lot of coffee is grown. There are regular minibuses between the two towns and seats can be booked in advance. There are also regular buses between Songea and Dar es Salaam, which take about 24 hours, but you must book three days in advance as this route is heavily subscribed.

In **Songea**, there's a good choice of accommodation. Cheapest, but dirty, is the *Songea Deluxe Hotel*, which offers singles/doubles with shared toilet for TSh 450/500. Much better, but noisy between 6 am and 10 pm, is the *New Rombo Guest House*, behind the Mossile Music studio at the bus station, which offers clean doubles with shared toilet and cold bucket showers for TSh 750.

Up in price, the *New Nipu Guest House*, at the bus station, is very popular. Clean singles/doubles with shared toilet and cold bucket showers cost TSh 800/1000. It's comfortable but fills up early in the day.

For good, cheap, tasty food try the *Salama Hotel*, up the hill from the New Rombo Guest House.

The next leg of the journey is from Songea to **Tunduru** on a terrible road which goes through some of the most deserted countryside in Tanzania. It can sometimes take a week to do the 272 km between the two towns in a truck, but with luck it won't take you more than a day. There is also a bus every second day but it's very overcrowded. The fare is TSh 6000 and the journey should take about 13 hours given ideal conditions. The rest of the time you'll have to hire private Land Rovers which are much more expensive but take about 10 hours. Lodgings are available in Tunduru for about TSh 1000 per person.

Between Tunduru and **Masasi**, there's an all-weather gravel road, but the bus service is erratic and always very crowded. It leaves very early in the morning (about 4 am), costs TSh 2000 and takes about 12 hours to do the 200 km (including repair time).

Once at Masasi, you're on the Makonde Plateau, and from here there are daily buses to Lindi and Mtwara on the coast along a sealed road.

There is a regular ferry between Mtwara and Dar es Salaam operated by Adecon Marine. The ship is the FB *Canadian Spirit*, which does the journey once a week departing Dar es Salaam on Wednesday at 9 am and departing Mtwara on Friday at 5 pm. The journey between Dar es Salaam and Mtwara takes about 18 hours. See the Tanzania Getting Around chapter for further details about this ferry.

National Parks & Reserves

Kenya may well have the better-stocked game parks, and easier access to them, but Tanzania has the world famous Serengeti National Park and Ngorongoro Crater, with the Olduvai Gorge sandwiched between them. It also has Mt Kilimanjaro. Less famous but no less of a drawcard are Arusha, Tarangire and Lake Manyara national parks. All of these are within striking distance of Arusha, though Kilimanjaro is generally more easily approached from Moshi.

Serengeti has a huge animal population, and they're easy to see in the flat grassland of the park, especially in the dry season. At Ngorongoro, the game reserve encompasses the crater and sides of a huge extinct volcano, said to be the world's largest caldera.

Tanzania has many other national parks, but getting to those in the more remote western or southern parts of the country can be problematical, expensive or both. Accommodation at these more remote parks also tends to be limited to expensive game lodges unless you plan on camping. This doesn't mean that they're not worth the effort – they certainly are, especially the Selous Game Reserve, which is Tanzania's largest park. The Selous was also the very first game park to be set up in Tanzania, yet it remains a vast wilderness with facilities available only on the north-eastern fringes.

The national parks are open from 6 am to 7 pm. You are not permitted to drive in the parks at any other time.

Conservation & Wildlife Groups

If you want to get involved in anti-poaching measures and conservation activities in Tanzania (and help is needed in a big way), contact either the Tanzania Wildlife Protection Fund, PO Box 1994, Dar es Salaam, or the African Wildlife Foundation, PO Box 48177, Nairobi, Kenya (also 1717 Massachusetts Ave NW, Washington DC 20036, USA). The Wildlife Conservation Society of Tanzania, PO Box 70919, Dar es Salaam, does similar work.

All these societies do their best to protect wildlife and their habitats, help the recovery of endangered animal and plant species, and fund research into the management of wildlife and the impact of human beings on their habitats. Enquiries are welcome.

Park Entry Fees

All national park fees must be paid in hard currency (cash or travellers' cheques) unless you are a Tanzanian citizen, in which case you pay in local currency. The following fees are for each 24-hour period or part thereof.

	Noncitizen	Citizen
Adult entry	US$20	TSh 1500
Child entry	US$5	TSh 100
Vehicle entry		
up to 2000 kg	US$30	TSh 1000
over 2000 kg	US$150	TSh 10,000
Camping		
established sites	US$20	TSh 1000
'special' sites	US$40	TSh 2000
Guide/Ranger	US$10	TSh 500

The only exception to this fee structure is at the Gombe Stream National Park on Lake Tanganyika, where the park entry fee is US$100, or TSh 1500 for citizens (and the fees for children are US$20, or TSh 200 for citizens).

Charges for vehicle recovery in the event of an accident are TSh 50,000 (up to 2000 kg) and TSh 100,000 (over 2000 kg).

On Mt Kilimanjaro and Mt Meru, there are additional fees for use of mountain huts, rescue fees and fees for guides and porters, but these are specific to those national parks (see relevant sections for details).

Since foreigners must pay the above fees in hard currency it's important to bear in mind that if you don't have the exact amount, the park officials are entitled to give you the

TANZANIA

change in local currency at the official rate of exchange (ie not at foreign exchange bureau rates). Usually, they're more accommodating than this *if* you pay in cash dollars. If that's the case, you can usually arrange for the change to be paid in cash dollars, *if* they have it. Rather than assume this, it's better to sort this out between yourselves before you arrive at a park entry gate.

You may well hear (as we do) of travellers who have managed to negotiate part or all payment in local currency at some entry gates. You can safely assume that they've been very lucky. At most entry gates,

attempting to do this would simply be a waste of time.

You should also take heed of the warning in the Organised Safaris section of the Getting Around chapter regarding companies which cater for budget travellers and their commitment to pay park entry fees as part of the price of a safari. Some of these companies are banned from entering the parks because their cheques have bounced.

Books & Maps

There's a considerable amount of literature available on the various national parks. The

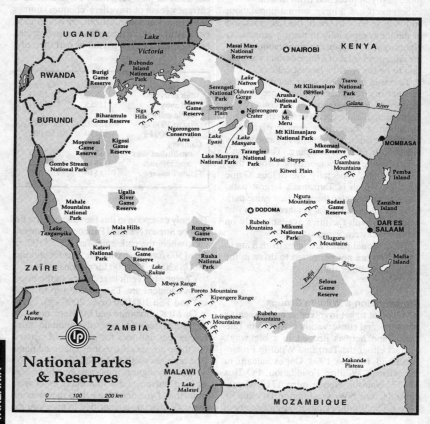

National Parks & Reserves

REGION	FEATURES
North-Eastern Tanzania	
Arusha National Park	With Ngurdoto Crater, Momela Lakes and Mt Meru, it is one of Tanzania's most beautiful and spectacular parks; a superb range of flora and fauna.
Lake Manyara National Park	Guaranteed sightings of giraffe, wildebeest, baboon and hippo and a chance of spotting elephant and the famous tree-climbing lion.
Mt Kilimanjaro National Park	The rainforest supports a wildlife population including elephant, buffalo, rhino, leopard and monkey but the grandeur of snowcapped Mt Kilimanjaro is the main drawcard.
Ngorongoro Conservation Area	The views from the crater rim are fantastic and the abundance of wildlife on the bottom is just as impressive, including thousands of flamingo wading in the shallow lake on the crater floor.
Serengeti National Park	Tanzania's most famous game park where you can see millions of hoofed animals, including up to two million wildebeest, on the move in search of grassland. It is one of the most amazing sights you'll ever see.
Tarangire National Park	During the dry season the park fills with herds of zebra, wildebeest and kongomi but you can see eland, lesser kudu, gazelle, buffalo, giraffe, waterbuck, impala, elephant, leopard and rhino all year round.
Lake Victoria	
Rubondo Island National Park	Sandy beaches, palm trees, forested rocky hills, papyrus swamps and lowland plains guarantee a terrific walking safari; rich in indigenous animal species.
Central & North Western Tanzania	
Gombe Stream National Park	The journey there by lake taxi is an experience in itself but the chimpanzee sanctuary, where groups of chimps are often seen at the research station, remains the major highlight.
Mahale Mountains National Park	A remote park with plenty of wildlife including chimpanzee, colobus monkey, guinea fowl and mongoose and in recent times leopard, lion and buffalo.
Ruaha National Park	Access is difficult and the place is undeveloped but it's swarming with elephant, hippo, crocodile, kudu, roan and sable antelope.
Southern Tanzania	
Mikumi National Park	Crawling with wildlife including elephant, hippo, lion, leopard, buffalo, zebra, impala, wildebeest and warthog all year round; includes a lush area of vegetation called Mkata River flood plain.
Selous Game Reserve	Huge, wild and largely untouched by humans, this reserve is teeming with wildlife. It's said to contain 100,000 elephants so there's every chance you'll see a herd of several hundred.

TANZANIA

best is a series of booklets written in association with the Tanzania National Parks, the African Wildlife Foundation or the Wildlife Conservation Society of Tanzania. These are priced between TSh 1000 and TSh 1500 and include detailed descriptions of the national parks, their geography, flora and fauna and tourist facilities, and include sketches and maps. The series includes *Kilimanjaro National Park, Ngorongoro Conservation Area, Serengeti National Park, Tarangire National Park, Arusha National Park, Mikumi National Park, Selous Game Reserve* and *Gombe Stream National Park.*

There's also an excellent series of booklets on various aspects of Ngorongoro Crater, published by the Ngorongoro Conservation Area Authority, which cover the geology, fauna and flora of the area though these are somewhat more expensive at TSh 4500 each. All these booklets are available at the book shops of the large hotels in Arusha and Dar es Salaam and sometimes at park entry gates.

The best maps of all to buy which cover the north-eastern parks are those put out by Gio (an Italian man) in association with Hoopoe Adventure Tours, Arusha. There are currently four of them: *Serengeti National Park, Lake Manyara National Park, Tarangire National Park* and *Ngorongoro Conservation Area.* All cost TSh 2500 each. These maps are literally works of art and in full colour and you'll see them pinned up in most safari company offices. You can find them for sale in many places but try Hoopoe Adventure Tours on India St in Arusha first. If, for some reason, you can't find them, they're distributed by Maco Ltd, PO Box 322, Zanzibar, Tanzania.

There's also an excellent large-scale (1:250,000) map of Serengeti National Park and Ngorongoro Crater put out by the Frankfurt Zoological Society (TSh 3500). It's hard to find these days but is very useful if you're driving your own vehicle.

Getting There & Around

You can safely assume that attempting to hitch into the national parks is a complete waste of time. You may well be able to get to the entry gates of the most popular parks but it's very unlikely you'll get any further. Most people arriving at a park entry gate will be either part of an organised safari group (in which case you've got next to no chance) or in their own vehicle (in which case they probably have lodge bookings and/or are loaded to the roof with supplies and camping equipment etc, so they'll be extremely reluctant to overload the vehicle with you and your gear or get involved in complications about where you're going to stay).

This being the case, there are basically only three ways to visit a national park: go on an organised safari, bring your own vehicle or rent your own vehicle. A list of recommended safari companies with a rundown of what they offer and their prices is given under Safaris in the Tanzania Getting Around chapter.

It's virtually impossible to rent a car for travel outside of Dar es Salaam, Arusha and Zanzibar. For more details, again see the Getting Around chapter.

As far as walking inside the parks goes, the only ones you're allowed to do this in are Kilimanjaro, Arusha, Selous, Mahale, Ruaha and Gombe Stream and, even here, it's compulsory to be accompanied by a guide or a ranger. There are, however, quite a number of walking safari options *outside* of the national parks especially in the north-east. For details, see under Other Safaris in the Tanzania Getting Around chapter.

The Parks & Reserves

ARUSHA NATIONAL PARK

Although it's one of Tanzania's smallest parks, Arusha is one of the most beautiful and spectacular. It's also one of the few that you're allowed to walk in (accompanied by a ranger). Yet, despite its attractions, few travellers appear to visit it, possibly because of their haste to press on to the more famous parks of Ngorongoro Crater, Serengeti and Mt Kilimanjaro. This is a profound mistake, since it has all the features of those three parks, including a superb range of flora and fauna.

The park's main features are Ngurdoto Crater (often dubbed Little Ngorongoro), the Momela Lakes and rugged Mt Meru (4556m), which overlooks the town of Arusha to the south. Because of the differing altitudes within the park (from 1500m to over 4500m) and the geological structure, there are several vegetation zones, which support different animal species.

The **Ngurdoto Crater** is surrounded by forest, while the actual crater floor is a swampy area. To the west of it lies Serengeti Ndogo (Little Serengeti), an extensive area of open grassland and the only place in the park where herds of Burchell's zebra can be found.

The **Momela Lakes**, like many in the Rift Valley, are shallow and alkaline and attract a wide variety of wader birds, particularly fla-

mingos. The lakes are fed largely from underground streams and, because of their different mineral content, each lake supports a different type of algal growth, which gives them each a different colour. As a result, the bird life varies quite distinctly from one stretch of water to another, even where they are separated by a strip of land only a few metres wide.

Mt Meru, which rivals Kilimanjaro, is a mixture of lush forest and bare rock and has a spectacular crater. On its eastern side is a sheer cliff face which rises over 1500m and is one of the tallest of its type in the world.

Animal life is abundant, and although it's impossible to predict what you will see and exactly where you will see it, you can be fairly certain of sighting zebra, waterbuck, reedbuck, klipspringer, hippopotamus, buffalo, elephant, hyena, mongoose, dik-dik, warthog, baboon, vervet and colobus monkeys. You might even catch sight of the

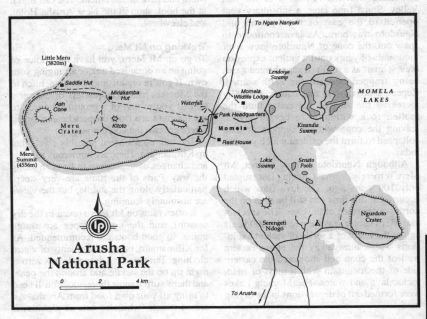

Arusha National Park

0   2   4 km

occasional leopard, but there are no lions in this park and, sadly, there are no rhinos due to poaching.

It's possible to see a good deal of the park in just one day – the Ngurdoto Crater, Momela Lakes and the lower slopes of Mt Meru – assuming you're in a vehicle. But this won't give you the chance to walk around, so it's much better to spend two days here, staying overnight at a camp site, the Momela Rest House or the Momela Game Lodge. A trek to the summit of Mt Meru usually takes three days, although the final day is very long. Alternatively you can split the trek over four days, or not go all the way to the summit (Rhino Point and Little Meru Peak make good intermediate places to aim for).

Park entry, hut and camping fees are exactly the same as those on Mt Kilimanjaro.

Geological Background
Mt Meru is a volcano formed about 20 million years ago during earth movements associated with the formation of the Rift Valley. Some time later, a subsidiary vent opened to the east of the volcano and Ngurdoto was born. As lava continued to spew out, the cone of Ngurdoto grew over thousands of years until a violent explosion blew it apart as a result of superheated gases being trapped beneath the earth's crust. Repeated activity of this nature gradually increased the size of the crater until the molten rock withdrew to deeper levels, leaving the cone without support. It then collapsed to form the caldera which you see today.

Although Ngurdoto is now extinct, Mt Meru is merely dormant, having last erupted only 100 years ago. The lava flow which occurred at this time can still be seen on the north-western side of the cone. The spectacular Meru Crater was formed 250,000 years ago as the result of a series of violent explosions which blew away the entire eastern wall of the cone and showered the eastern side of the mountain with a mass of mud, rocks, lava and water. The Momela Lakes were formed out of depressions in the drying mud.

History
The first European to sight Mt Meru was the Austrian Count Teleki von Szek, in 1876, at about the time of the volcano's last eruption. His comments about the prolific wildlife which he saw here suggest that it must once have rivalled Ngorongoro Crater as a sort of lost Garden of Eden. Later, in 1907, the Trappe family moved to the Momela region and set up a ranch and a game sanctuary, but when the park was created in 1960, it incorporated the ranch.

Information
Before visiting Arusha National Park, buy a copy of the booklet *Arusha National Park*, edited by Deborah Snelson and published by Tanzania National Parks in association with the African Wildlife Foundation. It contains an excellent description of the area and descriptions of all the animals, birds and plants to be found there, as well as notes on accommodation, transport, trekking Mt Meru and park management. You can find it at the book shop in the New Arusha Hotel, and elsewhere.

Trekking on Mt Meru
To go up Mt Meru, you have the choice of going on an organised trek or arranging your own. If you're organising your own, hitch to the Momela park headquarters or charter a taxi (if you're part of a group). The trek to the summit starts from the park headquarters. There are two huts on the way up.

The trek up Mt Meru possibly rivals that up Kilimanjaro. There are numerous animals and changes of vegetation to be seen along the way. Parts of the route are very steep, particularly along the saddle, but the views are absolutely stunning.

It often rains on Mt Meru (even in the dry season), and the upper slopes are rough going, so good boots are recommended. As for Kilimanjaro, bring along plenty of warm clothing. Temperatures drop to below zero at night up on the saddle and around the peak, and there's often snow there, too. You'll need to bring all your own food from Arusha. An armed ranger (who also acts as a guide) is compulsory and can be hired from the park headquarters at Momela. Porters are available and their fees are the same as for porters on Kilimanjaro, as are the expected tips at the end of the trek.

Bookings for the two mountain huts should be made in advance through the park warden (Arusha National Park, PO Box 3134, Arusha). It's also a good idea to book a guide in advance here so that you don't waste time waiting around park headquarters. If you go on an organised trek, the company will arrange all these bookings for you.

Organised Treks

Companies in Arusha which offer treks of Mt Meru include the following:

Hoopoe Adventure Tours
    PO Box 2047, India St, Arusha (☎ (057) 7011/7541; fax 8226). This company offers three-day Mt Meru treks for US$390 (minimum two people) all-inclusive.
Roy Safaris Ltd
    PO Box 50, Sokoine Rd, Arusha (☎ (057) 2115; fax 8892). This company offers the three-day trek for US$485 (minimum four people) or US$505 (minimum two people) all-inclusive.
Shidolya Tours & Safaris
    PO Box 1436, AICC, Serengeti Wing, Rooms 333-334, Arusha (☎ (057) 8506; fax 8242). Shidolya offers three-day treks of Mt Meru for US$330 regardless of numbers, which includes everything except tips.
Sunny Safaris Ltd
    PO Box 7267, Col Middleton Rd, Arusha (☎ (057) 7145; fax 8094). Sunny also offers three-day treks of Mt Meru for a comparable price to Roy Safaris and they're very reliable.
Tropical Tours
    PO Box 727, Goliondoi Rd (rear of Adventure Centre), Arusha (☎ (057) 8353; fax 8907). Tropical offers a slightly different trek of Mt Meru from the other companies by spending two nights at the Miriakamba Hut, once on the way up and again on the way down. The all-inclusive price of this four-day trek is US$480 (minimum two people).
Wild Spirit Safari Ltd
    PO Box 2288, India St, Arusha (☎ /fax (057) 4215). This comparatively new but enthusiastic company offers three-day treks of Mt Meru for US$280 (four people), US$285 (three people) and US$310 (two people). The price includes park entry, hut and rescue fees, food and one guide and two porters per person.

The Route

Assuming you take three days on the mountain, the usual route is:

Day 1 The first part of the walk is from the Momela park headquarters to Miriakamba Hut. This takes about three hours and leaves you the rest of the day to explore Meru Crater. The hut accommodates up to 48 people and firewood is provided.

Day 2 From Miriakamba Hut, it's a three hour walk to Saddle Hut and an afternoon trek up to the summit of Little Meru (3820m). Saddle Hut accommodates up to 24 people and firewood is provided.

Day 3 It's usual to start around 2 or 3 am. From Saddle Hut, you walk around the rim of Meru Crater to the summit of Mt Meru. This takes four to five hours. You then return to Saddle Hut (two to three hours) and then return all the way to Momela (another three to five hours). It's a long hard day.

It's obvious from the walking times mentioned that Mt Meru can be scaled in just two days, which makes this an option if your time and/or money is limited, but it does limit what you will see on the way and you need to be fairly fit. It may not be Kilimanjaro, but it's not that small either, so rushing up means altitude sickness is fairly likely.

Organised Day Trips

Several safari companies in Arusha arrange day trips to the park, but they're expensive unless you're part of a group of between five and seven people. Check out Sunny Safaris (around US$120 with five people), Peacock Tours & Safaris (US$115 with five people, US$110 with six people and US$105 with seven people – all-inclusive) and Hoopoe Adventure Tours (US$170 regardless of numbers plus US$20 park entry fee).

If you can't afford the above but would like to experience rural Tanzanian village life outside of the park boundaries yet still in the foothills of Mt Meru, get in touch with Japhet and Victor at Sunny Safaris. These two experienced guides offer a full day's hike taking in local Maasai villages, leaving Sunny Safaris at 8.30 am and returning to Arusha at around 4 pm. All you need to bring is water and a packed lunch and it's a bargain at just US$12 assuming a minimum of four people. They can also arrange longer walking safaris on request to places like Lake Eyasi via Ngorongoro.

Places to Stay

There are three *camp sites* at Momela (close to the park headquarters) and another at Ngurdoto. All cost the usual US$20 per person per night and all have water, toilet facilities and firewood.

There's also a very pleasant self-help *Rest House* near the Momela Gate which accommodates up to five people. There are superb views from here up tthrough Meru Crater to the peak of Mt Meru. Bookings can be made through the Warden, Arusha National Park, PO Box 3134, Arusha.

Just outside the park, north of the Momela Gate, is the *Momela Wildlife Lodge* (☎ (057) 6423), PO Box 999, Arusha, which can accommodate up to 40 people. Bed and breakfast costs US$56/74 for singles/ doubles with private bathroom or US$68/98 with half board. Lunch boxes can be arranged if ordered in advance. The lodge has excellent views of Mt Meru and Mt Kilimanjaro.

Getting There & Around

The park is 21 km from Arusha and is reached by turning off the main Arusha to Moshi road at the signpost for the national park and Ngare Nanyuki.

There's an excellent series of gravel roads and tracks within the park which will take you to all the main features and viewing points. Most are suitable for saloon cars, though some of the tracks get slippery in the wet seasons (October and November and between March and May). There are also a few tracks which are only suitable for 4WD vehicles.

When driving around the park you don't need a guide, but if you intend to walk, an armed guide/ranger is compulsory because of the danger of buffalo. A guide/ranger is also compulsory if you intend to trek Mt Meru. Guides/rangers can be hired for US$10 a day from the park headquarters at Momela. While you can drive or walk around the Ngurdoto Crater rim, you are not allowed to walk down to the crater floor.

GOMBE STREAM NATIONAL PARK

Primarily a chimpanzee sanctuary, this tiny park covers 52 sq km on the shores of Lake Tanganyika between Kigoma and the Burundi border, stretching between the lake shore and the escarpment a little further inland. In recent years, it has become very popular with travellers going north to or coming south from Burundi, although with Burundi basically a no-go area it's likely that visitor numbers will fall away sharply. It's well worth the effort to get here, and the journey by lake taxi makes an interesting alternative to the MV *Liemba*.

The park is the site of Jane Goodall's research station, which was set up in 1960. It's a beautiful place and the chimps are great fun. A group of them usually comes down to the research station every day, but if they don't, the rangers generally know where to find them. You must have a guide whenever you are away from the park headquarters at **Kasekela** on the lake shore. You can share the guide fee of US$10 between however many people are with you.

Entry to the park costs US$100 per person for each 24-hour period (US$20 for children between the ages of five and 16).

Places to Stay & Eat

Camping is only possible with special permission, which for most travellers means staying at the '*hostel*'. It consists essentially of caged huts, each with six beds and a table and chairs (they're caged to keep the baboons out). A bed costs US$10 per night.

Bring all your own food, though eggs and fish are sometimes available at the station. If you run out of food, you can get more at

TANZANIA

Mwamgongo village, about 10 km north of here at the northern extremity of the park. The village has a market twice a week (enquire at the station as to the days). Be careful when walking between the cookhouse and the huts at the station, especially if you are carrying food. Baboons have jumped on quite a few people and robbed them of food. The hostel also has a well-stocked library.

Getting There & Away

There are no roads to Gombe Stream, so the only way in is to take one of the lake taxis – small, motorised wooden boats – which service the lake-shore villages all the way from Kigoma to the Burundi border.

From Kigoma, the lake taxis leave from the small village of Kalalangabo, about three km north of town, usually between 9 and 10 am. The trips to Gombe Stream and from there to Kagunga (the last village in Tanzania) take about three hours each and cost TSh 250 per person for each leg of the journey. These boats do not operate on Sundays, and it is therefore important not to arrive on a Saturday, otherwise you'll be up for two days park entry fees (US$200) and hostel fees (US$40).

LAKE MANYARA NATIONAL PARK

Lake Manyara National Park is generally visited as the first stop on a safari which takes in this park and Ngorongoro and Serengeti. It's generally a bit of a letdown, apart from the hippos, since the large herds of elephant which used to inhabit the park have been decimated in recent years. Because the park is too small, the elephants invade adjoining farmland for fodder during the dry season. Naturally, local farmers have been none too pleased, and once outside the park boundaries, the elephants are fair game (and their ivory is worth a lot of money).

Even the water birds which come to nest here (greater and lesser flamingos in particular) can usually only be seen from a distance because there are no roads to the lake shore, though this may have changed recently as the level of the lake has shrunk and there are

large expanses of open sand. You will certainly see wildebeest, giraffe and baboon and you may well see the famous tree-climbing lion. The trouble is, most safaris to Manyara only spend a day here, so what you see is limited.

There is a reasonably interesting market in the nearby village of Mto-wa-Mbu – mainly fabrics and crafts – but they see a lot of tourists here, so it's very commercialised and bargains are hard to find. Indeed, it's possibly cheaper to buy the same thing in Arusha.

Places to Stay & Eat

There are two *camp sites* just outside the park entrance, which is just down the road from Mto-wa-Mbu (River of Gnats or Mosquito Village, according to various translations, and whichever one you choose, it's true). *Camp Site No 2* is probably the better. You can either pitch a tent here or rent one of the bandas, which contain two beds, blankets and sheets and have running water, a toilet and firewood. Insect repellent and/or a mosquito net would be very useful and you need to beware of thieving baboons.

Avoid camping at any sites within the park, as they're all so-called 'special camps', which will cost you US$40 per person per night.

Budget and mid-range accommodation is available in Mto-wa-Mbu village. There are several budget hotels around the market/craft square, including the *Rift Valley Bar & Hotel*, which has doubles with shared bathroom facilities for TSh 1500 per person including free condoms, and the *Camp Vision Traders Ltd*, which costs TSh 1500/2000 for singles/doubles with shared bathroom facilities. Despite the name, you cannot camp here and there's no restaurant.

There's also the *Kibo Guest House*, which has doubles for TSh 2000 without breakfast and a restaurant which offers nyama choma, and the *Rombo Star Guest House* (very basic).

The best place to stay in Mto-wa-Mbu, however, is the popular *Holiday Fig Resort* (☎ 2), which is set in its own leafy grounds off the main street and has a swimming pool, bar and restaurant. It's a very friendly place run by Zulekha and her daughter Shaina. The beds are large and clean and the rooms have private bathroom. It costs US$15/30 for singles/doubles including breakfast. You can also camp here for US$5 per person, and there's guarded parking as well as vehicles which can take you into the national park. Look for the hotel's signpost on the main street.

Further down the street which takes you to the Holiday Fig Resort are the *Manyara Guest House* and the *Lutheran Evangelical Guest House*. The latter offers full-board facilities. Up on top of the escarpment overlooking Lake Manyara is the *Starehe Bar & Hotel*. It's about 100m off to the left along the turn-off for the Lake Manyara Hotel (signposted) on the main road from Mto-wa-Mbu to Ngorongoro. It's rustic but very clean and comfortable and there are no bugs, mosquitoes or electricity (though candles are provided). There are hot showers, and the staff are eager to please and very friendly, and will cook you superb, generous meals. Accommodation costs TSh 3000 per person.

Lake Manyara Hotel (☎ (057) 3300) is the place to stay for luxury hotel accommodation. It sits right on the edge of the escarpment overlooking Lake Manyara, about three km along the same turn-off on which the Starehe Bar stands. It's part of the Accor/Tahi Hotel chain. Singles/doubles cost US$110/138 including breakfast. The hotel has flower gardens, a swimming pool, petrol pumps and a curio shop. Reservations can be made at the Novotel Mount Meru in Arusha.

Also up on top of the escarpment overlooking the lake, but on the opposite side of the main Lake Manyara to Ngorongoro road, is Hoopoe Adventure Tours' *Kirurumu Tented Camp* (☎ (057) 7011). It's about 13 km from the main road (signposted) and has become very popular with safari companies. The twin-bed tents are clean and comfortable and the showers (bucket hot water provided) and toilets are shared. It costs US$20/25 for singles/doubles (children under 10 years are half price), or you can camp for US$5 per

person (tent provided) or US$3 per person (own tent). Delicious meals are available in the mess tent for US$2.50 (breakfast) and US$7 (lunch/dinner), and there's a plentiful supply of cold beer.

MAHALE MOUNTAINS NATIONAL PARK

This national park, like Gombe Stream, is mainly a chimpanzee sanctuary but you won't find it marked on many maps since it was only created in 1985. It's on the knuckle-shaped area of land which protrudes into Lake Tanganyika about halfway down the lake, opposite the Zaïrese port of Kalemie.

The highest peak in the park, Nkungwe (2460m), ensures that moist air blowing in from the lake condenses there and falls as rain. This rain supports extensive montane forests, grasslands and alpine bamboo. Numerous valleys intersect the mountains, and some of these have permanent streams which flow into the lake. The eastern side of the mountains is considerably drier and supports what is known as miombo woodlands. It's a very isolated area.

The animals which live in this park show closer affinities with western rather than eastern Africa. They include chimpanzee, brush-tailed porcupine, various species of colobus monkey (including the Angolan black-and-white colobus), guinea fowl and mongoose. Scientists, mainly from Japan, have been studying the chimpanzees for 20 years, during which time more than 100 of the animals have been habituated to human contact. The population has dramatically increased since 1975, when local people were moved to villages outside the park, thus putting a stop to poaching and field-burning activities. This relocation has also led to the reappearance of leopard, lion and buffalo, which were never (or very rarely) seen in the past.

Mahale is also one of the parks which you can walk around – there are no roads in any case. Very few tourists come here because of the remoteness of the area, but it's well worth it if you have the time and initiative.

The best time to visit is between May and October.

Places to Stay

Camping is allowed in specific *camping areas* if you have equipment (otherwise there may be a limited amount for hire). Camping fees are US$20 per person per day. There's also a *guesthouse* at Kasiha village, though the facilities are very limited. Bring all your food from Kigoma, since meals are not available. It's a good idea to check with the park headquarters in Kigoma about current conditions, transport and accommodation before setting off.

Getting There & Away

The only way to get to the park is by lake steamer from Kigoma using either the MV *Liemba* or the MV *Mwongozo*. You have to get off at Lagosa (otherwise known as Mugambo), usually in the middle of the night, and take a small boat to the shore. From Lagosa, charter a small boat from the local fishers or merchants for the trip to Kasoge (about three hours). For the MV *Liemba* schedule, see the Tanzania Getting There & Away chapter. For the MV *Mwongozo* schedule, enquire in Kigoma.

Because you will be reliant on the lake steamers for getting into and out of Mahale, you may have to stay there for a whole week. This is obviously going to be expensive in terms of park entry and camping fees, so you need to think seriously about this before you go. It also means you'll have to bring enough food with you from Kigoma to last a week.

MIKUMI NATIONAL PARK

Mikumi National Park covers 3237 sq km and sits astride the main Dar es Salaam to Mbeya highway, about 300 km from Dar es Salaam. Not many budget travellers seem to visit this park, probably because of the lack of cheap accommodation, but there is a lot of wildlife to be seen. Elephant, lion, leopard, buffalo, zebra, impala, wildebeest and warthog can be viewed at any time of the year.

One of the principal features of Mikumi is the Mkata River flood plain, an area of lush vegetation which particularly attracts elephant and buffalo. Hippo can also be seen at Hippo Pools, about five km from the park entrance gate.

Mikumi is often visited as a weekend outing from Dar es Salaam. Most of the safari companies with branches in Dar es Salaam offer trips there.

Places to Stay

For those on a budget, there are three *camp sites* in the park (US$20 per person per night), as well as a *youth hostel* at the park headquarters, which has a capacity for 50 people. None of the camp sites has water, but they do have toilets and firewood. If you're staying at the youth hostel, bring your own bedding. There are toilet and cooking facilities. If you're camping, bring everything you need except firewood. Bookings for the youth hostel can be made through the Chief Park Warden, Mikumi National Park, PO Box 62, Mikumi, Morogoro.

Considerably higher in price is the *Mikumi Wildlife Tented Camp* (☎ (051) 68631 in Dar es Salaam), a luxury tented camp which costs slightly less than the lodge and has 10 tents at present. It's managed by the Oyster Bay Hotel in Dar es Salaam, through which bookings should be made.

The *Mikumi Wildlife Lodge* is built around a watering hole and is the place to stay if you're looking for creature comforts. It's owned by the TTC (☎ (051) 27671), PO Box 2485, Dar es Salaam, and costs US$45/55 a single/double including breakfast, plus 25% tax and service charges. Between Easter Monday and 30 June there's a 50% discount. The lodge has a swimming pool, gift shop and petrol station.

MT HANANG

Mt Hanang, at 3417m, is Tanzania's third-highest mountain but is not a national park. If mountain trekking is your passion but you can't afford the park entry and camping fees, then you could consider trekking Mt Hanang. See Walking Safaris in the Tanzania Getting Around chapter for full details.

MT KILIMANJARO NATIONAL PARK

An almost perfectly shaped volcano which

rises sheer from the plains, Mt Kilimanjaro is one of Africa's most magnificent sights. Snowcapped and not yet extinct, at 5895m it is the highest peak on the continent.

From cultivated farmlands on the lower levels, it rises through lush rainforest to alpine meadow and finally across a barren lunar landscape to the twin summits. The rainforest is home to many animals, including elephant, buffalo, rhino, leopard and monkey. You may encounter herds of eland on the saddle between the summits of Mawenzi and Kibo.

Geological Background

Kilimanjaro is a relative newcomer to the Rift Valley and didn't even exist between one and two million years ago. At that time, where Kilimanjaro now stands, there was just an undulating plain with a few old eroded mountains. But that all changed with movements of the earth's crust associated with the rift. Lava poured out from the fractures that were created and eventually gave rise to an enormous ridge, which is now represented by the nearby peaks of Ol Molog, Kibongoto and Kilema.

Kilimanjaro began to grow about 750,000 years ago as a result of lava spewing out of three main centres – Shira, Kibo and Mawenzi. It kept growing until their cones reached a height of about 5000m about half a million years ago. About this time, Shira collapsed into a caldera and became inactive, but Kibo and Mawenzi continued to erupt until their peaks reached about 5500m. Mawenzi was the next to die, but Kibo continued to be active until about 360,000 years ago, during which time there were some particularly violent eruptions, including one which filled the old eroded caldera of Shira with black lava.

From an estimated final height of 5900m, Kibo gradually fell silent, and though intermittent eruptions continued for thousands of years, the whole mountain began to shrink and Kibo's cone collapsed into a series of concentric terraces. Erosion, in the form of glaciers which came and went, wore the peaks down even more, as did a huge landslide about 100,000 years ago which created the Kibo Barranco.

Kibo finally died after a last fling of violent activity which created the present caldera and the lava flows known as the Inner Crater and Ash Pit. Then the glaciers returned to continue their work. Meanwhile, the forests and alpine vegetation claimed what they could of the mountain, and streams sculpted the sides of the massif into the shape it is today. Interestingly, it appears that Kilimanjaro, like Mt Kenya, is gradually losing its glaciers due to the gradual warming of the earth's atmosphere.

Trekking Kilimanjaro

Kilimanjaro can be trekked at any time of the year, but there's usually a lot of rain during April, May and November. It's also best to avoid trekking during the Christmas/New Year period, as all the huts will be fully booked.

It is a traveller's dream to scale the summit, watch the dawn break and gaze out over vast expanses of East African bushland. Nevertheless, it's going to cost you around US$400 minimum for a standard five-day trek along the Marangu route which most people do (plus US$70 to US$80 for each additional day) and considerably more than this if you make the ascent up any of the other routes. These costs include park entry fees, hut fees, rescue fees, food, guide, porters and, usually, transport to Marangu, but exclude the hire of camping gear and clothing/footwear. The bulk of this is payable in hard currency – cash or travellers' cheques – as it represents national park entry and hut fees. See later in this section for a list of tour companies.

Safety Too many people try to scale Mt Kilimanjaro without sufficient acclimatisation and end up with altitude sickness or, at the very least, nausea and headaches. This is obviously going to detract from your enjoyment and prevents quite a few people from reaching the summit. Scaling a 5895m mountain is no Sunday school picnic! See the health section in the Regional Facts for the Visitor chapter for more information about altitude sickness.

To give yourself the best chance of reaching the top, it's a very good idea to stay at the Horombo Hut for two nights instead of one, though this will not guarantee you plain sailing. You won't get the same benefits from staying two nights at the Kibo Hut as it's too high and you won't be able to sleep very much.

Also, whatever else you do, walk *pole pole* (slowly), drink a lot of liquid, suck glucose tablets and eat all you can to stay strong. Staying two nights at the Horombo Hut is going to make the trek into a six-day affair and increase your costs, so bear this in mind and make sure that the guides and porters understand what you have in mind before setting off.

There's a very funny but accurate description of what it's like trekking Kilimanjaro in Mark Savage's *Kilimanjaro – Map & Guide*. Make sure you read it!

Books & Maps The best map of Kilimanjaro is *Kilimanjaro – Map & Guide* (1:75,000), by Andrew Wielochowski. It has an excellent topographical map of Kilimanjaro on one side and details of the geology, flora and fauna, weather and climate, history, walking and trekking routes on the other. Similar is *Kilimanjaro – Map & Guide* (1:50,000), by Mark Savage, except that this cuts off the trailheads. Both are available from most book shops in Nairobi, or you may be able to get one from the book shop in the New Arusha Hotel in Arusha. They're not available in either Moshi or Marangu.

Lonely Planet's *Trekking in East Africa* covers Mt Meru, Kilimanjaro and other long walks through Tanzania, including a trek through the region north of Ngorongoro Crater.

An excellent booklet to take on your trek is *Kilimanjaro National Park*, which was written by Jeanette Hanby in association with the Tanzania National Parks and the African Wildlife

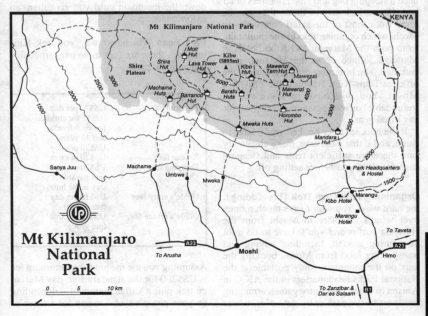

Foundation. It contains descriptions of all the possible routes up Kilimanjaro, the climate, flora and fauna, mountain medicine and tourist facilities, complete with maps and illustrations. It's for sale in Arusha (at book shops in the large hotels) and in Dar es Salaam.

For those intending to rock climb, as opposed to just walking, the *Guide to Mt Kenya & Kilimanjaro*, edited by Iain Allan, is worth chasing up. You won't be able to get a copy from the Mountain Club of Kenya (PO Box 45741, Nairobi) or from book shops in Nairobi. You won't be able to buy it in Tanzania.

For any other information, get in touch with the Kilimanjaro Mountain Club, PO Box 66, Moshi, Tanzania.

Clothing & Equipment No specialist equipment is required to trek Kilimanjaro but you do need a strong pair of boots, and plenty of warm clothing, including gloves, a woollen hat and waterproof overclothes. You also need a sleeping bag and small mattress or air bed. If you lack any of these, they can be hired from most of the safari companies in Moshi which organise treks up the mountain, from both the Marangu and Kibo hotels in Marangu village or at the Marangu park entrance. The hire rates are posted up in the office at Trans-Kibo Travels at the YMCA in Moshi. You will have to leave money (refundable) or your passport as a deposit for any hired gear.

If the huts are fully booked you'll have to camp, and if that's the case, make absolutely sure there are sufficient tents and sleeping bags for all of you *before* setting off.

Organising Your Own Trek This is doing it the hard way! You won't save much money over what's on offer in Moshi from the cheapest outfits and you'll have to do a lot of running around, including buying and transporting food from Moshi, booking the huts on the mountain (only possible at the National Parks headquarters in the AICC in Arusha or at the park entry gates), arranging transport to the park entry gate plus, where

necessary, hiring equipment or extra clothing.

A saving of US$50 overall is about all you can expect, and for that you'll have to carry all your own food and gear and do your own cooking on the trek. Nevertheless, if you're determined you can do it, as it's not compulsory to do the trek through a safari company. A guide (compulsory) and porters (optional) can be arranged at the park entry gate, but remember that even if you don't engage porters to carry your own gear, the guide will demand his own. Clothing and the like can be hired from the park entry gate or from the Marangu and Kibo hotels in Marangu.

Think seriously before doing it yourself because it can be a major hassle, the huts may be booked out, forcing you to camp, and you don't know who you're going to get as a guide. Some of them are good, especially when they work regularly for specific companies and are looking for continuous work; others can make your life a misery to the point of even refusing to guide you back down the mountain until you give them an extortionate tip.

Park Fees Whichever way you trek Kilimanjaro, there are fees to be paid since this is a national park.

Park entry fees	US$20 per day (US$5 for children between five and 16 years)
Hut fees	US$20 per day
Rescue fee	US$20 per trek
Camping fees	US$20 per day (not payable if you stay in the huts)
Guide's entry fees	US$10 per day (per group)
Guide's rescue fee	US$20 per trek (per group)

Assuming you use the huts, the minimum fee is US$200 for the standard five-day Marangu trek plus a variable amount – depending on your group's size – to pay for a share of the guide's entry and also for rescue fees, and all this must be paid in hard currency. It's considerably more on the other routes because the trek takes longer. To this minimum-fee figure you must add the entry fees (TSh 500 per day) of any porters you engage but this can be paid in Tanzanian shillings.

Guides & Porters Daily wages are negotiable but the less you pay, the more problems you'll have. Reputable safari companies pay, on average, around US$16 per day for guides and US$8 per day for porters on the Marangu route. On the Machame route it's more like US$22 per day for guides and US$11 per day for porters because it's a harder trek. If it's raining, guides and porters are entitled to demand a 50% increase in the wages which they've agreed to. Not all safari companies pay the sort of rates specified above but you can safely assume that no guide or porter will work for less than half these amounts.

Whether you take an organised trek or organise your own, the guide and porters will expect a tip at the end of the trek. Be generous about this but don't be profligate. Unfortunately, a lot of affluent tourists have been tipping excessively over the last few years so guides commonly attempt to squeeze outrageous amounts out of punters. We've heard figures as high as US$100 per day for the guide and US$50 per day for the porters! This is ridiculous when you consider the average wage levels in Tanzania. A reasonable guideline is US$10 per day for the guide and US$5 per day for each porter shared between however many of you there are in your group. Nevertheless, you can expect a hassle and even threats to abandon you on the summit unless you tip them *before* the descent and by an amount which the guide considers he can squeeze out of you. A lot of people have had nasty altercations about this.

You must head this sort of nonsense off before you start the trek. Have it clearly understood that the tips will be given *only on completion of the trek*, and don't compromise on this. Better still, negotiate a figure for tips *before even starting the trek*.

Another ruse which is becoming common is for the guide to claim that there were more porters than there actually were so your tip must be increased. Be sure how many porters there actually are, and if any of them 'disappear' during the trek, adjust your tip accordingly. And don't put up with any threats – tell the guide firmly to get his act together. And report it to the park authorities.

Accommodation The Marangu route is the most popular of all the trails up Kilimanjaro and most of those who take it find it convenient to stay in the village of Marangu the night before starting a trek. You don't have to do this unless you want to since the drive from Moshi only takes about one hour, but staying the night at Marangu generally guarantees you an early start the following morning. See the Marangu section in the North-Eastern Tanzania chapter for full details of the options.

On the other routes (Machame, Umbwe, Mweka, Shira and Rongai) accommodation near the trailheads is very limited so it's probably best to stay in Arusha or Moshi the night before starting a trek.

Organised Treks
Most people who trek Kilimanjaro, unlike Mt Kenya, opt to go on an organised tour. There are good reasons for this. Most of the charges are standard and a guide is compulsory in any case. Also, as the trek takes a minimum of five days, organising your own trek involves a lot of running around, which is difficult without your own transport.

Competition for business is fierce both in Moshi and Arusha, so it's easy to find a company which will offer you the trek for US$380 or even less, all-inclusive. Some people come out of these cheap deals smiling; most people definitely do not. A great deal depends on your own attitude. If you're very fit and prepared to carry your own gear the whole way, not fussy about food quality, don't care whether there's a bed for you at the huts and are used to roughing it, then you might come out smiling.

Ask yourself how a company can organise

TANZANIA

a trek for just US$380 per person when their minimum costs should be around US$320 per person, unless they are cutting corners. And there's the rub. The majority of companies offering US$380 treks do cut corners. That means basic food and grumbling porters and a guide who will hit you for an extortionate tip, and maybe even no transport back to Moshi or Arusha at the end of the trek. And if you think you're going to be compensated for any of this, forget it. No-one ever gets a refund let alone a sympathetic hearing of grievances on a US$380 trek.

If you want a well-organised trek with good food and your heavy gear carried by porters who don't 'disappear' halfway through the trip, as well as guaranteed transport back to Moshi or Arusha at the end of the trek, then think in terms of US$450 per person minimum.

It's probably true to say that the cheapest deals are available in Moshi rather than Arusha, but this is not always the case, particularly if you want good accommodation the night before and the night after a trek, as some safari companies in Arusha can offer deals on the hotel accommodation which you would not be able to match through your own efforts. Also some hotels which organise Kilimanjaro treks offer substantial discounts on their room rates if you book through them.

Moshi & Marangu Tour Companies Those in search of rock-bottom treks and negotiated prices should check out the following companies in Moshi:

Mauly Tours & Travels
PO Box 1315, Moshi (☎ (055) 52787; fax 53330). This outfit can offer you treks on any of the routes to the summit and quote US$420 for the standard five-day Marangu route (plus US$80 for each extra day), including transport to and from Marangu, but will negotiate down to US$380 in the low season. For the Machame route, they quote US$750 (seven days). They also have equipment for hire.

Kilimanjaro Guide Tours & Safaris
PO Box 210, Moshi (☎ (055) 50120; fax 51220). This outfit operates out of a wooden hut (signposted) directly opposite Moshi Hotel/Air Tanzania in Moshi. They offer the standard Marangu route for US$420 and the Machame route for US$600. The people are friendly, know the scene and will negotiate on prices.

Shah Tours & Travels Ltd
PO Box 1821, Moshi (☎ (055) 52370/52988; fax 51449). This company offers the Marangu route (five days, four nights) for a group of four at $450 per person, leaving from Marangu. Transport to/from Moshi, if required, is $35 for the vehicle (otherwise take the local bus). They offer the Machame route for six days, five nights at $700 per person, including transport from Moshi. For larger groups, or individuals wanting to join a group already going, Shah Tours will negotiate on price. Their office is in Moshi about 100m west of the clock tower.

Marangu Hotel
PO Box 40, Moshi (☎ (055) 50639; fax 51307). Although there is no negotiation on prices, this hotel (at Marangu) is quite willing to organise what it calls 'hard way' treks on the standard five-day Marangu route for US$335 per person including national park fees, hut bookings, a guide, two porters per trekker and transport to and from the park entry gate, but you must bring all your own food and equipment and cater for yourself. This is about the cheapest responsible offer you will find but it's definitely no-frills. How they do it at this price is beyond us.

Natural Action Ltd
PO Box 864, Marangu (☎ (055) 51309. This company offers budget treks for travellers. Their office is at the Hotel Capricorn, near the bus stand in Marangu – you can walk in and arrange things on the spot. They also offer more specialist, and more expensive, treks on the longer routes such as Machame and Umbwe.

Babylon Lodge
PO Box 227, Marangu (☎ 5 Marangu – go through the operator). This lodge offers the standard five-day Marangu trek for US$400 with extra days at US$70, excluding transport to Marangu and accommodation before and after a trek. This price is negotiable for large groups.

If you'd like a little more grease on the wheels and basic creature comforts without the organisational headaches, check out the following companies. You can safely assume that the prices quoted by all of these outfits include park fees, hut fees, guide and porters' fees and wages, food, guaranteed hut bookings and transport to and from the trailheads. Most of them will also endeavour to make up shortfalls in any equipment which you may be lacking but you should not take this for granted. Try to bring as much with you as possible.

Kilimanjaro-Serengeti Tours & Travels

PO Box 8213, Moshi (☎ (055) 51287). This company has its offices just off Kibo Rd not far from the clock tower at the back of Helen's Restaurant & Take-Away. It offers standard Marangu treks for US$420 per person (minimum four people) with extra days at US$70 per person including camping gear and one night's accommodation at a hotel either before or after a trek. They also offer the Machame route for US$800 per person or US$700 per person if there is a minimum of three to four people.

Key's Hotel

PO Box 933, Moshi (☎ (055) 52250; fax 50073). Key's offers the standard Marangu treks for US$445 per person (assuming a minimum of four people) with extra days at US$90 per person, as well as a six-day Machame route for US$740 per person (assuming a minimum of four people) with extra days at US$115 per person. All these prices include two nights half board at Key's Hotel. It's a popular company to go with and they're completely reliable.

Trans-Kibo Travels Ltd

PO Box 558, Moshi (☎ (055) 52017; fax 50096). This outfit, based at the YMCA in Moshi, has been in business for years and is very reliable. It has daily departures for Kilimanjaro at 10 am and quotes US$450 per person for the five-day Marangu trek (assuming three or more trekkers) with extra days at US$80 per person. These charges are exclusive of accommodation before and after the trek and any equipment you may need. For the Machame, Umbwe and Mweka routes they quote US$800 per person (six days) but this is exclusive of accommodation before or after the trek, food and any equipment you may need.

MJ Safaris International Ltd

PO Box 9593, Moshi (☎ /fax (055) 52017) or PO Box 6031, AICC, Ngorongoro Wing, Room 105, Arusha (☎ (057) 6863). This company offers the standard five-day Marangu route for the same price as Trans-Kibo Travels and can also arrange treks along the other routes for a comparable price.

Marangu Hotel

PO Box 40, Moshi (☎ (055) 50639). In addition to offering the 'hard way' treks, this outfit offers fully serviced treks for US$490 to US$570 (depending on numbers) plus US$130 for each extra day, including transport to and from the park entrance gate. Like the Key's Hotel, it offers concession rates for hotel accommodation if you go on one of its treks.

Kibo Hotel

PO Box 102, Marangu (☎ Marangu 4 – through operator; fax (055) 51308). The Kibo offers daily departures on the Marangu route for US$300 per person plus park fees (US$200). Extra days beyond the standard five cost US$60 per person per day. It also offers the Machame route at US$580 per person (six days) plus park fees (US$350). Extra days cost US$100 per person. The management at the Kibo are medically trained to treat altitude sickness should you have a bad case of it and they have the appropriate medication and oxygen. No other company, at present, offers this sort of facility.

Arusha Tour Companies If you book through an Arusha tour company on the Marangu route, make sure they're not going to subcontract it out to a Moshi company, as otherwise you'll have given up your ability to negotiate and will end up paying two lots of commission. On any of the other routes up Kilimanjaro, except Mweka, it's not a concern as the trailheads are all off the main Arusha-Moshi road so you don't go through Moshi to start a trek. The following lists some of the companies, arranged in alphabetical order not in order of preference or cost:

Hoopoe Adventure Tours

PO Box 2047, India St, Arusha (☎ (057) 7011; fax 82226). This long-established and very reliable company offers five-day treks of Kilimanjaro along the Marangu route for US$600 (minimum four people) including two nights half board at the Kibo Hotel. Extra days are US$80 per person. This is an excellent deal considering the normal price of accommodation at the Kibo Hotel. They also offer the Machame route (six days) for US$1110 (minimum two people) with extra nights at US$100 per person but this does not include accommodation before or after the trek.

Kibo Express Guide & Safaris

PO Box 11439, YMCA, India St, Arusha (☎ (057) 7460; fax 8220). Again, this is a small but reliable company which offers the standard five-day Marangu trek for US$500 excluding accommodation before or after a trek. Ask for Musa at the YMCA if you'd like more details.

Peacock Tours & Safaris Ltd

PO Box 10123, Arusha (☎ (057) 7884; fax 8256). This company offers six-day treks of Kilimanjaro along the Marangu route for US$800 regardless of numbers but the price does not include accommodation before or after a trek.

TANZANIA

Roy Safaris Ltd
  PO Box 50, Sokoine Rd, Arusha (☎ (057) 2115; fax 8892). This company has been in business for years and can arrange a standard five-day Marangu trek for US$550 (minimum three people).

Shidolya Tours & Safaris
  PO Box 1436, AICC, Serengeti Wing, Rooms 333-334, Arusha (☎ (057) 8506; fax 8242). This small but reliable company offers five-day Kilimanjaro treks along the Marangu route for US$420 all-inclusive or US$460 for a six-day trek. They also do a six-day trek along the Machame route for US$700 or US$780 for seven days. The price does not include accommodation before or after a trek.

Simba Safaris
  PO Box 1207, Arusha (☎ (057) 3509; fax 8207). This company offers what is possibly the most expensive trek available. Their seven-day treks via the Marangu route cost US$1150 but include transport from the Namanga border (Kenya/Tanzania) and two nights accommodation with half board at the Kibo Hotel. The price is negotiable, to an extent, if you don't need transport from Namanga to Arusha.

Sunny Safaris Ltd
  PO Box 7267, Col Middleton Rd, Arusha (☎ (057) 7145; fax 8094). This is an excellent and friendly company with a proven track record which you can rely on completely. It offers the standard five-day Marangu trek for US$475 with extra days at US$75 per person. Prices do not include accommodation before or after a trek.

Tropical Tours Ltd
  PO Box 727, Goliondoi Rd (rear of Adventure Centre), Arusha (☎ (057) 8353; fax 8907). This company, headed by a friendly Swiss and German couple, specialises in off-the-beaten-track safaris and is one of the best around. They offer a six-day special route trek of Kilimanjaro which takes in both the Machame and Mweka routes. The price is US$920 (minimum four people) including all camping equipment and sleeping bags. Radio contact with Moshi is maintained throughout the trek in case of emergency and the food is excellent; they will also cater for vegetarians.

Wild Spirit Safari Ltd
  PO Box 2288, India St, Arusha (☎ /fax (057) 4215). This is a fairly new company which can arrange a trek up any of the routes to the summit and their prices are competitive. A five-day/four-night trek via the Marangu route costs US$410 (four to six people), US$420 (three people) and US$460 (two people). A six-day trek on the Machame route costs US$670 (assuming a group of four to six people). An extra day on either of these routes costs US$70 per person. You'll find the prices for a trek along any of the other routes are comparable.

Getting to the Trekking Routes

The Marangu trail is the route most taken by tourists, being the easiest way up the mountain. The trailhead/park entry gate is five km above Marangu village. There are minibuses all day, every day until late in the afternoon between Moshi and Marangu via Himo, terminating in Marangu village at a spot below the post office. The fare is TSh 400 and the journey takes about one hour. A taxi over the same distance costs about TSh 19,000 shared between up to four people, though drivers' initial quotes are often higher.

Marangu Trail

Day 1 Starting from the Marangu park entry gate at 1800m, it's a fairly easy three to five-hour walk through thick rainforest to the Mandara Hut (2700m). (This hut and the Horombo Hut might be better described as lodges, since they consist of a large central chalet surrounded by many smaller huts.) There's often quite a lot of mud along this route, so wear good boots. The Mandara Hut consists of a group of comfortable wooden A-frame huts with bunk beds and mattresses and has a total capacity of 60. Water is piped in from springs above the hut and there are flush toilets. There's a dining area in the main cabin.

Day 2 The route treks steeply through giant heath forest and out across moorlands onto the slopes of Mawenzi and finally to the Horombo Hut (3720m). It's a difficult 14-km walk and you need to take it slowly. Reckon on five to seven hours. If your clothes are soaked through by the time you arrive at the Horombo Hut, don't assume you will be able to dry them there. Firewood is relatively scarce and is reserved for cooking. The Horombo Hut is similar to Mandara Hut but can accommodate 120. There are both earth and flush toilets.

Days 3 & 4 If possible, spend two nights at the Horombo Hut and on the fourth day go

TANZANIA

to Kibo Hut (4703m), about six to seven hours away. Porters don't go beyond the Kibo Hut, so you'll have to carry your own essential gear from here to the summit and back. Don't skimp on warm clothing. It's extremely cold on the summit (up to 5°C during the day but down to -22°C at night) and you'll freeze to death if you're not adequately clothed. Kibo Hut is a stone block house which is more like a mountain hut of the type you are likely to find on Mt Kenya. It has a small dining area and several dormitory rooms with bunk beds and mattresses (total capacity of 60). There are earth toilets but no water, so bring sufficient water from the stream above Horombo Hut.

Day 5 Most people find it difficult to sleep much at Kibo, so as you have to start out for the summit very early (1 or 2 am) to get to it just before sunrise, it's a good idea to stay awake the evening before. You'll feel better if you do this rather than try to grab a couple of hours of fitful sleep. The mist and cloud closes in and obscures the views by 9 am and sometimes earlier. The route over the snow to the summit is sometimes like a technicolour dream if it hasn't snowed recently, due to the deposits of those who have vomited as a result of trying to get to the top too quickly! Expect to take five to six hours from Kibo Hut to Gillman's Point and a further one to two hours from there to Uhuru Peak.

On the same day, you will descend from the summit to the Horombo Hut and spend the night there.

Day 6 On the last day, you return to the starting point at Marangu.

Mweka Trail

Starting from Mweka village directly north of Moshi, this is the most direct, fastest and steepest route to the summit.

To get to the trailhead, you will have to drive or get a lift from Moshi to Mweka village. Vehicles can usually be left safely at the College of Wildlife Management if you ask permission.

From here you follow an old logging

track, which is often very slippery. Two hours later the track turns into a path, which follows a gully. This path will take you up above the tree line to a ridge where the Mweka Huts (3000m) are situated. Expect this leg of the trek to take six to eight hours. The huts are two round metal constructions which each sleep eight people but they're pretty dirty, not furnished and there are no toilets. Camping is a better option. Water can be found below the huts.

From the Mweka Huts, continue up the ridge to the west until you reach the Barafu Huts (4600m). These are exactly the same as the Mweka Huts (no toilets and water, and pretty dirty) and sleep eight people, but you may prefer to camp. The walk will take six to eight hours.

From the Barafu Huts you can ascend straight up to the rim of Kibo, but the trail is very steep and will take you about six hours. Uhuru Peak is another hour away.

Umbwe Trail

This is another relatively short but steep route (west of Moshi), and it's probably better to descend it from either the Mweka or Machame trails rather than attempt the ascent.

To get to the trailhead, take the main Moshi to Arusha road and turn off right to Weru Weru and Mango. Drive past Weru Weru for some 15 km along the Lyamungu road and turn right at the T-junction towards Mango. About 150m after crossing the Sere River, turn left and you'll find the Umbwe Mission, where vehicles can be left (with permission).

From the mission, follow an old forestry track up to 2100m and then follow the path along a narrow ridge between the Lonzo and Umbwe rivers. If it's getting late by the time you get up here, stay at Bivouac I (2800m), an all-weather rock shelter with water close by. The walk up here from Umbwe village takes four to six hours.

From Bivouac I, continue up to Bivouac II (3780m), which is a rock overhang. Water is available from a spring about 15 minutes down the ravine to the west. Next go up the

...he end of the tree line. From here a ...ked by cairns goes up to Barranco Hut (3900m). This hut, an unfurnished metal cabin with a wooden floor, sleeps up to five people. There's an earth toilet and water is available from nearby streams. The walk from Bivouac I to here takes about five hours.

From Barranco Hut, head up to Lava Tower Hut and the summit via what's known as the Great Western Breach. The walk from Barranco to Lava Tower takes about three hours.

Machame Trail

Some people regard this as the most scenic of the trails up Kilimanjaro. The ascent through forest is gradual until you emerge onto the moorland of Shira Plateau, from which there are superb views of the Kibo peak and the Great Western Breach.

The turn-off on the main Moshi-Arusha road is even further west than that for Umbwe. Once you get there, head north for Machame village. If you have your own transport you can leave the vehicle at either the school or the hotel.

From the village, a track leads through coffee plantations and forest to the park entry gate (about four km). From the gate there's a clear track which continues up through more plantations and forest to a ridge between the Weru Weru and Makoa streams and on to the Machame Huts (3000m). These consist of two unfurnished metal huts which sleep up to six people but they're pretty dirty so camping might well be a better option. There are earth toilets and water is available about five minutes walk down the valley. From Machame village to the Machame Huts takes about nine hours, so an early start is recommended.

From Machame Huts, cross the valley and continue up the steep ridge, then west into a gorge and up again to the Shira Hut (3800m), an unfurnished metal cabin which sleeps up to eight people. There is no toilet, but water is available in the stream about 50m north of the hut. The walk takes about five hours.

From the Shira Hut you have the options of continuing on to the Barranco Hut (five to six hours), the Moir Hut (two hours) or the Lava Tower Hut (4600m, four hours). The Lava Tower Hut is an unfinished metal cabin which sleeps up to eight people. There are no toilets but water is available close by.

Loitokitok Trail

This trail is now open, but is only used by specialised tour groups.

NGORONGORO CONSERVATION AREA

There can be few people who have not heard, read or seen film or TV footage of this incredible 20-km-wide volcanic crater with its 600m walls packed with just about every species of wildlife to be found in East Africa. The views from the crater rim are incredible, and though the wildlife might not look too impressive from up there, when you get to the bottom you'll very quickly change your mind. It's been compared to Noah's Ark and the Garden of Eden, and though this is a little fanciful, it might have been just that around the turn of the century, before wildlife in East Africa was decimated by the 'great White hunters' armed with the latest guns and a total lack of concern and foresight regarding conservation.

It doesn't quite come up to Noah's Ark expectations these days, but you definitely see lion, elephant, rhino, buffalo and many of the plains herbivores such as wildebeest, Thomson's gazelle, zebra and reedbuck, as well as thousands of flamingos wading in the shallows of Lake Magadi – the soda lake on the floor of the crater.

Despite the steep walls of the crater, there's considerable movement of animals in and out – mostly to the Serengeti, since the land between the crater and Lake Manyara is intensively farmed. Yet it remains a favoured spot for wildlife because there's permanent water and grassland on the crater floor. The animals don't have the crater entirely to themselves. Local Maasai tribespeople have grazing rights, and you may well come across some of them tending their cattle. In the days when Tanzania was a German colony, there was also a settler's farm there, but that has long since gone.

You can visit Ngorongoro at any time of the year, but during the months of April and May it can be extremely wet and the roads difficult to negotiate. Access to the crater floor may be restricted at this time.

Geological Background

Ngorongoro and the nearby craters and volcanoes are fairly recent additions to the landscape, geologically speaking. Though

there has been a considerable amount of volcanic activity in the area for about 15 million years, Ngorongoro is thought to date back only 2.5 million years and may at one time have rivalled Mt Kilimanjaro in size. Its vents filled with solid rock, however, and the molten material was forced elsewhere. As the lava subsided, circular fractures developed and the cone collapsed inwards to form the caldera. Nevertheless, minor volcanic activity continued as lava found cracks on the caldera floor and in the flanks of the mountain, which created the small cones and

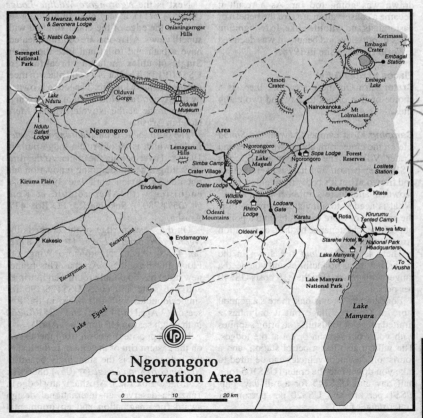

Ngorongoro
Conservation Area

0   10   20 km

693

...ich you can see on the floor of the

History

Only in the 1930s was a road constructed through Ngorongoro and a lodge built on the rim, but even before WWII the crater had acquired international fame as a wildlife area. In 1951 it was included in the newly created Serengeti National Park. It was hived off five years later due to conflict between the park authorities and the local Maasai, who felt that being excluded from the Serengeti was bad enough but that to have their grazing rights to Ngorongoro also withdrawn was going too far. As a result it became a conservation area for the benefit of pastoralists and wildlife alike. In recognition of its importance and beauty, it was declared a World Heritage site in 1978.

Places to Stay & Eat

Crater Rim On the crater rim, there is a choice of five places to stay and two camp sites.

Camping Most campers stay at the *Simba* site on the crater rim, about two km beyond Crater Village. The site is guarded, costs US$10 per person and has showers, toilets and firewood but it's badly maintained, often crowded and there's rubbish everywhere. What is needed to alleviate this problem is the creation of more camp sites and a policy of positive maintenance by the Conservation Area Authority.

There is also a *camp site* down in the crater, but it has no facilities and you need a ranger with you to stay there. It costs US$40 per person.

For campers' provisions, there's a general store at Crater Village but it only has a limited range of foodstuffs, so bring supplies with you from Arusha or eat at the lodges. The village also has a petrol station, and a tourist office where vehicles can be hired to take you down into the crater (US$105 for a half day and US$145 for a full day, plus US$1 per km and US$20 per person for crater/ranger fees).

Lodges Of the four lodges, the *Rhino Lodge* is the first one you come to, off to the left. It costs US$45/70 for singles/doubles including breakfast in the high season (1 July to 31 March) and half that price in the low season. Breakfast (for casual visitors) is US$7 and lunch/dinner is US$10. It's on a beautiful site but is somewhat out of the way and doesn't overlook the crater. You might be able to camp here if you have a tent. Bookings can be made in Arusha at the Ngorongoro Conservation Area Authority (☎ (057) 3339), PO Box 776, Arusha. Its office is by the roundabout at the junction of Makongoro and Goliondoi Rds.

Next is the *Ngorongoro Wildlife Lodge* (☎ (057) 2711), a very modern building set right on the edge of the crater rim and with superb views. All rooms are centrally heated, have a bath and toilet and face the crater. Singles/doubles including breakfast are US$110/138. The bar is a good place to meet people and has a log fire. The lodge is owned by the Accor/Tahi Hotels chain so bookings can be made at the Novotel Mount Meru Hotel in Arusha.

The third lodge is the *Ngorongoro Crater Lodge* which is an old rustic lodge built in 1937 and overlooking the crater. At the time of writing it was undergoing renovation and not due to reopen until late 1997. Make enquiries with Abercrombie & Kent (☎ (057) 7803), Sokoine Rd, PO Box 427, Arusha.

On the western edge of the crater is the *Ngorongoro Serena Lodge* (☎ (057) 8175; fax 4155), AICC, Ngorongoro Wing, 6th Floor, PO Box 2551, Arusha. This brandnew hotel has 66 double rooms, eight triples and one suite and costs US$128/195 for singles/doubles with full board in the low season (9 April to 14 June) and US$170/260 in the high season (15 June to 8 April).

In the opposite direction from the above, on the eastern rim of the crater, is the last of the lodges. This is the stunningly beautiful *Ngorongoro Sopa Lodge* (☎ (057) 6886; fax 8245), PO Box 1823, Arusha. If any lodge in Tanzania deserves an international design award for imagination and environmental sensitivity, it's this one. Built to resemble an African village, at least in layout, it consists of an interlocking series of stone-walled and shingle-roofed suites, each with its own verandah overlooking the crater and with palatial interiors. The vast reception, dining and bar areas are equally courageous and the landscaping excellent. There's also a swimming pool. It doesn't come cheap, but what an experience if you can afford it! In the high season (1 July to 4 April) half board costs US$132/194 for singles/doubles; in the low season the full-board rates are US$113/183. All the rates include tax and service charges. Meals are US$12.50 breakfast, US$25 lunch and US$30 dinner. The food is superb, the service is second to none and there's a log fire in the bar in the evenings.

Karatu Karatu (known to everyone as 'Safari Junction') is about halfway between Lake Manyara and Ngorongoro. Virtually all camping safaris out of Arusha use this place as an overnight stop in order to economise on park entry fees for Ngorongoro.

The cheapest place to stay here is *Safari Junction Camp* (☎ Karatu 50 – through operator), where you can either camp (with your own tents or hire one) or rent a log cabin, some of which have private bathroom. It's open all year, there's a restaurant and bar and they can also lay on 4WD vehicles for safaris in the adjacent national parks. Camping costs TSh 900 per person and the log cabins with shared toilet and bathroom are US$20/30 for singles/doubles. Log cabins with private bathroom are US$30/40. Meals cost TSh 700 breakfast, TSh 1500 lunch and TSh 1800 dinner. Land Rovers for touring Ngorongoro Crater cost TSh 45,000 per vehicle per day, excluding park entry and service fees.

Going up in price, there's the *Kifaru Lodge* (☎ Karatu 20 – through operator), PO Box 20, Karatu, managed by Big Game Safaris Ltd (☎ (057) 3181), PO Box 7553, Arusha. It offers singles/doubles with private bathroom for US$75/88, including taxes and service charges.

Top of the line and long-established is *Gibb's Farm* (☎ (057) 6702 or Karatu 25 – through operator), PO Box 6084, Arusha (or PO Box 2, Karatu). Here there are 15 double rooms, seven of them in separate cottages, all with private bathroom and maid service. The atmosphere is that of a family guesthouse and all the food is home-grown. The guesthouse is part of a coffee farm. Bed and breakfast costs US$96/118 for singles/doubles, with half board at US$120/166. The hotel is closed during April and May. The farm is signposted on the main road into Karatu coming from Lake Manyara.

Getting There & Away

If you are trying to get to the crater under your own steam, there are private buses from Arusha at least as far as Karatu but it may be difficult to find anything going beyond there. There are also plenty of trucks as far as Karatu.

Only 4WD vehicles are allowed down in the crater, except at times during the dry season when the authorities *may* allow conventional vehicles in. The roads into the crater, except from the Sopa Lodge, are very steep, so if you are driving your own vehicle, make sure it can handle the roads.

Whether you are driving your own vehicle or are on an organised tour, you must take a park ranger with you (US$20 per day). It's also possible to hire a 4WD Land Rover from the tourist office at Crater Village from the same place where you collect a ranger (prices above). The lodges also offer this service but they charge more than the tourist office.

RUAHA NATIONAL PARK

Ruaha National Park was created in 1964 from half of the Rungwa Game Reserve. It covers 13,000 sq km. Like the Selous, it's a wild, undeveloped area and access is difficult, but there's a lot of wildlife here as a result. Elephant, hippo and crocodile, and kudu, roan and sable antelope are particularly numerous. The **Great Ruaha River**, which forms the eastern boundary of the park, has spectacular gorges, though a lot of the rest of the park is undulating plateau

TANZANIA

averaging 1000m in height with occasional rocky outcrops.

Visiting the park is only feasible in the dry season, from June to December. During the rest of the year the tracks are virtually impassable. The grass is long between February and June, restricting game-viewing.

If you're interested in helping this park to expand facilities, control poaching, reduce fire risks, and provide suitable equipment to undertake park maintenance, contact the Friends of Ruaha Society (☎ (051) 20522), PO Box 60 in Mufindi or PO Box 786 in Dar es Salaam. These people are doing an excellent job to help the chief park warden and the 50 rangers to conserve the flora and fauna of this park (there's one ranger for every 260 sq km).

Places to Stay

Camping is permitted around the park headquarters at Msembe and at various other *camp sites* for the usual fee (US$20 per person per night). Also at the park headquarters is a permanent camp, consisting of bandas equipped with beds. Most of the essential equipment is provided but you must bring your own food and drink. This is also essential if you intend to camp. There are no shops in the vicinity, so bring supplies from Iringa, the nearest town. Bookings for the bandas can be made through the Park Warden, Ruaha National Park, PO Box 369, Iringa.

Possibly the most mellow place to stay if you have the money is *Ruaha River Camp*, which is constructed on and around a rocky kopje overlooking the Great Ruaha River. (Kopjes are slight rises strewn with huge, smooth granite boulders. They generally support a few trees and are often the lookouts of cheetah.) It consists of a number of beautiful bandas, which blend into their surroundings, and a central dining and bar area (in the same style) on an elevated position, from which there are spectacular views. The food is excellent and the owners have had over 25 years experience in Ruaha. A double banda with full board costs US$65. It's excellent value and highly recom-

mended. Game drives are available for US$60 per vehicle (two hours), US$90 per vehicle (half day) and US$150 per vehicle (full day). Transfers from the airstrip cost US$35. Reservations should be made through Foxtreks Ltd (☎ (0811) 327706), PO Box 10270, Dar es Salaam, or through Coastal Travels Ltd (☎ (051) 37479), Ali Mwinyi Rd, Dar es Salaam.

Equally pleasant is the small *Mwagusi Safari Camp* which has accommodation for 16 guests in twin-bed tents each with en suite bathroom facilities, hot water and flush toilet. Every tent overlooks the Mwagusi Sand River and provides superb views of the animal and bird life. Full board costs US$140/180. Game drives and game walks are available with knowledgeable guides. The game drives cost US$25 per person (three to four hours) or US$250 per vehicle for a full-day drive. Bookings should be made through Foxtreks or Coastal Travels (see above).

Getting There & Away

Air Coastal Travels Ltd (address and telephone number above) has departures by light plane from Dar es Salaam to Ruaha via Selous and vice versa three times a week (US$215).

Road There is a good all-weather road from Iringa to the park headquarters via Mloa (112 km). This involves crossing the Ruaha River by ferry at Ibuguziwa, which is within the park. The drive should take about four hours. Hitching isn't really feasible, so you'll need to have your own vehicle or go on an organised safari.

RUBONDO ISLAND NATIONAL PARK

This little-visited national park lies in the south-west corner of Lake Victoria and covers some 450 sq km, of which 240 sq km are made up of Rubondo island and various other islets. It consists of sandy beaches with palm trees, forested rocky hills, papyrus swamps and lowland plains. The park has no large predators and so offers excellent opportunities for foot safaris.

The area was declared a forest reserve during the German colonial period and later upgraded to a game reserve in 1965 and, finally, declared a national park in 1977. The park is rich in indigenous animal species which include sitatunga, bushbuck, hippo, crocodile, vervet monkey and rock python as well as introduced species such as black rhino, giraffe, chimpanzee, black and white colobus monkey, elephant, roan antelope and porcupine.

There is a network of motorable tracks on the main island and vehicles are available for game drives. Boats are also available which connect the island with the Tanzanian mainland. The park is open all year but the best time to visit is from June to October.

Places to Stay

There are two double bungalows which cost US$20 per person per night and include cooking utensils but you must bring all your own food with you. Advance booking is essential through either the Public Relations Officer, Tanzania National Parks, PO Box 3134, Arusha, or the Park Warden, Rubondo National Park, PO Box 111, Geita.

Getting There & Away

It's possible to get to Rubondo by boat if you can find transport from Mwanza to Mganza, from where the village chairman will arrange a boat to the island. Alternatively, contact Kijereshi Tented Camp Ltd (☎ (068) 41068; fax 50142), PO Box 190, Mwanza, who will put together a five-day safari ex-Mwanza for US$1600 (per person for two people) or US$2200 (four people) all-inclusive of food, accommodation, transport and park fees. These safaris start and end in Mwanza.

SELOUS GAME RESERVE

The little-visited, 54,600-sq-km Selous is probably the world's largest game reserve. It's the quintessential East African wilderness. Largely untouched by people, it is said to contain the world's largest concentration of elephant, buffalo, crocodile, hippo and hunting dog, as well as plenty of lion, rhino and antelope and thousands of dazzling bird species. Poaching probably makes the estimates of wildlife populations overly optimistic, but there are supposedly about 100,000 elephants in this reserve and there is a good chance of seeing a herd several hundred strong.

Established initially in 1905, for many years it remained largely the preserve of the trophy collectors and big-game hunters, even though only the northern tip of the reserve has ever been adequately explored. Most of it is trackless wilderness and is almost impossible to traverse during the rainy season, when floods and swollen rivers block access. Not only that, but it is almost devoid of human habitation due mainly to the presence of tsetse flies which prevent the herding of domestic livestock but which are harmless to wildlife.

One of the main features of the reserve is the huge **Rufiji River**, which has the largest water-catchment area in East Africa. Massive amounts of silt are dumped annually during the wet season into the Indian Ocean opposite Mafia island. For the rest of the year, when the floods subside and the water level in the river drops, extensive banks of shimmering white and golden sand are exposed.

In the northern end of the reserve, where the Great Ruaha River flows into the Rufiji, is **Stiegler's Gorge**, probably the best known feature of the park. On average it's 100m deep and 100m wide. A cable car spans the gorge, for those who are game enough to go across. It's in the area where most of the safari camps and the lodges are found. The gorge is named after the German explorer of the same name who was killed here by an elephant in 1907.

History

The Selous and the Rufiji River delta played an important part in the East African campaign between the British and German colonial authorities during WWI. It was during that campaign that Capt Frederick Courteney Selous, after whom the game reserve is named, met his end near Beho Beho in 1917 during a clash between the

German forces, under General von Lettow-Vorbeck, and the British Royal Fusiliers, a detachment of which was under Selous' command. By the time of his death, Selous had become a legend in his own time and it's said that von Lettow-Vorbeck sent a letter of condolence to the British military authorities on hearing of Selous' death in action. Selous' modest grave and those of his men who fell with him is to be found in the northern extremity of the game reserve.

Further to the east, the German light cruiser *Königsberg* was sunk by the British navy in the Rufiji delta, where it had sought shelter but not before the crew had removed 10 of its 4.1-inch guns. These they fitted with wheels and hauled around with them throughout the rest of the campaign. One of the guns is now in the National Museum in Dar es Salaam.

Information

The best time to visit is from July through to the end of March and during January and February. From the end of February to the end of May are the heavy rains when much of the reserve is inaccessible. The lodges and camp sites are closed during April and May.

The booklet *Selous Game Reserve* by Rolf D Baldus, put out by the Selous Conservation Programme, is an excellent buy before you come here but it's difficult to find. Try the book shops in Arusha and Dar es Salaam.

Activities

The Selous is one of the few national parks which are allowed to explore on foot. **Walking safaris** are conducted by all five camps in the reserve.

Boat trips up the Rufiji River are also offered by three of the camps (Rufiji River, Impala and Mbuyuni Safari Camps) and are a very popular way of exploring the area. Beho Beho also has a boat on Lake Tagalala.

Places to Stay

All the reserve's facilities are concentrated

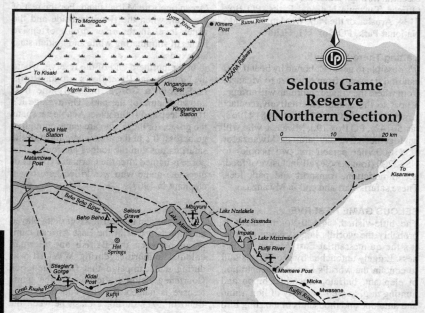

Selous Game Reserve (Northern Section)

in the extreme northern end, and consist of five luxury tented camps. There are no budget facilities other than two *camp sites*, one at Mtemere and another close to Matambwe at the Beho Beho bridge. If you plan on camping you must bring everything with you – camping equipment, cooking and eating utensils and food. Camping anywhere other than the official sites is prohibited.

All five of the luxury tented camps are sited along either the Rufiji or Beho Beho rivers and four of the camps have their own airstrips.

At Stiegler's Gorge itself is the *Stiegler's Gorge Safari Camp*, which was built in 1977 for Norwegian scientists and engineers who were working in the area, but it's currently closed.

North-east of here on the Beho Beho River is the *Beho Beho Tented Camp* (☎ (051) 68631), PO Box 2261, Dar es Salaam, or c/o Oyster Bay Hotel.

Next up on the Rufiji River is *Mbuyuni Luxury Tented Camp* (☎ (051) 37479), PO Box 3052, Dar es Salaam, which overlooks Lake Manze and offers full board for US$135/220. Game drives from this camp cost US$30 per person (two hours) or US$36 per person (three hours). Selous' grave site is close to this tented camp on the opposite side of the river.

East of here and also on the Rufiji River is the *Impala Safari Camp* which is run by Impala Tours & Safaris (☎ (051) 25779), Zanaki St, PO Box 4783, Dar es Salaam. Accommodation rates are much the same as at Mbuyuni Luxury Tented Camp.

Furthest east and also along the Rufiji River is the *Rufiji River Camp* which is run by Hippotours & Safaris (☎ (051) 36860; fax 75165), PO Box 1658, Dar es Salaam. Each tent at this camp (up to 40 guests) has twin beds with mosquito nets, private bathroom, a verandah and overlooks the Rufiji River. The food is excellent and ice-cold drinks are available. Charges are US$130 per person with full board. Boat trips or game drives are available for US$30 and walking safaris for US$15. Flights to the local airstrip from Dar es Salaam cost US$80 one way and depart regularly.

Getting There & Away

Air The most convenient way to get there is to fly. Four of the camps (Rufiji River Camp, Mbuyuni Luxury Tented Camp, Beho Beho and Sand River have an airstrip. Coastal Travels Ltd (☎ (051) 37479), Ali Mwinyi Rd, Dar es Salaam, has daily departures by light plane in either direction. The flight takes 45 minutes and the one-way fare is US$75.

Train Those going in by train should take the TAZARA line as far as Fuga railway station. From Fuga, the lodges will collect you in one of their vehicles, but you must make arrangements for this before you leave Dar es Salaam. Being collected won't be cheap unless you're sharing the cost with others.

Road Hitching to Selous Game Reserve is virtually out of the question. To get there, you'll need to join an organised safari or have your own vehicle which will have to be 4WD.

Those coming by road in their own vehicle have two options. The first is to take the Dar es Salaam to Mkongo road via Kibiti and then on to Mtemere. The road is sealed as far as Kibiti but badly potholed, after which it's a rough track to Mkongo. The remaining 75 km can become temporarily impassable during heavy rains between February and April. The last petrol station is in Kibiti and the distance from Dar es Salaam is about 250 km and the drive takes about seven to eight hours on average.

The alternative route is to take the northern Dar es Salaam to Kisaki road via Morogoro and then on to Matambwe but this is longer (350 km) and will take you eight to nine hours. The first 190 km is on a good tarmac road to Morogoro. From here you take the road in the direction of the teachers' training college and then turn right which will take you to Bigwa and Kisaki via the Uluguru Mountains. It's a steep and rough road so the going is slow. Allow around seven hours from Morogoro to Matambwe.

The companies which own the camps can

...oad transport if you don't have a
...ut it's an expensive option.

SERENGETI NATIONAL PARK

Serengeti, which covers 14,763 sq km, is
Tanzania's most famous game park and is
contiguous with the Masai Mara Game
Reserve in neighbouring Kenya. Here you
can get a glimpse of what a lot of East Africa
must have looked like in the days before the
'great White hunters'. Their brainless
slaughter of the plains animals began in the
late 19th century, but more recently, trophy
hunters and poachers in search of ivory and
rhino horn have added to the sickening toll.

On the seemingly endless and almost treeless plains of the Serengeti are literally
millions of hoofed animals. They're constantly on the move in search of grassland
and are watched and pursued by the predators which feed off them. It's one of the most
incredible sights you will ever see and the
numbers are simply mind-boggling.

Nowhere else will you see wildebeest,
gazelle, zebra and antelope in such concentrations. The wildebeest, of which there are
up to two million, is the chief herbivore of
the Serengeti and also the main prey of the
large carnivores such as lion and hyena. The
wildebeest are well known for the annual
migration which they undertake – a trek with
many hazards, not least of which is the crossing of large rivers, which can leave hundreds
drowned, maimed or taken by crocodile.
During the rainy season the herds are widely
scattered over the eastern section of the
Serengeti and the Masai Mara in the north.
These areas have few large rivers and
streams and quickly dry out when the rains
cease. When that happens the wildebeest
concentrate on the few remaining green
areas and gradually form huge herds which
move off west in search of better grazing. At
about the time the migration starts, the
annual rut also begins. For a few days at a
time while the herds pause, bulls establish
territories, which they defend against rivals,
and try to assemble as many females as they
can with which they mate. As soon as the

migration resumes, the female herds merge
again.

The dry season is spent in the western
parts of the Serengeti, at the end of which the
herds move back east in anticipation of the
rains. Calving begins at the start of the rainy
season, but if it arrives late, up to 80% of the
new calves may die from lack of food.

Serengeti is also famous for its lions,
many of which have collars fitted with trans-
mitters so that their movements can be
studied and their location known. It's also
famous for cheetah and remarkably large
herds of giraffe. You need to bring a pair of
binoculars with you to this park, as the distances are so great that you'll probably miss
out on a lot of the action unless it occurs close
to the road.

The main route from Ngorongoro to
Seronera village is a well-maintained gravel
road with the occasional kopje to one side or
the other. You'll see plenty of Maasai
herding cattle from Ngorongoro as far as the
Olduvai Gorge. A 1978 census of the largest
mammals in the Serengeti recorded 1.5
million wildebeest, one million Grant's and
Thomson's gazelle, 200,000 zebras, 75,000
impala, 74,000 buffalo, 65,000 topi, 18,000
eland, 9000 giraffe, 5000 elephant, 4000
hyena, 3000 lion, 500 cheetah and 100 rhino.

There hasn't been too much change in the
numbers since then, except that rhino and
elephant have suffered badly from poaching.
The hard-pressed but enthusiastic rangers
can do little about poaching, given the
extremely limited resources provided them
by the government. The animals are also
very easy to see, as the Serengeti is substantially flat grassland with bushes and trees
only in clumps, particularly along river
banks.

Hot-Air Ballooning

Serengeti National Park is the only Tanzanian park where you can take a hot-air
balloon flight similar to those available in
Masai Mara in Kenya. These can be booked
at either the Seronera Wildlife Lodge or the
Serengeti Sopa Lodge. They take off daily at
dawn from the Seronera Lodge. The balloons

can accommodate up to 24 passengers. The cost is US$300 per person, which includes a champagne breakfast after the approximately two-hour flight. You need to book them in advance, as there's heavy demand for places, through Serengeti Balloon Safaris (☎ (057) 8578; fax 8997) at the Adventure Centre, PO Box 12116, Goliondoi Rd, Arusha.

Places to Stay & Eat

Camping Most budget travellers stay at one or other of the *public camp sites* (US$20 per person). There are 12 of these – six at

Seronera, two at Kirawira, one at Ndabaka, two at Lobo and one at Bologonja – but facilities are minimal. Some don't even have water, so it's best to bring everything you'll need.

In addition, there are six *special camp sites* (US$40 per person): one at Seronera, two at Kirawira, two at Lobo and one at Bologonja; and 12 *wilderness camp sites* (US$40 per person): three at Moru, one at Hembe, one at Soit le Motonyi, two at Naabi Hill and five at Lake Lagarja (Ndutu).

Lodges In addition to Ndutu Safari Lodge

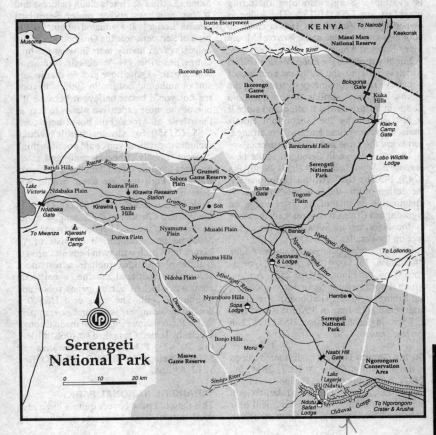

Serengeti National Park

0   10   20 km

i Gorge), there are four other
Serengeti. The *Seronera Wild-*
...Lodge is a stunningly beautiful and very
imaginative building constructed on top of
and around a kopje, with hyrax (a small
rodent-like creature) running around everywhere. The enormous bar and observation
deck at this lodge is right on top of the kopje,
with the boulders incorporated into the
design. Getting up to it on narrow stone steps
between massive rocks is like entering
Aladdin's Cave! The rooms are very pleasantly furnished and decorated and they all
have a bathroom with hot water – when water
is available. Singles/doubles including
breakfast are US$110/138. The lodge is
owned by the Accor/Tahi Hotels chain so
bookings can be made at the Novotel Mount
Meru Hotel in Arusha.

Equally superb is the *Lobo Wildlife Lodge*,
which is built into the faults and contours of
a massive rock promontory overlooking the
plains. It's very similar to the Seronera
Lodge in terms of what it offers and since it
is also owned by the Accor/Tahi Hotels
chain, the room prices and booking arrangements are the same as for the Seronera.

The other lodge in Serengeti is the new
Serengeti Sopa Lodge (☎ (057) 6886; fax
8245), PO Box 1823, Arusha. Unfortunately,
the design of this lodge is nowhere near as
imaginative as that of its sister lodge on
Ngorongoro Crater. It costs exactly the same
as the Ngorongoro Sopa Lodge (see that
section for details).

Lastly, there's the *Serengeti Serena Lodge*
(☎ (057) 8175; fax 4155), AICC, Ngorongoro Wing, 6th Floor, PO Box 2551, Arusha,
which is north-west of Seronera overlooking
the Mbingwe valley. Half board here in the
high season (15 June to 8 April) is US$158/
237 for singles/doubles and US$116/172 in
the low season.

Tented Camps The first of the tented camps
is the *Migration Camp* (☎ (057) 2814; fax
8997), Adventure Centre, Goliondoi Rd, PO
Box 12095, Arusha. The camp is built within
the rocks of a kopje on Ndassiata Hill near
Lobo and overlooking the Grumeti River.

Resident game including lion, leopard, elephant and buffalo are always present due to
permanent water, and the wildebeest migration masses around the site for several
months on its way to and from the southern
plains. The camp has 16 tents, all with mosquito nets, private bathrooms with hot water,
and electricity. Other facilities include a bar,
restaurant, library and swimming pool.
During the high season it costs US$295/460
for full board, dropping to US$185/270 in
the low season.

Another of the luxury tented camps is the
Kirawira Camp which is owned by the
Serena Lodges & Hotels chain (address and
☎/fax numbers above under Serengeti
Serena Lodge). It's situated about 90 km
west of Seronera near the Grumeti River and
consists of 25 luxury tents in what the brochure describes as 'a classic Victorian
atmosphere'. Quite how you do that in any
sort of authentic fashion in 1996 is beyond
me but you'd better believe it because it's
one of the most expensive places to stay in
the whole of Africa. Full board here costs
US$365/550 for singles/doubles which
includes everything you could possibly think
of from 'bubbly', shoe-cleaning and afternoon tea to game drives, laundry and airstrip
transfers. Park fees are extra, would you
believe.

Next up is the *Kijereshi Tented Camp* in
the Western Corridor of the Serengeti, about
16 km east of the road between Mwanza and
Musoma near Ramadi. It consists of 12
luxury tents each with twin beds and private
bathroom. Facilities include a restaurant
serving international cuisine, a barbecue
area, well-stocked bar, a games room and
swimming pool. The tents cost US$70 a
double including breakfast and government
taxes. Reservations should be made through
Kijereshi Tented Camp Ltd (☎ (068) 41068;
fax 50142), PO Box 190, Mwanza, or
Mamba Safaris (☎ (057) 2127), PO Box
1212, Arusha.

TARANGIRE NATIONAL PARK

This national park covers quite a large area
south-east of Lake Manyara, mainly along

the course of the Tarangire River and the swamp lands and flood plains which feed it from the east. During the dry season, the only water here flows along the Tarangire River. The park fills with herds of zebra, wildebeest and kongoni, which stay until October when the short rains allow them to move to new grasslands. Throughout the year, however, you can see eland, lesser kudu, various species of gazelle, buffalo, giraffe, waterbuck, impala, elephant and the occasional leopard and rhino. For ornithologists, the best season is from October to May.

Tsetse flies can be a pest in this park at certain times of year (February and March), so keep the windows of your vehicle closed when not taking photographs.

Places to Stay & Eat

There are two public *camp sites* where you can pitch a tent for the usual price (US$20 per person per night, US$5 for children between the ages of five and 16). Also, there are six so-called special camp sites at US$40 per person per night (US$10 for children).

The beautifully sited *Tarangire Safari Lodge* (☎ (057) 7182), PO Box 2703, Arusha, set on a bluff overlooking the Tarangire River, is run by Serengeti Select Safaris. It consists of 35 luxury double tents protected from the elements by makuti roofs. Each tent has comfortable beds, a solar-heated shower, a flush toilet, electricity until

midnight and a verandah, and there's a swimming pool. The rates for singles/doubles are US$52/65 and meals cost US$5 for breakfast, US$12 lunch and US$15 dinner.

Further into the park is the *Tarangire Sopa Lodge* (☎ (057) 6896; fax 8245), PO Box 1823, Arusha, which also has a great setting but is considerably more expensive. In the high season (1 July to 4 April) half board costs US$132/194 for singles/doubles. In the low season full board rates are US$113/183. All the rates include tax and service charges. Meals for non-guests are US$12.50 breakfast, US$25 lunch and US$30 dinner. The food is superb and the service is second to none.

Just outside Tarangire to the east is *Oliver's Camp* (☎ /fax (057) 3108), PO Box 425, Arusha. This is a luxury tented camp set among an almost two-km-long set of kopjes known as Kikoti by the Maasai. The camp takes a maximum of 12 guests at a time, thus ensuring intimacy and closeness to nature. The emphasis is on walking and observing, which you do with an armed ranger. The twin-bed tents are individually sited with all the necessary facilities, plus there's a large dining tent and a library tent where wildlife videos are shown in the evenings after dinner. Full board costs US$220/320 which includes all meals, service charges, government taxes, laundry service, wilderness conservation fees and a guided morning or afternoon walk.

Glossary

The following is a list of words and acronyms you are likely to come across when in East Africa.

ADFL – Alliance of Democratic Forces for the Liberation of Congo-Zaïre
askari – security guard, watchman

banda – thatched hut with wooden or earthen walls
boma – village
bui-bui – black cover-all garment worn by Islamic women outside the home

CCM – Chama Cha Mapinduzi, ruling political party in Tanzania
chai – tea, but also a bribe
chakula – food
choo – toilet (pronounced as 'cho')

dalla dalla – Tanzanian *matatu*
duka – small shop or kiosk selling household basics

forex – foreign exchange bureau
fundi – repair man/woman (eg clothing, building trades, cars etc)

hakuna matata – no problem. Watch out – there often is!
harambee – the concept of community self-help, voluntary fund-raising. A cornerstone of Jomo Kenyatta's ideology.
hoteli – restaurant (Swahili)

Interahamwe – Hutu militia in Rwanda
IZCN – Institut Zaïrois pour la Conservation de la Nature

jinga! – crazy! (also used as an adjective)
jua kali – literally, 'hot sun'. Usually an outdoor vehicle repair shop or market.

kabaka – king (Uganda)
kanga – printed cotton wrap-around incorporating a Swahili proverb. Worn by many women both inside and outside the home.
kikoi – printed cotton wrap-around
kiondas – woven baskets
kitu kidogo – 'a little something', a bribe

lugga – dry river bed, mainly in northern Kenya

makuti – roof made of palm leaves, mainly on the coast
malaya – prostitute
manamba – *matatu* tout, often a veritable Daddy Cool
manyatta – Maasai or Samburu livestock camp often surrounded by a circle of thorn bushes
matatu – Kenyan minibus with megadecibel sound system, seemingly unlimited carrying capacity and two speeds – stationary and flat out
miraa – leafy twig or stem of Kenyan plant which has stimulant and appetite suppressant qualities
moran – Maasai or Samburu warrior (pl *morani*)
murram – dirt or part-gravelled road
mwami – king (Rwanda and Burundi)
mwananchi – worker of any kind but usually agricultural (pl *wananchi*, which is also used to refer to 'the people')
mzungu – white person (pl *wazungu*)

NRA – National Resistance Army (Uganda)
NRM – National Resistance Movement (Uganda)
Nyayo – 'footsteps'. One of the cornerstones of Moi's political ideology. In other words, to follow in the footsteps of Kenyatta.

panga – machete, carried by many people in the East African countryside and often by thieves in the cities
parking boys – unemployed youths/young men in Kenya who offer various services
pesa – money

pirogue – dug-out canoe (Zaïre)

RMS – Ruwenzori Mountaineering Services (Uganda)
RPF – Rwandan Patriotic Front

shamba – small farm or plot of land
soukous – Zaïrean Lingala music

taka taka – rubbish
taxi – minibus (Uganda)
tilapia – Nile perch
TTC – Tanzania Tourist Corporation

Uhuru – freedom or independence

waragi – Ugandan millet-based alcohol
Watutsi – plural of Tutsi

Index

ABBREVIATIONS

MAPS

TEXT

Map references are in **bold** type.

Aberdare NP (K) 344-7, **345**
Aberdares (K) 284-9
accommodation 40
   Kenya 135
   Rwanda 482
   Tanzania 565
   Uganda 409
activities, see individual entries
Adamson, Joy 273, 363
air travel 44-7
   Africa 46-7
   Asia 47
   Australia & NZ 45
   Burundi 511, 513
   Eastern Zaïre 527, 529
   Kenya 140
   Rwanda 483, 484
   Tanzania 568, 574
   UK 45-6
   USA 44-5
   Uganda 410, 414
   within East Africa 51
Akagera, see Parc National de
   L'Akagera
Akamba people 105, 106, 301
altitude sickness 29-30
Amboni Caves (T) 604
Amboseli NP (K) 347-9, **348**
Amin, Idi 395-7
antelopes 54-66
archaeological sites (K)
   Hyrax Hill 278
   Kariandusi 275
   Olorgasailie 282
Arusha (T) 636-45, **638**
   entertainment 643
   getting around 644
   getting there & away 643-4
   places to eat 642-3
   places to stay 637-42
Arusha NP (T) 676-80, **677**
   trekking route 678-9

baboon 80-1
Baboon Cliffs (U) 466
Bagamoyo (T) 601-2
Bagaza, Jean-Baptiste 506
Bahima people 459
ballooning

Kenya 134, 160-1, 360
   Tanzania 584-5, 700-1
Bamburi Beach (K) 226-9
Bamburi Quarry Nature Trail
   (K) 226
Bantu people 556
Baragoi (K) 296, 334
Barsaloi, see Parsaloi
Basese people 443
Bawe Island (T) 622, 623
beaches, see individual entries
Beni (Z) 530-1, **531**
bicycling, see cycling
Bigodi (U) 458
bilharzia 34
birds, see fauna
Blixen, Karen 200
boat travel 52, see also dhow
   trips
   Burundi 511
   Eastern Zaïre 529
   Kenya 150
   Rwanda 485
   Tanzania 570-3, 577-8
   Uganda 413, 415
   Zambia 49
Bomas of Kenya, The 198
books 20-2, see also literature
   Kenya 208
   Rwanda 481
   Tanzania 563, 674-6
   Uganda 407
Boran (K) 337
border crossings
   Burundi 511
   Eastern Zaïre 527
   Ethiopia 47, 339
   Malawi 47-8
   Rwanda 483
   Somalia 48
   Sudan 48
   Uganda 410-3
   Zambia 48
Budadiri (U) 461
Budongo Central Forest
   Reserve (U) 455-6
buffalo 70
Buffalo Springs National
   Reserve (K) 381-4, **382**
Buggala Island (U) 444
Buhoma (U) 457

Bujagali Falls (U) 434-5
Bujumbura (B) 513-7, **515**
Bukasa Island (U) 444
Bukavu (Z) 534-7, **535**
Bukima (Z) 542-3
Bukoba (T) 658-9, **658**
Bunagana (Z) 542
Bundibugyo (U) 439
Bunia (Z) 530
Burundi 504-18, **505**
bus travel 51
   Burundi 513
   Kenya 140, 144
   Rwanda 484
   Tanzania 568-70, 574-5
   Uganda 410, 414
   Zambia 48
business hours 39
Busingiro (U) 455
Butare (R) 496-7, **496**
Butembo (Z) 531
Butiaba (U) 452
Butogota (U) 457
Buyangu (K) 352
Buyoya, Major Pierre 506-7
Bwejuu (T) 623-4
Bwindi NP (U) 456-7

camel safaris (K) 158-9,
   (T) 584
Camel Derby (K) 331
car & 4WD travel
   Kenya 146-50, 198
   Rwanda 485
   Tanzania 576
   Uganda 414
carnets 49-50
caving
   Mgahinga NP (U) 460
Central Highlands (K)
   283-302, **283**
Central Island NP (K) 327
Chake Chake (T) 629-30, **629**
Changuu Island (T) 622-3
cheetah 70-1
Cherangani Hills (K) 317-8, 325
children, travel with 38-9
chimpanzees
   Kibale NP (U) 458
   Queen Elizabeth NP Sanctuary
      (U) 466

THANKS

Thanks to the following travellers and others (apologies if we've misspelt your name) who took the time to write to us about their experiences in East Africa:

J Acker, Wolfgang Aichner, Coriina Alberg, Maureen Alcorn, Rory Allen, Nicki Anderson, R Andrews, Robert Anthony, Silvia Arduini, Marco Arpagus, Enid Atalyeba, Jonathon Badger, Edwin Bailey, Maggie Bangser, Guillanne Barbe, Efrat Barber, Simon Barne, M Bartick, Peter Beck, David Bergeron, AR Bland-Ward, Jeff Bogers, Byamukama Bonefence, Adam Booth, Michael Bourke, Richard Brandlon, Andie Brazewell, P Brown, Bill Brummond, Ewan Bryce, Desmond Bull, Patricio Bustos-Heppe, Bill Burt, D Butchart, Anja Buwalda, Scott Carlton, Rebecca Casson, Abbie Challanger, C Charsley-White, P Chasseriaud, Joan Clague, Erez Cohen, Ian Colclough, Caroline Coombs, Brian Cooper, Joseph Crapanzano, Matthew Croucher, P Cullinane, Stine Dahlgaard, Ralph Darbyshire, C Davies, Fia de Blok, Carrie de Carteret, Marny Dickson, James Doscher, Claire Durrant, Jamie Eisenfeld, S Endres, Janneke Erkelens, Gorrel Espelund, Jan Evans, Susan Evans, Ronald Fabel, A Fattoretti, Donald Feinberg, Laura Fied, A Finlay, Thea Fischer, Tone Fiskaa, Tom Fleming, Mike Foller, David Fox, Matt Francey, Bob Freeman, Doug Freemantle, Mark Furniss, Manuela Galaverni, Dr O Galili, A & L Gasquet, John Gaye, Pam Gilbert, E Gillespie, Tiffany Glass, Bill Glover, Peter Gomolka, Michael Graf, Maria Grascia Oddone, Pamela Greaces, K Grigat, Guido Groenen, Jan Grothe, David Hadley, Mat Hardy, Menno Harkema, Andy Harper, Paul Harper, P Harrison, Shane Harvey, Sam Hay, Ruth Hellier, Christen Henriksson, Elli Herczeg, Marko Heusala, Amelie Horgan, Mark Hornyansky, Mark Howard, Karen Hoy, Andrea Hubert, Rebecca Watts Hull, Ben Ingram, Robert Jackson, Ellen Jacobs, Ralph Jager, Wiegand Jahn, Christine & Paul Jarrett, Julie Jeffcott, Mark Jenkins, Henrik Jensen, Mai Britt L Jensen, Oluf Z Jessen, Tom Johnsen, Rob Johnson, Niaill Johnston, G Jones, Ivan Jones, W J Kar, Dave Kelly, Joan Kelly, H Kennedy, Charles Kimanthi, Christopher Kimball, Jenny Kimberlee, James King, Eva Kisgyorgy, Thomas Kjeldsen, Sue Knuse, Marjan Koerts, Pascal Kraemer, A Krock, Elizabeth Krol, Holger Kuhn, Marko Kuhn, Marielle Lapidaine,

S La Rosa, Beth Ann Larsen, Panayiotis Latsoudis, Bernard Leeman, Craig Lenske, Ken Leonard, Katherine Letchworth, A Levison, Ray Lewis, Rune Lindquist, Simon Linkin, Mike Linnett, Michele Lischi, Deborah Lodge, Joan Lynch, Karen Lyons, Judy Ma, Ruth Mackay-Shea, Karla Mader, Abby Magee, Scott Malone, Roger Mann, Nicolle Martindale, Angel Aznarez Masa, Jim Mauch, Shane McCarthy, Kris McElwee, Tom McGrath, Sue McIntosh, Derek McKee, B & C McLaren, R McSporran, Lailee Mendelson, Nicole Meyer, Biba Migliavacca, Phil Miller, Peter Moline, Heather Mosher, Anne Mosrat, Danny Nagtalin, Ignatius Nakishero, Chris Naylor, Michael Newman, G Nicholson, Victoria Nixon, Staffan Noreus, Fiona O'Brien, Mark Ogilvie, Cora Olsthoorn, Richard Owen, T Petal, Kate Phillips, Paul Phillips, Andrew Pickett, Robert Pitera, Richard Pledger, Paolo Possa, Keith Potts, M J Powley, Eckhard Radermacher, Dr Harald Rauer, Bridget Rawlings, Luke Rea, Klaus Rehe, Barbara Reissland, Helen Rhodes, Terri Rice, A Riley, Seppo Rinne, Mark Roberts, Daniel Rodriguez, Sandra & Richard Roik, Patricia & Marv Rosen, David Rowell, Michael Rutherford, Jenny Saar, Dr Alistair Santhouse, Karwan Sarai, Nathan Sato, Ulrich Schoene, Alan Schrager, Gregor Schwank, Erich Schwerd, Stanley Shayo, L Sheldon, Gillian Sheldrick, J Sidey, Paul Sigler, Jayne Slatcher, Ken Sloane, Gonneke Smeets, Steven Smith, Anthony Solomon, Jurgen Soltau, M Spurr, Andronico Ssemakula, Henrik Stabell, Jolanda Staman, Paul Gareth Steele, Sean Stratham, Martin Sturmer, Dave Stutz, Alkesh Sulanki, Dany Surralles, Steve Susswein, Elmer & Heidi Swanson, Sallie Sweet, R Sztorc, P & J Tanner, Jannie Klitsgaard Testrup, Andreas Thiele, Terry Thomas, Simon Thompson, Frank & Veronika Tiechs, Jacek Torbicz, Dr R F Trahan, Regina Treutien, Sharon Trevelyan, Alice Tulloch, Victoria Turnball, Linda Turner, Mark van der Wijh, John Jansen van Galen, Marie-Jeanne Vantuykom, Marian Verkade, C Visser, Satcy Vogan, Alexa Voight, S Wachsmuth, Susan Wagner, Tonia Walden, Ernst & Ursula Waldmann, J Walker, Sylvia Walter, Deborah Ward, Dr Louise Westrater, Clive Wilby, Helen Williams, Andrew Wilson, Therese Winfield, David Alain Wohl, James Wood, Susan Wood, Brian Woodward, David Wright, Gavin Wright, Gregory Wright, Robin Wright, Keiko Yamamoto, G Yates, Scott Zesch, Wolfgang Zilm, F Zitscher, Leszek Zubek, Rainer Zuszek.

LONELY PLANET JOURNEYS

JOURNEYS is a unique collection of travel writing – published by the company that understands travel better than anyone else. It is a series for anyone who has ever experienced – or dreamed of – the magical moment when they encountered a strange culture or saw a place for the first time. They are tales to read while you're planning a trip, while you're on the road or while you're in an armchair, in front of a fire.

JOURNEYS books catch the spirit of a place, illuminate a culture, recount a crazy adventure, or introduce a fascinating way of life. They always entertain, and always enrich the experience of travel.

THE RAINBIRD
A Central African Journey
Jan Brokken
translated by Sam Garrett

The Rainbird is a classic travel story. Following in the footsteps of famous Europeans such as Albert Schweitzer and H.M. Stanley, Jan Brokken journeyed to Gabon in central Africa. A kaleidoscope of adventures and anecdotes, *The Rainbird* brilliantly chronicles the encounter between Africa and Europe as it was acted out on a side-street of history. It is also the compelling, immensely readable account of the author's own travels in one of the most remote and mysterious regions of Africa.

Jan Brokken is one of Holland's best known writers. In addition to travel narratives and literary journalism, he has published several novels and short stories. Many of his works are set in Africa, where he has travelled widely.

SONGS TO AN AFRICAN SUNSET
A Zimbabwean Story
Sekai Nzenza-Shand

Songs to an African Sunset braids vividly personal stories into an intimate picture of contemporary Zimbabwe. Returning to her family's village after many years in the West, Sekai Nzenza-Shand discovers a world where ancestor worship, polygamy and witchcraft still govern the rhythms of daily life – and where drought, deforestation and AIDS have wrought devastating changes. With insight and affection, she explores a culture torn between respect for the old ways and the irresistible pull of the new.

Sekai Nzenza-Shand was born in Zimbabwe and has lived in England and Australia. Her first novel, *Zimbabwean Woman: My Own Story*, was published in London in 1988 and her fiction has been included in the short story collections *Daughters of Africa* and *Images of the West*. Sekai currently lives in Zimbabwe.

LONELY PLANET TRAVEL ATLASES

Lonely Planet has long been famous for the number and quality of its guidebook maps. Now we've gone one step further and in conjunction with Steinhart Katzir Publishers produced a handy companion series: Lonely Planet travel atlases – maps of a country produced in book form.

Unlike other maps, which look good but lead travellers astray, our travel atlases have been researched on the road by Lonely Planet's experienced team of writers. All details are carefully checked to ensure the atlas corresponds with the equivalent Lonely Planet guidebook.

The handy atlas format means no holes, wrinkles, torn sections or constant folding and unfolding. These atlases can survive long periods on the road, unlike cumbersome fold-out maps. The comprehensive index ensures easy reference.

- full-colour throughout
- maps researched and checked by Lonely Planet authors
- place names correspond with Lonely Planet guidebooks
  – no confusing spelling differences
- legend and travelling information in English, French, German, Japanese and Spanish
- size: 230 x 160 mm

Available now:
Chile & Easter Island • Egypt • India & Bangladesh • Israel & the Palestinian Territories •
Jordan, Syria & Lebanon • Kenya • Laos • Thailand • Vietnam • Zimbabwe, Botswana & Namibia

---

LONELY PLANET TV SERIES & VIDEOS

Lonely Planet travel guides have been brought to life on television screens around the world. Like our guides, the programmes are based on the joy of independent travel, and look honestly at some of the most exciting, picturesque and frustrating places in the world. Each show is presented by one of three travellers from Australia, England or the USA and combines an innovative mixture of video, Super-8 film, atmospheric soundscapes and original music.

Videos of each episode – containing additional footage not shown on television – are available from good book and video shops, but the availability of individual videos varies with regional screening schedules.

Video destinations include: Alaska • American Rockies • Australia – The South-East • Baja California & the Copper Canyon • Brazil • Central Asia • Chile & Easter Island • Corsica, Sicily & Sardinia – The Mediterranean Islands • East Africa (Tanzania & Zanzibar) • Ecuador & the Galapagos Islands • Greenland & Iceland • Indonesia • Israel & the Sinai Desert • Jamaica • Japan • La Ruta Maya • Morocco • New York • North India • Pacific Islands (Fiji, Solomon Islands & Vanuatu) • South India • South West China • Turkey • Vietnam • West Africa • Zimbabwe, Botswana & Namibia

The Lonely Planet TV series is produced by:
Pilot Productions
Duke of Sussex Studios
44 Uxbridge St
London W8 7TG UK

Lonely Planet videos are distributed by:
IVN Communications Inc
2246 Camino Ramon
California 94583, USA

107 Power Road, Chiswick
London W4 5PL UK

Music from the TV series is available on CD & cassette.
For video availability and ordering information contact your nearest Lonely Planet office.

PLANET TALK

Lonely Planet's FREE quarterly newsletter

We love hearing from you and think you'd like to hear from us.

*When...*is the right time to see reindeer in Finland?
*Where...*can you hear the best palm-wine music in Ghana?
*How...*do you get from Asunción to Areguá by steam train?
*What...*is the best way to see India?

For the answer to these and many other questions read PLANET TALK.

Every issue is packed with up-to-date travel news and advice including:

- a letter from Lonely Planet co-founders Tony and Maureen Wheeler
- go behind the scenes on the road with a Lonely Planet author
- feature article on an important and topical travel issue
- a selection of recent letters from travellers
- details on forthcoming Lonely Planet promotions
- complete list of Lonely Planet products

To join our mailing list contact any Lonely Planet office.

Also available: Lonely Planet T-shirts. 100% heavyweight cotton.

LONELY PLANET ONLINE

Get the latest travel information before you leave or while you're on the road

Whether you've just begun planning your next trip, or you're chasing down specific info on currency regulations or visa requirements, check out the Lonely Planet World Wide Web site for up-to-the-minute travel information.

As well as travel profiles of your favourite destinations (including interactive maps and full-colour photos), you'll find current reports from our army of researchers and other travellers, updates on health and visas, travel advisories, and the ecological and political issues you need to be aware of as you travel.

There's an online travellers' forum (the Thorn Tree) where you can share your experiences of life on the road, meet travel companions and ask other travellers for their recommendations and advice. We also have plenty of links to other Web sites useful to independent travellers.

With tens of thousands of visitors a month, the Lonely Planet Web site is one of the most popular on the Internet and has won a number of awards including GNN's Best of the Net travel award.

http://www.lonelyplanet.com

LONELY PLANET PRODUCTS

Lonely Planet is known worldwide for publishing practical, reliable and no-nonsense travel information in our guides and on our web site. The Lonely Planet list covers just about every accessible part of the world. Currently there are eight series: *travel guides*, *shoestring guides*, *walking guides*, *city guides*, *phrasebooks*, *audio packs*, *travel atlases* and *Journeys* – a unique collection of travel writing.

EUROPE

Austria • Baltic States & Kaliningrad • Baltic States phrasebook • Britain • Central Europe on a shoestring • Central Europe phrasebook • Czech & Slovak Republics • Denmark • Dublin city guide • Eastern Europe on a shoestring • Eastern Europe phrasebook • Finland • France • Greece • Greek phrasebook • Hungary • Iceland, Greenland & the Faroe Islands • Ireland • Italy • Mediterranean Europe on a shoestring • Mediterranean Europe phrasebook • Paris city guide • Poland • Portugal • Prague city guide • Russia, Ukraine & Belarus • Russian phrasebook • Scandinavian & Baltic Europe on a shoestring • Scandinavian Europe phrasebook • Slovenia • Spain • St Petersburg city guide • Switzerland • Trekking in Greece • Trekking in Spain • Ukrainian phrasebook • Vienna city guide • Walking in Britain • Walking in Switzerland • Western Europe on a shoestring • Western Europe phrasebook

NORTH AMERICA

Alaska • Backpacking in Alaska • Baja California • California & Nevada • Canada • Florida • Hawaii • Honolulu city guide • Los Angeles city guide • Mexico • Miami city guide • New England • New Orleans city guide • Pacific Northwest USA • Rocky Mountain States • San Francisco city guide • Southwest USA • USA phrasebook • Washington, DC & the Capital Region

CENTRAL AMERICA & THE CARIBBEAN

Bermuda • Central America on a shoestring • Costa Rica • Cuba • Eastern Caribbean • Guatemala, Belize & Yucatán: La Ruta Maya • Jamaica

SOUTH AMERICA

Argentina, Uruguay & Paraguay • Bolivia • Brazil • Brazilian phrasebook • Buenos Aires city guide • Chile & Easter Island • Chile & Easter Island travel atlas • Colombia • Ecuador & the Galápagos Islands • Latin American Spanish phrasebook • Peru • Quechua phrasebook • Rio de Janeiro city guide • South America on a shoestring • Trekking in the Patagonian Andes • Venezuela

Travel Literature: Full Circle: A South American Journey

ANTARCTICA

Antarctica

ISLANDS OF THE INDIAN OCEAN

Madagascar & Comoros • Maldives & Islands of the East Indian Ocean • Mauritius, Réunion & Seychelles

AFRICA

Arabic (Moroccan) phrasebook • Africa on a shoestring • Cape Town city guide • Central Africa • East Africa • Egypt • Egypt travel atlas • Ethiopian (Amharic) phrasebook • Kenya • Kenya travel atlas • Morocco • North Africa • South Africa, Lesotho & Swaziland • Swahili phrasebook • Trekking in East Africa • West Africa • Zimbabwe, Botswana & Namibia • Zimbabwe, Botswana & Namibia travel atlas

Travel Literature: The Rainbird: A Central African Journey • Songs to an African Sunset: A Zimbabwean Story

MAIL ORDER

Lonely Planet products are distributed worldwide. They are also available by mail order from Lonely Planet, so if you have difficulty finding a title please write to us. North American and South American residents should write to Embarcadero West, 155 Filbert St, Suite 251, Oakland CA 94607, USA; European and African residents should write to 10 Barley Mow Passage, Chiswick, London W4 4PH; and residents of other countries to PO Box 617, Hawthorn, Victoria 3122, Australia.

NORTH-EAST ASIA

Beijing city guide • Cantonese phrasebook • China • Hong Kong, Macau & Guangzhou• Hong Kong city guide • Japan • Japanese phrasebook • Japanese audio pack • Korea • Korean phrasebook • Mandarin phrasebook • Mongolia • Mongolian phrasebook • North-East Asia on a shoestring • Seoul city guide • Taiwan • Tibet • Tibet phrasebook • Tokyo city guide

Travel Literature: Lost Japan

MIDDLE EAST & CENTRAL ASIA

Arab Gulf States • Arabic (Egyptian) phrasebook • Central Asia • Iran • Israel & the Palestinian Territories • Israel & the Palestinian Territories travel atlas • Istanbul city guide • Jerusalem city guide • Jordan & Syria • Jordan, Syria & Lebanon travel atlas • Middle East • Turkey • Turkish phrasebook • Yemen

Travel Literature: The Gates of Damascus • Kingdom of the Film Stars: Journey into Jordan

ALSO AVAILABLE:

Travel with Children • Traveller's Tales

INDIAN SUBCONTINENT

Bangladesh • Bengali phrasebook • Delhi city guide • Hindi/Urdu phrasebook • India • India & Bangladesh travel atlas • Indian Himalaya • Karakoram Highway • Nepal • Nepali phrasebook • Pakistan • Rajasthan • Sri Lanka • Sri Lanka phrasebook • Trekking in the Indian Himalaya • Trekking in the Karakoram & Hindukush • Trekking in the Nepal Himalaya

Travel Literature: In Rajasthan • Shopping for Buddhas

SOUTH-EAST ASIA

Bali & Lombok • Bangkok city guide • Burmese phrasebook • Cambodia • Ho Chi Minh city guide • Indonesia • Indonesian phrasebook • Indonesian audio pack • Jakarta city guide • Java • Laos • Lao phrasebook • Laos travel atlas • Malay phrasebook • Malaysia, Singapore & Brunei • Myanmar (Burma) • Philippines • Pilipino phrasebook • Singapore city guide • South-East Asia on a shoestring •South-East Asia phrasebook • Thailand • Thailand travel atlas • Thai phrasebook • Thai audio pack • Thai Hill Tribes phrasebook • Vietnam • Vietnamese phrasebook • Vietnam travel atlas

AUSTRALIA & THE PACIFIC

Australia • Australian phrasebook • Bushwalking in Australia • Bushwalking in Papua New Guinea • Fiji • Fijian phrasebook • Islands of Australia's Great Barrier Reef • Melbourne city guide • Micronesia • New Caledonia • New South Wales & the ACT • New Zealand • Northern Territory • Outback Australia • Papua New Guinea • Papua New Guinea phrasebook • Queensland • Rarotonga & the Cook Islands • Samoa • Solomon Islands • South Australia • Sydney city guide • Tahiti & French Polynesia • Tasmania • Tonga • Tramping in New Zealand • Vanuatu • Victoria • Western Australia

Travel Literature: Islands in the Clouds • Sean & David's Long Drive

THE LONELY PLANET STORY

Lonely Planet published its first book in 1973 in response to the numerous 'How did you do it?' questions Maureen and Tony Wheeler were asked after driving, bussing, hitching, sailing and railing their way from England to Australia.

Written at a kitchen table and hand collated, trimmed and stapled, *Across Asia on the Cheap* became an instant local bestseller, inspiring thoughts of another book.

Eighteen months in South-East Asia resulted in their second guide, *South-East Asia on a shoestring*, which they put together in a backstreet Chinese hotel in Singapore in 1975. The 'yellow bible', as it quickly became known to backpackers around the world, soon became *the* guide to the region. It has sold well over half a million copies and is now in its 9th edition, still retaining its familiar yellow cover.

Today there are over 240 titles, including travel guides, walking guides, language kits & phrasebooks, travel atlases and travel literature. The company is the largest independent travel publisher in the world. Although Lonely Planet initially specialised in guides to Asia, today there are few corners of the globe that have not been covered.

The emphasis continues to be on travel for independent travellers. Tony and Maureen still travel for several months of each year and play an active part in the writing, updating and quality control of Lonely Planet's guides.

They have been joined by over 70 authors and 170 staff at our offices in Melbourne (Australia), Oakland (USA), London (UK) and Paris (France). Travellers themselves also make a valuable contribution to the guides through the feedback we receive in thousands of letters each year and on our web site.

The people at Lonely Planet strongly believe that travellers can make a positive contribution to the countries they visit, both through their appreciation of the countries' culture, wildlife and natural features, and through the money they spend. In addition, the company makes a direct contribution to the countries and regions it covers. Since 1986 a percentage of the income from each book has been donated to ventures such as famine relief in Africa; aid projects in India; agricultural projects in Central America; Greenpeace's efforts to halt French nuclear testing in the Pacific; and Amnesty International.

'I hope we send the people out with the right attitude about travel. You realise when you travel that there are so many different perspectives about the world, so we hope these books will make people more interested in what they see. These are guidebooks, but you can't really guide people. All you can do is point them in the right direction.'

– Tony Wheeler

LONELY PLANET PUBLICATIONS

Australia
PO Box 617, Hawthorn 3122, Victoria
tel: (03) 9819 1877 fax: (03) 9819 6459
e-mail: talk2us@lonelyplanet.com.au

USA
Embarcadero West, 155 Filbert St, Suite 251,
Oakland, CA 94607
tel: (510) 893 8555 TOLL FREE: 800 275-8555
fax: (510) 893 8563
e-mail: info@lonelyplanet.com

UK
10 Barley Mow Passage, Chiswick,
London W4 4PH
tel: (0181) 742 3161 fax: (0181) 742 2772
e-mail: 100413.3551@compuserve.com

France:
71 bis rue du Cardinal Lemoine, 75005 Paris
tel: 1 44 32 06 20 fax: 1 46 34 72 55
e-mail: 100560.415@compuserve.com

World Wide Web: http://www.lonelyplanet.com